THE PAPERS OF MARTIN LUTHER KING, JR.

Initiated by

The King Center

in association with

Stanford University

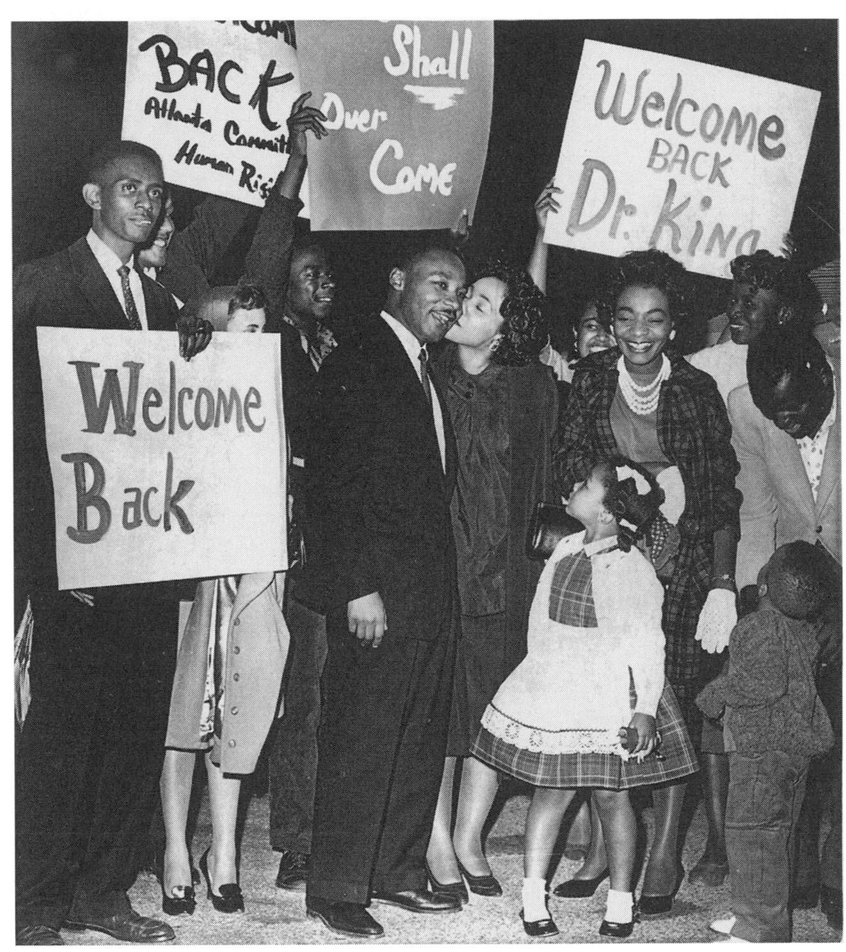

Upon his release from the Georgia State Prison at Reidsville, King is greeted by his wife, Coretta Scott King, his sister, Christine King Farris, and children Yolanda and Martin Luther King III on 27 October 1960. Courtesy of AP/Wide World Photos.

THE PAPERS OF MARTIN LUTHER KING, JR.

VOLUME V

Threshold of a New Decade

January 1959–December 1960

Senior Editor

Clayborne Carson

Volume Editors

Tenisha Armstrong
Susan Carson
Adrienne Clay
Kieran Taylor

UNIVERSITY OF CALIFORNIA PRESS

Berkeley Los Angeles London

University of California Press
Berkeley and Los Angeles, California

University of California Press, Ltd.
London, England

Library of Congress Cataloging-in-Publication Data
King, Martin Luther, Jr., 1929–1968.
The papers of Martin Luther King, Jr.
V. 5. Threshold of a new decade, January 1959–December 1960.
Contents: V. 1. Called to serve, January 1929–June 1951—V. 2. Rediscovering precious values, July 1951–November 1955—V. 3. Birth of a new age, December 1955–December 1956—V. 4. Symbol of the movement, January 1957–December 1958.
p. cm.
Includes bibliographical references and index.
ISBN 0-520-24239-4 (cloth: alk. paper).
1. Afro-Americans—Civil rights. 2. Civil rights movements—United States—History—20th century. 3. King, Martin Luther, Jr., 1929–1968—Archives. 4. United States—Race relations. I. Carson, Clayborne, 1944– . II. Armstrong, Tenisha. III. Carson, Susan. IV. Clay, Adrienne. V. Taylor, Kieran. VI. Title.
E185.97.K5A2 2005
323'092—dc22 91–42336
CIP

Manufactured in the United States of America
13 12 11 10 09 08 07 06 05
10 9 8 7 6 5 4 3 2 1

The paper used in this publication meets the minimum requirements of ANSI/NISO Z39.48-1992 (R 1997) (*Permanence of Paper*). ⊗

A civil rights crisis rocks the nation.
We are on the threshold of a new decade in which
the masses of Negro people are coming on to the stage of history
and demanding their freedom now.

MARTIN LUTHER KING, JR., & A. PHILIP RANDOLPH
9 June 1960

The editors of the Martin Luther King, Jr., Papers Project wish to acknowledge the generosity of the following major contributors, without whose support this volume would not have been possible.

Major Contributors

Betty A. Williams Curtis and G. Russell Curtis, Sr.
The Flora and William Hewlett Foundation
Lilly Endowment Inc.
Ronnie Lott / All Stars Helping Kids
National Endowment for the Humanities
National Historical Publications and Records Commission
The Peninsula Community Foundation
Stanford University
Woodside Summit Group, Inc.

Patrons

A. Greg Crossfield
Bonnie Fisher and Boris Dramov
Leonard Merrill Kurz and the Kurz Family Foundation

Donors

David and Susan G. Abernethy
Rabbi Sidney Akselrad, Congregation Beth Am
Bettina Aptheker
Herbert Aptheker
Sara and Harold Boyd
Harvey L. Cole
Nadine Cruz and Laurence Ulrich
Wayne Duckworth
Mary McKinney Edmonds
Candace Falk
George M. Fredrickson
Leola P. Graves
Lettie and Dr. Robert Green
Jenna Klein
Bernard and Kate B. Lafayette, Jr.
Ronald and Shoshana Levy
Patricia Margulies
Henry P. Organ
Mrs. Paprocki's Seventh Grade Social Studies Class,
Marie Murphy School, Wilmette, Illinois
Philadelphia Yearly Meeting of the Religious Society of Friends
Arnold Rampersad
Joan S. Reid
Viola M. C. White
Tyrone and Kim Willingham
Rosalind Wolf
Peter Zeughauser, the Zeughauser Group

The Papers of Martin Luther King, Jr.

CLAYBORNE CARSON,
Senior Editor

1. *Called to Serve, January 1929–June 1951*
Volume editors: Ralph E. Luker and Penny A. Russell

2. *Rediscovering Precious Values, July 1951–November 1955*
Volume editors: Ralph E. Luker, Penny A. Russell, and Peter Holloran

3. *Birth of a New Age, December 1955–December 1956*
Volume editors: Stewart Burns, Susan Carson, Peter Holloran, and Dana L. H. Powell

4. *Symbol of the Movement, January 1957–December 1958*
Volume editors: Susan Carson, Adrienne Clay, Virginia Shadron, and Kieran Taylor

5. *Threshold of a New Decade, January 1959–December 1960*
Volume editors: Tenisha Armstrong, Susan Carson, Adrienne Clay, and Kieran Taylor

ADVISORY BOARD

The publishers gratefully acknowledge the many individuals and foundations that have contributed to the publication of the Papers of Martin Luther King, Jr., and the General Endowment Fund of the Associates of the University of California Press for its contribution toward the publication of this volume.

Our special thanks to Maya Angelou, Sukey Garcetti, Maxine Griggs, Mary Jane Hewitt, Franklin Murphy, Joan Palevsky, and Marilyn Solomon for their leadership during the campaign.

Challenge Grant
Times Mirror Foundation

Leadership Grants
The Ahmanson Foundation
AT&T Foundation

Partners
ARCO Foundation
William H. Cosby and Camille O. Cosby
The George Gund Foundation
The Walter and Elise Haas Fund
LEF Foundation
Sally Lilienthal
J. Michael Mahoney
The Andrew W. Mellon Foundation
National Historical Publications and Records Commission
Peter Norton Family Foundation
Joan Palevsky
The Ralph M. Parsons Foundation

Benefactors
Anonymous
BankAmerica Foundation
Fleishhacker Foundation
David Geffen Foundation
Linda Johnson Rice—Johnson Publishing Company
Koret Foundation
Levi Strauss Foundation
Lilly Endowment Inc.
McDonnell Douglas Foundation
Foundations of the Milken Families
National Endowment for the Humanities
Pacific Telesis Group
Jocelyn, Drew, and Keith Reid
Charles H. Revson Foundation, Inc.
Ernst D. and Eleanor Slate van Löben Sels Foundation

Patrons
Earl and June Cheit
Berry Gordy—Jobete Music Publishing Co., Inc.
Frances and Kenneth Reid

Sponsors
Jacqueline and Clarence Avant
Edward R. Bradley, Jr.
Francine and Kevin Castner
Esther Gordy Edwards—Motown Museum
Susan and August Frugé
Deborah and Joseph Goldyne
Hugh Hefner
Beatrice and Richard Heggie
Quincy Jones—Quincy Jones Productions
Max Palevsky
The Roth Family Foundation
Sony Corporation of America

CONTENTS

ILLUSTRATIONS

Photographs

Facsimiles

Map

The Martin Luther King, Jr., Papers Project continues to rely on the generous contributions of many individuals who are drawn together by a common desire to disseminate the ideas of King and the social justice movements he inspired. The participants in the Project's editorial and research activities constitute a uniquely dedicated and talented community. As the Project's director, I have appreciated the opportunity to work closely with my colleagues, both staff members and students researchers, and with supporters who contributed funding, historical information, documents and permission to use them, and generous encouragement. In the previous four volumes of this edition, I have described the many individuals whose contributions to the Project have been long-term. Thus, I will focus attention here on those individuals whose contributions since the completion of *Volume IV: Symbol of the Movement* have been of particular significance during the final stages of preparation of *Volume V: Threshold of a New Decade.*

Institutional Support

The King Papers Project would not be possible without the support of the Martin Luther King, Jr., Estate and the continuing cooperation of the King Center in Atlanta. During recent years I have often relied upon the assistance and support of Coretta Scott King, the King Center's founding president, and that of Dexter King, her successor. Lynn Cothren, Mrs. King's assistant, has been consistently helpful, as have members of her office staff, including Patricia Latimore. They have been particularly helpful in providing access to documentary materials that are not part of the King collection at the King Center.

Staff members of the King Center administration supported the Project's work in various ways. In addition to Dexter King, we have appreciated the support of King Center administrators, including Chief Executive Officer Tricia Harris and her predecessor, Ana Mollinedo. We are also grateful for the support of the King Library and Archives staff, particularly Director of Archives Cynthia Lewis. Other King Center staff members who have been helpful to us include Alice Eason, Michael England, Barbara Harrison, Steve Klein, and Robert Vickers. I have also enjoyed working with Jennifer Quirk from Intellectual Properties Management.

We have benefited enormously from the research resources and administrative support of our sponsoring institution, Stanford University. The Project has received enthusiastic backing from President John Hennessy and Provost John Etchemendy as well as LaDoris Hazzard Cordell, Vice Provost and Special Counselor to the President for Campus Relations. Regarding the Project's ongoing needs, I have had the pleasure of consulting with Vice Provost for Undergraduate Education John Bravman and Director of Undergraduate Research Programs Susan Brubaker-Cole. Dean of Humanities and Sciences Sharon Long and former Dean Russell

Berman have been consistently gracious and supportive. We also appreciate the concern of Judith Goldstein, Cognizant Dean for Graduate and Undergraduate Studies, and Robert Gregg, former Cognizant Dean. We are also thankful for the encouragement of History Department chair Carolyn Lougee Chappell. On personnel matters, we have received vital assistance from Human Resource officer Lori Kohara. James Henry, Director of Finance, and Deborah Burgstrum, former Financial Management Analyst, were also helpful. In the Office of Sponsored Research we appreciate the assistance of Lillie Ryans-Culclager, Co-Director; Blanca Rebuelta, Grants Officer; Catherine Boxwell, Contract Officer; Linda Erwin, Assistant Director; Mila Dacorro, Senior Accountant; Cecile Imbert, Accounting Associate; and Diven Sharma, Research Accountant. Associate Dean of Development Robert Franklin and Assistant Development Officer Erica O'Neal have assisted the Project in its never-ending pursuit of additional funding. We are also deeply grateful for the continuing assistance of the staff at Stanford's Cecil H. Green Library, especially Mary-Louise Munill in the interlibrary borrowing office.

The King Papers Project has had a supportive relationship with the publisher of our edition, the University of California Press. We have enjoyed working with all of the staff members involved in the painstaking work of producing our volumes. Those involved with this volume include Director Lynne Withey, Randy Heyman, and Monica McCormick. Kathleen MacDougall's enthusiasm and organizational skills in coordinating this effort at UC Press are especially noteworthy.

The involvement of the Project's Advisory Board has declined in recent years, but we continue to appreciate the advice we receive from this extraordinary group of distinguished scholars and former associates of Dr. King, who are listed in this volume's opening pages. In addition to Mrs. King and Mrs. Farris, I wish to acknowledge in particular the critical comments regarding Volume V that we received from David Garrow and Preston N. Williams. Their thoughtful criticism on the manuscript drafts were invaluable.

In addition to benefiting from the advice of these members of the Advisory Board, the Project has also relied on its Stanford University Advisory Committee, which has expanded its role in recent years. They included the committee's chair, Harold Boyd, and the following members: Barton J. Bernstein, Vicki Brooks, Capri Silverstri Cafaro, Roy Clay, Greg Crossfield, Karl Cureton, G. Russell Curtis, Sr., George Fredrickson, Morris Graves, Julie Anne Henderson, Henry Organ, John Rickford, Betty A. Williams Curtis, Alene Smith, and David Tyack.

Financial Supporters

The King Papers Project could not have survived without funding from numerous generous donors. Major contributors to this volume include the Flora and William Hewlett Foundation, Lilly Endowment Inc., Ronnie Lott / All Stars Helping Kids the National Endowment for the Humanities (NEH), the National Historical Publications and Records Commission (NHPRC), the Peninsula Community Foundation, Stanford University, the Woodside Summit Group, and Betty A. Williams Curtis and G. Russell Curtis, Sr. Individuals at these institutions have often demonstrated a concern for the Project far outside the bounds of professional responsibilities. I acknowledge in particular NEH Chairman William R. Ferris, Grants Officer Alice Hudgins, and former Program Officer Daniel P. Jones. NHPRC Executive Director Ann C. Newhall, Deputy Executive Director Roger Bruns, Program Officer Daniel Stokes, and Archivist John W. Carlin have been generous in their assistance to the Project. In addition, I have appreciated the support of Lilly Endowment Program Director Jacqui Burton, and Program Officers Jeanne Knoerle and Jean Smith.

Patrons of this volume include A. Greg Crossfield, Bonnie Fisher and Boris Dramov, and Leonard Merrill Kurz and the Kurz Family Foundation.

Donors include David and Susan G. Abernethy, Rabbi Sidney Akselrad (Congregation Beth Am), Bettina Aptheker, Herbert Aptheker, Sara and Harold Boyd, Harvey L. Cole, Nadine Cruz and Laurence Ulrich, Wayne Duckworth, Mary McKinney Edmonds, Candace Falk, George M. Fredrickson, Leola P. Graves, Lettie and Dr. Robert Green, Jenna Klein, Bernard and Kate B. Lafayette, Jr., Ronald and Shoshana Levy, Patricia Margulies, Henry P. Organ, Mrs. Paprocki's Seventh Grade Social Studies Class (Maria Murphy School, Wilmette, Illinois), Philadelphia Yearly Meeting of the Religious Society of Friends, Arnold Rampersad, Joan S. Reid, Viola M. C. White, Tyrone and Kim Willingham, Rosalind Wolf, and Peter Zeughauser (the Zeughauser Group).

Sustainers include Bobbie J. Armstrong, Kimberley J. Baker, W. Todd Beaney, Rabbi Andrea Berlin (First Hebrew Congregation of Oakland, Temple Sinai), M. Robert Breslauer, Ellen Broms, Sharon H. Carson, Tina Ebey, Virginia and Frances Geddes, David Gelfand, Robert and Muriel Herhold, Steven F. Lawson, Judith Clay Lhamon, Catherine M. McCann, Delia McGrath, Kimberly Oden, M. Brigid O'Farrell, Steve Phillips, Sallie Reid, Joel and Rachel Samoff, Deborah A. Scalise, Matthew Scelza, Roland Shepard, Robert Tasto, Commicolla D. Thierry, Sheila Troupe, Unity Northwest Church of Des Plaines, Illinois, Amy Whitcomb, and L. A. Wright.

Staff Members

This volume, as with all the volumes of King's papers, has been the result of a long-term collaboration involving student and postdoctoral researchers, in which academic credentials counted for less than demonstrated ability and dedication. From its inception, the mission of the King Papers Project has not only been to produce a definitive edition of King's papers but to provide opportunities for able and dedicated students to acquire research skills and to increase their understanding of the modern African American freedom struggle. As the Project has evolved, a few veteran staff members have provided an essential degree of stability amid the continual turnover of student researchers and professionals. The editors listed on the title page have each made especially vital contributions to this volume.

Amid the many changes in the King Project's personnel, Susan Carson has continued to be a vital and steadfast source of guidance for me and for those who have joined the staff. Helping to train new staff members, Susan has been involved in every aspect of the Project's work, from preparation of grant proposals to document acquisition to manuscript preparation. She also supervised the Project's difficult but necessary transition from the mainframe database that the Project had used since its early years to the more powerful and versatile InMagic software that we currently use.

This volume could not have been completed without the contributions of several very talented and dedicated young editors. After finishing work on Volume IV in 1999, assistant editors Kerry Taylor and Adrienne Clay devoted their considerable energy to this volume. Kerry came to the Project after completing course work in southern studies at the University of Mississippi. Adrienne, a graduate of Colby College, was a King Summer Research Fellow before joining the staff. They established a model collaboration, working closely together on every aspect of the research and editing of the volume. Kerry left the Project after the summer of 2001 to pursue doctoral studies at the University of North Carolina, and Adrienne departed a year later for doctoral studies at Columbia.

During this period, research assistant Tenisha Armstrong, who first came to the Project as a King Summer Research Fellow in 1998, earned a well-deserved promotion to associate editor. After the departure of Kerry and Adrienne, Tenisha became the lead editor of this volume; her utter dedication to the Project's mission and to the highest of editorial standards have helped her to craft this manuscript into a splendid work of historical scholarship. All three of these editors took on responsibilities that were far more than could have been expected when they came to the Project, but each succeeded admirably in meeting the special research and editorial challenges of the volume.

Several new people joined the staff during the final year of work on this manuscript. Susan Englander, initially hired as the editor of Volume VI, was called upon to assist in many aspects of completing this manuscript. Elizabeth Brummel enthusiastically supervised the process of entering and verifying document records. Research assistants Stewart Walker and Andrea Dowdy demonstrated a keen eye for details and gladly performed any task given them. Damani Rivers ably digitized many of the documents included in this volume. No longer with the Project but contributing to this volume were Lauren Araiza, Elizabeth Baez, Alice Endamne, Rebecca Engel, Pete Holloran, Jennifer Trask, and Erin Wood.

In addition, the King Papers Project benefited tremendously from the volunteer labors of the late Herbert Aptheker, whose pioneering publications in the field of African American documentary history inspired our own work. We will miss him.

Although not directly involved in the research or writing of this volume, other staff members provided essential administrative support, especially Project Administrator Jane Abbott and Assistant Administrator Regina Covington. Terry McBride managed the transition of our database from the Stanford mainframe to a Web-based program, and Jesika Gandhi continued the supervision of our computer-related needs.

Student Researchers

The King Papers Project is immensely grateful for the many hours of thoughtful, sometimes tedious, work put in by undergraduate and graduate students over the years. These students, representing many disciplines, brought their methods and perspectives to bear upon the important task of locating King's words in time and place. They plotted his daily movements against the sweep of events in a region too often shadowed by racial violence. With diligence they discovered unknown documents and patiently deciphered recordings of King's voice, sometimes barely audible, to produce some of this volume's most distinctive documents. Their individual and collective contributions are many, as are their number.

The Project has always depended on the skills, dedication, and exceptional talents of Stanford students. These students, working as interns, volunteers, or for academic credit, have contributed much to our work through their deep interest in and enthusiasm for the material. Undergraduate researchers who worked on Volume V or whose work was not acknowledged in previous volumes include Sarah Allen, Brandis Anderson, Che Banjoko, Gina Bateson, Caitlin Callaghan, Jackie Chang, Harriet Clark, Jonathan Cohen, Dana Craig, Taya Cromley, Brannon Cullum, Lisa Ehrlich, Karis Eklund, Kristin Ferrales, Crystal Garland, Kelly Garrett, Melissa Ghoston, Cheryl Gladstone, Hanan Hardy, Adrianna Hernandez-Stewart, Sophia Hurd, Arthur-Damon Jones, Ahmad Khalil, Nicole Kief, Jessica Kim, Lynda Lao, Katrina Logan, Christy Machida, Sarah Mangin, Kalideidra Martin, Christallyn McCloud, Marina McCoy, Maria Medina, Gina Moon, Trevor Neeb, Becky Neil, Angel Page, Marissa Pareles, Celia Perry, Jedediah Peterson, Hari Raman, Meghana Reddy, Julia Mercedes Roy, Anna Sale, Christina Sauve, Sumit Shah, Rebecca Sheehan, Leroy Sims, Dwight Slater, Jolan Smith, Kate Stanley, Karen Tisdale, Serafina Uludong, Amorita Valdez, Annie Verderosa, Clara Webb, and Teresa Yeager. In addition, Jose Gordon, Chien Le, Shirley Lin, Andrew Mo, and Alan Yu provided the Project with dependable computer expertise, helping maintain our electronic databases and Web site, and addressing our endless questions. During this period the following volunteers have greatly enhanced the Project's work and productivity: Owen David, Jessica Feinstein, Lillian Hardy, Anthony Logan, Debra Messick, Susana Ortega, William Tucker, and Victoria Wobber.

King Summer Research Fellows

The Project has also gained immensely from the contributions of graduate and undergraduate students from other colleges and universities who worked at the Stanford office as part of the Martin Luther King, Jr., Summer Research Fellowship. The Summer Fellows from 1999 through 2002 are Juliana Boucher (North Carolina State University), Elizabeth Crocker (University of Virginia), Adrienne Denson (Williams College), Joshua Dougherty (Concordia University), Kristin Ferrales (Stanford University), Krystal Frazier (Florida A&M University), Dan Gilbert (Wesleyan University), Reygan Harmon (Spelman College), Jessica Harris (Dillard University), Demetrius Hobson (Morehouse College), Kristina Hoeppner (University of California, Davis), Tim Lake (Bowling Green University), Katrina Logan (Stanford University), Brad March (University of Northern Colorado), Vernon C. Mitchell, Jr. (University of Missouri, Columbia), Jedediah Peterson (Stanford University), Jennifer Sahrle (CUNY-Genesco), Anna Sale (Stanford University), Kate Stanley (Stanford University), Eric Stowe (University of Washington, Tacoma), Ben Wheeler (Columbia University), and Teresa Yeager (Stanford University).

Acquisition and Research Assistance

Volume V, like the volumes that preceded it, would not have been possible without the King-related documents that have been provided to us by numerous individuals and institutions. The King collections at Boston University and the King

Center have been at the core of our selection. We are especially grateful for the generous assistance of Boston University's Special Collections Director Howard Gotlieb, as well as Assistant Director Charlie Niles and Cynthia Lewis at the King Center.

In addition to documents obtained from the King Center and Boston University, we identified more than 150 manuscript collections with King-related material important for this volume. Institutions, archives, and libraries that assisted us in locating documents for this volume include the Alabama Department of Archives and History, American Baptist–Samuel Colgate Historical Library (Rochester, New York), the American Friends Service Committee, Amistad Research Center (Tulane University), AP/Wide World Photos, Archives of Labor History and Urban Affairs (Wayne State University), Atlanta Historical Society, Atlanta University Center, Bethel College, Black Star Publishing, California Labor Federation AFL-CIO Library, Canadian Broadcasting Corporation, Central United Methodist Church Archives, Chicago Historical Society, The Christopher Reynolds Foundation, Colgate-Rochester Divinity School, Columbia Broadcasting System, Corbis-Bettmann Archives, Cornell University, Dartmouth College, DePauw University, Dickinson College, Dillard University, Duke University, *Durham Herald Sun,* Dwight D. Eisenhower Library, Earlham College, Emory University, Georgetown University, Georgia Department of Archives, Georgia State University, Goshen College, Harvard University, Hawaii State Archives, *Honolulu Star-Bulletin,* Howard University, Indiana Historical Society, Indiana University, Iowa State University, John F. Kennedy Library, Library of Congress, Mani Bhavan Gandhi Sangrahalaya, McCormick Theological Seminary, George Meany Memorial Archives, Miami University, Mississippi Department of Archives and History, Montgomery County Courthouse, National Broadcasting Company, Nehru Memorial Museum and Library, New York Public Library, New York University, North Central College, Richard M. Nixon Library, Oberlin College, Ohio University, Pacifica Radio Archive, Presbyterian Department of History, Princeton University, Franklin D. Roosevelt Library, Shiloh Baptist Church, Swarthmore College, Tennessee State Library and Archives, Time Inc., Tougaloo College, Harry S. Truman Library, Tuskegee Institute, Unitarian Church of Germantown, United States National Archives, University of Arizona, University of Arkansas, University of California (Davis), University of California (Los Angeles), University of Georgia, University of Hartford, University of Maryland Eastern Shore, University of Massachusetts, University of Michigan, University of Minnesota, University of North Carolina, University of Northern Iowa, University of Oregon, University of South Carolina, University of Texas, Virginia Union University, War Resisters League, Waterloo Public Library, Wayne State University, Western Reserve Historical Society, Wisconsin Historical Society, and Yale University.

King's travels in India in 1959 opened new avenues of research and collaboration for us. With help from the Philadelphia Yearly Meeting of the Religious Society of Friends, assistant editor Adrienne Clay was able to travel to India for one month to explore King's trip and obtain useful research materials. In addition, we received advice and information from many sources in India and the United States to help us better contextualize King's trip and understand its significance. For that valuable assistance we would like to thank S. K. Bhatnagar, National Gandhi Museum and Library, New Delhi; S. K. De; O. P. Kejariwal, Nehru Memorial Museum and Library, New Delhi; Naresh Kunta and Manju Ruthod, Indian Council of World Affairs, New Delhi; Vinay Lal, UCLA; S. K. Mohan, Karnataka Gandhi Smarak Nidhi, Bangalore, India; Chris Rapoport; E. S. Reddy; Rita Roy, Gandhi Peace Foundation, New Delhi; Gandhi Smarak Nidhi, New Delhi; Usha Thakkar, Mani Bhavan Gandhi Sangrahalaya, Mumbai.

King's colleagues, acquaintances, and their families have been among the most important sources of King-related documents. Of those whom we were able to contact, many assisted us immeasurably in our research. Some graciously allowed us to make photocopies of the documents in their possession, which until now have not been available, and many kindly consented to interviews in connection with this volume. These individuals include Jeanne Adkins, Gilder Anderson, Thelma Archer, Randi Ashton-Pritting, Lewis Baldwin, Maude Ballou, Kathryn Barrett, Rose Blaney, Anne Braden, John Brooke, Candie Carawan, Constance Couts, Clarence Davis, Carla Drije, Patricia Stephens Due, Christine King Farris, Havert L. Fenn, Flora Flowers, David Garrow, Irwin Gellman, Johnnie Goodson, Edward Gottlieb, Dee Grimsrude, Wythe W. Holt, Jr., George Houser, Asbury Howard, Jr., Alberta Johnson (Stanley United Methodist Church), Corinne Johnson, W. T. Johnson, Coretta Scott King, Lonnie King, Jr., Margaret Larson, Tina Law, Earl W. Lawson, James Lawson, Edmund D. Livingston, Jerry Livingston, Shirley Livingston, Kathy Marquis, Michael Meeropol, Rebecca Dixon Mohr, Willie Morton, Gerald W. Musselman, John Patterson, James Robinson, Elsa Satchell, Julius Schatz, William X. Scheinmann, Evett L. Simmons, James Sleight, Irene Stevenson, Robert E. Sullivan, Nancy Taylor, William E. Taylor, E. M. Thorpe, Barry Tulloss, and Annette J. Winfrey. We continue to utilize the documents provided to us from the churches King pastored: Dexter Avenue King Memorial Baptist Church and Ebenezer Baptist Church.

Individuals who gave permission for publication of their documents or those of relatives include Jeanne Johns Adkins, Julius J. Alexander, Jr., Maude Ballou, Ramji Prasad Bhoop, Anne Braden, G. McLeod Bryan, Candie Carawan, Dorothy Cotton, Madeleine DeWolf, Andrew C. Faire, Walter Fauntroy, Norman Hill, Thorsten Horton, Joshua Javits, Muriel King, James Lawson, Andrew Levison, Michael Meeropol, S. K. Mohan, Douglas Moore, Christopher Niebuhr, E. D. Nixon, Jr., John Patterson, Rev. John Thomas Porter, Ram Chandra Rahi, Ella R. Reddick, James Robinson, Rachel Robinson, Richard Sears, Fred Shuttlesworth, Gloria Smart, Irene Stevenson, Glennette Tilley Turner, Wyatt Tee Walker, Priyanka Gandhi Vadra, and Harris Wofford.

Permissions were obtained with the assistance of Joellen El Bashir (Moorland-Spingarn Research Center, Howard University), Lolis Elie (Elie, Jones and Associates), Wayne Furman (Schomburg Center for Research in Black Culture), Norman Hill (A. Philip Randolph Institute), Gloria E. Karefa-Smart (James Baldwin Estate), Walter Naegle (Bayard Rustin Fund), Rev. Joseph L. Roberts (Ebenezer Baptist Church), and Jack Sutters (American Friends Service Committee).

Several institutions and individuals assisted the Project on our audiovisual acquisitions and research for this volume: the American Friends Service Committee Archives, Associated Press/Wide World Photos, Boston University, John Brooke, Canadian Broadcasting System, Lawrence Edward Carter, Central United Methodist Church Archives, Columbia Broadcasting System, Corbis-Bettmann Archives, DePauw University, *Durham Herald Sun*, Earlham College, Christine King

Farris, Indiana University, Alberta Johnson (Stanley United Methodist Church), Martin Luther King, Jr., Estate, Library of Congress, Gail Malmgreen (the Tamiment Library and Robert F. Wagner Labor Archives, New York University), Augustine Mensah (Ghana National Archives, Accra), Miami University, Harold Miller (Wisconsin Historical Society), Montgomery to Memphis Film Research Files, Cathy Lynn Mundale (Atlanta University Center), National Broadcasting Corporation, Nehru Memorial Museum and Library, *New York Times,* Patricia O'Donnell (Swarthmore College), Ohio University, Pacifica Radio Archives, Franklin D. Roosevelt Library, William X. Scheinman, Wallace Smith (Shiloh Baptist Church), Bart Sullivan (*Memphis Commercial Appeal*), Jack Sutters (American Friends Service Committee), Athan Theoharis (Marquette University), Time Inc., Tuskegee Institute, Unitarian Church of Germantown, University of Georgia, University of Hartford, University of Maryland Eastern Shore, Virginia Union University, and Wisconsin Historical Society.

Many scholars without official ties to the Project also provided assistance to the editors. These include John D'Emilio, Adam Fairclough, John M. Glen, Jacquelyn Hall, Reginald Hildebrand, Michael Honey, Troy Jackson, Sudarshan Kapur, Clifford Kuhn, Keith Miller, William Minter, and Gerald Smith. We are particularly grateful to Tom Jackson for his insightful criticisms on early drafts of the manuscript.

A few individuals have enhanced the work of the Project simply by visiting us and talking about their involvement with or scholarship on the civil rights movement or other movements for social change. Among the Project's recent invited guests have been Victoria Gray Adams, Chude Pam Allen, Bettina Aptheker, the late Herbert Aptheker, Dorothy Cotton, Jimmy Collier, Connie Curry, Dave Dennis, Betty Mae Fikes, John Hope Franklin, Haile Gerima, Rutha and Emory Harris, Bruce Hartford, Matt Herron, Darlene Clarke Hine, Ericka Huggins, Jesse Jackson, Matthew and Marshall Jones, Ed King, Benet Luchion, Doug MacAdam, Elizabeth Martinez, Steve McCutchen, Robert Moses, Chuck Neblett, Wazir Peacock, Bill Perlman, Fred Shuttlesworth, C. T. Vivian, Jean Wiley, Joy Williamson, and Gavin Wright.

Certainly there are other individuals and organizations that participated in and contributed to the success of the King Papers Project. Failure to mention them simply reflects the limits of my memory rather than of my gratitude.

CLAYBORNE CARSON

JANUARY 2004

INTRODUCTION

If my life, with the accompanying trials, tribulations, and difficulties that I have faced for my people have not proven my courage, then there is no way that I can convince anyone. I have lived amid threats, intimidation, physical violence, and even death, and yet I have never run from the situation. I have urged my people at all times to stand up against segregation, and even disobey the segregation laws in order to arouse and awaken the conscience of our nation. I will continue to do this, but I will do it in the right spirit. I will never allow any man to drag me so low as to make me hate him; and above all I will never become bitter.

Martin Luther King, Jr.
15 June 1959

When Martin Luther King, Jr. reviewed his activities in his 1958 annual report to Dexter Avenue Baptist Church, he referred with understatement to his "rather difficult year," during which he had endured police brutality, a groundless arrest, and a "near fatal stab wound by a mentally deranged woman." Nevertheless, he reported that the future was "filled with vast possibilities" and he urged his congregation to "move on into this uncertain but promising future with the faith that the dawn of a new day is just around the horizon."[1] It had been three years since King's leadership of the Montgomery bus boycott had propelled him into the national spotlight. His decision to remain a part of the young freedom struggle, with which he was becoming synonymous, had provided him a national pulpit from which to denounce racial injustice, afforded him access to the president, and garnered him considerable fame. At the same time, King and the organizations he led, the Montgomery Improvement Association (MIA) and the Southern Christian Leadership Conference (SCLC), had failed to build upon the success of the bus protest, and the Eisenhower administration remained impervious to their pleas for reform.[2] Moreover, his growing notoriety had endangered his safety and that of his family. The 20 September 1958 stabbing had forced King to reduce his relentless pace of activities and, following the advice of physicians,

1. King, Annual Report, Dexter Avenue Baptist Church, Presented on 18 November 1958, in *The Papers of Martin Luther King,* vol. 4: *Symbol of the Movement, January 1957–December 1958,* ed. Clayborne Carson, Susan Carson, Adrienne Clay, Virginia Shadron, Kieran Taylor (Berkeley and Los Angeles: University of California Press, 2000), pp. 538–539.

2. For a discussion of the MIA's and SCLC's stalled programs, see Introduction, *Papers* 4:21–26 and 36–37.

he cancelled or postponed nearly three months of speaking engagements, allowing his wife to deliver his prepared remarks at the national Youth March for Integrated Schools in late October.[3] By December King had returned to public life and political engagement, addressing the third annual MIA Institute on Nonviolence and Social Change and a rally in Atlanta.[4] With his closest associates, including New York attorney Stanley Levison and pacifist Bayard Rustin, King also continued discussions regarding the direction of SCLC and plans for a long-deferred trip to India that had been postponed several times since the conclusion of the bus boycott.

Traveling to India offered the hope of a break from the hectic pace King had maintained since his rise to prominence, but it would also serve as a transition to a still more demanding period when his efforts were confronted by new challenges. White intransigence would show no signs of abating over the coming months, and public officials in the South continued to tolerate and sometimes actively support acts of segregationist violence. The harassment from Georgia and Alabama officials would put King's commitment to nonviolent direct action to the test, and though the upcoming presidential elections promised the possibility of change, the major political parties appeared most concerned with accommodating their southern and conservative constituents. King's earlier clashes with NAACP general secretary Roy Wilkins and National Baptist Convention president J. H. Jackson continued, but for the first time he would face challenges from African American leaders who advocated alternative strategies for achieving equality.[5] SCLC colleagues Ella J. Baker, James Lawson, and Fred Shuttlesworth had long served as friendly foils, attempting to persuade King of the importance of developing local movement leadership and engaging in head-on confrontations with segregation. But they would soon be joined by challengers, such as Robert F. Williams, a North Carolina NAACP official who publicly advocated retaliatory violence, as well as other black community leaders who were growing impatient with the federal government's failure to protect civil rights. Amidst these challenges and against a backdrop of public indifference, a student-led movement unexpectedly infused the southern civil rights struggle with new energy and pushed King toward greater militancy.

As he completed his convalescence in Montgomery during the fall of 1958, King decided that the time had finally come to undertake a tour of India to deepen his understanding of Gandhian principles and to assess the movement's legacy

3. King was stabbed by Izola Ware Curry, a woman who was later determined to be mentally disturbed. For more on the stabbing and the Youth March, see Introduction and King, Address at Youth March for Integrated Schools in Washington, D.C., Delivered by Coretta Scott King, in *Papers* 4:34–35 and 514–515, respectively.

4. MIA, "Program, third Annual Institute on Nonviolence and Social Change," 1 December–7 December 1958; see also "Conference Condemns Alabama Officials," *New York Amsterdam News,* 20 December 1958.

5. For more on tension between King and other black leaders, see Introduction, *Papers* 4:17–18 and 26.

through conversations with Gandhi's associates and exposure to their social projects.[6] Two years earlier Indian prime minister Jawaharlal Nehru had indicated to a group of American pacifists that he would welcome such a visit.[7] King's associates Rustin and Lawson had traveled to India, and he also knew and admired a number of African American leaders who had met with Gandhi—notably Howard Thurman in 1935, Benjamin Mays the following year, and Howard University dean William Stuart Nelson in 1946. Securing funds from the Christopher Reynolds Foundation, the MIA, SCLC, and his own Dexter congregation, King invited Alabama State College professor Lawrence D. Reddick, author of the recently completed King biography *Crusader Without Violence,* to accompany him and Coretta and to assist in drafting public addresses and press releases while in India.[8]

While King made travel plans from Montgomery, representatives of the American Friends Service Committee (AFSC) and the Gandhi Smarak Nidhi (Gandhi Memorial Fund), the co-sponsors of the visit, began arranging for King to meet with Indian officials and Gandhian activists during the five-week tour.[9] The Nidhi offered the services of a guide, Swami Vishwananda, and helped secure a letter of welcome from Prime Minister Jawaharlal Nehru.[10] Vishwananda's AFSC counterpart, James E. Bristol, director of the Quaker Centre in New Delhi, arranged the itinerary in consultation with Friends in Philadelphia and Bayard Rustin, who served as King's representative. After a visit with American embassy officials who "were most emphatic that under no circumstances" was he to leave King's company, Bristol warned his AFSC colleagues in the United States that the visit was attracting considerable interest in India from "all sorts of forces and movements." He noted that the significance of King's tour was heightened by the possibility that it would coincide with the visit of controversial African American entertainer

6. From the early days of the Montgomery bus boycott, King had pointed to the Indian independence struggle as a model for his own efforts in the South (see King, "The Montgomery Story," Address Delivered at the Forty-seventh Annual NAACP Convention, 27 June 1956, in *The Papers of Martin Luther King, Jr.*, vol. 3: *Birth of a New Age, December 1955–December 1956,* ed. Clayborne Carson, Stewart Burns, Susan Carson, Peter Holloran, Dana L. H. Powell [Berkeley: University of California Press, 1997], p. 307).

7. See Homer Alexander Jack to King, 27 December 1956, in *Papers* 3:496, 498; Dorothy M. Steere to King, 5 January 1957, and King to Steere, 31 January 1957, in *Papers* 4:115–116.

8. See King, "My Trip to the Land of Gandhi," July 1959, pp. 231–238 in this volume, and "The Kings Leave Country," *Dexter Echo,* 11 February 1959. James E. Bristol of the American Friends Service Committee (AFSC) later indicated that the Reynolds grant resulted from "Libby Holman Reynold's friendship with the Kings" (Bristol to Corinne B. Johnson, 10 March 1959, p. 139 in this volume). Reddick's *Crusader Without Violence: A Biography of Martin Luther King, Jr.* (New York: Harper & Brothers) appeared later in 1959. King initially considered extending his trip by meeting with Christian leaders in the Soviet Union but changed his mind shortly before leaving the United States, citing "the state of his health and the urgency of the racial conflict in the South" ("Dr. King Calls Off Russian Part of Trip," *Los Angeles Tribune,* 6 February 1959). In a later letter to the general secretary of the American Baptist Convention, King mentioned that his decision came after failing to gain "assurance that the Russian Baptists were participating in my coming. Without this assurance, the visit to Russia would have taken on too many political connotations" (King to Reuben E. Nelson, 23 March 1959, p. 158 in this volume).

9. James E. Bristol to Corinne B. Johnson, 30 December 1958.

10. See G. Ramachandran to King, 27 December 1958, in *Papers* 4:552–553, and Nehru to King, 14 January 1959, pp. 107–108 in this volume.

Paul Robeson, who had been feted in the Soviet Union and other countries after the United States Supreme Court overturned a government decision denying him a passport due to his alleged Communist ties. Bristol explained that Robeson and King were "THE two most important American Negroes in Indian eyes."[11]

On the morning of 29 January, King departed Montgomery for several engagements, including a visit with AFSC officials in Philadelphia on 2 February to work out last-minute details of the trip. That evening in New York he addressed the annual dinner of the War Resisters League (WRL), during which he praised the league's work and linked the domestic struggle for racial justice with the campaign for global disarmament: "What will be the ultimate value of having established social justice in a context where all people, Negro and White, are merely free to face destruction by strontium 90 or atomic war?"[12] Late the following evening, King and his traveling companions boarded their overseas flight at New York's Idlewild Airport. Reddick recalled that they "chatted for an hour or so" before Coretta King noticed her husband dozing and cradled his head as he reclined over several seats on the uncrowded plane—"There she was: the serene Madonna, strong and protective."[13]

After a brief stopover in London, the King party continued on a 6 February flight to Paris where Reddick had arranged a meeting with Richard Wright, the expatriate African American novelist he had known during his years in New York. Reddick recalled a far-reaching discussion about race and politics at Wright's apartment: "Coretta and I threw in a point now and then but we were content to observe the giants in intellectual action. Both were short and brown-skinned but Dick was intense, always reaching for a thought or phrase while Martin was relaxed and un-spirited." As the group grew more comfortable, there was much "giggling and cutting up, imitating first one, then another personal friend or public figure."[14] Reddick recounted that Wright's response to King "was never more enthusiastic about any person that the two of us had known." Wright told Reddick that King lacked "that preacher fakery that I always look for in those sermon-on-the-mount boys," and King later indicated his own enthusiasm for Wright: "Now, I really understand his writings. He can tell a story as vividly as he writes it." King asked Reddick to arrange a visit to Montgomery, but Wright died the following year.[15]

From Paris the group traveled to Zurich, where they missed a connecting flight to New Delhi when fog prevented the plane from landing. While hundreds of Indians waited in vain for King's arrival in India's capital, a later flight took them to Bombay on 9 February. The three travelers were shocked by their initial encounter

---

11. Robeson cancelled his trip to India after becoming ill in Moscow; however, Bristol was still concerned about the repercussions of King's visit to a nation that was resolutely nonaligned in the Cold War and had mulled the possibility of using United States Information Service personnel to help prepare press releases (Bristol to Johnson, 16 January 1959).

12. King, Address at the Thirty-sixth Annual Dinner of the War Resisters League, 2 February 1959, p. 122 in this volume; see also "Martin Luther King Addresses War Resisters League Dinner," *WRL News,* March–April 1959.

13. Reddick, "With King through India: A personal memoir," 1968.

14. Reddick, "With King through India."

15. Reddick, "With King through India."

with Indian poverty on the drive to Bombay's Taj Mahal Hotel. "The sight of emaciated human beings wearing only a dirty loincloth, picking through garbage cans both angered and depressed my husband," Coretta King wrote in her memoir. "Never, even in Africa, had we seen such abject, despairing poverty."[16] Although told that the Indian government discouraged begging, King himself remembered finding it difficult to resist pleas of desperation: "What can you do when an old haggard woman or a little crippled urchin comes up and motions to you that she is hungry?"[17] As would often be the case in his comments about India, King combined his observations with implicit criticisms of his own country: "They are poor, jammed together and half starved but they do not take it out on each other," he generalized. "They do not abuse each other—verbally or physically—as readily as we do."[18]

By the time the King party arrived at New Delhi's Palam Airport on 10 February, there was a smaller crowd of well-wishers and curious onlookers than had been waiting two days earlier, but the "press, news photographers, and news-reel cameramen were there in full force."[19] G. Ramachandran and Sucheta Kripalani of the Gandhi Smarak Nidhi greeted the party with garlands as they disembarked from their plane. After being escorted to the Janpath Hotel, King conducted his first press conference. "To other countries I may go as a tourist," he announced, "but to India I come as a pilgrim."[20] King commented on the impact of Gandhi's ideas on the Montgomery bus boycott and other southern protests. "We have found them to be effective and sustaining—they work!" he was quoted as saying. Although King conceded that not all African Americans shared his views on nonviolence, he affirmed that he had "come to look at non-violence as a philosophy of life."[21]

That evening the Kings and Reddick drove through guarded iron gates past flowered lawns to Nehru's residence, Teen Murti Bhavan, a classic sandstone structure built by the British. Nehru had accommodated his delayed guests by inviting them to join a previously scheduled dinner with Lady Mountbatten, wife of the last viceroy of India, as well as her daughter and Nehru's daughter, Indira Gandhi.[22] Holding loosely to an agenda they had worked out beforehand, the Kings and Reddick spoke to Nehru about the potential for nonviolent resistance in the area of international politics.[23] Reddick recalled that the prime minister "re-

16. Coretta Scott King, *My Life with Martin Luther King, Jr.* (New York: Holt, Rinehart and Winston, 1969), p. 173.

17. King, Draft, "My trip to India," April 1959. According to Coretta King, "Martin soon disobeyed these instructions and gave all the money he could to the forlorn humans who beseeched us" (*My Life with Martin Luther King, Jr.*, p. 174).

18. King, "My Trip to the Land of Gandhi," July 1959, p. 235 in this volume.

19. Bristol, "Notes from My Tour-Diary," in *With the Kings in India: A Souvenir of Dr. Martin Luther King's Visit to India, February–March 1959* (New Delhi: Gandhi National Memorial Fund, 1959), p. 8.

20. Reddick, Account of Press Conference in New Delhi on 10 February 1959, p. 126 in this volume; see also "Martin Luther King, Negro Leader, Pays Tribute to Gandhi," *American Reporter*, 13 February 1959.

21. "Dr. King Will Make Study of Gandhism," *The Hindustan Times*, 11 February 1959.

22. See King, Palm Sunday Sermon on Mohandas K. Gandhi Delivered at Dexter Avenue Baptist Church, 22 March 1959, p. 151 in this volume.

23. See "Notes for Conversation between King and Nehru," 10 February 1959, p. 130 in this volume.

sponded by saying that as an individual and follower of Gandhi he favored non-violent resistance in every phase of life—between persons, groups and nations; but as a head of state, in a world that had not accepted the non-violent principle, it would be folly for one country to go very far down that road alone."[24] Nevertheless, Nehru declared, India "should never give up trying to persuade other countries to adopt the non-violent approach to international affairs."[25]

Nehru also informed his guests about India's efforts to eliminate discrimination based on caste and defended the policy of giving preference to untouchables in competition for university admission. King recalled that when Reddick asked whether this constituted discrimination, Nehru admitted, "It may be," but argued it was India's "way of atoning for the centuries of injustices we have inflicted upon these people."[26] King later remarked that he was "surprised and delighted" that Indian leaders had "placed their moral power" behind antidiscrimination laws protecting untouchables while "in the United States some of our highest officials decline to render a moral judgment on segregation and some from the South publicly boast of their determination to maintain segregation."[27] Following this discussion, Nehru considered the King party's suggestion of offering scholarships for black students to attend Indian universities but admitted he had not yet considered the notion of "poor" India offering scholarships to "rich" America.[28]

King came away from the discussion impressed by Nehru as "an intellectual and a man charged with the practical responsibility of heading the government" and someone seeking to "steer a middle course" between Gandhi's emphasis on local economic self-sufficiency and western-style modernization. Nehru, he explained, "felt that some industrialization was absolutely necessary" and believed that "pitfalls" could be avoided "if the state keeps a watchful eye on the developments."[29] Reddick remembered the four hours of conversation as "a wonderful evening" and contrasted the warm reception with the fact that "Martin had never been to dinner in the White House."[30]

Continuing on their busy schedule, the Kings visited Rajghat the following day to lay a wreath on the site of Gandhi's cremation. Bristol recalled that they were "obviously deeply moved" and that Martin "knelt in prayer" following the

---

24. Reddick, "With King through India." For more on the differences between Gandhi's belief in nonviolence and Nehru's, see King, "The Negro Is Part of That Huge Community Who Seek New Freedom in Every Area of Life," 1 February 1959, and King, Interview on "Front Page Challenge," 28 April 1959, pp. 119 and 193–194 in this volume, respectively.

25. Reddick, "With King through India"; see also "Notes for Conversation between King and Nehru," 10 February 1959, p. 130 in this volume.

26. King, *Why We Can't Wait* (New York: Harper and Row, 1963), p. 135.

27. King, "My Trip to the Land of Gandhi," July 1959, p. 236 in this volume. For more on King's admiration for Indian policies toward its untouchables, see note 4 to Address at the Religious Leaders Conference, 11 May 1959, and King, Palm Sunday Sermon on Mohandas K. Gandhi, 22 March 1959, pp. 197 and 145–157 in this volume, respectively.

28. Reddick, "With King through India"; see also "Notes for Conversation between King and Nehru," 10 February 1959, p. 130 in this volume.

29. King, "My Trip to the Land of Gandhi," July 1959, p. 236 in this volume.

30. Reddick, "With King through India."

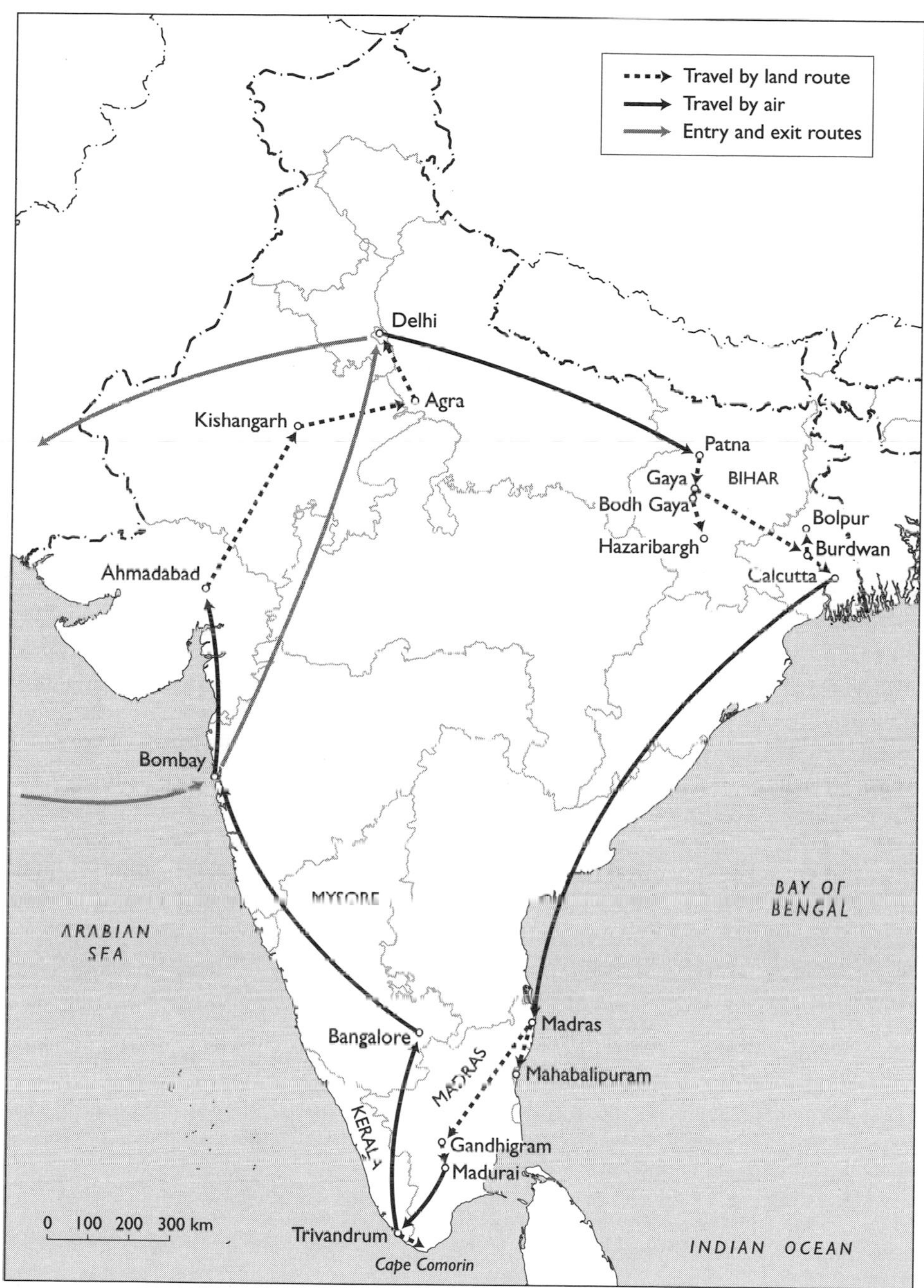

Map of India listing the stops King made during his 9 February to 10 March 1959 tour

ceremony.[31] In Delhi the King party also met with India's president, Rajendra Prasad, and its vice president, Sarvepalli Radhakrishnan.[32] Particularly impressed by the latter talk with the "philosopher-politician," Coretta King noted that her husband compared the sessions with India's leaders to "meeting George Washington, Thomas Jefferson, and James Madison in a single day."[33]

On 13 February the Kings left Delhi for Patna, and over the next week they visited a number of cities including Gaya, Calcutta, and Madras. Bristol recounted that during a train ride from Patna to Gaya, in the state of Bihar, King visited with socialist activist Jayaprakash Narayan, who outlined his ideas on decentralism.[34] Bristol also reported on the visits to two Gramdan (cooperatively owned) villages where the party experienced rural life, eating seated "on the ground from banana leaves," and a student meeting in Madras that was "among the best in the entire trip."[35] Vishwananda would later describe Martin King as "impressed" and Coretta "moved" by their visit to Gandhigram, an institute for rural development, where "five-hundred-strong *Shantisena* [Peace Army] in spotless white *khadi* received Dr. King and gave him the salute."[36]

The enthusiastic reception King received in Trivandrum on 22 February had special importance given its status as the capital of Kerala, the only Indian state with a Communist government and the only state not governed by Nehru's Congress Party. Bristol noted the contrast between the warm reception accorded King and that given to New York governor Averell Harriman's arrival two days later: "Then there was only the one government representative on hand; nobody else; no garlands, no bouquets, no photographers. King's tour was popular and triumphal as Harriman's was not."[37] Unplanned incidents made indelible impressions on King. Years later he recalled that when a principal of a school attended largely by children of former untouchables introduced him as "a fellow untouchable," he was at first "a bit shocked and peeved," but he then reflected on the "airtight cage of poverty" that afflicted African Americans "in rat-infested, unendurable slums in the big cities of our nation, still attended inadequate schools faced with improper recreational facilities. And I said to myself, 'Yes, I am an untouchable, and every Negro in the United States of America is an untouchable.'"[38]

---

31. Bristol, "Notes from My Tour-Diary." Reddick recalled of the wreath laying: "A picture of that went around the world and we were told that the 'Today,' morning TV show, had a five minutes clip about it" ("With King through India").

32. Bristol to Johnson, 20 March 1959.

33. Coretta Scott King, *My Life with Martin Luther King, Jr.*, p. 176.

34. For more on King's visit with Narayan, see King to Jayaprakash Narayan, 19 May 1959, pp. 209–211 in this volume.

35. Bristol to Johnson, 20 March 1959.

36. Vishwananda, "I Go Round with the Kings," in *With the Kings in India: A Souvenir of Dr. Martin Luther King's Visit to India, February–March 1959* (New Delhi: Gandhi National Memorial Fund, 1959), pp. 5–6; see also Bristol to Johnson, 20 March 1959.

37. Bristol to Johnson, 20 March 1959. Harriman, who had visited King in the hospital while he recuperated from his 1958 stabbing, was studying the Soviet Union's impact on India. He had met with the Kings in Delhi soon after their arrival. For coverage of the public meeting on 23 February, see "Emancipation of Negroes: 'Non-violence the Only Way,'" *The Hindu* (Madras), 25 February 1959; see also K. Krishnan Nair to King, 5 October 1959.

38. King, "The American Dream," Sermon delivered at Ebenezer Baptist Church, 4 July 1965.

King also had lasting memories of his brief journey to nearby Cape Comorin at India's southern tip late one afternoon: "It is one of the most beautiful points in all the world," he later told his Dexter congregation. At the convergence of the Bay of Bengal, the Indian Ocean, and the Arabian Sea, he remembered sitting on a rock, watching the sun set "like it was sinking in the very ocean itself." After the sky darkened, he noticed a full moon rising in the east: "This is one of the few points in all the world that you can see the setting of the sun and the emergence of the moon simultaneously." King drew spiritual significance from the serene surroundings: "For when it was dark and tragedy around, seemed that the light of day had gone out, darkness all around and sunlight passing away, I got enough strength in my being to turn around and only to discover that God had another light. This would be a tragic universe if God had only one light."[39]

By the time they flew to Bangalore on 24 February, Bristol recognized that their schedule had been too ambitious, resulting in cancelled or delayed meetings and some frustration on the part of Indians who were eager to meet King. In reports that evening and the following day that were forwarded to AFSC headquarters, he indicated that they had trimmed the itinerary into "the sort of schedule King had in mind." Bristol observed that "both the Kings (especially King himself) are JUST PLAIN EXHAUSTED and very understandably have been so for months before coming to India."[40] Bristol's account of the three days in Bombay suggests that the reduced schedule suited King. Moving from the luxurious accommodations they had in Calcutta and Madras, the party chose Mani Bhavan, Gandhi's Bombay residence, where they "enjoyed simple accommodations in an authentically Gandhian atmosphere." King left his impressions in the Mani Bhavan guest book: "To have the opportunity of sleeping in the house where Gandhiji slept is an experience that I will never forget."[41] A public meeting on 27 February attracted "about 400 really top-calibre people," including former U.S. ambassador G. L. Mehta, to King's "inspired" presentation.[42] The following day King met with African students studying in Bombay who challenged him regarding the effectiveness of nonviolence. "They felt that non-violent resistance could only work in a situation where the resisters had a potential ally in the conscience of the opponent," King later reflected in *Ebony* magazine. "We soon discovered that they, like many others, tended to confuse passive resistance with non-resistance."[43] Traveling north to Ahmadabad on 1 March, the King party went to the Sabarmati ashram, which had been founded by Gandhi and was where he began his 1930 Salt March to the sea to protest British taxation of salt. Vishwananda recalled that "the Kings had a great experience going round the hallowed place and meeting in prayer the six hundred" residents, many of whom were untouchables.[44]

On 3 March, King rose early for a drive toward Kishangarh, where the party was scheduled to meet with Acharya Vinoba Bhave, the leader of the Bhoodan

---

39. King, A Walk Through the Holy Land, Easter Sunday Sermon Delivered at Dexter Avenue Baptist Church, 29 March 1959, pp. 173–174 in this volume.

40. Bristol to Dorothy Bristol, 24 February–25 February 1959.

41. For a facsimile of King's 29 February guest book entry, see p. 134 in this volume.

42. Bristol to Johnson, 20 March 1959.

43. King "My Trip to the Land of Gandhi," July 1959, p. 234 in this volume.

44. Vishwananda, "I Go Round with the Kings," p. 7.

(land distribution) movement and Gandhi's spiritual successor. Just outside of town they met up with the peripatetic Vinoba and a group of his followers who traveled India on foot, persuading landlords to provide land to the poor. Reddick recalled that Vinoba embraced King, and the two men walked together, Vinoba shortening "his long strides in order that Martin could keep up."[45] After the marchers entered Kishangarh, Vinoba addressed local residents and then retired to his room in a school building, where King presented questions to him. During this structured exchange, which was later reported in the weekly *Bhoodan,* Vinoba replied to King's query about his "hopes for the future" by insisting that "either there will be 'Kingdom of Kindness' or there will be no society."[46] Vinoba declined King's request for a message "for the United States in terms of racial justice and world peace," stating that he would not "be so presumptuous as to send a message to a Christian nation." But Vinoba did advise Americans to "simply follow Jesus Christ" rather than "listen to flocks of sermons."[47]

Although Vinoba abruptly ended the morning interview by announcing, "I have finished your questions," King was granted a less formal audience in the evening. During this later meeting, King talked about Montgomery and pressed Vinoba about the limitations of nonviolence. Given that totalitarian regimes "are composed of human beings" rather than people of "a different species," Vinoba maintained that "non-violence and its effective appeal to others requires faith. Mere argument and persuasion is not enough."[48] King was greatly affected by the hours he spent with Vinoba, whom he later called "sainted." While conceding that his ideas "sound strange and archaic to Western ears," he was impressed that "millions of acres of land have been given up by rich landlords and additional millions of acres have been given up to cooperative management by small farmers." He also observed that "the Bhoodanists shrink from giving their movement the organization and drive that we in America would venture to guess that it must have in order to keep pace with the magnitude of the problems that everybody is trying to solve."[49]

As the visit entered its final week, Bristol had hoped that the Kings and Reddick would spend two more days with Vinoba, but the group went back to Delhi ahead of schedule. Disappointed that other events did not go as expected during the remaining four days of the tour, Bristol complained vehemently to Friends in Philadelphia that the trip had been "ARRANGED AT TOO SHORT NOTICE" and had suffered from "insufficient communication (worse than that, practically no communication) between [the] Kings and AFSC." Bristol observed that the Kings possessed a "fanatical interest in snapshots" and "newspaper publicity" and concluded that "one of the motives clearly appeared to be to build up King as a world figure, and to have this build-up recorded in the US." Both Bristol and his AFSC

---

45. Reddick, "With King through India."

46. Vinoba Bhave, "Dr. Martin Luther King with Vinoba," *Bhoodan* 3 (18 March 1959): 369–370.

47. Bristol to Johnson, 17 April 1959.

48. Bristol to Johnson, 17 April 1959; see also Bristol to Johnson, 16 April 1959.

49. King, "My Trip to the Land of Gandhi," July 1959, p. 237 in this volume. At his farewell press reception the following week, King called Vinoba "a great spiritual man, moving in a humble way to keep the spirit of Gandhiji's philosophy alive" ("Mahatma's Spirit Lives in India," *Hindustan Times,* 9 March 1959).

colleagues suspected Rustin's heavy hand in seeking to use the trip to enhance King's profile and increase his political capital.[50] Despite Bristol's criticisms of some aspects of the trip, he reported that "the net effect of the King trip seems to have been very, very good!"[51]

On 9 March, his last full day in India, King delivered a farewell address to reporters gathered at the Gandhi Smarak Nidhi and then recorded similar remarks for broadcast on All India Radio. Thanking those who had made his "short stay both pleasant and instructive," he remarked that he and his traveling companions would not be "rash enough to presume that we know India." Nonetheless, he suggested "that the spirit of Gandhi is much stronger today than some people believe." He then offered his most controversial public pronouncement of the India tour by repeating Vinoba Bhave's suggestion that India disarm unilaterally: "It may be that just as India had to take the lead and show the world that national independence could be achieved nonviolently, so India may have to take the lead and call for universal disarmament."[52]

Reflecting on his trip a few months later, King reiterated his call for aid to India: "It is in the interest of the United States and the West to help supply these needs and *not attach strings to the gifts*."[53] Touched by India's reception of him "with open arms," King related that Gandhians had "praised our experiment with the non-violent resistance technique at Montgomery." The tour party had been looked "upon as brothers with the color of our skins as something of an asset," but "the strongest bond of fraternity was the common cause of minority and colonial peoples in America, Africa and Asia struggling to throw off racialism and imperialism."[54] Buttressing his calls for nonviolence in the United States, King elaborated on his discussions with skeptical African students in India: "While I understand the reasons why oppressed people often turn to violence in their struggle for freedom, it is my firm belief that the crusade for independence and human

50. Bristol to Johnson, 10 March 1959, pp. 137–142 in this volume; see also Bristol to Johnson, 22 April 1959, and Johnson to Bristol, 26 March 1959. A subsequent AFSC report on the trip attributed some of the problems to the "last minute" changes and to the difficulty of scheduling because "communication had to be almost exclusively through a third person, Bayard Rustin" (AFSC, Report on Martin Luther King's trip to India," 4 May 1959).

51. Bristol to Johnson, 27 March 1959.

52. King, Farewell Statement for All India Radio, 9 March 1959, pp. 135–136 in this volume.

53. King, "My Trip to the Land of Gandhi," July 1959, p. 237 in this volume.

54. King, "My Trip to the Land of Gandhi," July 1959, pp. 233–234 in this volume; see also King, Draft, "My trip to India," April 1959. Bristol also remarked later that Indians had not regarded King as an American, but "as the champion of the oppressed peoples of the world—in America, Asia and Africa" (Bristol to Johnson, 11 March 1959). Reddick similarly returned convinced that King was "better understood in India than in America" and that King's experiences in India had caused him to "realize some of the changes that will be necessary if his movement in the South is to wipe out racial segregation without violence and bloodshed" (Press release, "Reddick returns from India; now understands King," 18 March–28 March 1959). In his 1968 memoir, "With King through India," Reddick concluded that India was "a turning point" in King's development. Previously King "had something of a reputation—especially with black folk and white liberals." But "he had reason to wonder how he would be received in Gandhi's homeland where the people really knew the meaning of nonviolence." Rather than an "impostor," Reddick concluded that King "was accepted as the real thing" and had become "the leading, living exponent of the Mahatma's theory and practice."

dignity that is now reaching a climax in Africa will have a more positive effect on the world, if it is waged along the lines that were first demonstrated in that continent by Gandhi himself." King also gave implicit support to India's effort to find a middle road between capitalism and communism, predicting that India could "be a boon to democracy" by proving "that it is possible to provide a good living for everyone without surrendering to a dictatorship of either the 'right' or 'left.'" King depicted India as "a tremendous force for peace and non-violence . . . where the idealist and the intellectual are yet respected. We should want to help India preserve her soul and thus help to save our own."[55]

Departing from Delhi on 10 March, the Kings flew to Karachi, Pakistan, and continued to Beirut, Lebanon, where they spent the night before traveling through Damascus to Jerusalem. His brief tour of the Middle East gave King an opportunity to increase his awareness of the ongoing conflict between Israel and the surrounding Arab states. In a sermon preached a few weeks after the trip, King avoided taking a stand on the Arab-Israeli conflict, but he noted its consequences in the partitioned city: "And so this was a strange feeling to go to the ancient city of God and see the tragedies of man's hate and his evil, which causes him to fight and live in conflict."[56]

King's pilgrimage to Jerusalem's holy sites was typical of the "Stations of the Cross" guided tours taken by Christian visitors, although his theological and biblical studies deepened the meaning of his observations and strengthened his identification with the travails of Jesus. King visited the Garden of Gethsemane, the reputed site of Jesus's betrayal by his disciple Judas Iscariot, and later reflected on tragic aspects of the garden of life when "even those people that we have confidence in and that we believe in and we call our friends fail to understand us. And in the most difficult moments of life they leave us going the road alone." The story of Simon of Cyrene helping Jesus carry the cross became a metaphor for the freedom struggles of the world's colored people: "And in all of our struggles for peace and security, freedom and human dignity, one day God will remember that it was a black man who aided his only begotten son in the darkest hour of his life." At the Church of the Holy Sepulchre, according to tradition the site of Jesus's crucifixion, King recalled an epiphany: "There was something that overwhelmed me, and before I knew it I was on my knees praying . . . I was weeping. This was a great world-shaking, transfiguring experience."[57]

Upon returning home from his travels on 21 March, King confronted SCLC's continued ineffectiveness. Fund-raising efforts had attracted only slightly more than two thousand dollars in contributions during the period from December 1958

55. King, "My Trip to the Land of Gandhi," July 1959, pp. 231–238 in this volume.

56. King, A Walk Through the Holy Land, 29 March 1959, p. 165 in this volume. In a letter to Bristol, he reported talking "with many people concerning the Arab Israeli problem," which he described as "still one of the most difficult problems of the world" (King to Bristol, 30 March 1959, p. 176 in this volume).

57. King, A Walk Through the Holy Land, 29 March 1959, pp. 164–175 in this volume.

through the end of March 1959, and the group's depleted financial resources were insufficient to cover the salaries of associate director Ella Baker and executive director John Tilley.[58] Much of the blame for SCLC failings fell on Tilley, who found it difficult to balance his organizational responsibilities in Atlanta with the needs of his congregation at Baltimore's New Metropolitan Baptist Church. When Jesse Hill, the chair of Atlanta's All-Citizens Registration Committee, reported to King early in 1959 on SCLC's local efforts, he pointedly called attention to Tilley's periods of absence from the city and noted that "registration efforts require experienced direction from day to day."[59] King defended Tilley, but the issue of his future was a prime topic for discussion when SCLC's administrative committee met on 2 April.[60] Lawrence Reddick's notes of the meeting suggest that King and other SCLC leaders had already decided that Tilley should be dismissed. The committee also recognized that SCLC's poor financial situation necessitated severe personnel cutbacks and decided that only Baker should be retained "at a reduced salary."[61]

The administrative committee also discussed the more general question of how to reinvigorate SCLC and the southern civil rights movement. Reddick's notes reveal that King's suggestion that Rustin join SCLC's staff prompted *Birmingham World* editor Emory O. Jackson to label Rustin a communist. Reddick recalled that he "pointed out the dangers of the 'enemy' using" Rustin's brief membership in the Communist Party and his homosexuality "to smear SCLC" and recommended using him exclusively in unofficial capacities.[62] Given their inability to find a minister to replace Tilley immediately, Baker again assumed the executive leadership of the organization, a capacity in which she had served before his hiring the previous year.

The following day SCLC leaders discussed King's own commitment to the organization. According to Reddick, Baker "really came to lay him out and abuse him" for not spending enough time on SCLC. King defended himself against the charge that he was spending too much time delivering speeches by insisting "that an artist . . . not be denied his means of expression," but Reddick noted that Baker's complaints resonated with his own suggestions to King—made while they were traveling in India—that he would have to choose between devoting himself "full time to Crusading" or retaining his salary as Dexter's pastor. Reddick predicted that King would never give up being a clergyman and thus would remain "a crusader in a gray flannel suit" rather than becoming "a Vinoba Bhave."[63]

After the meetings King quickly informed Tilley of the committee's decision and explained that it resulted from "the financial crisis confronting the organi-

58. Ralph Abernathy, Financial report, 2 April 1959.

59. Jesse Hill, Jr. to King, 19 January 1959.

60. See King to Hill, 28 January 1959, pp. 114–115 in this volume.

61. Reddick, Notes on SCLC Administrative Committee Meetings on 2 April and 3 April 1959, p. 177 in this volume.

62. Reddick, Notes, p. 177 in this volume. Rustin had briefly been a member of the Young Communist League in the 1930s and was convicted of engaging in a homosexual act in the 1950s.

63. Reddick, Notes, pp. 178–179 in this volume.

zation" and Tilley's failure "to achieve the public response expected."[64] As Tilley made clear when he submitted his resignation, SCLC's problems resulted from more than the deficiencies of one individual. Cautioning that the achievement of SCLC's goals would "require time and patience," Tilley offered a list of the daunting obstacles facing the group, including "the limited staff for the many varied demands, the non-spectacular nature of the educational process, and the lack of funds."[65]

Despite SCLC's internal crisis and Baker's criticisms, King resumed his busy speaking schedule as well as his pastoral obligations. On 18 April he was once again in the national spotlight as the concluding speaker at the second Youth March for Integrated Schools. Black labor leader A. Philip Randolph and Rustin had been sufficiently encouraged by the 1958 Youth March to plan a larger demonstration that would mobilize young people throughout the nation to circulate petitions urging the Eisenhower administration and Congress to implement the Supreme Court's *Brown v. Board of Education* decision.[66] Although Roy Wilkins feared that the Youth March might compete with the NAACP's efforts, Randolph assured him that the march was intended simply as "an ad hoc project" and would not result in a permanent organization.[67] With King's help, Randolph and Rustin managed to secure widespread support for the event, including the backing of the National Student Association and other campus-based groups.[68] Indeed, as support for the march increased during the spring of 1959, march organizers became concerned about the involvement of the Socialist Workers Party, prompting them to issue a statement repudiating rumors that "anti-American" demonstrators might picket the White House and discouraging "the participation of these groups" and "individuals or other organizations holding similar views."[69]

On the morning of the protest, a four-student delegation marched to the gates

---

64. King to Tilley, 3 April 1959, p. 180 in this volume. Writing to an associate a few months later, King was more frank regarding Tilley's departure: "The actual fact is that Rev. Tilley was forced to resign by the Board because he was not producing. We were kind enough not to let this out to the public, and we said to Rev. Tilley that we would protect his name and reputation at every point" (King to Theodore E. Brown, 19 October 1959, p. 311 in this volume).

65. Tilley to King, 13 April 1959, p. 000 in this volume.

66. Randolph and Rustin, "Interim report," 30 December 1958; see also "Expect 100,000 Signatures Urging Integrated Schools," *Chicago Defender*, 11 April 1959, and Youth March for Integrated Schools, "A call for a petition campaign and Youth March for Integrated Schools," January 1959. SCLC became a sponsor of the Youth March but did not provide financial support until after the march, when it agreed to send $200 to help cover the organizers' remaining debt (see King, Recommendations to the SCLC Executive Committee, 30 September 1959, pp. 295–297 in this volume). In contrast, the NAACP contributed $3,000 to the Youth March (Wilkins to Randolph, 14 April 1959).

67. Wilkins to Randolph, 26 May 1959, and Randolph to Wilkins, 5 June 1959.

68. Rustin to Friend, 19 February 1959, and Youth March for Integrated Schools, Press release, 16 March 1959.

69. The press release announced that the sponsors had "not invited Communists or communist organizations," adding that members of the Ku Klux Klan and White Citizens' Councils would also not be welcome at the march (Youth March for Integrated Schools, "Anti-American groups not invited to Youth March for Integrated Schools," 17 April 1959).

of the White House where Gerald Morgan, Eisenhower's deputy assistant, informed them that the president was not there but, nonetheless, shared their concerns and would not "be satisfied until the last vestige of discrimination has disappeared."[70] After a fifteen-minute conversation with Morgan, the delegation joined more than twenty thousand other marchers, including King, who sang "We Shall Not Be Moved" as they walked toward the Sylvan Theater on the grounds of the Washington Monument. Opening the program, Randolph promised to return to Washington "again and again" until blacks were given equal education and civil rights laws were passed.[71] After speeches by Wilkins, Kenyan labor leader Tom Mboya, and entertainer Harry Belafonte, King took the stage to give a brief address.[72] Returning to the theme of voting rights that had marked his speech at the 1957 Prayer Pilgrimage in Washington, he stated that SCLC intended to increase the number of black registered voters in the South to three million. This, he asserted, would "change the composition of Congress," opening the way for school desegregation. King acknowledged the students' growing interest in racial equality and declared that "a hundred years from now the historians will be calling this not the 'beat' generation, but the generation of integration."[73]

There is little evidence that the Youth March had much impact on Eisenhower or on Congress, which failed to pass proposed legislation that would have bolstered the 1957 Civil Rights Act. Nonetheless, the mobilization of protesters strengthened the organizational links between SCLC, the labor movement, and other social reform organizations. Furthermore, participation in the march provided thousands of young people with an outlet for their support of integration. Michael Harrington, Eleanor Norton, Jack O'Dell, Tom Kahn, Norman Hill, Robert Moses, and dozens of other young activists who would later become key figures in the civil rights movement gained important organizing experience working with Rustin and other organizers. King left Washington to deliver a series of sermons and speeches in the Chicago area and New York. Over the next several weeks he also appeared on the Canadian television program "Front Page Challenge" before returning to Washington to address the Conference of Religious Leaders sponsored by the President's Committee on Government Contracts.[74] Events in the South that spring, however, served as a reminder of racist intransigence while underscoring the need for SCLC to take bolder steps to force the federal government to protect black civil rights. On the evening of 24 April, a twenty-three-year-old rape suspect, Mack Charles Parker, was seized from a jail in Poplarville,

---

70. "Integration Rally Here Assured Ike Seeks End of Racial Bias," *Washington Post,* 19 April 1959; see also "Ike Won't See Belafonte with Youth Leaders," *Jet,* 23 April 1959, p. 3, and "Eisenhower Cites Integration Goal," *New York Times,* 19 April 1959.

71. Sara Slack, "30,000 in March: Belafonte, Mboya Stampede Crowd," *New York Amsterdam News,* 25 April 1959. Joining King at the front of the march were Randolph, Wilkins, Daisy Bates, Dorothy Height, Jean Noble, Joseph Overton, William Oliver, Gardner Taylor, and William Bowe.

72. Youth March for Integrated Schools, "Program at the Sylvan Theater," 18 April 1959, and Slack, "30,000 in March."

73. King, Address at the Youth March for Integrated Schools on 18 April 1959, p. 187 in this volume.

74. See King, Interview on "Front Page Challenge," 28 April 1959, and King, Address at the Religious Leaders Conference on 11 May 1959, pp. 191–194 and 197–202 in this volume, respectively.

Mississippi; his body was found ten days later in the Pearl River near the Louisiana border. A week later, a black college student in Tallahassee, Florida, was abducted while on a double date and brutally raped by four white men. From Birmingham Fred Shutlesworth, the embattled activist minister, reported on a rash of racist kidnappings and assaults over the previous few days. Urging SCLC to adopt more aggressive protest strategies, Shuttlesworth warned King: "I believe that time is running out for this thing to be done."[75]

King's meetings with Indian leaders and, earlier, with Ghanaian prime minister Kwame Nkrumah, strengthened his belief that the southern struggle was part of a worldwide movement against racist oppression and colonialism.[76] His identification with African freedom struggles was solidified in Atlanta on 13 May when he introduced Kenyan labor leader and legislator Tom Mboya during an SCLC-sponsored dinner honoring Mboya's work toward independence from Great Britain. King located the U.S. civil rights movement within the "worldwide revolution for freedom and justice" and explained "we are all caught in an inescapable network of mutuality. And whatever affects one directly affects all indirectly."[77] In his reply to a 16 June letter from Mboya, King continued this line of thought, noting that "there is no basic difference between colonialism and segregation. They are both based on a contempt for life, and a tragic doctrine of white supremacy. So our struggles are not only similiar; they are in a real sense one."[78] These links to anticolonial struggles were more than rhetorical expressions of goodwill; they fortified King's domestic civil rights agenda. King's

---

75. Shuttlesworth to King, 24 April 1959, p. 189 in this volume. King and SCLC demanded an investigation of Parker's lynching in two telegrams sent 25 April to attorney general William Rogers and Mississippi governor James P. Coleman. For more on the Parker case, see King to Coleman, 25 April 1959, pp. 190–191 in this volume. King also offered support to Florida A&M students who staged demonstrations in response to the rape (see King to Clifford Taylor, 5 May 1959, p. 196 in this volume).

76. Bayard Rustin, drawing upon his extensive links to non-Communist left movements, facilitated many of King's contacts with African, Indian, and European activists.

77. King, Remarks Delivered at Africa Freedom Dinner at Atlanta University, 13 May 1959, p. 204 in this volume.

78. King to Mboya, 8 July 1959, p. 243 in this volume. King later secured, at Mboya's urging and with support from SCLC and Dexter Church, a financial sponsorship for Nicolas W. Raballa, one of eighty-one Kenyan students receiving scholarships to American colleges and universities (Mboya to King, 31 July 1959; King to William X. Scheinman, 18 August 1959; and Harry Belafonte, Jackie Robinson, and Sidney Poitier to King, 13 November 1959). Raballa maintained an active correspondence with King while at Tuskegee Institute, mainly concerning his poor financial circumstances. King also maintained ties to the American Committee on Africa, lending his name to fund-raising appeals and protest statements. After his trip to Ghana, he was increasingly viewed by Africans as an international symbol for justice (see for example, King, Introduction to *Southwest Africa: The UN's Stepchild,* pp. 298–299 in this volume; King to Friend, 12 November 1959; and King to Homer Alexander Jack, 27 November 1959). Early in 1960 King became a signatory on a letter to the Eisenhower administration urging action against the government of South Africa after the Sharpeville Massacre (Americans for Democratic Action, Press release, 17 April 1960; see also King to Claude Barnett, 24 March 1960, pp. 399–400 in this volume). For King's growing stature among Africans, see King to Albert Lutuli, 8 December 1959, and King to Deolinda Rodrigues, 21 July and 21 December 1959, pp. 344–345, 250–251, and 345–346 in this volume, respectively.

speeches and correspondence with public officials during this period increasingly cited American cold war vulnerabilities as a reason for reform. Writing to Eisenhower shortly before Soviet premier Nikita Khrushchev's visit, King suggested that "it would be tragic should his visit coincide with tension and violence accompanying the desegregation of some schools." The following year he warned an audience in Charlotte that "the price that America must pay for the continued oppression of the Negro is the price of its own destruction." He added that his recent travels had left him convinced that "America is at its lowest ebb in international prestige; and most of this loss of prestige is due to our failure to grapple with the problem of racial injustice."[79]

Even as the international implications of nonviolent protest became a more central part of his oratory, King's long-term optimism was chastened by his realization that he must demonstrate that Gandhian principles could become a basis for an effective civil rights reform strategy. The steady prodding he received from Baker and Shuttlesworth only offered hints of the unexpected challenge he faced from Robert F. Williams, the NAACP branch leader who had organized an armed self-defense group in Monroe, North Carolina. In May Williams attracted considerable press attention when he called for retaliation when an all-white jury acquitted a white man accused of raping a black woman.[80] After the NAACP's national office suspended Williams, he appealed his case to delegates attending the group's national convention in July. King's address at the convention provided an opportunity to reaffirm his own commitment to nonviolence. "We all realize that there will probably be some sporatic violence during this period of transition, and people will naturally seek to protect their property and person," he explained, "but for the Negro to privately or publicly call for retaliatory violence as a strategy during this period would be the gravest tragedy that could befall us."[81]

Although Wilkins was able to convince delegates to uphold his suspension of Williams, King felt there was a need to elaborate on the issues that had been raised. He accepted an invitation from *Liberation* magazine to respond to Williams's article arguing that nonviolence was an unrealistic strategy for African Americans. While praising King as "a great and successful leader of our race," Williams insisted that nonviolence was "made to order" for the Montgomery bus boycott but cautioned that black southerners often confronted "the necessity of combating savage violence."[82]

Facing an articulate protagonist, King fashioned a thoughtful defense of his position. Conceding some ground to Williams, he acknowledged that the "principle of self-defense, even involving weapons and bloodshed, has never been condemned, even by Gandhi, who sanctioned it for those unable to master pure nonviolence." He nonetheless saw "incalculable perils" in Williams's approach, arguing

79. King to Dwight D. Eisenhower, 13 August 1959, and King, "The Negro and the American Dream," Excerpt from Address at the Annual Freedom Mass Meeting of the North Carolina State Conference of Branches of the NAACP, 25 September 1960, p. 263 and 509 in this volume, respectively.

80. "N.A.A.C.P. Leader Urges 'Violence,'" *New York Times,* 7 May 1959.

81. King, Address at the Fiftieth Annual NAACP Convention, 17 July 1959, p. 248 in this volume.

82. Williams, "Can Negroes Afford to Be Pacifists?" *Liberation* 4 (September 1959): 4–7.

that it would "mislead Negroes into the belief that this is the only path and place them as a minority in a position where they confront a far larger adversary than it is possible to defeat in this form of combat." King insisted that his own nonviolent approach offered a workable alternative to violence. Recognizing that armed self-defense and retaliation had long been accepted strategies for self-preservation among southern African Americans, King insisted that "persistent and unyielding" protest required "bold" and "brave" activists: "It requires dedicated people, because it is a backbreaking task to arouse, to organize, and to educate tens of thousands for disciplined, sustained action. From this form of struggle more emerges that is permanent and damaging to the enemy than from a few acts of organized violence." He concluded by defending himself against Williams's charge that his opposition to war should have included nuclear war. "I have unequivocally declared my hatred for this most colossal of all evils and I have condemned any organizer of war, regardless of his rank or nationality," he wrote. "I have signed numerous statements with other Americans condemning nuclear testing and have authorized publication of my name in advertisements appearing in the largest circulation newspapers in the country, without concern that it was then 'unpopular' to so speak out."[83]

King felt similarly compelled to respond to the growing notoriety of the black separatist group Nation of Islam, who were brought to the attention of the general public through a highly publicized television documentary and a *Time* magazine feature in the late summer. Speaking to the National Bar Association in Milwaukee, King warned against "hate groups arising in our midst" and cautioned that it was necessary to "avoid both external physical violence and internal violence of spirit."[84]

The challenges from the militants provided King another indication that he could not take for granted his preeminent position in the southern civil rights struggle. Looking to the end of its third year, SCLC had done little to stimulate mass protest and insurgency. King had applauded signs of increased student activism in his speeches at the second Youth March for Integrated Schools and at the NAACP convention on 17 July, but his own organization had not initiated or sustained any protest movements. His public statements continued to define a modest mission for the group. "This organization came into being in order to serve as a channel through which local protest organizations in the South could coordinate their ac-

83. King, "The Social Organization of Nonviolence," October 1959, pp. 299–304 in this volume. For more on King's support of antinuclear efforts, see Norman Cousins and Clarence Pickett to King, 9 March 1958, in *Papers* 4:379–380, and "Humanity Has a Common Will and Right to Survive," *New York Times,* 13 August 1959. Williams's challenge to King's nonviolent strategy would continue long after the exchange in *Liberation.* A few months after King's article appeared, the *Southern Patriot,* published by the Southern Conference Educational Fund (SCEF), ran it in its January 1960 issue alongside Williams's piece as a "great debate," with the headline "Is Violence Necessary to Combat Injustice?" For a facsimile, see p. 300 in this volume.

84. King, Address at the Thirty-fourth Annual Convention of the National Bar Association, 20 August 1959, pp. 268–269 in this volume.

tivities," he explained to a Mississippi audience during September. Although King ambitiously described SCLC's "basic aim" as the implementation of "the Supreme Court's desegregation decisions on the local level through mass, direct, non-violent action," he added that "at the present time" the group was "joining with other organizations to increase the number of Negro registered voters in the South."[85] But even in the field of voter registration, King could point to few achievements. When the executive committee met in Columbia, South Carolina, on 30 September he admitted to his colleagues that "we have not really scratched the surface in this area," blaming the failure on the lack of "any genuine cooperation and coordination between national and local organizations working to increase the vote," a reference to the continuing tensions in SCLC's relations with the NAACP.[86]

The discussion in South Carolina focused not only on SCLC's future direction but also on the concern Baker had raised the previous April—that is, King's part-time leadership. Committee members quickly agreed that King should "seriously consider giving the maximum of his time and energies" to SCLC.[87] They recognized, however, that SCLC required much more than simply King's full-time commitment. Having dismissed Tilley, they were still undecided about how to invigorate their organization. Ella Baker continued to press for a greater emphasis on local organizing and direct action. Her queries to the leadership in her director's report conveyed broad criticisms of the group's direction: "Have we been so busy doing the things that had to be done that we have failed to [do] what should be done? Have we really come to grips with what it takes to do the job for which SCLC was organized; and are we willing to pay the price?" Baker's list of three "basic aims of SCLC" suggested a redirection toward "coordinated action by local groups," the development of "potential leaders," and "a vital movement of nonviolent direct mass action." Deriding SCLC's lack of "reflective thinking and planning," she concluded her recommendations with a challenge: "I am convinced that SCLC can and should play a unique role in the struggle for human rights; but I am equally convinced that this can not be done by following, or even approximating 'usual procedures.' SCLC must present creative leadership that will bestir dynamic mass action." Baker complained that planning meetings and other events had "been not only physically exhausting, but intellectually frustrating and spiritually depleting."[88] The executive committee responded to Baker's report by authorizing a committee—Abernathy, Reddick, Shuttlesworth,

---

85. King, "Address at Public Meeting of the Southern Christian Ministers Conference of Mississippi," 23 September 1959, p. 282 in this volume.

86. King, Recommendations to the SCLC Executive Committee, 30 September 1959, p. 295 in this volume. After an October *Jet* magazine article pointed to the lack of progress in SCLC's "clergy-backed Dixie vote campaign," King defended his organization, suggesting that the article may have been spurred by the disgruntled Tilley. He conceded that "no organization has done enough in the area of registration and voting in the South" ("Ticker Tape U.S.A.," *Jet,* 12 October 1959, and King to Theodore E. Brown, 19 October 1959, p. 311 in this volume; see also King to Simeon Booker, 20 October 1959, pp. 313–315 in this volume).

87. Wyatt Tee Walker and Fred Shuttlesworth, "Resolutions adopted at Fall Session," 1 October 1959; see also SCLC, Recommendations adopted by the executive committee and delegates at Fall Session, 1 October 1959.

88. Baker, "Report of the executive director," 16 May–29 September 1959.

Samuel Williams, and Joseph Lowery—to meet with her and "work out the program for the next year."[89]

As King gradually recognized that he would have to leave Montgomery to devote more time to SCLC, he also decided that Rustin should be hired to assist him in handling press relations. Though the executive committee had approved the idea of hiring a part-time staff member, King did not announce his choice of Rustin until several weeks later. While acknowledging "the possible perils involved" he insisted that "Rustin's unique organizational ability, his technical competence, and his distinctive ability to stick with a job until it is thoroughly completed, justifies our willingness to take the risk."[90] Levison later reported in a 1 November letter to Rustin that Baker had expressed her opposition "firmly and unyieldingly," citing Rustin's vulnerabilities as a homosexual as well as an ex-communist and insisting that the hiring of a field secretary should take priority. "The substance and method of her argumentation became so provoking," Levison informed Rustin, that SCLC colleague Joseph Lowery "took Martin aside and suggested that they agree to hire you and simultaneously to fire" Baker.[91]

As news of his imminent departure from Montgomery leaked to the press during November, King considered how best to explain his decision to leave Dexter.[92] In a draft of his resignation statement to the congregation on 29 November, he admitted that he had been "unprepared for the symbolic role that history had thrust upon" him. As a result of the Montgomery bus boycott, he recalled, "new responsibilities poured in upon me in almost staggering torrents."[93] Speaking to a *Jet* reporter after the announcement, King confessed: "What I have been doing is giving, giving, giving and not stopping to retreat and meditate like I should—to come back. If the situation is not changed, I will be a physical and psychological wreck."[94] An SCLC press release described the move to Atlanta, where he would join his father as co-pastor of Ebenezer Baptist Church, as "a painful decision" made necessary because King needed to be closer to SCLC headquarters when "the time was right for expanded militant action across the South." The statement offered assurances that King would maintain his MIA ties and quoted one of Dexter's "oldest members" as saying, "Rev. King will not truly be leaving us because part of him always will remain in Montgomery, and at the same time, part of us will go with him."[95] As black leaders in Atlanta publicly applauded King's return to his birth-

---

89. King, Recommendations to the SCLC Executive Committee, 30 September 1959, p. 296 in this volume; see also SCLC, Recommendations adopted by the executive committee and delegates at Fall Session, 1 October 1959.

90. King, Recommendations to SCLC Committee on Future Program, 27 October 1959, pp. 315–318 in this volume.

91. Levison, Tom Kahn, and Joe Filner to Rustin, 1 November 1959.

92. Associated Negro Press, Press release, 18 November 1959, and SCLC, "Suggested draft for amplifying press release," 11 November–30 November 1959.

93. King, Draft, Resignation from Dexter Avenue Baptist Church, 29 November 1959, pp. 328–329 in this volume.

94. "Why Rev. M. L. King Is Leaving Montgomery: Leader Says Time Is Ripe to Extend Work in Dixie," *Jet,* 17 December 1959, pp. 14–15.

95. SCLC Press Release, "Dr. King Leaves Montgomery for Atlanta," 1 December 1959, pp. 330–331 in this volume.

place, Georgia governor Ernest Vandiver announced that King would face police surveillance upon his arrival, maintaining that "anyone, including King, who comes across our state lines with the avowed intention of breaking laws will be kept under surveillance at all times."[96] Ralph McGill, editor of the *Atlanta Constitution,* worried privately that King's return would lessen the chances for Atlanta to resolve the issue of school desegregation.[97] King spent much of the months of December and January planning details of the move and transferring the leadership of the MIA to Abernathy. On 3 December he delivered his final report as president of the MIA to an "emotionally charged crowd of 900 Negroes" at Bethel Baptist Church. King recounted the organization's recent achievements and defended it against accusations that the local movement had atrophied. "If you have any final doubts about our aliveness, talk with the candidates who ran for reelection in the city last spring and they will have to admit that they are out of business because the MIA is very much in business," King said, referring to the election defeats of segregationists mayor W. A. Gayle and city commissioner Clyde Sellers. He then endorsed the MIA's continuing efforts to desegregate the city's parks and schools and expressed his confidence in the group's future: "The freedom struggle in Montgomery was not started by one man, and it will not end when one man leaves. The Montgomery story was never a drama with only one actor. More precisely it was always a drama with many actors, each playing his part exceedingly well."[98]

Five days later King traveled to an SCLC board meeting in Birmingham, after which he endured blaring sirens from police and fire vehicles sent to disrupt his address at a mass meeting at St. James Baptist Church. King indicated that the southern movement had reached a decisive point, and he unveiled a program for "mass action" led by a "creative minority" willing to "take punishment in order to push into the promised land of freedom."[99] After delivering several speeches in Ohio and Illinois, King returned to Atlanta where he and other SCLC leaders met with their NAACP counterparts to discuss joining forces for a major voter registration campaign seeking to double the number of black voters before the November 1960 election.[100]

On the morning of 31 January King delivered his farewell sermon, "Lessons from History," and that evening Dexter members staged "A Salute to Dr. and Mrs. King," a scripted review of King's life, featuring appearances by his friends and

96. "Ga. Governor Warns Dr. King He'll Be Watched," *New York Amsterdam News,* 19 December 1959.

97. "I have the highest esteem for the Reverend, but he could not have come at a worse time," McGill confided in a 15 December letter to editor Harry S. Ashmore. The *Montgomery Advertiser* reacted to King's impending departure with a critical editorial that conceded that King was "a courageous man and was obviously prepared to die. His Gandhi peace talk was spurious, but it was peace talk nevertheless" ("King Returns to Atlanta," *Montgomery Advertiser,* 6 December 1959).

98. Dick Hines, "Farewell Talk: King Pledges to File Suit on School Mixing," *Montgomery Advertiser,* 4 December 1959, and King, Address at the Fourth Annual Institute on Nonviolence and Social Change at Bethel Baptist Church, 3 December 1959, p. 342 in this volume.

99. Emory O. Jackson, "King Says South Out to Kill 1954 Supreme Court Decision," *Atlanta Daily World,* 11 December 1959.

100. Charles Moore, "Drive Launched Here Seeks Million More Negro Voters," *Atlanta Constitution,* 29 December 1959.

relatives and modeled after the popular television program "This Is Your Life."[101] Following the skit, King expressed his appreciation for the support he had received from his wife, his family, and his congregation. Although he was leaving Montgomery, King insisted that he would remain active:

> I intend to stay with it until victory is won and until every black boy and black girl can walk the streets of Montgomery and the United States with dignity and honor, knowing that he's a child of the Almighty God and knowing that he has dignity and self-respect. It may not come in the next five years; I do not know. I hope it comes tomorrow morning by nine o'clock. But realism impels me to admit that there are still days of resistance ahead, difficult, dark days. I do not know what suffering we will have to go through. Some more bombings will occur, I'm sure. Some of us will have to go to jail some more. And I'm not so sure now that some of us may not have to pay the price of physical death, but I'm convinced that if physical death is the price that some must pay to free their children from a permanent life of psychological death, then nothing could be more Christian. And so let us go out with new and bold determination to make this old age—a new age.[102]

The following evening, King bid his followers a final public farewell at the MIA's "Testimonial of Love and Loyalty," held at Ralph Abernathy's First Baptist Church. In his address he urged the crowd to support newly elected president Abernathy, maintaining, as he passed him the MIA's gavel, that "not only, I say, is he a great soul, but he has great ability."[103]

On 7 February a "standing-room-only crowd of about 1,200" assembled at Ebenezer Baptist Church to hear King deliver his first sermon as co-pastor.[104] King, Sr., who had for years tried to entice his son to move back to Atlanta, introduced him to the congregation, beaming proudly: "You know how happy I am to have my child with me."[105] Amid shouts of "Amen" and "preach, preach," King delivered "Three Dimensions of a Complete Life." He declared that "our white brothers are only concerned with the length of life—their preferred economical position, their social status, their political power and their so-called 'way of life.'" A news report indicated that as King's sermon reached its climax, with his arms stretched outward "and his voice full of emotion," he asked, "Is my ultimate faith in America? Oh no. . . . America sometimes worries me. Is my ulti-

---

101. See "Dexter Honors Dr. & Mrs. King!!" 3 February 1960, and King, Address Delivered during "A Salute to Dr. and Mrs. Martin Luther King" at Dexter Avenue Baptist Church, 31 January 1960, pp. 364–365 and 351–357 in this volume, respectively.

102. King, "A Salute to Dr. and Mrs. Martin Luther King," 31 January 1960, pp. 354–355 in this volume; see also John Coombes, "Additional Boycotts Asked in King's Farewell Address," *Montgomery Advertiser,* 2 February 1960.

103. King, Address Delivered at the Montgomery Improvement Association's "Testimonial of Love and Loyalty," 1 February 1960, p. 361 in this volume.

104. "Dr. King Asks Love Returned for Hate," *Atlanta Constitution,* 8 February 1960; see also Martin Luther King, *Daddy King: An Autobiography,* with Clayton Riley (New York: William Morrow, 1980), p. 168.

105. "Dr. King Asks Love Returned for Hate," 8 February 1960.

mate faith in western civilization? Oh no. . . . My ultimate faith is in the eternal God!"[106]

When he announced his decision to leave Montgomery, King promised a new program for SCLC that would include "a full scale assault" on "discrimination and segregation in all forms," but neither King nor the SCLC initiated the wave of student sit-ins that began on 1 February in Greensboro, North Carolina.[107] Nonetheless, many of the youthful activists who spearheaded the protest campaign had been inspired by King and other SCLC leaders. Ezell Blair, one of the four students from North Carolina A&T College who conducted the first sit-in, had been deeply affected by a King speech at Greensboro's Bennett College.[108] In Durham, North Carolina, King's SCLC colleague Douglas Moore advised sit-in demonstrators; and in Tallahassee, Florida, another colleague, C. K. Steele, worked closely with student protesters, including his two sons Henry and Charles.[109] In Montgomery Ralph Abernathy advised student activists at Alabama State College. SCLC's Nashville affiliate had encouraged student activism even before the Greensboro sit-in, sponsoring an ongoing nonviolence workshop under the leadership of Vanderbilt divinity student James Lawson, who King had earlier encouraged to move to the South to support the movement.[110] Lawson's workshop, which began meeting in 1958 in the basement of SCLC executive committee member Kelly Miller Smith's church, attracted a cadre of student activists who would sustain the Nashville Student Movement after eighty-one students were arrested in that city's initial series of sit-ins on 14 February. Workshop participants included Diane Nash and Marion Barry of Fisk University and John Lewis and James Bevel of the American Baptist Theological Seminary. Despite these ties between SCLC and participants in the sit-ins, a widening gulf between King and the new student movement would soon emerge. King consistently expressed support for the sit-ins, but he remained largely on the sidelines of the new movement until the fall of 1960. Instead of leading the campaign of civil disobedience, he became preoccupied with defending himself against perjury charges that threatened his reputation. The sit-in movement was a manifestation of his Gandhian ideals, but it also led to the creation of a new civil rights group, the Student Nonviolent Coordinating Committee (SNCC), that would eventually challenge King and SCLC.

Two weeks after the sit-ins began, King traveled to Durham at Douglas Moore's request to offer support to the sit-in campaign that had closed the city's lunch counters. King held a press conference and then toured the downtown restaurants,

---

106. Paul Delaney, "'Follow Way of Love,' Dr. King Asks People," *Atlanta Daily World,* 9 February 1960.

107. SCLC Press Release, "Dr. King Leaves Montgomery for Atlanta," 1 December 1959, p. 331 in this volume.

108. Jibreel Khazan [Ezell Blair, Jr.], Interview by William H. Chafe, 27 November 1974; see also Introduction in *Papers* 4:38.

109. See King to Steele, 19 March 1960, pp. 391–392 in this volume. For Moore's protests in Durham, see Moore to King, 3 October 1956, in *Papers* 3:393–397.

110. See Lawson to King, 3 November 1958, in *Papers* 4:522–524.

where store employees and police scuffled briefly with press photographers covering the visit. He then discussed nonviolence in Durham with student groups from North and South Carolina as well as Virginia.[111] That evening, accompanied by Moore and Abernathy, King addressed about one hundred students gathered at White Rock Baptist Church, comparing them to the youthful activists he had encountered in Africa and Asia. "What is new is that American students have come of age," he remarked. "You now take your honored places in the world-wide struggle for freedom." King also advised against fearing arrest, explaining that "if the officials threaten to arrest us for standing up for our rights, we must answer by saying that we are willing and prepared to fill up the jails of the South."[112]

Returning to Atlanta on 17 February, King unexpectedly found himself facing a possible jail term when he was arrested on felony charges regarding alleged false statements in his 1956 and 1958 Alabama tax returns. Two Fulton County, Georgia, sheriff deputies entered his Ebenezer office and arrested him, citing the Alabama charges.[113] An audit of King's returns the previous month indicated that he had not reported funds he received on behalf of the MIA and SCLC, and thus he still owed the state more than seventeen hundred dollars. King immediately paid the disputed amount, but Alabama officials, nonetheless, obtained a grand jury indictment against him.[114] At the Fulton County courthouse, King posted $2,000 bail and was released. When asked by a reporter whether there was a connection between the arrest and his statement of support for student protesters in Durham, King responded that it was "a new attempt on the part of the State of Alabama to harass me for the role that I have played in the civil rights struggle." Immediately placing the arrest in the context of civil disobedience, he indicated his willingness to go to jail if necessary, explaining that "maybe through our willingness to suffer and accept this type of sacrifice we will be able to arouse and awaken the dozing conscience of many citizens of our nation."[115]

Nearly two weeks later, King surrendered to Alabama authorities and was again released on bond. At a press conference at Dexter, King refrained from commenting on his own case and instead directed attention to the Alabama State Col-

---

111. "Negro Told Not to Fear Jail Terms," *Greensboro Daily News,* 17 February 1960.

112. King, "A Creative Protest," 16 February 1960, pp. 367–370 in this volume; see also "Negro Told Not to Fear Jail Terms," *Greensboro Daily News,* 17 February 1960. In an interview with *Newsweek* conducted shortly after King's Durham speech, King suggested that the sit-ins might initiate "a full-scale assault on segregation" and were responses to the South's delaying actions following the Supreme Court's 1955 mandate calling for school desegregation with "deliberate speed" ("Integration: 'Full-Scale Assault,'" *Newsweek,* 29 February 1960).

113. See King, Interview on Arrest following Indictment by Grand Jury of Montgomery County, 17 February 1960, pp. 370–372 in this volume.

114. After King sent the Department of Revenue a check for the disputed amount on 16 February 1960, one day before his indictment for falsifying his returns, E. A. Erwin of the Department of Revenue informed him that a computation error indicated that he owed slightly less than had earlier been thought (King and Coretta Scott King to Erwin, 5 March 1960).

115. King, Interview on Arrest following Indictment by Grand Jury of Montgomery County, 17 February 1960, p. 371 in this volume. In a printed statement, King indicated that he was unlikely to get a "fair hearing" in Alabama. He further suggested that "a group of distinguished citizens of the highest integrity go over all of my books and make a report of their findings" (King, Statement on the indictment by grand jury of Montgomery County, 17 February 1960).

lege students who, a few days earlier, had launched sit-ins protesting segregated facilities at the Montgomery County courthouse. While offering SCLC's "moral support and our financial support," he asserted that the protests "have no direction from Martin Luther King."[116] The Montgomery protests soon attracted additional publicity when Alabama governor John Patterson ordered the president of Alabama State, H. Councill Trenholm, to expel student participants and fire faculty supporters. The latter threat had particular importance to King because of his close friendship with several targeted faculty members including Reddick and Dexter members Jo Ann Robinson and Mary Fair Burks.[117] King and other SCLC leaders sent a telegram to Patterson protesting the reported "purge" and affirming the teachers' "academic freedom and the right of citizenship."[118] In a letter to Burks, King was especially critical of Trenholm, also a member of his former Dexter congregation: "If he would only stand up to the Governor and the Board of Education and say that he cannot in all good conscience fire the eleven faculty members who have committed no crime or act of sedition, he would gain support over the nation that he never dreamed of."[119]

Meanwhile, friends, supporters, and other civil rights leaders mobilized on King's behalf in the tax case.[120] In late February, a group of King's supporters met in Harry Belafonte's New York apartment to form the Committee to Defend Martin Luther King and the Struggle for Freedom in the South, with A. Philip Randolph as chairman.[121] The committee immediately launched a fund-raising effort with the announced goal of $200,000 to support King's legal defense and SCLC's voter registration drive. On 3 March they issued a press release that denounced the charges against King as a "gross misrepresentation of fact" because

116. Dick Hines, "King Free on Bond; Denies Starting Sit In," *Montgomery Advertiser,* 1 March 1960. For more on the Montgomery protests, see King to Eisenhower, 9 March 1960, and King to Rebecca Dixon, 10 March 1960, pp. 385–387 and 388 in this volume, respectively.

117. "ASC Negroes Roar Approval of Campus Walkout Threat," *Montgomery Advertiser,* 1 March 1960; see also King to Burks, 5 April 1960, pp. 406–408 in this volume. Burks and Robinson were both past presidents of the Women's Political Council, the group that had written and distributed the leaflet that began the Montgomery bus boycott on 2 December 1955.

118. King to John Malcolm Patterson, 14 April 1960, pp. 425–426 in this volume.

119. King to Burks, 5 April 1960, p. 407 in this volume; see also King to Patterson, 9 August 1960, pp. 495–496 in this volume.

120. See letters from John Wesley Dobbs to King, 18 February 1960; A. Philip Randolph to King, 19 February 1960; E. D. Nixon to King, 20 February 1960, pp. 372–373 in this volume; and Kelly Miller Smith to King, 22 February 1960. The Dexter Avenue Baptist Church newsletter reported: "In a special joint meeting of the official staff of Dexter Avenue Baptist Church and the Montgomery Improvement Association held at Dexter . . . the officials of each organization gave a pledge of implicit confidence to Dr Martin Luther King, Jr in his recent embarrassment by the Department of Revenue of the State of Alabama" ("Dexter Official Staff Gives Vote of Confidence to Dr Martin Luther King," *Dexter Echo,* 2 March 1960, p. 5; see also Paul Delaney, "Atlanta Ministers Deplore Alabama Indictment Issued against Dr. M. L. King, Jr.," *Atlanta Daily World,* 23 February 1960).

121. Other members included Rustin, Levison, Belafonte, former baseball star Jackie Robinson, Brooklyn minister Gardner Taylor, Harry Emerson Fosdick (the former president of Union Theological seminary and minister of Riverside Church in New York), Ruth Harris Bunche (the wife of United Nations under-secretary Ralph Bunche), and Jerome Nathanson of the American Ethical Union (Committee to Defend Martin Luther King and the Struggle for Freedom in the South, Press release, Committee to undertake fundraising campaign, 3 March 1960).

King's income had never "even approached" the $45,000 that Alabama officials claimed King received in 1958. "The officials of Alabama reached their fantastic figure by the shoddy device of adding to Dr. King's personal income sums spent for transportation, hotels and other expenses in connection with his extensive travels on behalf of civil rights," they explained.[122]

When Rustin and others drafted a fund-raising appeal to appear in the *New York Times,* they sought to demonstrate that King's arrest was not only politically motivated but part of an effort "to destroy the one man who, more than any other, symbolizes the new spirit now sweeping the South." The decision to include the phrase "and the Struggle for Freedom in the South" as part of the committee's name reflected a desire to broaden its mission, as did the committee's statement that donations would support SCLC's voter registration program. The appeal, however, led to unexpected problems when Patterson and other Alabama officials filed libel suits against the *Times* and the ministers, including King, charging that it contained defamatory statements regarding the student protests.[123] The committee's decision to place King's arrest at the center of the appeal also alienated some of his allies, who recognized that the fund-raising effort had benefited from the widespread public sympathy for the students, many of whom were facing their own reprisals and legal difficulties. Soon after the ad appeared, Harris Wofford, who had served as an advisor during the bus boycott and had helped write sections of *Stride Toward Freedom,* voiced his concerns to King. "I do not think that your problem should be equated with that of the students and others who have been arrested in the demonstrations," Wofford wrote. He argued that the legal issues involved and your "stature—as the leader and symbol of this movement" differed from those of the students. "It seems to me that this turns you into a kind of Scottsboro boy, not a man who is master of his fate." While offering to assist in recruiting a legal defense team for King, Wofford advised King that his case would have "greater dignity" if he "did not permit solicitation of funds on your behalf, but conducted your own defense independently and courageously."[124]

Wofford's advice did not result in an immediate shift in the committee's approach, but it suggested the increasing difficulties facing King as he advised and spoke on behalf of student protesters while refraining from joining their sit-ins. Nevertheless, King accepted a proposal to sponsor a south-wide meeting of student protest leaders to be held Easter weekend at Shaw University in Raleigh, North Carolina. King co-signed an invitation drafted by Baker offering "youth leaders" from protest centers an opportunity to "chart new goals and achieve a more unified

---

122. Committee to Defend Martin Luther King and the Struggle for Freedom in the South, Press release, "Statement on the indictment of Martin Luther King, Jr.," 3 March 1960.

123. For a facsimile of the committee's appeal, "Heed Their Rising Voices" (published 29 March 1960 in the *New York Times*), see p. 382 in this volume; see also Patterson to King, 9 May 1960, pp. 456–458 in this volume.

124. Wofford to King, 1 April 1960, p. 403 in this volume. NAACP board member Jackie Robinson and CORE executive secretary James Robinson also voiced concerns about the appeal (see Jackie Robinson to King, 5 May 1960, and James R. Robinson to King, 13 May 1960, pp. 454–455 and 458–459 in this volume, respectively).

sense of direction for training and action in Nonviolent Resistance." Students were assured that, although adult leaders would be present to offer "counsel and guidance," the gathering would be "youth centered."[125]

On 15 April, the opening day of the conference, King read a statement to the press that applauded the students for having taken "the struggle for justice into their own strong hands." He offered the more than one hundred high school and college students six topics for discussion, including establishing a permanent organization, instituting a "selective buying" campaign, going to jail rather than paying bail, broadening the struggle into every Southern community, and studying nonviolence in order to "arouse vocal and vigorous support and place pressures on the federal government that will compel its intervention," and finally, deepening their commitment to the philosophy of nonviolence.[126] King's statement suggested the future direction of the student protest movement, but it also embraced tactics that went far beyond those that SCLC itself had utilized.

When King left the conference for an Easter morning appearance on NBC's "Meet the Press," he struggled to speak on behalf of the upsurge in student militancy. He fended off growing criticisms of the students, including former president Harry Truman's recent statement opposing sit-ins.[127] But he spent most of the program on the defensive. When asked to explain how "breaking local laws" could be justified, King remarked, "whenever a man-made law is in conflict with what we consider the law of God, or the moral law of the universe, then we feel that we have a moral obligation to protest. And this is in our American tradition all the way from the Boston Tea Party on down." King further maintained that the federal government "has the responsibility of protecting our citizens of this nation as they protest against . . . the injustices which they face."[128] Meanwhile, in Raleigh, the students established the Temporary Student Nonviolent Coordinating Committee.[129]

Despite King's verbal support for student activism, he was restrained by other concerns during the spring of 1960, especially the perjury trial that threatened his preeminent role in the southern civil rights struggle. In a reflective article published in April, King acknowledged the cumulative emotional strain of five arrests,

---

125. King and Baker, Announcement, "Youth leadership meeting, Shaw University, Raleigh, N.C., 4/15/1960–4/17/1960," March 1960. A month before the conference in Raleigh, Baker met with two adult advisors to the sit-in protesters, Glenn Smiley of the Fellowship of Reconciliation and Douglas Moore, an SCLC board member, who agreed that the conference "should be youth centered" with adults speaking "only when asked to do so" (Baker, Memo to King and Abernathy, 23 March 1960, p. 397 in this volume).

126. King, "Statement to the Press at the Beginning of the Youth Leadership Conference," 15 April 1960, p. 427 in this volume; see also Charles Craven, "Be Jailed If Necessary King Tells Negroes: Group Meets Here to Plan Future Move," *Raleigh News and Observer,* 16 April 1960; Claude Sitton, "Dr. King Favors Buyers' Boycott," *New York Times,* 16 April 1960; and SNCC, "Report of the Raleigh conference," 23 June 1960.

127. King, Interview on "Meet the Press," 17 April 1960, pp. 428–435 in this volume. Truman was quoted as saying, "If anyone came into my store and tried to stop business, I'd throw him out. The Negro should behave himself and show he's a good citizen. Common sense and goodwill can solve this whole thing" ("Truman Reiterates Views on Sitdowns," *New York Times,* 25 March 1960; see also King to Truman, 19 April 1960, pp. 437–439 in this volume).

128. King, Interview on "Meet the Press," 17 April 1960, pp. 428–435 in this volume.

129. "Negro Students Form Group to Guide Policies," *Washington Post,* 18 April 1960.

two bombings of his home, repeated death threats, and the near-fatal stabbing: "I must admit that at times I have felt that I could no longer bear such a heavy burden, and have been tempted to retreat to a more quiet and serene life."[130] Although he had moved to Atlanta in order to invigorate SCLC and to enjoy the reduced pastoral obligations of a co-pastor, he expressed a measure of discouragement in a letter to one of his Boston University professors, writing that "in many instances I have felt terribly frustrated over my inability to retreat, concentrate, and reflect." He had hoped to find "more time to meditate and think through the total struggle ahead" but had been unable to set aside the necessary time. "I know that I cannot continue to go at this pace, and live with such a tension filled schedule. My failure to reflect will do harm not only to me as a person, but to the total movement."[131] Coretta King would later remember the tax indictment as a low point in her husband's public career, writing that "despite all of the bravery he had shown before, under personal abuse and character assaults . . . this attack on his personal honesty hurt him most."[132] The family's peace of mind was not helped by the flaming cross burned in their yard late on the evening of 26 April. The cross was one of several burned in Atlanta that day.[133]

In May, the young activists met to discuss a more permanent organization, electing Fisk graduate student Marion Barry as the group's first chairman. The students named King as an advisor, but other individuals also exerted influence during subsequent months. Baker offered encouragement, providing office space in a corner of SCLC headquarters in Atlanta and helping SNCC's office administrator Jane Stembridge arrange meetings and prepare presentations to the upcoming Democratic and Republican Party platform committees.[134] Lawson's influence was considerable as well. He was also chosen as an advisor, and his role in training the Nashville protesters caused some student activists to look to him more than King for guidance regarding Gandhian principles. Lawson had become a center of controversy in March when he was expelled from Vanderbilt's Divinity School because of his support for the local protests.[135] The expulsion, along with Lawson's background as a conscientious objector to military service, a former missionary in India, and a representative of the Fellowship of Reconciliation, enhanced his credibility as an advocate of nonviolent resistance. It had been Lawson who prepared the succinct explication of Gandhian principles that became SNCC's official statement of purpose, affirming "the philosophical or religious ideal of nonviolence as the foundation of our purpose, the presupposition of our faith, and the manner

130. King, "Suffering and Faith," 27 April 1960, p. 444 in this volume.

131. King to Allan Knight Chalmers, 18 April 1960, p. 436 in this volume.

132. *My Life with Martin Luther King, Jr.*, p. 185.

133. "This, Son, Is a Klan Cross!" *Norfolk Journal and Guide*, 7 May 1960.

134. See articles in initial issue of the *Student Voice*, June 1960 (*The Student Voice, 1960–1965, Periodical of the Student Nonviolent Coordinating Committee*, compiled by the staff of the Martin Luther King, Jr., Papers Project [Westport, Conn.: Meckler, 1990]).

135. James W. Donaldson, a student with ties to Nashville, wrote King on 3 March to inform him of the school's efforts to oust Lawson. Following his dismissal, Lawson was allowed to reapply several months later after many Vanderbilt faculty members threatened to resign in protest (*The Lawson-Vanderbilt Affair: Letters to Dean Nelson*, August 1960).

of our action. Nonviolence as it grows from Judaic-Christian traditions seeks a social order of justice permeated by love."[136]

SNCC's statement of purpose was consistent with King's beliefs, but Lawson, despite being slightly older than King, was more in touch with the rebellious attitudes of the students. Lawson's remarks at the Raleigh conference had also generated controversy when he expressed the frustration felt by many students regarding the NAACP's reliance on litigation and lobbying. A *New York Times* article reported that Lawson called the NAACP's *Crisis* magazine a publication for the "black bourgeois club" and also referred to the group as "a fund-raising agency, a legal agency" that had "by and large neglected the major resource that we have—a disciplined, free people who would be able to work unanimously to implement the ideals of justice and freedom."[137] After learning of Lawson's remarks through press reports, Wilkins quickly contacted other NAACP officials and called a meeting to plan a response and to discuss why the comments had "not thus far been repudiated by Rev. Martin Luther King."[138] In a letter to King, Wilkins expressed his outrage, asking "how was it that Lawson claimed his views were shared by other leaders in the SCLC?" Wilkins further complained that the attack was unwarranted and reminded King that "SCLC did not initiate the sit-downs. That we know. CORE did not initiate them. That we know. The NAACP did not initiate the wave that began February 1, but the NAACP staged the only successful sit-down at lunch counters in Oklahoma City and in Wichita, Kansas, in 1958. That we do know." In order to avoid a split between the two organizations, Wilkins requested a private meeting with King to discuss the situation.[139]

Caught in the middle of the dispute, King forwarded Wilkins's letter to Lawson asking for advice before his 7 May meeting with the NAACP leader in Atlanta.[140] King's sympathies were clearly with Lawson and the student activists, having contrasted the potency of "direct action" to the possibility of "a century of litigation" when he appeared on "Meet the Press."[141] His article published in the May issue of *The Progressive* referred approvingly to the fearless young people who had brought about a shift "from the slow court process to direct action in the form of bus protests, economic boycotts, mass marches."[142] King's close associate Stanley Levison had privately identified Thurgood Marshall and other NAACP leaders as "gradualists in reality while they pretend to be uncompromising and firm" who were "using up the good will past victories in the courts brought them, and in-

---

136. James Lawson, "Statement of purpose," 17 April 1960; see also SNCC, "Report," 13 May–14 May 1960. Following the 13–14 May SNCC meeting, this draft statement was circulated among the group's state and local affiliates (*The Student Voice,* June 1960, p. 2).

137. Claude Sitton, "Negro Criticizes N.A.A.C.P. Tactics," *New York Times,* 17 April 1960.

138. Wilkins to Gloster Current et al., 18 April 1960.

139. Wilkins to King, 27 April 1960, pp. 444–446 in this volume.

140. King enclosed Wilkins's letter with a note to Lawson reading: "I would appreciate your reading it so that I can talk with you concerning the contents before I talk with Roy" (King to Lawson, 2 May 1960).

141. King, Interview on "Meet the Press," 17 April 1960, p. 432 in this volume.

142. King, "The Burning Truth in the South," May 1960, p. 449 in this volume.

creasingly criticism and cynicism about their motives is being expressed."[143] Despite King's own dissatisfaction with Wilkins and the NAACP's gradualist approach, he recognized the necessity of maintaining good relations with the nation's oldest and largest civil rights organization.

Lawson also sought to defuse the controversy, insisting in a 9 May letter to Wilkins that his remarks had been misinterpreted and pointing to his long association with the NAACP. Wilkins's anger was not readily assuaged, however, especially after he learned that Bernard Lee, a student leader from Alabama State, had expressed even stronger criticisms of the NAACP and CORE at an event sponsored by the Students for a Democratic Society (SDS) at the University of Michigan. CORE founder and NAACP officer James Farmer shared Wilkins's dismay, suggesting that Bayard Rustin had exerted a negative influence over the student movement. Farmer expressed difficulty in understanding "how anyone as vulnerable as Rustin can make such a target of himself."[144] While Wilkins briskly dismissed Lawson's attempted reconciliation—"Frankly, I do not know what you can do at this date to correct the impression that has been created"—NAACP stalwart Jackie Robinson wrote King to convey his dismay "that people who claim to represent the Southern Christian Leadership Conference are saying the N.A.A.C.P. has outlived its usefulness" and cautioned King to "not be a party to the old game of divide and conquer."[145]

While King struggled to mend fences with NAACP leaders, his perjury trial opened on 25 May. Despite the concern of King's lawyers that they had little time to prepare an adequate defense, they were able to expose weaknesses in the state's case and attack the prosecution for failing to disclose crucial evidence. During the four-day trial, the defense called the all-white jury's attention to the vagueness of the indictment and the fact that the expense reimbursements King received from SCLC were not taxable income.[146] On 27 May, King took the stand and testified that a state auditor examined the return and revealed that he was "under pressure by his supervisors" to find fault with it. The following day the jury found him not guilty.[147] King was elated, telling reporters that the verdict reaffirmed his "faith in the ultimate decency of man" and indicated "that there are hundreds and thousands of people, white people of goodwill in the South."[148] Writing to L. Harold

---

143. Levison to King, March 1960, p. 383 in this volume.

144. In a memo to Wilkins, Farmer and NAACP labor secretary Herbert Hill claimed that Lee derided them for including whites in their organizations. Farmer further explained that Lee subsequently apologized for his comment, stating that "he did not want anyone going from the conference telling people that he was the one who was trying to split the North from the South and keep the movement for fostering only black" (Hill and Farmer, Memo to Wilkins, 3 May 1960).

145. Wilkins to Lawson, 13 May 1960, and Robinson to King, 5 May 1960, p. 454 in this volume. Morehouse College president Benjamin Mays, who had deep ties to the King family, also entered the fray, complaining to Wilkins about the anti-King comments he had heard from NAACP state officials: "It is not enough for you and Martin Luther King, Jr. to work together harmoniously but the persons under your leaderships . . . must do the same" (Mays to Wilkins, 18 May 1960).

146. King, Defendant, "Demurrer to indictment," *State of Alabama v. Martin Luther King, Jr.*, 20 May 1960.

147. Arthur Osgoode, "Income Tax Case: Final Arguments Set Today in King Trial," *Montgomery Advertiser*, 28 May 1960.

148. King, Statement on verdict by jury of Montgomery County, 28 May 1960, and King, Statement on Perjury Acquittal, 28 May 1960, p. 462 in this volume.

DeWolf, his former Boston University advisor, King expressed his "real surprise . . . that an all white jury of Montgomery, Alabama would ever think of acquitting Martin Luther King." He told DeWolf that his supporters had "felt that it would have been necessary to go to the United States Supreme Court in order to finally receive justice."[149]

The successful perjury defense and a new wave of student protests goaded King to action in the spring of 1960. Wyatt Tee Walker resigned his pastorship in Petersburg, Virginia, on 29 May to accept King's offer to become SCLC's executive director.[150] King also met Democratic presidential hopeful John F. Kennedy for breakfast on 23 June at the Massachusetts senator's Manhattan apartment.[151] Kennedy, who was courting skeptical liberal voters put off by his tepid support of civil rights, had been encouraged by his advisors for several months to meet with King.[152] During their hour and a half meeting, the two men discussed civil rights and the role of the executive branch. Reflecting on their meeting several years later, King recalled confronting Kennedy for siding with segregationists to weaken the Civil Rights Bill of 1957. Kennedy admitted his vote was a mistake and explained that "the sit-in movement had caused him to reevaluate his thinking" and had made clear to him "the injustices and the indignities that Negroes were facing all over the South." King left the meeting "impressed" by his "forthright and honest manner," but he later recalled thinking that Kennedy had "intellectually committed himself to integration" without having "emotional involvement at that moment."[153]

News from Buffalo erased any guarded hope King may have gained from his Manhattan visit. Representative Adam Clayton Powell, the nation's most prominent African American politician, told a gathering of black Baptists that King and A. Philip Randolph were "captives" of outside interests. He named Stanley Levison and Bayard Rustin as the radicals behind the scenes. Powell also accused Randolph and King of dividing the movement by barring Roy Wilkins from their planning sessions to organize upcoming convention protests designed to press the political parties to adopt strong civil rights planks.[154] While not questioning

---

149. King to DeWolf, 16 June 1960, p. 473 in this volume.

150. "Negro Leader Urges Continued Struggle," *Richmond News Leader,* 2 June 1960. For King's job offer, see King to Walker, 5 March 1960, pp. 384–385 in this volume.

151. Anthony Lewis, "Kennedy Salutes Negroes' Sit-Ins," *New York Times,* 25 June 1960.

152. See King to Marjorie McKenzie Lawson, 4 September 1959, and King to Bowles, 24 June 1960, pp. 276–277 and 478–480 in this volume, respectively. King had also met with Kennedy advisor Harris Wofford just two weeks before the meeting with Kennedy.

153. King, Interview by Berl I. Bernhard, 9 March 1964, and King to Bowles, 24 June 1960, p. 480 in this volume; see also Anthony Lewis, "Kennedy Salutes Negroes' Sit-Ins," *New York Times,* 25 June 1960.

154. "Powell Insists Randolph, King Are 'Captives,'" *Pittsburgh Courier,* 25 June 1960. While there were tensions among the leaders of the March on the Conventions protests, Wilkins had been involved in the planning from the start (Levison, Kahn, and Filner to Rustin, 1 November 1959). King and Randolph officially announced the protests at a June press conference, but they had spoken about them publicly since January (see King, Outline, Remarks for "A Salute to A. Philip Randolph," 24 January 1960, and King and Randolph, Statement Announcing the March on the Conventions Movement for Freedom Now, 9 June 1960, pp. 350 and 467–469 in this volume, respectively).

King's and Randolph's "dedication" or "zeal," Powell explained to the gathering of church leaders that "we must be on guard against our best leaders being captured by anyone."[155] King quickly sent a telegram to Powell: "How you could say the malicious things that the press reported last week concerning two of your best friends is still mystery to me." He reminded Powell that he had defended him against the attacks of his "most severe critics" but pledged not to seek revenge: "I will hold nothing in my heart against you and I will not go to the press to answer or condemn you."[156]

King had dealt with previous conflicts within the movement and accusations of left-wing ties, but he was unprepared for Powell's follow-up. Through intermediaries, Powell demanded the cancellation of the convention protests and threatened to leak to the press accusations of a sexual relationship between Rustin and King.[157] Randolph refused to cancel the protests, but with pressure mounting, Rustin tendered his resignation as King's special assistant, director of the New York office of SCLC, and as executive director of the Committee to Defend Martin Luther King. He explained in a press release that he could not be responsible for causing problems when "the best elements of the Negro leadership are frustrated, diverted, and attacked as the result of my relationship to them."[158]

Delayed en route from Rio de Janeiro where he had attended a meeting of the Baptist World Alliance, King requested that a representative read his prepared remarks to the Democratic Party's platform committee, which had convened in Los Angeles on 7 July. Local minister and NAACP leader Maurice A. Dawkins delivered King's statement, which questioned the sincerity of the party "when sitting in your midst are delegates sworn to deny citizens their Constitutional rights." The statement further demanded that committee members "unseat and repudiate" segregationist delegates and other "such defilers of the law of the land."[159] A second representative, L. B. Thompson, presented platform proposals on behalf of King and Randolph including an endorsement of the sit-in protests, a presidential order banning discrimination in government jobs and housing, and a civil rights bill

155. "Powell Insists Randolph, King Are 'Captives,'" *Pittsburgh Courier,* 25 June 1960.

156. King to Powell, 24 June 1960, p. 481 in this volume. For King's public defense of Powell during the congressman's 1958 tax evasion trial, see King to Powell, 10 June 1958, in *Papers* 4:420–421.

157. By Rustin's later account, King found the threat debilitating: "Martin was so terrified by this that he, in fact, tried to get Randolph to call off the demonstrations" (Bayard Rustin, *The Reminiscences of Bayard Rustin* [New York: Oral History Research Office, Columbia University, 1988], p. 161). Nat Hentoff, writing in the *Village Voice,* criticized Powell for his divisiveness but also chided King for failing to support Rustin just as he had failed Lawson a month earlier: "King by temperament is not a fighter. He is appalled at prospects of 'division' within 'the movement.' Accordingly, he sometimes will not only not fight for himself, but he will also not support his subordinates" (Nat Hentoff, "Adam Clayton Powell: What Price Principle?" *Village Voice,* 14 July 1960).

158. SCLC, Press release, 27 June 1960; see also Rustin, Interview by T. H. Baker, 30 June 1969.

159. Introductory remarks to the 1960 Democratic Party platform committee, read by Maurice A. Dawkins, 7 July 1960.

that would provide stronger enforcement of the Supreme Court's school desegregation decision.[160]

On 10 July, King and student protest leaders Bernard Lee and Marion Barry led a march of several thousand demonstrators to the sports arena where the convention was to begin the following day.[161] At a brief outdoor rally near the arena, King explained that the purpose of the gathering was to "urge the great Democratic party" to treat racial injustice "as one of the basic moral issues facing the world today."[162] In a six-block-long column, marchers then proceeded to an NAACP meeting at the Shrine Auditorium where civil rights leaders and presidential hopefuls addressed the audience.[163] A disapproving chorus greeted Kennedy's remarks as well as those of a representative of Senator Lyndon Johnson, prompting NAACP Washington Bureau Director Clarence Mitchell to seize the microphone and admonish the audience: "This is not the NAACP way. We do not boo our invited guests."[164] According to a press account, Adam Clayton Powell received the most enthusiastic response from the crowd, despite his earlier opposition to the March on the Conventions Movement.[165] In an interview with a *Montgomery Advertiser* reporter, King expressed his mixed views of Senator Kennedy, who by this time had become the frontrunner for his party's nomination. King asserted that Alabama governor John Patterson's recent endorsement of Kennedy had added to his problems with black voters, and he suggested that his Roman Catholicism raised "legitimate questions" though "once he has answered them we should not cast him aside." King also expressed the hope that religion "doesn't become a major issue and ultimately a nasty issue in this campaign."[166]

The March on the Conventions Movement reprised its efforts two weeks later in Chicago, where King, Wilkins, and Randolph and more than five thousand protesters encircled the International Amphitheatre and congested local automobile and pedestrian traffic. Republican delegates were forced to cross lines of mostly black picketers until a party representative promised them a floor vote on a proposed civil rights plank the demonstrators considered too weak.[167] The demonstrations successfully prodded both parties to adopt their strongest civil rights planks in recent history, with the Democrats embracing several of the protesters' demands. When they spoke with reporters at Chicago's Conrad Hilton Hotel, King and Randolph applauded "the overall goals and principles in both party planks," but they questioned whether either party could deliver on its promises.[168]

Following the demonstrations, King left for speaking engagements in Oklahoma

160. See King and Randolph, Joint Platform Proposals to the 1960 Democratic Party Platform Committee, Read by L. B. Thompson, 7 July 1960, pp. 482–485 in this volume.

161. "Cheers and Boos Greet Kennedy at Rights Rally," *Los Angeles Times*, 11 July 1960.

162. Louis Lautier, "Rev. Powell Steals Show at NAACP Pre-Convention Rally," *Baltimore Afro-American*, 23 July 1960.

163. For King's remarks, see Address at NAACP Mass Rally for Civil Rights, 10 July 1960, pp. 485–487 in this volume.

164. Lautier, "Rev. Powell Steals Show," 23 July 1960.

165. Kenneth C. Field, "7,000 Boo, Cheer at 'Rights' Rally," *Los Angeles Sentinel*, 14 July 1960.

166. Bob Ingram, "Kennedy Out of Favor with Negro, King Says," *Montgomery Advertiser*, 14 July 1960.

167. Thomas Powers, "5,000 Demonstrate for Civil Rights Plank," *Chicago Tribune*, 26 July 1960.

168. Johnnie Moore, "King, Randolph Still Skeptical," *Chicago Defender*, 28 July 1960.

that marked the start of a series of addresses delivered over the next three months in which he peppered his standard remarks with appeals intended to boost black voter turnout.[169] Appearing on behalf of a Louisville voter registration drive that featured a downtown parade and rally, he encouraged his audience of nine thousand to make "wider use of the wonder drug of voting" and to build upon the courageous student "sit-ins, wade-ins, and kneel-ins" with the added dimension of "stand-ins at places of voter registration." Though Eisenhower had signed the Civil Rights Act of 1960 just four months earlier, King warned that "if the Democratic Party emerges from this session of Congress without supporting new civil-rights legislation merely to appease the Southern Dixiecrats, it may well be committing political suicide where the Negro vote is concerned."[170]

In the midst of the presidential campaign, King participated in what was becoming an annual fall drama at the National Baptist Convention. During the previous four conventions, J. H. Jackson, the autocratic president of the largest organization of black Baptists, had successfully dodged parliamentary, legal, and even physical challenges to his leadership.[171] King and other, mostly younger, ministers who doubted Jackson's commitment to civil rights had been privately plotting his ouster for several years, but the 1960 meeting in Philadelphia marked the first time that King publicly opposed him. In a tumultuous session during which podium addresses were interrupted by marching bands and mysteriously malfunctioning microphones, reporters spotted King huddling with Jackson's main rival, New York minister Gardner Taylor. The convention ended with the delegates electing two competing slates of officers, a situation that remained unresolved until the following year when King and the insurgents formed a splinter organization, the Progressive National Baptist Convention.[172]

The fall also witnessed renewed attempts by black parents to desegregate public schools, the return to campus of black student protesters, and heightened racist resistance to desegregation. On 27 August, a white mob in Jacksonville, Florida, armed with bats and ax handles, pummeled peaceful picketers affiliated with the NAACP's Youth Council. The mob pursued the students into a black neighborhood, where they clashed with black gang members. King appealed to the Jacksonville movement to remain nonviolent, but his offer to visit the city was rejected by a local NAACP official who explained that his group had not instigated the violence "and since our people are alert and responsible, we believe we are fully

---

169. In Tulsa, Oklahoma, on 28 July, King spoke before a crowd of 1,500 at a rally held at First Baptist Church ("Freedom Rally: Attended by 1,500 King Urges Sit-ins," *Oklahoma Eagle,* 4 August 1960).

170. "King Urges Negro Voter Registration Raps Both Parties," *Louisville Times,* 24 August 1960; see also King, Excerpts, Address at Jefferson County armory, 23 August 1960. For more on the Civil Rights Act of 1960, see Jacob K. Javits to King, 21 April 1960, pp. 439–440 in this volume.

171. For more on previous Baptist conventions, see Introduction, in *Papers* 4:17–18. Following the 1959 convention in San Francisco, King wrote to New York minister Thomas Kilgore, urging Jackson's ouster: "We can no longer passively accept the moral degeneracy which has infiltrated the top echelon of our convention. Let us go on to victory in 1960" (King to Kilgore, 6 October 1959, p. 305 in this volume).

172. "Baptists in Convention, Name Two," *Baltimore Afro-American,* 17 September 1960.

able to meet what ever situation that may arise."[173] Around the same time, three of Fred Shuttlesworth's children were arrested and beaten in jail after they refused to move to the back of a Greyhound bus near Gadsden, Alabama, on their way home from a youth workshop at the Highlander Folk School in Tennessee. King's demands to the attorney general for an "immediate investigation" were brushed off by Justice Department officials, who "assured" him that "appropriate action will be taken should it develop that violations of federal laws are involved."[174] A few weeks later, landowners in Fayette and Haywood counties in Tennessee began evicting black sharecroppers for attempting to register to vote. White bankers and merchants collaborated by refusing to trade with the evicted farmers, and hundreds of black families took refuge from the approaching winter in two tent cities that were kept supplied by civil rights supporters.[175] SCLC's own annual conference in Shreveport was marred by a shooting attack aimed at new field secretary Harry Blake.[176]

Returning to Atlanta on 14 October, King participated in a three-day SNCC conference intended to confirm the group's status as a permanent organization and to map its future direction. Roughly two hundred black and white students attended the opening session of the conference, held at Atlanta University, to hear King speak on "The Philosophy of Nonviolence."[177] On the program to address the conference was a mixture of movement veterans such as Ella Baker, Marion Wright of the Southern Regional Council, C. T. Vivian of the Nashville Christian Leadership Conference (NCLC), and student newcomers such as Marion Barry and Diane Nash.[178] SNCC chairman Barry, buoyed by his participation in the convention protests, effused that "for the first time in history, Negro students . . . are heard by the political parties, and our demands were written into their platforms." James Lawson struck a more sober note in his discussion of "Jail Versus Bail," arguing that the movement had lost its "finest hour . . . when so many hundreds of us left the jails across the South. Instead of letting the adults scurry around getting bail, we should have insisted that they scurry about to end the system which

173. Goodson to King, 2 September 1960; see also King to Johnnie H. Goodson, 29 August 1960, pp. 497–498 in this volume. For press coverage of the Jacksonville riot, see "Violence Flares in Jacksonville," *New York Times,* 28 August 1960, and "Violence in Jacksonville," *Southern Patriot,* October 1960.

174. King to William P. Rogers, 18 August 1960, p. 497 in this volume, and Harold R. Tyler to King, 2 September 1960.

175. "Negroes' Tent City Decried As Stunt," *New York Times,* 29 December 1960, and Anthony Lewis, "U.S. Suit Charges an Economic Bar to Negro Voting," *New York Times,* 14 September 1960; see also King to James F. Estes, December 1960, p. 567 in this volume, and Baker to Estes, 12 February 1960.

176. James Wood, "3500 Attend SCLC Annual Conference," *Southern Patriot,* November 1960. For more information on the meeting, see King, "Message from the President," 11 October–13 October 1960, pp. 517–518 in this volume, and Tyler to King, 17 October 1960.

177. See King, Outline, The Philosophy of Nonviolence, 14 October 1960, pp. 520–521 in this volume.

178. SNCC, Agenda, "Conference: nonviolence and the achievement of desegregation," 14 October–16 October 1960.

had put us in jail. If history offers us such an opportunity again, let us be prepared to seize it."[179]

History waited about five days. On 19 October King and fifty-one demonstrators were arrested for trespassing while attempting to obtain service at a restaurant in Rich's department store. King and thirty-five other protesters refused bond and chose to remain in custody for "a year or even ten years" if necessary.[180] At the new Fulton County jail, the students dined on liver and onions, while King, who was fasting, phoned Coretta before speaking to the press. He denied reporters' suggestions that he had led the protests and emphasized the students' initiative and leadership: "Last night they called me and asked me to join in it. They wanted me to be in it, and I felt a moral obligation to be in it with them. I had been in on this thing from the beginning, and I felt that when the actual moment came when somebody got arrested I should be in on it."[181] In jail the following day, King and the other young inmates shuttled notes amongst themselves to maintain their spirits, while outside two thousand students formed picket lines at other segregated downtown stores.[182] Police arrested a second round of demonstrators, including A. D. King, and telegrams from across the nation demanding the students' release began flooding Atlanta mayor William B. Hartsfield's office.[183] As protests continued into the weekend, store owners closed many downtown lunch counters, and reporters noted the appearance on the streets of white counter-protesters and Ku Klux Klansmen. King resisted pleas from both supporters and civic leaders to accept bail, declaring to a *Pittsburgh Courier* reporter that he and the students "will positively stay in jail unless the lunch counters are desegregated." He observed that his detention had caused him to miss several engagements, including a scheduled fund-raising address in Cleveland that would have netted SCLC several thousands of dollars. King asserted that he felt obliged to remain in jail "since this was what I had been preaching. I had to practice what I preached."[184]

On Saturday, 22 October, Hartsfield moved to broker a truce by calling sixty black leaders, including King, Sr. and student representatives, to City Hall. After

---

179. Anne Braden, "Student Movement: New Phase," *Southern Patriot,* October 1960.

180. King, Draft, Statement to Judge James E. Webb after Arrest at Rich's Department Store, 19 October 1960, p. 524 in this volume; see also Bruce Galphin and Keeler McCartney, "King, 51 Others Arrested Here in New Sit-In Push," *Atlanta Constitution,* 20 October 1960, and Wyatt Tee Walker to Hartsfield, 20 October 1960. Several student leaders would later recall that the effort to coax King into the protest required something of a campaign in itself; Morehouse student Lonnie King explained to King that he "was going to have to go to jail if he intended to maintain his position as one of the leaders in the civil rights struggle" (Lonnie King, Interview by John H. Britton, 29 August 1967).

181. Raleigh Bryans, "Negroes Count on Atlanta as Moderate, Dr. King Says," *Atlanta Journal,* 20 October 1960.

182. See King, To Female Inmates, 19 October–23 October 1960, pp. 527–528 in this volume; see also Mattie Cox et al. to Brothers, 19 October–23 October 1960, and Carolyn Long to Omega Brothers, 22 October 1960.

183. John Britton, "Mayor Suggests 'Truce' in Demonstrations Here," *Atlanta Daily World,* 22 October 1960; see also William H. Gray, Jr. to William Berry Hartsfield, 20 October 1960, and "Gate City 'Shook Up': 'Sit-Ins' Step Up Pressure in Atlanta," *Pittsburgh Courier,* 29 October 1960.

184. Trezzvant W. Anderson, "'I Had to Practice What I Preached,'" *Pittsburgh Courier,* 29 October 1960.

a nearly three-hour meeting, Hartsfield announced that local black leaders had agreed to halt the demonstrations for thirty days in exchange for the release of the jailed students. Hartsfield also pledged to open negotiations with the store owners to consider the students' demands.[185] The following day, the released protesters began making their way from jail to a celebration at Paschal's restaurant near the Morehouse campus. Coretta King waited anxiously among the well-wishers, but her husband never appeared.[186] King remained in custody awaiting a hearing to determine if his arrest had violated the conditions of his probation stemming from a May traffic violation in neighboring DeKalb County.[187]

King supporters, spectators, and reporters packed his 25 October hearing at the DeKalb County courthouse. Atlanta NAACP president Samuel Williams jostled with police before being arrested, while Coretta sat alongside King, Sr., A. D., and Christine on the "colored" side of the courtroom. King's attorney Donald Hollowell argued that the probation was excessive for a minor traffic offense, and King testified that he had been unaware of his probation until being notified of it in the Fulton County jail just three days earlier. DeKalb County judge J. Oscar Mitchell was unmoved by these arguments, and he was equally unpersuaded by pleas from six prominent character witnesses, including Benjamin Mays. He sentenced King to four months in Georgia state prison at Reidsville.[188] Roy Wilkins, who had flown in from New York to attend the hearing, decried the "shocking decision" and explained to reporters that it would have a "great impact upon all the colored people of this country emotionally." Shortly after the sentencing, Wilkins attempted to visit King to deliver him a copy of George Orwell's *1984*, but guards denied him access after he identified himself as a visitor from New York. "I should have said I came over from Savannah," he quipped.[189] Coretta, with Daddy King at her side, was allowed to see her husband for what was an emotional visit. She later recalled that he appeared "weakened by his days in jail" and that he was "greatly depressed" by the "unexpected shock" of his sentence.[190]

At 4 A.M. the following morning, guards woke King, ordering him to dress and gather his belongings. Before his attorney or any of his family received notification, King was transferred from his cell to the state penitentiary at Reidsville. Uncertain of his destination and finding his guards unresponsive to his queries, King was deeply

185. "Negroes Agree to Halt Sit-Ins for 30 Days Here," *Atlanta Journal*, 23 October 1960, and "Rev. King Freed in Fulton Sit-Ins but Must Face DeKalb Traffic Case," *Atlanta Constitution*, 25 October 1960; see also Hartsfield, Interview on Martin Luther King, Jr.'s arrest and student sit-ins, 24 October 1960.

186. Coretta Scott King, *My Life with Martin Luther King, Jr.*, p. 192.

187. King had been stopped by police on 4 May while driving white author Lillian Smith to Emory University Hospital. On 23 September he pled guilty to driving with an invalid license and was fined $25 and a twelve-month probation (John Britton, "Sentence Termed Excessive, Harsh, Cruel: Motion to Revoke Conviction of King Rejected Following Early Morning Transfer to Reidsville," *Atlanta Daily World*, 27 October 1960; see also Jack Strong, "King Gets 4 Months in DeKalb Court," *Atlanta Constitution*, 26 October 1960).

188. Jack Strong, "King Gets 4 Months in DeKalb Court," *Atlanta Constitution*, 26 October 1960; see also Coretta Scott King, *My Life with Martin Luther King, Jr.*, p. 193.

189. Roy Wilkins, Press conference, 25 October 1960.

190. Coretta Scott King, *My Life with Martin Luther King, Jr.*, p. 194.

unnerved by the situation. "On the way they dealt with me just like I was a hardened criminal," he later told an interviewer. "They had me chained all the way down there and—you know, the chains about my legs. They kind of tied my legs to . . . they had something in the floor where the chains were attached and I guess it's a method they use when they transport real criminals so it would be no way for me to escape—and I was handcuffed."[191] Escorted to a single cell, apart from the rest of the prison population, King penned a letter to Coretta, who was five months pregnant: "Hello Darling, Today I find myself a long way from you and the children." Acknowledging the inconvenience his arrest had caused his wife, he explained, "this excessive suffering that is now coming to our family will in some little way serve to make Atlanta a better city, Georgia a better state, and America a better country. Just how I do not yet know, but I have faith to believe it will."[192]

King's predicament spurred widespread sympathy and support. Receiving the brunt of an outpouring of political pressure from King's supporters, an exasperated Hartsfield issued a declaration to the press: "We wish the world to know that the City of Atlanta had no part in the trial and sentencing of Dr. Martin Luther King for a minor traffic offense. The responsibility for this belongs to DeKalb County and the State of Georgia."[193] Judge Mitchell, Georgia governor Ernest Vandiver, and President Eisenhower also received critical telegrams and phone calls, many of which argued that the incident was damaging the nation's global standing. The Jewish Labor Committee demanded that Vandiver issue a pardon immediately and warned that "the arrest and imprisonment of Dr. King will be played up in the Soviet and stooge press in order to buttress Khrushchev's contentions" about discrimination and bigotry in the United States. Two educators from New York lamented that the administration's efforts with unaligned African countries "will be canceled by wire photographs abroad of the Rev. King in handcuffs."[194]

With the election little more than a week away, King supporters also exerted substantial pressure on the presidential candidates, transforming what had begun as a local protest against segregation into a national campaign issue with international implications. SCLC and nearly twenty other civil rights groups wired Nixon and Kennedy explaining that white intransigence and government inaction in the South had threatened "the prestige of our nation and our moral integrity as a people." Among a list of ten demands, the organizations urged the candidates to "speak out against the imprisonment of Dr. Martin Luther King, Jr." before the election.[195] Following the announcement of King's removal to state prison, Harris Wofford and other intermediaries persuaded Senator Kennedy to telephone Coretta King to express his concern. On the day of King's transfer to Reidsville, Kennedy spoke with her briefly from Chicago, where he had been campaigning. Later that day Coretta King told a reporter that the Democratic candidate's call

---

191. Quoted in Interview by Berl I. Bernhard, 9 March 1964.

192. King to Coretta Scott King, 26 October 1960, pp. 531–532 in this volume.

193. "Trial Not City's, Mayor Emphasizes," *Atlanta Journal,* 26 October 1960.

194. "King's Imprisonment Stirs U.S.-Wide Wave of Criticism," *Atlanta Constitution,* 27 October 1960; see also Joachim Prinz to S. Ernest Vandiver, 26 October 1960.

195. SCLC and Southern Conference Educational Fund, Inc. to Kennedy and Nixon, 27 October 1960.

"certainly made me feel good that he called me personally and let me know how he felt." She also said that the call led her to believe that Kennedy "would do what he could to see that Mr. King is let out of jail."[196] Soon after this call, attorney general Robert Kennedy initiated a series of contacts with Vandiver that eventually led to King's release. In a 1964 interview Robert Kennedy described his conversation with Vandiver: "I talked to the governor. And he said that if I called the judge, that he thought that the judge would let Martin Luther King off."[197] Calling from a pay booth in Long Island, Robert Kennedy phoned Judge Mitchell, and on 27 October the judge freed King on a $2,000 appeal bond.[198] King emerged from prison and flew immediately to Peachtree-DeKalb airport, where he was greeted by his family, reporters, and cheering students. He told the gathered reporters that he owed "a great debt of gratitude to Senator Kennedy and his family" and downplayed the candidate's political motivations: "I'm sure that the senator did it because of his real concern and his humanitarian bent." Though pressed by reporters, King declined to endorse Kennedy, explaining that it would be in-

196. When asked if she had heard from Vice President Nixon, Coretta King replied that "he's been very quiet" ("Kennedy Phoned to Express Concern, King's Wife Says," *Atlanta Constitution,* 27 October 1960). Within the Nixon campaign, advisors drafted telegrams and support statements on King's behalf, including the following by deputy attorney general Lawrence E. Walsh: "It seems to me fundamentally unjust that a man who has peacefully attempted to establish his right to equal treatment free from racial discrimination be imprisoned on an old, unrelated and relatively insignificant charge, driving without a license. . . . Accordingly, I have asked the Attorney General to take all proper steps to join with Dr. King in an appropriate application to vacate this sentence" (Lawrence E. Walsh, Suggested statement on arrest of Martin Luther King, Jr., 31 October 1960). These proposals were pocketed by campaign organizers "to think about," as one black staff member would later recall (E. Frederic Morrow, Journal entry, 10 November 1960). E. Frederic Morrow would later tell an interviewer that his efforts were frustrated by campaign staff members and not the candidate: "It was his advisors who did me in rather than Nixon" (Morrow, Interview by Thomas Soapes, 23 February 1977). Speaking to an interviewer several years later, King blasted Nixon as a "moral coward" for failing to act on his behalf: "He had been supposedly close to me and he would call me frequently about things . . . getting . . . seeking my advice. And yet, when this moment came it was like he had never heard of me" (King, Interview by Berl I. Bernhard, 9 March 1964).

197. Kennedy further noted that he kept the conversation with Vandiver secret because he "thought it would destroy the governor!" (Robert F. Kennedy and Burke Marshall, Interview by Anthony Lewis, 4 December 1964). In a 1967 interview, Vandiver reiterated Kennedy's concern that it would have been "political suicide, with the temper of the times as it was, for it to have been publicized. . . . However, with my interest in seeing that Kennedy was elected president, I was willing to take that chance" (S. Ernest Vandiver, Interview by John F. Stewart, 22 May 1967). Various leaders began taking credit for Kennedy's election in November 1960, including Atlanta mayor William Hartsfield, who recalled receiving numerous telegrams and letters protesting King's arrest; realizing the political significance the arrest could have for the presidential election, he recalled exclaiming: "Great goodness, this presidential race is close. None of us knows which way New York's going; none of us knows which way Illinois is going and the Negro vote counts heavily" (William B. Hartsfield, Interview by Charles T. Morrissey, 6 January 1966).

198. Robert F. Kennedy and Burke Marshall, Interview by Anthony Lewis, 4 December 1964. To the press Robert Kennedy attempted to downplay the phone call's impact, explaining that he had been pressed to act by the requests that had "swamped" Kennedy headquarters. Governor Vandiver, who was intimately involved in the arrangements, blasted the Kennedys for their alleged meddling on behalf of "the foremost racial agitator in the country" (Bruce Galphin, "His Call Misinterpreted, Robert Kennedy Says," *Atlanta Constitution,* 1 November 1960).

appropriate for him to do so as the leader of the nonpartisan SCLC.[199] King's reluctance to take a formal stand was soon overshadowed, however, by Daddy King's announcement that he had switched his allegiance to Kennedy, despite his earlier concern that the candidate was Catholic. "I've got all my votes, and I've got a suitcase, and I'm going to take them up there and dump them in his lap," the elder King was quoted as saying.[200]

Over the next several days, Kennedy campaign workers distributed thousands of flyers at black churches all over the country contrasting "'No Comment' Nixon" with the "Candidate with a Heart." The pamphlet featured quotes from King, Abernathy—"it is time for all of us to take off our Nixon buttons"—as well as from King's wife and father.[201] These efforts among black voters may have given Kennedy his slim margin of victory over Nixon on 8 November.[202] The following day the chairman of the Republican National Committee explained that Nixon's defeat came about because the party "lost the Negro vote by a larger percentage" than in previous elections. President Eisenhower grumbled that a "couple of phone calls" made the difference, and the *Atlanta Journal* dubbed Judge J. Oscar Mitchell "president-maker."[203]

Soon after the election, King departed for Lagos, Nigeria, where he witnessed the inauguration of Nnamdi Azikiwe as governor-general.[204] Upon his return home he took part in a televised debate with segregationist newspaper editor James J. Kilpatrick. The latter event proved a serious test of King's ability to defend the principles of civil disobedience against an articulate opponent. King, shuffling through note cards during the broadcast, scarcely expanded his argument during the half-hour program. When Kilpatrick prodded King about legal issues and property rights, King sheepishly replied, "I go back to the argument, Mr. Kilpatrick, that an unjust law is no law at all."[205] According to one account, SNCC students who watched King's appearance on "The Nation's Future" were sorely disappointed

---

199. King, Interview on John F. Kennedy's role in release from prison, 27 October 1960; see also King, Interview after Release from Georgia State Prison at Reidsville, 27 October 1960, and King, Statement on Presidential Endorsement, 1 November 1960, pp. 535–536 and 537–540 in this volume, respectively.

200. Margaret Shannon and Douglas Kiker, "Out on Bond, King to Name Choice," *Atlanta Journal,* 28 October 1960.

201. For a facsimile of the Freedom Crusade Committee pamphlet, "The Case of Martin Luther King," see pp. 538–539 in this volume.

202. The following month, in Chattanooga, Tennessee, King addressed an audience at Memorial Auditorium, where he declared that the "Negro played a decisive role in electing the president" and remained optimistic about the "power of the ballot and what the ballot can do." King instructed the audience that "we must remind Mr. Kennedy that we helped him to get in the White House" and that "we are expecting him to use the whole weight of his office to remove the ugly weight of segregation from the shoulders of our nation" ("The Negro and the American Dream," Address delivered at the Memorial Auditorium, 30 December 1960).

203. Harold Davis, "Lodge Lost Negro Votes: Did Judge in King Case Supply Kennedy His Edge?" *Atlanta Journal,* 10 November 1960, and Anthony Lewis, "Protests over Dr. King's Arrest Was Drafted for President's Use," *New York Times,* 15 December 1960; see also Gloster B. Current, "Why Nixon Lost the Negro Vote," *The Crisis* (January 1961): 5–14.

204. See Nnamdi Azikiwe to King, 26 October 1960, pp. 533–534 in this volume.

205. Debate with James J. Kilpatrick on "The Nation's Future," 26 November 1960, p. 563 in this volume.

in his feeble defense of the sit-in movement. Ella Baker recalled that students left the room mid-debate and "their criticism of King . . . finally broke openly to the surface," illustrating the disconnect between the burgeoning student movement and its elders.[206]

King returned from Africa to a different freedom movement than the one he had rejoined after traveling to India in the spring of 1959. No longer broke and unable to meet its payroll, SCLC found itself, by virtue of the tax case and the Atlanta arrests, in the unaccustomed position of receiving sufficient contributions to expand its staff and develop new programs. King's endless run of speaking engagements and Levison's and Rustin's honing of the organization's direct appeals had also finally paid off; plans were under way to complement these efforts with grants from major foundations and donations from a benefit performance featuring top entertainers Sammy Davis, Jr. and Frank Sinatra.[207] The addition of Wyatt Tee Walker, as well as Atlanta staff members James Wood and Dorothy Cotton, regularized SCLC's day-to-day operations, allowing it to respond to the demands of its affiliates and the needs of a growing civil rights movement.[208] Wood and Cotton spent the last weeks of 1960 arranging to assume responsibility for the Highlander Folk School's citizenship education training program, as Harry Blake pressed SCLC's voting initiative in Louisiana, giving that campaign the full-time attention it required.[209]

Most importantly, the freedom movement had at last found a base. The murmur of discontent signaled by the Youth Marches had burst into a chorus of revolt in the spring of 1960. Black high school and college students from across the South had reclaimed the energy of Montgomery, extended it, and in the process captured the imagination of young people across the nation. Through the end of 1960 sit-ins were staged in more than one hundred southern cities, and the students' energy showed few signs of waning.[210] If Mayor Hartsfield had hoped that the approaching holidays would bring a tapering off of protest spirit in Atlanta, he would be sorely disappointed. At the end of the thirty-day truce on 23 November, youth leaders granted him two additional days to reach an agreement with the store owners, after which they resumed their pickets and demonstrations into the new year.[211] The students had added an important weapon to the movement's arsenal, which had relied heavily on moral suasion to this point. Practitioners of direct action possessed the power to disrupt the normal operation of segregation. SCLC and SNCC were becoming increasingly sophisticated at dramatizing the contradictions of southern racism for the nation and the world through their arrests, boycotts, and convention protests. For the new Democratic

206. James Howard Laue, "Direct Action and Desegregation: Toward a Theory of the Rationalization of Protest" (PhD diss., Harvard University, 1965), p. 169.

207. See King to Davis, 20 December 1960, pp. 582–583 in this volume.

208. Walker, "Report of the director to the executive board," 11 October 1960.

209. Wood, "Report, Leadership training program," 23 November 1960.

210. Martin Oppenheimer, "The Sit-In Movement of 1960" (Ph.D. diss., University of Pennsylvania, 1963), p. 268.

211. Bruce Galphin, "Negroes Resume Sit-Ins, End Truce," *Atlanta Constitution,* 26 November 1960.

administration, which had made the nation's loss of global prestige its central campaign theme and which may have owed its victory to African American voters, the demands of the black South could no longer go unheeded. New tactics and a shifting political climate offered King reason for hope as he looked to the coming year. Writing to Roy Wilkins shortly after the election, King observed that "although the problems which we face in Atlanta and in the South at the present time are somewhat gigantic in extent and chaotic in detail, I am convinced that we stand on the threshold of the world's bright tomorrows. I will continue to work with that faith."[212]

---

212. King to Wilkins, 1 December 1960.

1959

1 Jan King attends an Emancipation Day program in Mobile, Alabama. At the Prayer Pilgrimage for Public Schools in Richmond, Virginia, march organizers play a seven-minute pre-recorded message from King.

2–3 Jan King attends a meeting of the planning committee of the Southern Christian Leadership Conference (SCLC) at Atlanta's Ebenezer Baptist Church.

4 Jan King preaches "Inner Calm Amid Outer Tension" at Dexter Avenue Baptist Church in Montgomery.

11 Jan King preaches at Dexter.

14 Jan In New Haven, Connecticut, King meets with Yale University president Whitney Griswold and conducts an interview prior to delivering "The Future of Integration" at Yale's Woolsey Hall. During King's speech, police receive a bomb threat but no bomb is found. Later, King's hosts throw a surprise birthday party for him at the university's Pierson College.

15 Jan King speaks on the "Problems of the South" in the Yale University auditorium.

18 Jan King delivers "The Blinding Power of Sin" at Dexter.

20–23 Jan King attends the National Baptist Convention board of directors meeting in Hot Springs, Arkansas.

24 Jan At Montgomery's First Baptist Church, King is among seventy-five Alabama leaders who discuss strategies for increasing voter registration among African Americans.

26 Jan During a mass meeting at Dexter, Montgomery Improvement Association (MIA) members hold a "bon voyage" party for Martin and Coretta Scott King before their upcoming trip to India and the Middle East. The Kings are later feted at the home of congregation member J. T. Alexander.

28 Jan In the church auditorium, the Dexter Women's Council hosts a reception for the Kings on the night before their departure from Montgomery.

30 Jan Due to inclement weather King arrives in Gary, Indiana, after midnight, missing his scheduled appearance at a mass meeting sponsored by the Fair Share Organization. Prior to traveling to Detroit to meet with Walter Reuther of the United Auto Workers (UAW), King meets with officers of the Fair Share

Organization at Junior's Snack Shop and tape records a message to be played during a meeting of the organization.

1 Feb In the morning, he preaches at Bright Hope Baptist Church in Philadelphia. At Beaver College in Glenside, King receives the Anderson Memorial Award from the Berean Institute. At Philadelphia's National Freedom Day observance, King addresses the audience and lays a wreath at the Liberty Bell. King later attends dinner at the Sheraton Hotel and preaches at Philadelphia's Vine Memorial Baptist Church.

2 Feb King attends a luncheon given by India trip co-sponsors at the American Friends Service Committee (AFSC) in Philadelphia. He later addresses a meeting of the War Resisters League in New York.

3 Feb At New York's Idlewild Airport, the Kings and Lawrence Dunbar Reddick depart for a six-week visit to India and the Middle East.

4 Feb King arrives in London.

5 Feb In London, the Kings and Reddick see the play *Chrysanthemum.*

6 Feb King arrives in Paris; expatriate African American novelist Richard Wright meets King and his companions at the airport. They dine at Wright's home that evening.

7 Feb King arrives in Zurich, Switzerland.

8 Feb King's tape-recorded sermon "Looking Beyond Our Circumstances" is played during Sunday services at Dexter.

9 Feb King arrives in Bombay.

10 Feb Indian admirers present garlands to the Kings as they arrive at the Palam Airport in New Delhi two days late because of a missed flight in Zurich. King holds a press conference at the Janpath Hotel before having lunch with Rajkumari Amrit Kaur, secretary to Gandhi and India's first female cabinet minister. King then attends a reception at the Gandhi Smarak Nidhi, a co-sponsor of the visit. He later meets with India's vice president Sarvepalli Radhakrishnan and attends a reception at the Quaker Centre. In the evening, King has dinner with Indian prime minister Jawarharlal Nehru at the Teen Murti Bhavan, Nehru's residence.

11 Feb King visits Rajghat and lays a wreath on the Samadhi, the site of Gandhi's cremation. He has lunch at the New Delhi home of Indian independence leaders J. B. and Sucheta Kripalani before delivering "Achievement of Racial Justice in the World Today" to the Indian Council of World Affairs at Sapru House. King dines with Morarji Desai, the finance minister of India.

12 Feb After lunch with Kaka Kalelkar, a member of India's parliament, King addresses the Delhi University Students' Union at Ramjas College. He has tea with India's president Rajendra

Prasad before visiting the Moghul Gardens at the Rashtrapati Bhavan and addressing a meeting of Sarvodaya workers at the Gandhi Smarak Sangrahalaya building at Rajghat. That evening, King meets with former New York governor Averell Harriman at the Ashoka Hotel.

13 Feb King leaves New Delhi and arrives in Patna where he meets with Zakir Hussain, the governor of Bihar, and Sri Krishna Sinha, chief minister of the state. He attends a public meeting at the university before leaving for Gaya.

14 Feb King visits a Buddhist temple and monastery at Bodh Gaya, followed by a tour of an ashram founded by Vinoba Bhave, leader of the Bhoodan movement. He travels with Sarvodaya leader Jayaprakash Narayan to his ashram and attends a meeting with ashram workers.

15 Feb King arrives in Burdwan and drives to Shantiniketan, a school founded by Indian poet Rabindranath Tagore, where he addresses a small gathering. Later that evening, he arrives in Calcutta.

16 Feb King holds a press conference and attends a meeting at the Calcutta Gandhi Smarak Nidhi before dining at the home of Quakers Benjamin and Emily Polk. Twenty-five local leaders attend dinner, including Indian scholar Nirmal Kumar Bose.

17 Feb In Calcutta, King meets with students, followed by a public meeting.

18 Feb King holds a press conference after arriving in Madras. While there, he addresses two meetings and is a guest at Governor Bishnuram Medhi's residence, Raj Bhavan.

19 Feb King meets Chakravarti Rajagopalachari, first governor-general of independent India, before visiting the ancient stone temples at Mahabalipuram. King returns to Madras and meets with the Joint Development commissioner.

20 Feb King arrives at Gandhigram Rural Institute and attends a Shanti Sena (Peace Army) rally in the morning. At the conclusion of the Friday afternoon prayer, King delivers remarks. In the evening, he gives an address at Gandhigram and attends a cultural program.

21 Feb King visits two Gramdan (collective) villages and one village of untouchables. In Madurai, King visits a Hindu temple and attends a public meeting.

22 Feb In Trivandrum, King attends a luncheon hosted by E. M. S. Namboodiripad, the chief minister of the state of Kerala and India's communist leader. King rides to Cape Comorin, the southernmost tip of India, where some of Gandhi's ashes had been cast into the sea.

23 Feb King starts the day with a swim before taking a tour of Trivan-

drum. He attends the legislative assembly meeting and holds a press conference before speaking at a public meeting.

24 Feb In Bangalore, King meets with B. D. Jatti, chief minister of the state of Mysore.

25 Feb Still in Bangalore, King meets with Jaya Chamaraja Wadiyar, the governor of Mysore, before attending the All India Cattle Show.

26 Feb King attends a public meeting at the Institute of World Culture. At the airport in Bombay, King is greeted by Shantalal Shah, the city's labor minister. R. R. Diwakar, chairman of the Gandhi Smarak Nidhi, gives King a tour of the Mani Bhavan, Gandhi's residence in Bombay.

27 Feb In the evening King has dinner at Shah's home and attends a public meeting presided over by G. L. Mehta, former Indian ambassador to the United States, at Green's Hotel.

28 Feb At Mani Bhavan, King views *A Voice of India,* a film on Mahatma Gandhi. After meeting with Sri Prakasa, governor of Bombay, and Y. B. Chavan, the chief minister of the state, King meets with members of the Congress Party. In the evening, he spends time with a group of African students before attending a dance recital.

1 Mar King flies to Ahmadabad where he travels to Sabarmati ashram, the starting point of Gandhi's Salt March to the Sea. Following a visit to a second nearby ashram, King meets with associates of Navajivan Trust, a Gandhian publishing house.

2 Mar King travels by train to Kishangarh. He has lunch in a small village outside Kishangarh where he meets briefly with Vinoba Bhave, leader of the Bhoodan movement, and lunches with Jayaprakash Narayan.

3 Mar King joins Vinoba on a march of several miles back to Kishangarh. Following the march, King interviews Vinoba. Excerpts of the interview are later published in *Bhoodan,* the weekly newspaper of the Bhoodan movement. In the evening, Vinoba grants him an additional meeting.

4 Mar In Agra, King visits the Taj Mahal and the Agra Fort before departing for New Delhi.

5 Mar King spends much of the day at the Quaker Centre before attending a South Indian circus in New Delhi.

6 Mar King visits the office of Gandhi's secretary, Pyarelal Nayyar, and dines with G. Ramachandran, the director of the Gandhi Smarak Nidhi.

7 Mar At the Quaker Centre, King attends a discussion with representatives of the U.S. Embassy. After lunch with Rajkumari Amrit Kaur, King returns to the circus. Later, he has tea at the home of Gandhi's physician, Sushila Nayyar.

8 Mar Following worship service, King attends a farewell reception in his honor at the Gandhi Smarak Nidhi.

9 Mar On King's last day in New Delhi, he holds a press conference at the Gandhi Smarak Nidhi before attending a luncheon at the home of Ellsworth Bunker, U.S. ambassador to India. At the Quaker Centre, he records a message for broadcast on All India Radio. In the evening, King has dinner at the home of J. B. and Sucheta Kripalani.

10–17 Mar King departs from New Delhi and travels to Karachi, Beirut, Jerusalem, and Cairo before returning to New York.

18 Mar Upon his return from India, King holds a press conference at New York's Statler Hilton Hotel. He later attends a showing of the film *The Diary of Anne Frank* and visits the home of actor Harry Belafonte.

21 Mar King returns to Montgomery.

22 Mar King preaches a Palm Sunday sermon on Mahatma Gandhi at Dexter.

27 Mar In Montgomery, King conducts an interview with students from Baldwin-Wallace College. He later attends a birthday party at the home of a Dexter member.

29 Mar King preaches "A Walk Through the Holy Land" at Dexter.

Apr King's "The Future of Integration" appears in *Crises in Modern America.* Christian Education Press publishes King's *The Measure of a Man,* a book of two sermons.

2 Apr King convenes an SCLC administrative committee meeting in Montgomery, and they decide to request the resignation of SCLC executive director John Tilley.

3 Apr Administrative committee members meet with King at his Dexter office to discuss his commitment to SCLC.

5 Apr King preaches "Unfulfilled Hopes" at Dexter. He later delivers an address at Holt Street Baptist Church during a benefit for the Hale Infirmary.

12 Apr King delivers "Making Use of What You Have" at Dexter. At Mount Vernon First Baptist Church in Newnan, Georgia, he participates in his brother A. D. King's installation service.

16 Apr At Dexter, the Kings present a travelogue of their trip to India and the Middle East.

18 Apr King addresses the second Youth March for Integrated Schools at the Washington Monument.

19 Apr At Orchestra Hall, King delivers "The Dimensions of a Complete Life" before the Chicago Sunday Evening Club.

20 Apr King delivers "Paul's Letter to American Christians" at the McCormick Theological Seminary in Chicago.

22 Apr At Memorial Auditorium in Gary, Indiana, King signs copies of

Stride Toward Freedom before speaking on behalf of the Fair Share Organization.

23 Apr King delivers "Real Progress in the Area of Race Relations" at the Earlham College convocation in Richmond, Indiana.

26 Apr King preaches "The Art of Getting Along with Others" at Dexter.

28 Apr In Toronto, King appears on the Canadian television program "Front Page Challenge."

29 Apr King embarks on a speaking tour in New York sponsored by the Empire State Baptist Missionary Convention. He addresses a worship service at Concord Baptist Church of Christ in Brooklyn.

30 Apr King speaks at a rally held at Grace Baptist Church in Mount Vernon, New York.

1 May King addresses mass meetings at Harlem's Convent Avenue Baptist Church and Mount Olivet Baptist Church.

2 May At Dexter, King delivers the eulogy for church member Nellie Williams. In the evening, he attends a party sponsored by the church's April Club at the home of a Dexter member.

3 May King preaches "Sleeping Through a Revolution" at Dexter. In the afternoon he delivers a sermon for G. W. Smiley's 54th anniversary as pastor of Elizabeth Baptist Church in Union Springs, Alabama.

5 May King speaks at Calvary Baptist Church in New York City.

7 May In Connecticut, King delivers "The Future of Integration" at the University of Hartford's Bushnell Memorial Hall.

8 May King addresses a Negro Affairs rally at the New York office of District 65 of the Retail, Wholesale, and Department Store Union (RWDSU).

9 May At a press conference in New York, King comments on federal intervention into the Mack Charles Parker lynching in Mississippi and the rape of a black girl by white men in Tallahassee.

10 May King preaches "A New Challenge for Modern Mothers" at Dexter.

11 May At Washington's Sheraton Park Hotel, King addresses the Religious Leaders Conference, sponsored by the President's Committee on Government Contracts. He later addresses a mass meeting at Thessalonia Baptist Church in New York. *Stride Toward Freedom* is published in England by Victor Gollancz, Ltd.

13 May King greets Kenyan leader Tom Mboya at Atlanta Municipal Airport. He later delivers remarks at the SCLC-sponsored "Africa Freedom Dinner" in honor of Mboya, held at Atlanta

University. Following the dinner King and others socialize at Lawrence Dunbar Reddick's house.

14 May In Tallahassee, Florida, King presides over the two-day annual SCLC conference. He speaks at a mass meeting at Bethel Baptist Church.

15 May On the second day of the conference, SCLC demands that President Dwight D. Eisenhower investigate the lynching of Mack Charles Parker in Mississippi.

17 May King preaches at Dexter.

22 May King delivers the convocation address at Bishop College in Marshall, Texas.

24 May King delivers the commencement address at Maryland State College in Princess Anne.

31 May King preaches "The Service of the Church to Mental Health" at Dexter. After services he flies to New Orleans and delivers "The Dimensions of a Complete Life" at Dillard University's baccalaureate service.

1 June King delivers the commencement address at Talladega College's DeForest Chapel in Alabama.

2 June In Atlanta, King delivers "Remaining Awake Through a Great Revolution" at Morehouse College's commencement and speaks at a post-commencement banquet.

5 June King speaks at an SCLC fund-raiser at Third Baptist Church in Springfield, Massachusetts.

7 June King preaches at Twelfth Baptist Church in Roxbury, Massachusetts. At Boston University's commencement exercises, held at the Boston Garden, King recites the benediction and receives an honorary degree from his alma mater.

14 June King preaches "Unconditioned Faith" at Dexter.

16 June King speaks at the Emery Auditorium in Cincinnati to support a local register-to-vote campaign. He also speaks to the Council of Churches of Greater Cincinnati.

21 June King preaches " On Knowing How to Live with Prosperity" at Dexter.

22–28 June King is reelected vice president of the National Sunday School and Baptist Training Union (BTU) Congress at the group's annual meeting in Memphis.

25 June King speaks at an SCLC fund-raising rally held at Memphis's Metropolitan Baptist Church.

28 June At Dexter, King delivers "On Knowing How to Live with Poverty."

July *Ebony* publishes "My Trip to the Land of Gandhi," King's account of his India trip.

17 July At the New York Coliseum, King addresses the NAACP's fiftieth annual convention.

19 July King preaches at Dexter.

22 July At Spelman College, King speaks on the opening day of the First Southwide Institute on Nonviolent Resistance to Segregation.

23 July King leads a panel at the institute on "The Mass Process of Nonviolent Resistance"; he serves as an advisor during a subsequent discussion.

26 July King preaches at Dexter.

31 July King attends a meeting of the Public Advisory Review Commission of the United Packinghouse Workers of America (UPWA) at the Conrad Hilton Hotel in Chicago. At the Mason Temple in Memphis, King addresses a freedom rally on behalf of several black candidates for local office.

2 Aug King preaches at Dexter.

9 Aug King preaches "Man's Helplessness Without God" at Dexter.

16 Aug King preaches "The Conflict in Human Nature" at Dexter.

20 Aug In Milwaukee, Wisconsin, King addresses the National Bar Association convention.

21 Aug King delivers "The Future of Integration" at the Fellowship of Reconciliation (FOR) national convention in Green Lake, Wisconsin.

23 Aug King preaches "Loving Your Enemies" at Central Methodist Church in Detroit.

30 Aug King preaches "A Tough Mind and a Tender Heart" at Dexter.

2 Sept In Montgomery, King meets with black homeowners from Gadsden, Alabama, to discuss efforts to protect their houses from city demolition plans.

6 Sept King preaches at Dexter.

8 Sept King arrives in San Francisco for the annual meeting of the National Baptist Convention.

11 Sept King addresses the Laymen's Movement of the National Baptist Convention at Mount Pilgrim Baptist Church in San Francisco.

13 Sept King preaches at Victory Baptist Church in Los Angeles.

14 Sept King holds a press conference upon his arrival in Honolulu.

15 Sept King addresses the Honolulu Ministerial Union at the Armed Forces YMCA. He also speaks at Punahou School.

16 Sept At an event sponsored by the Honolulu Council of Churches, King delivers "A Pastor's Hope for America" in the McKinley High School auditorium.

17 Sept In the Iolani Palace, King addresses the House of Representatives of the Hawaiian State legislature. He tours the Pearl Harbor memorial aboard a private yacht.

20 Sept King delivers the Youth Day sermon at Second Baptist Church in Los Angeles. In Tucson that evening, he delivers "A Great Time to Be Alive" for the Sunday Evening Forum at the University of Arizona auditorium.

21 Sept At a mass meeting sponsored by the local SCLC affiliate, King speaks at the International Longshoremen's Association (ILA) Union Hall Auditorium in New Orleans.

23 Sept King gives a press conference prior to meeting with faculty members at Campbell College in Jackson, Mississippi. At Pearl Street AME Church, King speaks before the Southern Christian Ministers Conference of Mississippi.

27 Sept King preaches "Understanding Life's Injustices" at Dexter. In the evening he delivers the invocation and benediction at a concert at Dexter featuring Atlanta's Ebenezer Baptist Church choir.

30 Sept King presides over an SCLC executive board meeting at the organization's fall conference at First Calvary Baptist Church in Columbia, South Carolina. Conference delegates honor King and other civil rights leaders at a "Crusade for Citizenship Dinner" held at the Township Auditorium, followed by a mass meeting during which King speaks on "Rays of Hope."

Oct *Liberation* publishes King's "The Social Organization of Nonviolence."

1 Oct SCLC concludes its fall meeting in Columbia.

4 Oct King preaches at Dexter.

11 Oct King officiates at the funeral of church member P. H. Hobson and that evening delivers the invocation before Dexter's Women's Day program.

14 Oct At Denver's Manual High School, King speaks at an SCLC fund-raising event sponsored by the East Denver Ministerial Alliance.

16 Oct King delivers "The Future of Integration" at the American Studies Conference on Civil Rights held at the University of Minnesota's Northrop Auditorium. He then attends a luncheon in his honor at the Coffman Memorial Union. Later that afternoon, King tapes an interview for "That Free Men May Live," a national educational television program.

18 Oct King preaches at Dexter. He conducts a telephone interview with a committee of students and faculty from the United Campus Christian Fellowship at the University of North Dakota.

22 Oct King delivers "A Great Time to Be Alive" at the Majestic Theater Auditorium in Fort Worth, Texas.

25 Oct At the University of Chicago's Rockefeller Memorial Chapel,

King delivers "Remember Who You Are." After services, he attends a reception in his honor sponsored by the Hillel and Methodist Foundations.

29 Oct At New York City's Manhattan Center, King addresses a rally at an SCLC and NAACP joint fund-raising event sponsored by the Federation of Negro Civil Service Organizations.

1 Nov King preaches at Dexter.

2 Nov In Chester, Pennsylvania, Crozer Theological Seminary honors King with its first Alumni Achievement Award.

3 Nov King conducts a morning and an evening worship service during the Samuel A. Crozer lecture series at Crozer.

4 Nov King presides over morning worship services during the Crozer lectures. Later that evening, he addresses Chester's West Branch YMCA.

5 Nov At Philadelphia's Baptist Temple Church, King delivers an address at a Crusade for Citizenship rally.

8 Nov At White Rock Baptist Church, King is presented with the proceeds from the 5 November rally.

10 Nov King addresses the Waterloo, Iowa, NAACP.

11 Nov In Cedar Falls, Iowa, King delivers "The Montgomery Story" to students and faculty at Iowa State Teachers College. In the evening, he holds a press conference before delivering "The Future of Integration" at the State University of Iowa in Iowa City.

12 Nov At University Christian Church in Des Moines, Iowa, King addresses the local branch of the NAACP.

15 Nov King preaches at Dexter.

22 Nov In Columbus, Ohio, King speaks at the 71st anniversary of Union Grove Baptist Church.

29 Nov King announces his resignation from Dexter during Sunday morning services. In the evening he is the guest preacher at Ralph Abernathy's First Baptist Church in Montgomery.

30 Nov In New York, King discusses a voter registration campaign with NAACP executive secretary Roy Wilkins.

3 Dec King delivers the presidential address at the MIA's Fourth Annual Institute on Nonviolence and Social Change at Montgomery's Bethel Baptist Church.

6 Dec At Holt Street Baptist Church, King presides over the last day of the MIA's institute on nonviolence.

8 Dec At Birmingham's St. James Baptist Church, King convenes an SCLC board meeting. Following the meeting, he delivers "Freedom's Role" at a rally held at the church.

10 Dec Under the auspices of the Miami Independent Association, King delivers "The Future of Integration" at Miami University in Oxford, Ohio. Following the address, he meets with community members and university faculty.

11 Dec In Indianapolis, King delivers "Remaining Awake Through a Revolution" at the New Fall Creek Parkway YMCA.

14 Dec In Chicago, King is greeted by a 100-car motorcade at the Midway Airport. Prior to addressing an audience at Tabernacle Baptist Church, King attends a dinner in his honor at the Sherman Hotel.

15 Dec King attends a dinner in his honor at Ted's Diner in Chicago. He later speaks at Stone Temple Baptist Church.

20 Dec King preaches "The Significance of the Manger" at Dexter.

27 Dec At Dexter, King preaches "After Christmas, What?"

28 Dec After a meeting with SCLC and NAACP leaders at Atlanta's Waluhaje Hotel, King and Wilkins announce plans for a voter registration campaign.

30 Dec At Ohio University in Athens, King delivers the keynote address at the Eighteenth Ecumenical Student Conference on the Christian World Mission and holds a press conference.

1960

1 Jan At the Mosque Auditorium in Richmond, Virginia, King delivers the keynote address at the Second Annual Pilgrimage of Prayer for Public Schools. Following his address, King leads a two-mile march to the state capitol.

3 Jan King preaches at Dexter.

10 Jan At Harvard University's Memorial Church, King delivers "The Three Dimensions of a Complete Life." In the afternoon, King meets with students and faculty. That evening, King delivers "St. Paul's Letter to America" under the auspices of the Cambridge Council of Churches.

13 Jan In Washington, D.C., King attends a dinner with congressional leaders at the Willard Hotel.

14 Jan King attends a meeting of the Leadership Conference on Civil Rights in Washington, D.C.

17 Jan King delivers "The Dilemma of the Righteous Man" at Dexter.

21 Jan In North Newton, Kansas, King attends a tea in his honor before delivering "The Future of Integration" at Bethel College's Memorial Hall Series.

22 Jan At Iowa State University in Ames, Iowa, King delivers "The Moral Challenges of a New Age."

24 Jan In Charleston, West Virginia, King preaches at First Baptist

Church's morning worship service. That evening, King delivers greetings at the "Salute to A. Philip Randolph" at Carnegie Hall in New York City.

27 Jan The Kings attend a farewell party in their honor at Ralph and Juanita Abernathy's home.

30 Jan Members of the Alpha Phi Alpha fraternity hold a party in King's honor at the Montgomery home of J. Garrick Hardy.

31 Jan In his final sermon as pastor of Dexter, King delivers "Lessons from History." That evening, the Kings attend a farewell program in their honor at the church.

1 Feb At First Baptist Church, King offers his valediction at an MIA farewell celebration.

4 Feb King relocates to Atlanta, Georgia.

7 Feb King delivers "The Three Dimensions of a Complete Life," his first sermon as co-pastor of Ebenezer Baptist Church.

12 Feb A Montgomery County, Alabama, grand jury indicts King on two counts of perjury for falsifying his 1956 and 1958 tax returns.

14 Feb King delivers "Looking Beyond Difficult Circumstances" at Ebenezer.

15 Feb At Harry Belafonte's home in New York, King meets with Bayard Rustin, Ralph Abernathy, and Sidney Poitier to discuss financial support for SCLC.

16 Feb In Durham, North Carolina, King tours segregated stores that had been targeted by the city's sit-in protesters. He later delivers "A Creative Protest" at White Rock Baptist Church.

17 Feb In Atlanta, King is arrested on his Alabama tax violation.

19 Feb At Ebenezer, King and members of SCLC's personnel committee meet to interview Harry Blake for a field secretary position.

21 Feb At Chicago's Quinn Chapel AME Church, King preaches at a worship service before delivering "Going Forward by Going Backward" for the Chicago Sunday Evening Club.

23 Feb In Los Angeles, he delivers "The Struggle for Racial Justice" at Temple Isaiah.

25 Feb In Bakersfield, California, King delivers an address at Harvey Auditorium.

26 Feb King arrives in San Diego and attends a luncheon with city ministers. That evening, he addresses a rally at Calvary Baptist Church.

27 Feb In Los Angeles, King delivers "The Power Struggle and Security in a Nuclear Space Age" at Wilshire Methodist Church. At the home of George G. Smith, King discusses race relations and civil rights with other Morehouse College alumni.

28 Feb In the morning, King preaches "The Three Dimensions of a Complete Life" at Pasadena's Friendship Baptist Church. That afternoon, he speaks at Zion Hill Baptist Church in Los Angeles and later delivers "Going Forward by Going Backward" at Mt. Sinai Baptist Church.

29 Feb Facing Alabama perjury charges, King surrenders to state authorities in Montgomery and is released on $4,000 bail. Following his arraignment, King holds a press conference at Dexter and later addresses protesting Alabama State College students at Hutchinson Street Baptist Church and Bethel Baptist Church.

3 Mar King attends an SCLC board meeting at Tuskegee Institute in Alabama.

4 Mar King attends the second day of the SCLC board meeting. In the afternoon he speaks at a student rally at Beulah Baptist Church in Montgomery.

6 Mar King preaches at Ebenezer. He is later the guest speaker at New Pilgrim Baptist Church's annual Men's Day Celebration in Birmingham.

7 Mar King speaks at student rallies at Tuskegee Institute and Maggie Street Baptist Church in Montgomery.

10 Mar King delivers "The Future of Integration" at Goshen College in Indiana.

13 Mar King speaks at Princeton University's Chapel.

15 Mar King attends an executive committee meeting of the National Sunday School and BTU Congress at Mount Olivet Baptist Church in New York City.

20 Mar King preaches at Tabernacle Baptist Church in Detroit, Michigan. That evening, he delivers "Paul's Letter to American Christians" at First Methodist Church in Battle Creek, Michigan.

27 Mar King delivers "Rediscovering Lost Values" at Ebenezer.

31 Mar In Scarsdale, New York, King delivers "Loving Your Enemies" at Scarsdale Community Baptist Church. He has dinner with Eugene Exman of Harper & Brothers.

1 Apr King speaks at a fund-raising event at Salem Methodist Church in Harlem.

3 Apr King delivers "Love in Action" at Ebenezer. Later that day, he appears on "Open End," a television talk show, with segregationist editor James J. Kilpatrick.

10 Apr King delivers "The Tension Between Life's Palm Sunday and Life's Good Friday" at Ebenezer. In the afternoon, he delivers "Keep Moving from This Mountain" at the Spelman College Founder's Day.

13 Apr King's "Pilgrimage to Nonviolence" appears in *Christian Century*.

15 Apr King speaks to the press on the opening day of the Youth Leadership Conference at Shaw University in Raleigh, North Carolina.

16 Apr At Raleigh Memorial Auditorium, King addresses students attending the Youth Leadership Conference.

17 Apr King appears on "Meet the Press."

20 Apr At the Fisk University gymnasium in Nashville, a bomb scare delays King's address before a mass meeting sponsored by the Nashville Christian Leadership Conference.

21 Apr In Minneapolis, Minnesota, King addresses the local Urban League at the Leamington Hotel.

24 Apr King delivers "Three Dimensions of a Complete Life" at the morning worship service at Howard University's Andrew Rankin Memorial Chapel.

25 Apr At Howard University, King delivers "St. Paul's Letter to America" for the Washington Ministerial Association.

26 Apr A cross is burned on the front lawn of King's home in Atlanta.

27 Apr *Christian Century* publishes King's "Suffering and Faith."

29 Apr At Atlanta's First Congregational Church, King delivers "The Struggle for Racial Justice" at a human relations workshop.

May King's "The Burning Truth in the South" appears in *The Progressive*. *The Spelman Messenger* publishes King's "Keep Moving from This Mountain."

1 May King delivers "A Doing Religion" at Ebenezer.

4 May King is cited for driving with an invalid license and improper registration while taking white author Lillian Smith to Emory University Hospital in Atlanta.

5 May King holds a press conference with African independence leader Kenneth Kaunda at Ebenezer.

7 May In Atlanta, King meets with Wilkins to discuss alleged remarks made by James Lawson criticizing the NAACP.

8 May King speaks on the subject "The Church's Mission on the Frontier of Racial Tension" at University Baptist Church in Chapel Hill, North Carolina.

9 May Prior to delivering "The Struggle for Racial Justice" at the University of North Carolina at Chapel Hill, King speaks to an undergraduate sociology class and meets with members of the YMCA and YWCA.

10 May In New York, King meets with Stanley Levison, Bayard Rustin, and Wyatt Tee Walker to discuss SCLC.

11 May At New York's Trade Show Building, King is the guest of honor at a luncheon for the city's labor leaders.

13–14 May	At Atlanta University, King attends the first meeting of the Student Nonviolent Coordinating Committee (SNCC).
15 May	King delivers "Why Jesus Called a Man a Fool" at Ebenezer.
16 May	After appearing in a Montgomery courtroom, King's arraignment on perjury charges is postponed.
17 May	At Atlanta's Wheat Street Baptist Church, King addresses student protesters at an event commemorating the sixth anniversary of *Brown v. Board of Education.*
22 May	King delivers the baccalaureate sermon at Tuskegee Institute.
25–28 May	King's tax trial begins in Montgomery.
27 May	King testifies at his trial.
28 May	A jury of twelve white men acquits King of falsifying his 1956 tax return.
29 May	At Ebenezer, King delivers the "Autobiography of Suffering."
30 May	King delivers "A Great Time to Be Alive" at Knoxville College's commencement exercises in Tennessee.
June	King's "To Win Racial Justice" appears in the inaugural issue of the *Student Voice,* the SNCC newsletter. *AME Church Review* publishes King's "Going Forward by Going Backward."
1 June	In Virginia, King addresses a mass meeting of the Petersburg Improvement Association.
5 June	King preaches the "Tragedy of Almost" at Ebenezer.
9 June	At A. Philip Randolph's New York office, King and Randolph hold a press conference announcing protests at the Democratic and Republican National Conventions.
12 June	King preaches "Who Is Truly Great?" at Ebenezer.
14 June	King speaks to a group of clergy for the Council of Churches of Greater Cincinnati.
15 June	King is the keynote speaker at a public meeting at Zion Baptist Church in Cincinnati.
17 June	In Buffalo, King attends the National Sunday School and BTU Congress meeting.
18 June	Still in Buffalo, King addresses a youth rally.
19 June	In Pittsburgh, King speaks at a Freedom Jubilee at Forbes Field.
23 June	In New York, King discusses civil rights with Massachusetts senator John F. Kennedy.
24 June	En route to the Tenth Annual Baptist World Alliance in Rio de Janeiro, Brazil, King arrives in Miami for an overnight layover.
25 June	King leaves Miami and arrives in Nassau, Bahamas.
27 June	King leaves Nassau and arrives in San Juan, Puerto Rico. In the evening he leaves for Rio de Janeiro.
28 June–3 July	King attends the Tenth Annual Baptist World Alliance in Rio de Janeiro.

3 July King departs Rio de Janeiro and arrives in Buenos Aires, Argentina.

5 July King departs Buenos Aires and arrives in Caracas, Venezuela.

6 July King departs Caracas and arrives in New York before returning to Atlanta.

7 July After missing his scheduled appearance before the Democratic Party Platform Committee in Los Angeles, King's remarks are read by a representative.

8 July King arrives in Los Angeles for the March on the Conventions Movement at the Democratic National Convention.

9 July King and Congressman Adam Clayton Powell, Jr. lead a prayer rally at People's Independent Church in Los Angeles.

10 July King addresses protesters during an NAACP-sponsored march and rally on civil rights in Los Angeles.

13 July At the Watkins Hotel in Los Angeles, King is interviewed by a *Montgomery Advertiser* reporter regarding Senator John F. Kennedy's civil rights stance.

18 July Alabama officials drop charges related to King's 1958 income tax return.

24 July King delivers "Beyond Condemnation" at Ebenezer. King travels to Chicago to address a rally with New York governor and GOP presidential nominee Nelson Rockefeller at Liberty Baptist Church on the eve of the Republican National Convention. Later, he addresses a rally at Stone Temple Baptist Church on the West Side of Chicago.

25 July King, Wilkins, and Randolph lead protesters on a march to the International Amphitheater, site of the Republican Convention.

28 July At the conclusion of the March on the Conventions Movement, King and Randolph hold a press conference at Chicago's Conrad Hilton Hotel. King is later greeted by a 200-car motorcade at the airport in Tulsa, Oklahoma; that evening, King addresses a rally at First Baptist Church.

29 July The Tulsa Ministerial Alliance hosts a breakfast in King's honor at the YWCA. In Oklahoma City, King delivers "Our Role in the Freedom Struggle" at a rally at Calvary Baptist Church. King is awarded an inscribed plaque by local Morehouse alumni.

31 July King preaches "Making the Most of a Difficult Situation" at Ebenezer. At the evening worship service, King gives a report on the Baptist World Alliance conference he attended in June.

4 Aug At Atlanta's Butler Street YMCA, King delivers "Nonviolence: Its Basic Precepts" at SCLC's Second Statewide Institute on Nonviolent Resistance to Segregation.

5 Aug King delivers closing remarks at the final session of the Institute on Nonviolent Resistance to Segregation. He later attends a SNCC meeting at Morehouse College.

7 Aug King delivers "Does God Answer Prayer?" at Ebenezer.

14 Aug King delivers "Levels of Love" at Ebenezer. In the afternoon, King preaches at his brother A. D. King's Mount Vernon First Baptist Church in Newnan, Georgia.

19 Aug King and A. D. perform the marriage ceremony of their sister Christine to Isaac Farris at Ebenezer.

21 Aug King delivers "Why Jesus Called a Man a Fool" at Central Methodist Church in Detroit. Following the address, he participates in a question-and-answer session with the church's Young Adult Fellowship.

23 Aug Upon his arrival in Louisville, Kentucky, King holds a press conference at Standiford Field and later rides in a parade sponsored by the Non-Partisan Registration Committee. At Jefferson County Armory, King speaks before a crowd of 9,000 at a mass rally in support of voter registration efforts in the South.

28 Aug King preaches at Ebenezer.

31 Aug King conducts nonviolent training at CORE's Interracial Action Institute in Miami, Florida.

1 Sept King attends the second day of the CORE Institute.

4 Sept King preaches "Why God Called a Man a Fool" at Ebenezer.

5 Sept King delivers "Paul's Letter to American Christians" before five hundred ministers at DePauw University's School of the Prophets in Greencastle, Indiana.

6 Sept King delivers "The Rising Tide of Racial Consciousness" at the Golden Anniversary Conference of the National Urban League at Community Church of New York. Following his address, executives of the Harlem Labor Union present King with a $1,250 contribution for SCLC.

7 Sept In New York, King makes a guest appearance on "Today."

8 Sept Over two hundred people gather at Philadelphia's Benjamin Franklin Hotel to hear King address a dinner meeting sponsored by the Berean Institute.

9 Sept At Philadelphia's Municipal Auditorium, King speaks to the National Baptist Laymen's Movement at the 80th annual session of the National Baptist Convention.

11 Sept King is the guest speaker at Philadelphia's Pinn Memorial Baptist Church's morning worship service. In the afternoon, he is the featured speaker at Salem Baptist Church's annual Men's Day service, and later he addresses the congregation of Bright Hope Baptist Church.

12 Sept At the Howard High School auditorium in Wilmington, Dela-

ware, King speaks at a public meeting sponsored by the local NAACP.

14 Sept Speaking at a press conference at the Overseas Press Club in New York, King and Wilkins announce a nonpartisan crusade to register one million black voters.

18 Sept King preaches "The Goodness of the Good Samaritan" at Ebenezer.

21 Sept King delivers "Nonviolent Resistance to Segregation" at the fall session of the Southern Christian Ministers Conference in Jackson, Mississippi.

23 Sept King pleads guilty to driving with an improper license. He is fined $25 and given a twelve-month suspended sentence.

25 Sept In Charlotte, North Carolina, King delivers "The Negro and the American Dream" at a mass rally sponsored by the local NAACP.

30 Sept At Omaha's Civic Auditorium, King is the guest speaker at an event sponsored by the Western Baptist Bible College.

2 Oct King delivers "The Seeking God" at Ebenezer.

7 Oct In South Orange, New Jersey, King is the featured speaker at a mass meeting sponsored by the General Baptist Convention of New Jersey.

8 Oct At the Laurels Country Club in Sackett Lake, New York, King delivers "The Future of Integration" before District 65 of the RWDSU.

9 Oct King delivers "Why Jesus Called a Man a Fool" at Shiloh Baptist Church's Men's Day service in Washington, D.C. At Shiloh's afternoon service, King delivers "The Negro and the American Dream."

11 Oct At the Evergreen Baptist Church in Shreveport, Louisiana, King meets with the SCLC executive board prior to the start of the organization's annual conference.

12 Oct At Galilee Baptist Church in Shreveport, King speaks at a freedom rally.

13 Oct On the final day of SCLC's annual conference, King participates in a workshop held at Evergreen Baptist Church.

14 Oct King delivers "The Philosophy of Nonviolence" at a SNCC conference in Atlanta.

16 Oct King preaches at Ebenezer. Following the morning worship service, he meets with the chairman of the Gandhi Smarak Nidhi, R. R. Diwakar of Bangalore, India.

19 Oct King and dozens of others are arrested for participating in a sit-in demonstration at Rich's department store in Atlanta. King and others are taken to Fulton County jail after refusing to post bond.

20–24 Oct Although charges are dropped against King for his participation in the sit-in demonstration at Rich's, he remains in jail for violating the terms of a suspended sentence he received for his May traffic violation.

25 Oct At the DeKalb County courthouse, King is sentenced to four months in a public work camp at Georgia State Prison at Reidsville.

26 Oct Before daybreak, Georgia law officials transport King to Georgia State Prison at Reidsville where he is to begin serving his four-month term. In the evening, presidential candidate John F. Kennedy phones Coretta Scott King to express his concern over King's jailing.

27 Oct Following a call to Atlanta judge J. Oscar Mitchell by Robert F. Kennedy, brother and campaign manager to John F. Kennedy, King is freed on $2,000 bond. King flies back to Atlanta and addresses a mass rally at Ebenezer.

1 Nov In a press conference in Atlanta, King refuses to endorse either the Republican or Democratic presidential candidate.

2 Nov King meets with a committee of local college administrators in Atlanta to discuss the sit-in demonstrations.

4 Nov At Virginia Union University, King delivers "Education—The Road to Freedom" at the Virginia Teachers Association convention in Richmond.

6 Nov King delivers "Eight Days Behind Bars" at Ebenezer. Atlanta radio station WAOK airs a prerecorded interview with King in which he discusses the presidential election.

7 Nov In Atlanta's Auburn Avenue Casino, King speaks at a trade show sponsored by the Bronner Bros' Beauty Supply Company. At Atlanta University's Harkness Hall, King meets with local leaders to form a committee to assist the lunch counter desegregation efforts in the city.

9 Nov At Brown University, King delivers "The Future of Integration."

10 Nov In the morning, King holds a press conference before delivering "Facing the Challenge of the New Age" at Brown University.

13 Nov King delivers "The Dimensions of a Complete Life" at Cornell University's Sage Chapel. Following the speech, he answers questions by students before departing for Nigeria.

14–18 Nov In Lagos, Nigeria, King attends the inauguration festivities for Governor-General and Commander-in-Chief Nnamdi Azikiwe.

20 Nov King preaches at Ebenezer. At the Southern Regional Council office in Atlanta, King has lunch with Adlai Stevenson and trustees of the Field Foundation.

21 Nov King delivers "Strides Toward Freedom" at North Central

College in Naperville, Illinois. Following the worship service, he attends a luncheon at the student union and delivers a public lecture in the evening.

23 Nov King meets with Atlanta student leaders.

25 Nov King meets with the student advisory committee to discuss the protests in Atlanta.

26 Nov King debates the sit-in demonstrations with segregationist newspaper editor James J. Kilpatrick on NBC's "The Nation's Future" in New York.

27 Nov At St. Louis's United Hebrew Temple, King delivers "The Future of Integration" before the Liberal Forum of the Jewish Community Centers Association.

Dec The *YWCA Magazine* publishes King's "The Rising Tide of Racial Consciousness," an address delivered at the September 1960 Golden Anniversary of the National Urban League.

4 Dec King delivers "Pride Versus Humility" at Ebenezer.

5–7 Dec King is a National Baptist Convention delegate to the National Council of the Churches of Christ meeting in San Francisco.

10 Dec At New York City's Belmont Plaza Hotel, King meets with civil rights leaders to discuss current desegregation efforts in the South.

11 Dec In the morning, King delivers "The Three Dimensions of a Complete Life" at the Unitarian Church of Germantown in Philadelphia. Later, King delivers "The Future of Integration" at the Ford Hall Forum in Boston.

14 Dec At King's office in Atlanta, he meets with SCLC and Southern Conference Educational Fund (SCEF) leaders to discuss organizational cooperation.

15 Dec King attends a YWCA dinner meeting at Atlanta University's Bumstead Hall.

18 Dec King preaches "Christ Our Starting Point" at Ebenezer. Following the morning worship service, King meets with the church leadership.

19 Dec King addresses a rally at Wheat Street Baptist Church in Atlanta.

20 Dec In Atlanta, King meets with local ministers and college administrators to discuss the student sit-ins.

24 Dec King performs the wedding of former Morehouse classmate Barney Rutledge.

30 Dec After the Chattanooga, Tennessee, school board refused use of Howard High School, King speaks at Memorial Auditorium. Prior to his address, he attends a dinner in his honor held at the Henry Branch of the YMCA.

The central goal of the Martin Luther King, Jr., Papers Project is to produce an authoritative, multivolume edition of King's works. These chronologically arranged volumes contain accurate, annotated transcriptions of King's most important sermons, speeches, correspondence, published writings, unpublished manuscripts, and other papers.

We assign highest priority to King's writings, public statements, and publications, although such materials are not included when they repeat significant portions of the text of other documents from the period. When one of King's addresses or sermons is available in different versions, we prefer recordings rather than printed or published transcripts, complete versions rather than excerpts, and versions that have greater rather than lesser public impact. We also include correspondence containing significant information about King's thought or activities and incoming letters illuminating his relationships with or impact on others. We generally exclude office generated replies, mass mailings, and unsolicited incoming letters, except in the few instances when such letters are of exceptional interest or provoked a personal reply from King.

For this volume we have examined more than seven thousand King-related documents and recordings and selected those that are the most biographically or historically significant to King's life, thought, and leadership. We have selected for inclusion some documents that do not fit within the previously mentioned categories when they provide vital information regarding King's attitudes, activities, associations, and leadership. This category includes newspaper articles quoting King speeches or sermons for which the entire text is not available; recorded or transcribed interviews; and press releases or statements issued by King or jointly with others. We have included third party correspondence that describes events attended by King. For example, details on King's trip to India are revealed in correspondence written by individuals who accompanied him. Some sermons and homiletic material produced by King during this period will be included in our forthcoming thematic volume tracing King's early theological development, rather than in this volume.

This volume also contains other sections designed to provide information useful to lay and scholarly readers alike. The Chronology lists King's significant activities for the period. The Introduction is a narrative essay based on the documentary records assembled by the King Papers Project. It is intended to place King's papers in a historical context rather than to substitute for a thorough biographical or historical treatment of King's activities during 1959 and 1960. Finally, to assist scholars and others seeking further information regarding King-related primary documents, this volume includes a Calendar of Documents that provides full citations for items referred to in annotations. It also lists a selection of other significant King-related documents. King Papers Project descriptions of archival collections related to King are available in an electronic database of the Research Libraries Information Network (RLIN).

Documents are introduced by a title, date, and place of origin. Existing titles are used, when available, and are designated by quotation marks. When necessary in titles, we have corrected errors or irregularities in punctuation, capitalization, and spelling, and we have standardized names; these corrected titles are not designated by quotation marks. In addition, descriptive titles that appear on the document are similarly designated with quotation marks (e.g., "Address at Public Meeting of the Southern Christian Ministers Conference of Mississippi"). For untitled items, we have created descriptive titles reflecting content (e.g., Statement on Perjury Acquittal). Speech or sermon titles indicate the occasion of the address. In King's correspondence, the title contains the author or recipient (e.g., To Roy Wilkins), leaving King's participation implied. When the date was not specified in the document but has been determined through research, it is rendered in italics and enclosed in square brackets. When a specific date could not be determined through research, we have provided a range date. Documents are placed in the volume where they will provide the strongest narrative continuity. In some instances, the dateline of published documents is dropped when the date of delivery is indicated in the document's title and the actual publication date is given in the document's source line. If the place of origin appears on the document, it is included; if not and it could be determined through research, it is provided for King-authored documents only. (A more detailed explanation of procedures for assigning titles, dates, and other cataloging information appears at the end of the volume in the Calendar of Documents.)

Annotations are intended to enhance readers' understanding of documents. Headnotes preceding documents explain the context of their creation; in the case of longer documents a brief summary may be offered. Headnotes and editorial footnotes also identify individuals, organizations, events, literary quotations, biblical allusions, and other references in the document, as well as relevant correspondence or related documents. Biographical sketches describe the background and relationship to King of individuals who corresponded with him or are mentioned prominently in documents. We have not included such sketches for individuals described in previous volumes, nor have we annotated theological ideas and persons likely to be discussed in standard reference works. Editorial footnotes, on occasion, refer to alternative accounts of events and to variations among versions (e.g., sentences altered or added by King when he modified an address for a different occasion). Marginal notes on the document, particularly those written by King, are also noted. Annotations may contain implicit or abbreviated references to documents (e.g., "King replied on 9 February 1960"); full bibliographic information for such documents can be found in the Calendar of Documents.

The source note following each document provides information on the characteristics of the original document and its provenance. Codes are used to describe the document's format, type, version, and form of signature. The code "TLS," for example, identifies the document as a typed letter with a signature. The location of the original or source document is described next, using standard abbreviations from *USMARC Code List for Organizations.* (See List of Abbreviations for all codes used.)

To Alberta Williams King ——— Title

12 October 1959 — Date
[*Montgomery, Ala.*] — Place of Origin

King sends his mother, assistant director of the Ebenezer Baptist Church choir, the honorarium for the choir's 27 September concert at Dexter.[1] *The event, which King opened with an invocation, filled the church to capacity and included a solo by King's sister, Christine.*[2] ——— Headnote

Mrs. M. L. King, Sr.
2873 Dale Creek Road, N.E.
Atlanta, Georgia

Dear Mother:

Enclosed is a check in the amount of three hundred forty-five dollars and seventy-five cents which includes the expenses of one hundred ninety-five dollars and seventy-five cents plus a one hundred fifty dollar honorarium. This program was such a financial success that we felt compelled to add a little more to the honorarium. Already the receipts have reached around fifteen hundred dollars. The members of the committee asked me to express their deep gratitude to you and the overall choir for the great concert that you rendered. This was certainly one of the high points in the Montgomery Community. — Document

Give my regards to all. I will be seeing you soon.

Very sincerely yours,
M. L.

enc/1
MLK/lmh ——— Physical description codes

TLc. DABCC. ——— Document's archival code

---

1. See Dexter Avenue Baptist Church, Program, "The church choir of Ebenezer Baptist Church in concert," 27 September 1959. — Editorial footnote

2. Leonard Ballou, "Ebenezer Choir Pleases Large Audience," *Dexter Echo,* 7 October 1959. Coretta King served as co-chair of the event. — Brief reference; full citation in Calendar of Documents

Transcription Practices

Transcriptions are intended to reproduce the documents accurately, adhering to the exact wording and punctuation of the original. In general, errors in spelling, punctuation, and grammar, which may offer important insights into the author's state of mind and conditions under which a document was composed, have been neither corrected nor indicated by *sic*. Capitalization, boldface, underscores, subscripts, abbreviations, hyphenation, strikeouts, ellipses, and symbols are likewise replicated.

This rule has certain exceptions, however. Single-letter emendations by the author have been silently incorporated, and typographical errors, such as malformed and superimposed characters, have been corrected. In published documents, spelling and grammatical errors have been retained unless an earlier draft revealed the author's intention. Moreover, some formatting practices such as outlining, underscoring, paragraph indentation, and spacing between words or lines of text have been regularized to maintain consistency within the edition (e.g., continuous rather than discontinuous underscoring). Dashes, which appeared in several styles in the original manuscripts, have been regularized. The overall appearance of the source document (e.g., line breaks, pagination, vertical and horizontal spacing, end-of-line hyphenation) has not been replicated, and some features that could not be readily reproduced, such as letterheads and typographic variations, are described in annotations (in a few cases, visually interesting documents such as advertisements or postcards have been reproduced as facsimiles).The internal address, salutation, and complimentary closing of a letter have been reproduced left-aligned, regardless of the original format. Insertions in the text by the author (usually handwritten) are indicated by curly braces ({ }) and placed as precisely as possible within the text. Telegrams are rendered using small capital letters.

Editorial explanations are rendered in italics and enclosed by square brackets. Conjectural renderings of text are set in italic type followed by a question mark and placed within brackets: e.g., [*There's?*]. Instances of illegible text are indicated: e.g., [*strikeout illegible*] or [*word illegible*]. If the strikeout was by someone other than the author, it has not been replicated but instead is described in a footnote. If part of a document is lost, the condition is described: e.g., [*remainder missing*]. In some instances, long documents may be excerpted to highlight passages that are most significant with respect to King. Editorial deletions to eliminate repetitive or extraneous segments are explained by an editorial comment or are indicated by ellipses: [. . .]. Signatures that are identical with the typed name are reproduced as follows:

> Sincerely,
[*signed*]
Benjamin E. Mays

The King Papers Project's transcriptions of audio recordings are intended to replicate, to the extent possible, King's public statements as they were delivered, excluding only those utterings that do not convey significant meaning (e.g., unintentional stutters and pause words, such as "uh"). Certain sharply stressed phrases are rendered in italics to indicate the speaker's emphasis and non-English words are italicized as well. When available, King's written text is used to clarify ambiguous phrases and as a guide to delineating sentences, paragraphs, and punctuation. In cases where the written text is not available, we have supplied punctuation for clarity. Transcriptions also attempt to convey some of the quality of the speech event, particularly the interplay between speaker and audience. When practical, audience responses to King's orations are enclosed in parentheses and placed appropriately within King's text. Editorial descriptions of audience participation are enclosed in square brackets. The first instance of a verbal audience response to a speech is indicated as follows: e.g., [*Audience:*] (*Yes*). Subsequent audience interjections are enclosed, as is appropriate, in brackets or in parentheses: e.g., [*applause*] or (*Lord help him*). Multiple audience responses are indicated in order of occurrence, separated with commas: e.g., (*Tell it, Don't stop*). In addition, transcriptions occasionally suggest the loudness or duration of audience responses: e.g., [*sustained applause*]. In cases where a recording or its transcription is incomplete or unintelligible, that status is indicated within the text proper: e.g., [*gap in tape*] or [*words inaudible*].

Collections and Repositories

1960CR-MWalK	Records of the 1960 Campaign, Civil Rights Division (Marjorie Lawson), John F. Kennedy Library, Boston, Mass.
ACA-ARC-LNT	American Committee on Africa Papers, Amistad Research Collections, Tulane University, New Orleans, La.
ACCP-DAFL	A.F.L.-C.I.O. Office of the President, George Meany Memorial Archives, Silver Spring, Md.
ACLUC-NjP	American Civil Liberties Union Collection, Princeton University, Princeton, N.J.
AFLP-DAFL	American Federation of Labor and Congress of Industrial Organizations Papers, George Meany Memorial Archives, Silver Spring, Md.
AFSCR-PPAFS	American Friends Service Committee Records, American Friends Service Committee Archives, Philadelphia, Pa.
AJC-ICHi	Archibald James Carey Collection, Chicago Historical Society, Chicago, Ill.
AJMP-PSC-P	A. J. Muste Papers, Swarthmore College Peace Collection, Swarthmore, Pa.
APRC-DLC	A. Philip Randolph Collection, Library of Congress, Washington, D.C.
ASCL-OAU	Archives and Special Collections, Ohio University Library, Ohio University, Athens, Ohio
BJDP-NN-Sc	Benjamin J. Davis Papers, Manuscript, Archives and Rare Books Division, Schomburg Center for Research in Black Culture, The New York Public Library, New York, N.Y.
BRP-DLC	Bayard Rustin Papers, Library of Congress, Washington, D.C.
BSCP-DLC	Brotherhood of Sleeping Car Porters and Maids Records, Library of Congress, Washington, D.C.
BTC	Barry Tulloss Collection (in private hands)
CAABP-WHi	Carl and Anne Braden Papers, Wisconsin Historical Society, Madison, Wis.
CABP-ICHi	Claude A. Barnett Papers, Chicago Historical Society, Chicago, Ill.
CaOTBC	Canadian Broadcasting Corporation, Toronto, Canada
CB-CtY	Chester Bowles Collection, Yale University, New Haven, Conn.

CBSNA-NNCBS	Columbia Broadcasting System News Archives, Columbia Broadcasting System, Inc., New York, N.Y.
CCCSU	Clayborne Carson Collection (in private hands)
CJDP-A-Ar	Clifford Judkins Durr Papers, Alabama Department of Archives and History, Montgomery, Ala.
CKFC	Christine King Farris Collection (in private hands)
CLPAC	Pacifica Radio Archive, Los Angeles, Calif.
CLU-FT	University of California, Los Angeles, Film and Television Archive
CMCR-AMC	Circuit Court, Montgomery County Records, Montgomery County Courthouse, Montgomery, Ala.
COREP-A-GAMK	Papers of the Congress of Racial Equality: Addendum, 1944–1968, Martin Luther King, Jr., Center for Nonviolent Social Change, Inc., Atlanta, Ga.
COREP-WHi	Congress of Racial Equality Papers, Wisconsin Historical Society, Madison, Wis.
CSKC	Coretta Scott King Collection (in private hands)
CSKCH	Coretta Scott King Home Study Collection (in private hands)
CSfSFL	California Labor Federation A.F.L.-C.I.O. Library, San Francisco, Calif.
CTRP-OO	Carl T. Rowan Papers, Oberlin College, Oberlin, Ohio
CtWeharU	University of Hartford, West Hartford, Conn.
CUL-NIC	Cornell University Library, Cornell University, Ithaca, N.Y.
DABCC	Dexter Avenue King Memorial Baptist Church Collection (in private hands)
DBC-WHi	Daisy Bates Collection, Wisconsin Historical Society, Madison, Wis.
DDEP-KAbE	Dwight D. Eisenhower Miscellaneous Papers, Dwight D. Eisenhower Library, Abilene, Kan.
DGFBI-NN-Sc	David J. Garrow Federal Bureau of Investigation Collection, Manuscript, Archives and Rare Books Division, Schomburg Center for Research in Black Culture, The New York Public Library, New York, N.Y.
DJG-GEU	David J. Garrow Collection, Special Collections, Emory University, Atlanta, Ga.
DWW-ARC-LNT	Daniel Webster Wynn Papers, Amistad Research Collections, Tulane University, New Orleans, La.
EBCR	Ebenezer Baptist Church Miscellaneous Records (in private hands)
EFMP-KAbE	E. Frederic Morrow Papers, Dwight D. Eisenhower Library, Abeline, Kan.
EJBC-NN-Sc	Ella J. Baker Collection, Manuscript, Archives and Rare

	Books Division, Schomburg Center for Research in Black Culture, The New York Public Library, New York, N.Y.
ERC-NHyF	Eleanor Roosevelt Collection, General Services Administration, National Archives and Record Service, Franklin D. Roosevelt Library, Hyde Park, N.Y.
FLSC-GAMK	Fred L. Shuttlesworth Collection, Martin Luther King, Jr., Center for Nonviolent Social Change, Inc., Atlanta, Ga.
FORP-PSC-P	Fellowship of Reconciliation Papers, Swarthmore College Peace Collection, Swarthmore, Pa.
GCP-CRA-InU-N	George Chacharis Papers, Calumet Regional Archives, Indiana University, Northwest Regional Campus, Gary, Ind.
GGDP-GASU	Georgia Government Documentation Project, Special Collections Department, Pullen Library, Georgia State University, Atlanta, Ga.
GMF-DAFL	Office of the President, George Meany's Files, George Meany Memorial Archives, Silver Spring, Md.
GMWC-MiU-H	G. Mennen Williams Collection, Michigan Historical Collection, University of Michigan, Ann Arbor, Mich.
GRDJ-DNA	General Records for the Department of Justice, United States National Archives and Record Service, National Archives Library, Washington, D.C.
HG-GAMK	Hazel Gregory Papers, Martin Luther King, Jr., Center for Nonviolent Social Change, Inc., Atlanta, Ga.
HHSA	Hawaii State Archives, Iolani Palace Grounds, Honolulu, Hawaii
HJP-GAMK	H. J. Palmer Papers, Martin Luther King, Jr., Center for Nonviolent Social Change, Inc., Atlanta, Ga.
HRECR-WHi	Highlander Research and Education Center Records, Wisconsin Historical Society, Madison, Wis.
HSF-GAHi	Highlander Subject File, Atlanta Historical Society, Atlanta, Ga.
IaW	Waterloo Public Library, Waterloo, Iowa
IiMMBGS	Mani Bhavan Gandhi Sangrahalaya, Mumbai, India
IiNNMML	Nehru Memorial Museum and Library, Teen Murti Bhavan, New Delhi, India
InGrD	DePauw University, Greencastle, Ind.
JBC	John Brooke Collection (in private hands)
JFKOH-MWalK	John F. Kennedy Library Oral History Program, John F. Kennedy Library, Boston, Mass.
JLHP-CtY-BR	Langston Hughes Papers, James Weldon Johnson Collection in the Yale Collection of American Literature, Beinecke Rare Books and Manuscript Library, Yale University, New Haven, Conn.

JPCP-Ms-Ar	James P. Coleman Papers, Mississippi Department of Archives and History, Jackson, Miss.
LBJOH-TxU-J	Lyndon Baines Johnson Oral History Collection, University of Texas, Lyndon Baines Johnson Presidential Library, Austin, Texas
LDPF-GAMK	Library Documentation Project Files, Martin Luther King, Jr., Center for Nonviolent Social Change, Inc., Atlanta, Ga.
LDRP-NN-Sc	Lawrence Dunbar Reddick Papers, Manuscript, Archives and Rare Books Division, Schomburg Center for Research in Black Culture, The New York Public Library, New York, N.Y.
LewBP	Lewis Baldwin Papers (in private hands)
Lill-InRE	Lilly Library, Earlham College, Richmond, Ind.
LND	Special Collections and University Archives, Dillard University, New Orleans, La.
MiDCUMA	Central United Methodist Church Archives, Detroit, Mich.
MLKB-MsToT	Martin Luther King, Jr., Box, Tougaloo College, Tougaloo, Miss.
MLKEC	Martin Luther King, Jr. Estate Collection (in private hands)
MLKJP-GAMK	Martin Luther King, Jr., Papers, 1950–1968, Martin Luther King, Jr., Center for Nonviolent Social Change, Inc., Atlanta, Ga.
MLK/OH-GAMK	Martin Luther King, Jr., Oral History Collection, 1950–1968, Martin Luther King, Jr., Center for Nonviolent Social Change, Inc., Atlanta, Ga.
MLKP-MBU	Martin Luther King, Jr., Papers, 1954–1968, Boston University, Boston, Mass.
MMFR	Montgomery to Memphis Film Research Files (in private hands)
MWJP-DHU	Mordecai Wyatt Johnson Papers, Howard University, Washington, D.C.
NAACPP-DLC	National Association for the Advancement of Colored People Papers, Library of Congress, Washington, D.C.
NBCNA-NNNBC	National Broadcasting Company News Archives, National Broadcasting Company, Inc. General Library, New York, N.Y.
NBCTV-WHi	National Broadcasting Company Records, Wisconsin Historical Society, Madison, Wis.
NCCP-PPPrHi	National Council of the Churches of Christ in the United States of America Papers, Presbyterian Department of History, Philadelphia, Pa.
NcDurDHS	*Durham Herald Sun,* Durham, N.C.
NNAPWW	Associated Press/Wide World Photos, New York, N.Y.
NNCRF	The Christopher Reynolds Foundation, Inc. Collection, New York, N.Y.

NNTI	Time Inc., New York, N.Y.
NNU-T	Tamiment Library, New York University, New York, N.Y.
NULR-DLC	National Urban League Records, Library of Congress, Washington, D.C.
OClWHi	Western Reserve Historical Society, Cleveland, Ohio
OGCP-MBU	Office of General Counsel Papers, Boston University, Boston, Mass.
OH-KAbE	Oral Histories Collection, Dwight D. Eisenhower Library, Abilene, Kan.
OHP-ArU	Oren Harris Papers, University of Arkansas, Fayetteville, Ark.
OOxM	Miami University, Oxford, Ohio
PFC-WHi	Pamphlet File Collection, Wisconsin Historical Society, Madison, Wis.
PHTPG-MoIT	Papers of Harry S. Truman. Post Presidential General File, Harry S. Truman Library, Independence, Mo.
PP-WHi	Progressive Papers, Wisconsin Historical Society, Madison, Wis.
PPRN-CYINL	Pre Presidential Papers of Richard M. Nixon, Special Files, Series 320, Richard M. Nixon Library and Birthplace, Yorba Linda, Calif.
PPUCGC	Unitarian Church of Germantown Collection, Philadelphia, Pa
PSC-Hi	Friends Historical Library of Swarthmore College, Swarthmore, Pa.
RBOH-DHU	Ralph J. Bunche Oral History Collection, Howard University, Washington, D.C.
RKC-WHi	Richard Kaplan Collection, Wisconsin Historical Society, Madison, Wis.
RMP-GEU	Ralph McGill Papers, Special Collections, Emory University, Atlanta, Ga.
RPP-NN-Sc	Richard Parrish Papers (Additions), 1959–1976, Manuscript, Archives and Rare Books Division, Schomburg Center for Research in Black Culture, The New York Public Library, New York, N.Y.
RWP-DLC	Roy Wilkins Papers, Library of Congress, Washington, D.C.
SAVFC-WHi	Social Action Vertical File Collection, Wisconsin Historical Society, Madison, Wis.
SBCC-DSC	Shiloh Baptist Church Collection, Shiloh Baptist Church, Washington, D.C.
SCLCR-GAMK	Southern Christian Leadership Conference Records, Martin Luther King, Jr., Center for Nonviolent Social Change, Inc., Atlanta, Ga.
SNCCP-GAMK	Student Nonviolent Coordinating Committee Papers,

	Martin Luther King, Jr., Center for Nonviolent Social Change, Inc., Atlanta, Ga.
SOHP-NcU	Southern Oral History Program Collection, University of North Carolina, Chapel Hill, N.C.
SRCR-IaAS	Student Religious Council Records, Special Collections, Iowa State University, Ames, Iowa
SWWP-GAU	Samuel W. Williams Papers, Robert W. Woodruff Archives and Special Collections, Atlanta University Center, Atlanta, Ga.
T	Tennessee State Library and Archives, Nashville, Tenn.
TAP	Thelma B. Archer Papers (in private hands)
TCCU-AzU	Tucson Council for Civic Unity, University of Arizona, Tucson, Ariz.
TIA-ATT	Tuskegee Institute Archives, Tuskegee Institute, Tuskegee, Ala.
TxU-J	University of Texas, Lyndon Baines Johnson Presidential Library, Austin, Texas
UAWRCR-NNU-LA	United Automobile, Aircraft, and Vehicle Workers of America, District 65 Records, Cleveland Robinson Papers, New York University, Robert F. Wagner Labor Archives, New York, N.Y.
UMR-MnU-Ar	University of Minnesota Records, University of Minnesota Archives, Minneapolis, Minn.
UNCFR-GAU	United Negro College Fund Records, Robert W. Woodruff Library Archives and Special Collections, Atlanta University Center, Atlanta, Ga.
UPIR-NNBETT	United Press International and Reuters Photo Collection, Corbis-Bettmann Archives, New York, N.Y.
UPWP-WHi	United Packinghouse Workers Papers, State Historical Society of Wisconsin, Madison, Wis.
WCFG-KAbE	White House Central Files (General Files), Dwight D. Eisenhower Library, Abilene, Kan.
WCFO-KAbE	White House Central Files (Official File), Dwight D. Eisenhower Library, Abilene, Kan.
WCOH-NcD	William H. Chafe Oral History Collection, Duke University, Durham, N.C.
WEBD-MU	W. E. B. (William Edward Burghardt) DuBois Papers, University of Massachusetts, Amherst, Mass.
WMC-OrU	Wayne Morse Collection, University of Oregon, Knight Library, Eugene, Or.
WMP-MBU	Walter Muelder Papers, Boston University, Boston, Mass.
WONS-KAbE	White House Office, Office of the Special Assistant for National Security Affairs, Dwight D. Eisenhower Library, Abilene, Kan.

WPRC-MiDW-AL	Walter P. Reuther Collection, Wayne State University, Walter P. Reuther Library of Labor and Urban Affairs, Archives of Labor History and Urban Affairs, Detroit, Mich.
WRLC-NNWRL	War Resisters League Collection, War Resisters League, New York, N.Y.
WRMP-GAMK	William Robert Miller Papers, Martin Luther King, Jr., Center for Nonviolent Social Change, Inc., Atlanta, Ga.
WSBA-GU	WSB Newsfilm Collection, University of Georgia, Libraries, Athens, Ga.
WXSC	William X. Scheinman Collection (in private hands)

Abbreviations Used in Source Notes

The following symbols are used to describe the original documents:

Format

A	Autograph (author's hand)
H	Handwritten (other than author's hand)
P	Printed
T	Typed

Type

At	Audio tape
Aw	Art work
D	Document
F	Film
Fm	Form
L	Letter or memo
Ph	Photo
Ta	Audio transcript
Tv	Video transcript
Vt	Video tape
W	Wire or telegram

Version

c	Copy
d	Draft
f	Fragment

Signature

I	Initialed
S	Signed
Sr	Signed with representation of author

Photographs

The Kings and Lawrence Dunbar Reddick arrive at New Delhi's Palam Airport on 10 February 1959. King is flanked by Gandhi associates Sucheta Kripalani and G. Ramachandran. Courtesy of AP/Wide World Photos.

On their first day in India, the Kings meet Rajkumari Amrit Kaur, an associate of Mohandas Gandhi and the first woman to serve in the Indian cabinet. Courtesy of the American Friends Service Committee.

(Top left) The Kings meet with Indian vice president Sarvepalli Radhakrishnan on 18 February 1959. Courtesy of the American Friends Service Committee.

(Bottom left) King, tour organizer James Bristol, and G. Ramachandran talk during a 10 February reception at the Delhi Quaker Centre. Courtesy of the American Friends Service Committee.

(Above) The Kings meet with Prime Minister Jawaharlal Nehru at his residence on their first evening in New Delhi, 10 February 1959. ©Bettmann/CORBIS; copy at Teen Murti Bhavan, New Delhi.

The Kings lay a wreath on Gandhi's samahdi, the site of his cremation, at Rajghat in New Delhi on 11 February 1959. They are accompanied by Tina Bristol, James Bristol, Swami Vishwananda, and Lawrence Dunbar Reddick. Courtesy of the American Friends Service Committee.

The Kings at the home of Indian independence leader J. B. Kripalani (*third from left*) on 9 March 1959. Miss Shanta, Tina Bristol, and James Bristol join them. Courtesy of AP/Wide World Photos.

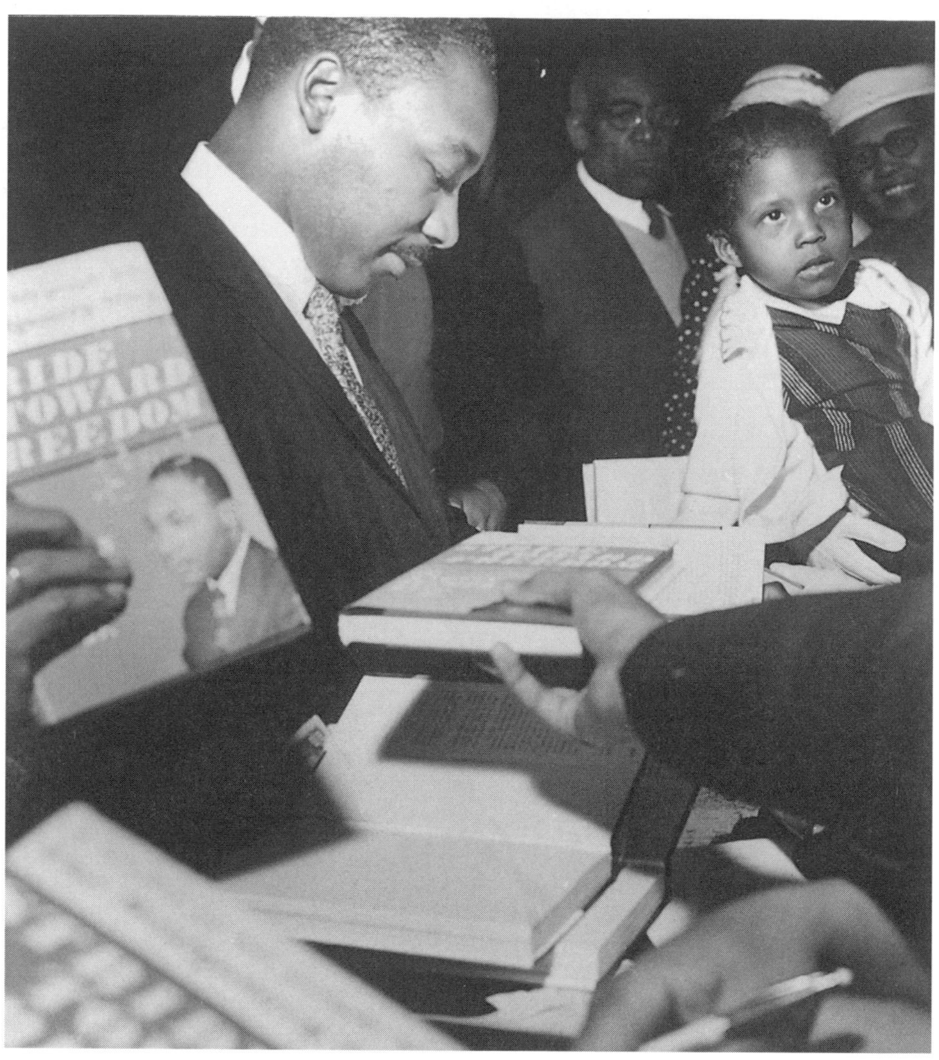

King autographs copies of *Stride Toward Freedom* prior to a 22 April 1959 speaking engagement sponsored by the Fair Share Organization at the Memorial Auditorium in Gary, Indiana. Courtesy of the Calumet Regional Archives, Indiana University Northwest.

King fields questions from the audience in Earlham College's Stout Meeting House in Richmond, Indiana, on 23 April 1959. Courtesy of Archives, Lilly Library, Earlham College, Richmond, Indiana.

King appears on Canada's popular current events quiz show, "Front Page Challenge," on 28 April 1959. © Canadian Broadcasting Company, Still Photo Collection, Toronto.

In December 1959 King meets with Nicholas Raballa, a Kenyan student whose Tuskegee Institute education was sponsored by SCLC and Dexter Avenue Baptist Church. Courtesy of the Tuskegee University Archives.

Coca-Cola

(Top left) Ralph Abernathy, King, Douglas Moore, and an unidentified student visit a closed Woolworth lunch counter in Durham, North Carolina, on a tour of sit-in sites on 16 February 1960. Courtesy of Jim Thornton/ *Durham Herald-Sun.*

(Bottom left) King leaves the Fulton County courthouse after posting bond for his 17 February 1960 arrest on charges of perjury in connection with his 1956 and 1958 Alabama state income tax returns. The men are laughing at King's remark to photographers: "If I had known you would be here I would have worn my Sunday suit." From left to right in the foreground are A. D. King, Martin Luther King, Sr., King, deputy Leroy Stynchcombe, and sheriff Ralph Grimes. Courtesy of AP/Wide World Photos.

(Above) King poses with a group of participants at the April 1960 Youth Leadership meeting at Shaw University in Raleigh, North Carolina. *Back row (L to R):* Bernard Lee, David Forbes (seated), Henry Thomas, Lonnie King, James Lawson. *Middle:* Virginius B. Thornton, Wyatt Tee Walker, King, Michael Penn. *Front row:* Clarence Mitchell, Marion Barry. Courtesy of Howard Sochurek/Timepix.

King and Kenneth Kaunda, nationalist leader of Northern Rhodesia, speak at a press conference at Ebenezer Baptist Church on 5 May 1960. Courtesy of Alfred Eisenstaedt/Timepix.

King stands with his lawyers outside the Montgomery County courthouse after being acquitted of all charges in his perjury case on 28 May 1960. From left to right: Hubert T. Delany, Arthur D. Shores, King, Fred D. Gray, William R. Ming, and Solomon S. Seay, Jr. Courtesy of Donald Uhrbrock/Timepix.

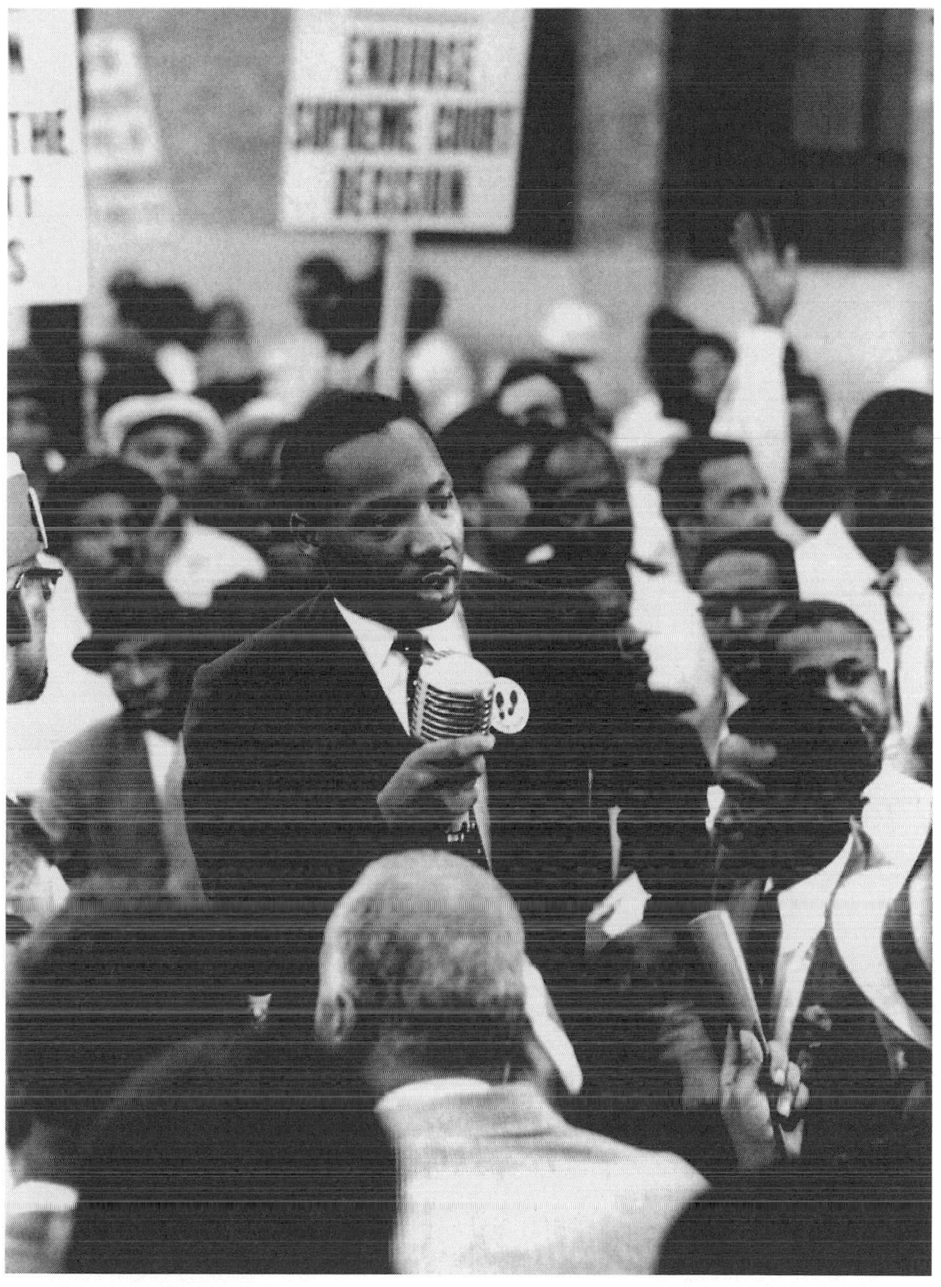

King speaks on 25 July 1960 at a demonstration for a strong civil rights plank outside the Republican National Convention held in Chicago. Courtesy of Francis Miller/Timepix.

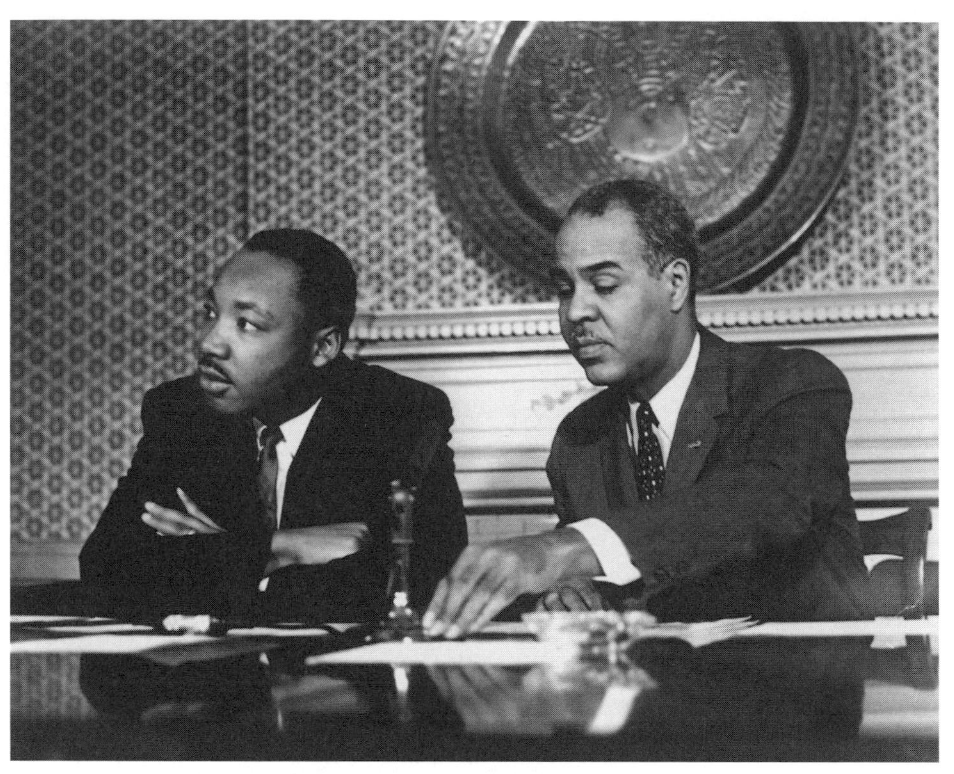

(Top left) At the New York Overseas Press Club on 14 September 1960, King and Roy Wilkins announce a nationwide, nonpartisan campaign to register one million new black voters. Courtesy of the Library of Congress.

(Bottom left) King, seated in his office, talks with a group of student sit-in organizers during an October strategy meeting to desegregate Atlanta's lunch counters. From left to right the students are Lonnie C. King, Edward B. King, Carolyn Banks, Julian Bond, and Alice Clopton. Courtesy of Donald Uhrbrock/Timepix.

(Above) King and Lonnie C. King pass a picketer in downtown Atlanta after being arrested by Atlanta police captain R. E. Little for staging a sit-in at Rich's department store on 19 October 1960. Courtesy of AP/Wide World Photos.

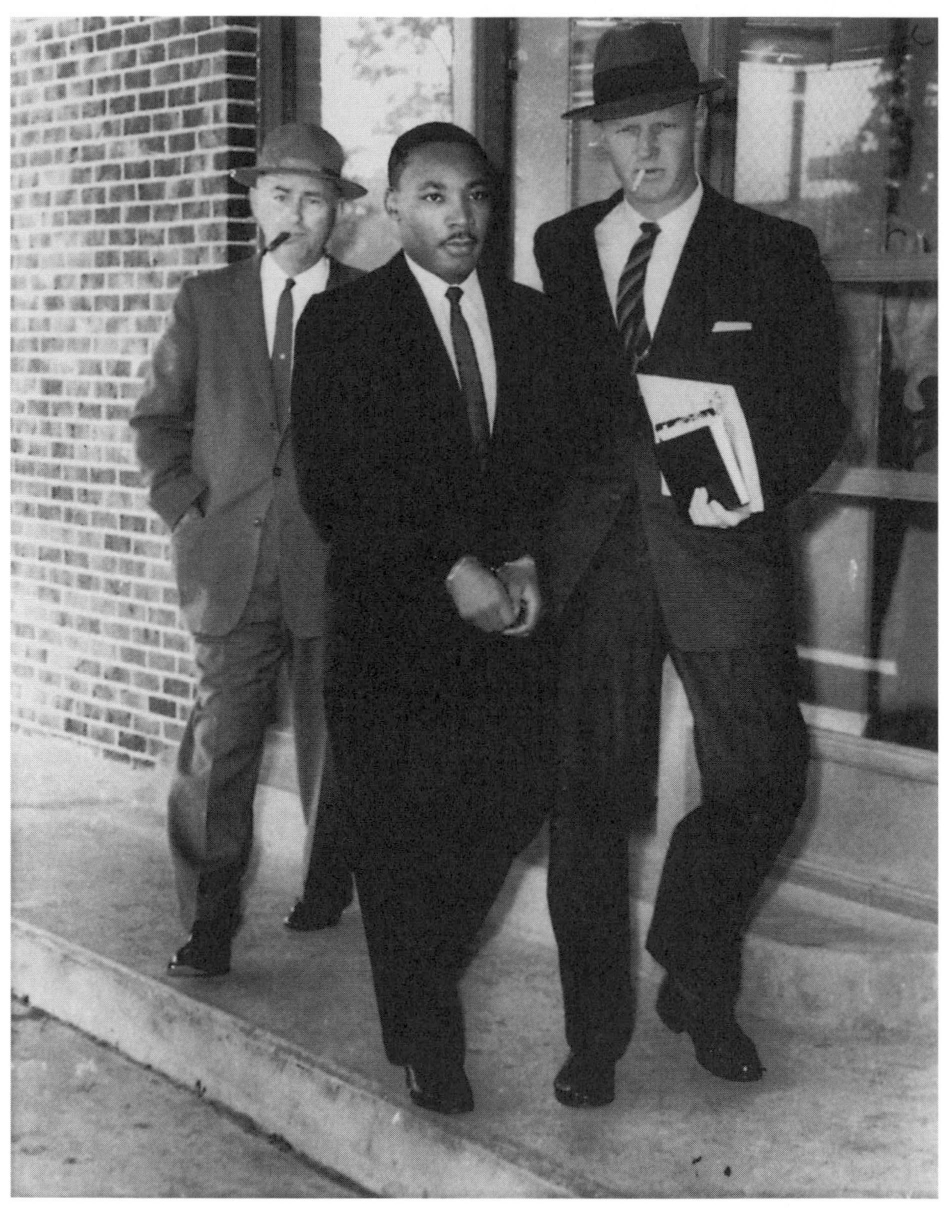

King is escorted by two unidentified police officers from the Atlanta jail to neighboring DeKalb County courthouse for his 25 October 1960 hearing to determine if his participation in the sit-in was a parole violation. Courtesy of AP/Wide World Photos.

King enjoys a moment with his wife, Coretta, and their two children, Martin III and Yolanda, at their Atlanta home in 1960. Courtesy of Donald Uhrbrock/Timepix.

The Papers

Foreword to *The Power of Nonviolence*

1959
Montgomery, Ala.

In his foreword to the second edition of Richard B. Gregg's The Power of Nonviolence, *King expresses his hope that the "classic book" will be widely read, especially among those who are "seeking ways of achieving full social, personal and political freedom in a manner consistent with human dignity."*[1] *Gregg expressed his thanks to King in a 2 May letter: "Your introduction will greatly help the sale of the book and thus spread further Gandhi's ideas and help solve conflicts of all kinds."*

When the great Quaker leader, Rufus Jones, wrote an introduction to the first edition of *The Power of Nonviolence,* he observed that "here is a new kind of book . . . a fine blend of *what is* and *what ought to be.* . . . There is as much realism in this book as there is idealism."[2]

That was in 1935. Since then history's most devastating war has swept the globe, and new weapons of terrifying dimensions have made it more clear than ever that war and civilization cannot both continue into man's future. New ways of solving conflicts, without violence, must be discovered and put into operation.

The years since 1935 have not only demonstrated how uncontrollable war is when it breaks out; they have shown also how right Richard Gregg was in preparing this perceptive study in the first place. The heroic, though unanticipated nonviolent resistance against the Nazis in Denmark and Norway, recounted in this new edition, and by smaller groups in France, the Netherlands and in Germany itself, was such a demonstration. So has been the struggle in South Africa against unjust laws, the winning of its freedom by the new nation of Ghana, and our own experience in Montgomery.

I am delighted that Richard Gregg, after spending another eighteen months in India in more research into this vital new kind of action, should have put the time and effort into this new version of his classic book. I hope it gets a wide readership, particularly among those, in this country and throughout the world, who are seeking ways of achieving full social, personal and political freedom in a manner consistent with human dignity.

—Martin Luther King Jr.
Montgomery, Alabama

PD. *The Power of Nonviolence* (Nyack, N.Y.: Fellowship Publications, 1959).

---

1. After reading the first edition during the Montgomery bus boycott, King wrote Gregg that he found the book "filled with lasting spiritual meaning" (King to Gregg, 1 May 1956, in *The Papers of Martin Luther King, Jr.*, vol. 3: *Birth of a New Age, December 1955–December 1956,* ed. Clayborne Carson, Stewart Burns, Susan Carson, Peter Holloran, Dana L. H. Powell [Berkeley and Los Angeles: University of California Press, 1997], p. 244). The two men met for the first time in February 1959 at a War Resisters League (WRL) event in New York (Gregg to King, 2 May 1959; see also King, Address at the Thirty-sixth Annual Dinner of the War Resisters League, 2 February 1959, pp. 120–125 in this volume).

2. Rufus M. Jones co-founded the American Friends Service Committee (AFSC) in 1917 and served as honorary chair of the Quaker organization until his death in 1948.

Montgomery Ala.
Jan. 1–1959

Rev. M. L. King.

I must warn you that my husband is being paid 5 hundred dollars from some of the members of your church to Kill you. they are tired of your lies and always making trouble for them. You have caused some of them to loose their jobs I ask my husband not to do it, but he said the world would be better of when You are in hell where you belong with the rest of the swine, that You was a disgrace to our race. Be careful.

Anonymous letter threatening King's life (1 January 1959)

To Aubré de L. Maynard

6 Jan 1959

6 January 1959
[*Montgomery, Ala.*]

On 20 September 1958 Izola Ware Curry, a mentally disturbed African American woman, stabbed King in a Harlem department store as he autographed copies of Stride Toward Freedom, *his memoir of the Montgomery bus protest.*[1] *At Harlem Hospital a team of physicians led by Maynard, the hospital's director of surgery, successfully removed a letter opener lodged perilously close to King's heart. King spent most of October recuperating in New York before returning to a reduced workload in Montgomery.*

In the following letter King thanks Maynard for his medical assistance and requests a check-up for 16 January.[2] *After the examination, Maynard informed King in a 23 January letter that he had fully recovered.*

Dr. Aubrey de L. Maynard
312 Manhattan Avenue
New York 39, New York

Dear Dr. Maynard:

I will be in New York for a few hours on Friday, January 16. I would appreciate it very much if I could talk with you for a few minutes and also have a physical check up. Please let me know by return mail whether this is a possibility and also the best time of day for you.

I have been intending to write you ever since I left New York to express my sincere appreciation to you for doing so much to preserve my life. I have no doubt that it was your skilled surgery and your genuine concern that brought me from a very low ebb to a healthy body again. Your thoughtful and considerate concern will remain dear to me so long as the cords of memory shall lengthen.

I hope you have received our Christmas gift by now. It is just a little expression of our appreciation to you for all that you did to ease the burden in a very difficult period in our lives.[3]

You have my prayers and best wishes for a continued success in the great work that you are doing, and for a new year packed with meaningful fulfillment.

---

1. *Stride Toward Freedom: The Montgomery Story* (New York: Harper & Brothers, 1958). For a full discussion of the stabbing, see Introduction, *The Papers of Martin Luther King, Jr.*, vol. 4: *Symbol of the Movement, January 1957–December 1958*, ed. Clayborne Carson, Susan Carson, Adrienne Clay, Virginia Shadron, Kieran Taylor (Berkeley and Los Angeles: University of California Press, 2000), pp. 34–35.

2. King wrote thank-you letters to the other physicians who had treated him in New York (King to Alphonzo Jordan, Emil Naclerio, John W. V. Cordice, all dated 6 January 1959; King to Helene D. Mayer, 7 January 1959; and King to Bernard B. Nadell, 8 January 1959).

3. King had sent Maynard a fountain pen (Aubré de L. Maynard, *Surgeons to the Poor: The Harlem Hospital Story* [New York: Appleton-Century-Crofts, 1978], p. 191).

Very sincerely yours,
Martin L. King, Jr.
MLK:mlb

TLc. MLKP-MBU: Box 31.

From Reinhold Niebuhr

6 January 1959
New York, N.Y.

Shortly after the September 1958 publication of Stride Toward Freedom, *King inscribed a copy for theologian Reinhold Niebuhr: "In appreciation for your genuine good-will, your great prophetic vision, your creative contribution to the world of ideas, and your unswerving devotion to the ideals of freedom and justice."*[1] *In* Stride *King wrote that Niebuhr's work had greatly influenced his own theology, though he disagreed with Niebuhr's critique of pacifism.*[2]

The Rev. Martin Luther King
Dexter Avenue Baptist Church
Montgomery, Alabama.

My dear friend Martin Luther King,

During the summer when I was absent in Princeton, New Jersey, you were good enough to send me your splendid book "Stride toward Freedom" with a very generous inscription.[3] I did not see this book until I returned because no books were forwarded to me and my secretary could not acknowledge it because she did not know your address. Indeed I do not know it either but I am taking the chance of sending it to your church. I want to say how grateful I am for the book and for the inscription and for the splendid example which you have given both to your people and to the Christian people of the nation. Incidentally I read your book with great enthusiasm before you sent me the inscribed copy, but I am just as well pleased to have an inscribed copy and to give the other copy to my son.[4]

1. King, Inscription to Reinhold Niebuhr, November 1958.

2. *Stride Toward Freedom,* p. 98: "True pacifism is not unrealistic submission to evil power, as Niebuhr contends. It is rather a courageous confrontation of evil by the power of love." For King's earlier graduate school writings on Niebuhr, see "Reinhold Niebuhr's Ethical Dualism," 9 May 1952, and "The Theology of Reinhold Niebuhr," April 1953–June 1954, in *The Papers of Martin Luther King, Jr.,* vol. 2: *Rediscovering Precious Values, July 1951–November 1955,* ed. Clayborne Carson, Ralph E. Luker, Penny A. Russell, Peter Holloran (Berkeley and Los Angeles: University of California Press, 1994), pp. 141–152 and 269–279, respectively.

3. Niebuhr, a professor at Union Theological Seminary in New York, was a visiting scholar at the Institute for Advanced Study in 1958.

4. Niebuhr refers to his son Christopher.

With cordial personal regards and best wishes for the new year.

Sincerely yours,
[*signed*]
Reinhold Niebuhr.

TLS. MLKP-MBU: Box 84.

From Stanley D. Levison

8 January 1959
New York, N.Y.

In December 1956 King met New York attorney Stanley Levison, who would become one of his primary legal, financial, and tactical advisors. In a 15 December 1958 letter, King invited Levison to submit a bill "for all of the things that you are doing to lessen my load and also to save me money."[1] *In this reply Levison explains that his participation in the struggle for civil rights "is payment enough," and adds, "I am indebted to you, not you to me." King replied on 12 January.*

Dear Martin:

Between holidays, colds, and Youth Marching for 1959, I've been dalayed in writing you about several matters, apart from those Bayard reports on to you.[2]

First, in your last letter you suggested that you should pay me for handling your taxes, the book, etc. It does you credit to make such a thoughtful offer but it is out of the question. I could wax philosophical on this subject at length but instead I'll put it simply. My skills to which you refer were acquired not only in a cloistered academic environment, but also in the commercial jungle where more violence in varied forms occurs daily than is found on many a battlefront. Although our culture approves, and even honors, these practices, to me they were always abhorrent. Hence, I looked forward to the time when I could use these skills not for myself but for socially constructive ends. The liberation struggle is the most positive and rewarding area of work anyone could experience. So the skills learned in basically destructive activity are employed here in constructive effort. That is payment enough for me and very seriously I am indebted to you, not you to me.

The national director of programs for the American Jewish Congress, Jules

1. See *Papers* 4:545.

2. With Levison's assistance, pacifist Bayard Rustin organized the 1958 Youth March for Integrated Schools, an effort to pressure the Eisenhower administration to enforce the Supreme Court's 1954 school desegregation ruling in *Brown et al. v. Board of Education of Topeka et al.* (347 U.S. 483). They also helped coordinate the 1959 march (for King's remarks, see Address at the Youth March for Integrated Schools on 18 April 1959, pp. 186–188 in this volume).

Schatz, (you met him in Miami), called me recently to say he was approached by the Canadian television network seeking your appearance on an interview program.[3] They ~~sai~~ will pay a fee of $500 and travelling expenses. They would like any Tuesday in April. This is an important program covering all of Canada. I think it would enhance your prestige, offer an important outlet, and since the fee is a good one plus expenses, you should accept it if it is at all possible. Your appearance on this television network increases the possibility of other paid appearances on U.S. networks. This should be pinned down before you leave and since Schatz must give them an answer, I'd appreciate hearing from you quickly.[4] No commission is involved for Schatz either from the network or from you.

I am also investigating another interesting project which has not yet jelled, but may shortly. This concerns the production of a recording to be distributed commercially through record shops nationally. The people discussing it are qualified to competently produce and distribute records in the best market areas. This can be another effective educational medium and would be handled on a commercial basis with proper royalties for you. We had talked of records when Bayard and I were in Montgomery last and if you remember, we spoke of you and Coretta being combined in an artistic presentation of readings and songs reflecting the Montgomery Story. I have not mentioned this earlier because I felt it was practical and useful only if a qualified firm could be involved to assure both a high standard product and distribution where it counts. The people presently interested seem to have both, so as soon as they are ready to talk concretely I'll advise you further.

I know how busy you've been since I've been working with Bayard on some of the aspects of your trip.[5] I hope you're not overdoing it—but I guess you are.

Give my best to Coretta (The Woman Behind Martin Luther King, Jr.) Tell her if she keeps growing someone will some day an article on you entitled "The Man Behind Coretta Scott King".[6]

Warmest and best.

Sincerely,
[*signed*] Stanley

P.S. Let me know as soon as possible on the Canadian engagement.

TLS. MLKP-MBU: Box 2.

---

3. King spoke to the American Jewish Congress (AJC) in Miami Beach the previous spring (see King, Address Delivered at the National Biennial Convention of the American Jewish Congress, 14 May 1958, in *Papers* 4:406–410).

4. In his 12 January reply to Levison, King agreed to appear on a Canadian Broadcasting Company program. For a transcript of the television show, see King, Interview on "Front Page Challenge," 28 April 1959, pp. 191–194 in this volume.

5. Rustin and Levison helped arrange King's 1959 visit to India.

6. Levison refers to a profile on Coretta Scott King in the January 1959 issue of *Ebony* magazine ("The Woman Behind Martin Luther King," pp. 33–38).

To George Meany

12 January 1959
New York, N.Y.

King, labor leader A. Philip Randolph, and Catholic priest John LaFarge invite AFL-CIO president George Meany to join them as chairmen of the Youth March for Integrated Schools and to endorse a petition to Congress and the White House demanding an end to school segregation.[1] *In his 16 January reply, Meany agreed to sign the petition but declined to co-chair the march, explaining that he would "be unable to take an active part in the committee's work."*

Mr. George Meany, President
American Federation of Labor–
Congress of Industrial Organizations
815 16th Street, N.W.
Washington 6, D.C.

Dear Mr. Meany,

At the now famous Youth March for Integrated Schools last October, you will recall that ten thousand young people gathered at the Lincoln Memorial, and there voted to return this spring to Washington "to press for the laws which will guide and sanction our advancement to a fuller, more just interracial democracy."[2]

The 1958 Youth Maarch for Integrated Schools was organized by an ad hoc committee of distinguished church, labor, school and community leaders who supported the young people in their epochal action.[3] We are now in the process of re-constituting and enlarging the committee to achieve the objectives of the Lincoln Memorial meeting through a Petition Campaign for hundreds of thousands of signatures and a Youth March carrying the Petitions to the Congress and the White House on April 18th, 1959. (Text of the petition is enclosed.)[4]

---

1. King sent similar invitations to other individuals, including Eleanor Roosevelt (King, A. Philip Randolph, and Ruth H. Bunche to Roosevelt, 12 January 1959). For King's remarks at the Youth March, see Address at the Youth March for Integrated Schools on 18 April 1959, pp. 186–188 in this volume. George Meany (1894–1980), born in New York City, became an apprentice plumber at age sixteen and served as business agent for Plumbers Union Local 463 from 1922 until 1934, when he became president of the New York State Federation of Labor. Meany was secretary-treasurer (1940–1952) and president (1952–1955) of the American Federation of Labor (AFL). In 1955 he became the president of the merged AFL and the Congress of Industrial Organizations (CIO), a position he held until his retirement in 1979. The AFL-CIO, under Meany's leadership, provided critical support for the Civil Rights Bill of 1964 and other civil rights initiatives although it did little to end racial discrimination in many of its member unions and refused to endorse the 1963 March on Washington for Jobs and Freedom.

2. King quotes the 25 October Youth March press release announcing the "Youth Pledge."

3. At the march Coretta Scott King delivered remarks on behalf of her husband, who was recuperating from his September 1958 stabbing (see King, Address at Youth March for Integrated Schools in Washington, D.C., Delivered by Coretta Scott King, 25 October 1958, in *Papers* 4:514–515).

4. Youth March for Integrated Schools, "A petition for integrated schools to the President and the Congress of the U.S.," January 1959.

12 Jan 1959

Young people, who are those primarily affected by school integration, have thus found a way to express their convictions, and participate actively in the struggle for equal educational opportunities for all. Negro leaders in the South have let us know that the morale of those working with them under the most trying circumstances was measurably uplifted by the outpouring of young people to Washington last October. They look forward hopefully to the Petition Campaign and the Youth March of 1959 as an event which will dramatize before the nation and the world, the support of young people for their heroic and often lonely struggle. The widespread newspaper coverage and the sympathetic treatment in editorials of the objectives and conduct of the 1958 March gives assurance that both the supporters and opponents of integration will regard our campaign in 1959 as one of the major events in the civil rights struggle this year.[5]

The enthusiasm with which thousands of young people responded to the 1958 March, and the eagerness with which they are working on the preparations for the Petition Campaign and Youth March of 1959 leads us to have high hopes for a really historic success. on this fifth anniversary year of the Supreme Court integration decision. Furthermore, we now have behind us the experience and demonstration of the Committee's ability to organize and conduct this kind of campaign in the responsible and dignified manner which our cause requires. (After the last March, we received a letter from Robert McLaughlin, president of the Board of Commissioners of the District of Columbia, in which he wrote in part: "I'd like to commend the group, also, on its decorum while in the D.C.")

The combination of a vast petition campaign and Youth March is indeed a prodigious task. We need the help of important Americans for whom the youth of the nation have respect. You are such an American. We would be honored if you would join us as a sponsor of the Petition, and as a co-chairman of our committee. An early reply will make it possible for us to complete our list of co-chairmen and get the petition campaign rolling.

Very truly yours,
[*signed*] Martin L. King Jr
REV. MARTIN LUTHER KING, JR.

[*signed*] John LaFarge S.J.
FATHER JOHN LAFARGE, S.J.[6]

[*signed*]
A. PHILIP RANDOLPH

THLS. GMF-DAFL: Box 41.

---

5. See for example "Integration March Staged in Washington," *Chicago Tribune,* 26 October 1958, and "'March' in Capital Asks Integration," *New York Times,* 26 October 1958.

6. Jesuit priest John LaFarge was one of the Catholic Church's foremost proponents of racial justice. In April 1957 he was co-recipient, with King, of the Social Justice Award from the Religion and Labor Foundation.

From Jawaharlal Nehru

14 January 1959
New Delhi, India

In December 1956, while meeting with a group of Quakers in New York City, Indian prime minister Jawaharlal Nehru "responded with enthusiasm" to the possibility of meeting King.[1] *Though King had hoped to travel to India in 1957, continuing southern racist violence and his obligations as president of the Southern Christian Leadership Conference (SCLC) forced him to postpone the trip until February 1959.*[2] *Intermediaries attempted to secure an official invitation from the Indian government but settled for this letter of welcome from the prime minister.*[3] *Nehru met with King in Delhi on 10 February.*[4]

Dr. Martin Luther King,
309 South Jackson,
Montgomery,
Alabama
(U.S.A.)

Dear Dr. King,

I have today received your book "Stride Towards Freedom" which you have kindly sent me. I am grateful to you for this.[5]

---

1. Dorothy M. Steere to King, 5 January 1957; see also Homer Alexander Jack to King, 27 December 1956, in *Papers* 3:496, 498. Jawaharlal Nehru (1889–1964), born in Allahabad, India, received a B.A. (1910) from Trinity College, Cambridge, and was accepted into the bar two years later before returning to India. Around 1918 Nehru joined the Indian National Congress and was soon recognized as a leader in the struggle for independence. Nehru spent more than thirteen years in prison for his protest activities. After serving as the chief negotiator during the transfer of power, Nehru was elected the first prime minister of independent India in 1947, a position he held until his death. Though he was a close associate of Gandhi's, the two leaders sometimes disagreed over strategies for bringing about independence and economic development. Upon Nehru's death, King remembered the prime minister as "a towering world force skillfully inserting the peace will of India between the raging antagonisms of the great powers of East and West" (K. Natwar-Singh, *The Legacy of Nehru: A Memorial Tribute* [New York: The John Day Company, 1965], p. 65).

2. King to The Christopher Reynolds Foundation, Inc., 7 March 1958, and King to Clarence Pickett, 17 October 1958.

3. Rajkumari Amrit Kaur to Stewart Meacham, 18 December 1958, and Corinne B. Johnson to Rustin, 31 December 1958. King received an invitation from the Gandhi Smarak Nidhi (Gandhi National Memorial Fund), which served as the official host of the visit (see G. Ramachandran to King, 27 December 1958, in *Papers* 4:552–553). The Nidhi was founded after Gandhi's 1948 assassination to promote charitable activities influenced by his ideals.

4. See "Notes for Conversation between King and Nehru," 10 February 1959, p. 130 in this volume.

5. In his inscription to Nehru, King thanked the Indian leader for providing inspiration to black Americans fighting segregation: "We hope that as the march to the sea ushered in mass action leading to India's independence, so our efforts here may become a part of the great liberation movement changing the face of the world" (King, Inscription to Jawaharlal Nehru, November 1958).

I have long been interested in the work that you have been doing and, more especially, in the manner of doing it. This book will give me a greater insight into this and so I welcome it.

I understand that there is a chance of your coming to India. I shall look forward to meeting you.

Yours sincerely,
[*signed*] Jawaharlal Nehru

TLS. MLKP-MBU: Box 32.

From Wyatt Tee Walker

16 January 1959
Petersburg, Va.

Walker, the pastor of Gillfield Baptist Church in Petersburg, reports on a 1 January Prayer Pilgrimage to protest the efforts of Virginia officials to block public school integration.[1] *He thanks King for providing prerecorded remarks that were played at the culmination of the demonstration outside the capitol in Richmond. King replied on 28 January, congratulating Walker on the success of the Pilgrimage: "Virginia and the nation will remain in debt to you for many years to come."*[2]

Dr. Martin L. King, Jr.
Dexter Avenue Baptist Church
454 Dexter Avenue
Montgomery, Alabama

Dear Mike,

Upon my return to Petersburg immediately following the Pilgrimage my first impulse was to call you and tell you the good news of how tremendously successful our protest was. After three calls or so, it dawned on me that you could not possibly have returned from Mobile.[3] Carey and I both tried the next day, but to no avail; thus we assumed that you were spending the holidays with your relatives in Atlanta.[4]

Friday and Saturday following the Pilgrimage we worked all day getting out our

---

1. For King's endorsement of the Prayer Pilgrimage, see To Brother in Christ, 3 December 1958, in *Papers* 4:542–543.

2. King later offered Walker the position of executive director of SCLC (see King to Walker, 5 March 1960, pp. 384–385 in this volume).

3. On New Year's Day King attended an Emancipation Day program in Mobile, Alabama.

4. Congress of Racial Equality (CORE) field secretary Gordon Carey helped Walker coordinate the Pilgrimage. In a 15 January 1959 letter, Carey also thanked King for his contribution to the march and praised Walker's efforts in Petersburg.

Surprise Birthday Party Given Rev. Martin Luther King

Register Photo—Child

Serving his birthday cake at a surprise birthday party in Pierson College is the Rev. Martin Luther King, who spoke on the problems of the integration at Woolsey Hall Wednesday night, under sponsorship of the Undergraduate Lecture Bureau. With him are Mrs. Lynne Clark and Merrell Clark (Yale '60).

A surprise birthday party honoring King following his address at Yale University (15 January 1959). Reprinted with permission from Bob Child, *New Haven Evening Register.*

final press release (we sent one to your Montgomery paper) and balancing the accounts. Sunday, of course, I was tied down with my pulpit work and left at 3:30 that afternoon for New York City. There I attended the Annual Meeting of the NAACP and on Tuesday, Carey and I were both honored at a luncheon of the National Action Committee of CORE, at which time we gave a first-hand report of the Pilgrimage.[5]

For the past week since my return I have resumed my regular duties as the Minister of Gillfield Church. I say all this to say this is why I haven't written sooner.

5. Hortense Sawyer, "Minutes, National Action Committee," 6 January 1959.

16 Jan 1959

I hesitated to write because I wanted to do it in a moment when I was not being pushed for time, because I felt such a letter should be written in a moment of leisure that I might adequately express my sincere appreciation for your endorsement and encouragement and, above all, your prayers. The tape recording arrived 9 o'clock on the morning of the Pilgrimage. There were so many last minute details to be looked after that I heard it for the first time when everyone else did.

I attended a National Emancipation Day program at 11 o'clock hoping that my appearance there would, in some little way, advertise our program at the Mosque to be held some time later in the day.

The newspaper accounts said that there was a steady drizzle, but believe you me, it was a steady downpour! There were many moments on January 1 when I wished that I had never heard of a Pilgrimage of Prayer for Public Schools. You can imagine my shock and surprise at 2:10 when I took a peek into the main auditorium of the Mosque and saw more than 1500 people. With the promise of bad weather we had not expected more than 500. I was really "shook".

Enclosed is a program.[6] Everything was orderly and of a very reverent tone. You could not have spoken more directly to the situation if you had been here yourself. This whole experience has persuaded me to renewed faith "that God knows what He is about". I did not think, after my first shock, that there could ever be anything comparable to it, yet, when we left the Mosque to march seventeen blocks across the city of Richmond in the rain, I felt within my own self that if one hundred persons or ministers would walk that far in that kind of weather it would be a significant demonstration. Two blocks from the Mosque it happened all over again. When I looked back across a small park that adjoins the Mosque I saw a number behind me that "no man could number".[7] We began singing, at this point, the great hymns of the church and Negro spirituals. It was in these moments that I felt keenest the solidarity of our struggle in the South. For twelve or thirteen blocks, men, women, and children; the halt and the lame; the young and the aged; orderly, and with dignity, making a non-violent protest against the evil of closed schools in our Commonwealth. It was really a sight to behold!

I had thought many times of being a part of something like this, and I imagined that I would have been very proud, but in the moments immediately following our service on the south portico of the Capitol steps, and in the intervening days since, it has had a very humbling effect upon me. I really lost myself in this protest and I have seen the words of Jesus come true in my own life—"He that loses his life for My sake shall surely find it".[8] I feel strengthened now more than I have ever felt before and I shall always cherish the personal inspiration you have afforded me in our very warm friendship. I earnestly solicit your prayers and counsel that I may keep my feet on the ground and allow the Good Lord to use me in some small way that our people may be truly freed in this generation from the shackles of prejudice and discrimination.

Our constant prayers are ever with you in your work and I look forward to see-

6. Pilgrimage of Prayer for Public Schools, Program, "State-Wide Emancipation Day service," 1 January 1959.

7. Cf. Revelations 7:9.

8. Cf. Matthew 16:25.

ing you at the War Resisters League Dinner in New York City on February 2.[9] My warm regards to Coretta and the children. 25 Jan 1959

Sincerely yours,
[*signed*] W. Tee
Wyatt Tee Walker, Coordinator
Pilgrimage of Prayer for Public Schools

WTW/nad
Enclosures

P.S. It is too early to tell just what the effects of the Pilgrimage will be, but certainly it was significant that as many pilgrims as did come were there to be counted for so vital an issue on such a bad day.

TLS. MLKP-MBU: Box 73A.

---

9. King delivered the keynote address at the WRL's thirty-sixth annual dinner on 2 February 1959 (see pp. 120–125 in this volume).

To Dwight D. Eisenhower

25 January 1959
Montgomery, Ala.

In December 1958 and January 1959 the United States Commission on Civil Rights held hearings into discriminatory voter registration practices. During the hearings, Alabama officials rebuffed the commission's attempts to access county voting records. At the conclusion of an SCLC-sponsored meeting on 24 January at Montgomery's First Baptist Church, King and other Alabama black leaders drafted the following telegram to Eisenhower protesting this defiance and petitioning him to "manifest more serious concern for the potentially dangerous state of racism in Alabama."[1]

THE PRESIDENT
THE WHITE HOUSE

75 NEGRO LEADERS FROM ALL SECTIONS OF ALABAMA MEETING IN MONT-

---

1. The black leaders sent similar telegrams to Attorney General William Rogers and congressional leaders (SCLC, Press release, 28 January 1959). The group sent Eisenhower an additional telegram urging him to name an African American member to the Civil Rights Commission in light of the death of its only black member, J. Ernest Wilkins (King to Eisenhower, 27 January 1959). Replying on behalf of the president, White House special assistant Robert E. Hampton assured W. C. Patton on 29 January that Eisenhower "intends to appoint a capable and highly respected negro" to the commission. Eisenhower nominated former Howard University Law School dean George M. Johnson, who was confirmed on 21 April 1959.

GOMERY SATURDAY JANUARY 24TH.[2] VOICED VIGOROUS PROTEST AGAINST CONTINUED EMASCULATION OF THEIR CITIZENSHIP RIGHTS, DEFIANCE OF FEDERAL COURTS AND BREAKDOWN OF LAW AND ORDER AS REGARDS RACIAL JUSTICE STOP THESE CITIZENS UNANIMOUSLY VOTED TO PETITION THE PRESIDENT THE CONGRESS AND THE DEPARTMENT OF JUSTICE TO MANIFEST MORE SERIOUS CONCERN FOR THE POTENTIALLY DANGEROUS STATE OF RACISM IN ALABAMA AND TO ACT WITH FIRMNESS CONSISTENT WITH THE NOBLEST DEMOCRATIC TRADITIONS OF AMERICA AND MAKE REAL FOR NEGROES THE RIGHTS GUARANTEED BY THE US CONSTITUTION STOP ESPECIALLY EMPHASIZED WAS THE NEED FOR FEDERAL PROTECTION OF NEGROES IN THEIR RIGHT TO VOTE WITHOUT FEAR OF BODILY HARM OR ECONOMIC REPRISAL, THEIR FREEDOM TO ASSEMBLE WITHOUT POLICE INTERFERENCE AND THE SANCTITY AND SECURITY OF THEIR HOMES STOP THE MEETING WAS CALLED JOINTLY BY THE UNDERSIGNED

REV K L BUFORD ACTING PRESIDENT TUSKEGEE CIVIC ASSOCIATION REV MARTIN LUTHER KING JR PRESIDENT SOUTHERN CHRISTIAN LEADERSHIP CONFERENCE MR W C PATTON PRESIDENT ALABAMA CO-ORDINATING ASSOCIATION ON REGISTRATION AND VOTING 208 AUBURN AVE NE ATLANTA GA RM 203 SOUTHERN CHRISTIAN LEADERSHIP CONFERENCE.[3]

PWSr. WCFO-KAbE: GF 124-A.

---

2. SCLC associate director Ella Baker began planning the meeting in early January (Baker to King and Baker to Kenneth L. Buford, both dated 8 January 1959; see also Baker, "Agenda, Meeting on registration and voting in Alabama," 24 January 1959).

3. Kenneth L. Buford (1917–), born in Pulaski, Virginia, received a B.A. (1939) from Livingston College and a B.Th. (1943) from the Bloomfield School of Religion. He served as pastor of Butler Chapel AME Zion Church from 1956 until 1966, and became Alabama state field director of the National Association for the Advancement of Colored People (NAACP) the following year. William C. Patton (1911–1997), born in Marion, Alabama, graduated from Alabama State College and worked as a high school teacher in the 1930s and 1940s. He served as leader of the NAACP Birmingham branch and was Alabama state conference president of the NAACP from 1947 to 1955. Patton later served as NAACP national director of voter education (1956–1978). He provided the NAACP national office with some of the first eyewitness accounts of the Montgomery bus protest and served as the association's liaison with the Montgomery Improvement Association (MIA) in the early days of the boycott.

To G. Mennen Williams

28 January 1959
Montgomery, Ala.

In a 25 November 1958 letter, Michigan governor G. Mennen Williams thanked King for sending him an inscribed copy of Stride Toward Freedom.[1] *Six weeks*

---

1. King's inscription praised Williams's "great humanitarian concern" and "unswerving devotion to the ideals of freedom and justice" (King, Inscription to G. Mennen Williams, November 1958).

later, Williams solicited King's appraisal of the Alabama Council on Human Relations (ACHR) after receiving a request for support from the organization's executive director.[2]

Governor G. Mennen Williams
State of Michigan
Lansing, Michigan

Dear Governor Williams:

I am in receipt of your letter of January 6, making inquiry of the work of the Alabama Council on Human Relations. I would strongly recommend this organization as one worthy of support. It is an affiliate of the Southern Regional Council and is by far the most effective interracial organization in the South working for better race relations. While it is not an action organization, it is doing a marvelous job in the educational realm. It is the one organization that is keeping the desperately needed channels of communication open to the races.

Rev. Robert E. Hughes, the Executive Director of the Alabama Council, is a very fine person, a dedicated Christian and a native white southerner who is deeply devoted to the principles of freedom and justice for all.[3]

I hope these brief comments will be of some help to you in making your decision.

Very sincerely yours,
[*signed*]
Martin L. King, Jr.

(Dictated, but not personally signed by Dr. King.)
MLK:mlb

TLS. GMWC-MiU-Hi: Box 676.

---

2. Williams to King, 6 January 1959. In a 19 March 1959 letter, Williams requested King's advice on a speech he was to give for Africa Freedom Day at Carnegie Hall in New York City. King, however, was out of town and unable to respond (Maude Ballou to Williams, 15 April 1959). Gerhard Mennen Williams (1911–1988), born in Detroit, Michigan, received an A.B. (1933) from Princeton University and a J.D. (1936) from the University of Michigan. During his tenure as governor of Michigan (1949–1961), Williams appointed African Americans to his cabinet and the courts and championed laws against racial discrimination in employment and housing. He later served as assistant secretary for African Affairs in the Kennedy administration and as a Michigan Supreme Court justice.

3. Hughes helped arrange the initial negotiations between the MIA and local white officials during the bus boycott.

To Jesse Hill, Jr.

28 January 1959
[*Montgomery, Ala.*]

On 10 December 1958, SCLC executive board members agreed to join the Atlanta All-Citizens Registration Committee to undertake a campaign to add fifty-seven thousand local African Americans to the voting rolls. SCLC assigned executive director John L. Tilley and office assistant Judith Fisher to coordinate the effort.[1] *The following month Hill, chairman of the Registration Committee, complained to King of Tilley's inability to devote sufficient time to the voting drive and requested that SCLC "consider providing only the services of Miss Judith Fisher."*[2]

Mr. Jesse Hill, Jr., Chairman
Atlanta All-Citizens
Registration Committee
148 Auburn Avenue, N.E.
Atlanta 1, Georgia

Dear Mr. Hill:

I am in receipt of your letter of January 19, outlining the details of why your committee found it necessary to discontinue the services of Rev. John L. Tilley as Director of the Atlanta Voting Drive. I have read the contents of this letter with scrutinizing care.

Naturally we were very sorry to know that Rev. Tilley's schedule made it impossible for him to give as much time as you thought was necessary in the early stages of the campaign. The Board of the Southern Christian Leadership Conference was under the impression that the Atlanta All-Citizens Registration Committee was aware of Dr. Tilley's part-time status from the beginning and that he would occasionally have to be out of the city. We regret very deeply that this misunderstanding arose.

May we assure you, however, that this in no way diminishes our interest in the Atlanta voting drive. The Southern Leadership Conference initiated its crusade for citizenship several months ago to function as a service agency, rendering assistance in various communities in any way that we possibly could. Our one big aim is to assist the whole South in doubling the number of Negro voters by 1960. In no way do we attempt to interfere with the work of existing local groups, but

1. "Tilley Named to Lead Drive Here for Registration," *Atlanta Daily World,* 14 December 1958. Spelman College graduate Judith Fisher was the daughter of A. Franklin Fisher, pastor of Atlanta's West Hunter Baptist Church. King's father, Martin Luther King, Sr., served on the executive committee of the All-Citizens Registration Committee.

2. Hill, a local black businessman who had donated money to the MIA during the bus boycott, also asked that King send a donation toward hiring a new coordinator: "Since we will have the new responsibility of providing a qualified director ourselves any additional contribution would be most effective and timely" (Hill to King, 19 January 1959).

only to assist and coordinate these groups when and wherever they desire. The job of registration is such a big one that no single group could cover the whole field. It will require the cooperative work of all existing organizations. We feel that one of the most decisive steps that the Negro can take at this time is that short walk to the voting booth. We were, therefore, especially delighted to join in the Atlanta drive because that community places no external resistance to registration. It appears that the only barrier to be overcome is that of apathy on the part of Negroes themselves. We feel that Atlanta is one of the communities of the South where a successful voting drive would lead to the election of Negroes to some important city positions. Since the Atlanta community is so important, we would not at all think of withdrawing our support. I hope that you will be able to work out a plan whereby Dr. Tilley can render some service within the limits of his schedule. As you know, Dr. Tilley is a man of wide experience in this area, having lead the city of Baltimore in one of the most successful voting drives to date. I am sure that he would be willing to cooperate at any point that he possibly can. We will also be happy to have Miss Fisher continue serving in her present capacity.[3]

May I add a personal word concerning the Atlanta drive. As you probably realize I have a rather selfish interest in this campaign because Atlanta is my home. When Dr. Tilley mentioned the proposed voting campaign in Atlanta, my heart immediately throbbed with joy. I took great pleasure in recommending our participation in this drive to the Executive Board.. Atlanta is a city with vast potentialities and great promise. Its is unique, economic and cultural prominence places it in a position to stand as a beacon light of hope to the whole South. If Atlanta succeeds, the South will succeed. If Atlanta fails, the South will fail, for Atlanta is the South in miniature. I hope for the Atlanta community a most successful and far reaching registration drive. If there is anything that I can do to assist you presently, please do not hesitate to call on me. I regret that I will be out of the country for the next two months, but on my return I will be looking to hear the results of your great work.

With every good wish, I am

Sincerely Yours,
Martin L. King, Jr.

MLK:mlb

TLc. MLKP-MBU: Box 28.

---

3. In a 23 April 1959 letter, Hill informed King that the committee's efforts had led to an increase of five thousand new voters. He also requested that Fisher remain with the campaign until "at least June 30, 1959." King replied on 5 May 1959, explaining that "budgetary limits" prevented SCLC from continuing its support for Fisher.

1 Feb
1959

"The Negro Is Part of That Huge Community Who Seek New Freedom in Every Area of Life"

1 February 1959
New York, N.Y.

In this interview from Challenge, *a publication of the Young People's Socialist League, King responds to questions regarding the broader implications of the civil rights struggle.*[1] *He argues that "complete political, economic and social equality" requires "a whole series of measures which go beyond the specific issue of segregation" and explains that the success of this struggle will depend on the realization of a "gigantic and integrated alliance of the progressive social forces in the United States."*

Martin Luther King, the leader of the Montgomery Bus Boycott is probably the best known leader of the historic struggle for Civil Rights in the United States today. He achieved this position through providing dynamic leadership to a movement which made a unique contribution to this American battle for human decency: the use of non-violent direct action against the power of Jim Crow.

Recently Dr. King published his first book, *Stride Toward Freedom* (Harper & Brothers, $2.95). It provides an excellent occasion for exploring the larger significance of the Montgomery victory. At least one reviewer, Conrad Lynn, writing in the *American Socialist,* raised a series of critical points with regard to King's point of view, implying that the Montgomery leader had refused the radical implications of his action, that non-violence will not work because American Negroes, unlike the Indians who followed Gandhi, are a minority of the population and so on.[2]

In this context, the editors of *Challenge* addressed three questions to Dr. King:[3]

How does the struggle for Civil Rights relate to the broader social issues of our time?

Is non-violent direct action inadequate because Negroes are a minority of the American population?

Does the Montgomery experience indicate that Negroes are being won to a principled pacifist point of view?

Following is Dr. King's reply.

---

1. See also King, Draft, The Negro Is Part of That Huge Community Who Seek New Freedom in Every Area of Life, 1 February 1959.

2. Lynn, a civil rights lawyer, cautioned King against repeating the mistakes of other black leaders who attempted "to keep the upsurge of his people within 'respectable' limits." Lynn predicted that, despite King's "martyr image" following his September 1958 stabbing, he faced an uphill battle because few whites in the South were "suffering any twinges of conscience yet over the new technique of pacifist action" (Lynn, "Negro Leadership," *American Socialist* 6 [January 1959]: 21–22).

3. Tom Marcel was the editor of *Challenge,* which had a six-member editorial board.

* * *

I am delighted to have the opportunity to answer your questions and thus to deepen the discussion of the struggle for Civil Rights in the United States. For I agree—and even with my critics—that we must carefully explore the potentialities and the limits of the kind of direct action which was successful in Montgomery.

In answer to your first question, I strongly believe that the fight for Civil Rights is an integral part of the over-all battle for social justice in [*the?*] United States. By its very nature, this movement for the human dignity of eighteen million Negroes raises problems and demands solutions which involve every American who is concerned with freedom and decency. And then, the very success of our cause depends upon our ability to fashion a gigantic and integrated alliance of the progressive social forces in the United States. Indeed, the very fact that we stand for "integration," for a society in which the Negro will have complete political, economic and social equality, commits us to fight for a whole series of measures which go beyond the specific issue of segregation.

For example, it is no accident that the forces of race hatred in the South are also the partisans of reaction on every other issue. The American labor movement has discovered this when it tries to organize workers or when it faces the fact that "Right-to-Work" laws are a favorite instrument of the leaders of the White Citizen Councils and the Klan. In the South itself, then, the broader implications of our struggle for Civil Rights are there for everyone to see—and are made most obvious by the supporters of discrimination themselves. As integration develops, the Negro will more and more face the social and political dimensions of the race issue. As a Southern *citizen,* he will discover an identity of interest with all those who champion decent conditions for all workers, adequate housing and medicine for the entire population, and so on.

Then, there is the political aspect of our fight. It is obvious to us that a political majority for Civil Rights will also be a majority in favor of many other social reforms. Those who already support our cause—the unions, the liberals, the more progressive farmers—represent a cross section of the great American majority. When this coalition becomes politically effective in its battle against minority rule and reaction, it will act on Civil Rights *and* on the many other problems confronting the American people, Negro and white.

Negroes and Labor

Perhaps a special word is in order here about the American labor movement. The unions in this country still have a considerable distance to travel before they root out racism in their own structure. The documentation of Herbert Hill, the labor secretary of the National Association for the Advancement of Colored People, is impressive and conclusive on this count.[4] And yet, with all of the changes which

4. The following year Hill, NAACP labor secretary since 1949, mailed King copies of his recent articles on the impact of racism on unionization and industrial development (Hill to King, 25 January 1960, and enclosures: Hill, "Labor Unions and the Negro," *Commentary* 28 [December 1959]: 479–488; Hill, "Recent Effects of Racial Conflict on Southern Industrial Development," *Phylon Quarterly* 20 [Winter 1959]: 319–326).

1 Feb 1959 must be made within the labor movement, the American unions represent a major and natural ally of the Negroes in their striving for equal rights. The Negro, it must be emphasized again and again, is not set apart from other Americans. The fact of race hatred imposes a terrible deformation upon his life, but it is not the only fact of his life. The vast majority of Negroes in the United States face the problems of poverty, of slum housing and inadequate medicine as well as those of Jim Crow.

Today, the real issue is to make this "natural" alliance real and effective. In the 1958 election, Negroes worked along with the unions against "Right-to-Work" laws, and the candidates of labor and liberalism stood for Civil Rights.[5] Yet it is clear that these forces have not yet really reached a level of effectiveness. Their majority mandate is subject to minority veto through the structure of our political parties and undemocratic rule in Congress, as the results of the recent Senate debate on Rule 22 points up.[6] It may well be that political realignment is a pre-condition for a real development of majority rule in the United States. But whatever the course of the struggle, there is no question that the fight for Civil Rights is integral to the indivisible cause of social justice in America. The Negro cannot win alone, or in a vacuum. The Negro is part of that huge community of Americans who seek new freedoms in every area of life.

I would summarize my answer to your first question this way: we stand for brotherhood, not for "Negro justice" and not for "white justice." We reject black supremacy at the same moment as we reject white supremacy. And this fundamental value, this spiritual commitment, obliges us to take our rightful place in the campaign for the advancement of every single human right.

The second problem which you raise—the fact that American Negroes are a minority of the population—is intimately related to the first. For if Negroes were isolated, if we thought of our cause apart from that of the majority, then this would be a compelling objection. But we don't think in these terms. As I see it, our problem is to make the majority of Americans who are willing to accept, and even to seek, integration aware of their responsibilities in this struggle.

Protest Minority Rule

Thus, the significance of actions like the Youth March for Integrated Schools or the Montgomery Bus Boycott, is not limited to a minority of Americans. On the contrary, these demonstrations are a means of making the majority conscious: they focus upon the moral principles involved. For it is an embattled minority

---

5. In 1958 King, National Baptist Convention president J. H. Jackson, and NAACP executive secretary Roy Wilkins issued statements opposing proposed right-to-work legislation in California and other states. King noted that such legislation was "backed by the same reactionary forces which flout the Supreme Court decision on school desegregation" and called such laws "inherently wrong in principle because they seek to circumvent the collective bargaining power of American workers, which is the fundamental keystone of free trade unionism" (National Council for Industrial Peace, Press release, 6 October 1958; see also NAACP, "Vote 'No' on Proposition 18," October–November 1958).

6. On 12 January 1959, the U.S. Senate amended Standing Rule 22, reducing the number of votes necessary to break a filibuster (*Congressional Record* 105 [12 January 1959]: 421–494). Segregationists had used the filibuster to stymie civil rights initiatives.

which seeks to thwart the fundamentals of human decency, the values of democracy, and the sentiment of the majority through a "century of litigation."

The arduous campaign in the courts has, of course, achieved magnificent victories. But now, precisely because the minority is organizing politically, economically and socially against these gains, we must seek new forms of struggle. That, to me, is the larger dimension of the non-violent action in Montgomery. Here, in the very midst of the South, we proved that the court decisions could be made real and meaningful. Here, in the very midst of the South, we proved that the people were prepared to accept integration on the buses—in short, we did awaken the conscience of the majority.

Here, again, we see that the Civil Rights issue refuses to be strait-jacketed as the narrow interest of a minority. It is a majority concern, and this means that non-violent actions like Montgomery, demonstrations like the Youth March, are an absolute essential to our cause, for they are the means of reaching the conscience of millions, not simply with the issue of integration, but with the fundamental values of brotherhood itself.

Finally, a few words about the tactical value of the non-violent approach. It is in the local community that Southern Negroes are under the most acute pressures and daily suffer the cumulative humiliations and, frequently, violence, which deprives them of dignity. Hence, it is in the local community that non-violent direct action is rooted and finds its most effective expression. For, in many Southern communities, the Negro is not in the minority, but in the majority, and is capable of exerting immovable force.

Inspired by Gandhi

Your third question is also quite important, for it is often a source of confusion. Non-violence can be approached on two levels, that of principle and that of action. Both are extremely important, yet they are distinct. I personally have been deeply moved and motivated by the inspiration of a teacher like Gandhi. To me, the non-violence we practiced in Montgomery is an application of my most profoundly held beliefs and Christian faith. I feel that we cannot organize ourselves on the basis of [*hatred?*], because if we do we will imitate the worst aspects of those who oppress us. Once again, for it cannot be repeated too often, we do not seek to counter white supremacy with black supremacy: we seek brotherhood.

In saying this, I am relating non-violence to my own most deeply-held values. But this does not mean that a principled commitment to non-violence, or even religious faith, is necessary before one can participate in a movement like the bus boycott. Far from it. It is quite possible, and even probable, that American Negroes will adopt non-violence as a means, an instrument, for the achievement of specific and limited ends. This was certainly true in the case of Gandhi himself, for many who followed him, like Nehru himself, did so on this kind of basis. Certainly, it would be wrong, and even disastrous, to demand principled agreement on non-violence as a pre-condition to non-violent action. What is required is the spiritual determination of the people to be true to the principle as it works *in this specific action.* This was the case in Montgomery, and it will continue to be the rule in further developments of our struggle.

At the same time, this emphasis upon the practical and tactical aspect of nonviolence in action should not be interpreted as a denigration of the spiritual values which must be present if non-violence is to work at all. Let me cite just one case in point. In Montgomery, crime among Negroes declined markedly during the course of the boycott. There was no organized campaign in this direction. What happened was that the very presence of a sense of social mission and human brotherhood worked tremendous changes in the personal lives of those involved. Thus, even when non-violence is accepted as a practical means, an instrument, it has profound spiritual consequences, it leads toward the consideration of non-violence as a principle.

A Visionary Struggle

But there is an even larger dimension to non-violence and it is with this point that I wish to close. When Negroes involve themselves in such a struggle, they take a radical step. Their rejection of hatred and oppression in the specific situation cannot be confined to a single issue. For it raises the question of hatred and oppression in the society as a whole, it moves toward an even deeper commitment to a pervasive social change. For out of this one problem, the sense of brotherhood springs as a practical necessity, and once this happens, there is revealed the vision of a society of brotherhood. We seek new ways of human beings living together, free from the spiritual deformation of race hatred—and free also from the deformations of war and economic injustice. And this vision does not belong to Negroes alone. It is the yearning of mankind.

PD. *Challenge,* 1 February 1959, p. 3; copy in NNU-T.

Address at the Thirty-sixth Annual Dinner of the War Resisters League

[2 *February 1959*]
[*New York, N.Y.*]

In this typed draft, King embellishes some of his standard remarks on nonviolence with a call for an end to war and an affirmation of the link between social justice at home and peace abroad: "No sane person can afford to work for social justice within the nation unless he simultaneously resists war and clearly declares himself for non-violence in international relations." He concludes with the hope that, through adherence to nonviolence, "the colored peoples" would so "challenge the nations of the world that they will seriously seek an alternative to war and destruction." The War Resisters League's newsletter reported that this event, held in honor of pacifist A. J. Muste, was the "most widely attended WRL dinner in recent years."[1] *The following day, King departed for India.*

---

1. "Martin Luther King Addresses WRL Dinner," *WRL News,* March–April 1959; see also War Resisters League, Program, "Thirty-sixth annual dinner," 2 February 1959. The War Resisters League, founded in 1923, emerged out of opposition to World War I. In 1956 Bayard Rustin, executive secretary of the WRL, arrived in Montgomery to offer assistance in the early days of the bus boycott.

I bring warm greetings from the embattled South—from {50},000 Negroes of Mongomery, Alabama, from the S.C.L.C., uniting Negro leadership in 12 southern states representing the millions of Americans not yet recipients of the rights guaranteed in their own Constitution. I also bring greetings from your friends, and my colleagues, who keep ~~an~~ {the} heroic struggle going regardless of its cost to them personally. ~~Rev. Fred Shuttelsworth of Birmingham, Mr. Asbury Howard of Bessemer, who only last week was brutally beaten by a mob shile leaving a court house.~~[2] Your sympathy and support mean a great deal to the fearless men who live daily with terror, and resist it with non-violent power and determination.

I would not want you to feel that the pressures which surround southern resistance leaders obscure the positive gains our harrassed movement is making. This week marks a turning point in our struggle. The defeat of massive resistance in Virinia is the Gettysbufg of today.[3] Gov. [*J. Lindsay*] Almond with his army of political forces has had his lines broken, and has tasted defeat. This is significant because their resistance was total, but met its match in the total and active resistance of our forces. It was not alone expressions of good will from white moderates which weakened their ranks. Nor alone was it the legal manipulations and the successful utilization of court orders.

In Virgina Negroes themselves took into their own hands through direct action, the mobilizing of public opiniion. CORE, NAACP, Ministers, and labor, organized and conducted a March on the State Capitol in Richmond on January 1.[4] Earlier in October the S.C.LC brought to Norfolk Negro leaders from all over the South for a two day conference on non-violence. Though I was scheduled to be the ~~leading~~ {principle} speaker my confinement in the hospital made this impossible, but your A. J. Muste took my place and deepened in his inimitable fashion the thinking of our leaders on non-violence.[5] At the conclusion of this conference over 4000 of the Negro citizens of Norfolk jammed the City Auditorium: the first demonstration of such numbers in the city's history, thus dramatizing the dynamic involvement of the community in this struggle. The whole press of Virginia front-paged this event making it umistakably clear that the Negro of Virginia was not waiting submissively or passively for his rights to be handed to him.[6] I have repeatedly warned my people that victory would not come if they wait for the white people to furnish the dinner while they merely furnish the apetite. The significant

---

2. Shuttlesworth was founder of the Alabama Christian Movement for Human Rights (ACMHR) and co-founder of SCLC. Howard was a Birmingham-area black labor leader. For more about Howard, see Statement Adopted at Spring Session of SCLC in Tallahassee, Florida, 15 May 1959, pp. 205–208 in this volume.

3. On 19 January, efforts to avoid integration by closing schools were frustrated by decisions from the state supreme court and the federal district court (*Albertis S. Harrison v. Sidney C. Day, Jr.*, 200 Va. 439, 106 S.E. 2d 636 [1959], and *Ruth Pendleton James et al. v. J. Lindsay Almond, Jr., et al.*, 170 F. Supp. 331 [1959]). On the day of King's address, schools in two Virginia cities opened on an integrated basis without incident.

4. For more on the Richmond protest, see Wyatt Tee Walker to King, 16 January 1959, pp. 108–111 in this volume.

5. Muste spoke at the October 1958 SCLC conference in Norfolk while King recuperated from the stabbing. For more on Muste's address, see SCLC, Minutes, Fall meeting, 2 October 1958.

6. See for example, "Non-Violent Protest Set on Schools," *Richmond News Leader*, 1 January 1959, and "Negro Protest Called a New 'Moral Force,'" *Richmond News Leader*, 2 January 1959.

victory in Virginia illustrates that this lesson was learned and the fruits of active struggle, as always, is victory.

Not only in the South, but throughout the nation and the world, we live in an age of conflict, an age of biological weapons, chemical warfare, atomic fallout and nuclear bombs. It is a period of conflict between the mammoth powers. It is an age of conformity. It is a period of uncertainty and fear. Every man, woman and child lives, not knowing if they shall see tomorrow's sunrise.

We are in a period when men who understand the dimensions of our tragic state must be heard. We must stand up and accept the consequences of our convictions. First of all, we must resist war. With all our energy we must find our alternative to violence as a means to deal with the terrible conflicts ~~conflicts~~ that beset us.

We must no longer cooperate with policies that degrade man and make for war. The great need in the world today is to find the means for the social organization of the power of non-violence.

In this connection, I salute the War Resisters League, which for 36 years ~~had~~ {has} courageously carried on the fight against war. I applaud its members, many of whom chose prison rather than break their faith in the power of love. {Some} chose to be ostracized rather than engage in the brutalization of their fellow man.

You have been prophetic and, as Albert Einstein once said, {"}you are part of the moral elite that may yet lead mankind from self-destruction{."}[7]

As you know, the establishment of social justice in our nation is of profound concern to me. This great struggle is in the interest of all Americans and I shall not be turned from it. Yet no sane person can afford to work for social justice within the nation unless he simultaneously resists war and clearly declares himself for non-violence in international relations.

What will be the ultimate value of having established social justice in a context where all people, Negro and White, are merely free to face destruction by strontium 90 or atomic war.

If we are to find a new method to avoid such terrible possibilities, it will be based on love not hate; it will be based on reconciliation and not retaliation; it will be based on forgiveness and not on revenge.

If we are to find an alternative to war, we must re-examine the assumptions of {th} pacifist position{:—}

My study of Gandhi convinced me that true pacifism is not non-resistance to evil; but non-violent resistance to evil. Between the two positions, there is a world of difference. Gandhi resisted evil with as much vigor and pwer as the violent resister, but he resisted with love instead of hate. True pacifism is not unrealistic submission to evil power. [*strikeout illegible*] It is rather a courageous confrontation of evil by the power of love, in the faith that it is better to ~~by~~ {be} the recipient of violence than the inflicter of it, since the latter only multiples the existence of violence and bitterness in the universe, while the former may develop

---

7. Einstein, a WRL member in the early 1930s, abandoned his strict pacifism following Hitler's ascension to power in Germany; he continued to press for peace and disarmament until his death in 1955.

a sense of shame in the opponent, and thereby bring about a transformation and change of heart.[8] However bringing about such a transformation is not a simple matter. It requires directness of purpose, dedication and above all humility of mind and spirit. Because our thinking is so close, and because the task before us is so great, I feel free to say that we who believe in non-violence often have an unwarranted optimism concerning man and lean unconsciously toward self-righteousness. It seems to me that we must see the pacifist position not as sinless but as the lesser evil in the circumstances. I have often felt that we who advocate non-violence would have a greater appeal if we did not claim to be free from the moral dilemmas that the nonpacifist confronts.

Dispite all short comings, the philosophy of non-violence played such a positive role in the ~~Montgomery movement~~ {southern struggle} that it may be wise to turn to a brief discussion of some basic aspects of ~~this philosophy~~ {non-violence} as they apply to Montgomery and may be applied to the quest for peace. First it must be emphasized that nonviolent resistance is not a method for cowards; it does resist. If one uses this method because he is afraid or merely because he lacks the instruments of violence, he is not truly nonviolent. This is why Gandhi often said that if cowardice is the only alternative to violence, it is better to fight.[9] He made this statement conscious of the fact that there is always another alternative: no individual or group need submit to any wrong, nor need they use violence to right the wrong; there is the way of nonviolent resistance. This is ultimately the way of strong men. It is not a method of stagnant passivity. The phrase "passive resistance" often gives the false impression that this is a sort of "do nothing method" in which the resister quietly and passively accepts evil. But nothing is further from the truth. For while the nonviolent resister is passive in the sense that he is not physically aggressive toward his opponent, his mind and emotions are always active, constantly seeking to persuade his opponent that he is wrong. It is not passive non-resistance to to evil; it is active nonviolent resistance to evil.

A second basic fact that characterizes nonviolence is that it does not seek to defeat or humiliate the opponent, but to win his friendship and understanding. The nonviolent resister must often express his protest through non-cooperation or boycotts, but he realizes that these are not ends themselves; they are merely means to awaken a sense of moral shame in the opponent. The end is redemption and reconciliation. The aftermath of nonviolence is the creation of the beloved community, while the aftermath of violence is tragic bitterness.

A third characteristic of this method is that the attack is directed against forces of evil rather than against persons who happen to be doing the evil. It is evil that

---

8. King published a similar discussion on Gandhi and nonviolence in *Stride Toward Freedom,* pp. 98–99. He additionally published an excerpt from *Stride* under the title "My Pilgrimage to Nonviolence" (see *Papers* 4:473–481).

9. In his 15 August 1920 essay "The Doctrine of the Sword," Gandhi wrote: "I do believe that where there is only a choice between cowardice and violence I would advise violence. . . . I would rather have India resort to arms in order to defend her honour than that she should in a cowardly manner become or remain a helpless witness to her own dishonour" (*The Collected Works of Mahatma Gandhi,* vol. 18, July–November 1920 [Delhi: The Publications Division, Ministry of Information and Broadcasting, Government of India, 1965], p. 132).

the nonviolent resister seeks to defeat, not the persons victimized by evil. If he is opposing injustice, the nonviolent resister must have the vision to see the real and not the apparent antagonisms. As I have said again and again, to the people in Montgomery, "The tension is, at bottom between justice and injustice, between the forces of light and the forces of darkness. And if there is a victory, it will be a victory not merely of 50,000 Negroes, but a victory for justice and the forces of light. We are out to defeat injustice and not white persons who may be unjust."

A fourth point that characterizes nonviolent resistance is a willingness to accept suffering without retaliation, to accept blows from the opponent without striking back. "Rivers of blood may have to flow before we gain our freedom, but it must be our blood," said Gandhi to his countrymen.[10] The non-violent resister is willing to accept violence if necessary, but never to inflict it. He does not seek to dodge jail. If going to jail is necessary, he enters it "as a bridegroom enters a bride's chamber."[11]

One may well ask: "What is the nonviolent resister's justification for this ordeal to which he invites men, for this mass political application of the ancient doctrine of turning the other cheek?" The answer is found in the realization that unearned suffering is redemptive. Suffering, the nonviolent resister realizes, has tremendous educational and transforming possibilities. "Things of fundamental importance to people are not secured by reason alone, but have to be purchased with their suffering," said Gandhi. He continues: "Suffering is infinitely more powerful than the law of the jungle for converting the opponent and opening his ears which are otherwise shut to the voice of reason.[12] But beyond its effect upon the aggressor, the voluntary suffering inspires respect from the uncommitted and ultimately leads to a growth of, and solidarity with, the ranks of the peacemakers. ~~This is the lesson of the experience of Jesus from the beginning of the modern era to the second half of the 20th century in Montgomery Alabama.~~

A fifth point concerning nonviolent resistance is that it avoids not only external physical violence but also internal violence of spirit. The nonviolent resister not only refuses to shoot his opponent but he also refuses to hate him. At the cen-

---

10. King's discussion of Gandhi in this draft may have been drawn from civil rights attorney Harris Wofford's address "Nonviolence and the Law," delivered at Howard University on 7 November 1957. Wofford: "'Rivers of blood may have to flow before we gain our freedom but it must be our blood,' he said to his countrymen." For an additional version of Wofford's address, see "Nonviolence and the Law," *Gandhi Marg* 3 (January 1959): 27–35. King had also relied on Wofford in his discussion of nonviolence in *Stride Toward Freedom* (see Introduction in *Papers* 4:31–32).

11. In Gandhi's 15 December 1921 "Young India" column, he wrote: "We must widen the gates of prisons and we must enter them as a bridegroom enters the bride's chamber" (*The Collected Works of Mahatma Gandhi,* vol. 22, December 1921–March 1922 [Delhi: The Publications Division, Ministry of Information and Broadcasting, Government of India, 1966], p. 10).

12. In 1931, Gandhi wrote: "And so, in 1920, I became a rebel. Since then the conviction has been growing upon me, that things of fundamental importance to the people are not secured by reason alone, but have to be purchased with their suffering. Suffering is the law of human beings; war is the law of the jungle. But suffering is infinitely more powerful than the law of the jungle for converting the opponent and opening his ears, which are otherwise shut, to the voice of reason" (*The Collected Works of Mahatma Gandhi,* vol. 48, September 1931–January 1932 [Delhi: The Publications Division, Ministry of Information and Broadcasting, Government of India, 1971], p. 189).

ter of nonviolence stands the principle of love. The nonviolent resister would content that in the struggle for human dignity, the oppressed people of the world must not succumb to the temptation of becoming bitter or indulging in hate campaigns. To retaliate in kind would do nothing but intensify the existence of hate in the universe. Along the way of life, someone must have sense enough and morality enough to cut off the chain of hate. This can only be done by projecting the ethic of love to the center of our lives.

On the eve of my departure for India, it is particularly appropriate that I have the privilege of being with the people who have had so long a dedicated concern for socal justice, racial equality and world peace. ~~This is the great hour for the Negro and the other colored peoples of the world.~~ {Let each of us go away this evening with a new determination to stand against the evils of our day.} The challenge is here. To become the instruments of a great idea is a privilege that history gives only occasionally.[13] Arnold Toynbee says in A Study of History that it may be the colored peoples who will give the new spiritual dynamic to western civilization that it so desperately needs to survive.[14] I hope this is possible. The spiritual power that the colored peoples can radiate to the world comes from love, understanding, goodwill, and nonviolence. It may even be possible for the colored peoples through adherence to nonviolence, so to challenge the nations of the world that they will seriously seek an alternative to war and destruction. In a day when Sputniks and Explorers dash through outer space and guided ballistic missles are carving highways of death through the stratosphere, nobody can win a war. Today the choice is no longer between violence and nonviolence. It is either nonviolence or nonexistence. The colored peoples may be God's appeal to this age—an age drifting rapidly to its doom. The eternal appeal takes the form of a warning: "All who take the sword will perish by the sword."[15]

TADd. MLKP MBU: Box 119.

13. Wofford, "Nonviolence and the Law": "It is a privilege that history gives only occasionally for men to become the instruments of a great idea."

14. Arnold Toynbee, *A Study of History*, vol. 2 (New York: Oxford University Press, 1934), pp. 219–220. See also note 7 to "'Mother's Day in Montgomery,' by Almena Lomax," 18 May 1956, in *Papers* 3:266.

15. Cf. Matthew 26:52.

Account by Lawrence Dunbar Reddick of Press Conference in New Delhi on 10 February 1959

[*1959*]

On 3 February King departed for India from New York's Idlewild Airport in the company of his wife, Coretta, and his biographer, Alabama State College history professor Lawrence D. Reddick. They arrived in New Delhi two days behind schedule due to a missed flight in Europe and were greeted at the airport by a group of reporters and well-wishers, as well as by James Bristol of the Quaker Centre, who would serve as King's travel guide along with Swami Vishwananda of the Gandhi Smarak Nidhi.[1] *This excerpt from an unpublished manuscript describes King's press conference at the Janpath Hotel the day of his arrival in New Delhi.*[2]

We finally made it to our hotel where, after checking in, a press conference was set up. Present were some twenty-odd Indian newspaper men and women, a man from the New York Times and another from the Baltimore Afro-American. Martin pulled out his prepared statement and said:

> My Friends,
>
> For a long while I have looked forward to visiting your great country.
>
> To other countries I may go as a tourist, but to India I come as a pilgrim.
>
> This is because India means to me Mahatma Gandhi, a truly great personality of the ages.
>
> India also means to me Pandit Nehru and his wise statesmanship and intellectuality that are recognized the world over.
>
> Perhaps, above all, India is the land where the techniques of non-violent social change were developed that my people have used in Montgomery, Alabama and elsewhere throughout the American South. We have found them to be effective and sustaining—they work!
>
> Accordingly, I bring greetings to the people of India—greetings and thanks for what your freedom movement has meant to ours.
>
> During our brief stay here, we hope that you will receive us as friends, will share with us your problems and aspirations and will let us share ours with you.
>
> We hope and pray that the bonds of friendship will be strengthened between us and among all men who dedicate their lives and possessions to justice, peace and brotherhood.
>
> In the name of my people and my country, America, I salute you and extend the hand of a brother.

After King had read this statement, I passed around copies of it to everyone. After a pause for a moment or two, the questions started coming. First, he was asked about the bus boycott. He told that story, at least as much of it as he could squeeze into a two-minute statement*[3]

Then he was asked how the desegregation of buses in Montgomery had affected

---

1. The King party had flown from London to Paris, where they visited Richard Wright, an expatriate African American novelist and friend of Reddick's. When the flight they expected to board in Zurich bypassed the city due to fog, the travelers flew to Istanbul, Beirut, and then Bombay before reaching New Delhi on 10 February.

2. Reddick, Draft, Martin Luther King, Jr.'s trip to India, 1959. Following King's death in 1968, Reddick wrote "With King through India: A personal memoir." For coverage of King's press conference, see "Martin Luther King, Negro Leader, Pays Tribute to Gandhi," *American Reporter,* 13 February 1959.

3. Reddick added a footnote at the bottom of the page: "For detailed account, see Stride Toward Freedom or Crusader Without Violence."

transportation services in other cities. King answered that some thirty-three cities had desegregated their buses, Atlanta, Georgia being the latest. The following question–answer sequence ensued.:

Q. How many Little Rocks are there in the U.S.?

A. In a sense Little Rock is symbolic of the whole non-complying South. This is not to say that the whole South is not complying but that those communities in the South that do not wish to implement the Supreme Court's desegregation decision are watching Little Rock and cheering from the side lines.

Q. Do you think that the Gandhian technique can work in Africa?

A. When I was visiting in Ghana, West Africa, Prime Minister Nkrumah told me that he had read the works of Gandhi and felt that non-violent resistance could be extended there.[4] We recall that South Africa has had bus boycotts also.[5]

Q. Can you say that you have transformed the hearts of the white people of Montgomery?

A. I wish that I could say that our movement has transformed the hearts of all of Montgomery—some, no doubt; but there is a degree of bitterness and a refusal to accept a new [*way?*] of human relations.

Q. How far would your movement have been successful without the Supreme Court decision?[6]

A. This is a difficult question but even aside from the court rulings, our movement gave the Negro people a deeper sense of dignity and destiny; gave new morale all over the South and America.

Q. Does your conception of non-violence include vegetarianism?

A. No.

Q. Is non-violence with you a creed or a policy?

A. I have come to believe in it as a way of life. Perhaps most people in America still treat it as a technique.

Q. Have many Negroes married white Americans?

A. Not many.

---

4. King met Prime Minister Kwame Nkrumah during Ghana's independence celebrations in March 1957 (see Introduction in *Papers* 4:7–8).

5. In 1957, over 60,000 South Africans participated in a bus boycott in Alexandra, a township near Johannesburg. For three months, protesters challenged the rising cost of bus fares until employers agreed to subsidize the transportation costs of their employees.

6. The U.S. Supreme Court ordered Montgomery's buses desegregated on 17 December 1956, and the MIA called off the boycott a few days later (*Gayle v. Browder* [352 U.S. 950] and King, Statement on Ending the Bus Boycott, 20 December 1956, in *Papers* 3:485–487).

10 Feb 1959

Q. Is intermarriage illegal in all Southern states?
A. Yes.[7]

Q. Do American Negroes look down upon Africans?
A. Maybe in times past but today there is a great deal of pride, mutual pride between Africans and Negro Americans, real sympathy in the common struggle.

Q. What is the number of Negroes moving North every year?
A. Sorry, I don't have the statistics. I may say, however, that the motivation is principally economic. Usually there are more jobs, for the major industries are in the North; also, greater civil liberty in the North.

Q. What is the position of Paul Robeson in America and in the Negro community?
A. There are mixed views. He has some supporters, many admire his artistry as an actor and singer and also his integrity but do not accept his political views.[8]

Q. What is your personal view of Robeson?
A. No comment.

Q. Do you note any marked leftist views among American Negroes or do they still believe in free enterprise? On the basis of their mistreatment, we should have expected a larger shift to the left.
A. My guess is that not more than one per cent of American Negroes have embraced definite extreme leftist views. Even during the depression the percentage was not very large. Negroes, like many other Americans, do want a wider distribution of wealth but the Negro still believes that he can get his economic and political rights under democracy without turning to other ideologies.[9]

Q. Now that you have won your case on the buses are you going to consolidate your gains and expand the movement.
A. It is my hope that the philosophy of non-violence will carry over into the

---

7. The U.S. Supreme Court declared "antimiscegenation" laws illegal in 1967; at that time, interracial marriage was illegal in sixteen states (*Loving v. Virginia* [388 U.S. 1]).

8. An outspoken supporter of the Soviet Union and critic of racial segregation, Robeson was forced to testify before the House Committee on Un-American Activities (HUAC) in 1956. At the hearings, Robeson refused to provide names of Communist Party members or to divulge his relationship with the organization.

9. According to the *American Reporter*, King replied that "the basic reason is that the American Negro has faith that he can get justice within the framework of the American democratic set-up" ("Martin Luther King, Negro Leader," 13 February 1960).

general struggle for full and complete rights for all. We have organized the Southern Christian Leadership Conference along this line. It is composed of major Negro leaders of the South and we will have a South-wide institute during the coming summer [1959] to discuss the theory and techniques of non-violent resistance.[10] We have had three such institutes in Montgomery.[11]

Q. Will non-violence be a permanent part of the struggle for justice in America?

A. I hope so and hope that it will be successful. Some of us believe in it strongly and you know that it is usually the creative minority at work who stand against the general trend.

Q. Do you function through political parties or churches?

A. Our movement is non-political in terms of any particular party. Our approach is through mass action as a majority of our people are affiliated with some church.

Q. What are the next burning issues in the Negro struggle in America?

A. It is difficult to say but school integration seems to be the biggest issue just now. There is also the question of voting throughout the South.

Q. Don't you have the vote already?

A. According to the federal Constitution and recent federal civil rights legislation in support of the 14th and 15th Amendments, theoretically there should be no denial of voting rights on the basis of race or color. But in the South today while more than fifty-per cent of the white people of voting age do vote only twenty-five per cent of the Negroes vote. The Civil Rights Commission is now making investigations of the nature and extent of disfranchisement and will report to the President, Congress and the public on its findings.[12]

TAD. LDRP NN Sc.

---

10. SCLC, the Fellowship of Reconciliation (FOR), and the Congress of Racial Equality (CORE) co-sponsored the Southwide Institute on Nonviolent Resistance to Segregation, which was held in Atlanta from 22 to 24 July. For more on the institute, see Resolutions, First Southwide Institute on Nonviolent Resistance to Segregation, held on 22 July–24 July 1959, 11 August 1959, pp. 261–262 in this volume.

11. King refers to the annual MIA-sponsored Institute on Nonviolence and Social Change (see King, "Facing the Challenge of a New Age," Address at the First Annual Institute on Nonviolence and Social Change, 3 December 1956, in *Papers* 3:451–463, and King, "Some Things We Must Do," Address Delivered at the Second Annual Institute on Nonviolence and Social Change at Holt Street Baptist Church, 5 December 1957, in *Papers* 4:328–343. For details on the 1958 institute, see Introduction in *Papers* 4:36–37).

12. U.S. Commission on Civil Rights, *Report of the United States Commission on Civil Rights, 1959* (Washington, D.C.: U.S. Government Printing Office, 1959), pp. 134–142.

"Notes for Conversation between King and Nehru"

[*10 February 1959*]

King's late arrival in New Delhi caused him to miss his meeting with Prime Minister Nehru on 9 February, but King soon learned that Nehru had agreed to reschedule for the following evening.[1] *Coretta King later recalled that her husband and the Indian leader discussed nonviolence and compared the struggles in India and the United States for four hours.*[2]

While it is uncertain who prepared these notes, Reddick's unpublished 1968 memoir of the India trip suggested that they reflect the points King had hoped to cover in his meeting with Nehru.[3] *A few weeks after the meeting, Nehru wrote to the secretary of the Gandhi Smarak Nidhi of his "great pleasure" in meeting King.*[4]

1. What is the present status of non-violent social change in the world today?
   a. for domestic problems
   b. for international relations
2. How vital and socially useful is Gandhianism in India's current struggle to improve the welfare of its people?
   a. what modifications are required?
   b. does it conflict with industrialization or national defense?
3. Can a nation committed to democracy make progress toward ma good life for all of its people fast enough for them not to desert democracy for the more rapid progress of communism?
   a. China or India?
   b. Which way will Africa go?
4. How can the bonds of friendship between the Negro people of America and the people of India be made stronger?
   a. exchange of students and professors and journalists
   b. visits to the South of Indian leaders and visits of Negro leaders to India.

THD. MLKP-MBU: Box 1.

---

1. Nehru's daughter, Indira Gandhi, and Lady Edwina Mountbatten, the last colonial vicereine in India, were also in attendance that evening at Teen Murti Bhavan, the prime minister's home.

2. Coretta Scott King, *My Life with Martin Luther King, Jr.* (New York: Holt, Rinehart and Winston, 1969), pp. 174–175.

3. Reddick recalled: "In our little caucus before the dinner, the Kings and I had decided to talk about non-violence, of course, but in its application to international affairs; also, we would ask of the possibility of scholarships in Indian universities for black American students" (Reddick, "With King through India: A personal memoir," 1968).

4. Nehru to G. Ramachandran, 5 March 1959.

From Wonwihari Prasad Bhoop

21 February 1959
Gaya, India

After leaving Delhi in the early hours of 13 February, King and his travel companions spent the morning in Patna, capital of the state of Bihar, before catching the train to Gaya. The following day, they toured the Buddhist holy sites of Gaya and Bodh Gaya before leaving for the rural ashram of Indian activist Jayaprakash Narayan.[1]

In the following letter Bhoop, who had met King in Gaya, offers to translate Stride Toward Freedom *into Hindi and arrange for its distribution.*[2] *King replied to this letter on 14 July: "I am greatly concerned about my book being read in India because of the inspiration that came to me from that great country, and above all because of the fact that I have tried in some little way to follow the noble insights and principles of Mahatma Gandhi." King, however, declined Bhoop's offer, stating that he had already signed a contract with Navajivan Press to translate his book into Hindi and Gujarati.*

My dear Friend,

It was such a pleasure to meet you and to be able to spend a few hours with you all at Gaya and Bodh-Gaya. Though it was only for a short period that I could be in your company yet, in fact, I spent two more days with you—the 16th & 17th Feb.—reading your book "Stride towards Freedom". Shri Jayaprakash Narayan gave me this book on his return from Calcutta on the 16th morning.[3] He had shown me the book and it was to remain with me only for a few hours that he was going to stay with us. But, by mistake it could not be returned to him and it is still with me. I was sorry to discover the mistake but on the other hand it saved me the delay ~~in~~ of a few days, in reading it, by which I would have got my own copy.

As I proceeded with the book I became more and more engrossed in it and I felt as if the Montgomery protest was going on before my eyes. When I had finished it, and seen in it the same unbending insistence—based on love—of man's equality, same dependence on God and other striking similarity of the events, narrated so nicely ~~in your book~~, with the Indian movement for Independence under the

1. Bodh Gaya, also in the state of Bihar, is considered the birthplace of Buddhism. King also visited the Samanvaya ashram in Bodh Gaya, established by Vinoba Bhave in 1954.

2. Wonwihari Prasad Bhoop (1913–1999) was born in Gaya, Bihar. A follower of Vinoba Bhave's Bhoodan movement, or land-gift campaign, Bhoop donated his land for distribution to India's landless poor in 1953.

3. Narayan, a Gandhian independence leader, was co-founder of the All India Congress Socialist Party in 1934 (for more on King's meeting with Narayan, see King to Narayan, 19 May 1959, pp. 209–211 in this volume). On 15 February King traveled to Burdwan and toured Shantiniketan, an open-air school founded by Indian nationalist poet Rabindranath Tagore on the site where his father, Maharshi Debendranath Tagore, had begun an ashram in 1863.

great leadership of Mahatma Gandhi, the victory of which was not the victory of one community or one country upon the other but, victory of Truth, of Mankind itself, I realized, that it was one of the books that deserved reproduction in all the languages of the world. I have, therefore, been tempted to do it myself in our Hindi language which will enable our countrymen to know more intimately the young leader of the epoch making struggle in the other end of the earth Montgomery, Alabama, and to realize how the same force of ultimate good is operating every where with the help of unseen power.

I have prepared myself to do this work though I am at present very busy with another important work, namely, reproduction of our Holy Scripture Shri Madbhagwat from Sanskrit into Hindi verse.[4] If I take up the book it shall necessarily mean postponement of the other work for sometime. But my satisfaction will be that the theme of complete faith in Almighty, the realisation, thereby, of the oneness of the whole unniverse as one brotherhood, the denunciation of injustice wherever it maybe, and the achievement of ultimate Truth which are so dear to Shri Madbhagwat, are also the basis and goal of your book.

I should also make it clear that no monetary gain is being sought through it. After I have completed it, I shall give it to All India Sarva Seva Sangh Prakashan the main publication centre of our Sarvodaya Movement, aim of which is to produce good books at cheap rates without profit motive for the sake of wide circulation.[5]

I shall begin this work as soon as I receive your permission. Please let me know if it is possible.

My wife Shyama is also happy meeting your wife and you all. Though there was the difference of language creating difficulties of expression, yet, the unspoken language of mankind—the language of goodwill and understanding—was there to help her.

Hoping this to find you all well.

With our best regards to you, your wife, and Dr. Reddick.

My address:—
Durga Koyhi,
P.O. Buniadgunj,
GAYA. (Bihar)

Yours Sincerely,
[*signed*] [*WP?*] Bhoop
(Wonwihari Prasad Bhoop).

TLS. MLKP-MBU: Box 26.

---

4. Bhoop refers to the Hindu text also known as the Bhagavat Purana or the Srimad Bhagavatam.

5. The Sarvodaya movement grew out of Gandhi's philosophy for rural development, emphasizing resource sharing, rural industry, and improvement of the position of the untouchables. After Gandhi's assassination, this program was continued by Vinoba Bhave and other Gandhi associates.

From R. S. Hukkerikar

24 Feb 1959

24 February 1959
Dharwar, India

The chairman of the Gandhi Smarak Nidhi in Mysore state sends a letter of welcome to King and his party.[1]

Rev. Dr. Martin Luther King,
Camp Bangalore.

My dear Dr. King,

I extend a warm welcome to you and Mrs. King on your first visit to this State. During the last 35 years in the Freedom-struggle, this State has played an important role under the guidance of Mahatma Gandhi. In fact, in the popular language, this State is known as Gandhi State. It is in this State that the 'NO TAX CAMPAIGN' was launched by the peasants of the Karwar district and it went on for more than 4 years and was closed only when Mahatmaji sent a letter to do so. In every phase of the War of Independence, the State responded liberally to the call of the Mahatma. I wish, during your stay here, you will meet some of the old workers who will be able to explain how we were able to do all this. Though we have won independence, we have to still fight many a battle in the social and the economic field. There may not be actually the need to offer Satyagraha.[2] But the discipline gained during the last 35 years will be of great avail to achieve our objects in these fields. Your experience in your own country will also be of great help to us. With mutual understanding and co operation, we can not only help people of our own country but also help a number of small countries which are still in a very backward condition.

I am extremely sorry that I am not able to meet you there because of my ill health. If you are going this side, I shall be very happy to meet you and spend some time with you.

I wish your stay in this State will be comfortable and useful.

With kind regards,

Yours sincerely,
[*signed*] R S Hukkerikar

TLS. MLKP-MBU: Box 1.

---

1. Ramarao S. Hukkerikar (1886–1963) was raised in Chincholi, Karnataka state (formerly Mysore). He received both a B.A. (1910) and an M.A. (1912) from Ferguson College in Pune. A schoolteacher and journalist, Hukkerikar joined the Indian National Congress in 1920 and was imprisoned a number of times for his activities in the independence movement. In 1952, Hukkerikar was elected to the Bombay Legislative Council. He served as chair of the Mysore Gandhi Smarak Nidhi from 1958 to 1963.

2. Gandhi defined *satyagraha* as "insistence on truth." The term came to be applied to Gandhi's policy of nonviolent resistance as a means of pressing for political reform.

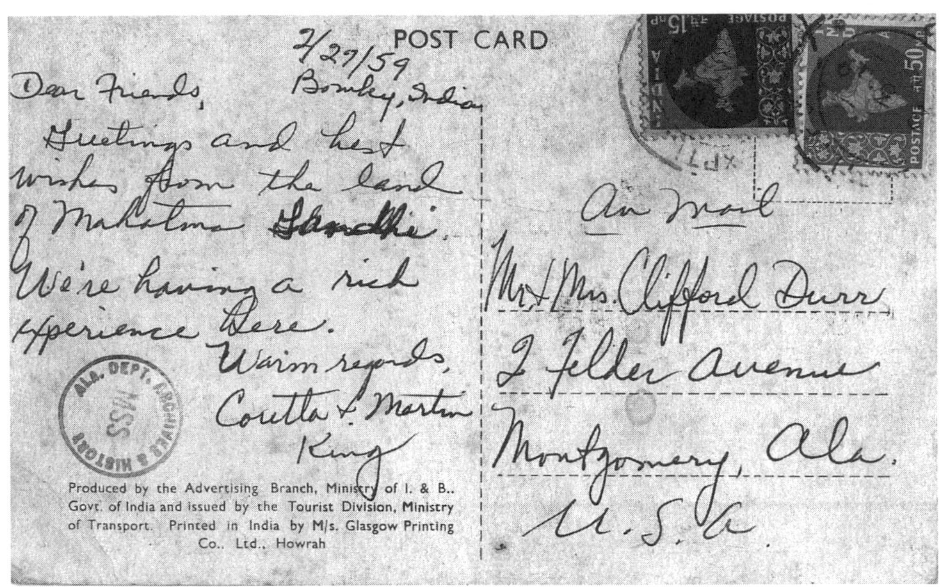

POST CARD

2/27/59
Bombay, India

Dear Friends,
Greetings and best wishes from the land of Mahatma Gandhi. We're having a rich experience here.
Warm regards,
Coretta & Martin King

Air Mail

Mr & Mrs. Clifford Durr
2 Felder Avenue
Montgomery, Ala.
U.S.A.

Produced by the Advertising Branch, Ministry of I. & B., Govt. of India and issued by the Tourist Division, Ministry of Transport. Printed in India by M/s. Glasgow Printing Co., Ltd., Howrah

From Bombay, India, the Kings write to Virginia and Clifford Durr, two white activists in Montgomery (27 February 1959)

तारीख DATE	नाम NAME	संख्या NOS.	पता ADDRESS	राय REMARKS
10-2-59	Naguedas J. Nalawalla	1	Continental Photo Store, 243 D.N. Road	Very happy to be here. Preserve it in the condition
12-2-59	Donald L. Baldwin	1	San Francisco, California	May India somehow be able to follow the Great man
	Rev. Donald H Baldwin	1	" "	
2/16/59	Mrs. George Slocum	1	965 E. Jefferson Detroit 7 Mich.	A truly great man. Can they say the same [illegible]
21-2-59	[illegible]	38	कर्नाटक भूदान कार्यालय हुबली	[illegible]
28-2-59	Martin L. King Jr.	2.	Montgomery, Ala USA	To have the opportunity of sleeping in the house where Gandhiji slept is an experience that I will never forget

King's signature in the guest book of the Mani Bhavan Gandhi Sangrahalaya in Bombay, India (28 February 1959); he writes, "To have the opportunity of sleeping in the house where Gandhiji slept is an experience that I will never forget." Reprinted with the permission of the Mani Bhavan Gandhi Sangrahalaya.

Farewell Statement for All India Radio

[9 March 1959]
[New Delhi, India]

During his final evening in India, King recorded this statement for broadcast on All India Radio. This transcript is drawn from an audio recording.[1]

Leaders in and out of government, organizations—particularly the Gandhi Smarak Nidhi and the Quaker Centre—and many homes and families have done their utmost to make our short stay both pleasant and instructive.

We have learned a lot. We are not rash enough to presume that we know India—vast subcontinent with all of its people, problems, contrasts, and achievements. However, since we have been asked about our impressions, we venture one or two generalizations.

First, we think that the spirit of Gandhi is much stronger today than some people believe. There is not only the direct and indirect influence of his comrades and associates but also the organized efforts that are being made to preserve the Mahatma's letters and other writings, the pictures, monuments, the work of the Gandhi Smarak Nidhi, and the movement led by the sainted Vinoba Bhave. These are but a few examples of the way Gandhiji will be permanently enshrined in the hearts of the people of India.

Moreover, many governmental officials who do not follow Gandhi literally apply his spirit to domestic and international problems.

Secondly, I wish to make a plea to the people and government of India. The issue of world peace is so critical that I feel compelled to offer a suggestion that came to me during the course of our conversations with Vinoba Bhave.[2]

The peace-loving peoples of the world have not yet succeeded in persuading my own country, America, and Soviet Russia to eliminate fear and disarm themselves. Unfortunately, as yet, America and the Soviet Union have not shown the faith and moral courage to do this. Vinobaji has said that India or any other nation that has a faith and moral courage could disarm itself tomorrow, even unilaterally.

It may be that just as India had to take the lead and show the world that na-

1. Earlier in the day King read a version of these remarks during a press conference at the Gandhi Smarak Nidhi. His typescript included two introductory sentences: "Our much too brief pilgrimage to India has regretfully come to a close. I wish to thank everyone for the way your doors and hearts have been opened to me, my wife and Dr. Reddick" (King, "Farewell statement," 9 March 1959; see also "Need for Universal Disarmament," *Hindustan Times*, 10 March 1959).

2. On 3 March, King walked for several miles on a *padayatra* (walking tour) with Vinoba, a disciple of Gandhi and founder of the Bhoodan movement, an effort to convince landowners to give land to the poor. King questioned Vinoba about his strategies for change and the future of India. For Vinoba's replies, see "Dr. Martin Luther King with Vinoba," *Bhoodan* 3 (18 March 1959): 369–370; see also Bristol to Johnson, 16, 17, and 22 April 1959.

tional independence could be achieved nonviolently, so India may have to take the lead and call for universal disarmament. And if no other nation will join her immediately, India may declare itself for disarmament unilaterally.[3]

Such an act of courage would be a great demonstration of the spirit of the Mahatma and would be the greatest stimulus to the rest of the world to do likewise.

Moreover, any nation that would take such a brave step would automatically draw to itself the support of the multitudes of the earth, so that any would-be aggressor would be discouraged from risking the wrath of mankind.

May I also say that since being in India, I am more convinced than ever before that the method of nonviolent resistance is the most potent weapon available to oppressed people in their struggle for justice and human dignity. In a real sense Mahatma Gandhi embodied in his life certain universal principles that are inherent in the moral structure of the universe, and these principles are as inescapable as the law of gravitation.

Many years ago when Abraham Lincoln was shot—and incidentally he was shot for the same reason that Mahatma Gandhi was shot for, namely, for committing the crime of wanting to heal the wounds of a divided nation. And when he was shot, Secretary Stanton stood by the dead body of the great leader and said these words: "Now he belongs to the ages." And in a real sense we can say the same thing about Mahatma Gandhi and even in stronger terms: "Now he belongs to the ages." And if this age is to survive, it must follow the way of love and nonviolence that he so nobly illustrated in his life.[4]

Mahatma Gandhi may well be God's appeal to this generation, a generation drifting again to its doom.[5] This eternal appeal is in the form of a warning: "They that live by the sword shall perish by the sword."[6] We must come to see in the world today that what he taught and his method throughout revealed to us that there is an alternative to violence and that if we fail to follow this we will perish in our individual and in our collective lives. For in a day when Sputniks and Explorers dash through outer space and guided ballistic missiles are carving highways of death through the stratosphere, no nation can win a war.

At. CLPAC (*Gandhi Centennial Radio Program,* 1968).

---

3. At the press conference this suggestion provoked a flurry of questions from reporters. When asked if he meant that the Indian army should disband, King told the press that he favored the elimination of "all major weapons of destruction" ("Need for Universal Disarmament").

4. King underlined the following passage in his copy of missionary E. Stanley Jones's *Mahatma Gandhi: An Interpretation* (New York: Abingdon-Cokesbury Press, 1948), p. 154: "When Lincoln was shot for the same reason that Gandhi was shot, namely, for the crime of wanting to heal the wounds of a divided nation, Secretary Stanton said as he stood beside the dead leader, 'Now he belongs to the ages.' Of Mahatma Gandhi it can also be said, and said with deeper meaning, 'Now he belongs to the ages'; for if there are to be any ages to come for man on this earth, we will have to apply his way of truth and nonviolence." Edwin M. Stanton was Lincoln's Secretary of War.

5. Jones, *Mahatma Gandhi: An Interpretation,* p. 159: "So Mahatma Gandhi is God's appeal to this age—an age drifting again to its doom."

6. Cf. Matthew 26:52.

James E. Bristol to Corinne B. Johnson

10 March 1959
Delhi, India

In this report to Johnson, an American Friends Service Committee (AFSC) colleague in Philadelphia, Bristol, who served as King's travel guide in India, suggests that the political and educational goals of King's visit to India were compromised by his traveling party's "fanatical interest in snapshots" and press coverage: "One of the motives clearly appeared to be to build up King as a world figure, and to have this build-up recorded in the US."[1] *Despite a divergence of goals and poor communication between King and his Quaker sponsors, Bristol concludes that the trip was overall "a good and positive experience as regards Martin's learning about India, and Indians learning about the non-violent movement in the United States."*[2]

Corinne Johnson
American Friends Service Committee
20 South 12th Street
Philadelphia 7 Pa USA

cc: Allen White
Roderick Ede
Lou Schneider[3]

---

1. James Ellery Bristol (1912–1992), born in Philadelphia, Pennsylvania, received a B.A. (1932) from Gettysburg College and a diploma of the seminary (1935) from the Lutheran Theological Seminary at Philadelphia. During World War II, Bristol spent eighteen months in prison for refusing to serve in the armed forces. In 1943 he resigned from the pulpit at Grace Lutheran Church in Camden, New Jersey, to work with several Philadelphia-based peace organizations. Bristol joined the AFSC in 1947 and served as director of its Community Peace Education Program until 1957. He began working for the Friends in Delhi in the fall of 1957. Corinne Benson Johnson (1929–), born in Boston, Massachusetts, received an A.B. (1950) from Smith College. Johnson was a mathematics teacher at Westover School (1950–1952) and an editorial assistant for *Harvard Business Review* (1953–1954) before serving as an administrator for the AFSC's Asia, Refugee, Family Planning and Population Education Programs (1957–1961 and 1968–1973). Johnson later served as the director of AFSC's Latin America/Caribbean Programs (1973–1979) and director of International Programs (1979–1997).

2. Bristol was similarly positive in a 27 March letter to Johnson: "The net effect of the King trip seems to have been very, very good! . . . People were generally impressed by King and by what he said." Bristol reported that Swami Vishwananda, who accompanied King during much of the trip, also felt the visit was a success, although he wondered if "perhaps King had not achieved prominence ~~a bit~~ too early." Bristol surmised that Vishwananda "and some others here wonder whether King can stand the adulation without having it go to his head."

3. White was AFSC business manager; Ede was director of the Asia desk of the Friends Service Council in London; and Schneider was Foreign Service Secretary of AFSC.

10 Mar 1959

Dear Corinne,

Martin Luther King

This will probably be the most disorganised letter on record. The Kings and Dr. Reddick left on the plane at 9.15 this morning. I had three things to take care of in New Delhi and since then I have been straightening up King finances with Arjan, and have had a long conference with Dee. It is already 4 P.M., and I am soon to confer with Philip.[4] I have had absolutely no time in which to organise my thoughts, but I do want to dash off some lines to you now.

Philip, Arjan, Dee and friends at the Gandhi Smarak Nidhi have insisted that I must take a short rest immediately. Accordingly this morning Dee and I made arrangements to fly to Jaipur tomorrow morning (Wednesday), returning to Delhi on Friday. Apparently I am very tired. I have been embarrassed several times during the past three days in Delhi because I could not keep my eyes open in private conversation. I cannot take more time off because I must plan for Bill Barton's visit, but these two days should prove helpful.[5]

Corinne, I would need to write a small book to report adequately on the King tour. In a way there are still many things I do not understand fully—many things which continue to mystify me. Of one thing, however, I am absolutely certain (I remember pointing this out to you once or twice in correspondence in January): THE KING TRIP WAS ARRANGED AT TOO SHORT NOTICE.[6] The result was insufficient communication (worse than that, practically no communication) between Kings and AFSC—at least this is what I have been told more than once here.

Frankly, Corinne, this has been the thorn in everyone's flesh. The trip fortunately has gone better and better, though there were improvements in the last ten day period which I ha~~ve~~d pressed for.** {**and which were not accepted by the Kings and Reddick.} Nonetheless, the overall experience has been increasingly good. The reason I did not make certain suggestions and urge certain changes was because of the resentment so evident from the beginning—resentment at having to fit into previously arranged schedules. I am certain that this is not a figment of my imagination I can document it from conversations with the Kings and Reddick, and if I was in any doubt, those doubts were removed by the conversation at breakfast this morning—a conversation which I did not initiate.

The Kings were in Delhi for five days at the end, having cut two days off the time with Vinoba Bhave (they and Dr. Reddick reached this decision alone without consulting me, and told me).[7] I planned nothing during these five days, except by agree-

---

4. Arjan Dass was Bristol's longtime assistant and manager of the Quaker Centre. Bristol also refers to his wife, Dorothy "Dee" Bristol, and Philip Zealey, a British Friend who worked for AFSC in India.

5. William Barton was general secretary of the Friends Service Council in London.

6. In a 24 December 1958 letter to Johnson, Bristol expressed his growing frustration with "the last minute nature" of the King visit. Bristol wrote Johnson several additional letters detailing arrangements for the trip (Bristol to Johnson, 16 and 28 January 1959).

7. Bristol later acknowledged that the planned three days with Vinoba were probably too long, but reported that one Indian leader "said quietly to me that he wished King had stayed longer, so that he might have gotten the feel of the Padyatra, and might have had opportunities for informal conversations with Vinoba" (Bristol to Johnson, 22 April 1959).

ment of the Kings, and even then very little. They filled up the time so that they were just as busy as before, in some cases with inconsequential (I am not thinking here of recreational experiences) appointments after having refused to accept more significant appointments which I put before them. At breakfast Coretta mentioned that they had been so busy and were so tired, but {that} it was their own doing, ~~she said,~~ and this made it much better than when planned by someone else.

The second thing that happened was a blast from Reddick against the Quakers. He has made it very clear since the day he arrived that he felt the AFSC had handled the whole trip badly. He has been very careful to pay every penny of his own way and to keep himself absolutely clear of any obligation to the Quakers. He said this morning that he thought the AFSC had been unfair in the publicity they had given to the trip; he felt they had exploited the Kings, and had put the Kings almost in a strait jacket (not his exact words, but this is the idea he was conveying); he said also that the AFSC had <u>not</u> relayed information properly to the Kings. He must be a free agent when he returns to the USA. He plans to write a long report on the trip, and to write several articles for publication (he has kept profuse notes). This report will <u>not</u> be shared with the AFSC, nor will he inform the AFSC of any articles prepared for publication.

Perhaps I said the wrong thing. I said nothing at all for a while, but then I did say that the AFSC would be very unhappy to have him doing all this as though the AFSC did not even exist. Obviously, he is a free agent, but I thought he could be a cooperative agent. I talked with him again at the airport, and there he told me that he was in no sense beholden to the Quakers, and would be a free agent, "but not a hostile agent". I am honestly certain that he has absolutely nothing against me or the Delhi Centre (he is really very appreciative of our help) but he certainly does have it in for Philadelphia. I did finally say to him (when he emphasised his lack of indebtedness to the Quakers) that as the Quaker representative in India I had spent considerable time and effort arranging for his part of the journey. And this is very true, for there were many extra hours required because of Reddick, certain meetings for him, his side trip to Hyderabad, his finances having to be kept separate, his telegrams to be sent, etc. I am afraid, however, that I should not have mentioned this because it produced a bad reaction. I honestly did not care for myself, but it seemed to me he was being unrealistic about the way in which he was involved in this Quaker-sponsor~~ship~~{ed} trip.[8]

I do not know whether the Kings felt this strongly or not, though it is obvious that they did feel this to a degree. I asked Reddick this morning whether he felt that the Reynolds Foundation had given the money to the Kings because of Libby Holman Reynold's friendship with the Kings.[9] The money had been given to the

8. In a letter written to Johnson the following day, Bristol elaborated on Reddick's behavior and noted that he "determined to a very great extent" King's schedule: "King leaned heavily on him for advice, with the result that Larry determined in probably 75% of the cases whom King would see or not see, which engagements would be kept or cancelled. Also I recall Larry's telling me that the AFSC did <u>not</u> consider it necessary at all for him to come along on the trip. Perhaps this has been eating him" (Bristol to Johnson, 11 March 1959).

9. Singer and philanthropist Libby Holman Reynolds was likely introduced to King by civil rights attorney Harris Wofford (Stanley Levison to Lawrence Dunbar Reddick, 27 November 1969). The Christopher Reynolds Foundation contributed $4,000 to King's trip to India (Jack Clareman to A. Philip

AFSC for ~~ei~~ income tax purposes, and then the AFSC which was in reality only serving as a channel for the money proceeded to take over. He agreed that I had stated the case correctly.

Our rapport had been ~~going~~ {growing} better and better as the trip went on and as we had all sorts of experiences {together,} both pleasant and arduous. ~~together.~~ I certainly was sad that this conversation took place this morning just prior to departure. I still feel as though someone had kicked me in the stomach. I do not know whether you wish to go into all this with the Kings or just forget it. I must report this to you, yet I hate to have it appear that I am tale-bearing. At the plane this morning, the Kings were most cordial and warm and friendly, and I am sure my relations with them are good. Reddick, however, was not cordial. Incidentally,—and this is important, Coretta overheard Dee asked Reddick, "Are you happy?" She asked Dee about the question, and Dee told her about much of this conversation. Coretta made no comment, but she seemed friendly to Dee.

Corinne, can you sort this all out? In a way the whole experience has been a nightmare since we met a plane at the airport on February 8 with no Kings on it and absolutely no explanation.[10] As far as the public is concerned, the trip was a huge success. Fortunately, it was also a rich and valuable experience for both Martin and Coretta, and clearly also for Lawrence Reddick. How I wish that matters could have been clear and understood before they left Philadelphia. This was like ~~the~~ {a} festering [*strikeout illegible*] {wound} through so much of the journey.

Both Kings and Reddick commented on the fact that they ~~made~~ met so many important and genuinely significant people. They said both publicly and privately that probably never before in India had any non-official guests met so many people of such high calibre. If I may pat myself on the back, we really made it possible for them to see the cream of India from one end of the land to the other. Newspaper coverage was excellent. It was really a triumphal tour, and King's speeches were good throughout, and on two occasions genuinely inspired.

Unfortunately, they were dead tired before they left the U.S. and this was a handicap throughout.[11] It meant tardiness in keeping many appointments (a King trait in the US also, I am now told from two reliable sources), and on occasions it meant the cancelling of appointments. ~~And~~ The lack of understanding with the AFSC, as well as a total lack of orientation about India, were also very serious handicaps.

Randolph, 5 February 1957, King to The Christopher Reynolds Foundation, 7 March 1958, and The Christopher Reynolds Foundation to Stephen Cary, 9 January 1959).

10. The Kings' arrival in Delhi was delayed by two days because they missed a flight in Zurich, Switzerland.

11. Bristol had commented on King's fatigue in an earlier report to his wife: "Both the Kings (especially King himself) are JUST PLAIN EXHAUSTED and very understandably have been so for months before coming to India. I know what Corinne means by their seeming to be 'bewildered'. I think they are drained terribly ~~seriously~~ {nervously} and emotionally as result of past few years, and the way Martin must drive himself in the States. What they both want to do is to get to their room and rest as much as possible—and Martin certainly so often wants to be left alone (very easy to understand and appreciate). He will even pick up a newspaper or magazine and read it in someone's home or some place else when a person (or persons) is (or are) talking to him, even when he is their guest. Reddick and Mrs. K then carry on the conversation with Martin hidden behind the newspaper" (James E. Bristol to Dorothy Bristol, 25 February 1959).

I might also mention that ~~they~~ all three had an~~me~~ almost fanatical interest in snapshots, pictures and newspaper publicity. Many Indians noticed this and even commented on it. Almost before greeting a person or group they were posing for {the} camera (they carried three wherever they went). You would have to see this to believe it. Constantly they had their eyes on the USA and the impact the trip would be making there. And so much of their conversation as we were travelling about concerned this same subject. I regret this paragraph, but in all honesty I must write it.

Now I must stop. This report is off the top of my mind, but it is all true, and it is obviously uppermost in my mind as I review the trip. Trust this will reach you in ample time for study and thought before the Kings arrive on March 20.

Best always.

Sincerely,
[*signed*] Jim
James E. Bristol
Director.

P.S. Philip, Dee and I have just spent an hour discussing the King trip. Four things to mention: 1) On the whole it was a good and positive experience as regards Martin's learning about India, and Indians learning about the non-violent movement in the United States. Excellent also that Martin challenged so many audiences to practice non-violence in today's conflict situations.[12] 2) Very many things that I shall never have time to report that could fill you in and document much of what I have written. 3) I should attempt next week to write an account, give you some idea of significant experiences, conversations, etc along the way. 4) A question: Whose idea was it for King to come to India? Was it Bayard Rustin's, Reddick's, the AFSC's, or Kings'? One of the motives clearly appeared to be to build up King as a world figure, and to have this build-up recorded in the US. Again we have just talked about the abnormal interest in the pictures and publicity, even to the extent of having Absalom Peters take movies of them boarding the plane this morning.[13] He took the pictures with their own camera and handed it into them just before the plane door closed. Actually, they delayed the departure of the plane with the motion picture and the still picture taking.

12. In a follow-up letter to Johnson, Bristol observed that King was consistently greeted by Indians "as the champion of the oppressed peoples of the world—in America, Asia and Africa, and never . . . thought of as an American." Bristol noted that "all the questions with which Americans are bombarded were missing in King's case, both in our public meetings and in private conversation" (Bristol to Johnson, 11 March 1959).

13. These observations echo Bristol's comments from an earlier report: "The Kings seem almost totally disinterested in sight-seeing, and shopping, and the remarkable art and craft work of India (I would say just about 100% disinterested). Our hosts and Indian friends get so discouraged receiving negative answers to all suggestions. Like going through India wearing <u>BLINDERS</u>. Ser[n]ap-shots, picture post-cards, <u>newspaper clippings</u> and news stories, any pictures taken by other photographers—here it all begins and ends. This whole trip is being thought of in terms of the <u>return</u> to U.S.A. and what will make an impact and produces an effect there" (Bristol to Bristol, 25 February 1959). Peters was an employee of the Quaker Centre in Delhi.

18 Mar 1959

PPS. We also wondered how the Gandhi Smarak Nidhi felt about the whole experience. I think they were unhappy at certain points, but my impression now is {that} they feel satisfied with the over-all experience. They gave the Kings and Reddick a reception on Sunday evening and all the appropriate words were certainly uttered.

Incidentally, they certainly have gotten a lot of publicity from the visit. Ranjit sent me a letter a day ago in which he mentioned the fact that all the publicity mentioned the Gandhi Smarak Nidhi as sponsoring organisation, and not one word was ever said about the American Friends Service Committee or the Quaker Centre in Delhi. Unfortunately, this is true. I was fully aware of this, but was not able to alter the situation. It seems to me the Gandhi Smarak Nidhi should have done something about this, but they did not.

PPPS. Reddick will not be coming to Philadelphia on March 20. He wants to keep as far away from the AFSC as possible.[14]

[*signed*] Jim
James E. Bristol
Director

TALS. AFSCR-PPAFS.

---

14. King was similarly unable to attend the scheduled meeting in Philadelphia (see King to Corinne B. Johnson, 23 March 1959, pp. 159–160 in this volume).

Statement upon Return from India

18 March 1959
New York, N.Y.

After six weeks abroad, King arrived in New York on the morning of 18 March and met with a small group of reporters at the Statler Hilton Hotel. Along with offering brief remarks to the press and answering their questions, King distributed copies of this statement in which he urges aid from the West to India to "help save one of the great nations of the World for democracy." He also praises India for "integrating its untouchables faster than the United States is integrating its Negro minority."[1]

I say upon returning to America as I said upon leaving India, that I would not be so rash as to presume to know India after a one-month tour of that vast coun-

---

1. These remarks may have been prepared by Reddick, who had returned to New York several days before the Kings (Johnson to Bristol, 26 March 1959). During the press conference, King also told reporters that the Little Rock, Arkansas, school integration crisis of 1957 had harmed U.S. prestige abroad ("Non-Violence Move More Imperative Now," *New York Amsterdam News,* 28 March 1959).

try. However, we are glad to say that while there we received a most enthusiastic reception and the most generous hospitality imaginable. Almost every door was open so that our party—Mrs. King, Dr. L. D. Reddick and myself—was able to see some of India's most important social experiments and talk with leaders in and out of Government, ranging from Prime Minister Nehru to village councilmen and Vinoba Bhave, the sainted leader of the land reform movement. We are most grateful to the Gandhi Smarak Nidhi which extended the official invitation and the American Friends Service Committee which helped to arrange the tour.[2]

Since we are often asked our impressions, we venture two generalization.

First, America and other nations of the West should extend generous economic and technical aid to India immediately. The Government and people of India are trying desperately to solve their grave problems of unemployment, food shortages, housing, etc., through democratic means. They need help but will not accept it if strings are attached to it. Our impression is that unless the problems of India can be solved through democratic means soon, the people there may turn to Communism or a Military dictatorship. America and the West should help India because she needs help; not as a part of an anti-communist campaign, even though the effect of this aid will help save one of the great nations of the World for democracy.

Secondly, we found the problem of the untouchables in India to be similar to the race problem in America. Even so India appears to be integrating its untouchables faster than the United States is integrating its Negro minority. Both countries have Federal Laws against discrimination but in India the leaders of Government, of religious, educational and other institutions have publicly endorsed the integration laws. This has not been done so largely in America. For example, today no leader in India would dare to make a public endorsement of untouchability. But in America, every day some leader endorses racial segregation

India's faster progress is thus a challenge to us, for many Indians are convinced that unless America solves its race problem soon, America will lose prestige greatly in the eyes of the World.

TD. MKLP-MBU: Box 1

2. Corinne Johnson later complained that AFSC had not received a copy of this statement beforehand and suggested "that the Kings and Bayard might have felt that we would have wanted a stronger exposition" of the committee's sponsorship of the trip (Johnson to Bristol, 26 March 1959).

From Myles Horton

20 March 1959
Monteagle, Tenn.

Highlander Folk School director Myles Horton updates King on the Tennessee legislature's investigation of the leadership training school. Shortly after King's September 1957 address at Highlander, the Georgia Commission on Education published a report alleging that the school was a Communist front organization.[1] *For the next several years, southern state officials and segregationist groups used the allegations to thwart Highlander's efforts to promote racial and economic justice.*

Dr. Martin Luther King
Dexter Avenue Baptist Church
454 Dexter Avenue
Montgomery, Alabama

Dear Martin:

I noticed that you had returned from your trip to India which I know you must have enjoyed.

While you were away, the Tennessee legislature investigated Highlander, as you will see from the enclosures. I am sending you a copy of the Nashville Tennessean which carries a feature story on the investigation and an article by Joe Hatcher, the Tennessean's veteran political reporter.[2]

There are two reasons why I think you will be interested. One, your interest in Highlander, and two, the fact that your name came up, both in the questioning and in the final report. You were listed along with Aubrey Williams, Jim Dombrowski, Pete Seeger and Abner Berry, as proof of Highlander's Communist connections.[3] I assured the committee that while we were very proud of your having been at Highlander, they were mistaken about your being subversive. Frankly however I do not think they were greatly impressed by my efforts to set the record straight.

The present status of the investigation is a recommendation from the state legislature that legal proceedings be taken to cancel Highlander's charter and to find me and put me in jail if the evidence warrants.[4] It will not be surprising to you to learn that they dropped the charges of subversion and just decided to close Highlander anyway.

I hope I will have an opportunity to sit down and talk to you about more important matters someday.

---

1. Georgia Commission on Education, "Highlander Folk School: Communist Training School, Monteagle, Tenn.," October 1957. For King's Highlander address, see "A Look to the Future," Address Delivered at Highlander Folk School's Twenty-fifth Anniversary Meeting, 2 September 1957, in *Papers* 4:269–276.

2. Horton probably enclosed the 5 March edition containing the articles "Horton Denies Bennett Charge" by Garry Fullerton and "Can Probers Prolong Dull Show?" by Joe Hatcher.

3. Barton Demet et al., "Committee report to the members of the eighty-first session of the general assembly of the state of Tennessee," 6 March 1959. Williams, a resident of Montgomery, was a former New Deal administrator and president of the Southern Conference Educational Fund (SCEF). Dombrowski, executive director of SCEF, had once served on Highlander's staff. Pete Seeger, a folk singer who was blacklisted in the 1950s for his political activities, helped popularize the civil rights anthem "We Shall Overcome." Berry was a reporter for the *Daily Worker,* a Communist Party newspaper. All were at Highlander during the weekend of King's 1957 address.

4. For more on the State of Tennessee's efforts to close Highlander, see Anne Braden to King, 23 September 1959, pp. 290–293 in this volume.

Cordially yours,
[*signed*] Myles
Myles Horton

TLS. MLKP-MBU: Box 28.

Palm Sunday Sermon on Mohandas K. Gandhi, Delivered at Dexter Avenue Baptist Church

[*22 March 1959*]
[*Montgomery, Ala.*]

Returning to his pulpit after an absence of nearly two months, King discusses the life of Gandhi, suggesting that "more than anybody else in the modern world" he had "caught the spirit of Jesus Christ, and lived it more completely in his life." Referring to Gandhi as one of Jesus's "other sheep," he observes that "it is one of the strange ironies of the modern world that the greatest Christian of the twentieth century was not a member of the Christian church." King continues by comparing the lives of three martyred leaders, Jesus, Gandhi, and Abraham Lincoln, noting that the latter two were shot for their efforts "to heal the wounds of a divided nation." He concludes with a warning: "God grant that we shall choose the high way. Even if it will mean assassination, even if it will mean crucifixion, for by going this way we will discover that death will be only the beginning of our influence." This transcript is drawn from an audio recording of the service.

To the cross and its significance in human experience. This is the time in the year when we think of the love of God breaking forth into time out of eternity. This is the time of the year when we come to see that the most powerful forces in the universe are not those forces of military might but those forces of spiritual might. And as we sing together this great hymn of our church, the Christian church, hymn number 191, let us think about it again:

When I survey the wondrous cross,
On which the prince of glory died,
I count my richest gains but loss
And pour contempt on all my pride.

A beautiful hymn. I think if there is any hymn of the Christian church that I would call a favorite hymn, it is this one. And then it goes on to say, in that last stanza:

Were the whole realm of nature mine,
That was a present far too small.
Love so amazing, so divine,
Demands my life, my all and my all.[1]

1. Isaac Watts, "When I Survey the Wondrous Cross" (1707).

We think about Christ and the cross in the days ahead as he walks through Jerusalem and he's carried from Jerusalem to Calvary Hill, where he is crucified. Let us think of this wondrous cross. [*congregation sings "When I Survey the Wondrous Cross"*]

This, as you know, is what has the traditionally been known in the Christian church as Palm Sunday. And ordinarily the preacher is expected to preach a sermon on the Lordship or the Kingship of Christ—the triumphal entry, or something that relates to this great event as Jesus entered Jerusalem, for it was after this that Jesus was crucified. And I remember, the other day, at about seven or eight days ago, standing on the Mount of Olives and looking across just a few feet and noticing that gate that still stands there in Jerusalem, and through which Christ passed into Jerusalem, into the old city.[2] The ruins of that gate stand there, and one feels the sense of Christ's mission as he looks at the gate. And he looks at Jerusalem, and he sees what could take place in such a setting. And you notice there also the spot where the temple stood, and it was here that Jesus passed and he went into the temple and ran the money-changers out.[3]

And so that, if I talked about that this morning, I could talk about it not only from what the Bible says but from personal experience, first-hand experience. But I beg of you to indulge me this morning to talk about the life of a man who lived in India. And I think I'm justified in doing this because I believe this man, more than anybody else in the modern world, caught the spirit of Jesus Christ and lived it more completely in his life. His name was Gandhi, Mohandas K. Gandhi. And after he lived a few years, the poet Tagore, who lived in India, gave him another name: "Mahatma," the great soul.[4] And we know him as Mahatma Gandhi.

I would like to use a double text for what I have to say this morning, both of them are found in the gospel as recorded by Saint John. One found in the tenth chapter, and the sixteenth verse, and it reads, "I have other sheep, which are not of this fold." "I have other sheep, which are not of this fold." And then the other one is found in the fourteenth chapter of John, in the twelfth verse. It reads, "Verily, verily, I say unto you, he that believeth on me, the works that I do, shall he do also. And greater works than these shall he do because I go unto my Father."

I want you to notice these two passages of scripture. On the one hand, "I have other sheep that are not of this fold." I think Jesus is saying here in substance that "I have followers who are not in this inner circle." He's saying in substance that "I have people dedicated and following my ways who have not become attached to the institution surrounding my name. I have other sheep that are not of this fold. And my influence is not limited to the institutional Christian church." I think this is what Jesus would say if he were living today concerning this passage, that "I have

---

2. For more on King's travels in the Middle East, see King, A Walk Through the Holy Land, Easter Sunday Sermon Delivered at Dexter Avenue Baptist Church, 29 March 1959, pp. 164–175 in this volume.

3. Cf. Mark 11:15.

4. Indian nationalist and poet Rabindranath Tagore (1861–1941) won the Nobel Prize for Literature in 1913. It is believed that he was the first to address Gandhi as Mahatma (see *The Collected Works of Mahatma Gandhi,* vol. 15, August 1918–July 1919 [Delhi: The Publications Division, Ministry of Information and Broadcasting, Government of India, 1965], pp. 495–496).

people who are following me who've never joined the Christian church as an institution."

And then that other passage, I think Jesus was saying this—it's a strange thing, and I used to wonder what Jesus meant when he said, "There will be people who will do greater things than I did."[5] And I have thought about the glory and honor surrounding the life of Christ, and I thought about the fact that he represented the absolute revelation of God. And I've thought about the fact that in his life, he represented all of the glory of eternity coming into time. And how would it be possible for anybody to do greater works than Christ? How would it be possible for anybody even to match him, or even to approximate his work?

But I've come to see what Christ meant. Christ meant that in his life he would only touch a few people. And in his lifetime—and if you study the life of Christ, and if you know your Bible you realize that Christ never traveled outside of Palestine, and his influence in his own lifetime was limited to a small group of people. He never had more than twelve followers in his lifetime; others heard about him and others came to see him, but he never had but twelve real followers, and three of them turned out to be not too good. But he pictured the day that his spirit and his influence would go beyond the borders of Palestine, and that men would catch his message and carry it over the world, and that men all over the world would grasp the truth of his gospel. And they would be able to do things that he couldn't do. They were able, be able to travel places that he couldn't travel. And they would be able to convert people that he couldn't convert in his lifetime. And this is what he meant when he said, "Greater works shall ye do, for an Apostle Paul will catch my work."

And I remember just last Tuesday morning standing on that beautiful hill called the Acropolis in Athens. And there, standing around the Parthenon, as it stands still in all of its beautiful and impressive proportions, although it has been torn somewhat through wars, but it still stands there. And right across from the Acropolis you see Mars Hill. And I remember when our guide said, "That's the hill where the Apostle Paul preached."[6]

Now when you think of the fact that Athens is a long ways from Jerusalem, for we traveled right over Damascus where Paul was converted, and Damascus is at least five hours by flight from Athens. And you think about the fact that Paul had caught this message and carried it beyond the Damascus Road all over the world, and he had gone as far as Greece, as far as Athens, to preach the gospel of Jesus Christ. This is what Jesus meant that "somebody will catch my message, and they would be able to carry it in places that I couldn't carry it, and they would be able to do things in their lives that I couldn't do."

And I believe these two passages of scripture apply more uniquely to the life and work of Mahatma Gandhi than to any other individual in the history of the world. For here was a man who was not a Christian in terms of being a member of the Christian church but who was a Christian. And it is one of the strange ironies of the modern world that the greatest Christian of the twentieth century

5. Cf. John 1:50.
6. Cf. Acts 17:22.

was not a member of the Christian church. And the second thing is, that this man took the message of Jesus Christ and was able to do even greater works than Jesus did in his lifetime. Jesus himself predicted this: "Ye shall do even greater works."[7]

Now let us look at the life, as briefly as possible, the life of this man and his work, and see just what it gives us, and what this life reveals to us in terms of the struggles ahead. I would say the first thing that we must see about this life is that Mahatma Gandhi was able to achieve for his people independence [*Congregation:*] (*Yes*) through nonviolent means. I think you should underscore this. He was able to achieve for his people independence from the domination of the British Empire without lifting one gun or without uttering one curse word. He did it with the spirit of Jesus Christ in his heart and the love of God, and this was all he had. He had no weapons. He had no army, in terms of military might. And yet he was able to achieve independence from the largest empire in the history of this world without picking up a gun or without any ammunition.

Gandhi was born in India in a little place called Porbandar, down almost in central India. And he had seen the conditions of this country. India had been under the domination of the British Empire for many years. And under the domination of the British Empire, the people of India suffered all types of exploitation. And you think about the fact that while Britain was in India, that out of a population of four hundred million people, more than three hundred and sixty-five million of these people made less than fifty dollars a year. And more than half of this had to be spent for taxes.

Gandhi looked at all of this. He looked at his people as they lived in ghettos and hovels and as they lived out on the streets, many of them. And even today, after being exploited so many years, they haven't been able to solve those problems. For we landed in Bombay, India, and I never will forget it, that night. We got up early in the morning to take a plane for Delhi. And as we rode out to the airport we looked out on the street and saw people sleeping out on the sidewalks and out in the streets, and everywhere we went to. Walk through the train station, and you can't hardly get to the train, because people are sleeping on the platforms of the train station. No homes to live in. In Bombay, India, where they have a population of three million people, five hundred thousand of these people sleep on the streets at night. Nowhere to sleep, no homes to live in, making no more than fifteen or twenty dollars a year or even less than that.

And this was the exploitation that Mahatma Gandhi noticed years ago. And even more than that, these people were humiliated and embarrassed and segregated in their own land. There were places that the Indian people could not even go in their own land. The British had come in there and set up clubs and other places and even hotels where Indians couldn't even enter in their own land. Gandhi

---

7. King may have been influenced by missionary E. Stanley Jones's book on the life of Gandhi: "One of the most Christlike men in history was not called a Christian at all. . . . God uses many instruments, and he has used Mahatma Gandhi to help Christianize unchristian Christianity" (Jones, *Mahatma Gandhi: An Interpretation,* p. 77). King owned and annotated a copy of Jones's book.

looked at all of this, and as a young lawyer, after he had just left England and gotten his law, received his law training, he went over to South Africa. And there he saw in South Africa, and Indians were even exploited there.[8]

And one day he was taking a train to Pretoria, and he had first-class accommodations on that train. And when they came to took up the tickets they noticed that he was an Indian, that he had a brown face, and they told him to get out and move on to the third-class accommodation, that he wasn't supposed to be there with any first-class accommodation. And Gandhi that day refused to move, and they threw him off the train. And there, in that cold station that night, he stayed all night, and he started meditating on his plight and the plight of his people. And he decided from that point on that he would never submit himself to injustice, or to exploitation.

It was there on the next day that he called a meeting of all of the Indians in South Africa, in that particular region of South Africa, and told them what had happened, and told them what was happening to them every day, and said that, "We must do something about it. We must organize ourselves to rid our community, the South African community, and also the Indian community back home, of the domination and the exploitation of foreign powers."[9]

But Mahatma Gandhi came to something else in that moment. As he started organizing his forces in South Africa, he read the Sermon on the Mount.[10] He later read the works of the American poet Thoreau. And he later read the Russian author Tolstoy. And he found something in all of this that gave him insights. Started reading in the Bible, "turn the other cheek," "resist evil with good," "blessed are the meek, for they shall inherit the earth."[11] And all of these things inspired him to no end. He read Thoreau as he said that no just man can submit to anything evil, even if it means standing up and being disobedient to the laws of the state. And so this he combined into a new method, and he said to his people, "Now, it's possible to resist evil; this is your first responsibility: never adjust to evil, resist it. But if you can resist it without resorting to violence or to hate, you can stand up against it and still love the individuals that carry on the evil system that you are resisting."[12]

And a few years later, after he won a victory in South Africa, he went back to India. And there his people called on him, called on his leadership, to organize

8. Gandhi was called to the bar in London in 1891 and traveled to South Africa two years later.

9. Gandhi describes these events in part 2, chapters 8 through 12, of his autobiography (Gandhi, *Gandhi's Autobiography: The Story of My Experiments with Truth* [Washington, D.C.: Public Affairs Press, 1948]).

10. Cf. Matthew 5–7.

11. Cf. Matthew 5:39, Romans 12:21, and Matthew 5:5. In his autobiography Gandhi recalled reading the Bible while a student in England (Gandhi, *Gandhi's Autobiography,* pp. 91–93).

12. Gandhi suggested that Thoreau's impact on him had been overstated: "The statement that I had derived my idea of civil disobedience from the writings of Thoreau is wrong. The resistance to authority in South Africa was well advanced before I got the essay of Thoreau on civil disobedience" (Gandhi to Kodanda Rao, 10 September 1935, in *The Collected Works of Mahatma Gandhi,* vol. 61, April 25–September 30, 1935 [Delhi: The Publications Division, Ministry of Information and Broadcasting, Government of India, 1975], p. 401).

22 Mar 1959 them and get ready for the trials ahead, and he did just that. He went back, and in 1917 he started his first campaign in India.[13] And throughout his long struggle there, he followed the way of nonviolent resistance. Never uttered a curse word, mark you. He never owned an instrument of violence. And he had nothing but love and understanding goodwill in his heart for the people who were seeking to defeat him and who were exploiting and humiliating his people.

And then came that day when he said to the people of India, "I'm going to leave this community." He had set up in a place called Ahmadabad, and there was the Sabarmati ashram. He lived there with a group of people; his ashram was a place of quiet and meditation where the people lived together. And one day he said to those people, "I'm going to leave this place, and I will not return until India has received her independence." And this was in 1930. And he had so organized the whole of India then; people had left their jobs. People with tremendous and powerful law practices had left their jobs. The president of India was a lawyer who had made almost a million rupees—a million dollars—and he left it, turned it all over to the movement. The father, the president of, the prime minister of India, Mr. Nehru, left his law practice to get in the freedom movement with Gandhi, and he had organized the whole of India.[14]

And you have read of the Salt March, which was a very significant thing in the Indian struggle. And this demonstrates how Gandhi used this method of nonviolence and how he would mobilize his people and galvanize the whole of the nation to bring about victory. In India, the British people had come to the point where they were charging the Indian people a tax on all of the salt, and they would not allow them even to make their own salt from all of the salt seas around the country. They couldn't touch it; it was against the law. And Gandhi got all of the people of India to see the injustice of this. And he decided one day that they would march from Ahmadabad down to a place called Dandi.

We had the privilege of spending a day or so at Ahmadabad at that Sabarmati ashram, and we stood there at the point where Gandhi started his long walk of two hundred and eighteen miles. And he started there walking with eighty people. And gradually the number grew to a million, and it grew to millions and millions. And finally, they kept walking and walking until they reached the little village of Dandi. And there, Gandhi went on and reached down in the river, or in the sea rather, and brought up a little salt in his hand to demonstrate and dramatize the fact that they were breaking this law in protest against the injustices they had faced all over the years with these salt laws.

And Gandhi said to his people, "If you are hit, don't hit back; even if they shoot at you, don't shoot back; if they curse you, don't curse back (*Yes, Yes*), but just keep

13. Gandhi returned to India in 1914 and in 1917 began his first protest movement on behalf of exploited indigo farmers in Champaran, Bihar. The campaign, which consisted of rent strikes, work boycotts, and community development, led to the signing of the Champaran Agrarian Act (1918).

14. In his autobiography, Nehru describes his father's immersion into the freedom movement: "Nonco-operation meant his withdrawing from his legal practice; it meant a total break with his past life and a new fashioning of it—not an easy matter when one is on the eve of one's sixtieth birthday" (Nehru, *Toward Freedom: The Autobiography of Jawaharlal Nehru* [New York: The John Day Co., 1941], p. 66).

moving. Some of us might have to die before we get there; some of us might be thrown in jail before we get there, but let us just keep moving." And they kept moving, and they walked and walked, and millions of them had gotten together when they finally reached that point. And the British Empire knew, then, that this little man had mobilized the people of India to the point that they could never defeat them. And they realized, at that very point, that this was the beginning of the end of the British Empire as far as India was concerned.

He was able to mobilize and galvanize more people than, in his lifetime, than any other person in the history of this world. And just with a little love in his heart and understanding goodwill and a refusal to cooperate with an evil law, he was able to break the backbone of the British Empire. And this, I think, is one of the most significant things that has ever happened in the history of the world, and more than three hundred and ninety million people achieved their freedom. And they achieved it nonviolently when a man refused to follow the way of hate, and he refused to follow the way of violence, and only decided to follow the way of love and understanding goodwill and refused to cooperate with any system of evil.

And the significant thing is that when you follow this way, when the battle is almost over, and a new friendship and reconciliation exists between the people who have been the oppressors and the oppressed. There is no greater friendship anywhere in the world today than between the Indian people and the British people. If you ask the Indian people today who they love more, what people, whether they love Americans more, British more, they will say to you immediately that they love the British people more.

The night we had dinner with Prime Minister Nehru the person who sat at that dinner table with us, as a guest of the prime minister at that time, was Lady Mountbatten with her daughter, the wife of Lord Mountbatten, who was the viceroy of India when it received its independence.[15] And they're marvelous and great and lasting friends. There is a lasting friendship there. And this is only because Gandhi followed the way of love and nonviolence, refusing to hate and refusing to follow the way of violence. And a new friendship exists. The aftermath of violence is always bitterness; the aftermath of nonviolence is the creation of the beloved community so that when the battle is over, it's over, and a new love and a new understanding and a new relationship comes into being between the oppressed and the oppressor.

This little man, one of the greatest conquerors that the world has ever known. Somebody said that when Mahatma Gandhi was coming over to England for the roundtable conference in 1932, a group of people stood there waiting.[16] And somebody pointed out, and while they were waiting somebody said, "You see around that cliff? That was where Julius Caesar came, the way he came in when he invaded Britain years ago." And then somebody pointed over to another place and

15. Louis Mountbatten (1900–1979) was the last viceroy of India. His wife, Edwina Mountbatten (1901–1960), and their daughter Pamela (1929–) were in attendance at the 10 February dinner with Nehru and the Kings.

16. Between 1930 and 1932, three roundtable conferences were held in London to consider a future constitution for India. Gandhi represented the India National Congress at the second roundtable in 1931.

22 Mar 1959

said, "That was the way William the Conqueror came in. They invaded years ago in the Battle of Hastings." Then somebody else looked over and said, "There is another conqueror coming in. In just a few minutes the third and greatest conqueror that has ever come into Great Britain." And strangely enough, this little man came in with no armies, no guards around him, no military might, no beautiful clothes, just loin cloth, but this man proved to be the greatest conqueror that the British Empire ever faced. He was able to achieve, through love and nonviolence, the independence of his people and break the backbone of the British Empire. "Ye shall do greater works than I have done." And this is exemplified in the life of Mahatma Gandhi.

Let me rush on to say a second thing: here is a man who achieved in his life absolute self-discipline. Absolute self-discipline. So that in his life there was no gulf between the private and the public; there was no gulf in his life between the "is" and the "oughts." Here was a man who had absolved the "isness" of his being and the "oughtness" of his being. And this was one of the greatest accomplishments in his life. Gandhi used to say to his people, "I have no secrets. My life is an open book." And he lived that every day. He achieved in his life absolute self-discipline.

He started out as a young lawyer. He went to South Africa, and he became a thriving, promising lawyer making more than thirty thousand dollars a year. And then he came to see that he had a task ahead to free his people. And he vowed poverty, decided to do away with all of the money that he had made, and he went back to India and started wearing the very clothes that all of these disinherited masses of people of India had been wearing. He had been a popular young man in England, worn all of the beautiful clothes and his wife the beautiful saris of India with all of its silk beauty, but then he came to that point of saying to his wife, "You've got to drop this." And he started wearing what was called the dhoti, loin cloth, the same thing that these masses of people wore. He did it, identified himself with them absolutely.

And he had no income; he had nothing in this world, not even a piece of property. This man achieved in his life absolute self-discipline to the point of renouncing the world. And when he died, the only thing that he owned was a pair of glasses, a pair of sandals, a loincloth, some false teeth, and some little monkeys who saw no evil, who said no evil, and who somehow didn't see any evil. This is all he had. And if you ask people in India today why was it that Mahatma Gandhi was able to do what he did in India, they would say they followed him because of his absolute sincerity and his absolute dedication. Here was a man who achieved in his life this bridging of the gulf between the "ought" and the "is." He achieved in his life absolute self-discipline.

And there is a final thing Mahatma Gandhi was able to do. He had the amazing capacity, the amazing capacity for internal criticism. Most others have the amazing capacity for external criticism. We can always see the evil in others; we can always see the evil in our oppressors. But Gandhi had the amazing capacity to see not only the splinter in his opponent's eye but also the planks in his own eye and the eye of his people.[17] He had the amazing capacity for self-criticism. And this

17. Cf. Luke 6:41–42.

was true in his individual life; it was true in his family life; and it was true in his people's life. He not only criticized the British Empire, but he criticized his own people when they needed it, and he criticized himself when he needed it.

And whenever he made a mistake, he confessed it publicly. Here was a man who would say to his people, "I'm not perfect. I'm not infallible. I don't want you to start a religion around me. I'm not a god." And I'm convinced that today there would be a religion around Gandhi if Gandhi had not insisted all through his life that "I don't want a religion around me because I'm too human. I'm too fallible. Never think that I'm infallible."

And any time he made a mistake, even in his personal life or even in decisions that he made in the independence struggle, he came out in the public and said, "I made a mistake." In 1922, when he had started one of his first campaigns of nonviolence and some of the people started getting violent, some of the Indian people started getting violent, and they killed twenty some, twenty-eight of the British people in this struggle. And in the midst of this struggle, Gandhi came to the forefront of the scene and called the campaign off. And he stood up before the Indian people and before the British people and said, "I made a Himalayan blunder. I thought my people were ready; I thought they were disciplined for this task."[18] And people around Gandhi were angry with him. Even Prime Minister Nehru says in *Toward Freedom* that he was angry. His father was angry. All of these people who had left their hundreds and thousands of dollars to follow Gandhi and his movement were angry when he called this movement off.[19] But he called it off because, as he said, "I've made a blunder." And he never hesitated to acknowledge before the public when he made a mistake. And he always went back and said, "I made a mistake. I'm going back to rethink it, I'm going back to meditate over it. And I'll be coming back. Don't think the struggle is over, don't think I'm retreating from this thing permanently and ultimately. I'm just taking a temporary retreat, because I made a mistake."

But not only that, he confessed the errors and the mistakes of his family. Even when his son, one of his sons, went wrong he wrote in his paper about it.[20] And his wife committed an act once that was sinful to him. He had pledged himself to poverty, and he would never use any of the money that came in for his personal benefit. And one day his wife, feeling the need for some of that money that had come in, decided to use it. And Gandhi discovered it, and he wrote in his paper that his wife had committed a grave sin.[21] He didn't mind letting the world know it. Here was a man who confessed his errors publicly and didn't mind if you saw

18. Gandhi admitted to making a "Himalayan miscalculation" in organizing a protest movement against the English repression of Indian civil liberties in 1919 (Gandhi, *Gandhi's Autobiography,* p. 469). Three years later Gandhi halted a non-cooperation movement after an Indian mob killed twenty-two British officials in Chauri Chaura, Uttar Pradesh.

19. Nehru, *Toward Freedom,* pp. 79–80.

20. Gandhi was responding to allegations that his eldest son, Harilal, operated a fraudulent business (*Young India,* 18 June 1925, in *The Collected Works of Mahatma Gandhi,* vol. 27, May–July 1925 [Delhi: The Publications Division, Ministry of Information and Broadcasting, Government of India, 1968], pp. 259–262).

21. Gandhi reflected on this incident in his autobiography (pp. 219–222).

22 Mar 1959

him fail. He saw his own shortcomings, the shortcomings of his family, and then he saw the shortcomings of his own people.

We went in some little villages, and in these villages we saw hundreds of people sleeping on the ground. They didn't have any beds to sleep in. We looked in these same villages; there was no running water there, nothing to wash with. We looked in these villages, and we saw people there in their little huts and in their little rooms, and the cow, their little cow, or their calves slept in the same room with them. If they had a few chickens, the chickens slept in the same room with them. We looked at these people, and they had nothing that we would consider convenient, none of the comforts of life. Here they are, sleeping in the same room with the beast of the field. This is all they had. Pretty soon we discovered that these people were the untouchables.

Now you know in India you have what is known as the caste system, and that existed for years. And there were those people who were the outcasts, some seventy million of them. They were called untouchables. And these were the people who were exploited, and they were trampled over even by the Indian people themselves. And Gandhi looked at this system. Gandhi couldn't stand this system, and he looked at his people, and he said, "Now, you have selected me and you've asked me to free you from the political domination and the economic exploitation inflicted upon you by Britain. And here you are trampling over and exploiting seventy million of your brothers." And he decided that he would not ever adjust to that system and that he would speak against it and stand up against it the rest of his life.

And you read, back in his early life, the first thing he did when he went to India was to adopt an untouchable girl as his daughter.[22] And his wife thought he was going crazy because she was a member of one of the high castes. And she said, "What in the world are you doing adopting an untouchable? We are not supposed to touch these people." And he said, "I am going to have this young lady as my daughter." And he brought her into his ashram, and she lived there, and she lives in India today. And he demonstrated in his own life that untouchability had to go. And one of the greatest tasks ever performed by Mahatma Gandhi was against untouchability.

One day he stood before his people and said, "You are exploiting these untouchables. Even though we are fighting with all that we have in our bodies and our souls to break loose from the bondage of the British Empire, we are exploiting these people, and we're taking from them their selfhood and their self-respect." And he said, "We will not even allow these people to go into temple." They couldn't go in the temple and worship God like other people. They could not draw water like other people, and there were certain streets they couldn't even walk on.

And he looked at all of this. One day he said, "Beginning on the twenty-first of September at twelve o'clock, I will refuse to eat. And I will not eat any more until the leaders of the caste system will come to me with the leaders of the untouch-

22. Gandhi adopted Lakshmi Dafda Sharma (1914–) in October 1920. Lakshmi and her parents, Dudabhai and Danibehn Dafda, became residents of the Satyagraha ashram near Ahmadabad in September 1915 at Gandhi's invitation.

ables and say that there will be an end to untouchability. And I will not eat any more until the Hindu temples of India will open their doors to the untouchables." And he refused to eat. And days passed. Nothing happened. Finally, when Gandhi was about to breathe his last, breathe his last breath and his body—it was all but gone and he had lost many pounds. A group came to him. A group from the untouchables and a group from the Brahmin caste came to him and signed a statement saying that we will no longer adhere to the caste system and to untouchability. And the priests of the temple came to him and said now the temple will be open unto the untouchables. And that afternoon, untouchables from all over India went into the temples, and all of these thousands and millions of people put their arms around the Brahmins and peoples of other castes. Hundreds and millions of people who had never touched each other for two thousand years were now singing and praising God together. And this was the great contribution that Mahatma Gandhi brought about.[23]

And today in India, untouchability is a crime punishable by the law. And if anybody practices untouchability, he can be put in prison for as long as three years. And as one political leader said to me, "You cannot find in India one hundred people today who would sign the public statement endorsing untouchability." Here was a man who had the amazing capacity for internal criticism to the point that he saw the shortcomings of his own people. And he was just as firm against doing something about that as he was about doing away with the exploitation of the British Empire. And this is what makes him one of the great men of history.

And the final thing that I would like to say to you this morning is that the world doesn't like people like Gandhi. That's strange, isn't it? They don't like people like Christ. They don't like people like Abraham Lincoln. They kill them. And this man, who had done all of that for India, this man who had given his life and who had mobilized and galvanized four hundred million people for independence so that in 1947 India received its independence, and he became the father of that nation. This same man because he decided that he would not rest until he saw the Muslims and the Hindus together; they had been fighting among themselves, they had been in riots among themselves, and he wanted to see this straight. And one of his own fellow Hindus felt that he was a little too favorable toward the Muslims, felt that he was giving in a little too much toward the Muslims.

And one afternoon, when he was at Birla House, living there with one of the big industrialists for a few days in Delhi, he walked out to his evening prayer meeting.[24] Every evening he had a prayer meeting where hundreds of people came, and he prayed with them. And on his way out there that afternoon, one of his fellow Hindus shot him. And here was a man of nonviolence, falling at the hand of a man of violence. Here was a man of love falling at the hands of a man of hate.[25] This seems the way of history.

23. King describes Gandhi's September 1932 fast, which was triggered by the British government's announcement of separate electorates for the untouchables.

24. Gandhi frequently stayed at the home of G. D. Birla in Delhi.

25. Gandhi was murdered on 30 January 1948 by Nathuram Vinayak Godse, a member of the Rashtriya Swayamsevak Sevak Sangh, a Hindu nationalist organization. Godse was later hanged with a co-conspirator.

And isn't it significant that he died on the same day that Christ died; it was on a Friday. This is the story of history. But thank God it never stops here. Thank God Good Friday is never the end. And the man who shot Gandhi only shot him into the hearts of humanity. And just as when Abraham Lincoln was shot—mark you, for the same reason that Mahatma Gandhi was shot, that is, the attempt to heal the wounds of a divided nation. When the great leader Abraham Lincoln was shot, Secretary Stanton stood by the body of this leader and said, "Now he belongs to the ages." And that same thing can be said about Mahatma Gandhi now.[26] He belongs to the ages, and he belongs especially to this age, an age drifting once more to its doom. And he has revealed to us that we must learn to go another way.

For in a day when Sputniks and Explorers are dashing through outer space and guided ballistic missiles are carving highways of death through the stratosphere, no nation can win a war. Today it is no longer a choice between violence and nonviolence; it is either nonviolence or nonexistence. It may not be that Mahatma Gandhi is God's appeal to this age, an age drifting to its doom.[27] And that warning, and that appeal is always in the form of a warning: "He who lives by the sword will perish by the sword."[28] Jesus said it years ago. Whenever men follow that and see that way, new horizons begin to emerge and a new world unfolds. Who today will follow Christ in his way and follow it so much that we'll be able to do greater things even than he did because we will be able to bring about the peace of the world and mobilize hundreds and thousands of men to follow the way of Christ?

I close by quoting the words of John Oxenham:

> To every man there openeth a way, and ways, and a way
> The high soul climbs the high way, and the low soul gropes the low,
> And in between on the misty flats, the rest drift to and fro.
> But to every man—to every nation, to every civilization—there openeth
> a high and a low way.
> Every soul decideth which way it shall go.[29]

And God grant that we shall choose the high way, even if it will mean assassination, even if it will mean crucifixion, for by going this way we will discover that death would be only the beginning of our influence.

"I have other sheep," says Jesus, "which are not of this fold. And if you will believe in me and follow my way, you will be even, you will be able to do even greater works than I did in my lifetime."

---

26. King used this same description in his 9 March "Farewell Statement for All India Radio" (see note 4, p. 136 in this volume).

27. Jones, *Mahatma Gandhi: An Interpretation,* p. 159: "So Mahatma Gandhi is God's appeal to this age—an age drifting again to its doom."

28. Cf. Matthew 26:52.

29. King paraphrases Oxenham's "The Ways," which was published in a collection of poems entitled *All's Well!* (New York: George H. Doran, 1916), p. 91. Allan Knight Chalmers, a professor of preaching and applied Christianity at Boston University and an acquaintance of King's, quoted Oxenham's verse in two of his books (Chalmers, *The Constant Fire* [New York: Charles Scribner's Sons, 1944], p. 104, and *High Wind at Noon* [New York: Charles Scribner's Sons, 1948], pp. 76–77).

O God, our gracious Heavenly Father, we thank Thee for the fact that you have inspired men and women in all nations and in all cultures. We call you different names: some call Thee Allah; some call you Elohim; some call you Jehovah; some call you Brahma; and some call you the Unmoved Mover; some call you the Archetectonic Good. But we know that these are all names for one and the same God, and we know you are one.

And grant, O God, that we will follow Thee and become so committed to Thy way and Thy kingdom that we will be able to establish in our lives and in this world a brotherhood. We will be able to establish here a kingdom of understanding, where men will live together as brothers and respect the dignity and worth of all human personality.

In the name and spirit of Jesus we pray. Amen. [*organ plays*]

We open the doors of the church now. Is there one who will accept the Christ this morning just as you are? Who will make that decision as we stand and sing together? One hundred and sixty-two. [*congregation sings "Just As I Am"*]

Let us remain standing now for the recessional hymn. We are grateful to God for these persons who have come to unite with the church. I might mention, just before leaving, that this afternoon the baby contest which is sponsored by the August club [*recording interrupted*]

At. MLKEC: ET 64.

To Reuben E. Nelson

23 March 1959
[*Montgomery, Ala.*]

Just prior to departing for India, King abandoned his plans for a Russian leg of the tour, citing health reasons and "the urgency of the racial conflict in the South."[1] *In the following letter, King thanks Nelson, the general secretary of the American Baptist Convention, for the organization's contribution to his trip to India and explains that a visit to the Soviet Union might "have taken on too many political connotations."*[2] *Nelson replied on 8 April.*

1. "King Postpones Planned Visit to Soviet Union," *Atlanta Daily World*, 3 February 1959. In November 1958, upon learning that the American Baptist Convention would finance his proposed trip to Russia, King wrote to an intermediary outlining his reasons for desiring such a visit (King to Darrell Randall, 13 November 1958, in *Papers* 4:533–535).

2. Reuben Emmanuel Nelson (1905–1960), born in Lake Elizabeth, Minnesota, received an A.B. (1927) from Des Moines University, a B.D. (1930) from Bethel Theological Seminary, and an S.T.M. (1933) from Andover Newton Theological Seminary. After serving as pastor of First Swedish Baptist Church in Brockton, Massachusetts, as a seminary professor and as an administrator in several Baptist bodies, Nelson became general secretary of the American Baptist Convention, the largest northern-based association of Baptist churches in the United States, in 1950.

23 Mar 1959

Dr. Reuben Nelson
The American Baptist Convention
152 Madison Avenue
New York, New York

Dear Dr. Nelson:

I am just returning to the country from a most rewarding experience in India. I had planned writing you while in India to express my appreciation to you and the Executive Board of the American Baptist Convention for the contribution of nine hundred dollars toward my trip, but my schedule was so heavy that I found it impossible. Please accept my rather belated thanks at this time. I can assure you that I will long remember this kind expression of Christian generosity.

I found India a most interesting country. The people gave us a very enthusiastic reception and showered upon us the most generous hospitality imaginable. While I would not be so rash as to pretend to know India after just a months visit, I do feel that I gained some meaningful insights that will strengthen me in my commitment to the way of nonviolence as a technique to social change.

I had a chance to talk to Dr. Hargroves before leaving concerning his views on the trip to Russia.[3] Maybe he was right in feeling that this was the wrong time for me to go. At any rate, I certainly did not want to go without the assurance that the Russian Baptists were participating in my coming. Without this assurance, the visit to Russia would have taken on too many political connotations. Maybe some time in the not-too-distant future it will be possible for me to make this trip.

Again, let me express my wholehearted appreciation to the American Baptists for making it possible for me to go to India without reversing my initial plans. If there is anything that I can do to assist in the great work that you are doing, please do not hesitate [*to?*] call on me.

Very sincerely yours,
Martin L. King, Jr.

P.S. I have been quite interested in having my church become a part of the American Baptist Convention. Is [*it?*] possible for a church in the South to join the American Baptist Convention? If so, please send me the necessary information.[4]

TLc. MLKP-MBU: Box 18.

---

3. King refers to Vernon Hargroves, who served as president of the American Baptist Convention (1954–1955) and was a missionary in the Soviet Union.

4. In his 8 April reply, Nelson explained that churches normally apply to an association or state convention: "However, where we do not have American Baptist churches you do not need to go through the procedure of application for membership." Almost two years after King became co-pastor of Atlanta's Ebenezer Baptist Church, the church members voted to affiliate with the American Baptist Convention (King to William H. Rhoades, 26 January 1962, and Rhoades to King, 31 January 1962).

To Corinne B. Johnson

23 March 1959
Montgomery, Ala.

On 19 March, Bayard Rustin telephoned Johnson to explain that King was "extremely tired" upon returning from India and planned "to go directly home to Montgomery" rather than stop in Philadelphia as scheduled to meet with AFSC officials.[1] *The following day Johnson wrote to King requesting that he come to Philadelphia in April to discuss problems related to his visit to India: "We are aware from our correspondence with Jim Bristol that there were some arrangements which were not entirely satisfactory to you. We would be glad to hear from you any comments you may have on either the positive or less good aspects of the trip."*[2]

Dear Miss Johnson:

Thank you very kindly for your letter of March 20. I, too, regret that circumstances made it necessary for me to cancel the engagement with the American Friends Service Committee on Friday, March 20. I hope it will be possible to arrange something at a later date. I am afraid that April 17, will be impossible for me because of a long standing commitment in another section of the country. Actually, I will not be able to get to the Youth March until the last minute.[3] I will be checking my schedule to see when I will be in that area again.

I had a marvelous experience in India. The people gave us a very enthusiastic reception and showered upon us the most generous hospitality imaginable. While I would not be so rash as to pretend to know India after such a short visit, I can say that I gained some meaningful insights while there and I am more convinced than ever before of the potency and rightness of the way of nonviolence as a method for social change. I believe I came away with a deeper understanding of nonviolence and also a deeper commitment. Very soon Dr. Reddick and I will do some writing on our impressions.[4] When this is done, I will be sure to send you a copy.

At first, we felt that the schedule was rather heavy, and that more time should have been provided for an opportunity to reflect over our many experiences and to properly digest them. However, we soon adjusted to the schedule and tried to

1. Johnson to Bristol, 26 March 1959.

2. Johnson to King, 20 March 1959. In her report on the trip to the AFSC Foreign Service Executive Committee, Johnson noted that "it was extremely difficult to communicate with Martin Luther King . . . almost exclusively through a third person, Bayard Rustin," and that King did not inform Bristol "of changes in transportation arrangements, so that there was a good deal of confusion as to dates and appointments." These administrative problems, Johnson continued, "should not obscure the real success of the visit and the opportunity provided to the Indians and to King to share insight on the non-violent approach to current problems" (AFSC, "Report on Martin Luther King's trip to India," 4 May 1959).

3. For King's remarks at the Youth March, see Address at the Youth March for Integrated Schools on 18 April 1959, pp. 186–188 in this volume.

4. See King, "My Trip to the Land of Gandhi," July 1959, pp. 231–238 in this volume.

make the best of it. Jim Bristol did an excellent job in making the necessary arrangements after we were in India.

Words are inadequate for me to express my appreciation to the American Friends Service Committee for sponsoring this trip. Without this tremendous assistance I am sure that I would have been wandering around in circles in India. As I just said, Jim Bristol was wonderful. He went far beyond the call of duty to make our trip enjoyable and rewarding. We also owe a great debt of gratitude to Mrs. Bristol and their two charming daughters for joining in and assisting at every point.[5]

Enclosed you will find a statement of additional expenses.[6] If there are any questions concerning them, please feel free to write me. I will send the medical forms as soon as we have an opportunity to see our physicians.[7] We found such a load of work on our return that we will be playing catch up for a long time.

Very sincerely yours,
[*signed*] Martin L. King Jr.
Martin Luther King, Jr.

MLK:mlb

TLS. AFSCR-PPAFS.

---

5. King refers to Bristol's wife, Dorothy, and their daughters Tina and Leigh. In her 26 March letter to Bristol, Johnson enclosed a copy of this letter and noted that King "certainly writes in this letter in a way in which he has not corresponded with us at all during this whole trip." She also pointed out that King had "great praise for the way you handled things for him in India, which may not have seemed so evident at the time."

6. In a 24 March letter, Maude Ballou forwarded Johnson a list of two additional travel expenses totaling just less than two hundred dollars.

7. King refers to medical forms Johnson had sent in her 20 March letter: "It is an AFSC policy to have all returning personnel who have been abroad examined medically immediately on their return."

To Harry Belafonte

25 March 1959
[*Montgomery, Ala.*]

After arriving in New York City from India on 18 March, the Kings spent an evening at the home of entertainer and civil rights supporter Harry Belafonte.

Mr. Harry Belafonte
300 West End Avenue
Apartment 5-C
New York, New York

Dear Harry:

This is just a note to again express our appreciation to you and Julie for so graciously entertaining us in your palatial apartment a few nights ago. We will long remember the enjoyable moments we spent together. It was also good to have seen the great movie, "The Diary of Anne Frank," with you, and to have met your many lovely friends afterwards.[1]

We are now fairly well rested up after our long flight across the Atlantic. However, we are now confronting a load of accumulated work at home, and I am sure we will be playing a game of catch up for many weeks to come. Give our best regards to Julie and to your handsome son, David. We will look forward to seeing you at the Youth March in Washington and also on "Person to Person" the night before.[2]

Very sincerely yours,
Martin and Coretta

TLc. MLKP-MBU: Box 21.

1. Among the people King met was actress Shelley Winters, who won an Academy Award for her role in the Anne Frank movie. The following day Winters sent King a copy of the book *The Diary of a Young Girl* with a note: "I know how tired you and your wife were last night so thanks again for coming to the film" (Winters to King, 19 March 1959). In 1942 Anne Frank, a thirteen-year-old Jewish girl, went into hiding during the Nazi occupation of Amsterdam. In March 1945, two months before the German surrender, Frank died of typhus in the Bergen-Belsen concentration camp. Her diary, originally published in Dutch in 1947, first appeared in English in 1952.

2. Belafonte helped promote the 1958 and 1959 Youth Marches for Integrated Schools (see King, Address at Youth March, 25 October 1958, in *Papers* 4:514–515, and Youth March for Integrated Schools, "A petition for integrated schools to the President and the Congress of the U.S.," January 1959). "Person to Person" was Edward R. Murrow's popular Friday evening interview program on CBS.

From Martin Luther King, Sr.

26 March 1959
Atlanta, Ga.

King's father informs him that he will be unable to attend an SCLC administrative committee meeting in Montgomery on 2 April.[1]

Dr. Martin Luther King, Jr.
454 Dexter Avenue
Montgomery 4, Alabama

Dear M. L.:

I very much regret that prior to receiving your letter on yesterday informing me of the forth-coming meeting in Montgomery, I had announced the board meet-

1. For more on the meeting, see Reddick, Notes on SCLC Administrative Committee Meetings on 2 April and 3 April 1959, pp. 177–179 in this volume.

ing of the Atlanta Baptist Association. You know then that I cannot make the Montgomery meeting, as much as I would like to.

My schedule follows:

Departing for Detroit—March 30th. . . . .

Will address the Baptist Ministers' Conference in an appeal for Southern Christian Leadership Conf., on March 31.

Returning to Atlanta—Wednesday, April 1

Atlanta Association board meeting—Thursday—April 2

You already know that you can count on me to assist in anyway that I can. Sorry I cannot make the meeting.

[*signed*] Daddy
Sincerely,

TLS. MLKP-MBU: Box 29.

From Ella J. Baker

26 March 1959
Atlanta, Ga.

SCLC's associate director updates King on recent civil rights efforts. Baker had spent the previous five weeks in Louisiana organizing a voter registration campaign and collecting evidence of electoral discrimination to present to the U.S. Commission on Civil Rights.

Rev. Martin Luther King, Jr.
309 South Jackson Street
Montgomery, Alabama

Dear Martin:

I returned to the Atlanta office, Tuesday, after a very meaningful stay in Shreveport. A detailed report will be sent the first of next week, but you will be interested to know that more than 65 voting complaints were sent to the Commission on Civil Rights, and 200 persons presented themselves at Caddo Parish Courthouse for registration last Thursday, March 19th.[1]

1. Baker later noted that only fifteen people were allowed to register that day (Baker, "Report of the director to the executive board," 15 May 1959). For more on Baker's activities in Louisiana, see Baker and R. C. Thomas to Registered voter, 14 March 1959, and Baker to R. C. Thomas, 21 March 1959.

Letters urging reports on books are now being sent out. However, we are without books to fill new orders, because the books from Houston have not been returned. We have written and called Rev. Hill several times, the last call was made in Shreveport, about a week ago.[2] He again promised to ship the books at once. But to date, they have not arrived. You know, of course, that the book fund has been transferred to the general account, except for $36.94.

26 Mar 1959

I stopped in Birmingham, Monday on my way from Shreveport to see what can be done there on a registration drive. Fred [*Shuttlesworth*] suggests that a letter from you to such key persons as Rev. Ware, Bishop Gibbs, and Attorney Billingsley, would be more productive than if he initated it.[3] They would be asked to contact other community representatives for a committee meeting to explore the possibilities of a coordinated, city-wide drive. I could go over for such a meeting and will send you a suggested letter on this tomorrow. It appears that S.C.L.C. will have to follow through on the program proposed at the January 24th meeting.[4]

I don't think that the initial letters for the May meeting have been sent out, and Rev. Tilley will not be back until April 5th or 6th, he said. Hence, I'll send a draft Friday for your consideration, and you can call me or drop me a note by Monday or Tuesday.[5]

Glad you had a nice trip—I found your card on my return to the office.

Best regards.

Sincerely yours,
[*signed*] Ella
Ella J. Baker

EJB/cb

TLS. MLKP-MBU: Box 20.

---

2. Baker refers to *Stride Toward Freedom,* which was often sold through churches and ministerial groups on consignment. Edward V. Hill was a Houston minister and SCLC member.

3. Baker refers to James Lowell Ware, pastor of Trinity Baptist Church in Birmingham; AME bishop Carey Abraham Gibbs; and Orzell Billingsley, Jr., who served on King's legal team during the Montgomery bus boycott.

4. Gathering in Montgomery on 24 January, SCLC representatives and Alabama black community leaders agreed to increase pressure on federal agencies to protect black voting rights and to organize voter registration drives (SCLC, Press release, 28 January 1959; see also King to Eisenhower, 25 January 1959, pp. 111–112 in this volume).

5. King to Friend of freedom, 13 April 1959. For more on the May meeting, see Statement Adopted at Spring Session of SCLC, 15 May 1959, pp. 205–208 in this volume.

29 Mar
1959

A Walk Through the Holy Land, Easter Sunday Sermon Delivered at Dexter Avenue Baptist Church

[*29 March 1959*]
[*Montgomery, Ala.*]

As King recounts his recent visit to the Middle East, he recalls falling to his knees and weeping during a visit to Calvary. He observes that Jesus's sacrifice on the cross was "something that nobody could demand him to do," making him "a man who had the amazing capacity to be obedient to unenforceable obligations." King tells his congregation that the cross is ultimately a symbol of hope: "We've been buried in numerous graves—the grave of economic insecurity, the grave of exploitation, the grave of oppression. We've watched justice trampled over and truth crucified. But I'm here to tell you this morning, Easter reminds us that it won't be like that all the way. It reminds us that God has a light that can shine amid all of the darkness." The following was transcribed from an audio recording.

It was on a beautiful afternoon a few weeks ago that we journeyed from our hotel in Beirut, Lebanon, to the airport to take a plane for Jerusalem. Lebanon is that beautiful country in the Middle East that we remember from biblical times, for occasionally we read about the cedars of Lebanon. And Beirut is that beautiful city that sits elevated on a hill overlooking the mighty Mediterranean Sea. Pretty soon we were in the air passing through places like Damascus. There again you remember Damascus, you remember it in modern days as the capital of the little country of Syria. But you remember Damascus as an ancient city, for it was on the Damascus road that the Apostle Paul was converted. You remember as he stood one day before King Agrippa, he said, "It was at noon day, oh King, that I saw a light, a light that outshines the radiance, the brilliance of the sun."[1] And after seeing that light and gaining a new vision, he was transformed from Saul the persecutor to Paul the Christian and became one of the great Christian saints of all generations.

After about two hours in the air we were notified to fasten our seat belts—we were beginning to descend, the descent for the airport in Jerusalem. Now, I must say that when you say "landing in Jerusalem" you must qualify what you are saying and tell what part of Jerusalem. That is because men have not solved their social problems, and we're still banned because in their Jerusalem, that ancient holy city has been divided and split up and partitioned. And before you can enter one side of the city, it must be clear that you will not enter the other because one side is Jerusalem, Israel, the other side is Jerusalem, Jordan. Because of the Arab-Israeli conflict this city has been divided. And if on your visa it is revealed that you are going into any Arab nation, you can only go to Israel without being able to ever go back to an Arab country in the life of your passport; the hate is

1. Cf. Acts 26:13.

intensified. And so this was a strange feeling to go to the ancient city of God and see the tragedies of man's hate and his evil, which causes him to fight and live in conflict.

But we were going to Jerusalem, Jordan. And it is in this section of Jerusalem that all of the ancient sites, on the whole, are preserved. Those sacred, holy sites. We landed there, in Jerusalem, Jordan, and in a few moments we had checked in our hotel, which was a YMCA hotel. Pretty soon we discovered, after checking in, that many other people were there from all over the world, many people from the United States, who were on tour through the world from various sections of the world. This is always one of the interesting things about traveling, that you learn to know people. You meet people of all races and of all cultures, and you tend to be lifted above provincialism, and chauvinism, and what the sociologists call ethnocentrism. You come to see a unity in mankind. If I had my way, I would recommend that all of the students who can afford it to go to college five years; they would study in that college four years, and they would use their tuition one year and their board and what have you to travel abroad. I think this is the greatest education that can ever come to an individual. I think if more of our white brothers in the South had traveled a little more, many of our problems would be solved today. So often we live in our little shells because we've never risen above the province. We've never risen above sectionalism. And so it was a great pleasure to meet people, various sections of the world, various sections of our own nation.

The next morning we rose early because we knew that this was the day that we would start our pilgrimage around this holy city and this was the day that we would tour Jerusalem itself. The next day we were to go to Hebron. There stands abound the points where Abraham stood. There we would see the tomb of Abraham, Isaac, and Jacob, and Sarah and others. And from there we moved to Bethlehem, that city, "oh little town of Bethlehem," we hear Phillips Brooks talking about it. We sing about it. We talk about "yet in the dark streets shineth the everlasting light." We think about it as that city where "the hopes and fears of all the years met in thee tonight."[2] And that city where the wise men decided to leave because an event was taking place, and they went to see it and be a part of it.[3] We were to stand there to see this spot and this place where our Christ was born. And to see the little inn, which is still preserved, where there was no room, no room for Christ, crowded out.[4] When one looks at that, he cannot help but think of the fact that this is the long story of human history. We crowd him out by being preoccupied with other things. It doesn't mean that we are preoccupied with bad things either. So often the choice in life is not between the bad and the good; it's between the good and the better. And so often we fail to make way for the better because we are bogged down in the good. Those were not bad people in that inn that night. They were good people, I'm sure, and they had noble purposes for being there; and the

2. Episcopalian minister and abolitionist Phillips Brooks wrote the hymn "O Little Town of Bethlehem" in 1868, recalling his visit to the Holy Land three years earlier. King paraphrases lines from the opening stanza of the hymn.

3. Cf. Matthew 2:9–12.

4. Cf. Luke 2:6–7.

innkeeper was good, but they didn't have room for the better. This is so often the tragedy of life. And this came back as we stood there.

A day later we were to journey into Samaria. There, I think about the ancient days when the Jews had no dealings with the Samaritans. We looked up in Mount Gerizim, where the temple of the Samaritans used to exist, and we attended a service one afternoon. There are only two hundred and thirty Samaritans left in the whole world, and they live right around that little ancient shore there. And there we went and saw those people, and they had preserved there in their little temple an ancient document known as the Pentateuch, the first five books of the Bible. And it is supposed to be the most ancient document in the world. And these five books of the Bible—Genesis, Exodus, Leviticus, Numbers, and Deuteronomy—we had a privilege, the privilege to see that, written in its old Hebrew.

Then we were to go later to Jericho and to see that great city. And to think of the Jericho road that Jesus had talked about, that winding road. And when you travel on that road you can see why a man could easily be robbed on that road. Jesus told a parable about it one day.[5] And then you see the walls of Jericho, which have recently been excavated. And you think about the walls of Jericho, and you think about Joshua, and you think about Joshua fighting the battle of Jericho.[6] And then around Jericho you go to the Dead Sea and also the river of Jordan. And all of these things were in store for us.

And we stood in the holy city, but this day we would only go around the city of Jerusalem. Our guide came early that morning immediately after we had eaten breakfast. We'd started out and, interestingly enough, our first stop that morning was a mountain, a mountain that we've all heard about called the Mount of Olives. We've heard about that mountain in our Bible; we've read about. And every night, every first Sunday night when we have communion we read about it. Well, you remember it says that after the last supper they had sung a hymn, and they went out into the Mount of Olives.[7] This was a significant mountain in the life of Christ. It has many interesting connotations. And you can stand there on the Mount of Olives and look over the whole of Jerusalem. Exalted that high, elevated that high, and you can look all around and see the old city and the new city. There we stood there on the Mount of Olives with all of its sacred meaning. Just below that mount at the bottom you see a little garden. It is known as the Garden of Gethsemane, and it's still preserved there with beautiful flowers; it's a beautiful garden.

But there is something about that garden that we must always remember. It is the garden where Christ agonized with his own soul.[8] It is the garden where Christ uttered a statement which reveals that he was amazingly human. He didn't want to die, for we read that he said, "Father, if Thy be willing, let this cup pass from me."[9] This is a painful, difficult cup. But then we see there the meaning of religion and all of its profound meaning, the transformation that comes about when

5. Cf. Luke 10:30–37.

6. Cf. Joshua 4:13–24.

7. Cf. Matthew 26:30–31.

8. King's 1957 Palm Sunday sermon focused on Jesus's experience in the garden (King, Garden of Gethsemane, Sermon delivered at Dexter Avenue Baptist Church, 14 April 1957).

9. Cf. Matthew 26:39.

you love God and when you know him. We hear them in that same garden, saying a few minutes later, "not my will but Thy will be done."[10] It was the same garden. And there is something else that you must remember about this garden. It was the garden where Jesus faced the most lonesome moments of his life. It was the garden where his three friends deceived him and were not concerned enough about him to stay awake while he was there praying. We read in the scripture that they went to sleep not concerned.[11] Isn't it tragic and dark in life when even those people that we have confidence in and that we believe in and we call our friends fail to understand us? And in the most difficult moments of life they leave us going the road alone. This is the story of life, though. So Gethsemane is not only a spot on the map. Gethsemane is an experience in the heart and the soul. Gethsemane is something that we go through every day. For whenever our friends deceive us, we face Gethsemane. Whenever we face great moral decisions in life and we find that we must stand there and people turn their backs on us and they think we are crazy, we are facing Gethsemane. Gethsemane is a story that comes to all of us in life. We looked at this garden, and all of these thoughts came back. 29 Mar 1959

Just over from Gethsemane we saw a gate. And our guide said to us that this is the gate where Jesus entered Jerusalem. This is the gate where Jesus made the triumphful entry. We read about this. We read about the triumphant entry that day when Jesus came into Jerusalem. He came by way of the Mount of Olives, by the way, and entered that holy city, that city where so many things stood in terms of the long history of Judaism. That city that had stoned its prophets, that city that had crucified men because they stood up for right. This is the city that Jesus entered, and he entered through that gate. Why did he enter in this triumphant entry? We don't know. Some scholars said that this was the moment that Jesus decided to let the secret out; the messianic secret had been a secret for a long time, and now he would let men know that he was Messiah. Others would say that Jesus was not doing this himself but his followers were doing it. Those that he had let in on the, allowed to know the secret, would now let men know it, and so they were the ones who precipitated the triumphant entry. Others would say that this was the day of the Feast of Tabernacles. And it so often happened that on that day there were great parades and great crowds. And so it happened that Jesus entered on the day of the Feast of Tabernacles, and the people decided that they wanted to honor this great prophet as he entered the city on the day of the Feast of Tabernacles.[12]

Maybe there is some truth in all three of these theories. But at least there is something more basic than all of this and that was that Jesus entered Jerusalem as a different kind of king. He didn't enter as David with great military power and great military might or as Saul with all of the military power [*word inaudible*]. Not even as Solomon with all of his wealth. But he entered on a lowly ass, which revealed that this was a new kind of king, not the same type of king that had come in the past but a king who had another type of kingdom. And so his escort would

10. Cf. Matthew 26:42.
11. Cf. Matthew 26:43–45.
12. Cf. Luke 19:28–38.

be not spear but palm. And he would enter by the voices of little children, not by the shouts of soldiers. A new kind of kingdom and a new kind of king.

And he entered this gate, and we walked around and through there and pretty soon, about fifty feet from the gate, we came to a spot and the guide said, "This is where the old temple stood, the Temple of Jerusalem." You remember that temple fell in 70 A.D. The Roman Empire came to stop an uprising in Palestine, and they destroyed the temple. But the spot is still reserved, and there is a big stone in the middle of that point where all of the sacrifices used to take place on the altar. This was the temple where Jesus entered as soon as he got to Jerusalem a few hours and ran the money-changers out of the temple.[13] This was where Jesus made his profound mistake. And what was his profound mistake? His profound mistake was that he went beyond the realm of talking about what he believed but he was willing to act about it. And he was willing to act on truth, and the world considers that a mistake.

We looked at this temple; then we started walking the ancient streets of Jerusalem. And you cannot walk those little narrow streets in that old city, as you move through the gate of Damascus and the gate of Corinth, without getting a real sense of history and the ancient qualities of that old city. We walked those narrow streets, and then finally that afternoon we came to another point. This was the point known as Pilate's judgment hall. In Jerusalem today all of the sacred points are enclosed, you see; they have churches around them now. Helena, the mother of Constantine, back in the fourth century went to Jerusalem. After finding all of these sacred points of the death and the life of Jesus and the Resurrection of Jesus, she had churches erected there. And so you will find a church erected around every sacred point in Jerusalem. And we stood there where the church stands now, that point known as Pilate's judgment hall. This was where Jesus was tried. This was where Jesus faced, on the outside, a crowd crying, "Crucify him."[14] This is where Jesus had to stand before a man who knew that he had no faults but who, willing to content the people, decided to crucify him. And one cannot leave that point without weeping for Pilate, for here is a man who sacrificed truth on the altar of his self-interest. Here was a man who crucified justice on the cross of his egotism.

Then you leave that point, which is the judgment hall, and you start a new walk. It is known as the Via Dolorosa. This is the way of sorrow. And it is the way Jesus walked from the judgment hall on to the cross. You walk there—it's about a mile—from that point up to Golgotha, the place of the skull, or Calvary. This is the walk that is a noble walk. It is a walk that does something to the soul because you know that as you walk there you're walking the way of sorrow that Christ walked. And they have, as you walk along the way, spots. They call them stations—station one, station two—and there are fourteen stations between the judgment hall of Pilate and the place where Jesus was brought and crucified. And at every station, some significant event occurred, something happened. At one station Jesus stumbled; at another station Jesus fell; at another station he got up; at another station some-

---

13. Cf. Luke 19:45–48.

14. Cf. John 19:6–15.

body came to help him along the way. And I will remember the experience that came when the guide said, "At this station Jesus stumbled and fell with that heavy cross on his shoulder." This was the tradition, you see, for when a person was crucified they made them carry the cross themselves. This was heavy, and Jesus had broken down under the load, and he'd fallen.

And I started thinking of something that I heard my friend Archibald Carey say some time ago.[15] The thing that I thought about at that moment was the fact that when Jesus fell and stumbled under that cross it was a black man that picked it up for him and said, "I will help you," and took it on up to Calvary. And I think we know today there is a struggle, a desperate struggle, going on in this world. Two-thirds of the people of the world are colored people. They have been dominated politically, exploited economically, trampled over, and humiliated. There is a struggle on the part of these people today to gain freedom and human dignity. And I think one day God will remember that it was a black man that helped His son in the darkest and most desolate moment of his life. It was a black man who picked up that cross for him and who took that cross on up to Calvary. God will remember this. And in all of our struggles for peace and security, freedom and human dignity, one day God will remember that it was a black man who aided his only begotten son in the darkest hour of his life.[16]

You keep walking on that way, that way of sorrow, that way of trials and tribulations, and you finally come to that church known as the Church of the Holy Sepulchre. And it's here, it is here within that church that you find the point where Jesus was crucified. It is here that you come to the cross of Jesus the Christ. Now certainly the cross that stands there today is not the same cross that Jesus was crucified on, but you forget that for the moment. You begin to feel the fact that you are around the spot where he was crucified. I never will forget the experience that came to me. And I stood before that cross and before the point, something within began to well up. There was a captivating quality there, there was something that overwhelmed me, and before I knew it I was on my knees praying at that point. And before I knew it I was weeping. This was a great world-shaking, transfiguring experience. And I remember we were with some other people and I, after that, went back to the hotel. And I left Coretta and the other people and said I was going in to the hotel, and I went on back alone. I walked back that same way and went back to the hotel alone and tried to meditate on the meaning of that cross and the meaning of the experience that I just had. And I started thinking in a way that I'd never thought before of the meaning of the cross.

And as I meditated on that cross, these things came to my mind. As I tried to calculate in my own mind and in my own limited way the meaning of this cross, these things came to my mind. That first, Jesus didn't have to go to this cross. He voluntarily did something that nobody could demand him to do. Nobody could ever demand that he sacrifice his life in a way like this. And he didn't have to do it. He could have recanted, and everything could have been all right. He could

15. Carey was pastor of Quinn Chapel AME Church in Chicago.

16. King refers to Simon of Cyrene, who was commanded by Pilate's soldiers to carry Jesus's cross (cf. Matthew 27:32).

29 Mar 1959

have gone back on the back side with the Mount of Olives and gone on back to Galilee, forgotten about the whole thing, and everything would have been all right. But here was a man who had the amazing capacity to be obedient to unenforceable obligations. I think this is what the cross says to us this morning. If there is any one thing that I would like for you to leave with this morning and that is that a man is not a man until he is obedient to the unenforceable.

There are three groups of people in the world. They are the lawless people on the one hand—people who break laws, people who are in our prisons, people who never follow the codes of society, whether they are written laws or customs. These are the lawless people. Then you have a second group—the law-abiding people whose standards of conduct come mainly from without. Their standards come from the man-made law, the law written on the book, or the customs and mores of society. So many people fit into this category. I would suspect that most of us here this morning would fit into this category. We are not lawless people; we are law-abiding. We follow what the law says, and we follow what the law without says; we are certainly true to the customs and mores of our community. There is a third group—those people who are committed to an inner law, those people who have an interior criteria of conduct. And this is the difference. These are the people who have an inner [*word inaudible*]. These are the people who are obedient to the unenforceable. These are the people who are obedient to something that the law without could never demand and could never write for you to do. These are the people who, in the words of, those beautiful words that Shakespeare said about Desdemona: "They hold it something of a vice in their goodness not to do more than is required."[17] These are the people who change history and who make history. They come occasionally.

It might be a Socrates who talks to his friend Crito who tells him that he can leave and everything can be all right and he need not face the tragedy of the hemlock. Socrates looks back and says to him, "I must stand on what I consider to be right and true, even if it brings death to me."[18] And now he said at the end of the *Apology,* "I go to life and, you—I go to death, and you go to life. Which of us goes to the better life, nobody knows but God. But I go because I believe finally in truth."[19]

It might be a Martin Luther who stands before the officials of the Catholic Church. They tried to get him to recant and take back everything that he said about the corruption in the system of indulgences, about the Ninety-five Theses that he tacked on the door of Wittenberg. And he stands before them and said, "Here I stand. I can do none other, so help me God."

It might be a Jesus of Nazareth who can leave and go back to Nazareth and become merely an insignificant character in history but who said to himself, "Oh no, I cannot follow this way. I must be true to what I know is truth and what I know is right. What I know will eventually be a part of the structure of the universe." And this is what the cross says to us this morning: greatness in life comes when we are obedient to the unenforceable.

---

17. William Shakespeare, *Othello,* act 2, scene 3.
18. Plato, *Crito.*
19. Plato, *Apology.*

A great nation is a nation that has citizens who are obedient not only to the laws written on the books but people who are obedient to those unenforceable laws. Great family, beautiful home life built not on the enforceable, on the unenforceable. Ultimately, there is a quality that can't be enforced. Whether a man is faithful to his wife or whether a wife is faithful to the husband is not enforceable. Ultimately, the individual must be obedient to the unenforceable. Whether a man will support his children and be true to them is unenforceable. The law can say you must support your children, but the law can't make you love your children. The law cannot make you give as much time to your children as you should. The law cannot keep you from going into endless activities and endless social functions while you neglect your children. The law can't make you stop doing that. Ultimately it is obedience to the unenforceable. And whenever a man rises to this point, he rises to the greatness of Jesus Christ on the cross. 29 Mar 1959

This is what the cross says to me more than anything else—that we find a man who had the amazing capacity to be obedient to unenforceable obligation. And this is what he meant in his life, he lived it in his life. You remember he said, "Go the second mile. If they compel you to go the first, go the second."[20] Now what was Jesus saying? He said it again, "If men ask you to forgive them, don't stop seven times; forgive seventy times seven."[21] Maybe they can require you to forgive seven times. But what he's saying is this—that the privilege of generosity begins when the requirement of the law ends. Jesus said this, and this is what he is doing on the cross. The cross is a climax of all that he had lived and expressed in his life. Going the second mile means merely being obedient to the unenforceable. This was the one thing that that cross said to me.

But it said something else to me which had great meaning as I thought about it. The cross is an eternal expression of the length to which God is willing to go to restore a broken community. Now this, I think is very vital. It tells us not only about the courage and the commitment, the moral commitment, of Jesus Christ, but it tells us about the love of God himself, the length to which God is willing to go to restore broken communities. Through our sins, through our evil and through our wickedness, we've broken up communities. We've torn up society. Families are divided, homes are divided; cultures are divided; nations are divided; generations are divided; civilizations are divided. Jesus experienced this in his day. He knew that, and God looked out, he looked back at Israel, and he knew that Israel had been a naughty child. She had gone whoring after other gods. She had brought about division in the very center of her being. And what is the cross but God's way of saying to a wayward child, "I still love you, and I am willing to go any length, including sacrificing the life of my only begotten son, in order to redeem you. And in order to come and to say to you that if you will see within that suffering Christ on the cross my power, you will be able to be transformed. And you will be redeemed." That cross is an expression of the eternal love of God our Father.

There is a final point. The cross is not only an expression of the love of God and the courage and moral commitment of Jesus Christ who is obedient to the

20. Cf. Matthew 5:41.

21. Cf. Matthew 18:21–22.

unenforceable. But I started thinking of the fact; as we stood at that cross, there was a little walk, maybe about sixty or seventy-five feet. They said to us that this is the tomb where Jesus was buried. Strangely enough, it was a borrowed tomb.[22] Borrowed tomb—he didn't have anything; he didn't have any money. He didn't have anywhere to lay his head.[23] Even when he died on a cross, one of the most ignominious deaths that we can ever point to in history, he had to be buried in a borrowed grave. We stood in there. But that guide began to talk, and he became eloquent when he talked about it. He said, "But I want you to know that this tomb is empty. He is not there now. This is just a symbol of where he was, but he isn't there now." And oh, that cross to me is a demonstration of something. It is triumph, isn't it? It is not only tragedy, but it is triumph. It is a revelation of the power of God to ultimately win out over all of the forces of evil.

Whatever you believe about the Resurrection this morning isn't important. The form that you believe in, that isn't the important thing. The fact that the revelation, Resurrection is something that nobody can refute, that is the important thing. Some people felt, the disciples felt, that it was a physical resurrection, that the physical body got up. Then Paul came on the scene, who had been trained in Greek philosophy, who knew a little about Greek philosophy and had read a little, probably, of Plato and others who believed in the immortality of the soul, and he tried to synthesize the Greek doctrine of the immortality of the soul with the Jewish-Hebrew doctrine of resurrection. And he talked, as you remember and you read it, about a spiritual body. A spiritual body. Whatever form, that isn't important right now. The important thing is that that Resurrection did occur. Important thing is that that grave was empty. Important thing is the fact that Jesus had given himself to certain eternal truths and eternal principles that nobody could crucify and escape. So all of the nails in the world could never pierce this truth. All of the crosses of the world could never block this love. All of the graves in the world could never bury this goodness. Jesus had given himself to certain universal principles. And so today the Jesus and the God that we worship are inescapable.

We can talk this morning about the inescapable Christ. We can get by and for all of the world he lives today. He lives today in society; he lives today in our lives; he lives today in the world. And this is our hope. This is what keeps us going. There is something in the cross that is not only an element of tragedy; there is an element of triumph within that cross. So you can go out this morning with new hope, new hope for the future. No matter how dark it gets, realize that God ultimately transforms Good Friday into Easter.

Some years ago, somebody asked William Howard Taft, "What about the League of Nations?" He said most good things in this world get crucified, eventually placed in a tomb.[24] There's always the third day. Isn't that true? That League of Nations that was one day crucified, today, [*gap in tape*] has been resurrected in the United Nations. Woodrow Wilson probably died unhappy and frustrated,

---

22. Cf. Matthew 27:59–60.

23. Cf. Matthew 8:20.

24. Taft was the twenty-seventh president of the United States (1909–1913). In 1921, Taft was appointed chief justice of the U.S. Supreme Court.

'cause men didn't have the vision to see it.[25] They didn't have the vision to follow it. But today there's the United Nations, which is nothing but the old League of Nations on a broader scale. And before there can ever be peace in this world, we must turn to an instrument like the United Nations and disarm the whole world and develop a world police power so that no nation will possess atomic and hydrogen bombs for destruction. This is our hope, isn't it? It was buried one day, but now it has been resurrected. Years ago, back in 1896, doctrine was crucified, the doctrine of righteousness, the doctrine of treating men as equals. The doctrine of integration, it was crucified. There was a man by the name of Justice [*Louis*] Harlan who was crucified along with it, I guess. He was condemned because he gave a dissenting vote when they set forth the *Plessy versus Ferguson* decision.[26] But thank God there came May seventeenth, 1954, and it was resurrected.[27] Given in a unanimous decision by the Supreme Court of the United Nations, here was a minority opinion in 1896 which became a majority opinion in 1954. What is this saying? The cross reveals to us that ultimately the impractical idealists of yesterday become the practical realists of today. The cross reveals to us that what was a minority opinion yesterday becomes a majority opinion tomorrow, and the world forgets that it ever trampled over it because it rises up with new truth and new meaning and new beauty. This is what the cross tells us. It brings hope to us.

And so this morning, let us not be disillusioned. Let us not lose faith. So often we've been crucified. We've been buried in numerous graves—the grave of economic insecurity, the grave of exploitation, the grave of oppression. We've watched justice trampled over and truth crucified. But I'm here to tell you this morning, Easter reminds us that it won't be like that all the way. It reminds us that God has a light that can shine amid all of the darkness. And he can bring all of the light of day out of the darkness of the midnight.

I close with this little experience some weeks ago, about four Sundays ago. Mrs. King and I journeyed down to a city in India called Trivandrum. It is a city in the last state, the southernmost point of the country of India. And then we went from Trivandrum on down to a point known as Cape Comorin. This is the point where the land of India ends and the vast and rolling waters of the ocean have their beginning. It is one of the most beautiful points in all the world. The point where three great bodies of water meet together in all of their majestic splendor: the Bay of Bengal, the Arabian Sea, the Indian Ocean.

I remember that afternoon how we went out there and we took a seat on a rock that slightly protruded itself out into the waters, out into the ocean. We looked at the waves of these great bodies of water as they unfolded in almost rhythmic procession. Then we looked at the beautiful skies, all of their radiant beauty. Then we looked over at the sun, as it stood like a great cosmic ball of fire, it started setting. And you know at the setting of the sun you see that glowing fusion of colors

25. In 1920, President Wilson failed in his efforts to gain Senate approval for U.S. membership in the League of Nations. He died four years later. The United States joined the United Nations in 1945.

26. The Supreme Court's 1896 *Plessy v. Ferguson* (163 U.S. 537) decision upheld a Louisiana law mandating separate but equal accommodations for blacks and whites on intrastate railroads.

27. In 1954, the Supreme Court unanimously reversed the doctrine of "separate but equal" and declared racial segregation in public schools unconstitutional (*Brown v. Board of Education*).

so characteristic of the setting of the sun. We watched it. It went down. We were sitting there on that rock as the waves were beating upon it, looking at the sun. And that sun started going down and down, and it looked like it was sinking in the very ocean itself. Finally, it had passed away so that we couldn't see any more of the sun. It started getting a little dark and hazy about. Then, right at that moment, I turned around, and I said to Coretta, "But look, there is another light." It was the light of the moon over there in the East. And this was an interesting thing; this is, as I said, one of the most beautiful points in all the world. And this happened to be one of those days when the moon was full. And this is one of the few points in all the world that you can see the setting of the sun and the emergence of the moon simultaneously. And I looked at that, and something came to my mind that I had to share it, Coretta and Dr. Reddick and the other people who were accompanying us around at that point. I said to myself there is something in this that is an analogy to life.

So often we come to those points when it gets dark. It seems that the light of life is out. The sunlight of day moves out of our being and out the rest of our faith. We get disillusioned and confused and give up in despair. But if we will only look around we will discover that God has another light. And when we discover that, we need never walk in darkness. I've seen this so often in my own personal experience. For when it was dark and tragedy around, seemed that the light of day had gone out, darkness all around and sunlight passing away, I got enough strength in my being to turn around and only to discover that God had another light. This would be a tragic universe if God had only one light. But I came to see in a way that I'd never seen it before, that God has another light, a light that can guide you through the darkness of any midnight. Are you disillusioned this morning? Are you confused about life? Have you been disappointed? Have your highest dreams and hopes been buried? You about to give up in despair? I say to you, "Don't give up, because God has another light, and it is the light that can shine amid the darkness of a thousand midnights." This is what the cross tells us. It reminds us that when men put the sunlight out, that God has the light of the moon. And no matter how dark it gets, God is still around with all of his power. They put the light out on Good Friday, but God brought it back on on Easter morning. They've put the light out so many times in history. I've seen empires and kings and rulers put it out. But God has another light. Go into the valleys, through the hedges, and into the highways and tell men that God has another light. You can turn the light off, but he has another light to turn on. And then you will discover that He even turns that light on that went out again.

For I started thinking finally that that light which went down in India, went up in Montgomery, Alabama. The minute that the light was going out in India, the light of the sun is getting up in Montgomery because there is twelve hours difference in the time. And even that same light that will get up in Montgomery and go down, will be getting up in India again. You don't block God's lights. He manipulates and controls them. And we never need walk in darkness because God has a light for the night and a light for the day, and he controls both. This is our hope. This is what the Resurrection tells us. This is what Easter tells us. And this is what I found as I walked around that holy land and stood around that cross.

Be obedient, not only to the external written law but to that law written in your heart, obedient to the unenforceable. Not only that, be grateful to God for his love. And even then you can't repay it. Because when you survey that wondrous cross on which the prince of glory died, there is something that reminds you that your greatest gain you must count as loss and pour contempt on all your pride. And then even after that you find yourself saying, "Were the whole realm of nature mine, that were a present far too small. Love so amazing, so divine, demands my life, my all, and my all."[28] But not only that. Know that God has the universe in His hands. And because of that, segregation will die one day. Because of that, all of the lands of Africa will be free one day. Several years ago, forty years ago, only two of them were free—that was Liberia and Ethiopia. Today eight of them have been added, and in 1960 some more will be added—Nigeria, Togoland, the Cameroons, and Somalia.[29] And then I predict that fifteen years from now, all of them will be free, and there will not be a colonial power existing anywhere in this world. Why is all of that? It is because God holds the reins of the universe in His hands, and when the light goes out at one hour, it comes on at another with the power of His being. And this is the hope that can keep us going and keep us from getting frustrated as we walk along the way of life. Let us pray. O God our gracious [*recording interrupted*]

At. MLKJP-GAMK: T-17.

---

28. King paraphrases the first and last stanzas of Isaac Watts's hymn "When I Survey the Wondrous Cross" (1707).

29. In addition to the four King mentions, thirteen other African nations gained their independence in 1960: Benin, Burkina Faso, Central African Republic, Chad, Congo, Cote d'Ivoire, Democratic Republic of Congo, Gabon, Madagascar, Mali, Mauritania, Niger, and Senegal.

To James E. Bristol

30 March 1959
[*Montgomery, Ala.*]

King thanks Bristol for his assistance in India and describes his subsequent trip to the Middle East. Bristol replied on 16 April.

Mr. James Bristol
24 Rajpur Road
DELHI, INDIA

Dear Jim:

This is just a note to again express my appreciation to you for making our recent visit to India such a meaningful one. I will long remember the fellowship we enjoyed together. There is a word in Catholic theology called supererogation which means in substance, more than justice requires. Certainly, the hospitality which you and your family showered on our party and the detail work you did to keep

30 Mar 1959

things smooth and orderly were acts of supererogation. I am sure that I will never be able to repay you for all that you did for us. However, I do hope that we can return some of the courtesy. Our unostentacious home in Montgomery, Alabama is always open to you and your family. I do hope that you will come to see us.

As expected, we found that our work had accumulated tremendously at home. This means that we will have to play a game of catch up for the next few months. We found things going very well in the South and although the forces of resistance are still strong, things are happening every day to diminish the barriers to an integrated society.

Our stops in the Middle East proved to be most profitable and rewarding. While in Jerusalem we had an opportunity to talk with many people concerning the Arab Israeli problem. This, as you know, is still one of the most difficult problems of the world. We enjoyed Cairo with its ancient pyramids and Athens with its towering acropolis. Our flight from Athens to New York, with intermediate stops, was about twenty-five hours. So when we arrived at Idlewild Airport, we were just about exhausted. It took us about two or three days to get ourselves together. Now we are doing very well and back on the job.

Coretta and Larry [*Reddick*] send their best regards. We are now in the process of getting our pictures developed, after which we will have about three evening discussions in the community on India.[1] We are looking forward to this with great anticipation.

Please give our best regards to your lovely wife, Dorothy, and your charming daughters Tina and Leigh. We were all greatly impressed with your family, and I hope the friendship between your family and ours will grow over the years.

Very sincerely yours,
Martin L. King, Jr.

MLK:mlb

TLc. MLKP-MBU: Box 26.

---

1. In his 16 April reply, Bristol wrote that he was "glad to hear" that King had enjoyed his Middle Eastern travels and continued: "You should have a wonderful collection of pictures, and I am sure that your discussion evenings on India should be both pleasurable and profitable for your friends in Montgomery." The Kings and Reddick shared travel photos and reflections with the Dexter congregation on 16 April (Program, Sunday services, 12 April 1959).

Notes by Lawrence Dunbar Reddick on SCLC Administrative Committee Meetings on 2 April and 3 April 1959

[*April 1959*]

Upon King's return from India, he attended two administrative committee meetings in Montgomery during which the organization grappled with its financial troubles and lack of direction. The committee decided to fire executive director John Tilley immediately and possibly hire Bayard Rustin. The following notes by Reddick recount a discussion between King and Ella Baker in which "she gave him the devil for not spending more time with the SCLC." Reddick recalls telling King in India that "he must devote himself full time to Crusading and thus give up his church and all other means of assured income" but concludes that "he will never do this. . . . He will continue to be a crusader in a gray flannel suit."

I'll have to check the dates a little later but two meetings have been held in Martin's office that revealed developments that should be noted. The first meeting was the administrative committee of SCLC on the question of what to do about the present problems and future of that organization. Present were [*I. M.*] Augustine and [*James A.*] Smith from New Orleans, Lowry [*Joseph Lowery*] from Mobile, Sam Williams from Atlanta, [*Fred*] Shuttlesworth and the man who drove him down from Birmingham, Abernathy, King and myself. Abernathy was so late that he held up the meeting at least an hour. He did the same thing the following day. The out-of-town people wondered why he right here in Montgomery could not get to the meetings on time. There was a good joke that when the chariot came to take Abernathy and King to town it would have to pick them up on a delayed schedule. Martin didn't like this too much and protested that he was ready to start the meeting on time but that the people did not get there so that he could do so.

It was decided that the office would be cut down one half, letting Tilley and Miss Fisher, who was working with the Atlanta ~~Board of~~ Voter Registration Committee, go, retaining Miss Baker at a reduced salary and the girl in the office.[1]

Martin brought up the question of using Bayard Rustin. He praised him for his ability and his contacts. I pointed out the dangers of the "enemy" using his record to smear SCLC and that if we used him it should be done unofficially.[2] In praising R, King and Abernathy recalled that he brought $10.000 down with him during the bus boycott. Abernathy said that he was afraid for him with so much money. I need to find out who sent that money and what became of it because I believe

1. For more on Judith Fisher's work for SCLC, see King to Jesse Hill, Jr., 28 January 1959, pp. 114–115 in this volume. The office "girl" is probably Ernestine Brown.

2. Rustin had been involved in the Young Communist League during the 1930s. In 1953, he was arrested for homosexual activity in Pasadena, California. SCLC leaders also discussed Rustin's hiring at their fall meeting (see King, Recommendations to SCLC Committee on Future Program, 27 October 1959, pp. 315–318 in this volume).

that Pierce or Nixon told me that they were afraid to accept the money because it had a red taint.[3] Emory O. Jackson at this point or later attacked R as a communist though this is not true.[4]

In our first days meeting Sam Williams' assault upon Tilley, I felt was too much. I feel that Americans abuse each other more than is necessary. Martin reported that a member of Tilley's church in Baltimore had taken a shot after him. I wondered how a man as mild as Tilley could make someone so angry as to shoot at him.

We had ~~list~~ missed two pay days, each of two weeks and upon my recommendation worked out a budget covering all debts due and expected for the next two or three months and on the basis of that float alone. This I learned was done subsequently.

Shuttlesworth now seems to be a little mature but he is still impulsive, over active and fearless. To my surprise he is actually devoted to non-violence than Sam Williams. Sam says that if he catches anybody "monkeying around" his yard he's going to take his gun and leave some of him there. While Suttlesworth says that we need to get non-violence into our preachers because most of them don't really understand it. This he said on his own initiative and I think he means it.

On the second day Ella Baker came down to see King and both of them privately had asked me to sit in and since some of the committee members were still in town Martin asked them to sit in, too. I had given her some indication of the line that I was going to persue and had done the same with Martin.

She really came to lay him out and abuse him. She gave him the devil for not spending more time with the SCLC. I raised the question as to whether, honestly, the director and his staff of SCLC felt free to go ahead for we at the Atlanta Board Meeting had specifically given Tilley and Miss Baker a blank check.[5] We told them to make statements to the press and that we would back them up in whatever they did or said even if they made mistakes. Still [*strikeout illegible*] almost nothing came out in the papers. She put the blame for this on Tilley.

Next when she was telling King [*strikeout illegible*] that perhaps she spent too much time in speaking everywhere on every subject, he protested. When I said that possibly she meant that aside from speaking to raise money for SCLC or MIA that he should reserve his time for working with SCLC, he protested with a feeling of hurt. He said that an artist shoudl not be denied his means of expression. That he liked to preach and felt that he should do it. It was almost touching the way he said it and at that point I became convinced that he of himself does not have the [*toughness?*] to say no when these invitations flood in on him. He keeps saying that he wants an administrative assistance but as Miss Baker told him Roy Wilkins, A. Philip Randolph and all the other big shots have the same problem and they themselves have to decide to say no to most of the invitations they re-

3. James E. Pierce was a member of the MIA executive board, and E. D. Nixon was the group's first treasurer.

4. Jackson was the managing editor of the *Birmingham World*, Alabama's leading black newspaper.

5. Reddick likely refers to the 2–3 January meeting of the Committee on the Future Program of SCLC held at Ebenezer Baptist Church.

ceive; that nobody else but them can make that decision. I don't believe that Martin will be able to severly discipline himself this way.

Over seas when he raised the question with me I had said to him that either he must devote himself ~~to~~ full time to Crusading and thus give up his church and all other means of assured income and let his family and himself depend upon whatever people would do for him for his and their lively-hood. I know that he will never do this. ~~so~~ So M. L. K will never become a Vinoba Bhave.[6] He will continue to be a crusader in a gray flannel suit.

Now that Ella is in charge herself, she cannot put the blame on anybody. She will have to reduce. I believe that she has more ability [*than?*] Tilley but I wonder if she hasn't complained so long in life that it has become a habit with her. She, too, has a tendency to come ~~to~~ late to things and we'll see how she promotes the Mboya dinner, the Tallahassee Conference and whether she is able to get the sororities of Atlanta make sizable contributions.[7]

TD. LDRP-NN-Sc: Box 3.

6. Vinoba Bhave was widely considered to be Gandhi's spiritual successor. King met Vinoba on 2–3 March in India. For more on their meeting, see King, Farewell Statement for All India Radio, 9 March 1959, pp. 135–136 in this volume; see also Vinoba Bhave, "Dr. Martin Luther King with Vinoba," *Bhoodan* 3 (18 March 1959): 369–370.

7. Kenyan independence leader Tom Mboya addressed an SCLC-sponsored dinner in Atlanta on 13 May. In notes written following the event, Reddick mentioned that "in so far as I know no money has come in from the frats and sororities" (Reddick, "Mboya dinner at Atlanta," 14 May 1959; see also King, Remarks Delivered at Africa Freedom Dinner at Atlanta University, 13 May 1959, pp. 203–204 in this volume). For more on the Tallahassee Conference, see Statement Adopted at Spring Session of SCLC, 15 May 1959, pp. 205–208 in this volume.

To John Lee Tilley

3 April 1959
[*Montgomery, Ala.*]

With SCLC's Crusade for Citizenship stalled and its treasury overextended, King asks its first executive director to resign.[1] *Tilley complied on 13 April.*[2]

1. Tilley sent a letter to SCLC board members on 17 March in which he noted that "the success of our organization is being threatened by a rapidly dwindling bank account. . . . we are hard pressed, and will be greatly embarrassed, if further funds are not available from some source, immediately." SCLC treasurer Ralph Abernathy sent out a mass appeal for funds on the same day (Abernathy to Friend of freedom, 17 March 1959).

2. See pp. 182–184 in this volume. SCLC's associate director Ella Baker served as interim executive director until Wyatt Tee Walker of the Petersburg Improvement Association was hired to replace Tilley in mid-1960 (see King to Walker, 5 March 1960, pp.384–385 in this volume).

3 Apr 1959

Dr. John L. Tilley
2101 Whittier Street
Baltimore, Maryland

Dear Dr. Tilley:

In a meeting of the Administrative Committee of the Southern Christian Leadership Conference which was held on Thursday, April 2, in Montgomery, Alabama, several important matters were discussed which the Committee asked me to bring to your attention immediately.

First, the financial crisis confronting the organization was seriously analyzed. As you well know, our treasury is almost empty and we are now operating in the red.[3] In the last few months our disbursements have far exceeded our income. In order to assure the continued existence of the organization, we concluded that our budget must be cut immediately. This automatically means cutting the staff. I am sure that you can understand both the necessity and the wisdom of this.

Secondly, it was the feeling of the committee that the organization has not had a dynamic program commensurate with the amount of money that it is spending. It was also felt that the Executive Director had not been able to achieve the public response expected. We had hoped that our program would be well developed by now, and that the aims and purposes of the Southern Christian Leadership Conference would have been well established in the minds and hearts of the people all over the nation by this time. Of course, we were not unmindful of the factors that were probably responsible for this failure in implimentation. We were cognizant of the fact that your responsibilities as a pastor had to continue along with your work with us, and it was probably too much to expect the full implimentation of our program from a person who could only give part-time to it.[4]

In the light of the factors here enumerated, the Administrative Committee has instructed me to request your resignation to become effective April 15. We are certainly grateful to you for the work that you have given to our youthful organization. The fact that you were willing to take a partial leave from your church and come to us at a time when we were in desperate need of assistance is something that we will never forget. We hope that this move, which has been precipitated by our present crisis, will not in any way cause you to sever your interest and affection from our conference.[5]

In the next four or five days I will mail you a check for all that the organization owes you up through the fifteenth of April. If you feel that it is necessary, I will be very happy to discuss this matter with you.

---

3. SCLC's funds had dwindled to $163.75 and it owed over sixteen hundred dollars to Tilley and Baker (Abernathy, Financial report, 2 April 1959).

4. After becoming executive director of SCLC in 1958, Tilley continued to serve as part-time pastor of New Metropolitan Baptist Church in Baltimore.

5. King later suspected that Tilley may have contributed to an unfavorable article on SCLC that appeared in the October issue of *Jet* (see King to Theodore E. Brown, 19 October 1959, pp. 310–312 in this volume).

Yours very truly,
Martin L. King, Jr.

MLK:mlb

TLc. MLKP-MBU: Box 72.

To William Stuart Nelson

7 April 1959
[*Montgomery, Ala.*]

King asks Howard University dean William Stuart Nelson for reading material on the caste system in India. Nelson, an advocate of Gandhian nonviolence who had been in India just prior to King's visit, sent the requested material on 10 April. He added that the civil rights movement in the United States "is proving a source of great encouragement to and re-awakening of people in India . . . thereby serving the cause of nonviolence in the very country which has witnessed its most significant demonstration."[1]

Dr. William S. Nelson
Howard University
Washington, D.C.

Dear Dr. Nelson:

I trust that you are now settled down after your six month stay in India. We met many people in India who knew you and they never tired of mentioning your name in the most favorable manner.

In a real sense my visit to India was one of the most rewarding experiences of my life. While I would not be so rash as to pretend to know India after such a brief visit, I do feel that I gained many meaningful insights that will deepen my understanding of nonviolence, and also my commitment to it. I hope that we will have an opportunity to sit down and talk about the trip in the not-too-distant-future.

I am writing you mainly to inquire whether you have any books or pamphlets on untouchability. If so, I would like to borrow them for about two weeks. I am in the process of making a study of untouchability, and unfortunately, I left India without securing any material on it.[2] If you have such material, and can find it possible to mail it to me, I would be more than happy to reimburse you for the costs involved. And you can expect me to return it within two weeks.

---

1. King had hoped that Nelson would serve as his guide in India, but Nelson left the country before King arrived. Nelson did consult on some of the arrangements for King's visit before returning to Howard University (Stewart Meacham to King, 12 December 1958, and Bristol to Johnson, 24 December 1958).

2. In his travel account published in *Ebony,* King compared the caste system in India with American segregation (see King, "My Trip to the Land of Gandhi," July 1959, pp. 235–236 in this volume).

There is another matter that I would like to explore with you which I will be writing you about in a few days.[3]

With best wishes, and warm personal regards, I am

Very sincerely yours,
Martin L. King, Jr.

MLK:mlb

TLc. MLKP-MBU: Box 32A.

---

3. In a 24 April letter, King invited Nelson to participate in a nonviolent institute being planned by SCLC for July 1959. Nelson agreed to do so in a 30 April reply. For more on the institute, see Resolutions, First Southwide Institute on Nonviolent Resistance to Segregation held on 22 July–24 July 1959, 11 August 1959, pp. 261–262 in this volume.

From John Lee Tilley

13 April 1959
Atlanta, Ga.

Tilley resigns as executive director of SCLC in response to King's 3 April request. He calls his work with the organization a "privilege and pleasure" but suggests that "fear and apathy . . . in regard to voting, jealousies, and the attitude of competition on the part of many individuals and organizations," as well as a lack of sufficient funds and staffing, pose barriers to SCLC's success.

Dr. Martin Luther King, Jr.
309 South Jackson Street
Montgomery, Alabama

Dear Dr. King:

In April of 1958, the Southern Christian Leadership Conference invited me to become its Executive Director.[1] I was, at the time, serving as pastor of the New Metropolitan Baptist Church of Baltimore, Maryland. I stated that I could consider the position, only on the condition that I might serve on a part-time basis; continuing to serve the church also, part-time. It was agreed by both the Executive Board, and myself that this relationship would be temporary.

Upon my request, the New Metropolitan Baptist Church granted me a part-time

---

1. Tilley met with SCLC's personnel committee in Atlanta on 29 April 1958 and was likely offered the executive director post at that time; formal confirmation followed shortly thereafter (Baker to King, 24 April 1958 and 9 May 1958, and King, Draft, Letter to John Lee Tilley, 9 May 1958).

leave of absence to serve S.C.L.C., despite the hardship which this arrangement would impose upon the church. So great was the concern of the membership of the church in the program and objectives of S.C.L.C., a trial period of three months was agreed upon, and was later extended.

Before giving my answer to S.C.L.C. officials regarding accepting the position offered, the Baltimore Branch of the NAACP, and Mr. Carl Murphy, president of Afro-American Newspaper, asked me to accept a position to promote voter-registration, and train persons in citizenship, in Baltimore, and the State of Maryland. This meant a continuation, on a more intensive basis, work in which I had been engaged. Although the salary offered was the same as that offered by S.C.L.C., and I could have remained at home and avoided the inconveniences and expense of living away from home, so intense was my concern and interest for the problems of Negroes in the deep South, and the challenge which S.C.L.C. presented, that I felt obligated to do what I could.

I agreed to relieve the church of financial obligations, to me, except the equivalent to the cost of my transportation to and from Atlanta. It was necessary for someone to serve in my absence. I, therefore, accepted the offer to serve as Executive Director of S.C.L.C. on a part-time basis, for a limited time. I agreed, also, to give from two-thirds to three-fourths of my time to S.C.L.C., and I have given more than three-fourths or three weeks or more per month.

During the fall of 1958, I presented my resignation to the church in order that I might give full time to the work of S.C.L.C., with no suggestion of additional salary. The church almost unaminously voted not to accept my resignation. The church asked me to propose such plans as would enable me to continue my relationship with them, even if it necessitated giving them less time, rather than sever the relationship.

In recent months, evidence of the need of the church for me to give more time than I am giving, have been apparent. At the same time, the demands of S.C.L.C. for more concentrated work, are evident. There is naturally an increased taxation upon my energies and time. This poses a problem which I had hoped to discuss with you at the first opportunity after your return from India.

For the period of approximately ten and one half (10 1/2) months that it has been my privilege and pleasure to serve and be associated with S.C.L.C., some progress has been made toward its goals. However, much remains to be achieved.

Fear and apathy on the part of the great majority of Negroes in the South in regard to voting, jealousies, and the attitude of competition on the part of many individuals and organizations, the unwillingness of many people to accept and support a new social action organization, the lack of the dramatic appeal which voting and the philosophy of non-violence present, the limited staff for the many varied demands, the non-spectacular nature of the educational process, and the lack of funds, are some factors that must be considered in working successfully to realize the goals of S.C.L.C. Like a farmer clearing a forest to plant his crops, or an engineer clearing the land and laying a foundation to construct a skyscraper building, builders of education and social action organizations such as S.C.L.C., require considerable time in laying a foundation for their work.

S.C.L.C. has the philosophy, the organizational pattern and approach which will ultimately deal effectively with the basic problems of voting and resistance to segregation, but the process will be gradual, and will require time and patience.

15 Apr 1959

As you stated in your letter of April 3rd, the present status of the treasury is such, that a drastic cut in the budget, is necessary, and that the staff must be reduced. In the light of the budgetary situation, and the necessity for me to give more time to my church, I present my resignation as Executive Director, to become effective as of April 15th.

If it is your desire, at any time, that I serve S.C.L.C. in any way, such as field work in conducting a voter-registration program, or assist in clinics or workshops, or make any contacts in your behalf, feel free to call upon me.

The experience of working with you has been a pleasant and profitable one.

Respectfully yours,
[*signed*]
John L. Tilley

JLT/eb

TLS. MLKP-MBU: Box 72.

To Branch Rickey

15 April 1959
[*Montgomery, Ala.*]

King thanks baseball executive Branch Rickey, who in an earlier letter had praised Stride Toward Freedom *as a "Christ-like document from beginning to end."*[1] *Rickey replied to King on 18 June: "I am down-right proud to have a corresponding acquaintanceship with you."*

Mr. [*Branch?*] Rickey
Silver Springs Farm
Old Mill Road
Pittsburgh 38, Pennsylvania

Dear Mr. Rickey:

On returning to the country, I found your very kind letter of January 28, on my desk. Words are inadequate for me to express my appreciation to you for your encouraging words concerning my book, Stride Toward Freedom. This book is simply my humble attempt to bring Christian principles to bear on the difficult

1. Rickey to King, 28 January 1959. Wesley Branch Rickey (1881–1965), born in Stockdale, Ohio, graduated from Ohio Wesleyan University (1904) and the University of Michigan Law School (1911). Beginning in 1905, Rickey worked for several professional baseball teams in a variety of capacities, among them player, scout, and general manager. As general manager of the Brooklyn Dodgers, Rickey signed Jackie Robinson to one of the organization's minor-league teams in 1945. Two years later Robinson was promoted to the Dodgers, thus integrating major league baseball.

problem of racial injustice which confronts our nation. I am happy to know that you found it helpful. 17 Apr 1959

May I say in passing that I have long had a tremendous admiration for you. Your dedicated spirit, your humanitarian concern, and your unswerving devotion to the principles of freedom and justice for all men will remain an inspiration to generations yet unborn. I do hope that in the not-too-distant future we will get a chance to meet personally and talk over some of the issues that are close to our hearts.[2]

With best wishes and warm personal regards, I am

Sincerely yours,
Martin L. King, Jr.

MLK:mlb

TLc. MLKP-MBU: Box 68.

---

2. King and Rickey probably met at a 19 June 1960 "Freedom Jubilee" in Pittsburgh, where both men received plaques for their contributions "to the cause of world-wide freedom" (Central Baptist Church, Program, "Tri-State's Freedom Jubilee," 19 June 1960).

To Kwame Nkrumah

17 April 1959
[*Montgomery, Ala.*]

King thanks Ghana's prime minister for the courtesies he extended during the Ghanaian independence celebrations in March 1957.[1]

Dr. Kwame Nkrumah, Prime Minister
Ghana
ACCRA, GHANA

Dear Dr. Nkrumah:

I have been intending to write you ever since I left Ghana in 1957 after having a most rewarding experience at your independence celebration. Words are inadequate for me to express my appreciation to you for the hospitality that you extended to me and my wife. It was most gracious of you to take time out of your extremely busy schedule and receive us for lunch at your residence. These things will remain in my thoughts so long as the cords of memory shall lengthen.

---

1. King sent a similar letter to Ghana's finance minister (see King to K. A. Gbedemah, 4 May 1959, pp. 194–195 in this volume). For more information about King's trip to Ghana, see Introduction in *Papers* 4:7–9.

Since that time I have watched you and the growth of your nation with great pride. I am sorry that I was in Mexico last summer when you were in the United States and did not have an opportunity to attend any of the affairs in your honor.[2] I have just returned to the United States from India and I was more than delighted to learn from Prime Minister Nehru and many others that you had been in India a month or so earlier and that your impact on the Indian people was tremendous.

I am sending you, under separate cover, a copy of my book, Stride Toward Freedom, which was published a few months ago. It is an account of our bus boycott in Montgomery, Alabama and also an exposition of my philosophical and theological convictions on nonviolence.

I certainly hope that our paths will cross again in the not-too-distant future. If I come to Nigeria next year for the independence celebration, I will certainly plan to stop by Ghana.[3]

Very sincerely yours,
Martin Luther King, Jr.

MLK:mlb
(Dictated, but not personally signed by Dr. King.)

TLc. MLKP-MBU: Box 26.

---

2. On the eve of an NAACP-sponsored dinner in Nkrumah's honor, King cabled his regrets from Mexico City, where he was vacationing (King to Roy Wilkins, 28 July 1958; see also American Committee on Africa, NAACP, and National Urban League, Invitation, Dinner in honor of Kwame Nkrumah, July 1958).

3. On 16 November 1960, King attended the inauguration of Nnamdi Azikiwe as governor-general and commander-in-chief of Nigeria (see Azikiwe to King, 26 October 1960, pp. 533–534 in this volume). Leaving Nigeria on 18 November, King had planned a seven-hour stopover in Accra (Itinerary for Martin Luther King, Jr., 9 November–19 November 1960). Although the *Atlanta Daily World* suggested that King would spend a day with Nkrumah on his way home, it is unclear whether or not this occurred ("Dr. King Will Visit Nigeria Next Week," *Atlanta Daily World,* 11 November 1960).

Address at the Youth March for Integrated Schools on 18 April 1959

Washington, D.C.

Almost six months after the first Youth March for Integrated Schools, King addresses some twenty-six thousand people at the Sylvan Theater on the grounds of the Washington Monument.[1] *This effort, spearheaded by A. Philip Randolph and coordinated by*

---

1. King's stabbing had prevented him from addressing the 1958 Youth March in person (see King, Address at Youth March, Delivered by Coretta Scott King, 25 October 1958, in *Papers* 4:514–515).

Bayard Rustin, drew support from a wide array of religious, civil rights, peace, and labor leaders.[2] *The program at the Washington Monument followed the presentation of petitions to the president and Congress calling for the "orderly and speedy" integration of schools.*[3] *In his remarks at the event's conclusion, King urges the young people to "make a career of humanity. . . . you will make a greater person of yourself, a greater Nation of your country and a finer world to live in."*[4] *This speech was published in the* Congressional Record.[5]

As I stand here and look out upon the thousands of Negro faces, and the thousands of white faces, intermingled like the waters of a river, I see only one face—the face of the future.

Yes, as I gaze upon this great historic assembly, this unprecedented gathering of young people, I cannot help thinking—that a hundred years from now the historians will be calling this not the "beat" generation, but the generation of integration.[6]

The fact that thousands of you came here to Washington and that thousands more signed your petition proves that this generation will not take "No" for an answer—will not take double talk for an answer—will not take gradualism for an answer.[7] It proves that the only answer you will settle for is—total desegregation and total equality—now.

I know of no words eloquent enough to express the deep meaning, the great

2. Two days before this event, FBI director J. Edgar Hoover forwarded a confidential report to an Eisenhower aide alleging Communist connections to the Youth March (Hoover to Gordon Gray, 16 April 1959, and FBI, "Youth March on Washington," 16 April 1959). On the eve of the march, chairmen King, Wilkins, and Randolph issued a statement stressing that "the sponsors of the March have not invited Communists or communist organizations" (Youth March for Integrated Schools, "Anti-American groups not invited to Youth March for Integrated Schools," 17 April 1959).

3. The students at the first march were turned away by a guard at the White House gate, but the interracial delegation bearing the 1959 petitions met with deputy presidential assistant Gerald D. Morgan (Associated Negro Press, Press release, 20 April 1959; see also Youth March for Integrated Schools, "A petition for integrated schools to the President and the Congress of the U.S.," January 1959). Eisenhower was vacationing in Georgia the day of the 1959 demonstration.

4. Also addressing the crowd were AFL-CIO civil rights chair Charles Zimmerman, NAACP executive secretary Roy Wilkins, and Kenyan nationalist leader Tom Mboya (Youth March for Integrated Schools, "Program at the Sylvan Theater," 18 April 1959).

5. Michigan congressman Charles Diggs submitted King's address and several other Youth March documents for publication in the *Congressional Record;* Georgia congressman E. L. Forrester had earlier inserted material into the *Record,* implying a link between the Youth March and the Communist Party (*Congressional Record* 105 [20 April 1959]: 6352–6353).

6. The term "Beat," coined by writer Jack Kerouac and popularized by John Clellon Holmes's 16 November 1952 article "This Is the Beat Generation" in the *New York Times Magazine,* labeled a social and literary movement that rejected the conventional values of postwar America in favor of a defiant and celebratory individualism. Coretta Scott King referred to the Beats when she delivered remarks on King's behalf at the 1958 Youth March (see *Papers* 4:514–515).

7. In a form letter that was circulated with the petition, the Youth March was hailed as "the only major social action project that is contributing to the development of a youth movement that may yet embrace many other areas of social concern" (King, Ruth H. Bunche, and Bayard Rustin, Form letter to Friend, March 1959).

18 Apr 1959

power, and the unconquerable spirit back of this inspiringly original, uniquely American march of young people. Nothing like it has ever happened in the history of our Nation. Nothing, that is, except the last youth march. What this march demonstrates to me, above all else, is that you young people, through your own experience, have somehow discovered the central fact of American life—that the extension of democracy for all Americans depends upon complete integration of Negro Americans.

By coming here you have shown yourselves to be highly alert, highly responsible young citizens. And very soon the area of your responsibility will increase, for you will begin to exercise your greatest privilege as an American—the right to vote. Of course, you will have no difficulty exercising this privilege—if you are white.

But I wonder if you can understand what it feels like to be a Negro, living in the South, where, by attempting to exercise this right, you may be taking your life in your hands.

The denial of the vote not only deprives the Negro of his constitutional rights—but what is even worse—it degrades him as a human being. And yet, even this degradation, which is only one of many humiliations of everyday life, is losing its ability to degrade. For the southern Negro is learning to transform his degradation into resistance. Nonviolent resistance. And by so doing he is not only achieving his dignity as a human being, he is helping to advance democracy in the South. This is why my colleagues and I in the Southern Leadership Conference are giving our major attention to the campaign to increase the registration of Negro voters in the South to 3 million. Do you realize what would happen in this country if we were to gain 3 million southern Negro votes? We could change the composition of Congress. We could have a Congress far more responsive to the voters' will. We could have all schools integrated—north and south. A new era would open to all Americans. Thus, the Negro, in his struggle to secure his own rights is destined to enlarge democracy for all people, in both a political and a social sense.

Indeed in your great movement to organize a march for integrated schools you have actually accomplished much more. You have awakened on hundreds of campuses throughout the land a new spirit of social inquiry to the benefit of all Americans.

This is really a noble cause. As June approaches, with its graduation ceremonies and speeches, a thought suggests itself. You will hear much about careers, security, and prosperity. I will leave the discussion of such matters to your deans, your principals, and your valedictorians. But I do have a graduation thought to pass along to you. Whatever career you may choose for yourself—doctor, lawyer, teacher—let me propose an avocation to be pursued along with it. Become a dedicated fighter for civil rights. Make it a central part of your life.

It will make you a better doctor, a better lawyer, a better teacher. It will enrich your spirit as nothing else possibly can. It will give you that rare sense of nobility that can only spring from love and selflessly helping your fellow man. Make a career of humanity. Commit yourself to the noble struggle for equal rights. You will make a greater person of yourself, a greater Nation of your country, and a finer world to live in.

 PD. *Congressional Record* 105 (1959): 8696–8697.

From Fred L. Shuttlesworth

24 April 1959
Birmingham, Ala.

Birmingham's leading civil rights advocate reiterates his desire for more concrete action in response to southern intransigence: "I have often stated that when the flowery speeches have been made, we still have the hard job of getting down and helping people to work to reach the idealistic state of human affairs which we desire."[1]

Dear Martin,

I am writing you this letter because I feel that the leadership in Alabama among Negroes is, at this time, much less dynamic and imaginative than it ought be. More than this, there have been several serious incidents of beatings and kidnappings in the last few days; plus the fact that very much publicity is being given by our governor and the legislative forces to the forthcoming batch of segregation bills; and nothing has been said or done by us as leaders together to protest on an organized basis or to make Negroes who follow us believe that we are watching carefully these tactics, and making plans to meet them.[2]

I am sure that none know, more than you of my desire to cooperate fully with all areas in Alabama that are putting any kind of fight at all for Civil Rights. Surely you know of how I have plugged over and over again in our meetings for some type of set up so that we could make organized protests and take organized actions when something happens in our state. To date this has not been done, nor does there seem to be any way of getting the leaders of movements in Alabama together to such an extent. But I believe that time is running out for this thing to be done.

1. For similar correspondence, see Shuttlesworth to King, 27 July 1957, in *Papers* 4:240–241; see also Shuttlesworth to King, 15 June 1959.

2. On 10 April, civil rights worker Charles Billups and two other black men were taken to a wooded area in Birmingham where they were robbed and beaten by at least three white men ("Three Negroes Said Robbed, Beaten Here," *Birmingham News*, 10 April 1959). On 13 April, the U.S. Department of Justice denied Shuttlesworth's request for an investigation ("Robbed, Beaten Minister Home from Hospital," *Birmingham World*, 18 April 1959). The following week, African American activist O'Hara M. Prewitt was abducted and beaten in Tuscaloosa, Alabama, allegedly by Ku Klux Klan and White Citizens' Council members ("Push Probe of Alabama Attack," *Birmingham World*, 22 April 1959).

Shuttlesworth also refers to several recent proposals aimed at strengthening Alabama's segregation laws. These included provisions to grant full control of public education to the states, to dispose of voter applicant rejection records within thirty days, to keep voter registration records away from federal investigators, and to "create a standby legislative committee to watch racial developments in heavily Negro populated Macon County" (Hugh W. Sparrow, "Bills Offered to Tighten Laws on Segregation," *Birmingham News*, 1 February 1959). A few days before Shuttlesworth wrote this letter, the *Birmingham News* reported on a bill being drafted to "give state and local authorities ample power to crack down on racial agitators" by requiring persons "agitating for boycotts or otherwise endeavoring to provoke a breach of the peace" to reveal their supporters (Hugh W. Sparrow, "Bill Would Hold New Club over Race Agitators," *Birmingham News*, 19 April 1959).

Neither have I any doubt that conferences once in a while without positive action to follow will help us to reach the goal we are seeking. And I have often stated that when the flowery speeches have been made, we still have the hard job of getting down and helping people to work to reach the idealistic state of human affairs which we desire. Even in our Southern Christian Leadership Conference, I believe we must move now, or else the hard put in the not too distant future, to justice our existence. Thus, I hope that our forthcoming gathering in Talahasse on May 13–14 will be the best, and that we can really lay some positive plans for action.[3] Events of the past few days—actions named above and Appellate dismissal on technicalities of our bus appeal make me believe that now is the time for serious thinking and practical resulting actions.[4]

Sincerely yours,
[*signed*]
Fred

TLS. MLKP-MBU: Box 71.

---

3. For more on SCLC's Tallahassee meeting, see Statement Adopted at Spring Session of SCLC, 15 May 1959, pp. 205–208 in this volume.

4. On 25 April, the Alabama Court of Appeals in Montgomery refused to review the appeal of Shuttlesworth and twelve other demonstrators arrested in Birmingham for an October 1958 bus integration protest. Shuttlesworth and J. S. Phifer received fines and jail sentences of ninety and sixty days, respectively, for disorderly conduct; the other protesters received fines. Shuttlesworth and Phifer were freed on appeal bonds after serving five days in jail ("Negro Clerics Freed," *New York Times,* 29 October 1958, and "Shuttlesworth, Other Leaders Denied Review," *Birmingham World,* 29 April 1959).

To James P. Coleman

25 April 1959
Montgomery, Ala.

King protests the lynching of Mack Charles Parker in Poplarville, Mississippi.[1] *Mississippi governor James P. Coleman replied rapidly, assuring King that "every possible effort" was being made to find the perpetrators.*[2] *King also wired Attorney General William P. Rogers, seeking federal intervention.*[3]

---

1. Parker, an African American, was abducted from the local jail late in the night of 24 April, just hours after his arrest for the alleged kidnapping and rape of a white woman. His body was found ten days later in the Pearl River, near the Louisiana border. Though the FBI conducted an extensive investigation, two grand juries failed to charge anyone with Parker's murder.

2. Coleman to King, 25 April 1959. King and the governor had first corresponded during the Montgomery bus boycott, when Coleman requested that King not appear at a public rally in Mississippi (see Coleman to King, 23 April 1956, and King to Coleman, 24 April 1956, in *Papers* 3:220 and 221, respectively; see also King to Coleman, 7 June 1958, in *Papers* 4:419–420).

3. King to Rogers, 25 April 1959. In a 15 May report to the SCLC executive board, Ella Baker noted that Eisenhower was also sent a telegram protesting the lynching; neither this telegram nor any

GOVERNOR COLEMAN=
JACKSON MISS=

28 Apr 1959

NEWS REPORTS ETATE THAT A YOUNG NEGRO, CHARLES PARKER, AGE 23, WAS ABDUCTED FROM JAIL IN POPLARVILLE, MISSISSIPPI EARLY SATURDAY MORNING BY A HOODED GROUP OF MEN WHO WORE GLOVES TO AVOID FINER PRINTS. A TRAIL OF BLOOD FROM THE JAIL TO THE CURB IS ALLEDGEDLY ALL THE EVIDENCE OF WHAT MIGHT HAVE HAPPENED TO YOUNG PARKER. HE NOR HIS BODY HAS BEEN FOUND. THIS APPARENT LYNCHING SHOCKINGLY DEMONSTRATES AGAIN THE ALL-TOO-FEQUENT FAILURE OF SOUTHERN LAW OFFICERS TO PROVIDE " EQUAL PROTECTION OF THE LAW" FOR NEGROES IN THEIR CUSTODY. ALTHOUGH PARKER WAS CHARGED WITH RAPE, NO JAILER WAS ON DUTY LAST NIGHT. IT IS UNTHINKABLE THAT ANY LAW OFFICER CONCERNED WITH THE SAFETY OF HIS PRISONER WOULD HAVE LEFT A NEGRO CHARGED WITH RAPE OF A WHITE WOMAN IN AN UNGUARDED JAIL IN ANY SOUTHERN TOWN AND IN MISSISSIPPI IN PARTICULAR. IT WOULD ALMOST APPEAR THAT MOB ACTION WAS BEING INVITED. WE STRONGLY URGE YOU TO USE ALL OF THE CONSTITUTIONAL RESOURCES AT YOUR DISPOSAL TO INVESTIGATE THIS OUTRAGEOUS DEED AND BRING THOSE WHO COMMITTED IT TO THE BAR OF JUSTICE–

MARTIN LUTHER KING JR PRESIDENT THE SOUTHERN CHRISTIAN LEADERSHIP CONFERENCE–

PWSr. JPCP-Ms-Ar.

---

response from the president has been located. However, in what may have been a draft of the wire to Eisenhower, King noted the damage this incident would do to America's international prestige and called for "forthright federal civil rights legislation" (King, Statement on apparent lynching of Mack Charles Parker, 25 April 1959).

Interview on "Front Page Challenge"

[*28 April 1959*]
[*Toronto, Canada*]

On a popular Canadian television quiz show and interview program, King distinguishes between legal desegregation, which he believes may be achieved in "ten or fifteen years," and "genuine, inter-group, interpersonal living," which will take much longer. Appearing as a mystery guest, King was hidden from the panel, who attempted to guess his identity before this interview took place.[1] *This*

---

1. Stanley Levison had helped arrange the appearance (see note 4 to Levison to King, 8 January 1959, p. 104 in this volume). Soon after its premiere in the summer of 1957, the Canadian Broadcasting Corporation's "Front Page Challenge" became Canada's most popular television program. James L. Gray, president of Atomic Energy of Canada, appeared in the first half of the 28 April program.

transcript was taken from Canadian Broadcasting Company film footage of the program.

[*Fred Davis*]:[2] Tonight, "Front Page Challenge" welcomes, in person, Reverend Martin Luther King. [*applause*]

[*Toby Robins*]:[3] Dr. King, if you were in charge of rectifying this situation, what decisions would you make? How can we best rectify the whole problem of segregation?

[*King*]: Well, I think it will entail many forces working together. There isn't one answer or one force that will solve the problem. I think it will, it means that the federal government will have to do a great deal in taking a positive, forthright stand. The moderates of the white South will have to become more courageous and positive in their stands, and liberals all over the country. And, I think, the church, religious organizations have a great deal to do in this period of transition. And the attitude of the Negro himself. He must be firm. He must work continuously for first-class citizenship, but certainly he must not use second-class methods to gain it. I think the methods are very important in thinking in terms of the end.

[*Robins*]: Well, what do you mean by "second-class methods?"

[*King*]: Well, I would think of violence as a second-class method. I would think of hatred as a second-class method. It seems to me that it is possible to move on toward the goal of justice with wise restraint and calm reasonableness, not compromising principles and never capitulating to the whims and caprices of the guardians of the deadening status quo, but at the same time, maintaining a positive attitude of goodwill.

[*Frank Tumpane*]:[4] Dr. King, how long do you think it will be before the Negro in the southern states attains racial equality? Social equality?

[*King*]: Well, I would have to make a distinction here between desegregation and integration. Now, on the question of desegregation, I think within ten or fifteen years we will achieve desegregation. We will break down the legal barriers in almost all areas, except in the most remote situations. Now, when we think in terms of integration, which is genuine, inter-group, interpersonal living, that will take longer. I think, however, before the turn of the century we will have moved a great deal toward an integrated society.

[*Tumpane*]: Do you believe, Dr. King, that racial and religious prejudice, generally speaking, feeds on ignorance?

[*King*]: Well, I think so. I think this is certainly a . . . .

---

2. Fred Davis was the host of "Front Page Challenge" from its inception in 1957 until it was canceled in 1995.

3. Canadian actress Toby Robins was a panelist on the show from 1957 until 1961.

4. *Toronto Telegram* columnist Francis M. Tumpane appeared as the program's guest panelist.

[*Tumpane*]: Ignorance on both sides, I mean.

[*King*]: Pardon?

[*Tumpane*]: Ignorance on both sides.

[*King*]: Yes, yes, I think so.

[*Pierre Berton*]:[5] Dr. King, you mentioned the church's role in this. Some of the churches in the South are still segregated, aren't they?

[*King*]: Oh yes, by and large, the churches in the South are segregated.

[*Berton*]: How can they preach the Christian religion and segregate people? This must seem ironic to you as a minister yourself.

[*King*]: Yes, it is, but this is a perennial problem. This whole problem of the gulf or the gap between our profession and our practice.

[*Berton*]: Billy Graham changed his mind on this thing, didn't he?

[*King*]: Yes, he has taken, in recent years, a very active, I mean, a very strong stand against segregation. There was a time that he would even preach before segregated audiences. But now he refuses to preach to any audience that is segregated, which, I think, is a marvelous step.[6]

[*Berton*]: Am I right in suspecting there's a large body of the white South who do not raise their voice but who have more liberal views than we get in Canada from the newspaper reports?

[*King*]: Oh yes, I think you're quite right. I'm convinced that there are many more moderates and people of goodwill in the white South than we are able to see on the surface. But they are afraid to speak out today—the fear of social, political, and economic reprisals.

[*Gordon Sinclair*]:[7] Dr. King, you recently visited India and had talks with Mr. Nehru, and tonight you tell us it's useful and desirable that there should be no violence in your cause. Did you get these ideas from Mahatma Gandhi?

[*King*]: Yes, I would say from Mahatma Gandhi and Jesus. My whole Christian background had a great deal to do with my coming to this conclusion that love and nonviolence should be the regulating ideals in any struggle for human dignity. And, along with this, I read Mahatma Gandhi in my student days and got a great deal from him.

[*Sinclair*]: This last visit to India, did you discuss these things with Mr. Nehru?

[*King*]: Yes, I did.

[*Sinclair*]: Is he a nonviolent type also?

[*King*]: Yes, he was. He followed Gandhi quite closely through the independence struggle, and he believed in the way of nonviolence, certainly in that par-

5. Canadian columnist and commentator Pierre Berton was a panelist for the show's entire run.

6. King had delivered an invocation at one of evangelist Billy Graham's 1957 campaigns in New York City (King, Invocation Delivered at Billy Graham Evangelistic Association Crusade, 18 July 1957, in *Papers* 4:238).

7. Gordon Sinclair, a reporter with the *Toronto Daily Star* and a radio personality, appeared regularly on "Front Page Challenge" until his death in 1984.

ticular instance. Mr. Nehru would say that violence would have been both immoral and impractical in their struggle in India. Now, I think he would make some difference when it comes to the question of international relations. Gandhi believed in absolute nonviolence in all situations; when I think Nehru would believe in it in internal situations within nations, but when it comes to international conflicts, then he believes that a nation has to maintain an army.

[*Davis*]: Thank you. Dr. King, I'm sorry to interrupt, but our time is running out. We thank you very much, and may we wish you continued success in your most worthwhile endeavors. Thank you for coming to the program. [*applause*]

F. CaOTBC.

To K. A. Gbedemah

4 May 1959
[*Montgomery, Ala.*]

King thanks Ghana's finance minister for his hospitality during the March 1957 Ghanaian independence ceremonies and laments Gbedemah's encounter with segregation during a visit to the United States. He also promises to send him a copy of Stride Toward Freedom. *In his 3 August reply, Gbedemah indicated that he had received the book and planned to read it during an upcoming holiday.*

Mr. K. A. Gbedemah
Minister of Finance
GHANA

Dear Mr. Gbedemah:

I have been intending to write you ever since I left Ghana in 1957 after having a most rewarding experience in your country during the Independence Celebration. Words are inadequate to express my appreciation to you for the personal courtesies that you extended to me and my wife. It was certainly gracious of you to take time out of your extremely busy schedule to entertain us in your lovely home. All of these things will remain in our thoughts so long as the cords of memory shall lengthen.

I am sorry that I missed seeing you when you were in the United States last year. I am also sorry that you faced such a humiliating experience in our country. But in spite of the odious effects of that experience, I think that it helped in the sense that it served to dramatize the absurdity of the whole system of segregation. The fact that the President hastily invited you to the White House reveals that America is now more sensitive to the rolling tide of world opinion than ever before.[1]

---

1. In October 1957, Eisenhower hosted a breakfast for Gbedemah after the African leader had been denied service at a Howard Johnson restaurant in Dover, Delaware (W. H. Lawrence, "Ghanan Is Served White House Meal," *New York Times*, 11 October 1957).

I am deeply grateful to you for sending me a telegram when I was in Harlem Hospital a few months ago. Your encouraging words came as a great spiritual lift to me.[2] I am happy to say that I am doing very well now and have about recovered completely. As you well know, in this struggle for freedom and human dignity we must be prepared for sacrifices and suffering at all levels. Therefore, I am still moving on in the struggle with the conviction that unearned suffering is redemptive. 4 May 1959

I am sending you under separate cover a copy of my book, <u>Stride Toward Freedom</u>. It was published a few months ago. It is a rather detailed account of our bus boycott here in Alabama and also an exposition of my philosophical and theological thinking on nonviolent resistance. I know that your schedule is extremely heavy, but if you have time to read it, I hope you will find it helpful. Since I only have a limited number of extra copies, I hope you can let our friend, Bill Sutherland read it.[3]

Please give my best regards to Bill and tell him that I will be writing him in the not too distant future. Also extend my best wishes to Mrs. [*Adelaide Plange*] Gbedemah.

Very sincerely yours,
Martin Luther King, Jr.

TLc. MLKP-MBU: Box 26.

---

2. Gbedemah wrote that he was "shocked" by King's near-fatal stabbing and extended his "best wishes for speedy recovery" (Gbedemah to King, [illegible] September 1958).

3. African American pacifist William Sutherland was Gbedemah's secretary and had helped with arrangements for King's visit to Ghana.

To Clifford C. Taylor

5 May 1959
Atlanta, Ga.

On 2 May, a nineteen-year-old student at Florida A&M University was abducted while on a double date and raped by four white men. Students staged demonstrations and a one-day classroom boycott, which ended when officials announced that a grand jury would consider charges against the men who had confessed to the crime.[1] *In the following telegram to the student body president, King applauds the students' "courageous, dignified and effective demonstration."*[2] *At the bottom of this copy of the telegram, Ella Baker added the following: "We will write Mr. Taylor a note, inviting him and other students to participate in our Tallahassee Conference. EJB."*[3]

Mr. CLIFFORD TAYLOR
President, Student Body
Florida A & M University
Tallahassee, Fla.

THE SOUTHERN CHRISTIAN LEADERSHIP CONFERENCE COMMENDS YOU AND YOUR FELLOW STUDENTS FOR YOUR COURAGEOUS, DIGNIFIED AND EFFECTIVE DEMONSTRATION, PROTESTING THE MASS RAPE OF YOUR SCHOOLMATE AND WARNING AGAINST "DOUBLE STANDARDS OF JUSTICE".[4] YOUR DETERMINED BUT NON-VIOLENT DEMANDS CERTAINLY ADDED [*strikeout illegible*] VIGOR TO THE PROSECUTION OF THE CASE AND HAVE GIVEN NEW HOPE TO ALL OF US WHO STRUGGLE FOR HUMAN DIGNITY AND EQUAL JUSTICE. GOD BLESS ALL OF YOU.

REV. MARTIN LUTHER KING, JR.
PRESIDENT
SOUTHERN CHRISTIAN LEADERSHIP CONFERENCE, Inc.
208 Auburn Avenue, N.E.
Atlanta, Ga.

TWc. MLKP-MBU: Box 70.

---

1. "A&M Student Strike Ends; Jury Recalled," *St. Petersburg Times,* 5 May 1959, and "Leon Grand Jury Meets Tomorrow," *Tallahassee Democrat,* 5 May 1959.

2. In a telegram to Florida governor Leroy Collins two days earlier, SCLC associate director Baker noted that "with memories of Negroes who have been lynched and executed on far less evidence, Negro leaders from all over the South will certainly examine every development in this case. . . . What will Florida's answer be?" In Collins's 4 June reply he explained to Baker that "all judicial processes have proceeded efficiently and expeditiously." The four white men, who ranged in age from sixteen to twenty-four, received life sentences for the rape (Hallie Boyles, "Life Sentences Given to All 4 Youths for Rape," *Tallahassee Democrat,* 22 June 1959).

3. For more on the Tallahassee conference, see Statement Adopted at Spring Session of SCLC, 15 May 1959, pp. 205–208 in this volume.

4. Student protesters carried signs demanding that "double standards of justice must be eliminated" ("Negroes Ask Justice for Co-Ed Rapists," *Atlanta Constitution,* 4 May 1959).

Address at the Religious Leaders Conference on 11 May 1959

Washington, D.C.

In a 17 April 1959 letter, Vice President Richard Nixon invited King to a conference to discuss how religious leaders might support the President's Committee on Government Contracts "in advancing its program of elimination of discrimination in employment in government contracts."[1] Four hundred religious leaders representing twenty-two denominations attended the gathering at Washington's Sheraton Park Hotel.[2] In this published transcript of his remarks, King decries the "injurious effect" of discrimination upon black workers and declares that "to deny any group honest work and fair pay is not only immoral, it is almost murderous." He calls on his fellow clergy to help "break the deadening silence which engulfs the well-meaning white people of the South" who fear to "speak or act in the absence of respected company." King notes that "the Government alone has the power to establish the legal undergirding that can insure progress" and concludes by describing his dream of an America "where men do not argue that the color of a man's skin determines the content of his character."[3] Two drafts of King's address vary significantly from this version, published in 1960.

I warmly welcome the opportunity to be with you on this occasion because the subject of our discussion has such profound implications of human and economic importance. I am sure that a group of such distinguished leaders of thought will be able to develop constructive and lasting proposals.[4]

---

1. King accepted Nixon's invitation on 24 April. At Nixon's request, King had delivered the invocation at a previous meeting of the President's Committee on Government Contracts on 15 January 1958 (King to C. E. Ryan, 9 January 1958). For a typescript of King's address, see King, Address at the Religious Leaders Conference, 11 May 1959.

2. "Fight on Jobs Bias Spurred by Nixon," *New York Times*, 12 May 1959, and President's Committee on Government Contracts, Program, "Religious Leaders Conference," 11 May 1959.

3. In an 18 June 1959 letter, Nixon thanked King for attending the conference and noted that "the real success of the meeting will depend in large measure on the follow-up action taken by all of us to implement the concept of equal opportunity for employment and training for all groups." The following year, King declined an invitation to serve on a Religious Advisory Council to the President's Committee (King to George O. Butler, 18 April 1960).

4. A draft of this address that King deposited at Boston University [MLKP-MBU] included editorial comments made by an unknown person, some of which were incorporated in the published version. King's draft: "The problem we are dealing with is part of a world wide problem of man's failure to apply Judeo-Christian ethics to his every day life. It is part of our failure to conquer the evil of discrimination not only in so-called backward countries, but in the most advanced and civilized nations in the world. Indeed it is paradoxical that some less developed nations are more creative and resolute in attacking discrimination than are we with our long heritage of democracy. [¶]In my recent trip to India [*strikeout illegible*] I was profoundly struck by the approach of the Indian government to the question of untouchability. Not only is such discrimination a violation of law punishable by imprisonment but so great a general social attitude prevails that no public figure anywehre would dare to defend the discrimination of untouchability. It would be considered little short of barbaric to oppose the efforts toward progress in this regard. But beyond this a unique underlyging moral philosophy gives strength to positive sentiment. India holds the view that there is a deep ethical

Unfortunately, in our nation the moral determination to deal with the evil of discrimination has been neither deep enough nor consistent enough.[5] There has been some progress, but even the most casual observer must admit that we are far from the Promised Land in the area of equal job opportunity.[6] The tragic truth is that discrimination in employment is not only dominant throughout the South, but is shamefully widespread in the North, particularly in great urban communities which often pride themselves as liberal and progressive centers in government and economics.[7]

This discrimination in employment has resulted in an appalling gap between the living conditions of whites and members of minority groups.[8]

We need not look very far to see the injurious effect that discrimination in employment has upon the psychological and moral life of the victims. To deny any group honest work and fair pay is not only immoral, it is almost murderous. It is a deliberate strangulation of the physical and cultural development of the victims! Few practices are more detrimental to our national welfare than the discrimination with which the economic order is rife. Few practices are more thoroughly sinful.

---

responsibility and obligation of the whole people toward the untouchables for the centuries of injustice they were made to suffer. Consequently, as atonement for society's sins toward these people, they are granted special help and given special advantages to ensure their rapid advancement. These take the form of special scholarships, grants, special status for employment and other similar measures. I submit to you that while India may have to learn much in technology from us, we can learn much of moral attitude from her."

5. King's draft [MLKP-MBU] included this additional sentence: "It is, therefore, gravely ineffective."

6. The draft [MLKP-MBU] included this additional sentence: "One must measure what could have been accomplished against what ought to have been accomplished."

7. King's draft [MLKP-MBU]: "Even more serious is the fact that [*strikeout illegible*] the failure to make adequate progress is but one facet of the problem. The problem is compounded by the fact that new features are emerging which are forcing us backwards at a time when we should be speeding ahead. [¶] To illustrate; in many southern states great new industrial plants have developed employing hundreds of thousands. The jobs in these factories are and will increasingly become the most desirable forms of employment in the South. However, for the Negro they are as unavailable as if they were built on the planet Mars. Thus, the future is already passing the Negro by, and he remains condemned to ~~the~~ second, third or tenth class employment. Tragically, this occurs at a time when democracy needs the skills, and maximum capacity of every American. [¶]Furthermore, [*strikeout illegible*] in recent years there has emerged the development of a stubborn tenancious level of unemployment presently totalling 4 1/2 million wage earners. The special tragedy for Negroes is that they constitute some 25% of the total unemployed although they are only 10% of the whole population. [*strikeout illegible*] Discrimination hits the Negro with a double blow: He is excluded from desirable employment and he is proportionately the greatest victim of unemployment. [¶]This brings us to the effect upon moral life of a man whose most elementary necessities are denied and frustrated by his need for adequate employment."

8. King's typescript included these additional remarks: "For instance, recent statistics revealed that 43 per cent of the Negro families of America earn less than $2,000 a year, while just 17 per cent of the white families earn less than $2,000 a year. Twenty-one per cent of the Negro families of America earn less than $1,000 per year, while only 7 per cent of the white families earn less than $1,000 per year. Eighty-eight per cent of the Negro families of America earn less than $5,000 per year, while only 60 per cent of the white families earn less than $5,000 annually. Or to put it another way: only 12 per cent of the Negro families of America earn $5,000 a year or more, while 40 per cent of the white families earn $5,000 a year or more. Similar statistics can be recorded for other minority groups."

The churchman who ministers to the poor or economically insecure section of the population knows well that morality is influenced by poverty. It is infinitely harder for hungry men with hungry children to respect the property of others than it is for the well-fed and the well-housed.[9]

But there is more than poverty which corrodes morality. When an individual is subjected to systematic humiliation, contempt and ridicule as an everyday feature of his life, it is hard for him to think of his tormentors as brothers.[10] Moreover, under the incessant beating of effective propaganda drums, many members of minority groups become convinced of their inferiority.[11] With the destruction of their self-respect there follows a loss of respect for others and a deterioration of moral values generally.[12]

This festering sore of discrimination also debilitates the white person. It so often victimizes him with a false sense of superiority, thus depriving him of genuine humility, honesty and love. It causes him to treat his brother as a means to an end, substituting an "I-It" relationship for the "I-Thou" relationship.[13] At its lowest level, this evil results in brutality, and its most inhuman expression in lynchings, bombings, and outrageous terrorism.

It is clear from all of this that the problem of discrimination in employment is not merely a political issue; *it is a profound moral issue.* Since the Church is the guardian of the morals of the community, it cannot look with indifference upon this pressing problem. A religion true to its nature must always be concerned about man's social conditions. Religion operates not only on the vertical plane but also on the horizontal. It seeks not only to integrate men with God, but to integrate men with men and each man with himself.

This means, at bottom, that true religion is a two-way road. On the one hand it seeks to change the souls of men, and thereby unite them with God; on the other hand it seeks to change the environmental conditions of men so that the soul will

---

9. King further elaborated in his draft [MLKP-MBU]: "For the hungry man the temptation to sin is far more intense than for any other. Indeed, as a representative of the poorest section of the population I am proud that under pressures, often inhuman, so few succumb, and so many are deeply attached to high moral principles, and to their churches. This point needs to be emphasized when sensation seeking newspapers exaggerate crime and with deliberate [*remainder missing*].

10. In a second draft of this address, from the Coretta Scott King Collection [CSKC], King made handwritten insertions and added paragraphs not included in the published version. In this draft, King substituted "Negro" for "individual." At the end of the sentence, King added the phrase "or as children of God."

11. In King's draft [CSKC], he substituted "some Negroes" for "many members of minority groups."

12. At the end of this paragraph King handwrote "despite these conditions." The succeeding paragraph reads [CSKC]: "This degenration occurs equally in the white person. Arrogance, false superiority, deprive him of Christian humility, honesty and love. In its worst form, at its lowest level, these evils murge into brutality and its most inhuman expression, in lynchings, bombings and terroristic outrages." King began the following paragraph: "It is then that the light of the Christian ethic burns so ~~fully~~ feebly {that} we must wonder if it exists at all."

13. King refers to the work of Jewish philosopher Martin Buber (*I and Thou* [Edinburgh: T. and T. Clark, 1937]).

have a chance after it is changed. Any religion that professes to be concerned with the souls of men and is not concerned with the slums that damn them, the economic conditions that strangle them, and the social conditions that cripple them, is a spiritually moribund religion in need of new blood.[14]

This, therefore, becomes a grave challenge to the Church and to churchmen. To meet it, all churches must accept the obligation to create the moral climate in which fair employment practices are viewed positively and accepted willingly. We must utilize the vast resources of the churches and synagogues for the many educational functions they can employ, and for which they have highly developed skills, facilities and experience. However, to possess resources is worthless without the will to be effective. The time has come when the churches are needed by their people and their nation as never before. They, uniquely, can break the deadening silence which engulfs the well-meaning white people of the South.

Everywhere, the white Southerner who deplores the evils of discrimination and segregation complains that, to speak honestly, or to employ Negroes, or to work side-by-side with them, will incur community hostility and scorn. He fears to speak or act in the absence of respected company. No one fills this need so perfectly as the clergyman. If he speaks out not once, not guardedly, but with the firm and eloquent confidence that truth provides, a small stream of support will grow gradually to a mighty river. I have said many times that I have faith that millions of white Southerners want to end the dying order of discrimination. They need spiritual leadership and guidance. The churches must provide it because they possess it, and have the moral duty to do it. If they fail, history will record that, in this tumultuous era of change, the churches were unable or unwilling to furnish moral leadership. This would be a grave indictment, and must not be the judgment for our age.[15]

While the churches have a moral responsibility to create an atmosphere conducive to fair employment, the Government alone has the power to establish the legal undergirding that can insure progress.[16] We appreciate that the Government

---

14. King may have adopted this passage from Harry Emerson Fosdick's *The Hope of the World* [New York: Harper & Brothers, 1933], p. 25: "Any church that pretends to care for the souls of people but is not interested in the slums that damn them, the city government that corrupts them, the economic order that cripples them . . . that kind of church, I think, would hear again the Master's withering words: 'Scribes and Pharisees, hypocrites!'"

15. King's draft [CSKC]: "Every church, and church organization should honestly reevaluate its programs to determine if a moral and social problem of these immense dimensions is adequately reflected in the life of their institution. Support for missionary work is noble and important. Support for community charities, socials and religious euducation are eminently worthwhile. But, is there a fair and proper degree of concern for practical brotherhood as a vital and every day activity. Is there some zeal and fervor behind such concern. I think if all of us elevate this burning issue to its proper level an infinite variety of creative applications can be developed because we have among us some of the nations finest minds. But the central and [*strikeout illegible*] urgent necessity is to recognize that in these turbulent days religious duty cannot truly be fulfilled without dedicated, courageous, consistent activity to give living meaning to brotherhood."

16. King's draft [CSKC] included the following additional sentences: "In this connection as in all other aspects of social progress, the government has two areas of responsibility: Firstly, the responsibility to establish in law the democratic ethical principle. Secondly, the obligation to maintain compliance with the law."

has made some moves in this direction.[17] We rejoice that Federal Government contracts clearly define the principle of non-discrimination.[18] Now it is our task to support the government in its responsibility to enforce compliance with the law.

As churchmen, we naturally would prefer that men would voluntarily comply with the requirements of such contracts, but no one knows better than we do the problems and limitations of maintaining order and moral growth merely by means of persuasion and convincement. Love and persuasion are virtues that are basic and essential, but they must forever be complimented by justice and moral coercion.[19] Without love, justice becomes cold and empty; without justice, love becomes sentimental and empty. We must come to see that justice is love, correcting and controlling all that stands against love.

Precisely because we cannot endure in love or justice the erosion and demoralization to minority groups that spring from discrimination in employment, the Church must be the first segment in the nation to stand firmly, not merely for the enunciation of the moral principle of non-discrimination, but it must also encourage and stand behind the Government when it carries out its obligation in refusing or withdrawing Federal contracts from those employers who do not in fact live up to the letter and spirit of the non-discrimination clause.

The Church must have the courage and the resoluteness to support the Government when it determines to make examples of industries in dramatically cancelling large contracts where the principle of brotherhood is violated. For, in refusing to operate strictly within the framework of the contract, employers violate and degrade human personality—and our most sacred trust.

Beyond this, there is a major job for all of us to tackle. We must work for the enactment of Federal and State fair employment practices laws. The existence of such F.E.P.C. laws, at state and national levels, is not merely for economic benefit of minority groups. Such laws are essential if our nation is to maintain its economic growth and prosperity.[20]

I cannot close without stressing the responsibility laid upon leaders of minority groups to stimulate their youth to prepare themselves for better jobs. Doors are opening now that were not opened in the past, and the great challenge facing minority groups is to be ready to enter these doors as they open. No greater tragedy can befall minority groups at this hour than to allow new opportunities to emerge, without the concomitant preparedness and readiness to meet them.

Ralph Waldo Emerson said in a lecture back in 1891 that "if a man can write a better book, or preach a better sermon, or make a better mousetrap than his neighbor, even if he builds his house in the woods the world will make a beaten path to

17. In his draft [CSKC], King worded this sentence differently: "We appreciate that certain limited efforts within the area of federal competence have been taken."

18. In his draft [CSKC], King quoted a nondiscrimination clause from an employment contract.

19. The CSKC draft included an additional sentence: "However, love and reconciliation are considerations that must be applied to all men—the oppressed as well as the oppressors."

20. From 1941 to 1946 the Fair Employment Practices Committee monitored discrimination in the federal government, the armed forces, and defense industries. After its demise, several states outside of the South established agencies to monitor employment discrimination.

his door."[21] Certainly this has not always been true. But we have reason to believe that, because of the shape of the world today and the fact that we cannot afford the luxury of an anemic democracy, this affirmation will become increasingly true. So we must strongly urge our youth to achieve excellence in their various fields of endeavor.

Throughout this talk I have spoken repeatedly of the need for action in the area of job discrimination. The words are not spoken lightly. I am not unmindful of the price that those must pay who act. It will often be high in inconvenience and unpopularity. But we must not allow *anything* to prevent us from making the ideal of brotherhood a reality. We cannot be a sheltered group of detached spectators, chanting and singing on sequestered corners, in a world that is being threatened by the forces of evil. We must work assiduously, and with determined boldness, to remove from the body politic this cancerous disease of discrimination, which is preventing our democratic and Christian health from being realized. Then and only then will we be able to bring into full realization the dream of our American democracy—a dream yet unfulfilled. A dream of equality of opportunity, of privilege and property widely distributed; a dream of a land where men will not take necessities from the many to give luxuries to the few; a dream of a land where men do not argue that the color of a man's skin determines the content of his character, where they recognize that the basic thing about a man is not his specificity but his fundamentum; a dream of a place where all our gifts and resources are held, not for ourselves alone, but as instruments of service for the rest of humanity; the dream of a country where every man will respect the dignity and worth of all human personality, and men will dare to live together as brothers—*that* is the dream. Whenever it is fulfilled we will emerge from the bleak and desolate midnight of man's inhumanity to man into the bright and glowing daybreak of freedom and justice for all of God's children.

PD. *Faiths: Joined for Action* (Washington, D.C.: U.S. Government Printing Office, 1960).

---

21. This quotation may have originated from a journal entry of Emerson's (see note 6 to "Mother's Day in Montgomery," by Almena Lomax, 18 May 1956, in *Papers* 3:266).

Remarks Delivered at Africa Freedom Dinner at Atlanta University

[*13 May 1959*]
Atlanta, Ga.

King delivers remarks before the keynote address of Kenyan nationalist leader Tom Mboya, who was nearing the end of a five-week tour of the United States.[1] *"Our struggle is not an isolated struggle," King insists. "We are all caught in an inescapable network of mutuality." Mboya defended Kenya's policy of non-alignment, chided the West for spending too much money on defense, and accused the developed nations of failing to understand the needs of Africa: "When we are talking about how best to preserve human life . . . you are talking about how to project the first person into space. These two languages are essentially different, and consequently sometimes it is difficult for some people to understand our very simple aspirations, our very simple demands, our very simple human needs." The following transcription of King's introduction is drawn from an audio recording of the event.*[2]

[*words inaudible*] question why we invited Mr. Mboya to Atlanta and to the South because that is very obvious. As you well know there is a great revolution going on all over our world. And we think of the fact that just thirty or forty years ago there were only two countries in Africa that had independence at that particular time—that was Liberia and Ethiopia. And today eight countries have been added to that number, and in 1960 four more will be added: Somalia, Togoland, the Cameroons and the largest country in Africa, Nigeria. This reveals that an old order is passing away. And our guest speaker is one of the great leaders in this struggle for freedom and independence.

And in a real sense what we are trying to do in the South and in the United States is a part of this worldwide struggle for freedom and human dignity. Our

1. Thomas Joseph Odhiambo Mboya (1930–1969), born in Kilima Mbogo, Kenya, founded the Kenya Local Government Workers' Union, a union of government workers. After many of its leaders were jailed, Mboya assumed the leadership of the Kenya Federation of Labour in 1953, distinguishing himself by mediating the Mombasa dock workers' strike in 1955. Returning to Kenya after studying at Ruskin College in Oxford, England, Mboya was elected to Kenya's Legislative Council in 1957. The same year he formed the People's Convention Party, over which he presided. After assuming a leading role in the negotiations preceding Kenyan independence in 1963, Mboya was named minister of labor. In 1965 Kenya's president Jomo Kenyatta promoted Mboya to the Ministry of Economic Planning. He was assassinated in 1969. For additional details on King's relationship with Mboya, see King to Mboya, 8 July 1959, pp. 242–243 in this volume.

2. Following the address, Morehouse College professor Samuel Williams presented Mboya with copies of King's *Stride Toward Freedom*, Lawrence D. Reddick's *Crusader Without Violence* (New York: Harper & Brothers, 1959), and Horace Mann Bond's *The Search for Talent* (Cambridge: Harvard University Press, 1959). Prior to the event, King greeted Mboya's plane at Atlanta Municipal Airport (Reddick, "Mboya dinner at Atlanta," 14 May 1959, and John Britton, "No Compromise on Fight for Equality—Mboya," *Atlanta Daily World*, 14 May 1959; see also SCLC, Program, "Africa Freedom Dinner honoring Mr. Tom Mboya," 13 May 1959).

struggle is not an isolated struggle; it is not a detached struggle, but it is a part of the worldwide revolution for freedom and justice. We are not sitting here detached, as I said, but we are all caught in an inescapable network of mutuality. And whatever affects one directly affects all indirectly. So we are concerned about what is happening in Africa and what is happening in Asia because we are a part of this whole movement. And we want Mr. Mboya to know, as he prepares to go back to Africa, that we go back with him in spirit and with our moral support and even with our financial support.[3] Certainly injustice anywhere is a threat to justice everywhere. And so long as problems exist in Africa, or in Asia, or in any section of the United States, we must be concerned about it.

And through our Southern Christian Leadership Conference we are trying to implement the Supreme Court's decision on the local level through nonviolent means. This is a big job; it is not an easy job. It will call for sacrifice and even some suffering. It will call for hard work. It will call for dedicated leaders. This organization came into being to serve as a channel through which the Negro leaders of the South could coordinate their local protest actions. And we hope to work together and to stick together until this problem is solved. How many years it will take we don't know. Predictions are very difficult to make, but I'm sure that we are committed to the ideal of achieving first-class citizenship all over America in general and in the South in particular.

And we are deeply grateful to our guest speaker for coming here this evening, and I'm sure that he will be a great inspiration to us, for he is a symbol of the longings and aspirations of oppressed people for freedom and human dignity. And again I say we are very happy to see each of you, and I hope as a result of this meeting we will go out with grim and bold determination to make the ideal of first-class citizenship a reality. And that we will go away with a new concern for Africa and Asia and all of the oppressed peoples over the world as they struggle to realize the dream of brotherhood and man's love for all men. Thank you very kindly. [*applause*]

At. WXSC.

---

3. In a 29 September financial report, SCLC treasurer Ralph Abernathy noted that a disbursement of $514.38 was allocated to the Mboya dinner.

Statement Adopted at Spring Session of SCLC in Tallahassee, Florida

15 May 1959
Atlanta, Ga.

On 14–15 May, eighty-five SCLC members convened at Tallahassee's First Baptist Church for the organization's first meeting of 1959.[1] *In the wake of SCLC executive director John Tilley's departure, Ella Baker reported on the organization's activities of the past seven months and its future plans.*[2] *On the first day of the conference, King addressed a mass meeting at Bethel Baptist Church. SCLC approved this statement deploring recent acts of racist terror and urging Eisenhower to travel to Mississippi to "assume personal command of the investigation" into the lynching of Mack Charles Parker.*[3] *They request that the attorney general "saturate danger areas" in the South with federal agents, and they threaten to appeal to the United Nations if the administration fails to act.*

"The Southern Christian Leadership Conference has the unwelcomed and grim satisfaction of noting that for several years we have repeatedly called to the attention of the President, the Attorney General and the nation that violence in the South can not merely be deplored or ignored. We have emphasized that without effective action led by the President, himself, the situation would worsen. Today, the outrageous record speaks for itself.

"The barbaric lynching of young Mack Charles Parker, in Poplarville, Miss., while he was in the custody of law officials, has shocked the civilized world. In Tallahassee, Florida, a Negro girl has been abducted at gun-point and viciously raped by four white men.[4] In Bessemer, Alabama, a respected leader and colleague of

1. The meeting was delayed to accommodate the 13 May Africa Freedom Dinner in Atlanta.

2. In her report to the executive board, Baker called for the distribution of "thousands of pieces of literature in the North, urging Negro voters not to let their Southern brothers and sisters down by failing to vote," and stressed the need of promoting "the participation of women and youth in the Southern civil rights struggle" (Baker, "Report of the director to the executive board," 15 May 1959). The board also voted for officers and executive board members. Following the Tallahassee meeting, Baker sent King and the SCLC board members the results of the election, noting that the selection of National Beauty Culturist League president Katie Wickham as SCLC's first female officer was "in keeping with the expressed need to involve more women in the movement" (Baker to King, 28 May 1959).

3. On 25 April, Parker was abducted and killed while he awaited trial for allegedly raping a white woman. King sent an immediate wire to the governor of Mississippi (see King to James P. Coleman, 25 April 1959, pp. 190–191 in this volume). Though scores of FBI agents investigated the case, no one was indicted for the murder.

4. In his address at Bethel Baptist Church, King reportedly remarked that he did not believe in capital punishment but was hoping for a "punishment suited to the crime." He also praised students from Florida A&M for drawing attention to the case. "If the court fails now Florida will be condemned in the eyes of the nation" ("Eyes of the World Waiting to See if Justice Will Be Done in Tallahassee—King," *Atlanta Daily World*, 16 May 1959). For more on this case, see King to Clifford C. Taylor, 5 May 1959, p. 196 in this volume.

ours, Asbury Howard was beaten by some forty white men in the presence of police officers; and while the attackers have not been arrested, Asbury Howard was jailed and sentenced without proper recourse to appeal; and his son has been condemned to the chain gang for the manly act of defending his father. Their only "crime" was that of the simple exercise of freedom of speech in an effort to encourage Negroes to register and vote.[5]

"In Birmingham and Tuscaloosa, Alabama, four men, two of them ministers, have been brutally beaten by white men with chains and other heavy instruments.[6] In many areas of the South there has been a general breakdown of law and order which we attribute to the resurgence of the Ku Klux Klan and the status of respectability given to the White Citizens Councils by some law officers, elected public officials, and "solid citizens" of the South. The unholy attitude of certain Governors, state officials and United States Congressmen from the South in calling for open defiance of law and constituted authority, have done much to inflame and incite those who committed these attrocities.

"It is ironical that these Un-American outrages occur as the representatives of our nation confer in Geneva to argue for the extension of democratic principles in the conduct of international affairs.[7] Sitting as a silent, but weighty judge, at the Geneva roundtable is the ghost of the mutilated, bullet ridden, water soaked body of young Parker. His death alone explodes the arguments of the gradualists that Federal legislative and executive action should be delayed until the white South is ready to accept change. As we have repeatedly warned, delay encourages defiance of law, rather than compliance with it.

"We can not ignore the fact that opponents of racial justice have moved from vocal defiance of constitutional edict to an avowed reliance upon terror. This low level of lawlessness is expressed in brutal acts, deliberately designed not only to crush or destroy the immediate victim, but to intimidate and silence the millions of oppressed Negroes of the South.

"But, we will not be terrorized or silenced. We will demand and act until the latent decency, and intelligent self-interest of the American people forces an end to this disgraceful breakdown of law and order. We urge Negroes and other concerned Americans to speak forthrightly to their Government for action, now.

---

5. Howard, vice president of the International Union of Mine Mill and Smelter Workers, was attacked inside Bessemer City Hall, where he had just been found guilty of "breach of the peace" for attempting to display a poster urging people to vote. He was sentenced to six months on the chain gang and his son, Asbury Howard, Jr., received five years probation. Writing on behalf of the Alabama Christian Movement for Human Rights (ACMHR), Fred Shuttlesworth and King sent telegrams to Alabama governor John Patterson and U.S. Attorney General William P. Rogers, demanding an investigation of the Howard case (Emory O. Jackson, Press release, 4 February 1959; see also "Negro Labor Leader Hurt During Attack," *Montgomery Advertiser,* 25 January 1959, and "Alabama Negro Leader Beaten, Jailed in 1st Amendment Case," *Civil Liberties,* March 1959).

6. King refers to the 9 April kidnapping, robbery, and beating of minister Charles Billups, a member of the ACMHR, and two coworkers by a group of white men in Birmingham. One week later, minister O'Hara M. Prewitt was similarly abducted and beaten in Tuscaloosa.

7. During the 11 May through 5 August meeting of the Council of Foreign Ministers in Geneva, the United States pressed for the continued occupation of Berlin until Germany could be democratically reunited.

"In this tense and frustrating period, some Negroes have been driven to advocate violence to meet the violence perpetrated upon them.[8] While we thoroughly understand their outrage and despair, we must reaffirm our fundamental conviction that violence is neither a practical nor a moral force for the establishment of justice. We pray that those advocating violence to meet violence, will come to embrace our unshaken belief that continued and firm resistance, based upon the spirit of nonviolence, is the only constructive course.

"Because the Federal Government has both the moral obligation to protect all citizens and the power to right many wrongs, this conference of Southern leaders calls upon it to take these step:

"1. The immediate enactment by Congress of legislation, such as the Douglas civil rights bill to strengthen the authority of federal agencies to act with vigor in enforcing law.[9] Congress should also enact a definite anti-lynch law that would cover all mob imposed deaths, and thus end a barbaric practice which is worse than murder.

"2. As a means of changing the climate of opinion, the president should go to Poplarville, Mississippi and assume personal command of the investigation of the Parker case. He would thus vitalize the efforts to apprehend the lynchers and demonstrate his human concern as he has done in travelling to disaster areas caused by floods and other catastrophies. The mob-inflicted death of Mack Charles Parker and the outrages it represents are catastrophic to millions of Negroes whose physical safety is threatened throughout the South.[10]

"3. The office of the Attorney General of the United States should treat the resurgence of mob violence in the South as a national calamity, and should use existing legal powers, afforded by present laws, to saturate danger areas such as Mississippi and Alabama with sufficient Federal marshals and special agents to apprehend those who have broken the law and to anticipate future crimes. There are federal violations justifying such steps, and historically our government, when it had to tame the frontier West, utilized federal marshals when local law and order broke down and citizens lived in daily terror.

---

8. King's statement was probably provoked by recent remarks made by Monroe, North Carolina, NAACP leader Robert F. Williams. For more on Williams, see King, Address at the Fiftieth Annual NAACP Convention, 17 July 1959, pp. 245–250 in this volume.

9. Senate Bill 810, co-sponsored by Illinois senator Paul Douglas, would have hastened the enforcement of the Supreme Court's school desegregation decision and allowed the U.S. attorney general to initiate lawsuits to protect civil rights. It was not approved by the Judiciary Committee.

10. At a 5 May press conference, Eisenhower rejected a reporter's suggestion that the Parker case underscored the need for new civil rights legislation: "I don't know how you can make law stronger except to . . . make certain that its violation will bring about punishment." Eisenhower expressed his confidence that the FBI and Mississippi authorities "will find some way of punishing the guilty, if they can find them" (*Public Papers of the Presidents of the United States: Dwight D. Eisenhower, 1959* [Washington, D.C.: U.S. Government Printing Office, 1960], p. 364).

"In the name of justice and decency, we appeal for action NOW. As reasonable people, we can wait a reasonable period of time, ~~but~~ {But} if these atrocities continue and nothing is done to stop them, we have no choice ~~by~~ {But} to present our plight to the President in person, through a southwide delegation of Negro leaders. And it well might be necessary and expedient to appeal to the conscience of the world through the Commission on Human Rights of the United Nation."[11]

Signed: Rev. Martin L. King, Jr.
President

THD. MLKP-MBU: Box 4.

---

11. The commission was formed in 1947 to draft a Universal Declaration of Human Rights.

To Thomas Jovin

19 May 1959
[*Montgomery, Ala.*]

California Institute of Technology student Thomas Jovin hosted King's 25–27 February 1958 visit to the campus.[1] *In a 7 May 1959 letter Jovin, who had been elected student body president, asked King's advice on recruiting black students to Caltech.*

Mr. Tom Jovin

Dear Tom:

On returning to the office after a rather lengthy speaking tour, I was very happy to find your letter on my desk. I still remember with pleasant thoughts the moments that I spent on the campus of Caltech.

It is very heartening to know that you are greatly concerned about the fact that there are no colored undergraduate students at Caltech. This is certainly a manifestation of your genuine goodwill and your basic humanitarian concern.

Certainly, I can understand some of the reasons that Negro students are not presently in the studentbody of Caltech. The two reasons that you listed in your

---

1. Jovin to King, 23 January 1958. Thomas M. Jovin (1939–), born in Buenos Aires, Argentina, received a B.S. (1960) from the California Institute of Technology. In 1964, he received an M.D. from Johns Hopkins University and later became the chairman of the department of molecular biology at the Max Planck Institute for Biophysical Chemistry in Göttingen, Germany.

letter are probably foremost.[2] On the other hand, I am sure that there are several Negro students around the country who could qualify and who would be interested if the proper approach is made. I would suggest that you seek to develop some type of scholarship program which would assist Negro students in their tuition, and then follow through with a recruiting program in some of the more advanced Negro high schools in the South and other sections of the country. I think your idea of a summer visitation program is very good indeed. So often Negro students are not in some of the major institutions of learning because no determined effort has been made to get them. And there is always the unconscious fear that they are not wanted. Once the ice is broken, however, it is not difficult to get students to continue to come.

As I travel around the country I will certainly keep this matter in the forefront of my mind. If I run across promising students who are academically qualified for studies at Caltech I will certainly encourage them to apply.

Again, let me express my appreciation to you for your interest at this point. I am sure that something meaningful will come out of it.

Give my best regards to all of my friends on the campus. You have my best wishes for a most profitable visit to India and the Far East.[3] I have just returned from India after a month's visit and it was certainly one of the most rewarding experiences of my life.

Very sincerely yours,
Martin L. King, Jr.

TLc. MLKP-MBU: Box 28A.

2. In his 7 May letter, Jovin had suggested that the "failing lies in the fact that our tolerance, though real, is of a distinct passive nature." He also noted that most people attributed the absence of black students to the school's competitive admissions standards and that most "qualified colored students" regard "their chances of admission and financial support to be poor."

3. Jovin's letter concluded by noting that he had received a summer travel grant.

To Jayaprakash Narayan

19 May 1959
[*Montgomery, Ala.*]

While visiting the Indian state of Bihar, King spent 14 February at the ashram of Gandhian independence leader Jayaprakash Narayan, an advocate of hand labor and a decentralized economy. According to James Bristol, King "found J. P.'s decentralist ideas challenging, but he could not go as far as J. P. is prepared to."[1]

1. Bristol, Notes from the tour diary, 10 February–10 March 1959. Jayaprakash Narayan (1902–1979), born in the Sarah district of Bihar, studied political science and economics for seven years in

During a jeep ride to the ashram, King reportedly noted Narayan's dependence "upon a factory-produced vehicle to keep his Ashram in touch with the surrounding community."[2]

Sri Jayaprakash Narayan
Mahila Charkha Samithi
Kadam Kua, PATNA 3,
INDIA

Dear Sri Narayan:

I have written you over and over again in my mind, but I am just getting to the point of putting it on paper. Actually, when I returned to my office, I found such an accumulation of mail and other organizational problems that I have been playing a game of catch up ever since.

Words are inadequate for me to express my appreciation to you for making our recent visit to India such a meaningful and enjoyable one. I will long remember our moments together. Your deep sense of dedication, your warm personality, and your devotion to God and man, tremendously impressed me from the very beginning. I was deeply moved by the powerful and positive manner that you are going about the task of serving humanity.

I regret very deeply that problems here at home made it impossible for me to spend more time in India, but I am consoled by the fact that this does not necessarily mean my last visit to India. I hope to come back some day when I can spend much more time.

I returned to the United States more convinced than ever before that nonviolent resistance is the most potent weapon available to oppressed people in their struggle for freedom and human dignity. As a result of my visit to India, I believe that my understanding of nonviolence is greater and my conviction deeper. I hope to spread this message all over the United States.

Please give my best regards to all of the friends that I had an opportunity to meet through you, and especially the members of your Ashram. We are looking forward with great anticipation to your visit to the United States. I hope you will consider it a must to visit us when you come.[3] My wife, Coretta, and Dr. Reddick,

---

the United States. Returning to India in 1929, he joined the Indian National Congress and was frequently imprisoned for his anti-colonial activities, which included acts of sabotage. An ally of both Gandhi and Nehru, Narayan was widely regarded as the successor to the prime minister, but he gave up politics in 1954 to join the land redistribution movement headed by Vinoba Bhave. In 1975, Narayan was jailed for leading a protest campaign targeting corruption within the government of prime minister Indira Gandhi.

2. According to Bristol's tour diary, the visit with Narayan was "both a revelation and a revolution-in-the-process for Martin and Coretta King." At the ashram, Bristol also observed King's "great love for children," referring to him as a "Pied Piper" who "moved about the Ashram with several children clutching his arm or holding his hand."

3. King had recently agreed to serve on an advisory committee for Narayan's planned visit, which was canceled the following month (Ballou to Clarence Pickett, 14 May 1959, and Pickett to King, 8 June 1959).

join me in extending best wishes to you. We have talked about nothing but India since we have been back.

With warm personal regards, I am

Sincerely yours,
Martin L. King, Jr.

MLK:mlb

TLc. MLKP-MBU: Box 26.

To G. Ramachandran

19 May 1959
[*Montgomery, Ala.*]

King thanks the secretary of the Gandhi Smarak Nidhi for his hospitality in India and commends his "concise, and profound interpretations" of Gandhi, which "left an indelible imprint" on his thinking. After Ramachandran extended the initial invitation to King, the Nidhi co-sponsored the visit and assisted with the coordination of King's itinerary.[1]

Mr. G. Ramachandran
Gandhi Smarak Nidhi
Rajghat
New Delhi, INDIA

Dear Mr. Ramachandran:

Ever since returning from India, I have been intending to write you, but an extremely busy schedule has stood in the way of my intention. I came back to the office and found a flood of mail that had accumulated in my absence, plus several organizational matters that needed my attention.

Words are inadequate for me to express my appreciation to you personally, and the Gandhi Smarak Nidhi for making my trip to India such a meaningful one. I will long remember the fellowship we enjoyed together, and the whole experience will remain in my thoughts so long as the cords of memory shall lengthen. I only regret that circumstances made it necessary for me to spend only one month in your great country, but I gain consolation in the fact that this does not have to be my last trip to India. I hope to return again when I can spend much more time.

I left India more convinced than ever before that the method of nonviolent resistance is the most potent weapon available to oppressed people in their strug-

1. See Ramachandran to King, 27 December 1958, in *Papers* 4:552–553.

gle for freedom and human dignity. In fact, there is no other lasting way. I have returned to America with a greater determination to achieve freedom for my people through nonviolent means. As a result of my visit to India, I believe that my understanding of nonviolence is greater and my commitment deeper. I have tried to get this message over America since I have returned to the country.

I might say to you that I was greatly impressed with your ability to interpret Gandhi. Out of the many people that I talked with in India, I left with the feeling that you had interpreted the life and teachings of Gandhi to us better than anybody else. Your clear, concise, and profound interpretations left an indelible imprint on my thinking. For this, I am deeply grateful to you.

You have my prayers and best wishes for continued success in the great work that you are doing through the Gandhi Smarak Nidhi. I was tremendously moved by the powerful, aggressive, and positive manner that the Gandhi Smarak Nidhi is going about to preserve the works and philosophy of the great saint. I will certainly want to keep in touch with you and your colleagues.

Please give my best regards to all of the fine people that it was my privilege to meet in India. I hope to get around to writing most of them personally very soon. Be sure to extend my best wishes to your charming and scholarly wife. It was a great delight to spend a few hours with her at Gandhigram.[2] My wife, Coretta, and Dr. L. D. Reddick, join me in sending their best regards.

With warm personal regards, I am

Sincerely yours,
Martin Luther King, Jr.

MLK:b

TLc. MLKP-MBU: Box 26.

2. Ramachandran and his wife, T. S. Soundram, founded Gandhigram at Madurai as a rural college rooted in Gandhian principles.

From Hilda S. Proctor

22 May 1959
Honolulu, Hawaii

Proctor, who served as King's secretary in the spring of 1958 while Maude Ballou was on maternity leave, reports attending a Fellowship of Reconciliation (FOR) meeting in Hawaii, where she had recently relocated. Those in attendance discussed FOR field secretary Glenn Smiley's contribution to the Montgomery bus protest. King replied on 1 June.[1]

1. See pp. 218–219 in this volume.

Dear Martin:

22 May 1959

I have just come from an FOR meeting where your book was reviewed by one Reverend Donald Gaylord of the Pearl Harbor Community Church. I was invited to tell the people "just what is Martin Luther King like?", or I should say, to answer that question.

It is odd that all across the country, in places where I have stopped, people have asked me that question more than any other. . . . like, "do you think they are making any progress down there?"

As you have said to me, I am, at times, inclined to be cynical . . . This might come from my long experience with people. Anyway, I have detected a note of reluctance on the part of many white people to come right out and declare that what you represent is not only for "you people" but for all mankind.

Today, at this meeting, a Haole (white) woman said. "Of course, you know that Glenn Smiley was down there for a long time working with the people and teaching them about passive resistence, so that when this bus problem arose, it was just the culmination of his work and Martin Luther King's work was made easier for Glenn having been there.

I don't know whether or not I was wrong, but I told them all that I doubted that any of the people in Montgomery had even heard of non-violence until Martin Luther King taught it to them. I explained that white people just do not go into Mountgomery and teach the Negroes anything . . that is live among them, organize them and teach them non-violence. Then a Chinese or oriental woman spoke up and said that she agreed that Glenn had laid the foundation for your boycott success. The only other Negro there, Shelton Hale Bishop, retired from St. Philips Church in Harlem spoke up and said that he doubted seriously if the people had heard anything about Glenn Smiley until AFTER THE BUS BOYCOTT.[2]

This is one of the things that I do not like about the FOR and why I resigned. It is a parasite organization . . . moves in on something that someone else has done. I have found this to be true since I joined the Fellowship of Youths for Peace in my 'teens.

I am sending, under separate cover, a book which belongs to the Rev. Gaylord and which he would like to have you autograph and return to him directly at Pearl Harbor.[3]

Also, I am enclosing a check for two books and postage. Please autograph them and send them to

Mrs. Aiko T. Reinecke[4]
1555 Piikor Street
Honolulu 14, Hawaii

---

2. Shelton Hale Bishop, a priest and chairman of the Honolulu chapter of FOR, moved to Hawaii in 1957 after retiring from St. Philip's, the largest Episcopal church in the country. He hosted King during his September visit to Hawaii (see King, Address to the House of Representatives of the First Legislature, State of Hawaii, on 17 September 1959, pp. 277–281 in this volume).

3. Donald F. Gaylord was the minister at Pearl Harbor Community Church in Honolulu, Hawaii. In a 27 July 1959 letter, he thanked King for his "kindness in autographing my copy of your book."

4. Aiko Reinecke and her husband, John, longtime civil rights and civil liberties activists, were fired from the Honolulu schools in 1948 for their suspected affiliation with the Communist Party.

25 May 1959

Mr. Zenichi Abe[5]
P.O. Box 88
Waipahu, Oahu

They are going to try to raise some money to have you come to Hawaii to speak in the fall when you are in California. Can you do it?

If it will make Maud feel "any ways happy", they asked how come you did not mention me in your book for credit-giving as they did her. I told them that she was the REAL secretary. . . . . I was just a sort of stop-gap.

Please give my love to Coretta and tell her to come here with you and sing. She has all the ingredients that make up a breathtaking Hawiian lass. . . . long "blow" hair; color, beauty, smile and. . . . hips to swing to the hula-hula.

Please also give my best to Betty. I wanted to send her a card from here, but forgot her last name.

I know you haven't the time to read all this, but I'll send it anyway.

Cordially,
[*signed*] Hilda

P.S. My black ribbon has a hole in it, hence the red.

TLS. MLKP-MBU: Box 33A.

---

5. Abe was a trade union activist and a pacifist.

To Lewis Happ

25 May 1959
[*Montgomery, Ala.*]

In a 9 May letter, Happ wrote of his hurt and frustration at reading stories of racist incidents in the Montgomery Improvement Association's newsletter: "I begin to read where that some injustice have been done to my peoples and there is absoluty nothing done about it but singing and praying and reading scripture lessions." Happ continued, "its just makes my heart ach to just see us drift back in to slavery agane."[1]

---

1. The 30 April issue of the newsletter described two incidents of racist violence that would not be prosecuted because black victims and witnesses feared retribution (MIA, "Fear—A Road-Block to Freedom," *Newsletter,* 30 April 1959; see also "Police Brutality as a Pattern" in the same issue).

Mr. Lewis Happ
766 Lafayette Avenue
Brooklyn 21, New York

25 May 1959

Dear Mr. Happ:

This is to acknowledge receipt of your letter of May 9. I am very happy to know that you have been receiving the MIA Newsletter. I can well understand how you feel concerning the situation here in the South. But let me assure you that we are not merely singing and praying about our problems, we are engaged in positive action every day to solve it. I don't think any leader of the South has ever suggested singing and praying as a substitute for positive action, and certainly this is why we are suffering and being brutalized as leaders. If we were passively and silently accepting evil, we would not be facing the condemnation that we are facing today from the die hards in the white community.

As you probably know, I believe firmly in nonviolence as a way to solve our problem. And I further believe that love must be our guiding ideal. But this does not imply that we are to do nothing. It simply means that we must stand up and resist the system of segregation and all of the injustices which come our way and at the same time refuse to hate our opponents and use violence against them. For I still believe with Jesus that "He who lives by the sword will perish by the sword."[2] And he who hates does as much harm to himself as to the person that he hates.

And so I would urge you to continue to support us in our struggle and be assured that we will be on the firing line doing all that we can to solve these problems.

Very sincerely yours,
Martin L. King, Jr.

(Dictated, but not personally signed by Dr. King.)

TLc. MLKP-MBU: Box 28.

---

2. Cf. Matthew 26:52.

To John Malcolm Patterson

28 May 1959
Montgomery, Ala.

In the following letter to the governor of Alabama, King and other MIA leaders protest the recent racist beatings of three Montgomery men and the suspicious disappearance of MIA member Horace G. Bell at a newly opened public lake in Selma.[1] *An accompanying report detailed the incidents.*[2]

Honorable John Patterson, Governor
State of Alabama
State Capitol
Montgomery, Alabama

Dear Governor Patterson:

The attached document relates several tragic incidents which have occurred in the State of Alabama within recent days. These unfortunate acts of violence which have been inflicted upon several Negroes of Montgomery are so shameful that we feel the need of calling them to your immediate attention. The mob which attacked these persons in Dallas County should be apprehended and brought before the bar of justice and the whereabouts of Mr. Horace G. Bell revealed. To allow these incidents to go without public cognizance of them will encourage greater and more frequent acts of violence by these irresponsible persons.

The disappearance of Mr. Bell is a great shock to Montgomery. The failure to act now will deny all our claims for law and order and make meaningless our profession of Christian principles.

It is to you that we look for protection and your failure to respond in this instance would give encouragement to those who seek to take the law into their own hands and administer it according to their own brand of justice. The state of Alabama has the power and the laws on the statue books to remedy these injustices. As law abiding citizens who are interested in the good name of the State of Alabama, we urge you to order the necessary investigation and bring to justice those

1. King also sent a telegram to Attorney General William P. Rogers demanding an investigation of the assaults and warning that "if the Federal Government fails to take a forthright stand against these evils our Southland is in danger of drifting into a Hitler like fanaticism which will bring our whole nation to shame" (King, Abernathy, and S. S. Seay to Rogers, 28 May 1959). Replying on behalf of Rogers, Assistant Attorney General W. Wilson White suggested that King present evidence of any violations of federal law to local FBI officials (White to King, 29 May 1959; see also Memos to J. Edgar Hoover, 28 May and 8 July 1959).

2. According to the report, on 24 May, a white mob at the lake forced Quintus Hooten from his car, beat him severely, and ordered him to leave the county. E. L. Carl and Johnny Foster were similarly attacked the same day. Bell had disappeared the previous day and was found dead on 29 May of an apparent drowning ("Facts relating to recent violence inflicted upon Negro citizens of Montgomery, Ala.," 28 May 1959; see also "Patterson Asks Record School Budget, Also Closing Authority," *Southern School News,* June 1959).

who are guilty of these acts of violence. We also urge you to use every resource at your disposal to locate Mr. Horace G. Bell, whose strange disappearance, has caused many to suspect foul play. The location of this man will either confirm or dispel this suspicion.

We sincerely hope that you will immediately take a strong stand on these pressing issues. We also urge you to publicly declare the policies of the state regarding the use of the lake. Your forthright action at this point will help to assure the safety of all citizens in the enjoyment of the resources of this state.

Very sincerely yours,
Martin Luther King, President
Southern Christian Leadership Conference

Ralph D. Abernathy, Chairman of the
Board of Directors, Montgomery Improvement Association

S. S. Seay, Sr., Executive Secretary
Montgomery Improvement Association, Inc.

enclosure: 1

THLc. MLKP-MBU: Box 33A.

To Hilda S. Proctor

1 June 1959
[*Montgomery, Ala.*]

King replies to Proctor's 22 May letter in which she complained about FOR's exaggeration of Glenn Smiley's contributions to the Montgomery bus boycott.[1]

Mrs. Hilda S. Proctor
2088 Kuhio Avenue
Apartment #10
Honolulu, Hawaii

Dear Hilda:

You are really a great globe trotter. I guess next time I hear from you, you will be in Japan or maybe India.

I am happy to know that things are going well with you and you are liking our new state so well.[2] From all reports it is certainly one of the most beautiful points in the world.

I am seriously considering coming to Hawaii after the National Baptist Convention in San Francisco.[3] This will be about the second week of September. If the jets are running out by that time I will probably come out and spend four or five days.[4] Because of an extremely busy schedule I cannot stay longer. Do you plan to be there that long?

I am glad that you straightened the people out on the FOR. I fear that this impression has gotten out in many quarters because members of the staff of the FOR have spread the idea.[5] While I hate to believe this, it seems to be true.

Things are going as well as can be expected here. We are still engaged in a difficult struggle. The forces of resistance are as strong as ever. However, there are some hopeful signs. Brother Faubus seems to be losing ground in Little Rock and the moderates in the white south are speaking out a little more.[6] If we can keep

---

1. See pp. 212–214 in this volume.

2. On 21 August 1959, Hawaii became the fiftieth state admitted to the Union.

3. King traveled to Honolulu in mid-September (see King, Address to the House of Representatives of the First Legislature, State of Hawaii, on 17 September 1959, pp. 277–281 in this volume).

4. Regular jet service to Honolulu began on 7 September 1959.

5. In a letter to an associate following the conclusion of the Montgomery bus boycott, Smiley had written: "While I do not know that you would want to say it, it seems clear to me that the FOR has developed in the south a self-conscious, nonviolent movement with King at the head" (Smiley to William Robert Miller, 14 January 1957).

6. Following the closing of Little Rock public schools in September 1958, local business and civic leaders withheld their support for Arkansas governor Orval Faubus and organized Stop This Outrageous Purge (STOP), a group committed to protesting the firing of pro-integration teachers and to reopening the schools. STOP and the Women's Emergency Committee succeeded in winning the local school board election in mid-1959, replacing three segregationist with moderate members.

the Negroes from falling into a state of apathy I believe that the south will be a different place in which to live ten years from now.

All of your friends here are doing fine. Maude [*Ballou*] and Lillie [*Hunter*] are on the job everyday and working hard as usual. They send their best regards. Coretta and the children are fine. They too send their regards.

I have autographed the books for your friends.[7] They should be arriving in a few days. As soon as I definitely know whether or not I will be coming to Hawaii in September, I will let you know. Be sure to keep in touch with me.

Very sincerely yours,
Martin L. King, Jr.

TLc. MLKP-MBU: Box 33A.

7. In Proctor's 22 May letter, she asked that King autograph books for three of her associates in Hawaii.

"Remaining Awake Through a Great Revolution," Address at Morehouse College Commencement

[*2 June 1959*]
[*Atlanta, Ga.*]

In a 22 December 1958 letter, Morehouse president Benjamin Mays invited King to address the graduating class of 1959; King accepted six days later. In these prepared remarks—his earliest known usage of this title—King invokes his common themes of anticolonialism and black self-respect.[1] *He places the domestic "social revolution" in a global context and urges the graduates of his alma mater to rise above the limits of "individualistic concerns," submitting that all people are "caught up in an inescapable network of mutuality."*

News coverage of the speech indicates that King modified this handwritten text at several points. He advised his audience to adhere to nonviolence, for the "oppressors would be happy" if black Americans "would resort to physical violence" and reminded them of progress already made: "We've broken loose from the Egypt of slavery . . . and

1. The text of this address resembles one that King gave at a 1957 NAACP rally (see "Facing the Challenge of a New Age," Address Delivered at NAACP Emancipation Day Rally, 1 January 1957, in *Papers* 4:73–89). A month prior to the Morehouse speech, King had delivered a sermon at Dexter titled "Sleeping Through a Revolution" that contained similar allusions (Napoleon N. Vaughn to King, 9 May 1959). King would continue to deliver variations on this theme throughout the 1960s (see for example, "Remaining Awake Through a Great Revolution," 12 October 1964 and 31 March 1968).

Remaining Awake Through A Great Revolution

There can be no gainsaying of the fact that we are experiencing today one of the greatest revalutions that the world has ever known. Indeed there have been other revalutions, but they have been local and isolated. The distinctive feature of the present revalution is that it is worldwide. It is shaking the foundations of the east and the west. It has engulfed every continent of the world. You can hear its deep rumblings from the lowest village street to the highest intellectual ivory tower. Every segment of society is being

First page from handwritten draft of "Remaining Awake Through a Great Revolution"

we stand on the border of the promised land in integration."[2] *King reportedly closed with a warning against inaction: "If you go home, sit down and do nothing about the revolution which we are witnessing you will be the victims of a dangerous optimism."*[3]

There can be no gainsaying of the fact that we are experiencing today one of the greatest revolutions that the world has ever known. Indeed there have been other revolutions, but they have been local and isolated. The distinctive feature of the present revolution is that it is worldwide. It is shaking the foundations of the east and the west. It has engulfed every continent of the world. You can hear its deep rumblings from the lowest village street to the highest intellectual ivory tower. Every segment of society is being swept into its mainstream. The great challenge facing every member of this graduating class is to remain awake, alert and creative through this great revolution.

In thinking of the challenge which this revolution brings to each of us, I am reminded of a familiar story that comes down to us from the pen of Washington Irving. It is the story of Rip Van Winkle.[4] The one thing that ~~most of us us~~ we all remember about this story is the fact that Rip Van Winkle slept twenty years. But there is another significant fact in this story that is often over looked. It is the change that took place in ~~that~~ the pictures ~~that~~ [*strikeout illegible*] on of wall of the little inn in the ~~Hudson~~ town on the Hudson from which Rip went up into the ~~mountains~~ mountains for his long sleep. When he went up the wall had a picture of King George III of England. When he came down it had the picture of another George, George Washington. Rip looking up at the picture of George Washington was completely lost. When he started his quiet sleep America was still under the domination of the British Empire. When he came down she was a free and independent nation. This incident suggest that the most striking thing about the story of Rip Van Winkle was not that he slept twenty years, but that he slept through a great revolution. While he was peacefully snoring up in the mountain a revolution was taking place which completely changed the face of the world. Rip knew nothing about it. He was asleep. There is nothing more tragic than to sleep through a revolution.[5]

---

2. "Rev. King Urges Negro Goodwill," *Montgomery Advertiser,* 3 June 1959.

3. Marion E. Jackson, "'Remain Awake,' Dr. King Tells Morehouse Graduates," *Atlanta Daily World,* 3 June 1959; see also "'Native Son' Delivers Ninety-second Anniversary Commencement Address: Dr. M. L. King, Jr., Makes Epochal Speech," *Morehouse College Bulletin,* July 1959.

4. "Rip Van Winkle" was New York author Washington Irving's best-known story. It first appeared in 1819 in *The Sketch Book of Geoffrey Crayon, Gent.* King adopted this illustration from Methodist minister Halford Luccock's sermon "Sleeping Through a Revolution" (Luccock, *Marching Off the Map and Other Sermons* [New York: Harper & Brothers, 1952], pp. 129–130).

5. Luccock, *Marching Off the Map,* pp. 129–130: "I was startled by something . . . that I had never thought of before. That was the sign on the inn in the little town on the Hudson from which Rip went up into the mountains for his long sleep. When he went up the sign had a picture of George III of England. When he came down, it had a picture of George 'the first'. . . . Rip, looking up at that picture of George Washington, was completely lost. The incident suggests that the most striking thing about the story of Rip Van Winkle was not that he slept twenty years (almost anyone could do that!) But that he *slept through a revolution.* While he was peacefully snoring up in the mountains, there had been a great turnover which completely changed the face of his world. But Rip did not know anything about it. He had been asleep."

We do not have to look very far to see signs of the ~~present revolution.~~ revolution that is taking place in our world today. There is a revolution in the social and political structure of our world on the question of the equality of man. The great masses of people are determined to end the explotation of their lives, and share in their own future and destiny. They are moving toward their goal like a tidal wave. They are saying in no uncertain terms that colonialism and racism must go.

~~There are approximately two billion five hundred million (2,500,000,000) people in this world, and the vast majority of these~~

The practical consequences of this revolution are clearly seen. For ~~insta~~ example; twenty five years ago most of the one billion six hundred million (1,600,000,00) colored peoples of Asia and Africa were dominated politically, exploited economically, segregated and humiliated by some foreign power. Just fourteen years ago the British had under her control more than five hundred million people in Asia and Africa. ~~Twenty~~ Thirty years ago there were only two independent countries in the whole of Africa—Liberia and Ethiopia. But today the picture has greatly changed. More the one billion three hundred million (1,300,000,000) of the former colonial subject have their independence, and the British Empire now has less than ~~80 eighty~~ sixty million people under her control in Asia and Africa. [*strikeout illegible*] In less than three decades eight independent countries have arisen in Africa, and in 1960 four more will be added—Nigeria, The Camaroons, Togoland and Somalia. I predict that in ten years the vast majority of the countries of ~~continental~~ Africa will be independent, and that the funeral procession~~al~~ will be forming for the eternal burial of colonialism and imperialism in that section of the world.

This world shaking revolution which is engulfing our world is seen in the United States in the transition from a segregated to an integrated society. The social revolution which is taking place in this country is not an isolated, detached phenomenon. It is a part of the world wide revolution that is taking place.

It is impossible to understand the revolution in America without understanding the great change that has taken place in the Negro's evaluation of himself. Living through the long night of slavery and segregation many Negroes lost faith ~~it~~ in themselves. Many came to feel that perhaps they were inferior, for they were forced to live with a system that continually stared them in the face saying; "you are less than, you are not equal to." Then something happened to the Negro. Circumstances made it possible and necessary for him to travel more—to spread of the automobile, the upheavels of two world wars, and the great depression. His rural plantation background was gradually supplanted by migration to urban and industrial communities. His cultural life gradually rose through the steady decline of crippling illiteracy. His economic ~~life~~ security gradually rose through the growth of industry and the influnce of organized labor. All of these forces conjoined to cause the Negro to take a new look at himself. Negro masses all over began to reevaluate themselves. He came to feel that he was somebody. His religion revealed to him that God loves all of his children and that the important thing about a man is not "his specificity but his fundamentum" [*strikeout illegible*] not the texture of his hair or the color of his skin, but the texture and quality of his soul.

With this new sense of self-respect and new sense of dignity, a new Negro emerged. The tension which we are witnessing in race relation today can be explained in part by the revolutionary change in the Negroes evaluation of ~~himself~~ his nature and destiny, and his determination to struggle and sacrifice until the walls of segregation have finally been crushed by the battering rams of surging justice.

Along with the Negro's changing image of himself came the supreme courts momentous decision of May 17, 1954 outlawing segregation in the public schools. In this decision the Supreme Court of this nation unanimously affirmed that the old Plessy Doctrine must go.[6] It affirmed in unequivocal terms that separate facilities are inherently unequal and that to segregate a child on the basis of his race is to deny that child equal protection of the law. As a result of this decision a revolution change is taking place in the structure of American society. Let nobody fool you, all of the loud noises that we hear today in terms of "nullification" and "interposition" and "massive resistance" are merely the death groans from a dying system.

There is not only a revolution taking place in the social and political structure of man's being, but there is a revolution taking place in the external physical structure of his being. In other words, a revolution is taking place in man's scientific and technological development. Man through his scientific genius has been able to dwarf distance and place time in chains. He has been able to carve highways through the stratosphere, and is now making preparations for a trip to the moon. These revolutionay changes have brought us into a space age. The world is now geographically one.[7] Jet planes have compressed into minutes distances that a few years ago took weeks. Bob Hope has described this new jet age in which we live.[8] He says it is an age in which we will be able to take a non stop flight from Los Angeles to New york city, and if by chance we develop hiccups on taking off, we will "hic" in Los Angeles and "cup" in New york city. It is an age in which one will be able to leave ~~toyko~~ Tokyo on Sunday morning and, because of the time difference, arrive in Seattle Washington on the preceding Saturday night. When your friends meet you at the airport in Seattle inquiring when you left Toyko, you will have to say, "I left tomorrow". This is a bit humorous, but it reminds us that a great revolution is taking place in the physical structure of our universe.

Now the great question facing us today is whether we will remain awake through this worldshaking revolution, and achieve the new mental attitudes which the situations and conditions demand.[9] There would be nothing more tragic

---

6. King refers to the 1954 ruling in *Brown v. Board of Education* and the 1896 *Plessy v. Ferguson* decision.

7. An *Atlanta Daily World* reporter quoted King: "We have carved highways through the stratosphere for a trip to the moon. This has brought about a geographical oneness and an end to the narrow confines of individualistic concerns to the broader concerns of humanity. This geographical oneness means that our very existence will be determined by our coexistence. It has forcibly demonstrated that our bases in space must be built on the general concerns and understanding that all life is interrelated and we must keep our moral and spiritual advances within our scientific and technological growth" (Jackson, "'Remain Awake,' Dr. King Tells Morehouse Graduates").

8. Hope, a British-born American comedic actor, made numerous film and television appearances during this period.

9. Luccock, *Marching Off the Map*, p. 130: "That is one of the great liabilities of life, is it not, of sleeping through a time of great change, and failing to achieve the new mental attitudes which the new situations and conditions demand?"

during this period ~~of social change~~ than to allow our mental and moral attitudes to sleep while this tremendous social change takes place. May I suggest a few of the the changed responses that we must make in order to remain awake during this great revolution

First, we are challenged to rise above the narrow confines of our individualistic concerns to the broader concerns of all humanity. The individual or nation that feels that it can live in isolation has allowed itself to sleep through a revolution. The geographical togetherness of the modern world makes our very existence dependent on co-existence. We must all learn to live together as brothers or we will all perish together as fools. Because of our involvement in humanity we must be concerned about every human being.

I have just returned to the country from a memorable [*strikeout illegible*] visit to India. Although I had a most rewarding experience in that great country, there were those depressing moments. For how can one avoid being depressed when he sees with his own eyes millions of people sleeping on the sidewalks, and discovers that millions go to bed hungry at night? How can one avoid being depressed when he discovers that out of India's population of 400 million people, more than 300 million make an annual income of less than $70 per year, and most of them have never seen a doctor or dentist? All of this has resulted from the centuries of exploitation and oppression inflicted upon the India people by foreign powers.

As I observed these conditions I found myself asking: "Can we in America stand idly by and not be concerned? The answer is an emphatic no, because the destiny of America is tied up with the destiny of India. As long as India, or any other nation, is insecure we can never be totally secure. We must use our vast resources of wealth to aid the undeveloped nations of the world. To often have we used our wealth to establish military bases, while neglecting the need of establishing bases of genuine concern and understanding.

All of this amounts to saying that in the final analysis all life is interrelated. No nation or individual is independent; we are interdependent. We are caught up in an inescapable network of mutuality.

As long as there is poverty in the world I can never be rich, even if I posses a billion dollars. As long as millions of people are inflicted with debilitating diseases and cannot expect to live more than thirty-five years, I can never be totally healthy even if I receive a perfect bill of health from Mayo Clinic. Strangely enough, I can never be what I ought to be until you are what you ought to be. John Donne placed this truth in graphic terms when he affirmed, "No man is an island entire of itself. Every man is a piece of the continent, a part of the maine." Then he goes on to say, "Any man's death diminishes me because I am involved in mankind, and therefore never send to know for whom the bell tolls; it tolls for thee."[10]

A second challenge facing us in this day of revolution is to keep our moral and spiritual development in line with our scientific and technological growth. Certainly, one ~~of our failures in the past has been~~ of the tragedies of the present era is modern man's blatant failure to bridge the gulf between scientific means and moral ends. Unless the gap is filled we are in danger now of destroying ourselves

---

10. King recites a section from John Donne's "Meditation XVII" (1624).

by the misuse of our own instruments. Moral stagnantcy is not only intolerable, but suicidal in a day when the rivers of science and technology are constantly to larger oceans of fulfillment.

An understanding of man's present predicament [*strikeout illegible*] may be found in the distinction between civilization and culture. Professor Maciver of Columbia University, following the German sociologist, Alfred Weber, has clearly set forth the distinction.[11] Civilization refers to the things we use; culture, to what we are. Civilization is the complex of devices, mechanisms, techniques, and instrumentalitism by means of which we live. Culture is the realm of spiritual ends, expressed in art, literature, morals, and religion, for which at best we live. The great problem confronting man today is that he has allowed his civilization to outdistance his culture. He has allowed his mentality to outrun his morality. He has allowed his technology to outdistance his theology. He has allowed the means by which he lives to tower above the ends for which he lives. How much of our modern life can be summarized in the shewd diction of the poet thoreau, "Improved means to an unimproved end."[12] So we have ended up producing a generation of guided missels and misguided men. Unless [*strikeout illegible*] we awake and solve this problem soon our ~~generation~~ civilization will not only be indicted for sleeping through a revolution; it may well be destroyed before it has the opportunity to arise from its complacent slumber.

A third response that this revolutionary period demands is that of achieving [*strikeout illegible*] excellence in our various fields of endeavor. This is particularly true for those of us who are emerging from the yoke of oppression as a result of the present revolution. If we allow ourselves to be content with shear mediocrity, we will be sleeping ~~through the~~ at a time when we should be fully awake.

Today many doors will be opening to us that were not opened in the past, and the great challenge which we confront is to be prepared to enter these door as they open. Ralph Waldo Emerson said in a lecture in 1871;

> If a man can write a better book, or preach a better sermon, or make a better mouse trap than his neighbor, even if he builds his house in the woods the world will make a beaten path to his door[13]

This has not always been true us, but the social revolution that is taking place will make it increasingly true.

---

11. Sociologist Robert Morrison MacIver (1882–1970) wrote several books on the complexities of political and social organization. German economist Alfred Weber (1868–1958) is best known for his *Theory on the Location of Industries* (Chicago: The University of Chicago Press, 1929). He also authored *Fundamentals of Culture-Sociology: Social Process, Civilizational Process and Culture-Movement* (New York: Columbia University, 1939).

12. Henry David Thoreau, *Walden; or, Life in the Woods* (1854), p. 57: "Our inventions are wont to be pretty toys, which distract our attention from serious things. They are but improved means to an unimproved end, an end which it was already but too easy to arrive at; as railroads lead to Boston or New York."

13. The source of this quotation, generally attributed to Emerson, is uncertain (see note 6 to "Mother's Day in Montgomery," 18 May 1956, in *Papers* 3:266).

In this new age that is emerging we will be forced to compete with people of all races and nationalities. Therefore, we cannot aim merely to be good Negro teachers, good Negro doctors, good Negro ministers, good Negro skilled labours. Maybe that was alright in the past. But today if you are merely seeking to do a good Negro job, you have already failed your [*strikeout illegible*] matriculation examination for entrance into the university of integration. You have failed to remain awake through a great revolution.

We must broaden our interest to include fields that we have not persued in the past. While we must to make strides in the relatively secure professions, we must produce more scientist & engineers. These are demands of the space age.

Above all, whatever your life's work happens to be, do it well. Do it with such dedication and thoroughness that even God almighty will have smile with approval. If it falls in the category of an ordinary job, do it in an extraordinary way. In the words of Douglas Malloch:[14]

AD. MLKP-MBU: Box 119.

14. King probably intended to quote lines from Douglas Malloch's "Be the Best of Whatever You Are" (1926), as he did in "The Three Dimensions of a Complete Life," Sermon Delivered at the Unitarian Church of Germantown, 11 December 1960, p. 573 in this volume.

Statement on House Committee on Un-American Activities Hearings on the United Packinghouse Workers of America

11 June 1959
Atlanta, Ga.

Following accusations of Communist Party involvement in the United Packinghouse Workers of America (UPWA), the House Committee on Un-American Activities (HUAC) held investigatory hearings on the union in May 1959.[1] *King enclosed this statement of support from SCLC in an 11 June letter to UPWA official Russell Lasley.*[2] *King*

1. "6 Accused as Reds Balk at Hearing," *New York Times,* 6 May 1959. UPWA president Ralph Helstein denied any Communist influence within the union. Following the HUAC hearings, the union distributed a questionnaire to union members accused of being Communist Party members prior to 1949 and who may have been in violation of the AFL-CIO's Ethical Practices Codes. The codes stipulated that "no person should hold or retain office or appointed position in the AFL-CIO or any of its affiliated national or international unions or subordinate bodies thereof who is a member, consistent supporter or who actively participates in the activities of the Communist Party or of any fascist or other totalitarian organization" (Russell Lasley to Sir and Brother, 10 July 1959). HUAC was established as a standing committee in the U.S. House of Representatives in 1938 to investigate Communist and fascist influence within American institutions.

2. Russell R. Lasley (1914–1989) was an officer in UPWA Local 46 in Waterloo, Iowa, and served as UPWA international vice president from 1948 until 1968.

assured Lasley that "we are with you absolutely" and encouraged him to use this statement "as you see fit." The union had been an early supporter of SCLC, providing the bulk of the organization's initial budget in 1957.[3]

After discovering that the House Committee on Un-American Activities had conducted hearings in the matter of alleged Un-American activities in the Union of the United Packing House Workers of America, the Executive Committee of the Southern Christian Leadership Conference voted unanimously to publicly express its confidence in the integrity of this union.

The officers and members of the United Packing House Workers Union have demonstrated a real humanitarian concern. They have worked indefatiguably to implement the ideals and principles of our democracy. Their devotion to the cause of civil rights has been unswerving. This union has stood out against segregation and discrimination not only in public pronouncements, but also in actual day to day practice. They have given thousands of dollars to aid organizations that are working for freedom and human dignity of the South. Because of the forthright stand of the Packing House Workers in the area of civil rights, they have aroused the ire of some persons who are not so commited. But in spite of this they have continued to work courageously for the ideal of the brotherhood of man. It is tragic indeed that some of our reactionary brothers in America will go to the limit of giving Communism credit for all good things that happen in our nation. It is a dark day indeed when men cannot work to implement the ideal of brotherhood without being labeled communist.

We sincerely hope that nothing will happen to deter the significant work being done by this dedicated labor organization. Again we express our confidence in the integrity and loyalty of the officers and members of the United Packing House Workers of America.

TD. UPWP-WHi: Box 389.

---

3. At the third meeting of the fledgling civil rights group on 8 August 1957, King announced the start of a voter registration campaign. SCLC treasurer Ralph Abernathy estimated that $200,000 was needed to finance the campaign. In October, UPWA president Ralph Helstein presented King with a check for $11,000 at their convention in Chicago (Art Osgoode, "Negroes Rap State Solons in Resolution," *Montgomery Advertiser*, 9 August 1957; Ralph Helstein, Remarks at the fourth biennial wage and contracts, third national anti-discrimination, and third national women's activities conference of the United Packinghouse Workers, 2 October 1957; see also UPWA, "Program proposals for 1957," 21 June 1957). King later agreed to serve on the UPWA's Advisory Review Commission of Public Citizens set up to monitor the union's compliance with the AFL-CIO Ethical Practices Codes (Helstein to King, 8 July 1959).

To G. W. Sanders

15 June 1959
[*Montgomery, Ala.*]

During a 14 May address in Tallahassee, King voiced his opposition to the death penalty for four white men accused of raping a black teenager in Florida.[1] *Two weeks later Sanders chastised King for his remarks, reminding him that "just before you came to Tallahassee to talk clemency for four white men, two colored men sat in the death chair about forty-five minutes behind each other." Sanders also questioned King's right to "speak out in terms for clemency for guilty white men for raping a colored college girl?"*[2] *In the letter below, King defends himself against the charge of being one of those "highbrow intellectuals" and explains his reasoning: "I have always felt that the purpose of punishment is to improve the character and life of the person punished, rather than pay him back for something that he has done to society."*

Mr. G. W. Sanders
1080 West Adams Street
Jacksonville, Florida

Dear Mr. Sanders:

I am in receipt of your letter of May 29, some misgivings about a statement that I made incident to my visit to Tallahassee, Florida for a meeting of the Southern Christian Leadership Conference.

I fear that you might have misunderstood my statement or that it may have been misquoted. I never suggested that the men who committed this tragic crime should not be punished. I made it emphatically clear that they should be punished on the basis of the crime they had committed, and that failure of the jury to do this would bring shame to the whole state of Florida and the United States. I went on to say that this was a time and opportunity for the white South to prove that it did not adhere to a double standard of justice. After that I went on to say that some of us were not necessarily calling for capital punishment. Even though we ourselves have been the victims of capital punishment for much less crimes and even in cases where it hasn't been proved that we were guilty. I am certainly as aware as you are of the fact that many Negroes have been the victims of capital punishment in most of the southern states for the sheer accusation of rape, rather than the actual proving of it.

I made the statement about capital punishment for two reasons. First, I am absolutely convinced that no jury in the state of Florida will render a verdict calling

---

1. "Eyes of the World Waiting to See if Justice Will Be Done in Tallahassee—King," *Atlanta Daily World,* 16 May 1959; see also Statement Adopted at Spring Session of SCLC, 15 May 1959, pp. 205–208 in this volume. For more on King's reaction to this rape case, see King to Clifford C. Taylor, 5 May 1959, p. 196 in this volume. A few months after this letter, King responded to another rape incident of a black girl by a white man (King to Lottie Lett, 8 October 1959).

2. Sanders to King, 29 May 1959.

for capital punishment for four white men on a rape case on a Negro, so that by not calling for capital punishment I felt that it might be possible to reach the hearts and souls of some of the white people who would see that our aim was not to retaliate and pay back for all of the injustices that have been heaped upon us. The second reason that I made this statement was that I sincerely believe that capital punishment is wrong. Let me assure you that I say this in all humility because I am still humbly groping for truth. It is certainly possible that I am wrong in my position. But I have always felt that the purpose of punishment is to improve the character and life of the person punished, rather than pay him back for something that he has done to society. Now if the ultimate aim is to improve the character of the person, how can their character be improved when the person is inflicted with death? So on the basis of this I don't believe in capital punishment for white people or Negro people. It was as a result of this general principle that I made my assertion.

I can understand how you feel at this time because so many Negroes have been the victims of capital punishment. I realize that the first thing that comes to your mind as well as many other people is that the same thing that has been done to the Negro should be done to these white men. But I still feel the need of bringing the Christian ethic of love in all of my dealings in the area of race relations. And when I follow Christ to the end I find myself willing to forgive, to refuse to retaliate, and to refuse to hate. I know this is difficult and sometimes it sounds unrealistic, but I am still convinced that love is the most durable power in all the world. Consequently I would rather be the reciepient of violence than the inflictor of it. I would rather be hated than to hate. I would rather be the victim of injustice than the inflictor of injustice upon another. And I am foolish enough to believe that in the long run it is through this approach that we will be able to create a society of brotherhood based on the principle of mutual respect, and man's humanity to man.

Again, I say although the white man has done us wrong it is our Christian obligation not to do them wrong. We must work passionately and unrelentingly for first-class citizenship. We must stand up positively, courageously, with bold and grim determination to be free. But I think it is possible to do this with love in our hearts and the willingness to forgive. If we seek to do the same thing to the white man that he has done to us over the years, the new order which is emerging will be nothing but a duplicate of the old order. Someone must have religion enough and morality enough to meet hate with love, to meet physical force with soul force. This has been my contention all along, and I am willing to tread the road alone feeling that ultimately my faith will be vendicated.

Let me close by saying that I regret very deeply that you feel that I am one of those highbrow intellectuals who knows nothing about history and what the white man has done to the Negro. And even more I was shocked to read your statement that I had given aid to the white man, thereby exalting white supremacy.[3] If my

3. In his letter, Sanders stated that "some of our high, educated men and women do not take time to re-read their text books. They go along telling the southern white man, by action, that he is your white supremacy."

life, with the accompanying trials, tribulations, and difficulties that I have faced for my people have not proven my courage, then there is no way that I can convince anyone. I have lived amid threats, intimidation, physical violence, and even death, and yet I have never run from the situation. I have urged my people at all times to stand up against segregation, and even disobey the segregation laws in order to arouse and awaken the conscience of our nation. I will continue to do this, but I will do it in the right spirit. I will never allow any man to drag me so low as to make me hate him; and above all I will never become bitter.

Let us pray and hope that the light of God will shine in our situation, so that in the not too distant future we will be able to emerge from the bleak and desolate midnight of man's inhumanity to man into the bright and glittering daybreak of freedom and justice.

Very sincerely yours,
Martin L. King, Jr.

MLK:mlb

TLc. MLKP-MBU: Box 68.

"My Trip to the Land of Gandhi"

July 1959
Chicago, Ill.

In this account of his India tour published in Ebony *magazine, King notes that Gandhi's spirit is still alive though "some of his disciples have misgivings about this when . . . they look around and find nobody today who comes near the stature of the Mahatma."*[1] *Lamenting India's pervasive economic inequalities, King observes that "the bourgeoise—white, black or brown—behaves about the same the world over," and he calls upon the West to aid India's development "in a spirit of international brotherhood, not national selfishness."*

For a long time I had wanted to take a trip to India. Even as a child the entire Orient held a strange fascination for me—the elephants, the tigers, the temples, the snake charmers and all the other storybook characters.

While the Montgomery boycott was going on, India's Gandhi was the guiding light of our technique of non-violent social change. We spoke of him often. So as soon as our victory over bus segregation was won, some of my friends said: "Why don't you go to India and see for yourself what the Mahatma, whom you so admire, has wrought."

In 1956 when Pandit Jawaharlal Nehru, India's Prime Minister, made a short visit to the United States, he was gracious enough to say that he wished that he and I had met and had his diplomatic representatives make inquiries as to the possibility of my visiting his country some time soon. Our former American ambassador to India, Chester Bowles, wrote me along the same lines.[2]

But every time that I was about to make the trip, something would interfere. At one time it was my visit by prior commitment to Ghana.[3] At another time my publishers were pressing me to finish writing *Stride Toward Freedom.* Then along came Mrs. Izola Ware Curry. When she struck me with that Japanese letter opener on that Saturday afternoon in September as I sat autographing books in a Harlem store, she not only knocked out the travel plans that I had but almost everything else as well.

After I recovered from this near-fatal encounter and was finally released by my doctors, it occurred to me that it might be better to get in the trip to India before plunging too deeply once again into the sea of the Southern segregation struggle.

---

1. Four weeks after returning from India, King prepared a draft of this article (Draft, "My trip to India," April 1959; see also Maude L. Ballou to Lerone Bennett, 17 April 1959). Nine photographs accompanied it, including pictures of King meeting Prime Minister Nehru and the Kings and traveling companion Lawrence Reddick placing a wreath at the site of Gandhi's cremation.

2. Bowles to King, 28 January 1957; see also Homer Alexander Jack to King, 27 December 1956, in *Papers* 3:496, 498.

3. In March 1957 King attended the Ghanian independence celebrations. For more on King's trip to Ghana, see Introduction in *Papers* 4:7–9.

I preferred not to take this long trip alone and asked my wife and my friend, Lawrence Reddick, to accompany me. Coretta was particularly interested in the women of India and Dr. Reddick in the history and government of that great country. He had written my biography, *Crusader Without Violence,* and said that my true test would come when the people who knew Gandhi looked me over and passed judgment upon me and the Montgomery movement. The three of us made up a sort of 3-headed team with six eyes and six ears for looking and listening.

The Christopher Reynolds Foundation made a grant through the American Friends Service Committee to cover most of the expenses of the trip and the Southern Christian Leadership Conference and the Montgomery Improvement Association added their support.[4] The Gandhi Memorial Trust of India extended an official invitation, through diplomatic channels, for our visit.[5]

And so on February 3, 1959, just before midnight, we left New York by plane. En route we stopped in Paris with Richard Wright, an old friend of Reddick's, who brought us up to date on European attitudes on the Negro question and gave us a taste of the best French cooking.[6]

We missed our plane connection in Switzerland because of fog, arriving in India after a roundabout route, two days late. But from the time we came down out of the clouds at Bombay on February 10, until March 10, when we waved goodbye at the New Delhi airport, we had one of the most concentrated and eye-opening experiences of our lives. There is so much to tell that I can only touch upon a few of the high points.

At the outset, let me say that we had a grand reception in India. The people showered upon us the most generous hospitality imaginable. We were graciously received by the Prime Minister, the President and the Vice-President of the nation; members of Parliament, Governors and Chief Ministers of various Indian states; writers, professors, social reformers and at least one saint.[7] Since our pictures were in the newspapers very often it was not unusual for us to be recognized by crowds in public places and on public conveyances.[8] Occasionally I would take a morning walk in the large cities, and out of the most unexpected places someone would emerge and ask: "Are you Martin Luther King?"

Virtually every door was open to us. We had hundreds of invitations that the

---

4. The Reynolds Foundation provided $4,000 for the trip, SCLC provided an additional $500, and the MIA and Dexter Avenue Baptist Church presented the Kings with a money tree at a "bon voyage" celebration in their honor on 26 January (AFSC, "Budget: leadership intervisitation, visit to India by Martin Luther and Coretta King," February–March 1959, and "The Kings Leave Country," *Dexter Echo,* 11 February 1959).

5. See G. Ramachandran to King, 27 December 1958, in *Papers* 4:552–553.

6. Wright, an African American novelist, had lived in Paris since 1947. In a draft of this article, King had crossed out the reference to Wright. For more on King's visit with Wright, see Introduction, p. 4 in this volume.

7. Among those King met were Nehru, President Rajendra Prasad, Vice President Sarvepalli Radhakrishnan, and member of Parliament Sucheta Kripalani. King also refers to Gandhi's disciple Vinoba Bhave.

8. King's draft phrased this differently: "Our pictures were in the newspapers very often and we were recognized by crowds at the circus and by pilots on the planes." The draft did not include the subsequent sentence or the following two paragraphs.

limited time did not allow us to accept. We were looked upon as brothers with the color of our skins as something of an asset. But the strongest bond of fraternity was the common cause of minority and colonial peoples in America, Africa and Asia struggling to throw off racialism and imperialism.

We had the opportunity to share our views with thousands of Indian people through endless conversations and numerous discussion sessions. I spoke before university groups and public meetings all over India. Because of the keen interest that the Indian people have in the race problem these meetings were usually packed. Occasionally interpreters were used, but on the whole I spoke to audiences that understood English.

The Indian people love to listen to the Negro spirituals. Therefore, Coretta ended up singing as much as I lectured. We discovered that autograph seekers are not confined to America. After appearances in public meetings and while visiting villages we were often besieged for autographs. Even while riding planes, more than once pilots came into the cabin from the cockpit requesting our signatures.

We got a good press throughout our stay. Thanks to the Indian papers, the Montgomery bus boycott was already well known in that country. Indian publications perhaps gave a better continuity of our 381-day bus strike than did most of our papers in the United States. Occasionally I meet some American fellow citizen who even now asks me how the bus boycott is going, apparently never having read that our great day of bus integration, December 21, 1956, closed that chapter of our history.

We held press conferences in all of the larger cities—Delhi, Calcutta, Madras and Bombay—and talked with newspaper men almost everywhere we went. They asked sharp questions and at times appeared to be hostile but that was just their way of bringing out the story that they were after. As reporters, they were scrupulously fair with us and in their editorials showed an amazing grasp of what was going on in America and other parts of the world.

The trip had a great impact upon me personally. It was wonderful to be in Gandhi's land, to talk with his son, his grandsons, his cousin and other relatives; to share the reminiscences of his close comrades; to visit his ashrama, to see the countless memorials for him and finally to lay a wreath on his entombed ashes at Rajghat.[9] I left India more convinced than ever before that non-violent resistance is the most potent weapon available to oppressed people in their struggle for freedom.[10] It was a marvelous thing to see the amazing results of a non-violent campaign. The aftermath of hatred and bitterness that usually follows a violent campaign was found nowhere in India. Today a mutual friendship based on complete equality exists between the Indian and British people within the commonwealth. The way of acquiescence leads to moral and spiritual suicide. The way of violence leads to bitterness in the survivors and brutality in the destroyers. But, the way of non-violence leads to redemption and the creation of the beloved community.

The spirit of Gandhi is very much alive in India today. Some of his disciples have misgivings about this when they remember the drama of the fight for na-

---

9. See King to Ramdas M. Gandhi, 8 August 1959, pp. 255–256 in this volume.

10. This sentence and the remainder of the paragraph were not included in King's draft.

tional independence and when they look around and find nobody today who comes near the stature of the Mahatma. But any objective observer must report that Gandhi is not only the greatest figure in India's history but that his influence is felt in almost every aspect of life and public policy today.

India can never forget Gandhi. For example, the Gandhi Memorial Trust (also known as the Gandhi Smarak Nidhi) collected some $130 million soon after the death of "the father of the nation." This was perhaps the largest, spontaneous, mass monetary contribution to the memory of a single individual in the history of the world. This fund, along with support from the Government and other institutions, is resulting in the spread and development of Gandhian philosophy, the implementing of his constructive program, the erection of libraries and the publication of works by and about the life and times of Gandhi. Posterity could not escape him even if it tried. By all standards of measurement, he is one of the half dozen greatest men in world history.

I was delighted that the Gandhians accepted us with open arms. They praised our experiment with the non-violent resistance technique at Montgomery. They seem to look upon it as an outstanding example of the possibilities of its use in western civilization. To them as to me it also suggests that non-violent resistance *when planned and positive in action* can work effectively even under totalitarian regimes.

We argued this point at some length with the groups of African students who are today studying in India.[11] They felt that non-violent resistance could only work in a situation where the resisters had a potential ally in the conscience of the opponent. We soon discovered that they, like many others, tended to confuse passive resistance with non-resistance. This is completely wrong. True non-violent resistance is not unrealistic submission to evil power. It is rather a courageous confrontation of evil by the power of love, in the faith that it is better to be the recipient of violence than the inflictor of it, since the latter only multiplies the existence of violence and bitterness in the universe, while the former may develop a sense of shame in the opponent, and thereby bring about a transformation and change of heart.

Non-violent resistance does call for love, but it is not a sentimental love. It is a very stern love that would organize itself into collective action to right a wrong by taking on itself suffering. While I understand the reasons why oppressed people often turn to violence in their struggle for freedom, it is my firm belief that the crusade for independence and human dignity that is now reaching a climax in Africa will have a more positive effect on the world, if it is waged along the lines that were first demonstrated in that continent by Gandhi himself.[12]

India is a vast country with vast problems. We flew over the long stretches, from North to South, East to West; took trains for shorter jumps and used automobiles and jeeps to get us into the less accessible places.

---

11. King's draft added the following sentence: "They, like many others, seem to feel that nonviolent resistance means non-resistance, do nothing." The remainder of the paragraph and the following paragraph were not included in the draft.

12. King's draft included the following paragraph: "We also learned a lot from the India journalists. Our practice was to divide the time of our press conferences between questions they asked us and questions we asked them."

India is about a third the size of the United States but has almost three times as many people. Everywhere we went we saw crowded humanity—on the roads, in the city streets and squares, even in the villages.[13]

Most of the people are poor and poorly dressed. The average income per person is less than $70 per year. Nevertheless, their turbans for their heads, loose flowing, wrap-around *dhotis* that they wear instead of trousers and the flowing saries that the women wear instead of dresses are colorful and picturesque. Many Indians wear part native and part western dress.

We think that we in the United States have a big housing problem but in the city of Bombay, for example, over a half million people sleep out of doors every night. These are mostly unattached, unemployed or partially employed males. They carry their bedding with them like foot soldiers and unroll it each night in any unoccupied space they can find—on the sidewalk, in a railroad station or at the entrance of a shop that is closed for the evening.

The food shortage is so widespread that it is estimated that less than 30% of the people get what we would call three square meals a day. During our great depression of the 1930's, we spoke of "a third of a nation" being "ill-housed, ill clad and ill fed." For India today, simply change one third to two thirds in that statement and that would make it about right.

As great as is unemployment, under-employment is even greater. Seventy per cent of the Indian people are classified as agricultural workers and most of these do less than 200 days of farm labor per year because of the seasonal fluctuations and other uncertainties of mother nature. Jobless men roam the city streets.

Great ills flow from the poverty of India but strangely there is relatively little crime. Here is another concrete manifestation of the wonderful spiritual quality of the Indian people. They are poor, jammed together and half starved but they do not take it out on each other. They are a kindly people. They do not abuse each other—verbally or physically—as readily as we do. We saw but one fist fight in India during our stay.[14]

In contrast to the poverty-stricken, there are Indians who are rich, have luxurious homes, landed estates, fine clothes and show evidence of over-eating. The bourgeoise—white, black or brown—behaves about the same the world over.

And then there is, even here, the problem of segregation. We call it race in America; they call it caste in India. In both places it means that some are considered inferior, treated as though they deserve less.

---

13. King's draft added the following: "The people have a way of squatting, resting comfortably (it seemed) on their haunches. Many of the homes do not have chairs and most of the cities have very few park or street benches."

14. In King's draft, he had stricken the following two paragraphs: "There is great consideration for human life but little regard for labor and time. We saw men mending shoes almost without tools. Five persons may be sent to bring down a package that one could carry. Human muscles there do many jobs that our machines do here. Moreover, nobody seems to be in a hurry and it is surprising when arrangements and appointments come off according to schedule. [¶] Young boys accost you everywhere, persistently offering to supply you with just about anything your heart could desire and your pocket book can pay for. Begging is widespread though the government has done much to discourage it. But what can you do when an old haggard woman or a little crippled urchin comes up and motions to you that she is hungry?"

We were surprised and delighted to see that India has made greater progress in the fight against caste "untouchability" than we have made here in our own country against race segregation. Both nations have federal laws against discrimination (acknowledging, of course, that the decision of our Supreme Court is the law of our land). But after this has been said, we must recognize that there are great differences between what India has done and what we have done on a problem that is very similar. The leaders of India have placed their moral power behind their law. From the Prime Minister down to the village councilmen, everybody declares publicly that untouchability is wrong. But in the United States some of our highest officials decline to render a moral judgment on segregation and some from the South publicly boast of their determination to maintain segregation. This would be unthinkable in India.

Moreover, Gandhi not only spoke against the caste system but he acted against it. He took "untouchables" by the hand and led them into the temples from which they had been excluded. To equal that, President Eisenhower would take a Negro child by the hand and lead her into Central High School in Little Rock.

Gandhi also renamed the untouchables, calling them "Harijans" which means "children of God."

The government has thrown its full weight behind the program of giving the Harijans an equal chance in society—especially when it comes to job opportunities, education and housing.

India's leaders, in and out of government, are conscious of their country's other great problems and are heroically grappling with them. The country seems to be divided. Some say that India should become westernized and modernized as quickly as possible so that she might raise her standards of living. Foreign capital and foreign industry should be invited in, for in this lies the salvation of the almost desperate situation.

On the other hand, there are others—perhaps the majority—who say that westernization will bring with it the evils of materialism, cut throat competition and rugged individualism; that India will lose her soul if she takes to chasing Yankee dollars; and that the big machine will only raise the living standards of the comparative few workers who get jobs but that the greater number of people will be displaced and will thus be worse off than they are now.

Prime Minister Nehru, who is at once an intellectual and a man charged with the practical responsibility of heading the government, seems to steer a middle course between these extreme attitudes. In our talk with him he indicated that he felt that some industrialization was absolutely necessary; that there were some things that only big or heavy industry could do for the country but that if the state keeps a watchful eye on the developments, most of the pitfalls may be avoided.

At the same time, Mr. Nehru gives support to the movement that would encourage and expand the handicraft arts such as spinning and weaving in home and village and thus leaving as much economic self help and autonomy as possible to the local community.

There is a great movement in India that is almost unknown in America. At its center is the campaign for land reform known as Bhoodan. It would solve India's great economic and social change by consent, not by force. The Bhoodanists are led by the sainted Vinoba Bhave and Jayaprakash Narayan, a highly sensitive intellectual, who was trained in American colleges.[15] Their ideal is the self-sufficient village. Their program envisions

1. *Persuading* large land owners to give up some of their holding to landless peasants;
2. *Persuading* small land owners to give up their individual ownership for common cooperative ownership by the villages;
3. *Encouraging* farmers and villagers to spin and weave the cloth for their own clothes during their spare time from their agricultural pursuits.

Since these measures would answer the questions of employment, food and clothing, the village could then, through cooperative action, make just about everything that it would need or get it through barter or exchange from other villages. Accordingly, each village would be virtually self sufficient and would thus free itself from the domination of the urban centers that are today like evil loadstones drawing the people away from the rural areas, concentrating them in city slums and debauching them with urban vices. At least this is the argument of the Bhoodanists and other Gandhians.

Such ideas sound strange and archaic to Western ears. However, the Indians have already achieved greater results than we Americans would ever expect. For example, millions of acres of land have been given up by rich landlords and additional millions of acres have been given up to cooperative management by small farmers. On the other hand, the Bhoodanists shrink from giving their movement the organization and drive that we in America would venture to guess that it must have in order to keep pace with the magnitude of the problems that everybody is trying to solve.

Even the government's five year plans fall short in that they do not appear to be of sufficient scope to embrace their objectives. Thus, the three five-year plans were designed to provide 25,000,000 new jobs over a 15 year period but the birth rate of India is 6,000,000 per year. This means that in 15 years there will be 9,000,000 more people (less those who have died or retired) looking for the 15 million new jobs.[16] In other words, if the planning were 100 per cent successful, it could not keep pace with the growth of problems it is trying to solve.

As for what should be done, we surely do not have the answer. But we do feel certain that India needs help. She must have outside capital and technical know-how. It is in the interest of the United States and the West to help supply these needs and *not attach strings to the gifts.*

Whatever we do should be done in a spirit of international brotherhood, not national selfishness. It should be done not merely because it is diplomatically expedient, but because it is morally compelling. At the same time, it will rebound

---

15. For King's 1959 interview with Vinoba Bhave, see Vinola, "Dr. Martin Luther King with Vinoba," *Bhoodan* 3 (18 March 1959): 369–370; see also King to Narayan, 19 May 1959, pp. 209–211 in this volume.

16. King's draft indicated that ninety million more people would be looking for work.

to the credit of the West if India is able to maintain her democracy while solving her problems.[17]

It would be a boon to democracy if one of the great nations of the world, with almost 400,000,000 people, proves that it is possible to provide a good living for everyone without surrendering to a dictatorship of either the "right" or "left." Today India is a tremendous force for peace and non-violence, at home and abroad. It is a land where the idealist and the intellectual are yet respected. We should want to help India preserve her soul and thus help to save our own.

PD. *Ebony,* July 1959, pp. 84–92.

---

17. In his draft, King marked the following sentence for deletion: "Her people are remarkably patient but many of them are looking toward their neighbor to the North and noting that China under the discipline of communism seems to be moving ahead more rapidly than India."

From Swami Vishwananda

2 July 1959
New Delhi, India

In a 19 May letter, King thanked Vishwananda, secretary of the Delhi branch of the Gandhi Smarak Nidhi, for serving as his guide through India and commented that he had "never been showered with such hospitality" nor "met people more genuine and loving."[1] King concluded: "I am almost driven to say that I have an affection for the Indian people unlike that that I have for any other people in the world."[2]

Dr. Martin Luther King Jr.,
Dexter Ave., Baptist Church,
454 Dexter Avenue,
Montgomery-4, ALABAMA.

{My} Dear Dr. King,

It was kind of you to have written such a sweet letter. Many who saw the letter have appreciated it deeply, particularly your expression of affection for the people of India.

---

1. Swami Vishwananda (1910–) served as secretary of the Gurukul ashram (1935–1955) and of the Harijan Sevak Sangh (1942–1955), an organization dedicated to the nonviolent eradication of untouchability. He worked at Gandhigram (1955–1958), when he began a two-year stint with the Delhi Gandhi Smarak Nidhi. He returned to Gandhigram in 1962.

2. In a booklet published to commemorate the visit, Vishwananda recalled King's departure from Delhi: "Some of us were very silent; the relationship that had developed was too sacred. When the heart speaks the tongue is silent. Our eyes searched the skies until the plane that carried the Kings to Pakistan disappeared over the horizon" (*With the Kings in India: A Souvenir of Dr. Martin Luther King's Visit to India, February 1959–March 1959* [New Delhi: Gandhi National Memorial Fund, 1959]).

I am grateful to you for what you said about me personally and shall strive to deserve it better. The thirty years and odd I have given to the service of humanity, I feel, have not been as complete as they should have been, nor adequate enough, though intentions all along have been good. But it is in His hands to use this humble instrument for what it is worth.

I hope you would not mind this deviation as it has been provoked by your letter.

The correct way my name is written is Swami Vishwananda.

Please convey my affection to Mrs. King, the children and Dr. Reddick.

Yours sincerely,
[*signed*] Vishwananda
(Swami Vishwananda)

TALS. MLKP-MBU: Box 26.

To Ella J. Baker

3 July 1959
[*Montgomery, Ala.*]

King suggests that Baker prepare a series of press releases for the upcoming "Institute on Non-Violent Resistance to Segregation" at Spelman College. In her 7 July reply, Baker detailed plans for the conference and informed King that his "suggestions regarding press releases will be followed." On 22 July, King delivered the keynote address at the conference, which was co-sponsored by SCLC, the Congress of Racial Equality (CORE), and FOR.[1]

Miss Ella J. Baker
Executive Director
The Southern Christian Leadership Conference
208 Auburn Ave, N.E.
Atlanta, Georgia

Dear Ella:

Enclosed is a copy of the letter that I have just received from the Indian Ambassador. Since we cannot get a figure of his caliber I suggest that we dispense with the mass meeting.[2] This means that the conference will close after Friday afternoon's session.

1. For more information on the institute, see Resolutions, First Southwide Institute on Nonviolent Resistance to Segregation, 11 August 1959, pp. 261–262 in this volume.

2. The Indian ambassador to the United States, M. C. Chagla, declined King's invitation to address the institute, explaining in a 1 July letter that it would be inappropriate for him "to intervene on a question which solely concerns the Government of this country and its people." He added: "I must keep aloof from all controversies and . . . the question of segregation is one of the most controversial subjects to-day" (see also King to Chagla, 19 June 1959).

M E M O R A N D U M

FROM: Ella J. Baker

To: Rev. M.L.King, Jr, and Rev. Ralph D. Abernathy

R E: * SCHEDULE OF NONVIOLENT INSTITUTE

The following skeletal draft was drawn up by Dr. Reddick and myself just prior to my trip to New York. It was my hope that it could ~~have~~ have been discussed with Bayard Rustin and Glenn Smiley while there. However this did not work out. So it is being submitted for your thinking:

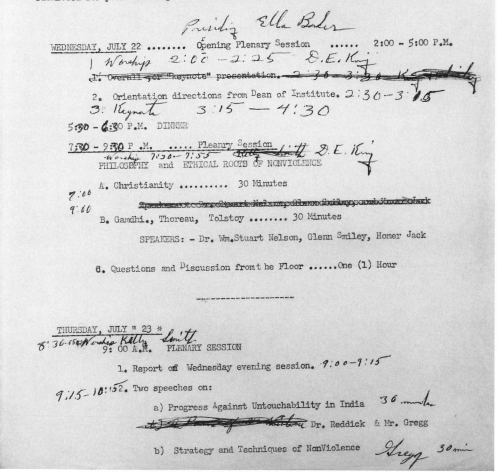

Presiding Ella Baker

WEDNESDAY, JULY 22 .... Opening Plenary Session ...... 2:00 - 5:00 P.M.

1 Worship 2:00 -2:25 D.E. King

~~1. Overall or "keynote" presentation. 2:30-3:30 K~~

2. Orientation directions from Dean of Institute. 2:30-3:15

3. Keynote 3:15 — 4:30

5:30 - 6:30 P.M. DINNER

7:30 - 9:30 P .M. ..... Pleanry Session ~~Kelly Smith~~ D. E. King

Worship 7:30-7:55

PHILOSOPHY and ETHICAL ROOTS OF NONVIOLENCE

A. Christianity .... 30 Minutes

7:00 ~~Speakers: Dr. Stuart Nelson, Glenn Smiley, and Homer Jack~~

9:00

B. Gandhi., Thoreau, Tolstoy .... 30 Minutes

SPEAKERS: - Dr. Wm.Stuart Nelson, Glenn Smiley, Homer Jack

C. Questions and Discussion fromt he Floor ......One (1) Hour

---

THURSDAY, JULY " 23 *

8:30-55 Worship Kelly Smith

9: 00 A.M. PLENARY SESSION

1. Report on Wednesday evening session. 9:00-9:15

9:15-10:15 2. Two speeches on:

a) Progress Against Untouchability in India 30 minutes

~~a) The Power of Non-Violence~~ Dr. Reddick & Mr. Gregg

b) Strategy and Techniques of NonViolence Gregg 30 min

King writes handwritten comments on Ella Baker's proposed schedule for SCLC's July 1959 First Southwide Institute on Nonviolent Resistance to Segregation (July 1959)

FRIDAY, JULY 24, 1959

MORNING SESSION
Dr. C. O. Simpkins, Presiding

8:30 - 8:55	WORSHIP SERVICE	Dr. Harry Richardson
9:00 - 9:15	Report on Thursday evening session	
9:15 - 10:15	PANEL DISCUSSION -	Allies and Opponents of Negroes Drive for Equality (Participants- Will Campbell, "The White Church," and Ella J. Baker, "Power Structure of the South."
10:15 - 10:30	Brief question period.	
10:30 - 12:30	Break up into small groups.	

AFTERNOON SESSION
Dr. Charles Lawrence, Presiding

2:00 - 4:00	Summary Session. (Reports on morning session, overall reports, recommendations, etc.)

EVENING SESSION

PUBLIC MASS MEETING

In order to keep the conference before the public I would suggest getting a press release out every week leading up to the conference. In one of them you may stress the fact that Dr. Nelson will be one of the key speakers.[3] This will give you an opportunity to make a statement about his background and his broad knowledge about the Gandhian philosophy. You may get another release out on Charles Lawrence and Richard Gregg.[4] Another one might deal with the whole question of violence which has become a live issue as a result of the Williams case, making it clear that this conference will emerge with some answer to the pressing questions on the lips of people all over this nation.[5]

Very sincerely yours,
Martin

MLK:mlb
Enc

TLc. MLKP-MBU: Box 20.

---

3. An article that was likely drawn from a Baker press release appeared in the *Atlanta Daily World* before the conference ("Dr. William Stuart Nelson to Address Leadership Institute," *Atlanta Daily World*, 14 July 1959). Nelson, the dean of Howard University, was an expert on Gandhi and had recently returned from an extended stay in India (see King to Nelson, 7 April 1959, pp. 181–182 in this volume).

4. SCLC, Press release, 3 July–22 July 1959. Lawrence was the national chairman of FOR (1955–1963); Gregg was a Gandhian scholar and a member of FOR.

5. SCLC, Press release, 25 July–28 July 1959. Union County, North Carolina, NAACP leader Robert F. Williams had recently advocated that African Americans defend themselves with weapons because of the failure of white authorities to protect black civil rights. For more on Williams, see King, Address at the Fiftieth Annual NAACP Convention, 17 July 1959, pp. 245–250 in this volume.

To Tom Mboya

8 July 1959
[*Montgomery, Ala.*]

On 16 June, shortly after attending an SCLC-sponsored "Africa Freedom Dinner," Kenyan nationalist leader Mboya wrote King requesting financial assistance for a Kenyan student who was to enter Tuskegee Institute in the fall.[1]

---

1. See King, Remarks Delivered at Africa Freedom Dinner at Atlanta University, 13 May 1959, pp. 203–204 in this volume.

Tom Mboya, [*M.?*]L.C.
P.O. Box 10818
Nairobi, Kenya

8 July 1959

Dear Tom Mboya:

I am in receipt of your very kind letter of recent date thanking the leaders of the Southern Christian Leadership Conference for the dinner in your honor. I should have written you before you wrote me to thank you for giving us the opportunity to honor ourselves in bringing you to Atlanta. Because of your distinguished career and dedicated work, the honor was ours and not yours. I will long remember the moments that we spent together. I am sure that you could sense from the response that you gained all over the United States that your visit here made a tremendous impact on the life of our nation. Your sense of purpose, your dedicated spirit, and your profound and eloquent statement of ideas all conjoin to make your contribution to our country one that will not soon be forgotten.

Thank you for your very kind comments concerning my book, Stride Toward Freedom.[2] This book is simply my humble attempt to bring moral and ethical principles to bare on the difficult problem of racial injustice which confronts our nation. I am happy to know that you found it helpful. I am absolutely convinced that there is no basic difference between colonialism and segregation. They are both based on a contempt for life, and a tragic doctrine of white supremacy. So our struggles are not only similiar; they are in a real sense one.

I am happy to know that you will have a student enrolled in Tuskegee Institute in the next few months. I will be happy to make some move in the direction of assisting this student. Please give me some idea of the amount of money that he will need over and above the aid that he will get from Tuskegee Institute itself.[3] Also let me know whether the money should be sent directly to you or given to him in person.

With warm personal regards, I am,

Sincerely yours,
Martin L. King, Jr.

MLK:mlb

TLc. MLKP-MBU: Box 26.

---

2. Mboya had written that he had never found himself "so completely captured by a book and ideas" (Mboya to King, 16 June 1959).

3. In a 31 July reply, Mboya indicated that the student would need $1,000. King arranged for Dexter Church and SCLC to support Nicholas W. Raballa, who was among an initial group of eighty-one Kenyan students flown to the United States on 7 September 1959 under a program organized by Mboya. More than one thousand Kenyan students would eventually take part in the "airlifts" to the United States (S. F. Yette, "M. L. King Supports African Student," *News of Tuskegee Institute,* December 1959; see also King to Raballa, 11 January 1960, and photograph of King and Raballa, p. 87 in this volume).

From Lynward W. Stevenson

11 July 1959
Chicago, Ill.

Stevenson, the pastor of Chicago's Parkway Garden Christian Church, asks King to speak at his church and reminisces about their days together at Morehouse College: "I recall Dr. Tillman's observation of you when you attempted to read LEAR for him: 'King, you are illiterate.'"[1]

Dr. Martin Luther King
Minister, Dexter Ave. Church
Montgomery, Alabama

Dear M. L.:

Our church is celebrating its 40th anniversary during the month of October. We would be extremely happy if we could involve you in this celebration as a speaker. If you can come, our Program Committee makes an initial offer of $100. and expenses. You, of course, can set your own fees if their offer is inadequate.

We have in mind a banquet setting in one of the Loop hotels on either the 16th or 23rd of October, depending on the date acceptable to you. If neither date is convenient for you we will take any date in October when you can come.

I hope that you can come to us. For forty years this church has wandered in the wilderness of petty things. Since my ministry began here, I have been pointing to wider horizons. We have moved into our first unit of a three-unit church; our membership has increased 50%. Two Palm Sundays ago we re-located in the new Parkway Garden Community under an arrangement of commity set up by the Church Federation of Greater Chicago. We are still small (only 350 members) but we aim at big things. Your coming would be our biggest undertaking.

I have never had the opportunity to tell you how proud I am of you. I boast of the fact that you and I took the same class in Shakespeare. Incidentally, I recall Dr. Tillman's observation of you when you attempted to read LEAR for him: "King, you are illiterate."[2] Of course even then he was far from the truth. I often wonder if Tillman himself recalls this. You have gone on to become our most articulate and thought-provoking American.

---

1. King declined the invitation in a 20 July letter, explaining that he had already accepted more speaking engagements than his doctors felt advisable. Lynward Willard Stevenson (1923–1982) was born in Louisville, Kentucky. After receiving a B.A. (1947) from Morehouse College, he taught English at Alabama State College. He received a B.Div. (1956) from the University of Chicago and shortly thereafter became the pastor of Parkway Garden Christian Church. He later served as pastor of Bethlehem Covenant Baptist Church (1962–1967) and Calvary Presbyterian Church (1967–1969). A longtime Chicago activist, Stevenson was president of the Woodlawn Organization (1964–1966) and assisted King's integration efforts in the city during the mid-1960s.

2. Nathaniel P. Tillman gave King a "B" during both semesters of the 1946–1947 school year (see Introduction, *The Papers of Martin Luther King, Jr.*, vol. 1: *Called to Serve, January 1929–June 1951*, ed. Clayborne Carson, Ralph E. Luker, Penny A. Russell [Berkeley: University of California Press, 1992], p. 40).

How is Dexter Ave. Church? When I taught at Alabama State, I worshipped at Dexter. Vernon Johns was then the pastor. As you know he has a sharp tongue. He told the congregation once that there were greater men than he, but they could not get them. But "One greater than John(S) has come."[3]

These little memories are not flatteries—you don't need this. This is my way of saying that I identify myself in the setting of your past and hope this fact will help you to decide to take time from a busy schedule to share with my people the riches of your life. May I hear from you?

Sincerely,
Lynward W. Stevenson

TL. MLKP-MBU: Box 50.

3. Cf. Luke 7:28; Matthew 11:11. Vernon Johns was King's immediate predecessor at Dexter.

Address at the Fiftieth Annual NAACP Convention

17 July 1959
New York, N.Y.

In June, NAACP executive secretary Roy Wilkins suspended Union County, North Carolina, branch president Robert F. Williams for public remarks he made following the acquittal of a white man accused of raping a black woman. Williams had asserted that the failure of the courts demanded that African Americans "meet violence with violence," and added: "We are going to have to try and convict these people on the spot."[1]

On 17 July, delegates at the association's convention overwhelmingly affirmed Wilkins's decision after a heated floor debate. Speaking that evening at a Youth Night program honoring young NAACP activists, King condemns Williams's comments and warns that resorting to retaliatory violence "would be the gravest tragedy that could befall" African Americans. He argues that "many of our oppressors would be more than happy for us to turn to violence" because "it would give them an opportunity to wipe out many innocent Negroes."[2]

Mr. Chairman, my good friend Mr. Wilkins, delegates to this Golden Anniversary celebration of the National Association for the Advancement of Colored People, ladies and gentlemen:

1. "N.A.A.C.P. Leader Urges 'Violence,'" *New York Times*, 7 May 1959; see also Wilkins, Telephone conversation with Robert F. Williams, 6 May 1959.

2. In a 3 August letter, Wilkins thanked King for his remarks to the NAACP: "No one in the country could have exposed the folly of violence as a weapon as crushingly and as convincingly as you did." For further discussion of King's views on the Williams case, see King, "The Social Organization of Nonviolence," October 1959, pp. 299–304 in this volume.

I am indeed honored to have the opportunity of sharing in the 50th anniversary observance of this great organization. I bring sincere and hearty greeting to you from the Montgomery Improvement Association and the Southern Christian Leadership Conference.

We salute you not merely because you have existed fifty years, but because your fifty years have been filled with creative purpose, calm dignity, determined courage, and meaningful fulfillment. The work of the NAACP is one of the glowing epics of our time. Your aims have been noble and your ideals have been sublime; your dedication has been inspiring and your achievements have been amazing. Your work has served as a great beacon light of hope to all men who have been caught in the stormy seas of oppression. Some day all of America will take pride in your achievements.

I have been asked to present to this convention a group of young people whose achievements have been outstanding examples of NAACP youth in action.[3] I am delighted beyond the power of expression to have this responsibility. These young people have given Negroes everywhere a new sense of dignity and destiny. They have manifested a maturity beyond their years. Their noble activities have already been stenciled on millions of mental sheets, and their names have been etched in innumerable hearts.

With this general background, let me state the specific reasons why we pause to recognize these youth.

First, we honor these young people because of their quiet, yet intrepid, courage. There is nothing more admirable in all the world than true courage. Without it, nations are pushed into the valley of social stagnation and individuals are plunged into the abyss of moral cowardice; without it, social change would be a floating dream and progress a glorified illusion. Without courage, noble yesterdays can never unfold into glorious tomorrows. So, in a real sense, the courage of these young people has contributed to the survival of the ideals and values of our nation. They have walked with fortitude through hostile and jeering mobs, and they have stood firm when the clouds of physical danger were hovering mighty low. I know that the bravery, the dignity, and the suffering of these Negro youth will be an inspiration to generations yet unborn.

Second, through their powerful positive action these young people have made it palpably clear that segregation is a moral and social evil that they will never passively accept. They have made it clear that they will not take no for an answer, they will not take a do-nothing gradualism for an answer, they will not take evasive schemes for an answer. They are saying in no uncertain terms, "We want integration now."

No well thinking person can deny the essential rightness of this position. If democracy is to live, segregation must die. Segregation is a cancer in the body politic which must be removed before our democratic health can be realized. It is a festering sore that debilitates the white man as well as the Negro. Therefore, we can

3. On a copy of an NAACP memorandum forwarded to King outlining the achievements of the young people, King wrote that their "activity during 1958–59 made them outstanding examples of NAACP youth in action" (Herbert L. Wright, Memo to John A. Morsell, 8 July 1959).

never be content with an outmoded doctrine of separate-but-equal. In the area of race relations the separate is inherently unequal. And above all segregation is morally wrong. It relegates persons to the status of things and leaves their personalities distorted and their souls damaged. The underlying philosophy of segregation is diametrically opposed to the underlying philosophy of Christianity and all the dialectics of the logicians cannot make them lie down together.

Third, we honor these young people because they conducted their courageous struggle against segregation on the highest level of dignity and discipline. They avoided both external physical violence and internal violence of the spirit. By their very action they recognized that there is a necessary correlation between means and ends, and that a moral end does not justify immoral means, because the end is pre-existent in the means.

There is something basic that we must all learn from this. There has been considerable talk recently on the question of whether the Negro should meet violence with violence. It has been suggested that maybe the doctrine of love and non-violence are weak and cowardly positions which have no place in the present struggle for racial justice. I would like to take a few minutes to seriously discuss this matter with you.

First, it must be clearly stated that the method of non-violence does not mean doing nothing; it does resist. If non-violence meant passive do-nothingism and complacent adjustment to evil, I would be the first to condemn it. No righteous man can fail to resist evil. Non-cooperation with evil is as much a moral obligation as is cooperation with good. It is at this point that non-violence comes in as a powerful method. It makes it possible for individuals to stand up against evil and yet not resist it with physical weapons or inner feelings. of bitterness. Certainly, no one fully understanding this approach would call it a method of weakness. Would you say that these young people from Oklahoma, Kansas and Virginia followed a weak course of action simply because they did not use violence and bitterness as their approach?[4] Would you call the powerfully organized protest of the 50,000 Negroes of Montgomery, Alabama, weak simply because they walked and sacrificed 381 days without retaliating with a single act of violence? Of course not. These were dramatic acts of strength. It is the strong man who can resist evil without violence.

Yes, non-violence calls for love, but it is not a weak and sentimental love; it is a strong love that organizes itself into positive social action.

It is my prayerful hope that our natural resentment over the injustices that are constantly heaped upon us will not cause us to stoop to the low and primitive methods of some of our opponents. I know how we feel as we face the viciousness of lynch mobs and the tragic midnight of unjust southern courts. I know how patient we have been, and how the cup of endurance can eventually run over. But in spite of all, we must not allow ourselves to become bitter.

---

4. Among those honored during the program were members of NAACP Youth Councils from Oklahoma City and Wichita who had led sit-in protests at local restaurants and department stores and fifty-five students attending newly integrated schools in Virginia. The Laurel, Mississippi, Youth Council was also honored for attending NAACP meetings in defiance of their principal's orders. According to a press report, King requested that the Oklahoma City group stand up for recognition during his address ("'Hallelujahs' Greet King's NAACP Speech," *New York Amsterdam News,* 25 July 1959).

We all realize that there will probably be some sporatic violence during this period of transition, and people will naturally seek to protect their property and person, but for the Negro to privately or publicly call for retaliatory violence as a strategy during this period would be the gravest tragedy that could befall us. It would be most impractical. Many of our oppressors would be more than happy for us to turn to violence. It would give them an opportunity to wipe out many innocent Negroes under the pretence that they were inciting a riot. I am convinced that if we had resorted to violence in Montgomery, Alabama, our protest would have ended in utter defeat. Our opponents were always disappointed when we refused to retaliate with violence. The power of non-violence is that it presents the opponent with a method that he does not know how to handle. The opponent always knows how to deal with violence because oppressors always control the instruments and techniques of violence.

Violence is also impractical as a method because it would only serve to increase the fears of the white South, and thereby increase the resistance. It must also be stressed that there are more and more white persons of goodwill who are willing to be our allies in this struggle, and certainly we need them if we are to win. But the minute we call for violence as a method, that support would almost completely disappear. So even if we cannot go to the point of accepting non-violence as a philosophy of life, we must admit that it is the best strategy for the present situation.

But beyond this there are some of us who still believe that violence is immoral. It is immoral because it seeks to humiliate the opponent rather than win his friendship and understanding; it seeks to annihilate rather than convert. It is immoral because it thrives on hatred rather than love. It destroys the community and makes brotherhood impossible.

Fourth, the young people that we pause to honor tonight have demonstrated a willingness to pay whatever price is necessary for freedom. They have recognized that freedom is a priceless possession which every man must possess if he is to be truly human.

Tolstoy, the Russian writer, said in War and Peace: "I cannot conceive of a man not being free unless he is dead."[5] While this statement sounds a bit exaggerated, it gets at a basic truth. What Tolstoy is saying in substance is that the absence of freedom is the presence of death. Any nation or government that deprives an individual of freedom is in that moment committing an act of moral and spiritual murder. Any individual who is not concerned about his freedom commits an act of moral and spiritual suicide. He, at that moment, forfeits his right to be. The struggle for freedom is not a struggle to attain some ephemeral desire; it is a struggle to maintain one's very selfhood. It is a struggle to avoid a tragic death of the spirit. It is no wonder that there have been those discerning individuals throughout history who have been willing to suffer sacrifice and even face the possibility of physical death in order to gain freedom. They have had the vision to realize that physical death may be more desirable than a permanent death of the spirit.

5. Leo Tolstoy, *War and Peace* (New York: Heritage Press, 1938), p. 826: "A man having no freedom cannot be conceived of except as deprived of life."

It was under the spell of this conviction that our forefathers would cry out: Oh, freedom, Oh, freedom, and before I'll be a slave, I'll be buried in my grave and go home to my Father and be saved.[6]

Ans so our most urgent message to this nation can be summarized in these simple words: "We just want to be free." We are not seeking to dominate the nation politically or to hamper its social growth; we just want to be free. Our motives are not impure and our intentions are not malicious; we simply want to be free. We are not seeking to be professional agitators or dangerous rabblerousers; we just want to be free. As we struggle for our freedom, America, we are struggling to prevent you from committing a continuous act of murder. Moreover, we are struggling for the very survival of our selfhood. To paraphrase the words of Shakespeare's Othello: "Who steals my purse steals trash; tis something, nothing; twas mine, tis his, and has been slave to thousands. But he who filches from me my freedom robs me of that which not enriches him and makes me poor indeed."[7] We simply want to be free.

America, in calling for our freedom we are not unmindful of the fact that we have been loyal to you. We have loved you even in the moments of your greatest denial of our freedom. In spite of all of our oppression, we have never turned to a foreign ideology to solve our problem. Communism has never invaded our ranks. And now we are simply saying we want our freedom. We have stood with you in every major crisis. For you, America, our sons sailed the bloody seas of two world wars. For your security, America, our sons died in the trenches of France, in the foxholes of Germany, on the beachheads of Italy and on the islands of Japan. And now, America, we are simply asking you to guarantee our freedom.

I must come to a close now. In conclusion I would like to say to these young, valiant freedom fighters and to everybody assembled here that we must struggle with the faith that our cause is destined to be vindicated in the future of mankind. Sometimes I know that it is difficult to believe this. When we notice the prodigious hilltops of opposition and stand before gigantic mountains of opposition, we are moved to give up in despair. But my advice to you is to fight on. Yes, we will face temporary setbacks and moments of frustration. Before the victory is won some of us may have to be bruised and scarred. Some will probably have to face the howl of evening winds of adversity.

But let us realize that this is only temporary. It is probably true that there can be no social gain without some individual pain. Growth and progress come through struggle. And it is still true that often the darkest moments of life are just before dawn. Fight on, my friends. We will win. We will win because our cause is right. Since justice is God's will, the stars in their courses support what we stand for. The arch of the moral universe is long, but it bends toward justice.[8] Therefore, I can see something marvelous unfolding and a future filled with vast possibilities.

---

6. These lines are from the spiritual "Oh Freedom."

7. Cf. William Shakespeare, *Othello,* act 3, scene 3.

8. King may have adopted this phrase from an article by John Haynes Holmes (see note 5 to Statement on Ending the Bus Boycott, 20 December 1956, in *Papers* 3:486).

Mine eyes have seen the glory of the coming of the Lord
He is trampling out the vintage where the grapes of wrath are stored
He has loosed the fateful lightning of His terrible swift sword
His truth is marching on.
He has sounded forth trumpet that shall never call retreat
He is sifting out the hearts of men before His Judgment seat,
Oh, be swift, my soul, to answer him! Be jubilant, my feet!
Our God is marching on![9]

PD. NAACPP-DLC: Group III-A177.

---

9. King recites the first and fourth verses of Julia Ward Howe's "The Battle Hymn of the Republic" (1862).

To Deolinda Rodrigues

21 July 1959
[*Montgomery, Ala.*]

In a 30 May letter Rodrigues, a twenty-year-old Angolan student living in Brazil, requested King's advice and support for the independence movement in her native country but admonished: "Please just do what You really can with no harm for You. . . . If some people have to pay with their lives . . . let it be ourselves."[1] *In his reply below, King suggests that the Angolan movement needs a "person or some few persons" to symbolize the struggle: "As soon as your symbol is set up it is not difficult to get people to follow, and the more the oppressor seeks to stop and defeat the symbol, the more it solidifies the movement."*[2]

---

1. Rodrigues also wrote that she would "pay a high price for it if portugueses know I have written you about this" and added: "It would be good because it is easier for me to suffer with my People than to be well here. Just I have to do something to help ANGOLA before I am jailed too." Deolinda Rodrigues Francisco de Almeida (1939–1967), born in Catete, Angola, studied sociology in São Paulo, Brazil, after receiving a Methodist mission scholarship in 1959. She left São Paulo for the United States in 1960, fearing that she would be deported under the terms of an extradition treaty between Portugal and Brazil. She studied at Drew University before returning to Africa in 1962 to direct the Angolan Volunteer Corps for Refugee Assistance in Congo (Leopoldville). As an activist in the Popular Movement for the Liberation of Angola (MPLA), Rodrigues worked as a poet, translator, teacher, and radio host. She was killed in prison after being captured by the Congo-based Front for the National Liberation of Angola, an opposing political group backed by the United States.

2. In her 26 September reply, Rodrigues wrote: "I aggre that a symbol for our independence movement is really necessary. Our leaders are not boast widely and openly but I know we have at Home a hidden political party working to awake my People and which is getting more and more followers. Some of these leaders are already arrested and surely their imprisonment is awakening more people. [¶]Indeed it hurts more than I thought it could for me to be away from Home and be well here while

Miss Deolinda Rodrigues

21 July 1959

Dear Miss Rodrigues:

Thank you for your very kind letter of recent date. I have read every line with great interest. It is indeed encouraging to know of your interest in the freedom of the people of your country. I am very glad to get firsthand information about the situation in Angola. I have heard about it from others who live outside of the country, but there is nothing like getting a firsthand report.

It seems that the Portuguese are some of the slowest people to give up their possessions in foreign territories. It is very unfortunate that they lack the vision to see the handwriting on the wall. It is always tragic to see an individual or nation seeking to stand up and stop an irristable tidal wave.

I do not know if I can give you any concrete suggestion as to what to do in your particular situation because it is often necessary to see it for yourself before you can give a definite answer. I would say, however, that the first step toward rectifying the situation is to develop real leadership in your country. Some one person or some few persons must stand as a symbol for your independence movement. As soon as your symbol is set up it is not difficult to get people to follow, and the more the oppressor seeks to stop and defeat the symbol, the more it solidifies the movement. It would be a wonderful thing for you to return to your country with this idea in mind. Freedom is never achieved without suffering and sacrifice. It comes through the persistent work and tireless efforts of dedicated individuals. You must also know that what is happening in other countries of Africa will inevitably have repercussions in your own country. It is impossible for Angola to stand in Africa and not be affected by what is happening in Nigeria and Kenya and Rhodesia. And so your real hope lies in the fact that independence will be a reality in the whole of Africa in the next few years. You have my prayers and best wishes for God's blessings in all that you are doing. I hope that your studies ahead will be most fruitful and rewarding.

Under separate cover I am sending a copy of my book, Stride Toward Freedom. Please accept this as a gift from me. I hope that you will find this humble work of mine somewhat helpful.[3]

Very sincerely yours,
Martin L. King, Jr.

TLc. MLKP-MBU: Box 25.

---

my People is having harder tryings there. The only thing which becomes me glad is that after prepare myself better I can also serve better my People at Home. This thought and God's presence help me a great deal to bear homesickness." For additional correspondence, see King to Rodrigues, 21 December 1959, pp. 345–346 in this volume.

3. In her 30 May letter, Rodrigues had inquired about obtaining a copy of *Stride Toward Freedom* and asked King to find someone with whom she might exchange her "whole, little African stamps collection" for a subscription to *Ebony:* "It is pretty wonderful that here I may get Ebony by mail with no censorship and no risk of being questioned or arrested because of it."

From Lawrence Dunbar Reddick

31 July 1959
Montgomery, Ala.

Reddick comments on the recent NAACP convention and offers suggestions for King's forthcoming article, "Pilgrimage to Nonviolence." The article was published as part of a series entitled "How My Mind Has Changed" in Christian Century.[1]

Reverend Martin L. King
454 Dexter Avenue

Dear Martin,

Many thanks for copies of the speeches and the English edition of Stride.[2] Please let me forward a couple of suggestions that may escape me before I see you in person.

In the first place, the victory for non-violence at the recent NAACP convention is very important. Not only was a crushing defeat dealt violence but some of the NAACP leaders were forced to do much more thinking on this subject than ever before and I do believe that they have come out now with a deeper conviction than they have previously held. We should encourage them in this and I believe that in our speeches and writings we should emphasize the importance of the full embracing of non-violent resistance by the most important civil rights organization America has.

As for your piece for the Christian Century, I believe that it should be a bit more personal than your Yale speech.[3] I believe that you told me over the telephone that it is to indicate wherein you have changed your mind on important issues of the day and on your general approach to moral problems—socially and personally. I suggest that the experience of the Montgomery boycott re-inforced certain preliminary intellectual convictions that you had before coming to the local situation.

Furthermore, as of your Yale speech, I think that the word "only" should be inserted after the word "America" on page 7 in the second paragraph. This helps the transition. In the next paragraph on that same page, please note that the term "maladjusted" is not "the ringing cry of the new child psychology." This is rather old stuff now. Moreover, in this paragraph I think that you should tie up

---

1. See King, "Pilgrimage to Nonviolence," 13 April 1960, pp. 419–425 in this volume. King had previously published an excerpt from *Stride Toward Freedom* under the title "My Pilgrimage to Nonviolence" (see *Papers* 4:473–481).

2. *Stride Toward Freedom* was published in England by Victor Gollancz in 1959.

3. On 14 January 1959, King delivered "The Future of Integration" at Yale University.

your use of maladjusted with the phrase "until the good society is realized." Otherwise, it might appear that you are simply endorsing maladjusted people in general.[4]

31 July 1959

If you give me a buzz next week, we can talk further about these and other matters.

Sincerely yours,
[*signed*] Lawrence
L. D. Reddick

LDR:bcd

TLS. MLKP-MBU: Box 68.

---

4. While King did not use the material from his Yale address for the article, he did follow Reddick's suggestion to qualify his endorsement of maladjustment in at least two subsequent versions of the address. King continued, however, to characterize maladjustment as "the ringing cry of modern psychology" ("The Future of Integration," Address at the National Convention of the Fellowship of Reconciliation, 21 August 1959, and "The Future of Integration," Address at the American Studies Conference on Civil Rights, 16 October 1959).

To James O. Grigsby

7 August 1959
[*Montgomery, Ala.*]

On 15 March Grigsby, a white Tennessean, asked King for advice on getting involved in the struggle for racial justice and wrote that "the South has been waiting a long time for a leader such as you!"[1] *King replies that he has "longed for a white southerner to come into some predominantly Negro organization and work side by side with Negro leaders."*

Mr. J. O. Grigsby
5951 Skyland Drive
Kingsport, Tenn.

Dear Mr. Grigsby:

I have just come across your letter of March 15. I regret very much that my reply is so late. When the letter came I was out of the country on a rather extended tour of India and the Middle East. On returning to the office my mail had accumulated to such a point that some letters were misplaced in the process. I think this happened in the case of your letter, and I just happened to have been looking back through some old folders and found it. Please accept my apologies for this misplacement.

First, I must express appreciation to you for reviewing my book. I am deeply moved by your encouraging words concerning it. Stride Toward Freedom is simply my humble attempt to bring Christian principles to bear on the [*difficult?*] problems of racial injustice which confronts our nation. I am happy to know that you found it helpful.[2]

It is deeply consoling to me to know of your interest in our struggle for freedom and human dignity. Such moral support and Christian generosity are of inestimable value in the continuance of our humble efforts. It is so seldom that you find a person of true dedication and real courage that when one comes along you are almost carried away with joy. I do not know exactly what to suggest to you in terms of your future helpfulness in the struggle. It might be good to find some organization that is working in the area of human rights and seek to express your

1. Grigsby added that he had been receiving MIA mailings since the days of the bus boycott: "Probably nowhere in the South or in the whole world, for that matter, was there another person watching the struggle with more intense interest than was I, nor prouder at the victorious outcome." James O. Grigsby (1917–) was born in Whitesburg, Tennessee, and served as a technical sergeant and pilot training instructor at Turner Field in Albany, Georgia, during World War II. He received a B.S. (1949) from the Georgia Institute of Technology. His opposition to racial injustice began during the war when he witnessed the beating of a black soldier by a white policeman; Grigsby later helped found a biracial community group under the auspices of the Unitarian Fellowship of Kingsport, Tennessee. He began working at Kingsport Press in 1949 and retired as a project engineer in 1970.

2. Grigsby mentioned in his letter that he had reviewed *Stride Toward Freedom* in March for a publication of the Holston Valley Unitarian Fellowship.

ideas through this channel. While an individual witness is important and absolutely necessary, we know that it is possible to do more through organized efforts. I have always longed for a white southerner to come into some predominantly Negro organization and work side by side with Negro leaders. This would lift it above a mere racial struggle, and people would come to see that the tension is at bottom between justice and injustice rather than between Negro people and white people. This was one of the most inspiring things that I saw in India. When Mahatma Gandhi was involved in the independence struggle many of the British people joined his movement and worked side by side with him to throw off British imperialism. This made the struggle more than a struggle of Indian people against British people, but one of the forces of light against the forces of darkness. If you could find an organization in the South through which you could work, you would make a contribution that is desperately needed. I am the president of an organization known as the Southern Christian Leadership Conference which seeks to implement the Supreme Court's Desegregation Decision on the local level through nonviolent means. So far, we only have Negro participants in this organization, or I should say by and large Negro participation (there are a few white persons who have joined up with us). We would be happy to have you work with us and give your moral support wherever possible. Of course there are interracial organizations such as the Southern Regional Council with its affiliates in each state of the South. I am sure that you could make a valuable contribution in this organization. You may consider these suggestions, and I hope they will be of some help.

Again, thank you for your interest and concern. I hope it will be possible for us to meet personally in [*the?*] not-too-distant future. Enclosed is the very interesting material which you were gracious enough to send me.

Very sincerely yours,
Martin Luther King, Jr.

Enc.

TLc. MLKP-MBU: Box 27.

To Ramdas M. Gandhi

8 August 1959
[*Montgomery, Ala.*]

King replies to an 11 May letter from Mohandas Gandhi's third son, whom he had met in India. Gandhi had sent King biographical information on his father's personal secretary Mahadev Desai and reported losing a memo book containing autographs from King and his traveling party.[1]

1. Mahadev Desai worked with Gandhi for over twenty years and translated several of Gandhi's writings into English. Desai died in the Aga Khan Palace jail in August 1942, a few days after being arrested by the colonial government for his political activities.

8 Aug 1959

Mr. Ramdas M. Gandhi
P.O. Sevagram
Dist. Vardha, INDIA

Dear Mr. Gandhi:

I am very sorry that I am just getting to the point of answering your letter of several weeks ago. Absence from the city and many other pressing responsibilities account for the delay. I hope you will accept my apologies.

It was certainly a rich experience to meet you in India. Since I did not have the opportunity to meet your great and immortal father, I considered it something of a blessing to be able to meet one so close to him in blood and kinship.[2] My trip to India was one of the most rewarding experiences in my life. I came back with a new love and affection for the Indian people. I will never forget the warm hospitality extended to Mrs. King and me during our visit there. I am more convinced than ever before that nonviolence resistance is the most potent weapon available to oppressed people in our struggle for freedom and human dignity.

Enclosed you will find three cards with the autographs of me, Mrs. King, and Dr. Reddick. I am very sorry that your memo pocket diary was misplaced.

Please extend our best regards to all of our friends in your area. Tell them that we long to see them again. We hope that it will be possible to come back to India in the not-too-distant future.

With warm personal regards.

Sincerely yours,
Martin Luther King, Jr.

MLK:mlb

TLc. MLKP-MBU: Box 17.

---

2. Ramdas Mohandas Gandhi (1897–1969), born in Johannesburg, was imprisoned in South Africa at the age of fourteen for his political activity. He later moved to India and became involved in the independence movement; he was arrested in Champaran during his father's first protest campaign in India. For a time, Ramdas Gandhi served as the editor of the weekly *Navjivan* newspaper, founded by his father in 1919, and managed the ashram at Bardoli, established by Indian independence leader Sardar Patel.

To Joseph Tusiani

8 August 1959
[*Montgomery, Ala.*]

On 2 August Italian-born poet Joseph Tusiani requested that King respond to a set of questions for an article to be published in the Italian-language magazine Nigrizia.[1] *In this reply, King suggests that the Little Rock school integration conflict may have been "a blessing in disguise" because it forced people to recognize that the desegregation problem "had to be met forthrightly." He also blames the federal government, "especially the president," for failing to take a "strong, moral stand" after the Supreme Court's 1954 desegregation decision. Tusiani's questions and King's translated answers appeared at the end of the article in the January 1960 edition of* Nigrizia.[2]

Dr. Joseph Tusiana
553 East 188th Street
New York 58, New York

Dear Dr. Tusiani:

I am in receipt of your letter of August 2, and I hasten to answer it before leaving town in a few hours. I regret that a very tight schedule at this moment will not permit me to give detail answers to your questions.

Answer to question number 1.[3] In my opinion the main obstacle to the realization of brotherhood in the United States and other parts of the world is man's failure to respect the dignity and worth of all human personality. The problems facing our world in the area of human relations are chiefly moral. They are not merely economic and political, but they are basically moral. Actually, moral value is supreme and gives worth to all others. That is why personality as the locus of moral value has irreplaceable worth and must be respected. Segregation, colonialism, and economic imperialism all violate that principle. Any society degrades itself when it heaps indignities upon persons.

---

1. *Nigrizia,* a magazine dedicated to "Africa and the black world," had been published by the Comboni Missionaries since 1882. Giuseppe (Joseph) Tusiani (1924–) was born in San Marco in Lamis, Italy. He received his Ph.D. (1947) from the University of Naples and emigrated to the United States that year. He served as the chair of the Italian department at the College of Mount Saint Vincent (1948–1971) and also taught at Hunter College (1950–1963) and New York University (1956–1963). Tusiani published numerous volumes of poetry and other works in English, Italian, and Latin. Prior to this interview with King, Tusiani had written on African American spirituals for *Nigrizia.* He later published *Influenza Cristiana nella Poesia Negro-Americana* (Bologna: Nigrizia, 1971).

2. "La Non Violenza Del Dott. King," *Nigrizia* (January 1960): 23–24. Tusiani was pleased with the "enthusiastic" response to the article and requested a second interview with King; Maude Ballou replied that King was too preoccupied with the southern struggle to respond at the time (Tusiani to King, 20 April 1960, and Ballou to Tusiani, 5 May 1960).

3. Tusiani had asked: "What, in your opinion, constitutes the main obstacle to the realization of brotherhood on earth and, especially, in U.S.A."

Answer to question number 2:[4] I was certainly disappointed when the Little Rock incident occured some time ago. It was a shocking demonstration of how one man, through irresponsible action and demagogic tendencies, can lead a whole state into acts of meaness that no normal or rational person would commit.[5] Moreover, it was a tragic revelation of what prejudice can do to blind the visions of men and darken their understanding. However, there are two other things that must be said about Little Rock. It might have been a blessing in disguise in that for the first time this issue was brought to the forefront of the conscience of the nation, and men of goodwill came to see that this problem had to be met forthrightly. Too long had we been dealing with it in a light, easy going manner. It must also be admitted that if the Federal Government, especially the president of our country, had taken a strong, moral stand when the Supreme Court rendered it's decision in 1954, federal troops probably would not have had to stand in Little Rock. But the tragic fact is that while the forces of goodwill in our nation remained silent, the forces of opposition mobilized and organized.

Answer to question number 3:[6] I definitely feel that the present situation is brighter than it was a few years ago. We are nearer the promised land of integration than we were ten years ago. It is true that we have more tension in some areas of the South than we had a few years ago, but this tension is a necessary phase of the transition. It is a sign of the progress that we have made, rather than tragic retrogression. It is indicative of the fact that a new order is being born in America and the old order of segregation and paternalism is passing away.

Answer to question number 4:[7] If I added a chapter to my book, Stride Toward Freedom, I would probably turn to a discussion of the effectiveness of nonviolence in international relationships. It would be my contention that this method must be adopted not merely on the local level in struggles between relatively small groups, but even between nations. In a day when nuclear weapons are plentiful and guided ballistic missles are carving highways of death through the stratosphere, no nation can win a war. It is no longer a choice between violence and nonviolence; it is either nonviolence or nonexistence. If mankind feels that it has a right to exist, then we must find some alternative to war. I would contend that the only true way to peace is the way of love, patience, understanding, goodwill, and an adherence to principles of justice.

As I said, these answers are briefer than I would ordinarily make them and they were given in a great deal of haste. However, I hope they will serve your purpose and I am happy to know that you have chosen me as a subject for your article in the Italian magazine, Nigrizia.

With every good wish.

---

4. "The grievous incident of Little Rock must have wounded your heart immensely; what was your reaction to it?"

5. King refers to resistance by Arkansas governor Orval Faubus to school desegregation in Little Rock.

6. "Would you call the present situation brighter than it was a few years ago?"

7. "Should you add a chapter to your Stride Toward Freedom, what would you like the world to know?"

Sincerely yours,
Martin L. King, Jr.

P.S. I would appreciate your sending me a copy of the article when it is written. Although I don't read Italian, I would appreciate having it in my files.

MLK:mlb

TLc. MLKP-MBU: Box 6.

To Tracy D. Mygatt

8 August 1959
[*Montgomery, Ala.*]

King replies to a 3 August request for an endorsement from Mygatt, New York secretary of the Campaign for World Government.[1] *In the letter below King expresses his support for the concept. On 20 August, Mygatt thanked King for his "ringing declaration of your belief in world government" and added, "I believe I am correct in assuming that I am at liberty to quote you, as occasion offers."*

Miss Tracy D. Mygatt
Campaign for World Government, Inc.
333 Park Avenue
Glencoe, Illinois

Dear Miss Mygatt:

I have read both of your letters with great interest. I am sorry that I was out of the country when the first letter arrived, but my secretary was thoughtful enough to call it to my attention on my return.[2] I had intended answering it before now, but absence from the city and the pressures of other responsibilities delayed my reply.

I am deeply sympathetic with your campaign for world government. I have come to see that the geographical oneness of our world and the potential destructiveness of modern weapons of war make it necessary for us to move in the direction

1. Mygatt enclosed an article she had written for a Methodist student magazine ("World Federation—A Must" *Motive* [October 1957]: 9–11). Mygatt met King on 2 February 1959, when he addressed the War Resisters League in New York. Tracy Dickinson Mygatt (1885–1973), born in Brooklyn, New York, graduated from Bryn Mawr College (1909). Soon after graduating she helped organize a woman suffrage movement in eastern Pennsylvania. In 1913 she joined the Socialist Party and two years later founded the Anti-Enlistment League to promote unconditional opposition to war. Mygatt was among the founders of the War Resisters League in 1923, serving as an honorary chairwoman of the organization until her death. She worked for the Campaign for World Government, Inc., from 1941 until 1969 when she began to work part-time from a retirement home in Philadelphia.

2. Mygatt had initially written King on 20 January 1959.

of a world government if we are to survive. There can hardly be any gainsaying of the fact that war is now obsolete as a way of dealing with world problems. It can only lead to mutual annihiliation.

I am not unmindful of the fact that there are many practical problems involved in the whole idea of world government, but in spite of this we must continue to work in this direction. Certainly, world government is the ideal toward which men of goodwill should work passionately and unrelentingly. So I want you to know that I am deeply concerned about what you are seeking to do. While my many responsibilities in the South at this time will not allow me the time to be of any assistance to you, I can at least say that you have my moral support.

I am happy to know of your interest in our struggle here in the South. Such moral support is of inestimable value in the continuance of our humble efforts.

With every good wish.

Yours very truly,
Martin L. King, Jr.

MLK:mlb

TLc. MLKP-MBU: Box 31.

To Juanita Jelks

8 August 1959
[*Montgomery, Ala.*]

King replies to Jelks's 6 August request to discuss the Greater Gadsden Housing Authority's plan to demolish the homes of black residents in Gadsden, Alabama, as part of an urban renewal project.[1] *As secretary of the Citizen's Protective Association of Gadsden, Jelks pleaded: "We need help from all sources of strength, spiritual, mental, and financial."*[2] *In a 9 September letter, Jelks thanked King for meeting with the committee from Gadsden on 2 September.*

Mrs. Juanita Jelks
525 Lamar Street
Gadsden, Alabama

Dear Mrs. Jelks:

Thanks for your very kind letter of August 6. I have read the contents very scrutinizingly. Certainly, I am deeply sympathetic with the plight of Negroes in Gads-

1. Earlier in the summer, Jelks and four other plaintiffs had lost their case against the City of Gadsden and the Housing Authority (*Barnes et al. v. The City of Gadsden, Alabama, et al.*, 268 F.2d 593 [1959]).

2. Jelks informed King that she was referred to him by NAACP Legal Defense and Educational Fund attorney Constance Baker Motley. Juanita Jeanette Jelks (1916–1980), born in Atalla, Alabama, worked as a bookkeeper for the Atlanta Life Insurance Company. She was a member of the Gadsden NAACP and the Etowah County Voters League.

den in the efforts of the segregationists to uproot your home and preserve a system that is destined to die.

I am sorry that I did not know about this situation before. I am sure that it is due to my own oversight. We have been involved in recent months with so many responsibilities I have often overlooked many important things in our home state.

I will be more than happy to talk with you about the situation in Gadsden. Unfortunately, however, my calendar reveals that I will have to be out of the office for the next three weeks. This means that the only time that I can possibly see you and your committee would be the week of September 1st. Any day that week would be satisfactory to me with the exception of Tuesday. I will have to be leaving town again on the sixth of September for a three week lecture in California and Hawaii. Please let me know by return mail whether it will be possible for you to come one day that week (September 2, 3, or 4) and I will be happy to place it on my calendar.

Please know again that I am deeply sympathetic and concerned about your present plight. I hope I can be of some assistance.

Very sincerely yours,
Martin L. King, Jr.

TLc. MLKP-MBU: Box 15

Resolutions, First Southwide Institute on Nonviolent Resistance to Segregation held on 22 July–24 July 1959

11 August 1959
Atlanta, Ga.

Sixty ministers and activists attended the institute at Atlanta's Spelman College and heard addresses by such advocates of nonviolence as King, William Stuart Nelson, Richard Gregg, and James Lawson.[1] *The following resolutions were approved at the conclusion of the gathering, which was sponsored by SCLC, FOR, and CORE.*[2]

1. SCLC, Press release, 3 July–22 July 1959. For King's handwritten draft of the program, see King, "Proposed schedule for Institute on Nonviolent Resistance to Segregation," 22 July 1959. According to MIA secretary H. J. Palmer's notes from the proceedings, King applauded the participation of women activists and distinguished the civil rights movement from struggles in other countries for "we must live with" the opposition (Palmer, Notes, Program on First Southwide Institute on Nonviolent Resistance to Segregation, 22 July–24 July 1959). For an additional account of the meeting, see Reddick, "Report, Nonviolent Institute," 22 July–24 July 1959.

2. Those in attendance also approved a statement that pledged the group's adherence "to the practice of Christian love and nonviolence, not simply as a tactical measure, but always moving towards it as an all embracing rule of conduct" (SCLC, "Manifesto, Institute on Nonviolent Resistance to Segregation, 7/22/1959–7/24/1959," 11 August 1959).

1. We thank President [*Albert*] Manley, the faculty and staff of Spelman College for so graciously opening its facilities to our institute.
2. The Institute re-affirms our dedication to the principles and practices of nonviolent resistance as the supreme instrument of social change.
3. We recommend that this institute be held annually and that similar institutes and workshops should be held nationally, regionally, and locally as the opportunity arises. We call upon the sponsoring organizations to initiate plans to implement this resolution.[3]
4. We commend the several local organizations who have been engaged in nonviolent direct action projects.
5. We commend the 50th Anniversary Convention of the NAACP for reaffirming its position of rejecting the use of violence in securing social change.[4]
6. We urge the sponsoring organizations to produce a handbook on: The Principles and Techniques of Nonviolence, as related to social change in race relations.
7. We recognize the importance of legislation as an instrument of social change, and the use of constitutional procedures. We further recognize the responsibility of a democracy to insure the equal rights of all citizens. We therefore call upon the Congress and the President to support and implement the desegregation decisions of the Supreme Court.
8. We make common cause with the oppressed and submerged peoples of the world—particularly the unfreed peoples of Africa and the former "untouchables" of India. We call upon them to adhere to the principles of nonviolence in our common world struggle.
9. We call upon organizations active in the field of social action and civil rights to initiate plans for a nation-wide demonstration against all forms of racial discriminations and segregations.

TD. MLKJP-GAMK: Box 33.

---

3. SCLC held a second institute the following year (SCLC, Program, "Second Statewide Institute on Nonviolent Resistance to Segregation," 4 August–5 August 1960). SCLC also co-sponsored a number of regional workshops and institutes over the next several months.

4. The preamble to the NAACP's convention resolutions rejected violence as a strategy for challenging segregation but reaffirmed the right to self-defense (NAACP, "Fiftieth annual convention resolutions," 13 July–19 July 1959).

To Dwight D. Eisenhower

13 August 1959
New York, N.Y.

King urges Eisenhower to endorse school desegregation prior to Soviet premier Nikita Khrushchev's September visit to the United States, noting that "it would be tragic should his visit coincide with tension and violence accompanying" the start of another school year.[1] *Gerald D. Morgan, deputy assistant to President Eisenhower, responded to this wire on 27 August: "The President has repeatedly declared and reaffirmed his determination that the law as set forth in the Constitution, statutes and decisions of the courts must be respected and obeyed, and feels that nothing could be added by a Proclamation to the same effect."*

THE PRESIDENT
THE WHITE HOUSE

DEAR MR PRESIDENT, MY COLLEAGUES AND I RECOGNIZE THAT THE COMING EXCHANGE OF VISITS BETWEEN YOU AND MR KHRUSHCHEV HAS INTRODUCED A NEW ELEMENT IN THE INTERNATIONAL SITUATION INSPIRING HOPE THAT CONSTRUCTIVE STEPS TOWARD PEACE MAY RESULT. EVERYONE MUST APPLAUD AND RESPECT THIS INITIATIVE WHICH AN ANXIOUS WORLD HAS LONG AWAITED.

IT IS UNIVERSALLY AGREED THAT MR KHRUSHCHEV MUST BE IMPRESSED WITH OUR ECONOMIC AND TECHNOLOGICAL ACHIEVEMENTS. HE UNDOUBTEDLY WILL BE AS THE OVERWHELMING EVIDENCE PRESENTS ITSELF ON EVERY SIDE. IT IS LESS CERTAIN THAT SO CLEAR AND INSPIRING A PICTURE OF OUR DEMOCRATIC UNITY AND IDEALS WILL EMERGE. MR KHRUSHCHEV WILL ARRIVE IN OUR COUNTRY JUST AS SCHOOLS ARE REOPENING IN SEPTEMBER. IT WOULD BE TRAGIC SHOULD HIS VISIT COINCIDE WITH TENSION AND VIOLENCE ACCOMPANYING THE DESEGREGATION OF SOME SCHOOLS. AS SUCH SITUATIONS HAVE OCCURED ANNUALLY FOR THE PAST FIVE YEARS, CAUSING OUR NATION GRAVE EMBARRASSMENT

THEREFORE WE RESPECTFULLY SUGGEST THAT BEFORE THE OPENING OF SCHOOLS YOU ISSUE A PRESIDENTIAL PROCLAMATION DECLARING THAT IN THE INTEREST OF THE MORAL INTEGRITY OF OUR NATION AND AS A CONTRIBUTION TO WORLD PEACE EVERY CITIZEN SHALL PEACEFULLY ABIDE BY THE DECISIONS OF THE SUPREME COURT AND OTHER FEDERAL COURTS FACILITATING INTEGRATION OF PUBLIC SCHOOLS ACROSS THE NATION. MAY WE HAVE YOUR REACTION TO THIS PROPOSAL AFTER YOU HAVE AN OPPORTUNITY TO REFLECT UPON IT

<u>MARTIN LUTHER KING PRESIDENT</u>
SOUTHERN CHRISTIAN LEADERSHIP CONFERENCE

PWSr. WCFG-KAbE.

---

1. Khrushchev arrived in the United States on 15 September for a thirteen-day visit. Nikita Sergeyevich Khrushchev served as Soviet premier from 1958 until 1964.

Address at the Thirty-fourth Annual Convention of the National Bar Association

20 August 1959
Milwaukee, Wis.

In this typescript of an address to the oldest and largest federation of African American lawyers, King reemphasizes the importance of nonviolence and denounces the "hate groups arising in our midst" that advocate "a doctrine of black supremacy." He reminds his audience that "we must not try to leap from a position of disadvantage to one of advantage, thus subverting justice."[1] *King's remarks may have been prompted by the July 1959 television broadcast of "The Hate That Hate Produced," which drew public attention to the Nation of Islam, a black separatist religious group.*[2]

Mr. Chairman, delegates to this session of the National Bar Association, ladies and gentlemen:

I am indeed happy to have the opportunity of being with you on this significant occasion. To speak before such a distinguished group of legal minds is a rare privilege and a great pleasure.

Words are inadequate for me to express the great debt of gratitude that we owe the lawyers of our race for bringing us to this significant point in our struggle. It goes without saying that some of the most momentous achievements in the civil rights struggle have come through the courts. These victories would never have been achieved without the assiduous labors, courageous stands, and brilliant arguments of our dedicated lawyers. Many of you have never received adequate recognition or proper financial returns for your work, but you have continued to give yourselves unstintingly to a cause that you know is right. One day all of America will take pride in your achievements. Long after the names of Governor Faubus and Senator Eastland will be forgotten in shame, the names of Charles Houston, Thurgood Marshall and a host of others will be creatively stenciled on the mental sheets of succeeding generations.[3]

---

1. King's appearance was initiated by his friend Miami lawyer Henry Arrington (Arrington to King, 3 April 1959, and King to Arrington, 11 April 1959). A few months after accepting the invitation, King expressed concern to National Bar Association president William S. Thompson that the event might interfere with SCLC's planned fund-raising efforts in Milwaukee: "I was under the impression that the meeting . . . would be a banquet meeting limited to the lawyers and their guests." Thompson assured King that they would do their "utmost to raise a substantial sum of money for your organization" (King to Thompson, 1 July 1959, and Thompson to King, 13 July 1959).

2. Reporter Mike Wallace's documentary was followed by a *Time* magazine article on the Nation of Islam. Earlier in the month King told a Montgomery reporter he doubted the "Moslems" had much of a presence outside larger northern cities (Dick Hines, "Black Supremacy Cult Grows but Any Activity Here Doubtful," *Montgomery Advertiser,* 6 August 1959; see also "The Black Supremacists," *Time,* 10 August 1959, pp. 24–25).

3. Orval Faubus and James Eastland had become international symbols of segregation. Charles Hamilton Houston served as the NAACP's first full-time legal counsel from 1935 until 1940. Chief NAACP counsel Thurgood Marshall, Houston's successor, addressed the National Bar Association one day after King ("King and Marshall Assail Eisenhower," *Baltimore Afro-American,* 5 September 1959).

I bring warm and sincere greetings to you from two organizations. The first is the Montgomery Improvement Association—the organization which guided and directed the bus boycott in Montgomery, Alabama. The second is the Southern Christian Leadership Conference. This organization came into being in order to serve as a channel through which local protest organizations in the South could coordinate their activities. Our basic aim is to implement the Supreme Court's desegregation decisions on the local level through mass, direct non-violent action. One of our most specific undertakings at the present time is that of increasing the number of Negro registered voters in the South. This is a big job, and one that cannot be tackled without hard work and great financial resources. Whatever support you can give in this difficult, yet challenging task ahead will give us renewed courage and vigor to carry on. 20 Aug 1959

We have come to a very decisive moment in our struggle for racial justice. As we look over the long sweep of race relations in our nation, we notice, broadly speaking, three distinct periods, each representing growth over a former period. It is interesting to note that in each period the Supreme Court of the nation rendered a decision that gave legal and constitutional validity to the dominant thought patterns of that particular period.

The first period in the area of race relations extended from 1619 to 1863. This was the era of slavery. During this period the Negro was considered a thing to be used rather than a person to be respected. He was a depersonalized cog in a vast plantation machine. In 1857 there finally came a decision from the Supreme Court to give constitutional validity to the whole system of slavery. This decision, known as the Dred Scott decision, stated in substance that the Negro was not a citizen of this nation; he was merely property subject to the dictates of his owner.

The second period in the development of race relations in America extended, broadly speaking, from 1863 to 1954. This was the period of restricted emancipation. We must admit that this stage was something of an improvement over the first stage of race relations, because it at least freed the Negro from the bondage of physical slavery, and accepted him as a legal fact. But it was not the best stage, because it failed to accept the Negro as a person. It was, therefore, very easy for the ethos of segregation to emerge as the basic principle and practice of this period. In 1896, through the famous Plessy versus Ferguson decision, the Supreme Court established the doctrine of separate but equal as the law of the land. Through this decision the dominant thought patterns of the second stage of race relations were given legal and constitutional validity. But because segregation is at bottom a form of slavery covered up with certain niceties of complexity, the end results of the period of restricted emancipation was that of plunging the Negro into the abyss of oppression where he experienced the bleakness of nagging injustice.

The third period in the development of race relations in America had its beginning on May 17, 1954.[4] This is the period of constructive integration. It is the period in which men seek to rise to the level of genuine intergroup and interpersonal living. The Supreme Court's decision which came to give legal and constitutional validity to the dominant thought patterns of this period stated that the

4. King refers to *Brown v. Board of Education.*

old Plessy doctrine must go, that separate facilities were inherently unequal, and that to segregate a child on the basis of his race is to deny that child equal protection of the law. As a result of this decision we find ourselves standing on the threshold of the most creative period in the development of race relations in the history of our nation. To state it figuratively in biblical language: We have broken loose from the Egypt of slavery; We have moved through the wilderness of "separate but equal;" and now we stand on the border of the promised land of integration.

The great challenge facing America at this hour is to bring into full realization the ideals and principles of this third period. The shape of the world today does not permit us the luxury of an anemic democracy. In a world where three-fourths of the people are colored, it is not only practically inexpedient, but rationally illogical, to defend a doctrine of segregation.

But we must face the painful fact that there are still those enemies of democracy in our nation who are seeking to defend segregation. These persons have joined in a campaign of defiance. The legislative halls of the South ring loud with such words as interposition and nullification. The dark and agonizing story of the White Citizens Councils and the Ku Klux Klan is a familiar one. Their methods range from intimidation and economic reprisals to outright physical violence. The recent mob demonstration in Little Rock is a clear manifestation of the tragic ends to which some will go to preserve a dying order.

But in spite of this defiance, there are some hopeful signs. Even in Little Rock we must commend the police force for its forthright and determined action in handling the mob that assembled around Central High School last week.[5] Their actions made it palpably clear that they were determined to keep the episode of 1957 from becoming a repeat performance. We must also commend the majority of white citizens of Little Rock for finally repudiating the irresponsible leadership of Governor Faubus. Actually, what we now see in both Little Rock and Virginia is something very revealing.[6] Two powerful institutions have collided in the South—the institution of segregation and the institution of public schools. And the people have made it clear that when the final moment of choice comes they will choose public schools rather than segregation.

So maybe we pro-integrationist shouldn't be so hard on Governor Faubus after all, for, however ironical it may sound, he has done more to promote the cause of integration than almost any personality of this decade. His irresponsible actions brought the issue to the forefront of the conscience of the nation, and allowed people to see the futility of attempting to close the public school.

Now what of the future? First, let me answer this question by attempting to give the lie to an attitude that is too often prevalent in society—the feeling that social

5. On 12 August, while two black students entered the building for classes, Little Rock police restrained several hundred white protesters at Central High School. On the same day, Little Rock's Hall High School was uneventfully integrated by three black students (Roy Reed, "Police Rout March on Central, Arrest 24; Hall Opening Quiet," *Arkansas Gazette,* 13 August 1959).

6. During the convention the association honored two Virginia attorneys, Oliver W. Hill, Jr. and Victor J. Ashe, for their efforts to desegregate Virginia's schools ("Curb on Vote Is Denounced: A Key Racial Issue," *Milwaukee Journal,* 23 July 1959).

progress is an automatic phenomenon that can emerge without human effort. To believe this is to be victimized with an illusion wrapped in superficiality. Human progress in neither automatic nor inevitable. Even a casual look at history reveals that no social advance rolls in on the wheels of inevitability. Every step toward the goal of justice requires sacrifice, suffering and struggle; the tireless exertions and passionate concern of dedicated individuals. Without this persistent effort, time itself becomes an ally of the insurgent and primitive forces of irrational emotionalism and social stagnation.

In the final analysis integration will become a reality in America only when enough people come to believe that is is morally right and are willing to work passionately for its fulfillment.

Many agencies and groups must work constructively together in order to achieve the ideals and principles of an integrated society—the Christian Church, organized labor, liberal whites, North and South, the federal government and the Negro himself. While time will not permit me to discuss the role of all of these groups, I would like to elaborate on the last two.

There is the need for strong and aggressive leadership from the federal government. So far, only the judicial branch of the government has given this type of leadership. The executive branch of our government has been all too silent and apathetic during this period of transition; the legislative branch has been all too stagnant and hypocritical. I fear that future historians will have to record that when America came to its most progressive moment of creative fulfillment in the area of human relations, it was temporarily held back by a chief executive who refused to make a strong positive statement morally condemning segregation. Much of the terror and confusion that we are now facing in the South might have been avoided if the office of the president had just given an occasional word counseling the nation on the moral aspects of integration and the need for complying with the law. I submit to you that the president is as obligated to go to the television and plead for strong civil rights legislation as he is to plead for the passage of his labor bill.[7] Indeed the civil rights issue is not some evanescent political issue that can be conveniently ignored by our highest officials, it is an eternal moral issue that may well determine the destiny of our nation.

I must hasten to say that the dearth of positive leadership from Washington is not confined to one political party. The cause of justice has been betrayed by both political parties. Many Democrats have betrayed it by capitulating to the undemocratic practices of the southern Dixiecrats. Many Republicans have betrayed it by capitulating to the hypocrisy of right-wing northerners. Sometimes I am prone to feel that this hypocrisy in the Republican Party is more dangerous than the undemocratic practices of the southern Dixiecrats. At least you know where the Dixiecrats stand. One can deal better with an Eastland because he airs his vicious prejudice all the time, and makes it clear that he stands against the more enlightened conscience of our time. But the individual who dresses his words up in the garments of enlightenment in order to get votes when at bottom he is actu-

7. King refers to the Landrum-Griffin Act (1959), which provided for increased regulation of internal union affairs and finances.

ally reactionary is a dangerous menace, not only to his party, but to democracy itself. It is difficult to understand how many of the Republican politicians are as reactionary as they are on the question of Civil Rights when they do not confront the sectional pressures and prejudices that the southern politicians face. Hypocrisy, whether in politics or ordinary human relations, is a tragic vice that can lead only to moral degeneration.

We see obvious signs of this Republican laxity in the present civil rights debate in Congress. The failure of the House Judiciary Committee to go along with the language of the Civil Rights Bill authorizing "the attorney general to act in all types of denial of civil rights" revealed the same old coalition of southern Democrats and ultra conservative Republicans that has defeated every progressive move in the area of civil rights.[8] The southern Democrats could not have removed the language by themselves. They had to receive help from the Republicans.

All of this prompts me to say that the Negro must make it palpably clear that he is not inextricably bound to either political party. In 1960 we must affirm that we are aware of the fact that we hold the balance of power in several key states, and that we will not blindly support any party that refuses to take a forthright stand on the question of civil rights.

Government action is not the whole answer to the present crisis, but it is an important partial answer. Morals cannot be legislated, but behaviour can be regulated. The law cannot make an employer love, but it can keep him from refusing to hire me because of the color of my skin. We must depend on religion and education to alter the errors of the heart and mind; but meanwhile it is an immoral act to compel a man to accept injustice until another man's heart is straight. As the experience of several northern states has shown, anti-discrimination laws can provide powerful sanctions against this kind of immorality. The habits if not the hearts of people have been and are being altered every day by federal action.

The Negro himself has a decisive role to play if integration is to become a reality. Realism impels me to admit that if first-class citizenship is to become a reality for the Negro he must assume the primary responsibility for making it so. One of the most damaging effects of past segregation on the personality of the Negro may well be that he has been victimized with the delusion that others should be more concerned than himself about his citizenship rights.

There are several specific things that we must do. (1) We must put forth a determined effort to gain the ballot. One of the most important steps that the Negro can take at this hour is that short walk to the voting booth. (2) We must give strong financial support to civil rights organizations. We have done far too little in this area. (3) We must maintain a sense of "somebodiness" and self respect. (4) We must continue to produce courageous, dedicated and intelligent leaders who avoid the extremes of hotheadedness and Uncle Tomism. (5) We must make it clear that the system of segregation is a social and moral evil that we will no longer passively accept. (6) We must conduct our struggle against segregation on the highest level of dignity and discipline. We must avoid both external physical violence

---

8. On 5 August, the House Judiciary Committee approved a civil rights bill after dropping the provision allowing the attorney general to initiate civil rights suits (Richard L. Lyons, "House Unit Votes 5-Point Rights Bill; 'Unholy Alliance' Kills School Aid," *Washington Post*, 6 August 1959).

and internal violence of spirit. I must stress this point a bit because of a dangerous philosophy that is being taught by some elements of the Negro community. There are hate groups arising in our midst which would preach a doctrine of black supremacy. It is my prayerful hope that our natural resentment over the injustices that are constantly heaped upon us will not cause us to stoop to the law and primitive methods of some of our opponents. I know how we feel as we face the brutality of lynch mobs, the viciousness of economic exploitations, and the constant oppression of unjust southern courts. I know how patient we have been, and how the cup of endurance can eventually run over. But in spite of all, we must not allow ourselves to become bitter. We must become strong enough to meet hate with love, physical force with soul force. Our aim must not be to defeat or humiliate the white man, but to win his friendship and understanding. In an effort to achieve freedom in America, we must not try to leap from a position of disadvantage to one of advantage, thus subverting justice. We must seek democracy and not the substitution of one tyranny for another. Black supremacy is as bad as white supremacy. God is not interested merely in the freedom of black men and brown and yellow men, God is interested in the freedom of the whole human race.

So I would recommend to you a way of love. I still believe that love is the most durable power in all the world. Hate is a cancerous disease which distorts the personality and scars the soul. To return hate for hate only intensifies the existence of hate in the universe. Hate seeks to annihilate rather than convert. It destroys community and makes brotherhood impossible. We must learn that it is possible to stand up courageously and positively against an evil system and yet not resist it with physical weapons and inner feelings of hatred. (7) Finally, we must be willing to suffer and sacrifice in order to achieve our freedom. We must recognize that freedom is a priceless possession which every man must possess if he is to be truly human.

Tolstoy, the Russian writer, said in War and Peace: "I cannot conceive of a man not being free unless he is dead."[9] While this statement sounds a bit exaggerated, it gets at a basic truth. What Tolstoy is saying in substance is that the absence of freedom is the presence of death. Any nation or government that deprives an individual of freedom is in that moment committing an act of moral and spiritual murder. Any individual who is not concerned about his freedom commits an act of moral and spiritual suicide. He, at that moment, forfeits his right to be. The struggle for freedom is not a struggle to attain some ephemeral desire; it is a struggle to maintain one's very selfhood. It is a struggle to avoid a tragic death of the spirit. It is no wonder that there have been those discerning individuals throughout history who have been willing to suffer, sacrifice and even face the possibility of physical death in order to gain freedom. They have had the vision to realize that physical death may be more desirable than a permanent death of the spirit. It was under the spell of this conviction that our forefathers would cry out: Oh, Freedom, Oh, Freedom, and before I'll be a slave, I'll be buried in my grave and go home to my Father and be saved.[10]

And so our most urgent message to this nation can be summarized in these sim-

9. Leo Tolstoy, *War and Peace,* p. 826: "A man having no freedom cannot be conceived of except as deprived of life."

10. King invokes the traditional spiritual "Oh Freedom."

ple words: "We just want to be free." We are not seeking to dominate the nation politically or to hamper its social growth; we just want to be free. Our motives are not impure and our intentions are not malicious; we simply want to be free. We are not seeking to be professional agitators or dangerous rabblerousers; we just want to be free. As we struggle for our freedom, America, we are struggling to save your soul. We are struggling to prevent you from committing a continuous act of murder. Moreover, we are struggling for the very survival of our selfhood. To paraphrase the words of Shakespeare's Othello: "Who steals my purse steals trash; tis something, nothing; twas mine, tis his, and has been slave to thousands. But he who filches from me my freedom robs me of that which not enriches him and makes me poor indeed."[11] We simply want to be free.

America, in calling for our freedom we are not unmindful of the fact that we have been loyal to you. We have loved you even in the moments of your greatest denial of our freedom. In spite of all of our oppression, we have never turned to a foreign ideology to solve our problem. Communism has never invaded our ranks. And now we are simply saying we want our freedom. We have stood with you in every major crisis. For you, America, our sons sailed the bloody seas of two world wars. For your security, America, our sons died in the trenches of France, in the foxholes of Germany, on the beachheads of Italy and on the islands of Japan. And now, America, we are simply asking you to guarantee our freedom.

If this is done we will be able to emerge from the bleak and desolate midnight of man's inhumanity to man into the bright and glittering daybreak of freedom and justice. This will be a great day, not only for America, but for the whole human family.

TD. MLKP-MBU: Box 2.

---

11. Cf. William Shakespeare, *Othello,* act 3, scene 3.

To the Montgomery County Board of Education

28 August 1959
Montgomery, Ala.

King and other members of the MIA's executive committee request that the Montgomery Board of Education begin good-faith efforts to desegregate local schools.[1]

---

1. In a typewritten draft of this statement King wrote: "Therefore be it resolved that: 1. the Board of Education announce it plans not later than January 1, 1960 for conforming with the mandate of the Supreme Court of the United States" (King, Draft, Proposed statement to the board of education, 28 August 1959). King later complained to a northern supporter that "there is no integrated school in the whole state of Alabama" and that state officials "say in no uncertain terms that they will never comply" with federal desegregation laws (King to Linda Carver, 16 November 1959).

The Board of Education
Montgomery County
Mr. Harold Harris, Chairman
305 South Lawrence Street
Montgomery, Alabama

28 Aug 1959

Dear Sirs:

The era following World War II finds the United States catapulted into the forefront of world affairs. Through the forces of history, she has been thrust into the lofty and responsible position of leader and defender of the democratic nations. One of the cardinal principles of the democratic creed is that the individual has inherent dignity and worth that is neither derivative from nor subjected to the state. But today the United States and all the free nations are challenged by a strange philosophy of communism which would relegate the individual to the status of a cog in the wheel of the state, and leave man's sacred destiny in the hands of a small ruling clique.

To properly combat this foreign ideology the United States must create the conditions for its citizens to achieve both spiritual maturity and technical competence. We are challenged more than ever before to achieve excellence in our various fields of endeavor. The public school system is the free societies' response to this important challenge. It is, therefore, mandatory for this system to be preserved if we are to continue to progress as a nation. In the face of the responsibilities that have come to our nation as a result of its unique niche in history, it becomes increasingly necessary for us to strengthen our public school system, and provide the millions of youth of our nation with educational opportunities that are non-discriminatory.

On May 17, 1954, the Supreme Court of our nation rendered a momentous decision declaring segregation unconstitutional in the public schools. The decision stated in substance that separate facilities are inherently unequal, and that to segregate a child on the basis of his race is to deny that child equal protection of the law. A year after the supreme court rendered this decision, it handed down a decree outlining the details by which integration should proceed "with all deliberate speed."[2] While the court did not set a definite deadline for the determination of this process, it did set a time for the beginning. It was clear that the court had chosen this reasonable approach with the expectation that the forces of good will would immediately get to work and prepare the communities for a smooth and peaceful transition.

When the decision was rendered seventeen (17) states and the District of Columbia practiced segregation in the public schools. Today, the process of integration has started in all but five (5) of these states. In some cases—such as Kentucky, Kansas, Missouri, West Virginia, Oklahoma, Maryland and the District of Columbia—the public schools have been almost completely desegregated. In most cases the transition took place smoothly and peacefully. Contrary to the thinking of some southerners, integrated schools have tended to lift the moral and cultural standards of both races rather than pull them down—a fact which was positively

2. *Brown et al. v. Board of Education of Topeka et al.*, 349 U.S. 294 (1955).

affirmed by the superintendent of the Washington, D.C. school system in a recent speech in Atlanta, Georgia.

Five (5) years have elapsed and no discernable move has been made toward integrating the schools of Montgomery, Alabama. We feel that this is contrary not only to the constitution of our nation, but also to the best interest of our children. We would, therefore, like to humbly request that you announce your plan of integration to the community. We make this request because already Negro parents and students are making inquiries relative to the desegregation of schools in Montgomery, and several of them are already prepared to apply for formerly all white schools.[3] We are also mindful of the fact that Alabama's Placement Act, which has been declared constitutional on its face, has not been implemented.[4] In order for our state to be true to its face, we are obliged to start the process of integration in the public schools.

We know that there are some problems involved in changing from a segregated to an integrated school system and we realize that mores are not changed without difficulty. Therefore, we are simply calling on you to begin in good faith to study the idea, and then provide a reasonable start. We hope that this problem can be worked out in our community through voluntary goodwill; and that it will not be necessary to carry it into the courts. Since our aim is to presuade, and our end is a community at peace with itself, we will always be willing to talk with you and seek fair adjustment.

Please know that the foregoing is neither a threat nor an ultimatum. It is rather a sincere effort to urge you to begin some reasonable compliance with the "law of the land," and to cease the maintenance of a system which is injurious to both Negro children and white. We urgently request that you let us hear from you on this matter in a few days.[5]

Sincerely yours,
Executive Committee of the
Montgomery Improvement Association
Reverend Martin L. King, Jr.
Reverend Robert E. DuBose, Jr.
Reverend H. J. Palmer
Reverend Ralph D. Abernathy
Reverend H. H. Hubbard
Reverend S. S. Seay

TLc. MLKP-MBU: Box 20.

---

3. Following the start of the 1959 fall term, the *Montgomery Advertiser* reported that "Negroes heeded the advice of their leaders and made no effort to enroll in all-white schools" ("Enrollment Shows Rise in Montgomery Schools," *Montgomery Advertiser,* 4 September 1959).

4. Passed in the wake of the *Brown* decision, the placement law allowed Alabama school boards wide latitude in assigning students to schools. Fred Shuttlesworth challenged this law, but the Supreme Court ruled that it was not discriminatory "upon its face" (*Shuttlesworth et al. v. Birmingham Board of Education of Jefferson County, Alabama,* 358 U.S. 101 [1958]).

5. In his annual address to the MIA in December, King complained that the local board of education "has not even given us the courtesy of an answer" (Address at the Fourth Annual Institute on Nonviolence and Social Change at Bethel Baptist Church, 3 December 1959, p. 337 in this volume).

To J. Charles Whitfield

31 August 1959
[*Montgomery, Ala.*]

Texas state representative J. Charles Whitfield wrote King an admiring letter on 5 August and requested advice on dealing with school desegregation in Houston.[1]

Mr. J. Charles Whitfield
The State of Texas
House of Representatives
Austin, Texas

Dear Mr. Whitfield:

On returning to the office I found your letter of August 5, on my desk. I deeply regret that absence from the city for several days has delayed my reply.

I am happy to know of your concern over the question of school integration in Houston, Texas. I have always felt that if people of good will really take the leadership in this area, the transition from the segregated to an integrated society would be much smoother and peaceful. I do not know if I can give any specific suggestions concerning the Houston situation since I am not too familiar with the pulse of the community. There are certain unique situations within every community which cannot fit into a general pattern. However, there are one or two things that I would like to suggest which might make for a transition devoid of extreme ten sion. The first one is the necessity of preparing the community to accept the inevitable. This means that the religious and civic leaders of the community should seek to work through their congregations and organizations to mitigate the fears that many white persons have concerning integration. So many half truths and false ideas have been dessiminated concerning integration that many white people sincerely feel that it is a design of the devil [*so?*] to speak. It is at this point that I think respected and influential community leaders can be of tremendous service. This has happened in other communities and in almost every case the situation worked out very well

I would also suggest that the community leaders urge the political leaders of the city to take a definite stand in urging the people to accept law and order. This means that they must not predict that violence will emerge as a result of integration. Actually, the constant prediction of violence is a conscious or unconscious invitation to it. But it has been proven that where governors, mayors and other officials have made it clear that they would not stand for violence to break out dur-

1. Joseph Charles Whitfield (1921–1997) was born in Beaumont, Texas, and received a B.B.A. (1943) from the University of Texas School of Business Administration. After serving in the U.S. Navy during World War II, Whitfield received a J.D. (1957) from the South Texas College of Law and practiced law until he was elected to the Texas House of Representatives in 1958. A liberal Democrat concerned with civil rights, Whitfield represented Harris County until 1966. He ran for the State senate in 1965 and U.S. Congress in 1976, losing to his opponent on both occasions.

ing the integration process there has been no violence. The police force must also be alerted so that they will be determined to keep down any real incidents. It has been proven that mobs only take over when they feel that they are aided and abetted by the police force. Once they discover that they do not have the support of the police force they fade away. This was vividly revealed at Central High School a few days ago when integration took place again.[2] After the mob discovered that they did not have the support of the police force we have heard no more from them.

I do not want to give the impression that there is nothing that the Negro must do himself. Certainly, Negro leaders must stress the importance of nonviolence and love during this period of transition. They must urge the children who are entering integrated schools to go with a spirit of humility and also of forgiveness in case some incident develops. In the final analysis, this whole problem is a moral problem and it will depend on the commitment that individuals have toward the moral ideals of religion and the great creed of our democracy.

I don't know if these suggestions are at all pertinent, but I hope they will be helpful. I would also suggest that you read the last chapter of a book that I wrote a few months ago entitled, Stride Toward Freedom. There I have elaborated my philosophy, and also attempted to give some direction to the question of school integration. You may secure this book from Harper and Brothers at 49 East 33rd Street, New York 16, New York.

Thank you for writing me, and whenever I can be of any assistance please feel free to call on me.

Very sincerely yours,
Martin L. King, Jr.

MLK:mlb

TLc. MLKP-MBU: Box 73.

---

2. On 12 August five black students attended previously all-white high schools in Little Rock.

From Norman Thomas

1 Sept 1959

1 September 1959
New York, N.Y.

Thomas, a Socialist Party leader who had corresponded with King during the bus boycott, invites him to co-sponsor a public forum to discuss world peace and human rights during Soviet premier Nikita Khrushchev's visit to the United States.[1] *In his 5 September reply, King indicated that he would "be happy to serve" as a sponsor.*[2]

Martin Luther King, Jr.
301 S. Jackson
Montgomery, Ala.

Dear Martin Luther King, Jr.

The impending Khrushchev-Eisenhower talks are of profound importance to all of us. Certainly any discussion in the present tense situation is a healthy thing.

There is a danger, however, that in all the discussion of the pros and cons of the visit, certain key issues may be overlooked. The point which some of us believe should be emphasized is that while the talks are a good thing, they cannot end the Cold War until both major powers are prepared to deal with the basic issues.

We are arranging for a large public meeting at Community Church here in New York the night of September 20—following immediately after Khrushchev's visit to this city. We hope at that time to raise the basic issues of disarmament, disengagement, ending nuclear tests, human rights, national self-determination, etc., that must be discussed if peace is to become a reality.

In a sense we plan to discuss a possible "agenda" for these two leaders to concentrate on—we want to use the visits not to attack or to praise one side or the other, but to focus public attention on the basic problems underlying the Cold War.

I am writing to ask if you would agree to serve on the Ad Hoc Sponsoring Committee—being formed for the sole purpose of sponsoring this one public meeting. The suggested list of sponsors is enclosed with this letter, with asterisks indicating those who have already agreed to serve.[3]

Speakers being invited include Eleanor Roosevelt, James P. Warburg, Roger

---

1. One month earlier, King declined Thomas's invitation to be interviewed for a nationally distributed radio program, citing scheduling conflicts (King to Thomas, 31 July 1959).

2. King was among the signatories of a 3 September *New York Times* advertisement applauding the Khrushchev-Eisenhower talks (Clarence Pickett to King, 27 August 1959). He also agreed to sign a statement drafted by the National Committee for a Sane Nuclear Policy calling for arms control (Maude L. Ballou to Norman Cousins, 11 September 1959).

3. The list of fifty-two proposed members included labor leader A. Philip Randolph, sociologist C. Wright Mills, urban planner Lewis Mumford, psychologist Erich Fromm, and playwright Tennessee Williams ("Proposed members of the ad hoc committee on the Eisenhower-Khrushchev talks," 1 September 1959).

4 Sept 1959

Baldwin, George Kennan, A. J. Muste, Rep. William Myers, and myself.[4] We had hoped you might be able to speak but Bayard Rustin tells me that you cannot make it that evening. Stanley Issacs, the Republican member of the New York City Council, has agreed to chair the meeting.

May we hear from you immediately—by collect wire—to know if you will agree to serve.

Sincerely,
[*signed*]
Norman Thomas

NT/dmc

TLS. MLKP-MBU: Box 72.

---

4. Warburg served as a financial advisor to the Roosevelt administration; Baldwin co-founded the American Civil Liberties Union (ACLU) in 1920; Kennan was a historian, diplomat, and U.S. ambassador to the Soviet Union in 1952; Muste was a leading pacifist; William Meyer was a congressman from Vermont.

To Marjorie McKenzie Lawson

4 September 1959
[*Montgomery, Ala.*]

Following Massachusetts senator John F. Kennedy's failed bid for the vice presidency at the 1956 Democratic National Convention, he asked Washington attorney Marjorie Lawson and her husband, Belford, to help boost his profile among African Americans.[1] *At the 20 August meeting of the National Bar Association in Milwaukee, Marjorie Lawson approached King about the possibility of meeting Kennedy.*[2] *In the following letter King informs Lawson that he is unable to meet with Kennedy until after October.*[3]

---

1. Belford V. Lawson, Interview by Ronald J. Grele, 11 January 1966. Marjorie McKenzie Lawson (1912–1980), born in Pittsburgh, received a B.A. (1933) from the University of Michigan and law degrees from Terrell Law School (1939) and Columbia University School of Law (1950). For several years preceding Kennedy's successful 1960 presidential bid, Lawson represented him at national gatherings of black religious, political, and women's organizations, and she managed his 1958 senatorial reelection campaign in Boston's black community. In 1962 Kennedy appointed Lawson to his Commission on Equal Employment Opportunities and to serve as judge of the Juvenile Court of the District of Columbia. During the 1950s and 1960s, she wrote a weekly public affairs column for the *Pittsburgh Courier*.

2. For King's remarks at the event, see Address at the Thirty-fourth Annual Convention of the National Bar Association, 20 August 1959, pp. 264–270 in this volume.

3. See also Kennedy to King, 10 November 1959, p. 319 in this volume.

Mrs. Marjorie M. Lawson
2001–11th Street, N.W.
Washington, D.C.

17 Sept 1959

Dear Mrs. Lawson:

Ever since returning home from Milwaukee I have been attempting to rearrange my schedule in order to make a trip to Washington to meet with Senator Kennedy. Unfortunately, however, it just hasn't worked out. I found several important organizational matters and a good deal of accumulated mail that needed my immediate attention on my return. In the light of this it will not be possible for me to see Senator Kennedy before I leave for California and Hawaii. I would appreciate your speaking to him to ascertain when it would be possible for him to see me after the first of October.

I am deeply grateful to you for your interest in our coming together and I hope something fruitful can grow out of this proposed conference.

It was certainly a real pleasure to see you in Milwaukee. Give my best regards to your husband. Both of you are doing a marvelous job, and whenever you need me, please feel free to make it known.

Yours very truly,
Martin L. King, Jr.

MLK:mlb

TLc. MLKP-MBU: Box 29A.

Address to the House of Representatives of the First Legislature, State of Hawaii, on 17 September 1959

Honolulu, Hawaii

After attending the National Baptist Convention in San Francisco and speaking in Los Angeles, King flew to Hawaii for several engagements and a brief vacation.[1] *Arriving just three weeks after Hawaii became the fiftieth state, he addresses the legislature at the state capitol, the Iolani Palace.*[2] *King thanks the Hawaiians for offer-*

1. King had received invitations from Ellen J. Watumull of the Watumull Foundation, whom he had met in India, and Shelton Hale Bishop of the Honolulu Council of Churches (Watumull to King, 21 May 1959, and Bishop to King, 1 July 1959). On 15 September King spoke to members of the Honolulu Ministerial Union about the lack of support for integration among white clergy ("King Says Alabama White Pastors Fight Integration," *Honolulu Star-Bulletin,* 16 September 1959). The following day he delivered "A Pastor's Hope for America" at the McKinley High School auditorium in Honolulu (Hubert H. White, "Dr. M. L. King Wins Friends in 50th State," *Los Angeles Sentinel,* 24 September 1959).

2. For King's invitation to address the House of Representatives, see "House Resolution no. 30," 16 September 1959.

ing the nation "a noble example" of progress "in the area of racial harmony and racial justice."[3] *King's appearance triggered an argument on the house floor when a state representative denounced Hawaii's Republican U.S. senator Hiram L. Fong for his opposition to civil rights legislation.*[4] *This text was published in Hawaii's* Journal of the House of Representatives.[5]

"Mr. Speaker, distinguished menbers of the House of Representatives of this great new state in our Union, ladies and gentlemen:

It is certainly a delightful privilege and pleasure for me to have this great opportunity and, I shall say, it is a great honor to come before you today and to have the privilege of saying just a few words to you about some of the pressing problems confronting our nation and our world.

I come to you with a great deal of appreciation and great feeling of appreciation, I should say, for what has been accomplished in this beautiful setting and in this beautiful state of our Union. As I think of the struggle that we are engaged in in the South land, we look to you for inspiration and as a noble example, where you have already accomplished in the area of racial harmony and racial justice what we are struggling to accomplish in other sections of the country, and you can never know what it means to those of us caught for the moment in the tragic and often dark midnight of man's inhumanity to man, to come to a place where we see the glowing daybreak of freedom and dignity and racial justice.

People ask me from time to time as I travel across the country and over the world, whether there has been any real progress in the area of race relations and I always answer it by saying that there are three basic attitudes that one can take toward the question of progress in the area of race relations. One can take the attitude of extreme optimism. The extreme optimist would contend that we have come a long, long way in the area of race relations and he would point proudly to the strives that have been made in the area of civil rights in the last few decades. And from this, he would conclude that the problem is just about solved now and that we can sit down comfortably by the wayside and wait on the coming of the inevitable.

And then there is the extreme, the attitude of extreme pessimism, that we often find. The extreme pressimist would contend that we have made only minor strives in the area of human relations. He would contend that we have created many more problems than we have solved. He would look around and see the tensions in certain sections of the country; he would listen to the rhythmic beat of the deep rumblings of discontent; he would point to the presence of Federal troops in Little Rock, Arkansas; he would point to schools being closed in some states of the Union

3. He later shared his impressions of Hawaii's multi-ethnic society with his congregation: "As I looked at all of these various faces and various colors mingled together like the waters of the sea, I could see only one face—the face of the future!" ("Dr. King Reports on Trip to Hawaii," *Dexter Echo,* 4 November 1959).

4. Shortly after his arrival in Hawaii, King criticized Fong's gradualist approach to civil rights ("King Criticizes Fong's Civil Rights Stand," *Honolulu Star-Bulletin,* 14 September 1959).

5. According to the journal, the address was followed by much applause.

and from all of this, he would conclude that we have retrogressed instead of progressed. And then he would go on later and contend that a monster human nature cannot be changed. Sometimes he will turn to the realm of theology and talk about the tragic taint of original sin hovering over every individual, or he might turn to psychology and talk about the inflexibility of certain habit structures once they have been molded and from all of this, he would conclude that there can be no progress in the area of human relations because human beings cannot be changed once they have started on a certain road.

Now, it is interesting to notice that the extreme optimist and the extreme pessimist have at least one thing in common. They both agree that we must sit down and do nothing in the area of race relations. The extreme optimist says do nothing because integration is inevitable. The extreme pessimist says do nothing because integration is impossible. But I think there is a third position, a third attitude that can be taken, namely, the realistic position. The realistic attitude seeks to reconcile the truths of two opposites while avoiding the extremes of both. So the realist in the area of race relations would agree with the optimist that we have come a long, long way, but he would balance that by agreeing with the pessimist that we have a long, long way to go. And so this is my answer to the question of whether there has been any progress in the area of race relations. I seek to be realistic and say we have a long, long way to go.

Now, it is easy for us to see that we have come a long, long way. Twenty-five years ago, fifty years ago, a year hardly passed that numerous Negroes were not brutally lynched in our nation by vicious mobs. Lynchings have about ceased today. We think about the fact that just twenty-five years ago, most of the Southern states had a system known as a poll tax to prevent Negroes from becoming registered voters. The poll tax has been eliminated in all but four states.[6] We think about the fact that the Negro is voting now more than he has ever voted before. At the turn of the century, there were very few Negro registered voters in the South. By 1948 that number had reached to 750,000 and today it stands at about 1,300,000.

And even in the area of economic justice, we have seen a good deal of progress. The average Negro wage earner in the South today and over the nation makes four times more than the average Negro wage earner of ten years ago and the national income of the Negro is now $17 billion a year. That is more than all of the exports of the United States and more than the national income of Canada. So, we've come a long, long way.

Then we've come a long, long way in seeing the walls of segregation gradually crumble. When the Supreme Court rendered its decision in 1954, seventeen states and the District of Columbia practiced segregation in the public schools but today, most of these states have complied with the decision and just five states are left that have not made any move in the area of compliance and two of these states are now under orders to integrate—Atlanta, Georgia and New Orleans, Louisiana.[7]

6. At the time of this address, five states required a poll tax: Virginia, Alabama, Texas, Mississippi, and Arkansas. In 1964, the 24th Amendment to the U.S. Constitution eliminated the poll tax in federal elections.

7. King refers to the Supreme Court's school desegregation ruling in *Brown v. Board of Education.*

17 Sept 1959

So after next September, that will only leave Mississippi, Alabama and South Carolina as the states that have not complied with the Supreme Court's decision.

So you can see that we have come a long, long way. But before stopping—it would be wonderful if I could stop here—but I must move on for two or three more minutes and say that there is another sign.

You see, it would be a fact for me to say we have come a long, long way but it wouldn't be telling the truth. A fact is the absence of contradiction but truth is the presence of coherence. Truth is the relatedness of facts. Now, it is a fact that we have come a long, long way but in order to tell the truth, it is necessary to move on and say we have a long, long way to go. If we stop here, we would be the victims of a dangerous optimism. We would be the victims of an illusion wrapped in superficiality. So, in order to tell the truth, it's necessary to move on and say we have a long, long way to go.

Now, it is not difficult to see that. We know that the forces of resistance are rising at times to ominous proportions in the South. The legislative halls of many of our states ring loud with such words as 'interposition' and 'nullification.' While lynchings have ceased to a great extent, other things are happening. Churches are being bombed; homes are being bombed; schools are being bombed; synagogues are being bombed by forces that are determined to stand against the law of the land.

And although the Negro is voting more than ever before, we know that there are still conniving forces being used to keep the Negro from being a registered voter. Out of the potential 5,000,000 Negro registered voters in the South, we only have 1,300,000. This means that we have a long, long way to go in order to make justice a reality there in the registration of voting. And although we have come a long, long way in the economic realm, we have a long, long way to go there in order to make economic justice a reality.

And then segregation is still with us. Although we have seen the walls gradually crumble, it is still with us. I imply that figuratively speaking, that Old Man Segregation is on his death bed but you know history has proven that social systems have a great last-minute breathing power and the guardians of the status quo are always on hand with their oxygen tents to keep the old order alive and this is exactly what we see today. So segregation is still with us. We are confronted in the South in its glaring and conspicuous forms and we are confronted in almost every other section of the nation in its hidden and subtle forms. But if democracy is to live, segregation must die. Segregation is a cancer in the body politic which must be removed before our democratic health can be realized. In a real sense, the shape of the world today does not permit us the luxury of an anemic democracy. If we are to survive, if we are to stand as a force in the world, if we are to maintain our prestige, we must solve this problem because people are looking over to America.

Just two years ago I traveled all over Africa and talked with leaders from that great continent. One of the things they said to me was this: No amount of extensive handouts and beautiful words would be substitutes for treating our brothers in the United States as first-class citizens and human beings. This came to me from the mouth of Prime Minister Nkrumah of Ghana.[8]

---

8. For more on King's March 1957 trip to the Ghanian independence celebration, see Introduction in *Papers* 4:7–9.

Just four months ago, I traveled throughout India and the Middle East and talked with many of the people and leaders of that great country and other people in the Middle East and these are the things they talked about: That we must solve this problem if we are to stand and to maintain our prestige. And I can remember very vividly meeting people all over Europe and in the Middle East and in the Far East and even though many of them could not speak English, they knew how to say, 'Little Rock.'

And these are the things that we must be concerned about—we must be concerned about because we love America and we are out to free not only the Negro. This is not our struggle today to free 17,000,000 Negroes. It's bigger than that. We are seeking to free the soul of America. Segregation debilitates the white man as well as the Negro. We are to free all men, all races and all groups. This is our responsibility and this is our challenge and we look to this great new state in our Union as the example and as the inspiration. As we move on in this realm, let us move on with the faith that this problem can be solved and that it will be solved, believing firmly that all reality hinges on moral foundations and we are struggling for what is right and we are destined to win.

We have come a long, long way. We have a long, long way to go. I close, if you will permit me, by quoting the words of an old Negro slave preacher. He didn't quite have his grammar right, but he uttered some words in the form of a prayer with great symbolic profundity and these are the words he said: 'Lord, we ain't what we want to be; we ain't what we ought to be; we ain't what we gonna be, but thank God, we ain't what we was.' Thank you."

PD. *Journal of the House of Representatives of the First Legislature State of Hawaii: First Special Session of 1959* (Honolulu: Fisher Corporation, 1960), pp. 56–59; copy in HHSA.

"Address at Public Meeting of the Southern Christian Ministers Conference of Mississippi"

23 September 1959
[*Jackson, Miss.*]

Closing a two day session on nonviolent resistance at Pearl Street AME Church, King praises Mississippi's civil rights leaders who "have stood in this state like courageous Davids amid the giants of resistance and the Goliahs of injustice."[1] *After reflecting on the current state of race relations, King outlines the responsibilities*

1. W. H. Hall, chairman of the Southern Christian Ministers Conference of Mississippi, confirmed the speaking engagement in a 21 May 1959 letter. Earlier in the conference, James Lawson addressed "The Biblical-Theological Basis to Nonviolence" and Ella Baker spoke on "Allies and Opponents of the Negro's Drive for Equality" (Hall to Fellow minister, 17 August 1959). At a press conference preceding his address, King warned that "it is likely that Communist Russia would take over as the world leader" should the United States not solve its racial problems ("Rev. King Sees Resistance to Integration Nearing End," *Montgomery Advertiser,* 24 September 1959).

of African Americans interested in social change. He predicts "a season of suffering" and warns that "as victories for civil rights mount in the federal courts, angry passions and deep prejudices are further aroused." In the face of continuing attacks, King asserts that "the Negro needs the vision to see the ordeals of the generation as the opportunity to transfigure himself and American society." A handwritten draft included corrections that King incorporated into this typescript.[2]

Mr. Chairman, members of the Southern Christian Ministers Conference of Mississippi, fellow workers for freedom:

I am delighted to have the opportunity of being with you in this significant meeting. It is through conferences of this nature that we gain new insights, new inspiration, and, indeed, new courage to carry on in the mighty struggle in which we are engaged.

I come to Mississippi with nothing but praise for the fearless and dedicated leaders that have stood in this state like courageous Davids amid the giants of resistance and the Goliahs of injustice. As we all know, it is not easy to take a stand in Mississippi, for the possibilities of economic reprisals and bodily harm are much greater here than in any other section. In a real sense there is nothing more majestic and sublime than the determined courage of individuals willing to suffer and sacrifice for their freedom. This is what your leaders exemplify. God grant that new dedicated leaders will rise up and join the ranks of the few who have already given so much of their time and energy to a cause that we know is right.

I bring warm and sincere greetings to you from the Montgomery Imporvement Association and the people of Montgomery. I bring special greetings from the 50,000 Negro people of Montgomery who, through their words and deeds, revealed that it is ultimately more honorable to walk in dignity than ride in humiliation. I also bring greetings from the Southern Christian Leadership Conference. This organization came into being in order to serve as a channel through which local protest organizations in the South could coordinate their activities. Our basic aim is to implement the Supreme Court's desegregation decisions on the local level through mass, direct, non-violent action. One of our most specific undertakings, at the present time, is that of joining with other organizations to increase the number of Negro registered voters in the South. This is a big job, and one that cannot be tackled without hard work and great financial resources.

On May 17, 1954, the Supreme Court of this nation rendered in simple, eloquent and unequivocal language a decision that was destined to change the future course of American history.[3] It declared segregation unconstitutional in the public schools, and made it palpable clear that to segregate a child on the basis of his race meant denying that child equal protection of the law. This decision came as a joyous daybreak to the long night of enforced segregation. It came as a

2. King, Draft, Address at public meeting of the Southern Christian Ministers Conference of Mississippi, 23 September 1959. In composing his remarks, King drew upon several earlier addresses, including "Give Us the Ballot," his speech delivered at the 17 May 1957 Prayer Pilgrimage for Freedom in Washington, D.C. (see *Papers* 4:208–215).

3. King refers to *Brown v. Board of Education.*

legal and sociological death-blow to the old Plessy doctrine of "separate-but-equal".[4] The rendering of this decision did far more to advance the prestige of the United States than all of her astounding achievements in the scientific and technological realm.

Since the 1954 decision was rendered, many notable advances have taken place. Out of the seventeen states and the District of Columbia that practiced segregation when the Supreme Court handed down its edict, all but five have made some move toward compliance. Integration is definitely gaining ground in the Deep South, and with less violence than at any time since the momentous 1954 decision outlawing "separate-but-equal" schools.

One of the most hopeful signs of our time is the breakdown of massive resistance in Virginia and Arkansas. Interestingly enough, this massive resistance has crumbled as a result of the massive insistence of white southerners to keep the public schools open. What we now see in both Little Rock and Virginia is something very revealing. Two powerful institutions have collided in the South—the institution of segregation and the institution of public schools. And the people have made it clear that when the final moment of choice comes, they will choose public schools rather than segregation.

So maybe we pro-integrationists shouldn't be so hard on Governor [*Orval*] Faubus after all, for, however ironical it may sound, he has done more to promote the cause of integration than almost any personality of this decade. His irresponsible actions brought the issue to the forefront of the conscience of the nation, and allowed people to see the futility of attempting to close the public schools. The price to be paid by school closing, it has been found, is much too high. Business suffers. Children receive an inferior education. Many responsible persons move away. The cultural life of the community lags.

All of this has made it possible for the cooler heads to gain ground. The moderates in the white South are being heard. They are no longer voices crying in the wilderness.

Despite these definite signs of progress, the forces of resistance are still active. The South is not letting down the barriers willingly. Except in the District of Columbia and the border states, such as Delaware, Maryland, Missouri, Kentucky, Oklahoma and West Virginia, full-scale integration is still a long way off. Virginia, North Carolina, Tennessee, Texas, Arkansas and now Florida have accepted integration on a token basis only. Five states—South Carolina, Georgia, Alabama, Mississippi and Louisiana—are still fighting to keep even token mixing of classes out of their schools.

All of this reveals that we have a great deal of positive work to do before the ideals and principles of an integrated society are brought into full realization. Let me hasten to say that this problem will not just work itself out. It is a fallacy to say that time will cure all problems. If time is not aided by human effort, it becomes a powerful ally of the insurgent and primitive forces of irrational emotionalism and social stagnation. Even a casual look at history reveals that no social advance rolls in on the wheels of inevitability. Every step toward the goal of justice requires

4. King refers to the U.S. Supreme Court's 1896 decision in *Plessy v. Ferguson* (163 U.S. 537).

sacrifice, suffering and struggle; the tireless exertion and passionate concern of dedicated individuals.

We must also realize that privileged groups never give up their privileges voluntarily. If we are victimized with the feeling that we can sit down comfortably by the wayside and wait for the white man to voluntarily give us our justly deserved freedom, we will be the victims of a dangerous illusion, which can only end up in tragic disillusion. If we are waiting for our rights to be given to us without any determined effort to gain them, I fear that we will still be waiting when our great grand children make their entrance on the stage of history. All of the gains that we have made thus far, in the area of civil rights, have come through legal and moral pressure.

In the final analysis, integration will become a reality in America only when enough people come to believe that it is morally right and are willing to work passionately for its fulfillment.

Many agencies and groups must work constructively together in order to achieve the ideals and principles of an integrated society—the Christian church, organized labor, liberal whites, North and South, the federal government and the Negro himself. Since time will not permit me to discuss the role of all of these groups, I would like to take the moments left in discussing the role of the Negro.

Certainly, if first class citizenship is to become a reality for the Negro, he must assume the primary responsibility for making it so. One of the most damaging effects of past segregation on the personality of the Negro may well be that he has been victimized with the delusion that others should be more concerned than himself about his citizenship rights. There are several specific things that we must do:

1. We must maintain a sense of somebodiness and self-respect. One of the great tragedies of the system of segregation is that it so often robs its victims of a sense of dignity and worth. It tends to develop a false sense of inferiority in the segregated. But despite the existence of a system that denies our essential worth, we must have the spiritual audacity to assert our somebodiness. We must no longer allow our physical bondage to enslave our minds. He who feels that he is nobody eventually becomes nobody. But he who feels that he is somebody, even though humiliated by external servitude, achieves a sense of selfhood and dignity that nothing in all the world can take away.

2. We must make a vigorous effort to improve our standards wherever they lag behind. We must not be afraid to admit our own shortcomings. One of the sure signs of maturity is the ability to rise to the point of self-criticism. Whenever we are objects of criticism from white men, even though the criticisms are maliciously directed and mixed with half-truths, we must pick out the elements of truth and make them the basis of creative reconstruction. We must not let the fact that we are the victims of injustice lull us into abrogating responsibility for our own lives.

We must make full and constructive use of the freedom we already possess. We must not allow our oppression and lack of full freedom to drive us into a state of contentment with the mediocre and satisfaction with the non-productive. History has proven that inner determination can often break through the outer shackles of circumstance. Take the Jews for an example. For years they have been forced to walk through the dark night of oppression. They have been carried through the fires of affliction, and put to the cruel sword of persecution. But this did not keep them from rising up with creative genius to plunge against cloud-filled nights of affliction, new and blazing stars of inspiration. Being a Jew did not keep [*Baruch*] Spinoza from rising from a proverty stricken ghetto to a place of eminence in philosophy. Being a Jew did not keep [*George Frideric*] Handel from lifting his vision to high heaven and emerging with creative and melodious music that sill shakes the very fiber of men's souls. Being a Jew did not keep [*Albert*] Einstein from using his profound and genius-packed mind to challenge an axiom and add to the lofty insights of science a theory of relativity. Being a Jew did not prevent Karl Marx from adding to the accumulated knowledge of political science, making it necessary for men to study his theories whether they agree with him or not. Being a Jew did not keep Sigmund Freud from delving into the inner chambers of the subconscious, making it easier for man to discover the source of his inner conflicts and the roots of his personality disintegration. Being Jews did not prevent Amos and Hosea, Ezekial, Isaiah and Jeremiah from standing up amid forces of religious idolatry and unjust power structures and declaring with prophetic urgency the eternal word of God, and the never ceasing necessity of being obedient to his will.

23 Sept 1959

So we too can make creative contributions, even though the door of freedom is not fully opened. We need not wait until oppression ceases before we seek to make creative contribution to our nation's life. We must seek to rise above the crippling restrictions of circumstance. Already we have a host of Negroes whose inspiring achievements have proven that human nature cannot be catalogued, and that we need not postpone the moment of our creativity until the day of full emancipation. From an old slave cabin in Virginia's hills, Booker T. Washington rose to the statue of one of America's greatest leaders; he lit a torch and darkness fled. From the red hills of Gordon County, Georgia, Roland Hayes rose to the palace of King George the Fifth and the mansion of Queen Mother of Spain. From a poverty stricken area in Philadelphia, Pennsylvania, Marion Anderson rose up to be the world's greatest contralto, so that Toscaninni could say, "A voice like this comes only once in a century," and Sabelius of Finland could say, "My roof is too low for such a voice." From oppressive and crippling surroundings, George Washington Carver lifted his searching, creative mind to the ordinary peanut, and found therein extraordinary possibilities for goods and products unthinkable by minds of the past. These was a star in the sky of female leadership, and Mary McCloud Bethune grabbed it and used it. There was a star in the diplomatic sky; Ralph Bunche caught it and allowed it to shine in his life, in spite of the fact that he was the grandson of a slave preacher. There was a star in the athletic sky; then came Joe Louis with his educated fist, Jessie Owens with his fleet and dashing feet, and Jackie Robinson with his calm spirit and powerful bat.[5] There are many others.

5. Booker T. Washington (1856–1915) founded Tuskegee Institute. Roland Hayes (1887–1977) was a well-known lyric tenor. Marian Anderson (1897–1993) was an internationally acclaimed opera singer. Arturo Toscanini (1867–1957) was an Italian conductor who led the New York Philharmonic-Symphony Orchestra (1928–1936), and Jean Sibelius (1865–1957) was a Finnish composer. George Washington Carver (1864?–1943) was a scientist particularly famed for his agricultural research. Mary McLeod Bethune (1875–1955) was a pioneering educator who founded the National Council of Negro Women. Ralph Bunche (1904–1971) was a United Nations diplomat who became the first African

The names are too numerous to list. But these are sufficient to demonstrate the fact that we need not wait until the day of complete freedom before we seek to achieve excellence in our various fields of endeavor.

3. We must make a determined effort to achieve the ballot. One of the most important steps that the Negro can take at this hour is that short walk to the voting booth. As you know, there are two problems that we must deal with in this area. One is the problem internal apathy. This is where people out of sheer laziness and a lack of interest fail to register in areas where there are no real barriers. We all know that there are some cities in the Deep South where the Negro faces only the obstacle of his own laxity. The other problem that we confront in seeking to obtain the ballot is that of external resistance. This resistance includes threats and intimidation from white extremists, conniving methods set up by boards of registrars, such as, literacy tests, written and oral, and occasional physical violence against Negroes seeking to vote. The story of Gus Courts and the Rev. George Lee here in Mississippi is a familiar one, and the violence inflicted upon these men constitutes one of the most shameful stories of American history.[6] It is a shame before this nation and the world that less than twenty thousand Negroes are registered in Mississippi because of the forces of resistance.

If this problem of injustice at the ballot box is to be solved, we must press for stronger civil rights legislation. In passing, I would like to commend the members of the Civil Rights Commission who recommended such powerful and constructive proposals in the area of civil rights. I am certain that if these recommendations are enacted into law we will see a new birth of freedom and a new day of justice in the South.[7]

Our most urgent plea to the federal government is to guarantee our voting rights. We must cry out to the federal government in firm and positive terms, give us the ballot. Give us the ballot and we will creatively join in the freeing of the soul of America. Give us the ballot and we will transform the silent misdeeds of blood-thirsty mobs into the blessed good deeds of orderly citizens. Give us the ballot and we will no longer worry you about a federal anti-lynching law; we will, by the power of vote, write such a law on the statue books of the South, and bring an end to the dastardly acts of hooded perpetrators of violence who have left wounded justice lying prostrate in the streets of our cities. Give us the ballot and we will keep the sublime name of shame in the newspapers of Europe, in the market places of Asia, and in the discussion groups of Africa. We will bring before

---

American to win the Nobel Peace Prize in 1950. Joe Louis (1914–1981) held the world heavyweight championship from 1937 to 1949. Jesse Owens (1913–1980) was a track and field star who won four gold medals in the 1936 Berlin Summer Olympics. Jackie Robinson (1919–1972) was the first African American to play modern major league baseball.

6. In separate incidents in 1955, Courts and Lee were shot after registering black voters in Belzoni, Mississippi. Lee was killed and Courts relocated to Chicago.

7. Among the commission's recommendations were that all registration and voting records be made public, that the commission be bestowed with the authority to investigate and dismiss allegations of disenfranchisement, and that the president be allowed to designate temporary registrars in localities with more than nine complaints (U.S. Commission on Civil Rights, *Report of the United States Commission on Civil Rights, 1959* [Washington, D.C.: U.S. Government Printing Office, 1959], pp. 134–142).

the bar of justice the brutal murderers of little Emmitt Till and the vicious lynchers of Mack C. Parker.[8] Give us the ballot and we will house our courts with judges who will do justly, love mercy, and walk humbly with God, and we will send to the sacred halls of Congress men who will not sign a Southern Manifesto because they are committed to a higher manifesto of justice and love. Give us the ballot and we will quietly and non-violently implement the Supreme Court's decision of May 17, 1954.[9]

23 Sept 1959

4. We must give generous financial contributions to civil rights organizations. Massive resistance must be met by massive financial assistance. It is appalling to discover how little money we are willing to invest in the struggle for our own freedom and dignity. The excuse that we don't have the money is no longer valid or acceptable. The annual income of the Negro is now about 17 billion dollars a year, which is more than the national income of Canada and all the exports of the United States. We have money for almost everything else that we want, including insignificant things. I submit to you that we spend far too much on frivolities and far too little on worthwhile causes. It will be tragic indeed if future historians are able to record that the Negro spent more on transitory pleasure than he spent on the eternal values of freedom and justice.

5. We must continue to produce intelligent, dedicated and courageous leaders. We need leaders who avoid the extremes of hotheadedness and "uncle-tomism", leaders who, on the one hand, embrace wise restraint and calm reasonableness and, on the other hand, reveal a courageous determination to press on until the victory for justice is won. We need leaders not in love with money, but in love with justice; leaders not in love with publicity, but in love with humanity to paraphase the great words of Holland: God give us leaders; a time like this demands great leaders; leaders whom the spoils of office cannot buy; leaders who have honor; leaders who will not lie; leaders who possess opinions and a will; leaders who can stand before a demagogue and damn his treacherous flatteries without winking; tall leaders, sun crowned in public duty and in private thinking.[10]

6. We must possess the firm conviction that segregation is an evil that we cannot passively accept. Segregation is evil because it seeks to repudiate the principle that all men are created equal. Segregation is wrong because it relegates men to the status of things, and makes them objects to be used, rather than persons to be respected. Segregation is wrong because it gives the segregated a false sense of inferiority, while leaving the segregator confirmed in a false sense of superiority.

---

8. Fourteen-year-old Emmett Till was murdered in Mississippi in August 1955 for allegedly whistling at a white woman. Two white men were acquitted of Till's murder the following month. For more details on the murder of Mack Charles Parker, see King to James P. Coleman, 25 April 1959, pp. 190–191 in this volume.

9. In March 1956 ninety Southern congressmen and all but three Southern senators signed the "Declaration of Constitutional Principles," popularly known as the "Southern Manifesto," in which they pledged to resist desegregation, asserting that it was a subversion of the Constitution.

10. King paraphrases Josiah Gilbert Holland's poem "Wanted" (1872).

Segregation is wrong because it assumes that God made a mistake and stamped upon certain men an eternal stigma of shame because of the color of their skin.[11]

Therefore, we must not rest until segregation is removed from every area of our nation's life. Segregation is a cancer in the body politic, which must be removed before our democratic health can be realized. We must not be deluded into complacent acceptance of an outmoded doctrine of separate-but-equal because of the present erection of beautiful school buildings. The fact remains that separate facilities are inherently unequal, and so long as segregated schools exist the South can never reach its full economic, political and moral maturity.

7. We must be willing to suffer and sacrifice in order to achieve our freedom. It is trite but true that freedom is never handed out on a silver platter, and that the road to progress is never a smooth and easy road. The flight from the Egypt of slavery to the glorious promised land is always temporarily interrupted by a bleak and desolute wilderness, with its prodigious mountains of opposition and gigantic hilltips of evil. The triumphant drums of Easter are never allowed to beat until the desolate moments of life's Good Friday have plucked the radiant star of hope from the sky of human experience. This is the story of life. Too many of us want the fruits of integration but we are not willing to courageously challenge the roots of segregation. But let me assure you that it does not come this way.

We must gird our courage and stand firm for an integrated society. We must tell our white brothers that the few Uncle Toms who will sill their souls for a mess of economic pottage do not speak for the Negro. We must let them know that we are determined to be free, and that we are willing to pay the price in terms of suffering and sacrifice. We must never adjust to segregation, because it deprives us of our selfhood, and robs us of our dignity and self respect. Once more we must have the courage to cry out with our forefathers: "Oh freedom, oh freedom, before I'll be a slave, I'll be buried in my grave and go home to my Father and be saved".[12]

8. Finally, we must conduct our struggle on the highest level of dignity and discipline. We must rise to the creative level of being able to resist the evil system, and yet not hate the persons who are responsible for the system. We must not allow ourselves to become bitter. Hate is a cancerous disease that debilitates the hater as well as the hated. I am still convinced that love is the most durable power in all the world, and that Jesus was right when he said to the men and women of his generation, "Love your enemies, bless them that curse you, pray for them that despitefully use you".[13]

---

11. King may have drawn the preceding two sentences from Benjamin E. Mays's 1955 speech, "The Moral Aspects of Segregation": "If the strong handicaps the weak on the grounds of race or color, it is all the more immoral because we penalize the group for conditions over which it has no control, for being what nature or nature's God made it. And that is tantamount to saying to God, 'You made a mistake, God, when you didn't make all races white'. . . . It gives the segregated a feeling of inherent inferiority which is not based on facts, and it gives the segregator a feeling of superiority which is not based on facts" (Mays's speech was published in *The Three Views of the Segregation Decisions* [Atlanta: Southern Regional Council, 1956], pp. 13 and 15).

12. King quotes a verse from the spiritual "Oh Freedom."

13. Cf. Matthew 5:44.

I know that some of you are asking me, what is the Negro's best defense against acts of violence inflicted upon him? His only defense is to meet every act of cruelty and injustice toward an individual Negro with the fact that 100 more Negroes will present themselves in his place as potential victims. Every time one Negro school teacher is fired for believing in integration, a thousand others should be ready to take the same stand. If the oppressors bomb the home of one Negro for his protest, they must be made to realize that to press back the rising tide of the Negro's courage they will have to bomb hundreds more, and even then they will fail.

Faced with this dynamic unity, this amazing self respect, this willingness to suffer, and this refusal to hit back, the oppressor will find that he is glutted with his own barbarity. Forced to stand before the world and his God splattered with the blood and reeking with the stench of his Negro brother, he will call an end to his self-defeating massacre.

It is becoming clear to me that the Negro is in for a season of suffering. As victories for civil rights mount in the federal courts, angry passions and deep prejudices are further aroused. The mountain of state and local segregation laws still stands. Negro leaders continue to be arrested and harassed under city ordinances, and their homes continue to be bombed. I pray that, recognizing the necessity of suffering, the Negro will make of it a virtue. To suffer in a righteous cause is to grow to our humanity's full stature. If only to save himself from bitterness, the Negro needs the vision to see the ordeals of this generation as the opportunity to transfigure himself and American society.

And now let us go out looking to a future filled with vast possibilities. I know you are asking, when will that future fulfilled itself? When will our suffering in this righteous struggle come to an end? ~~When will evening winds of adversity be transformed into soothing breezes~~ of peace? When will the ~~dark and~~ desolate valleys of oppression be transformed into sun lit paths of justice? When will the radiant star of hope be plunged against the nocturnal bosom of this lonely night, and plucked from weary souls the chains of fear and the manacles of death? I must confess that I cannot give you the exact date. But I have no doubt that the midnight of injustice will give way to the daybreak of freedom. My faith in the future does not grow out of a weak and uncertain thought. My faith grows out of a deep and patient ~~faith~~ {trust} in God who leaves us not alone in the struggle for righteousness, and whose matchless power is a fit contrast to the sordid weakness of man. I am certain of the future because:

> Mine eyes have seen the glory of the coming of the Lord;
> He is trampling out the vintage where the grapes of wrath are stored;
> He hath loosed the fateful lightning of His terrible swift sword:
> His truth is marching on.
>
> I have seen Him in the watch-fires of a hundred circling camps;
> They have builded Him an altar in the evening dews and damps;
> I can read His righteous sentence by the dim and flaring lamps;
> His day is marching on.
>
> He has sounded forth the trumpet that shall never call retreat;
> He is sifting out the hearts of men before His judgment seat:
> O be swift, my soul, to answer Him! Be jubilant, my feet!
> Our God is marching on.

Refrain:
Glory! Glory, Hallelujah! Glory! Glory, Hallelujah!
Glory! Glory, Hallelujah! His truth is marchin on.[14]

TAD. SAVFC-WHi.

---

14. Julia Ward Howe, "The Battle Hymn of the Republic" (1862).

From Anne Braden

23 September 1959
Louisville, Ky.

Southern Conference Educational Fund (SCEF) field secretary Anne Braden informs King that a witness in the state of Tennessee's case against the Highlander Folk School testified that he had heard King declare: "White people should be murdered to force the Federal Government to support integration."[1] King replied to Braden on 7 October.[2]

Dr. Martin Luther King, Jr.
Dexter Avenue Baptist Church
454 Dexter Avenue
Montgomery, Alabama

Dear Dr. King:

Last week I went down to Altamont, Tenn., to cover the hearings on the petition to padlock Highlander Folk School for The Southern Patriot.[3]

Your name came into the testimony, and you were badly misquoted on the witness stand. After the hearing, I talked to the witness who had given the testimony,

---

1. For nearly two years, Tennessee authorities had campaigned to close Highlander for violating the state's segregation laws. After a 31 July 1959 raid on the school, the charge of unlawful sale of alcohol was added to the state's grievances (Mouzon Peters, "Highlander Case Opened; Beer Sales Labeled Issue," *Chattanooga Daily Times,* 15 September 1959). While King declined a request from Highlander's director to testify on the organization's behalf during the November hearings, he did sign a petition "affirming the right of the School to exist and to do its educational work without recurrent intimidation" (King to Myles Horton, 19 October 1959, and Petition in support of Highlander Folk School, November 1959). In February 1960 a judge ruled against Highlander and, after numerous appeals that reached the Supreme Court, the school closed in October 1961 ("Charter Is Lost by Mixed School," *New York Times,* 17 February 1960; see also *Highlander Folk School et al. v. Tennessee Ex Rel. Sloan, District Attorney General,* 368 U.S. 840 [1961]).

2. See pp. 306–307 in this volume.

3. For Braden's coverage of the trial, see "Partial Victory at Highlander," *Southern Patriot,* October 1959.

and I am writing you because I think you will want to have full information on this episode in case the segregationists attempt to use it against you in some way. 23 Sept 1959

It happened this way:

One of the witnesses presented by the state against Highlander was Ed Friend, of Georgia. You may recall that he was the man sent by Former Governor [*Marvin*] Griffin of Georgia to cover the 25th anniversary celebration of Highlander on Labor Day Weekend in 1957. You remember he represented himself to school officials as a free lance photographer and stayed around all weekend taking pictures. Later these pictures were used in that four-page slanderous brochure about Highlander published by the Georgia Education Commission and sent out all over the country.[4]

Last week he testified mainly about how he had seen people at Highlander drinking beer—since this was the line the state was taking in its current efforts to close the school. However, in the course of his testimony he got in some other points too. During cross-examination by Highlander's lawyer, Cecil Branstetter of Nashville, this exchange took place (the following is not an exact word-for-word account—you'd have to get that from the official transcript—but this is the gist):

Branstetter: You came there because you wanted to know what discussions were taking place about how to bring about integration, didn't you?

Friend: Yes, I did.

Branstetter: If there were any instructions being given on bringing about integration, you wanted to know about it?

Friend: Yes, I did. We still want to know.

* * * *

Branstetter: And the only thing you saw you didn't like was Negroes and whites dancing together, is that right?

Friend: The greatest objection I had was that one of the Negro preachers who was there said that white people should be murdered to force the Federal Government to support integration in the South—that was Martin Luther King.

By this time, the courtroom was in a good bit of confusion. It was late in the afternoon, and everybody was anxious to get away, anyway. There followed an exchange, of which I am sorry I did not get the wording, in which Branstetter asked Friend if Martin Luther King had made such a statement at Highlander and Friend replied no, that it wasn't at Highlander. But unfortunately, Branstetter did not pursue the matter further or pin him down as to just what the statement was supposed to have been or when it had allegedly been made. Many people in the courtroom apparently did not hear this latter exchange and some left with the impression that Friend was quoting from a speech you had made.

The next day, the Nashville Tennessean in its Sept. 15 issue, reported the incident with this paragraph:

---

4. Georgia Commission on Education, "Highlander Folk School: Communist Training School, Monteagle, Tenn.," October 1957. In September 1957, King delivered the closing address at Highlander's twenty-fifth anniversary celebration (King, "A Look to the Future," 2 September 1957, in *Papers* 4:269–276).

23 Sept 1959

"Highlander students and staff members in the courtroom burst into a roar of laughter when Friend testified, 'the biggest objection I had was that one of the Negro ministers there at that time—Martin Luther King—advocated the murder of white people to force intervention of the federal government on the South.'"[5]

The Chattanooga Times for Sept. 15 reported it with this paragraph:

"He [Friend] said he came to Highlander also in the hope of meeting the Rev. Martin Luther King of Montgomery and to investigate what he said were charges that the Alabama Negro leader 'was advocating murder to force Federal intervention to bring about public school integration.'"[6]

Meantime, immediately after Friend testified that afternoon, I followed him out of the courtroom to try to pin him down and get the straight story on this alleged quote from you. He was hurrying to get away, because Highlander lawyers were having a subpoena issued to hold him there for further cross-examination and he wanted to leave before it could be served. So I didn't have long to talk to him. This exchange took place between us:

Me: Did you say Martin Luther King made that statement about murder that you quoted at Highlander?

Friend: I didn't say he made it at Highlander.

Me: Well, did he make it anywhere?

Friend: Yes.

Me: Did you hear him make it?

Friend: I certainly did.

Me: When?

Friend: Just a couple of months ago.

Me: Where?

Friend: At Spellman College in Atlanta, at a meeting there. [Apparently he was referring to the Institute on Non-Violence in July, wouldn't you suppose?][7]

Me: Well, what did he say, exactly?

Friend: Pretty much what I testified. That was just about it.

Me: No, that couldn't have been it, exactly. That's not a natural way for somebody to word something in a speech. Even if you wanted to express that thought, you wouldn't say in a speech, "I advocate that white people be murdered to force the Federal Government to support integration in the South.' That's too stilted. What were his exact words?

Whereupon Friend pulled out of his pocket a piece of paper on which he had some notes written and read to me what he represented as a quote from you. I was not taking notes so I'm sorry I don't have the exact wording for sure, but it was some thing similar to this:

---

5. Rudy Abramson, "State Witnesses Rap Folk School," *Nashville Tennessean,* 15 September 1959.

6. Braden enclosed Friend's name in brackets in original. Peters, "Highlander Case Opened; Beer Sales Labeled Issue."

7. Braden enclosed her inference in brackets in original. For information about the institute, see Resolutions, First Southwide Institute on Nonviolent Resistance to Segregation, 11 August 1959, pp. 261–262 in this volume.

Friend: This is what he said: "In order to get the Federal Government into Alabama, some of my group are saying that white people must be killed."

23 Sept 1959

[A far cry, certainly, from what he had said on the stand and what got quoted in the press the next day.]

I commented: "Well, that certainly doesn't sound to me as if he were advocating Murder."

To which Friend replied: "Well, he was the one who was up there making the speech and agitating the people." With that, he dashed off—trying to get away from the subpoena.

So there you have it. It certainly shows how false rumors and cruel lies can get started.

* * * *

Hope things are going well with you generally. By the way, Carl is planning to be in Columbia next week when the Southern Christian Leadership Conference meets there and is looking forward to seeing you.[8]

Please give Coretta my love. I so much enjoyed getting to know her a little better when I was in Montgomery in the summer. Sorry I missed you.

Kindest regards,
[*signed*] Anne
Anne Braden

P.S.: Could you see that we are put on the mailing list to get any news releases either you or the Montgomery Improvement Association sends out? We would like to publicize these things in the Southern Patriot, which has a wide readership both South and North. Every once in a while we see things in other papers that we didn't receive—for example, stories on your recent communications to school officials in Montgomery.[9]

TALS. MLKP-MBU: Box 20.

---

8. Braden's husband, Carl, attended the SCLC conference in Columbia, South Carolina, on 30 September and 1 October 1959. For Braden's notes on the conference, see Notes on SCLC Fall Session, 30 September–1 October 1959.

9. See King to the Montgomery County Board of Education, 28 August 1959, pp. 270–272 in this volume.

To Adlai E. Stevenson

25 September 1959
[*Montgomery, Ala.*]

In an 8 September letter, former Illinois governor Adlai Stevenson invited King to co-sponsor a tribute dinner for Eleanor Roosevelt.[1] *King agrees to the request in the letter below. The 7 December dinner in New York City, which King did not attend, was a fund-raiser for the Democratic National Committee and a showcase for the party's presidential hopefuls, including Stevenson, G. Mennen Williams, and John F. Kennedy.*[2]

Governor Adlai E. Stevenson
135 South LaSalle Street
Chicago 3, Illinois

Dear Governor Stevenson:

On returning to the office I found your letter of September 8, inviting me to join the National Sponsors Committee of the dinner in tribute to Eleanor Roosevelt. I will be more than delighted and honored to do this. To my mind Mrs. Roosevelt is one of the truly great persons of the world.

Very sincerely yours,
Martin L. King, Jr.

MLK:mlb

TLc. MLKP-MBU: Box 69.

---

1. Adlai Ewing Stevenson (1900–1965), born in Los Angeles, earned an A.B. (1922) from Princeton University and a J.D. (1926) from Northwestern University. Stevenson served in several governmental positions before his election as governor of Illinois in 1948. He received the Democratic presidential nomination in 1952 and in 1956, but lost to Eisenhower both times and chose not to run again in 1960 despite the encouragement of his supporters. In 1960 Kennedy appointed him ambassador to the United Nations, a position he held until his death in 1965.
2. Leo Egan, "Mrs. Roosevelt Disputes Truman on Liberals' Role," *New York Times,* 8 December 1959.

Recommendations to the SCLC Executive Committee

[*30 September 1959*]
[*Columbia, S.C.*]

Postponed one day by Hurricane Gracie, SCLC convened its fall meeting on 30 September at First Calvary Baptist Church in Columbia. The executive committee approved each of these eight recommendations from King but referred the proposal to hire a new executive director to the administrative committee. The following day, the SCLC delegates accepted the executive committee's recommendations and adopted ten resolutions, one of which called on King to "seriously consider giving the maximum of his time and energies to the work" of SCLC.[1]

Recommendations

1. I recommend that the conference will hold one annual meeting instead of two meetings anually. This will provide the opportunity for more effective response on the part of potential delegates and more long range, detailed planning on the part of the staff. This will mean revising Article II, section 4 of the Constitution dealing with the annual meeting, Article IV, section 3 concerning meetings of executive board, and Article IV, section 9 concerning the Nominating Committee. There will be only two meetings of the executive board anually instead of three, one in conjunction with the annual meeting of the conference and one in Atlanta during another period of the year. If it is the consensus that the annual meeting be held in May, then the Atlanta board meeting will continue to meet after the first Sunday in December. If it is the consensus that the conference should be held in October, the Atlanta board meeting shall be held in May.[2]
2. Since one of the basic concerns of [*strikeout illegible*] SCLC at the present time is that of increasing the number of Negro registered voters, we must seek to use every resource at our disposal to make this possible. Honesty impells us to admit that we have not really scratched the surface in this area. One of the reasons for this lack of success is that there has never been any genuine cooperation and coordination between national and local organizations working to increase the vote. I, therefore, recommend that the

---

1. The executive committee also recommended that the next annual meeting be held in Shreveport, Louisiana (SCLC, Recommendations adopted by the executive committee and delegates at Fall Session, 1 October 1959). An additional resolution urged King to join other national efforts to develop "an appropriate mass action program" aimed at affecting the 1960 political conventions (Wyatt Tee Walker and Fred L. Shuttlesworth, "Resolutions adopted at Fall Session," 1 October 1959; see also SCLC, Program, "Fall Session," 29 September–1 October 1959). For more details on King's move to Atlanta, see King, Draft, Resignation from Dexter Avenue Baptist Church, 29 November 1959, pp. 328–329 in this volume.

2. The committee's decisions on these recommendations were written by an unknown person. Next to this recommendation was written: "1—accepted—time left to administrative committee."

SCLC call a meeting of persons directing voting campaigns in southern communities and seek to work out some clearly defined areas of work. As we all know, the job is to big to be carried out by any one organization. ~~Every~~ All organizations must work creatively together to prevent needless overlapping.[3]

3. There can be no gainsaying of the fact that the SCLC has not been publized through the press or otherwise. The aims and purposes of the Conference have not ~~been~~ gotten over to a large ~~se~~ number of people, north and south. I therefore recommend that a person be employed on a part time basis (possibly six months) to carry out the all important task of placing the organization before the public through intelligent publicity. We should seek to secure for this job a person who already has good contact with the press and who has real ability as a writer. This person would work under the supervision of the president and the executive secretary. No writings would be released without their approval. One of the obvious gains that would come to the organization as a result of hiring such a part time worker is that of leaving the executives free to give full time to the larger job of implimenting the total program of the organization. We must not overlook the fact that, in the final analysis, the greatest channel of publicity for the organization is the existence of a positive, dynamic, and dramatic program.[4]
4. In order to keep a sense of direction and meet the many challenges ahead, a committee shall be appointed to sit down with the executive secretary in the next three weeks and work out the program for the next year. This committee shall consist of: Samuel W. Williams, L. D. Reddick, Ralph Abernathy, Fred Shuttlesworth, J. E. Lowery.[5]
5. In order to meet the demands and needs for a dynamic program, the personal committee shall immediately seek to employ a second executive to replace Rev. Tilley.[6]
6. One of the shameful tragedies of the south is the continued existence of segregated waiting rooms, restaurants, and rest rooms in airport terminals. This, as we know, is far behind the railroads, for at least in interstate travel ~~segregation has~~ the once existent signs have been removed. I feel certain that segregation can be removed from our Airport terminal without any great emotional reaction from the white community. Therefore, I recommend that a committee from the SCLC go to Washington and ~~present~~ lay this issue squarly before the civil Aearonautics Board. This board has the

---

3. This recommendation was "approved."

4. This recommendation was "approved."

5. Williams was King's philosophy teacher at Morehouse College and pastor of Friendship Baptist Church in Atlanta. Lowery was the pastor of Mobile's Warren Street Methodist Church. This recommendation was "approved."

6. For an account of the deliberations of the personnel committee, see note 5 to Recommendations to SCLC Committee on Future Program, 27 October 1959, p. 318 in this volume. For more on John Tilley's resignation, see Tilley to King, 13 April 1959, pp. 182–184 in this volume. This recommendation was referred to the administrative committee.

power to hand down a ruling, similar to that of the interstate commerce commision, and thereby bring an end to segregation in airport terminals. While the legal [*phase?*] of this problem must be left to the NAACP, this is one of those extra-legal things that we can do. Maybe through the power of moral persuasion, we will be able to save many dollars which would be necessary to fight this battle out in the courts.[7]

7. In order to express our deep sympathy for ~~the~~ our African brothers in the struggle for freedom and human dignity, and in order to reveal ~~the~~ our awareness of the oneness of our struggle, I recommend that we give a scholarship of at least 500.00 per year to assist in the education of some African student. This will do a great deal to develop a sense self respect within African students, and contribute in some little way toward the developing of persons to take over leadership responsibilities in that great continent.[8]

8. A few months ago several organizations joined in the sponsoring of the youth march for integrated schools in Washington D.C. This event was a great success, and I am sure it did a great deal to arrouse the conscience of the nation on this important issue. Like all undertakings of this kind, there was need for real financial resources. After checking up on the expense involved, it was revealed that there was a deficit of some $2000.00 Since the SCLC had some part in the sponsorship of the March and since we have not made any financial contribution to it, I recommend that we give 200.00 in order to assist the committee in meeting its obligations.[9]

AHD. MLKP-MBU: Box 48.

---

7. The executive board modified this proposal to include a similar approach to the Interstate Commerce Commission (ICC). Shortly after the Columbia conference, King requested the meeting with the Civil Aeronautics Board but was informed that the agency lacked jurisdiction over airports (James R. Durfee to King, 29 October 1959; for King's letter to the ICC, see King to Kenneth H. Tuggle, 19 October 1959, pp. 309–310 in this volume) Next to this recommendation was written. "Amended to include approach ICC as well as CAB—FOR ALL [*word illegible*]."

8. SCLC made its first contribution to Kenyan student Nicholas Raballa, who also received a contribution from Dexter Church. For more on Raballa, see King to Tom Mboya, 8 July 1959, pp. 248–249 in this volume; see also S. F. Yette, "M. L. King Supports African Student," *News of Tuskegee Institute,* December 1959. This recommendation was "approved."

9. A request for funds from A. Philip Randolph prompted this recommendation (Randolph et al. to All Youth March supporters, April 1959). This recommendation was "approved."

Introduction to *Southwest Africa: The UN's Stepchild*

[*October 1959*]
Montgomery, Ala.

On 31 July 1959 Homer Jack, associate director of the American Committee on Africa, asked King to write an introduction for a pamphlet to "inform the American people about South West Africa—a subject about which they know practically nothing."[1] *King agreed to provide the introduction on 5 August and sent it to Jack on 31 August, observing that the pamphlet will serve an important purpose: "I, myself, learned a lot by reading it, for my knowledge of Southwest Africa has been quite limited."*[2]

Africa is today a continent in transition. It is the land in which a great social revolution is taking place. You can hear the deep rumbling of this from the Sahara Desert to the Cape of Good Hope. Africans are united in their deep yearning for freedom and human dignity. They are determined to end the exploitation of their lives and to have a full share in their own future and destiny. The story of this struggle for freedom and independence is a familiar one. It has been told by every major American periodical and dramatized on practically every television channel. It is the theme of numerous speeches and the subject of many fireside discussions.

Despite this unusual coverage of African affairs, there are still areas in this vast and complex continent whose problems and conditions are little known to Americans. One such area is South West Africa. About the only thing most of us Americans know about South West Africa is its geographical location in the emerging continent; northwest of apartheid.

This tragic land for many years was a German colony. After World War I it was a League of Nations mandate under the Union of South Africa. After World War II and the demise of the League, South Africa tried to annex South West Africa. The League's legal successor—the United Nations—so far has prevented this action.[3] The U.N. has not, however, yet been able to prevent South Africa from treating the Africans in this territory with the same regime of oppression and segregation as it gives the non-whites in its own territory.

While Christianity has been timid in too much of Africa, I am glad that Michael Scott—a clergyman—for more than a decade has represented the Herero people of South West Africa when South Africa refused to allow their representatives to

1. Jack also indicated that the pamphlet would be distributed at the fourteenth session of the United Nations General Assembly.

2. In his 31 July request, Jack enclosed "the kind of ideas one might put into an introduction" but added that King was "perfectly free to write anything you want" (see also King to Jack, 5 August 1959).

3. Portions of South West Africa—later known as Namibia—were first declared a German colony in 1884. South Africa seized the region during World War I and was granted a League of Nations mandate to manage the territory following the war. After World War II, the newly created United Nations formed a Trusteeship Council for territories that were not self-governing. South Africa, hoping to annex the territory, refused to place South West Africa under United Nations trusteeship, beginning a struggle that did not end until Namibia gained independence on 21 March 1990.

appear before the U.N.[4] Now two or three residents have managed to tell the U.N. their own story.[5] It is not a pleasant story. At places, it has a nightmarish effect and points up some of the most tragic expressions of man's inhumanity to man. It is the story of more than 450,000 people constantly being trampled over by the iron feet of injustice.

This is the story the American people should know—one which their delegates at the U.N. should act upon. If for no other reason, we should know this story and act upon it because injustice anywhere is a threat to justice everywhere.

—Martin Luther King, Jr.
Montgomery, Alabama, U.S.A.

PD. *Southwest Africa: The UN's Stepchild* (New York: American Committee on Africa, 1959).

4. Jack had arranged a meeting between King and Scott in March 1957 during the Ghanaian independence ceremonies (see Introduction in *Papers* 4:8–9).

5. In the late 1950s Hereros Fanuel Jariretundu Konzonguisi and Mburumba Kerina testified before the United Nations Committee on South West Africa.

"The Social Organization of Nonviolence"

October 1959
New York, N.Y.

This defense of nonviolent resistance appeared in Liberation *as a response to an essay by North Carolina NAACP leader Robert F. Williams that challenged the strategy of "turn-the-other-cheekism" in the face of racist terror.*[1] *In his September article, Williams had argued that "nonviolence is a very potent weapon when the opponent is civilized, but nonviolence is no match or repellent for a sadist."*[2]

Though King points out that the principle of self-defense "has never been condemned, even by Gandhi," he rejects Williams's suggestion that black people take up arms: "There is more power in socially organized masses on the march than there is in guns in the hands of a few desperate men."[3]

1. Williams, "Can Negroes Afford to Be Pacifists?" *Liberation* 4 (September 1959): 4–7. Williams had been suspended from the NAACP in May 1959 for allegedly advocating violence (for more on Williams's suspension, see King, Address at the Fiftieth Annual NAACP Convention, 17 July 1959, pp. 245–250 in this volume). King had previously published three articles in *Liberation* ("Our Struggle," April 1956, and "We Are Still Walking," December 1956, in *Papers* 3:236–241 and 445–451, respectively; and "Who Speaks for the South?" *Liberation* 3 [March 1958]: 13–14).

2. Williams praised King as "a great and successful leader of our race" and explained that nonviolence was "made to order" for the Montgomery bus boycott, but he cautioned against conflating the various aspects of the southern struggle: "In a great many localities in the South. Negroes are faced with the necessity of combating savage violence. The struggle is for mere existence."

3. A. J. Muste originally solicited King's article for inclusion in the September issue of *Liberation* (Muste to King and "Draft of prospectus for September issue of *Liberation*," both dated 10 June 1959). King

★ THE SOUTHERN PATRIOT

The Great Debate

Is Violence Necessary to Combat Injustice?

Editor's Note

The great debate in the integration movement in recent months has been the question of violence vs. nonviolence, as instruments of social change. The non-violent way was brought dramatically to the public consciousness by the successful Montgomery bus protest of 1955-56. The debate, long smoldering under the surface, was precipitated last spring when Robert Williams, Negro leader of Monroe, N. C., made his much-publicized statement that Negroes must "meet violence with violence." Much misunderstanding of both positions has followed. In the opinion of Patriot editors, the most meaningful and enlightening discussion of the issue was presented in the September and October issues of the pacifist publication, Liberation, in the form of articles by Mr. Williams and by Dr. Martin Luther King, Jr., leader of the non-violent movement. We reprint excerpts from both articles here.

For the Positive: Williams Says 'We Must Fight Back'

By ROBERT F. WILLIAMS

In 1954, I was an enlisted man in the United States Marine Corps . . . . I shall never forget the evening we (heard) the historic Supreme Court decision that segregation in the public schools is unconstitutional . . . .

At last I felt that I was a part of America and that I belonged. That was what I had always wanted, even as a child.

I returned to civilian life in 1955 and the hope I had for Negro liberation faltered . . . . Acts of violence and words and deeds of hate and spite rose from every quarter . . . . There is open defiance to law and order throughout the South today . . . . I have become disillusioned . . .

What Will Deter?

Laws serve to deter crime and protect the weak from the strong in civilized society. Where there is a breakdown of law . . . . where is the force of deterrent? . . . . Only highly civilized and moral individuals respect the rights of others . . . . The Southern brute respects only force. Nonviolence is a very potent weapon when the opponent is civilized, but nonviolence is no repellent for a sadist . . . .

I have great respect for the pacifist, that is, for the pure pacifist . . . . I am not a pacifist and I am sure I may safely say most of my people are not. Passive resistance is a powerful weapon in gaining concessions from oppressors, but I venture to say that if Mack Parker had had an automatic shotgun at his disposal, he could have served as a great deterrent against lynching . . . .

In 1957 the Klan moved into Monroe and Union County (N.C.) . . . . Their numbers steadily increased to the point

Robert Williams

wherein the local press reported 7500 at one rally. They became so brazen that mile-long motorcades started invading the Negro community.

These hooded thugs fired pistols from car windows . . . . On one occasion they caught a Negro woman on the street and tried to force her to dance for them at gun point . . . . Drivers of cars tried to run Negroes down . . . . Lawlessness was rampant . . . . instead of cowing, we organized an armed guard . . . . On one occasion, we had to exchange gunfire with the Klan.

Each time the Klan came on a raid they were led by police cars. We appealed to the President of the United States to have the Justice Department investigate the police. We appealed to Governor Luther Hodges. All our appeals to constituted law were in vain . . .

A group of nonviolent ministers met the City Board of Aldermen and pleaded with them to restrict the Klan from the colored community. The city fathers advised these cringing, begging Negro ministers that the Klan had constitutional rights to meet and organize in the same way as the NAACP.

Not having been infected by turn-the-other-cheekism, a group of Negroes who showed a willingness to fight caused the city officials to deprive the Klan of its constitutional rights after local papers told of dangerous incidents between Klansmen and armed Negroes. Klan motorcades have been legally banned from the City of Monroe . . . .

'Sick Inside'

On May 5, 1959, while president of the Union County branch of the NAACP, I made a statement to the United Press International after a trial wherein a white man was supposed to have been tried for kicking a Negro maid down a flight of stairs in a local white hotel. In spite of the fact that there was an eyewitness, the defendant failed to show up for his trial, and was completely exonerated.

Another case in the same court involved a white man who had come to a pregnant Negro mother's home and attempted to rape her. In recorder's court the only defense offered for the defendant was that "he's not guilty. He was just drunk and having a little fun." . . . A white woman neighbor testified that the woman had come to her house excited, her clothes torn, her feet bare and begging her for assistance; the court was unmoved . . . .

This great miscarriage of justice left me sick inside, and I said then what I say now. I believe Negroes must be willing to defend themselves, their women, their children and their homes. They must be willing to die and to kill in repelling their assailants . . . . Negroes *must* protect themselves, it is obvious that the federal government will not put an end to lynching; therefore it becomes necessary for us to stop lynching with violence . . . .

Taught to Fight

Some Negro leaders have cautioned me that if Negroes fight back, the racist will have cause to exterminate the race . . . . This government is in no position to allow mass violence to erupt, let alone allow twenty million Negroes to be exterminated . . . .

. . . . it is instilled at an early age that men who violently and swiftly rise to oppose tyranny are virtuous examples to emulate. I have been taught by my government to fight . . . . nowhere in the annals of history does the record show a people delivered from bondage by patience alone.

For the Negative: King Sees Alternative in Mass Actions

By MARTIN LUTHER KING, JR.

Paradoxically, the struggle for civil rights has reached a stage of profound crisis, although its outward aspect is distinctly less turbulent and victories of token integration have been won in the hard-resistance areas of Virginia and Arkansas.

The crisis has its origin in a decision rendered by the Supreme Court more than a year ago which upheld the pupil placement law. Though little noticed then, this decision fundamentally weakened the historic 1954 ruling of the Court. It is imperceptibly becoming the basis of a *de facto* compromise between the powerful contending forces . . . .

Token integration is a developing pattern. This type of integration is merely an affirmation of principle without the substance of change . . . . Full integration can easily become a distant or mythical goal . . . .

'No Compromise'

The Negro was the tragic victim of another compromise in 1878, when his full equality was bargained away by the Federal Government . . . . There is reason to believe that the Negro of 1959 will not accept supinely any such compromises in the contemporary struggle for integration . . . .

It is axiomatic in social life that the imposition of frustrations leads to two kinds of reactions. One is the development of a wholesome social organization to resist with effective, firm measures any efforts to impede progress. The other is a confused, anger-motivated drive to strike back violently, to inflict damage . . . . It is punitive—not radical or constructive. The current calls for violence have their roots in this latter tendency.

Here one must be clear that there are three different views on the subject of violence. One is the approach of pure nonviolence, which cannot readily or easily attract large masses, for it requires extraordinary discipline and courage.

The second is violence exercised in self-defense, which all societies, from the most primitive to the most cultured and civilized, accept as moral and legal.

The third is the advocacy of violence as a tool of advancement, organized as in warfare, deliberately and consciously. To this tendency many Negroes are being tempted today.

Violence Confuses

There are incalculable perils in this approach . . . . The greatest danger is that it will fail to attract Negroes to a real collective struggle, and will confuse the large uncommitted middle group, which as yet has not supported either side . . . .

It is unfortunately true that however the Negro acts, his struggle will not be free of violence initiated by his enemies, and he will need ample courage and willingness to sacrifice to defeat this manifestation of violence. But if he seeks it and organizes it, he cannot win.

Does this leave the Negro without a positive method to advance? Mr. Robert Williams would have us believe that there is no effective and practical alternative. He argues that we must be cringing and submissive or take up arms. To so place the issue distorts the whole problem. There are other meaningful alternatives.

The Negro people can organize socially to initiate many forms of struggle which can drive their enemies back without resort to futile and harmful violence . . . . many creative forms have been developed—the mass boycott, sitdown protests and strikes, sit-ins,—refusal to pay fines and

Martin Luther King, Jr.

bail for unjust arrests—mass marches—mass meetings—prayer pilgrimages, etc.

There is more power in socially organized masses on the march than there is in guns in the hands of a few desperate men. Our enemies would prefer to deal with a small armed group rather than with a huge, unarmed but resolute mass of people.

However, it is necessary that the mass-action method be persistent and unyielding. Gandhi said the Indian people must "never let them rest," referring to the British. He urged them to keep protesting daily and weekly, in a variety of ways. This method inspired and organized the Indian masses and disorganized and demobilized the British. It educates its myriad participants, socially and morally.

It is this form of struggle—non-cooperation with evil through mass actions—"never letting them rest"—which offers the more effective road for those who have been tempted and goaded to violence.

Boldness Needed

It needs the bold and the brave because it is not free from danger . . . . It requires dedicated people, because it is a back-breaking task to arouse, to organize, and to educate tens of thousands for disciplined, sustained action.

Our present urgent necessity is to cease our internal fighting and turn outward to the enemy, using every form of mass action yet known—create new forms—and resolve never to let them rest. This is the social lever which will force open the door to freedom.

Our powerful weapons are the voices, the feet, and bodies of dedicated, united people . . . . Greater tyrants than Southern segregationists have been subdued and defeated by this form of struggle. We have not yet used it, and it would be tragic if we spurn it because we have failed to perceive its dynamic strength and power . . . .

3

The Louisville-based newspaper *The Southern Patriot* features articles by King and Robert F. Williams debating the role of violence in the struggle for integration (January 1960). Reprinted with permission from Anne Braden.

Paradoxically, the struggle for civil rights has reached a stage of profound crisis, although its outward aspect is distinctly less turbulent and victories of token integration have been won in the hard-resistance areas of Virginia and Arkansas.

The crisis has its origin in a decision rendered by the Supreme Court more than a year ago which upheld the pupil placement law. Though little noticed then, this decision fundamentally weakened the historic 1954 ruling of the Court. It is imperceptibly becoming the basis of a *de facto* compromise between the powerful contending forces.

The 1954 decision required for effective implementation resolute Federal action supported by mass action to undergird all necessary changes. It is obvious that Federal action by the legislative and executive branches was half-hearted and inadequate. The activity of Negro forces, while heroic in some instances, and impressive in other sporadic situations, lacked consistency and militancy sufficient to fill the void left by government default. The segregationists were swift to seize these advantages, and unrestrained by moral or social conscience, defied the law boldly and brazenly.

The net effect of this social equation has led to the present situation, which is without clearcut victory for either side. Token integration is a developing pattern. This type of integration is merely an affirmation of a principle without the substance of change.

It is, like the Supreme Court decision, a pronouncement of justice, but by itself does not insure that the millions of Negro children will be educated in conditions of equality. This is not to say that it is without value. It has substantial importance. However, it fundamentally changes the outlook of the whole movement, for it raises the prospect of long, slow change without a predictable end. As we have seen in Northern cities, token integration has become a pattern in many communities and remained frozen, even though environmental attitudes are substantially less hostile to full integration than in the South.

Three Views of Violence

This then is the danger. Full integration can easily become a distant or mythical goal—major integration may be long postponed, and in the quest for social calm a compromise firmly implanted in which the real goals are merely token integration for a long period to come.

The Negro was the tragic victim of another compromise in 1878, when his full equality was bargained away by the Federal Government and a condition some-

---

consented on 22 June but was tardy in producing this article, which Stanley Levison may have helped him prepare (Levison to King, 1 September 1959; see also Muste to King, 27 July 1959). In a 29 October letter, SCEF's Anne Braden asked King's permission to publish excerpts of this article alongside portions of Williams's article, noting that she found King's essay "one of the best brief statements of the case for non-violence" she had ever read; King consented on 2 November ("The Great Debate: Is Violence Necessary to Combat Injustice?" *Southern Patriot* 18 [January 1960]: 3). King's essay was later reprinted, with minor changes, in Williams's book *Negroes with Guns* (New York: Marzani & Munsell, 1962), pp. 11–15.

what above slave status but short of genuine citizenship become his social and political existence for nearly a century.[4]

There is reason to believe that the Negro of 1959 will not accept supinely any such compromises in the contemporary struggle for integration. His struggle will continue, but the obstacles will determine its specific nature. It is axiomatic in social life that the imposition of frustrations leads to two kinds of reactions. One is the development of a wholesome social organization to resist with effective, firm measures any efforts to impede progress. The other is a confused, anger-motivated drive to strike back violently, to inflict damage. Primarily, it seeks to cause injury to retaliate for wrongful suffering. Secondarily, it seeks real progress. It is punitive—not radical or constructive.

The current calls for violence have their roots in this latter tendency. Here one must be clear that there are three different views on the subject of violence. One is the approach of pure nonviolence, which cannot readily or easily attract large masses, for it requires extraordinary discipline and courage. The second is violence exercised in self-defense, which all societies, from the most primitive to the most cultured and civilized, accept as moral and legal. The principle of self-defense, even involving weapons and bloodshed, has never been condemned, even by Gandhi, who sanctioned it for those unable to master pure nonviolence.[5] The third is the advocacy of violence as a tool of advancement, organized as in warfare, deliberately and consciously. To this tendency many Negroes are being tempted today. There are incalculable perils in this approach. It is not the danger or sacrifice of physical being which is primary, though it cannot be contemplated without a sense of deep concern for human life. The greatest danger is that it will fail to attract Negroes to a real collective struggle, and will confuse the large uncommitted middle group, which as yet has not supported either side. Further, it will mislead Negroes into the belief that this is the only path and place them as a minority in a position where they confront a far larger adversary than it is possible to defeat in this form of combat. When the Negro uses force in self-defense he does not forfeit support—he may even win it, by the courage and self-respect it reflects. When he seeks to initiate violence he provokes questions about the necessity for it, and inevitably is blamed for its consequences.[6] It is unfortu-

---

4. King refers to the Compromise of 1877, in which the disputed outcome of the 1876 presidential election was resolved in favor of Republican Rutherford B. Hayes. To placate southern Democrats, Republicans agreed to withdraw remaining federal soldiers from the South, effectively ending the era of Reconstruction.

5. In an 11 August 1920 essay, "The Doctrine of the Sword," Gandhi wrote: "I do believe that where there is only a choice between cowardice and violence I would advise violence. . . . I would rather have India resort to arms in order to defend her honour than that she should in a cowardly manner become or remain a helpless victim to her own dishonour" (*The Collected Works of Mahatma Gandhi,* vol. 18, July–November 1920 [Delhi: The Publications Division, Ministry of Information and Broadcasting, Government of India, 1965], p. 132).

6. The October issue of *Liberation* included an NAACP rejoinder to Williams, which explained that Williams's disciplinary suspension was "based upon his call for aggressive, premeditated violence. . . . No action was taken against Mr. Williams for the advocacy of self-defense" (NAACP, "The Single Issue in the Robert Williams Case," *Liberation* 4 [October 1959]: 7–8). In his article, Williams rejected the

nately true that however the Negro acts, his struggle will not be free of violence initiated by his enemies, and he will need ample courage and willingness to sacrifice to defeat this manifestation of violence. But if he seeks it and organizes it, he cannot win. Does this leave the Negro without a positive method to advance? Mr. Robert Williams would have us believe that there is no effective and practical alternative. He argues that we must be cringing and submissive or take up arms. To so place the issue distorts the whole problem. There are other meaningful alternatives.

The Negro people can organize socially to initiate many forms of struggle which can drive their enemies back without resort to futile and harmful violence. In the history of the movement for racial advancement, many creative forms have been developed—the mass boycott, sitdown protests and strikes, sit-ins,—refusal to pay fines and bail for unjust arrests—mass marches—mass meetings—prayer pilgrimages, etc. Indeed, in Mr. Williams' own community of Monroe, North Carolina, a striking example of collective community action won a significant victory without use of arms or threats of violence. When the police incarcerated a Negro doctor unjustly, the aroused people of Monroe marched to the police station, crowded into its halls and corridors, and refused to leave until their colleague was released. Unable to arrest everyone, the authorities released the doctor and neither side attempted to unleash violence.[7] This experience was related by the doctor who was the intended victim.

There is more power in socially organized masses on the march than there is in guns in the hands of a few desperate men. Our enemies would prefer to deal with a small armed group rather than with a huge, unarmed but resolute mass of people. However, it is necessary that the mass-action method be persistent and unyielding. Gandhi said the Indian people must "never let them rest," referring to the British. He urged them to keep protesting daily and weekly, in a variety of ways. This method inspired and organized the Indian masses and disorganized and demobilized the British. It educates its myriad participants, socially and morally. All history teaches us that like a turbulent ocean beating great cliffs into fragments of rock, the determined movement of people incessantly demanding their rights always disintegrates the old order.

It is this form of struggle—non-cooperation with evil through mass actions—"never letting them rest"—which offers the more effective road for those who have been tempted and goaded to violence. It needs the bold and the brave because it

---

accusation that he was promoting anything other than self-defense: "How can an individual defend his person and property from attack without meeting violence with violence? . . . I could never advocate that Negroes attack white people indiscriminately. Our branch of the N.A.A.C.P. in Union County is an interracial branch."

7. Albert Perry, Williams's vice president in the Union County NAACP, was arrested and charged with performing an abortion on a white woman in October 1957. Assuming the arrest to be retaliation for Perry's efforts to desegregate the local swimming pool, a large crowd of black residents gathered at police headquarters and successfully demanded his release. According to one account, the armed crowd "surged against the doors, fingered their guns and knives until Perry was produced" ("Is North Carolina NAACP Leader a Marked Man?" *Jet,* 31 October 1957, pp. 10–11).

is not free of danger. It faces the vicious and evil enemies squarely. It requires dedicated people, because it is a backbreaking task to arouse, to organize, and to educate tens of thousands for disciplined, sustained action. From this form of struggle more emerges that is permanent and damaging to the enemy than from a few acts of organized violence.

Our present urgent necessity is to cease our internal fighting and turn outward to the enemy, using every form of mass action yet known—create new forms—and resolve never to let them rest. This is the social lever which will force open the door to freedom. Our powerful weapons are the voices, the feet, and the bodies of dedicated, united people, moving without rest toward a just goal. Greater tyrants than Southern segregationists have been subdued and defeated by this form of struggle. We have not yet used it, and it would be tragic if we spurn it because we have failed to perceive its dynamic strength and power.

Cashing In on War?

I am reluctant to inject a personal defense against charges by Mr. Williams that I am inconsistent in my struggle against war and too weak-kneed to protest nuclear war.[8] Merely to set the record straight, may I state that repeatedly, in public addresses and in my writings, I have unequivocally declared my hatred for this most colossal of all evils and I have condemned any organizer of war, regardless of his rank or nationality. I have signed numerous statements with other Americans condemning nuclear testing and have authorized publication of my name in advertisements appearing in the largest circulation newspapers in the country, without concern that it was then "unpopular" to so speak out.[9]

PD. *Liberation* 4 (October 1959): 5–6.

8. Williams titled the final section of his article "King Cashes in on War" and criticized King's inconsistent stance on violence: "Even Negroes like King who profess to be pacifists are not pure pacifists and at times speak proudly of the Negro's role of violence in this violent nation's wars. . . . King may not be willing to partake in expeditions of violence, but he has no compunction about cashing in on the spoils of war. There are too many Negro leaders who are afraid to talk violence against the violent racist and are too weak-kneed to protest the warmongering of the atom-crazed politicians of Washington." Williams referred to remarks King made on black participation in World War II at the 17 July 1959 NAACP convention (see p. 249 in this volume).

9. In the 1962 reprint of this article in Williams's *Negroes with Guns,* this paragraph began: "To set the record straight on any implications that I am inconsistent in my struggle against war and too weak-kneed to protest nuclear war, may I state that repeatedly, in public addresses and in my writings, I have unequivocally declared my hatred for this most colossal of all evils and I have condemned any organizer of war, regardless of his rank or nationality." For more on King's support of anti-nuclear efforts, see Norman Cousins and Clarence Pickett to King, 9 March 1958, in *Papers* 4:379–380, and King to Cousins, 1 April 1959; see also "Humanity Has a Common Will and Right to Survive!" *New York Times,* 13 August 1959.

To Thomas Kilgore

6 October 1959
[*Montgomery, Ala.*]

For several years King had been involved in discussions with other Baptist ministers, including Kilgore and Gardner Taylor, about their dissatisfaction with the leadership of the National Baptist Convention.[1] *A month after their annual meeting, held in San Francisco in early September, King expresses his disgruntlement with the organization.*[2] *Kilgore replied on 13 October suggesting that they immediately begin organizing against the convention's president, J. H. Jackson: "Silence and inactivity at this time are but adding to the total climate of moral degeneracy in our Convention."*

Rev. Thomas Kilgore, Jr.
Friendship Baptist Church
144 West 131st Street
New York 27, New York

Dear Tom:

I am happy to know that Mrs. English will be able to study in Vienna this year, and I want to share in some little way.[3] Enclosed you will find a check in the amount of $15.00. I am sorry that some heavy financial obligations at the present time stand in the way of my contributing more. As I said to you once before Mrs. English possesses a voice of rare quality and unusual beauty.

I missed seeing you in California at the convention. We must move Dr. Jackson in Philadelphia next year.[4] It can be done through an organized effort. Philadelphia is a good setting and the time is right. We must get behind a man and do the job. That man is Gardner Taylor. We can no longer passively accept the moral degeneracy which has infiltrated the top echelon of our convention. Let us go on to victory in 1960.

Very sincerely yours,
Martin L. King, Jr.

Enclosure

TLc. MLKP-MBU: Box 29.

---

1. For earlier accounts of the conflicts within the National Baptist Convention, see Introduction in *Papers* 4:17–18, and J. Pius Barbour to King, 3 October 1957, in *Papers* 4:281–283.

2. In an earlier letter King complained to theologian Howard Thurman, who had been unable to attend, about "the sometimes meaningless outbursts" at the San Francisco meeting (King to Thurman, 30 September 1959).

3. In a 22 September letter Kilgore had requested contributions to send Rose Battle English, a member of his congregation who had sung the national anthem at the 17 May 1957 Prayer Pilgrimage for Freedom, in Washington, D.C., to Vienna to study music. English thanked King for his contribution in a 12 January 1960 letter from Vienna.

4. At the Philadelphia convention in 1960, both Taylor and Jackson declared victory, and the contested presidency remained unresolved until 1961 when Taylor, King, and other dissident ministers disaffiliated from the National Baptist Convention and formed the Progressive National Baptist Convention ("Baptists in Convention, Name Two," *Baltimore Afro-American*, 17 September 1960).

To Anne Braden

7 October 1959
Montgomery, Ala.

King responds to Braden's 23 September letter and relays information about Ed Friend, a segregationist operative who attended an SCLC event. He also expresses his hope that Braden and her husband Carl would become "permanently associated" with SCLC.[1] *On the day that King wrote this letter, Carl Braden appeared before the U.S. Court of Appeals in Atlanta at a hearing to overturn his 1958 conviction for refusing to testify before the House Committee on Un-American Activities (HUAC).*[2]

Mrs. Anne Braden
Southern Conference Educational Fund, Inc.
4403 Virginia Avenue
Louisville 11, Kentucky

Dear Anne:

This is just a note to acknowledge receipt of your letter of September 23, which came to the office in my absence.

I am deeply grateful to you for sending me the information concerning Mr. Ed Friend. I am quite familiar with him, and realize that he is a very dangerous character. He attended many of the sessions of our institute on nonviolence in Atlanta this summer before anybody recognized him.[3] I finally became suspicious and had a committee to question him to see if he was the same person that was at Highlander on Labor Day weekend in 1957. It turned out that he was. I knew that from that moment on that he would do something in a malicious manner. It turned out just as I had expected. I will certainly keep your letter on my file, since it might be necessary to refer to it some day.

It was certainly good to have Carl in Columbia last week. He added a great deal to the meeting.[4] I hope both of you will find it possible to become permanently associated with the Southern Christian Leadership Conference. It is my firm belief that our movement must be interracial to be thoroughly effective. This will keep the struggle over and above a mere racial struggle, for as I have said so often, the tension in the South is between justice and injustice rather than white people

---

1. In a 10 October reply, Carl Braden conveyed his delight in affiliating with SCLC but expressed his uncertainty as to what "qualifications" or "dues" were necessary for membership. On 22 October King answered that because SCLC was not a membership organization "in a real sense you are already a part of" the organization.

2. King, Sr. and Ella Baker attended Braden's 7 October hearing (SCEF, Press release, 8 October 1959, and Carl Braden to King, Sr., 10 October 1959).

3. SCLC, CORE, and FOR co-sponsored the 22–24 July institute at Spelman College (see Resolutions, First Southwide Institute on Nonviolent Resistance to Segregation, 11 August 1959, pp. 261–262 in this volume).

4. Carl Braden took detailed notes at SCLC's fall conference (Braden, Notes on SCLC Fall Session, 30 September–1 October 1959).

or Negro people. We will be keeping in touch with you concerning future meetings, and we will definitely put you on the mailing lists of both the Southern Christian Leadership Conference and the Montgomery Improvement Association.

Very sincerely yours,
[*signed*]
Martin

TLS. CAABP-WHi: Box 31.

From G. McLeod Bryan

10 October 1959
Umuahia, Nigeria

After meeting with Albert Lutuli in South Africa, Bryan, a professor at Wake Forest College, reports on the African National Congress (ANC) president's great esteem for Stride Toward Freedom*: "He wished for copies to put into the hands of his African National Congress leaders."*[1] *King wrote Lutuli on 8 December.*[2]

Dr. Martin Luther King, Jr.
Montgomery, Ala.

Dear Martin Luther,

Just getting out of South Africa after three months in that tense atmosphere, I am fulfilling a promise I made to Chief Luthuli within the past fifteen days. He as you know is under ban, for the third time in 10 years. But without knowledge of your and my friendship, he told me that the greatest inspiration to him was your Stride Toward Freedom (that Bishop Reeves had put into his hands).[3] Luthuli had been reading it in his cane fields the very day I visited him. He wished for copies

---

1. Bryan had written King in late 1958 for advice before leaving to teach in South Africa and to tour the continent. King and Bryan first met during Religious Emphasis Week at Georgia's Fort Valley State College in October 1955 (Bryan to King, 20 November 1958). In April 1959, Bryan had requested that King provide him a letter of introduction, acknowledging that while the Africans would not know King personally, "they of course link your name with American friendship for the rising peoples of the earth" (Bryan to King, 21 April 1959, and King, Letter of introduction for G. McLeod Bryan, 30 April 1959). In a 4 May 1959 letter, King had encouraged Bryan to meet with Kwame Nkrumah and K. A. Gbedemah of Ghana and Tom Mboya of Kenya. George McLeod Bryan (1920–), born in Garner, North Carolina, received a B.A. (1941) and M.A. (1944) from Wake Forest College and a B.D. (1947) and Ph.D. (1951) from Yale University. He served as pastor of Olivet Baptist Church in New Haven, Connecticut, from 1945 to 1948. Bryan became a professor of Christian social ethics at Wake Forest College in 1956 and later worked for Volunteers for Africa.

2. See pp. 344–345 in this volume.

3. Bryan refers to Ambrose Reeves, Anglican bishop of Johannesburg, whom King had met on 25 July 1957 at a church event in New York City ("Dr. King Meets Bishop," *New York Times,* 28 July 1957).

to put into the hands of his African National Congress leaders. I told him I would put the request to you, believing that you would contribute this much and more to South African freedom. His eyes were the brightest when I referred to him as the "King" of S.A. His odds are so much greater, but he is a Profound Christian sharing your views. If only the world knew with whom it dealt!

I am at the moment lecturing in East Nigeria, for two months, completing my eight months tour of all-Africa. I hope you are getting my lengthy newsletters to close friends—

Send to:
Chief Luthuli
Groutville, Natal
South Africa

Your friend,
[*signed*] G. McLeod Bryan
Box 97
Trinity College
Umuahia
E. Nigeria

ALS. MLKP-MBU: Box 25.

To Alberta Williams King

12 October 1959
[*Montgomery, Ala.*]

King sends his mother, assistant director of the Ebenezer Baptist Church choir, the honorarium for the choir's 27 September concert at Dexter.[1] *The event, which King opened with an invocation, filled the church to capacity and included a solo by King's sister, Christine.*[2]

Mrs. M. L. King, Sr.
2873 Dale Creek Road, N.E.
Atlanta, Georgia

Dear Mother:

Enclosed is a check in the amount of three hundred forty-five dollars and seventy-five cents which includes the expenses of one hundred ninety-five dollars and seventy-five cents plus a one hundred fifty dollar honorarium. This program

1. Dexter Avenue Baptist Church, Program, "The church choir of Ebenezer Baptist Church in concert," 27 September 1959.

2. Leonard Ballou, "Ebenezer Choir Pleases Large Audience," *Dexter Echo,* 7 October 1959. Coretta King served as co-chair of the event.

was such a financial success that we felt compelled to add a little more to the honorarium. Already the receipts have reached around fifteen hundred dollars. The members of the committee asked me to express their deep gratitude to you and the overall choir for the great concert that you rendered. This was certainly one of the high points in the Montgomery Community.

Give my regards to all. I will be seeing you soon.

Very sincerely yours,
M. L.

enc/1
MLK/lmh

TLc. DABCC.

To Kenneth H. Tuggle

19 October 1959
[*Montgomery, Ala.*]

Acting on a resolution from SCLC's executive committee, King requests a meeting with the chair of the Interstate Commerce Commission to discuss "discriminatory practices" faced by black interstate travelers.[1] *Tuggle replied on 28 October and agreed to a 25 November meeting in Washington, D.C.*[2] *A press report indicated that Tuggle assured King that "action would be taken . . . upon receipt of complaints of discrimination."*[3]

Mr. Kenneth H. Tuggle, Chairman
The Interstate Commerce Commission
Constitution Avenue and 12th Street, N.W.
Washington, D.C.

Dear Mr. Tuggle:

A small committee from the Southern Christian Leadership Conference, Inc. would like to meet with members of the Interstate Commerce Commission to dis-

---

1. King, Recommendations to the SCLC Executive Committee, 30 September 1959, pp. 295–297 in this volume.

2. The 1946 Supreme Court decision in *Morgan v. Virginia* (328 U.S. 373) declared segregation in interstate travel unconstitutional. The ICC did not enforce the decision until 1955, when the commission banned segregation in interstate trains, buses, and waiting rooms. Kenneth Herndon Tuggle (1904–1978), born in Barbourville, Kentucky, received an A.B. (1926) from the University of Kentucky. A businessman and attorney, Tuggle served as lieutenant governor of Kentucky (1943–1947). President Eisenhower appointed him to the ICC in 1953. In 1959 Tuggle served a one-year term as chair of the ICC and remained on the commission until retiring in 1975.

3. "Rival Faction Plans Boycott of King Talk," *Montgomery Advertiser*, 3 December 1959. In 1960 King corresponded with Tuggle's successor at the ICC on the arrest of Fred Shuttlesworth's children in Gadsden, Alabama, for refusing to move to the back of a bus on an interstate route (King to John H. Winchel, 18 August 1960; see also King to William P. Rogers, 18 August 1960, pp. 496–497 in this volume).

19 Oct 1959

cuss the discriminatory practices which Negro interstate passengers still experience in this area.

Wednesday, November 25th is the date we would prefer. However, if that is not convenient with your office, please indicate other dates later in November or in December that are convenient, and we will select one on which our committee can come to Washington.

We should appreciate hearing from you at the earliest possible date.

Sincerely yours,
Rev. Martin L. King, Jr.
President

MLK/eb

TLc. SCLCR-GAMK: Box 5.

To Theodore E. Brown

19 October 1959
[*Montgomery, Ala.*]

In this letter to Ted Brown, the assistant director of the AFL-CIO's civil rights department, King criticizes an article in Jet *that described SCLC's "clergy-backed Dixie vote campaign" as having made little progress, while trumpeting the NAACP's efforts.*[1] *King insists that the information is largely false and suggests it is part of an effort to divide SCLC and the NAACP: "There is nothing that arouses my ire more than those individuals in distant cities who will use the power of their pens to create jealouses, conflicts, and confusion." He details SCLC's plans to "rise up more aggressively" and adds that he would "hate to feel that" former SCLC executive director "Rev. Tilley was behind the writing of this in any way."*[2]

---

1. "Ticker Tape U.S.A.," *Jet,* 12 October 1959, pp. 10–11. Theodore E. Brown (1915–1983), born in New Brunswick, New Jersey, received a B.A. (1936) from Northwestern University and an M.O.C (1944) from Harvard University. Brown worked as A. Philip Randolph's administrative assistant from 1946 to 1956 before joining the AFL-CIO's civil rights department. Brown was appointed secretary of the Negro American Labor Council in 1961. As president of the American Negro Leadership Conference on Africa (1962–1968), Brown campaigned to bar American warships from refueling at South African ports. He later worked for the U.S. Department of State and the Agency for International Development. In the preface to *Stride Toward Freedom,* King acknowledged Brown's "significant suggestions and real encouragement" (p. 11).

2. The *Jet* article featured a photo of Tilley and noted his departure from SCLC. For more on Tilley's resignation, see King to Tilley, 3 April 1959, pp. 179–181 in this volume.

Mr. Theodore E. Brown
AFL-CIO
815–16th Street, N.W.
Washington 6, D.C.

19 Oct 1959

Dear Ted:

On returning to the office I found your letter of October 13, with the enclosed letter from Mrs. Margaret Bush Wilson.[3] From your letter I am not clear on the question of whether you wrote Mrs. Wilson stating that it would not be possible for me to accept the invitation. As I said to you, I have a long standing commitment in Philadelphia on November 8, which makes it impossible for me to go to St. Louis. Please let me know whether you answered to that effect.

I am quite anxious to have the get together to discuss trade union cooperation with the program of the Southern Christian Leadership Conference. At the present time I am making some arrangements to be in the New York area for a series of business discussions around the middle of November. This might be our best time to talk. I will let you know as soon as my schedule has been cleared.

If you have not read the Jet for this week, I wish you would look at the lead column of Ticker Tape U.S.A. I think it is very unfortunate that Mr. Booker would stoop to such tragic methods.[4] First, almost everything he says in the article is false, and he did not take the time to consult with any officials of SCLC to corroborate his statements. Second, it gives the impression that the voting drive in the South is not going because Rev. Tilley left, when the actual fact is that Rev. Tilley was forced to resign by the Board because he was not producing. We were kind enough not to let this out to the public, and we said to Rev. Tilley that we would protect his name and reputation at every point. Third, the article says that we have only raised $25,000.00, and there is nothing further from the truth. Our financial statements will show that we have raised well over $25,000.00, and we are still raising fairly good money in the light of the fact that we have never really seriously developed a fund raising program. More than $3,000.00 was reported in the Columbia, South Carolina meeting, and I have just returned from Denver where more than a thousand dollars was raised for the Conference and I will go to Fort Worth, Texas where another thousand dollars is guaranteed. The fourth thing that is very bad in the column is a continuation of the diliberate attempt to divide the Southern Christian Leadership Conference and the NAACP. One can easily see that the article leans toward justifying the NAACP and ridiculing the SCLC. Now the fact is that no organization has done enough in the area of registration and voting in the South. If we are honest and really concerned about solving the problem we will have to admit this. And if there is any comparison, I would venture to say that

3. In a 13 October letter to King, Brown had enclosed a 29 September letter from Wilson, president of the St. Louis NAACP, in which she requested that Brown ask King to speak at their annual Freedom Fund Tea on 8 November.

4. King refers to Simeon Booker, Washington bureau chief for Johnson Publishing Co., publisher of *Jet.*

SCLC has done much more than the NAACP. I am convinced that if we are to solve our problems in the South, we need the cooperation and support of all agencies, particularly the press, and there is nothing that arouses my ire more than those individuals in distant cities who will use the power of their pens to create jealouses, conflicts, and confusion. Anybody knows that the NAACP cannot do this job alone, and this is true for many reasons. For instance, in Alabama there is not even an NAACP in operation, and the question is can we afford to wait and hold back the onward move of progress until the NAACP is restored.[5] The job of registration and voting is so big that it will take the concerted effort of every organization. This is no time for small things and small actions. It is a time for positive, powerful, and determined cooperation.

In the Columbia meeting of SCLC we decided to do several things to expand the work of the organization. So instead of fading away as Mr. Booker implies in Jet, we are really planning to rise up more aggressively. We voted to enlarge our staff. We also voted to employ a person part-time in the area of public relations who can publicize the work of the organization. I have felt all along that that we have been weak in this area.

Well I guess I should close now and get on with some other important matters on my desk. I did not mean to burden you with this situation, but I felt that you might be interested in knowing the facts, and certainly Mr. Booker should be interested. At points the article gives the impression that there is an attempt to justify Rev. Tilley's leaving. I would hate to feel that Rev. Tilley was behind the writing of this in any way.

Very sincerely yours,
Martin L. King, Jr.

MLK:mlb

TLc. MLKP-MBU: Box 20.

---

5. In June 1956, an Alabama circuit judge ordered the NAACP to cease operations within the state for the organization's failure to comply with state law requiring organizations to properly register. In 1964, the Supreme Court overturned the Alabama court's decision (*National Association for the Advancement of Colored People v. Alabama Ex Rel. Flowers, Attorney General,* 377 U.S. 288).

To Simeon Booker

20 October 1959
[*Montgomery, Ala.*]

After reading an unfavorable article on SCLC in Jet, *King called the magazine's Washington bureau chief to rebut the charges.*[1] *Following up in this letter, King asserts that SCLC's "aim is neither to grab headlines nor have a multiplicity of mass meetings" and notes that some members have "taken time out of extremely busy schedules to actually knock on doors" to encourage voter registration. King admits, however, that he is "all too conscious and even ashamed of our occasional apathy, complacency, irresponsibility." He concludes with an affirmation of his respect for Johnson Publishing Company and observes that "unity is still that magical something that will be necessary to finally crush the walls of segregation."*

Mr. Simeon Booker
Washington Bureau Chief
Jet Magasine
Johnson Publishing Company
Washington, D.C.

Dear Mr. Booker:

As a follow-up of our telephone conversation a few hours ago I would like to submit the following facts concerning the Southern Christian Leadership Conference:

1. Far from halting its efforts and program, the Southern Christian Leadership Conference is actually expanding. In the recent meeting of the Conference at Columbia, South Carolina, we voted to add two persons to our staff in Atlanta and expand our general program throughout the South.

2. While it is true that there have been changes in personnel, these changes were made to strengthen the organization instead of diminishing its effectiveness. As far as Rev. Tilley is concerned, my only comment is that he is a very fine man with a dedicated spirit, and one whom I have warm affections for.

3. It is true that we have not raised $250,000.00 as we had initially contemplated, but we have raised much more than $25,000.00. Our secretary-treasurer is out of the city now and I do not have the figures before me, but I would ven-

1. A subsequent news item in *Jet* reflected King's refutation and included information on SCLC's financial condition and expansion plans ("Ticker Tape U.S.A.," *Jet,* 12 November 1959, pp. 10–11). Simeon S. Booker (1918–), born in Baltimore, received a B.A. (1942) from Virginia Union University. In 1950 he was awarded Harvard's Nieman Fellowship in journalism and worked as the first full-time black reporter at the *Washington Post* from 1952 until 1954. Booker became the Washington bureau chief for Johnson Publishing Co. in 1955 and traveled to Ghana's independence celebrations in March 1957 as part of Vice President Nixon's delegation. Booker covered the Selma to Montgomery march for *Ebony* and in 1967 was part of a panel that interviewed King on "Meet the Press."

ture to say that we have raised approximately $50,000.00. Actually, our organization is in better financial shape at the present time than it has ever been, and we are getting support from many new sources.

4. Our aim is neither to grab headlines nor have a multiplicity of mass meetings on the question of registration and voting; we are concerned about getting the job done. We have been so concerned about this that we have tried to employ people to head the administrative staff of our organization with technical know how and competence. I may say further that some of us have been so concerned about this pressing problem of getting our people registered that we have taken time out of extremely busy schedules to actually knock on doors. More than fifteen of the leading ministers of Montgomery, Alabama took a day off and went into numerous homes to determine how many people were registered and encourage those who were elligible to do so.[2]

A further illustration of our concern with technical know how and concrete results is the fact that one of the most important sessions of our Columbia meeting was given to a practical discussion of political action on the part of the Negro in Memphis, Tennessee. We had Attorney Sugarmon and Attorney Hooks to lead the discussion, both of whom ran for public offices in Memphis in the recent municipal election.[3]

As I said to you on the telephone, I do not want to give the impression that we have done any herculean job in the area of registration and voting. We are quite conscious of the fact we have not scratched the surface in the South in this all-important area of voting. Moreover, we do not feel that our organization is above criticism, nor any individual connected with it, for it is often through constructive criticism that we grow, correct our errors, and improve our shortcomings. I for one am not the minister with a holy art thou attitude, feeling that we are above reproach. I am all too conscious and even ashamed of our occasional apathy, complacency, irresponsibility. But in spite of all of this, I am sure that destructive criticism will do the cause of freedom no good. Neither will it help for any individual or publication to sow seeds of dissention. The job ahead is difficult, and our opponents are willing to use any technique to prevent our advances. In order to meet this massive resistance we will need the massive assistance of every segment of Negro society. This is a time for big things and big action. Individuals and organizations must submerge their petty jealouses, envies, and quests for recognition in the glowing commitment to the overall cause. The fact remains that no organization has done an adequate job in the area of registration and voting. The job is too big for any single organization. What we must do now is come together on all levels and coordinate our efforts. Unity is still that magical something that will be necessary to finally crush the walls of segregation.

---

2. King and other MIA ministers walked door to door in Montgomery's Victor Tulane housing project to encourage voter registration ("Montgomery Launches New Voter Registration Drive," *Birmingham World,* 26 September 1959).

3. Attorney Russell B. Sugarmon ran for Memphis city commissioner during the summer of 1959. Benjamin L. Hooks, an attorney and ordained minister who went on to become the executive director of the national NAACP, ran for juvenile court judge in the same year.

Again, I must say that I am sorry that this situation developed, and above all, I am sorry that we were misrepresented in the article. I am sure that it will cause my associates and me some embarrassment and lay upon us the burden of some unnecessary explaining; and I am sure it will make it much more difficult for us to raise funds for our humble and struggling efforts. But in spite of that we will continue to move on. And let me assure you that this in no way lessens my regards for you and Johnson Publication, for I have been so inspired by the good that has come to the Negro and the nation as a result of the creative contribution made by Johnson Publication—nothing less than a tour de force—that I would be an ingrate to fail to appreciate it.

Very sincerely yours,
Martin Luther King, Jr., President
The Southern Christian Leadership
Conference, Inc.

MLK:mlb

TLc. MLKP-MBU: Box 30.

Recommendations to SCLC Committee on Future Program

27 October 1959

King offers several proposals to offset criticisms that SCLC's voter registration efforts had faltered. He recommends publicizing the group's recent achievements and hiring Bayard Rustin "with the understanding that if any undue criticism" arose "that would prove embarrassing to him or the organization, he would quietly resign."

1. In order to counteract some false ideas that have been disseminated concerning the program of SCLC, a press release shall be immediately prepared by the Executive Director stating in positive terms the plans and future program of the Conference. It should be made palpably clear that instead of halting its activities the Conference is actually expanding its activities. Something should also be said concerning things that have already been accomplished by the Conference. This release should reach the press before Friday of this week in order to get good coverage.[1]
2. Immediately prepare a newsletter to be mailed to at least five thousand persons. The mailing list would be secured from minutes of church groups,

1. In a statement released to the press on 10 November, SCLC announced plans for "a stepped up action program" to include expanded efforts in "voter-registration, leadership training and nonviolent resistance to segregation." The release indicated that registration efforts in northern Louisiana and Birmingham would continue (SCLC, Press release, 2 November 1959).

thus covering a large number of ministers, the MIA files, select group from In Friendship, and persons who wrote to the President during his illness.[2] This newsletter should clearly express the aims and purposes of the Conference, its past accomplishments and future proposals. The section in the last letter dealing with the history of the organization and the names of officers and board members should be repeated since it only reached five or six hundred people.[3] An appeal should be made at the end of the letter for financial aid to carry on the work of the organization.

3. In order to attempt once more to coordinate the activities of the NAACP and the SCLC in the vote drive, and clear up what appears to be seeds of dissention being sown by persons in the top echelon in the NAACP, the President, accompanied by one person from the official family of SCLC, should immediately have a Conference with Roy Wilkins and other NAACP staff members whose presence Mr. Wilkins may deem necessary.[4]
4. Select some few cities where intensified voting drives can be conducted without any resistance from state or local authorities. Immediately seek to set dates when the SCLC can assist in setting up such drives. Since we are a service agency we would naturally seek to work through and coordinate the activities of already existing groups.
5. In order to seriously think through the total freedom struggle, and the role that we should continually play, a two-day retreat should be held during the Christmas holidays. This retreat should consist of about ten persons, and a place should be secured that would be conducive to deep thinking and serious discussion.
6. While the voting drive still holds a significant place in our total program, we must not neglect other important areas. Therefore, I recommend that we begin thinking of some of the other areas that should gain our immediate attention.
7. In order to give Miss Baker an opportunity to set up voting drives in various cities and impliment the larger program of SCLC, I recommend that we seek to secure by December 1, the services of the person in public relations whom we voted to employ in our Columbia meeting. This person would assist in carrying out the day to day details of the office and start the all-important job of presenting our organization more adequately to the public. After prayerful and serious consideration, I would like to recommend Bayard Rustin to this position. I make this recommendation not unmindful of the possible perils involved. But I feel that Mr. Rustin's unique organizational ability, his technical competence, and his distinctive ability to stick with a job until it is thoroughly completed, justifies our willingness

---

2. King received thousands of letters from well-wishers in the wake of his September 1958 stabbing. In 1956, Rustin, Levison, and Baker formed In Friendship to provide support for the Montgomery bus boycott and other southern desegregation struggles.

3. The inaugural issue of SCLC's *The Crusader* had appeared in February 1959, but the next issue was not published until May 1961.

4. King met with Wilkins on 30 November in New York City (King to Wilkins, 18 November 1959).

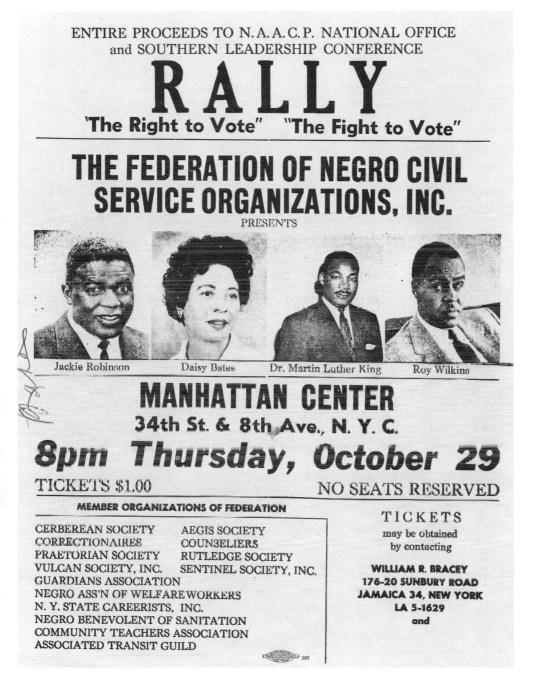

ENTIRE PROCEEDS TO N. A. A. C. P. NATIONAL OFFICE
and SOUTHERN LEADERSHIP CONFERENCE

RALLY

'The Right to Vote" "The Fight to Vote"

THE FEDERATION OF NEGRO CIVIL SERVICE ORGANIZATIONS, INC.

PRESENTS

Jackie Robinson | Daisy Bates | Dr. Martin Luther King | Roy Wilkins

MANHATTAN CENTER

34th St. & 8th Ave., N. Y. C.

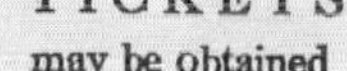

8pm Thursday, October 29

TICKETS $1.00 NO SEATS RESERVED

MEMBER ORGANIZATIONS OF FEDERATION

CERBEREAN SOCIETY
AEGIS SOCIETY
CORRECTIONAIRES
COUNSELIERS
PRAETORIAN SOCIETY
RUTLEDGE SOCIETY
VULCAN SOCIETY, INC.
SENTINEL SOCIETY, INC.
GUARDIANS ASSOCIATION
NEGRO ASS'N OF WELFARE WORKERS
N. Y. STATE CAREERISTS, INC.
NEGRO BENEVOLENT OF SANITATION
COMMUNITY TEACHERS ASSOCIATION
ASSOCIATED TRANSIT GUILD

380

TICKETS
may be obtained
by contacting

WILLIAM R. BRACEY
176-20 SUNBURY ROAD
JAMAICA 34, NEW YORK
LA 5-1629
and

Flyer by the Federation of Negro Civil Service Organizations announcing New York City rally 29 October 1959 on the right to vote and the fight to vote. Courtesy of Wisconsin Historical Society.

27 Oct 1959

to take the risk. We may employ him for a period on a trial basis, with the understanding that if any undue criticism that would prove embarrassing to him or the organization, he would quietly resign.[5]

TD. MLKP-MBU: Box 47A.

---

5. In a 1 November letter, Stanley Levison wrote Rustin attempting to persuade him to return from Africa, where he was working with the Sahara Project, a campaign to protest French nuclear testing in North Africa. According to Levison, over the protests of Ella Baker, the SCLC ministers backed King's proposal to hire Rustin, despite his earlier arrest for homosexual activity and his involvement with the Communist Party in the 1930s: "The person who played the role of firmly and unyieldingly opposing you was our buddy, Ella. She used the fears as well as the argument that the organization didn't need someone like you, but a field secretary." A few weeks later King asked Levison when Rustin might be expected to return to the United States: "Please let me hear from you as soon as Bayard gets back in the country. We are in desperate need of his services" (King to Levison, 19 November 1959). Rustin went to work with SCLC in early 1960 but was forced to resign in June 1960 due to claims that he unduly influenced King (see King to Adam Clayton Powell, Jr., 24 June 1960, pp. 480–481 in this volume).

From John F. Kennedy

10 November 1959
Washington, D.C.

During the fall of 1959 Marjorie Lawson, a supporter of presidential hopeful Kennedy, attempted several times to arrange a meeting between King and the Massachusetts senator.[1] *They met in June 1960.*[2]

Rev. Martin Luther King
454 Dexter Avenue
Montgomery, Alabama

Dear Rev. King:

Our mutual friend, Mrs. Marjorie McKenzie Lawson, has suggested to me that you might be interested in the enclosed statement concerning my record in civil rights and race relations.

Mrs. Lawson has suggested further that we put your name on our mailing list to receive other material which we send out from time to time.

With every good wish, and in appreciation for your interest, I am

Sincerely,
[*signed*]
John F. Kennedy

JFK:cjr
jms 21
Enclosure 1

TLS. MLKP-MBU: Box 90.

---

1. See King to Lawson, 4 September 1959, pp. 276–277 in this volume, and Lawson to King, 18 November 1959.
2. See King to Chester Bowles, 24 June 1960, pp. 478–480 in this volume.

To Friend

12 November 1959
New York, N.Y

In a 16 October letter George M. Houser, executive director of the American Committee on Africa (ACOA), requested that King sign an enclosed form letter "to rally support for the new Africa Defense and Aid Fund."[1] *King agreed and indicated that the appeal could be distributed without changes.*[2] *After making slight modifications to the draft, the ACOA sent this letter to potential supporters.*

Dear Friend:

I think I can say, as one well aware of the problems we still face in the United States, that the problems of Africa are of utmost importance in the world today. The people of Africa are struggling for independence and equal rights. There is no question that they will get them—but how? I am convinced that our future as well as theirs depends on what you and I do right now to make the transition peaceful and democratic.

In Central Africa at this moment there are over 600 Africans imprisoned, their families deprived of income.[3] Their "crime" is that they are members of African organizations—legal at the time of their arrest—which seek greater political rights for the African majority, and an end to the color bar. The Nyasaland government (part of the Central African Federation), alleging a "massacre plot," rounded up some 1300 Africans early this year and declared a state of emergency.[4] The British government sent in an investigating commission which reported that not only was there no evidence of such a plot, but that under present conditions Nyasaland is a police state.

Urgent appeals have come to the American Committee on Africa to help the families of these Africans who are being held indefinitely and without specific charges. A responsible channel exists for us to give help. Through the South Africa Defense Fund, set up by the Committee three years ago when 156 opponents of

---

1. Draft, King to Friend, 16 October 1959. Earlier in the year King had served as an honorary chairman of the "Africa Freedom Day" event in New York sponsored by the American Committee on Africa on behalf of victims of racist violence in South Africa (ACOA, Program, "Africa Freedom Day," 15 April 1959). George Mills Houser (1916–), born in Cleveland, Ohio, received a B.A. (1938) from the University of Denver and an M.Div. (1942) from Chicago Theological Seminary. In 1940 Houser was sentenced to one year in prison for draft resistance. He worked for the Fellowship of Reconciliation (1942–1955). In 1942 he co-founded the Congress of Racial Equality (CORE), serving as its executive secretary (1945–1955). He helped organize the Journey of Reconciliation in 1947 to protest segregation on buses and trains in the South. Houser was also a co-founder of the American Committee on Africa and served as its executive director from 1955 until 1981.

2. King to Houser, October 1959. In a 9 November letter Houser thanked King for his "immediate response and willingness to sign the appeal letter."

3. The draft of this letter referred to five hundred jailed Africans.

4. The draft reported that two thousand Africans had been arrested.

apartheid were arrested, the American Committee of Africa sent $50,000 for aid in the extensive legal costs and family hardships of the accused.[5] Now through the new Africa Defense and Aid Fund, the needs forced by the continuing trial in South Africa and the emergencies in Central Africa, as well as those described in the enclosed folder, can be met by one concerted effort.

The American Committee on Africa is the only organization in this country today which is actively trying to channel American aid in support of Africa's struggle for greater democracy. If you and every one of the people to whom I am writing would respond with a check of at least $10, the American Committee on Africa could launch the Africa Defense and Aid Fund effectively and send immediate aid to those in need. Your support will help serve justice in Africa today, and build our friendship with Africans in the crucial period ahead. We need your help.[6]

Sincerely yours,
[*signed*] Martin L. King Jr.
Martin Luther King, Jr.

P.S. Because I am trying to reach many people with this letter, and it is very expensive to check lists for duplications, you may receive more than one. If so will you please forgive us and pass the additional letter on to a friend.

TLS. MLKP MBU: Box 88A.

---

5. For King's support of this earlier ACOA effort, see King to Chester Bowles, 8 November 1957, in *Papers* 4:311–314.

6. This sentence and the postscript were not included in the draft.

To Paul G. Landis

17 November 1959
[*Montgomery, Ala.*]

Landis, the director of the Mennonite Voluntary Service, wrote King of the progress of his church's ministry to black migrant workers in the South in a 24 September letter.[1] *He explained that some Mennonite youth wished to "do more in a tangible way to carry out our position against racial prejudice and segregation" and asked King for "suggestions as to how we might be able to assist on a 'grass roots' level in some of these poor rural communities." In this reply, King admits his limited knowledge of the rural South.*

---

1. Paul Groff Landis (1932–), born in Lancaster, Pennsylvania, became camp chaplain with the Florida Christian Ministry to Migrants in 1952. From 1954 until 1963 he served as director of the Mennonite Voluntary Service. Landis was ordained a Mennonite minister in 1958 and became a bishop in 1962.

17 Nov 1959

Mr. Paul G. Landis, Director
Mennonite Voluntary Service
The Lancaster Conference
Salunga, Pennsylvania

Dear Mr. Landis:

I am in receipt of your letter of September 4. First, let me apologize for being so tardy in my reply. Absence from the city for several weeks and the accumulation of a flood of mail account for the delay.

I read your letter with great interest, and I am happy to know that you have developed a program called Voluntary Service to help your young people find a positive expression to Christian love. Certainly, this is a noble venture.

I regret to say that my suggestions of how you may be able to assist on the "grass roots" level in some of the poorer communities of the South are very limited. I have very little knowledge of rural communities in Alabama. In the last few years I have been so involved in the struggle to break down the barriers of segregation and discrimination in the urban South that I have not had a chance to look into the rural situation. Of course, this is not something of which I am very proud, because the economic injustices in the rural South are much greater than the justices in the urban South. But I must confess that I have not gotten around to this area as yet.

However, the job is there to be done, and you are to be commended for seeing the need. Since I do not have any concrete suggestions to send you I would like to suggest an agency that you can write and possibly get some positive ideas concerning the rural situation. It is the America's Farm Workers Union, Suite 1106, 112 East 19th Street, New York 3, New York. Dr. Frank P. Graham is the Chairman of this committee.[2] Here, you can probably find more about the plight of the Negro in rural communities than anywhere else. I am sure that they can also suggest the best areas of concentration. I have had some little contact with this organization, and I know how intensely concerned they are about the problem.

You mention in your letter that you will be in this area in the not-too-distant future.[3] If that time has not already passed, please feel free to let me know when you are coming, and I will be more than happy to talk with you. I am sure that we will find many issues of mutual interest to us. Incidentally, I am quite familiar with the Mennonites. I have had many creative contacts with your denomination in the past few years.

Very sincerely yours,
Martin L. King, Jr.

MLK:mlb

TLc. MLKP-MBU: Box 31.

---

2. King refers to the National Agricultural Workers Union (NAWU). He agreed to an 11 August request from Eleanor Roosevelt to serve as a sponsor for the union's twenty-fifth anniversary celebration. United Nations mediator Frank Graham was on the advisory committee for SCLC's Crusade for Citizenship and served as chairman of the NAWU celebration.

3. Landis visited King in Montgomery in December and attended a session of the MIA's Institute on Nonviolence and Social Change (Elmer Neufeld to King, 17 December 1959).

From Ebenezer Baptist Church

17 November 1959
Atlanta, Ga.

Ebenezer Baptist Church leaders inform King that the congregation voted unanimously to request that he join his father as co-pastor. King replied two days later.[1]

Dr. Martin Luther King, Jr.
309 South Jackson
Montgomery, Alabama

Dear Doctor King:

The Ebenezer Baptist Church met in a called business meeting on November 16. The item on the agenda was the consideration of a recommendation brought by the Trustee Board and the Board of Deacons that you would be extended a call to Ebenezer Baptist Church as active Co Pastor. The recommendation was read and accepted unanimously by the church.

We are therefore extending to you a call to come to Ebenezer Baptist Church to become the Co Pastor with Dr. M. L. King, Sr.

Please advise us as to your decision, and also, let us know when we may expect you in a business meeting with the official Board and the Church.

We would appreciate a reply at your earliest possible convenience.

Yours truly,
[*signed*] P. O. Watson
P. O. Watson, Church Clerk[2]

[*signed*] Robert J. Collier
Robert J. Collier, Acting Chmn.
Board of Deacons[3]

[*signed*] J. H. Reese
J. H. Reese, Chmn. Trustee Board[4]

[*signed*] M. L. King Sr
M. L. King, Sr., Pastor

TLS. MLKP-MBU: Box 24.

---

1. See pp. 326–327 in this volume.
2. Peter O. Watson (1883–1967) was an insurance salesman.
3. Robert J. Collier (1913–1983) was a real estate agent.
4. John Horton Reese (1892–1982) was a self-employed salesman.

EBENEZER BAPTIST CHURCH

407-413 AUBURN AVENUE, N. E.

ATLANTA 12, GEORGIA

MURRAY 8-7263

M. L. KING, SR., Pastor
Res.: 193 Boulevard, N. E.
JA. 2-7164

November 17, 1959

Dr. Martin Luther King, Jr.
309 South Jackson
Montgomery, Alabama

Dear Doctor King:

The Ebenezer Baptist Church met in a called business meeting on November 16. The item on the agenda was the consideration of a recommendation brought by the Trustee Board and the Board of Deacons that you would be extended a call to Ebenezer Baptist Church as active Co Pastor. The recommendation was read and accepted unanimously by the church.

We are therefore extending to you a call to come to Ebenezer Baptist Church to become the Co Pastor with Dr. M. L. King, Sr.

Please advise us as to your decision, and also, let us know when we may expect you in a business meeting with the official Board and the Church.

We would appreciate a reply at your earliest possible convenience.

Yours truly,

P. O. Watson
P. O. Watson, Church Clerk

Robert J. Collier
Robert J. Collier, Acting Chmn.
Board of Deacons

J. H. Reese
J. H. Reese, Chmn. Trustee Board

M. L. King Sr
M. L. King, Sr., Pastor

/s

Letter extending call to King to serve as co-pastor with his father, M. L. King, Sr. Reproduced by permission. Courtesy of Ebenezer Baptist Church.

To Nettie K. Hurlburt

18 November 1959
[*Montgomery, Ala.*]

In a 29 October letter, Hurlburt expressed her ambivalence over the jail sentences given to two segregationists for their roles in the 7 September bombing of the Little Rock Board of Education building.[1] *Hurlburt explained that as a FOR member she supported integration but "the idea of these two young, ignorant, and impetuous (to say nothing of the fact that they were probably being 'used') men going to the penitentiary for many years, doesn't seem to be the answer either." She asked that King write the judge recommending probation "to redeem some of the miseries we are all sharing."*

Mrs. G. W. Hurlburt
2269 Grandview Avenue
Cleveland Heights 6, Ohio

Dear Mrs. Hurlburt:

On returning to the office I found your letter of October 28, on my desk making inquiry of my attitude concerning the penalties given the young men for bombing the Little Rock Board of Education Building.

This is certainly an important issue that you raise and one that would require a very detailed discussion. However, I will try to give you my views in as simple a statement as possible. It seems to me that the court system with its juries and judges is the best answer that society has worked out to deal with an offender. This does not mean that the system is perfect, for ultimately judgement is left in the hands of God. But society must have some system by which it controls and regulates behaviour. Those individuals who trespass the laws of society are arrested to demonstrate to others that no one is to go beyond certain fixed boundaries. Now I must stress the fact that when an individual is arrested for a criminal act he is not being paid back for what he has done, but he is being placed in a position to be improved. Ultimately punishment must be for the improvement of the criminal rather than an act of retribution. This is the view of modern criminology and I wholeheartedly agree with it.

Now I certainly agree with you that these men are not wholeheartedly responsible for their acts. They are the victims of the system. And in a sense Gov-

1. On 28 October the court sentenced Jesse Raymond Perry to three years in prison; J. D. Sims had earlier turned state's evidence, pled guilty, and was sentenced to five years. Three more men were tried later and also found guilty of participating in the bombings. Governor Orval Faubus commuted the sentences of the convicted men, while Sims served nearly two years before being released on parole ("Little Rock Bomber Given 3-Year Term," *New York Times*, 29 October 1959, and "Bombing Case Figure's Rights Are Restored," *Arkansas Gazette*, 13 April 1962). Antoinette Katherine Bolek Hurlburt (1892–1977) was born in Cleveland, Ohio, and attended Ohio University.

ernor Faubus and all of the other people who have made irresponsible statements and resisted integration are responsible for the acts of violence that some people commit. I also agree with you that justice must be tempered with mercy. But even after conceding these points I think it would have been a mistake to allow these men to go scotch free. Such an act would only have given other violent forces in the community an excuse, and even a justification to follow through on acts of terror.

This is about as simple an answer as I can give. I hope that it will prove helpful in some way. I appreciate your great moral concern and your deep commitment to the ideal of brotherhood.

Very sincerely yours,
Martin L. King, Jr.

MLK:mlb

TLc. MLKP-MBU: Box 27A.

To P. O. Watson

19 November 1959
[*Montgomery, Ala.*]

King replies to the call to serve as co-pastor of Ebenezer Baptist Church. Ten days later he resigned his position at Dexter Avenue Baptist Church.[1]

Mr. P. O. Watson, Clerk
The Ebenezer Baptist Church
407–413 Auburn Avenue, N.E.
Atlanta 12, Georgia

Dear Mr. Watson:

I am in receipt of your letter of November 17, informing me that I have been unanimously called to serve as Co-Pastor of the Ebenezer Baptist Church.

First, let me say how honored I am to be invited to fill such a significant position, and to serve such a great church. To know that the members voted unanimously to extend this call to me is indeed gratifying. It makes me feel both humble and grateful.

Please let me assure you that I will give this invitation my most prayerful and serious consideration. I hope it will be possible for me to give you a definite an-

1. See King, Draft, Resignation from Dexter, 29 November 1959, pp. 328–329 in this volume.

swer in the next few days. I will be very happy to meet with the official board to discuss this call in detail on Wednesday evening, November 25. If this date is acceptable to you, Mr. Collier, Mr. Reese, and Dr. King, Sr., I would appreciate your letting me know immediately.

With every good wish, I am

Yours in the Cause of Christ,
Martin Luther King, Jr.

cc: Mr. Robert J. Collier
Mr. J. H. Reese
Dr. M. L. King, Sr.

MLK:mlb

TLc. MLKP-MBU: Box 24.

To William P. Rogers

[*19 November 1959*]
[*Montgomery, Ala.*]

King lauds Attorney General Rogers for advocating the integration of a Huntsville, Alabama, elementary school that excluded the children of black military personnel.[1] *Acting Assistant Attorney General Joseph M. F. Ryan thanked King on Rogers's behalf.*[2] *The Huntsville schools remained segregated until 1963.*

ATTORNEY GENERAL WILLIAM P ROGERS
THE JUSTICE DEPARTMENT
WASHINGTON, D.C.

MAY I COMMEND YOU FOR YOUR FORTHRIGHT STAND FOR INTEGRATED SCHOOLING AT THE ARMY' S REDSTONE MISSLE CENTER IN ALABAMA. IT IS CER-

1. At a news conference, Rogers claimed that because the school was built with federal funds the "Negro youngsters on the base should be permitted to go to that school" ("Rogers Says Steps Planned to Lift Redstone Race Bars," *Montgomery Advertiser,* 19 November 1959). Objecting to Rogers's statements, Governor John Patterson told the press that he found it "inconceivable that the federal government would go so far as to jeopardize its missile program at such a time of national peril" ("Governor Blasts Plan to Mix Huntsville School," *Birmingham News,* 10 November 1959). William Pierce Rogers (1913–2001), born in Norfolk, New York, received an A.B. (1934) from Colgate University and an LL.B. (1937) from Cornell University. Rogers became deputy attorney general in 1953 and was named attorney general after Herbert Brownell resigned in October 1957. While in private practice, Rogers successfully represented King before the U.S. Supreme Court in *New York Times v. Sullivan* (376 U.S. 254 [1964]). Rogers later served as U.S. secretary of state from 1969 until 1973.

2. Ryan to King, 24 November 1959.

TAINLY UNJUSTIFIABLE FOR MILITARY PERSONNEL TO BE ORDERED AROUND VARIOUS STATIONS AND THEN CONFRONT A DENIAL OF EDUCATIONAL OPPORTUNITIES FOR THEIR CHILDREN ON THE BASES. I STRONGLY IMPLORE YOU AND THE MILITARY AUTHORITIES TO FOLLOW THROUGH WITH THE INTEGRATION OF SCHOOLS AT REDSTONE CENTER. A RETREAT AT THIS POINT WOULD ONLY CONFIRM STATE OFFICIALS IN THEIR UNDEMOCRATIC DEFIANCE OF THE LAW AND MAKE THEM MORE DETERMINED IN THEIR RESISTANCE. IT WILL ALSO MAKE IT MORE DIFFICULT FOR THOSE MODERATE WHITES IN THE SOUTH WHO ARE WILLING TO JOIN WITH NEGRO LEADERS IN WORKING TOWARD PEACEFUL COMPLIANCE WITH THE SUPREME COURT'S DECISION OUTLAWINGS SEGREGATION IN THE PUBLIC SCHOOLS.

MARTIN LUTHER KING, JR., PRESIDENT
SOUTHERN CHRISTIAN LEADERSHIP CONFERENCE

TWc. MLKP-MBU: Box 24.

Draft, Resignation from Dexter Avenue Baptist Church

[*29 November 1959*]
[*Montgomery, Ala.*]

King announced his resignation following Sunday services at Dexter and may have used this handwritten draft to frame his remarks. According to a news account, after King spoke three elderly women stood up in protest and looked about "to see if others would join them." Twelve parishioners eventually rose to demonstrate. One man explained: "We weren't just going to give him up without some kind of a fight. But we were not against him, we just wanted to show our regret."[1]

A little more than five years ago I accepted the patorate of this Church. We started out at that moment on a great and creative spiritual venture. You responded to my program with a cooperative spirit that could hardly be duplicated anywhere. At that time my only desire was to serve the Dexter Avenue Baptist Church to the best of my ability

Little did I know when I came to Dexter that in a few months a movement would commence in Montgomery that would change the course of my life forever. But history ~~always preserves for itself unpredictable~~. [~~*acts*~~*?*] still has its unpredictable

1. "Why Rev. M. L. King Is Leaving Montgomery: Leader Says Time Is Ripe to Extend Work in Dixie," *Jet,* 17 December 1959, p. 16.

qualities and it reserves for itself elements of creative. Unknowingly and unexpectedly, I was catapulted into the leadership of ~~a movement whose~~ the Montgomery movement. At points I was unprepared for the symbolic role that history had thrust upon me ~~But there was~~ [*strikeout illegible*]

Everything happened so quickly {& spontaneously} that I had no time to think through the implications of such leadership. At points I was unprepared for the symbolic role that history had thrust upon me. But there was no way out. I, like [*everything?*] in Montgomery, was pulled into the mainstream by the rolling tide of historical necessity.

As a result of my leadership in the Montgomery movement my duties and [*strikeout illegible*] activities tripled. A multiplicity of new responsibilities poured in upon me in almost staggering torrents. So I ended up ~~in the~~ futily attempting to be four or five men in one.

One would have expected that many of these responsibilities would have tapered off after the boycott. But now three years after the termination of the bus struggle the same situaton stands. At points the demands have increased.

ADf. MLKJP-GAMK

SCLC Press Release, "Dr. King Leaves Montgomery for Atlanta"

1 December 1959
Atlanta, Ga.

In the following press release, King explains that his decision to leave Montgomery was a response to pleas from his SCLC colleagues, and he links his move with the announcement that "a full scale assault will be made upon discrimination and segregation in all forms." The news of King's relocation to Atlanta prompted Georgia governor Ernest Vandiver to vow that King would be kept under surveillance and prosecuted if he were "responsible for strife involving law violations."[1]

Southern Christian Leadership Conference, Inc.
208 Auburn Avenue, N.E.
Atlanta, Georgia

For immediate release:

Atlanta, Georgia—"The time has come for a broad, bold advance of the southern campaign for equality," declared Dr. Martin Luther King as he announced that he is shifting his base of operation from Montgomery, Alabama to Atlanta, Georgia.

Dr. King is resigning as pastor of Montgomery's historic Dexter Avenue Baptist Church and moving his family to Atlanta, where he will become co-pastor with his father in the 4,000 member Ebenezer Baptist Church. This new post will give the "American Gandhi" more time and a much better location to direct the southwide campaign of the Southern Christian Leadership Conference of which he is head.

Dr. King will remain associated with the Montgomery Improvement Association, which launched and directed the world-famous bus boycott. He has assured it's members that he will be in and out of Montgomery "almost as much as ever."

For the past year, the Southern Christian Leadership Conference has been pleading with Dr. King to give it the maximum of his invaluable leadership.[2] Dr. King emphasized his change of residence was a painful decision, but came in response to the appeal of the SCLC that the time was right for expanded militant action across the South, and for which his presence closer to headquarters was in-

---

1. "Vandiver Says Rev. King Not 'Welcome' Here," *Atlanta Daily World,* 2 December 1959. King reflected on Vandiver's statement in a letter to a supporter: "Why Governor Vandiver made such an extreme accusation I do not know, other than the fact that he probably felt the need to appeal to some of the reactionaries who vote to keep him in office" (King to Lee Peery, 23 December 1959).

2. A late November SCLC document detailed the need for King's "close presence virtually on a day to day basis" and called upon him "to take up the new and enlarged mission by a rearrangement of his schedules and if necessary by a change of his residence" (SCLC, "Suggested draft for amplifying press release," 11 November–30 November 1959; see also Associated Negro Press, Press release, 18 November 1959).

dispensable. In responding to this urgent request, he said: "After prayerful consideration, I am convinced that the psychological moment has come when a concentrated drive against injustice can bring great tangible gains. We must not let the present strategic opportunity pass. 1 Dec 1959

"Very soon our new program will be announced. Not only will it include a stepped-up campaign of voter registration, but a full scale assault will be made upon discrimination and segregation in all forms. We must train our youth and adult leaders in the techniques of social change through non-violent resistance. We must employ new methods of struggle, involving the masses of our people. At the same time, we must realize that our crusade for citizenship is also for integrity. We cannot lay the whole blame for our short-comings upon those who oppose us. We must purge ourselves of internal jealousies, defeatism and criminal behaviour.

"Atlanta is perhaps the most strategic location for the headquarters of this expedition. We intend that it shall reach the far corners of every state of the South.

"I hate to leave Montgomery, but the people here realize that the call from the whole South is one that cannot be denied."[3]

One of the oldest members of Dr. King's church in Montgomery, speaking for his fellow members stated that "Rev. King will not truly be leaving us because part of him always will remain in Montgomery, and at the same time, part of us will go with him. We'll always be together, everywhere. The history books may write it Rev. King was born in Atlanta, and then came to Montgomery, but we feel that he was born in Montgomery in the struggle here, and now he is moving to Atlanta for bigger responsibilities."[4]

In emphasizing the importance of extending voter registration to all parts of the South, Dr. King stated that in 1960 Negroes and their allies are planning a huge and dramatic demonstration on a national scale. The foremost leaders, North and South, will collaborate to insure the presidential candidates are committed to a vigorous program to achieve concrete progress in every area of life.[5] Further details will be forthcoming after the first of the year from a national coordinating committee.

TD. MLKP-MBU: Box 35.

3. In a subsequent interview King elaborated on his feelings about leaving: "I have a sort of nagging conscience that someone will interpret my leaving Montgomery as a retreat from the civil rights struggle. Actually, I will be involved in it on a larger scale. I can't stop now. History has thrust something upon me from which I cannot turn away" ("Why Rev. M. L. King Is Leaving Montgomery: Leader Says Time Is Ripe to Extend Work in Dixie," *Jet*, 17 December 1959, p. 15).

4. Richard Harris, an MIA activist, indicated to a reporter that he was proud of King's move: "He's a big league ball player who has been batting .1000 in the minors. I'd rather see him in the majors, even if he bats only .350. Montgomery can't be selfish about Rev. King because we've never really owned him. He belongs to the whole country" ("Why Rev. M. L. King Is Leaving Montgomery," p. 17).

5. For more on the demonstrations at the Democratic and Republican national conventions, see King and Randolph, Statement Announcing the March on the Conventions Movement for Freedom Now, 9 June 1960, pp. 467–469 in this volume.

From T. H. Randall

1 December 1959
Montgomery, Ala.

Church deacon T. H. Randall reflects on King's pastorate two days after the announcement of his resignation from Dexter.

REPORT FOR NOVEMBER

Dr. Martin L. King, Jr., Pastor
Dexter Avenue Baptist Church
Montgomery, Alabama

Dear Dr. King:

The church year ended today—hence this report. In the first place I want to express to you my thanks and appreciation for the opportunity to visit the sick, shut-in and the members generally—which has meant so much to me.[1] To visit the sick, shut-in and the church generally, to hear them talk and to have the privilege of talking with them I find that my own experience has been enriched with a deeper sense of my own responsibility as a Christian.

Moreover, I want you to know, also, that the kind of life you have lived as our pastor, the sermons and talks have served as a compelling force in our life—urging us to live the full life thus broadening the hoizons of our responsibilities beyond our own church.

In closing I wish to say that your coming as pastor of Dexter Avenue Baptist Church and Mrs. Coretta King as first lady of the Dexter family has meant more to us than you ever will know. Under your leadership the spirit of togetherness and fellowship is evidenced throughout the church.

I trust that God will continue to bless you in every endeavor. I trust, also, that life will continue to bring things to your liking.

[*Randall lists twenty-two church members visited and indicates eleven who took communion*]

Respectfully submitted,
[*signed*]
T. H. Randall
Church Visitor

THR:lmh

TLS. MLKP-MBU: Box 23A.

---

1. In November 1958 King appointed Randall "church visitor," a position newly created "to give the pastor some assistance in the multiplicity of duties that have accumulated as a result of his larger ministry to the community and nation" (King, "Annual Report, Dexter Avenue Baptist Church," November 1957–30 November 1958).

Address at the Fourth Annual Institute on Nonviolence and Social Change at Bethel Baptist Church

3 December 1959
Montgomery, Ala.

In this typescript of his final address as president of the MIA, King summarizes the past year's accomplishments, highlighting attempts to desegregate the city's public schools and parks: "I think this is enough to say to the cynics, skeptics, and destructive critics that the MIA is still in business, and that while it does not have the drama of a bus boycott, it is doing a day to day job that is a persistent threat to the power structure of Montgomery." He outlines the MIA's "threefold task": challenging segregation, suffering and sacrificing for freedom, and making full and constructive use of existing freedoms. King discusses "the painful experience" of leaving Montgomery and admits that he had "not accomplished for you all that I desired, but I have tried to do my best." King pledges to remain "actively associated" with the MIA and reminds the members that "the freedom struggle in Montgomery was not started by one man, and it will not end when one man leaves."

I. Introduction

Presiding officer, members of the Montgomery Improvement Association, visiting friends, ladies and gentlemen.

Four years ago we assembled in the Holt Street Baptist Church and expressed in strong and courageous terms our determination to be free.[1] When we came together on that brisk and cold night in December our minds were filled with the dark memories of past oppression. We knew that the shadow of injustice was still athwart our path, and the dust of discrimination had not been removed from our longing souls. The result of our determination to organize against these evils, particularly as they expressed themselves in bus segregation, was the Montgomery Improvement Association. Little did we know when we brought this organization into being that we were starting a movement whose influence would be felt in large cities and small villages of America, in the sunny climes of Africa, and the rich soils of Asia, indeed throughout the whole civilized world. Little did we know on that night that we were starting a movement that would change the face of Montgomery forever and leave for unborn generations an imperishable legacy of creative nonviolent struggle.

The achievements of the bus boycott are so well known that we need not pause to mention them in great detail at this time. Suffice it to say that our year long united struggle gave Negroes everywhere a new sense of dignity and destiny and provided a powerful and creative approach to the crisis in race relations. I firmly believe that one day all of America—including those who have opposed us—will be proud of our achievements.

1. See King, MIA Mass Meeting at Holt Street Baptist Church, 5 December 1955, in *Papers* 3:71–79.

II. The MIA Today

But we have not been content to live merely on past accomplishments. He who lives only in the past has a doubtful present and an unattainable future. No greater tragedy can befall a people than to rest complacently on some past achievement. Noble yesterdays must always be challenges to more creative tomorrows. So the Montgomery Improvement Association is still attempting to make this community a better place in which to live. It has served as a continuing influence for good in Montgomery. In spite of negative cries of "What are you doing now?", the MIA is still active and deeply committed to its task. We are still courageously challenging the system of segregation. We are making it clear through our words and actions that segregation in any area of Montgomery life is an undue luxury that the community can ill afford.

We have used our financial resources to generously aid community projects. At the end of the boycott we had several thousands of dollars left in our treasury as a result of the generous gifts that people sent to us from every section of this country. And may I say in passing that every penny that came to Montgomery to assist in the bus struggle was used wisely and honestly. As president of the MIA I can truthfully say that I do not know of a single instance of mishandling or misappropriation of funds.[2] Our books have been audited every year by competent certified public accountants, and I am sure that if funds had been mishandled they would have notified us by now. But back to the main point. We have used the money remaining in our treasury to do many worthwhile things. The YMCA, which is presently under construction, would be an unfulfilled dream and a blasted hope if the MIA hadn't come to its rescue by making the sizable contribution of twenty thousand dollars ($20,000.00).[3] This money could have very easily been placed in reserve to finance many of the court suits that await us in the future. But we were willing to overlook this to meet the pressing need of the YMCA.

Along with our concern for the YMCA, we have taken great interest in Farm and City Enterprise, the cooperative grocery store in Mobile Heights. We came to the rescue of this institution to the tune of eleven thousand dollars ($11,000.00).[4] This was done because of our interest in seeing Farm and City survive and stand as a symbol of what the Negro could do by pooling his economic resources.

Not only have we given to collective community enterprises, but we have given economic aid to individuals who have faced reprisals as a result of their participation in our movement.[5] When the needs have been made known, we have always responded with immediate help.

We have made a determined effort to get our members to patronize Negro busi-

---

2. During the bus boycott, MIA secretary U. J. Fields accused the organization of mishandling funds; he later retracted his remarks (see Introduction in *Papers* 3:24–25).

3. See King to Royce Kershaw, 17 December 1958, in *Papers* 4:546–547.

4. For more on Farm and City Enterprises, Inc., see Vernon Johns to King, 8 May 1960, pp. 455–456 in this volume.

5. For example, the MIA relief committee gave $300 to Rosa Parks (see King to Abernathy, 26 February 1957, in *Papers* 4:143–144).

ness. As a result of this continual plea in mass meetings and other channels we have made it possible for Negro business and professional people to know more prosperity than they have ever known before. Almost any Negro business and professional person who is honest will have to admit that his business has taken a decisive turn upward since the boycott. I submit to you that the MIA is largely responsible for this.

Since the NAACP is not operating in Alabama at this time many of the court cases that would ordinarily fall under her domain are taken up by our association. We contributed more than one thousand dollars ($1,000.00) to the Jeremiah Reeves case. We threw the full resource of our office and legal counsel behind the Jimmie Wilson case and contributed in some little way to the saving of his life. We have already put more than fifteen hundred ($1,500.00) in the Aaron case.[6]

Above all the MIA has provided the Negro community with an agency to which individuals can come to air their grivances and complaints when they have been mistreated. To know that we have an organization in our community that is daily concerned with the injustices that we continually confront is a source of great hope and deep consolation. The MIA is that institution in our community which stands as an eternal reminder of the fact that as we walk through the dark night of oppression we do not walk alone, but a host of others are walking with us. Every Negro in Montgomery now knows that he has an organization, with its doors opened everyday in the week, that will fight for his rights.

I think this is enough to say to the cynics, skeptics, and destructive critics that the MIA is still in business, and that while it does not have the drama of a bus boycott, it is doing a day to day job that is a persistent threat to the power structure of Montgomery. If you have any final doubts about our aliveness, talk with the candidates who ran for reelection in the city last spring and they will have to admit that they are out of business because the MIA is very much in business.[7]

III. A Word About the Park Situation

It goes without saying that the Negroes of Montgomery have been the victims of the most glaring forms of injustice in park and recreational facilities. All the Negro Parks in Montgomery put together could hardly meet the specifications

6. Alabama officials succeeded in banning the NAACP from the state in 1956 on the grounds that it had failed to register properly with the secretary of state. Reeves was executed on 28 March 1958 following his conviction for attacking several white Montgomery women (see King, "Statement Delivered at the Prayer Pilgrimage Protesting the Electrocution of Jeremiah Reeves," 6 April 1958, in *Papers* 4:396–398). In September 1958 Wilson was sentenced to die for stealing $1.95 from an eighty-two-year-old white woman in Marion, Alabama; his sentence was commuted to life imprisonment. For King's earlier reference to the Wilson case, see note 5 to Statement to Eugene Loe, 5 September 1958, in *Papers* 4:488. Drewey Aaron was given the death penalty after he was convicted of raping a white Montgomery woman. In 1973, his sentence was commuted to life in prison (*Aaron v. State*, 49 Ala. App. 402).

7. In its 30 April newsletter, the MIA asserted that a relatively strong black turnout in the March elections helped defeat two ardent segregationists who had led the opposition to the Montgomery bus boycott, mayor W. A. Gayle and city commissioner Clyde Sellers (MIA, "The City Election," *Newsletter*, 30 April 1959).

for one good park. It is indeed shameful that there is not a single public swimming pool or tennis court for Negroes in the city of Montgomery.

For many years Negroes protested these blatant expressions of discrimination. Committee after committee called these oppressive conditions to the attention of the city commissioner. But all of this was to no avail. Finally, after serious and prayerful discussion, we decided to take this issue into the federal courts. Being mindful of the Supreme Court's affirmation of the inherent inequality of separate facilities, we naturally decided to challenge the constitutionality of segregated parks. The result was a favorable decision from the federal district court declaring segregation unconstitutional in the public parks of Montgomery.[8] This was a significant victory, and one that left every person of goodwill throbbing with inner joy. This decision means in simple terms that public parks never can be operated in Montgomery on a segregated basis.

As you recall, when we first decided to take this issue into the federal courts the city commission responded by closing all of the parks. Up to now the parks are still closed, and the new commissioners have not made it known whether or not they will open them. Naturally, we want to see the parks opened, for recreation is a vital part of the total welfare of the individual and the community. But we cannot in all good conscience make an agreement to accept a new form of segregation in order to entice the city commission to open the parks. While compromise is an absolute necessity in any moment of social transition, it must be the creative, honest compromise of a policy, not the negative and cowardly compromise of a principle.

IV. The Question of School Integration

On May 17, 1954, the Supreme Court of our nation rendered a momentous decision declaring segregation unconstitutional in the public schools. The decision stated in substance that separate facilities are inherently unequal, and that to segregate a child on the basis of his race is to deny that child equal protection of the law. A year after the Supreme Court rendered this decision, it handed down a decree outlining the details by which integration should proceed "with all deliberate speed."[9] While the court did not set a definite deadline for the termination of this process, it did set a time for the beginning. It was clear that the court had chosen this reasonable approach with the expectation that the forces of goodwill would immediately get to work and prepare the communities for a smooth and peaceful transition.

Five years have elapsed and no discernable move has been made toward integrating the schools of Montgomery, Alabama. Realizing that this was not only contrary to the Constitution of our nation, but to the best interest of our children, we in the MIA decided to request that the school board announce its plan of in-

---

8. On 9 September 1959, a federal district court ruled on behalf of eight black residents who had sued the previous December to desegregate the city's parks. City authorities, who had responded to the initial suit by closing the parks, successfully thwarted the district court's ruling by keeping the parks closed for several years. The case was not ultimately decided until 1974 by the U.S. Supreme Court (*Gilmore v. City of Montgomery*, 417 U.S. 556 [1974]).

9. King refers to *Brown v. Board of Education*, 349 U.S. 294 (1955).

tegration to the community.[10] In making this request we made it clear that we were issuing neither a threat nor an ultimatum. We were simply urging them to begin some reasonable compliance with the "law of the land," and to cease the maintenance of a system which was injurious to both Negro children and white.

Three months have passed since we made this request to the board of education, and it has not even given us the courtesy of an answer. It seems now that we have no alternative but to carry this issue into the federal courts. We have said all along that we would make the courts a last resort, and this we sincerely meant. But when the school board absolutely refuses to acknowledge your letter and act on your request the last resort stage has already emerged.

The governor of our state has promised to close the school if we continue our moves toward integration. Such a big threat, however, will not in the least deter us from our righteous efforts.

Our governor has also predicted violence if schools are integrated.[11] Of course the continuous prediction of violence is a conscious or unconscious invitation to it. But even so, it should now be clear to the reactionaries of the white South that we fear neither bodily injury nor physical death, because we know that we are engaged in a cause that is right. We will not allow threats or vitriolic words to frighten us into a position of retreat.

In spite of the threats and loud noises we know that the idea of closing the public schools is a fanatical proposal which is both rationally absurd and practically inexpedient. The absurdity of this approach was clearly seen in the breakdown of massive resistance in Virginia and Arkansas. Interestingly enough, this massive resistance has crumbled as a result of the massive insistence of white southerners to keep the public schools open. What we now see in both Little Rock and Virginia is something very revealing. Two powerful institutions have collided in the South—the institution of segregation and the institution of public schools. And the people, on the whole have made it palpably clear that when the final moment of choice comes, they will choose public schools rather than segregation. People are gradually coming to see the futility of attempting to close the public schools. The price to be paid by school closing is much too high. Business suffers. Children receive an inferior education. Many responsible persons move away. The cultural life of the community lags.

So if our governor is driven to the extreme of closing the public schools, as he has so earnestly promised to do, he will do more to promote integration in Alabama in a few hours than the most powerful integrationist could do in ten years.

V. Our Threefold Task

1. We must continue ~~to~~ courageously {to} challenge the system of segregation. It must be our firm conviction that segregation is an evil that we cannot passively

10. See King to the Montgomery County Board of Education, 28 August 1959, pp. 270–272 in this volume.

11. Governor John Patterson warned the state's African Americans that pushing for school integration would "lead to chaos and disorder and violence and the destruction of our public school system" ("Governor Makes Plea to Negroes," *Montgomery Advertiser,* 6 September 1959).

accept. Segregation is evil because it seeks to repudiate the principle that all men are created equal. Segregation is wrong because it relegates men to the status of things and makes them objects to be used, rather than persons to be respected. Segregation is wrong because it gives the segregated a false sense of inferiority, while leaving the segregator confirmed in a false sense of superiority. Segregation is wrong because it assumes that God made a mistake and stamped upon certain men an eternal stigma of shame because of the color of their skin.[12]

Therefore, we must not rest until segregation is removed from every area of our nation's life. Segregation is a cancer in the body politic, which must be removed before our democratic health can be realized. And may I say to you that we must not be deluded into complacent acceptance of an outmoded doctrine of separate-but-equal because of the present erection of beautiful school buildings in many southern communities. The fact remains that separate facilities are inherently unequal, and so long as segregated schools exist the South can never reach its full economic, political and moral maturity.

2. We must be willing to suffer and sacrifice in order to achieve our freedom. It is trite, but true that freedom is never handed out on a silver platter, and the road to progress is never a smooth and easy road. The road from the Egypt of slavery to the Cannah of freedom is an often lonely and meandering road surrounded by prodigious hilltops of opposition and gigantic mountains of evil. The triumphant beat of Easter's drum is never allowed to sound until the bleak and desolate moments of life's Good Friday have plucked the radiant star of hope from the sky of human experience. Yes, even dawn must temporarily hide itself behind some distant horizon until the deep darkness of the midnight has had its opportunity to reign supreme. This is the story of life. There is rarely ever any social gain without some individual pain. I am afraid that too many of us want the fruits of integration but are not willing to courageously challenge the roots of segregation. But let me assure you that it does not come this way. Freedom is not free. It is always purchased with the high price of sacrifice and suffering.

We must gird our courage and stand firm for a better world for our boys and girls. We must tell our white brothers that the few Uncle Toms who will sell their souls for a mess of economic pottage do not speak for the Negro. We must let them know that we are determined to be free, and that we are willing to pay the price.

And so our most urgent message to this nation must be summarized in these simple words: "We just want to be free." We are not seeking to dominate the nation politically or hamper its social growth; we just want to be free. Our motives are not impure and our intentions are not malicious: we simply want to be free. We are not seeking to be professional agitators or dangerous rabblerousers: we just want to be free. America, in calling for our freedom we are not unmindful of the fact that we have been loyal to you. We have loved you even in the moments of your greatest denial of our freedom. And now we are simply saying we want to be free. We have stood with you in every major crisis. Since Crispus Attucks gave

---

12. The preceding two sentences are similar to several lines from Benjamin E. Mays's 1955 speech, "The Moral Aspects of Segregation" (see note 11 to King, "Address at Public Meeting of the Southern Christian Ministers Conference of Mississippi," 23 September 1959, p. 288 in this volume).

his life on Boston's Commons black men and women have been mingling their blood with other Americans in defense of this republic.[13] For the protection of our honored flag which still floats untarnished in the breeze, Negro men and women have died on the far flung battle fields of the world. And so America we think we have a right to insist on our freedom. For your security, America, our sons sailed the bloody seas of two world wars. For you, America, our sons died in the trenches of France, in the foxholes of Germany, on the beachheads of Italy, and on the islands of Japan. And now, America, we are simply asking you to guarantee our freedom.

This must be our message to America. Freedom is that vital, intrinsic value which determines ones selfhood. It is worth suffering for: it is worth losing a job for: it is worth going to jail for. I would rather be a poor free man than a rich slave. I would rather live in a humble dwelling by the side of the road with my freedom and a sense of dignity than to live on some palatial hillside a mental slave. Once more every Negro must be able to cry out with his forefathers: "Before I'll be a slave, I'll be buried in my grave and go home to my Father and be saved."[14]

3. We must make full and constructive use of the freedom we already possess. We must not allow our oppression and lack of full freedom to drive us into a state of contentment with the mediocre and satisfaction with the non-productive. History has proven that inner determination can often break through the outer shackles of circumstance. Take the Jews for example. For years they have been forced to walk through the dark night of oppression. They have been carried through the fires of affliction, and put to the cruel sword of persecution. But this did not keep them from rising up with creative genius to plunge against cloud-filled nights of affliction, new and blazing stars of inspiration. Being a Jew did not keep Handel from lifting his vision to high heaven and emerging with the inspiration to leave for unfolding generations the glad thunders and gentle sighings of the great Messiah.[15] Being a Jew did not keep [*Albert*] Einstein from using his profound and genius-packed mind to challenge an axiom and add to the lofty insights of science a theory of relativity. Being Jews did not prevent Amos and Hosea, Isaiah and Jeremiah from standing up amid forces of religious idolatry and unjust power structures and declaring with prophetic urgency the eternal word of God, and the never ceasing necessity of being obedient to his will.

So we too can make creative contributions, even though the door of freedom is not fully opened. We need not wait until oppression ceases before we seek to make creative contributions to our nation's life. Already we have a host of Negroes whose inspiring achievements have proven that human nature cannot be catalogued, and that we need not postpone the moment of our creativity until the day of full emancipation. From an old slave cabin in Virginia's Hills, Booker T. Washington rose to the stature of one of America's greatest leaders; he lit a torch in the state of Alabama and darkness fled. From the red hills of Gordon County, Georgia, Roland Hayes rose up to be one of the world's great singers, and carried his

13. Attucks was killed by British troops in 1770 during the Boston Massacre.

14. This verse is from the spiritual "Oh Freedom."

15. King refers to George Frideric Handel, composer of "Messiah" (1741).

melodious voice to the palace of King George the fifth and the mansion of Queen Mother of Spain. From a poverty stricken section of Philadelphia, Pennsylvania, Marian Anderson rose up to be the world's greatest contralto, so that Toscanini could say, "A voice like this comes only once in a century," and Sabelius of Finland could cry out, "My roof is too low for such a voice." From oppressive and crippling surroundings, George Washington Carver lifted his searching, creative mind to the ordinary peanut, and found therein extraordinary possibilities for goods and products unthinkable by minds of the past, and left for succeeding generations an inspiring example of how an individual could rise above the paralyzing conditions of circumstance. There was a star in the sky of female leadership, and Mary McCloud Bethune grabbed it and allowed it to shine in her life with scintillating beauty. There was a star in the diplomatic sky, and Ralph Bunche, the grandson of a slave preacher, reached up and brought its radiant outpour into the center of his life. There was a star in the athletic sky; then came Joe Louis with his educated fists; Jessie Owens with his fleet and dashing feet, and Jackie Robinson with his calm spirit and powerful bat. These are but few of the Negroes whose epic making contributions have justified the conviction of the poet:

> Fleecy locks and black complexion
> cannot forfeit nature's claim
> Skin may differ, but affection
> dwells in black and white the same
> And were I so tall as to reach
> the pole or to grasp the ocean at a span,
> I must be measured by my soul,
> the mind is the standard of the man.[16]

VI. A Plea to the White Community

There is great need for positive leadership from the moderates of the white South in this tense period of transition. Unfortunately today, the leadership of the white South is by and large in the hands of close-minded extremists. These persons gain prominence and power by the dissemination of false ideas, and by appealing to the deepest fears and hates within the human mind. But they do not speak for the South; of that I am convinced.

There are in the white South millions of people of goodwill whose voices are yet unheard, whose course is yet unclear, and whose courageous acts are yet unseen. Such persons are in Montgomery today. These persons are often silent today because of fear of social, political, and economic reprisals. In the name of God, in the interest of human dignity, and for the cause of democracy, I appeal to these white brothers to gird their courage, to speak out, to offer the leadership that is needed. Here in Montgomery we are seeking to improve the whole community, and we call upon the whites to help us. Our ~~little~~ message to the white commu-

---

16. The first four lines are quoted from "The Negroes Complaint" (1788) by William Cowper, and the remaining lines are quoted from *Horae Lyricae*, "False Greatness" (1706) by Isaac Watts; see note 5 to "The 'New Negro' of the South: Behind the Montgomery Story," June 1956, in *Papers* 3:283.

nity is simply this: We who call upon you are not so-called outside agitators. We are your Negro brothers whose sweat and blood ~~has~~ {have} also built Dixie. We yearn for brotherhood and respect and want to join hands with you to build a freer, happier land for all. If you fail to act now, history will have to record that the greatest tragedy of this period of social transition was not the strident clamor of the bad people, but the appalling silence of the good people.

VII. A Parting Word

I cannot close without expressing my sincere gratitude to you for giving me the privilege to serve as your president for the past four years. You have been indeed kind to trust me with so great a responsibility, and to honor me with so lofty a task. I have not accomplished for you all that I desired, but I have tried to do my best.

Thanks to the members of the executive board of the MIA who have done all within their power to help carry the burden of this responsibility. Some have answered every call and responded to every demand of duty. Thanks to the faithful members of the Dexter Avenue Baptist Church who have been generous in allowing me the time to carry on the work of the MIA and the Southern Christian Leadership Conference. They have encouraged me with the warmth of their fellowship and have sustained me by their earnest prayers.

And now I have the painful experience of having to say to you that after four years as your president and five years as a citizen of this community, I will leave Montgomery for Atlanta.[17] The pain is somewhat relieved when I realize that Atlanta is such a short distance from here, and that I will have the privilege of remaining actively associated with the MIA.

For the past year the Southern Christian Leadership Conference has been pleading with me to give it the maximum of my time, since the time was ripe for expanded militant action across the South. After giving the request serious and prayerful consideration, I came to the conclusion that I had a moral obligation to give more of my time and energy to the whole South. This was only possible by moving closer to the headquarters where transportation was more flexible and time hitherto consumed in longer travel could be saved and utilized for planning, directing and supervising.

It was not easy for me to decide to leave a community where bravery, resourcefulness and determination had shattered the girders of the old order and weakened confidence of the rulers, despite their centuries of unchallenged rule. It was not easy to decide to leave a city whose Negroes resisted injustice magnificently and followed a method of nonviolent struggle that became one of the glowing epics of the twentieth century.

---

17. In a later interview, King detailed some of his personal reasons for the move: "For almost four years now, I have been faced with the responsibility of trying to do as one man what five or six people ought to be doing. . . . What I have been doing is giving, giving, giving and not stopping to retreat and meditate like I should—to come back. If the situation is not changed, I will be a physical and psychological wreck. I have to reorganize my personality and re-orient my life" ("Why Rev. M. L. King Is Leaving Montgomery: "Leader Says Time Is Ripe to Extend Work in Dixie," *Jet,* 17 December 1959, pp. 14–15).

3 Dec 1959

Now let me assure you that my leaving Montgomery should in no way slow up or end the struggle for first-class citizenship. Things will proceed just as they have been going. The freedom struggle in Montgomery was not started by one man, and it will not end when one man leaves. The Montgomery story was never a drama with only one actor. More precisely it was always a drama with many actors, each playing his part exceedingly well.

As I said earlier I will still remain associated with the MIA and will often come into the community to lend my assistance wherever it is needed. But the important thing is that you get behind the person who is elected president, and be as loyal to him as you have been to me. Indeed he will need more of your loyalty than I needed, because I started out with certain advantages that he will not have. When I became your president I did not have to create unity; you had already been brought together by the forces of history. And there was always the drama of the boycott which caused us to submerge our individual egoes in the greatness of the cause. But the new president will have neither this preexistent unity nor the powerful aid of a dramatic boycott. Therefore, he will need your backing and support at every point.[18] New divisive forces are at work in our community. In the mad quest to conquer us by dividing us they are working through some Negroes who will sell their race for a few dollars and cents. We must make it clear that we never intend to go back to the days when all of our efforts were paralyzed by the nagging virus of division. We never intend to go back to the days when the white community could pick our leaders for us and give them a few measly handouts to keep their mouths shut. We never intend to go back to the days when our children suffered discrimination because of our negligence, and our own lives were inflicted with a lack of self respect because of our complacency.

We have gone too far now to turn back. We owe it not only to this community, but to this nation and the world to keep the MIA a live and energetic organization.

I urge you above all to continue the struggle on the highest level of dignity and discipline. You have given to the world a marvelous demonstration of the power of nonviolence. Turn not your backs on this creative method. We must keep it at the center of this movement. The days ahead will be difficult. As victories for civil rights mount in the federal courts, the angry passions and deep prejudices of the diehards will be further aroused. These persons will do all within their power to provoke us and make us angry. But we must not retaliate with external physical violence or internal violence of spirit. We must not allow ourselves to become bitter. As we continue the struggle for our freedom we will be persecuted, abused and called bad names. But we must go on with the faith that unearned suffering is redemptive, and love is the most durable power in all the world. I am convinced that Jesus was right when he uttered in words lifted to cosmic proportions: "Love your enemies, bless them that curse you, pray for them that despitefully use you."[19]

---

18. On 31 January 1960, King formally announced Ralph Abernathy as the new president of the MIA (see King, Address Delivered during "A Salute to Dr. and Mrs. Martin Luther King" at Dexter Avenue Baptist Church, p. 354 in this volume).

19. Cf. Matthew 5:44.

This is a great hour for the Negro. To become the instruments of a great idea is a privilege that history gives only occasionally.[20] As I tried to say in Stride Toward Freedom: "It may even be possible for the Negro, through adherence to nonviolence, so to challenge the nations of the world that they will seriously seek an alternative to war and destruction. In a day when Sputniks and Explorers dash through outer space and guided ballistic missiles are carving highways of death through the stratosphere, nobody can win a war. Today the choice is no longer between violence and nonviolence. It is either nonviolence or nonexistence. The Negro may be God's appeal to this age—an age drifting rapidly to its doom. The eternal appeal takes the form of a warning: "All who take the sword will perish by the sword."[21]

And now let us go out looking to a future filled with vast possibilities. I know you are asking, when will that future fulfill itself? When will our suffering in this righteous struggle come to an end? When will the desolate valleys of oppression be transformed into sun lit paths of justice? When will the radiant star of hope be plunged against the nocturnal bosom of this lonely night, and plucked from weary souls the chains of fear and the manacles of death? I must confess that I cannot give you the exact date. But I have no doubt that the midnight of injustice will give way to the daybreak of freedom. My faith in the future does not grow out of a weak and uncertain thought. My faith grows out of a deep and patient trust in God who leaves us not alone in the struggle for righteousness, and whose matchless power is a fit contrast to the sordid weakness of man. I am certain of the future because:

> Mine eyes have seen the glory of the coming of the Lord;
> He is trampling out the vintage where the grapes of wrath are stored;
> He hath loosed the fateful lightening of His terrible swift sword:
> His truth is marching on.
> I have seen Him in the watch-fires of a hundred circling camps;
> They have builded Him an altar in the evening dews and damps;
> I can read His righteous sentence by the dim and flaring lamps;
> His day is marching on.
> He has sounded forth the trumpet that shall never call retreat;
> He is sifting out the hearts of men before His judgment seat:
> O be swift, my soul, to answer Him! Be jubilant, my feet!
> Our God is marching on.
>
> Refrain:
> Glory! Glory, Hallelujah! Glory! Glory, Hallelujah!
> Glory! Glory, Hallelujah! His truth is marching on.[22]

TAD. MLKP-MBU: Box 3.

---

20. In a 7 November 1957 address titled "Nonviolence and the Law," Harris Wofford used a similar phrase: "It is a privilege that history gives only occasionally for men to become the instruments of a great idea." King owned a typewritten copy of Wofford's address.

21. Cf. Matthew 26:52.

22. Julia Ward Howe, "The Battle Hymn of the Republic" (1862).

To Albert J. Luthuli

8 December 1959
[*Montgomery, Ala.*]

In a 10 October letter, G. McLeod Bryan conveyed African National Congress president Albert Lutuli's desire for copies of Stride Toward Freedom *to give to other anti-apartheid leaders.*[1] *King responds below, sending a copy of his book and expressing admiration for the South African leader: "I admire your great witness and your dedication to the cause of freedom and human dignity. . . . One day all of Africa will be proud of your achievements."*

Chief Luthuli
Groutville, Natal
SOUTH AFRICA

Dear Chief Luthuli:

My good friend Dr. McLeod Bryan wrote me the other day and said he had an opportunity to talk with you when he was in South Africa. He spoke of you in very glowing and warm terms. In fact, he said one of the greatest experiences he has had in all of Africa came when he spent those creative moments with you. May I say that I too have admired you tremendously from a distance. I only regret that circumstances and spacial divisions have made it impossible for us to meet. But I admire your great witness and your dedication to the cause of freedom and human dignity. You have stood amid persecution, abuse, and oppression with a dignity and calmness of spirit seldom paralleled in human history. One day all of Africa will be proud of your achievements.

Dr. Bryant mentioned to me that you are interested in having copies of my book, Stride Toward Freedom. I am sending you, under separate cover, one copy of my book, and if you are desirous of having additional copies please feel free to write me and I will be more than happy to send them.[2] I will appreciate knowing whether you receive this copy alright.

You have my prayers and best wishes in the days ahead.

---

1. See pp. 307–308 in this volume. In 1957 King served as a sponsor of the 10 December 1957 "Day of Protest" decrying the jailing of 156 South African political activists, including Lutuli (see King to Chester Bowles, 8 November 1957, in *Papers* 4:311–314). Albert John Mvumbi Lutuli (1898?–1967), born in Southern Rhodesia, graduated from South Africa's Adams College (1921) and taught there until 1935. He was chief of the Umvoti Reserve community near Groutville, South Africa. Lutuli was elected provincial executive secretary for the Natal branch of the African National Congress (ANC) in 1945 and became provincial president in 1951. The following year he assumed the presidency of the ANC, a position he held until his death. In 1960, he was awarded the Nobel Peace Prize for his anti-apartheid activism; he was the first African to receive the honor.

2. In March 1960, King asked his graduate school advisor L. Harold DeWolf for advice about delivering the books to ANC leaders and learned that "it would be impossible to get a shipment of books to [Lutuli] directly," as he had been arrested in a March 1960 state of emergency called by the South African government following the Sharpeville massacre (DeWolf to King and Coretta Scott King, 1 April 1960). Responding to DeWolf on 10 May, King concluded that "the South African situation is truly the most difficult in the world, and we must pray and hope that something will happen to bring the leaders to a reasonable position."

Very sincerely yours,
Martin L. King, Jr.

MLK:mlb

TLc. MLKP-MBU: Box 25.

To Deolinda Rodrigues

21 December 1959
[*Montgomery, Ala.*]

King responds to a 28 November letter from an Angolan student in Brazil who had written of her anticipated imprisonment upon her return home: "Of course, I hope to do my best while jailed and I need your advice about: if I say nothing about other Persons who have cooperated at Home for my Country, is it a sin? But I don't want portuguese to know about them. What do you think, Dr. King, please?"[1] *He advises Rodrigues against giving Angolan officials the names of her associates, reasoning that "such persons should be allowed to give themselves in." She replied on 30 December.*[2]

Miss Deolinda Rodrigues
Instituto Metodista
Caixa Postal 12.681
Santo Amaro-Sao Paulo
BRASIL

Dear Miss Rodrigues:

I am in receipt of your letter of recent date. Please excuse me for being rather slow in my reply. Absence from the city accounts for the delay.

You have a very difficult problem. It is not easy to decide whether to go to jail or seek asylum in some foreign embassy. However, we must realize that in the struggle for freedom and independence there must always be a willingness to sacrifice and suffer. You must decide whether your going back to prison will in some way serve to speed up the cause of independence for your country. If it does, then your going to prison will not be in vain. If it does not, I can see why you would seek refuge in a foreign embassy. I don't feel that you should tell the officials the names of persons who have been associated with you in the independence strug-

---

1. Rodrigues also wrote of her jailing that "it will be wonderful since it can help Angola and I have been wondering about the kind of tortures they have and use for 'political' Africans arrested." For their earlier correspondence, see King to Rodrigues, 21 July 1959, pp. 250–251 in this volume.

2. Rodrigues thanked King for his advice and told him that she would continue her studies in Brazil for two years instead of returning to Angola to face imprisonment (Rodrigues to King, 30 December 1959). Fearing deportation, Rodrigues left Brazil for the United States in February 1960. She later returned to work with Angolan refugees in Congo (Leopoldville) and was killed in 1967 while imprisoned by an opposing Angolan political group.

gle. Such persons should be allowed to give themselves in. I think it would be much better if it came from them rather than you. However, all of these are things that you must decide for yourself. I do hope that the best for your country will work out, and you certainly have my prayers and best wishes.

I am wondering if you have received my book, Stride Toward Freedom yet.[3] Please let me know so that I can be sure that you have it before you leave.

Very sincerely yours,
Martin L. King, Jr.

MLK:mlb

TLc. MLKP-MBU: Box 20.

3. In her 28 November letter, Rodrigues wrote that she did not want to be arrested before reading *Stride Toward Freedom.* After finally receiving a copy from King, she thanked him and noted the "wonderful lesson I have and am learning from your life and book" (Rodrigues to King, 29 February 1960).

To Ingeborg Teek-Frank

23 December 1959
[*Montgomery, Ala.*]

On 1 December Teek-Frank wrote King about her interest in Gandhian nonviolence and asked him for his opinion on whether China should be admitted to the United Nations.[1]

Mrs. Ingeborg Teek-Frank
30 Fifth Avenue
New York 11, New York

Dear Mrs. Frank:

This is just a note to acknowledge receipt of your letter of December 1. It is always good to hear from you. I am deeply grateful to you for enclosing a copy of Gandhi's Selected Letters.[2] You mentioned the book Gandhi's Letters to a Disciple. Unfortunately, I do not have a copy of this book and I would certainly ap-

1. Teek-Frank initiated correspondence with King after receiving a fund-raising letter he wrote on behalf of CORE (Teek-Frank to King, 2 November 1959). In 1971, the United Nations recognized the People's Republic of China as that nation's sole representative, displacing the anti-communist government in Taiwan. Ingeborg Teek-Frank (1918–) published several German-language books, including *Schriftwechsel mit beruhmten Personlichkeiten* (Correspondence with famous personalities).

2. Gandhi, *Selected Letters: First Series* (Ahmadabad: Navajivan Publishing House, 1949).

preciate it if you could find it for me.[3] I am happy to say that I have read most of Gandhi's works and I have most of them in my library.

Incidentally, I have written a book entitled <u>Stride Toward Freedom.</u> One of the chapters is devoted to my pilgrimage to nonviolence. Here I try to show the Gandhian influence in my thinking. I regret that I sent my last copy out a few days ago. If you are interested, however, you may secure a copy from Harper and Brothers. It was published in September, 1958. I will highly appreciate your comments.

In answer to your question concerning China, I definitely feel that it should be admitted to the United Nations. We will never have an effective United Nations so long as the largest nation in the world is not in it.

Thanks again for your kind letter, and I hope for you a joyous Christmas season and a blessed new year.

Yours very truly,
Martin L. King, Jr.

(Dictated, but not personally signed by Dr. King.)

TLc. MLKP-MBU: Box 72.

---

3. Gandhi, *Gandhi's Letters to a Disciple* (New York: Harper, 1950). In a 2 November 1960 letter to King, Teek-Frank indicated that she had learned that the book was out of print but offered to lend him her copy the next time he visited New York.

To Langston Hughes

29 December 1959
Montgomery, Ala.

King thanks Hughes for contributing a poem to A. Philip Randolph's upcoming birthday celebration.[1] In "Poem for a Man," Hughes wrote: "Poem for a man / Who plays the checkered game, / Of king jump king / And jumps a President. / That <u>order 8802</u> / For me and you."[2] Hughes replied on 18 January 1960.[3]

---

1. Stanley Levison forwarded Hughes's poem to King in a 22 December letter (for more on the Randolph tribute, see King, Outline, Remarks for "A Salute to A. Philip Randolph," 24 January 1960, p. 350 in this volume). James Mercer Langston Hughes (1902–1967), born in Joplin, Missouri, received a B.A. (1929) from Lincoln University. Hughes first received attention for his poem "The Negro Speaks of Rivers," which appeared in the NAACP's *Crisis* magazine in 1921. One of the leading figures of the Harlem Renaissance, Hughes published numerous books of poetry, fiction, and plays and wrote newspaper columns for the *Chicago Defender* and the *New York Post.*

2. Under pressure from Randolph, President Franklin D. Roosevelt signed Executive Order 8802 prohibiting racial discrimination in defense industries in 1941.

3. Hughes thanked King and sent a copy of "Prayer for the Mantle-Piece," an arietta from his work-in-progress opera titled "Five Wise, Five Foolish."

29 Dec 1959

Mr. Langston Hughes
20 East 127th Street
New York 35, New York

Dear Mr. Hughes:

I cannot say more to express both my appreciation of your poem to Phil Randolph and of your generosity in writing it, than to say it is just what I expected from you.

You have added another weapon of the pen to our struggle. We are sincerely sorry you cannot read it, but it will be delivered by Ossie Davis who, as you undoubtedly know, is currently starring in "A Raisin in the Sun."[4]

With warmest thanks and good wishes,

Sincerely yours,
[*signed*]
Martin L. King, Jr.

MLK:mlb

(Dictated, but not personally signed by Dr. King.)

THLS. JLHP-CtY-BR.

---

4. Lorraine Hansberry's 1959 Broadway play *A Raisin in the Sun* took its title from a line in Hughes's poem "Harlem" (1951).

Introduction to *Cracking the Color Line: Non-Violent Direct Action Methods of Eliminating Racial Discrimination*

[*1960*]
[*New York, N.Y.*]

In 1958 King wrote the foreword to a CORE pamphlet on school integration.[1] *The following year, CORE officials arranged for King, a member of the organization's advisory committee, to write this introduction to a follow-up booklet, detailing the group's activities and strategies for ending segregation.*[2]

I like what CORE is doing. The techniques so graphically described in "Cracking The Color Line" should be widely studied by all who work to achieve a just and democratic America. You—the people who carry on CORE action—realize the difficulty of achieving full integration and use brains and imagination as well as good-will, self-discipline and persistence.

I especially like the non-violent CORE approach. I cannot see how means can be separated from ends, how the process can be judged in one light, and the goal in another.

We can and must win the mind of the prejudiced person. Force doesn't change minds. Anger reinforces fears. And that is why it is so terribly urgent to work out the techniques of changing people's minds, of allaying their fears about integration.

CORE puts before people's eyes a new way of acting. You say and you show that feelings about segregation are silly, that customs can change without disaster following, and that this is the time to change them. And you proceed to demonstrate. Here is a method of achieving social change which we all may use.

[*signed*] Martin L. King Jr.
—Martin Luther King, Jr.

PDS. James Peck, *Cracking the Color Line: Non-Violent Direct Action Methods of Eliminating Racial Discrimination* (New York: CORE, ca. 1960).

1. King, Foreword to *A First Step Toward School Integration,* May 1958, in *Papers* 4:403–404.
2. In a 30 December 1959 letter, CORE executive secretary James R. Robinson enclosed the text of this introduction, thanked King for signing it, and assured him that it would "not be used for fund appeals" (King, Introduction, "Cracking the Color Line," 30 December 1959). King later allowed this text to be used as an endorsement letter to a foundation interested in underwriting the booklet's publication (Maude L. Ballou to Marvin Rich, 8 January 1960).

Outline, Remarks for "A Salute to A. Philip Randolph"

[*24 January 1960*]

During a Carnegie Hall birthday celebration for Randolph, King praised the black leader's refusal "to sell his race for a mess of pottage."[1] *This handwritten outline may have framed King's remarks, which directly preceded an address by Randolph announcing plans for protests at the Democratic and Republican national conventions.*[2]

1. He has always had the penetrating insight to dream when the time for a great idea had appeared
2. He has recognized the power of mass non-violent action
3. He has never been afraid to challenge an unjust state power speak out against the power structure
4. He is a symbol, dedicated and courageous leadership

AD. CKFC.

---

1. Louis E. Burnham, "The Spectator: One Man's Stature," *National Guardian*, 1 February 1960. In addition to remarks from Eleanor Roosevelt and Minnesota senator Hubert Humphrey, the audience heard a tribute to Randolph from President Eisenhower: "In this great unfinished business, your spirit and ability provide a major resource to your fellow men" (Eisenhower to Randolph, 18 January 1960). Entertainers Ossie Davis and Ruby Dee dramatized Randolph's life, and Juanita Hall sang selections from the hit musical "South Pacific" (Program, "Salute to A. Philip Randolph," 24 January 1960). As a member of the event's sponsoring committee, King thanked Roosevelt on 4 December 1959 for agreeing to attend: "Unquestionably your presence as America's First Citizen will heighten the significance of the occasion and serve to dramatize the profound meaning for all Americans of Mr. Randolph's dedicated decades of service."

2. "Pullman Union Leader Urges Negro Marches on Conventions," *New York Times*, 25 January 1960. For more on the protests, see King and Randolph, Statement Announcing the March on the Conventions Movement for Freedom Now, 9 June 1960, pp. 467–469 in this volume. The ideas outlined in this document correspond to those suggested in a 16 January telegram to King, probably sent by Bayard Rustin.

Address Delivered during "A Salute to Dr. and Mrs. Martin Luther King" at Dexter Avenue Baptist Church

31 Jan 1960

[*31 January 1960*]
Montgomery, Ala.

At the end of King's final day as Dexter's pastor, congregation members gathered in the sanctuary for a tribute and farewell. After an introductory statement from Board of Deacons vice chair William E. Anderson, church members performed a skit, "This is Your Life," that included roles for King's children and friends. His mother, sister, and brother traveled from Atlanta to surprise him and also participated in the sketch, which was modeled after the popular TV show of the same name.[1]

In his remarks, King thanks his parishioners and admits: "I have not been able to do all that I had hoped to do at Dexter. When I came here in 1954, I had a program that I put on paper, and I regret to say that much of that program is still on paper." Asking the congregation to pray for him and Coretta, King reflects on the increasing importance of a "personal God" in his life: "I have felt His power working in my life in so many instances, and I have felt an inner sense of calmness in dark and difficult situations, an inner strength that I never knew I had." The following transcript is drawn from an audio recording of the event.

Dr. Anderson and to the members of our family who have been gracious enough to surprise us this evening, at least surprise me, and to the beloved members and friends of the Dexter Avenue Baptist Church, I think Coretta has well stated what I need to say and what I would like to say: I have been deeply moved tonight.[2] Often in life, we have those moments, transfiguring moments, that we are able to rise above the dull monotony of sameness and the miasma of everyday life and experience those periods of unutterable joy. Such a moment and such a period we experience tonight. And I do not have words to thank you for this creative program that you have presented. I cannot claim to be worthy of such a tribute and such kind and gracious expressions, but I can assure you that these moments have strengthened me. And they will give me renewed courage and vigor to carry on in the struggle for freedom and human dignity.

As Coretta said to you, you have been amazingly patient in moments that I have not been able to be here. You have carried on, and you have not complained. And I must thank you once more for that. Then I want to thank the men who have worked and the women who have worked very closely with me and the official board, and the chairman of the Deacon's Board, Brother [*T. H.*] Randall. And to

1. Dexter Avenue Baptist Church, A Salute to Dr. and Mrs. Martin Luther King, Jr., 31 January 1960. Prior to the event, Anderson solicited telegrams from friends and associates that were bound in a book and presented to the Kings (Anderson, Memo to Eleanor Roosevelt, 13 January 1960).

2. In her remarks following the skit, Coretta expressed "deep and sincere appreciation" for the evening's program. She thanked the church members for the presentation of a silver service given to her by the church: "I never thought that I would own anything this fine."

all of the other associates: the vice chairman, Dr. Anderson; the clerk of the church, Brother [*R. D.*] Nesbitt; the choir director, Brother [*J. T.*] Brooks; the chairman of the finance committee, Brother [*F. W.*] Taylor; and the treasurer of the church, Brother [*J. H.*] Gilchrist; and the custodian, Brother [*William*] McGhee, and I could go on down the line. I just mention these names because I have worked very closely with them, members of the official board. And we have worked together for these five years as a unit. As I said to you this morning, I cannot remember one second of disharmony, one second of conflict that we've had, and I'm deeply grateful to all of these men.[3]

I should have mentioned also Professor [*Richmond*] Smiley, who is the chairman of the trustee board. And all of the heads of auxiliaries of our church: Mrs. [*Elizabeth M.*] Arrington, the head of our missionary society; Mrs. [*Louvenia*] Herring, the head of our Baptist Training Union; Brother J. T. Alexander, the head of the Sunday School; and all of the heads of month clubs and other organizations that I cannot pause to name at this time. But I'm sure you know that I'm deeply grateful to each of you for your cooperative spirits and the support that you have given me over these years.

Certainly, I have not been able to do all that I had hoped to do at Dexter. When I came here in 1954, I had a program that I put on paper, and I regret to say that much of that program is still on paper because, after I got here, I was still in the process of writing a dissertation, which took a great deal of my time, and you were gracious enough to allow me to do that and go back and forth to Boston.[4] And then, immediately after finishing my dissertation, our struggle started against the injustices and humiliating experiences that we had faced on the buses. And so this took my time. My duties overnight were multiplied, and it made it necessary, it became necessary for me to travel a good deal and to give a great deal of time to the community. And in the midst of all of this, you encouraged me and gave me great and lasting support. And then in those dark and desolate days when we experienced violence occasionally, living every day under the threat of death, you were always on hand, not only with your prayers but with your physical presence and with your support at every point. And so again, I want to thank you for that.

I could thank you also for the many things that you have given us along the way, the many gifts that you've given. All week long, we have been in the midst of affairs that were given by friends, and I will not take time to name them at this point. But I want all of you to know, all of those persons who entertained us all week long, we want you to know how grateful we are to you. I also want to say for the young lady who talked a few minutes ago that I'm so happy that, as a part of this tribute, you made it a joint one, for I know that I could not have done this job if

3. For more on King's morning sermon, "Lessons From History," see "Dexter Honors Dr. & Mrs. King!!" *Dexter Echo,* 3 February 1960, pp. 364–365 in this volume.

4. See King, "Recommendations to the Dexter Avenue Baptist Church for the Fiscal Year 1954–1955," 5 September 1954, in *Papers* 2:287–294. For King's dissertation, see King, "A Comparison of the Conceptions of God in the Thinking of Paul Tillich and Henry Nelson Wieman," 15 April 1955, in *Papers* 2:339–544.

I had not had Coretta behind me. She has given me words of encouragement when I needed them most, and she has presented a calm spirit in the most difficult and trying situations. A spirit that made it possible for me to stand up and made it possible for me to be calm. And that is why, when I wrote *Stride Toward Freedom,* and the publishers mentioned to me that "I'm sure you would want to dedicate this book to someone," I dedicated it to the person who has been closest to me. And I referred to her not only as my wife but as my coworker, for this is what she has been for these years that we have lived together. And I want to thank her publicly for that, and I'm always thanking her privately.

You see to my right a lot of people, and I could talk all night about them. There is the darling lady who brought me into the world. She is the sweetest lady in all the world, equal to Coretta King. [*laughter*] They are the two sweetest ladies in all the world. [*laughter*] But very seriously, my mother has been a great inspiration. Somebody tried to describe my personality at one time, and they said that I have something of the gentleness of my mother and the hard, courageous spirit of my father. This is what the French philosopher meant when he said that, "In order to do anything constructive, you must bear in your character antitheses strongly marked."[5] And so the gentle sweetness of my mother and the strong, hard, rough courage of my father; I hope one day that I will be able to attain and keep them in a sort of harmonious balance.

And then there is my darling sister who has been a real sister all across the years. You know her; she's been with us before. She has been here to sing for us with her beautiful voice. And as you know, she is on the faculty at Spelman College now. And she has a young man sitting here on the front who will confer the M.R.S. degree upon her in a few months. [*laughter*] And we are very happy to see Isaac along, also.[6]

And then there is my brother, my brother in the ministry and also my biological brother. There again we have had a wonderful, intimate family relationship. We have lived together as a family, and he was not kidding you when he said he has four children.[7] And I just discovered, A. D., that a fifth one is on the way. [*laughter*] You hadn't told me about it. Coretta was in Atlanta over the weekend, and she told me that A. D. and Naomi were expecting another baby, and they had hid this from me.[8] But one of the things that he said, and it's certainly true, that when he decided to go in the ministry and go back to Morehouse College—he's finished Morehouse now, and he's in the Interdenominational Theological Center in Atlanta—we said that we wanted him to be able to get to work and do the studying, and that as a family,

5. This statement, often attributed to French mathematician and theologian Blaise Pascal (1623–1662), mirrors lines from missionary E. Stanley Jones's book on Gandhi, a copy of which King owned: "A French philosopher once said that 'no man is strong unless he bears within his character antitheses strongly marked'" (Jones, *Mahatma Gandhi: An Interpretation,* p. 17).

6. In 1958, King's sister, Willie Christine, began teaching in the education department at Spelman. She married Isaac Newton Farris on 19 August 1960.

7. King refers to Alveda, Derek, Esther, and Alfred Daniel Williams King, Jr.

8. Vernon Christopher King was born on 6 September 1960.

31 Jan 1960

we didn't want him to have financial worries, that we would get together.[9] And there were no strings attached. He doesn't have to pay any of us back in doing nothing but being a good preacher, as he has already proven to be.

And then there are these two wonderful persons, my mother-in-law and my father-in-law.[10] You might not know the Scotts, but they are persons of great spirit. And it has been great to have them as a new mother and a new father. And I'm so happy that they came tonight, and I assure all of you that I knew nothing about it. [*laughter*]I went to hang my coat, try to get in my office, and they blocked me; they wouldn't let me go in the office. And I knew something, but I just assumed, I said maybe they have a gift in there and they don't want me to see it. So, I didn't know any of this was here. Nobody, they really kept this a secret. And even Coretta, who will share all of the intimate secrets of life with me, was able to hold this back. [*laughter*] And when a woman can hold a secret, it's a great secret. [*laughter*] So this was really a wonderful surprise to me.

And then my great friend and my brother, Ralph Abernathy. I will not leave Ralph because we will be together forever. He has been a great companion and a great associate. We have worked together across these years and have developed a relationship that nothing in all the world can separate. And although we will be separated by a few miles, just a hundred and seventy-five, we will still be working together. And I ask *you* tonight, and all of the people of Montgomery, to join Ralph Abernathy as the president of the Montgomery Improvement Association. He has already proven his ability as a leader; he has already proven his ability as a thinker; and he has already proven his ability as a detail worker and as a great administrator. And so Montgomery will not suffer at all. And I predict that under his leadership, Montgomery will grow to higher heights and new and creative things will be done. I hope that you will be able to find a pastor of this church who will join him and the movement in this city and will carry you on to higher heights and do many of the things that I wanted to do and that I couldn't do. I will be praying as I leave you, as you embark upon this serious and important responsibility of calling a pastor. And as I know Dexter, I know you will get a good one because you have proven your ability to do that across the years.[11]

I close now by saying that I solicit your prayers as we go to a new field of labor. I do not know what the future holds for us. When you move into another area, there is always an element of risk involved when you move to a new job. I only know that I'm trying to serve a call, being catapulted into the leadership of a movement that has profound implications for the growth and the development of our democracy. I do not intend to desert that call to that movement. I intend to stay with it until victory is won and until every black boy and black girl can walk the streets of Montgomery and the United States with dignity and

9. A. D. King earned a B.A. from Morehouse College in 1960.

10. King refers to Obie and Bernice Scott.

11. For more on Dexter's search for a new pastor, see King to Earl Wesley Lawson, 23 April 1960, pp. 441–442 in this volume.

honor, knowing that he's a child of the Almighty God and knowing that he has dignity and self-respect. It may not come in the next five years; I do not know. I hope it comes tomorrow morning by nine o'clock. But realism impels me to admit that there are still days of resistance ahead, difficult, dark days. I do not know what suffering we will have to go through. Some more bombings will occur, I'm sure. Some of us will have to go to jail some more. And I'm not so sure now that some of us may not have to pay the price of physical death, but I'm convinced that if physical death is the price that some must pay to free their children from a permanent life of psychological death, then nothing could be more Christian. And so let us go out with new and bold determination to make this old age—a new age.

As somebody has said, "I know not what the future holds, but I know who holds the future."[12] And I know this God enough to know that He's with us. I've come to believe in prayer stronger, stronger than ever before, since I've been in Montgomery. And I'm convinced that when we engage in prayer, we are not engaging in just the process of autosuggestion, just an endless soliloquy or a monologue, but we are engaged in a dialogue. And we are talking with a Father who is concerned about us. And I've come to believe that. Maybe this is rationalization. Maybe I have believed more in a personal God over these last few years because I needed Him. But I have felt His power working in my life in so many instances, and I have felt an inner sense of calmness in dark and difficult situations, an inner strength that I never knew I had. And so I say to you: continue to pray for us. And if we will take God with us, I know we will make it, no matter what comes.

In closing, I'd like to mention three other people. Names, it's always perilous to mention names. I could call all of the names here, but I do see three young ladies who have worked very closely with me over the last few years. They have worked with me in difficult periods, and they have proved their concern and loyalty. First is my personal secretary, Mrs. Maude Ballou, who has been a loyal secretary and who has worked long and difficult hours when I needed her most, and she has been a real associate and a real encouraging person in this total struggle. I'm happy to say that, for at least a period, Mr. [*Leonard*] Ballou has been gracious enough to release Mrs. Ballou to go to Atlanta to help us get adjusted. It's difficult to adjust to a new secretary, and I will have to be in the process of finding a new one, but she will be there for a few months with us. And then there is Mrs. [*Lillie*] Hunter, who has served as the church secretary, and as the church secretary she's had to work very closely with me. And, there again, she has been a very loyal worker, and I want to express my appreciation to her publicly. For you know, when you have to work with people like me, you have to have a lot of patience. And running all over the country and being in the midst of things all the time, you are always flying off and all that. People don't think I fly off, but I occasionally do. If you don't believe it, ask Mrs. Ballou and Mrs. Hunter. [*laughter*] And then,

12. Country and gospel singer Stuart Hamblen included this phrase in his hit song from the 1950s "Known Only to Him."

there is Mrs. Hazel Gregory, who is the secretary of the Montgomery Improvement Association and who also has been a very loyal worker in our association and with me. At times when Mrs. Ballou has been away on vacations and been out, she has worked with me, and she has never said, even though most of her work was to carry on work in the office of the MIA, that she was too busy to do something that I asked her to do. So, I'm grateful to these three ladies, and I'd like to ask them to stand so that everybody can see them. [*applause*] These are very wonderful ladies.

I could mention my biographer, but enough has been said about him, and it has been said well. I think we all know Lawrence D. Reddick. He's been a friend, not only to me and to Coretta, but to our total movement. And he is revealing that continual interest through his relationship with the Southern Christian Leadership Conference and through his relationship with Ralph as the new president of the Montgomery Improvement Association.

And let us never forget that behind Ralph is a strong, encouraging, fine wife. And that's our good friend Juanita, who just thought of the idea of giving something in our honor. And she had an affair at their home on Wednesday night and invited about eighteen of our most intimate friends. And there they gave us one of the most beautiful, useful gifts. And we can never totally thank Juanita for thinking of this idea. And Ralph admits that he didn't do any of the work to get it ready. She did all of it.

Finally, let me thank you for what you have already been thanked for. I, like Coretta, never knew and never thought that anything this fine and this beautiful [*laughter*], I don't know if you're supposed to, are you supposed to touch it? That's the, so beautiful that I'm afraid to touch it. [*laughter*] It's really, this is really wonderful. I don't know who conceived of the idea to have this as the gift, but it's something that will last through the generations. And even Yoki and Yoki's children [*laughter*] will, and Marty's children, will be able to look back across the years and think of Dexter as results of this beautiful gift, which we will take to Atlanta.[13] Now, I assure you that the house that we will be living in will in no way match and fit anything this beautiful; [*sustained laughter*] but it will really be something to point to. Thank you very much.

And may I say to you as I said to my fraternity brothers last night—Dr. [*R. D.*] Crockett was gracious enough, who's president of our fraternity, to have an affair in my honor where the brothers assembled at the home of Dr. [*J. Garrick*] Hardy.[14] Large numbers of them assembled and presented me a beautiful picture with a beautiful inscription there in beautiful words. And as I talked with them, I closed with these words: We must keep going in our struggle with the faith that God lives. And they that stand with Him stand in the glow of the world's bright tomorrows.

---

13. On behalf of the congregation, Elizabeth Arrington had presented King with an inscribed silver service and remarked: "May you find it useful and may it serve as a reminder of your years here as our pastor. And finally, and finally, may Yoki and her family have a service of it. And Marty may borrow it, if Yoki gives the consent. May God's richest blessings rest upon you and yours always."

14. King was a member of Alpha Phi Alpha.

And they that stand against Him stand in a tragic and an already-declared minority. This is our hope, and this is our witness.

31 Jan 1960

One or two other people that I should mention I think I forgot to mention Reverend B. J. Johnson. Is he still there? Yes. Of Atlanta, Georgia. His father pastors in Atlanta, and he is now pastoring.[15] He is a very good friend of our family and very good friend of my brother's, and he came down with him tonight. We're very happy to have all of these friends come and be with us, and God bless you.

And God grant that Dexter will continue to move on and go to higher heights. And one day, when you get tired of hearing good preaching and you want to hear a fellow still trying to learn how to preach, invite me back and I'll try to do it for you. [*sustained applause*]

[*congregation sings "Blessed Be the Tie That Binds"*]

At. MLKEC: ET-56.

15. B. Joseph Johnson, Jr. served as pastor of First Baptist Church in Clarkston, Georgia, and succeeded his father, B. Joseph Johnson, Sr. (1927–1977) as pastor of Greater Mt. Calvary Baptist Church. Johnson, Jr. was also an SCLC field secretary (1962–1971).

1 Feb 1960

Address Delivered at the Montgomery Improvement Association's "Testimonial of Love and Loyalty"

[*1 February 1960*]
Montgomery, Ala.

Shortly before King's departure to Atlanta, the MIA honored him and his family at Ralph Abernathy's First Baptist Church. The Kings were treated to music from at least ten local church choirs, expressions of support and appreciation from area clubs and businesses, and testimonials from several SCLC and MIA associates.[1] *Preceding her husband's address, Coretta King thanked the audience for inspiring her by their example: "For when I see you stand up with courage and face the things that you have had to face, it has given me courage to do my little bit." Looking forward to continuing the struggle in Atlanta, she surmises that "perhaps we will have some more bombing, but I don't mind that because I know that you will be behind us."*

In his remarks below, King thanks the crowd for the generous financial gift presented to his family but insists there is "no greater gift to be purchased than the gift of freedom." He immediately turns the money over to the treasurers of SCLC and the MIA and encourages them to "protest till all of your sons and daughters can walk the streets with dignity and honor knowing that they are children of almighty God." As the crowd's cheers build, King promises to return to Montgomery "if you want to boycott a little more," and he turns the presidency over to Abernathy. King urges the MIA to recognize that Abernathy won't have the same advantages he had enjoyed: "Martin Luther King didn't bring about the hour. Martin Luther King happened to be on the scene when the hour came." These remarks are drawn from an audio recording of the evening's proceedings.

Dr. Hubbard and my associates in the ministry and in the struggle for freedom, members and friends of the Montgomery Improvement Association. And first, I want to thank you for this generous contribution that you have so graciously given tonight.[2] And I say generous not because I know the amount, but I saw the box, and I noticed that the box was filled, and I noticed that in the envelopes dollars were present rather than coins. So I say that I thank you for the generous contribution. I know you want us to use this money to purchase some cherished gift that will be meaningful to us for years and years to come. And I know no greater gift to be purchased than the gift of freedom. [*Audience:*] (*Freedom*) Sometimes freedom has to be purchased through suffering. But I am convinced that freedom is not free, and if we are to achieve freedom in this nation, in general and this community in particular, we will have to give. I see sitting before me the financial sec-

1. Among those honoring King were Fred Shuttlesworth, C. K. Steele, and C. O. Simpkins representing SCLC, Solomon S. Seay and Ralph Abernathy from the MIA's executive board, and Robert D. Nesbitt of Dexter Avenue Baptist Church (MIA, Program, "A Testimonial of Love and Loyalty," 1 February 1960).

2. H. H. Hubbard, MIA treasurer and pastor of Bethel Baptist Church, presided over part of the evening's program and presented the financial gift to the Kings.

retary and treasurer of the Southern Christian Leadership Conference (*Amen*), an organization representing thousands and millions of people in eleven southern states. That person is the Reverend Ralph David Abernathy. (*Amen*) [*applause*] I see behind me [*applause*], I see behind me the treasurer of the organization that, to a large extent, gave impetus to the southern struggle and the Southern Christian Leadership Conference, namely the Montgomery Improvement Association. That is the Reverend Dr. H. H. Hubbard. (*Amen*) [*applause*] And so when the members of the finance committee come up tonight, I would like to ask them to turn that box over to Reverend Abernathy and to Reverend Hubbard, and every penny of this money will be divided between the Southern Christian Leadership Conference and the Montgomery Improvement Association. [*applause*] I understand that Reverend Hubbard has the money in his hands already, so we are very happy. (*He's got it*) [*laughter*] And I say that very seriously, I mean *every* penny of it (*Yes*) will go to the work of these organizations that are so close to my heart.

My friends, I have been deeply moved tonight, and I could stand here for a long, long time and thank you for these meaning-packed statements that have left me with unutterable gratitude. (*Yes, Lord*) But I'm not going to be here but just a few minutes, and I want to stand here and thank you not only for your words and your contributions tonight but for the inspiration that you have given me and my family over the years that we have struggled together. I will never forget Montgomery, for how can one forget a group of people who took their passionate yearnings and deep aspirations and filtered them into their own souls and fashioned them into a creative protest, which gave meaning to people and gave inspiration to individuals all over the nation and all over the world. I will forever forget the bright luminous witness of nonviolent resistance that you left shining not only in this community but for the whole nation to see. (*That's right*) Not only have I read about nonviolence, but I have been able to live it with you. (*Amen, Amen, Amen*) And I will take it wherever I go (*Amen*), for I'm still convinced that although we must work passionately and unrelentingly for first-class citizenship that we must never use second-class methods to gain it. (*That's right*) And I still go down the road of life believing, even though violence is often inflicted upon us and even though we are the recipients of abuses and persecution, that love is the only absolute and that it is the most durable power in all the world. (*Amen*) And I still believe that the most ardent segregationist can be transformed into a genuine integrationist. I believe that because I believe in the new birth (*Amen*) and because I believe in this way of love and nonviolence. (*Amen*) And so I would urge you, on the one hand, to continue protesting. Protest until the walls of segregation (*Yes*) have been finally crushed by the battering rams of surging justice. Protest (*Amen, All right, That's right*) until all of the segregation in parks, all of the segregation in the airport, all of the segregation in the public schools of Montgomery will have passed away.[3] (*Yeah*) Protest

3. One month after King's departure, Abernathy and MIA secretary Robert DuBose led a march from Dexter Church to the state capitol protesting the expulsion of several black student protesters at Alabama State. The 750 marchers were forced to retreat back to Dexter when more than four hundred police, some on horseback, and an estimated five thousand white demonstrators blocked streets around the church ("Police Thwart Negro Services at Capitol," *Montgomery Advertiser,* 7 March 1960). For more on these events in Montgomery, see King to Eisenhower, 9 March 1960, pp. 385–387 in this volume.

(*Protest*) till all of your sons and daughters can walk the streets with dignity and honor (*Well*), knowing that they are children of almighty God, knowing that they are made in His image (*Yeah*), knowing that every man from a bass black to a treble white is significant on God's keyboard. [*applause*] (*Go ahead*)

But there is another side to this coin and that is reconciliation. (*Yeah, That's right*) And so not only must we protest, but I urge you to continue to follow the path of reconciliation as you protest (*Yeah*), for our aim must never be to defeat or to humiliate the white man. No matter what he says about us, no matter if he misunderstands us, no matter if he bombs us, no matter what he does to us, our aim must never be to defeat him or to humiliate him, but to win his friendship and understanding. (*Yeah*) And this is the end which we seek. [*applause*] We might have to boycott in Montgomery some more. (*Yeah*) And if you want to boycott a little more, I will certainly be willing to come down and help you. [*applause*] And may I say to you that as we boycott (*Yeah*), let us remember that a boycott is not an end within itself. A boycott is merely a means through which we seek to awaken a sense of shame in the opponent (*Yeah*) and to lift him to a new level of his own humanity. But the end which we seek is reconciliation. The end which we seek is the creation of the beloved community. The end which we seek to create is a society in which all men will be able to live together as brothers and respect the dignity and worth of all human personality. And finally I say to you that you will not be able to protest or to follow the path of reconciliation unless you get behind the leadership of the community and follow that leadership. (*That's right*) Let nobody fool you. Without this unity between leaders and followers, we will not be able to do the job. (*Well*)

And I've listened to all of your kind and marvelous expressions tonight. But I want to say to you that the new president of the Montgomery Improvement Association will not have some of the advantages that I had, not because he doesn't have the ability, for I know him and I know that he has great ability. But you must remember that I came to Montgomery when the hour was here (*Yeah*), and when the hour comes (*Yeah*), nothing can stop it (*Amen*) [*applause*] when the hour comes. [*applause*] (*That's right*) And so although you've been kind enough to say nice things about me, Martin Luther King didn't bring about the hour. (*Amen*) Martin Luther King happened to be on the scene (*Amen*) when the hour came. (*All right, All right*) And you see my friends [*applause*], when the hour comes (*All right*) you are just projected into a symbolic structure. (*That's right, That's right*) And even if Martin Luther King had not come to Montgomery, the hour was here. (*Yeah*) This was what the Old, the New Testament referred to as the *kairos* in the Greek language. (*Yeah*) It talked about it as the fullness of time. (*Amen, All right*) [*laughter*] And there are times in history (*Well*) that we face the fullness of time, when history is pregnant (*Yes*), ready to give birth to a great idea and a great movement. (*Yeah*) On December the fifth, nineteen-fifty-five we experienced the *kairos* (*Yeah*), the fullness of time. (*Well*) And Martin Luther King just happened to been here. (*Yeah*) And so there was a preexisting unity that Martin Luther King didn't create. [*laughter*] It was created by the fullness of time. (*Yeah*) [*laughter*] There was a preexisting unity here (*Yes*) that caused you to substitute tired feet for tired souls (*Yes, All right*) and walk the streets of Montgomery (*Yeah*) until segregation (*Well*) had to fall before the great and courageous witness (*Yeah*) of a marvelous people. (*Yes, Amen*)

Therefore, I say to you that the new president will not have these advantages. And I say to you that you must get behind him (*Oh yes*) and give him that unity (*Yes*) and give him that support and that following which will make for a great movement. (*Yes, Well*) Montgomery is fortunate to have Ralph Abernathy. (*Amen*) [*applause*] (*Amen*) Ralph Abernathy [*applause*], Ralph Abernathy is a great soul. (*Yes*) And I can say that because I think I know him better than anybody in here but Juanita [*Abernathy*]. (*Amen*) He's a great soul. (*Amen*) And not only that, Ralph Abernathy is a man of great ability. (*That's right*) Ralph Abernathy has proved his administrative ability. I have worked very closely with him not only in the Montgomery Improvement Association but in the Southern Christian Leadership Conference. And since he's been executive, I mean secretary, financial secretary-treasurer of the Southern Christian Leadership Conference, he has handled thousands and thousands of dollars. (*Yes*) And I have looked at the honesty and the accuracy which he's kept the records. (*Yes*) Not only, I say, is he a great soul, but he has great ability. (*Yes*) And I urge you to get behind him. Give him your backing, give him your support and so that he will be able to do this job (*Yes*) which is ahead.

1 Feb 1960

It gives me great pleasure at this time, before presenting him to you, to present the other leaders, the other officers of the Montgomery Improvement Association. And in presenting them as they come forward, I say to you that although we are moving to Atlanta, Georgia, we are not moving from Montgomery. [*applause*] We are going [*applause*], we are going to a broader base to have more time and a better location to give to the total southern struggle, but I'm happy that the Montgomery Improvement Association saw fit to keep me a member of the executive board.[4] [*applause*] And if I don't get to twelve board meetings a year, I will, at least, get to six of them. (*Yeah*) [*applause*] So that I'll be here. [*applause*] And I want you to know that we will be remembering you, and we will be thinking about you. (*Yes*) And, as my wife said, when you come through Atlanta, we will be looking for you. (*Yes, Lord*)

First, I want to present to you a man who has been with us since the beginning of our struggle. He is a man who's always on hand to give whatever he can give so that we can carry on. I have enjoyed working with him. I have enjoyed his companionship. He is the Reverend H. J. Palmer, who is the chaplain of the Montgomery Improvement Association. (*All right*) Give him a hand. [*applause*]

The next man is a man that we all love. He has given dignity to our movement, and he has worked assiduously to keep things going on so many levels. Since he is older than I am in age, on the one hand, I have considered him a father, but since he's such a gracious companion I also consider him a brother. And that is the treasurer of the Montgomery Improvement Association, Dr. H. H. Hubbard. [*applause*]

Sometimes you don't hear about some of the people who are in our struggle as much as you hear about others because these are the people who work in the background, and they do a lot of the day-to-day work that must be done. And I'm thinking of a lady who was with us when we organized on December the fifth, and

---

4. The evening's program listed King as a member of the MIA's executive board; he was reelected to a three-year term (Ralph Abernathy, Form letter to Friend, 30 December 1960).

a lady who's been with us ever since, keeping the records, on hand in every meeting. (*Yes*) And she's done it, not because there was any tremendous salary involved in it because it's nothing, but she's done it because of her dedication to the work of the Montgomery Improvement Association. And one of the things I like about her is that, even if we differ on a point, she certainly isn't a fighter; when the majority rules, she follows the majority. (*Amen*) And she has been a wonderful person to work with. I refer to you, I mention, I refer, rather, to Mrs. Erna Dungee, the wife of a prominent physician in our community and the person who is the financial secretary of this association and who has been reelected for this year.[5] Erna's back in the back if we can all see her. [*applause*]

There is another person that I would like to introduce to you. He, too, has been a very loyal supporter. He was not in Montgomery when we started; he was pastoring in Tuskegee. But when he came to this community, he started working just as he had been here all of the years. And he's gotten into our hearts, into the hearts of the members of the executive board, and I have greatly appreciated his commitment and his stick-to-itness, his willingness to stick to a job until it is completed. He is a person that we all love and admire, Father Robert E. DuBose [*applause*], who is our new secretary. [*applause*] He is the new secretary of the Montgomery Improvement Association.

There is another young man whom I consider a personal friend. I would like to tell you a little secret. A few weeks ago I started thinking about this young man, and he was in our home, in the parsonage. And I told him I wanted, that I wanted to talk with him about something very seriously. I had mentioned this to the nominating committee. I said I feel that you should be one of the vice presidents of the Montgomery Improvement Association because I have seen something within you. I have noticed your ability, not only as a physician, but your ability to work with people. And not only that, I have followed your dedication, and in the midst of your busy schedule you take time to come to our mass meetings, Monday after Monday. And I said, "I believe you can give something to the MIA that it needs at this hour along with the other dynamic leadership." And he said, "I can't do that." He said, "I just can't do it. You need a person as vice president who can talk and who can make a good speech and who can move the people." And when I heard him speaking tonight I said to myself, he certainly didn't know what he was talking about. [*laughter*] And he was either telling an untruth. (*That's right*) Because I can agree, I think you can agree with me (*Yeah*), that he made a sincere, a thought-provoking (*That's right*), and a well-stated speech. I refer to Dr. Jefferson Underwood [*sustained applause*], who is the second vice president [*applause*], the second vice president [*applause*] of the Montgomery Improvement Association.

There is another man. He has been with us from the beginning. I think I said in *Stride Toward Freedom* that one of the things I like about him is that he is always calm (*That's right*) and that he is a man of deep convictions and sober thoughts. And whenever this man speaks, I pause to listen because he has something to say, he knows how to say it (*Amen*), and he's always thinking (*Yes*) in terms of the total situation. And I would like to present to you now the first vice president of the

---

5. King refers to Dungee's husband, Dr. A. C. Dungee.

Montgomery Improvement Association, the Reverend Dr. W. J. Powell, a minister of the Old Ship AME Zion Church.[6] [*applause*]

And finally, I would like to ask my brother. Last night, my church gave a program I guess entitled "This is Your Life," a beautiful program, as a testimonial for our family. And they really surprised me; they had my mother here, my sister, my brother. And they had been in town all day, and I didn't know a thing about it. [*laughter*] But I say that only to say that my brother was here, Alfred Daniel King, whom I love. But the man that I'm about to present now is a man that I love as much as I love A. D. King, for he too has been a real brother. (*Yeah*) Not only has he been a brother in Christ, but he's been a true brother in all of the situations and all of the struggles of life. And it gives me great pleasure to take this, which is a symbol of the leadership, which is a symbol of the authority, of the presidency (*Amen*) of the Montgomery Improvement Association, and I take great pleasure now in turning it over (*Yes*) to one who is able to do the job. (*Amen*) And as John the Baptist said [*applause*], and I hand it over by saying sincerely as John the Baptist said on the coming of Jesus, "I must decrease in order that he may increase."[7] (*Amen*) God bless you, Ralph. [*applause*]

At. MLKEC: ET-53, ET-54.

---

6. In *Stride Toward Freedom*, King characterized Powell as having a "cool head and an even temper" (p. 73).

7. Cf. John 3:30. Accepting the MIA gavel from King, Abernathy declared, "Definitely, I am not Martin Luther King." He promised that he would lead the MIA to the best of his ability. Identifying police brutality, school upkeep, and integration of public facilities as top priorities, the new MIA president promised ultimate victory (Ralph Abernathy, "Inaugural statement upon assumption of the presidency of the MIA," 1 February 1960).

To Martin Luther King, Sr.

1 February 1960
[*Montgomery, Ala.*]

King writes his father in preparation for his first sermon as co-pastor at Ebenezer. On 7 February, a standing-room-only crowd filled the sanctuary and overflowed into the basement where loudspeakers had been set up for King's return to the church in which he had grown up.[1] *Preaching "Three Dimensions of a Complete Life," King reportedly explained that "many of today's problems are because our white brothers*

---

1. King's father introduced him as "a grown man, whose decisions have been respected the world over" and remarked: "We can't look on him as little M. L. now. To all of us he is now Dr. Martin Luther King, Jr." (Paul Delaney, "'Follow Way of Love,' Dr. King Asks People," *Atlanta Daily World*, 9 February 1960).

are only concerned with the length of life—their preferred economical position, their social status, their political power and their so-called 'way of life.'"[2]

Rev. M. L. King, Sr.
The Ebenezer Baptist Church
407 Auburn Avenue, N.E.
Atlanta, Georgia

Dear Dad:

Enclosed is a biographical sketch which Esther can use in preparing her article for my first sermon as new Co-Pastor of Ebenezer Baptist Church on Sunday.[3] Tell her to feel free to use as much of this material as she desires. You may request Scott to put the article in a prominent place. It may be better to put the longer article with the picture in the Thursday or Friday paper and then have another short notice in the Saturday paper.[4]

I will look forward to seeing you Thursday.

Very sincerely,
M. L.

Enc.
MLK:mlb

TLc. MLKP-MBU: Box 24.

---

2. Delaney, "'Follow Way of Love,' Dr. King Asks People." King delivered similar sermons in January and February (Harvard University Memorial Church, Program, "Order of worship," 10 January 1960, and King, "The Three Dimensions of a Complete Life," Sermon delivered at Friendship Baptist Church, 28 February 1960; see also "The Three Dimensions of a Complete Life," Sermon Delivered at the Unitarian Church of Germantown, 11 December 1960, pp. 571–579 in this volume).

3. King may refer to Esther M. Smith, Ebenezer's Social Action Committee chair and director of Christian Education.

4. C. A. Scott, editor and publisher of the *Atlanta Daily World,* was a member of Ebenezer's congregation. An article announcing King's return to Ebenezer appeared in the paper the day before his Sunday sermon ("Dr. M. L. King Jr. Preaches at Ebenezer Church Sunday," *Atlanta Daily World,* 6 February 1960).

"Dexter Honors Dr. & Mrs. King!!"

3 February 1960
Montgomery, Ala.

The Dexter Echo *recounts King's final sermon as pastor.*

Sunday, January 31, 1960 was a great day in Dexter! It was the final official day for Dr Martin Luther King as Minister. And a glorious occasion it was—beginning at the morning worship hour and continuing through the evening hour featuring "A SALUTE TO DR & MRS MARTIN LUTHER KING, Jr, a joint production from the matchless pens of Dr W E Anderson and Mrs Mary Fair Burks and followed by a fellowship dinner in our dining room directed by our social committee headed by Mrs F W Taylor, SR.[1]

At the morning hour, Dr King spoke to a capacity audience which filled the balcony and all extra chairs which could be placed in the auditorium. Using as his Scriptural reference St Luke 12:54–56, Dr King chose as the subject of his final message "Lessons from History."[2] One of the unique aspects of mankind, stated he, is that man has a history and can comprehend history. Lower animals, caught in the clutches of the moment, have no yesterdays and no tomorrows. On the other hand, man has yesterdays and therefore a tomorrow—he can commune with the past and think on the future. One of the great tragedies of our times, however, is the fact that too often man does not make use of this unique ability with which he is endowed.

He listed three lessons to be learned from history: (1) He who oppresses another will ultimately be cut down as a result of such oppression. No oppressor, he stated, can permanently survive. In this connection, he listed as examples France under the Louises, England, Germany under Hitler, and America with her problems of discrimination and segregation.

(2) Militarism is ultimately suicidal. Referring to militarism as 'the twin of imperialism', Dr King used Napoleon to show that military genius is not the answer and declared that he who lives by the sword shall die by the sword.

(3) A great creative idea whose time has come can not be stopped. The quest for human freedom and dignity is the great idea of this day, stated he; and the quest is evident whether in Accra, Johannesburg, Berlin, New York, of Montgomery. He declared that whenever the secular superstructure is cut off from its moral and spiritual foundation, disintegration sets in—whether in society or whether in individual life. The man who allows PRELIMINARY concerns to take precedence over ULTIMATE concerns is doomed. Man must live by the WITHIN as well as by the WITHOUT. Whenever STRUCTURE absorbs DESTINY, we are in chaos. He reiterated his worry about America and her practical atheism—where we deny by our lives the very existence of God and where the materialistic is what is important. [*The article continued with excerpts from Anderson's remarks at the church tribute to the Kings*]

TD. *Dexter Echo,* 3 February 1960, DABCC.

1. Anderson was vice chair of the church's Board of Deacons. Burks was chair of Dexter's Social-Political Action Committee. Cleonia K. Taylor served as chair of the Courtesy Committee, and her husband, Franklyn W. Taylor, was the chair of Dexter's Finance Committee.

2. Luke 12:54–56: "And he said also to the people, When ye see a cloud rise out of the west, straightway ye say, There cometh a shower; and so it is. And when ye see the south wind blow, ye say, There will be heat; and it cometh to pass. Ye hypocrites, ye can discern the face of the sky and of the earth; but how is it that ye do not discern this time?"

From Roy Wilkins

8 February 1960
New York, N.Y.

Wilkins thanks King for participating in the 13–14 January Leadership Conference on Civil Rights meeting with congressional leaders regarding pending civil rights legislation.[1]

Reverend Martin Luther King
Montgomery Improvement Association
530-C South Union Street
Montgomery, Alabama

Dear Martin:

This is a somewhat delayed word of personal thanks for the enormous help you gave to the cause of civil rights legislation by your participation last month in our conferences with the congressional leadership I have wanted for some time to say this, but the heavy duties attendant upon the legislative battle have been overwhelming.

The delay has at least made it possible to witness the concrete evidence that our joint activity has had valuable results. At the time we journeyed to Washington everyone was painfully conscious of the low level of public awareness of, and involvement in, the civil rights legislative effort. Bulding upon our conferences and on the widespread stimulus provided thereby to our respective organizations, a highly encouraging response has been developed from the grass-roots. We are sparing no effort to see to it that this response continues to expand so that the pressure of public opinion will be manifest to all members of Congress until the job is properly done.

I hope to be able to inform you from time to time of the situation as it unfolds. The action this week by the House Rules Committee is only the first step in what we hope will be a major victory.[2]

---

1. Wilkins invited King to the meeting in an 18 December telegram, stating that the Washington meeting would be "confined to top leaders." Civil rights proponents met with Senate Majority Leader Lyndon B. Johnson (D-Texas), Senate Minority Leader Everett Dirksen (R-Ill.), House Speaker Sam Rayburn (D-Texas), House Majority Leader John McCormack (D-Mass.), and House Minority Leader Charles Halleck (R-Ind.). Other participants included officials from the National Urban League, Brotherhood of Sleeping Car Porters, American Jewish Congress, National Council of Negro Women, Women's International League for Peace and Freedom, Japanese American Citizens League, American Civil Liberties Union (ACLU), and the United Auto Workers (UAW) ("Participants in civil rights legislative conference," 13 January–14 January 1960, and "Rights Bloc Fails to End Deadlock," *New York Times,* 15 January 1960).

2. A civil rights bill had languished in committee since August 1959. On 1 February 1960 the House Rules Committee voted to act on the pending legislation after 190 members of Congress petitioned to release the measure. The committee sent the civil rights legislation to the floor on 18 February with a seven-to-four vote. For more on the bill's progress, see Jacob K. Javits to King, 21 April 1960, pp. 439–440 in this volume.

Very sincerely yours,
[*signed*]
Roy Wilkins
Chairman

Rw:erb

TLS. MLKP-MBU: Box 64A.

"A Creative Protest"

16 February 1960
Durham, N.C.

On 1 February four black college students in Greensboro, North Carolina, took seats at the F. W. Woolworth lunch counter.[1] *Refused service on the basis of a custom that reserved seats for white patrons, the students continued to sit at the counter until closing time. Within a week, several hundred Greensboro-area students were participating in sitdown demonstrations, which had expanded to another downtown store. This tactic rapidly spread across North Carolina and into other southern states, and the Woolworth chain faced picketing at their northern stores.*

In the midst of the swelling movement, Durham minister and SCLC board member Douglas Moore telephoned King and invited him to speak with students involved in the protest.[2] *On 16 February, King and Abernathy toured downtown Durham lunch counters that had closed the previous week as a result of the demonstrations.*[3] *King's address to a large rally that evening at White Rock Baptist Church was later printed as this pamphlet.*[4] *Pledging SCLC's full support, he advises the students to remain nonviolent and accept jail willingly: "Let us not fear going to jail. If the officials threaten to arrest us for standing up for our rights, we must answer by saying that we are willing and prepared to fill up the jails of the South." Commenting on this new dimension of the southern struggle, King observes: "What is fresh, what is new in your fight is the fact that it was initiated, fed and*

1. The four protesters were North Carolina A&T College students David Richmond, Joseph McNeil, Franklin McCain, and Ezell Blair, Jr. Two years earlier Blair had attended a King speech at Bennett College in Greensboro (Jibreel Khazan [Ezell Blair, Jr.], Interview by William H. Chafe, 27 November 1974; see also Introduction in *Papers* 4:38).

2. Moore, Interview by Robert Wright, 12 December 1968. Moore later asked King to write to students arrested at a lunch counter protest in Raleigh and suggested a "non-violent workshop for students for either the easter weekend or at the close of school" (Moore to King, 18 February 1960). Moore had also corresponded with King during the Montgomery bus boycott (see Moore to King, 3 October 1956, in *Papers* 3:393–397).

3. A scuffle broke out when Woolworth employees and local police tried to prevent news photographers from taking pictures of King in the store ("Negro Told Not to Fear Jail Terms," *Greensboro Daily News*, 17 February 1960).

4. Prior to his address, King met with students to discuss techniques of nonviolence. A student spokesman indicated that a "coordinating council" had been organized for the demonstrations ("Negro Told Not to Fear Jail Terms").

sustained by students. What is new is that American students have come of age."[5]

Victor Hugo once said that there is nothing in all the world more powerful than an idea whose time has come.[6] The dynamic idea whose time has come today is the quest for freedom and human dignity. Men are tired of being trampled over by the iron feet of oppression. They are tired of being plunged into the abyss of exploitation where they experience the bleakness of nagging despair. And so all over the world formerly oppressed people are making it palpably clear that they are determined to be free.

You students of North Carolina have captured this dynamic idea in a marvelous manner. You have taken the undying and passionate yearning for freedom and filtered it in your own soul and fashioned it into a creative protest that is destined to be one of the glowing epics of our time. For the past few days, you have moved in a uniquely, meaningful orbit imparting heat and light to distant satellites.

In this period when civil rights legislation hangs in an uncertain balance in the congress—when the recalcitrance of some public officials in the South instills us with frustration and despondency, the spectacular example of determined and dedicated young people demanding their rights gives glorious inspiration to all decent persons not only of our nation, but throughout the world. You have taken hold of the tradition of resolute non-violent resistance and you are carrying it forward toward the end of bringing all of us closer to the day of full freedom.

In my recent travels in Africa and Asia, I was struck by the youthfulness of the leaders in the struggle for liberation and by the immensely responsible role of students. What is fresh, what is new in your fight is the fact that it was initiated, fed and sustained by students. What is new is that American students have come of age. You now take your honored places in the world-wide struggle for freedom.

This creative protest against segregated eating facilities again highlights the fact that segregation is the Negro's burden and America's shame.

You have given an additional death blow to the once prevalent idea that the Negro prefers segregation. You have also made it clear that we will not be satisfied with token integration, for token integration is nothing but a new form of discrimination covered up with certain niceties of complexity. Separate facilities, whether in eating places or public schools, are inherently unequal. The underlying philosophies of segregation are diametrically opposed to democracy and Christianity, and all the dialectics of all the logicians of the world cannot make them lie down together.

So, I would call upon all of the people of goodwill in this community to support the efforts of these students. I would also call upon the white people of this

5. At a press conference earlier that day, King refrained from predicting how long the protests would last and asserted that "the continued existence of segregation in any form in North Carolina and the United States can have a much more devastating effect than the sitdowns" ("Negro Told Not to Fear Jail Terms").

6. Hugo, *The History of a Crime: Deposition of a Witness* (New York: P. F. Collier & Son, 1877), p. 429.

State to back-up the marvelous protest of these students. What they are doing is significant not only for North Carolina, not only for the Negro, but for the whole of America.

I'm convinced more white people must join the movement against segregation in this country. The tensions in race relations in the United States today are not tensions between white and black people; they are tensions between justice and injustice, between light and darkness. If there is a victory, it will not be for just seventeen million Negroes; it will be a victory for justice, democracy and freedom. The festering sore of segregation debilitates the white man as well as the Negro. So long as America is burdened down with the ugly weight of segregation, she cannot expect to have the respect of the peoples of the world. Indeed the shape of the world today does not permit us the luxury of an anemic democracy. America must either achieve racial justice or face the ultimate social psychosis that can lead to domestic suicide.

May I say to you as you continue your protest, you will confront moments of difficulty. But let us realize that no great and lasting gain comes in history without suffering and sacrifice. I have prayed much over our Southern situation, and I have come to the conclusion that we are in for a season of suffering. Now I pray that, recognizing the necessity of suffering, the Negro will make of it a virtue. To suffer in a righteous cause is to grow to our humanity's full stature. If only to save ourselves from bitterness, we need the vision to see the ordeals of this generation as an opportunity to transfigure ourselves and American society. Let us not fear going to jail. If the officials threaten to arrest us for standing up for our rights, we must answer by saying that we are willing and prepared to fill up the jails of the South. Maybe it will take this willingness to stay in jail to arouse the dozing conscience of our nation.

May I also urge you to continue the struggle on the highest level of dignity. You have rightly chosen to follow the path of non-violence. As we protest, our ultimate aim is not to defeat or humiliate the white man but to win his friendship and understanding. We have a moral obligation to remind him that segregation is wrong. Let us protest with the ultimate aim of being reconciled with our white brothers. As we sit down quietly to request a cup of coffee, let us not forget to drink from that invisible cup of love, which can change a segregationist into an integrationist. Let us keep our eyes on the end we seek, but let us never forget the significance of proper means. There is a success of history and a success of eternity. Right methods to achieve a right objective is itself a coming together of history and eternity, and where one uses right methods there is, even if obscured in history, a spiritual victory. Let us avoid not only external physical violence but also internal violence of the spirit. We can build an empire depending on Love. In that way, we may be able to not only teach ourselves something, but we may be able also to teach others something. The choice is no longer between violence and non-violence; it is between violence and non-existence. All the darkness in the world cannot obscure the light of a single candle.

And so I would urge you to continue your just struggle until the people with whom you trade will respect your person as much as they respect your dollar. May I assure you that you have the full weight of the Southern Christian Leadership Conference behind you in your struggle. At a certain point in every struggle of great importance, a moment of doubt or hesitation develops. Some voices declare,

"Let us stop here, we have gone far enough." We confronted this crisis in Montgomery—we had these doubts. Despite the debates, the confusion and the uncertainty we carried on. If there is one lesson experience taught us which I would hope to leave with you, it is that when you have found by the help of God a correct course, a morally sound objective, you do not equivocate, you do not retreat—you struggle to win a victory.

Let nobody stop you; you are doing something that will ultimately save the soul of America. If you continue to struggle, there will be a new day in America.

We're not rabble rousers; we're not dangerous agitators, nor do we seek political dominance. Black supremacy is as bad as white supremacy. But freedom is necessary for one's selfhood, for one's intrinsic worth. Let us say to the white people, we're not going to take bombs into your communities. We will not do anything to destroy you physically. We will not turn to some foreign ideology. Communism has never invaded our ranks. We've been loyal to America. Now we want to be free.

And remember that both history and destiny are on your side. All the stars in their course are supporting you. Go out with the attitude that God is with us and we have cosmic companionship. And one day, historians of this era might be able to say, there lived a great people, a black people who injected new meaning into civilization.[7]

PD. MLKJP-GAMK.

---

7. King echoes a statement he made in his address at the first mass meeting during the Montgomery bus boycott (MIA Mass Meeting at Holt Street Baptist Church, 5 December 1955, in *Papers* 3:74).

Interview on Arrest following Indictment by Grand Jury of Montgomery County

[17 February 1960]
[Atlanta, Ga.]

Upon King's return from North Carolina, two Fulton County sheriff deputies appeared at his Ebenezer office and took him into custody on the afternoon of 17 February. A grand jury in Alabama had issued a warrant for his arrest on two counts of felony perjury for signing fraudulent tax returns for 1956 and 1958.[1] *Accompanied to*

---

1. The Montgomery County Grand Jury handed down the indictments on 12 February after state tax officials had conducted an audit of King's tax records (Indictment, *State of Alabama v. Martin Luther King, Jr.*, 12 February 1960). In a typed statement of the same date as this interview, King voiced his frustration at the tendency in the South "to misrepresent and frustrate the moves of persons working to achieve the ideal of freedom and brotherhood" (King, Statement on indictment by grand jury of Montgomery County, 17 February 1960).

the Fulton County courthouse by his father and brother, King was arraigned and released on $2,000 bond.[2] *In the WSB-TV film footage from which this interview fragment was taken, King responds to the questions of a male reporter who remains off-camera.*[3]

[*King*]: No, I didn't have the slightest idea that I would be arrested today. I had no idea that the grand jury would indict me. I have always said that if it is necessary for us to go to jail in the midst of this struggle we should do it willingly and we should do it with love in our hearts. And maybe through our willingness to suffer and accept this type of sacrifice we will be able to arouse and awaken the dozing conscience of many citizens of our nation.

[*Interviewer*]: You spoke in Durham, North Carolina, and said at that time that the Negro should be willing to go to jail, if necessary, to support his cause.[4] Had you [*recording interrupted*] that you would be arrested? What do you believe lies at the root of the indictment against you?

[*King*]: Well, I feel that it is just a new attempt on the part of the state of Alabama to harass me for the role that I have played in the civil rights struggle. This seems to be a pattern in many areas of the South now as evidenced by the fact that the Highlander Folk School was closed a few days ago by an order, a court order.[5] It seems to be a pattern to harass individuals working in the area of freedom and integration and brotherhood.

[*Interviewer*]: Are you ever afraid?

[*King*]: Well, I wouldn't say that I have totally risen above the shackles of fear, but I live every day under the threat of death almost and with constant harassment, so that I have had to develop something within to keep me going amid all of these difficulties. And I think that something has come from the realization that in the struggle we have cosmic companionship and that the cause is right. And there is a great spiritual power that comes to an individual when he feels that he's engaged in a struggle and in a cause that is right and that will ultimately win.

[*Interviewer*]: There was a published story that you moved into an eighty five thousand dollar home when you moved to Atlanta.[6]

---

2. Two days later, Alabama governor John Patterson signed papers for King's extradition to stand trial in Montgomery. After turning himself in to Alabama authorities on 29 February, King posted an additional $4,000 bond, and his trial was set for May.

3. According to one news account of the interview, King also denied any "pretense to absolute goodness" but maintained that if he possessed "one virtue, it's honesty" (Marion Gaines, "Rev. King Arrested in Perjury Case," *Atlanta Constitution,* 18 February 1960).

4. The interviewer refers to King's 16 February speaking engagement (see King, "A Creative Protest," pp. 367–370 in this volume).

5. A Tennessee Circuit Court judge revoked Highlander Folk School's charter on 16 February for violating state segregation and liquor laws ("Charter Is Lost by Mixed School," *New York Times,* 17 February 1960). King had signed a petition in 1959 to prevent Highlander's closure (Petition in support of Highlander Folk School, November 1959). The school officially closed in October 1961, but the institution's staff had already opened the Highlander Research and Education Center in Knoxville.

6. Speaking on behalf of the MIA executive committee, Ralph Abernathy dismissed the charge that King "purchased an $85,000 home" in Atlanta and vouched for King's "honesty, sincerity, integrity and leadership" ("Montgomery Supports King," *Atlanta Daily World,* 20 February 1960).

[*King*]: Yes, it is true that that came out. I own only one piece of property in the world, and that is a 1954 Pontiac. I am renting the house that we live in at the present time. And I have no plans to buy a house, and I have no plans to build a house in the foreseeable future.

[*Interviewer*]: Have your income tax returns been investigated before?

[*King*]: Oh yes, they have been investigated two or three times before. This is nothing new. Investigations have taken place before. And the last time the state came and said that since I was leaving the state they wanted to make this audit. And the man who made the audit made it very clear to me, over and over again, that my returns were thoroughly honest and as accurate as anyone could make returns, but he also admitted that he was under pressure from his superiors to bring some charge.[7] This was one of the last things I heard from him when we were [*recording interrupted*]

F. WSBA-GU.

---

7. King refers to the investigation conducted by Alabama state revenue agent Lloyd Hale. Hale later testified that he did not believe King had committed fraud on his tax returns (Arthur Osgoode, "State Rests King Trial Testimony," *Montgomery Advertiser*, 27 May 1960).

From E. D. Nixon

20 February 1960
Montgomery, Ala.

The former treasurer of the MIA affirms his support for King and challenges any suggestion that King improperly handled funds intended for the civil rights struggle.[1]

Dr. M. L. King,
563 Johnson Avenue, N.E.
Atlanta, Georgia

Dear Sir;

How are you and Mrs King and the whole family fine I hope aside from a little cold we are fair, well I visited last evening with Rev. Abernathy, in his office and I

---

1. Nixon had resigned his position as MIA treasurer in 1957. Many years later, Nixon recalled leaving the organization because he "disagreed with how the records were kept" (Steven M. Millner, "The Montgomery Bus Boycott, A Case Study in the Emergence and Career of a Social Movement," in *The Walking City*, ed. David J. Garrow [Brooklyn, N.Y.: Carlson Publishing, 1989], p. 550; see also note 1 to Nixon to King, 3 June 1957, in *Papers* 4:217).

talk to Atty. [*Fred*] Gray, and Mrs [*Erna*] Dungee, to see if there is anything that I can do, because I feel that you is charge with Money that was not yours, for an instance the $5000.00 that we draw out of the Alabama National Bank, you got the Money but it was not yours, the Money we sent you or was paid to you to go to places was not your money, and some time you paid bills with your money and was rembursed for the money you spent that would mean that you would be charge twice,

Now you must check everything there is to check, keep your mind open do not feel bad about these white people my Lord and your is able to over all unjust, keep the faith, Two things I can Say is that you did not handle any money of the Organization, you did not pay any bill's and the only money that was paid to you was for Organization expense.

You have my pray, and more than me have complete faith in you with reference to any money Matters.

Youre In Christ
[*signed*]
E. D. Nixon

TLS. MLKP-MBU: Box 49A.

From Cynthia and Julius Alexander

[*14 February–21 February 1960*]
Montgomery, Ala.

The Alexanders, Dexter Church congregants, share with King their response to his first sermon as co-pastor of Ebenezer Baptist Church.[1] *They also report hearing news that King had been indicted on 17 February for perjury.*[2] *The Alexanders bemoan King's perjury indictment, commenting "that many months ago you said we must be prepared to face some real dark days ere freedom comes."*

Dear Pastor,

This has been a rather dreary Sunday, raining continuously; Sunday School attendance was fair, so was Church attendance. Our minister for the morning ser-

1. Julius J. Alexander (1901–1983) was born in Montgomery and left home to complete high school in Washington, D.C. He returned to Montgomery to join his father's construction contracting firm and eventually set up his own business in specialty carpentry work. Alexander served as a church deacon and participated in several church committees during King's tenure. His wife, Cynthia Drake Smith Alexander (1899–1991), was secretary to Alabama State College president H. Councill Trenholm and served as vice chair of Dexter's Courtesy Committee.

2. Although the letter is dated 14 February, many of the events described in it, including King's 17 February arrest, took place after that date.

21 Feb 1960

vice was Chaplain B. C. Trent, of Maxwell Air Force Base.[3] He brought what I considered a challenging and inspiring message. The text was taken from that passage of Scripture which deals with the reports of the spies sent into the promised land prior to itss conquest; and the text specifically was one from which you have preached "and we were in our own sight as grasshoppers, and so were we in their sight."[4] His central theme was relative to one's image of himself, which necessarily determined the image others would have of him. He also dealt with the immediate importance of the here and now as well as the ultimate importance of the hereafter. In summarizing his admonition was that the time now is and always has been for the Negro to appraise himself without thought of inferiority, and to go in and "possess the land", for in no instance did God intimate to the Children of Israel that the land would be "handed over to them".

It was indeed a privilege to be present in Ebenezer of the occasion of your initial sermon as co-pastor, and to share the rich spiritual experience of the morning worship.[5] At the next meeting of the January Club it was my privilege to tell about it and share the experience with our fellow club members. It was also a pleasant treat to run across Mrs. King downtown the Saturday we were there, and ~~slo~~ {also} to see your parents. Since returning we have both been hit by "flu". I was out for a few days and my wife is still convalescent from that and her eye ailment.

We were looking at the Dave Garroway show when the neqs came thru, relative to your indictment and subsequent arrest.[6] Although I had put nothing beneath the enemies of right and justice, and had been expecting some sort of action against us on the part of the state, I was not quite prepared for this "new low". To say that we have not the slightest doubt of your innocence, your honesty, and your integrity would superfluous. That is without question. So I am making no attempt to reassure you of a fact you know so well. I do wish you and Mrs. King and your family to know you have our prayers, and our support, in this another attempt to destroy a cause by hitting at the leader. I was disturbed at the first report that you would fight extradition, yet I realized that any decision you made would be the result of careful and prayerful consideration.[7] Yet, I felt that this would give the enemy an opportunity to say you had something to hide, and also the chance to hang the brand of "fugitive" on you, with the attendant condition of every law enforcement agent in Alabama waiting for the chance to pounce on you once you crossed the state line. The whole thing is a rather ugly

3. According to the 3 February *Dexter Echo,* B. C. Trent was scheduled to preach at Dexter on 21 February 1960.

4. Cf. Numbers 13:33.

5. According to a 9 February 1960 article in the *Atlanta Daily World,* a group of visitors from Montgomery, including Lawrence D. Reddick, attended King's first service as Ebenezer's co-pastor. King introduced them to his new congregation after his sermon (Delaney, "'Follow Way of Love,' Dr. King Asks People").

6. Dave Garroway hosted NBC's "Today Show" from 1952 until 1961.

7. On 18 February King announced he would not fight extradition but would "honorably go back to Alabama to face trial" ("King Won't Fight Extradition," *Atlanta Constitution,* 19 February 1960).

picture, but we take consolation in the fact that the same God, who early one morning in the kitchen at 309 S. Jackson said "Lo, I am with you always, even unto the end of the world" still lives and "has the whole world in his hand".[8] The message of "Non Violent Resistance" which sounded in Montgomery is reverberating all over the world. Every day the papers are full of the echoes and re-echoes. We happened to catch a great portion of Eric Severid's T.V. program a few days ago showing Freedom Bursting Forth in Africa (it was last Sunday).[9] It was a moving thing to witness. Truly God is Marching On.

I cannot help but recall that many months ago you said we must be prepared to face some real dark days ere freedom comes, and more and more I realize that, and the outlook from the forces of government is not too encouraging, for the moral aspect of right and justice has been eclipsed by the shadow of political expediency. Yet if I may quote you "Beyond the dim unknown God keeps watch over His own".[10]

In behalf of my wife and my parents I bid you faint not.[11] We believe in you and the God you serve. Our homes are open to you and to yours always.

Devotedly yours,
[*signed*] Cynthia & Julius
Cynthia and Julius Alexander

TALS. MLKP-MBU: Box 18.

---

8. The Alexanders recall King's 27 January 1957 sermon at Dexter, when he recounted that a divine presence had comforted him during the Montgomery bus boycott (see "King Says Vision Told Him to Lead Integration Forces," 28 January 1957, in *Papers* 4:114–115).

9. CBS aired "Nigeria: The Freedom Explosion," hosted by Eric Sevareid on Monday, 15 February 1960.

10. The Alexanders refer to a stanza from James Russell Lowell's poem *The Present Crisis* (1844), which King often quoted in his public addresses.

11. Alexander refers to his parents, James and Hattie.

To Daniel W. Wynn

24 February 1960
Atlanta, Ga.

Wynn, a fellow graduate of Boston University, who occasionally served as guest preacher at Dexter, wrote King on 18 February calling himself "one of the thousands of friends who believe in your integrity and who can understand . . . the cross that you have borne since 1954." He encouraged King to remain strong: "The Master is certainly with you as you walk through another Calvary."[1]

---

1. See also Wynn to King, 7 June 1955, in *Papers* 2:561–562, and King to Wynn, 27 January 1959.

24 Feb 1960

Dr. Daniel W. Wynn, Chaplain
Tuskegee Institute
Tuskegee Institute, Alabama

Dear Dan:

Thank you for your most encouraging and consoling words. I needed them very much.[2] So often in my dark and dreary moments I end up asking concerning my involvement in the civil rights struggle, "Is it worth it?" At other times I find myself asking, "Are you able?" In the midst of all of this an answer always comes back stating: Yes it is worth it and you are able if you will only realize that some individual pain is necessary for any ultimate social gain and that the cause which you represent is destined to win. So I go on living by the faith that God lives. They that stand against Him stand in a tragic and an already declared minority. But they that stand with Him stand in the glow of the world's bright tomorrow.

Best wishes to all of the members of your family.

Very sincerely yours,
[*signed*] Martin/b
Martin L. King, Jr.

TLSr. DWW-ARC-LNT.

---

2. Coretta King recalled that the tax case "caused Martin more suffering than any other event of his life" and that he worried that "many people will think I am guilty" (*My Life with Martin Luther King, Jr.*, p. 185).

"Recommendations to the Ebenezer Baptist Church for the Fiscal Year 1960–1961"

[*February–March 1960*]
[*Atlanta, Ga.*]

As co-pastors, King and his father present their recommendations to the congregation. Their proposals seek to boost the social life of the congregation, educate new members, and promote the social gospel through the work of the NAACP and SCLC: "The membership should unite with these organizations in a solid block." All but two recommendations—to form a credit union and a recreation committee—parallel King's proposals to Dexter Avenue Baptist Church during his first year as pastor.[1]

I. In order that every member of the Church shall be identified with a smaller and more intimate fellowship of the Church, Clubs representing the twelve months of the year shall be organized. Each member of the Church will automatically become a member of the Club of the Month in which he was born. Each month club shall choose its own officers. Each club shall meet once per month, with the exception of the month in which the club is named. In the month for which the club is named, each club shall meet weekly. So the January Club, for example, shall meet once monthly until January. In January, it shall meet each week. Each club shall be asked to make a special contribution of Four Hundred ($400.00) Dollars to the Church on the last Sunday of the month for which it is named.

II. It is both appalling and tragic that the average member of a Baptist Church has no conception of the doctrines of his faith. This doctrinal illiteracy has left many Protestant with a faith devoid of substance and meaning. Indeed, many do not know what they believe. As a result of this lack of doctrinal training many people take their Church Loyalty all too lightly and irresponsibly. In order to deal constructively with this problem a New Member Committee shall be formed. This committee shall conduct three classes per month for new members. Each person joining the church will be required to attend three classes before he can have the right hand of fellowship. When the member has fulfilled these requirements, the Chairman of the Committee shall notify him of his eligibility to be fellowshipped. On the Wednesday before the 1st Sunday in each month the Chairman of the Committee shall turn over to the Church Secretary the names of all persons eligible for the right hand of fellowship so that they can be officially reminded of their needed presence on the 1st Sunday Evening. In addition to the job of acquainting each member with the doctrines of the Church, the New Members Committee shall do the following:

1. See King, "Recommendations to the Dexter Avenue Baptist Church for the Fiscal Year 1954–1955," 5 September 1954, in *Papers* 2:287–294.

Mar 1960

A. Interview all new members concerning their particular areas of interest in the Church. If they have no particular interest, be sure to give them one. Place them in the particular department or club of the month of the new member's birth and assign him to his proper Month Club.

B. Acquaint each new member with the total program of the Church.

C. Explain the meaning of Christian Stewardship. Encourage each new member to tithe. Explain the budget and financial system to each new member. See that each new member makes a pledge and has a box of envelopes.

D. All names and vital statistics should be written plainly and turned over to the Office Secretary in order that she may make an orderly transfer of such information to the permanent files of the Church.

The NEW MEMBERS COMMITTEE shall consist of the following persons: Miss W. Christine King, Chairman, Mrs. Laura Henderson, Miss Dolores Robinson, Rev. Paul Anderson, Mrs. Wilhelmina H. Scretchin, and Mr. Melvin R. Waples.

III. In order that there may be a reliable and orderly record of the Church's origin, growth and future development, a Committee on the History of Ebenezer shall be organized. This Committee shall be requested to present a summary of the history of Ebenezer each year at the Church Anniversary. This Committee shall be requested to keep on file at least three weekly bulletins, and look into the possibility of having them bound at the end of each Church year. These records shall be carefully preserved in the Church library. This Committee shall consist of the following persons: Mrs. Nellie Perry, Chairman, Mrs. Ruth Parks Greene, Mr. Jethro English, Mrs. Mary Marshall, Mrs. Odessa Jones, Mrs. Sarah Reed, Mrs. Janie B. Lowe and Mrs. Emma Clayton.

IV. A Scholarship Fund Committee shall be established. It shall be the responsibility of this Committee to choose each year for scholarship awards the two high school graduates in Ebenezer's membership who posses the highest scholastic rating as well as unusual possibilities for service to humanity; students who have been actively engaged in some phase of church life and who plan to attend college. The scholarship award for this year shall be Four Hundred ($400.00) Dollars for the student with the highest scholastic rating, and Two Hundred ($200.00) Dollars for the other student. The members of this committee shall consist of the following persons: Mr. William Nix, Chairman, Mrs. Eva Williams, Vice Chairman, Mr. William Wilder, Mrs. Nannien W. Crawford, and Miss Doris Coleman.

V. A Cultural Committee shall be established consisting of the following persons: Mrs. Alberta Williams King, Chairman, Mr. Hampton Z. Barker, Mrs. Wilhelmina Scretchin, Mrs. Coretta King, Mr. David Stills and Mr. Henry Griffin. In addition to the concert that is given by the Ebenezer Choir each year, this committee shall sponsor another big cultural event by some outside group or individual. Such an undertaking will have a four-fold purpose: (a) To lift the general cultural appreciation of our church and community. (b) To give encouragement to our school groups. (c) To give encouragement to promising artists. (d) To give financial aid to the church.

VI. In order to assist the Director of Christian Education in implementing the program in this area, a Board of Christian Education shall be organized. This

Board shall immediately meet with the Pastors and the Director of Christian Education to discuss ways and means of strengthening the program of Christian Education. Obviously, this should be one of the strongest boards in the church. This Board shall consist of the following persons: Miss Lucile Harris, Chairman, Miss Lillian D. Watkins, Mrs. Elise Gilham, Rev. Paul Anderson, Mrs. N. W. Crawford, Miss W. Christine King, Mrs. A. W. King, Mrs. A. L. Neal, and Mrs. Nellie Perry

VII. Since the Gospel of Jesus is a social Gospel, as well as a personal Gospel, seeking to save the whole man, a Social Action Committee shall be established for the purpose of keeping the congregation informed (intelligently) concerning the social, poltical, and economic situation. This committee shall keep before the congregation the importance of supporting such civil rights organizations as the NAACP and the Southern Christian Leadership Conference. The membership should unite with these organizations in a solid block. This committee shall also keep before the congregation the necessity of being registered voters. Every member of Ebenezer must be a registered voter. During elections, both state and national, this committee will sponsor forums and mass meetings to discuss the relative merits of candidates and the major issues involved. This committee shall consist of the following persons: Mrs. Esther M. Smith, Acting Chairman, Mr. C. A. Scott, Mr. Timothy Gilham, Mr. Isaac Farris, Rev. Otis Burnett, Rev. Mancy Brown, Mr. Robert Norwood, Miss Lornell McCullough, Mrs. Vashti Ellis.

VIII. In order to instill the idea of thrift in our members and reveal the concern of the Church for the economic life of man, a committee shall be appointed to organize a Credit Union.[2] This Committee will immediately seek to secure a federal charter. It is hoped that every member will become associated with this Credit Union, and that it will become a powerful economic agency in the community. The need for such an institution in our Church is unquestioned. It will serve as a channel through which members can save money, and it prevents them from having to go to downtown finance companies to make loans for exploitative interest rates. Actually when the individual makes a loan from the Credit Union of which he is a member, he is borrowing from himself. The committee to begin setting up the Credit Union shall consist of the following persons: Mr. Robert Collier, Chairman, Mr. J. H. Reese, Mr. T. S. Gentry, Mr. Herbert Woods, Mr. Gartrell Williams, Mr. Clarence Mizzelle, Vice Chairman, Mrs. Venice Nash and Mrs. Robbie Mae Bell.

IX. In order to provide the Youth of the Church and community with a sound recreational outlet and strengthen the total program of recreation, a Recreation Committee shall be organized. This Committee shall immediately study the present recreational program and make recommendations to the Pastors concerning additional equipment that should be purchased. The Committee should look into the possibility of having a Church baseball and basket ball team. This committee shall consist of the following persons: Mr. Melvin R. Waples, Chairman, Mrs. Mildred Elder,

2. In 1957 and 1959 the MIA had sought to establish a credit union for its membership. The Bureau of Federal Credit Unions denied both requests, citing policies prohibiting charters for civic groups (Harold B. Wright to King, 28 March 1957, and J. Theodore Rutland to King, 28 July 1959).

Co-Chairman, Mr. John Bates, Mrs. Carrie Buggs Mrs. Renetta Chapman, Mrs. Clara Mizzelle and Mrs. Vivian Thomas.

X. In order to increase the feeling of real fellowship in the Church and make visitors feel a hearty welcome, a Courtesy Committee shall be organized. It will be the purpose of this committee to make its way to the visitors on Sunday and give them a sense of real welcome. Also, this Committee shall sponsor Coffee Hours at least once monthly, immediately after Morning Service. At this time both visitors and members shall be invited to the Fellowship Hall (Basement) of the Church for a moment of fellowship and getting acquainted. This Committee shall consist of the following persons: Mrs. Coretta King, Chairman, Mrs. Earnestine Brooks, Vice Chairman, Mrs. Katie Taylor, Miss Lornell McCullough, Mrs. Hazel Taylor, Mrs. Mellie Thomas, Mrs. Ruth Davis, Mrs. Marjorie McCrary, Mrs. Eunice Simmons, Mrs. Mattie Hodges, and Mrs. Lucile Crosby.

XI. The Church Membership Roll shall be divided into an active and in-active list. Those members who fail to register for the year and who contribute nothing to the financial upkeep of the Church, shall be placed on the Roll as inactive members, unless some satisfactory explanation be given to the officers. An inactive member shall have no voting privileges in the Church.

XII. The Membership shall be divided into districts of (30) persons. Each district shall have a Captain and a Co-Captain. Each district shall be worked out on the basis of geographical proximity so that every person in a particular district will live in a small geographical radius. It will be the duty of the Co-Captains constantly to call and visit members in their district. Members that are slack in Church attendance and general Church responsibilities should be persuaded to improve. At the end of every (2) months, each Captain shall receive from the Office Secretary the names of members in his group who might be behind in their pledges. It shall be the duty of the Captain to persuade the member to bring up his or her pledge.

TD. EBCR.

From Stanley D. Levison

[*March 1960*]

Levison reports on the progress of the Committee to Defend Martin Luther King and the Struggle for Freedom in the South, a legal defense group formed in response to King's Alabama perjury indictment.[1] *He also decries the recent statement of Thurgood*

1. A 3 March press release announced the formation of the committee and its plans to launch a "national fund-raising campaign" aimed at raising $200,000 to defend King and support SCLC's voter registration drives in the South (Committee to Defend Martin Luther King and the Struggle for Freedom in the South, Press release, Committee to undertake fundraising campaign, 3 March 1960). In addition to Levison, the press release listed over forty other members including Bayard Rustin, A. Philip

Marshall, head of the NAACP Legal Defense and Education Fund, that "the first stage of demonstrations should be ended" in favor of courtroom challenges.

Dear Martin,

Enclosed is a suggested draft for a fund appeal.[2] It is somewhat long but I think the vital charcater of the moment will hold the attention of readers. Furthermore it is important that the meaning of the events be clearly spelled out. I have not made separate drafts for the churchs, directors and individuals because I think the one message is suitable f for all. If you feel a specific point needs to be made for the different groups it can be added as a sentence which you or Ralph [*Abernathy*] would better be able to compose than I.

We are inundated with tasks. To organize a new committee is a complex job, but simultaneously we are thrown into a series of fund raising projects each of which is complicated. However, the response is heartwarming. Harry Belafonte has stirred the cultural forces as never before and they should become a new and increasing source of strength.[3] For the first time we have gotten the official leadership of the N.Y. Central Labor Council to come into the work with more than mere token endorsements of paper resolutions. Last week they had delivered to their meeting a full report of our Defense Committee with its objective of defending you, backing the students, and the S.C.L.C.[4] The entire delegated body endorsed the report voted to stage a huge demonstration on May 17th in the garment center, and to raise funds through the unions.[5] They are setting up a committee of their own to carry through these purposes. We are particularly encouraged because they appear willing to back up the method of going to the shops for

---

Randolph, Gardner C. Taylor, Mordecai Johnson, Harry Emerson Fosdick, Lorraine Hansberry, Jackie Robinson, and Ruth H. Bunche (Committee to Defend Martin Luther King and the Struggle for Freedom in the South, Press release, "Statement on the indictment of Martin Luther King, Jr.," 3 March 1960).

2. Levison likely enclosed an appeal for King's legal defense that eventually appeared in the *New York Times.* The statement was endorsed by supporters of King, including SCLC ministers, black entertainers, and prominent liberals (see "Heed Their Rising Voices," *New York Times,* 29 March 1960; see also Wofford to King, 1 April 1960, pp. 403–405 in this volume).

3. The committee was founded in late February in the New York apartment of Belafonte, who chaired the group's cultural committee.

4. The Labor Council's actions were reported in the 28 March minutes of the committee to defend Martin Luther King.

5. Among the speakers at the union-sponsored rally marking the sixth anniversary of the *Brown* decision were Morris Iushewitz, secretary of the New York Central Labor Council; Cleveland Robinson, secretary-treasurer of District 65 of the Retail, Wholesale, and Department Store Union (RWDSU); and David Livingston, president of District 65 ("15,000 Attend Garment Center Civil Rights Rally," *New York Times,* 18 May 1960). Following the rally the committee sponsored a benefit at New York City's 369th Armory. Sidney Poitier and Dorothy Dandridge emceed the event, which included performances by Belafonte, folk singer Odetta, and jazz vocalist Sarah Vaughn ("New Negro Is Key in Struggle," *New York Amsterdam News,* 21 May 1960). The committee later reported that the benefit netted over $10,000 (A. Philip Randolph and Gardner C. Taylor, Press release, and Committee to Defend Martin Luther King and the Struggle for Freedom in the South, "Statement of income and expenditure for period ending 7/31/1960," both dated 7 October 1960).

Heed Their Rising Voices

"The growing movement of peaceful mass demonstrations by Negroes is something new in the South, something understandable. . . . Let Congress heed their rising voices, for they will be heard."

—New York Times editorial
Saturday, March 19, 1960

As the whole world knows by now, thousands of Southern Negro students are engaged in widespread non-violent demonstrations in positive affirmation of the right to live in human dignity as guaranteed by the U. S. Constitution and the Bill of Rights. In their efforts to uphold these guarantees, they are being met by an unprecedented wave of terror by those who would deny and negate that document which the whole world looks upon as setting the pattern for modern freedom. . . .

In Orangeburg, South Carolina, when 400 students peacefully sought to buy doughnuts and coffee at lunch counters in the business district, they were forcibly ejected, tear-gassed, soaked to the skin in freezing weather with fire hoses, arrested en masse and herded into an open barbed-wire stockade to stand for hours in the bitter cold.

In Montgomery, Alabama, after students sang "My Country, 'Tis of Thee" on the State Capitol steps, their leaders were expelled from school, and truck-loads of police armed with shotguns and tear-gas ringed the Alabama State College Campus. When the entire student body protested to state authorities by refusing to re-register, their dining hall was padlocked in an attempt to starve them into submission.

In Tallahassee, Atlanta, Nashville, Savannah, Greensboro, Memphis, Richmond, Charlotte, and a host of other cities in the South, young American teenagers, in face of the entire weight of official state apparatus and police power, have boldly stepped forth as protagonists of democracy. Their courage and amazing restraint have inspired millions and given a new dignity to the cause of freedom.

Small wonder that the Southern violators of the Constitution fear this new, non-violent brand of freedom fighter . . . even as they fear the upswelling right-to-vote movement. Small wonder that they are determined to destroy the one man who, more than any other, symbolizes the new spirit now sweeping the South—the Rev. Dr. Martin Luther King, Jr., world-famous leader of the Montgomery Bus Protest. For it is his doctrine of non-violence which has inspired and guided the students in their widening wave of sit-ins; and it this same Dr. King who founded and is president of the Southern Christian Leadership Conference—the organization which is spearheading the surging right-to-vote movement. Under Dr. King's direction the Leadership Conference conducts Student Workshops and Seminars in the philosophy and technique of non-violent resistance.

Again and again the Southern violators have answered Dr. King's peaceful protests with intimidation and violence. They have bombed his home almost killing his wife and child. They have assaulted his person. They have arrested him seven times—for "speeding," "loitering" and similar "offenses." And now they have charged him with "perjury"—a *felony* under which they could imprison him for *ten years*. Obviously, their real purpose is to remove him physically as the leader to whom the students and millions of others—look for guidance and support, and thereby to intimidate *all* leaders who may rise in the South. Their strategy is to behead this affirmative movement, and thus to demoralize Negro Americans and weaken their will to struggle. The defense of Martin Luther King, spiritual leader of the student sit-in movement, clearly, therefore, is an integral part of the total struggle for freedom in the South.

Decent-minded Americans cannot help but applaud the creative daring of the students and the quiet heroism of Dr. King. But this is one of those moments in the stormy history of Freedom when men and women of good will must do more than applaud the rising-to-glory of others. The America whose good name hangs in the balance before a watchful world, the America whose heritage of Liberty these Southern Upholders of the Constitution are defending, is our America as well as theirs . . .

We must heed their rising voices—yes—but we must add our own.

We must extend ourselves above and beyond moral support and render the material help so urgently needed by those who are taking the risks, facing jail, and even death in a glorious re-affirmation of our Constitution and its Bill of Rights.

We urge you to join hands with our fellow Americans in the South by supporting, with your dollars, this Combined Appeal for all three needs—the defense of Martin Luther King—the support of the embattled students—and the struggle for the right-to-vote.

Your Help Is Urgently Needed . . . NOW!!

Stella Adler
Raymond Pace Alexander
Harry Van Arsdale
Harry Belafonte
Julie Belafonte
Dr. Algernon Black
Marc Blitztein
William Branch
Marlon Brando
Mrs. Ralph Bunche
Diahann Carroll
Dr. Alan Knight Chalmers
Richard Coe
Nat King Cole
Cheryl Crawford
Dorothy Dandridge
Ossie Davis
Sammy Davis, Jr.
Ruby Dee
Dr. Philip Elliott
Dr. Harry Emerson Fosdick
Anthony Franciosa
Lorraine Hansbury
Rev. Donald Harrington
Nat Hentoff
James Hicks
Mary Hinkson
Van Heflin
Langston Hughes
Morris Iushewitz
Mahalia Jackson
Mordecai Johnson
John Killens
Eartha Kitt
Rabbi Edward Klein
Hope Lange
John Lewis
Viveca Lindfors
Carl Murphy
Don Murray
John Murray
A. J. Muste
Frederick O'Neal
L. Joseph Overton
Clarence Pickett
Shad Polier
Sidney Poitier
A. Philip Randolph
John Raitt
Elmer Rice
Jackie Robinson
Mrs. Eleanor Roosevelt
Bayard Rustin
Robert Ryan
Maureen Stapleton
Frank Silvera
Hope Stevens
George Tabori
Rev. Gardner C. Taylor
Norman Thomas
Kenneth Tynan
Charles White
Shelley Winters
Max Youngstein

We in the south who are struggling daily for dignity and freedom warmly endorse this appeal

Rev. Ralph D. Abernathy (*Montgomery, Ala.*)
Rev. Fred L. Shuttlesworth (*Birmingham, Ala.*)
Rev. Kelley Miller Smith (*Nashville, Tenn.*)
Rev. W. A. Dennis (*Chattanooga, Tenn.*)
Rev. C. K. Steele (*Tallahassee, Fla.*)
Rev. Matthew D. McCollom (*Orangeburg, S. C.*)
Rev. William Holmes Borders (*Atlanta, Ga.*)
Rev. Douglas Moore (*Durham, N. C.*)
Rev. Wyatt Tee Walker (*Petersburg, Va.*)
Rev. Walter L. Hamilton (*Norfolk, Va.*)
I. S. Levy (*Columbia, S. C.*)
Rev. Martin Luther King, Sr. (*Atlanta, Ga.*)
Rev. Henry C. Bunton (*Memphis, Tenn.*)
Rev. S. S. Seay, Sr. (*Montgomery, Ala.*)
Rev. Samuel W. Williams (*Atlanta, Ga.*)
Rev. A. L. Davis (*New Orleans, La.*)
Mrs. Katie E. Whickham (*New Orleans, La.*)
Rev. W. H. Hall (*Hattiesburg, Miss.*)
Rev. J. E. Lowery (*Mobile, Ala.*)
Rev. T. J. Jemison (*Baton Rouge, La.*)

COMMITTEE TO DEFEND MARTIN LUTHER KING AND THE STRUGGLE FOR FREEDOM IN THE SOUTH
312 West 125th Street, New York 27, N. Y. UNiversity 6-1700

Chairmen: A. Philip Randolph, Dr. Gardner C. Taylor; *Chairmen of Cultural Division:* Harry Belafonte, Sidney Poitier; *Treasurer:* Nat King Cole; *Executive Director:* Bayard Rustin; *Chairmen of Church Division:* Father George B. Ford, Rev. Harry Emerson Fosdick, Rev. Thomas Kilgore, Jr., Rabbi Edward E. Klein; *Chairman of Labor Division:* Morris Iushewitz

Please mail this coupon TODAY!

Committee To Defend Martin Luther King
and
The Struggle For Freedom In The South
312 West 125th Street, New York 27, N. Y.
UNiversity 6-1700

*I am enclosing my contribution of $*__________
for the work of the Committee.

Name__________ (PLEASE PRINT)
Address__________
City______ Zone____ State______

☐ I want to help ☐ Please send further information

Please make checks payable to:
Committee To Defend Martin Luther King

This advertisement, endorsed by supporters of King, including SCLC ministers, black entertainers, and prominent liberals, appeared in the *New York Times* on 29 March 1960. The ad states that the funds would be distributed three ways: King's defense for his Alabama perjury trial, support for student protesters, and the voting rights struggle.

individual collections. This means larger sums than we normally get from the union treasuries. I don't think we will accomplish this easily but up to now we have never been able to get the officials to think this way. Too often they considered a fifty or one hundred dollar contribution as meeting the responsibility. With this new thinking we are starting down the right road.

All of this illustrats the point Bayard [*Rustin*] and I were attempting to make last week. This is a new stage in the struggle. It begins at the higher point where Montgomery left off. The students are taking on the strongest state power and demonstrating real will and deter~~i~~m~~a~~{i}n{a}tion. By their actions they are making the shadow boxing in Congress clear as a farce. They are by contrast exposing the lack of real fight that exists among allegedly friendly Congressmen and Presidential aspirants. And by example they are demonstrating the bankruptcy of the policy of relying upon the courts and legislation to acheive real results. The country is stirred by them and sickened by the feebleness of the foolishness in Congress.[6] It is interesting and very significant that this weekend Thurgood Marshall has called a conference of lawyers in Washington and has been quoted as saying that the first stage of demonstrations should be ended and a new one in the courts now {is} to be developed.[7] Characteristically, they want to give a tranquilizer or pacifier to the whole movement and send the people back to their ordinary preoccupations. More and more they are revealing themselves as gradualists in reality while they pretend to be uncompromising and firm. But they are not taking into account that people cannot and will not accept this policy. They are using up the good will past victories in the courts brought them, and increasingly crictism and cynicism about their motives is being expressed. It is not yet on a broad public scale because there is fear of appearance of disunity. But the clouds of distrust and opposition are gathering. Sooner or later their policy will have to change or their influence will sharply diminish and the true forces of struggle will move into effective leadership

Please forgive this sloppy typting. I am doing this late at night at home and both the hour and my abilities are fighting me. Please be careful in copying my draft to see that it is checked for spelling. I learned how to write but neglected to learn how to spell. Love to Coretta and your family,

Fondly
[*signed*] Stanley

TALS. MLKP-MBU: Box 2.

---

6. Levison refers to the filibuster of the 1960 civil rights legislation. For more on the filibuster, see Jacob K. Javits to King, 21 April 1960, pp. 439–440 in this volume.

7. The meeting was held 18–20 March at Howard University in order to discuss legal questions related to the arrests of student demonstrators. At the end of the three-day meeting, a news report quoted Marshall: "The right of protest is traditional, going back to dumping tea in Boston Harbor because we didn't like certain things. These kids have a right to have their say. The right to carry a picket sign is the most precious right we have" ("NAACP Sits Down with the 'Sit-Inners,'" *New York Amsterdam News,* 26 March 1960).

To Wyatt Tee Walker

5 March 1960
[*Atlanta, Ga.*]

Nearly eleven months after John Tilley's resignation as SCLC executive director, King offers Walker the position and expresses his hope that the Virginia minister will "bring into full grown maturity an organization that is presently a sleeping giant."[1] *Shortly after Walker resigned from his pastorate on 29 May, King announced his hiring, describing it as SCLC's "most significant move since its beginning in 1957."*[2]

Rev. Wyatt Tee Walker, Minister
The Gillfield Baptist Church
Petersburg, Virginia

Dear Wyatt:

After careful and serious deliberations, the Personnel Committee of the Southern Christian Leadership Conference has authorized me to offer you the position of Executive Director of the Southern Christian Leadership Conference. All of the members of the Committee were tremendously impressed with your interview, and strongly felt that you could give a leadership to the Conference which would lift it to one of the most significant movements in our nation today. The Committee was greatly impressed with your technical know-how, sincerity of purpose, general creativity, radiating personality, and willingness to stick with a job until it is finished, and felt that all of these factors coupled with your ability as a preacher and pastor would conjoin to produce the type of inimitable executive that is needed to carry on the challenging work of our organization.

We feel that the potentialities of the Conference are now greater than ever before. The recent developments with the student sit downs, and the centrality of the civil rights issue in Congress offer the SCLC a unique opportunity for leadership in the field of mass nonviolent direct action. People over the country are looking to the Southern Christian Leadership Conference for this type of leadership, and they are expressing every day a new willingness to support our efforts.

---

1. For Tilley's resignation letter, see Tilley to King, 13 April 1959, pp. 182–184 in this volume. King and Walker may have discussed the SCLC position when King spoke at a Richmond Emancipation Day rally organized by Walker (Program, "Second annual Pilgrimage of Prayer for Public Schools," 1 January 1960). Walker, who was also state director of CORE and president of the Petersburg NAACP, had led a number of protests directed at segregated schools and public accommodations. Two days after King's letter was written, Walker was among a group of eleven black protesters jailed for trespassing in the "whites only" section of the Petersburg Public Library (Robert Gordon, "11 Negroes Are Arrested at Petersburg Library," *Richmond Times-Dispatch,* 8 March 1960). King wired Walker words of encouragement: "Your determined courage and Christian methods are inspiring to all men of goodwill" (King to Walker, 8 March 1960).

2. Addressing a mass meeting on 1 June at Gillfield Baptist Church, King told the Petersburg Improvement Association that Walker "is not leaving Petersburg but is going to a larger job to serve a better Petersburg" ("Negro Leader Urges Continued Struggle," *Richmond News Leader,* 2 June 1960). Walker assumed the position in August 1960.

A case in point is my recent trip to California. I addressed two or three fund raising rallies, and at the end of the meetings more than $6,000.00 was raised for our work.[3] In each instance the people expressed an enthusiastic desire to give even greater financial support to our work. Now that we are opening our fund raising office in Atlanta on a full time basis, I am sure that our finances will triple. I mention all of these things to simply say that the opportunities are unlimited, and the financial resources will be available for you to do the job in a monumental way.

While there are several details concerning the job that cannot be adequately discussed until the position is accepted, I would like to say that the Committee agreed to offer a beginning salary of $8,000.00 a year. I don't think you would face any difficulties finding housing accommodations for your family in Atlanta. I am sure that you would find Atlanta a most interesting city in which to live. Its central location would greatly aid you in the travelling that you would have to do, and its urban sophistication (greater Atlanta has a population of more than one million), cultural outlet (there are six colleges and universities in Atlanta for Negroes alone and five for whites), and unique achievements of Negroes in the economic sphere would provide an atmosphere that would be very meaningful and enjoyable to your family.

All of the board members are eagerly awaiting your decision. We are confident that your acceptance of this position would bring into full grown maturity an organization that is presently a sleeping giant, and will add to your already emerging stature as a Christian minister, and as a social reformer.

I will await your reply with great anticipation. We would hope that you can make some decision within the next two weeks so that we may proceed with the other basic business details if your answer is in the affirmative.

Very sincerely yours,
Martin Luther King, Jr.

MLK:mlb

TLc. MLKP-MBU: Box 74.

---

3. On 23 February King spoke at Los Angeles's Temple Isaiah; on 27 February he delivered "The Power Struggle and Security in a Nuclear Space Age" for the Church Federation of Los Angeles, and the following day he delivered "The Three Dimensions of a Complete Life" at Friendship Baptist Church in Pasadena.

To Dwight D. Eisenhower

9 March 1960
Atlanta, Ga.

On 8 March, following two weeks of student-led protests against segregation, Montgomery police arrested thirty-seven demonstrators near the Alabama State College campus.[1] *In the telegram below, King warns Eisenhower: "Lest bloodshed stains the streets of America we ask that the American people through you be made aware of the brutal and flagrant violation of constitutional rights." He requests that Eisenhower instruct "the Attorney General to take immediate action . . . to restore law and order."*[2] *In a 17 March reply, Eisenhower's deputy assistant Gerald Morgan highlighted recent statements by the president expressing support for the protests sweeping the South.*[3]

THE PRESIDENT
THE WHITE HOUSE

A REIGN OF TERROR HAS BROKEN OUT IN MONTGOMERY, ALABAMA. GESTAPO LIKE METHODS ARE BEING USED BY POLICE AND CITY AUTHORITIES TO INTIMIDATE NEGROES WHO HAVE BEEN PURSUING PEACEFUL AND NON VIOLATE TECHNIQUES TO ACHIEVE THEIR MORAL AND CONSTITUTIONAL RIGHTS. WHILE STUDENTS OF ALABAMA STATE COLLEGE WERE CONVENED IN AN ORDERLY PROTEST ON THEIR CAMPUS, CITY OFFICIALS AND POLICE LAUNCHED AN INCREDIBLE ASSAULT, AND INFILTRATED THE COLLEGE CAMPUS WITH POLICE ARMED WITH RIFLES SHOTGUNS AND TEAR GAS. YESTERDAY THEY ARRESTED MORE THAN 35 STUDENTS, A FACULTY MEMBER, AND A PHYSICIAN.[4] TODAY THEY HAD NUMEROUS TRUCKS PARKED NOT FAR FROM THE CAMPUS WITH THE THREAT OF

---

1. Reporters estimated that one thousand students, about half the student body, attended the protest (Dick Hines and Arthur Osgoode, "City Police Arrest 37 Negro Agitators for Demonstration," *Montgomery Advertiser,* 9 March 1960). The demonstrations began on 25 February when several students staged a sit-in demonstration at the snack-bar of the Montgomery courthouse. The following day more than two hundred and fifty students held a rally outside the courthouse (John Coombes, "Rally Held by Negroes at College," *Montgomery Advertiser,* 27 February 1960).

2. Other civil rights proponents joined King's appeal including UAW president Walter Reuther, who informed the president: "The struggle of our Negro citizens for equality and dignity under law has focused the eyes of the world upon America. The image of our country—already defaced by violent and lawless segregationist elements—must not be permitted to suffer further damage. If American democracy is to provide inspiration, hope and leadership in the world struggle against communism, then America must first get its moral credentials in order by bridging the gap between our noble promises and our ugly practices in the field of civil rights" (Reuther to Eisenhower, 11 March 1960; see also Randolph to Eisenhower, 10 March 1960).

3. At a 16 March press conference, Eisenhower told reporters that some of the student protests "are unquestionably a proper expression of a conviction of the group which is making them." He also expressed his deep sympathy "with the efforts of any group to enjoy the rights, the rights of equality that they are guaranteed by the Constitution," adding "that if a person is expressing such an aspiration as this in a perfectly legal way, then I don't see any reason why he should not do it" (*Public Papers of the Presidents of the United States: Dwight D. Eisenhower, 1960–1961* [Washington, D.C.: U.S. Government Printing Office, 1961], p. 294). The day after the press conference, King sent Eisenhower a telegram commending his "recent statement declaring the present demonstrations . . . constitutional and proper," and explaining that they "are not ends in themselves, but a means to awaken the dozing consciences of those who oppress us, and urge them to respect our selfhood as much as they respect our dollars."

4. Montgomery police also arrested faculty member Olean Underwood and her husband, physician Jefferson Underwood, when he arrived at the city jail to inquire about his wife. After their arrest, King sent the Underwoods, who were members of the MIA, a telegram expressing "absolute support in all that you face" (King to Jefferson and Olean Underwood, 10 March 1960).

ARRESTING THE ENTIRE STUDENT BODY. POLICE ARE PARADING IN FRONT OF CHURCHES THEY INHIBIT THE HOLDING OF MEETINGS AND RELIGIOUS SERVICES. THEY HAVE ACTUALLY PHYSICALLY INTRUDED THEMSELVES INTO THESE RELIGIOUS SERVICES. YESTERDAY A BISHOP WAS CONDUCTING A CHURCH MEETING WHEN POLICE INVADED THE MEETING IN A RAID[5] TELEPHONES ARE BEING TAPPED AND TELEPHONE LINES OF NEGRO LEADERS ARE LEFT DISCONNECTED SO THAT THEY CANNOT MAKE NOR RECEIVE CALLS. THIS CALCULATED AND PROVOCATIVE CONDUCT OF THE POLICE BACKED BY THE MUNICIPAL AND STATE AUTHORITIES LEADS INESCAPABLY TO THE CONCLUSION THAT THEY ARE TRYING TO INCITE A RIOT IN THE HOPE THAT THE RESPONSIBILITY FOR THE INJURIES AND DEATHS THAT MIGHT RESULT WILL BE FASTENED ON THE NEGROES. THE NEGRO COMMUNITY AND STUDENTS CANNOT PERMIT THEMSELVES TO BE INTIMIDATED. THEY WILL NOT TURN AWAY FROM THE PURSUIT OF JUSTICE. THEY MUST AND WILL PURSUE THEIR RIGHTEOUS AND NON VIOLATE COURSE. LEST BLOODSHED STAINS THE STREETS OF AMERICA WE ASK THAT THE AMERICAN PEOPLE THROUGH YOU BE MADE AWARE OF THE BRUTAL AND FLAGRANT VIOLATION OF CONSTITUTIONAL RIGHT. MR PRESIDENT WE APPEAL TO YOU TO INTERVENE BY INSTRUCTING THE ATTORNEY GENERAL TO TAKE IMMEDIATE ACTION IN YOUR NAME TO RESTORE LAW AND ORDER IN THE CAPITAL OF ALABAMA. WE ARE PREPARED TO GO WITH THE ATTORNEY GENERAL INTO THE FEDERAL COURT FOR INJUNCTIVE RELEASE. WE APPEAL TO YOU TO URGE THE CITY AUTHORITIES TO PUT DOWN THEIR GUNS, TO GARAGE THEIR VEHICLES OF AGGRESSION WE ARE UNARMED AND DEDICATED TO NON VIOLENCE THOUGH DETERMINED TO RESIST EVIL. WE PRAY THAT NO HARM MAY COME EITHER TO OUR PEOPLE OR TO THOSE WHO OPPRESS US. THOUGH IT APPEARS THAT THE AGGRESSORS MAY UNLEASH VIOLENCE AGAINST US NO MATTER HOW RESTRAINED OUR CONDUCT. MAY GOD HELP US TO MAINTAIN OUR ENDURANCE AGAINST PROVOCATIONS WE ARE CONSCIOUS OF THE MANY PRESSING DUTIES OF YOUR OFFICE, BUT WE FEEL THIS TERROR WHICH GRIPS A WHOLE COMMUNITY IN AN AMERICAN CITY VIOLATING ELEMENTARY CONSTITUTIONAL RIGHTS REQUIRES IMMEDIATE FEDERAL EMERGENCY ACTION. OUR CONCERN FOR THE HONOR OF THE NATION WHICH WE LOVE DESPITE OUR SUFFERING IMPELS US TO MAKE THIS PUBLIC OUTCRY AND APPEAL FOR JUSTICE AND HUMAN DECENCY.[6]

MARTIN LUTHER KING, JR PRESIDENT
THE SOUTHERN CHRISTIAN LEADERSHIP CONFERENCE.

PWSr. WCFG-KAbE.

5. On 6 March police broke up a march and prayer vigil protesting the expulsion of nine student leaders ("Police Thwart Negro Services at Capitol: Whites Held at Distance by Officials," *Montgomery Advertiser,* 7 March 1960; see also Reddick, "The Montgomery situation," April 1960).

6. After this telegram was publicized in the press, Montgomery police commissioner L. B. Sullivan responded that "we have made every effort to maintain law and order here, and to protect the rights and property of all our citizens in what we feel is a tense situation. We would welcome any type of unbiased, unprejudiced investigation" ("King Asks Ike to Act in Montgomery," *Atlanta Journal,* 10 March 1960).

To Rebecca Dixon

10 March 1960
[*Atlanta, Ga.*]

King sends a telegram to an Alabama State College student who was among the thirty-seven people arrested for protest activities on 8 March.[1] *Dixon, whose mother was a member of Dexter Avenue Baptist Church, had attended MIA mass meetings during the bus protest. In her 22 March reply, Dixon related the details of her trial, stating that she and other student protesters were found guilty of disorderly conduct and disobeying a police officer: "I knew I hadn't done anything wrong so why should I be afraid. But after we got to Court, it was a different story, the arresting officer said I did have a sign stating, 'Who's Next?' My only regret was I didn't have one. Rev. King it was a total disgrace to see those police officers stand under oath and lie. I really got sick, but I guess I should have expected it."*[2]

MISS REBECCA DIXON
427 ROSS STREET
MONTGOMERY, ALABAMA

DEEPLY SHOCKED TO LEARN OF THE SHAMEFUL AND UNJUST ARREST WHICH YOU HAD TO FACE. HOWEVER, I AM GREATLY INSPIRED BY THE DIGNITY AND COURAGE THAT YOU AND YOUR FELLOW STUDENTS HAVE MANIFESTED BY STANDING UP FOR A RIGHTEOUS CAUSE. YOU HAVE MADE JAIL GOING A BADGE OF HONOR AND DIGNITY. YOU ALREADY STAND IN THE GLOW OF THE WORLD'S BRIGHT TOMORROWS. PLEASE KNOW THAT YOU AND YOUR FELLOW STUDENTS HAVE MY ABSOLUTE SUPPORT IN THESE DIFFICULT HOURS.

MARTIN LUTHER KING, JR.

TWc. MLKP-MBU: Box 23A.

---

1. Rebecca Dixon Mohr (1941–), born in Montgomery, earned a B.S. (1963) from Alabama State College and an M.S.L.S. (1967) from Atlanta University. Mohr worked as a librarian at Florida A&M University (1967–1971) and at Florida State University (1971–1978). She then served as grants administrator at Norfolk State University and Talladega College before returning to Alabama State in 1989 to work as a circulation librarian.

2. Montgomery Recorders Court judge Eugene Loe ordered the students to pay $100 fines (Herschel Cribb, "32 Students Given Fines; File Appeals," *Montgomery Advertiser,* 12 March 1960). In his 18 April reply to Dixon, King sent words of encouragement: "Be sure to keep your chin up. In spite of the tensions and difficulties of these days I am convinced that we are living in one of the most exciting periods of history. You should feel privileged to be able to live at such a time as this."

From Rosa Parks

14 March 1960
Detroit, Mich.

King receives a supportive letter from Parks, who refers obliquely to medical problems she had suffered since leaving Montgomery in 1957.[1] *A month after receiving this letter, King provided a statement of support for a fund-raising effort to benefit Parks: "Millions of Negroes all over this nation have a new sense of dignity and destiny because Mrs. Parks inspired an event which in turn inspired them. Now that she is facing her moments of suffering as a results of the reprisals that she faced, I know that all people of goodwill will come to her rescue."*[2]

Dr. Martin Luther King, Jr.
407 Auburn Avenue
Atlanta, Georgia

Dear Dr. King:

I was so sorry to hear of your being arrested for Alabama Income Tax. I hope this clipping from the Michigan Chronicle will be of some interest and comfort to you.[3]

It is good to know that you are going on with the movement for freedom in spite of the segregationists attempts to intimidate and embarrass you.

I am not so well, but better than I was some time ago. My mother and husband are quite well.[4] They join me in sending kindest regards to you and Mrs. King and wish for you much happiness in your new home.

Please ask Miss Ella J. Baker to send me her address. I would like to write to her. I will ever remember her kindness to me in 1957.

Sincerely yours,
[*signed*] Rosa Parks

ALS. MLKP-MBU: Box 56.

---

1. A July 1960 magazine profile described Parks as "just a tattered rag of her former self—penniless, debt-ridden, ailing with stomach ulcers and a throat tumor, compressed into two rooms with her husband and mother" (Alex Poinsett, "The Troubles of Bus Boycott's Forgotten Woman: Montgomery, Ala., Heroine Now Ill, Poverty-Stricken," *Jet*, 14 July 1960, p. 12; for earlier press criticism of the MIA's failure to assist Parks, see note 1, Parks to King, 23 August 1957, in *Papers* 4:261). An article in the MIA newsletter expressed the organization's shock and its resolve to provide more for Parks: "All freedom fighters should know that temporary relief will not meet the great need of Mrs. Parks. There must be some long-ranged planning" (MIA, "The Rosa Park's Case," *Newsletter*, 21 September 1960).

2. King to Maxcine Young, 29 April 1960. King may have also alerted the MIA to Parks's need; the organization sent a donation in March, and Abernathy phoned to assure her of the MIA's continuing support ("The Rosa Park's Case").

3. Parks likely enclosed an editorial denouncing the case against King ("Alabama Die-Hards Try Another Trick," *Michigan Chronicle*, 27 February 1960).

4. Parks refers to Leona McCauley and Raymond Parks.

18 Mar 1960

To Edward P. Gottlieb

18 March 1960
[*Atlanta, Ga.*]

At A. Philip Randolph's request, the War Resisters League granted Rustin, the organization's executive secretary, a one-year leave of absence to organize protests at the upcoming Democratic and Republican national conventions and to serve as King's special assistant.[1] *In a 2 March letter, WRL chairman Edward Gottlieb explained to King that the decision was made with the understanding that "nonviolent action" would be central to Rustin's assignment: "We know that Bayard has a unique contribution to make in this field."*[2] *In the following letter King assures Gottlieb that Rustin's assistance "will be of inestimable value" to the civil rights struggle.*

Mr. Edward Gottlieb, Chairman
War Resisters League
Five Beekman Street
New York 38, New York

Dear Mr. Gottlieb:

This is to acknowledge receipt of your letter of March 2, concerning the decision which your executive committee recently made in relation to the request of Mr. Randolph and myself to secure the services of Bayard Rustin. I have read your letter with scrutinizing care, and [*word illegible*] in full agreement with all of the decisions reached. We are deeply grateful to you for giving Bayard this leave of absence to work in the integration movement. We are thoroughly committed to the method of nonviolence in our struggle and we are convinced that Bayard's expertness and commitment in this area will be of inestimable value in our future efforts.

Business appointments and other concerns are constantly bringing me to New York. So I will be more than happy to find some time during some of these visits to discuss with your committee Bayard's work and any questions that you may have to raise.

Again, let me thank you for your cooperation and support, and I am sure that the gains that will come from Bayard's work in this field will in some way compensate for the real loss that you are facing at this time.

---

1. Gottlieb to Randolph, 2 March 1960.

2. Gottlieb also indicated that he was pleased that Randolph and King would occasionally meet with WRL officials "to discuss Bayard's work and any questions we may have about it, so that our Executive Committee may be in a position to make its own evaluation of the contribution Bayard is making to the cause of nonviolence." Edward P. Gottlieb (1905–), born in New York City, earned a B.S. (1925) from the City College of New York. He was a public school teacher (1925–1943) and principal (1952–1967) in the New York City public schools and served as chairman of the WRL (1960–1968). Gottlieb helped mobilize students to attend the 1958 and 1959 Youth Marches for Integrated Schools.

Very sincerely yours,
Martin L. King, Jr.

MLK:mlb

TLc. MLKP-MBU: Box 27.

To C. Kenzie Steele

19 March 1960
[*Atlanta, Ga.*]

On 20 February eleven Tallahassee demonstrators were arrested and charged with disturbing the peace for protesting at a local chain store. After Judge John Rudd ordered the protesters to either pay a $300 fine or serve a sixty-day jail sentence, eight of the eleven elected jail.[1] *Two days after the verdict, King sends encouragement to the eight students via SCLC vice president C. K. Steele, whose sixteen-year-old son Henry was among those jailed.*[2]

REV. C. K. STEELE
(FOR 8 JAILED STUDENTS)
TALLAHASSEE, FLORIDA

I HAVE JUST LEARNED OF YOUR COURAGEOUS WILLINGNESS TO GO TO JAIL INSTEAD OF PAYING FINES FOR YOUR RIGHTEOUS PROTEST AGAINST SEGREGATED EATING FACILITIES. THROUGH THIS DECISION YOU HAVE AGAIN PROVEN THAT THERE IS NOTHING MORE MAJESTIC AND SUBLIME THAN THE DETERMINED COURAGE OF INDIVIDUALS WILLING TO SUFFER AND SACRIFICE FOR THE CAUSE OF FREEDOM. YOU HAVE DISCOVERED ANEW THE MEANING OF THE CROSS, AND AS CHRIST DIED TO MAKE MEN HOLY, YOU ARE SUFFERING TO MAKE MEN FREE. AS YOU SUFFER THE INCONVENIENCE OF REMAINING IN JAIL, PLEASE REMEMBER THAT UNEARNED SUFFERING IS REDEMPTIVE. GOING TO JAIL FOR A RIGHTEOUS CAUSE IS A BADGE OF HONOR AND A SYMBOL OF DIGNITY. I ASSURE YOU THAT YOUR VALIANT WITNESS IS ONE OF THE GLOWING EPICS OF OUR TIME AND YOU ARE BRINGING ALL OF AMERICA NEARER THE THRESHHOLD OF THE WORLD'S BRIGHT TOMORROWS.

---

1. At a 17 March hearing Rudd gave the demonstrators a thirty-day suspended sentence and placed those attending Florida A&M University on probation for one year or until graduation ("Tallahassee Sitdown Sentences Are Suspended," *Miami Herald,* 18 March 1960).

2. The other students who chose jail with Henry Steele were Priscilla G. Stephens, William H. Larkins, Clement C. Carney, Angelina Nance, Barbara Joan Broxton, John A. Broxton, and Patricia G. Stephens, who later remarked: "We strongly believe that Martin Luther King was right when he said: 'We've got to fill the jails in order to win our equal rights'" (Stephens, "Letter from a Jailed Student," *CORE-lator,* April 1960; see also "8 Florida Negro Demonstrators Choose 60 Days in Jail over Fines," *Washington Post,* 19 March 1960).

TWc. MLKP-MBU: Box 70.

"Revolt Without Violence— The Negroes' New Strategy"

21 March 1960
Washington, D.C.

In this interview for U.S. News & World Report, *King predicts that the sit-in demonstrations, which had spread to more than thirty southern cities, will extend beyond dining facilities.*[1] *He stresses that no organization planned the protests; rather, they were "spontaneous" and "initiated by students," who then "asked for the advice and counsel and direction from organizations and individuals who had been more experienced in this area." King further claims that earlier protests, such as the Montgomery bus boycott, had influenced the students: "I am sure that many of the forces of history and many things that have happened in the United States at least inspired these young people to start them, because they had been hearing about nonviolent resistance."*[2]

Q: Dr. King, is the protest movement of Negroes in the South going to continue and grow greater?

A: I can say this—that the Negro is no longer willing to accept segregation in any area of life, whether it's in public eating places; whether it's in public transportation; whether it's in public schools. There is a strong revolt against the whole system of segregation on the part of Negro people all over the South and all over the nation.

It is natural and possible that this movement will go beyond eating places. For the moment it is being centered on eating places—and I'm not saying that it will go into another area the next week after we've finished working in this area.

But I do feel that, ultimately, the movement will dramatize the problem of segregation in every area and any other areas with which we are confronted.

Q: What would you say is the basic purpose of this campaign?

A: Well, the real purpose is to use a creative method to achieve full citizenship rights for the Negro people of the United States.

---

1. In an earlier letter to a supporter, King accused the magazine of having a racially biased editorial slant: "It has proved to be anti-Negro through and through and seeks to play up the ideas that are quite precious to the segregationists in the South" (King to Shirley A. Livingston, 30 May 1959).

2. King's interview was preceded by a photo essay that included remarks about race relations in Montgomery from SCLC secretary-treasurer Ralph Abernathy, Alabama governor John Patterson, and *Montgomery Advertiser* editor Grover C. Hall, Jr.

I am convinced that the method of nonviolent resistance is the most potent weapon available to impress people in their struggle for freedom and human dignity. Therefore, I have advised all along that we follow a path of nonviolence, because, if we ever succumb to the temptation of using violence in our struggle, unborn generations will be the recipients of the long and desolate night of bitterness—and our aim is not to defeat or to humiliate the white man, but to win his friendship and understanding.

One of the ways we seek to do this is through this nonviolent protest, thereby arousing the dozing conscience of the white community and hoping to ultimately achieve the beloved community and the type of brotherhood that is necessary for us to survive in a meaningful manner.

Q: Is it difficult for a Negro to find a good place to eat in the downtown area of a Southern city?

A: It is extremely difficult in the average Southern city. Negroes can't find eating places. Occasionally, they have segregated facilities, but these facilities for Negroes are usually very inadequate, very limited.

This is one of the reasons—I think probably more than anything else—that the protest moved in the area of eating facilities, because the conditions are, in many instances, appalling. In many of these stores, since they are stores with lower prices—and the Negro is still low on the economic ladder; he has to buy in these stores—the clientele is predominantly Negro.

This is why we feel that this protest is not only righteous from a moral point of view, but it is righteous from a practical point of view. It is justifiable in the sense that we spend a lot of money in these stores, and the young people are simply saying now: "We want you to respect our person and our selfhood as much as you respect our dollars."

Q: Are you saying that there is a real problem involved and this is not just a dramatic movement to get attention?

A: Oh, no—it's a real problem, a problem of accumulated injustices over the years.

Q: Is there danger, in your mind, that the picketing and the "sit-ins" may lead to violence?

A: Well, I certainly hope not. On the part of the Negro community, I think violence will remain at a minimum—that is to say I don't believe the Negro people will precipitate the violence, that they will inflict violence upon the white community, because we have stressed over and over again the need for nonviolence. And I'm proud that, by and large, the Negro students have followed a very disciplined course of action and a way of nonviolence.

Now, as far as the white community goes, I cannot give an absolute answer. I would say this: It depends on the law-enforcement agencies in the particular community. If the law-enforcement agencies are concerned about keeping peace and preventing mobs and the unlawful elements in the community from taking over, I don't think there will be any real violence. But, if the law-enforcement agencies continue to predict violence—as they do in so many cases—this will turn out to be an unconscious invitation to violence.

We know that violence develops in the whole racial struggle only when the violent forces feel they have support and that they are aided and abetted by the law-enforcement agencies. Wherever the law-enforcement agencies and the public officials have made it clear that they would not have violence, it hasn't emerged.

If the law-enforcement agencies are not really concerned, then there is a possibility that violence will emerge.

Q: How powerful is the Negroes' economic weapon, as used in these sit-downs, in your opinion?

A: I think it's a very sizable weapon. We haven't achieved economic justice in its total meaning in the United States as a race, but we have made real progress in the area of economic justice, and it has come to the point now that the national income of the Negro, collectively, is about 18 billion dollars a year—which is more than all the exports of the United States or total wages and salaries paid in Canada.

Now, with this much economic intake, so to speak, I think the Negro has a great weapon, and, in many of these areas, particularly in stores that have public eating places, Negroes are spending a lot of money. Many of these firms and many of these businesses would really suffer if the Negro decided to withdraw his support and refused to trade with them. So that I think it's really a powerful weapon and it's not to be underestimated, and, whenever the Negro can use it creatively, I think it is possible to bring amazing results.

Q: Do you expect the demonstrations and the present movement to continue over an extended period?

A: Well, I can't say. It depends on what breaks through in terms of achieved victory. If, in the next few weeks, some of the stores will come to the point of saying, "We will break down the barriers of segregation and allow people to eat on an integrated basis," then I believe this will stimulate many of the communities to slow up on the demonstrations and do more in terms of negotiation. It just depends on what we are able to achieve.

I do think it is a spreading movement, and it is still spreading. The Negro students are greatly concerned about their civil rights, and naturally the whole struggle in the world today has its implications in this country. I think this is really a part of the world-wide movement for freedom and human dignity. This isn't an isolated struggle, it's a part of the world-wide movement. And I'm sure that it will not automatically cease. It will cease only when the Negro people feel that they have achieved something.

Q: How many ministers are members of your organization—that is, the Southern Christian Leadership Conference?

A: We are not a membership organization. Our organization is an organization of organizations. We have affiliate organizations, rather than having memberships.

Now, in terms of our affiliates, I really don't have the number of ministers that would be involved; but in terms of our affiliates, that would bring in many, many ministers from across the South. In most States I would say the organization would cover the vast majority of Negro ministers. But I do not have the exact number.

Q: Are Negro educators members of the organization also?

A: Yes, we have some Negro educators who are working with us very closely—some on the executive board. One of our officers is the chairman of the department of history of Alabama State College in Montgomery.[3] He's quite a writer and has given active support. And we have other Negro educators and more are coming in, to share with us and give us their broad experience as we go on.

TRAINING IN NONVIOLENCE—

Q: How are the college students reached and trained for the demonstrations?

A: Well, by and large they have read literature on nonviolence and used that as a guide before they moved out. The leaders of the movements have stressed it over and over again, and we have had several of our board members in the situation and on hand to give assistance—as in North Carolina, the Rev. Douglas Moore, who is a member of our board, was on hand to guide the North Carolina students.

The Rev. Jim Lawson, who was expelled from Vanderbilt [University] a few days ago, a very dedicated Christian gentleman, was on hand in Nashville. He's a member of our organization, and he gave advice and direction.[4]

The Rev. Mr. [*Ralph*] Abernathy in Montgomery, who is the secretary-treasurer of our organization, the Rev. Mr. [*C. K.*] Steele, who is one of our vice presidents, in Tallahassee—all of these men have been disciplined in nonviolence, because we have had institutes constantly in our organization, and they have been on hand to give the students a sense of direction and a sense of the meaning of nonviolence.

And I shouldn't say only our organization, but other national organizations like the Congress of Racial Equality [CORE].[5] CORE has worked in this field for many years and has had members of its national staff going in local communities, guiding the students in the whole area of nonviolence.

Q: Have there been training courses for leaders?

A: Yes. Last year we had a South-wide institute on nonviolent resistance to segregation. It was here in Atlanta. We brought leaders in from all over the South—all of the Southern States.[6] And we have had local institutes—that is, in the States or in particular cities—so that we have men on hand who have been trained in nonviolence and, as I said, CORE has also come in and has given invaluable advice because of its long history and work in this area.

Q: So the demonstrations are not entirely spontaneous?

A: Well, I would say that, in the beginning, they were spontaneous—that is, there was no organization that sat down and planned these demonstrations on a national scale.

They were initiated by students; they have been fed and sustained by students. Once they started, however, the students asked for the advice and counsel and direction from organizations and individuals who had been more experienced

---

3. King refers to SCLC historian Lawrence D. Reddick.

4. Lawson, who had been conducting workshops on nonviolent protest with Nashville students for several months, was expelled on 3 March for his role in the city's sit-in demonstrations. "University" bracketed in original.

5. Acronym bracketed in original.

6. SCLC, FOR, and CORE sponsored the three-day nonviolent institute in July 1959 (see Resolutions, First Southwide Institute on Nonviolent Resistance to Segregation, 11 August 1959, pp. 261–262 in this volume).

in this area. But I think it is important that they were spontaneous in the beginning and initiated by the students. No organization started the demonstrations directly.

I am sure that many of the forces of history and many things that have happened in the United States at least inspired these young people to start them, because they had been hearing about nonviolent resistance. There was the Montgomery bus boycott, which was based on the whole nonviolent approach.[7]

PROGRESS FOR NEGROES—

Q: Do you feel that the position of the Negro in the South is changing?

A: Well, I definitely think the position of the Negro is changing in the South. We have made some very meaningful strides, I think, in past years. And I am sure that, as the years unfold, we will continue to make greater strides.

We are gradually gaining more economic security. The educational standards are rising. Even specific areas in the civil-rights struggle are moving and developing. Therefore, I think the Negro is gaining something very definite in the South.

Now, I am convinced there are many forces working in our world today, and in our nation in particular, that will bring about an even greater movement toward our goal in the next few years. There is, first, the rolling tide of world opinion which will make it necessary for the country to do something about this problem if it is to maintain its moral leadership in a world that is two-thirds colored.

The South is gradually industrializing, and this industrialization of the South, with its concomitant urbanization, will inevitably break down the mores of white supremacy.

Then, many forces of good will are at work in the South—and I'm not talking merely about Negro forces, but millions of white people who have been silent because of fear, fear of political, social and economic reprisals. But, I think, more and more, the liberals of the white South are going to be forced to come out, if for no other reason than to keep their schools open.

So this type of backing and support from the moderates of the white South and from the church—the church is coming out more than before—and, finally, the determination of the Negro himself will serve to make conditions better for the Negro in the next few years.

I feel that we are now moving toward the last days of the strong resistance in the South. I can't say exactly how many years, but I do feel that the forces of resistance are on their last legs and that, in a few years, even in the most recalcitrant State, the officials will recognize that it is necessary to come to terms with what is now the law of the land, and what is necessary to become a reality if we are to survive.

PD. *U.S. News & World Report,* 21 March 1960, pp. 76–78.

---

7. In August 1956 *U.S. News & World Report* published a version of King's "The Montgomery Story," an address delivered at the June 1956 annual NAACP convention, and a rebuttal to it from Grover C. Hall, Jr. (King and Hall, "Pro and Con, Alabama's Bus Boycott: What It's All About," *U.S. News & World Report,* 3 August 1956, pp. 82–89). For reactions to King's 1956 article, see King to William Cooper Cumming, 18 September 1956, and King to Sally Canada, 19 September 1956, in *Papers* 3:371–372 and 373, respectively.

From Ella J. Baker

23 Mar 1960

23 March 1960

Baker updates King and Abernathy on plans for a conference to assess the state of the student movement and to coordinate desegregation efforts.[1] *She reports on a conversation she had with Glenn Smiley and Douglas Moore, who "agreed that the meeting should be youth centered, and that the adults attending would serve in an advisory capacity, and should mutually agree to 'speak only when asked to do so.'"*

TO: Dr. Martin L. King, Jr. and Rev. Ralph D. Abernathy
FROM Miss Ella J. Baker
RE: Student Conference, April 15–17

The following developments have taken place in connection with the student conference on Non-Violent Resistance to Segregation, to be held at Shaw University, Raleigh, N.C., April 15–17:

I. VISIT TO RALEIGH–DURHAM

Last Wednesday evening, March 16, I went to Raleigh–Durham to consumate agreements on holding the student conference at Shaw University. By a favorable [*coincidence?*], Glenn Smiley arrived in Durham about the same time as I did, and I was able to discuss in some detail, the conference plans with him and Rev. Douglas Moore, simultaneously.[2]

They agreed that the meeting should be youth centered, and that the adults attending would serve in an advisory capacity, and should mutually agree to "speak only when asked to do so". However, to avoid any conflicting points of view among adults, it is hoped that we might meet for a couple of hours prior to the opening session of the conference. I am mentioning this at this point, so that those of us who are planning to attend might schedule ourselves to arrive by noon of Friday, April 15.

I Spoke with President [*William R.*] Strassmer, his administrative assistant, Mr. [*D. H.*] Keck, Dr. Grady W. Davis, Dean of the School of Religion, and Mr. [*Harvey*] Alexander, the Business Manager, regarding housing and eating facilities. Although Shaw University will only be able to accomodate about 40 students, the Dean of St. Augustine College, and the student leadership were pledged to cooperate on housing.[3]

In addition, the YMCA is only 2 blocks away from Shaw campus, and with the combined facilities of Shaw—St. Augustine, and the 'Y', ample housing can be provided.

---

1. For more on the conference, see King, "Statement to the Press at the Beginning of the Youth Leadership Conference," 15 April 1960, pp. 426–427 in this volume.

2. In addition to making arrangements for a conference on nonviolence in March, FOR field secretary Glenn Smiley had been in the state consulting with sit-in protesters and sympathizers (Smiley, To Members and Friends of FOR in North and South Carolina, 24 February 1960).

3. Prezell R. Robinson was the dean of St. Augustine College.

23 Mar 1960

II. CONFERENCE COST:

a. Housing — $1.00 per night

b. Meals — $4.30 for six (6) meals (Supper, Friday night, three meals Saturday, and breakfast and lunch, Sunday)

c. Transportation — The details of the transportation costs will have to be worked out, and will be based on bus fares from Raleigh to the various cities from which representatives are expected. I expect to have this completed by the end of the week.

III. PROMOTION AND FINANCIAL SUPPORT

1. Pledges of cooperation have been volunteered by FOR, CORE, and the Southeaster Regional Office of the American Friends Service Committee. This cooperation will include financial assistance, I understand, from both CORE and FOR, and probably from AFSC. The details of this will be determined after the total promotional cost has been estimated.

2. Contact with students. In addition to mail from our office, CORE has agreed to send out material for us, and Rev. Douglas Moore will personally visit the key areas in North Carolina to stimulate both youth delegations to the conference, and possible adult delegations to attend the Saturday evening mass meeting.

3. Mass Meeting — The Memorial Auditorium has been secured for a public mass meeting to be held Saturday evening, April 16. This meeting will be co-sponsored by SCLC and the Raleigh Citizens Association, of which Dr. Grady W. Davis is executive secretary. The Citizens Association negotiated the arrangement, and when Dr. Davis returns to Raleigh, this week-end, He and Rev. Moore will follow through on getting out the necessary placards and leaflets.

   Dr. Martin L. King, Jr. will be principle speaker, and other freedom fighters, and key student leaders will share the mass meeting program. Weekly news releases have been sent to the weekly and daily papers, and will continue to be sent.[4]

IV. PROGRAM

Program details have not been completed, but the following suggestions are under consideration:

a) Dean of Conference: Rev. J. M. [*James*] Lawson, Jr.
   Assistant Dean: Rev. Douglas E. Moore

SCHEDULE

FRIDAY

7:30 P.M. KEYNOTE SESSION

SATURDAY

Morning Workshop

Afternoon Workshop

4. "Youth Leadership Retreat Planned," *Baltimore Afro-American,* 12 March 1960.

SUNDAY

Morning | Committee Session
Plenary Session
Findings and Recommendations

ADJOURNMENT At Lunch

NOTE:

We should like to be able to print a program for this meeting.

TL. SCLCR-GAMK: Box 32.

To Claude Barnett

24 March 1960
[*Atlanta, Ga.*]

On 21 March South African police in the black township of Sharpeville killed more than sixty peaceful protesters who had been demonstrating against pass laws, which required blacks to carry identification. The incident sparked a massive outbreak of strikes, demonstrations, and riots in South Africa and focused international criticism on the apartheid regime. In a telegram sent the following day, Claude Barnett, head of the Associated Negro Press (ANP), requested that King wire him a "brief reaction to slaughter by police troops and planes of [Negroes] in South Africa conducting peaceful mass demonstration against restrictive law." Barnett queried, "Is there a lesson for USA where protests are also in progress"? He released excerpts of the following draft over the ANP wire on 28 March.[1]

MR. CLAUDE BARNETT
ASSOCIATED NEGRO PRESS
3531 SOUTH PARKWAY
CHIAGO, ILLINOIS

THE RECENT MASS MURDER OF AFRICANS ENGAGED IN ★ {the} PEACEFUL PROTEST AGAINST RESTRICTIVE LAW IS A TRAGIC AND SHAMEFUL EXPRESSION

1. Barnett also published reactions from William V. S. Tubman, president of Liberia, and Senator John F. Kennedy, chairman of the subcommittee on African Affairs (Associated Negro Press, Press release, 28 March 1960). King was later among the signatories of a letter to U.S. secretary of state Christian A. Herter, urging him to recall the ambassador to South Africa and to suspend purchases of South African gold (Samuel H. Beer et al. to King, 8 April 1960, and Americans for Democratic Action, Press release, 17 April 1960). Claude Albert Barnett (1889–1967), born in Sanford, Florida, graduated from Tuskegee Institute in 1906 and moved to Chicago, where he worked as a postal clerk. In 1919 he founded the Associated Negro Press, a wire service for African American newspapers. Barnett traveled to the Ghanian independence celebration in 1957 with his wife, who recorded a radio interview with King while there (King, Interview by Etta Moten Barnett, 6 March 1957, in *Papers* 4:145–148).

26 Mar 1960

OF MAN'S INHUMANITY TO MAN. SUCH BARBARIC AND UNCIVILIZED ACTS ARE SHOCKING TO ALL MEN OF GOODWILL. THIS TRAGIC MASSACRE BY POLICE TROOPS IN SOUTH AFRICA SHOULD AROUSE THE CONSCIENCE OF THE WHOLE WORLD. THIS TRAGIC OCCURRENCE IN SOUTH AFRICA SHOULD ALSO SERVE AS A WARNING SIGNAL TO THE UNITED STATES WHERE PEACEFUL DEMONSTRATIONS ARE ALSO BEING CONDUCTED BY STUDENT GROUPS. AS LONG AS SEGREGATION CONTINUES TO EXIST; AS LONG AS GESTAPO-LIKE TACTICS ARE USED BY OFFICIALS OF SOUTHERN COMMUNITIES; AND AS LONG AS {there are} GOVERNORS AND UNITED STATES SENATORS ARROGANTLY DEFY THE LAW OF THE LAND, THE UNITED STATES IS FACED WITH A POTENTIAL REIGN OF TERROR MORE BARBARIC THAN ANYTHING WE SEE IN SOUTH AFRICA.

MARTIN LUTHER KING, JR., PRESIDENT
THE SOUTHERN CHRISTIAN LEADERSHIP CONFERENCE

TAWc. MLKP-MBU: Box 35.

To Dwight D. Eisenhower

26 March 1960
New York, N.Y.

King and other civil rights supporters applaud the State Department's protest of the Sharpeville massacres and urge Eisenhower to issue a declaration "placing the administration firmly on the side of Negroes" in the South, adding: "Africans are turning to the UN for moral support and encouragement; must we?" In response, Gerald Morgan, deputy assistant to the president, referred to Eisenhower's earlier expression of sympathy for the "efforts of any group to enjoy the rights of equality."[1]

THE PRESIDENT
THE WHITE HOUSE

WE ARE GRATEFUL THAT OUR STATE DEPARTMENT HAS PROTESTED THE MASS KILLINGS OF OUR SOUTH AFRICAN BROTHERS AND WE ARE PLEASED THAT THE UN SECURITY COUNCIL WILL MEET MARCH 29TH TO CONSIDER THAT OUTRAGE.[2]

---

1. Morgan to Abernathy, 11 April 1960.

2. Noting that the United States "does not ordinarily comment on the internal affairs of governments with which it enjoys normal relations," a State Department representative expressed "regret" for "the tragic loss of life resulting from the measures taken against the demonstrators in South Africa" (Dana Adams Schmidt, "Police Violence in South Africa Criticized by U.S.," *New York Times,* 23 March 1960). On 1 April, following four days of discussion, the United Nations Security Council blamed the violence on South Africa's "continued disregard" of United Nations resolutions "calling upon it to

WE URGE THAT BEFORE MARCH 29TH OUR GOVERNMENT ISSUE A STATEMENT PLACING THE ADMINISTRATION FIRMLY ON THE SIDE OF NEGROES IN THE SOUTHERN STATES IN THEIR PRESENT STRUGGLE FOR THEIR CONSTITUTIONAL RIGHTS, SINCE THEY ARE SUBJECTED TO INTIMIDATION, THREATS AND VIOLENCE WHEN THEY CLAIM THESE RIGHTS.

26 Mar 1960

FURTHERMORE, VOTING LAWS ARE USELESS TO SOUTHERN NEGROES WHO FEAR FOR THEIR LIVES AND FOR THE SAFETY OF THEIR FAMILIES IF THEY TRY TO REGISTER AND VOTE.

SUCH A STATEMENT FROM THE ADMINISTRATION WOULD STRENGTHEN THE POSITION OF OUR DELEGATION BEFORE THE NATIONS OF THE WORLD.

SOUTH AFRICANS CANNOT HOPE FOR HELP FROM A GOVERNMENT COMMITTED TO "APARTHEID" ; NOR CAN WE HOPE FOR HELP FROM LOCAL AND STATE GOVERNMENTS COMMITTED TO "WHITE SUPREMACY" .

AFRICANS ARE TURNING TO THE UN FOR MORAL SUPPORT AND ENCOURAGEMENT; MUST WE?

SIGNED:
THE REVEREND R. O. ABERNATHY, MONTGOMERY, ALABAMA;
PRESIDENT, MONTGOMERY IMPROVEMENT ASSOCIATION.
DR. JOHN S. CHAMBERS, LEXINGTON, KENTUCKY; EXECUTIVE SECRETARY,
KENTUCKY COUNCIL OF CHURCHES.
JOHN WESLEY DOBBS, ATLANTA, GEORGIA; GRAND MASTER,
PRINCE HALL MASONS.
DR. CHARLES G. GOMILLION, TUSKEGEE, ALABAMA; PRESIDENT,
TUSKEGEE CIVIC ASSOCIATION.
DR. EDWIN B. HENDERSON, FALLS CHURCH, VIRGINIA;
AUTHOR AND EDUCATOR.
JOHN L. LEFLORE MOBILE, ALABAMA; PRESIDENT,
MOBILE CIVIC ASSOCIATION.
THE REVEREND MARTIN LUTHER KING, ATLANTA, GEORGIA;
PRESIDENT, SOUTHERN CHRISTIAN LEADERSHIP CONFERENCE.
DR. HERMAN H. LONG, NASHVILLE, TENNESSEE; FISK UNIVERSITY.
BISHOP EDGAR H. LOVE, BALTIMORE, MARYLAND; PRESIDENT,
COLLEGE OF BISHOPS, THE METHODIST CHURCH, CENTRAL JURISDICTION.
HERBERT MARSHALL III, M.D., WASHINGTON, D.C.; PAST PRESIDENT,
NATIONAL MEDICAL ASSOCIATION.
E. D. NIXON, MONTGOMERY, ALABAMA; PRESIDENT, INTERNATIONAL
BROTHERHOOD OF SLEEPING CAR PORTERS, MONTGOMERY DIVISION.
DR. M. D. PERDUE, LOUISVILLE, KENTUCKY; CHAIRMAN, COMMISSION
ON STATE OF THE NATION AND NEEDS OF THE RACE,
GENERAL ASSOCIATION OF KENTUCKY BAPTISTS.

---

revise its policies and bring them into conformity with its obligations and responsibilities under the Charter of the United Nations" (United Nations Security Council, 15th Year, *Official Records of the Security Council,* Supp. April, May and June 1960 [S/4300]).

26 Mar 1960

THE REVEREND FRED L. SHUTTLESWORTH, BIRMINGHAM, ALABAMA; PRESIDENT, ALABAMA CHRISTIAN MOVEMENT FOR HUMAN RIGHTS.
DR. C. O. SIMPKINS, SHREVEPORT, LOUISIANA; PRESIDENT, UNITED CHRISTIAN MOVEMENT.
THE REVEREND C. K. STEELE, TALLAHASSEE, FLORIDA; PRESIDENT, INTER-CITY COUNCIL.
BISHOP C. EUBANK TUCKER, LOUISVILLE, KENTUCKY; PRESIDING BISHOP, AME ZION CHURCH.
W HALE THOMPSON, NEWPORT NEWS VIRGINIA; ATTORNEY.
CARTER WESLEY, HOUSTON, TEXAS; PUBLISHER, THE INFORMER NEWSPAPERS.
AUBREY W. WILLIAMS, MONTGOMERY, ALABAMA; PUBLISHER, SOUTHERN FARM AND HOME; PRESIDENT, SOUTHERN CONFERENCE EDUCATIONAL FUND, INC.
BISHOP SMALLWOOD E. WILLIAMS, WASHINGTON, D.C. PRESIDING BISHOP, BIBLE WAY CHURCH, WORLDWIDE.
DEAN GRADY D DAVIS, RALEIGH NC SCHOOL OF RELIGION, SHAW UNIVERSITY.

PWSr. WCFG-KAbE.

From Harris Wofford

1 Apr 1960

1 April 1960
Notre Dame, Ind.

Civil rights attorney Harris Wofford offers "sharp criticism" of an appeal for funds that appeared in the 29 March New York Times.[1] *Placed by the Committee to Defend Martin Luther King and the Struggle for Freedom in the South, the advertisement described King as "the one man who, more than any other, symbolizes the new spirit now sweeping the South." Wofford suggests that the fund-raising effort should focus on student activists and argues that "the very name of the committee is a mistake and demeans you." He urges King to demonstrate his "confidence and independence, showing that you are not in any sense the puppet of a northern organization."*[2]

Rev. Martin Luther King, Jr.
The Ebenezer Baptist Church
407 Auburn Avenue, N.E.
Atlanta, Georgia

Dear Martin:

I have been trying to get you for a couple of days on the telephone. The March 29 full-page ad in the New York Times is a significant move, and I trust on balance a good one. Of course I support strongly an appeal for support from the North. But I am most concerned by the way part of this ad—fortunately only part of it—is pegged on you and your tax case. It seems to me that this turns you into a kind of Scottsboro boy, not a man who is master of his fate.[3]

I do not think that your problem should be equated with that of the students and others who have been arrested in the demonstrations. Not only are the legal problems different, but your stature—as the leader and symbol of this movement—is different. The students will need a battery of lawyers and the widespread legal defense will require adequate financing.

But I think you would give greater dignity to your case if you did not permit solicitation of funds on your behalf, but conducted your own defense independently and courageously. I do not mean to suggest that you should not have adequate le-

1. The advertisement, titled "Heed Their Rising Voices," also rankled NAACP officials (for a facsimile of the advertisement, see p. 382 in this volume). In an 8 April memo to Wilkins, NAACP program director James Farmer characterized it as "a thoroughly dishonest and deceptive appeal" and suggested that Randolph and King "be privately taken to task." For further reactions, see John Malcolm Patterson to King, 9 May 1960, pp. 456–458 in this volume.

2. The appeal indicated that any monies raised would be divided among King's defense, support for the student protesters, and the voting rights struggle. For more on the disbursement of funds, see King to Jackie Robinson, 19 June 1960, pp. 475–478 in this volume.

3. The "Scottsboro boys" were nine black youths aged thirteen to twenty, who in 1931 were accused of rape by two white women. Their case became a cause célèbre after the Communist-affiliated International Labor Defense (ILD) took over their legal defense and initiated an international protest campaign.

gal counsel. In a complicated case such as this you need the best counsel possible. But I am sure that you could get distinguished leaders of the American Bar to join in your legal defense without any such solicitation of funds or reimbursement to them. A friend of mine is convinced that Thomas K. Finletter, one of New York's top lawyers, former Secretary of the Air Force, would serve as counsel, and I am sure that a distinguished Republican lawyer would be prepared to join Finletter if that seemed indicated. Shad Polier, who is one of the men signing the appeal in the Times is himself a sharp lawyer.[4] I would think that a good lawyer from my former firm, Covington and Burling, might be available. I think such an unpaid legal committee in this situation would be far, far better than the approach suggested by the "Committee To Defend Martin Luther King and the Struggle for Freedom in the South."

How I wish we were closer or that we used the telephone more to each other! Because I am convinced that the tone of the ad, when it touches you, and the very name of the committee is a mistake and demeans you. If we were talking I would try to make the case for the following immediate action on your part: A letter to the New York Times and to the committee stating that you do not want any of the funds collected to be used for your own legal defense, that you deeply appreciate the support being offered to you but that on reflection you feel that the focus of the committee should be wholly on the defense of the students and others arrested in the demonstrations, and that you are asking that this be made clear to all contributors. You could add your own strong plea for support to the demonstrators. If you want to arrange in advance for the organization of a separate legal defense committee for you, I think that could be done promptly.

One reason I urge such action is that I think the one damaging part of your Alabama tax case is the implication to the public that, according to the "Where there is smoke there is fire" reasoning, you may have appropriated some of the funds collected for the bus boycott for your own purposes. I am sure there is not a penny of truth in this, but I think an appeal for funds for your defense compounds any suspicion that has been cast by this strategem of the State of Alamama.

I think an action on your part demonstrating your confidence and independence, showing that you are not in any sense the puppet of a northern organization appearing to be running your affairs, and renouncing any financial aid for yourself, would add to your stature, and would in fact contribute to the success of the committee soliciting support from the public. In fact, if I were a member of the committee I would use such a renunciation by you as the occasion for another ad strengthening the appeal for support to the students.

Let me suggest that some time soon you try to talk with a good friend of mine, a very astute public relations man, Ed Greenfield, who would be a good one for you to talk over things like this {with} from time to time. Greenfield could help you with your money-raising and other problems. He is the one who was, and I think still is, interested in our old idea of an institute for the study of race rela-

---

4. Polier was one of the lawyers in the Scottsboro case and later served on the executive board of the NAACP Legal Defense and Educational Fund. During the 1940s he became involved with the American Jewish Congress (AJC). His wife, Justine Wise Polier, who served as judge of the New York state family court from 1935 to 1973, was the daughter of prominent rabbi and AJC founder Stephen Wise.

tions ~~and~~ {in} their world wide aspects, and was instrumental in getting Finletter to propose this in his commencement address at Hampton Institute several years ago. Greenfield's number and address is as follows in case you want to get in touch with him directly;

Edward L. Greenfield
Edward L. Greenfield & Co.
501 Madison Avenue
N.Y. 22, N.Y.
Phone: PLaza 9–6535

Forgive the sharp criticism in this note at a moment when something big has happened, but I trust that you expect from me a full and honest reaction.

Thanks for calling me from Chicago the other day. It was great hearing your voice. These are historic days in the South, and I have confidence that the creative role you are playing is just beginning.

Love to Coretta.

As ever,
[*signed*] Harris
Harris Wofford
Associate Professor

HW:mh

TALS. MLKP-MBU: Box 71.

To Fred L. Shuttlesworth

4 April 1960
[*Atlanta, Ga.*]

After Shuttlesworth's second arrest during the student sit-ins in Birmingham, King pledges SCLC's support and praises the minister's "epic making career."[1]

REV FRED SHUTTLESWORTH
3191 NORTH 29TH AVE

HAVE JUST LEARNED OF YOUR RECENT ARREST ON TRUMPED UP CHARGES BY CITY OFFICIALS OF BIRMINGHAM YOU HAVE THE ABSOLUTE SUPPORT OF THE

---

1. On 31 March, the first day of a student sit-in campaign that resulted in ten arrests, Birmingham police also arrested Shuttlesworth for giving false information regarding an alleged incident of police brutality. Two days later he was arrested for vagrancy as well as aiding and abetting civil disobedience. Shuttlesworth was found guilty on both charges on 4 April; his conviction was reversed by the U.S. Supreme Court in 1963 (*Shuttlesworth v. City of Birmingham*, 373 U.S. 262; "Shuttlesworth Charged with False Information," *Birmingham World*, 6 April 1960; and "Youths Given $100 Fines and 180 Days in Jail Each," *Birmingham World*, 6 April 1960; see also Shuttlesworth to William P. Rogers, 4 April 1960).

SOUTHERN CHRISTIAN LEADERSHIP [*strikeout illegible*] CONFERENCE AS YOU FACE THIS HOUR.[2] WE ARE ALWAYS ~~INSPIRR~~ INSPIRED BY YOUR COURAGEOUS WITNESS, AND YOUR WILLINGNESS TO SUFFER IN THIS RIGHTEOUS CAUSE. YOU' VE TRANSFORMED THE JAIL FROM A DUNGEON OF SHAME INTO A HAVEN OF FREEDOM AND A BADGE OF HONOR. I KNOW THAT YOU WILL FACE THIS SITUATION WITH THE SAME COURAGE THAT HAS ALWAYS GUIDED YOUR EPIC MAKING CAREER CONTINUE YOUR GREAT WORK WITH THE CONVICTION ~~OF~~ THAT UNEARNED SUFFERING IS REDEMPTION

(GIVEN BY MRS [*Maude*] BALLOU)

MARTIN LUTHER KING JR

PWc. MLKP-MBU: Box 72.

---

2. A week after this telegram was sent, King and SCLC associates Joseph Lowery, Kelly Miller Smith, C. K. Steele, and Ralph Abernathy wrote Attorney General William P. Rogers urging an immediate investigation of Shuttlesworth's arrests: "Regard for legal rights of Negroes have sunken to a new low even for Birmingham when a full time pastor of a church can be jailed held incommunicado for hours and charged with vagrancy to prevent him from securing early bail" (King et al. to Rogers, 11 April 1960). Acting Assistant Attorney General Joseph Ryan replied on 25 April and maintained that the situation "is presently receiving this Department's careful attention."

To Mary Fair Burks

5 April 1960
[*Atlanta, Ga.*]

Under pressure from state officials, Alabama State College president and Dexter deacon H. Councill Trenholm announced on 26 March that he would purge the college of "disloyal faculty members" who had supported the student protests.[1] *Among those targeted were Lawrence D. Reddick, head of the history department, and English teachers and MIA stalwarts Mary Fair Burks and Jo Ann Robinson.*[2] *On 31 March, Burks wrote King and requested his assistance in finding work for the fall. In this reply, King*

---

1. "Trenholm Plans Purge of 'Disloyal' Faculty," *Montgomery Advertiser*, 27 March 1960.

2. Burks and Robinson resigned at the close of the spring semester; Reddick was fired in June (see King to Patrick Murphy Malin, Roy Wilkins, and Carl J. Megel, 16 June 1960, pp. 471–472 in this volume, and MIA, "Repercussions at Alabama State College," *Newsletter*, 21 September 1960). Mary Frances Fair Burks (1914–1991), born in Montgomery, received a B.A. (1933) from Alabama State College, an M.A. (1934) from the University of Michigan, and an Ed.D. (1975) from Columbia University. Following an automobile accident in 1946, Burks was struck by a policeman and arrested on false charges. This incident led her to become the founding president of the Women's Political Council, the organization that later initiated the Montgomery bus protest. In the late 1940s Burks became chair of the English department at Alabama State College and served in that capacity until her resignation in 1960. She then taught at the University of Maryland Eastern Shore from 1960 until 1986.

reassures Burks that he "will do all that I possibly can to assist you and your colleagues" and expresses his disapproval of Trenholm's treatment of the faculty.

Mrs. Mary Fair Burks
1215 Tuscaloosa Street
Montgomery, Alabama

Dear Frankie:

Thank you for calling me Martin in your recent letter. It is always good to break the chain of formality. Now I can call you Frankie without any sense of guilt.

Although I have been separated from you and my other friends by many miles I have been with you every minute in concern and genuine sympathy. I know what you are going through and be assured that you have been much in my prayers. I fear that you are right in saying that President Trenholm will ease the eleven teachers out quietly at the end of the semester rather than facing it head on at this moment. The unfortunate aspect to this approach is that if you are not fired outright at this time it will lose the drama and it will be much more difficult for the individuals involved to find work. I had hoped that Dr. Trenholm would emerge from this total situation as a national hero. If he would only stand up to the Governor and the Board of Education and say that he cannot in all good conscience fire the eleven faculty members who have committed no crime or act of sedition, he would gain support over the nation that he never dreamed of. And indeed jobs would be offered to him overnight if he were fired. But apparently he doesn't see this, and realism impels us to admit that he probably will not travel this road.[3]

Please know that I will do all that I possibly can to assist you and your colleagues in getting work for the Fall.[4] My contacts are not too great, but at least I have some and I will be using the contacts that I have to the highest degree. I do not know exactly what fellowship or scholarship agency to suggest to you at this time. But I will be making some preliminary contacts, and as soon as I come up with something I will let you know. Your interest in teaching in Ghana sounds very interesting. I know that there are great possibilities in that area.

Give my best regards to all of my friends in Montgomery. I hope to be coming down that way in the not too-distant future. In the meantime, I will be at work on the possibilities for next school year. Let me assure you once more that you have my prayers and support at every point. I am so sorry that such a fine and devoted person as you has to suffer so much. I hope, however, that you will go on living with the conviction that unearned suffering is redemptive, and that to suffer in a righteous cause is one of the most sublime experiences known to man. Since we

---

3. The day after writing this letter, King criticized Trenholm in a letter to a Kenyan student who was hoping to attend Alabama State. King apologized that Trenholm "has not stuck with his promise" to facilitate the student's admission and added that, given the "turmoil" at Alabama State fueled by Trenholm's decision to appease the governor rather than aid the students, he could "not advise you to come at this point" (King to Justus M. Kitonga, 6 April 1960).

4. The following fall Robinson taught at Grambling College, and Reddick began teaching at Coppin State Teachers College.

6 Apr 1960 are in the midst of the Easter Season you may find some consolation here. The darkness of Good Friday has its day for a while, but ultimately there is a third day which is a day of resurrected hopes and aspirations. Maybe we are experiencing now the darkest hour which is just before the dawn of freedom and human dignity. This is my faith.

With warm personal regards, I am

Sincerely yours,
Martin L. King, Jr.

MLK:mlb

TLc. MLKP-MBU: Box 20.

To William H. Gray, Jr.

6 April 1960
[*Atlanta, Ga.*]

On 24 March Gray, pastor of Philadelphia's Bright Hope Baptist Church, mailed King a New York Times *article about protests on northern campuses that highlighted the role of Gray's daughter Marian, a student at Vassar College. Gray chided King for being a "bad influence" on his daughter and warned: "If you don't watch out, my daughter will put you and me off of the front page, and I am just waiting until your daughter gets two years older and she will probably be running for president."*[1] *In his reply below, King predicts that the student protesters "will knock some of the oldsters out of their state of apathy and complacency."*

Dr. William H. Gray, Jr.
Bright Hope Baptist Church
Twelfth and Oxford Streets
Philadelphia 22, Pennsylvania

Dear Bill:

I read of the courageous activities of your daughter in the New York Times before you sent the article to me. When I read it my heart was throbbing with joy. You see my friend that is that old fighting spirit in you coming out anew. Be sure to tell Marian that when she gets ready to run for President of the United States I will be on hand to make the nominating speech.[2] In all seriousness, I think she

1. McCandlish Phillips, "Campuses in North Back Southern Negro Students," *New York Times,* 20 March 1960. King first met Gray in 1949 while King was studying at Crozer Theological Seminary; Gray later helped raise funds for the Montgomery bus boycott (see Gray to Martin Luther King, Sr., 8 October 1949, in *Papers* 1:210, and Gray to King, 29 February 1956). King's daughter Yolanda Denise was born on 17 November 1955.

2. Marian Gray Secundy (1938–), born in Baton Rouge, Louisiana, received an A.B. (1960) from Vassar College, an M.S.S. (1962) from Bryn Mawr College, and a Ph.D. (1980) from the Union In-

is to be highly commended. The students of our generation have now come of age, and they are manifesting a maturity far beyond their years. The most significant aspect of this student movement is that the young people will knock some of the oldsters out of their state of apathy and complacency.

I look forward to seeing you soon. I plan to be in Washington in about two weeks, and I will be sure to call you. It was good seeing you in New York.[3]

Very sincerely yours,
Martin L. King, Jr.

MLK:mlb

TLc. MLKP-MBU: Box 27.

---

stitute. She served as associate director, then director, of the American Friends Service Committee from 1965 until 1967. In 1971 she became the first African American elected to Vassar's board of trustees.

3. In a second letter from 24 March, Gray mentioned meeting with King and Gardner C. Taylor on "Monday," which probably refers to 21 March.

"Keep Moving from This Mountain," Address at Spelman College on 10 April 1960

Atlanta, Ga.

In this Founder's Day address at Spelman College, King identifies four symbolic mountains—relativism, materialism, segregation, and violence—that must be overcome "if we are to go forward in our world and if civilization is to survive." He also criticizes the "profit-making and profit-getting aspects of capitalism" and warns of the danger of being "more concerned about making a living than making a life." This speech was published in the May issue of the Spelman Messenger.[1]

Thank you, President Manley, members of the faculty, and students of Spelman College, ladies and gentlemen. I need not pause to say how delighted I am to be here this afternoon and to be a part of this occasion. Founders Day is always a significant day and I join you in paying tribute to those persons who through their dedication and their tireless effort brought this institution into being. In a real sense you are the heirs of a legacy of goodwill and sacrifice on the part of the founders of this institution. Of course there is also one basic reason why I am happy to be here, and that is because I happen to be a Morehouse man and Morehouse

---

1. Spelman College president Albert Manley had initially invited King to address the college in 1959 (Manley to King, 16 October 1958; see also Ballou to Manley, 10 November 1958, and Program, "Founders Day, seventy-ninth anniversary," 10 April 1960).

men always consider it a privilege to speak to Spelman ladies.[2] I'm deeply grateful to the president of this institution, Dr. Manley, for inviting me to be here today, and it is a great privilege to see each of you.

I would like to use as a subject for my address this afternoon, "Keep Moving From This Mountain." For the moment, I would like to take your minds back many, many centuries to a group of people whose exploits and adventures have long since been meaningfully deposited in the hallowed memories of succeeding generations. At a very early age in their history, these people were reduced to the bondage of physical slavery. They found themselves under the gripping yoke of Egyptian rule. But soon a Moses appeared on the scene who was destined to lead them out of the Egypt of slavery to a bright and glowing promised land. But as soon as they got out of Egypt by crossing the Red Sea, they discovered that before they could get to the promised land they would have to go through a long and difficult wilderness. And after realizing this, three groups, or rather three attitudes, emerged. One group wanted to go back to Egypt: they felt that the fleshpots of Egypt were more to be desired than the ordeals of emancipation. Then you had a second group that abhored the idea of going back to Egypt and yet could not quite attain the discipline and the sacrifice to go on to Canaan. These people chose the line of least resistance. There was a third group, probably the creative minority, which said in substance, "We will go on in spite of the obstacles, in spite of the difficulty, in spite of the sacrifices that we will have to make."

In every movement toward freedom and fulfillment we find these three groups. But this afternoon, I am concerned mainly with the second group, the individuals who didn't want to go back to Egypt necessarily and yet didn't want to go on to the Promised Land, the individuals who chose the line of least resistance.

As Moses sought to lead his people on, he discovered that there were those among them who would occasionally become emotionally and sentimentally attached to a particular spot so that they wanted to stay there and remain stationary at that point. One day when Moses confronted this problem, he wrote in the book of Deuteronomy, the first chapter and the fifth verse: "You have been in this mountain long enough, turn ye and go on your journey, move on to the mount of the Amorites."[3] This was a message of God through Moses. And whenever God speaks he says go forward, saying in substance that you must never become bogged down in mountains and situations that will impede your progress. You must never become complacently adjusted to unobtained goals; you have been in this mountain long enough, "turn ye and take your journey."[4]

---

2. In a typescript of this speech, King elaborated: "I was thinking yesterday that I would say that it was just a few years ago that I used to assemble in Sisters Chapel, in fact I used to sing in the chorus and the glee club at Morehouse, so I had the priviledge of coming here quite frequently. But then I got a little worried when I looked back and noticed how many years ago I came to this chapel and how many years ago I studied at Morehouse, I discovered that I finished about twelve years ago, thirteen years ago almost, and I got a little worried thinking that the years were going a little too fast for me and that age is piling up. But I'm still young so that doesn't particularly matter" (King, "Founders Day address," 10 April 1960).

3. Cf. Deuteronomy 1:6–7.

4. Cf. Deuteronomy 1:7.

In a real sense, each of us assembled here today is in a wilderness moving toward some promised land of freedom and fulfillment. In every age and every generation men have envisioned some promised land. Plato envisioned it in his republic as a time when justice would reign throughout society and philosophers would become kings and kings philosophers. Karl Marx envisioned it as a classless society in which the proletariat would finally conquer the reign of the bourgeoisie; out of that idea came the slogan, "from each according to his ability, to each according to his need."[5] Bellamy, in *Looking Backward,* thought of it as a day when the inequalities of monopoly capitalism would pass away.[6] Society would exist on the basis of evenness of economic output. Christianity envisioned it as the kingdom of God, a time when the will of God will reign supreme, and brotherhood, love, and right relationships will be the order of society. In every age and every generation men have dreamed of some promised land of fulfillment of freedom. Whether it was the right promised land or not, they dreamed of it. But in moving from some Egypt of slavery, whether in the intellectual, cultural or moral realm, toward some promised land, there is always the same temptation. Individuals will get bogged down in a particular mountain in a particular spot, and thereby become the victims of stagnant complacency. So, this afternoon, I would like to deal with three or four symbolic mountains that we have been in long enough—mountains that we must move out of if we are to go forward in our world and if civilization is to survive.

10 Apr 1960

First, I think we have been in the mountain of moral and ethical relativism long enough. To dwell in this mountain has become something of a fad these days, so we have come to believe that morality is a matter of group consensus. We attempt to discover what is right by taking a sort of gallup poll of the majority opinion. Everybody is doing it, so it must be all right, and therefore we are caught in the clutches of conformity. We've been in this mountain long enough—the feeling that there is nothing absolutely right and nothing absolutely wrong, that right is a matter of customs and tastes and appetites and what happens in a particular community. Nothing is absolutely right. To put it in sociological lingo, we follow the mores of the right way.

Another consequence of this moral and ethical relativism is that we have developed a sort of pragmatic test for right and wrong. According to this view, anything that works is all right if you can get by with it. We don't talk much any more about the Darwinian survival of the fittest, it is now the survival of the slickest. Whoever can slick his way through makes it through all right, according to this

5. Karl Marx, *Critique of the Gotha Programme* (Moscow, 1947), p. 17.

6. Edward Bellamy, *Looking Backward 2000–1887* (New York: Modern Library, 1951). Shortly after they had begun dating, Coretta Scott gave King a copy of Bellamy's book with the inscription: "I should be interested to know your reaction to Bellamy's predictions about our society," and added: "In some ways it is rather encouraging to see how our social order has changed since Bellamy's time. There is still hope for the future . . . Lest we become too impatient" (Coretta Scott, Inscription to Martin Luther King, Jr., 7 April 1952). King replied in an 18 July letter: "I welcomed the book because much of its content is in line with my basic ideas. I imagine you already know that I am much more socialistic in my economic theory than capitalistic. And yet I am not so opposed to capitalism that I have failed to see its relative merits."

theory. In a sense, we are no longer concerned about the ten commandments—they are not too important. Everybody is busy, as I have said so often, trying to obey the eleventh commandment: "Thou shalt not get caught." And so, according to this view, it is all right to lie with a bit of finesse. It's all right to exploit, but be a dignified exploiter. It's all right to even hate, but dress your hate up into garments of love and make it appear that you are loving when you are actually hating. This type of moral and ethical relativism is sapping the very life's blood of the moral and spiritual life of our nation and our world. And I am convinced that if we are to be a great nation, and if we are to solve the problems of the world we must come out of this mountain. We have been in it too long. For if man fails to reorientate his life around moral and ethical values he may well destroy himself by the misuse of his own instrument.

Now education has a great role to play at this point. You see, education has a two-fold function. The one is utility and the other culture. Education must give an individual efficiency, but it must also humanize the individual. On the one hand education must give us the power to concentrate, the faculty for intensive thinking; this is a basic function of education. On the other hand, education must help us to think critically. And so education helps to lift an individual from the bondage of legends and half truths to the unfettered realm of objective analysis and creative appraisal. If an individual can't think critically he really isn't educated. Of course I'm sure all the Spelmanites and Morehouse men and Morris Brown and Clark and Atlanta University students and all the other people present here are educated, but I've found a lot of people who have been to school who are not educated. I'm sure that does not apply to you. So many people can't think critically. Thinking critically means that the individual must think imaginatively, creatively, originally. Originality is a basic part of education. That does not mean that you think something altogether new; if that were the case Shakespeare wasn't original, for Shakespeare depended on Plutarch and others for many of his plots.[7] Originality does not mean thinking up something totally new in the universe, but it does mean giving new validity to old form. In a real sense, education must help an individual think intensively, critically, imaginatively.

But this isn't enough. Any education that stops at this point is a dangerous education. An individual who is properly educated must have more than efficiency. The proper education will not only give the individual the power of concentration but worthy objectives upon which to concentrate. It will give him not only critical faculty for precise judgment, but profound sympathies with which to temper the asperity of his judgment. It will not only quicken his imagination but kindle his enthusiasm for the objects of his imagination. True education helps us on the one hand to know truth, but more than that it helps us to love truth and sacrifice for it. It gives us not only knowledge, which is power, but wisdom, which is control. I am convinced that if we are to move forward, that if we are to face the many problems of our world, education must take on this two-fold role as it has traditionally done, and give the individual a sense of moral and ethical values along with his efficiency, so that he will go out of his college classroom knowing that

---

7. Plutarch (ca. AD 46–120) was a Greek essayist and biographer.

there are certain moral laws in the universe just as there are basic physical laws. For in a real sense there is something in this universe that justifies Carlyle saying, "No lie can live forever."[8] There is something in this universe that justifies William Cullen Bryant in saying, "Truth crushed to earth will rise again."[9] There is something in this universe which justifies James Russell Lowell saying,

> Truth forever on the scaffold,
> Wrong forever on the throne,
> Yet that scaffold sways the future,
> And behind the dim unknown
> Standeth God within the shadows,
> Keeping watch above His own.[10]

There is even something in this universe which justifies Greek mythology in talking about a goddess of Nemesis.[11] There is something here in the structure of our universe that justifies the Biblical writer in saying, "You shall reap what you sow."[12] This is a law-abiding universe, and we must move out of the mountain of moral and ethical relativism that we have been in all too long.

We must also move out of the mountain of practical materialism. We have been in it long enough. I am not speaking now of metaphysical materialism—the materialism which says in substance that all reality can be explained in terms of matter in motion and that life is merely a physiological process with a physiological meaning. We need to move out of that mountain also, I guess, but I am talking about another type of materialism—not a theoretical materialism, which is usually confined to a sophisticated few. I am speaking of a practical materialism, which means living as if there were nothing else that had reality but fame and material objects. We operate, or we live, rather, in two realms, so to speak—the *within* of a man's life, which is the realm of culture, and the *without* that is the realm of civilization. There is structure, which is the realm of means, and destiny, which is the realm of ends, preliminary concerns which are the realm of science and technology, ultimate concerns which are the realm of morals and ethical religion. The great danger that faces our civilization is that we will allow the *without* of life to absorb the *within*—that we will allow destiny to get tied up in structure—that we will allow our preliminary concerns to take precedence over ultimate concern. We have been in this mountain long enough.

One of the dangers we must always watch in our nation and in the system un-

8. King paraphrases Thomas Carlyle, *The French Revolution* (1837), part 1, book 3, chap. 1: "No lie you can speak or act but it will come, after longer or shorter circulation, like a bill drawn on Nature's Reality, and be presented there for payments—with the answer, No effects."

9. William Cullen Bryant, *The Battlefield* (1839), stanza 9.

10. James Russell Lowell, *The Present Crisis* (1844), stanza 8. King's phrasing closely resembles a sermon by Harry Emerson Fosdick (see note 21 to "Facing the Challenge of a New Age," 1 January 1957, in *Papers* 4:82–83).

11. Nemesis was the goddess of retributive justice or vengeance. King included a fuller discussion of the Goddess of Nemesis in an earlier sermon at Dexter Avenue Baptist Church (King, "Conquering Self-Centeredness," 11 August 1957, in *Papers* 4:256).

12. Cf. Galatians 6:7.

der which we live is known as capitalism. As you know, capitalism stresses the profit motive. Of course capitalism has done some marvelous things for our nation and the world. Through this economic system we have been able to build up the greatest system of production that the world has ever known, and we have become the richest nation in the world. All of this is marvelous. But the danger point is that we will become so involved in the profit-making and profit-getting aspects of capitalism that we will forget certain ends of life. There is always the danger that we will become more concerned about making a living than making a life—that we will not keep that line of division between life and one's livelihood.

And there is also the danger that our system can lead to tragic exploitation. We must come out of the mountain and be concerned about a more humane and just economic order. And I say, this afternoon, that we cannot solve this problem by turning to Communism. Communism is based on an ethical relativism and a metaphysical materialism that no Christian can accept. I do believe that in America we must use our vast resources of wealth to bridge the gulf between abject, deadening poverty and superfluous, inordinate wealth. God has left enough space in this universe for all of his children to have the basic necessities of life. As I have travelled around the Middle East and in India and Africa, I have always been moved and deeply concerned about the poverty in those countries. Poverty there is so widespread, because these people have been exploited economically and dominated politically by foreign powers. Every time I look and notice these conditions I start thinking about the fact that in the United States of America we spend almost ten billion dollars a year to store the surplus food that we have in the nation. And I say to myself as I look at these conditions, "I know where we can store that food free of charge, in the wrinkled stomachs of hungry men and women and children of God all over the world." If the United States is to survive, along with all the citizens of the world, we must come out of this mountain of practical materialism which can be transformed from a legitimate individualism into a rugged individualism, and we must move out of that into a proper concern for all humanity and into a proper concern for every individual, and a proper concern in our individual lives for what I call the *within* of life—the realm of destiny.

There is another mountain we have been in long enough. We have been in the mountain of racial segregation long enough. We all know how long we have been in this mountain, so I need not go back and give the historical development of it. It is now time for us to turn and take our journey toward the promised land of integration. In a real sense, segregation in any form is wrong. Segregation is wrong because it substitutes an I-it relationship for the I-thou relationship.[13] Segregation is wrong because it relegates individuals to the status of things rather than taking the high moral position of elevating them to the status of persons. Segregation is wrong because it assumes that God made a mistake—and finally, it is wrong because it stands in the face of the great American creed "that all men are created equal and endowed by their creator with certain inalienable rights." And so we must go out and say to our nation and say to South Africa and say to the world, that we have been in the mountain of segregation too long and now we must move out.

---

13. Martin Buber, *I and Thou* (1937).

Segregation is a cancer in the body politic which must be removed before our democratic health can be realized. The underlying philosophy of segregation is diametrically opposed to the underlying philosophy of democracy and Christianity and all the sophisms of the logicians cannot make them lie down together. We must make it clear that in our struggle to end this thing called segregation, we are not struggling for ourselves alone. We are not struggling only to free seventeen million Negroes. The festering sore of segregation debilitates the white man as well as the Negro. We are struggling to save the soul of America. We are struggling to save America in this very important decisive hour of her history. 10 Apr 1960

This is why the student movement that has taken place at this time all over our country is so significant. Let nobody fool you, this movement is one of the most significant movements in the whole civil rights struggle. For you students, along with other students all over the nation, have become of age, and you are saying in substance that segregation is wrong and that you will no longer accept it and adjust to it. This movement says, more clearly than was ever said before, that segregation cannot be maintained in the South without leading to chaos and social disintegration. The beautiful thing about it is that you are not merely demanding service at the lunch counter, though that is a basic part of it. You're not merely demanding a cup of coffee and a hamburger here and there.[14] You are demanding respect. You are saying in substance, "if you respect my dollar you will also have to respect me as a person." An individual who is not concerned about his selfhood and his freedom is at that moment committing moral and spiritual suicide, and you are standing up to the great determination. You have taken up the deep groans of the century. The students have taken the passionate longings of the ages and filtered them in their own souls and fashioned a creative protest. It is one of the glowing epics of the time and I predict that it will win—that it will have to win, because this demand is a basic American demand.

Victor Hugo said many years ago, "There is nothing more powerful than an idea whose time has come."[15] The idea whose time has come is in the idea of freedom and human dignity. Wherever men are assembled today, whether they are in Johannesburg, Nairobi, Accra, Berlin, Atlanta, New York, Montgomery, or Little Rock the cry is always the same: "We want to be free." And so, today, let men everywhere join in this quest for freedom by moving out of the mountain of racial segregation. This is the mountain that we must leave we have dwelt in it long enough. On this Founders Day, if you forget all I have said, I hope you won't forget this mountain.

Finally, we have been in the mountain of corroding hatred and crippling vio-

14. King's associates James Lawson and Ella Baker had expressed similar thoughts in their own public remarks on the sit-ins. Speaking at a student conference, Lawson questioned whether the protests were "just a lot of nonsense over a hamburger? Or is it far more?" ("We Are Trying to Raise the 'Moral Issue,'" in Francis L. Broderick and August Meier, eds., *Negro Protest Thought in the Twentieth Century* [Indianapolis: The Bobbs-Merrill Company, 1965], p. 275). Baker published "Bigger than a Hamburger" in the May 1960 issue of the *Southern Patriot:* "The Student Leadership Conference made it crystal clear that current sit-ins and other demonstrations are concerned with something much bigger than a hamburger or even a giant-sized coke."

15. Hugo, *The History of a Crime,* p. 429.

lence long eough. We have been in this mountain for centuries because men have gone to war and they have fought numerous wars; battle fields of the world have been painted with blood. We know about it—we know about this mountain because violence is the inseparable twin of western materialism, the hallmark of its grandeur. We know about this mountain, we have been in it long enough. I am convinced if we fail to move out of this mountain we will be plunged into the abyss of annihilation. This means not only on the local scale; we must move out of it on the international scale. There was a time when we fought wars and felt they were just wars. I must admit that at one point in my intellectual pilgrimage I justified war, certainly as a sort of negative good in the sense that it blocked an evil force, a totalitarian force. I have come to believe firmly now that war can no longer serve even as a negative good because of the potenital destructiveness of modern war. There was a time when we had a choice of violence or nonviolence, but today it is either nonviolence or nonexistence.

And so the nations of the world must get together. In Geneva they must get together; at the Summit Conference they must get together, to bring an end to the armament race, to bring about universal disarmament and set up a sort of world police force.[16] This is a matter of survival now. Talk about love and nonviolence may have been merely a pious injunction a few years ago; today it is an absolute necessity for the survival of our civilization.

Also in the racial struggle, this is vitally important to our nation and to other nations: we must come out of the mountain of hatred and violence. This is why I am convinced that as we stand up for freedom and as we stand up for justice we must always struggle with the highest weapons of dignity and discipline. We must never use weapons of hatred and violence. Men have thought over the years that either they would have to fight their oppressions or they would have to acquiesce and surrender. You have seen the type of people who felt that the only way to deal with oppression was to accept it. Sometimes you will hear somebody singing, "been down so long that down don't bother me."[17] That is how some people adjust, they get exhausted in the struggle, and they give up and they are free—they achieve the freedom of exhaustion. Then others have felt that the only way to deal with oppression is to stand up with violence and get ammunition and weapons of violence to deal with an evil system and an evil opponent. I say to you, today, there is another way that combines the best points of both of these and avoids the evil points of both, and that is what we call *nonviolent resistance.* For here you have discovered a way of struggle which combines the militant and the moderate; a way of struggle that combines the realistic and the idealistic; a way of struggle that combines the calm and courageous. You need not now bow to hate, you need not now bow to violence, for you have now discovered another way and another approach. It comes to us from the long Christian tradition, Jesus of Nazareth himself, com-

16. King refers to the summit meeting of representatives from the Soviet Union, the United Kingdom, and the United States in Geneva, Switzerland, to discuss a permanent nuclear test ban. For more on King's involvement with nuclear disarmament campaigns, see Norman Cousins and Clarence Pickett to King, 9 March 1958, in *Papers* 4:379–380.

17. Blues singer Ishman Bracey's 1928 recording of "Trouble Hearted Blues" included the following lyric: "Down so long, down don't worry me."

ing down through Mahatma Gandhi of India, who took the love ethic of Jesus Christ and made it effective as a sociopolitical force and brought about the transformation of a great nation and achieved freedom for his people.

I know you are asking, "What do you mean about this love thing—you are talking about people who oppose you, loving people who are trying to misuse you, seeking to defeat you—what in the world are you trying to say? That is impossible!" Since these questions are often raised, I have to pause quite often to explain the meaning of love in this context. It is interesting that the Greek language comes to our rescue and our aid at this point. You know in the Greek language there are three words for love. One is *Eros.* Eros is a sort of aesthetic love. Plato talked about it a great deal in his dialogue, "the yearning of the soul for the realm of the divine." It has come to us to mean a sort of romantic love; in that sense we all know Eros because we have experienced it and we have lived with it, we have read about it in all of the beauties of literature. I would imagine Edgar Allen Poe was talking about Eros when he talked about his beautiful Annabelle Lee with a love surrounded by a halo of eternity.[18] In a sense Shakespeare was talking about Eros when he aid, "Love is not love which alters when it's alteration finds or bends with the remover to remove. Oh no! it is an everfixed mark that looks on tempests and is never shaken. It is a star to every wandering bark."[19] These are beautiful words of Shakespeare's. They express something of the meaning of love. Then there is another word, *philia,* which is a sort of intimate affection between personal friends. In a sense, this is the sort of love that you have for your roommate, the persons that you like and eat dinner with and the persons you like to talk to on the telephone. You have this intimate feeling of love because you like them and because there is something that you have in common on this level; you love because you are loved. It is a reciprocal love. Then the Greek language comes out with another word, *agape. Agape* is more than Eros. It is more than philia. It is understanding, creative, redemptive goodwill for all men. It is a spontaneous love which seeks nothing in return. Theologians would say it is the love of God operating in the human heart. When you rise to love on this level, you love men not because you like them, not because their ways appeal to you, not because they have any particular meaning to you at the moment, but you love them because God loves them. And so you rise to the point of loving the individual who does the evil deed while hating the deed that he does.

I think this is what Jesus meant when he said, "Love your enemies."[20] I am very happy he did not say like your enemies, because it is very hard to like some people. It is hard to like some senator who waters down the civil rights bill in Congress; it is pretty hard to like him. It is hard to like somebody who is bombing your house, who is seeking to kill you and defeat and destroy your children. It is difficult to like them. But Jesus says "Love them," and *love* is greater than *like.* Love is creative, redemptive goodwill for all men. When men rise to live on this level, they come to see all men as children of the almighty God, and they can look in the eyes of the opponent and love him in spite of his evil deed.

18. Poe's "Annabel Lee" (1849) was written in memory of his wife, who died of tuberculosis in 1847.
19. William Shakespeare, "Sonnet 116" (1609).
20. Cf. Luke 6:27.

10 Apr 1960

I believe if we will follow this way, we will be able to achieve not only desegregation, which will bring us together, physically but also integration, which is true intergroup, interpersonal living. I believe if we will follow this type of love we will go into the new age with the proper attitude. We will not go, believing in any philosophy of black supremacy, for black supremacy is as dangerous as white supremacy. God is not interested merely in the freedom of the whole human race. It is this type of love which will keep our attitudes right so that we will continue to struggle for first-class citizenship, never using second-class methods to gain it. We will move out of these mountains that have so often impeded our progress, the mountain of moral and ethical relativism, the mountain of practical materialism, the mountain of corroding hatred, bitterness and violence, and the mountain of racial segregation. We will be able to build a new world, and I say to you this afternoon as you look ahead to the days to come, always have faith in the possibility of getting over to the promised land. Don't become a pessimist and feel that we cannot get there; it is difficult sometimes, it is hard sometimes, but always have faith that the promised land can be achieved and that we can possess this land of brotherhood and peace and understanding.

I do not give you this element of faith and superficial optimism. I do not stand here as a detached spectator. As I say to you this afternoon, have faith in the future, I speak as one who lives every day amidst the threat of death. I speak as one who has had to stand often amidst the surging murmur of life's restless sea, I speak as one who has been battered often by the jostling winds of adversity, but I have faith in the future. I have faith in the future because I have faith in God and I believe that there is a power, a creative force in this universe seeking at all times to bring down prodigious hilltops of evil and pull low gigantic mountains of injustice. If we will believe this and struggle along, we will be able to achieve it.

Keep moving, for it may well be that the greatest song has not yet been sung, the greatest book has not been written, the highest mountain has not been climbed. This is your challenge! Reach out and grab it and make it a part of your life. Reach up beyond cloud-filled skies of oppression and bring out blazing stars of inspiration. The basic thing is to keep moving. Move out of these mountains that impede our progress to this new and noble and marvelous land. Langston Hughes said something very beautiful in "Mother to Son."

> Well son, I'll tell you
> Life for me ain't been no crystal stair.
> It's had tacks in it, splinters,
> Boards torn up, places with no carpets on the floors, bare!
> But all the time, I'se been a-climbing on and reaching landings
> And turning corners and sometimes going in the dark where there ain't been no light.
> So boy, don't you stop now.
> Don't you sit down on the steps cause you find it's kinda hard.
> For I'se still goin boy, I'se still climbing,
> And life for me ain't been no crystal stair.[21]

21. Langston Hughes, "Mother to Son," in *The Weary Blues* (New York: Knopf, 1926), p. 107.

Life for none of us has been a crystal stair, but there is something we can learn from the broken grammar of that mother, that we must keep moving. If you can't fly, run; if you can't run, walk; if you can't walk, crawl; but by all means keep moving.

PD. *Spelman Messenger,* May 1960, pp. 6–17.

"Pilgrimage to Nonviolence"

13 April 1960
Chicago, Ill.

On 10 July 1959, Christian Century *editor Harold Fey asked King to write an article for "How My Mind Has Changed," a series of "statements by significant thinkers" reflecting their intellectual and spiritual development over the previous ten years. In this essay, King stresses the academic influences that have led him to embrace nonviolence as "a way of life."*[1] *He also relates that his "involvement in a difficult struggle" had changed his conception of God from a "metaphysical category" to "a living reality that has been validated in the experiences of everyday life." God had become "profoundly real" to him: "In the midst of outer dangers I have felt an inner calm and known resources of strength that only God could give."*

Ten years ago I was just entering my senior year in theological seminary. Like most theological students I was engaged in the exciting job of studying various theological theories. Having been raised in a rather strict fundamentalistic tradition, I was occasionally shocked as my intellectual journey carried me through new and sometimes complex doctrinal lands. But despite the shock the pilgrimage was always stimulating, and it gave me a new appreciation for objective appraisal and critical analysis. My early theological training did the same for me as the reading of [*David*] Hume did for [*Immanuel*] Kant: it knocked me out of my dogmatic slumber.

At this stage of my development I was a thoroughgoing liberal. Liberalism provided me with an intellectual satisfaction that I could never find in fundamentalism. I became so enamored of the insights of liberalism that I almost fell into the trap of accepting uncritically everything that came under its name. I was absolutely convinced of the natural goodness of man and the natural power of human reason.

I

The basic change in my thinking came when I began to question some of the theories that had been associated with so-called liberal theology. Of course there

1. This essay bears similarities to chapter six of *Stride Toward Freedom,* a shortened version of which was reprinted in *Fellowship* (see King, "My Pilgrimage to Nonviolence," 1 September 1958, in *Papers* 4:473–481). A revised version of King's essay was later reprinted in a collected volume edited by Fey (*How My Mind Has Changed* [Cleveland: Meridian Books, 1961], pp. 105–115).

13 Apr 1960

is one phase of liberalism that I hope to cherish always: its devotion to the search for truth, its insistence on an open and analytical mind, its refusal to abandon the best light of reason.[2] Liberalism's contribution to the philological-historical criticism of biblical literature has been of immeasurable value and should be defended with religious and scientific passion.

It was mainly the liberal doctrine of man that I began to question. The more I observed the tragedies of history and man's shameful inclination to choose the low road, the more I came to see the depths and strength of sin. My reading of the works of Reinhold Niebuhr made me aware of the complexity of human motives and the reality of sin on every level of man's existence.[3] Moreover, I came to recognize the complexity of man's social involvement and the glaring reality of collective evil.[4] I came to feel that liberalism had been all too sentimental concerning human nature and that it leaned toward a false idealism.

I also came to see that liberalism's superficial optimism concerning human nature caused it to overlook the fact that reason is darkened by sin.[5] The more I thought about human nature the more I saw how our tragic inclination for sin causes us to use our minds to rationalize our actions. Liberalism failed to see that reason by itself is little more than an instrument to justify man's defensive ways of thinking. Reason, devoid of the purifying power of faith, can never free itself from distortions and rationalizations.

In spite of the fact that I had to reject some aspects of liberalism, I never came to an all-out acceptance of neo-orthodoxy. While I saw neo-orthodoxy as a helpful corrective for a liberalism that had become all too sentimental, I never felt that it provided an adequate answer to the basic questions. If liberalism was too optimistic concerning human nature, neo-orthodoxy was too pessimistic. Not only on the question of man but also on other vital issues neo-orthodoxy went too far in its revolt.[6] In its attempt to preserve the transcendence of God, which had been neglected by liberalism's overstress of his immanence, neo-orthodoxy went to the extreme of stressing a God who was hidden, unknown and "wholly other." In its revolt against liberalism's overemphasis on the power of reason, neo-orthodoxy

---

2. In notes that King may have written in preparation for this article, he stated: "Of course if by liberalism is meant merely an open and critical mind which refuses to abandon the best light of reason, I hope that I shall always remain a liberal" (King, Notes, "How My Mind Has Changed" series, 13 April 1960). In composing his notes, King may have borrowed language from a brief report written by one of his Boston University classmates on Nels Ferré (Roland Kircher, "Nels Ferré," 27 February 1952).

3. For more on King's reactions to Niebuhr, see "Reinhold Niebuhr's Ethical Dualism," 9 May 1952, and "The Theology of Reinhold Niebuhr," April 1953–June 1954, in *Papers* 2:141–152 and 269–279, respectively.

4. Cf. *Stride Toward Freedom,* p. 99.

5. King, Notes: "Liberalism failed to acknowledge that man is mostly a sinner, actually though not essentially, and that with regard to religion his reason is darkened by sin. . . . Neither did liberalism sense that the key to correct reasoning lies in the relation between God's eternal purpose and the historic process, that is, in the relation between eschatology and epistemology."

6. King, Notes: "Neo-orthodoxy came close to being a wounded wing of faith, representing mostly a general mood of irrationalism, despair, and existentialist revolt against an inadequate liberalism. It tended therefore to stress an unknown God, an absurd faith, and a narrow, self-sufficient Biblicism . . . Whether for the Church or for personal life, it lacked the serene faith in the Holy Spirit which can bring strength out of weakness and clarity out of confusion."

fell into a mood of antirationalism and semifundamentalism, stressing a narrow, uncritical biblicism. This approach, I felt, was inadequate both for the church and for personal life.

13 Apr 1960

So although liberalism left me unsatisfied on the question of the nature of man, I found no refuge in neo-orthodoxy. I am now convinced that the truth about man is found neither in liberalism nor in neo-orthodoxy. Each represents a partial truth. A large segment of Protestant liberalism defined man only in terms of his essential nature, his capacity for good. Neo-orthodoxy tended to define man only in terms of his existential nature, his capacity for evil. An adequate understanding of man is found neither in the thesis of liberalism nor in the antithesis of neo-orthodoxy, but in a synthesis which reconciles the truths of both.[7]

During the past decade I also gained a new appreciation for the philosophy of existentialism. My first contact with this philosophy came through my reading of [*Søren*] Kierkegaard and [*Friedrich*] Nietzsche. Later I turned to a study of [*Karl*] Jaspers, [*Martin*] Heidegger and [*Jean Paul*] Sartre. All of these thinkers stimulated my thinking; while finding things to question in each, I nevertheless learned a great deal from study of them. When I finally turned to a serious study of the works of Paul Tillich I became convinced that existentialism, in spite of the fact that it had become all too fashionable, had grasped certain basic truths about man and his condition that could not be permanently overlooked.[8]

Its understanding of the "finite freedom" of man is one of existentialism's most lasting contributions, and its perception of the anxiety and conflict produced in man's personal and social life as a result of the perilous and ambiguous structure of existence is especially meaningful for our time. The common point in all existentialism, whether it is atheistic or theistic, is that man's existential situation is a state of estrangement from his essential nature. In their revolt against [*Georg Wilhelm Friedrich*] Hegel's essentialism, all existentialists contend that the world is fragmented. History is a series of unreconciled conflicts and man's existence is filled with anxiety and threatened with meaninglessness. While the ultimate Christian answer is not found in any of these existential assertions, there is much here that the theologian can use to describe the true state of man's existence.

Although most of my formal study during this decade has been in systematic theology and philosophy, I have become more and more interested in social ethics. Of course my concern for social problems was already substantial before the beginning of this decade. From my early teens in Atlanta I was deeply concerned about the problem of racial injustice. I grew up abhorring segregation, considering it both rationally inexplicable and morally unjustifiable. I could never accept the fact of having to go to the back of a bus or sit in the segregated section of a train. The first time that I was seated behind a curtain in a dining car I felt as if the curtain had been dropped on my selfhood. I had also learned that the inseparable twin of racial

7. In *Stride Toward Freedom,* King used similar terms to compare Marxism and capitalism (p. 95). In his notes for this article he wrote: "The fluctuating pendulum of my mind seems most merely content to rest in a position between liberalism and neoorthodoxy, which I have sometimes called Christian Realism and sometimes Evangelical Catholicism."

8. King wrote his doctoral dissertation on Tillich (see "A Comparison of the Conceptions of God in the Thinking of Paul Tillich and Henry Nelson Wieman," 15 April 1955, in *Papers* 2:339–544).

injustice is economic injustice.[9] I saw how the systems of segregation ended up in the exploitation of the Negro as well as the poor whites. Through these early experiences I grew up deeply conscious of the varieties of injustice in our society.

II

Not until I entered theological seminary, however, did I begin a serious intellectual quest for a method to eliminate social evil. I was immediately influenced by the social gospel. In the early '50s I read Rauschenbusch's *Christianity and the Social Crisis,* a book which left an indelible imprint on my thinking.[10] Of course there were points at which I differed with Rauschenbusch. I felt that he had fallen victim to the 19th-century "cult of inevitable progress," which led him to an unwarranted optimism concerning human nature. Moreover, he came perilously close to identifying the kingdom of God with a particular social and economic system—a temptation which the church should never give in to. But in spite of these shortcomings Rauschenbusch gave to American Protestantism a sense of social responsibility that it should never lose. The gospel at its best deals with the whole man, not only his soul but his body, not only his spiritual well-being, but his material well-being. Any religion that professes to be concerned about the souls of men and is not concerned about the slums that damn them, the economic conditions that strangle them and the social conditions that cripple them is a spiritually moribund religion awaiting burial.[11]

After reading Rauschenbusch I turned to a serious study of the social and ethical theories of the great philosophers. During this period I had almost despaired of the power of love in solving social problems. The "turn the other cheek" philosophy and the "love your enemies" philosophy are only valid, I felt, when individuals are in conflict with other individuals; when racial groups and nations are in conflict a more realistic approach is necessary. Then I came upon the life and teachings of Mahatma Gandhi. As I read his works I became deeply fascinated by his campaigns of nonviolent resistance. The whole Gandhian concept of *satyagraha* (*satya* is truth which equals love, and *graha* is force; *satyagraha* thus means truth-force or love-force) was profoundly significant to me. As I delved deeper into the philosophy of Gandhi my skepticism concerning the power of love gradually diminished, and I came to see for the first time that the Christian doctrine of love operating through the Gandhian method of nonviolence was one of the most potent weapons available to oppressed people in their struggle for freedom. At this time, however, I had a merely intellectual understanding and appreciation of the position, with no firm determination to organize it in a socially effective situation.

When I went to Montgomery, Alabama, as a pastor in 1954, I had not the slight-

---

9. *Stride Toward Freedom,* p. 90.

10. Walter Rauschenbusch, *Christianity and the Social Crisis* (New York: Macmillan, 1907).

11. Harry Emerson Fosdick, *The Hope of the World,* p. 25: "Any church that pretends to care for the souls of people but is not interested in the slums that damn them, the city government that corrupts them, the economic order that cripples them, and international relationships that, leading to peace or war, determine the spiritual destiny of innumerable souls—that kind of church, I think, would hear again the Master's withering words: 'Scribes and Pharisees, hypocrites!'" (see also *Stride Toward Freedom,* p. 91).

est idea that I would later become involved in a crisis in which nonviolent resistance would be applicable. After I had lived in the community about a year, the bus boycott began. The Negro people of Montgomery, exhausted by the humiliating experiences that they had constantly faced on the buses, expressed in a massive act of noncooperation their determination to be free. They came to see that it was ultimately more honorable to walk the streets in dignity than to ride the buses in humiliation. At the beginning of the protest the people called on me to serve as their spokesman. In accepting this responsibility my mind, consciously or unconsciously, was driven back to the Sermon on the Mount and the Gandhian method of nonviolent resistance. This principle became the guiding light of our movement. Christ furnished the spirit and motivation while Gandhi furnished the method.[12]

The experience in Montgomery did more to clarify my thinking on the question of nonviolence than all of the books that I had read. As the days unfolded I became more and more convinced of the power of nonviolence. Living through the actual experience of the protest, nonviolence became more than a method to which I gave intellectual assent; it became a commitment to a way of life. Many issues I had not cleared up intellectually concerning nonviolence were now solved in the sphere of practical action.

A few months ago I had the privilege of traveling to India. The trip had a great impact on me personally and left me even more convinced of the power of nonviolence. It was a marvelous thing to see the amazing results of a nonviolent struggle. India won her independence, but without violence on the part of Indians. The aftermath of hatred and bitterness that usually follows a violent campaign is found nowhere in India. Today a mutual friendship based on complete equality exists between the Indian and British people within the commonwealth.

I do not want to give the impression that nonviolence will work miracles overnight. Men are not easily moved from their mental ruts or purged of their prejudiced and irrational feelings. When the underprivileged demand freedom, the privileged first react with bitterness and resistance. Even when the demands are couched in nonviolent terms, the initial response is the same. I am sure that many of our white brothers in Montgomery and across the south are still bitter toward Negro leaders, even though these leaders have sought to follow a way of love and nonviolence. So the nonviolent approach does not immediately change the heart of the oppressor. It first does something to the hearts and souls of those committed to it. It gives them new self-respect; it calls up resources of strength and courage that they did not know they had. Finally, it reaches the opponent and so stirs his conscience that reconciliation becomes a reality.

III

During recent months I have come to see more and more the need for the method of nonviolence in international relations. While I was convinced during my stu-

---

12. Cf. *Stride Toward Freedom,* p. 85. During the editing of the manuscript for *Stride,* King incorporated his former professor George D. Kelsey's suggestion to stress Christianity as the motivating force behind the Montgomery protest (Kelsey to King, 4 April 1958, in *Papers* 4:394–395).

dent days of the power of nonviolence in group conflicts within nations, I was not yet convinced of its efficacy in conflicts between nations. I felt that while war could never be a positive or absolute good, it could serve as a negative good in the sense of preventing the spread and growth of an evil force. War, I felt, horrible as it is, might be preferable to surrender to a totalitarian system. But more and more I have come to the conclusion that the potential destructiveness of modern weapons of war totally rules out the possibility of war ever serving again as a negative good. If we assume that mankind has a right to survive then we must find an alternative to war and destruction. In a day when sputniks dash through outer space and guided ballistic missiles are carving highways of death through the stratosphere, nobody can win a war. The choice today is no longer between violence and nonviolence. It is either nonviolence or nonexistence.[13]

I am no doctrinaire pacifist. I have tried to embrace a realistic pacifism. Moreover, I see the pacifist position not as sinless but as the lesser evil in the circumstances. Therefore I do not claim to be free from the moral dilemmas that the Christian nonpacifist confronts. But I am convinced that the church cannot remain silent while mankind faces the threat of being plunged into the abyss of nuclear annihilation. If the church is true to its mission it must call for an end to the arms race.[14]

In recent months I have also become more and more convinced of the reality of a personal God. True, I have always believed in the personality of God. But in past years the idea of a personal God was little more than a metaphysical category which I found theologically and philosophically satisfying. Now it is a living reality that has been validated in the experiences of everyday life. Perhaps the suffering, frustration and agonizing moments which I have had to undergo occasionally as a result of my involvement in a difficult struggle have drawn me closer to God. Whatever the cause, God has been profoundly real to me in recent months. In the midst of outer dangers I have felt an inner calm and known resources of strength that only God could give. In many instances I have felt the power of God transforming the fatigue of despair into the buoyancy of hope. I am convinced that the universe is under the control of a loving purpose and that in the struggle for righteousness man has cosmic companionship. Behind the harsh appear-

---

13. King, Notes: "During this decade I also turned pacifist. Previously I had repudiated aggressive warfare as unChristian. I still acce~~pted~~ accept the Christian responsibility for constructive force. To accept non-violence as the solely Christian method is to limit our obedience to God to the level of redemption, whereas God has first of all made us creatures in an actual world where, under him, we are responsible for the exercise of constructive compulsion. Christians are not exempt from the disagreeable choices and chores of ordering life, which is dominated more by what men fear than by what they love. But more and more I have come to the conclusion that modern warfare is on such a scale and of such a nature that, regardless of what might be said of wars in the past, future wars can no longer be classified as constructive."

14. King, Notes: "I am no pacifist doctrinaire. I do not believe in the all-inclusiveness of the method of nonviolence, and deplore its being made the center of the gospel, but I believe that the Church cannot dodge taking a stand on the war issue by first finding for itself its own distinctive dimension."

In a revised version of this article sent to Fey on 7 April, King inserted additional material at this point. King's revisions arrived too late for inclusion, but *Christian Century* later published King's addendum as "Suffering and Faith," 27 April 1960, pp. 443–444 in this volume. King's complete essay appeared in Fey's anthology, *How My Mind Has Changed.*

ances of the world there is a benign power. To say God is personal is not to make him an object among other objects or attribute to him the finiteness and limitations of human personality; it is to take what is finest and noblest in our consciousness and affirm its perfect existence in him. It is certainly true that human personality is limited, but personality as such involves no necessary limitations. It simply means self-consciousness and self-direction. So in the truest sense of the word, God is a living God. In him there is feeling and will, responsive to the deepest yearnings of the human heart: this God both evokes and answers prayers.

The past decade has been a most exciting one. In spite of the tensions and uncertainties of our age something profoundly meaningful has begun. Old systems of exploitation and oppression are passing away and new systems of justice and equality are being born. In a real sense ours is a great time in which to be alive. Therefore I am not yet discouraged about the future. Granted that the easygoing optimism of yesterday is impossible. Granted that we face a world crisis which often leaves us standing amid the surging murmur of life's restless sea. But every crisis has both its dangers and its opportunities. Each can spell either salvation or doom. In a dark, confused world the spirit of God may yet reign supreme.

PD. *Christian Century* 77 (13 April 1960): 439–441.

To John Malcolm Patterson

14 April 1960
[*Atlanta, Ga.*]

King and the SCLC executive board write the governor of Alabama to protest an anticipated "purge" of activist faculty at Alabama State College.[1]

HON JOHN PATTERSON
GOV STATE OF ALABAMA

WE VIEW WITH DEEP CONCERN THE PUBLISHED REPORTS THAT CERTAIN MEMBERS OF THE FACULTY OF ALABAMA STATE COLLEGE ARE INVOLVED IN A "PURGE" OR "CLEAN UP"[2] THESE REPORTS STATE THAT THE CHARGES AGAINST THESE TEACHERS ARE THAT THEY HAVE ATTENDED MEETINGS OR OTHERWISE EXPRESSED APPROVAL OF THE WAVE OF SIT IN DEMONSTRATIONS THAT STUDENTS ARE PRESENTLY STAGING IN ALL PARTS OF THE COUNTRY WE AFFIRM THAT TEACHERS ARE ALSO CITIZENS AND AS SUCH HAVE THE RIGHT OF PEACEFULLY ASSEMBLING DEMONSTRATING, OR OTHER FORMS OF PROTESTING WHAT THEY BELIEVE ARE SOCIAL EVILS. ACCORDINGLY, WE CALL UPON YOU TO IN-

1. A similar telegram was also sent on 14 April to Alabama superintendent of education Frank Stewart.
2. "Trenholm Plans Purge of 'Disloyal' Faculty," *Montgomery Advertiser,* 27 March 1960.

SURE THE PROTECTION OF TEACHERS AGAINST SUCH FANTASTIC CHARGES AND A FAIR TRIAL FOR THEM IN THE EVENT SUCH CHARGES SHOULD BE RAISED. MOREOVER WE PLEDGE OUR AID AND SUPPORT TO ANY VICTUM OF THE VIOLATION OF ACADEMIC FREEDOM AND THE RIGHT OF CITIZENSHIP. PLEASE HELP US KEEP OUR NATION FROM BEING HELD UP FOR SHAME BEFORE THE WORLD.

EXECUTIVE BOARD
THE SOUTHERN CHRISTIAN LEADERSHIP CONFERENCE
MARTIN LUTHER KING JR PRES

PWc. MLKP-MBU: Box 21A.

"Statement to the Press at the Beginning of the Youth Leadership Conference"

15 April 1960
Raleigh, N.C.

Over two hundred student and adult activists gathered at Shaw University for an Easter weekend youth conference to discuss the growing sit-in movement.[1] King issued this statement at a press conference on the opening day of the meeting.[2] Among his five suggestions for "a strategy for victory," King recommends that the students form a permanent nonviolent organization to "take the freedom struggle into every community in the South without exception."[3] The following day, King addressed a mass meeting at the Raleigh Memorial Auditorium and reportedly characterized the student movement as "a revolt against those Negroes in the middle class who have indulged themselves in big cars and ranch-style homes rather than in joining a movement for freedom."[4] During the three-day conference, youth leaders voted to create the Temporary Student Nonviolent Coordinating Committee.[5]

This is an era of offensive on the part of oppressed people. All peoples deprived of dignity and freedom are on the march on every continent throughout the world.

1. King and Baker had issued the call for the meeting (Announcement, "Youth leadership meeting, Shaw University, Raleigh, N.C., 4/15/1960–4/17/1960," March 1960; see also SCLC and Raleigh Citizens Association, Program, "Mass meeting featuring Dr. Martin Luther King," 16 April 1960, and SCLC, "Northern students and observers to Southwide Youth Leadership Conference, Shaw University, Raleigh, N.C.," 22 April 1960).

2. On the back of King's copy of this document was a list of five names, the last two of which—Elroy Embry of Montgomery and Paul LaPrad of Fisk University—were handwritten by King.

3. According to a newspaper account, King also explained that the protests were "a spontaneous movement without any national organization" (Guy Munger, "Students Begin Strategy Talks on Integration," *Greensboro Daily News,* 16 April 1960).

4. Claude Sitton, "Negro Criticizes N.A.A.C.P. Tactics," *New York Times,* 17 April 1960.

5. The students also voted that the temporary committee, composed of representatives from thirteen southern states and established student organizations, would be headquartered in Atlanta. King and James Lawson were to be "present in an advisory capacity" (Southwide Youth Leadership Conference, "Recommendations of the findings and recommendations committee," 15 April–17 April 1960).

The student sit-in movement represents just such an offensive in the history of the Negro peoples' struggle for freedom. The students have taken the struggle for justice into their own strong hands. In less than two months more Negro freedom fighters have revealed to the nation and the world their determination and courage than has occurred in many years. They have embraced a philosophy of mass direct nonviolent action. They are moving away from tactics which are suitable merely for gradual and long term change.[6]

Today the leaders of the sit-in movement are assembled here from ten states and some forty communities to evaluate these recent sit-ins and to chart future goals. They realize that they must now evolve a strategy for victory. Some elements which suggest themselves for discussion are: (1) The need for some type of continuing organization. Those who oppose justice are well organized. To win out the student movement must be organized. (2) The students must consider calling for a nation-wide campaign of "selective buying." Such a program is a moral act. It is a moral necessity to select, to buy from these agencies, these stores, and businesses where one can buy with dignity and self respect. It is immoral to spend one's money where one cannot be treated with respect.[7] (3) The students must seriously consider training a group of volunteers who will willingly go to jail rather than pay bail or fines.[8] This courageous willingness to go to jail may well be the thing to awaken the dozing conscience of many of our white brothers. We are in an era in which a prison term for a freedom struggle is a badge of honor. (4) The youth must take the freedom struggle into every community in the South without exception. The struggle must be spread into every nook and cranny. Inevitably this broadening of the struggle and the determination which it represents will arouse vocal and vigorous support and place pressures on the federal government that will compel its intervention.[9] (5) The students will certainly want to delve deeper into the philosophy of nonviolence. It must be made palpably clear that resistance and nonviolence are not in themselves good. There is another element that must be present in our struggle that then makes our resistance and nonviolence truly meaningful. That element is reconciliation. Our ultimate end must be the creation of the beloved community. The tactics of nonviolence without the spirit of nonviolence may indeed become a new kind of violence.

TAHD. MLKP-MBU: Box 2.

---

6. During the question and answer portion of the press conference, King elaborated on this point: "I'm not saying this brings about a cessation of legal activities. But the Negro students are saying, 'We will not wait for long litigation . . . delaying tactics.'" He also contrasted the "non-creative sitdown in Congress" with the "creative sitdown by Negro students" (Munger, "Students Begin Strategy Talks").

7. King explained that "if a store opens itself to the public, it is not private property in the sense that it may deny accommodations," and concluded: "We are not trying to put a store out of business. We are seeking to put justice into business" (Munger, "Students Begin Strategy Talks").

8. At the weekend's close, the coordinating committee adopted a number of resolutions, including one which read: "This conference recognizes the virtue of the movement and endorses the practice of going to jail rather than accepting bail" (Southwide Youth Leadership Conference, "Recommendations of the findings and recommendations committee," 15 April–17 April 1960).

9. According to a press account, King elaborated on this point when he explained that he was not defining federal government intervention "in physical terms" but as providing "moral support to the movement" ("Sit-in Meeting Fights Erupt," *Nashville Tennessean,* 16 April 1960).

Interview on "Meet the Press"

[*17 April 1960*]
[*Washington, D.C.*]

Three years after he initially agreed to be a guest on the show, King makes his first appearance on the National Broadcasting Company television program "Meet the Press."[1] *King addresses the legal and moral justifications for the student sit-ins and the federal government's "responsibility of protecting our citizens of this nation." This transcription was drawn from NBC film footage.*

[*Announcer*]: Now "Meet the Press," produced by Lawrence E. Spivak. Remember that the questions asked by the members of the panel do not necessarily reflect their point of view. It is their way of getting the story for you. Now, here is the moderator of "Meet the Press," Mr. Ned Brooks.[2]

[*Ned Brooks*]: Welcome once again to "Meet the Press." For the past several months, a new strategy to end racial segregation has been spreading through the South. It takes the form of sit-in demonstrations by Negro students against segregation in public eating places. It is part of a broader campaign of nonviolent resistance led by the Reverend Dr. Martin Luther King, Jr., who is our guest today. Dr. King is a Baptist minister and head of the Southern Christian Leadership Congress, Conference rather, which is spearheading the passive resistance movement. Dr. King first attracted nationwide attention in 1956 when he led the boycott against segregation in public buses in Montgomery, Alabama. His activities have resulted five times in his arrest, and his home and his church were bombed. Early this year, Dr. King moved his base of operations from Montgomery to Alabama, to Atlanta, Georgia. He is thirty-one-years old. He was born in the South, educated for the ministry in the North.

And now seated around the press table ready to interview Dr. King are Frank Van Der Linden of the *Nashville Banner,* May Craig of the *Portland* (Maine) *Press Herald,* Anthony Lewis of the *New York Times,* and Lawrence E. Spivak, a regular member of the "Meet the Press" panel.[3] Now, Dr. King, if you're ready, we'll start the questions with Mr. Spivak.

---

1. On 4 March 1957, the show's producer Lawrence Spivak approached King about appearing on the show "some Sunday in the future." King agreed in a 29 March 1957 letter, but scheduling conflicts delayed his appearance. He appeared on the show four other times: 25 August 1963, 28 March 1965, 21 August 1966, and 13 August 1967. Spivak described "Meet the Press" as being "conducted exactly like a press conference with four newsmen to do the questioning. The questions, of course, are in the area of the guest's interest and knowledge" (Spivak to King, 15 April 1957).

2. Ned Brooks (1901–1969) served as moderator for "Meet the Press" from 1953 to 1965.

3. Frank Van Der Linden (1919–) was a White House correspondent for major newspapers, a columnist, and author of several books on U.S. presidents. Elisabeth May Adams Craig (1889–1975) served as the Washington correspondent for the Gannett newspaper syndicate and wrote the column "Inside in Washington" that ran for nearly fifty years. Anthony Lewis (1927–) was a Pulitzer Prize-winning reporter who covered the Supreme Court for the *New York Times* from 1955 to 1964, including *New York Times Co. v. Sullivan* (1964). Lawrence Edmund Spivak (1900–1994) created the radio program "Meet the Press" in 1945; the television program followed two years later. He served as the moderator or a panelist until he retired in 1975. For more on King's involvement in the *Sullivan* case, see John Malcolm Patterson to King, 9 May 1960, pp. 456–458 in this volume.

[*Lawrence Spivak*]: Dr. King, the former president, Harry Truman, recently said this, and I quote, "If anyone came to my store and sat down, I would throw him out. Private business has its own rights and can do what it wants."[4] Now, President, former President Truman is an old friend of the Negro, I believe. Isn't this an indication that the sit-in strikes are doing the race, the Negro race, more harm than good? 17 Apr 1960

[*King*]: No, I don't think so, Mr. Spivak. First, I should say that this was an unfortunate statement, and we were very disappointed to hear the president, the former president of the United States, make such a statement.[5] In a sense a statement like this serves to aid and abet the violent forces in the South, and even if Mr. Truman disagreed with the sit-ins he should certainly disagree with them on a higher level. Following his past record, it seems to me that Mr. Truman wouldn't have faced such a situation because there wouldn't have been a segregated store in the beginning if he were running it, according to his statements in the past. Now, I do not think this movement is setting us back or making enemies; it's causing numerous people all over the nation, and in the South in particular, to reevaluate the stereotypes that they have developed concerning Negroes, so that it has an educational value, and I think in the long run it will transform the whole of American society.

[*Spivak*]: Well now you have yourself have said that the aim of your method of nonviolent resistance is not to defeat or to humiliate the white man but to win his friendship and understanding. How successful do you think you have been, or are being, in winning the friendship and understanding of the white men of the South?

[*King*]: Well, I should say that this doesn't come overnight. The nonviolent way does not bring about miracles, in a few hours, or in a few days, or in a few years, for that matter. I think at first, the first reaction of the oppressor, when oppressed people rise up against the system of injustice, is an attitude of bitterness. But I do believe that if the nonviolent resisters continue to follow the way of nonviolence they eventually get over to the hearts and souls of the former oppressors, and I think it eventually brings about that redemption that we dream of. Of course, I can't estimate how many people we've touched so far; this is impossible because it's an inner process. But I'm sure something is stirring in the minds and the souls of people, and I'm sure that many people are thinking anew on this basic problem of human relations.

[*Spivak*]: Well now, Dr. King, you speak of your movement as a nonviolent movement, and yet the end product of it has been violence. You've also called upon the white people, of the South particularly, to live up to the law as the Supreme Court has interpreted. Don't you think you would have more standing in your fight if you, yourself, if you called upon your people to live up to the law rather than to break the law and to risk jail in this sit-in?

[*King*]: Well, I would say two things to that, Mr. Spivak. First, the end result has not been a violent result. I would say that there has been some violence here and there, but the nonviolent resister does not go on with the idea that there will not be any violence inflicted upon him. In other words, he is always willing to be

4. Perry Mullen, "Reactions Have No Pattern," *Atlanta Journal*, 28 April 1960.

5. See King to Truman, 19 April 1960, pp. 437–439 in this volume.

17 Apr 1960

the recipient of violence but never to inflict it upon another. He goes on the idea that he must act now against injustice with moral means, and he feels that in acting against this injustice that he must never inflict injury upon the opponent. But he is always prepared to absorb the violence which emerges, if such violence emerges in the process.

[*Spivak*]: But aren't you urging him to break the local laws when you're asking the white people to live up to the laws? And is this a good method of procedure?

[*King*]: I think we will find that the law of the land is a law which calls for integration. This has been affirmed by the Supreme Court of the nation, mainly in the 1954 decision outlawing segregation in the public schools. It made it palpably clear that separate facilities are inherently unequal. So that in breaking local laws we are really seeking to dignify the law and to affirm the real and positive meaning of the law of the land.

[*Brooks*]: Mr. Lewis.

[*Anthony Lewis*]: Dr. King, in connection with the sit-in movement and other aspects of the racial question, there has certainly been an increase in tension in various parts of the South, what Mr. Spivak was speaking of, regardless of the motivation. During the last week, the *New York Times* has run some stories about Birmingham, Alabama, suggesting that a kind of reign of terror is taking place there with the officials on the side of those terrorizing those who believe in racial equality.[6] Now, my question is what role you see for the federal government in this situation? Do you think the federal government has a place to play in, say, Birmingham, or in connection with your sit-in demonstrations?

[*King*]: Yes, I do. I think the federal government has the responsibility of protecting our citizens of this nation as they protest against unjust, the injustices which they face. I also feel that the executive branch of the government should do more in terms of moral persuasion. The legislative branch should certainly do more in giving the proper legislation, so that the transition will be made in a much smoother manner than we are facing now.

[*Lewis*]: We've just had a civil rights bill passed. You speak of the legislative branch. I wonder what you think of that and what more you would have had Congress do.

[*King*]: Well, I must confess that I was disappointed with the final bill because so many things that I felt were basic happened to have been deleted or omitted. And the whole question of school integration I'm convinced that the nation, the federal government, will have to face it in a much more forthright and courageous manner than it has in the past. And by omitting this section of the bill, I think we face something very disappointing.[7] Or, even in the area of voter registration, I

---

6. In a 12 April 1960 *New York Times* article, "Fear and Hatred Grip Birmingham," Harrison E. Salisbury reported that "every channel of communication, every medium of mutual interest, every reasoned approach, every inch of middle ground has been fragmented by the emotional dynamite of racism, reinforced by the whip, the razor . . . the mob, the police and many branches of the state's apparatus." Three Birmingham city commissioners later demanded a retraction from the newspaper ("3 in Birmingham Ask a Retraction," *New York Times*, 27 April 1960).

7. For further discussion of the civil rights bill, see Jacob K. Javits to King, 21 April 1960, pp. 439–440 in this volume.

think there is much more that can be done. Now, the bill that we have, which is mainly in the area of voter registration, will help, particularly in some communities, but it is not at all a panacea. It has certain red tape, complex qualities about it which will still make the process a long one, and I think ultimately the federal government should set forth a uniform pattern of registration and voting, so that no citizen will have a problem at this point.

[*Lewis*]: You spoke of the executive branch, also, and moral leadership being needed. What precisely would you have the president do? President Eisenhower or his successor?

[*King*]: Well, Mr. Lewis, I think there are several things. Certainly, the president can do a great deal in the area of executive orders. He has certain executive powers where orders can be made and the country must follow [*them?*] and comply with these orders. On the other hand, there is a great deal that a man as powerful as the president of the United States can do in the area of moral persuasion, by constantly speaking to the people on the moral values involved in integration, and urging the people to comply with the law of the land.

[*Brooks*]: Mrs. Craig.

[*May Craig*]: Well, Dr. King, there have been court decisions saying that a storekeeper can select his customers. Are you saying that the end justifies the means and you're apparently breaking local laws, hoping for a better conclusion?[8]

[*King*]: Well, I would say, first, that the Supreme Court has not rendered a decision at this point. It is true that there have been other decisions. But I think on the basis of the 1954 decision if the Supreme Court follows what it set forth in 1954, it would have to uphold the law in this area, that segregation is wrong even in lunch counters and public places because that decision said in substance that segregation generates a feeling of inferiority within the segregated and, thereby, it breaches the equal protection clause of the Fourteenth Amendment. Now, I'm sure that if we follow this through in this area the same thing will follow. On the other hand, if you're saying are we breaking laws because we feel that the end justifies the means, we feel that there are moral laws in the universe just as valid and as basic as man-made laws, and whenever a man-made law is in conflict with what we consider the law of God, or the moral law of the universe, then we feel that we have a moral obligation to protest.[9] And this is in our American tradition all the way from the Boston Tea Party on down. We have praised individuals in America who stood up with creative initiative to revolt against an unjust system. So that this is all we're doing. In our institutions we give the Boston Tea Party as an example of the initiative of Americans, and I think this is an ex-

8. See for example, *Hodges v. United States,* 203 U.S. 1 (1906).

9. *Baltimore Afro-American* columnist Louis Lautier criticized King for making these comments. Arguing that the sit-downs were legal, Lautier wrote that "any of the 62 lawyers who met with Thurgood Marshall, director-counsel of the NAACP Legal Defense and Educational Fund, Inc., which is undertaking the legal defense of the approximately 1,500 students who have been arrested, could have informed Dr. King that there is nothing illegal in a student's peaceably and orderly taking a seat at a lunch counter in a variety store and ordering a hamburger." In the same article Lautier said that King possessed "the uncanny knack of muffing his big opportunities to show qualities of leadership on a national scale" ("Says King 'Muffed' Leadership Chance," *Baltimore Afro-American,* 7 May 1960).

ample of the initiative and the great creative move of the young people of our nation.

[*Craig*]: But Dr. King, this is a nation that lives under law. Above the Supreme Court is graven "Equal Justice Under Law." Are each of us to decide when it's all right to break a law?

[*King*]: I would say that when, as I said a few minutes ago, Mrs. Craig, when the law of our nation stands in conflict with the higher moral law and when a local law stands in conflict with the federal law, then we must resist that law in order to dignify and give meaning in the full outpour of the federal law and the moral law.

[*Craig*]: But sir, we have Congress to change a law. We have the courts to interpret the law. Are you going beyond them?

[*King*]: Well, we have discovered that in any nonviolent movement you have a way of direct action. In many instances the courts have made for slow movement, so to speak. As one attorney general says, "We are prepared for a century of litigation." We have observed the sometimes hypocritical attitudes in Congress and the slow movements there, the apathy. So that this is a direct-action approach, and the whole aim, the end result will be to arouse the conscience of those who are using these stalling and delaying methods to block our advance.

[*Brooks*]: Mr. Van Der Linden.

[*Frank Van Der Linden*]: Dr. King, in your own book, *Stride Toward Freedom,* you say you thoroughly studied the writings of Karl Marx and the teachings of communism and you don't agree with everything that the father of communism said. But you do say this, and I quote from page 95 of your book, "In so far as Marx pointed to the weaknesses of traditional capitalism and challenged the social conscience of the Christian churches," you responded with a definite "yes."[10] Now, I'd like to know just where does communism or collectivism fit into your program of resistance here?

[*King*]: Well, it doesn't fit in this particular program of resistance at all. I have made it crystal clear on many occasions that I feel that communism is based on an ethical relativism and a metaphysical materialism that no Christian can accept. I do not feel that the end justifies the means because the end is preexistent in the means, and I believe firmly that we must follow moral means to secure moral ends. So that, that particular quotation does not apply to this particular struggle. I was referring to something else altogether.

[*Van Der Linden*]: But sir, you said also in your book on page 220: "Our ultimate goal is integration which is genuine intergroup and interpersonal living." You also soft pedal as so-called irrational fears, that this program might lead to racial intermarriage. You say that marriage is an individual matter. Now, is it correct to say that you don't oppose racial intermarriage?

---

10. *Stride Toward Freedom,* p. 95: "In so far as Marx posited a metaphysical materialism, an ethical relativism, and a strangulating totalitarianism, I responded with an unambiguous 'no'; but in so far as he pointed to weaknesses of traditional capitalism, contributed to the growth of a definite self-consciousness in the masses, and challenged the social conscience of the Christian churches, I responded with a definite 'yes.'"

[*King*]: Well, I would certainly say, properly speaking, individuals marry and not races. And therefore, I cannot, I would not at all say that the laws prohibiting individuals of different races to marry, because this is an individual matter. It is not a matter of a group marrying another group but an individual marrying an individual.

[*Van Der Linden*]: Would you, then, attack next the state laws against such intermarriage?

[*King*]: Well, I haven't planned a particular attack on that, but I don't think America will ever come to its full maturity until every state does away with laws prohibiting individuals to marry on the basis of race. But I think basically this is an irrational fear because it is an individual matter. And I think the question here, at bottom, is a question of illicit miscegenation, and if you will follow the record there I think you will discover that illicit miscegenation has existed more in the South, where you have had rigid segregation laws, than it has existed in the North, where you don't have such barriers. It hadn't been the Negro who is the aggressor at this point. We just need to look around, and we can see that.

[*Brooks*]: Mr. Spivak.

[*Spivak*]: Dr. King, you say that the Negroes have a moral right to occupy the restaurant seats. Now, you've had a Supreme Court edict on the school integration. Would you say that your children, the Negro children, have a right to occupy the seats in classrooms, too, and would you consider that form of nonviolence?

[*King*]: Well, I'm sure that Negroes have this right on the basis of the Supreme Court, to go into schools. I haven't gone into, I haven't thought through the strategy at this point, how nonviolence, how nonviolent resistance can apply in the school integration struggle. I do think it can apply, and I think we need to think through some of these methods. The main thing is that the methods must always be nonviolent, and they must always be based on the principle of love. But the specific application I'm not prepared to say at this time. I do know that we have that right on the basis of the decision from the Supreme Court.

[*Spivak*]: Wouldn't you be on better ground, both legal and moral, if you occupied school seats than by occupying a few restaurant seats?

[*King*]: I'm not sure about that, Mr. Spivak, because I think we have an economic factor involved here, and even if one denied the legal aspect or the legal right to do it, there is a deeper moral right. As Governor Collins of Florida said, "It is a blatant injustice to welcome individuals into a store at all of the counters but the eating counter." This is a blatant injustice, and it is very unfair, so that we have not only legal rights involved here, but also moral rights.[11]

[*Spivak*]: But wouldn't you be on stronger grounds, though, if you refused to buy at those stores and if you called upon the white people of the country to follow you because of both your moral and your legal right not to buy?

---

11. Responding to the sit-ins in Florida, Governor LeRoy Collins remarked: "I don't mind saying that if a man has a department store and he invites the public generally to come in his department store and trade, I think then it is unfair and morally wrong for him to single out one department, though, and say he does not want or will not allow Negroes to patronize that one department. Now he has a legal right to do this. But I still don't think he can square that right with moral, simple justice" ("Collins Criticizes Stores in Florida Racial Strife," *Washington Post,* 21 March 1960).

17 Apr 1960

[*King*]: I think, Mr. Spivak, sometimes it is necessary to dramatize an issue because many people are not aware of what's happening. And I think the sit-ins serve to dramatize the indignities and the injustices which Negro people are facing all over the nation. And I think another reason why they are necessary, and they are vitally important at this point, is the fact that they give an eternal refutation to the idea that the Negro is satisfied with segregation. If you didn't have the sit-ins, you wouldn't have this dramatic, and not only this dramatic but this mass demonstration of the dissatisfaction of the Negro with the whole system of segregation.

[*Brooks*]: Mr. Lewis.

[*Lewis*]: You've just had a strategy meeting in Raleigh, North Carolina, Dr. King, on this whole question, and I notice that one speaker was quite critical of the National Association for the Advancement of Colored People, speaking of it as too conservative and too slow moving.[12] Do you share that view, and just what was the feeling at this strategy meeting? What was the conclusion—that you've got to move more quickly than you have been?

[*King*]: Well, I should say, first, that I didn't hear a speaker say, make that particular point, so that I can't speak on that—whether the speaker said it or whether he didn't say it. I heard all of the speakers, and I didn't hear that. I didn't find any anti-NAACP attitude at the strategy meeting. All of the leaders from the South, the southern sit-in movement, assembled there and they assembled there, with the awareness of the fact that the NAACP has given absolute support to the sit-ins. And the NAACP has made it very clear that this is a good movement, a positive movement, that it will support throughout. Now, there was some criticism, not of the NAACP but of the snail-like pace of the implementation process—the implementation of the Supreme Court's decision—and dissatisfaction with the conniving methods and evasive schemes used to avoid following the law of the land. This isn't a criticism of the NAACP; it's a criticism of the agencies and the courts that will use the law to delay and get it bogged down in complex litigation processes.

[*Brooks*]: Mrs. Craig.

[*Craig*]: Dr. King, I have been told that there are places in Harlem which refuse to serve white customers. Do you know if that's true? If so, do you justify it as either morally or legally right?

[*King*]: I am very sorry, I didn't get the first part of the question.

[*Craig*]: I say, I understand there are places in Harlem, in New York, where they will not serve white customers. Do you know if that's true or not?

[*King*]: I am very sorry, I do not, Mrs. Craig.

[*Craig*]: I have been so told.

[*King*]: I don't know of places in Harlem that will not serve white customers. If such places exist, I think it's a blatant injustice and just redevelopment of the thing we are trying to get rid of, so I certainly wouldn't go along with that.

[*Brooks*]: Mr. Van Der Linden.

---

12. For more on criticisms of the NAACP at the Raleigh Youth Leadership Conference, see Roy Wilkins to King, 27 April 1960, pp. 444–446 in this volume.

[*Van Der Linden*]: Dr. King, how many white people are members of your church in Atlanta? 18 Apr 1960

[*King*]: I don't have any white members, Mr. Van Der Linden.

[*Van Der Linden*]: Well sir, you said integration is the law of the land, and it's morally right, whereas segregation is morally wrong, and the president should do something about it. Do you mean the president should issue an order that the schools and the churches and the stores should all be integrated?

[*King*]: I think it is one of the tragedies of our nation, one of the shameful tragedies, that eleven o'clock on Sunday morning is one of the most segregated hours, if not the most segregated hours, in Christian America. I definitely think the Christian church should be integrated, and any church that stands against integration and that has a segregated body is standing against the spirit and the teachings of Jesus Christ, and it fails to be a true witness. But this is something that the Church will have to do itself. I don't think church integration will come through legal processes. I might say that my church is not a segregating church. It's segregated but not segregating. It would welcome white members.

[*Brooks*]: I think at this point I'll have to interrupt. I see that our time is up. Thank you very much, Dr. King, for being with us. We'll be back with "Meet the Press" in just a moment, but first, this message.

F. NBCNA-NNNBC.

To Allan Knight Chalmers

18 April 1960
[*Atlanta, Ga.*]

Upon returning from a meeting in New York about southern civil rights efforts, Boston University theology professor and civil rights advocate Allan Knight Chalmers relayed to King that "several of your close friends" expressed concern that the "constant pressure. . . . has filled your program so full that your opportunities for reflection have been taken away."[1] *In this response, King acknowledges being frustrated with his hectic schedule: "My whole life seems to be centered around giving something out and only rarely taking something in."*

1. Chalmers to King, 6 March 1960. Chalmers also wrote: "'Thinking time' has been filched from you. A man gets thin if he does not read, becomes inaccurate if he does not write, but most of all loses a profoundness if he does not think; or if he is deep he may only be in a rut because he has not had time to think anew as time and circumstances have gone on." Among those Chalmers mentioned as present at the meeting were United Nations diplomat Ralph Bunche, New York minister Harry Emerson Fosdick, and federal appellate judge William Hastie. In his capacity as NAACP treasurer, Chalmers had sent King a supportive letter during the bus boycott (Chalmers to King, 14 March 1956, in *Papers* 3:173–174).

18 Apr 1960

Dr. Allan Knight Chalmers
Boston University School of Theology
745 Commonwealth Avenue
Boston 15, Massachusetts

Dear Dr. Chalmers:

Thank you for your very kind letter of March 6. I have been intending to answer it for several weeks now, but an extremely crowded schedule has stood in my way. Please accept my apologies for being so tardy in my reply.

I am happy to know of the important meeting which you had in New York, and to know of the top flight people that you were able to bring together to discuss the southern situation. I am convinced that the student movement that is taking place all over the South at the present time is one of the most significant developments in the whole civil rights struggle. It finally refutes the idea that the Negro is content with segregation, and we are seeing through this movement that segregation cannot be maintained in the South devoid of social disintegration.

The other main point that you raise in your letter is a matter that I have been grappling with over the last three or four years. I must admit that in many instances I have felt terribly frustrated over my inability to retreat, concentrate, and reflect. My whole life seems to be centered around giving something out and only rarely taking something in. One of my reasons for moving to Atlanta was to meet this problem head on. I felt that by coming here I would have more time to meditate and think through the total struggle ahead. Unfortunately, however, things have happened as you know which have made my schedule more crowded in Atlanta than it was in Montgomery. I have also tried to deal with the problem in another way. After returning from India I decided that I would take one day a week as a day of silence and meditation. This, I attempted on several occasions, but things began to pile up so much that I found myself using that particular day as a time to catch up on so many things that had accumulated. And so in a real sense I am in about the same position now as I was two or three years ago. But I know that I cannot continue to go at this pace, and live with such a tension filled schedule. My failure to reflect will do harm not only to me as a person, but to the total movement. For that reason I feel a moral obligation to do it.

Thank you very much for the suggestions concerning places that I may go to take the much needed retreat.[2] I may well take you up on some of this. This summer I plan to take about a month off from everything in order to rest, think, and write. If I can get around to doing this it will be the first time that it has really occurred in my life. I certainly can say in recent years. Even when I was writing <u>Stride Toward Freedom</u> I would only take off one or two weeks at a time.

---

2. Chalmers suggested the over-garage apartment at the home of philanthropists Albert and Jessie Danielsen in Wellesley, Massachusetts, which many Boston University professors used as a retreat. He also offered his own coastal Maine home. Harold DeWolf had suggested King consider a stay at the Danielsen's guest house for "rest, spiritual renewal and writing" during the Montgomery bus boycott (DeWolf to King, 9 November 1956, in *Papers* 3:423).

Again, let me say how deeply grateful I am to you for your concern and suggestions. Always feel free to write me about these matters. I cherish your advice. I hope things are going well with you. Do let me know when you plan to be in this section of the country again so that we will have an opportunity to have a long talk.

Give my best regards to all. We had the privilege of having Harold DeWolf in our home a few days ago.[3] It was certainly wonderful to have him.

Very sincerely yours,
Martin L. King, Jr.

MLK:mlb

TLc. MLKP-MBU: Box 22.

3. DeWolf, King's graduate school advisor, visited Atlanta on 26 and 27 March 1960 (see King to DeWolf, 16 June 1960, pp. 472–474 in this volume).

To Harry S. Truman

19 April 1960
Atlanta, Ga.

At an 18 April news conference in Ithaca, New York, former president Truman declared that the southern lunch counter demonstrations were engineered by Communists.[1] Truman later reportedly stated: "If anyone came into my store and tried to stop business I'd throw him out. The Negro should behave himself and show he's a good citizen. Common sense and good will can solve this whole thing."[2] In the letter below a "baffled" King admonishes Truman: "Of course, we in the South constantly hear these McCarthy-like accusations and pay little attention to them; but when the accusations come from a man who was once chosen by the American people to serve as the chief custodian of the nation's destiny then they rise to shocking and dangerous proportions."[3] No reply from Truman has been located.

1. Clayton Knowles, "Truman Believes Reds Lead Sit-Ins," *New York Times,* 19 April 1960. Truman later explained that, while he had no proof of Communist influence, "usually when trouble hits the country the Kremlin is behind it" ("Truman Is Asked to Prove Charge," *New York Times,* 20 April 1960). In 1958 King had sent Truman an inscribed copy of *Stride Toward Freedom.* Truman thanked King for the book on 10 December 1958.

2. Perry Mullen, "Reactions Have No Pattern," *Atlanta Journal,* 28 April 1960.

3. Kennedy campaign aide Harris Wofford echoed King's concerns in a 20 April 1960 letter to Truman. Wofford sent a copy of the letter to King, adding a handwritten suggestion that he invite Truman to discuss the matter, "one Baptist to another" (Wofford to King, 20 April 1960; see also "King Asks Truman to Apologize to Nation and Negro," *Birmingham World,* 23 April 1960).

19 Apr 1960

Mr. Harry Truman
Independence, Missouri

Dear Mr. Truman:

For many years I have admired you. Like many other Negroes I have deeply appreciated your civil rights record.[4] But I must confess that some of your recent statements have completely baffled me, and served as an affront and disappointment to millions of Negroes of America. Your statement that appeared in the morning paper affirming that the "sit-ins" were Communist inspired is an unfortunate misrepresentation of facts. The more you talk about the sit-ins the more you reveal a limited grasp and an abysmal lack of understanding of what is taking place. It is a sad day for our country when men come to feel that oppressed people cannot desire freedom and human dignity unless they are motivated by Communism. Of course, we in the South constantly hear these McCarthy-like accusations and pay little attention to them; but when the accusations come from a man who was once chosen by the American people to serve as the chief custodian of the nation's destiny then they rise to shocking and dangerous proportions. We are sorry that you have not been able to project yourself in our place long enough to understand the inner longing for freedom and self respect that motivate our action. We also regret that you have not been able to see that the present movement on the part of the students is not for themselves alone, but a struggle that will help save the soul of America. As long as segregation exists, whether at lunch counters or in public schools, America is in danger of not only losing her prestige as a world leader, but also of losing her soul.

I have worked very closely with the students in this struggle and the one thing that I am convinced of is that no outside agency (Communist or otherwise) initiated this movement, and to my knowledge no Communist force has come in since it started, or will dominate it in the future. The fact that this is a spiritual movement rooted in the deepest tradition of nonviolence is enough to refute the argument that this movement was inspired by Communism which has a materialistic and anti-spiritualistic world view. No, the sit-ins were not inspired by Communism. They were inspired by the passionate yearning and the timeless longing for freedom and human dignity on the part of a people who have for years been trampled over by the iron feet of oppression. They grew out of the accumulated indignities of days gone by, and the boundless aspirations of generations yet unborn. We are very sorry that you have missed this point, and that you have been mislead either by your own analysis of the struggle or by misinformation that has come to you. If you feel that this movement is Communist inspired we feel that you should give the public some proof of such a strong indictment. If you cannot render such proof we feel that you owe the nation and the Negro people a public apology. Believing in your sense of goodwill and

4. In 1946 President Truman issued Executive Order 9808, which established the President's Committee on Civil Rights. Two years later, Truman issued Executive Order 9980, establishing a fair employment board to eliminate discriminatory hiring within the federal government concurrently with Executive Order 9981, which desegregated the United States armed forces.

humanitarian concern, we are confident that you would want to make such an apology.

I would appreciate hearing from you on this matter if you find it possible.

Yours for the Cause of Freedom,
[*signed*] Martin L. King Jr.
Martin Luther King, Jr., President
The Southern Christian Leadership Conference

MLK:mlb

TLS. PHTPG-MoIT.

From Jacob K. Javits

21 April 1960

In the midst of a months-long filibuster over a bill that would eventually become the Civil Rights Act of 1960, SCLC urged passage of "a strong, clear-cut provision for federal referees or registrars" to protect voting rights in the South.[1] *In the telegram SCLC stated that "time has run out when watered-down or hamstrung proposals, claiming to remedy violations of Negro voting rights . . . can be considered progress."*[2] *Senator Javits (R-NY) replies below.*

Rev. M. L. King, Jr., President
The Southern Christian Leadership Conference, Inc.
208 Auburn Ave., N.E.
Atlanta, Georgia

Dear Rev. King:

Thank you for your recent communication regarding Senate action on civil rights legislation. On April 8, 1960, after eight weeks of debate, the Senate passed H.R. 8601, the Civil Rights Act of 1960. This bill now goes back to the House of

1. Ella J. Baker to Richard M. Nixon, 30 March 1960. Introduced in the Senate on 8 February 1960 by Everett Dirksen (R-Ill.), the legislation consisted of seven sections, only five of which were ultimately passed in a 71–18 Senate vote on 8 April 1960. Jacob Koppel Javits (1904–1986), born in New York City, earned an LL.B. (1926) from New York University and began practicing law in 1927. After working for the Chemical Warfare Service during World War II, Javits was elected to the House of Representatives in 1946. He resigned in 1954 and served as New York City district attorney general from 1955 to 1957. Javits became a U.S. senator in 1957, serving until 1980. A supporter of civil rights, Javits authored several books, including *Discrimination, U.S.A.* (1960).

2. Baker to Nixon, 30 March 1960. SCLC also sent telegrams to Attorney General William P. Rogers, Senate majority leader Lyndon B. Johnson, and Senate minority leader Everett M. Dirksen (Southern Christian Leadership Conference, Press release, 5 April 1960; see also Ella J. Baker, "Ninety years—long enough!" 28 March 1960).

21 Apr 1960

Representatives, where early action on the amendments made by the Senate is expected.[3]

I have attached a memorandum showing the provisions in the bill as passed by the Senate.[4] However, the bill omitted a number of provisions which I felt were necessary in any civil rights bill in order to comprise meaningful and effective legislation. Among the important provisions which were omitted were those for assistance by the Federal Government to school desegregation and statutory authority for a Commission to seek to eliminate discrimination in employment by government contractors, both requested by the President. Also omitted were other proposals which I had urged, including measures to give power to the Attorney General to bring civil injunction cases for the protection of civil rights, elimination of the poll tax, and making lynching a federal crime.

I shall continue the fight in the next Congress for meaningful legislation which would fulfill our solemn obligation to make the constitutional guarantees of equal protection under the laws a reality to every individual, regardless of race, religion, color or national origin. You may be sure of my unstinting support for measures which will assure these rights to all our citizens.

Thank you for letting me have the benefit of your views on this vital national issue.

Sincerely,
[*signed*] J Javits
Jacob K. Javits, U.S.S.

JKJ:ml
Enclosure

TLS. MLKP-MBU: Box 28A.

---

3. The Senate made sixteen amendments to the bill the House passed in March. The House of Representatives further amended the bill prior to passing it on 21 April. The *New York Times* reported that southern representatives "won minor victories" as they successfully changed sections that affected school desegregation (Russell Baker, "Senate Votes Rights Bill, 71–18, after 8-Week Fight; House Approval Is Likely: Dirksen Also Hailed for Role—Referee Plan Is the Key," *New York Times,* 9 April 1960). President Eisenhower signed the Civil Rights Act of 1960 on 6 May.

4. Javits attached a five-item summary of the Civil Rights Act of 1960 (H.R. 8601) that included provisions to make "hate bombings" a federal crime, to make voting records available for inspection for twenty-two months, and to appoint "voting referees" to register people who had been denied the right to vote because of their race. In his summary, Javits also wrote that the act would permit "the Federal Government to provide schooling for children of members of the Armed Services, where local schools are closed to avoid compliance with the Supreme Court's decree against segregation" ("Summary of major provisions of Civil Rights Act of 1960," 8 April 1960).

To Earl Wesley Lawson

23 April 1960
[*Atlanta, Ga.*]

King replies to a letter from Lawson, whom he had recommended as a possible successor at Dexter.[1] *King comments on Lawson's 27 March visit to Montgomery and jokes that, although Dexter was known as "the 'big folks' church," he had learned during his time there "that some professional people have religion also."*[2]

Rev. Earl Wesley Lawson
The Emmanuel Baptist Church
Hillside and Eastern Avenues
Malden, Mass.

Dear Earl:

This is just a note to acknowledge receipt of your letter of April 2, and to say how good it was to hear from you.[3] I have heard nothing but glowing echoes from your visit to Montgomery and Dexter. The members were carried away and I mean just that. So it seems that if you want the church you have it in your hands. I understand that they are inviting you back for another sermon, and I certainly hope you will see your way clear to return. As I said to you before, Dexter is a good church with even greater possibilities. It is often referred to as the "big folks" church. But you will find that it has some of the finest people that you will ever meet in its membership. It is true that most of them are professional people. But I discovered at Dexter that some professional people have religion also.

As I said, Dexter has real possibilities for further development. I had many things in mind when I went there, and I regret that I never brought them into full realization because of my being catapulted into a leadership position which kept me out of the city so much. I am convinced, however, that a new man of dedication and ability such as yourself can carry Dexter to higher and higher heights.

I don't know when you will come this way again, but if you are in through Atlanta,

---

1. In a 21 March letter, Dexter deacon R. D. Nesbitt informed King of Lawson's upcoming trial sermon and expressed the hope that "he will do a good job and will be the man" (see also King to Nesbitt, 18 April 1960). Earl Wesley Lawson (1919–) was born in New Orleans, Louisiana. He received a B.Th. (1941) from the American Theological Seminary and later received an A.B. (1945) from Morehouse College. Lawson also obtained a B.D. and S.T.M. (1948) from Andover Newton Theological School. From 1947 until 1978, he served as pastor of Emmanuel Baptist Church in Malden, Massachusetts.

2. Lawson returned to Dexter in late May for another engagement, but in a 13 July letter he told King that he had heard nothing further from the church: "I guess the 'pulpit call' is out. Thanks for recommending me anyway." Dexter later called Herbert Eaton to its pulpit (see King to Eaton, 30 September 1960, pp. 513–514 in this volume).

3. In addition to describing his visit to Montgomery in his 2 April letter, Lawson informed King that the Girls' Guild at his church was named "Coretta" and requested a large photo of her.

please feel free to stop in to see me. I am on the road quite a bit, but it is altogether probable that I will be in town if you happen to come through.

Best wishes and God's blessings upon you in all of your endeavors.

Very sincerelyy yours,
Martin

TLc. MLKP-MBU: Box 8.

To Benjamin J. Davis

23 April 1960
[*Atlanta, Ga.*]

Following King's perjury indictment, black Communist Benjamin Davis reminded him that threats of imprisonment used to silence dissent have "never succeeded in stopping the march forward of the people."[1] *Davis assured King that, "while we struggle to save this Martin Luther King, others will arise from your example, until they do not have enough prisons to hold the Martin Luther Kings." In this response, King thanks Davis for his encouragement and promises to write the federal parole board in support of parole for Communist Party leader Henry Winston.*[2]

Mr. Benjamin J. Davis
710 Riverside Drive
New York 31, New York

Dear Mr. Davis:

This is just a note to acknowledge receipt of your kind letter of recent date. I would have answered it long before now, but an extremely crowded schedule stood in my way.

Your words are always encouraging, and although we do not share the political views I find a deeper unity of spirit with you that is after all the important thing. In the midst of the constant harrassment and intimidations and threats that I face as the result of my involvement in the civil rights struggle I often find myself ask-

1. Davis to King, April 1960. Davis, an Atlanta native and acquaintance of King, Sr., wrote King in September 1958 following his arrest in Montgomery for loitering (see Davis to King, 4 September 1958, in *Papers* 4:485–486).

2. On the same day he wrote this reply to Davis, King urged the chair of the U.S. Board of Parole to release Winston; less than two weeks later King received word from the Board of Parole that Winston's application had been denied (King to George J. Reed, 23 April 1960, and William K. McDermott to King, 3 May 1960). In letters of 20 August 1959 and 12 February 1960, Davis had solicited King's aid in the campaign to free Winston, who was among eleven leaders of the Communist Party convicted in 1949 for violating the Alien Registration (Smith) Act of 1940 for advocating the overthrow of the U.S. government. President Kennedy commuted Winston's sentence in 1961. By that time Winston had lost his eyesight due to a untreated brain tumor.

ing "Is it worth it?" But then a friend like yourself comes along with an encouraging word and this gives me renewed courage and vigor to carry on. So I have learned to live now with the conviction that unearned suffering will in some way contribute to the ultimate realization of the ideal of brotherhood and human dignity.

Please forgive me for not writing the letter on the Winston matter. I have been planning to do it for lo these many weeks, but the pressures of recent events have caused me to overlook so many things that I should have done. I will get this letter off immediately. I think it is both immoral and tragic for a nation to allow any human being to face such an inhuman situation.

Very sincerely yours,
Martin L. King, Jr.

MLK:mlb

TLc. MLKP-MBU: Box 23A.

"Suffering and Faith"

27 April 1960
Chicago, Ill.

Upon reading the draft of King's essay "Pilgrimage to Nonviolence," Christian Century *editor Harold Fey urged him to include material drawn from personal experiences: "You have been maligned, arrested and detained. You were stabbed. You say nothing about such sufferings, which must surely have had some influence on your thought."[1] King added these four paragraphs, but they arrived too late for inclusion in the article published on 13 April.[2]*

Some of my personal sufferings over the last few years have also served to shape my thinking. I always hesitate to mention these experiences for fear of conveying the wrong impression. A person who constantly calls attention to his trials and sufferings is in danger of developing a martyr complex and of making others feel that he is consciously seeking sympathy. It is possible for one to be self-centered in his self-denial and self righteous in his self-sacrifice. So I am always reluctant to refer to my personal sacrifices. But I feel somewhat justified in mentioning them in this article because of the influence they have had in shaping my thinking.

Due to my involvement in the struggle for the freedom of my people, I have

1. Fey to King, 31 December 1959.

2. An editor's note preceded the essay: "In his article for the series titled 'How My Mind Has Changed,' Martin Luther King, Jr., said nothing about his reaction to his personal perils (see the *Century* for 13 April). Before publishing the article, we asked him to consider whether or not his experience with danger and suffering had affected his thinking, and if it had, to add comments along this line. His comments arrived after his article had gone to press, so we publish them herewith" (see also Ballou to Fey, 7 April 1960).

known very few quiet days in the last few years. I have been arrested five times and put in Alabama jails. My home has been bombed twice. A day seldom passes that my family and I are not the recipients of threats of death. I have been the victim of a near fatal stabbing. So in a real sense I have been battered by the storms of persecution. I must admit that at times I have felt that I could no longer bear such a heavy burden, and have been tempted to retreat to a more quiet and serene life. But every time such a temptation appeared, something came to strengthen and sustain my determination. I have learned now that the Master's burden is light precisely when we take his yoke upon us.[3]

My personal trials have also taught me the value of unmerited suffering. As my sufferings mounted I soon realized that there were two ways that I could respond to my situation: either to react with bitterness or seek to transform the suffering into a creative force. I decided to follow the latter course. Recognizing the necessity for suffering I have tried to make of it a virtue. If only to save myself from bitterness, I have attempted to see my personal ordeals as an opportunity to transform myself and heal the people involved in the tragic situation which now obtains. I have lived these last few years with the conviction that unearned suffering is redemptive.

There are some who still find the cross a stumbling block, and others consider it foolishness, but I am more convinced than ever before that it is the power of God unto social and individual salvation. So like the Apostle Paul I can now humbly yet proudly say, "I bear in my body the marks of the Lord Jesus."[4] The suffering and agonizing moments through which I have passed over the last few years have also drawn me closer to God. More than ever before I am convinced of the reality of a personal God.

PD. *Christian Century* 77 (27 April 1960): 510.

---

3. Cf. Matthew 11:30: "For my yoke is easy, and my burden is light."
4. Galatians 6:17.

From Roy Wilkins

27 April 1960
New York, N.Y.

Wilkins complains about James Lawson's reported criticisms of the NAACP at the SCLC-sponsored youth leadership conference. Lawson was quoted in the New York Times *as calling the NAACP "a fund-raising agency" that had "neglected the major resource that we have—a disciplined, free people who would be able to work unanimously to implement the ideals of justice and freedom."*[1] *On 2 May King mailed*

---

1. Claude Sitton, "Negro Criticizes N.A.A.C.P. Tactics," *New York Times*, 17 April 1960. According to a SNCC report of the conference, Lawson remarked: "The legal question is not central. There has

a copy of this letter to Lawson: "I would appreciate your reading it so that I can talk with you concerning the contents before I talk with Roy. I will call you tomorrow evening (Tuesday) at your residence."[2]

Dr. Martin Luther King
Southern Christian Leadership Conference
407 Auburn Avenue, N.E.
Atlanta, Georgia

Dear Martin:

We were puzzled and greatly distressed at the criticism of the NAACP voiced by the Rev. James Lawson at the Raleigh meeting April 16–17 called by the Southern Christian Leadership Conference.

This has caused considerable discussion among our members.[3] In one way or another they have stated that since they understood that the NAACP had cooperated with the SCLC how did the Lawson blast come about, and how was it that Lawson claimed his views were shared by other leaders in the SCLC?

This last brings you into the matter, of course. Miss Baker evidently thought the situation serious enough to volunteer to newspapermen that Mr. Lawson was voicing a personal opinion.[4]

I know that you join me in the determination not to have a break between our

---

been a failure to implement legal changes and custom remains unchanged. Unless we are prepared to create the climate . . . the law can never bring victory" (SNCC, "Report on the Raleigh conference," 19 June 1960). Lawson's address was later reprinted as "We Are Trying to Raise the 'Moral Issue,'" in Broderick and Meier, eds., *Negro Protest Thought in the Twentieth Century*, pp. 274–281. King had been asked to comment on Lawson's statement during an appearance on "Meet the Press" (see Interview on "Meet the Press," 17 April 1960, p. 434 in this volume).

2. King penned Lawson's name and telephone number on the top of this letter. King and Wilkins met in Atlanta on 7 May (Wilkins to Mays, 19 May 1960). Two days later, Lawson sent Wilkins a typescript of his address and insisted that it was not "an attack on the NAACP at all" but was intended "to indicate how the sit in movement is a critique of all efforts to bring creative social change" (Wilkins to Lawson, 9 May 1960). In Wilkins's response to Lawson, which he also forwarded to King, he rejected Lawson's explanation and stated that the NAACP's work "made the happenings of the past few months possible" and concluded that "the tone, wording and course of your Raleigh speech are cause for as much disappointment as irritation" (Wilkins to King and Wilkins to Lawson, both dated 13 May 1960).

3. After receiving reports of Lawson's address, Wilkins invited several NAACP officials to provide reactions to the speech, noting that "the criticisms of the NAACP which emanated from this conference and which have not thus far been repudiated by Rev. Martin Luther King would seem to pose a situation to which I think we should give careful consideration" (Wilkins, Memo to Gloster Current et al., 18 April 1960). In a 20 April reply, John M. Brooks, director of the NAACP voter registration committee, commented: "Rev. Lawson's alleged statements certainly reflect the attitude of some of the Southern Christian leadership groups in the south, in spite of the fact that the whole movement is using the foundation built by the NAACP" (see also Henry Lee Moon to Wilkins, 18 April 1960).

4. According to the *Greensboro Daily News*, Ella Baker told a reporter that "there is no fight between the NAACP and the Southern Christian Leadership Conference" and acknowledged that "there is naturally a difference in emphasis." She also reportedly explained that the "comment reflected Lawson's opinion and 'certainly does not represent a policy opinion' of the student group" ("Negroes Organize Coordinating Body," *Greensboro Daily News*, 18 April 1960).

27 Apr 1960

groups. We seek the same goals and we have the same enemies. Those enemies would be happier than they have been for forty years if a split should develop.

At the same time we feel aggrieved over this unwarranted attack. The SCLC did not initiate the sit-downs. That we know. CORE did not initiate them. That we know. The NAACP did not initiate the wave that began February 1, but the NAACP staged the only successful sit-down at lunch counters in Oklahoma City and in Wichita, Kansas, in 1958.[5] That we do know.

But in the present case we did what SCLC and CORE did. We rushed in to help the youngsters. Upon what basis does Mr. Lawson speak so bitterly? If the NAACP had condemned the sit-down tactic and had refused to permit its youth units to participate or if the NAACP had remained outside, we could understand Mr. Lawson.

The Memphis NAACP Branch alone put up $3,400 in bail; the whole Orangeburg operation was an NAACP operation with bail money being furnished by us; we arranged for bail of the last students in Baton Rouge; it was the NAACP legal defense fund which called the lawyers conference in Washington and coordinated the complicated and varied strategy of defense; it was the NAACP youth group in San Antonio who won the battle without firing a shot, just by announcing their intention to sit down.[6] I am hopeful that you can help clarify the situation. I know you will want to.

There are some other disturbing elements in the picture which I would not care to go into here, but which I feel you and I should discuss privately as soon as possible.

Very sincerely yours,
[*signed*] Roy
Roy Wilkins,
Executive Secretary

RW/emb

THLS. MLKJP-GAMK: Box 17.

---

5. Lawson conducted nonviolent workshops with members of the Oklahoma City NAACP Youth Council before their 1958 protest. For more on the Oklahoma sit-ins, see Barbara Ann Posey, "Why I Sit In," September 1960.

6. The lawyers' conference was held 18–20 March at Howard University (Richard L. Lyons, "Dime Store Food Service Held a 'Right,'" *Washington Post,* 20 March 1960).

"The Burning Truth in the South"

May 1960
Madison, Wis.

In the following article published in The Progressive, *King predicts that "time will reveal that the students are learning lessons not contained in their textbooks."*[1] *He places the sit-ins within the context of a historic and international drive for equality: "Young people have connected up with their own history—the slave revolts, the incomplete revolution of the Civil War, the brotherhood of colonial colored men in Africa and Asia. They are an integral part of the history which is reshaping the world, replacing a dying order with modern democracy."*

An electrifying movement of Negro students has shattered the placid surface of campuses and communities across the South. Though confronted in many places by hoodlums, police guns, tear gas, arrests, and jail sentences, the students tenaciously continue to sit down and demand equal service at variety store lunch counters, and extend their protest from city to city. In communities like Montgomery, Alabama, the whole student body rallied behind expelled students and staged a walkout while state government intimidation was unleashed with a display of military force appropriate to a wartime invasion.[2] Nevertheless, the spirit of self-sacrifice and commitment remains firm, and the state governments find themselves dealing with students who have lost the fear of jail and physical injury.

It is no overstatement to characterize these events as historic. Never before in the United States had so large a body of students spread a struggle over so great an area in pursuit of a goal of human dignity and freedom.

The suddenness with which this development burst upon the nation has given rise to the description "spontaneous." Yet it is not without clearly perceivable causes and precedents. First, we should go back to the ending of World War II. Then, the new will and determination of the Negro were irrevocably generated. Hundreds of thousands of young Negro men were mustered out of the armed forces, and with their honorable discharge papers and G.I. Bill of Rights grants, they received a promise from a grateful nation that the broader democracy for which they had fought would begin to assume reality. They believed in this promise and acted in the conviction that changes were guaranteed. Some changes did appear—but commensurate neither with the promise nor the need.

Struggles of a local character began to emerge, but the scope and results were

1. On 4 April 1960 King sent his draft to editor Morris H. Rubin and invited him to edit as he saw fit: "I had to do the article in such haste that I did not have time to proof read it." In his 13 April reply, Rubin praised King's "excellent job" and informed him the article would be "leading off" the May issue. The article was later reprinted as a fund-raising brochure (Committee to Defend Martin Luther King and the Struggle for Freedom in the South, "The Burning Truth in the South by Martin Luther King," May 1960).

2. For more on the Montgomery protests, see King to Eisenhower, 9 March 1960, pp. 385–387 in this volume.

limited. Few Americans outside the immediately affected areas even realized a struggle was taking place. One perceptible aspect was the steady, significant increase in voting registration which took place, symbolizing the determination of the Negro, particularly the veteran, to make his rights a reality. The number of registered voters reached a point higher than exists today.

The United States Supreme Court decision of 1954 was viewed by Negroes as the delivery of part of the promise of change. In unequivocal language the Court affirmed that "separate but equal" facilities are inherently unequal, and that to segregate a child on the basis of his race is to deny that child equal protection of the law. This decision brought hope to millions of disinherited Negroes who had formerly dared only to dream of freedom. But the implementation of the decision was not to be realized without a sharp and difficult struggle. Through five years of turmoil some advances were achieved. The victory is far from complete, but the determination by Negroes that it will be won is universal.

What relation have these events to the student sit-downs? It was the young veteran who gave the first surge of power to the postwar civil rights movements. It was the high school, college, and elementary school young people who were in the front line of the school desegregation struggle. Lest it be forgotten, the opening of hundreds of schools to Negroes for the first time in history required that there be young Negroes with the moral and physical courage to face the challenges and, all too frequently, the mortal danger presented by mob resistance.

There were such young Negroes in the tens of thousands, and no program for integration failed for want of students. The simple courage of students and their parents should never be forgotten. In the years 1958 and 1959 two massive Youth Marches to Washington for Integrated Schools involved some 40,000 young people who brought with them nearly 500,000 signatures on petitions gathered largely from campuses and youth centers.[3] This mass action infused a new spirit of direct action challenging government to act forthrightly.

Hence for a decade young Negroes have been steeled by both deeds and inspiration to step into responsible action. These are the precedents for the student struggle of today.

Many related, interacting social forces must be understood if we are to understand history as it is being made. The arresting upsurge of Africa and Asia is remote neither in time nor in space to the Negro of the South. Indeed, the determination of Negro Americans to win freedom from all forms of oppression springs from the same deep longing that motivates oppressed peoples all over the world.

However inadequate forms of education and communication may be, the ordinary Negro Jim Smith knows that in primitive jungle villages in India still illiterate peasants are casting a free ballot for their state and federal legislators. In one after another of the new African states black men form the government, write the laws, and administer the affairs of state. But in state after state in the United States the Negro is ruled and governed without a fragment of participation in civic

---

3. For more on King's participation in the Youth Marches, see King, Address at Youth March for Integrated Schools, 25 October 1958, in *Papers* 4:514–515, and King, Address at the Youth March for Integrated Schools on 18 April 1959, pp. 186–188 in this volume.

life. The contrast is a burning truth which has molded a deep determination to end this intolerable condition.

Negroes have also experienced sharp frustrations as they struggle for the realization of promises expressed in hollow legislative enactments or empty electoral campaign oratory. Conferences from the lowest levels of officialdom up to the Chief Executive in the White House result in the clarification of problems—but not their solution. Studies by many commissions, unhappily devoid of power, continue to pose problems without any concrete results that could be translated into jobs, education, equality of opportunity, and access to the fruits of an historic period of prosperity. In "the affluent society," the Negro has remained the poor, the underprivileged, and the lowest class.[4] Court actions are often surrounded by a special type of red tape that has made for long drawn-out processes of litigation and evasive schemes. The Negro has also become aware that token integration was not a start in good faith but a new form of discrimination covered up with certain niceties.

It was inevitable, therefore, that a more direct approach would be sought—one which would contain the promise of some immediate degree of success based upon the concrete act of the Negro. Hence, a period began in which the emphasis shifted from the slow court process to direct action in the form of bus protests, economic boycotts, mass marches to and demonstrations in the nation's capital and state capitals.

One may wonder why the present movement started with the lunch counters. The answer lies in the fact that here the Negro has suffered indignities and injustices that cannot be justified or explained. Almost every Negro has experienced the tragic inconveniences of lunch counter segregation. He cannot understand why he is welcomed with open arms at most counters in the store, but is denied service at a certain counter because it happens to be selling food and drink. In a real sense the "sit-ins" represent more than a demand for service; they represent a demand for respect.

It is absurd to think of this movement as being initiated by Communists or some other outside group.[5] This movement is an expression of the longing of a new Negro for freedom and human dignity. These students were anchored to lunch counter seats by the accumulated indignities of days gone by and the boundless aspirations of generations yet unborn.

In this new method of protest a new philosophy provided a special undergirding—the philosophy of nonviolence. It was first modestly and quietly projected in one community, Montgomery, when the threat of violence became real in the bus protest. But it burst from this limited arena, and was embraced by masses of people across the nation with fervor and consistency.

The appeal of non-violence has many facets:

First—It proclaims the sincere and earnest wish of the Negro that though

4. *The Affluent Society,* John Kenneth Galbraith's best-selling economic and social critique, was published in 1958 (Boston: Houghton Mifflin).

5. Former president Harry Truman had recently stated that the demonstrations were Communist-inspired (see King to Truman, 19 April 1960, pp. 437–439 in this volume).

changes must be accomplished, there is no desire to use or tolerate force. Thus, it is consistent with the deeply religious traditions of Negroes.

Second—It denies that vengeance for past oppression motivates the new spirit of determined struggle.

Third—It brings to the point of action a great multitude who need the assurance that a technique exists which is suitable and practical for a minority confronting a majority often vicious and possessed of effective weapons of combat.

Fourth—Many Negroes recognize the necessity of creating discord to alter established community patterns, but they strongly desire that controls be built in, so that neither they nor their adversaries would find themselves engaged in mutual destruction.

Fifth—Having faith that the white majority is not an undifferentiated whole, Negro leaders have welcomed a moral appeal which can reach the emotions and intellect of significant white groups.

The appeal of the philosophy of non-violence encompasses these many requirements. The key significance of the student movement lies in the fact that from its inception, everywhere, it has combined direct action and non-violence.

This quality has given it the extraordinary power and discipline which every thinking person observes. It has discredited the adversary, who knows how to deal with force but is bewildered and panicky in the face of the new techniques. Time will reveal that the students are learning lessons not contained in their textbooks. Hundreds have already been expelled, fined, imprisoned, and brutalized, and the numbers continue to grow. But with the punishments, something more is growing. A generation of young people has come out of decades of shadows to face naked state power; it has lost its fears, and experienced the majestic dignity of a direct struggle for its own liberation. These young people have connected up with their own history—the slave revolts, the incomplete revolution of the Civil War, the brotherhood of colonial colored men in Africa and Asia. They are an integral part of the history which is reshaping the world, replacing a dying order with modern democracy. They are doing this in a nation whose own birth spread new principles and shattered a medieval social society then dominating most of the globe.

It is extremely significant that in many places the Negro students have found white allies to join in their actions. It is equally significant that on a mass scale students and adults in the North and elsewhere have organized supporting actions, many of which are still only in their early stages.

The segregationists now face some hard alternatives: They can continue to seek to maintain segregated facilities. In this event they must live with discord or themselves initiate, and be responsible for, violence with all its evil consequences. They may close the facilities as they have done in many places. But this will not end the movement; rather, it will spread to libraries, public parks, schools, and the like, and these too will have to be closed, thus depriving both white and Negro of necessary cultural and recreational institutions. This would be a step backward for the whole of society. Or finally, they can accept the principle of equality. In this case they still have two alternative approaches. They may make the facilities equally bad for both white and Negro or equally good. Thus finally simple logic and justice in their own interests should direct them to the only acceptable solution—to accept equality and maintain it on the best level for both races.

The outcome of the present struggle will be some time in unfolding, but the line of its direction is clear. It is a final refutation of the time-honored theory that the Negro prefers segregation. It would be futile to deplore, as many do, the tensions accompanying the social changes. Tension and conflict are not alien nor abnormal to growth but are the natural results of the process of changes. A revolution is occurring in both the social order and the human mind. One hundred eighty-four years ago a bold group of men signed the Declaration of Independence. If their struggle had been lost they had signed their own death warrant. Nevertheless, though explicitly regretting that King George had forced them to this extreme by a long "train of abuses," they resolutely acted and a great new society was born.[6] The Negro students, their parents, and their allies are acting today in that imperishable tradition.

PD. *The Progressive* 24 (May 1960): 8–10.

6. King quotes from the Declaration of Independence.

To Kivie Kaplan

3 May 1960
[*Atlanta, Ga.*]

In a 25 April 1960 letter, NAACP board member Kivie Kaplan renewed his attempts to recruit King to serve as an officer or board member of the organization.[1] *In the letter below, King agrees to "give very serious consideration" to serving on the board. He eventually declined Kaplan's offer, explaining "that it would probably be too much added to my schedule."*[2]

Mr. Kivie Kaplan
Colonial Tanning Company, Inc.
195 South Street
Boston 11, Mass.

Dear Kivie:

I am in receipt of your letter of April 25, again making inquiry of my availability to serve on the Board of the NAACP. As I have said to you before, I would give

1. Kaplan had discussed this idea with King on several occasions, beginning at the NAACP's July 1958 national convention (Kaplan to King, 10 December 1958). King, a lifetime NAACP member, had initially declined Kaplan's offer because he did not want to risk serving in an official capacity in an organization that had been declared illegal in Alabama in 1956 (Kaplan to King, 25 April 1960). On 28 January of the following year, King wrote Kaplan that he had received conflicting advice regarding the offer: "With these divided opinions, I am still left somewhat in a state of confusion."

2. King to Kaplan, 6 March 1961.

very serious consideration to the position of Board Member of the NAACP if it came to me. However, I would not want to be placed in the position of giving the impression that I am seeking to put myself on the Board. This I feel is a matter for the board members themselves to decide. So you can feel free to bring the matter up in the board meeting.

I am deeply grateful to you for your interest and concern. As I have said to you so often, your constant support is of inestimable value for the continuance of my humble efforts.

With warm personal regards, I am

Sincerely yours,
Martin

MLK:mlb

TLc. MLKP-MBU: Box 29.

To Benjamin Elijah Mays

4 May 1960
[*Atlanta, Ga.*]

In this letter to Morehouse College's president, King encloses a $100 payment of his $300 pledge to the institution. Citing exorbitant legal fees, stemming from his February indictment for perjury, King reconsiders his plan to donate a portion of the royalties from Stride Toward Freedom *to the college: "I felt that it would be wise for me to hold on to the book money until the case is over since it appears that I will have to spend more of my personal money." King remains hopeful that "when the case is over I will still be able to give Morehouse a sizable contribution over and above my pledge." Mays replied on 6 May.*[1]

Dr. B. E. Mays, President
Morehouse College
Atlanta, Georgia

Dear Dr. Mays:

In going through my file of unanswered letters I found your letter of November 20, making an appeal for pledges for Morehouse College.[2] I regret that an extremely crowded schedule made it impossible for me to get around to answering your letter before now. Enclosed is my check of one-hundred dollars which is the first payment on my pledge of $300.00 a year.

---

1. In his reply, Mays enclosed a receipt for King's contribution and assured him "that I stand back of you in what you will be facing in the Montgomery trial and that means finances as well as good wishes."

2. Mays, To Alumnus and Friend, 20 November 1959.

I think I mentioned to you once before that I plan to give all of the royalties accruing from my book to institutions and charitable causes.[3] I already have several thousand dollars set aside in the bank for just that purpose. I had planned to give Morehouse two thousand of this on the last founders day observance, but as you know, the Alabama case broke just a few days before, and this disrupted my total program.[4] Since the Alabama case developed, I have had to spend a great deal of unexpected money. I never felt that lawyers and accountants would charge such exhorbitant fees.[5] Already we have had to spend almost ten thousand dollars in this case and it has not even gotten to the first court yet. In the light of this, I felt that it would be wise for me to hold on to the book money until the case is over since it appears that I will have to spend more of my personal money than I had expected.[6] Although the defense committee is at work and doing a good job, I feel that it is both immoral and impractical to spend all of the money raised for my case when there is such a great need for funds for student defense, and the voter registration drive in the South. I hope, however, when the case is over I will still be able to give Morehouse a sizable contribution over and above my pledge of {three} hundred dollars a year.

With warm personal regards.

Very sincerely yours,
Martin L. King, Jr.

Enclosure: 1
MLK:mlb

TALc. MLKP MBU: Box 31.

---

3. The previous month, King received over $3,000 in royalties from *Stride* (Dolores Gentile to King, 6 April 1960).

4. King was arrested at his Ebenezer office on 17 February, on charges of filing fraudulent tax returns in 1956 and 1958 (see King, Interview on Arrest following Indictment by Grand Jury of Montgomery County, 17 February 1960, pp. 370–372 in this volume).

5. King's legal team included Hubert Delany of New York, William R. Ming of Chicago, Arthur Shores of Birmingham, and Fred Gray and Solomon S. Seay, Jr., both of Montgomery. In an 22 April letter to Fred Gray, Hubert Delany outlined the legal team's financial agreement with King and the Committee to Defend Martin Luther King and the Struggle for Freedom in the South, which he reported was "a substantial reduction in the fees we would normally charge." In a form letter to King's attorneys, A. Philip Randolph and Gardner Taylor, chairmen of the committee, set a $20,000 legal budget with the "understanding that the attorneys will administer the division of these funds amongst themselves" (Randolph and Taylor to Gentlemen, April–May 1960).

6. In her 1969 memoir, Coretta King recalled that her husband conceded that he did not "have the money to fight such a charge in the courts," but he vowed that he would not "under any circumstances use any funds from the Movement for such a purpose" (*My Life with Martin Luther King, Jr.*, p. 185; see also King, Statement on Perjury Acquittal, 28 May 1960, p. 462 in this volume).

From Jackie Robinson

5 May 1960
New York, N.Y.

Robinson, a member of the NAACP board of directors best known for integrating major league baseball in 1947, expresses concern over public criticisms of the veteran civil rights organization.[1] *Probably referring to James Lawson's comments a few weeks earlier, Robinson advises, "let's not be a party to the old game of divide and conquer."*[2] *King replied on 19 June.*[3]

Reverend Martin L. King
208 Auburn Avenue, N.E.
Atlanta, Georgia

Dear Martin:

First, let me say how much I respect and appreciate all the good you are doing. You have gained the confidence of people the world over, and for that reason I am concerned about the committees that have sprung up to raise money for your defense in the coming farce trial in Alabama.[4]

I am also quite disturbed because of reports I have been receiving that people who claim to represent the Southern Christian Leadership Conference are saying the N.A.A.CP. has outlived its usefulness. Let's not be a party to the old game of divide and conquer. The N.A.A.C.P., as any group, has its faults, but the good the organization has done cannot be measured. Talk like this sets our cause back.

I know you would not be party to any individual or group that would use your misfortune for their own selfish interest. We must be wary of groups who may be doing so.

Please let me know what groups you have authorized to solicit funds in your behalf and what you know about individuals who are knocking the N.A.A.C.P. in promoting the Southern Christian Leadership Conference.

I hope you know I am not questioning the need. It's only that I am concerned.

---

1. Jack Roosevelt Robinson (1919–1972), born in Cairo, Georgia , attended the University of California at Los Angeles (1939–1941) before serving in the United States Army (1942–1945). In 1947 Robinson became the first African American in the modern era to play major league baseball. In his first year with the Brooklyn Dodgers, Robinson was voted Rookie of the Year, and in 1949 he was presented with the National League's Most Valuable Player award. Following his retirement from baseball in 1957, Robinson served as the vice president of Chock Full O' Nuts, a restaurant chain. He was elected to the Baseball Hall of Fame in 1962. Robinson served on the NAACP board of directors (1958–1967).

2. For more on Lawson's remarks, see Wilkins to King, 27 April 1960, pp. 444–446 in this volume; King to Lawson, 2 May 1960; and Wilkins to King, 13 May 1960.

3. See p. 475–478 in this volume.

4. Other movement supporters voiced similar concerns to King regarding the activities of the Committee to Defend Martin Luther King and the Struggle for Freedom in the South (see Harris Wofford to King, 1 April 1960, and James R. Robinson to King, 13 May 1960, pp. 403–405 and 458–459 in this volume, respectively).

Sincerely yours,
[*signed*] Jackie
Jackie Robinson

JRR:cbc

TLS. MLKP-MBU: Box 84.

From Vernon Johns

8 May 1960
Petersburg, Va.

King's predecessor at Dexter Avenue Baptist Church requests support for his business cooperative, Farm and City Enterprises, and asks for assistance in arranging speaking engagements.[1]

{Written in a crowd, would [*re?*] copy—but difficulty in reading may make you reflect on it!}

Good Doctor—

If you could see what I have done with a dozen or more swank audiences over the US that tried to get you and couldnt—you would start referring them to me when you couldn't accept. Maybe not. It takes a mighty big man to enjoy hearing an audience say how glad it is the invited speaker couldn't get there! You will take this of course with a pound of salt!

I am going to Montgomery May 22 to preach at Dexter. My real mission concerns Farm & City. M.I.A has several thousand invested in F&C.[2] Not the least reason for non profit!!! By way of argument I want you to remember they ~~may~~ made ~~600%~~ 300% on the land I bought on the Atlanta highway!

It is just as clear to me how the rest of it can be profitable as it was how that ~~was~~ highway investment could be ~~possible~~ profitable—They have one of the finest walk in meat boxes in the country with not even a pig foot in it.

I want to increase the capital a little to enable them to take cows and hogs right from the pasture and pen as you see them in this picture and transfer them to the meat boxes. [The pictures are from my farm][3] This with buying at the

1. Johns also sent a statement by several of the board members of the Virginia Farm and City Enterprises detailing incidents of alleged mismanagement at the company and appended at the top a note: "I am enclosing this in case some religious SOB around Norfolk has 'informed' you" (F. J. Boddie et al., "Resume, Facts and events pursuant to present condition of Virginia Farm and City Enterprises," July 1959).

2. The MIA invested $11,000 in Montgomery Farm and City Enterprises (see King, Address at the Fourth Annual Institute on Nonviolence and Social Change at Bethel Baptist Church, 3 December 1959, p. 334 in this volume).

3. Johns enclosed a printed sermon ornamented with photos of livestock (Johns, "Children, Have Ye Any Meat?" 8 May 1960).

sources {SOURCES} of commodities instead of a shirt tail full in town will do the rest.

I am concentrating my engagements along the Route from here to Birmingham and New Orleans— ~~into to~~ in order to be there Montgomery often enough to keep in touch. Would appreciate—if you and Wyatt Tee [*Walker*] would plug me in for an engagement as often as your Movement could stand a top flight speaker without too much deflection!

Seriously—

Would you ask Abernathy to let me address the MIA the night after I am at Dexter—on—Economics For Freedom

—I really believe there is the opportunity here with your patronage to recreate both Farm & City and the Montgomery movement. Please do me the honor of a reply to this letter which is much more important than it will appear unless you can find time for a little reflection on it!

Yours Faithfully
[*signed*] Vernon Johns

Will be down for the Baccalaute of Atlanta U.[4] Hope to see you going or coming.

AHLS. MLKP-MBU: Box 28A.

4. Johns delivered the baccalaureate sermon at Atlanta University on 29 May 1960.

From John Malcolm Patterson

9 May 1960
Montgomery, Ala.

Alabama governor John Patterson demands that King publish a retraction of the "false and defamatory" statements in a 29 March 1960 fund-raising appeal titled "Heed Their Rising Voices."[1] *The text of the advertisement detailed the conditions that King and student protesters faced and criticized "the Southern violators" who "have answered Dr. King's peaceful protests with intimidation and violence."*

Patterson and other Alabama officials later filed libel suits against the New York Times *and several Alabama ministers who appeared as signatories of the ad.*[2] *The*

1. For a facsimile of the advertisement, see p. 384 in this volume. The *New York Times,* which published the advertisement, printed a retraction after Patterson sent them a similar letter ("Times Retracts Statement in Ad," *New York Times,* 16 May 1960).

2. Although Montgomery's mayor Earl James, city commissioner Frank Parks, and former city commissioner Clyde Sellers all filed suit shortly after Patterson, only the governor included King in his suit.

first of the plaintiffs was awarded $500,000 in a decision that was upheld by the state courts; it was eventually overturned by the U.S. Supreme Court in a landmark free speech case, New York Times Co. v. Sullivan.[3] 9 May 1960

Rev. Martin Luther King
563 Johnson Avenue
Atlanta, Georgia

Dear Sir:

You will hereby take notice that under and by virtue of the Laws of Alabama, I demand that you publish a retraction of certain false and defamatory matter published by you in The New York Times of Tuesday, March 29, 1960, on page 25, published under the heading, "Heed Their Rising Voices," and particularly the following false and defamatory matter therein contained,

> "In Montgomery, Alabama, after students sang 'My Country 'Tis of Thee' on the State Capitol steps, their leaders were expelled from school, and truckloads of police armed with shotguns and tear-gas ringed the Alabama State College campus. When the entire student body protested to state authorities by refusing to re-register, their dining hall was padlocked in an attempt to starve them into submission.
>
> "Again and again the Southern violators have answered Dr. King's peaceful protests with intimidation and violence. They have bombed his home almost killing his wife and child. They have assaulted his person. They have arrested him seven times—for 'speeding,' 'loitering' and similar 'offenses.' And now they have charged him with 'perjury'—a felony under which they could imprison him for ten years."[4]

The foregoing matter and the publication as a whole charge me with grave misconduct and of improper actions and omissions as Governor of Alabama and Ex-Officio Chairman of the State Board of Education of Alabama.

I further demand that you publish in as prominent and as public a manner as the foregoing false and defamatory material contained in the foregoing publication, a full and fair retraction of the entire false and defamatory matter so

---

3. *New York Times Co. v. Sullivan* (1964). For more on King's involvement in the case, see King to Fred D. Gray, 14 December 1960, p. 580 in this volume.

4. Attorneys for the Alabama officials argued that the statement was libelous because it contained false information and made reference to their clients, although it did not specifically name them. They noted several errors in the article: students sang the national anthem, not "My Country 'Tis of Thee"; students were expelled after attempting to eat at the Montgomery County courthouse, not for singing on the capitol steps; police never "ringed" the campus, nor were the dining halls padlocked; and King had been arrested only four times at the time of publication (see *New York Times Co. v. Sullivan* [1964]).

far as the same relates to me and to my conduct and acts as Governor of Alabama and Ex-Officio Chairman of the State Board of Education of Alabama.

Very truly yours,
[*signed*]
John Patterson
Governor

JP:k
REGISTERED MAIL
RETURN RECEIPT REQUESTED

TLS. MLKP-MBU: Box 5.

From James R. Robinson

13 May 1960
New York, N.Y.

Robinson, CORE's executive secretary, requests that King appear at a fund-raising event because the organization had "suffered considerably" as a result of the appeal from the Committee to Defend Martin Luther King and the Struggle for Freedom in the South.[1] *King, a member of CORE's advisory board since 1957, had recently expressed support for the organization and in August 1960 spoke at the group's nonviolent training institute in Miami.*[2]

The Rev. Martin Luther King, Jr.
563 Johnson Avenue
Atlanta, Georgia

Dear Dr. King:

It was certainly good to talk with you last evening. For weeks I have been in a state of indecision—feeling that you should know the reactions here in New York to the operation of Mr. Rustin and Mr. Levinson, and yet hesitating to make comments which could not escape questioning their integrity.

---

1. James R. Robinson (1918–), born in Rochester, New York, received a B.A. (1939) from Columbia University and an M.A. (1942) from the University of Chicago. As a graduate student Robinson co-founded the Chicago Committee of Racial Equality, CORE's forerunner. From 1945 until 1947, Robinson fulfilled his conscientious objector obligation by working in civilian public service camps in Tennessee and Colorado. Robinson was CORE's executive secretary (1957–1960) and membership secretary (1961) before becoming a fund-raiser for the American Committee on Africa (1961–1964) and the NAACP Legal Defense and Education Fund (1964–1993).

2. King to J. Holmes Ford, 17 August 1959; King, Introduction to *Cracking the Color Line*, 1960, p. 349 in this volume; and Phil Meyer, "Non-Violence Held the Best Strategy," *Miami Herald*, 1 September 1960.

Some of the activities of the Rustin Committee have been deliberately calculated to cut into the fund-raising of other organizations. The use of "Combined Emergency Appeal" on direct-mail appeals gave many people the impression that the money was to be divided between the various organizations in the field.[3]

Our fund-raising for CORE has apparently suffered considerably. In order to give greater service in the field, the field staff has been increased from two to six. In addition to Leonard Holt, the new additions are Ulysses Prince (Atlanta U. student), Major Johns (expelled Baton Rouge leader), and Darwin Bolden, Yale law graduate who is concentrating on the Woolworth boycott coordination.[4]

We need, and the movement needs, these men.

In order to keep them, however, a major fund-raising event must be held. To run such an event, we need your help. Would you give us one day in New York City in June between June 10th and June 24th? We are counting on having at least one other person of national stature, plus two student leaders. But the whole idea is dependent upon your participation.

Please call me COLLECT this weekend if possible. The home telephone is OR 4–6250. I certainly hope you will give us your help.

Sincerely yours,
[*signed*]
James R. Robinson
Executive Secretary

JRR/ckh

TLS. MLKP-MBU: Box 23.

3. The mailing stated: "This Combined Appeal gives you the opportunity to support both needs—the Student Defense Fund and the Committee to Defend Martin Luther King, Jr." (Abernathy et al., Form letter to Friend, April 1960).

4. On 3 April, King had appeared with Virginia attorney Leonard Holt and James J. Kilpatrick, editor of the *Richmond News Leader*, on "Open End," a New York television talk show. King later debated Kilpatrick (see Debate with James J. Kilpatrick on "The Nation's Future," 26 November 1960, pp. 556–564 in this volume).

To William P. Rogers

18 May 1960
[*Atlanta, Ga.*]

King informs U.S. attorney general William Rogers of voting rights violations in Lawrenceville, Georgia. In a 21 June 1960 reply, acting assistant attorney general of the Civil Rights Division Joseph M. F. Ryan thanked King and assured him that the matter "is being given careful attention."

26 May 1960

Attorney-General William Rogers
Department of Justice
Washington, D.C.

Dear Attorney-General Rogers:

I have been informed by an anonymous white person that the names of several Negro citizens of Lawrenceville, Georgia have been removed from the voting list.[1] This person tells me that no cause was given for the removal. It seems that almost every name that had colored marked after it was removed. The anonymous writer stated that he or she was afraid to sign their name for fear of possible reprisal. Listed below are the names of the persons who were excluded from the voting list. I would appreciate your investigating the matter at your earliest convenience.

Very sincerely yours,
Martin Luther King, Jr.

ENC.
MLK:mlb
(Dictated, but not personally signed by Dr. King.)

TLc. MLKP-MBU: Box 24.

---

1. Although the alleged purge of black voters from the county records may have occurred in late 1959, the Justice Department did not begin an investigation until August 1960 ("FBI Continues Its Probe into Voting Records Here," *Lawrenceville News-Herald*, 18 August 1960).

From James Baldwin

[*26 May 1960*]
Tallahassee, Fla.

After being asked by Harper's Magazine *to profile King, writer James Baldwin requests a meeting and raises the possibility of being "allowed to follow you about for a day or two" in order "to convey some dim approximation of what it is like to be in your position." He added: "I am one of the millions, to be found all over the world but more especially here, in this sorely troubled country, who thank God for you." Baldwin's essay appeared in the February 1961 issue of* Harper's.[1]

---

1. Baldwin, "The Dangerous Road Before Martin Luther King," *Harper's Magazine,* February 1961, pp. 33–42. Following the article's publication, King wrote Baldwin that his article had allowed readers to appreciate "the dilemma that I confront as a leader in the civil rights struggle" (King to Baldwin, 26 September 1961). James Arthur Baldwin (1924–1987) was born in Harlem, New York. In 1946 Baldwin published his first article in *The Nation* and by 1948 had become a well-known essayist. That same year he received a Rosenwald Fellowship, which enabled him to move to Paris where he completed his first novel, *Go Tell It On the Mountain* (1953). In 1957 he returned to the United States, be-

Dear Reverend King:

26 May 1960

I certainly do not expect you to remember it, but we met over two years ago, in Atlanta. I was then doing a couple of articles about the South, and I am in the South again, for the same purpose.[2]

I am writing you now because Harpers Magazine has asked me to do a profile of you, and I am coming to Atlanta—I do not know whether you are there or not, but one must start somewhere—to see if this can be done. I know that you are extremely busy and my effort would be to bother you as little as possible. I have read your book, and Reddick's book, so there are many things I will not need to ask you.[3] If you will permit it, and if it is possible, I would simply like to be allowed to follow you about for a day or two, or longer, in order to be made able to convey some dim approximation of what it is like to be in your position.

The effect of your work, and I might almost indeed, say your presence, has spread far beyond the confines of Montgomery, as you must know. It can be felt, for example, right here in Tallahassee.[4] And I am one of the millions, to be found all over the world but more especially here, in this sorely troubled country, who thank God for you.

I will be in your church on Sunday, and if you recieve this letter, and if you are there, I trust we will be able to talk.

Very sincerely,
[*signed*]
James Baldwin

TALS. MLKP-MBU: Box 20.

---

coming a commentator on the civil rights movement. Baldwin established a reputation as a social critic, traveling on a 1963 lecture tour with CORE and publishing *The Fire Next Time* (1963), a collection of essays. In November 1968 Baldwin spoke at a tribute to King. When he died Baldwin was working on a play and a biography on King.

2. Baldwin, "The Hard Kind of Courage," *Harper's Magazine,* October 1958, pp. 61–65, and "Nobody Knows My Name: Letter from the South," *Partisan Review* 26 (Winter 1959): 72–82. In Baldwin's 1961 essay he reported that he had been surprised that King was unlike "any preacher I have ever met before. For one thing, to state it baldly, I liked him. It is rare that one *likes* a world-famous man—by the time they become world-famous they rarely like themselves, which may account for this antipathy."

3. Baldwin refers to King's *Stride Toward Freedom* (1958) and Reddick's biography of King, *Crusader Without Violence* (1959).

4. Baldwin was in Tallahassee to conduct research for an article on the city's sit-in movement (Baldwin, "They Can't Turn Back," *Mademoiselle,* August 1960, pp. 324–325, 351). For more on the demonstrations in Tallahassee, see King to C. Kenzie Steele, 19 March 1960, pp. 391–392 in this volume.

Statement on Perjury Acquittal

[*28 May 1960*]
[*Montgomery, Ala.*]

After deliberating for three hours and forty-three minutes, an all-white jury acquitted King of perjury for signing a false state income tax return. A news report indicated that King seemed "stunned" by the verdict, while his parents "collapsed in tears."[1] *Outside the Montgomery courtroom, King delivers this statement to the press. This transcript was drawn from television news footage.*

[*King*]: Just a moment, now do you want me to just make a statement and not interview? You don't want an interview?

[*King*]: There are two or three things that I can say at this point. First, as any person in such a situation I am very happy to know that the jury came back with a verdict of not guilty. I certainly want to commend the jury for what I consider a fair, honest, and just verdict. And I want to commend the judge for the way he handled the case, for the high and noble manner that he used in the whole proceeding.[2] And I certainly want to commend all of the lawyers, this brilliant array of lawyers who represented me in this case.[3] And I'm sure that their brilliant and profound arguments and that factual evidence played a great part in the ultimate decision, which was one of not guilty. This represents to my mind great hope, and it reveals that said on so many occasions, that there are hundreds and thousands of people, white people of goodwill in the South, and even though they may not agree with one's views on the question of integration, they are honest people and people who will follow a just and righteous path. And so this rea [*break in film*][4]

[*question inaudible*]

[*King*]: Well, I knew all along that the evidence was clear. I knew all along that the facts in the case were on my side in the sense that I had never filed a fraudulent return, but I didn't know what the outcome would be. I didn't know how the jury was taking this, so that I just didn't know. This was purely a speculative period, not knowing what the outcome would be.

F. NBCNA-NNNBC.

---

1. John Coombes, "King Cleared of Falsifying Income Tax," *Montgomery Advertiser,* 29 May 1960. Returning to the Ebenezer pulpit on 29 May, King delivered an "Autobiography of Suffering," a sermon that highlighted his recent trial in Alabama ("King Sees 'Hope' in Verdict," *Montgomery Advertiser,* 30 May 1960). King reportedly told the congregation: "Something happened to that jury. It said no matter how much they must suppress me they must tell the truth" ("White Jury Obeyed Truth, King Asserts," *Atlanta Constitution,* 30 May 1960). Several years later, King reminisced on his acquittal, calling it "a turning point in my life as a participant in the Negro struggle in the South" (King, Foreword to *Deep in My Heart,* by William Kunstler [New York: William Morrow, 1966]).

2. Judge James Carter presided over King's trial.

3. King refers to Hubert Delany of New York, William R. Ming of Chicago, Arthur Shores of Birmingham, and Fred Gray and Solomon S. Seay, Jr., both of Montgomery.

4. In a transcript drawn from news footage of the statement, King continued: "And so this reaffirms my faith in the ultimate decency of man" (King, Statement on verdict by jury of Montgomery County, 28 May 1960).

From Wyatt Tee Walker and Dorothy Cotton

28 May 1960
Petersburg, Va.

Following the announcement of his acquittal, King receives a congratulatory telegram from SCLC's newly appointed executive director and the secretary of the Petersburg Improvement Association.[1]

REV MARTIN LUTHER KING JR
408 AUBURN AVE NORTHEAST ATLA

OUR BEST WISHES ON YOUR VENDICATION FOR THE STATE COURTS OF ALABAMA GOD IS NOT DEAD TRUTH CRUSHED TO THE EARTH WILL RISE AGAIN GOD BLESS YOU AND YOUR SPIRITUAL LEADERSHIP TO THE SOUTH AND TO AMERICA

THE THREE THOUSAND MEMBERS OF THE PETERSBURG IMPROVEMENT ASSOCIATION
REV WYATT T WALKER PRES MRS DOROTHY F COTTON SECTY.

PWSr. MLKP-MBU: Box 73A.

1. Among the congratulatory messages King received was a 31 May telegram from O. Clay Maxwell, the president of the National Sunday School and Baptist Training Union Congress: "Thanks be to God the victory through his servant." Dorothy Foreman Cotton (1931–), born in Goldsboro, North Carolina, received a B.A. (1957) from Virginia State College and an M.A. (1960) from Boston University. As a member of the Petersburg Improvement Association during the 1950s, Cotton helped organize protests against segregation at the city's public library and dining facilities. She moved to Atlanta to join the staff of SCLC in September 1960 and soon became a member of the executive staff. In 1963, Cotton was appointed director of SCLC's Citizenship Education Program, a position she held until her departure from the organization in 1972.

From Clennon King

2 June 1960
Albany, Ga.

The presidential candidate for the Afro-American Unity Party congratulates King on his vindication in the Alabama perjury trial but complains that the hardships of "noted Negro integrationists" have been exaggerated. "Have you suffered in any way by having been falsely charged?" he asks.[1]

Rev. Martin Luther King, Jr.
Assistant Pastor
Ebenezer Baptist Church
Atlanta, Georgia

Dear Brother King,

This is to congratulate you and thank God that you were exonerated. I hope the charges still held will cause you even less difficulty by being withdrawn forthwith, therefore making it unnecessary for you to be again brought to trial.[2]

My major concern however is the view which is so rampantly held among our people that you are a victim of some horrible persecution and that your adversaries are ignorant, villanous Simon Legrees.[3] Obviously you have not been treated without prejudice, but equally obvious essentials have been industriously camouflaged.

1.) Did you ever go to prison on the charges for which you are now exonerated? (In fact, have you ever spent as much as a day of your life in jail?)

2.) Were you ever seriously in danger of Imprisonment even had you not been ~~freed~~ {exonerated}?

3.) Can any state court normally expect to successfully convict an innocent man in your affluential category without the concurrence of the Federal courts?

4.) Have you suffered in any way by having been falsely charged?

5.) Have you gained by having been falsely charged?

---

1. King had written a letter on Clennon King's behalf after he was denied admission to the University of Mississippi in 1958 (see King to James P. Coleman, 7 June 1958, in *Papers* 4:419–420). Clennon W. King, Jr. (1920–2000).

2. The charges against King in connection with his 1956 and 1958 income tax returns had been separated. King was acquitted on 28 May of the 1956 charges; the second set of charges, related to his 1958 return, were dropped on 18 July 1960 ("Alabama Drops Second Charge against King," *Atlanta Daily World,* 19 July 1960).

3. Simon Legree, a character in Harriet Beecher Stowe's novel *Uncle Tom's Cabin; or, Life Among the Lowly,* was a cruel northern slave trader turned plantation owner. Stowe's book, which originally appeared as a series in the abolitionist newspaper *The Washington National Era,* was published in 1852 (Boston: John P. Jewett).

I believe that if these five questions are honestly answered, only the fifth can be answered in the affirmative.

Consequently, the most significant aspect of this matter is, "Why would Alabama officials prosecute this case when they had no practical hope of winning?" If the truthful answer is not that "they were trying to put Rev. M. L. King in jail", it must be something else these officials desired to unleash against the present integration struggle. And I suspect that this "something else" was achieved. Especially since its recognition has been so unexplainably ignored by your elite forces.

No matter what side the truth favors, we should tell the Negro people the truth. The Negro people are given the impression that the side of integration is unpopular and that its great leaders, such as you, are persecuted and undergo unremitting suffering from the whites, and that the "Toms" are the real financial beneficiaries. The larger significance of your case is that our great Negro integration leaders have grown wealthy through gifts, etc from whites as well as Negroes. [*word illegible*] Our great integration leaders are most influential with whites. {Your side was abetted by some of the biggest white names in America.}

In my own very trying experience, as one who would serve as a ~~mighty~~ voice of conscience to our people, I have constantly run into trouble raising {mere} subsistance money, while you people's personal incomes have quadrupled and more. Neither am I able to stay out of jail on false misdemeanor charges, while you noted Negro integrationists can even beat the felonies.

Yours in Unity,
[*signed*] Clennon
Rev. Clennon King
United States Presidential Candidate[4]

TALS. MLKP-MBU: Box 29.

---

4. In the 1960 presidential election, nearly 1,500 votes were cast in support of Clennon King and his running mate, Reginald Carter.

To Kelly Miller Smith

9 June 1960
[*Atlanta, Ga.*]

In the letter below, King responds to SCLC executive committee member Kelly Miller Smith's request for King to send a congratulatory message to Nashville's sit-in protesters.[1] *King explains that his response was delayed while he dealt with his perjury case in Alabama.*

Rev. Kelly Miller Smith
319 Eighth Avenue, North
Nashville 4, Tennessee

Dear Kelly:

On returning to the office I found your letter of May 24, on my desk asking me to send a message of congratulations to the students of Nashville who did such a magnificent job in their nonviolent campaign against lunch counter segregation. I regret so much that I was out of place at the time this letter came in. It so happened that I was facing the ordeals of an Alabama court at that time. I can assure you that I would have been more than happy to send a message if I had known about it before going into court. As I have said before, Nashville provided the best organized and best disciplined group in the whole southern student movement.[2] I have said this publicly and privately. And so I would like to give the students a belated message of congratulations and I would also like to express once more my appreciation to you for your magnificent leadership in the whole struggle.

Very sincerely yours,
Martin L. King, Jr.

MLK:mlb

TLc. MLKP-MBU: Box 69.

---

1. Smith's letter followed closely on the heels of the successful conclusion of the Nashville sit-in and boycott campaign. Following months of training by James Lawson, the Nashville sit-ins were launched on 13 February; lunch counters in the city began operating on a nonsegregated basis on 10 May 1960 ("Six Lunch Counters Here Serve Negroes," *Nashville Tennessean,* 11 May 1960).

2. During a 20 April 1960 address at Fisk University, King praised the Nashville students as "the best organized and the most disciplined in the Southland" and explained that he had come "not to bring inspiration but to gain inspiration from the great movement that has taken place in this community." King's speech was delayed nearly an hour by a bomb threat made credible by the previous day's bombing at the home of Nashville city councilman Z. Alexander Looby, an attorney who had defended students arrested during the protests (Garry Fullerton, "King Delayed by Bomb Scare," *Nashville Tennessean,* 21 April 1960).

Statement Announcing the March on the Conventions Movement for Freedom Now

[*9 June 1960*]
[*New York, N.Y.*]

The following statement, released during a press conference at Randolph's New York City office, announces plans for "massive" demonstrations at the upcoming Republican and Democratic national conventions.[1] *King and Randolph demand that the major political parties recognize the "revolutionary mood and determination of the Negro people," and they contrast the courage of the southern student protesters with presidential candidates who "have looked the other way when their parties have tolerated racists or made deals with racists."*

A civil rights crisis rocks the nation. We are on the threshhold of a new decade in which the masses of Negro people are coming on to the stage of history and demanding their freedom now.

We have witnessed the first stage of a revolution in the South against segregation and discrimination. Heroic Southern students have injected their very bodies into the non-violent struggle for freedom and have declared undying battle against Jim Crow. In recent years scores of thousands of Negroes and their white allies have converged on the nation's capital to demand an end to gradualism in all of its forms.[2]

These historic actions have been expressions of the profound political and social frustration of our people. Their demands have been met with the condescending smile of inert government, by incredible political deception and double-dealing, by an ingrained indifference to the democratic ideals of equality and freedom. Everywhere we look, the cry for justice is answered by a shrug, by business-as-usual. Government, far from meeting the needs of the times, has retreated. School integration has virtually ground to a halt. Six years after the Supreme Court decision, only 6% of Southern Negro students attend integrated classes. Congressmen of both parties this year conspired to deprive the Negro of his right to vote, for the 1960 Civil Rights Bill obstructs the voting process by placing overwhelming burdens of prosecution on the Negro rathern than on those who oppress him.

---

1. Rustin coordinated arrangements and publicity for the press conference (Rustin to Press agencies, 8 June 1960; see also Press release, Demonstrations to occur at the Democratic and Republican conventions, 9 June 1960). For more on the demonstrations, see King, Address at NAACP Mass Rally for Civil Rights, 10 July 1960, and Interview by Lee Nichols at Republican National Convention, 25 July 1960, pp. 485–487 and 492–493 in this volume, respectively.

2. King refers to the 1957 Prayer Pilgrimage for Freedom and the two Youth Marches for Integrated Schools. For more information on these events, see King, "Give Us the Ballot," 17 May 1957, and King, Address at Youth March for Integrated Schools, 25 October 1958, in *Papers* 4:208–215 and 514–515, respectively; and King, Address at the Youth March for Integrated Schools, 18 April 1959, pp. 186–188 in this volume.

9 June 1960

In our travels throughout the length and breadth of this country over the months, Negroes from every walk of life have repeatedly asked us: what is to be done this election year to cease the equivocation of both political parties on the issue of civil rights? What is to be done to register our insistence that both political parties repudiate the segregationists within their ranks or any political alliances with segregationists?

The time has come when the political parties of this country must feel this revolutionary mood and determination of the Negro people. We have therefore wired prominent community leaders, Negro and white, in Los Angeles and Chicago, informing them that we intend to be present at both the Democratic and Republican Conventions.[3] We are asking them to cooperate with us in a massive non-violent "March on the Conventions Movement for Freedom Now!"[4] The millions of Negroes denied the right to vote in the South are appealing to the people of Los Angeles and Chicago to represent them before the Conventions.

We believe that if the candidates and parties expect Negroes and their white allies to have any confidence in them, they must make a forthright declaration that racial segregation and discrimination in any form is unconstitutional, un-American, and immoral. The Supreme Court decision on integration can become the law of the land, and the elementary requirements of democracy be satisfied, only if both parties repudiate the minorities in their ranks who have combined in Washington to thwart the Supreme Court decision and the cry for justice of the Negro people. Unless the two major parties make such a declaration, the Negro people will remain doubly disfranchised: first, because they are barred from the polls, and secondly, because they are denied political representation through the existing parties. In the spirit of the Southern students, we shall march on the conventions in mass to serve notice that we will no longer endure this double disfranchisement, and that no party which ignores the just demands of our 18 million people can look to a long future.

At present, no candidate for the presidency has measured up to the courage of the Southern students.[5] All of them have looked the other way when their parties have tolerated racists or made deals with racists. We are going to present a list of questions to all the candidates. We are going to demand specific answers and a specific program to implement them. The time of compromise and empty gen-

---

3. Rustin may have prepared the text of a telegram regarding the protest (King and Randolph, To Los Angeles community leaders, June 1960; see also Randolph to Maurice Dawkins and Augustus F. Hawkins, 17 June 1960). In CBS film footage of the press conference, King estimated that "five thousand or more" protesters would participate in the demonstrations (Press conference on the March on the Conventions Movement for Freedom Now, 9 June 1960).

4. In his comments to reporters, King underscored the protesters' commitment to "the philosophy and the technique of nonviolence" and guaranteed that it will be made "clear to all of the persons who will assemble for the demonstration, for the march, that the movement is to be nonviolent through and through" (Press conference, 9 June 1960).

5. After accusing both political parties of failing to understand that "civil rights should constitute an issue in this election," Randolph concluded that no "single candidate for the presidency has completely earned the right to expect the support of Negro voters in this campaign" (Press conference, 9 June 1960).

eralities is over. The time for action is now.[6] The heroic students of the South have shown the way, and the least we can do is to carry their demands, and those of all Negroes who are denied the right to vote, directly to the political conventions.

TD. BRP-DLC.

---

6. At the conclusion of the press conference, Randolph acknowledged that "the probability of a candidate emerging which would reflect the spirit and purpose of our position on civil rights seems quite unlikely" (Press conference, 9 June 1960).

From Walter E. Fauntroy

10 June 1960
Washington, D.C.

Fauntroy, pastor of New Bethel Baptist Church in Washington, D.C., recalls the "lasting effect" of King's 1953 visit to his alma mater, Virginia Union University. He also proposes linking his organizing efforts with those of SCLC: "Our Washington experience indicates that after desegregation we must be prepared to combat . . . attempts to make Negro life in the New South but a replica of life in the massive racial ghettos that dot the North."[1] In his 18 June reply, King indicated that Fauntroy might serve "a most meaningful role" in SCLC, and the following year he appointed him a regional representative of SCLC.

Dr. Martin Luther King, Jr.
193 Boulevard, N.E.
Atlanta, Georgia

Dear Dr. King:

It was indeed a pleasure to see and hear you in Petersburg last week.[2] Your mention of the Interseminary Conference at Virginia Union in 1953 brought to mind the lasting effect your visit had upon me, then a sophomore at Union, when you spent that weekend with us in our guest suite.[3]

---

1. Walter E. Fauntroy (1933–), born in Washington, D.C., graduated from Virginia Union University in 1955 and received a B.D. (1958) from Yale Divinity School. The following year he was called to the pulpit of New Bethel Baptist Church. Fauntroy served as the District of Columbia's representative in Congress from 1971 until 1990.

2. Fauntroy refers to a meeting of the Petersburg Improvement Association on 1 June at which King was the featured speaker.

3. Fauntroy later recalled that King had spent the night in a dormitory guest room at Virginia Union. Wyatt Tee Walker had helped make the arrangements by contacting Fauntroy, who was then director of the freshman dormitory (Fauntroy, Interview with King Papers Project staff, 6 March 2002).

I recall quite vividly two sermons you shared with us then: one, a very humorous caricature on the subject "Is"; the other, Howard Thurman's treatment of the story of Elijah at Mt. Horeb as illustrating the "quiet power of love."[4] For months after you left, the latter was the subject of some of the most fruitful periods of meditation that I have ever spent. Its message became the sounding board against which all of my later exposure to theological thought was tested. When first I heard your name mentioned in connection with the Montgomery boycott, I thanked God that He had placed in that crisis the man with the message for our time.

I have been interested in talking to you about the situation here in Washington because I think it is a harbinger of the kind of challenge the Negro must be prepared to meet in other Southern cities as they become ostensibly desegregated. After our emancipation nearly 100 years ago came the Reconstruction Era with its carpetbag exploitation of the Negro situation that resulted in the yoke of segregation from which we are only now beginning to emerge (c.f. Lillian Smith, Killers of the Dream, chp. on "The Bargain").[5] Our Washington experience indicates that after desegregation we must be prepared to combat equally as sinister attempts to make Negro life in the New South but a replica of life in the massive racial ghettos that dot the North where self perpetuating sub-cultures are developed which then become formidable barriers to first class citizenship. I wish I could go into details here.

We are trying to develop in D.C. a kind of organization which may cope successfully with our problems in newly desegregated municipalities.[6] The gray sheet gives you a bit of the background of our group, while the white sheet explains how we are attempting to organize. Also find enclosed a letter to the editor of our local Afro.

When you are in Washington again and can spare an hour or so, I would like very much to go over the picture in more detail with you. Affiliated with SCLC, our work might serve as a pilot project for meetin similar challenges later on in the newly desegregated cities of the South.

Regards and best wishes to Tee Walker when you see him again and may God continue to bless you in your work.

Very sincerely yours,
[*signed*]
Walter E. Fauntroy

WEF/dsf
ENCLOSURES

TLS. MLKP-MBU: Box 25.

---

4. Cf. 1 Kings 19:8–18.

5. The chapter, "Two Men and a Bargain," describes a Reconstruction-era agreement reached between "Mr. Rich White" and "Mr. Poor White" to exclude "the Negro" (Smith, *Killers of the Dream* [New York: W. W. Norton, 1949]).

6. As part of his effort to form the "Citizen's Committee on Metropolitan Problems" for the District of Columbia, Fauntroy had written Ralph Abernathy on 17 February seeking information on the MIA's structure, objectives, and guiding principles.

To Patrick Murphy Malin, Roy Wilkins, and Carl J. Megel

16 June 1960
[*Atlanta, Ga.*]

King alerts the heads of the ACLU, NAACP, and American Federation of Teachers (AFT) regarding Lawrence Reddick's termination from Alabama State College and alleges that state officials are "seeking to halt the southern nonviolent student movement by making an example of Dr. Reddick."[1] *King characterizes Alabama as "a Gestapo state with no respect for decency, justice and fair play" and calls on Malin, Wilkins, and Megel to issue public statements in protest.*[2]

MR. PATRICK MURPHY MALIN
AMERICAN CIVIL LIBERTIES UNION
170 FIFTH AVENUE
NEW YORK, NEW YORK

MR. ROY WILKINS
THE NATIONAL ASSOCIATION FOR THE ADVANCEMENT OF COLORED PEOPLE
20 WEST 40TH STREET
NEW YORK, NEW YORK

MR. CARL J. MEGEL, PRESIDENT
AMERICAN FEDERATION OF TEACHERS
28 EAST JACKSON BOULEVARD
CHICAGO 4, ILLINOIS

THE GOVERNOR OF ALABAMA HAS ORDERED PRESIDENT TRENHOLM OF ALABAMA STATE COLLEGE TO FIRE DR. L. D. REDDICK IMMEDIATELY. HE HAS AT-

---

1. King also prepared a statement calling Alabama "an ugly symbol of injustice and immorality" and expressed his "unqualified confidence" in Reddick (King, Statement on the firing of Lawrence Dunbar Reddick by Alabama State College, 16 June 1960). On 14 June the Alabama State Board of Education, acting on a recommendation from Governor John Patterson, had ordered Alabama State College president H. Councill Trenholm to fire Reddick "before sundown." Though Reddick, who had served for six years as chair of the history department, had already submitted his resignation effective 31 August, Trenholm discharged him immediately (Bob Ingram, "Negro Teacher Linked to Reds, Ordered Fired: ASC Ouster Given Push by Governor," *Montgomery Advertiser,* 15 June 1960). Patrick Murphy Malin (1903–1964) obtained a B.S. (1924) from the University of Pennsylvania and taught economics at Swarthmore College from 1930 until 1950. Malin became the executive director of the ACLU in 1950 and held this position until 1962. Carl J. Megel (1899–1992) earned a B.A. (1923) from Franklin College. He became active in the Chicago Teachers Union (CTU) in the 1930s and served as president of the AFT from 1952 until 1964.

2. The three men all complied with King's request (ACLU, Press release, 17 June 1960; "Firing of Reddick Hit by Leader of Teachers," *Birmingham World,* 16 July 1960, and Wilkins to Patterson, 17 June 1960). Faculty reprisals had been threatened as early as March following a wave of student protests at Alabama State, and Reddick had written King twice about the importance of support from the ACLU and AFT (Reddick to King, 13 and 25 April 1960). Both Wilkins and Malin had also condemned threatened teacher firings (Malin to Patterson, 14 April 1960, and Reddick to King, 13 April 1960).

TEMPTED TO USE TRUMPTED UP CHARGES OF COMMUNIST ASSOCIATION AS THE BASIS OF THE FIRING. THERE IS NOT ONE SCINTILLA OF TRUTH IN THESE CHARGES. THE FACT IS THAT THE STATE IS SEEKING TO HALT THE SOUTHERN NONVIOLENT STUDENT MOVEMENT BY MAKING AN EXAMPLE OF DR. REDDICK BECAUSE OF HIS SYMPATHY FOR AND SUPPORT OF THE STRUGGLE FOR RACIAL JUSTICE. DR. REDDICK IS AN ABLE SCHOLAR AND DEDICATED HUMANITARIAN. HIS DEVOTION AND LOYALTY TO THE IDEALS OF AMERICAN DEMOCRACY ARE UNQUESTIONED. THE FIRING OF DR. REDDICK IS A TRAGIC MISCARRIAGE OF JUSTICE AND AN ASSAULT ON ACADEMIC FREEDOM. IT IS AN ATTEMPT TO DEPRIVE TEACHERS OF THEIR CONSTITUTIONAL RIGHTS OF FREE SPEECH AND FREE ASSEMBLY. I HOPE YOU CAN SEE YOUR WAY CLEAR TO ISSUE A STRONG STATENENT TO GOVERNOR PATTERSON IMMEDIATELY. GOVERNOR PATTERSON ALSO URGED THE BOARD OF EDUCATION TO SERIOUSLY CONSIDER FIRING ALABAMA STATE COLLEGE' S PRESIDENT, DR. H. COUNCIL TRENHOLM BECAUSE HE HAD NOT REMOVED THE FACULTY MEMBERS WHO EXPRESSED SYMPATHY FOR THE STUDENT SIT-INS. DR. TRENHOLM HAS BEEN ORDERED TO APPEAR BEFORE BOARD NEXT MONTH WITH PERSONAL FILES OF ALL FACULTY MEMBERS. ALL THIS IS INDICATIVE OF THE FACT THAT ALABAMA IS NOW A GESTAPO STATE WITH NO RESPECT FOR DECENCY, JUSTICE AND FAIR PLAY. THIS SHOULD BE CALLED TO ATTENTION OF WHOLE NATION. RELEASE STATEMENT YOU HAVE TO PRESS.

MARTIN LUTHER KING, JR.

THWc. MLKP-MBU: Box 68.

To L. Harold DeWolf

16 June 1960
Atlanta, Ga.

In a 10 May letter DeWolf, King's dissertation advisor, informed him that the Boston University Civil Rights Scholarship Fund had raised $2,500 for "any Negro or white student, who has been expelled from college for non-violent protest against discrimination."[1] King expresses enthusiasm for the scholarship fund and shares his surprise at the outcome of his perjury trial.

Dr. L. Harold DeWolf
Boston University
Boston, Massachusetts

Dear Dr. DeWolf:

Please accept my apologies for just getting to the point of answering your letter of May 10th. As you probably know, I was tied up in court most of the month

1. DeWolf was treasurer of the fund.

of May in the case brought against me by the State of Alabama. This inevitably threw me a great deal behind in my correspondence. I am happy to report that an all white jury rendered a verdict of not guilty in this case. I must say that this was a real surprise. We had no idea that an all white jury of Montgomery, Alabama would ever think of acquitting Martin Luther King. Even though we knew that the State had no case, and that all of their charges were false, we felt that it would have been necessary to go to the United States Supreme Court in order to finally receive justice. So this was a most significant decision. I hope that it represents a dawn of a new hope.

I am certainly happy to know of the Boston University Civil Rights Scholarship Fund. As I said to you in my last letter, the setting up of this fund is unprecedented and I know that it will serve a great purpose.[2] I will be very happy to pass the word along to college students and their advisors throughout the South that any Negro or white student who has been expelled from college because of their participation in the nonviolent protest against discrimination is invited to apply for assistance in carrying on his studies at Boston University. I have already spoken to the expelled students of Alabama State College concerning this scholarship fund, and I will get the word to the other expelled students that I know throughout the South.

I am very glad to know that Jim Lawson is at Boston University.[3] It is quite a tribute to Boston University that in spite of all of the other offers that came to Jim from other schools he chose to complete his education there. I can assure you that the great role that B.U. is playing in this whole struggle is most encouraging and consoling.

Before closing, I must mention something that grew out of your Atlanta visit which is profoundly meaningful. You will remember the evening that we had the small gathering at our home you constantly suggested to the faculty members of Emory University and the students of I.T.C. (The Negro theological seminary) that they should come together in small groups for the purpose of fellowship and discussion.[4] Upon the basis of your suggestion, two or three of them said that night that they planned to follow it through. I am happy to report that they did follow it through, and it has developed into one of the most creative groups imaginable. Some thirty white and Negro students from Emory and the Interdenominational Theological Seminary respectively joined in the group, and they have met almost weekly since you left Atlanta. They meet in various homes and all of them have said that the experience has totally transformed their lives. Most of the white students in the group are from the South, and they admitted that they had never had an experience with Negroes before in this type of situation. Several of them have

---

2. Upon hearing of the scholarship fund, King conveyed his pride in being an alumnus in a 10 May letter to DeWolf.

3. James Lawson was expelled from Vanderbilt University's Divinity School in March 1960 due to his protest activities in Nashville; he graduated with an S.T.B. from Boston University later that year. In a 13 March letter to King, DeWolf had denounced Lawson's expulsion. Upon his arrival in Nashville in 1958, Lawson was appointed social action leader of the Nashville Christian Leadership Conference (NCLC), the local SCLC affiliate. The following year, Lawson became SCLC's director of nonviolent education.

4. During DeWolf's March 1960 visit to Atlanta, King hosted a small interracial gathering that included some of DeWolf's acquaintances. In anticipation of his visit, DeWolf had written King that he knew a number of "white church people" in Atlanta who "might both gain and give most in co-operation with you" (DeWolf to King, 12 February 1960).

gone out with a new dedication and determination. I wanted to mention this to you because I am sure that it came directly out of your visit to Atlanta and your suggestion on the evening that we assembled at my home.

Please give my best regards to all. As soon as I get some more information on interested students I will be writing you.

Very sincerely yours,
[*signed*] Martin
Martin L. King, Jr.

MLK:mlb

TLS. OGCP-MBU.

To T. Y. Rogers

18 June 1960
[*Atlanta, Ga.*]

King congratulates Rogers, his former assistant at Dexter, on his graduation from seminary. King cautions Rogers on his interest in the vacant pulpit at Dexter, explaining that he might have difficulty gaining respect from the congregation: "It is one of the most difficult things in the world for a group of people who once taught you to accept you as their spiritual shepherd."[1]

Rev. T. Y. Rogers
Dear T. Y.:

First, I must apologize for being so tardy in replying to your letter of April 14th.[2] Actually, my involvement in the present student movement, a court case in Montgomery, Alabama, and other pressing responsibilities have kept me out of the office almost consistently for two months. Therefore, I am just getting to your letter.

I assume that the financial problems that you were confronting at the time that your letter was written are now taken care of, at least I hope so. If not, you can write me again and I will see what I can do to help. I am getting ready to leave the country to attend the Baptist World's Alliance in the next three or four days, and I will not return until after the middle of July. Please feel free to contact me after that time.[3]

Congratulations upon your graduation from Crozer Seminary. I am very happy

1. King wrote letters of recommendation for Rogers, calling him "a good and dynamic preacher" (King to Phinehas Smith, 29 September 1960; see also King to Horace G. Robson, May 1960).

2. In Rogers's 14 April letter he asked King for a loan to cover some final school bills.

3. King attended the Tenth Annual Baptist World Alliance in Rio de Janeiro, Brazil, from 24 June until 3 July.

to know of all of your accomplishments. You are doing a marvelous job, and we all expect a great future for you. Do keep in touch with me and let me know what you are doing.[4]

Incidentally, Dexter has not called a pastor yet. They are in the process of hearing men now. You may have noticed a bit of hesitation in my mind when you spoke to me concerning the possibility of your coming to Dexter. I can assure you that the hesitation was never a result of my feeling that you were not adequate for the job, but I did have then, and I still have the feeling that because you went to school in the community many of the members would not give you the respect and support that you would need as a pastor. In a sense Dexter is a peculiar church, and it is one of the most difficult things in the world for a group of people who once taught you to accept you as their spiritual shepherd. So I did not want to see you start your ministry in a situation that could so easily disillusion you. Of course, if Dexter had the proper vision at this point they would realize that they could not find a better person in the country than you. You would have the opportunity of growing with them, and they with you. But sometimes cold blooded intellectuals cannot see all of the facts.

Again, let me bid you Godspeed in all of your endeavors, and I hope things will continue to work in your behalf. Give my best regards to La Pelzia, and give your beautiful little daughter a big kiss for me.[5]

Very sincerely yours,
Martin L. King, Jr.

Signed in the absence of Rev. King.

TLc. MLKP-MBU: Box 68.

4. Rogers served as pastor of Galilee Baptist Church in Philadelphia for four years (1960–1964) before returning to the South as the pastor of First African Baptist Church in Tuscaloosa, Alabama, in order to work more closely with SCLC. At the time of his death in 1970, he was SCLC's director of affiliates.

5. King refers to Rogers's wife and their daughter, Gina.

To Jackie Robinson

19 June 1960
[Atlanta, Ga.]

King responds to Robinson's accusations that SCLC supporters had engaged in divisive fund-raising efforts and made derogatory comments about the NAACP. King states that he would rather "retire from the civil rights struggle" than "become a symbol of division."[1] *He reaffirms his support for the NAACP but notes that he has remained*

1. See also Robinson to King, 5 May 1960, pp. 454–455 in this volume.

silent in the face of "efforts on the part of NAACP officials to sabotage our humble efforts." Robinson thanked King for this "reassuring letter" on 29 June.

Mr. Jackie Robinson
425 Lexington Avenue
New York 17, New York

My dear Friend Jackie:

This is to acknowledge receipt of your letter of May 5. First, I must apologize for being so tardy in my reply. Actually, the southern student movement, the court case in Montgomery, Alabama, and other pressing responsibilities have kept me out of my office almost consistently for the last two months. Therefore, I have been thrown almost hopelessly behind in my correspondence. Even when I am in a desperate attempt to play a game of catch up, something else emerges to hold me back. I am sure that you can understand this with all of your busy responsibilities.

I am deeply grateful to you for calling my attention to some maladjustments and unfortunate situations that have developed around fund raising for my defense. Frankly, I did not know about these things, and I would want to investigate them immediately. I would certainly not be a party to anything that would damage fund raising for all organizations in the future.

The only organization raising money for my defense is the Defense Committee which was formed in the home of Harry Belafonte the week after I was indicted in Alabama. As you know, this committee was set up to raise funds for a three-fold purpose, namely, my defense, the student movement, and the voter registration drive of the Southern Christian Leadership Conference. Therefore, the committee had the joint name of "Committee to Defend Martin Luther King and the Struggle for Freedom in the South." The committee took on this three-fold responsibility because of a strong appeal that I made the night of the forming of the committee. I tried to make it palpably clear that it was not enough to defend me because in the long run of history it does not matter whether Martin Luther King spends ten years in jail, but it does matter whether the student movement continues, and it does matter whether the Negro is able to get the ballot in the South. I made it clear that I would not be so selfish as to be concerned merely about my defense and not be concerned about the great creative causes that were taking place in the South. And so I said to them that it would not be enough to defend me and then let the organization die which is a projection of me and my personality. I also made the suggestion because I knew that I would be out of circulation for a while, and that I could not raise as much money for the Southern Christian Leadership Conference as I would ordinarily raise. Therefore, to keep things moving, I felt that it was absolutely imperative that funds be raised for this purpose. Fortunately, the persons present agreed with me. They set up the committee and went out to raise money for these three causes. As you know the committee has made appeals through ads in newspapers, direct mail order appeals, mass meetings, and benefit concerts. As far as I have been able to discern, this committee has operated on the highest level of honest and integrity. There will be a public accounting of all the money that has been raised and spent in the next few days, and I am sure that the public will agree that it has handled the money [*properly?*].[2] As you know, there are always those later problems of organizational differences and the fear on the part of some that something new is offering competition. But I hope no one will get this impression. I have said both publicly and privately that before I become a symbol of division in the Negro community I would retire from the civil rights struggle because I think the cause is too great and too important for a few individuals to halt things by engaging in minor ego battles. 19 June 1960

Now to say just a word concerning the second question that you raised with reference to SCLC leaders making derogatory statements concerning the NAACP. I have always stressed the need for great cooperation between SCLC and the NAACP. I have made it clear in all of our board meetings and conference meetings that the NAACP is our chief civil rights organization, and that it has done more to achieve the civil rights of Negroes than any other organization. It, therefore, justifiably deserves our support and respect, and I have constantly said that any Negro who fails to give the NAACP this backing is nothing less than an ingrate. I have always felt that the SCLC could serve as a real supplement for the work of the NAACP, and not a substitute. In areas where the NAACP cannot operate the SCLC can. Also, with the number of ministerial leaders involved in SCLC it has an opportunity to get to the masses in order to mobilize mass action, and assist the NAACP in implementing its great program. So I have never seen any conflict between the two organizations. I only see the possibility of the greatest harmony. If there are those individuals who move under the name of SCLC and say derogatory things about the NAACP I can assure you that they do not speak for me or the organization. They are expressing individual positions which I can not control. I absolutely agree with you that we cannot afford any division at this time and we cannot afford any conflict. And I can assure you that as long as I am President of SCLC it will not be a party to any development of disunity.

The days ahead are challenging indeed. The future has vast possibilities and I am convinced that if we will gird our courage and move on in a sense of togetherness and goodwill we will be able to crush the sagging walls of segregation by the battering rams of the forces of justice. In my little way I am trying to help solve this problem. I have no Messiah complex, and I know that we need many leaders to do the job. And I am convinced that with the leadership of integrity, humility, and dedication to the ideals of freedom and justice we will be able to bring into full realization the principles of our American Democracy. Please be assured that you can count on me to give my ultimate allegiance to the cause. Even if it means pushing myself into the background. I have been so concerned about unity and the ultimate victory that I have refused to fight back or even answer some of the unkind statements that I have been informed that NAACP officials said about me and the Southern Christian Leadership Conference. Frankly, I hear these statements every day,

---

2. According to a 31 July financial report, of the over $85,000 raised by the committee, more than $51,000 went toward costs incurred during King's perjury trial and other expenses of the southern struggle (Committee to Defend Martin Luther King and the Struggle for Freedom in the South, "Statement of income and expenditure for the period ending 7/31/60," and A. Philip Randolph and Gardner C. Taylor, Press release, both dated 7 October 1960).

and I have seen efforts on the part of NAACP officials to sabotage our humble efforts. But I have never said anything about it publicly or to the press. I am sure that if criticisms were weighed it would turn out that persons associated with the NAACP have made much more damaging statements about SCLC than persons associated with SCLC have made concerning the NAACP. But I will not allow this to become an issue. The job ahead is too great, and the days are too bright to be bickering in the darkness of jealousy, deadening competition, and internal ego struggles.

I hope that I have in some way answered your very important questions. I am deeply grateful to you for your concern and interest, and always know that I, along with millions of Americans, are deeply indebted to you for your unswerving devotion to the cause of freedom and justice and your willingness at all times to champion the cause of the underdog.

With warm personal regards, I am

Sincerely yours,
Martin L. King, Jr.

MLK:mlb
Dictated, but not signed by Rev. King.

TLc. MLKP-MBU: Box 68.

To Chester Bowles

24 June 1960
Atlanta, Ga.

King reports on his first meeting with Democratic presidential hopeful John F. Kennedy on 23 June at the senator's New York apartment.[1] *King describes the encounter as "fruitful and rewarding" and expresses confidence that Kennedy would "do the right thing" on civil rights. He also conveys his ideas on the Democratic Party's civil rights platform to Bowles, who served as chair of the Democratic Platform Committee.*[2] *Bowles thanked King for his "excellent suggestions" on 29 June.*[3]

---

1. The meeting followed several attempts to get the two men together (see King to Marjorie McKenzie Lawson, 4 September 1959, pp. 276–277 in this volume). King later recalled his first meeting with Kennedy: "At that time I was impressed with his concern and I was impressed with his willingness to learn more about civil rights." King came away from the encounter with the impression that Kennedy had "a long intellectual commitment" to civil rights but hadn't yet developed "the emotional commitment" (King, Interview by Berl I. Bernhard, 9 March 1964).

2. King and Bowles had previously corresponded regarding travel in India and efforts to end apartheid in South Africa (King to Bowles, 28 October 1957 and 8 November 1957, in *Papers* 4:303–305 and 311–314, respectively).

3. In a 15 June letter, Bayard Rustin enclosed a list of seven points that SCLC should demand from the platform committees of both parties and requested to speak to King about it before it was sent to Bowles. The six points King outlines in this letter closely follow Rustin's suggestions, though King does modify the order and language. King and A. Philip Randolph included all seven of Rustin's points in their presentation to the Democratic convention (see Joint Platform Proposals to the 1960 Democratic Party Platform Committee, Read by L. B. Thompson, 7 July 1960, pp. 482–485 in this volume).

Congressman Chester Bowles
Essex, Conn.

24 June 1960

Dear Congressman Bowles:

I intended writing you immediately after our telephone conversation a few days ago, but several unexpected developments called me away from my desk. I also had to attend a Church meeting in Buffalo, New York which kept me out of the city almost a week.[4] In the next few hours I will be leaving for South America, so I hasten to give you some of my ideas on the Democratic platform before leaving.[5] The main point that I feel the platform committee should consider on the questions of civil rights are as follows:

1. That the 1954 Supreme Court Decision be explicitly endorsed as morally right and the law of the land. A forthright declaration should be made that the racial segregation and discrimination in any form is unconstitutional, un-American and immoral.
2. That Section 3, empowering the Federal Government to bring suits on behalf of Negroes denied their civil rights be enacted into law.[6]
3. That Congress pass the Federal Registrar Plan of the President's Civil Rights Commission, and that the responsibility for the protection of voting rights be placed squarely with the President and not with southern courts. (This would eliminate red tape complex qualities found in the present referee plan.)[7]
4. That in accordance with the Fourteenth Amendment Congressional responsibilities be reduced in those areas where Negroes are denied the right to vote.
5. That the party endorse the spirit and tactics of the sit-ins as having the same validity as labor strikes.
6. That the party and its candidates take a clear moral stand against colonialism and racism in all its forms, East and West, and especially in Africa where apartheid has lead to the massacre of hundreds of people seeking only to live in freedom in their own land.

These are just some of the things I think are quite significant. I know that most of them would be strongly opposed by the South, but I think they are important enough to at least reach the discussion stage.

---

4. King attended the National Sunday School and Baptist Training Union (BTU) Congress in Buffalo on 17 and 18 June.

5. King traveled to Brazil on 24 June to participate in the Tenth Annual Baptist World Alliance meeting.

6. Section III, deleted from the Civil Rights Bill of 1957, would have allowed the Justice Department to initiate lawsuits to desegregate schools and public facilities.

7. A September 1959 commission report included a recommendation that would allow the president to provide federal registrars to communities where citizens had been prevented from voting (U.S. Commission on Civil Rights, *Report of the United States Commission on Civil Rights, 1959* [Washington, D.C.: U.S. Government Printing Office, 1959], pp. 134–142). The Voting Rights Act of 1965 included a provision that allowed for the appointment of temporary federal registrars in cases where the right to vote was denied.

I had a very fruitful and rewarding conversation with Senator Kennedy yesterday. We talked about an hour and a half over the breakfast table. I was very impressed by the forthright and honest manner in which he discussed the civil rights question. I have no doubt that he would do the right thing on this issue if he were elected president. Of course, I am sure that you have been a great influence on Mr. Kennedy at this point. It may interest you to know that I had very little enthusiasm for Mr. Kennedy when he first announced his candidacy. When I discovered, however, that he had asked you to serve as his foreign advisor my mind immediately changed. I said to myself, "If Chester Bowles is Mr. Kennedy's advisor he must be thinking right on the major issues."[8]

Thank you for giving me the opportunity to make these few suggestions, and I hope you will find them helpful. I will look forward to seeing you in Los Angeles.

Very sincerely yours,
[*signed*]
Martin Luther King, Jr.

MLK:mlb
Dictated, but not signed by Rev. King.

TLSr. CB-CtY.

---

8. From 1961 until 1963, Bowles served as Kennedy's advisor on African, Asian, and Latin American affairs.

To Adam Clayton Powell, Jr.

24 June 1960

Shortly before leaving for the Tenth Annual Baptist World Alliance in Rio de Janeiro, King assails Powell's allegations that he and Randolph were "'captives' of behind-the-scenes interests" and that King had "been under undue influences ever since Bayard Rustin . . . went to Alabama to help in the bus boycott."[1] *Powell also reportedly accused them of excluding the NAACP from their plans to protest the upcoming political conventions.*[2] *King entreats Powell to "publicly correct these false charges with as much vigor as they were made."*

On 27 June, Rustin announced his resignation as King's special assistant and

---

1. Powell, who made his claims during a speech to the National Sunday School and Baptist Training Union Congress in Buffalo on 19 June, reportedly claimed Randolph was beholden to socialists, "guided principally" by Stanley Levison ("Powell Insists Randolph, King Are 'Captives,'" *Pittsburgh Courier,* 25 June 1960).

2. Powell may have felt the picketing would jeopardize his chances of becoming chair of the House labor and education committee (Nat Hentoff, "Adam Clayton Powell: What Price Principle?" *Village Voice,* 14 July 1960).

director of SCLC's New York office, citing Powell's claims that he had become a divisive force in the civil rights struggle.[3] *Rustin stated that he could not "permit a situation to endure" in which his relationship to SCLC "is used to confuse and becloud the basic issues confronting the Negro people today."*[4]

REV DR. ADAM CLAYTON POWELL
ABYSYNNIAN BAPTIST CHURCH 138TH ST & 7TH AVE

AS I LEAVE COUNTRY I AM STILL SOMEWHAT DISTRESSED. HOW YOU COULD SAY THE MALICIOUS THINGS THAT THE PRESS REPORTED LAST WEEK CONCERNING TWO OF YOUR BEST FRIENDS IS STILL MYSTERY TO ME. I HAVE ALWAYS ~~VIGIOU~~ VIGORIOUSLY DEFENDED YOU AGAINST YOUR MOST SEVERE CRITICS EVEN WHEN THEY WERE NAACP OFFICIALS. I HAVE PUBLICLY SUPPORTED YOU IN YOUR CAMPAIGN.[5] PHIL RANDOLPH HAS DONE EVEN MORE TO SUPPORT YOU ACROSS YEARS. IF YOU HAD ONLY CHECKED WITH ME OR RANDOLPH YOU WOULD HAVE DISCOVERED THAT WE TALKED WITH ROY ON THIS AT LEAST THREE TIMES. IF I AM A CAPTIVE OF BAYARD RUSTON IT IS BECAUSE HE CAME TO ME SO HIGHLY RECOMMENDED BY YOU. BECAUSE OF MY RESPECT FOR YOU AND YOUR JUDGMENT I ACCEPTED HIM AS ONE OF MY ASSISTANTS. IN SPITE OF ALL I WILL HOLD [*strikeout illegible*] NOTHING IN MY HEART AGAINST YOU AND I WILL NOT GO TO THE PRESS TO ANSWER OR CONDEMN YOU. I ONLY HOPE THAT SOMETHING WITHIN WILL CAUSE YOU TO PUBLICLY CORRECT THESE FALSE CHARGES WITH AS MUCH VIGOR AS THEY WERE MADE. MAY GOD EVER BLESS YOU IN YOUR ~~HEORIC HEORIC WORK~~ HEROIC WORK

MARTIN LUTHER KING JR.

PWc. MLKP-MBU: Box 21A.

---

3. Rustin later recalled that Powell had also threatened to allege a sexual relationship between King and Rustin if the protests at the Democratic convention were not called off (*The Reminiscences of Bayard Rustin* [New York: Oral History Research Office, Columbia University, 1988], pp. 160–161, 267).

4. SCLC, Press release, 27 June 1960. King continued to consult Rustin on plans for the political conventions, but the two men had little contact until early 1963 (see Rustin to King, 14 July 1960).

5. King had expressed his support for Powell during the New York congressman's 1958 reelection campaign (King to Powell, 10 June 1958, in *Papers* 4:420–421).

7 July
1960

Joint Platform Proposals to the 1960 Democratic Party Platform Committee, Read by L. B. Thompson

7 July 1960

L. B. Thompson, a representative of the March on the Conventions Movement, presented these proposals on behalf of King and Randolph to the Democratic Party's platform committee.[1] *On 11 July the Democrats adopted a civil rights plank that included an acknowledgment of the recent demonstrations in the South and a pledge to give the attorney general power to obtain injunctions against public officials accused of racial discrimination.*[2] *Several of the following proposals paralleled those adopted by the platform committee.*

JOINT PLATFORM PROPOSALS OF
MARTIN LUTHER KING, JR. AND A. PHILIP RANDOLPH
CO-CHAIRMEN, MARCH ON THE CONVENTIONS MOVEMENT

To: The 1960 Democratic Party Platform Committee

(These proposals will be submitted to the Republican platform committee in Chicago. They will be read today by Mr. L. B. Thompson, personal representative of Rev. King and Mr. Randolph, and Los Angeles Chairman of the March on the Conventions Movement.)

We submit these proposals to this national convention on behalf of the Constitutional rights and human dignity of 18 million Negro Americans. We believe they are supported by the overwhelming majority of the American people of all races, creeds and colors and from every walk of life.

We urge your convention to adopt these proposals—which are tryly minimal—to make them a part of your platform and to carry them into life. While these recommendations are limited to the matter of civil rights—which is the decisive domestic issue of our time—we are interested in seeing your convention adopt a

1. L. B. Thompson was a member of the Los Angeles branch of the Brotherhood of Sleeping Car Porters. In Los Angeles, SCLC representative Maurice Dawkins delivered remarks before the Democratic Party Platform Committee on behalf of King, who was returning from a conference in Rio de Janeiro, Brazil (Introductory remarks to the 1960 Democratic Party platform committee, read by Maurice A. Dawkins, 7 July 1960).

2. Paul A. Smith and Richard E. Mays, eds., *Official Report of the Proceedings of the Democratic National Convention and Committee* (Washington, D.C.: National Document Publishers, 1964), pp. 64–74. In an interview conducted in his Los Angeles hotel suite, King expressed his approval of the Democratic Party's civil rights plank: "I think it's the most positive, dynamic and meaningful civil rights plank that has ever been adopted by either party and I'm sure if the party goes through with the implementation of it we will go a long, long way toward solving the civil rights problems of the United States." King criticized the Democrats' failure to be more specific while conceding that "at least it gives the impression that the party stands in sympathy with sit-in demonstration" (Bob Ingram, "Kennedy Out of Favor with Negro, King Says," *Montgomery Advertiser,* 14 July 1960).

socially progressive position on all other international and national issues before the American people.

We warn you, gentlemen, that platforms and promises are no longer sufficient to meet the just and insistent demands of the Negro people for immediate free and unconditional citizenship. The time has come for action—action not only by this convention and its candidates who may prove successful in the November elections. We insist upon action now by the present Federal Government, especially by its Executive and Legislative branches which are still in power and in session. It is well-known that the Republican Party is in control of the executive branch of the government and the Democratic Party, of the legislative. The Congress is scheduled to reconvene in August following the national conventions of both parties. We shall judge the seriousness and sincerity of the platforms and candidates which you approve in your July convention by what the Congress and the White House do in August: first, to guarantee the right of the Negro people in the deep South to vote in the 1960 elections; secondly, to stop the brutal terror against peaceful Negro citizens and their supporters in the deep South; thirdly, to enforce the 1954 Supreme Court decision against school segregation in September; and, fourthly, to uphold the lawful, peaceful and non-violent picketing of Negro students and their supporters who seek to exercise their constitutional rights.

Our proposals follow:

1) We demand that this convention go on record as fully endorsing the great, peaceful democratic sit-in movement in the South, led by the heroic Negro students, supported by increasing numbers of their white fellow students.[3] This movement seeks not alone the constitutional rights of Negroes; but it aims at the moral regeneration of America. It should be endorsed by this convention both as to its non-violent methods and to its ennobling spirit. It is the responsibility of this convention and of its representatives in the federal government in Washington to speak out against, and to halt, the lawless terror, intimidation, brutality, false arrests and violence upon these students as they seek to exercise their constitutional rights against the degradation of segregation, discrimination and Jim Crow.[4]

2) The 1960 elections will be a farce unless more than 10 million Negroes in the South have the opportunity to vote. We demand that this convention go on record for establishing a federal registration apparatus in the deep South, in which the victims—the Negro people—shall serve. This apparatus should be put into effect now for the 1960 elections—and not be postponed until after the elections when the Negro people will have been ef-

3. On a typed draft of these proposals, King handwrote several minor changes that were not incorporated into the final version (Draft, "Proposals to both parties," 1 July–7 July 1960). In the draft of this document, King struck out "demand" and handwrote "strongly urge."

4. The Democratic Party adopted the following resolution, p. 72: "The peaceful demonstrations for first-class citizenship which have recently taken place in many parts of this country are a signal to all of us to make good, at long last the guarantees of the American Constitution."

fectively disfranchised in this year's election. Moreover, the entire federal apparatus should be drawn into guaranteeing the right of the Negro people in the South to vote.[5]

3) We demand the enactment as the law of the land of Section III of the 1957 Civil Rights Bill authorizing the Federal Department of Justice to intervene to uphold the 1954 U.S. Supreme Court decision outlawing segregation in all public school systems.[6] We recommend that 1961 be the target for completion of school integration in accordance with the Supreme Court decision of six years ago.[7]

4) We demand that the President of the United States—the present incumbent and the newly-elected candidate—issue an executive order barring all discrimination in government employment, in all employment policies of firms doing business with the government and in all forms of public supported housing.[8]

5) We demand that this convention go on record to pass at the next session of Congress an anti-lynch law with teeth in it.

6) We call upon your Party and National Convention to repudiate and condemn the segregationists, white supremacists, racists and Dixiecrats in your ranks—and to unseat and expel them. The Negro people nor any other democratic-minded Americans can have any confidence in a Party which seats a [*Orval*] Faubus or an [*James*] Eastland, or that contains within its ranks those who make alliances with such racists. We demand a pledge to unseat Senator Eastland from the United States Senate as being elected from the state of Mississippi where Negro citizens—the majority of the

---

5. Adopted resolution, p. 72: "The Democratic Administration which takes office next January will therefore use the full powers provided in the Civil Rights Act of 1957 and 1960 to secure for all Americans the right to vote. . . . If these powers, vigorously invoked by a new Attorney General and backed by a strong and imaginative Democratic President, prove inadequate, then further powers will be sought. We will support whatever action is necessary to eliminate literacy tests and the payment of poll taxes as requirements for voting."

6. In the draft, King crossed out "demand" and handwrote "earnestly request." Section III was deleted from the 1957 Civil Rights bill shortly before its passage.

7. Adopted resolution, p. 72: "A new Democratic administration will also use its full powers—legal and moral—to ensure the beginning of good faith compliance with the Constitutional requirement that racial discrimination be ended in public education. . . . We believe that every school district affected by the Supreme Court's school desegregation decision should submit a plan providing for at least first step compliance by 1963, which is the one hundredth anniversary of the Emancipation Proclamation. . . . To facilitate compliance, technical and financial assistance should be given to school districts facing special problems of transition."

8. Adopted resolution, p. 73: "The Democratic Administration will use its full executive powers to assure equal employment opportunities and to terminate racial segregation throughout federal services and institutions, and on all government contracts. The successful desegregation of the armed services took place through such decisive executive action under President Truman. Similarly the new Democratic Administration will take action to end discrimination in federal housing programs, including federally-assisted housing. To accomplish these goals will require executive orders, legal actions brought by the Attorney General, legislation, and improved Congressional procedures to safeguard majority rule."

state's population—are disfranchised in violation of the 13th, 14th, and 15th Amendments.

7) We demand that this convention go on record to uphold the second section of the 14th Amendment to the U.S. Constitution, which calls for the reduction of representation of states in accordance with their disfranchisement of qualified voters.

8) We demand that Section IV of Article IV of the U.S. Constitution be upheld guaranteeing every state a republican form of government. We submit that states in the deep South which disfranchise 40 to 52% of their populations do not have a republican form of government. Negroes are denied both the exercise of the vote and representation.

9) As an earmark of the fulfillment of these Constitutional rights, we demand that a Negro citizen be included as a full-fledged member of the Presidential cabinet. The lily-white exclusion of Negro citizens from the top policy-making levels of government must be ended. It is the source-pattern of white-supremacy state and city governments which exist in the 50 states of the Union.

10) We demand that this convention and its candidates take a clear moral stand against colonialism and racism of all kinds, everywhere, and especially in Africa where apartheid has led to the massacre of hundreds of people seeking only to live in freedom in their own land.[9]

TD. OHP-ArU.

9. Adopted resolution, p. 73: "In this spirit, we hereby rededicate ourselves to the continuing service of the Rights of Man—everywhere in America and everywhere else on God's earth." King may refer to the March 1960 massacre in Sharpeville, South Africa, against which he had protested (see King to Claude Barnett, 24 March 1960, pp. 399–400 in this volume).

Address at NAACP Mass Rally for Civil Rights

10 July 1960
Los Angeles, Calif.

On the eve of the Democratic National Convention, demonstrators marched to the convention site where they held a brief rally. King, Roy Wilkins, Adam Clayton Powell, and presidential hopeful John F. Kennedy were among those who addressed the marchers that day. Facing scattered boos because of his uneven record on civil rights, Kennedy told the audience that "the next President of the United States cannot stand above the battle, engaging in vague sermons on brotherhood."[1] *In this typescript of his remarks,*

1. "Cheers and Boos Greet Kennedy at Rights Rally," *Los Angeles Times,* 11 July 1960.

10 July 1960

King declares: "The cause of justice and freedom has been betrayed by both political parties."[2]

Occasionally we hear both political parties talking of adopting a policy of moderation in the civil rights struggle. Our answer to this is simple. If moderation means pressing on toward the goal of justice with wise restraint and calm reasonableness, then moderation is a great virtue which all men should seek to achieve in this tense period of transition. But if moderation means slowing up in the move toward justice and capitulating to the undemocratic practices of the guardians of a deadening status quo, then moderation is a tragic vice which men of good will must condemn. The fact is that we cannot afford to slow up. The shape of the world today does not afford us the luxury of "standstillism" and token democracy.

Most of the glaring denials of basic freedoms in the south are done in the name of "states' rights". But "states' rights" are only valid as they serve to protect larger human rights. I have no opposition to state government. I believe firmly in Jeffersonian democracy, and would not advocate a centralized government with absolute sovereign powers. But I do feel that the doctrine of states' rights must not be an excuse for insurrection.

States should have rights, but no state should have the right to do wrong. There are schools in the south presently closed to Negro students, because the particular state governments refuse to comply with the Supreme Court's decision. In my own state of Georgia, the governor and the legislature are threatening to close the schools next fall in order to avoid complying with a federal court order to desegregate.[3] In such situations, I think the national government has a moral and practical responsibility to <u>federalize</u> the schools and make it palpably clear to the world that no state will be permitted to deprive its students, Negro and white, of an equal education.

The Negro, in his efforts to achieve his rights, is determined to employ only the highest weapons of dignity and discipline. We will not succumb to the temptation of flirting with violence or indulging in hot campaigns. In seeking strong civil rights legislation, we are not seeking to defeat the white man, but to help him as well as ourselves. The festering sore of segregation debilitates the white man as well as the Negro.

---

2. According to a press account, King also stated that the demonstration was "indicative that we consider civil rights one of the most significant and vital issues facing our nation today." He added that the protesters had come "to urge the great Democratic party to take this issue seriously and earnestly plead with them to deal with this issue as one of the basic moral issues facing the world today" (Louis Lautier, "Rev. Powell Steals Show at NAACP Pre-Convention Rally," *Richmond Afro-American,* 23 July 1960).

3. In 1959, Atlanta district court judge Frank A. Hooper ordered the local board of education to prepare a plan to desegregate the city's schools. The board proposed gradual desegregation, but this plan met opposition from Georgia governor Ernest Vandiver. The following year, Vandiver created the General Assembly Committee on Schools, chaired by Georgia lawyer John A. Sibley, to investigate options to resolve the school crisis. In April 1960, the committee was unable to reach an unanimous decision and released two different plans.

The cause of justice and freedom has been betrayed by both political parties. We have looked patiently to Washington for our Constitutional rights, and then we have found a conspiracy of apathy and hypocrisy. Now we are tired. We are compelled to take the struggle into our own limited hands because for 100 years successive Republican and Democratic national administrations have failed to enforce our Constitutional liberties. We cannot in all good conscience wait any longer. In the spirit of the students, we continue our "sit-ins" against segregation until our national government begins it "stand ups" for justice.

TD. NAACP DLC. Group III-A175.

To Friend of Freedom

18 July 1960
Atlanta, Ga.

In the following form letter, King requests money to expand SCLC's program and to cover legal fees for student protesters and the ministers who had been charged with libel by Alabama officials.[1] *King asks that potential donors "think of a few of our heroic board members such as Daisy Bates, Fred Shuttlesworth, C. K. Steele, Ralph D. Abernathy," as well as the student activists: "If they can face jeering and hostile mobs and suffer brutal and nightmarish bombings to advance justice, how can you and I be less generous in our support?"*

Dear Friend of Freedom:

This is a form letter. But, I want you to know that it is as personal and serious as anything I have ever written. It is an appeal for your support for the Southern freedom struggle.[2] Therefore, I hope you will read every word of this letter with deep and sympathetic concern.[3]

---

1. For more on the libel case, see John Malcolm Patterson to King, 9 May 1960, pp. 456–458 in this volume.

2. King's handwritten draft of this letter included the following additional sentence: "It is an appeal for your backing in one of the most decisive moment in our quest for justice and human dignity" (King, Draft, Form letter to Friend of freedom, 18 July 1960).

3. In King's draft, he ended this sentence with "reverent attention." He continued: "The struggle for freedom in the south has entered upon a new stage, presenting us with unprecedented opportunities to advance. The ~~student sit-in movement has~~ young students of the south, through sit-ins and other demonstrations, have ~~demonstrated~~ given to America a glowing example of disciplined, dignified non-violent action against the system of segregation. Indeed, they have courageously grappled with a new and creative method in the crisis in race relations. I know that you have followed these activities with a great sense of pride and appreciation. [¶]You must know, however, that the people of the south have not engaged in this great movement without difficulties and trying moments. Scores of students have been arrested. In most instances they have ~~been~~ been inflicted with heavy fines. At times they have faced jeering and hostile mobs, and police forces that sought to block their peacefuls efforts with tear gas, night sticks, and fire hoses. [¶]As the student movement gained

In recent months, several developments have combined to create a "civil rights crisis" of historic depth and magnitude:

> First, southern Negro students launched a mass offensive that is cracking the walls of segregation. Their courageous and non-violent spirit has awed millions and given a new dignity to the cause of freedom. In retaliation, the southern racists have expelled them from schools, arrested and jailed them, denied them bail, and visited violence upon them.
>
> Second, the Southern Christian Leadership Conference is spearheading a crusade to bring hundreds of thousands of new Negro votes into the 1960 election.[4] The success of this campaign would, we are convinced, be one of the most important steps toward winning the Negro's equal rights in America.
>
> Third, as the student sit-ins and voting crusade struggled on with grim determination, a vicious attack was directed against me by the State of Alabama. With calculation, the State indicted me on obviously false charges of perjury. When they moved to aid me, four of my close associates were also struck by the State. Having endorsed an advertisment in the New York Times appealing for funds on my behalf and the students, four SCLC board members, Reverends Ralph D. Abernathy, J. E. Lowery, Fred Shuttlesworth, and S. S. Seay, are being sued by the City Commissioners of Montgomery and the Governor of Alabama for two and one half million dollars for libel.
>
> It is clear what the segregationists are attempting to do. Faced with the ending of their old order they would delay their demise by destroying the heroic mass student movement, by destroying uncompromising Negro leadership, and by demolishing our organizations of struggle and protest.

You can prevent this by giving your moral and financial support. Each of the aforementioned developments has given to the Southern Christian Leadership Conference new and heavy responsibilities. Funds are desparately needed NOW for legal defense; for the student movement which constantly calls on our organization for aid and guidance; for carrying our message of non-violence across the South thru institutes and workshops; and for continuing our voting crusade. We need to expand our staff and to put experienced students and adults on the field to propagate an understanding of non-violent resistance.[5] Please help us make the Southern Christian Leadership Conference strong for our battle.

---

momentum, the Rev. Martin Luther King Jr, spiritual leader and guide of the southern non-violent movement, was indicted by the State of Alabama on charges of perjury in connection with his state income tax return. Although he has been acquitted on one count of these false charges by an all white jury of Montgomery county, there is still need for financial aid to meet the legal expenses involved."

4. In December 1959, SCLC and the NAACP announced plans for a voter registration campaign aimed at registering over one million additional black voters before the 1960 presidential election (Charles Moore, "Drive Launched Here Seeks Million More Negro Voters," *Atlanta Constitution,* 29 December 1959).

5. King's draft: "We are constantly called upon to assist the students in financing their heroic movement. In some instances we are called upon to assist students in paying fines, attorney fees, and scholarship aid. At the same time we hope during the summer to employ students in various communities throughout the south to keep burning the spirit of the sit-ins, so that the movement may press forward in September when [*school?*] resumes."

I appeal to you to hlep us make the most of the historic opportunities before us. PLEASE SEND WHATEVER CONTRIBUTION YOU CAN AFFORD TODAY. Speed your gift now in the enclosed envelope. NO POSTAGE IS NECESSARY. In addition to your immediate contribution, I would also like to urge you to make an annual pledge to our organization. Also, have your church, club, or other organization to do likewise. This will keep our work going on a substantial basis. The pledge card is enclosed—please return it today with your contribution. As you write your check think of a few of our heroic board members such as Daisy Bates, Fred Shuttlesworth, C. K. Steele, Ralph D. Abernathy, only to mention a few, and the heroic students of the South. If they can face jeering and hostile mobs and suffer brutal and nightmarish bombings to advance justice, how can you and I be less generous in our support?

Yours for the cause of freedom,
[*signed*] Martin Luther King Jr.
Martin Luther King, Jr.
President

Attest: Ralph D. Abernathy
Financial Secretary-Treasurer

MLK:lmh
Enclosures: 2

P.S. If you receive more than one of these letters, then please pass it on to a friend.

THLS. ERC-NHyF.

From Ella J. Baker

20 July 1960

Shortly before resigning as executive director, Baker recommends that Bob Moses be sent to assist leaders of SCLC's Louisiana affiliate, the United Christian Movement.[1] *Moses, a high school math teacher, had come to know Baker while volunteering at*

1. Baker cited "the need for some extended rest" and upcoming cataract surgery as reasons for her 1 August resignation (Baker, Form letter to Friend, 31 July 1960). Robert Parris Moses (1935–), born in New York City, received a B.A. (1956) from Hamilton College and an M.A. (1957) from Harvard University. While teaching math at Horace Mann School in New York City from 1958 to 1961, Moses volunteered for SCLC and other civil rights organizations. He began working full-time for SNCC in 1961, moving to southwestern Mississippi to develop voter registration and education projects, and was named co-director of the Council of Federated Organizations (COFO) in 1962. Moses developed the idea that germinated into the 1964 Mississippi Summer Project and the Mississippi Freedom Democratic Party (MFDP). Following the MFDP's failure to unseat the state's all-white delegates at the 1964 Democratic National Convention in Atlantic City, Moses left Mississippi. In 1966, he went to Canada to avoid the draft, and two years later traveled to Tanzania to teach mathematics. He returned to the United States in 1976 and founded a math literacy program, the Algebra Project, with a five-year MacArthur fellowship he was awarded in 1982.

SCLC's Atlanta headquarters during the summer; he had previously worked with Bayard Rustin in New York on behalf of SCLC.[2] *Later that summer, Moses traveled to Louisiana, Mississippi, and Alabama recruiting students to attend the fall SNCC conference.*[3]

TO: Dr. Martin L. King
FROM: Ella J. Baker
RE: Mr. Robert Moses—Shreveport, La.

I talked with Dr. Simpkins in Shreveport, last night, and he indicated that special voter-registration efforts will be made during the month of August, covering the North Louisiana area.[4] Simultaneously, the United Christian Movement will be helping to process complainants who might be used if a hearing by the Civil Rights Commission is re-scheduled.[5] Representatives from the Commission presently, are in the area, and it appears that a hearing might be held later. In light of this, Mr. Robert Moses might be helpful, and gain some value experience, working with Rev. Blake and Dr. Simpkins.[6]

It is planned that students will be used in the person-to-person contacts for voter-registration in the area.

Attached hereto is a memorandum on the comparative cost of, and time involved in travelling from Atlanta to Shreveport, Louisiana, in the event you wish to consider having Mr. Moses go.[7]

TL. MLKP-MBU: Box 31.

---

2. Moses had been encouraged by Wyatt Walker to become involved with SCLC's New York office during a spring 1960 mass meeting in Newport News, Virginia (Moses, Interview by Clayborne Carson, 29 March 1982).

3. For more on SNCC's fall conference, see King, Outline, The Philosophy of Nonviolence, 14 October 1960, pp. 520–521 in this volume.

4. Cuthbert O. Simpkins, a Shreveport dentist, was a member of SCLC's executive board. He helped co-found the United Christian Movement in the spring of 1957 and shortly thereafter became the organization's president.

5. SCLC, the United Christian Movement, and other Louisiana-based organizations had sent seventy-eight "complaints of denial of voting rights" to the Civil Rights Commission in late 1959. A public hearing was scheduled to take place in Shreveport on 13 July 1959 but was blocked by the State of Louisiana (SCLC, *The Crusader,* November 1959). The Civil Rights Commission held hearings in New Orleans in September 1960 and May 1961.

6. Harry Blake became SCLC's first field secretary in March 1960.

7. Ernestine Brown, Memo to Baker, 20 July 1960.

From Malcolm X

21 July 1960
East Elmhurst, N.Y.

Nation of Islam minister Malcolm X invites King "as a spokesman and fellow-leader of our people" to a Harlem rally.[1] *In a 10 August reply, King's secretary Maude Ballou informed Malcolm X that this invitation, forwarded from the NAACP office in New York, "arrived after your program was held."*

Rev. Martin Luther King
NAACP
21 West 40th Street
New York, N.Y.

Dear Rev. King:

An "Education" Rally" will be held Sunday, July 31st at 1 PM in the 369th Armory, 5th Avenue and 142nd Street.[2]

Mr. Elijah Muhammad, the spiritual head of the fastest growing group of Moslems in the Western Hemisphere will be the principle speaker.

Since so much controversy has been spoken and written about Mr. Muhammad and his "Black Muslims," we invite you as a spokesman and fellow-leader of our people to be among our invited guests, so you can see and hear Mr. Muhammad for yourself and then make a more intelligent appraisal of his teachings, his methods and his program.[3]

All invited guests will be given time to make any statements, comments or observations that they may desire. If you plan to attend, please write me at the above address, or call OLympia 1–6320.

Sincerely,
[*signed*]
Malcolm X,

1. A newspaper advertisement for the rally listed King as one of the "invited guest speakers" ("Muhammad Is Coming to Harlem," *New York Amsterdam News,* 23 July 1960). An earlier advertisement indicated that King had been invited to a Nation of Islam rally in May 1960 ("Harlem Freedom Rally," *New York Amsterdam News,* 21 May 1960). Shortly after the conclusion of the Montgomery bus protest, Ballou had thanked Malcolm X for sending several letters and articles to King (Ballou to Malcolm X, 1 February 1957, in *Papers* 4:117).

2. For more on the rally, see "8,500 Crowd Armory to Hear Muhammad," *New York Amsterdam News,* 6 August 1960.

3. A week before the rally Malcolm X publicly "challenged Roy Wilkins, Martin Luther King, Thurgood Marshall and Jackie Robinson" to attend the event to "prove they weren't acting as 'paid parrots' for their white 'liberal bosses,' when they accused the Muslims of being a 'Black Ku Klux Klan, Black Supremists, and Racial Extremists'" ("A Switch—Muslims to Admit Whites to Rally!" *New York Amsterdam News,* 30 July 1960).

25 July 1960

Minister of Muhammad's New York Temple of Islam

MX:nx

TLS. MLKP-MBU: Box 10.

Interview by Lee Nichols at Republican National Convention

[25 July 1960]
[Chicago, Ill.]

Delegates attending the opening session of the Republican National Convention at Chicago's Amphitheater waded through five thousand picketers led by King, Randolph, and Wilkins. The protesters shouted "Jim Crow must go" and snarled area traffic until a Republican official promised a convention floor debate over the party's civil rights plank.[1] *The following transcript was drawn from NBC film footage of the demonstration.*

[*Announcer*]: [*words inaudible*] Beside him is the Reverend Martin Luther King, one of the leaders of this march. Lee is going to ask him what this is all about—what they hope to accomplish. So let's go outside the amphitheater to the street corner and to Lee Nichols.[2]

[*Nichols*]: [*words inaudible*] about five thousand marchers. How's this [*words inaudible*] compare to the one in Los Angeles?

[*King*]: It's about the same. We urged five thousand people to participate. We had about five thousand in Los Angeles, and I understand we have five thousand or more today. So I think it's equally successful.

[*Nichols*]: What's the purpose of the demonstration? What do you hope it would achieve?

[*King*]: Well, we are here to dramatize the significance of the civil rights issue. We feel that this is the most pressing moral issue facing our nation, and we are here to urge the Republican Party to come out with a strong, forthright civil rights plank in the platform.

[*Nichols*]: Do you consider that a specific mention, support of the sit-in demonstrations is important in the plank?

---

1. Thomas Powers, "5,000 Demonstrate for Civil Rights Plank," *Chicago Tribune*, 26 July 1960.

2. Leland L. Nichols (1929–), born in Hawthorne, California, earned a B.A. (1950) and an M.S. (1952) from the University of California at Los Angeles. Nichols began his career in broadcasting as an intern at NBC in 1954 and was hired as a reporter and commentator, covering political news and the 1960 Democratic and Republican national conventions. Nichols later worked in California state government and public broadcasting before teaching at California State University, Sacramento (1970–1992).

[*King*]: Yes, I think it's very important. As you know the Democratic Party in its plank at least expressed sympathy for the sit-ins, and I think the Republican Party should do the same. In fact, I would like to see the Party come out with an explicit statement endorsing the sit-in demonstration.[3] 25 July 1960

[*Nichols*]: There's been a suggestion that the Republican platform not promise more than can be delivered. Do you think that the Democratic plank on civil rights promise more than can be delivered?

[*King*]: Well, this is difficult to say. We will have to wait to see. They have promised to deliver it. We would hope so, and we will certainly demand and urge the leaders of the party to come out with it. Whether this will be done is something else, but the implementation is certainly the important issue now.

[*Nichols*]: Have you had a chance to compare the points of those fourteen points approved by Vice President Nixon and Nelson Rockefeller?[4] How does that point compare to the Democratic platform plank?

[*King*]: Well, I think it's [*break in tape*] very well. Mr. Rockefeller and Mr. Nixon came out with something very significant and important, and I think it [*words inaudible*] with it very well. Now, whether this will come out as the final statement of the final plank is not known yet, but I think this would be very important if it does emerge.

[*Nichols*]: Well, I thank you very much, Reverend Martin Luther King. This is Lee Nichols in front of the amphitheater with the NBC mobile unit.[5]

F. NBCNA-NNNBC.

3. The final draft of the 1960 Republican platform reaffirmed "the constitutional right to peaceable assembly to protest discrimination by private business establishments" and applauded "the action of the businessmen who have abandoned discriminatory practices in retail establishments." The platform also pledged "the full use of power, resources and leadership of the Federal Government to eliminate discrimination based on race, color, religion or national origin" (*Official Report of the Proceedings of the Republican National Convention* [Washington, D.C.: Republican National Committee, 1960], p. 256).

4. On 22–23 July, Vice President Richard Nixon met with New York governor and Republican candidate Nelson A. Rockefeller to draft a platform to be ratified by the convention's platform committee (William Fulton, "Platform Views Outlined by Nixon and Rockefeller: 14 Points Agreed Upon Called a Basis for Victory Planks," *Chicago Tribune*, 24 July 1960).

5. As the camera pulls away, the film focuses on a large group of protesters carrying signs that read "End School Segregation—Endorse Supreme Court Decision" and "End Your Equivocation—Oppose Job Discrimination—Support FEPC."

To William Michelson

3 August 1960
[*Atlanta, Ga.*]

King thanks New York labor official William Michelson for his 22 July letter and financial contribution.[1] *On 18 July, King had wired Michelson and his union colleague Cleveland Robinson requesting help to cover legal costs and fines incurred by students and ministers working to end segregation in Alabama.*[2]

Mr. William Michelson
Organization Director
District 65
Retail, Wholesale and Department Store Union
13 Astor Place
New York 3, New York

Dear Mr. Michaelson:

This is to acknowledge receipt of your very kind letter of July 22, with the enclosed check of three thousand dollars ($3,000.00) for the southern struggle which we discussed by telephone.

It is difficult to express the depth of appreciation which we in the South so warmly feel for support of this kind. The students and I have in common not only the objectives we seek, but we have both tasted the fierce onslaughts of the official machinery of government here in the South. Thousands of students were subjected to brutality, arrests and jailings which they faced with quiety heroism. It is probably unnecessary to say more in their praise than that both the Democratic and Republican National Conventions knew they had to give recognition to these student actions and each convention advanced a considerable distance in its platform promises. In the attack on me, which was in reality an attack on all militant Negro leadership in the South, a significant victory was scored when the jury rendered a verdict of acquittal.[3] None of these successes would have been possible had not devoted people like yourself and your associates organized support so promptly and so effectively.

I hope you will convey my deepest gratitude to all those who worked with you. Our fight continues and we here in the South are strengthened by the knowledge

---

1. William Michelson (1914–1989), born in Chelsea, Massachusetts, was an organizer and official of several New York unions, including the Storeworkers Union Local 2, the Retail, Wholesale and Department Store Union (RWDSU), and the United Store Workers Union. Michelson was elected a member of the New York City Central Labor Council's executive board in 1959 and received their Distinguished Service Award in 1962. A member of the Board of Trustees of New York City's Health and Hospitals Corporation, Michelson helped develop health care benefits for unionized workers.

2. King sent a similar telegram to UPWA international vice president Russell Lasley on 19 July.

3. See King, Statement on Perjury Acquittal, 28 May 1960, p. 462 in this volume.

that your determination, like ours, will continue until democratic rights become a reality for every person in our land.

I will certainly look forward to hearing from you as soon as our good friend Cleveland Robinson returns.[4] Whatever additional {funds} you can send will be of tremendous help in the days ahead. I can never tire of saying that District 65 has proved to be one of the most invaluable friends for those of us who are struggling in the South to make Democracy and justice a reality.

Very sincerely yours,
Martin L. King, Jr.

TLc. MLKP-MBU: Box 31.

4. In his 22 July letter, Michelson expressed certainty that upon the return of secretary-treasurer Robinson, the union's Negro Affairs Committee would arrange "to send some additional funds." Cleveland Robinson became secretary-treasurer of District 65, RWDSU in 1952. He was elected vice president of the Negro American Labor Council in 1960.

To John Malcolm Patterson

9 August 1960
[*Atlanta, Ga.*]

King writes Alabama's governor, expressing "astonishment" that Alabama State College president H. Councill Trenholm had pledged to suppress student and faculty activism. Governor Patterson had earlier threatened to fire Trenholm if he proved unable to maintain order on campus.[1] *At King's request, Maude Ballou forwarded a copy of this telegram to Trenholm.*[2]

1. Trenholm assured the Alabama State Board of Education that he would "redouble" efforts to prevent further demonstrations and that those remaining at Alabama State "will do so because of proper conduct." He also submitted a report detailing the changes at the college since the protest began as well as the precautions taken to prevent a reoccurrence. A news report indicated that Patterson "was satisfied with the work Trenholm has done" ("Bridle on Outbreaks Pledged by Trenholm," *Montgomery Advertiser,* 21 July 1960; see also King to Patrick Murphy Malin, Roy Wilkins, and Carl J. Megel, 16 June 1960, pp. 471–472 in this volume). In an October article in *Ebony,* King said that the student sit-ins would force college presidents "to make a choice between expediency and a course of action based on principle and morality." He further asserted "that there is no painless way to effect social change" and maintained that "every president must realize that he, too, is involved in this great struggle and that in the process he may lose his job" (Lerone Bennett, Jr., "The Plight of Negro College Presidents," *Ebony,* October 1960, p. 144).

2. Ballou to Trenholm, 9 August 1960. King also sent copies to Randolph and Wilkins explaining that he had "felt compelled to get some word to the Governor which would indirectly condemn Mr. Trenhom for taking such a cowardly position" and asking that they send similar messages to Patterson (King to Wilkins and King to Randolph, both dated 9 August 1960). Wilkins had previously wired Patterson on 17 June, conveying his dismay at the governor's handling of the Alabama State situation. Randolph wrote Patterson on 15 August.

GOVERNOR JOHN PATTERSON

WE HAVE LEARNED WITH ASTONISHMENT OF THE PLEDGE THAT YOU EXTRACTED FROM PRESIDENT H C TRENHOLM OF ALABAMA STATE COLLEGE THAT THE STUDENTS OF THAT COLLEGE WOULD NOT PARTICIPATE IN ANY MORE ANTI SEGREGATION DEMONSTRATIONS AND THAT THE FACULTY OF THAT COLLEGE WOULD REMAIN LOYAL TO ALABAMA SEGREGATION LAWS. YOU MUST KNOW THE PRESIDENT OF THIS COLLEGE DOES NOT POSSESS THE AUTHORITY TO PLEDGE AWAY THE RIGHTS OF THE AMERICAN CITIZENS WHO HAPPEN TO BE ATTENDING OR TEACHING AT ALABAMA STATE COLLEGE. THE AMERICAN PEOPLE REPUDIATE THIS IMPOSSIBLE PLEDGE AND DENOUNCE THOSE WHO ARE RESPONSIBLE FOR IT. STUDENTS AND FACULTY MEMBERS NOT ONLY HAVE THE RIGHT OF PEACEFUL ASSEMBLY AND PROTEST BUT HAVE THE OBLIGATION TO OPPOSE THE EVIL SYSTEM OF RACIAL DISCRIMINATION AND SEGREGATION THAT HAS BEEN CONDEMNED BY BOTH NATIONAL POLITICAL PARTIES. WE CALL UPON YOU TO RELEASE DR. TRENHOLM FROM THIS HUMILIATING PLEDGE THAT YOU HAD HIM GIVE AT YOUR STATE BOARD OF EDUCATION MEETING JULY 20TH.

MARTIN LUTHER H KING JR PRESIDENT
THE SOUTHERN CHRISTIAN LEADERSHIP CONFERENCE

PWc. MLKP-MBU: Box 73A.

To William P. Rogers

18 August 1960
[*Atlanta, Ga.*]

King requests that the U.S. attorney general initiate an "immediate investigation" into the mistreatment of Fred Shuttlesworth's three teenage children, who were arrested on 16 August for refusing to move to the back of an interstate bus in Gadsden, Alabama.[1] *On 2 September assistant attorney general Harold Tyler replied: "You may be assured that the matter is receiving the Department's careful attention and that appropriate action will be taken should it develop that violations of federal laws are involved." Two weeks later, Alabama juvenile court judge W. W. Rayburn found*

1. King sent similar telegrams to the chairman of the Interstate Commerce Commission and the president of Greyhound Lines (King to John H. Winchel and King to F. W. Ackerman, both dated 18 August 1960). The wire to the Greyhound official included an additional line: "If some positive action is not forthcoming it may be necessary to call on leaders across the country to join in boycott of Greyhound to make it undeniably clear we will not spend our dollars with a company that does not respect our person." Greyhound official H. Vance Greenslit replied that it was "not the policy of Greyhound Lines to interfere with the seating of interstate passengers" (SCLC, Press release, August 1960). In a 24 August letter to Roy Wilkins, Wyatt Tee Walker broached the idea of a conference between representatives from the NAACP, CORE, and SCLC to discuss ideas "to correct the many discrepancies of interstate and intrastate travel in the South with Greyhound."

the Shuttlesworth children guilty of delinquency and placed them on indefinite probation.[2]

TO: ATTY. GENL. WILLIAM P. ROGERS
DEPARTMENT OF JUSTICE
WASHINGTON, D.C.

REQUEST IMMEDIATE INVESTIGATION OF VIOLATION CIVIL RIGHTS CHILDREN AGED 13, 14 & 17 YEARS OF REV. FRED SHUTTLESWORTH WHILE ENROUTE FROM MONTEAGLE, TENN. TO BIRMINGHAM, ALA. AUG 16, 1960 VIA GREYHOUND BUS.[3] CHILDREN WERE ASKED TO MOVE TO REAR OF BUS FOR SEGREGATED SEATING AT CHATANOOGA, TENN. THEY REFUSED. AT GADSEN, ALA. DRVER CALLED POLICE AND HAD CHILDREN ARRESTED. WERE SUBJECTED TO POLICE BRUTALITY IN JAIL.[4] THESE FACTS CONFIRMED. FORTHRIGHT ACTION BY YOUR OFFICE MOST NECESSARY IN VIEW OF OBVIOUS INTENT BY SOME PERSONS, AND PUBLIC AND PRIVATE AGENCIES TO CONTINUE DENIAL OF CIVIL RIGHTS FOR THE NEGRO AND HIS EQUAL PROTECTION AND JUSTICE UNDER LAW.

MARTIN LUTHER KING, JR., PRES
SCLC
208 AUBURN AVE. — ROOM 203

TWc. RWP-DLC.

---

2. Immediately following the 16 September hearing, Len Holt, the attorney for the three Shuttlesworth children—Patricia Anne, Ruby Fredericka, and Fred Lee, Jr.—announced that he would file an appeal ("Delinquency—Alabama Style," *Southern Patriot*, October 1960). On behalf of his daughter Patricia, Shuttlesworth filed a nine million dollar lawsuit against Southeastern Greyhound, but the suit was dismissed in November 1961 (*Shuttlesworth v. City of Birmingham*, 273 Ala. 713).

3. When arrested, the children were traveling from a youth workshop at Tennessee's Highlander Folk School to their home in Birmingham. In 1946, the U.S. Supreme Court had ruled segregation on interstate buses unconstitutional (*Morgan v. Virginia*, 328 U.S. 373).

4. An SCLC press release detailed the physical abuse of the children: "One of the girls was slapped by policemen and Fred, Jr. was choked when he came to the defense of his sister." Wyatt T. Walker, in Alabama at the time of the arrests, saw the children and reported that "there was an obvious swelling and bloodshot condition of the younger daughter's eye that required medical attention" (SCLC, Press release, 29 August 1960). For additional details on the children's arrest, see Patricia Shuttlesworth et al., Interview, 20 August 1960.

To Johnnie H. Goodson

29 August 1960
[*Atlanta, Ga.*]

King urges Jacksonville, Florida, NAACP president Johnnie H. Goodson to "adhere strictly to non violence" two days after violence erupted between local civil rights demonstrators and segregationists.[1] *In Goodson's 2 September reply, he denounced violence as a means to achieve justice but affirmed "the right of individual and collective self-defense against unlawful assaults."*

JOHN J GOODSON
PRES JACKSONVILLE NAACP
1505 WEST 15 ST

AM DEEPLY SYMPATHETIC TO STRESS AND STRAIN ENCOUNTERED IN YOUR STRUGGLE FOR HUMAN DIGNITY. STRONGLY URGE THAT EVEN IN THE FACE OF SEVERE OR AGGRESSIVE VIOLENCE THAT YOU ADHERE STRICTLY TO NON VIOLENCE IN EVERY CIRCUMSTANCE VIOLENCE IN OUR STRUGGLE, AGGRESSIVE OR RETALITORY IS IMMORAL AND IMPRACTICABLE. AS DIFFICULT AS IT MAY BE TOTAL COMMITMENT TO NON VIOLENCE IN OUR STRUGGLE WILL ALONE SUFFICE TO REDEEM THE SOUL OF AMERICA. HEED NOT THE CALL TO ARMS. PLEAD EARNESTLY WITH YOUTH TO PUT UP THEIR WEAPONS EVEN THOUGH OUR LONG YEARS OF OPPRESSION SOME TIMES AROUSES AN UNCONSCIOUS RESENTMENT WITHIN WE MUST NOT SUCCUMB TO THE TEMPTATION OF BECOMING BITTER OR OF MEETING VIOLENCE WITH VIOLENCE. THERE IS NO POWER ON EARTH WHICH CAN OVER COME THE MAJESTIC OR GRANDEUR EVIDENCED IN THE CHALLENGEING WILLINGNESS OF A PEOPLE TO SACRIFICE AND SUFFER FOR THEIR RIGHTS. IF I CAN BE ON ANY ASSISTANCE IN THIS MOMENT OF CRISIS EVEN IF IT MEANS MAKING A PERSONAL VISIT TO JACKSONVILLE PLEASE FEEL FREE TO CALL ON ME[2]

MARTIN LUTHER KING JR
PRESIDENT
SOUTHERN CHRISTIAN LEADERSHIP CONFERENCE

PHWc. MLKP-MBU: Box 73A.

---

1. On 27 August, in response to sit-in demonstrations in downtown Jacksonville, whites armed with "baseball bats, ax handles, and heavy walking sticks" attacked black citizens and protesters. The Klansmen chased the demonstrators into black neighborhoods, where local black youth gangs retaliated. During the riot, more than one hundred people were arrested and approximately sixty-five were injured. Following the violent weekend, the local NAACP youth chapter postponed sit-in demonstrations scheduled for 29 August ("Violence Flares in Jacksonville," *New York Times,* 28 August 1960, and "Sit-Ins Halted in Jacksonville," *Atlanta Daily World,* 30 August 1960). Johnnie Hamilton Goodson, Sr. (1914–1992) was born in Gadsden County, Florida. A veteran of World War II, Goodson taught tailoring at Walker's Business College in Florida. A Prince Hall Free Mason, he was an active member of the Jacksonville NAACP and served briefly as the organization's president in 1960.

2. Goodson also expressed appreciation for King's offer of assistance but assured him that "we are fully able to meet what ever situation that may arise." King's assistant James Wood responded on his behalf and conveyed "hopes for an early restoration of relief from tension in your city" (Wood to Goodson, 23 September 1960).

"The Rising Tide of Racial Consciousness," Address at the Golden Anniversary Conference of the National Urban League

6 September 1960
New York, N.Y.

In this typed draft of his address, King asserts that "there need be no essential conflict" between the Urban League's efforts to help "the Negro adjust to urban living" and the need for "more militant civil rights organizations" to present a "frontal attack on the system of segregation." He advises that "the NAACP'er must not look upon the Urban Leaguer as a quiet conservative and the Urban Leaguer must not look upon the NAACP'er as a militant troublemaker. Each must accept the other as a necessary partner in the complex yet exciting struggle to free the Negro." King concludes by calling for the realization of democratic American ideals in a land "where men do not argue that the color of a man's skin determines the content of his character."[1] *King delivered his remarks before an overflow audience of nearly three thousand at the Community Church of New York.*[2]

I am indeed happy to have the opportunity of being with you on this auspicious occasion. I bring warm and sincere greetings to you from the Southern Christian Leadership Conference and all of its affiliate organizations. For fifty long years you have worked assiduously to improve the social and economic conditions of Negro citizens through interracial teamwork. Under the dedicated leadership of Lester B. Granger your purposes have always been noble and your work has always been creatively meaningful. One day all of America will take pride in your achievements. Now as you face the unfolding sixties with the problems of urban dislocation mounting on every hand, your work will be even more necessary. It is my hope and prayer that all people of goodwill will join and support you as you face the difficult, yet challenging days ahead.

I have been asked to speak this evening from the subject "The Rising Tide of Racial Consciousness." While I feel that a social scientist would be much more competent to interpret the emotions, the economics and the politics that have pro-

1. An abridged version of this address was later published in the December 1960 issue of the *YWCA Magazine.*

2. "King Stirs Urban League N.Y. Meet," *Atlanta Inquirer,* 14 September 1960. Following the event King thanked Lester Granger, who served as executive director of the National Urban League from 1941 until 1961, for arranging the speech. King also apologized for inadvertently disclosing to a reporter that the Urban League intended to give him a $500 honorarium for his appearance, despite the organization's policy against contributing to other civil rights causes (King to Granger, 28 September 1960, and Trezzvant W. Anderson, "The Truth about Earnings of Dr. Martin Luther King," *Pittsburgh Courier,* 18 June 1960). Granger reassured King that he was not "upset" over the statement and explained that "while our honorarium did violate the spirit of our organization's policy, it did not violate the letter—for we have a right to determine our honoraria." Granger further conveyed that he was "glad that the incident happened" because "it gave me a chance to get a letter from you which I treasure very much" (Granger to King, 30 September 1960).

duced the tide of racial pride and self-consciousness sweeping through the Negro group, I will seek to bring my limited insights to bare on this important theme.

We are all familiar with the historical circumstances and the psychological conditions that gave many Negroes a sense of inferiority. From 1619 through 1862 the Negro was forced to live through the long night of slavery. He was little more than a depersonalized cog in a vast plantation machine. After slavery ended the Negro found himself shackled with the cruel chains of segregation. Living with these conditions many Negroes lost faith in themselves and came to feel that perhaps they were less than human. But as the years unfolded something happened to the Negro. He began to look at himself in a new light. He came to feel a new sense of "somebodiness."

What are the factors that have led to this new sense of dignity and self-respect on the part of the Negro?

First, we must mention the population shift from rural to urban life. For many years the vast majority of Negroes were isolated on the rural plantation. They had very little contact with the world outside their geographical boundaries. But gradually circumstances made it possible and necessary for them to migrate to new and larger centers—the spread of the automobile, the great depression, and the social upheavals of the two world wars. These new contacts led to a broadened outlook. These new levels of communication brought new and different attitudes.

A second factor that has caused the Negroes' new self consciousness has been his rapid educational advance. Over the years there has been a steady decline of crippling illiteracy. At emancipation only five percent of the Negroes were literate. Today more than ninty-five percent are literate. Constant streams of Negro students are finishing colleges and universities every year. More than sixteen hundred Negroes have received the highest academic degree bestowed by an American university. These educational advances have naturally broadened his thinking. They have given the Negro not only a larger view of the world, but also a larger view of himself.

A third factor that produced the new sense of pride in the Negro was the gradual improvement of his economic status. While the Negro is still the victim of tragic economic exploitation, significant strides have been made. The annual collective income of the Negro is now approximately 18 billion dollars, which is more than the national income of Canada and all of the exports of the United States. This augmented purchasing power has been reflected in more adequate housing, improved medical care and greater educational opportunities. As these changes have taken place they have driven the Negro to change his image of himself.

A fourth factor that brought about the new sense of pride in the Negro was the Supreme Court's decision outlawing segregation in the public schools. For all men of goodwill May 17, 1954, came as a joyous daybreak to end the long night of enforced segregation. In simple, eloquent and unequivocal language the court affirmed that "separate but equal" facilities are inherently unequal, and that to segregate a child on the basis of his race is to deny that child equal protection of the law. This decision brought hope to millions of disinherited Negroes who had formerly dared only to dream of freedom. Like an exit sign that suddenly appeared to one who had walked through a long and desolate corridor, this decision came as a way out of the darkness of segregation. It served to transform the fatigue of despair into the bouyancy of hope. It further enhanced the Negro's sense of dignity.

A fifth factor that has accounted for the new sense of dignity on the part of the Negro has been the awareness that his struggle for freedom is a part of a world wide struggle. He has watched developments in Asia and Africa with rapt attention. On these vast prodigious continents dwell two-thirds of the world's people. For years they were exploited economically, dominated politically, segregated and humiliated by foreign powers. But there comes a time when people get tired of being trampled over by the iron feet of oppression. So the wind of change began blowing in Asia and Africa—and what a mighty wind it is! Fourteen years ago the British Empire had under her domination more than six hundred million people in Asia and Africa. But that number will be reduced to less than forty million (40,000,000) after Nigeria receives her independence a few days from now.[3] Thirty years ago there were only three independent countries in the whole of Africa—Liberia, Ethopia and South Africa. By 1962 there may be as many as thirty independent nations in Africa. These rapid changes have naturally influenced the thinking of the American Negro. He knows that his struggle for human dignity is not an isolated event. It is a drama being played on the stage of the world with spectators and supporters from every continent.

These are the factors which have conjoined to cause the Negro to take a new look at himself. He has come to feel that he is somebody. He is no longer ashamed of the color of his skin or the texture of his hair. He has come to see the meaning of the words of the eloquent poet:

Fleecy locks and black complexion
Cannot forfeit nature's claim
Skin may differ, but affection
Dwells in black and white the same.
And were I so tall as to reach the pole
Or to grasp the ocean at a span
I must be measured by my soul,
The mind is the standard of the man.[4]

This growing self-respect has inspired the Negro with a new determination to struggle and sacrifice until first-class citizenship becomes a reality. This is at bottom the meaning of what is happening in the South today. Whether it is manifested in nine brave children of Little Rock walking through jeering and hostile mobs, or 50,000 people of Montgomery, Alabama, substituting tired feet for tired souls and walking the streets of that city for 381 days, or thousands of courageous students electrifying the nation by quietly and non-violently sitting at lunch counters that have been closed to them because of the color of their skin, the motivation is always the same—the Negro would rather suffer in dignity than accept segregation in humiliation.

This new determination on the part of the Negro has not been welcomed by

---

3. Nigeria gained its independence on 1 October 1960; the following month, King attended the inauguration of Nnamdi Azikiwe, Nigeria's governor-general and commander-in-chief (see Azikiwe to King, 26 October 1960, pp. 533–534 in this volume).

4. The first four lines are quoted from "The Negro's Complaint" (1788) by William Cowper, and the remaining lines are quoted from *Horae Lyricae,* "False Greatness" (1706) by Isaac Watts.

some segments of the nation's population. In some instances it has collided with tenacious and determined resistance. This resistance has risen at times to ominous proportions. A few states have reacted in open defiance. The legislative halls of the South ring loud with such words as "interposition" and "nullification." Many public officials are going to the absurd and fanatical extreme of closing the schools rather than to comply with the law of the land.

This resistance to the Negroes' aspirations expresses itself in the resurgence of the ku klux klan and the birth of white citizens councils. Both of these organizations are determined to preserve segregation at any cost. Members of the klan often publicly admit that they will use violence if necessary to block integration. Many of the bombings of homes, schools, churches and synogogues can be traced directly to the klan's activities. The citizens councils often argue piously that they abhor violence, but their defiance of the law and their vitriolic public pronouncements inevitably create the atmosphere in which violence thrives.

The fact is that many of these men are desperate men, they are fanatical men willing to go to any extreme to obtain their ends. Under the proud banner of white supremacy, they have proved that they will murder little children, deprive men and women of meat and bread, and initiate a reign of terror reminiscent of the gestapo practices of Adolph Hitler. They are the high priests of the false religion of racism. They would baptize their converts in the polluted waters of hate and serve them the poisonous wine of defiance.

The resistance to the Negroes' aspirations does not only express itself in obvious method of defiance, but in the subtle and skillful method of truth distortion. In an attempt to influence the minds of northern and southern liberals, the segregationists will cleverly disseminate half truths. Instead of arguing for the validity of segregation and racial inferiority on the basis of the Bible, they set their arguments on cultural and sociological grounds. The Negro is not ready for integration, they say; because of academic and cultural lags on the part of the Negro, the integration of schools will pull the white race down. They are never honest enough to admit that the academic and cultural lags in the Negro community are themselves the result of segregation and discrimination. The best way to solve any problem is to remove the cause. It is both rationally unsound and sociologically untenable to use the tragic effects of segregation as an argument for its continuation.

All of these calculated patterns—the defiance of southern legislative bodies, the activities of white supremacy organizations, and the distortions and rationalizations of the segregationists—have mounted up to massive resistance. This resistance grows out of the desperate attempt of the white south to perpetuate a system of human values that came into being under a feudalistic plantation system and which cannot survive in a day of growing urbanization and industrial expansion.

The great challenge facing the nation today is to solve this pressing problem and bring into full realization the ideals and dreams of our democracy. How we deal with this crucial situation will determine our political health as a nation and our prestige as a leader of the free world. The price that America must pay for the continued oppression of the Negro is the price of its own destruction. The hour is late; the clock of destiny is ticking out. We must act now! It is a trite yet urgently true observation that if America is to remain a first-class nation, it cannot have second-class citizens.

But after saying this I would like to make it clear that our primary reason for bringing an end to racial discrimination in America must not be the communist challenge. Nor must it be merely to appeal to Asian and African peoples. The primary reason for our uprooting racial discrimination from our society is that it is morally wrong. It is a cancerous disease that prevents us from realizing the sublime principles of our Judeo-Christian tradition. Racial discrimination substitutes an "I-it" relationship for the "I-thou" relationship.[5] It relegates persons to the status of things. Whenever racial discrimination exists it is a tragic expression of man's spiritual degeneracy and moral bankruptcy. Therefore, it must be removed not merely because it is diplomatically expedient, but because it is morally compelling.

Given this appraisal of the situation, what can be done?

Of course there is need for strong and aggressive leadership from the Federal Government. So far only the judicial branch of our government has rendered strong leadership. The executive and legislative branches have all too often been engaged in a conspiracy of silence and apathy. There must be a determined effort to arouse our government out of this apathetic slumber. In the past apathy was a moral failure. Today, it is a form of moral and political suicide.

I must make it palpably clear that the dearth of positive leadership from Washington is not confined to one political party. The fact is that both major parties have been hypocritical on the question of civil rights. Each of them has been willing to follow the long pattern of using the Negro as a political football.

It is noteworthy that both political parties have emerged with the strongest civil rights platforms in their history. They have signed huge promissory notes. But we must not be content with empty promises. We know that platforms in the past have too often been used to get elected on and not to stand on. We must demand implementation. We must make it clear that neither political party can deliver its platform promises alone. The job can only be done through a sincere determined bi-partisan effort. Both parties missed a marvelous opportunity to demonstrate their good faith on the civil rights issue by failing to pass desperately needed civil rights legislation in the post convention session of Congress.[6] Here we saw a vivid example of the same old game of hypocrisy, immoral compromises, and political chicanery. The fact remains, however, that the issue of racial injustice cannot be successfully evaded nor will it disappear with double-talk.

Another group with a vital role to play in the struggle for racial justice and equality is the white northern liberals. The racial issue that we confront in America is not a sectional but a national problem. Injustice anywhere is a threat to justice

5. Martin Buber, *I and Thou* (1937).

6. In an address two weeks earlier in Louisville, Kentucky, King had also criticized the Democratic and Republican parties: "Already the democratic majority in the senate has made a tragic blunder by allowing civil rights legislation to be tabled. I submit that if the democratic party [*strikeout illegible*] emerges from this session of Congress without supporting new civil rights legislation, merely to appease the southern Dixiecrats, it may well be committing political sucide where the negro vote is concerned" (King, Excerpts, Address at Jefferson County Armory, 23 August 1960).

everywhere. Therefore, no American can afford to be apathetic about the problem of racial justice. It is a problem that meets every man at his front door.

There is a pressing need for a liberalism in the North which is truly liberal, a liberalism that firmly believes in integration in its own community as well as in the deep South. There is need for the type of liberal who not only rises up with righteous indignation when a Negro is lynched in Mississippi, but will be equally incensed when a Negro is denied the right to live in his neighborhood, or join his professional association, or secure a top position in his business. This is no day to pay mere lip service to integration, we must pay life service to it.

There are several other agencies and groups that have significant roles to play in this all important period of our nation's history. Time will not permit me to discuss them at this point. Suffice it to say that the problem of racial injustice is so weighty in detail and broad in extent that it requires the concerted efforts of numerous individuals and institutions to bring about a solution.

In the final analysis if first-class citizenship is to become a reality for the Negro he must assume the primary responsibility for making it so. The Negro must not be victimized with the delusion of thinking that others should be more concerned than himself about his citizenship rights. Neither the white liberal nor the federal government will pass out the Negroes' rights on a silver platter.

In this period of social change the Negro must work on two fronts. On the one hand we must continue to break down the barrier of segregation. We must resist all forms of racial injustice. This resistance must always be on the highest level of dignity and discipline. It must never degenerate to the crippling level of violence. There is another way—a way as old as the insights of Jesus of Nazareth and as modern as the methods of Mahatma Gandhi. It is a way not for the weak and cowardly but for the strong and courageous. It has been variously called passive resistance, non-violent resistance or simply Christian love. It is my great hope that as the Negro plunges deeper into the quest for freedom, he will plunge deeper into the philosophy of non-violence. As a race we must work passionately and unrelentingly for first-class citizenship, but we must never use second class methods to gain it. Our aim must not be to defeat or humiliate the white man, but to win his friendship and understanding. We must never become bitter nor should we succumb to the temptation of using violence in the struggle, for if this happens, unborn generations will be the recipients of a long and desolate night of bitterness and our chief legacy to the future will be an endless reign of meaningless chaos.

I feel that this way of non-violence is vital because it is the only way to reestablish the broken community. It is the method which seeks to implement the just law by appealing to the conscience of the great decent majority who through blindness, fear, pride or irrationality have allowed their consciences to sleep.

The non-violent resistors can summarize their message in the following simple terms: we will take direct action against injustice without waiting for other agencies to act. We will not obey unjust laws or submit to unjust practices. We will do this peacefully, openly and cheerfully because our aim is to persuade. We adopt the means of non-violence because our end is a community at peace with itself. We will try to persuade with our words, but if our words fail, we will try to persuade with our acts. We will always be willing to talk and seek fair compromise, but we are ready to suffer when necessary and even risk our lives to become witnesses to the truth as we see it.

I realize that this approach will mean suffering and sacrifice. It may mean going to jail. If such is the case the resistor must be willing to fill the jail houses of the South. It may even mean physical death. But if physical death is the price that a man must pay to free his children and his white brethren from a permanent death of the spirit, then nothing could be more redemptive. This is the type of soul force that I am convinced will triumph over the physical force of the oppressor.

This approach to the problem of oppression is not without successful precedent. We have the magnificent example of Gandhi who challenged the might of the British Empire and won independence for his people by using only the weapons of truth, non-injury, courage and soul force. Today we have the example of thousands of Negro students in the South who have courageously challenged the principalities of segregation. These young students have taken the deep groans and the passionate yearnings of the Negro people and filtered them in their own souls and fashioned them in a creative protest which is an epic known all over our nation. For the last few months they have moved in a uniquely meaningful orbit imparting light and heat to distant satellites. Through their non-violent direct action they have been able to open hundreds of formerly segregated lunch counters in almost eighty cities. It is no overstatement to characterize these events as historic. Never before in the United States has so large a body of students spread a struggle over so great an area in pursuit of a goal of human dignity and freedom. I am convinced that future historians will have to record this student movement as one of the greatest epics of our heritage.

Now that I have discussed the need for the Negro to work courageously to remove the barriers of segregation, let me mention another front on which he must work that is equally significant. The Negro must make a vigorous effort to improve his personal standards. I know that this is one of those matters that we often hesitate to mention publicly for fear that it will serve to aid and abet the enemy in his mad quest to convince the nation that the Negro is neither ready for nor capable of facing the responsibilities of integration. The only answer that we can give to those who through blindness and fear would question our readiness and capability is that our lagging standards exist because of the legacy of slavery and segregation, inferior schools, slums, and second-class citizenship, and not because of an inherent inferiority. As I said earlier, there is no more torturous logic than to take the tragic effects of segregation and use them as an argument for the need of its continuation. The fact that so many Negroes have made lasting and significant contributions to the cultural life of America in spite of these crippling restrictions if sufficient to refute all of the myths and half truths disseminated by the segregationist.

Yet we cannot ignore the fact that our standards do often fall short. Therefore I take the bold risk of being misquoted by the enemy in order to lay before you a fact that we must honestly face. One of the sure signs of maturity is the ability to rise to the point of self criticism. Whenever we are objects of criticism from white men, even though the criticisms are maliciously directed and mixed with half truths, we must pick out the elements of truth and make them the basis of creative reconstruction.

Let us face it. We have been affected by our years of economic deprivation and social isolation. Some Negroes have become cynical and disillusioned. Some have so conditioned themselves to the system of segregation that they have lost that creative something called initiative. So many have used their oppression as an excuse for mediocrity. Many of us live above our means, spend money on non-essentials and frivolities, and fail to give to serious causes, organizations, and educational institutions that so desperately need funds. Our crime rate is far too high.

Therefore there is a pressing need for the Negro to develop a positive program through which these standards can be improved. After we have analyzed the sociological and psychological causes of these problems, we must seek to develop a constructive action program to solve them. By improving our standards here and now we will go a long way toward breaking down the arguments of the segregationist.

We must constantly stimulate our youth to rise above the stagnant level of mediocrity, and seek to achieve excellence in their various fields of endeavor. Doors are opening now that were not open in the past, and the great challenge facing minority groups is to be ready to enter these doors as they open. No greater tragedy could befall us at this hour but that of allowing new opportunities to emerge without the concomitant preparedness to meet them. Ralph Waldo Emerson said in a lecture back in 1871 that "if a man can write a better book, or preach a better sermon, or make a better mousetrap than his neighbor, even if he builds his house in the woods the world will make a beaten path to his door."[7] This has not always been true. But I have reason to believe that because of the shape of the world today and the fact that we cannot afford the luxury of an anemic democracy, this affirmation will become increasingly true. We must make it clear to our young people that this is an age in which they will be forced to compete with people of all races and nationalities. We cannot aim merely to be good Negro teachers, good Negro doctors, or good Negro skilled laborers. We must set out to do a good job irrespective of race. We must seek to do our life's work so well that nobody could do it better. The Negro who seeks to be merely a good Negro, whatever he is, has already flunked his matriculation examination for entrance into the university of integration.[8]

This is the challenge of the hour. It seems to me that in this two-fold job ahead we see the role of an organization like the Urban League and that of the more militant civil rights organizations like the NAACP, CORE and the Southern Christian Leadership Conference. Just as there must be a division of labor in organizational work. It appears to me that there is no organization more uniquely equipped in structure, technical know how and program than the Urban League to carry out this all important job of helping the Negro adjust to urban living and improve his general standards. Naturally, this job will call for imaginative, bold and constructive action. It will call for thorough community organization. As the problem of urban dislocation becomes more critical the Urban League must intensify its program, and justifiably expect new and larger financial support.

While the Urban League works creatively and constructively on this front, the more militant civil rights organizations must continue the frontal attack on the

---

7. The source of this quotation, generally attributed to Emerson, is uncertain (see note 6 to "Mother's Day in Montgomery," 18 May 1956, in *Papers* 3:266).

8. In an earlier speech, King attributed this advice to Morehouse College president Benjamin Mays. For the entire quote, see King, "Facing the Challenge of a New Age," 1 January 1957, in *Papers* 4:79.

system of segregation. Although there will be some inevitable overlapping, there need be no essential conflict. The NAACP'er must not look upon the Urban Leaguer as a quiet conservative and the Urban Leaguer must not look upon the NAACP'er as a militant troublemaker. Each must accept the other as a necessary partner in the complex yet exciting struggle to free the Negro, and thereby save the soul of America.

In thinking of this two-fold task ahead, I would like to again suggest the role of the Federal government. This is based on some recent insights that I gained while traveling in India. I discovered that the Indian government had made much more progress in eliminating caste untouchability than we have made in eliminating segregation. This is because the national government of India has worked vigorously on two fronts. First the government set forth a constitutional provision making untouchability illegal. To discriminate against an untouchable is a crime punishable by imprisonment. But the government does not stop here. It carries on an active program of education and propaganda to get these ideas over. Moreover, the government spends millions of dollars a year in scholarships, housing, and community development to lift the standards of the untouchables. This is the government's way of atoning for the long years of demoralization inflicted upon these people by the system of untouchability.

So when our government takes this matter seriously it will continue to use its constitutional authority to end the system of segregation. But it will go beyond this. Through the Department of Health, Welfare and Education it will carry on an active program of propaganda to promote the idea of integration. Moreover the government should seriously consider making federal funds available to do this tremendous job of lifting the standards of a people too long ignored by America's conscience.

This then must be our present program; non-violent resistance to all forms of racial injustice, even when this means going to jail, and bold, constructive action to end the demoralization caused by the legacy of slavery and segregation. The non-violent struggle, if conducted with the dignity and courage already shown by the sit-in students of the South, will in itself help end the demoralization; but a new frontal assault on the poverty, disease, and ignorance of a people too long deprived of the God-given rights of life, liberty and the pursuit of happiness, will make the victory more certain.

We must work assiduously and with determined boldness to remove from the body politic this cancerous disease of discrimination which is preventing our democratic and Christian health from being realized. Then and only then will we be able to bring into full realization the dream of our American democracy—a dream yet unfulfilled. A dream of equality of opportunity, of privilege and property widely distributed; a dream of a land where men will not take necessities from the many to give luxuries to the few; a dream of a land where men do not argue that the color of a man's skin determines the content of his character, where they recognize that the basic thing about a man is not his specific but his fundamentum; a dream of a place where all our gifts and resources are held not for ourselves alone but as instruments of service for the rest of humanity; the dream of a country where every man will respect the dignity and worth of all human personality, and men will dare to live together as brothers—that is the dream. Whenever it is fulfilled we will emerge from the bleak and desolate midnight of man's inhumanity to man into the bright and glowing daybreak of freedom and ~~in~~justice for all of God's children.

THD. UAWRCR-NNU-LA.

"The Negro and the American Dream," Excerpt from Address at the Annual Freedom Mass Meeting of the North Carolina State Conference of Branches of the NAACP

25 September 1960
Charlotte, N.C.

In this typed draft of his address, King shares his dream of a nation "where men of all races, colors, and creeds will live together as brothers" but warns that American racism has put the country's international standing "at its lowest ebb."[1] He further recommends five ways that black people can continue "to remind America" of the dream: continue to challenge segregation, utilize the freedom blacks currently enjoy, obtain the ballot, "suffer and sacrifice" to achieve freedom, and use nonviolent methods in the struggle. A newspaper account reported that King was introduced by author and editor Harry Golden to a crowd of 2,700 people at Charlotte's Park Center.[2]

This afternoon I would like to speak from the subject, "The Negro and the American Dream." In a real sense America is essentially a dream—a dream yet unfilfilled. It is the dream of a land where men of all races, colors and creeds will live together as brothers. The substance of the dream is expressed in these sublime words: "We hold these truths to be self-evident, that all men are created equal, that they are endowed by their creator with certain unalienable rights, that among these are life, liberty and the pursuit of happiness." This is the dream. It is a profound, eloquent and unequivocal expression of the dignity and worth of all human personality.

But ever since the founding fathers of our nation dreamed this dream, America has manifested a schizophrenic personality. She has been torn between {two} selves—a self in which she has proudly professed democracy and a self in which she has sadly practiced the antithesis of democracy. Slavery and segregation have been strange paradoxes in a nation founded on the principle that all men are created equal.

Now more than ever before America is challenged to bring her noble dream into reality. The shape of the world today does not permit America the luxury of

---

1. In a 22 August telegram, King had accepted North Carolina NAACP president Kelly Alexander's invitation to address the organization.

2. Don Seaver, "King Tells Negroes to Start Voter Registration Protests," *Charlotte Observer,* 26 September 1960.

exploiting the Negro and other minority groups. The price that America must pay for the continued opression of the Negro is the price of its own destruction. My recent travel in Asia, Africa, the Middle East and South America have convinced me that America is at its lowest ebb in international prestige; and most of this loss of prestige is due to our failure to grapple with the problem of racial injustice. We must face the painful fact that we are losing out in the struggle to win the minds of the uncommitted peoples of the world. Just this week the most eloquent spokesman of the Communist bloc, Nikita Khruschev, suggested in his speech to the U.N., among other things, that the headquarters of this great organization be moved from the United States. The American press generally was very careful to conceal one of the reasons Mr. Khruschev gave for suggesting this move. His direct words were: "Facts are known . . . of representatives of young African and Asian states being subjected to racial discrimination in the United States."[3] While we are used to Mr. Khruschev's inteperate and sometimes irresponsible words, we cannot dismiss these as totally false. The hour is late: the clock of destiny is ticking out. We must act now! It is a trite yet urgently true observation that if America is to remain a firstclass nation it cannot have secondclass citizens.

25 Sept 1960

But after saying this I would like to make it clear that the primary reason for bringing an end to racial discrimination in America must not be the Communist challange. Nor must it be merely to appeal to Asian and African peoples. The primary reason for uprooting racial discrimination from our society is that it is morally wrong. It is a cancerous disease that prevents us from realizing the sublime principles of our Judeo-Christian tradition. It relegates persons to the status of things. Therefore, those persons who are working courageously to break down the barriers of segregation and discrimination are the real saviors of democracy.

So many forces in our nation have served to scar the dream of our democracy. The Klu Klux Klan, the White Citizens Council and other extremists groups have scarred the dream by their fanatical acts and bitter words. But our federal government has also scarred the dream through its apathy and hypocricy, its betrayal of the cause of justice. And even many white people of good-will have scarred the dream through silence and fear. In the midst of this conspiracy of silence and apathy the Negro must act. It may well be that the Negro is God's instrument to save the soul of America.

* * *

What can the Negro do to contimue to remind America of the necessity of realizing its dream?:

1. We must continue courageously to challenge the system of segregation. We must not rest until segregation is removed from every area of our nation's life. Segregation, whether at a lunch counter, in a public park. In a school

3. Khrushchev addressed the United Nations General Assembly on 23 September. A complete transcript of his speech appeared in the *New York Times* the following day.

room, or in the Christian church, is a cancer in the body politic which must be removed before our moral and democratic health can be realized.

We must also make it palpably clear that we can never settle for token integration. If token integration is a good faith start, it may have some merit: but too often it is nothing but a bad faith evasive scheme. Ultimately, token integration is no more than token democracy.

2. We must make full and constructive use of the freedom we already possess. We must not use our oppression as an excuse for mediocrity. History has proven that inner determination can often break through the outer shackles of circumstance.

3. We must make a determined effort to gain the ballot. One of the most significant steps that the Negro can take at this hour is that short walk to the voting booth. I propose that the creative movement that has electrified our nation as a result of the courageous student sit-ins, wade-ins, and kneel-ins will now add the deminsion of stand-ins at places of voter registration. Even in counties of the deep South where resistance is great, Negroes must organize themselves by the hundreds and thousands to stand nonviolently and peacefully for hours in the corridors and on the sidewalks of places of registration.[4] Such a movement may be the only thing that will dramatize the continued injustices the Negroes face in the area of voter registration, and the only thing that will arouse the conscience of our nation on this pressing issue.

   External resistance is not the only present barrier to Negro voting. Apathy among Negroes themselves is also a factor. Even where the polls are open to all Negroes have shown themselves too slow to exercise their voting privileges.

4. We must be willing to suffer and sacrifice to achieve our freedom. Our freedom will never be handed out on a silver platter. Freedom is not free. It is always purchased with the high price of sacrifice and suffering.

5. We must be sure that our struggle is conducted on the highest level of dignity and discipline. Our method must be nonviolent to the core. We must not flirt with retaliatory violence or drink the poisonous wine of hate. Our aim must not be to defeat the white man or pay him back for past injustices heaped upon us.

   I feel that this way of nonviolence is vital because it is the only way to reestablish the broken community. It is a powerful way to take direct action against injustice without waiting for other agencies to act.

   This approach to the problem of oppression is not without successful precedent. We have the magnificent example of Gandhi who challenged the might of the British Empire and won independence for his people by using only the

4. An article in the *Charlotte Observer* reported that King encouraged mass "stand-ins" at voter registration places throughout the South (Seaver, "King Tells Negroes to Start Voter Registration Protests," *Charlotte Observer,* 26 September 1960).

weapons of truth, noninjury, courage and soul force. Today we have the example of thousands of Negro students in the South who have courageously challenged the principalities of segregation. These young students have taken the deep groans and the passionate yearnings of the Negro people and filtered them in their own souls and fashioned them in a creative protest which is an epic known all over the nation. For the last few months they have moved in a uniquely meaningful orbit imparting light and heat to distant satellites. Through their nonviolent direct action they have been able to open hundreds of formerly segregated lunch counters in almost eighty cities. It is no overstatement to characterize these events as historic. Never before in the United States has so large a body of students spread a struggle over so great an area in pursuit of a goal of human dignity and freedom. I am convinced that future historians will have to record this student movement as one of the greatest epics of our heritage.

TAD. CSKC: Sermon file.

To George W. Lee

27 September 1960
[*Atlanta, Ga.*]

In an 18 September telephone conversation with George W. Lee, an officer of the Benevolent and Protective Order of the Elks, King requested assistance for Atlanta student movement leader Lonnie King, whose participation in the city's sit-in protest had provoked reprisals from creditors.[1] *Lee sent King a check on 19 September. King wrote this letter in response to Lee's request for a written record.*

1. King and Lee were among the speakers at a 31 July 1959 political rally in Memphis ("Dr. King Urges Memphians to Elect Candidates," *Birmingham World*, 5 August 1959). George Washington Lee (1894–1976), born in Indianola, Mississippi, was an author, politician, civic leader, and businessman. A World War I veteran, Lee was one of the few black officers in the American Expeditionary Forces, where he obtained the rank of lieutenant. As a member of the Republican Party, Lee served as national director of "Veterans For Hoover" during the 1928 presidential campaign. In the 1930s Lee became a member of Memphis's Benevolent Order of the Elks and later became the organization's Grand Commissioner of Education in 1951. In 1952, Lee was a delegate to the Republican National Convention, where he delivered the seconding speech for Senator Robert Taft. He was also the author of several books on Memphis, including *Beale Street: Where the Blues Began* (1934) and *Beale Street Sundown* (1942). Lonnie Cecil King, Jr. (1936–), born in Arlington, Georgia, earned a B.A. (1969) from Morehouse College and an M.A. (1998) from the University of Baltimore. In 1960, King and other Atlanta students founded the Committee on Appeal for Human Rights (COAHR) to coordinate the city's student sit-in demonstrations. King served as chairman of the organization until his departure from Atlanta in 1961. That same year, he enrolled at Howard University Law School and began organizing protests against the university's administrative policies. He left the university in 1962. From 1969 to 1973, he served both as president of the Georgia chapter of the NAACP and the principal organizer and chairman of the Community Coalition on Broadcasting.

27 Sept 1960

Mr. George W. Lee
Grand Commissioner of Education
Elks Department of Education
Lee Station
Memphis 5, Tennessee

My Dear Mr. Lee:

This is to acknowledge receipt of your letter of September 19 with the enclosed check of two hundred and fifty dollars for Lonnie King. This gesture of good will on your part will go a long, long way in helping Lonnie adjust to a difficult situation.

As I said to you over the telephone, Lonnie is a very dedicated young man with a real sense of commitment to the civil right struggle. He has done a very significant job here in Atlanta, and the community now has a sense of involvement in the total struggle that it has lacked so long. Since circumstances have catapulted Lonnie into the leadership of the Atlanta Student Movement we feel a moral responsibility to protect him from all situations that may jeopardize his unenviable position. As you know he is a student at Morehouse College and his wife [*Alice*] is a student at Spelman. In an attempt to keep himself and wife in school and meet other family responsibilities that naturally face them as a result of having a child [*Kimberly Jeanine*], Lonnie got behind in several bills. Although he works at the Post Office, and makes a fairly good salary I am sure you can realize how easily one can over spend when he has so many responsibilities. After Lonnie started receiving publicity as being head of the Student Movement many of his creditors demanded immediate payment of certain outstanding bills. This was obviously an attempt to retaliate for the leadership he had rendered in the Movement. Realizing the extent to which some of our opponents will go and the embarrassment they will seek to cast upon our leadership, a few of us, after becoming aware of the problem, decided to sit down with Lonnie and seek to work out some plan whereby he could pay these various bills immediately. It was out of this situation that my request came to you. I am happy to say that we have been able to meet the problem and Lonnie is now free to continue his leadership without having financial worries.

Please know that we would not have called on you in this way if we had not felt that we were dealing with an emergency situation. We realized that this was somewhat irregular, but we felt that the situation justified our making this special request. I said to the Committee when the issue came up the following words, "Although this will be something of an unusual request to make to the Elks Department of Education my knowledge of George W. Lee's sense of good will and commitment to the civil right struggle convinces me that he will give a sympathetic ear." So you did just as I expected. Again let me thank you for your cooperation and great concern. You have my prayers and best wishes for your contimued success in all of the significant work that you are doing.

Very sincerely yours,
Martin Luther King, Jr.

MLK:lmh

TLc. MLKP-MBU: Box 29A.

To Herbert H. Eaton

30 Sept 1960

30 September 1960
[*Atlanta, Ga.*]

King replies to a 28 September letter from Herbert H. Eaton, the pastor who replaced him at Dexter.[1] *Eaton wrote that he could not "help but feel proud at succeeding" King and welcomed advice "so as to profit from some of your experiences."*[2] *He also invited King to speak at the church's anniversary celebration on 11 December.*

The Reverend Herbert H. Eaton, Minister
Dexter Avenue Baptist Church
454 Dexter Avenue
Montgomery 4, Alabama

Dear Brother Eaton:

First let me extend my sincere congratulation to you for being called to the pastorate of Dexter Avenue Baptist Church. Although this is a little belated, my congratulation is as much from the heart as it would have been if it had come earlier. I know that you will have a rich and rewarding experience in your pastorate at Dexter. I can assure you that you have some of the finest people in the world to work with. Dexter is indeed fortunate to have a man of your training, background and Christian commitment. I will be more than happy to talk with you concerning some of my experiences at Dexter. and give you whatever counsel that I possibly can. If you are ever planing to be in Atlanta, please feel free to stop in our home.

I know nothing that would please me more than the opportunity of coming back to Dexter in December to preach the Anniversary sermon. Unfortunately, however, my calendar reveals that I have a long standing commitment to speak in Boston on the second Sunday in December.[3] Please know that I regret this very deeply. I hope it will be possible to serve you and my warm friends of Dexter on some other occasion. Please do not hesitate to call on me.

Again, let me thank you for the invitation. Give my best regards to the entire membership, and do stop in to see me when you are up this way so that we can

---

1. For more on Dexter's search for a minister, see King to Earl Wesley Lawson, 23 April 1960, pp. 441–442 in this volume.

2. Herbert Hoover Eaton (1928–), born in North Carolina, received a B.S. (1951) from North Carolina College at Durham, a B.D. (1956) from Howard University, an S.T.M. (1957) from Boston University, and an M.A. from Howard University (1972). Prior to his arrival at Dexter, Eaton worked as an administrative assistant to the dean of the School of Religion at Howard University from 1957 to 1960. In 1963, he was chairman of the board of directors of the MIA. Eaton served as Dexter's pastor until 1965, when he accepted the pastorate at Kenwood United Church of Christ in Chicago.

3. On 11 December, King delivered "The Future of Integration" at the Ford Hall Forum in Boston.

have a talk. If I can ever be of help to you from a distance, remember that I am as close as the telephone.

Very sincerely yours,
Martin L. King, Jr.

MLK:lmh

TLc. MLKP-MBU: Box 24.

From Maude L. Ballou

3 October 1960
Petersburg, Va.

Ballou, who became King's secretary soon after the Montgomery bus boycott began, relocated to Atlanta in January 1960 to help establish his new office.[1] *She writes following her family's move to Petersburg, Virginia.*

Dear Martin,

The campus and buildings here are lovely. The atmosphere is really collegiate. From all indications Virginia State is a well organized school. I went to work the Tuesday after I arrived in the Registrar's office. Dr. Daniel sent for me to have a conference that Sunday night, and wanted me to go to work that Monday, but I waited until Tuesday since registration was Monday.[2]

—Hope all is well with you, the office and family. Len and the children are fine, and send their regards.[3] I like it here. But I do not like the "temporary" housing—it is awful! Vicki is still in Norfolk with Mom and Dad. Len likes his work, the school, etc. The children like it here very much. Last week E. Franklin Frazier was here. Enjoyed him. He made an excellent reference to you in his lecture.[4] After the lecture we went to a lovely reception. This week we went to see two operas presented by the New York Opera Festival (The Wagner Opera Co., Inc.)—Cavalleria Rusticana and Pagliacci. I am really enjoying being here with Len and the children although I am kept busy trying to find a place to put various things in this terrible, terrible apartment. You will have to see it to appreciate how undesirable it is (smiles). We do not have a telephone yet. We just applied for one last week.

---

1. Ballou lived with the Kings in Atlanta until leaving for Petersburg in August 1960 (Ballou, Interview by King Papers Project staff, 6 February 2002).

2. Robert P. Daniel was president of Virginia State College from 1950 until 1968.

3. Ballou refers to her husband, Leonard, and their four children, Vicki, Joyce, Howard, and Leonard, Jr.

4. Franklin, a pioneering African American sociologist, delivered the main address at the college's formal opening convocation on 30 September.

I miss you very, very much, the office and general routine that had become a part of me and my life.

How are the ladies downstairs? Miss Watkins and Mrs. Reid?[5] My regards to them. Please write me because I would like to hear from you. How is Lillie?[6] I am sure she is doing fine and still enjoying Atlanta. Hello to Coretta. Will write her soon.

Sincerely,
[*signed*] Maude

P.S. Howard, Lenny and Joyce have asked about you many, many times. We have had such a nice time since being here. I took them to a football game last week (Saturday). The people here have been wonderful. Am looking forward to hearing from you soon!

[*signed*] M

ALS. MLKP-MBU: Box 20.

5. Lillian Watkins served as Ebenezer's senior secretary from 1928 until 1975. Sarah A. Reed began working as a church secretary in 1943.

6. Lillie M. Hunter, a church secretary at Dexter, also moved to Atlanta in 1960, where she worked with SCLC until 1970.

To Eleanor Roosevelt

6 October 1960
Atlanta, Ga.

SCLC's New York office sent this letter conveying King's thanks to the former First Lady for serving as a member of the Committee to Defend Martin Luther King and the Struggle for Freedom in the South. He asks her to endorse an enclosed mailing announcing that the temporary committee had become "a permanent body, to be known as the Emergency Committee for the Southern Freedom Struggle."[1] *Roosevelt expressed her "wholehearted approval" in a 17 October reply.*[2]

Mrs. Eleanor Roosevelt
55 East 74th Street
New York, New York

Dear Mrs. Roosevelt:

The days and nights have been so crowded with the unbroken chain of pressures and the urgent planning of new south-wide struggles, that I have been unable to do many things I have wanted to do,—foremost among which is to adequately thank you for your invaluable assistance and support in connection with my recent legal battle with the State of Alabama.[3]

Considering that I was exonerated by an all white jury in the heart of the deep south, the victory of course had a significance far beyond my personal vindication. It was a resounding defeat of the Reaction's all out attempt to crush any and all southern leadership. Beyond that our joint support of the student sit-ins resulted in intergration of lunch counters in 70 southern cities in a period of less than six months.

Because of all this the stage has been set for the next dramatic leap forward and everything indicates that the south is ready to move—Now.

In this connection, I am enclosing a draft of self-explanatory letter which I plan to send to all the sponsors and friends of the Defense Committee. In as much as I have taken the liberty of mentioning your name in it, as you can see, I will not send it out until it meets with your approval. To expedite matters I will have Miss Maya Angelou, the Co-ordinator of our New York office contact you.[4]

---

1. King to Friend, 6 October 1960. The finished mailing probably went out on 10 November (Willoughby Abner to King, 1 December 1960).

2. After learning that Roosevelt had replied directly to King in Atlanta, Jack Murray of the New York office forwarded this letter and its enclosed draft to King: "We learned that [*Roosevelt*] has written you in answer. Sending you these copies so you will know what it is all about" (Murray to King, 18 October 1960).

3. For more on King's trial in Alabama, see King, Statement on Perjury Acquittal, 28 May 1960, p. 462 in this volume.

4. Angelou became coordinator of SCLC's New York office in the summer of 1960 following the departure of Bayard Rustin. She resigned in January 1961 (Maya Angelou to King and Wyatt Tee Walker, 31 January 1961).

Once again, for all you have done, and I'm sure will continue to do to help extend the fruits of Democracy to our southern brothers, please accept my deep and lasting gratitude.

With thoughts of the very best warmest personal regards.

Very truly yours,
[*signed*] Martin Luther King Jr.
Martin Luther King, Jr.

TLSr. ERC-NHyF.

"Message from the President"

11 October–13 October 1960
Shreveport, La.

The typed program for SCLC's annual conference featured these comments. Held in Shreveport, the conference was hosted by the United Christian Movement, under the theme "The Southern Struggle and the American Dilemma."[1] Before the proceedings began, King told a reporter that support among Shreveport African Americans symbolized "their determination to move on to the better way of life that offers human dignity for all."[2] During the opening session, Gardner Taylor addressed the conferees and Guy Carawan of the Highlander Folk School led a "freedom sing." King spoke at a freedom rally on the second night.[3]

I am convinced beyond the shadow of a doubt that the philosophy of nonviolence will redeem the soul of America. There is a great temptation to accept nonviolence solely as a stratedy, a device; this we must guard against. This is one of the chief aims of the Southern Christian Leadership Conference: To broadly disseminate through intensive training the heart of nonviolence, that our commitment to nonviolence will not only be as a technique, but shall become for us a away of life with love and redemption as its center.

The other chief aim of SCLC is in the area of voter-registration. Here again, it must be recognized that the right and proper use of the ballot is vital in our struggle for first-class citizenship. The SCLC stands ready to serve in developing and

1. At Evergreen Baptist Church, on the first afternoon of the conference, King told SCLC's executive board that the organization "must do something creative this year" (Dorothy Cotton, "Minutes of annual board meeting," 11 October 1960). SCLC's new executive director Wyatt Tee Walker reported that the organization has successfully implemented "some of the basic organizational structure that SCLC has so sorely needed" (Walker, "Report of the director to the executive board," 11 October 1960).

2. "Shreveport Cops Arrest 4 Top Civil Rights Leaders," *Louisiana Weekly*, 22 October 1960.

3. After the conference closed, SCLC field secretary and conference organizer Harry Blake was shot at from a passing vehicle ("Assassin's Bullet Misses SCLC Secretary," *Pittsburgh Courier*, 22 October 1960).

organizing grassroots voter registration programs. One of the most significant steps that the Negro can take at this hour is that short walk to the voting booth.

[*signed*] M. L. King Jr

TDS. PFC-WHi.

From Stanley D. Levison

13 October 1960
New York, N.Y.

In this letter concerning SCLC's fund-raising efforts, Levison stresses the importance of King maintaining a nonpartisan position in the 1960 election. Levison also warns him to beware of "heavy pressure" from some of Kennedy's Hollywood supporters who perceive King "as a personality of glamour not as a leader whose responsibilities will continue over decades and through changes of great magnitude."

Dr. Martin L. King
The Ebenezer Baptist Church
407 Auburn Avenue, N.E.
Atlanta, Georgia

Dear Martin,

I hope the conference went well.[1] I have a few items which need your attention so that we can move on with some of the projects we've been discussing.

First: I am enclosing a draft of the appeal letter which we will get out shortly. My thought in developing it in this fashion takes advantage of the limited action you staged, in the "Stand-Ins", while not relying on it for the whole emotional appeal.[2] The recipient with this approach can feel he is part of the movement because he is in it from the experimental stage to the developmental period. This sense of participation from the beginning is the substitute for the drama we lack at this moment.

Second: I am enclosing a draft of a letter to go to Atty. Clarence Jones.[3] He

1. Levison refers to SCLC's annual conference, held 11–13 October in Shreveport, Louisiana.

2. On 3 October SCLC staged "stand-ins" at the Fulton County registrar's office, which King described as a "pilot project" to determine the "feasibility of a national program of voter registration protest" ("'Stand-Ins' Aim Is Told by Dr. King," *Atlanta Daily World,* 6 October 1960).

3. In a 13 October letter, Levison thanked Jones and his colleagues for their offer to raise funds for SCLC, describing the "electrifying actions" of student protesters as inspiration for a new initiative to protest for voting rights through "mass non-violent 'stand-ins' at the polling places in the south."

will need it when he reassembles the group of Hollywood lawyers in order to move them from the discussion stage to concrete action. By disclosing your agreement, the urgent need, and the importance of the venture, they can be stimulated to begin planning at once. Beyond this dinner also lies the organization of a permanent support committee which can develop other types of affairs. We have been talking of the practicability of a big mass affair in the spring in the Hollywood Bowl.[4] Given the presence on the coast of so many stars such an event should have real possibilities of success. It would attract a different group than a dinner encompassing the great number who can't afford expensive dinner prices. 13 Oct 1960

Third: Sammy Davis Jr., talked to Maya Angelou on the phone yesterday and confirmed arrangements for the January 27th Carnegie Hall affair.[5] He said everyone was set. In the same conversation he said he was trying to reach you to have you attend a big rally on the West Coast with him for Kennedy. Here we go again! Maya [*Angelou*] indicated to him very briefly that you necessarily held to a non-partisan position, but he said he wanted to talk to you, anyhow. In thinking of the conversation, and taking into account that Sammy is a Negro I think he will understand more than Harrison and Dave Livingston.[6] One point might be stressed with Sammy. Since you are concentrating on getting the vote in the south, the effectiveness of your efforts would be diminished if you were identified as an adherent of one party. You can't be as pursuasive to particularly apathetic Negroes, if they feel you are appealing to them as a partisan person who may be seeking to build up voters for his own future candidacy. A long view must be taken which sees that no matter what immediate advantages can be gained by having you speak for one party now, what is lost is a rare leader whose selflessness has been long established and highly prized by the people.

I am not so much concerned that Sammy will not understand as that Sinatra and the others we are counting on will not rise above superfically and grasp the essential points. As we have seen when people get deeply involved with a party's fortunes they sometimes lose perspective; see only that which they want to see.

Sometimes I think these people see you too much as a personality of glamour

4. On 18 June 1961, the Western Christian Leadership Conference sponsored a Freedom Rally at the Los Angeles Sports Arena, featuring King, Mahalia Jackson, Sammy Davis, Jr., California governor Edmund Brown, and other state and local politicians (Western Christian Leadership Conference, Announcement, Martin Luther King, Jr. to speak at freedom rally, 18 June 1961; see also Maurice Dawkins to King, 27 February 1961).

5. Angelou assisted in the organization of the January 1961 Carnegie Hall "Tribute to Martin Luther King, Jr." Frank Sinatra, Dean Martin, Sammy Davis, Jr., Tony Bennett, Nipsey Russell, and Jan Murray performed at the tribute (Sara Slack, "'Rat Pack' Raises $35,000 for King," *New York Amsterdam News*, 4 February 1961). King thanked Davis for his support in a 20 December letter (see pp. 582–583 in this volume).

6. George M. Harrison was the president of the Brotherhood of Railway and Steamship Clerks in Cincinnati and vice president of the AFL-CIO. David Livingston was president of District 65 of the Retail, Wholesale, and Department Store Union (RWDSU) in New York.

not as a leader whose responsibilities will continue over decades and through changes of great magnitude. There is probably some identification of themselves with you and though they can come and go, change horses, all as merely an avocation, for you the taking of a position is an immensely important step affecting millions deeply and lastingly. Frank, Sammy and the others are not intellectual leaders nor moral leaders so their decisions can be more easily arrived at without the singular weight that attaches to a decision or stand by you. I mention these thoughts because they may subject you to heavy pressure. I'll be calling you to find out about Friday. Warmest personal regards,

Sincerely,
[*signed*] Stan

SDL/ah
enclosures

TLS. MLKP-MBU: Box 2.

Outline, The Philosophy of Nonviolence

[*14 October 1960*]
[*Atlanta, Ga.*]

Some three hundred students and observers from across the country gathered in Atlanta from 14 to 16 October for the first major Student Nonviolent Coordinating Committee (SNCC) meeting since its founding at Shaw University in April. King may have used this handwritten outline as the basis for "The Philosophy of Nonviolence," his keynote address on the opening day of the SNCC conference.[1] *In it he endorses nonviolence as "the relentless pursuit of truthful ends by moral means" and asserts that there are "amazing potentialities for goodness" in human nature. King concludes by warning against "ego struggles" and other "pitfalls."*

The history of mankind is replete with ~~n~~ innumerable conflict-situation

I First and foremost in the philosophy of non-violence is the affirmation that means must be as pure as the end. Means and ends are convertible terms. [*They?*] are inseparable
{The means represent the end in process and the ideal in the making}
(1) This automatically sets non-violence against war and communism. Both says that the end justifies the means.

1. Other conference speakers included James Lawson, Lillian Smith, Ella Baker, Richard Gregg, and William Stuart Nelson (*Student Voice*, October 1960). King had been invited to deliver the keynote address in a 22 August letter from Marion S. Barry and Jane Stembridge, who also suggested the title.

(2) So non-violence seeks to achive moral ends through moral means. It is the relentless pursuit of of truthful ends through moral means. 14 Oct 1960

II A second basic fact in this philosophy is the consistent refusal to inflict injury upon another. There are to aspects to this There is first the external,

(1) This means that you dont use aggressive or retaliatory violence.

(2) But there is the internal. It deals with the way you talk, the way you make a press release

(3) The highest expression of non-injury is love

(4) This love means that you center your attention on the evil system and not the evil dooer. The non-violent resister separates the evil from the evildoor and while trying to eradicate the evil tries to save the evil doer

1. Means must be as pure as the end.
2. There must be no dual code of ethics for individual and group conduct.
3. Non-violence seeks to [*confuse?*] evil by truth, to resist physical foce by soul-force.

*4. Non-violence is the relentless pursuit of truthful ends by moral means.

5 The non violent resister ~~does not~~ is not victimized with the illusion that all conflicts will be eliminated; he aims at raising them from the destructive physical plane to the constructive moral plane [*where?*] differences can be peacefully adjusted. Thus, he seeks to eliminate antagonisms rather than antagonists.

6 The non-violent resister is prepared to suffer even unto death. He believes that by suffering alone he can bridge the gulf between himself and his opponent and reach his heart.

*7 Non violent resistance means a refusal to cooperate with evil

8 Non violence appeals not to physical might, but to moral right by making him cognizant of the evil.
{efforts must be intensified in deep south.}

III Another basic point in non-violence is ~~the courageoush willingness to accept suffering~~ that suffering may become a source of human and social force. It thwarts the oppositions efforts, exposes his moral defense and therby breaks his morale.

IV The belief that there is within human nature amazing potentialities for goodness.

V It is not only a philosophy, but a technique of action.

1 Some pitfalls to watch

(1) [*miscellaneous?*] activity—without planning

(2) publicity

(3) ego struggles

You will be misunderstood

AD. CSKC.

Draft, Statement to Judge James E. Webb after Arrest at Rich's Department Store

[*19 October 1960*]
[*Atlanta, Ga.*]

On 19 October—three days after the close of the SNCC conference—Atlanta police arrested King and student activists who had requested service at the Magnolia Room, a segregated restaurant at Rich's department store in downtown Atlanta.[1] *Organized by the Atlanta Committee on Appeal for Human Rights, the sit-in was one of several conducted simultaneously at lunch counters throughout the city.*[2] *After charges were dropped against many of the demonstrators, King and thirty-five others remained in custody, refusing to post bond.*[3] *King proclaims his willingness to remain "in jail a year or even ten years." King may have used this draft, handwritten in a spiral-bound notebook, to form his remarks during his arraignment later that day before Judge Webb.*[4]

Your Honor, I would simply like to say that I dont think we have done anything wrong in seeking to be served at the Magnolia Tea Room of Rich's. We assembled quietly, peacefully and non-violently to ~~secure~~ seek service just as any other citizen. If we lived in a totalitarian regiem or a gestapo system I could see how we might have been wrong. But one of the great glories of democracy is the right to protest for right. So we do not feel that we have violated the law.

If by chance, your honor, we are guilty of violating the law please be assured that we did it to bring the whole issue of racial injustice under the scrutiny of the conscience of Atlanta. I must honestly say that we firmly believe that segregation is evil, and that our southland will never reach its full economic, political and moral maturity until this cancerous disease is removed. We do not seek to remove this unjust system for ourselves alone but for our white brothers as well. The festering sore of segregation debilitates the white man as well as the Negro. So if our action in anyway served to bring this issue to the forefront of the conscience of the community ~~it could~~ it was not undertaken in vain.

We are not dangerous rabblerousers or ~~nagging~~ professional agitators. ~~Our actions grow out of a deep seated con~~ Our actions grow out of a deep seated concern for the moral heath of our community. We have not been motivated by some foreign ideology—communistic or any other. We did it because of our love for America, our southland and our white brothers.

---

1. Although reporters credited King with igniting the protest, he maintained that "the students asked me to come" ("More Sitdowns Rumored Today," *Atlanta Journal*, 20 October 1960).

2. Demonstrations took place at seven other Atlanta department and variety stores, but arrests occurred only at Rich's.

3. King and the students were charged under a new state anti-trespassing law (Bruce Galphin and Keeler McCartney, "King, 51 Others Arrested Here in New Sit-In Push," *Atlanta Constitution*, 20 October 1960).

4. The notebook may have belonged to a student jailed with King. A handwritten title, "Great Issues," was on its cover and inside was a page of notes dated 3 October 1960. Atlanta's Morris Brown College offered a course called Great Issues, which was mandatory for students in their senior year (*Morris Brown College Catalog*, 1960–1961).

Your Honor, I would simply like to say that I don't think we have done anything wrong in seeking to be served at the Magnolia Tea Room of Rich's. We assembled quietly, peacefully and non-violently to seek service just as any other citizen. If we lived in a totalitarian regime or a gestapo system I could see how we might have been wrong. But one of the great glories of democracy is the right to protest for right. So we do not feel that we have violated the law.

If by chance, your honor, we are guilty of violating the law, please be assured that we did it to bring the whole issue of racial injustice under the scrutiny of the conscience of Atlanta. I must honestly say that we firmly believe that segregation is evil, and that our southland will never reach its full economic, political and moral maturity until this cancerous disease is removed. We do not seek to remove this unjust system for ourselves alone but for our white brothers as well. The festering sore of segregation debilitates the white man as well as

Handwritten page from King's statement to Judge James E. Webb

And sir I know you have a legal obligation facing you at this hour. This judicial obligation may cause you to bound us over to another court rather than dismiss the charge. But sir I must say that I have a moral obligation facing me at this hour. This divine imperative drive me to say that if you find it necessary to set a bond, I cannot in all good conscience have anyone go my bail. I will coose jail rather than bail, even if it ~~takes re~~ means remaining in jail a year or even ten years. Mayby it will take this type of self suffering on the part of numerous Negroes to finally expose the moral defenses of ~~the~~ our white brother who happen to be misguided and therby awaken the doazing conscience of our community.[5]

AD. CSKC: M2.

---

5. According to the *Chicago Defender* King told the judge: "I cannot in all good conscience accept bail . . . I will stay in jail a year if necessary. It is our sincere hope that the acceptance of suffering on our part will serve to awaken the dozing consciousness of our community ("King Opens New Integration Fight," *Chicago Defender*, 22–28 October 1960). In a 19 October telegram, SCLC public relations director James Wood alerted J. Oscar Lee of the National Council of Churches to King's arrest and included portions of King's courthouse statement: "We do not seek publicity. We do not seek to disturb the city. We come in humility, in search of the same treatment accorded other patrons. I love my white brother. I cannot in good conscience accept bond or bail. I will stay in jail as long as is necessary." A similar wire was sent to Roy Wilkins (Wood to Wilkins, 19 October 1960).

From Nashville Nonviolent Student Movement

19 October 1960
Nashville, Tenn.

King's incarceration prompted numerous messages of support.[1]

MARTIN L KING JR
193 BLVD NE ATLA

COMMEND YOU & OTHERS FOR COURAGEOUS STAND PLEASE REMAIN IN JAIL FOR THE SAKE OF THE MOVEMENT

NASHVILLE NV STUDENT MOVEMENT.

PHWSr. CSKC: M2.

---

1. Correspondents included David Livingston and Cleveland Robinson of District 65, RWDSU (20 October 1960), the Emergency Committee for the Southern Freedom Struggle (20 October 1960), Carl and Anne Braden (24 October 1960), and L. C. and Daisy Bates (27 October 1960). In addition, SNCC officials Marion Barry and Ed King, and NAACP executive secretary Roy Wilkins urged individuals and organizations to write letters and send protest telegrams to Atlanta mayor William Hartsfield (Barry and King to Fellow students, 20 October 1960, and Wilkins to NAACP branch officers, 21 October 1960).

Why We Chose Jail Rather Than Bail

I Appeal to conscience of opponent.
  a. Change of attitude
  b. Very few people fail to be moved when they notice others suffering

II An expression of the extreme lengths that one is willing to go in agonizing inconvenience in order to convince the nation that the Negro is determined to be free.

III To open channels of negotiation where such has broken down.

IV To disarm the opponent of one of the chief weapons that he has held over the Negro namely the threat of arrest

V The highest expression of non-violence is self suffering

VI A willingness to accept penalty for breaking unjust law. So it is a matter of conscience.

VII A money saving device. It seems needless

This handwritten outline of "Why We Choose Jail Rather Than Bail" may have been written following King's October 1960 arrest at Rich's department store in Atlanta. On the second page of this document, King wrote, "VIII· It puts the opponent on the defensive. It exposes his moral defenses and weakens his morale."

From Candie Anderson

20 October 1960
Claremont, Calif.

Candie Anderson, a Pomona College student who had attended the Atlanta SNCC conference, writes King and the other jailed Atlanta protesters.[1]

Rev. Martin Luther King, Jr.
and other sit-in participants
c/o Atlanta City Jail (?)

Dear Rev. King & cohorts:

Congratulations on your most recent action against Atlanta's segregation policy. When I left the Conference Sunday evening I didn't realize there would be such immediate action right there in Atlanta. I think that most of us came away with enthusiasm & determination which we hope we can channel into something tangible, but your demonstration will provide further stimulation.

From what news we can get here it sounds as though some of you will remain in jail until trial. More power to you. I really do hope it has the effect of forcing the community to face the issue squarely.

The students here who sent me to the Atlanta Conference are very much interested in what was discussed there and now in the action you have taken. I hope their concern can be directed toward some very real problems of discrimination right here in California as well as in sympathy for the movement in the South.

My thoughts are with you. I think of what helped me more than once when I was in Nashville last year . . . "Walk together, Children . . . don't you get weary . . ." and I am encouraged by what this movement is doing for America.

Best wishes—
[*signed*] Candie Anderson

AHLS. SCLCR-GAMK: Box 5.

---

1. Carolanne (Candie) Marie Anderson Carawan (1939–), born in Los Angeles, California, received a B.A. (1961) from Pomona College. While an exchange student at Fisk University during the spring of 1960, she attended James Lawson's nonviolent training workshops and participated in sit-ins. At a gathering of southern student activists at Highlander Folk School that April, she met singer and songwriter Guy Carawan, whom she married the following year. In the mid-1960s, the Carawans organized a number of "Sing for Freedom" workshops around the South that SCLC helped sponsor. They later worked at Highlander as cultural organizers and educators, producing four books and a dozen documentary albums on the traditional music of the Deep South's African American and Appalachian communities.

"Press Release from Dr. King (Inside Fulton County Jail)"

21 October 1960
[*Atlanta, Ga.*]

Two days after his arrest, King comments on jailhouse conditions.[1]

"Much to my chagrin, the jail is segregated, also. I suppose the thing that wears on me most is the dread monotony. Sixteen hours is a long time to spend within a few square feet with nothing creative to do.

"My personal staying power is buttressed by the courage and dedication of my fellow jail-mates and the concern that has been shown around the nation and the world for this moral stand we have taken."

Upon being asked how long he would remain in jail, Dr. King replied "as long as is necessary."

TD. SCLCR-GAMK: Box 36.

1. In a newspaper interview conducted the same day, King, who is described as "in shirtsleeves, tieless and unshaven," characterized his jailers as "very courteous." King reaffirmed his determination to refuse bail and explained that "when the students called me at the last minute to go with them, I felt I had a moral obligation to take part, since this was what I had been preaching" (Trezzvant W. Anderson, "I Had to Practice What I Preached," *Pittsburgh Courier*, 29 October 1960).

To Female Inmates

[*19 October–23 October 1960*]
[*Atlanta, Ga.*]

This handwritten letter, composed on lined paper from the same notebook in which King drafted his arraignment statement, may have been intended for the female protesters arrested during the Atlanta sit-ins.[1]

1. Jacqueline Kay Anderson, Blondeen Arbert, Ann Ashmore, Diane Attaway, Charlotte Cherry, Mattie Cox, Gwendolyn Iles, Carolyn Long, Wylma Long, Johnnie Price, Marilynn Pryce, Minnie Riley, Patricia Simon, Patricia Ann Smith, Christine Sparks, Herschelle Sullivan, Lana Taylor, Yvonne Tucker, Laurine Weaver, and Bettye Williamson were reportedly arrested at Rich's department store and bound over to criminal court on the first day of demonstrations (Bruce Galphin and Keeler McCartney, "King, 51 Others Arrested Here in New Sit-In Push: Further Protests Foreseen," *Atlanta Constitution*, 20 October 1960). In a 22 October letter to the male prisoners, Carolyn Long wrote: "Tell M. L. that his dear cousins are fine." She also reported that King, Sr. had visited her in jail and is "going to bring me some cigarettes" (see also Ashmore to All my friends in the pokey, 22 October 1960, and Cox et al. to Brothers, 23 October 1960). All the student protesters were released on or before 23 October.

24 Oct 1960

Hello girls,

Words can never adequately express appreciation. Real appreciation must flow from the deep seas of the heart.[2] But in my stumbling words I would like to thank you for your intrepid courage, your quiet dignity, and your undaunted faith in the power of non-violence. Never before have I been more proud to be a Negro. Never before have I had more faith in the future. It is inspiring enought to see the fellows ~~a~~ willingly accepting jail rather than bail, but when young ladies are willing to accept this type of self suffering for the cause of freedom it is both majestic and sublime.

AL. CSKC: M2.

---

2. King began this letter one page earlier in the notebook but stopped in the middle of the second sentence (King, Draft, To female inmates, 19 October–23 October 1960).

From Dexter Avenue Baptist Church

24 October 1960
Montgomery, Ala.

On 23 October, after black community leaders and white business owners agreed to a thirty-day halt to student-led demonstrations, charges stemming from the Atlanta sit-ins were dropped and all protesters except King were released from the Fulton County jail. King remained in custody awaiting a 25 October hearing to determine if his sit-in arrest violated the terms of a suspended sentence imposed on him in September when he was convicted of a minor traffic violation in DeKalb County.[1] *The Dexter congregation sends the following telegram of support to the King home.*

DR AND MRS MARTIN LUTHER KING JR
363 JOHNSON AVE NORTHEAST ATLA

DEAR FRIENDS AS IN THE PAST WE WANT YOU TO KNOW THAT THE ENTIRE MEMBERSHIP OF DEXTER AVENUE BAPTIST CHURCH STILL FEELS STRONGLY ATTACHED TO YOU AND TO THE GREAT MINISTRY WHICH YOU ARE PERFORMING WE WANT YOU TO KNOW THAT OUR PRAYERS ARE WITH BOTH OF YOU DOING

---

1. While driving with white author Lillian Smith on 4 May, King was stopped by police and charged with having an improper driving license. Pleading guilty in Judge J. Oscar Mitchell's court on 23 September, King was fined $25.00 and sentenced to a twelve-month probation. King later told reporters that he had not been informed about the suspended sentence ("Dr. King Is Accused under Old Charge," *New York Times,* 25 October 1960; see also Frank Wells, "King Held on Old Count As Sit-Inners Leave Jail," *Atlanta Constitution,* 24 October 1960).

Hello girls,

Words can never adequately express appreciation. Real appreciation must flow from the deep seas of the heart. But in my stumbling words I would like to thank you for your intrepid courage, your quiet dignity, and your undaunted faith in the power of non-violence. Never before have I been more proud to be a Negro. Never before have I had more faith in the future. It is inspiring enough to see the fellows willingly accepting jail rather than bail, but when young ladies are willing to accept the cup of self suffering for the cause of freedom it is truly majestic and sublime.

Letter written in jail to women arrested with King during the October 1960 Atlanta sit-ins

THIS PRESENT MOMENT OF CRISIS THROUGH WHICH YOU ARE PASSING OUR PRAYER IS THAT TRUE JUSTICE AND GOOD WILL, WILL PREVAIL

DEXTER AVENUE BAPTIST CHURCH HERBERT M EATON PASTOR.

PWSr. SCLCR-GAMK: Box 5.

From the Student Nonviolent Coordinating Committee

26 October 1960
Atlanta, Ga.

At a packed public hearing on 25 October, DeKalb County judge J. Oscar Mitchell declared King's involvement in the Rich's sit-in a violation of his probation and sentenced him to four months hard labor at the Georgia State Prison in Reidsville. An SCLC press release issued the following day reported that Mitchell's decision "struck the hundreds of King supporters like a bombshell. Mrs. King wept quietly, Dr. King, Sr. was visibly moved; many of the coeds of the Atlanta University system burst into tears. Faces that reflected shock and horror were innumerable."[1] Following sentencing, SNCC officers Marion Barry and Edward King sent this note of support.[2] It is not likely that this wire, sent at 12:34 A.M. on the 26th, reached King before he was moved a few hours later from DeKalb County jail to the state prison; a handwritten note on the telegram reads "Not there."

DR MARTING LUTHER KING JR
DEKALB COUNTY JAIL DEKALB COUNTY GA

THE STUDENT NON VIOLENT COORDINATING COMMITTEE, SPEAKING FOR STUDENTS ALL OVER AMERICA, REACHES ACROSS THE BARS OF THE DEKALB COUNTY

1. Roy Wilkins, also present in the courtroom, predicted that the verdict would "be felt all over the country as a persecution rather than a satisfaction of a violation of a traffic rule" ("King Given 4 Months Hard Labor," *Montgomery Advertiser*, 26 October 1960).

2. Marion Shepilov Barry, Jr. (1936–), born in Itta Bena, Mississippi, received a B.A. (1958) from Le Moyne College and an M.S. (1960) from Fisk University. At Le Moyne Barry became active in the NAACP and at Fisk participated in the Nashville sit-ins. He was elected SNCC's first chairman in April 1960 but resigned the following November to focus on academics. Barry left a doctoral program in 1964 to return to SNCC's staff. Two years later he founded the Free D.C. Movement and organized a boycott of the city's public transportation. In 1974, Barry was elected to D.C.'s first city council and served as mayor (1979–1991). After serving six months in prison on drug charges, he was reelected in 1994 and served as mayor until 1999. Edward Biking King, Jr. (1939–1982), born in Roanoke, Virginia, was a Kentucky State College student when he was elected SNCC historian at the group's founding in April 1960; he later served as SNCC's first administrative secretary. King was expelled from Kentucky State in the spring of 1960 for his protest activities. He resigned from SNCC in September 1961 to attend Wilberforce University, where he obtained a B.S. (1963) in education. He later became a business executive and served as associate director of the Association of American Publishers' Office of Minority Manpower.

JAIL, IN THANKS TO YOU FOR YOUR DEEP COMMITMENT TO THE CONCEPT OF NO VIOLENCE, AND YOUR VISION OF A FREE SOCIETY WHICH MAKES POSSIBLE THIS STUDENT MOVEMENT. YOU SAT IN WITH US, YOU WENT TO JAIL WITH US, WE WANT YOU TO KNOW THAT THE FIGHT WILL NOT END FOR WE HAVE TAKEN UP THE TORCH FOR FREEDOM, WE WILL NOT FORGET THAT YOU ARE BEHIND IRON BARS. WE ASK THAT YOU REMEMBER US AS WE TRY TO REMOVE THE BARS THAT EXIST IN THE HEARTS OF MEN. YOURS IN THE CAUSE FOR FREEDOM

THE STUDENT NON VIOLENT COORDINATING COMMITTEE MARION S BARRY JR—CHAIRMAN—EDWARD BIKING JR—ADMINISTRATIVE SECRETARY.

PHWSr. MLKJP-GAMK: Vault Box 5.

To Coretta Scott King

[26 *October 1960*]
Reidsville, Ga.

King writes to his wife from the Georgia State Prison at Reidsville. He tells her "that it is extremely difficult for me to think of being away from you and my Yoki and Marty for four months" but that his ordeal "is the cross that we must bear for the freedom of our people."

Hello Darling,

Today I find myself a long way from you and the children. I am at the State Prison in Reidsville which is about 230 miles from Atlanta. They picked me up from the DeKalb jail about 4 'o clock this morning.[1] I know this whole experience is very difficult for you to adjust to, especially in your condition of pregnancy, but as I said to you yesterday this is the cross that we must bear for the freedom of our people.[2] So I urge you to be strong in in faith, and this will in turn strengthen me. I can assure you that it is extremely difficult for me to think of being away from you and my Yoki and Marty for four months, but I am asking God hourly to give me the power of endurance. I have the faith to believe that this excessive suffer-

1. King's attorney Donald Hollowell, who expected to see his client at the county jail that morning, complained that the pre-dawn transfer "came with astonishing . . . and unnecessary swiftness" (John Britton, "Motion to Revoke Conviction of King Rejected Following Early Morning Transfer to Reidsville," *Atlanta Daily World,* 27 October 1960). In a 1964 interview, King recalled the transfer: "They dealt with me just like I was a hardened criminal. They had me chained all the way down there, you know, the chains around my legs which kind of tied my legs" (King, Interview by Berl I. Bernhard, 9 March 1964).

2. In her memoir, Coretta King recalled speaking with her husband shortly after he had been sentenced: "I was trying not to cry when we went into the cell, but the tears were streaming down my face. When Martin saw me he said, 'Corrie, dear, you have to be strong. I've never seen you like this before. You have to be strong for me'" (*My Life with Martin Luther King, Jr.,* pp. 193–194). Dexter Scott, the Kings' third child, was born on 31 January 1961.

ing that is now coming to our family will in some little way serve to make Atlanta a better city, Georgia a better state, and America a better country. Just how I do not yet know, but I have faith to believe it will. If I am correct then our suffering is not in vain.

I understand that I can have visitors twice a month—the second and fourth Sunday. However, I understand that everybody—white and colored—can have visitors this coming Sunday. I hope you can find some way to come down. I know it will be a terrible inconvenience in your condition, but I want to see you and the children very badly. Also ask Wyatt to come. There are some very urgent things that I will need to talk with him about.[3] Pleas bring the following books to me: Stride Toward Freedom, Paul Tillich's Systematic Theology Vol 1&2, George Buttrick The Parables of Jesus E. S. Jones Mahatma Gandhi, Horns and Halo, a Bible, a Dictionary and my reference dictionary called Increasing your Word Power.[4] This book is an old book in a red cover and it may be in the den or upstairs in one of my [*strikeout illegible*] bags. Also bring the following sermons from my file: "What is Man" "The Three Dimensions" "The Death of Evil" "Why could not we cast him out?" "Why Jesus called A man A Fool" "The God Samaritan" "The Peril of the Sword" "Our God is Able" "Levels of Love" "Loving your enemies" "God of the Lost" "Vision of A world made New" "Keep moving From this Mountain" "A Religion of Doing" "Looking Beyond you circumstances" The Impassable Gulf" "Love for Action" "Christ The Center of our Faith" Some of these are in the file; others are on the desk.[5] Also bring a radio

Give my best regards to all the family. Please ask them not to worry about me. I will adjust to whatever comes in terms of pain. Hope to see you Sunday.

Eternally yours
[*signed*] Martin

ALS. MLKJP-GAMK: Vault Box 1.

---

3. In a 26 October telegram Walker wrote to King: "I will be to see you tomorrow afternoon."

4. King annotated his personal copies of E. Stanley Jones's *Mahatma Gandhi: An Interpretation* (New York: Abingdon-Cokesbury Press, 1948) and J. Wallace Hamilton's *Horns and Halos in Human Nature* (Westwood, N.J.: Fleming H. Revell Company, 1954).

5. Several of these titles also appeared as chapters in King's 1963 book of sermons *Strength to Love* (New York: Harper & Row).

From Michael Meeropol

26 October 1960
Swarthmore, Pa.

This postcard of support from the elder son of Julius and Ethel Rosenberg—the first American civilians executed for conspiracy to commit espionage—arrived among a batch of correspondence from Swarthmore college students who wished to express "moral support to the jailed student demonstrators in Atlanta."[1]

26 Oct 1960

Dear Rev. King:

I am a freshman at college, and I'd like to express my personal feelings and the feelings of my classmates about you and your work.[2] Our hearts go out to you and the brave Southern students. Anything that we can do, we'll be more than happy to. We are with you all the way.

Very sincerely,
[*signed*] Michael Meeropol 1964

ALS. SCLCR-GAMK: Box 5.

---

1. In 1951 the Rosenbergs were found guilty of conspiracy to commit espionage on behalf of the Soviet Union. Despite an international campaign for clemency, they were executed at New York's Sing Sing Prison in 1953. Michael A. Meeropol (1943–) was born Michael Rosenberg in New York City. In 1957 he and his brother Robert were adopted by Abel Meeropol (also known as Lewis Allan), who wrote the lyrics and co-wrote the music to the classic anti-lynching song "Strange Fruit," and his wife, Anne. The Meeropols were longtime Communist Party members. Michael Meeropol earned a B.A. (1964) from Swarthmore College, a B.A. (1966) and an M.A. (1970) from King's College, Cambridge University, and a Ph.D. (1973) from the University of Wisconsin. In 1970 Meeropol became a professor of economics at Western New England College.

2. In an October 1960 meeting, the Swarthmore Student Council unanimously adopted a proposal "to appropriate money for the purchase of postcards to be distributed to and sent" to the jailed sit-in participants (Swarthmore College, Minutes, Student council meeting on 23 October 1960, 28 October 1960).

From Nnamdi Azikiwe

26 October 1960
Lagos, Nigeria

Nnamdi Azikiwe, the newly appointed governor-general of Nigeria, writes in the hope that King will attend his inauguration.[1] *King traveled to Lagos in November to*

---

1. Nnamdi Azikiwe (1904–1996), born in Zungeru, Nigeria, attended missionary schools in Lagos before receiving a B.A. (1930) and an M.A. (1932) from Lincoln University in Chester County, Pennsylvania. He also received an M.S. (1933) from the University of Pennsylvania. Azikiwe edited the Gold Coast's *Africa Morning Post* in the mid-1930s and was convicted of sedition by the colonial government for an article appearing therein; the conviction was later overturned on appeal. Returning to Nigeria in 1937, he founded the *West African Pilot* and four other periodicals, which he used to agitate for independence from Britain. In 1944 he helped found the National Council of Nigeria and

26 Oct 1960

attend the festivities, which included several luncheons and a dance performance in honor of the African independence leader and his wife.[2]

The Rev. Martin Luther King, Jnr,
c/o Dr. Marguerite Cartwright,
57 Fifth Avenue,
New York 3, N.Y.

My dear Reverend King:

This is to inform you that I have included your name in the list of invitees to attend my inauguration on November 16, 1960, when I will be sworn in as Governor-General and Commander-in-Chief of the Federation of Nigeria.

The occasion will be of historic interest because it will be the first time in our national history when a person of African descent will be assuming the high office of Head of State in Nigeria, as representative of Her Majesty the Queen, Head of the Commonwealth.

I hope that when the official invitation reaches you, you will be disposed to accept same.[3] I am looking forward to an early reunion with you.

With kind wishes.

Sincerely yours,
[*signed*]
NNAMDI AZIKIWE

TLS. MLKP-MBU: Box 53A.

---

the Cameroons and in 1947 was elected to the Nigerian Legislative Council. Azikiwe was appointed to the honorary post of governor-general of Nigeria by Queen Elizabeth II in 1960. In 1963 Nigeria became a republic with Azikiwe as its first president; he served until deposed by a military coup in 1966.

2. Azikiwe, Invitation to the state luncheon, 18 November 1960; Azikiwe, Invitation to a display of national traditional dances, 18 November 1960; and K. O. Mbadiwe, Invitation to Martin Luther King, Jr., 19 November 1960.

3. A formal invitation to King was sent in care of *Pittsburgh Courier* columnist Marguerite Cartwright by the office of independent Nigeria's first prime minister, Abubakar Tafawa Balewa (Secretary to the Prime Minister of Nigeria to King, 23 October 1960). In her 23 October letter Cartwright forwarded the invitation and urged King to accept. In her 10 December 1960 article, Cartwright reported on the planning of the inauguration festivities: "Lucky candidates for the coveted invitations were personally selected by the then Governor General Designate. A number of the cables and invitations were directed to my home for forwarding" ("World Backdrop," *Pittsburgh Courier,* 10 December 1960).

Interview after Release from Georgia State Prison at Reidsville

27 Oct 1960

[*27 October 1960*]
[*Reidsville, Ga.*]

On 26 October, Massachusetts senator and presidential candidate John F. Kennedy telephoned Coretta Scott King from Chicago and expressed his concern about her husband's imprisonment.[1] *Kennedy's brother and campaign manager Robert initiated a series of calls to Georgia officials, including Judge J. Oscar Mitchell, reportedly to inquire into King's right to bail.*[2] *The following day, King was released on a $2,000 appeal bond after eight days imprisonment.*[3] *In this interview, King concedes that Kennedy "served as a great force in making the release possible." While King maintained a nonpartisan stance in the presidential race, his father publicly announced he was switching his support from Nixon to Kennedy in light of the Democratic candidate's call to his daughter-in-law.*[4] *This transcript is drawn from television news footage.*

[*King*]: I understand from very reliable sources that Senator Kennedy served as a great force in making the release possible. [*gap in film*] I think a great deal of Senator Kennedy. I have met him, and I've talked with him on three different occasions since the nomination, and I think a great deal of him. But I would not, at this point, endorse any candidate because of the nonpartisan position that I follow.

[*Interviewer*]: Some who say that you espouse the Supreme Court as being the law of the land and yet you break another law by taking part in sit-ins. What comment have you on that?

[*King*]: I would simply say that a law can only be a valid law if it is a just law, as St. Augustine said centuries ago. If a particular law is not in line with the moral laws of the universe, then I think a righteous and just person has no alternative but to protest against that unjust law. I urge people to follow the Supreme Court's

1. Coretta Scott King later recalled that Kennedy had said: "I want to express to you my concern about your husband. I know this must be very hard for you. I understand you are expecting a baby, and I just wanted you to know that I was thinking about you and Dr. King. If there is anything I can do to help, please feel free to call on me" (*My Life with Martin Luther King, Jr.*, p. 196).

2. Following King's release, Kennedy campaign headquarters confirmed Robert Kennedy's call to the judge but insisted that "any suggestion that interference was involved is untrue" (Charles Moore and Gene Britton, "King Freed on $2,000 Bond, Flies Home from Reidsville," *Atlanta Constitution*, 28 October 1960; see also Bruce Galphin, "His Call Misinterpreted, Robert Kennedy Says," *Atlanta Constitution*, 1 November 1960). For further discussion of Robert Kennedy's efforts on King's behalf, see Introduction, pp. 38–40.

3. Harold Ross, owner of the Fulton Bonding Company, provided the money for King's release (John Britton, "Minister Flies Back to Atlanta from Reidsville," *Birmingham World*, 2 November 1960).

4. Moore and Britton, "King Freed on $2,000 Bond." In a second interview, King acknowledged that he was "deeply indebted" to Kennedy for his help (King, Interview on John F. Kennedy's role in release from prison, 27 October 1960). For more on King and the presidential election, see King, Statement on Presidential Endorsement, 1 November 1960, and King to Ray A. Burchfield, 5 November 1960, pp. 537–540 and 542–544 in this volume, respectively.

27 Oct 1960

decision of 1954 because I think that particular decision is in line with the moral law of the universe. That decision establishes a fact that persons should be treated as persons and not things, so that I would urge everybody to follow that law. But if there are laws that are out of harmony with the moral law of the universe then I think we have a moral obligation to disobey those unjust laws in order to bring man-made laws into harmony with the law of God or the moral laws of the universe.

[*Film shows King's release from the Georgia State Prison at Reidsville*]

[*Interviewer*]: Dr. King, have you heard anything from Vice President Nixon or any of his supporters?

[*King*]: No, I haven't. I've been confined for the last eight days, and I haven't talked with anybody, actually, from Washington or from the campaign.[5]

[*Interviewer*]: Do you know whether any efforts were made on behalf of the Republican headquarters to help you?

[*King*]: No, I don't. I haven't heard of any efforts being made, and I don't know of any personally.

[*Interviewer*]: Do you know of any efforts made on behalf of the Kennedy group?

[*King*]: Well, I understand that the Kennedy group did make definite contacts and did a great deal to make my release possible. I don't know all of the details of this just coming out of [*gap in film*]

[*Interviewer*]: [*words inaudible*] you to vote for Kennedy?

[*King*]: Well, I would not like to make a public statement concerning the person for whom I will vote because I follow a nonpartisan course and, heading a non-partisan organization, namely the Southern Christian Leadership Conference [*film interrupted*]

F. NBCNA-NNNBC.

---

5. Following reports of Kennedy's role in King's release, Republican nominee Richard Nixon was criticized in some circles for his silence. Gloster B. Current, an NAACP official, commented at a conference that "Vice President Nixon may have thrown away a large segment of the Negro vote by his failure to speak out on the King arrest" ("NAACP Says Nixon Hurt in King Case," *Atlanta Constitution,* 31 October 1960). E. Frederic Morrow, the first African American appointed to an executive position in the White House, similarly recalled that Kennedy's phone call "won the election" and that the newly elected president "had keen, intelligent Negro advisers" that "he obviously listened to" (Morrow, *Black Man in the White House* [New York: Coward-McCann, 1963], p. 296).

Statement on Presidential Endorsement

1 November 1960
Atlanta, Ga.

One week before the presidential election, King announces that he has no plans to endorse a candidate but expresses gratitude for the Democratic nominee's concern about his imprisonment: "I hope that this example of Senator Kennedy's courage will be a lesson deeply learned."[1]

I have been asked from many quarters whether it is my intention to endorse one of the presidential candidates. The organization of which I am president, the Southern Christian Leadership Conference, from its inception and in its constitution has been non-partisan.[2] Accordingly, as its titular head, I am unable to endorse a political party or its candidate.[3] Moreover, the role that is mine in the emerging social order of the South and America demands that I remain non-partisan. This, devoid of partisan political attachments, I am free to be critical of both parties when necessary.[4]

But for fear of being considered an ingrate, I want to make it palpably clear that I am deeply grateful to Senator Kennedy for the genuine concern he expressed in my arrest. When reactionary forces sought to crush our movement for desegregation by methods so unjust and unwise that millions were inflamed with indignation, Senator Kennedy exhibited moral courage of a high order. He voluntarily expresses his position effectively and took an active and articulate stand for a just resolution. I hope that this example of Senator Kennedy's courage will be

1. This statement was distributed at an afternoon press conference (John Britton, "King Not Backing Either Candidate," *Atlanta Daily World*, 2 November 1960). Just prior to the election, Kennedy supporters in Philadelphia produced a pamphlet aimed at black voters that featured positive statements on Kennedy from King, King Sr., Coretta King, Ralph Abernathy, and Gardner Taylor. The pamphlet quoted Abernathy: "It is time for all of us to take off our Nixon buttons." King, Sr. acknowledged that he had been planning to vote against Kennedy "because of his religion" but had decided that "now he can be my President, Catholic or whatever he is" (Freedom Crusade Committee, Pamphlet, "The Case of Martin Luther King," 27 October–7 November 1960). For more on King, Sr.'s support of Kennedy, see King to Ray A. Burchfield, 5 November 1960, pp. 542–544 in this volume.

2. SCLC's constitution does not refer to the organization's nonpartisan status but states that SCLC is a charitable organization with an orientation toward "improving the Civic, Religious, Economic, and Cultural Conditions in the South and in the Nation" (SCLC, "Constitution and by-laws," November 1958).

3. Three days before the election, King's secretary Dora McDonald responded to Luvenia Springfield's 18 October request for advice on the "best" way to vote. McDonald acknowledged that as SCLC's president King "does not publicly endorse any candidates for political office" but privately "Dr. King intends to support Senator Kennedy—feeling that he has the best program for the hour" (McDonald to Springfield, 5 November 1960).

4. In response to a 1 November letter from Emory University theology professor Claude Thompson, King reiterated his nonpartisanship: "While I felt compelled to thank Senator Kennedy for his call to my wife and other expressions of concern, I wanted to make it clear that this should not be construed in any way as an endorsement" (King to Thompson, 5 November 1960). For King's political positions during the 1956 presidential campaign, see King to Viva O. Sloan, 1 October 1956, and King to Earl Kennedy, 30 October 1956, in *Papers* 3:383–384 and 408–409, respectively.

not only has he a great mind—but now I am convinced that he also has a great heart. This is the kind of man we need at this hour."

DR. GARDNER TAYLOR

President of The Protestant Council of New York

"All Americans can rejoice that Dr. Martin Luther King and all the sit-in students are now out of jail. We can also be proud that during these days of moral crisis one of the candidates for the Presidency showed that he had the heart and the American sense of fair play to take the initiative in expressing his concern and contributing to a just solution.

"This is the kind of moral leadership and direct personal concern which this problem has lacked in these last critical years. I was pleased to learn from Mrs. Coretta King herself that it was the candidate of my choice, Senator Kennedy, who personally telephoned Mrs. King and who took direct action to bring about the release of Dr. King and the students.

"*I am disappointed that when this time for plain speaking and action was at hand, there was nothing but silence from Mr. Nixon. I find it incredible that any candidate for the Presidency would be so insensitive to a case which has world-wide implications as to say that he has no comment about it.* I hope that Mr. Nixon will correct this report in The New York Times.

"My disappointment is doubled by the fact that Mr. Nixon did not respond to the request for a message of support to the Atlanta convention of the Student Non-Violent Coordinating Committee two weeks ago. Senator Kennedy sent a stirring message saying that 'The human rights for which you strive are the definite goal of all America.' "

FROM N.Y. POST EDITORIAL

It was Senator Kennedy who responded . . . He did so presumably with full awareness that his words and deeds would inflame the Southern racists and multiply his difficulties in Dixie.

Throughout this interval Mr. Nixon remained passive and silent, ignoring a plea from the sit-in group for a comparable declaration of support and articulating no sentiment about the harassment of Rev. King.

Mr. Nixon may have some pious afterthoughts to offer now that Rev. King has been released. But in this dramatic human episode Senator Kennedy has looked a lot larger and warmer—and bolder—than his opponent.

"No Comment" Nixon

versus

A Candidate With a Heart, Senator Kennedy

THE CASE OF MARTIN LUTHER KING

•

The following statements have been issued to or appeared in the press on a case of international significance testing American justice.

Sponsored by:
THE FREEDOM CRUSADE COMMITTEE
5536 Poplar Street, Philadelphia, Pa.
Rev. Marshall L. Shepard and Dr. William A. Gray, Co-Chairmen

Pamphlet endorsing John F. Kennedy's presidential campaign, sponsored by the Freedom Crusade Committee (7 November 1960)

American Justice on Trial

MRS. MARTIN LUTHER KING:

"*It certainly made me feel good that he called me personally and let me know how he felt.* Senator Kennedy said he was very much concerned about both of us. He said this must be hard on me. He wanted me to know he was thinking about us and he would do all he could to help.

"I told him I appreciated it and hoped he would help. I had the feeling that if he was that much concerned he would do what he could so that Mr. King would be let out of jail.

"I have heard nothing from the Vice President or anyone on his staff. *Mr. Nixon has been very quiet.*"

REV. MARTIN LUTHER KING, SR.:

"I had expected to vote against Senator Kennedy because of his religion. But now he can be my President, Catholic or whatever he is.

"It took courage to call my daughter-in-law at a time like this. He has the moral courage to stand up for what he knows is right. He has shown his sympathy and concern and his respect for the Constitutional rights of all Americans.

"I've got all my votes and I've got a suitcase and I'm going to take them up there and dump them in his lap."

REV. RALPH ABERNATHY

President, Montgomery Improvement Association; Secretary-Treasurer, Southern Christian Leadership Conference

"I earnestly and sincerely feel that it is time for all of us to take off our Nixon buttons. I wish to make it crystal clear that I am not hog-tied to any party. My first concern is for the 350-year long struggle of our people.

"Now I have made up my mind to vote for Senator Kennedy because I am convinced he is concerned about our struggle.

"*Senator Kennedy did something great and wonderful when he personally called Mrs. Coretta King and helped free Dr. Martin Luther King.* This was the kind of act I was waiting for. It was not just Dr. King on trial—America was on trial.

"Mr. Nixon could have helped, but he took no step in this direction. It is my understanding that he refused even to comment on the case.

"I learned a long time ago that one kindness deserves another. Since Mr. Nixon has been silent through all this, I am going to return his silence when I go into the voting booth.

"Senator Kennedy showed his great concern for humanity when he acted first without counting the cost. He risked his political welfare in the South. We must offset whatever loss he may sustain.

"He has my wholehearted support because

Dr. Martin Luther King, Jr.

"I am deeply indebted to Senator Kennedy who served as a great force in making my release possible. It took a lot of courage for Senator Kennedy to do this, especially in Georgia. For him to be that courageous shows that he is really acting upon principle and not expediency. He did it because of his great concern and his humanitarian bent.

"*I hold Senator Kennedy in very high esteem. I am convinced he will seek to exercise the power of his office to fully implement the civil rights plank of his party's platform.*

"I never intend to be a religious bigot. I never intend to reject a man running for President of the United States just because he is a Catholic. Religious bigotry is as immoral, un-democratic, un-American and un-Christian as racial bigotry."

a lesson deeply learned and consistently applied by all as we move forward in a non violent but resolute spirit to achieve rapidly proper standards of humanity and justice in our swiftly evolving world.

I would also like to express my appreciation to Mayor Hartsfield for his constrictive leadership throughout this whole struggle. I have always argued that the silent multitude of the South, who sincerely want fair play to be the hallmark of our society, needed support and encouragement available only from its major leadership to enable them to give open expression to their belief. I consider that Mayor Hartsfield's action illustrates the soundness of this course.[5] The best antidote to degeneration of conflict of opinion into maliciousness and violence is statesmanlike, firm, expressions of the moral issues giving active support to proper resolution.

This is not the time to look back, but to look forward. I am full of hope for the future because of the goodwill and concern shown by so many people in Georgia and all over the country.

Now let us use this period for genuine negotiations so that Atlanta can take a step forward toward the society of "wisdom, justice and moderation" which the Seal of the State of Georgia and the Constitution of the United States promised.

TD. MLKP-MBU: Box 2.

---

5. King refers to the thirty-day "sit-in truce" arranged by William B. Hartsfield to secure the release of the student protesters arrested in late October. On 22 November, Hartsfield reported that the merchants were still unwilling to desegregate their lunch counters. The students granted the merchants an extension, but talks fell apart on 24 November and the protests resumed ("Hartfield Wins New Sit-In Truce, *Atlanta Constitution,* 23 November 1960, and "Truce Talk on Sit-Ins Canceled," *Atlanta Constitution,* 29 November 1960).

"Special Meeting with Doctors M. L. King, Jr. and Samuel W. Williams"

2 November 1960
[*Atlanta, Ga.*]

On 2 November King met with Atlanta black college administrators to discuss the "coordination of student and adult leadership" in the local sit-in movement. The next day Benjamin Mays sent King these notes from the meeting, which was held at Atlanta University.

Present: Messrs. Rufus E. Clement, Frank Cunningham, M. L. King, Jr., Albert Manley, Benjamin E. Mays, A. A. McPheeters, Harry Richardson and Samuel W. Williams.[1]

---

1. Clement served as president of Atlanta University (1937–1967), Cunningham as president of Morris Brown College (1958–1965), Manley as president of Spelman College (1953–1976), Mays as

The main concern is how to coordinate protests and sit-in demonstrations with academic excellence. Doctor King expressed appreciate for the conference and said that he is definitely concerned with what we are concerned with. He too is in favor of coordination of student and adult leadership.

All aspects of the protest movement were explored and there was a meeting of minds in several areas. The Reverend Mr. Williams suggested that there should be an over-all committee on which Dr. King would sit to advise on all future actions in the area of protest demonstrations. Doctor King raised the question as to the function of such a committee. "Will it be advisory or policy making?" It was clear the committee would be primarily advisory.

A new committee will be set up as an advisory committee with Rev. S. W. Williams and Dr. M. L. King, Jr. being requested to convene the new committee after the Council of Presidents have had an opportunity to talk with the students on the All University Center Committee on An Appeal for Human Rights. November 4, we will invite the students to meet with the Council of Presidents at 2:30 p.m. Next Monday, November 6, at 3 p.m. the new committee will meet.[2]

Meeting adjourned.

TD. MLKP-MBU.

---

president of Morehouse College (1940–1967), McPheeters as dean of Academic Affairs at Clark College (1941–1962), Richardson was founding president of Atlanta's Interdenominational Theological Center (1959–1969), and Samuel Williams was chairman of the Department of Philosophy and Religion at Morehouse College (1947–1970).

2. King met with the students and adult leaders on 7 November but plans to form an overall advisory committee stalled because of opposition from student and adult leaders (Minutes, Meeting on advisory committee on desegregation of lunch counters, 7 November 1960; and J. H. Calhoun, "Notes on conference with college presidents," 8 December 1960).

To Walter R. Chivers

5 November 1960
[*Atlanta, Ga.*]

In a 4 October letter, King's Morehouse sociology professor recommended that he cosponsor a Planned Parenthood study on contraception. Chivers, who had volunteered with the organization for sixteen years, vouched "for it's integrity, honesty, and complete lack of racial prejudice." In the letter below, King agrees to become a member of the sponsoring committee.[1]

---

1. The study was published several years later (Lee Rainwater, *Family Design: Marital Sexuality, Family Size, and Contraception* [Chicago: Aldine, 1965]). The birth control pill was introduced in the United States in 1960.

5 Nov 1960

Mr. Walter R. Chivers
Morehouse College
Atlanta, Georgia

Dear Professor Chivers:

Please forgive me for being so tardy in my reply to your letter of October 4.[2] Several unforeseen circumstances, including an eight-day sojourn in Georgia jails, account for the delay.

After giving the matter serious consideration, I am happy to say that it will be possible for me to serve on the sponsoring committee of the new study being made by the Planned Parenthood Federation of America. I must say that the decision was based on your high recommendation of this agency. Of course, I have always been deeply interested in and sympathetic with the total work of the Planned Parenthood Federation so you may feel free to write Miss Snyder concerning my acceptance.[3]

I will look forward to receiving additional information as time goes on.

Very sincerely yours,
Martin Luther King, Jr.

MLK.m

TLc. MLKP-MBU: Box 34.

---

2. After receiving no response to his initial letter, Chivers sent King a reminder on 2 November.

3. After receiving a copy of this letter from Chivers, Margaret Snyder of Planned Parenthood expressed her appreciation for King's support (Snyder to King, 14 November 1960). In a 1957 advice column in *Ebony,* King wrote that he did "not think it is correct to argue that birth control is sinful" and called "birth control rationally and morally justifiable" (King, "Advice for Living," December 1957, in *Papers* 4:326).

To Ray A. Burchfield

5 November 1960
[*Atlanta, Ga.*]

King rejects an Indiana minister's charge that he is being used by the Democratic Party "as a tool for their selfish designs."[1] *Burchfield had voiced his opinion that King ought "to go the press and tell them that as an American Negro you will not be used by any political party for its benefit."*[2] *King dismisses Burchfield's concerns about King, Sr.'s*

---

1. Burchfield to King, 28 October 1960.

2. Burchfield to King, 1 November 1960; see also Burchfield to King, 3 November 1960. Ray A. Burchfield (1916–1981), born in Toronto, Ohio, received a B.A. (1948) from Marion College and a B.D. (1952) from the Christian Theological Seminary. Burchfield was a member of the board of directors of the Anderson, Indiana, Urban League from 1958 until 1962 and served as chairman of the Committee on Scholarships and Student Aid.

recent statements in support of Kennedy: "I am sure you will agree with me that my father, being sixty-two years old, is capable of making his own decisions and should have the freedom to vote any way that he chooses."[3]

Rev. Ray A. Burchfield
Fifth Street Methodist Church
Anderson,
Indiana

Dear Rev. Burchfield:

I am about to leave town and I hasten to drop this note to you before leaving.

I am very sorry that you have been misinformed concerning my political views at this time. I have not in the past and I will not in the next few days endorse Senator Kennedy or Vice President Nixon for the position of President of the United States. It has been my policy all along to follow a non-partisan course.

I am sure you will agree with me that my father, being sixty-two years old, is capable of making his own decisions and should have the freedom to vote any way that he chooses. His position does not in any way need to be construed as my position.

If this letter appears rather blunt, please forgive me, but I am sure that you know by now that a person in my position is constantly misquoted by the press and misrepresented. I think the enclosed statement, which I made just three days ago, will clarify my position.[4]

I must confess that I am very disappointed with your whole letter, and particularly the implication that I am seeking to strengthen the Southern Christian Leadership Conference financially with some of the Kennedy millions. In fact, I am so disappointed with this implication that I will not bother to answer it.

If, in this time, my integrity as a person and the integrity of the Southern Christian Leadership Conference have not been established, I am convinced that all of my words of explanation would be null and void. We certainly appreciate whatever support that you have given to the Southern Christian Leadership Conference, and other humanitarian organizations.

Concerning your resignation from the groups that you mentioned, I can only say, without seeking to offend you in any way, that if such a misunderstanding causes you to resign, you may not have been as committed to their purposes and goals as you thought you were.[5]

I am afraid I must close. I wish I had more time to discuss this matter with you.

---

3. At a mass meeting welcoming his son home from prison, King, Sr. reportedly told an audience: "I've got all my votes, and I've got a suitcase, and I'm going to take them up there and dump them in his lap" (Margaret Shannon and Douglas Kiker, "Out on Bond, King to Name Choice," *Atlanta Journal,* 28 October 1960).

4. King may refer to his Statement on Presidential Endorsement, 1 November 1960, pp. 537–540 in this volume.

5. In his 1 November letter to King, Burchfield threatened to resign from his positions with the Urban League if King did not "make a statement and give the American public some satisfaction other than the partisan bias you have given to Senator Kennedy."

Again I must ask you to forgive me if I have written too boldly, but believe me, it is humbly sincere and with Christian love.

Very sincerely yours,
Martin Luther King, Jr.

MLK:m

TLc. MLKP-MBU: Box 21.

Interview by Zenas Sears on "For Your Information"

[*6 November 1960*]
Atlanta, Ga.

Two days before the presidential election, Atlanta radio station WAOK broadcasted King's reflections on the candidates and his recent arrest.[1] *In this transcript of an audio recording of the interview, King rejects the suggestion that he has a "martyr complex," explaining: "I don't enjoy suffering and I don't have any desire to die."*[2]

[*Sears*]: This is Zenas Sears, program director of radio station WAOK. The program is "For Your Information." The opinions expressed on this program are those of the individual expressing them and not necessarily those of the radio station. Today, we are recording this program before broadcast time in the office of Reverend Martin Luther King, Jr., co-pastor of the Ebenezer Baptist Church here in Atlanta and president of the Southern Christian Leadership Conference. I hope I got that full title of the Conference out properly, Reverend King. I

[*King*]: Yes, that is exactly right.

[*Sears*]: It's, as your staff has expressed to me a couple times, rather a mouthful, but I think we're beginning to get it right now. [*laughs*]

[*King*]: Right.

[*Sears*]: Very nice for you to let us come and talk with you. There's some burning questions on the minds of many people in this country, I'd say a great majority of the country, and we hope that maybe you'll be kind enough to answer a few of those questions for us today. In reading the paper, in, where your name has

1. King's interview was recorded sometime between 28 October and 4 November ("Dr. King Airing Views on Rights," *Atlanta Constitution,* 4 November 1960).

2. Zenas Sears (1913–1988), born in Akron, Ohio, was a radio announcer and disc jockey who helped introduce African American music to Atlanta radio in the late 1940s. Sears, who received a B.S. (1936) from Johns Hopkins University, worked at several Atlanta stations before purchasing WATL in 1954 and renaming it WAOK. His support of both black music and SCLC often put him at odds with his employers, public officials, and the Ku Klux Klan. Sears also promoted the careers of many Georgia rhythm and blues artists, including Ray Charles, James Brown, and William "Piano Red" Perryman (Dr. Feelgood).

been so constantly in print in the last few days [*telephone rings*] and talking to people, it seems that one of the main questions, particularly in the area of the white moderate, if you, the mass of white citizens who may or may not be sympathetic, basically, with the cause espoused by the Southern Christian Leadership Conference, are disturbed over the, over the method used of breaking the law, various laws. And we'd like to ask you why it is necessary to break the law rather than to use the legal or lawful methods of picketing, boycotting, especially in regard to the business, restaurants in businesses?

[*King*]: Well, I would say, first, that when one moves into the whole question of breaking the law it brings up a very broad discussion because, first, in some situations, picketing is law-breaking. There are states and there are communities that have made laws against picketing. In Montgomery, Alabama, I was indicted and later convicted on the basis of what they call the anti-boycott law, so that even boycotting may be unlawful in some situations.[3] Therefore, I take the general position, following the words of Saint Augustine centuries ago, that an unjust law is no law at all and that a righteous man has a moral obligation to stand up and courageously protest against an unjust, man-made law in order to bring the law in line with the moral law of the universe.[4] If a man-made law is in conflict with what one's conscience reveals is a law of God, or the moral law of the universe, then he has a moral obligation, it seems to me, to break the unjust law and through self-suffering to accept whatever penalty comes. He's not seeking to evade the law as some of the extremist groups would do. He is not seeking to defy the law, but he is in a patient, loving, nonviolent way, consciously breaking the law in order to bring the law itself in line with the moral law of the universe. And I think, as I said, this is a moral responsibility.

[*Sears*]: Now, I've heard it said, mostly by the legal mind, that this is not necessary with any law. There is a legal, there is, there are legal recourses within the Constitution of the United States to attack any law outside of actually breaking it and testing it.

[*King*]: Well, there are certainly legal ways to do it. One can go into court and test the validity of the law. On the other hand, it seems to me that we have to bring into the equation the whole problem of using the courts to perpetuate an unjust law and to delay the ultimate implementation of a just law. Now, this is what we have seen in the South a great deal. The delaying tactics, the snail-like pace, for instance, of the implementation of the Supreme Court's decision is something that we are all familiar with, and it seems to me that the nonviolent, direct-action approach is one way that one can at least counteract this delaying method that is so often used by the reactionaries in the white South. As the attorney general of Georgia said on one occasion, "We are prepared for a century of litigation."[5] Now, I think he's quite true in stating that, that they would try to stall this whole issue a century through the litigation process. But the virtue of the nonviolent, direct-

3. For more on King's 1956 arrest in connection with the Montgomery bus boycott, see Testimony in *State of Alabama v. M. L. King, Jr.*, 22 March 1956, in *Papers* 3:183–196.

4. Cf. Augustine, *The City of God*, 19.21.

5. Eugene Cook was Georgia's attorney general from 1945 until 1965.

action approach is that it brings the issue directly to the center of community life, and it causes all people to at least look the issue squarely in the face and make some decision, for or against, but at least they are forced to the position of having to decide and seeing the issue first hand.

[*Sears*]: Now, you have, of course, in your discussions of the nonviolent method, direct-approach method have followed Gandhi, Mahatma Gandhi of India, whose course is now quite a person in history. And we forget that when he was using this method, he created, by nonviolence, a considerable amount of violence. Do you feel that this is, that this could possibly happen in your efforts?

[*King*]: Well, I don't, I don't at all throw this out as a possibility. This is *always* a risk that the nonviolent resister takes. He knows that violence is a possibility, but he feels justified in his course of action because the presence of injustice in society is already the presence of violence. Now, that violence, for the moment, may be lost beneath the surface, but it is still there. The presence of injustice is already the presence of potential of violence. And what the nonviolent resister does is to bring the whole issue to the surface so that society can be rid of all violence, and he feels justified in doing this because he's willing to absorb himself whatever violence emerges in the situation. So if any violence emerges, he's willing to take it among, upon himself. If it means being stabbed, if it means being shot, if it means his home being bombed, he takes that. His basic position is that he will never inflict violence upon another but that he will take it upon himself if it emerges in the situation.

[*Sears*]: We've had a great many people, and you've seen it in print of course, say that the action of the DeKalb County judge in forcing that little issue there, the traffic violation, created, at a time when it was very, very unfortunate from his point of view I would say, created more an image of the Reverend King, Martin Luther King, Jr., as a martyr almost overnight. Again, perhaps, this image has been created before, but this certainly, was this your intent when you, when this series of events started in the sit-in? Do you feel that you should become the image of the martyr in this country?

[*King*]: Well, I would hasten to say that I have no desire to be a martyr. I don't have a martyr complex. I don't enjoy suffering, and I don't have any desire to die. I'd like to live as long as anybody. My only concern is that we solve this problem of racial injustice, which, to my mind, is one of the most difficult, if not the most difficult, problems facing our nation today. It is certainly America's greatest moral dilemma, and my involvement in the struggle is not merely for Martin Luther King. It isn't merely for the Negro. It is to save the soul of America and because I think the whole struggle is morally right. Now, being involved in it will inevitably bring some suffering, and I will try to take that with all of the strength and all of the power of endurance that God will give me in the process, as I constantly pray. The prayers give me the power of endurance. But the basic aim, and certainly my basic concern, is that the problem will be solved and that it will be solved in a moral way. Therefore, it is as important for me to have moral means as it is to achieve a moral end.

[*Sears*]: Now, along this line, may I ask you one more question? How, and I don't mean this to sound sarcastic, but only, it is a sarcastic question in essence [*laughs*], but it does not come through, it comes merely through me. How can you decide which law is moral and which law is immoral?

[*King*]: Only on the basis of conscience. I am not as an individual, and certainly the Negro people collectively are not in a position to say they have absolute truth. I would never have any pretense to omniscience; I don't know everything, so that one has to be guided on the question of conscience here. Now, going beyond that, it seems to me that once the individual on the basis of conscience, and conscience develops in many ways through what we consider the religious insights of the ages. And it seems to me, from a religious point of view, segregation is wrong, and all of the laws that surround segregation and perpetuate the system would inevitably be wrong if the system itself is wrong. And then just on the basis of certain humanitarian insights that come to all of us, I think it would be wrong. And sometimes the majority opinion can be right, and I think the majority of people in the United States feel that segregation is wrong. I think the majority of the peoples of the world feel this, so that all of these things tend to substantiate one in a position of conscience. And the individual goes on out feeling that he's right on that basis. But it's possible that I'm wrong; it's possible that the other people in the struggle for freedom and human dignity are wrong. I don't know. Therefore, this is why I insist that we must follow moral means. We must always be nonviolent. The end is absolute, certainly. And we must also know and we must also follow means that for us are absolutely right. And I think violence is wrong, and I think nonviolence is right. Therefore, the means will be the guiding principle in all of our activities, or at least it should be.

[*Sears*]: Let me pin you down on one more question that comes to many people's minds. Should there be the occasion, in Atlanta or anywhere else, where a boycott or a nonviolent action on the part of students plus yourself and your group possibly, would throw a great many Negroes out of work on a reprisal basis, would you consider this a moral action on your part if you went ahead with that particular nonviolent action? I'm making it very loose, but we'll say that a certain store is under attack through sit-ins and you know that if the attack continues that maybe five hundred employees of that store will be thrown out of work. Is this, is your action in this case morally justified?

[*King*]: Now, do you mean all people working in the store or just Negro people?

[*Sears*]: Just the Negro people. A definite racial reprisal.

[*King*]: Yes. I would say this: first, the nonviolent resister must never be so lofty in his idealism that he doesn't come down to earth and consider certain practical problems of strategy and certain practical everyday problems that people confront. And this to me would be a matter of comparing the relative losses in the particular situation at the moment with the possible gains for the future. Now, it's never my desire to see people out of work, whether it's Negroes or white people, and if it means a lot of people losing jobs I would have to look at the total situation. I do feel that if one is right as an individual and if a community is moving out on a right course, then the individuals involved must be willing to face some suffering and sacrifice. And I've said constantly that freedom is not free. It may mean losing some jobs. It may even mean that some of us will have to spend some time in jail or somebody may have to die in the process. But I think all of this serves to redeem the social situation because I'm absolutely convinced that unearned suffering is redemptive, whether it's losing a job or whether it's suffering in another way. So it would depend, to answer the question, on my analysis of the situ-

6 Nov 1960

ation at the moment. If it means losing a few jobs here but ultimately gaining more jobs for everybody, then I would say that we should be willing to sacrifice those few jobs. Frankly, I don't have too many fears about losing jobs in any big sense. In Montgomery, for instance, we always had this threat from the white reactionaries that there would be a mass firing of Negroes

[*Sears interrupts*]: There was some

[*King continues*]: but it never happened.

[*Sears*]: But it didn't. Yes.

[*King*]: Yes.

[*Sears*]: There was very little. Pardon me, sir. What time do you have, Paul? How long have we gone? I wanted to get on another subject.

[*Paul?*]: Just about half.

[*Sears*]: Just about half. Good. Oh, by the way, Reverend King, did I hear that there is definitely going to be a debate on NBC? Did they find somebody to debate with you yet?

[*King*]: Well, I understand only through the newspaper [*Sears laughs*] that Mr. Kilpatrick of Virginia, the editor of the paper in Richmond, has consented to debate me. They, we've had a hard, they've had a hard time getting anybody.

[*Sears*]: They sure have.

[*King*]: So, I don't know.

[*Sears*]: Mr. Grays of . . .

[*King*]: Mr. Kilpatrick may back out later on also.[6]

[*Sears*]: Is he the *Times-Dispatch,* do you recall? Is he editor?

[*King*]: Yes.

[*Sears*]: Yes.

[*King*]: He's editor of *Times, Richmond Times-Dispatch.*[7]

[*Sears*]: I noticed a reprint in the *Constitution* this week from the *Richmond Times-Dispatch,* and I don't think you two are possibly too far separated.[8] I think it's, I think there's going to be some basis for understanding before the debate begins. If you recall

[*King interrupts*]: Well, I think so. I have been on the program before with Mr. Kilpatrick, and he's a very intelligent and enlightened man.[9] While I disagree with his views on segregation, I think he's at least an intelligent segregationist.

---

6. James H. Gray, editor of the *Albany Herald* and Georgia's Democratic Party chairman, reneged on an earlier agreement to debate King, explaining to the press that King had "violated his parole and probation of a Georgia court (and) apparently contends that state laws are not valid as they apply to him" ("Virginian to Debate Rev. King on TV," *Atlanta Constitution,* 2 November 1960). King reportedly suggested that Gray's refusal to debate him "may be an unconscious admission of the untenability of his position" ("King Hits Demo's Debate Refusal," *Montgomery Advertiser,* 1 November 1960).

7. Kilpatrick was editor of the *Richmond News Leader.*

8. On 3 November the *Atlanta Constitution* printed a short editorial from the *Richmond Times-Dispatch* criticizing Georgia authorities for treating King "as though he were one of the FBI's 'most wanted' criminals" ("Manacles for the Rev. Dr. King," *Richmond Times-Dispatch,* 28 October 1960).

9. King had previously debated Kilpatrick on "Open End," a New York television program, on 3 April 1960 (David Susskind to King, 13 April 1960). They debated again on national television later in the month (see Debate with James J. Kilpatrick on "The Nation's Future," 26 November 1960, pp. 556–564 in this volume).

[*Sears*]: Yes, he said, as I today, he was one of the people who said, and we quote the paper: "If Dr. King could have asked for the treatment most calculated to win him sympathy, not only in the North, but in the South, this knuckle-headed performance in Georgia is precisely right." 6 Nov 1960

[*King*]: Oh yeah.

[*Sears*]: Yes, well I left Montgomery the, yesterday, and you might be amused to know that everybody's being very self-righteous over in Montgomery. They say they never would have treated you like they did in Decatur, in Decatur, Georgia. [*laughs*]

[*King*]: Is that so? [*laughs*] That's very interesting.

[*Sears*]: [*laughs*] "Our courts never would have done that." Well, let's get on to the political situation. We're right in the middle of it now, and there's just two more days from this broadcast, well one more day [*laughs*], to make up our minds on the day to vote. I am not going to ask you how you're going to vote because I also see in the paper that, possibly, you are not going to be able to vote this year.

[*King*]: Yes, according to the state of Alabama [*Sears laughs*], I won't be able to get an absentee ballot, and I haven't lived in Georgia long enough to vote.[10]

[*Sears*]: You moved here, you have to be here a year before you can register, I understand.

[*King*]: That's right. Yes.

[*Sears*]: And then, of course, the registration is quite a ways off. So we'll discount who you're going to vote for, and let's discuss, if we may, the civil rights platforms, platform of both parties. I just happened to notice, we'll start off with the Democrats, if you don't mind. [*laughs*] I happened to notice that Mrs. Eleanor Roosevelt said she feels Senator Kennedy can bring about integration in the South much faster than the Eisenhower administration has done, and I wonder if we could take that as a starter.[11] Do you agree with Mrs. Roosevelt?

[*King*]: Well, I would say that not only Senator Kennedy, I think the next administration will do much more, and not only will do but will be all but forced to do much more than we have seen in the last eight years. I would not hesitate to say, in all honesty I will have to say, that I don't think President Eisenhower has given the leadership that this great problem demands. I am absolutely convinced that if we had had a very strong man in the White House on this issue many of the problems and even the tensions that we face in the South at this time would not exist.

[*Sears*]: Why do you say that? What could President Eisenhower have done to implement the Supreme Court decision, as I assume you're speaking on that.

---

10. After King announced his plans to vote absentee in Alabama, state officials informed him that he was ineligible to do so because of unpaid Alabama poll taxes ("King Loses His Vote in Alabama," *Atlanta Constitution*, 3 November 1960).

11. In April Roosevelt criticized President Eisenhower "as lacking leadership on civil rights" ("Democrats Map Plank on Rights," *New York Times*, 23 April 1960). A televised campaign advertisement for Kennedy, that ran in October and November, featured her endorsement: "I urge you to vote for John F. Kennedy for I have come to believe that as a president he will have the strength and the moral courage to provide the leadership for human rights we need in this time of crisis" (Eleanor Roosevelt, "The make-up of America: a majority of minorities," October–November 1960).

[*King*]: Well, I think he could have done several things. First, Mr. Eisenhower came in office and he, he's still a very popular man. With that tremendous popularity, he could have used his office a great deal. He could have at least used moral persuasion to get people to see that this is the law of the land, it is morally right, and this is something that we as a nation must do in order to maintain our position in the world. Just constantly counseling the nation on the moral implications involved and the moral values involved in the whole integration struggle

[*Sears interrupts*]: Do you think

[*King continues*]: would have been useful.

[*Sears*]: Do you think the present administration has recognized the world situation in respect to civil rights in this country—the lack of a good image in Africa and Europe and Asia? Do you think the Eisenhower administration has realized the importance of this problem?

[*King*]: Well, I think to a degree but certainly not enough. I don't think we've had enough vigorous action from the present administration to, at least, cause people in Asia and Africa to be convinced that we are serious in our determination to do away with segregation and discrimination in all of their dimensions.

[*Sears*]: Do you feel that the Democratic Party with the, under Kennedy will make progress in this line?

[*King*]: As I said, I think in the new administration will naturally do more. I don't know how much Senator Kennedy would do, but I'm sure he would take a pretty forthright position. I have talked with Senator Kennedy twice since the nomination about civil rights, and I was very impressed with his intelligence and, on this problem, his understanding of the problem and his honesty in discussing it, and I think he would take a pretty forthright position.[12] He doesn't hide it; he's made it clear in the campaign that there is a great deal that the president can do and that he intends to use the weight of his office to get behind the struggle for civil rights and to mobilize forces in the nation for implementation of the Supreme Court's decision on desegregation.

[*Sears*]: Have you talked to Vice President Nixon since the nomination?

[*King*]: Not since the nomination. I have talked with him, though, at length on the civil rights issue, and there again I was impressed with his understanding of the depths and dimensions of this problem, and I feel that he would take a forthright position.[13] Now, which man would take the stronger position, I don't know. I'm not in a position to say at this point. But I can say that I feel that both men would take a stronger stand than President Eisenhower has taken.

[*Sears*]: Let's get down to some practical politics starting with the first event that I'd like bring up is when vice president, or rather, the vice president nominee in the Republican Party, Mr. Lodge, promised, in essence, a Negro in the cabinet.[14] Forgetting whether or not he can deliver his promise or whether he intended

12. King met with Kennedy before his nomination on 23 June 1960 (see King to Chester Bowles, 24 June 1960, pp. 478–480 in this volume). In a 1964 interview, King recalled meeting Kennedy again in Washington during September (Interview by Berl I. Bernhard, 9 March 1964).

13. King and Nixon first met in Ghana in 1957.

14. During a Harlem campaign stop, Nixon's running mate Henry Cabot Lodge promised that the Republican administration would name an African American to the cabinet. The following day he retracted his statement prior to an appearance before a group of Virginia Republicans (Edward C. Burks,

to promise it or whatever, what effect do you think this statement and the resulting publicity has had with the Negro vote?

[*King*]: Well, frankly, I think there has been a little too much disagreement in the Republican ranks on this question and a little too much double talk to really strongly influence Negro voters. I feel that if there had been unity and agreement between Mr. Nixon and Mr. Lodge on this, and if it had been followed through, if Mr. Lodge and Mr. Nixon had made this clear and stated it in the South as well as the North, I believe that it would have strongly influenced Negro voters. But at the present time with all of the double talk and some of the developments that have taken place since the statement was made, I don't believe many Negro voters have been moved by this point alone.

[*Sears*]: You think it has been a reverse effect?

[*King*]: Well, I don't know if it has hurt the party as far as Negro voters go, but I don't think it has helped it tremendously. I don't think there had been any great gains as a result of it.

[*Sears*]: Mrs. Roosevelt said, also, last evening that Senator Kennedy appeared to be ignorant about the importance of the Negro vote early in the campaign but that he has shown great interest in civil rights in recent weeks. Of course she's talking, I think, primarily about his interest and the Kennedy campaign interest in your problem. Do you think that interest has affected Kennedy's chances with the Negro vote, as such?

[*King*]: Well, I have no doubt that Senator Kennedy has gained a great deal in recent weeks, not only with Negro voters but with voters generally.

[*Sears*]: Why?

[*King*]: He, well, he has made a very impressive presentation, several impressive presentations on television in the debates, and I think more and more he has demonstrated a good deal of courage. Now, there were some people who had doubts about Senator Kennedy's courage from the beginning, including Mrs. Roosevelt (*Yes*), which was (*Yeah*) one thing that she strongly stated before the convention—that Senator Kennedy lacked courage.[15] But I think more and more he has demonstrated a great deal of courage, and this has been impressive. He has spoken to the issues in a very articulate manner, and he has made it clear that he would be a strong president in many areas. Now, on the civil rights issue, I think he has taken a much more forthright stand within recent weeks than he did before the nomination or right after it.

[*Sears*]: Do you think that's practical politics, vote-getting, or is it sincere?

[*King*]: Well, this is something that I wouldn't be able to say. I guess it's this

"Negro in Cabinet Pledged by Lodge," *New York Times,* 13 October 1960, and Edward C. Burks, "Pledge on Negro Diluted by Lodge," *New York Times,* 14 October 1960).

15. In a 1958 televised appearance on "College News Conference," Eleanor Roosevelt discussed the 1960 Democratic presidential candidates. The following day a *New York Times* article reported that Roosevelt called Kennedy "a young man with an enormous amount of charm," but she was hesitant "to place the difficult decisions that the next President will have to make with someone who understands what courage is and admires it, but has not quite the independence to have it" ("Mrs. Roosevelt Lauds Humphrey," *New York Times,* 8 December 1958). Roosevelt later complained in her nationally syndicated column that this comment had been misrepresented by Kennedy's opponents to imply she did not support his candidacy ("My Day," 8 June 1960).

whole question of human motives. It's something [*Sears laughs*] (*Yeah*) that we (*Yes*) just can't, we can't answer. (*Yeah*) I would hope that it's sincere. [*Sears laughs*] Sometimes a thing can be expedient and morally right at the same time. And I do think it's rather expedient to take this position because in many of the large, urban, industrial areas the Negro vote is a very important vote, possibly the balance of power. So this may be the expedient course, but I think it's right, and sometimes in history the expedient and the right way tend to join hands.

[*Sears*]: Yes. I think you said that rather clearly in the first part of our interview. The congressman Adam Clayton Powell described Democratic vice presidential nominee Lyndon Johnson as "a great man of the South and the surprise hit of the campaign." Dr. Powell spoke in Detroit and praised Johnson for directing the 1960 civil rights bill and for opposing what he called a "Dixie-crat manifesto."[16] I think such a statement by Congressman Powell, if anybody before the nomination of Senator Johnson, if, anybody'd said that Reverend Powell would have come out for Senator Johnson at this time it would be a little surprising. How, what do you feel about that and about Johnson in general?

[*King*]: Well, I have, what I should say I had certain doubts, and I was certainly disappointed when Senator Johnson was nominated to run for vice president. But I, being a minister, I guess I will have to believe in the possibility of being converted and [*Sears laughs*] regenerated, and I hope Senator Johnson has changed at many points. Now, he has done some good things, but he's been a very shrewd maneuverer, and I think at times he has compromised basic principles. There is no doubt about the fact that he has not been a strong civil rights man, and yet, he hadn't been the reactionary. Now, I think more and more Senator Johnson will take a strong position. I think he took the nomination in order to become an American rather than a Texan with the sectional yoke of the South. And I believe more and more he will move toward liberal positions on the Negro question, on labor questions, and other things.[17]

[*Sears*]: That's very interesting. I, we have sort of run out of time here, and I'm going to ask you just one more question, sir. And that is, would you be willing to sort of say who you think will win the election two days from now? Have you a good prognostication?

[*King*]: Well, I'll tell you the truth, I have, I just don't have the political astuteness or the ability of the prognosticator at this point [*Sears laughs*] because I think there are so many intangible factors that it's very difficult. The religious issue's there, and it's a very important issue.

[*Sears*]: Yes.

[*King*]: And there are still undecided voters, more than probably before, so that it's just difficult to say. I think it will probably be a close election and, at least from the popular votes, and I just find it difficult to make any prediction at this point.

[*Sears*]: I think you're one of the few smart people in the United States. Everybody else has predicted at this time, except you and I, and off the air I am predict-

---

16. "Powell Lauds Johnson," *Washington Post*, 3 November 1960.

17. See Lyndon B. Johnson to King, 28 November 1960, p. 565 in this volume.

ing, but I won't say who. I want to thank you very much, sir. This program today has featured Reverend Martin Luther King, Jr., co-pastor of the Ebenezer Baptist Church and president of the Southern Christian Leadership Conference. This is Zenas Sears, program director of radio station WAOK. The program has been "For Your Information." The opinions expressed on it were those of the individual and not necessarily those of the radio station. Again, our thanks to our guest, one of the busiest man in United States today, for taking this half hour with us.

At. MLKEC: ET-35.

From L. Harold DeWolf

15 November 1960
Boston, Mass.

DeWolf suggests that Kennedy's role in King's release from prison was "decisive" in the presidential election. He also requests that King call him and his wife, Madeleine, by their first names: "I am sure that the respect which you feel for me as your old teacher cannot exceed the respect bordering on reverence which I feel for you."

Dr. Martin Luther King, Jr.
Ebenezer Baptist Church
407–413 Auburn Avenue, N.E.
Atlanta 12, Georgia

Dear Martin,

Thank you for your letter of November 2nd.[1]

Madeleine and I are sorry that your coming trip to Boston must be in such a rush, but, of course, we understand your many responsibilities are heavy in these days.

Recently I had the great pleasure to meet for a few minutes of conversation Coretta's sister, Edith.[2] Incidentally, although I know her first name and know that she was a Scott before her marriage, I should appreciate a note from you or Coretta, telling me her last name. I am much embarrassed in having forgotten it, and I want to get in touch with her again. If you have her present residential address, I should also be grateful for that. I know that she is studying in the School of Fine and Applied Arts.

It is one of the ironies of these times that the action of a judge in Atlanta, expressing his hostility to you and the cause which you represent, may have deter-

---

1. In the letter King had declined his dissertation advisor's invitation to stay at his home during an upcoming visit to Boston.

2. Edythe Scott Bagley attended Boston University intermittently from January 1957 until August 1965, when she was awarded an M.F.A. degree.

15 Nov 1960

mined the result of the recent national election.[3] I notice that high authoritative sources in both the Republican and Democratic National Committees have reported that their analyses show that the result was determined by the Negro vote in the large cities of the North, a vote which is believed on the basis of analysis to have gone almost totally to Kennedy's support. Of course, there were many factors in this, but I believe the decisive one was the picture of Martin Luther King in handcuffs, with expressions of concern and genuine efforts to correct this injustice coming from Senator Kennedy and from Nixon only a terse "No comment."[4] That had an important impact not only on the vote of many Negroes, but also on the decision of many liberals who were having great difficulty in deciding between various perplexing factors. About three weeks before those events, I had decided to cast my vote for Kennedy because of what seemed to be a much more promising outlook on foreign affairs. I believe that your unjust suffering in Georgia has rendered a genuine service to the peace of the world through the effect of this injustice and the response of the two candidates to it on our national affairs.

I shall look forward to hearing from you by telephone when you are in Boston. Of course, Madeleine and I will plan to hear you at Ford Hall, but it may not be possible to speak to you there.[5]

We hope that before long you will be coming to Boston again. If so, do please let us know well in advance so that if possible we can plan for you to spend some time in our home with us.

By the way, both Madeleine and I would much prefer to be called by our first names when you are addressing us. We think of ourselves as colleagues and friends. I am sure that the respect which you feel for me as your old teacher cannot exceed the respect bordering on reverence which I feel for you as one who has taught me very much and who is today one of the most creative persons in this land. I know also how deeply Coretta shares in all that you are and I feel a similar respect for her.

With warm regards to you both, I am

Most cordially yours,
[*signed*] Harold.
L. Harold DeWolf

LHD:dn

TALS. MLKP-MBU: Box 23.

---

3. DeWolf refers to Judge J. Oscar Mitchell's decision to release King on bond.

4. When asked for a statement regarding King's arrest in Atlanta, a Nixon aide reportedly responded that "the Vice President would have no comment" ("Kennedy Calls Mrs. King," *New York Times*, 27 October 1960).

5. King delivered "The Future of Integration" at the Ford Hall Forum on 11 December 1960.

From James M. Lawson

17 November 1960
Nashville, Tenn.

Lawson urges King to resume plans for a "direct action project in Montgomery."

Dr. Martin L. King, Jr.
Southern Christian Leadership Conference
208 Auburn Avenue, N.E.
Atlanta 3, Georgia

Dear Martin:

First I should like to say that your recent bout with the powers of darkness in Georgia have only served to strengthen the struggle of the Negro for social justice and to increase the impact of nonviolence in the world and to further establish your stature as the mature voice of love in the world. That means much to us all and will mean even more to the hope for a new day across the world.

Wyatt [*Walker*] tells me that our plans for the SCLC direct action project in Montgomery are off because of your involvement with the so-called traffic case in Georgia. I simply want to register my feelings with you; namely, that this direct non-violent project remains an utter necessity for the present time and I believe that in your case there would be no confusion in the mind of the country or the world between it and the Georgia case. In fact, while the State of Georgia screamed about the traffic violation most people across the earth intuitively recognized your innocency which to me demonstrates a major fact of nonviolence. That is to say, it doesn't matter which law is used to intimidate or subjugate the struggle; what matters is the approach of innocency of the non-violent practitioner. I say this to reiterate that we should go ahead with the non-violent direct project in December.[1]

Incidentally, I also want to say that the Shreveport meeting was by all odds the best that I have attended in the past two years of SCLC.[2] The whole spirit was one which made me deeply proud to be related to the SCLC and the struggle.

Best wishes to you.

---

1. It is unclear what project Lawson refers to, but in an 8 December speech to the MIA's annual nonviolence institute, Ralph Abernathy called for a boycott of Montgomery's segregated stores and business districts ("Local Negro Leader Asks Store Boycott," *Montgomery Advertiser,* 9 December 1960). On 9 December, Lawson addressed the institute's "Youth and Student Night" (MIA, "Program, Fifth anniversary and the Annual Institute on Nonviolence," 5 December–11 December 1960).

2. Lawson delivered "The Struggle and the Stone of Stumbling" and facilitated a workshop with King on nonviolence at SCLC's 11–13 October meeting in Shreveport, Louisiana (SCLC, Program, "Annual conference," 11 October–13 October 1960). For more on the meeting, see King, "Message from the President," 11 October–13 October 1960, pp. 517–518 in this volume.

Cordially yours,
[*signed*] Jim
J. M. Lawson, Jr.

JML:ddl

TLS. MLKP-MBU: Box 54A.

Debate with James J. Kilpatrick on "The Nation's Future"

[*26 November 1960*]
[*New York, N.Y.*]

King debates segregationist editor James J. Kilpatrick on a live, nationally televised program.[1] *They appeared before a studio audience of representatives from several civil rights and conservative groups as well as mayors attending the American Municipal Association Convention.*[2] *Defending the student protesters, King insists that "they respect law so much that they want to see all laws just and in line with the moral law of the universe." Kilpatrick calls it "an interesting experience to be here tonight and see Mr. King assert a right to obey those laws he chooses to obey and disobey those that he chooses not to obey and insist the whole time that he has what he terms the highest respect for law." Kilpatrick further describes the sit-ins as "a boorish exhibition of what seems to me plain bad manners in crashing into a place where they are not welcome."*[3] *Host John McCaffery moderates.*[4] *This transcription was taken from NBC television footage.*

---

1. In a 7 November letter to Robert Allison, the program's producer, Kilpatrick requested details as to the structure of the program, explaining that "the last time I appeared on television with Martin Luther King, I got boobytrapped by David Susskind into the short end of 5–1 odds. I don't propose to walk into a rigged situation again if I can avoid it." On 3 April 1960, Kilpatrick had debated King on "Open End," a New York television program. James Jackson Kilpatrick, Jr. (1920–), born in Oklahoma City, received a B.J. (1941) from the University of Missouri. Kilpatrick began working as a reporter for the *Richmond News Leader* in 1941. He became the paper's chief editorial writer in 1949 and its editor in 1951. Kilpatrick was frequently featured on television for his defense of segregation, and he wrote several books on the South and the law, including *The Sovereign States: Notes of a Citizen of Virginia* (1957) and *The Smut Peddlers* (1960).

2. Robert Allison to King, 12 October 1960 and List of New York audience for "The Nation's Future," 26 November 1960.

3. King's performance disappointed some members of SNCC, who watched the debate with Ella Baker during a meeting of SNCC's executive council. Baker criticized King's lack of preparation: "It was almost in the cards that he would muff it . . . for he had not forced himself to analytically come to grips with these issues. The students were sitting there in front of the TV, waiting for him to 'take care' of Kilpatrick. Finally some got up and walked away" (quoted in James Howard Laue, "Direct Action and Desegregation: Toward a Theory of the Rationalization of Protest" [Ph.D. diss., Harvard University, 1965], p. 169). At SNCC's November 1960 meeting, the group discussed King's performance and voted to contact the show and suggest that a "student involved in the movement be included in a future program of this type" (SNCC, Minutes of meeting, 25 November–27 November 1960).

4. John Kerwin Michael McCaffery (1913–1983), born in Moscow, Idaho, received a B.A. (1936) from the University of Wisconsin and an M.A. (1938) from Columbia University. McCaffery worked in radio and television as a newscaster, master of ceremonies, and game show host. His program, "Eleventh Hour News," ran on WNBC-TV from 1952 until 1963.

[*McCaffery*]: Ladies and gentlemen, welcome to this special half-hour edition of The Nation's Future. Now, every third week we concentrate on issues of national impact which have special local importance, and our subject tonight is, "Are Sit-In Strikes Justifiable?" 26 Nov 1960

Now, this question, with its overtones of racial segregation, is one of the most disturbing that we Americans have ever faced. Just today in Atlanta, for instance, klansmen and Negro demonstrators demonstrated in the city, each walking up and down one side of the street. They did not speak to each other; they did not exchange any words; there was certainly no violence, and finally both groups dispersed. As a result of this, all the lunch counters in Atlanta were closed.[5] This was the first time that we have had a white group and a Negro group demonstrating with no violence at the same time.

Now, of course, in a question like this there are moral problems involved, there are legal problems involved. Our first speaker, Reverend Martin Luther King, Jr., introduced the technique of direct nonviolent action in the South five years ago. He's an ordained minister, a Doctor of Philosophy. He is president of the Southern Christian Leadership Conference. He is particularly well-known as an outstanding leader in the anti-segregation battle.

Reverend Martin Luther King, Jr., then, will you state your position?

[*King*]: The position that I am attempting to present tonight is one that presents itself or commends itself both in its goals and its methods. The goals of the sit-in movement can scarcely be debatable in a society founded on the principle that all men are created equal. This movement seeks to remove from the body of our nation a cancerous disease which prevents our democratic health from being realized. It seeks to remove those barriers between men and men, barriers between color, dealing with color, barriers dealing with caste, which prevent us from realizing the ideals of human brotherhood. And so I would say that the sit-in demonstrations are justifiable because their ends are humanitarian, constructive, and moral.

But happily, the means toward these ends are consonant with the highest ideals of man in that they are peaceful and non-violent. The sit-in demonstrations seek to secure moral ends through moral means. And ever so often in history when men seek to achieve the splendid goals of freedom, human dignity, and justice, they resort to methods of violence, such as guerilla warfare, such as assassination, and other methods of bloody revolution. But we know that this isn't true of the sit-ins. We see here a crusade without violence, and there is no attempt on the part of those who engaged in sit-ins to annihilate the opponent but to convert him. There is no attempt to defeat the segregationists but to defeat segregation, and I submit that this method, this sit-in movement, is justifiable because it uses moral, humanitarian, and constructive means in order to achieve the constructive end.

And of course, this approach, the sit-in demonstrations, call upon the best in man. They somehow challenge his moral sense. They require action. And they do not merely wait and deal with a century of litigation. And they do not involve them-

5. For newspaper coverage of the demonstrations, see Bruce Galphin, "Negroes Resume Sit-Ins, End Truce," *Atlanta Constitution*, 26 November 1960.

selves in endless debates. But we see here real action working to bring about the realization of the ideals and principles of democracy.

Now, there are those who would argue that these demonstrations are unconstitutional and that they are illegal. They would go on to argue that they have no respect for law. But I would say that this is absolutely wrong. The individuals engaged in sit-in demonstrations are revealing the highest respect for law. And they respect law so much that they want to see all laws just and in line with the moral law of the universe. They're willing to suffer and sacrifice in order to square local custom, customs and local laws with the moral law of the universe. And they are seeking to square these local laws with the federal Constitution and with what is the just law of the land.

Therefore, I am sure, I am convinced, that they are just and that they are truly American, that somehow these sit-in demonstrations send us back to the deep wells of democracy that were dug by the Founding Fathers of our nation in formulating the Constitution and the Declaration of Independence. And so in sitting down, these students are in reality standing up for the highest and the best in the American tradition. And I think it is justifiable because it isn't a selfish movement. It isn't based on seeking merely rights for Negroes or seeking to secure those things that would apply only to one minority group, but they're seeking to save the soul of America.

Truly, America faces today a rendezvous with destiny, and I think these students, through their nonviolent, direct, courageous action have met the challenge of this destiny-packed moment in a very majestic and sublime way.[6]

[*McCaffery*]: Thank you, Dr. King. And now [*applause*] our second guest. [*sustained applause*] Mr. James J. Kilpatrick for the past nine years has been editor of the *Richmond News Leader* of Richmond, Virginia. He is a member of the Virginia Commission on Constitutional Government, an agency set up in 1956 by the State of Virginia to promote the role of the state in relation to the federal government. In addition to his award-winning accomplishments as an editorial writer, Mr. Kilpatrick is the author of *The Sovereign State* and a just-published work called *The Smut-Peddlers,* an investigation of the obscenity racket and censorship. Mr. Kilpatrick, may we have your position, please?

[*Kilpatrick*]: Mr. Chairman, these sit-ins, it seems to me, must be viewed in terms of the total problem of race relations that has occupied the South not merely since 1954 but for a very long period in our history. And seen in this larger perspective, the question of who eats integrated hot dogs seems to me greatly exaggerated, and both sides, I believe, have shared in this exaggeration, both the Negroes and the whites. The business of who sits where to eat the blue plate special in Woolworth's on Broad Street in Richmond seems to me to rank somewhat lower in this scale of values than voting rights or the right to own property or the right to serve on juries. And when some of my opponents tend to equate lunch counters with public education, it seems to me it reflects a rather

6. Portions of King's opening remarks closely follow his handwritten note cards. Video footage reveals King periodically referring to notes (King, Notes for debate on "The Nation's Future," 26 November 1960).

poor opinion of public education—though from what I have seen of public education here and there, perhaps the comparison with lunch counters may not be wholly inapropos at that.

These sit-ins, it seems to me, find their chief significance in very large, broad patterns of social and constitutional questions, and these divide us grievously. On that point I might make one thing plain. Contrary to recent high example, Mr. King and I do not agree on our objectives and disagree only on means of reaching them. He would accept racial separation nowhere; he would have integration everywhere. His aim, as I comprehend it, is the obliteration of race altogether. At the end of his line of argument, I submit, lies what has been termed the "coffee-colored compromise," a society in which every distinction of race has been blotted out by this principle of togetherness.

Now, I am opposed to this Waring blender process on our society. In common with most southerners, I believe, I take pride in our race, and we are often puzzled—perhaps Mr. King will comment upon this—that Negroes by and large seem to take so little pride in theirs.

We believe it is an affirmatively good thing to preserve the predominant racial characteristics that have contributed to Western civilization over the past two thousand years, and we do not believe that the way to preserve them lies in fostering any intimate race mixing by which these principles and characteristics inevitably must be destroyed. Toward that end, we believe in public policies that promote separation of the races in those few essential social areas where intimate personal association, long continued, would foster a break-down, especially among young people, of those ethnic lines that seem to us important.

Now, to the extent that integrated lunch counters and tea rooms in our department stores would contribute toward that breakdown, I would regard them as unwise. But I would say that as a practical matter I am inclined to believe this extent is relatively small. The business of eating lunch in a big city dime store, so far as I can see, is a largely impersonal exercise in indigestion. It involves no long-continued intimacy, and I would suppose that in the course of time most of the South's larger cities could adjust to this change as they have adjusted to an end of segregation on public transportation lines and in their parks. Indeed, my impression is that more than a hundred public eating facilities in private stores in the South already have taken this step.

Now, in his opening remarks, Mr. King dwelt at length upon the point that these are peaceful and nonviolent demonstrations. I would like, if I may, to present another side of that picture because I have seen these demonstrations as he has been involved in them and I know that they involve a great deal of tense pushing and shoving in an atmosphere that is electric with restrained violence and hostility, and in one city after another these demonstrations—they are more accurately described as disciplined and planned invasions—have resulted in riot and disorder. In one city after another there have been bomb threats, and melees, and disturbances, and the police called in. Peaceful demonstrations may be fine, but what we've seen in Tallahassee, Chattanooga, and elsewhere are far from peaceful.

I want principally to discuss, as our program goes along this evening, the legal and constitutional issues that seem to me so important in this because the key thing that is involved are questions of property rights. These are the rights of the store owners. I want to ask Mr. King if he would direct some comment to this question: Whence come the right that he asserts in these southern states on the part of the Negroes to eat in privately-owned lunch counters and department stores?

Other subjects I will touch on—my opening statement time is exhausted.

[*McCaffery*]: Thank you very much, Mr. Kilpatrick. [*applause*] Now, gentlemen, you both have an opportunity for discussion, for cross-examination, if you will, for rebuttal. And Dr. King, to you first, then.

[*King*]: I would like to mention just two or three things, or rather answer two or three things that you raised, Mr. Kilpatrick. First, I would like to deal with this whole question of violence. You contend that violence has always followed the sit-ins, that the sit-ins have led to riots and what-have-you. I would submit to you that if there has been any violence it has not come from the sit-inners themselves but from the opponents and the extremist groups in the white community. But the sit-inners have been amazingly disciplined. They have evinced dignity; and they have been non-violent at every point, so that we cannot hold the Negro students and the sit-inners responsible for the violence, but we must hold the individuals in the white community who have precipitated the violence responsible for it. [*one person applauds*]

I would like to also say [*applause*] that on the question of property rights, I would be the first one to contend that there are certain sacred and basic rights that should be protected concerning private property, but I do not think this is the issue at this point. We are not dealing with property that is exclusively private. We are dealing with property that is privately owned but supported by, sustained by the public and which depends on the public for its very existence, and I think we have a great difference here.

[*Kilpatrick*]: I would say on that point that as a matter of law, whatever rights are asserted by the sit-downers in these matters presumably come from the 14th Amendment, which applies to the States only, and court after court has said that.

I would like to go back to something that you said in your opening remarks about how moral all this is, that this was moral ends, it was a moral end that would be reached by moral means. It occurs to me on that point that there is a pretty high degree of morality involved in simply abiding by the law, and I would wonder, rhetorically, if a high degree of morality is not involved in obedience to law as such. Certainly, we of the South were told that over and over at the time of our early resistance to school integration. We were exhorted on every hand to abide by the law, and people were aghast at what they termed the southern resistance and southern defiance, southern, indeed, southern anarchy, and it is therefore an interesting experience to be here tonight and see Mr. King assert a right to obey those laws he chooses to obey and disobey those that he chooses not to obey and insist the whole time that he has what he terms the highest respect for law, because he is abiding by the moral law of the universe. I would [*word inaudible*] here on earth if we try to abide by the law of the land, by the statutes, by the court decisions, by the other acts that establish law here on earth. There will be time enough later on to get to the moral law of the universe. And I got one more thing I want to say on this question of morality

[*McCaffery interrupts*]: You can ask it right directly of Reverend King. This isn't a segregated discussion at all. [*laughter*] You don't have to make it a rhetorical discussion.

26 Nov 1960

[*Kilpatrick*]: He has based this on the moral question, and I simply submit to you, sir, that when this disciplined platoon comes in—in one of your letters you described them as your forces engaged in what you call a foray, very military language—when this disciplined platoon comes into a store, occupies all of the seats at the lunch counter, displaces the white patrons, makes it impossible for them to sit down. They occupy these lunch counter stools; they say, "We will sit here all day." They refuse to move on the request of the store owner; the police are called in; they disrupt the store's entire law-abiding operation; they put on a boorish exhibition of what seems to me plain bad manners in crashing into a place where they are not welcome. I submit to you, sir, it comes with singularly poor grace for their spokesman to then charge the store owner with bad behavior.

[*King*]: Mr. Kilpatrick, I think on this point you would have to agree with me that most of these local laws that have been set up are certainly contrary to the federal law.

[*Kilpatrick*]: Oh, I don't agree with that at all.

[*King*]: To the Constitution of our United States.

[*Kilpatrick*]: I don't agree with that at all.

[*King*]: I think they are. And I think in disobeying these laws, the students are really seeking to affirm the just law of the land and the Constitution of our United States. I would say this—that all people should obey just laws, but I would also say, with St. Augustine, that an unjust law is no law at all. And when we find an unjust law, I think we have a moral obligation to take a stand against it, and I think these local laws that have been set up are unjust.[7] Now, in many instances there were no laws—they were just customs—and the students were not breaking laws; they were just going against local customs.

I would also like to deal with another question that you raised, namely the resistance of the segregationists to the Supreme Court's decision of 1954.

[*Kilpatrick*]: We thought we were resisting an unjust law, you see.

[*King*]: But I think, there is [*laughter, applause*], I think. Mr. Kilpatrick [*applause*], I think, Mr. Kilpatrick, you would have to agree that there is a great distinction between the immoral, the hateful, the violent resistance of many of the white segregationists and the nonviolent, peaceful, loving, civil resistance of the Negro students. I think one is uncivil disobedience; the other is civil disobedience, if you will. [*applause*]

[*Kilpatrick*]: [*words inaudible*] Well, these are very interesting viewpoints on your part. Let me ask this question: Suppose that—let me precede it by saying this: within the past two years, five courts have passed upon this very point of the property rights of the store owner that I have been trying to defend here tonight. In every single one of these five cases, the courts have upheld the right of the property owner to say he will serve whom he pleases and will not serve whom he pleases. These are the Supreme Courts of Delaware, Virginia, North Carolina, a United States District Court in Maryland, and the Fifth United States Circuit Court of Appeals. Now, two of these cases are on appeal now, one coming out of Delaware and one coming out of Virginia. In one case, the Delaware case, involves a restaurant

7. Cf. Augustine, *The City of God,* 19.21.

in a publicly owned building; the Virginia case involves a bus terminal that's involved in interstate commerce. But let me suppose for a moment that a case should get up to the Supreme Court of the United States on a Woolworth's, or on a Kress's, or on a Thalheimer's Department Store in Richmond, not involved in interstate commerce, not involved in a publicly owned facility, and let me suppose further that the Supreme Court of the United States were to adopt the opinion of the Fourth United States Circuit Court of Appeals in this Howard Johnson's case.[8] Then, wouldn't it be your view that that became the supreme law of the land? Would you feel any higher moral duty to obey it then?

[*King*]: I think, first, on the question of the courts passing on this issue, I think again you would have to agree that no court has given the state the right to deny individuals their constitutional rights. Certainly this hasn't

[*Kilpatrick interrupts*]: Oh, no

[*King continues*]: happened with the federal court and it hasn't happened with the Supreme Court.

[*Kilpatrick*]: No, that is not what we are talking about.

[*King*]: I think it was made palpably clear that no court has the power or the authority to use its power, whether it is in the form of a legislative act, an anti-trespass law, or an executive decree, to deny an individual his constitutional rights.

I would say also that on this question of whether individuals have a moral right to obey what they consider just law, I think we all should do that, but I think the individual who discovers, on the basis of conscience, that a law is unjust and is willing, in a very peaceful sense, to disobey that unjust law and willingly and voluntarily suffer the consequence, I think at that moment he is expressing the highest respect for law. [*applause*]

[*Kilpatrick*]: Wouldn't you say that the legislature of Louisiana right now, do you believe that they are motivated by what they regard sincerely as the impulses of their conscience in conceiving these things to be wrong and unjust and that, therefore, they are justified in taking the actions they're taking?[9]

[*King*]: I would be the first one to say that there are some people in the white South who sincerely believe segregation is right. Some of them believe that it is morally right, I imagine, and I would call upon these people, if they want to resist, that they should resist nonviolently and peacefully and in a loving spirit. And I believe with this type of resistance we will ultimately come to a just resolution of the problem, and I think the right point of view will ultimately win. But I repeat that the resistance that I see is an unloving, impatient, uncivil resistance, which can only lead to chaos and anarchy.

---

8. In the case of *Williams v. Howard Johnson's Restaurant,* the Fourth Circuit United States Court of Appeals found that an Alexandria, Virginia, restaurant's refusal to serve Charles E. Williams was not a violation of federal laws prohibiting discrimination in businesses engaged in interstate commerce, as it engaged only in local commerce (268 F.2d 845 [1959]).

9. On 13 November1960, the Louisiana legislature attempted to block the New Orleans public school desegregation plans by seizing control of the school system. When a federal district court issued a restraining order against legislators, state police arrived at the forty-eight elementary schools and ordered a school holiday. School principals ignored the directive and held classes as usual (Claude Sitton, "Pupils Integrate in New Orleans as Crowd Jeers," *New York Times,* 15 November 1960).

[*Kilpatrick*]: Well, I'm the most loving, peaceful anarchist you ever likened to meet. [*laughter*] But going back to the question, which you didn't answer a minute ago when I put it to you, because I am probing to find out your sense of obedience or dedication to the Supreme Court of the United States, whose pronouncements we're so often told are the supreme law of the land. Should the Supreme Court of the United States affirm such an opinion as was written in that Williams case involving the Howard Johnson's restaurant? Would you, then, abandon all of your further efforts to sit in? Would you say the supreme law of the land has been settled and we have a duty to obey it?

[*King*]: I would answer that by asking you a question.

[*Kilpatrick interrupts*]: No, that's no way to answer a question. Why don't you answer first and then ask me a question?

[*King*]: And then I would come back to answering the question.

[*Kilpatrick*]: All right.

[*King*]: If the United States Supreme Court of the government of our nation issued a law, set forth a law or a decision stating that the public worship of God is unconstitutional, there would be a denial of the right of freedom of religion and to worship God publicly. Would you urge people to obey that and to be obedient to it and wait fifty or a hundred years through the century of litigation before protesting this?

[*Kilpatrick*]: No, sir, I would take the recourses that are provided under the law. I would try to impeach the Justices, for one thing, but I would go through legal procedures to try to do something about it. Though I may say on that very point, since you bring it up, that there is very high example in this country, in the Thomas Jefferson, whom you recite in one of your letters or that famous March 29th ad.[10] In 1798, when the Supreme Court of the United States, through Washington and Justice [*Samuel*] Chase, had overthrown freedom of speech and freedom of press absolutely, exactly as you talk about overthrowing freedom of religion, and they drew up the Kentucky and Virginia Resolutions of 1798, saying that a state had a right—had a right, and a power, and a duty—to put its sovereign powers between the court and, in this case the Congress also, and the people, so that that was a technique of resistance that was advocated by Jefferson whom you seem to admire a good deal.[11]

Now, let me go back to the question I put to you a while ago. If the Court should say this, would you be inclined to call off all your troops and disband your school down there where you're teaching them these techniques and so on?

[*King*]: I go back to the argument, Mr. Kilpatrick, that an unjust law is no law at all.

[*Kilpatrick*]: And you

[*King interrupts*]: And I think any law

---

10. Kilpatrick refers to the 29 March fund-raising advertisement placed in the *New York Times* by the Committee to Defend Martin Luther King and the Struggle for Freedom in the South. For a facsimile of the ad, "Heed Their Rising Voices," see p. 382 in this volume.

11. Jefferson authored the Kentucky resolution of 1798 in response to the Alien and Sedition Acts, designed to silence criticism of the Federalist government. The Kentucky resolution and its succeeding Virginia resolution of 1799 served as precedents for the nullification of federal law by the states.

[*Kilpatrick continues*]: reserve the right to say whether it is just or unjust?

[*King*]: Well, I think this, that on the basis of conscience—and how do we test conscience? On the basis of the insights of the ages through saints and prophets, on the basis of the best evidence of the intellectual disciplines of the day, psychology, sociology, anthropology, and what have you, on the basis of all that we find in the religious insights of the ages—and I think we will all agree that any law that degrades human personality is an unjust law, and one's conscience should reveal that to him.

[*Kilpatrick*]: Would you extend the right, the same right to everyone else that you claim for yourself, to decide what is just and what is unjust?

[*King*]: I would extend that right only if individuals will do it on the basis of conscience and in resisting it will do it in what I call a loving, nonviolent, peaceful sense, and not in terms of a violent, unloving, and uncivil sense.

[*Kilpatrick*]: This is the most remarkable exposition of obedience to law that I ever remember taking part in, in which everyone has the right to decide for himself on the basis of his conscience what laws he regards as just and what he regards as unjust.

Let me ask you about the boycott business since we have two or three minutes left. You've used the boycott as a very effective weapon, and you regard that certainly as the right of your forces not to buy and so on. Do you see any right comparable on the part of the store owner not to sell? Do you see in your freedom to associate any right of others not to associate?

[*King*]: I would say that on the one hand those individuals who are in the common market with their stores should not deny individuals access to the common market. I think, on the other hand, we must see that the boycott method as used by the students is not a negative thing.

[*McCaffery*]: Gentlemen, I'm sorry; we didn't have that two minutes. Our time is already up. I am afraid that you have been unkind to lawyers in how well you have taken care of the legal aspects of this.

It is obvious that we haven't enough time to take care of all of the ramifications of this, but we promise you that we will return to it in a future program.[12]

This is John McCaffery. Good night. [*applause*]

F. NBCNA-NNNBC.

12. In a 14 December letter, King thanked Allison for the opportunity to appear on the show and offered to participate in a future debate. King further commended the network for airing "a program of this nature" and stated that "I have always felt that news media could be a tremendous force in helping our nation to realize its unfulfilled dream."

From Lyndon B. Johnson

28 November 1960

Vice President-elect Lyndon B. Johnson thanks King for his support.[1] *Just prior to the election, King, who refrained from endorsing either ticket, had expressed his disappointment in the nomination of the Senate Democratic majority leader from Texas because of his position on civil rights.*[2]

Rev. Martin Luther King
407 Auburn Ave.
Atlanta, Georgia

Dear Dr. King:

Now that the election is over and our Democratic Party has won, I want to let you know how much I particularly appreciate having had your support.

The election was close and hard-fought. I am proud it was a clean and high-level campaign, and our country emerges from it without scars or embitterments that would keep us from working together in the crucial years lying ahead.

I want you to know that you may look to me for cooperation in those years, and I know that I can expect the same from you.

With best wishes, always,

Sincerely,
[*signed*]
Lyndon B. Johnson

TLS. MLKP-MBU: Box 90.

---

1. The Kings were later invited to Kennedy and Johnson's inauguration festivities (Edward H. Foley, Invitation to the inauguration of John F. Kennedy and Lyndon B. Johnson, 20 January 1961, and Stanley Woodward and Lindy Boggs, Invitation to the inaugural ball of John F. Kennedy and Lyndon B. Johnson, 20 January 1961).
2. See King, Interview by Zenas Sears on "For Your Information," 6 November 1960, p. 552 in this volume.

To Marie F. Rodell

30 November 1960
[*Atlanta, Ga.*]

In a 31 October letter, King's literary agent informed him that Coronet, *a family magazine, wished to have journalist Louis Lomax collaborate with him on an article about "the young American Negro of the next generation." In this reply, King explains*

30 Nov 1960

that in light of Lomax's recent criticisms of the NAACP—with which King admits he agrees—it would not be "judicious to undertake the project at this time."[1]

Miss Marie F. Rodell
15 East 48th Street
New York 17, New York

Dear Marie:

I regret that absence from the country for a few days, and an extremely crowded schedule made it impossible for me to get to your letter of October 31 before the present time.[2]

I am quite interested in the article proposed by CORONET magazine. I am sure that it could serve a real purpose. However, there is one little problem that I face at this time. It grows out of the person that CORONET has chosen to assist in writing the article.

Some months ago Mr. Louis Lomax wrote an article for HARPER's magazine strongly criticising the N.A.A.C.P.[3] As you can well imagine, this brought about a great uproar from N.A.A.C.P. officials. Actually, the article aroused the ire of N.A.A.C.P. supporters probably more than anything in recent years. While I privately agreed with many things that Mr. Lomax said in the article, I feel a moral obligation to preserve a public image of unity in our organizational work.

I am afraid that my writing an article with Mr. Lomax will be construed by N.A.A.C.P. officials as an endorsement of his views. Consequently, I do not think it will be judicious to undertake the project at this time. I might say, however, I will be more than happy to do the article with someone else. Or, as an alternative, I would be happy to take a few days off during the Christmas holidays to write it myself.[4]

I will look forward to hearing from you concerning your reaction.

Very sincerely yours,
Martin Luther King, Jr.

MLK.m

TLc. MLKP-MBU: Box 61.

---

1. In her 1 December reply, Rodell informed King that she understood his reluctance to work with Lomax.

2. King was out of the country from 13 to 18 November to attend Nnamdi Azikiwe's inauguration as governor-general of Nigeria (see Azikiwe to King, 26 October 1960, pp. 533–534 in this volume).

3. In his article, Lomax called the student-led protests "proof that the Negro leadership class, epitomized by the National Association for the Advancement of Colored People, was no longer the prime mover of the Negro's social revolt" and concluded that "these militant young people completely reversed the power flow within the Negro community." Lomax described King as one of the major prophets of the "new gospel of the American Negro" (Lomax, "The Negro Revolt Against 'The Negro Leaders,'" *Harper's Magazine,* June 1960). Regarding the tension between the NAACP and student activists, see Roy Wilkins to King, 27 April 1960, pp. 444–446 in this volume.

4. After Rodell wrote King on 2 December that *Coronet*'s senior editor would be "delighted" to have an article, King worked on a piece until Rodell informed him on 21 June of the following year that the magazine would discontinue publication in October and "we might just as well forget it" (King, "After Desegregation—What?" April 1961).

To James F. Estes

[*December 1960*]
[*Atlanta, Ga.*]

In this draft letter to the lawyer for the Fayette County Civic and Welfare League, King commends the organization's "unfaltering perseverance" in its grassroots voting rights campaign in western Tennessee.[1] *Ella Baker had previously corresponded with Estes regarding assistance SCLC might provide in Fayette and Haywood counties, and on 22 December SCLC sent $800 to support their struggle.*[2]

Jas. S. Estes, Esq.
777 Hamilton Street
Memphia

In our move toward the threshold of equality the time has come to re-double our efforts to stem the tide of segregationists retaliation and persecution in Fayette and Heywood Counties. The Southern Christian Leadership Conference has been able to raise $800 to serve this end. It will be mailed at once. We have gained new courage and determination from your unfaltering perseverance in the face of overwhelming odds. May you continue in the faith that unearned suffering is redemptive. At this festive season celebrating the birth of our Saviour, let us rededicate our faith in Him and our allegiance to the cause of freedom. Merry Christmas and may God bless all of you.

MLKjr

THL. MLKP-MBU: Box 24.

---

1. The Fayette County League and a similar organization in Haywood County were founded and began a voter registration drive in mid-1959 after an all white jury convicted Burton Dodson, a seventy-year old black man, of murder (Wayne Phillips, "Court Again Bars Negro Evictions," *New York Times*, 6 January 1961). Economic retaliation against black activists in the region had escalated in September 1960 when white landowners evicted several hundred sharecroppers from their homes and many businesses refused to buy, sell, or trade with blacks; this led to the establishment of a tent city composed of hundreds of families (James Talley, "Fayette Invokes Economic Force," *Nashville Tennessean*, 8 May 1960, and *Tent City . . . : "Home of the Brave"* [Washington, D.C.: AFL-CIO Industrial Union Department, 1961]). On 13 September 1960, the Justice Department charged twenty-seven individuals and two banks in Haywood County with using economic pressure to keep blacks from voting in violation of the Civil Rights Act of 1957, the first such suit to be filed against private individuals under this legislation (Anthony Lewis, "U.S. Suit Charges an Economic Bar to Negro Voting," *New York Times*, 14 September 1960).

2. King's assistant James Wood mailed the check to John McFerren, chairman of the Fayette County Civic and Welfare League (see also Baker to Estes, 12 February 1960 and 21 July 1960). James F. Estes was born near Madison County, Tennessee. He earned his undergraduate degree from Lane College and an L.L.B. degree (1948) at Marquette University. Estes was an Army officer during World War II and in 1955 formed the Veterans Benefit of America to help African American veterans obtain their benefits. When he served as Burton Dodson's attorney in 1959, Estes became the first black lawyer to try a case in Tennessee since Reconstruction.

"A Talk with Martin Luther King"

December 1960
Ithaca, N.Y.

King answers questions from students and faculty in Cornell University's Straight Memorial Room on 13 November 1960 after delivering "The Dimensions of a Complete Life" at Sage Chapel.[1] *Excerpts from the session were published the following month in* Dialogue, *a Cornell student publication. King acknowledges that some in the black community "do not share my views about nonviolence because they do not think it is militant enough" but emphasizes that, despite differences in approach, "there can be unity when there isn't uniformity."*

Question: Will the results of the recent election have any significance in the South?

Dr. King: We have seen some thing very significant in this election. Both parties had the strongest civil rights planks in their histories. Pressure in this nation and the current weight of world opinion will do a great deal to implement their programs. I have spoken to Senator Kennedy and I am very impressed with his grasp of the problem. I will be very disappointed if he does not take a forthright stand in this field. I am sure that we will have stronger action in his administration than we have had in the past eight years.

Question: When do you think integration will be realized in the South?

Dr. King: The struggle is to be a long and hard one and will continue until victory is won. If we continue to have the willingness to suffer and struggle creatively, integration will be a reality in the not-too-distant future I think we are beginning to see the end of the days of massive resistance in the South; by that I mean states saying that they will resist at any cost. They are beginning to see that this is a futile cause although many governors threaten to close the schools when they get an order to integrate. Little Rock taught us a lesson.[2] Two powerful forces have collided in the South—the force of segregation and the force of public schools. By having these two institutions collide we have seen something very interesting. The people have made it clear that when the final choice approaches they will choose their schools open, with token integration, rather than closed schools. So I think that desegregation, which is not necessarily integration, will be a reality in most of the South, certainly the urban areas, in less

1. In a 4 April 1959 letter, Cornell president Deane W. Malott invited King to campus. Malott had suggested 22 November 1959, but King cited a scheduling conflict and proposed two alternative dates for November of the following year (King to Malott, 21 April 1959; for a similar address, see King, "The Three Dimensions of a Complete Life," 11 December 1960, pp. 571–579 in this volume).

2. In an effort to avoid desegregation orders, Little Rock high schools were closed during the 1958–1959 school year. A federal mandate reopened the schools in June 1959.

than ten or twelve years. And by desegregation I mean a breakdown of all legal barriers. Integration, we know, is more than breaking down legal barriers; it is true interpersonal, intergroup living which takes place not because the law says so, but because it is natural and right. This will take a lot longer, but we are moving in the right direction, and we are very hopeful about the future. I hope that we will see true integration before the turn of the century.

Question: Is there any real disunity in the Negro community about the current struggle

Dr. King: You can never stand in a position of leadership without opposition. My attitude is that this can sometimes be healthy because it keeps you in a constant state of examining your self, your motives and methods. I always try to take criticism in a positive sense. I have not faced any vocal opposition in the Negro community. Some do not share my views about nonviolence because they do not think it is militant enough, but there is no real disunity. There can be unity when there isn't uniformity.

Question: What influenced your nonviolent approach and how is it implemented?

Dr. King: I cam to the philosophy of nonviolence as a way of life after a careful study of Mahatma Gandhi and other social philosophers. Of course, my whole religious background had something to do with it. The whole spirit of nonviolence came to me from Jesus of Nazareth. Its central idea is that you counteract an unjust system through direct action and love your opponents at the same time. You implement the philosophy through sit-ins and boycotts. You hope to be able to bring an end to your opponent's self-defeating massacre and that he will change his attitude.

Question: What can Northern students do to help integration?

Dr. King: All students should fight discriminatory barriers wherever they face them in their communities. The best way to help in the South is to make sure there is no discrimination in the North. Injustice anywhere is a threat to justice everywhere. Northern students can relate themselves to the Southern struggle by participating in sympathetic protest movements. One of the most encouraging developments in helping the sit-ins in the South has been the hundreds of students in the North who have joined in sympathetic protest to inform the chain variety stores that they need to have a unified program throughout the nation. I am sure that these demonstrations helped a great deal, along with the demonstrations in the South, to bring about desegregation in more than one hundred twelve cities within the past five months. Students in the North can also give very important financial support.

TD. *Dialogue,* December 1960, pp. 1, 4.

To the Montgomery Improvement Association

8 December 1960
[*Atlanta, Ga.*]

King sends greetings to the MIA's fifth annual Institute on Nonviolence and Social Change.[1]

MEMBERS OF THE MONTGOMERY IMPROVEMENT ASSOCN
CARE DR RALPH D ABERNATHY
1327 SOUTH HALL ST

PLEASE ACCEPT MY SINCERE FELICITATIONS AS YOU OBSERVE THE FIFTH ANNIVERSARY OF MIA DEEPLY REGRET ~~MY~~ THAT LEGAL COMPLICATIONS MAKE IT IMPOSSIBLE FOR ME TO BE WITH YOU IN PERSON[2] YOU MUST KNOW THAT I AM ALWAYS WITH YOU IN SPIRIT AND SUPPORT. YOU ARE DOING SUCH MARVELOUS THINGS FOR THE WHOLE ~~CASU~~ CAUSE OF FREEDOM AND DEMOCRACY. UNDER THE DYNAMIC AND DEDICATED LEADERSHIP OF MY FRIEND AND CLOSE ASSOCIATE RALPH ABERNATHY YOU ARE DESTINED AN EVEN GREATER FRONTAL ATTACK ON THE SYSTEM OF SEGREGATION. YOUR COURAGEOUS NON VIOLENT ACTION WILL CERTAINLY BE RECORDED AS ONE OF THE GLOWING EPICS OF RECENT HISTORY AS YOU CONTINUE THE STRUGGLE THERE WILL BE INEVITABLE MOMENTS OF SUFFERING SACRIFICE AND TENSION BUT MAY YOU GO ON WITH THE FAITH THAT UNEARNED SUFFERING IS REDEMPTIVE AND THAT BEYOND THE PRESENT DARKNESS THERE IS AN EMERGING DAYBREAK THAT WILL USHER IN THE WORLDS BRIGHT TOMORROW.

MARTIN LUTHER KING JR

PHWc. MLKP-MBU: Box 59.

---

1. The week-long institute opened on 5 December with an address by Anna Hedgeman, the first black woman to serve in the New York mayor's cabinet; Jackie Robinson was scheduled to give the closing speech on 11 December. Ralph Abernathy also spoke during the institute ("MIA Speaker Asks Negroes to Aid Youth," *Montgomery Advertiser,* 6 December 1960, and "Local Negro Leader Asks Store Boycott," *Montgomery Advertiser,* 9 December 1960; see also MIA, Program, "Fifth anniversary and the Annual Institute on Nonviolence," 5 December–11 December 1960). King had resigned as MIA president before moving to Atlanta in early 1960 and was listed as "president emeritus" in the institute's program (see King, Address Delivered at the Montgomery Improvement Association's "Testimonial of Love and Loyalty," 1 February 1960, pp. 358–363 in this volume).

2. King refers to the pending libel case brought by Alabama governor John Patterson.

"The Three Dimensions of a Complete Life," Sermon Delivered at the Unitarian Church of Germantown

[*11 December 1960*]
Philadelphia, Pa.

In this sermon, versions of which King had preached as early as 1954, King laments that "too many of our white brothers are concerned merely about the length of life rather than the breadth of life."[1] He suggests that with reordered priorities "the jangling discords of the South would be transformed into a beautiful symphony of brotherhood." King's theme and content reflect the influence of abolitionist minister Phillips Brooks's sermon "The Symmetry of Life."[2] After this morning sermon, King traveled to Boston to deliver "The Future of Integration" at the Ford Hall Forum. The following transcript was drawn from an audio recording.

Reverend Daskam and members and friends of this great church, ladies and gentlemen.[3] I need not pause to say how very delighted I am to be here today and to be with you and this community and to have the opportunity of sharing this great ecumenical pulpit. It is always a real pleasure to come back to Philadelphia and this area. I never feel like a stranger when I return because I lived in this community some three years, and I was a student in theological seminary.[4] At that time I met many, many people in this area, and I feel that I have some real genuine friends in Philadelphia. So it is always a rewarding experience to come back to this area. And it is a great pleasure to be in this pulpit, and I want to express my personal appreciation to Reverend Daskam for extending the invitation.

And this morning I would like to have you think with me on the subject, "The Three Dimensions of a Complete Life." The three dimensions of a complete life. Many, many centuries ago a man by the name of John was in prison out on a lonely obscure island called Patmos. While in this situation, John imagined that he saw the new Jerusalem descending out of heaven from God. One of the greatest glories of this new city of God that John saw was its completeness. It was not partial and one sided, but it was complete in all three of its dimensions. So in describing the city in the sixteenth chapter of the book of Revelation, John says this: "The

1. King, "The Dimensions of a Complete Life," Sermon at Dexter Avenue Baptist Church, 24 January 1954. King also preached a version of this sermon on his first Sunday as co-pastor at Ebenezer on 7 February 1960 (Paul Delaney, "'Follow Way of Love,' Dr. King Asks People," *Atlanta Daily World,* 9 February 1960). A published version appeared in King's book *The Measure of a Man* (Philadelphia: Christian Education Press, 1959).

2. Brooks, "The Symmetry of Life," *Selected Sermons,* ed. William Scarlett (New York: E. P. Dutton, 1949), pp. 195–206. In a later interview King acknowledged that Brooks's sermon was the inspiration for "Three Dimensions" (Mervyn A. Warren, "A Rhetorical Study of the Preaching of Doctor Martin Luther King, Jr., Pastor and Pulpit Orator" [PhD diss., Michigan State University, 1966], p. 105).

3. In a 24 May letter to Max Daskam, who had been pastor of the church since 1929, Maude Ballou relayed King's consent to preach. Daskam first invited King on 24 March 1959.

4. King attended nearby Crozer Theological Seminary in Chester from 1948 until 1951.

11 Dec 1960

length and the height and the breadth of it are equal."[5] In other words, of this new city of God, this city of ideal humanity is not an unbalanced entity, but it is complete on all sides. And John is saying something quite significant here. So many of us the book of Revelation is a difficult book, puzzling to decode. We see it as something of an enigma wrapped in mystery. And I guess the book of Revelation is a difficult book, shrouded with impenetrable mysteries, if we accept everything in the book as a record of actual historical occurrences. But if we will look beneath the peculiar jargon of the author, what theologians call the prevailing apocalyptic symbolism, we will find there many eternal truths which forever confront us, and one such truth is the truth of this text. For what John is really saying is this: that life at its best and life as it should be is three-dimensional; it's complete on all sides. So there are three dimensions of any complete life, for which we can certainly give the words of this text: length, breadth, and height.[6]

The length of life, as we shall use it here, is not its longevity, its duration, not how long it lasts, but it is a push, the push of a life forward to achieve its personal ends and ambitions. It is the inward concern for one's own welfare. The breadth of life is the outward concern for the welfare of others. The height of life is the upward reach for God. So these are the three dimensions. On one hand, we find the individual person; on the other hand, we find other persons; at the top we find the supreme infinite person. These three must work together; they must be concatenated in an individual life if that life is to be complete, for the complete life is the three-dimensional life.

Now, let us think, first, of the length of life, and this is that dimension of life, as I've said, in which the individual is concerned with developing his inner powers. In a sense this is the selfish dimension of life. There is such a thing as rational, healthy, and moral self-interest. If an individual is not concerned about himself, he cannot really be concerned about other selves. Some years ago a brilliant Jewish rabbi, the late Joshua Liebman, wrote a book entitled *Peace of Mind*. And he has a chapter in that book entitled "Love Thyself Properly."[7] What he says in that chapter in substance is this: that before we can love other selves adequately we must love our own selves properly. And many people have been plunged into the abyss of emotional fatalism because they didn't love themselves properly. So we have a legitimate obligation: be concerned about ourselves. We have a legitimate obligation to set out in life to see what we are made for, to find that center of creativity, for there is within all of us a center of creativity seeking to break forth, and we have the responsibility of discovering this, discovering that life's work.

Then once we discover what we are made for, what we are called to do in life,

---

5. Cf. Revelation 21:16.

6. Brooks, *Selected Sermons*, p. 195: "St. John in his great vision sees the mystic city, 'the holy Jerusalem,' descending out of heaven from God. It is the picture of glorified humanity, of humanity as it shall be when it is brought to its completeness by being thoroughly filled with God. And one of the glories of the city which he saw was its symmetry. Our cities, our developments and presentations of human life, are partial and one-sided. This city out of heaven was symmetrical. In all its three dimensions it was complete. Neither was sacrificed to the other. 'The length and the breadth and the height of it are equal.'"

7. Joshua Loth Liebman, *Peace of Mind* (New York: Simon and Schuster, 1946), pp. 38–58.

we must set out to do it with all of the strength and all of the power that we can muster up. Individuals should seek to do his life's work so well that the living, the dead, or the unborn couldn't do it better. He must see it as something with cosmic significance; no matter how small it happens to be, or no matter how insignificant we tend to feel it is, we must come to see that it has great significance, that it is for the upbuilding of humanity. So to carry it to one extreme, if it falls one's lot to be a street sweeper, he should at that moment seek to sweep streets like Michelangelo carved marble, like Rafael painted pictures. He should seek to sweep streets like Beethoven composed the music or like Shakespeare wrote poetry. He should seek to sweep streets so well that all the hosts of heaven and earth will have to pause and say, "Here lived a great street sweeper, and he swept his job well."[8] And I think this is what Douglas Malloch meant when he said, "If you can't be a pine on the top of the hill, be a shrub in the valley—but be the best little shrub on the side of the rill; be a bush if you can't be a tree. If you can't be a highway just be a trail, if you can't be the sun be a star, for it isn't by size that you win or you fail—be the best of whatever you are."[9] This power to discover what you are made for, this onward push to the end of personal achievement, the length of a man's life.

11 Dec 1960

We must not stop here. It's dangerous to stop with the length of life. Some people never get beyond this first dimension of life, they're often brilliant people. They develop their inner powers. They do extraordinarily well in their fields of endeavor. They live life as if nobody else lived in the world but themselves. Other people become mere means by which they climb to their personal ends or their personal ambitions. Their love is only a utilitarian love. There is nothing more tragic in life to find an individual bogged down in the length of life, devoid of the breadth.

The breadth of life is that outward concern for the welfare of others. I should submit to you this morning that unless an individual can rise above the narrow confines of his individualistic concerns to the broader concerns of all humanity he hasn't even started living.[10] You remember a man went to Jesus one day to raise some serious questions; he was interested about life and all of its eternal meaning. Finally he got around to the question, "Who is my neighbor?"[11] Now it could've very easily ended up in a sort of philosophical debate, in an abstract discussion. Jesus immediately pulled that question out of mid-air and placed it on a dangerous curve between Jerusalem and Jericho. He talked about a certain man that fell

---

8. In an earlier speech King attributed this quotation to Morehouse College president Benjamin Mays (see King, "Facing the Challenge of a New Age," Address Delivered at NAACP Emancipation Day Rally, 1 January 1957, in *Papers* 4:79).

9. King paraphrases the poem "Be the Best of Whatever You Are" (1926) by Douglas Malloch.

10. Brooks, *Selected Sermons,* p. 196: "The Breadth of a life, on the other hand, is its outreach laterally, if we may say so. It is the constantly diffusive tendency which is always drawing a man outward into sympathy with other men. And the Height of a life is its reach upward towards God; its sense of childhood; its consciousness of the Divine Life over it with which it tries to live in love, communion, and obedience. These are the three dimensions of a life,—its length and breadth and height,—without the due development of all of which no life becomes complete."

11. This question was asked of Jesus, who replied with the parable of the Good Samaritan (see Luke 10:29).

among thieves. Three men passed, you remember. One was a Levite; one was a priest. And they passed by on the other side; they didn't stop to help the man. And finally a man of another race came by. The Samaritan, you remember. He stopped; he administered first aid; he helped the man in need. Jesus implied that this Samaritan was good, that he was great, because he had the capacity to project the I into the Thou.

Now, when we read this parable we tend to use our imagination a great deal. I know I do when I read it. We begin to wonder why the priest didn't stop and why the Levite didn't stop. Now, there are many reasons when we begin to use our imagination about it. It's possible that they were busy and they were in a big hurry because they had some ecclesiastical meeting to attend. That's a possibility. And so they just didn't have time; they had to be there on time; they didn't want to be late; they considered the duties of ecclesiastical concerns more important. Now, there is also a possibility that they were going down to Jericho to organize the Jericho Road Improvement Association. That's another, a real possibility.

Well, you know there is another possibility that I often think about when I think about this parable. It's really possible that those men were afraid. You know, the Jericho road is a dangerous road. A few months ago Mrs. King and I were in Jerusalem, and we rented a car and drove down the Jericho road from Jerusalem to Jericho.[12] And I said to her as we went around this road—it's a meandering, curvy road—and I said I can easily see why Jesus used this as a setting for the parable because there is something dangerous about this road, and it's conducive for robbery. Here is Jerusalem, some twenty-six-hundred feet above sea level, and here is Jericho, some one thousand feet below sea level, and you go that distance within about fifteen or sixteen miles. Mountainous, dangerous, meandering road, and so it is possible that the priest and the Levite had a little fear. The robbers could have still been around, and they could have raised this question. Maybe they are still around; or maybe the man on the ground is faking, and he's just trying to get us over there to end up robbing us in the long run. So may it not be that the first question that the priest raised or the first question that the Levite raised was this: "If I stop to help this man, what will happen to me?" Then the Good Samaritan came by, and in the very nature of his concern reversed the question: "If I do not stop to help this man, what will happen to him?"[13] And so he was a great man because he had the mental equipment for a dangerous altruism. He was a great man because he not only ascended to the heights of economic security but because he could condescend to the depths of human need. He was a great man because he discovered in his own life that he who would be greatest among you must be your servant.[14]

Now this text has a great deal of bearing, this whole question of the breadth of life has a great deal of bearing on the crisis which we face in race relations in our own nation. I am absolutely convinced that the problems which we face today in

12. In a 29 March 1959 Easter Sunday sermon at Dexter, King recalled his recent visit to Jericho (see King, A Walk Through the Holy Land, pp. 164–175 in this volume).

13. Cf. Luke 10:30–37.

14. Cf. Matthew 23:11.

the Southland grow out of the fact that too many of our white brothers are concerned merely about the length of life rather than the breadth of life, concerned about their so-called way of life, concerned about perpetuating a preferred economic position, concerned about preserving a sort of political status and power, concerned about preserving a so-called social status. As we look to these problems we find ourselves saying, if they would only add breadth to length, the other-regarding dimension to the self-regarding dimension, the jangling discords of the South would be transformed into a beautiful symphony of brotherhood.

We look at New Orleans today—what do we see there? We find hundreds, hundreds and thousands of people infiltrated with hatred. We find a legislative body using all of the fears and all of the emotions to keep the people confused.[15] In many instances these political leaders are concerned merely about perpetuating their political power. So we see many irresponsible leaders of states in the South using this issue merely to keep the people confused and arousing their fears just to get elected, concerned merely about the length of life, not the breadth. For you see in a real sense the system of segregation itself is wrong because it is based on the question of length and not breadth, it is exclusive and not inclusive. Segregation is wrong because it substitutes an I-it relationship for the I-Thou relationship.[16] Segregation is wrong because it relegates persons to the status of things. Segregation is wrong because it assumes that God made a mistake and stamped a badge of inferiority on certain people because of the color of their skin.[17] Therefore, all men of goodwill have a moral obligation to work assiduously to remove this cancerous disease from the body of our nation. It must be done not merely to meet the Communist challenge, although it will be diplomatically expedient to do it. It must be done not merely to appeal to Asian and African people, although it would be expedient to do it. In the final analysis segregation and discrimination must be removed from our nation because they are morally wrong. They stand in conflict with all of the noble principles of our Judeo-Christian heritage. They must be removed because they are wrong at the very core.

I don't want to give the impression that those individuals who are working to remove the system and those individuals who have been on the oppressed end of the old order must not themselves be concerned about breadth. But I realize that so often in history when oppressed people rise up against their oppression they are too concerned about length too often. It is my firm conviction those of us who have been on the oppressed end of the old order have as much responsibility to be concerned about breadth as anybody else. This is why I believe so firmly in nonviolence. Our aim must not be merely to achieve rights for Negroes or rights for

15. Judge J. Skelly Wright had ordered the New Orleans public schools to desegregate on 14 November 1960, prompting whites to mob city hall and withdraw children in large numbers from the local schools (Claude Sitton, "Pupils Integrate in New Orleans as Crowd Jeers," *New York Times,* 15 November 1960).

16. Cf. Martin Buber, *I and Thou* (1937).

17. King's discussion of the effects of segregation is similar to Benjamin E. Mays's treatment in a 1955 speech, "The Moral Aspects of Segregation" (see note 11 to "Address at Public Meeting of the Southern Christian Ministers Conference of Mississippi," 23 September 1959, p. 288 in this volume).

colored people. We are concerned about this only, we will seek to rise from a position of disadvantage to one of advantage, thus subverting justice. The aim must never be to do that but to achieve democracy for everybody. And this is why I disagree so firmly with any philosophy of black supremacy, for I am absolutely convinced that God is not interested merely in the freedom of black men and brown men and yellow men. But God is interested in the freedom of the whole human race, the creation of a society where all men will live together as brothers and *every* man will respect the dignity and worth of all human personality. And a doctrine of white supremacy is concerned merely about the length of life, not the breadth of life. So the aim of the Negro never be to defeat or humiliate the white man but to win his friendship and understanding.

As I said, the tension which we face in America today, not so much a tension between black men and white men, but it's a tension between justice and injustice, a struggle between the forces of light and the forces of darkness. And, if there is a victory, it will be a victory not merely for seventeen or eighteen million Negroes. It will be a victory for democracy, a victory for justice, a victory for freedom. And this is why I admire so much these hundreds and thousands of students all across our Southland not merely because they are working for constructive ends but because they have decided to use means that have the element of breadth. For all of these months they have taken the deep groans and the passionate yearnings of the Negro people and filtered them in their own souls, fashioned them into a creative protest, which is an epic known all over our nation. Yes, they have moved in a uniquely meaningful orbit, [*imparting?*] light and heat to distant satellite. And I am convinced that when the history books are written the historians will have to record this movement as one of the most significant epics of our heritage, not merely because it seeks to bring about humanitarian ends, because it also has humanitarian means.

And not only does this text have bearing on our struggle in America in the area of race relations, but it has a great deal of bearing on the crisis in the world in international relations. This text says to us, in substance, that every nation must be concerned about every other nation. No nation can live in isolation today. We live in a world that is geographically one now. We have the job of making it spiritually one. A few months ago Mrs. King and I journeyed to that great country in the Far East known as India. I never will forget the experience; it was a most rewarding experience, one that I will remember as long as the chords of memory shall lengthen, experience of talking with the great leaders of government, meeting hundreds and thousands of people all over India, most rewarding experience. And I say to you this morning that there were those depressing moments. How can one avoid being depressed when he sees with his own eyes millions of people going to bed hungry at night? How can one avoid being moved and concerned when he sees with his own eyes millions of people sleeping on the sidewalks at night? In Calcutta alone more than a million people sleep on the sidewalk every night. In Bombay more than five hundred thousand people sleep on the sidewalk every night, no houses to go in, no beds to sleep in. How can one avoid being depressed, he discovers that out of India's population of four hundred million people, more than three hundred and fifty million of these people make an annual income of less than sixty dollars a year? Most of these people have never seen a doctor or a dentist. Many of these conditions exist because these people for many, many years were dominated politically, exploited economically, segregated and humiliated by foreign power. 11 Dec 1960

As I watched these conditions, I found conditions, I found myself asking, can we in America stand idly by and not be concerned? I thought of the fact that we spend millions of dollars a day to store surplus food, and I started thinking to myself, I know where we can store this food free of charge—in the wrinkled stomachs of the hundreds and thousands and millions of people all over the world who are hungry. Maybe in America we spend too much of our money establishing military bases around the world rather than establishing bases of genuine concern and understanding. And all I'm saying is simply this, that all life is interrelated. Somehow we are tied in a single garment of destiny, caught in an inescapable network of mutuality, where what affects one directly affects all indirectly. As long as there is poverty in this world, you can never be totally rich, even if you have a billion dollars. As long as diseases are rampant and millions of people cannot expect to live more than thirty or thirty-two years, you can never be totally healthy, even if you just got a clean bill of health from Mayo Clinic or John Hopkins Hospital. Strangely enough I can never be what I ought to be until you are what you ought to be, and you can never be what you ought to be until I am what I ought to be. This is the way the world is made; I didn't make it that way, but it's like that. And John Donne recorded it years ago and placed it in graphic terms: "No man is an island, entire of itself; every man is a piece of the continent, a part of the main." And then he goes on toward the end to say: "Any man's death diminishes me because I am involved in mankind. Therefore never send to know for whom the bell tolls; it tolls for thee."[18] Only by discovering this are we able to master the breadth of life.

Finally, there is another dimension. We must not stop with length and breadth. There is another dimension. Now some people never get beyond the first two. They are brilliant people, and in many instances they love humanity. They have active social concerns. They stop right there, so they seek to live life without a sky. They live only on the horizontal plane with no real concern for the vertical. Now I know that there are many reasons why people neglect this third dimension, this point of reaching up for the eternal God.[19] Some people, I'm sure, have honest reasons for, for not pursuing the ends of the third dimension. Some people have looked out into the world, and they have noticed evil in all of its glaring and colossal dimensions. That's something that the poet Keats called "the giant agony of the world."[20] They found themselves asking how is it that a good God who is at the same time an all-powerful God, how is it that such a God will allow all of this evil to exist in the world? And so they find themselves caught up in the problem of evil. Because of that they end up neglecting the third dimension.

And others who've gotten disgusted with organized religion and as a result of

18. King quotes lines from John Donne's "Meditation XVII" (1624).

19. Brooks, *Selected Sermons*, p. 202: "So much I say about the length and breadth of life. One other dimension still remains. The length and breadth and height of it are equal. The Height of life is its reach upward toward something distinctly greater than humanity. . . . The reaching of mankind towards God!"

20. King quotes from John Keats's "The Fall of Hyperion: A Dream" (1819).

their disgust with organized religion, and those people who claim that they believe in God living contrary to all of the demands of religion, they have decided that the third dimension is a waste of time. And we must admit that so often the church has been the arch conserver of the status quo. The church has too often been that institution that serves to crystallize the patterns of society through often evil patterns. How often in the church have we had a high blood pressure of creeds and an anemia of deeds? People looking out at that, seeing that the church has often gone out in society with no social consciousness, they've decided to neglect the third dimension. And then there are others who find it difficult to square their intellectual world view to the sometimes unscientific dogmas of religion.

But I imagine that most people fit in another category all together. They are not theoretical atheists; they are practical atheists. They are not the people who deny the existence of God with their minds and their lips, but they are the people who deny God's existence with their lives. For some of these other people who have the theoretical doubts and honest doubts reveal a deeper commitment in so many instances because while they deny God's existence with their minds they affirm God's existence in the bottom of their hearts and with their lives. But there is another type of atheism that is much more damaging. And so there are so many people that have neglected this third dimension just because they've become so involved in things [*gap in tape*] Greek civilization, unconsciously believing that only those things which we can see and touch, apply the five senses to, their existence.

But in spite of our theoretical denial, we still feel in life another order impinging upon us. In spite of our doubts, we go on in life having spiritual experiences that cannot be explained in materialistic terms. In spite of our inordinate worship of things, something keeps reminding us that the eternal things of the universe are never seen. We go out at night and look up at the beautiful stars as they bedeck the heavens like swinging lanterns of eternity; for the moment we think we see all. Then something comes to tell us, "Oh no." We can never see the law of gravitation that holds them there. We look at this beautiful church building, and we see the beautiful architecture, and we think for the moment we see all. Oh no. We can never see the mind of the architect who drew the blueprint; we can never see the love and the faith and the hope of the individuals who made it so. You look here this morning, and I know you're saying, "we see Martin Luther King." I hate to disappoint you. You merely see my body. You can never see my mind; you can never see my personality; you can never see the me that makes *me* me. So in a real sense everything that we see in life is something of a shadow cast by that which we do not see. Plato was right: "The visible is a shadow cast by the invisible."[21]

And so in spite of our denials we are still reminded of this, and may it not be that God is still around? And all of our new knowledge will not diminish his being one iota. All of our new developments can banish God neither from the microcosmic compass of the atom nor from the vast unfathomable ranges of interstellar space, living in a universe in which we are forced to measure stellar distance by light years, confronted with the illimitable expanse of the universe in which

21. King refers to Plato's allegory of the cave, from *The Republic:* "The truth would be literally nothing but the shadows of the images" (514a–c, 521a–e).

stars are five hundred million billion miles from the Earth, which heavenly bodies travel at incredible speed and in which the ages of planets are reckoned in terms of billions of years. Modern man is forced to cry out with the solace of old: "When I behold the heavens, the work of thy hands, the moon, the stars, and all that thou hast created, what is man that thou art mindful of him and the son of man that thou remembereth him?"[22] And so it may well be that God is still around. So let us go out with a cultivation of the third dimension, for it can give life new meaning. It can give life new zest, and I can speak of this out of personal experience.

Over the last few years, circumstances have made it necessary for me to stand so often amid the surging [*moment?*] of life's restless sea.[23] Moments of frustration, the chilly winds of adversity all around, but there was always something deep down within that could keep me going, a strange feeling that you are not alone in this struggle, that the struggle for the good life is a struggle in which the individual has cosmic companionship. For so many times I have been able with my people to walk and never get weary because I am convinced that there is a great camp meeting in the promised land of God's universe.[24] Maybe St. Augustine was right: we were made for God; we will be restless until we find rest in him.[25]

Love yourself if that means rational, healthy, and moral self-interest. You are commanded to do that; that is the length of life. Love your neighbor as you love yourself. You are commanded to do that; that is the breadth of life. But never forget there is a first and even greater commandment. Love the Lord thy God with all thy heart and with all thy soul and with all thy mind.[26] That is the height of life. When an individual does this, he lives a complete life. Thank God for John, who centuries ago caught vision of the New Jerusalem; and grant to those of us who are left to walk the streets and the highways of life will also catch vision of the New Jerusalem, decide to move toward that city of complete life in our individual lives, in our national lives, in which the length and the breadth and the height are equal.

Let us pray. Eternal God, our Father, we thank thee for the insights of old, the insights of prophets and those who have lived near to thee. Grant that as we continue to live we will seek to develop all of those dimensions that will bring completeness to us. Grant somehow that we will learn to be concerned about ourselves, but at the same time give us that great concern for other selves. At the same time, help us to be concerned about thee and to worship thee in spirit and truth.[27] Grant that somehow we will come to the great conclusion that unless we have all three of these we somehow live lives that are incomplete. Amen.

At. PPUCGC.

---

22. Cf. Psalm 8:3–4.

23. King may have borrowed the phrase "restless sea" from Cecil F. Alexander's 1852 hymn "Jesus Calls Us": "Jesus calls us o'er the tumult of our life's wild, restless sea; day by day his sweet voice soundeth, saying, 'Christian, follow me!'"

24. King adapts the lyrics of the spiritual "There's a Great Camp Meeting": "Walk together children, Don't you get weary, Don't you get weary, There's a great camp meeting in the Promised Land."

25. *The Confessions of St. Augustine,* 1.1: "Thou madest us for Thyself, and our heart is restless, until it repose in Thee."

26. Cf. Matthew 22:37.

27. Cf. John 4:24.

To Fred D. Gray

14 December 1960
[*Atlanta, Ga.*]

Several months after being served with a complaint in connection with Alabama governor John Patterson's libel suit, King forwarded it to his attorney, Fred Gray.[1] *On 9 December Gray responded that he was "very sorry that you did not send us this complaint immediately," noting that "the law requires that some type of answer or responsive pleading be filed in matters of this sort within thirty days." In the letter below, King explains why he did not respond more promptly. Patterson's attorneys later advised him to drop his case after the Supreme Court ruled against another Alabama official in 1964.*[2]

Attorney Fred D. Gray
34 North Perry Street
Montgomery, Alabama

Dear Fred:

I am in receipt of your letter of recent date concerning the copy of the complaint that was sent me through the mail. Frankly, I did not pay any real attention to this complaint when it was received for two reasons. First, I had been told that I could not be served since I lived outside of the State of Alabama. Second, I knew that I had not signed the ad in the New York Times, and, therefore, felt that the whole thing was a mistake. If I had known that the papers constituted a legitimate service, I would have immediately sought legal advice.

I would like for you to look into this matter immediately. Although I do not have the definite time that the papers came to Atlanta, I do remember picking the letter up from the Post Office on May 17, 1960. Consequently, it must have been mailed five or six days before that time.

Please let me know as soon as possible what I will be expected to do when the trial comes up. I am sure you can understand how anxious I am to have this whole matter cleared up because I have several speaking commitments in Alabama next year.[3]

Very sincerely yours,
Martin Luther King, Jr.

MLK.m

TLc. MLKP-MBU: Box 27.

---

1. Dora McDonald to Gray, 5 December 1960. On 30 May Patterson filed suit against the *New York Times*, King, Joseph Lowery, Fred Shuttlesworth, Ralph Abernathy, and S. S. Seay. For more on the libel charge, see Patterson to King, 9 May 1960, pp. 456–458 in this volume.

2. Patterson, Interview with King Papers Project staff, 18 July 2001 (see also *New York Times Co. v. Sullivan*, 376 U.S. 254 [1964]).

3. In his 12 January 1961 reply Gray assured King that his legal team was working on the matter but advised him not "to come into the state."

To Samuel L. Spear

16 December 1960
[*Atlanta, Ga.*]

Following the death of the pastor at Atlanta's West Hunter Baptist Church, Spear, a Philadelphia minister and longtime West Hunter member, asked King if he might be interested in filling the vacancy.[1] *King declines, reasoning that he has "certain advantages" as co-pastor at Ebenezer, and recommends Abernathy for the job.*[2] *Abernathy accepted the position at the church in August 1961 and moved to Atlanta the following November.*

Mr. Samuel L. Spear
7036 Lincoln Drive
Philadelphia 19, Pennsylvania

Dear Brother Spear:

This is just a note to acknowledge receipt of your very kind letter of recent date. I am indeed flattered to know that you are interested in my going to West Hunter to become your pastor. It makes me feel humble indeed to know that you have such trust and confidence in me. Let me assure you that I think a great deal of West Hunter Baptist church and I am greatly impressed with its potentialities. However, I feel that for the present at least, I should remain here at Ebenezer. I am sure that you can see how there are certain advantages that I have here that would not exist in a situation where I am the only pastor.

I do have another person that I am convinced would make West Hunter a great pastor. I speak of Rev. Ralph David Abernathy, who is presently pastor of First Baptist Church in Montgomery, Alabama. Ralph is a dynamic and able preacher, an exceptionally good administrator and organizer, and a great community leader. I am sure that he could give to West Hunter a type of leadership that would both double its membership and its spiritual impact in the community. I believe he would accept if a call were extended, although I cannot state this as a fact.

I would appreciate any good word that you could say for Ralph Abernathy, and I am sure that it would have an impact. I have not spoken to any of the officers about this yet because I am not sure whether they have started hearing prospective candidates.

Thank you again for your interest, and I will join you in praying that West Hunter

---

1. Spear to King, 5 December 1960. A. Franklin Fisher was pastor of West Hunter until his death in November 1960; King wired condolences to Fisher's widow on 9 November. Samuel L. Spear (1920–1986), born in Carlton, Georgia, attended Morehouse College from 1939 until 1941. In 1954, he accepted the pastorate of Ebenezer Baptist Church in Philadelphia, where he remained until his death.

2. King later wrote the chairman of the church board, giving Abernathy "an unqualified recommendation" as "one of the most capable men in our nation today" (King to J. R. Butts, 8 February 1961).

will have God's guidance as she sets out on this sacred and serious responsibility of calling a pastor.

Sincerely yours,
Martin Luther King, Jr.

MLK.m

TLc. MLKP-MBU: Box 69.

To Sammy Davis, Jr.

20 December 1960
[*Atlanta, Ga.*]

King thanks Davis for his "wonderful support" of the upcoming 27 January 1961 Carnegie Hall "Tribute to Martin Luther King, Jr."[1] *King also praises aspiring playwright Oscar Brown's musical* Kicks & Co. *for its portrayal of "the conflict of soul, the moral choices that confront our people, both Negro and white."*

Mr. Sammy Davis, Jr.
Sherry-Netherland Hotel
5th Avenue at 59th Street
New York 22, New York

Dear Sammy:

I have been meaning to write you for quite some time. A sojourn in jail and a trip to Nigeria among other tasks have kept be behind.

When I solicited your help for our struggle almost two months ago, I did not expect so creative and fulsome a response. All of us are inspired by your wonderful support and the Committee is busily engaged in the preparations for January 27th. I hope I can convey our appreciation to you with the warmth which we feel it.

In the midst of one of my usual crowded sojourns in New York, I had the opportunity to hear the play, "Kicks and Co." by Oscar Brown at the invitation of the Nemiroffs, at whose home I have previously been a guest.[2] I learned of your interest in it and I am deeply pleased.

---

1. On 5 December, Stanley Levison sent King a draft of this letter and invited King to "change or adapt it any way you see fit." King did not change the text before sending it to Davis. Sammy Davis, Jr. (1925–1990), born in New York City, studied tap dancing under Bill "Bojangles" Robinson. He served in the U.S. Army for two years during World War II. A popular performer, Davis appeared on Broadway and in motion pictures. In the 1960s, he became associated with the Rat Pack, a group of Hollywood entertainers including Frank Sinatra and Dean Martin. Davis wrote two autobiographies, *Yes I Can* (1965) and *Why Me?* (1989). In 1968, he was awarded the NAACP's Spingarn Medal.

2. Robert Barron Nemiroff, husband of playwright Lorraine Hansberry, co-produced "Kicks & Co." and helped arrange Oscar Brown's recording contract with Columbia Records.

To my knowledge, rarely has there come upon the American scene a work which so perceptively mirrors the conflict of soul, the moral choices that confront our people, both Negro and white, in these fateful times. And yet a work which is at the same time, so light of touch, entertaining—and thereby all the more persuasive.

Art can move and alter people in subtle ways because, like love, it speaks through and to the heart. This young man's work will, in its own special way, affect the conscience of vast numbers with the moral force and vigor of our young people. And coming as it does from a source so eminently influential, the Broadway theat~~are~~{re}, and an actor of such stature as yourself, it will be both an inspiration and a sustenance to us all.[3]

In that context, let me share with you again my appreciation for the motives and the wisdom that have led you to it.

Very sincerely yours,
Martin Luther King, Jr.

MLK.m

THLc. MLKP MBU: Box 23.

---

3. In January 1961 Nemiroff sent King a copy of Brown's latest album and reported that Davis would most likely be unable to star in the anticipated Broadway production of *Kicks & Co.* (Nemiroff to King, 19 January 1961). The play opened in Chicago in 1961 but never appeared on Broadway.

Each volume of *The Papers of Martin Luther King, Jr.* includes a Calendar of Documents that provides an extensive list of significant King-related material for the period. The calendar includes research material relevant to the study of King's life and work that was not selected for publication in the volume. It is generated from an online database maintained at the King Project's Stanford University office.

Space limitations prevent the listing of all 7,000 documents from the online database; only the most important (approximately 1,550) have been selected by the editors for inclusion in the calendar. This inventory includes not only notable documents in the King collections at Boston University and the King Center, but also those obtained from King's relatives and acquaintances and material gathered during an intense search of over sixty-five archives such as the Dwight D. Eisenhower Library.

Owing to space constraints, full bibliographic citations are not provided in editorial annotations: complete references for individual documents mentioned in headnotes, footnotes, and the Introduction are found only in the calendar. The calendar includes significant King-authored material such as speeches, sermons and articles; selected correspondence and other ephemera regarding events in which King participated; press releases and notes of meetings he attended. Relatively mundane documents such as routine office correspondence and most unsolicited letters of support are not listed in the calendar, though they remain available in the online database. The calendar also includes a sampling of the following types of documents: correspondence with friends, religious leaders, political leaders, and activists in civil rights organizations; historically significant MIA and SCLC documents such as financial material and correspondence with committee members; contemporary interviews; published articles with extensive King quotations; internal White House and Federal Bureau of Investigation memos; and other material documenting King's activities. The calendar also includes citations to documents that became available after the publication of the volume of the King Papers covering that time period. The listings of photographs and illustrations that appear in the current volume are printed in boldface type.

Each calendar entry provides essential bibliographic information about the document. Italics and brackets indicate information determined by the editors based on evidence contained in the document; when the evidence is not conclusive question marks are used as well. The entry adheres to the following format:

Date	Author (Affiliation). Document title. Date. Place of origin. (Physical description codes) Number of pages. (Notes.) Archival location. King Papers Project identification number.
4/7/1960	King, Martin Luther, Jr. "How My Mind Has Changed in the Last Decade." 4/7/1960. [*Atlanta, Ga.*] (THD) 10 pp. (Enclosed in 600407–014.) MLKP-MBU: Box 89. 600407–015.

DATE. The date in the left margin is intended to aid the reader in looking up specific documents. Complete date information is provided in the entry. In those cases where the original bears no date the editors have assigned one and enclosed it in brackets. Those documents bearing range dates appear after precisely dated documents and are arranged by end date in the range, unless logic dictates another order. The date of photographs is presented without brackets if the donor provided a date. The date of published or printed papers is the date of publication or public release rather than the date of composition.

AUTHOR. A standardized form of an individual's name (based on *Anglo-American Cataloging Rules,* 2d ed.) is provided in both the author and title fields. Forms of address are omitted unless necessary for identification, such as a woman who used only her husband's name. For photographs, the photographer is considered the author. Since King's script is distinctive, his unsigned handwritten documents are identified as of certain authorship. Institutional authorship is provided when appropriate.

AFFILIATION. Affiliation information is provided if the author wrote in his or her capacity as an official of an organization. No brackets or italics have been used in the affiliation field.

TITLE. Titles enclosed in quotation marks have been drawn directly from the document with minor emendations of punctuation, capitalization, and spelling for clarity. Phrases such as "Letter to," "Photo of," are used to create titles for otherwise untitled documents; in such titles, words are generally not capitalized and names are standardized. The use of the word "delivered" in the titles of speeches and sermons connotes an audio version. Published versions of earlier speeches contain the date of delivery in the title.

PLACE OF ORIGIN. This field identifies where the document was completed or, in the case of a published document, the place of publication. If the document does not contain the place of origin and the information can be obtained, it is provided in brackets; such information is offered only for documents written by King or those written on his behalf.

PHYSICAL DESCRIPTION. This field describes the format of presentation, type of document, version of document, and character of the signature (see List of Abbreviations, pp. 69–75). Documents that consist of several formats are listed with the predominant one first.

LENGTH. The number of pages or the duration of a recording is indicated.

NOTES. In this optional field, miscellaneous information pertaining to the document is provided. This information includes enclosures to a letter, routing information (e.g., "Copy to King") since King often received copies of correspondence addressed to others, and remarks concerning the legibility of the document or the authorship of marginalia. For tapes, information about the media used is also indicated in this field.

ARCHIVAL LOCATION. The location of the original document is identified using standard abbreviations based on the Library of Congress's codes for libraries and archives (see List of Abbreviations, pp. 69–75). When available, box numbers or other archival location identification are provided.

IDENTIFICATION NUMBER. The nine-digit identification number, based on the date, uniquely identifies the document. Documents of the same date are listed in order of their identification number.

1948 Jones, E. Stanley. *Mahatma Gandhi: An Interpretation*. New York: Abingdon-Cokesbury Press, 1948. (PD) (Marginal comments by King.) CSKCH. 480000–033.

1/1946–6/1948 King, Martin Luther, Jr. Notes on marriage. [*1/1946–6/1948*]. [*Atlanta, Ga.*] (AD) 1 p. MLKP-MBU: Box 113. 480600–005.

1949 Gandhi, Mahatma. *Selected Letters*. Ahmedabad: Navajivan Publishing House, 1949. (PHD) (Enclosed in 601102–012. Inscription by Ingeborg Teek-Frank, 11/2/1960.) CSKCH. 490000–037.

1951 Bellamy, Edward. *Looking Backward 2000–1887*. New York: Modern Library, 1951. (PHD) (Marginal comments by King. Inscription by Coretta Scott, 4/7/1952.) CSKCH. 510000–030.

2/27/1952 Kircher, Roland. "Nels Ferre." [*2/27/1952*] (THD) 1 p. (Marginal comments by King.) MLKP-MBU: Box 114. 520227–001.

4/7/1952 Scott, Coretta. Inscription to Martin Luther King, Jr. 4/7/1952. (ALS) 1 p. CSKCH. 520407–000.

7/18/1952 King, Martin Luther, Jr. Letter to Coretta Scott King. [*7/18/1952*]. [*Atlanta, Ga.*] (ALS) 13 pp. CSKC. 520718–000.

1954 Hamilton, James Wallace. *Horns and Halos in Human Nature*. Westwood, N.J.: Fleming H. Revell Company, 1954. (PHD) (Marginal comments by King. Inscription by Hamilton.) CSKCH. 540000–031.

1/24/1954 King, Martin Luther, Jr. "The Dimensions of a Complete Life," Sermon at Dexter Avenue Baptist Church. [*1/24/1954*]. [*Montgomery, Ala.*] (AD) 8 pp. CSKC: Sermon file. 540124–002.

4/4/1954 King, Martin Luther, Jr. "Going Forward by Going Backward," Sermon at Dexter Avenue Baptist Church. [*4/4/1954*]. [*Montgomery, Ala.*] (TD) 5 pp. CSKC: Sermon file. 540404–001.

1956 Southern Regional Council. *The Segregation Decisions*. Atlanta, Ga.: Southern Regional Council, 1956. (PHD) (Marginal comments by King.) CSKCH. 560000–154.

2/29/1956 Gray, William H. (William Herbert) (Bright Hope Baptist Church). Letter to Martin Luther King, Jr. 2/29/1956. Philadelphia, Pa. (TLS) 1 p. MLKP-MBU: Box 91. 560229–000.

8/3/1956 King, Martin Luther, Jr., and Grover C. Hall. "Pro and Con, Alabama's Bus Boycott: What It's All About." 8/3/1956. Washington, D.C. From: *U.S. News and World Report,* 3 August 1956, pp. 82–89. (PD) 8 pp. MLKJP-GAMK. 560803–000.

1/5/1957 Steere, Dorothy M. (Haverford College). Letter to Martin Luther King, Jr. 1/5/1957. Haverford, Pa. (TLS) 2 pp. MLKP-MBU: Box 65. 570105–002.

1/14/1957 Smiley, Glenn E. Memo to William Robert Miller. 1/14/1957. (TL) 1 p. FORP-PSC-P. 570114–007.

1/28/1957 Bowles, Chester. Letter to Martin Luther King, Jr. 1/28/1957. New Delhi, India. (TLS) 1 p. MLKP-MBU: Box 89. 570128–004.

2/5/1957 Clareman, Jack (The Christopher Reynolds Foundation, Inc.). Letter to A. Philip (Asa Philip) Randolph. 2/5/1957. New York, N.Y. (TLS) 1 p. APRC-DLC. 570205–008.

2/21/1957 Hill, Daniel G. (Howard University). Letter to Martin Luther King, Jr. 2/21/1957. Washington, D.C. (THLS) 1 p. (600413–014 on verso.) CSKC. 570221–008.

3/4/1957 Spivak, Lawrence E. (Lawrence Edmund) ("Meet the Press"). Letter to Martin Luther King, Jr. 3/4/1957. New York, N.Y. (TLS) 1 p. MLKP-MBU: Box 62. 570304–013.

3/28/1957 Wright, Harold B. (U.S. Dept. of Health Education and Welfare). Letter to Martin Luther King, Jr. 3/28/1957. Atlanta, Ga. (TLS) 2 pp. HG-GAMK. 570328–000.

3/29/1957 King, Martin Luther, Jr. (Dexter Avenue Baptist Church). Letter to Lawrence E. (Lawrence Edmund) Spivak. 3/29/1957. [*Montgomery, Ala.*] (TLc) 1 p. MLKP-MBU: Box 62. 570329–006.

4/5/1957 Minutes, Conference on Prayer Pilgrimage for Freedom. 4/5/1957. (THD) 7 pp. NAACPP-DLC: Group III-G2. 570405–012.

4/14/1957 King, Martin Luther, Jr. Garden of Gethsemane, Sermon delivered at Dexter Avenue Baptist Church. [*4/14/1957*]. [*Montgomery, Ala.*] (At) 37 min. (1 sound cassette: analog.) MLKEC: ET-66. 570414–004.

4/15/1957 Spivak, Lawrence E. (Lawrence Edmund) ("Meet the Press"). Letter to Martin Luther King, Jr. 4/15/1957. New York, N.Y. (TLS) 1 p. MLKP-MBU: Box 65A. 570415–004.

6/21/1957 United Packinghouse Workers of America, AFL-CIO. "Program proposals for 1957." [*6/21/1957*]. (TD) 9 pp. UPWP-WHi: Box 373. 570621–009.

10/1957 Georgia Commission on Education. "Highlander Folk School: Communist Training School, Monteagle, Tenn." [*10/1957*]. Atlanta, Ga. (PD) 3 pp. HSF-GAHi. 571000–013.

10/1/1957 Bowles, Chester. Letter to Martin Luther King, Jr. 10/1/1957. Essex, Conn. (TLS) 3 pp. MLKP-MBU: Box 20. 571001–000.

10/2/1957 Helstein, Ralph. Remarks at the fourth biennial wage and contracts, third national anti-discrimination, and third national women's activities conference of the United Packinghouse Workers. [10/2/1957]. Chicago, Ill. (TTa) 4 pp. UPWP-WHi: Box 526. 571002–001.

11/7/1957 Wofford, Harris. "Nonviolence and the Law." 11/7/1957. (TAD) 16 pp. CSKC. 571107–002.

1/9/1958 King, Martin Luther, Jr. Telegram to C. E. Ryan. 1/9/1958. [*Montgomery, Ala.*] (TWc) 1 p. MLKP-MBU: Box 34. 580109–004.

1/23/1958 Jovin, Thomas (Young Men's Christian Association (YMCA)). Letter to Martin Luther King, Jr. 1/23/1958. Pasadena, Calif. (THLS) 3 pp. (Marginal comments by King) MLKP-MBU: Box 37. 580123–002.

3/7/1958 King, Martin Luther, Jr. (Dexter Avenue Baptist Church). Letter to The Christopher Reynolds Foundation, Inc. 3/7/1958. Montgomery, Ala. (TLS) 2 pp. NNCRF. 580307–000.

3/13/1958 Diggs, Charles C. Telegram to Martin Luther King, Jr. 3/13/1958. Washington, D.C. (PWSr) 1 p. MLKP-MBU: Box 23. 580313–008.

4/24/1958 Baker, Ella J. (SCLC). Letter to Martin Luther King, Jr. 4/24/1958. Atlanta, Ga. (TLS) 1 p. MLKP-MBU: Box 68. 580424–002.

5/9/1958 Baker, Ella J. (SCLC). Letter to Martin Luther King, Jr. 5/9/1958. Atlanta, Ga. (TLSr) 1 p. (Contains enclosure 580509–005.) MLKP-MBU: Box 71. 580509–004.

5/9/1958 King, Martin Luther, Jr. (SCLC). Draft, Letter to John Lee Tilley. 5/9/1958. [*Montgomery, Ala.*] (THLd) 1 p. (Enclosed in 580509–004.) MLKP-MBU: Box 71. 580509–005.

6/16/1958 Clareman, Jack (The Christopher Reynolds Foundation, Inc.). Letter to Martin Luther King, Jr. 6/16/1958. New York, N.Y. (TLS) 1 p. MLKP-MBU. 580616–000.

7/1958 American Committee on Africa, NAACP, and National Urban League. Invitation, Dinner in honor of Kwame Nkrumah. [*7/1958*]. New York, N.Y. (PD) 2 pp. MLKP-MBU: Box 26A. 580700–007.

7/16/1958 Baker, Ella J. (SCLC). Letter to Bayard Rustin and Stanley D. Levison. 7/16/1958. Atlanta, Ga. (THLS) 2 pp. BRP-DLC. 580716–002.

7/16/1958 Baker, Ella J. (SCLC). Memo to Martin Luther King, Jr. 7/16/1958. Atlanta, Ga. (TL) 2 pp. BRP-DLC. 580716–005.

7/28/1958 King, Martin Luther, Jr. Telegram to Roy Wilkins. 7/28/1958. Mexico City, Mexico. (PHWSr) 1 p. NAACPP-DLC: Group III-A177. 580728–000.

9/22/1958 Gbedemah, K. A. (Ghana. Office of the Minister of Finance). Telegram to Martin Luther King, Jr. [*9/22/1958*]. Montreal, Canada. (PWSr) 1 p. CSKC. 580922–023.

10/1/1958 SCLC. Minutes, Executive board meeting. 10/1/1958. Norfolk, Va. (TD) 3 pp. EJBC-NN-Sc. 581001–000.

10/2/1958 SCLC. Minutes, Fall meeting. 10/2/1958. (AD) 3 pp. EJBC-NN-Sc. 581002–017.

10/6/1958 National Council for Industrial Peace. Press release, Martin Luther King, Jr., J. H. (Joseph Harrison) Jackson, and Roy Wilkins denounce right-to-work laws. [*10/6/1958*]. Washington, D.C. (TD) 7 pp. MLKP-MBU: Box 24. 581006–003.

10/16/1958 Manley, Albert E. (Spelman College). Letter to Martin Luther King, Jr. 10/16/1958. Atlanta, Ga. (THLS) 1 p. MLKP-MBU: Box 46. 581016–009.

10/17/1958 King, Martin Luther, Jr. Letter to Clarence E. Pickett. 10/17/1958. [*Brooklyn, N.Y.*] (TLc) 1 p. MLKP-MBU: Box 19. 581017–017.

10/25/1958 Youth March for Integrated Schools. Press release, "Youth Pledge." [*10/25/1958*]. (TD) 2 pp. APRC-DLC. 581025–010.

11/1958 King, Martin Luther, Jr. Inscription to Jawaharlal Nehru. [*11/1958*]. [*Montgomery, Ala.*] (ALS) 1 p. LDPF-GAMK. 581100–015.

11/1958 SCLC. "Constitution and by-laws." [*11/1958*]. Atlanta, Ga. (PD) 18 pp. MLKP-MBU. 581100–016.

11/1958 King, Martin Luther, Jr. Inscription to Reinhold Niebuhr. [*11/1958*]. [*Montgomery, Ala.*] (ALS) 1 p. CNP. 581100–020.

11/1958	King, Martin Luther, Jr. Inscription to G. Mennen Williams. [*11/1958*]. [*Montgomery, Ala.*] (ALS) 1 p. NWGP. 581100–024.
10/1958–11/1958	NAACP. "Vote 'No' on Proposition 18." [*10/1958–11/1958*]. San Francisco, Calif. (PD) 6 pp. CSfSFL. 581100–019.
11/8/1958	King, Martin Luther, Jr. Letter to Howard Thurman. 11/8/1958. [*Montgomery, Ala.*] (TLc) 1 p. MLKP-MBU: Box 72. 581108–008.
11/10/1958	Ballou, Maude L. Letter to Albert E. Manley. 11/10/1958. [*Montgomery, Ala.*] (TLc) 1 p. MLKP-MBU: Box 46. 581110–008.
11/20/1958	Bryan, G. McLeod (Wake Forest College). Letter to Martin Luther King, Jr. 11/20/1958. Winston-Salem, N.C. 2 pp. (Includes enclosure.) MLKP-MBU: Box 73. 581120–004.
11/25/1958	Williams, G. Mennen (Michigan. Office of the Governor). Letter to Martin Luther King, Jr. 11/25/1958. Lansing, Mich. (TLS) 1 p. MLKP-MBU: Box 31A. 581125–001.
11/28/1958	Levison, Stanley D. Letter to Martin Luther King, Jr. 11/28/1958. (TALS) 2 pp. MLKP-MBU: Box 2. 581128–002.
11/1/1957–11/30/1958	King, Martin Luther, Jr. "Annual Report, Dexter Avenue Baptist Church." 11/1/1957–11/30/1958 Montgomery, Ala. (TAD) DABCC. 581130–002.
12/1/1958–12/7/1958	MIA. Program, "Third annual Institute on Nonviolence and Social Change." 12/1/1958–12/7/1958. Montgomery, Ala. (PD) 7 pp. MLKJP-GAMK: Box 80. 581207–001.
12/10/1958	Kaplan, Kivie (Colonial Tanning Company, Inc.). Letter to Martin Luther King, Jr. 12/10/1958. Boston, Mass. (TLS) 2 pp. MLKP-MBU: Box 29. 581210–002.
12/10/1958	Truman, Harry S. Letter to Martin Luther King, Jr. 12/10/1958. Independence, Mo. (TLS) 1 p. MLKP-MBU. 581210–003.
12/12/1958	Meacham, Stewart (American Friends Service Committee). Letter to Martin Luther King, Jr. 12/12/1958. Philadelphia, Pa. (TLS) 1 p. MLKP-MBU: Box 19. 581212–005.
12/16/1958	Randolph, A. Philip (Asa Philip). Letter to Martin Luther King, Jr. 12/16/1958. New York, N.Y. (TLS) 2 pp. MLKP-MBU: Box 64A. 581216–000.
12/18/1958	Kaur, Rajkumari Amrit. Letter to Stewart Meacham. 12/18/1958. New Delhi, India. (TL) 1 p. (Enclosed in 581231–001.) MLKP-MBU: Box 1. 581218–007.
12/22/1958	Mays, Benjamin Elijah (Morehouse College). Letter to Martin Luther King, Jr. 12/22/1958. Atlanta, Ga. (TLS) 1 p. MLKP-MBU: Box 31A. 581222–002.
12/24/1958	Bristol, James E. (Quaker Centre). Letter to Corinne B. Johnson. 12/24/1958. New Delhi, India. (TALS) 4 pp. AFSCR-PPAFS. 581224–008.
12/25/1958	Bristol, James E. (Quaker Centre). Letter to Corinne B. Johnson. 12/25/1958. New Delhi, India. (TLS) 1 p. AFSCR-PPAFS. 581225–000.
12/28/1958	King, Martin Luther, Jr. Letter to Benjamin Elijah Mays. 12/28/1958. [*Montgomery, Ala.*] (TLc) 1 p. MLKP-MBU: Box 31A. 581228–001.
12/30/1958	Randolph, A. Philip (Asa Philip), and Bayard Rustin (Youth March for Integrated Schools). "Interim report." 12/30/1958. New York, N.Y. (THDS) 3 pp. (Contains enclosure 581230–006.) FORP-PSC-P. 581230–005.
12/30/1958	[*Youth March for Integrated Schools*]. Draft, "Petition to the President and to the Congress." [*12/30/1958*]. (TDd) 1 p. (Enclosed in 581230–005.) FORP-PSC-P. 581230–006.
12/31/1958	Johnson, Corinne B. (American Friends Service Committee). Letter to Bayard Rustin. 12/31/1958. Philadelphia, Pa. (TLc) 2 pp. (Contains enclosure 581218–007.) MLKP-MBU: Box 1. 581231–001.
1959	King, Martin Luther, Jr. "Hopeful Signs on the Human Relations Horizon," Sermon outline. [*1959*]. [*Montgomery, Ala.*] (AD) 5 pp. MLKJP-GAMK: Box 108. 590000–000.
1959	Reddick, Lawrence Dunbar. Draft, Chapter IX, Decision at Montgomery, *Crusader Without Violence*. 1959. (TADd) 39 pp. LDRP-NN-Sc. 590000–050.
1959	*With the Kings in India: A Souvenir of Dr. Martin Luther King's Visit to India, February 1959–March 1959*. New Delhi: Gandhi National Memorial Fund, 1959. 26 pp. WRMP-GAMK. 590000–070.
1958–1959	SCLC. List of officers and executive board members. [*1958–1959*]. Atlanta, Ga. (THD) 2 pp. MLKP-MBU: Box 48. 590000–095.
1959	King, Martin Luther, Jr. *The Measure of Man*. Philadelphia: Christian Education Press, 1959. (PD).
1959	SCLC. "Names for consideration for advisory committee." [*1959*]. (TD) 1 p. MLKP-MBU. 590000–105.

1959	King, Martin Luther, Jr. Excerpt, Address at Clarksdale, Mississippi. 1959. Clarksdale, Miss. (TD) 1 p. MLKB-MsToT. 590000–129.
1959	Reddick, Lawrence Dunbar. Draft, Martin Luther King, Jr.'s trip to India. [*1959*]. (TADdf) 31 pp. LDRP-NN-Sc: Box 3. 590000–132.
1/1959	Youth March for Integrated Schools. "A petition for integrated schools to the President and the Congress of the U.S." [*1/1959*]. (PD) 2 pp. (Enclosed in 590112–005 pp. 105–106 in this volume, 590206–005, 590300–028, & 590418–000.) GMF-DAFL: Box 41. 590100–026.
1/1959	Davis, Benjamin J. (Benjamin Jefferson). Letter to Martin Luther King, Jr. [*1/1959*]. New York, N.Y. (TLS) 3 pp. MLKP-MBU. 590100–028.
1/1959	Youth March for Integrated Schools. "A call for a petition campaign and Youth March for Integrated Schools." [*1/1959*]. New York, N.Y. (PD) 2 pp. (Enclosed in 590112–005 pp. 105–106 in this volume & 590300–028.) GMF-DAFL: Box 41. 590100–032.
1/1959	SCLC. "Introducing *The Crusader*." [*1/1959*]. (TD) 4 pp. SCLCR-GAMK: Box 32. 590100–034.
1/1959	Youth March for Integrated Schools. "Why we march." [*1/1959*]. (TD) 2 pp. (Enclosed in 590408–006.) APRC-DLC. 590100–035.
1/1/1959	**Anonymous. Letter to Martin Luther King, Jr. 1/1/1959. Montgomery, Ala. (AL) 1 p. MLKP-MBU: Box 19. 590101–000.**
1/1/1959	Walker, Wyatt Tee (Pilgrimage of Prayer for Public Schools). "Statement of purpose." 1/1/1959. Richmond, Va. (TD) 2 pp. MLKP-MBU. 590101–003.
1/1/1959	Pilgrimage of Prayer for Public Schools. Program, "State-Wide Emancipation Day service." 1/1/1959. Richmond, Va. (TD) 3 pp. (Enclosed in 590116–008, pp. 108–111 in this volume.) MLKP-MBU: Box 73A. 590101–004.
1/4/1959	Dexter Avenue Baptist Church. Program, Sunday services. 1/4/1959. Montgomery, Ala. (TD) 4 pp. DABCC. 590104–000.
1/5/1959	Dinkins, Charles L. (Sunday School Publishing Board). Letter to Martin Luther King, Jr. 1/5/1959. Nashville, Tenn. (TLS) 1 p. MLKP-MBU: Box 69. 590105–007.
1/6/1959	Williams, G. Mennen (Michigan. Office of the Governor). Letter to Martin Luther King, Jr. 1/6/1959. Lansing, Mich. (TLS) 1 p. MLKP-MBU: Box 31. 590106–003.
1/6/1959	King, Martin Luther, Jr. Letter to Emil Naclerio. 1/6/1959. [*Montgomery, Ala.*] (TLc) 1 p. MLKP-MBU: Box 32A. 590106–004.
1/6/1959	King, Martin Luther, Jr. Letter to Alphonzo Jordan. 1/6/1959. [*Montgomery, Ala.*] (TLc) 1 p. MLKP-MBU. 590106–015.
1/6/1959	King, Martin Luther, Jr. Letter to John W. V. Cordice. 1/6/1959. [*Montgomery, Ala.*] (TLc) 1 p. MLKP-MBU: Box 22A. 590106–016.
1/6/1959	Sawyer, Hortense. "Minutes, National Action Committee." 1/6/1959. (THD) 6 pp. COREP-A-GAMK: Reel 9. 590106–019.
1/7/1959	King, Martin Luther, Jr. Letter to Helene D. Mayer. 1/7/1959. [*Montgomery, Ala.*] (TLc) 1 p. MLKP-MBU: Box 31. 590107–003.
1/8/1959	King, Martin Luther, Jr. Letter to Bernard B. Nadell. 1/8/1959. [*Montgomery, Ala.*] (TLc) 1 p. MLKP-MBU: Box 32A. 590108–007.
1/8/1959	Smiley, Glenn E. (FOR). Letter to Martin Luther King, Jr. 1/8/1959. Nyack, N.Y. (THLS) 1 p. MLKP-MBU: Box 39. 590108–008.
1/8/1959	Baker, Ella J. Letter to Nannie Helen Burroughs. 1/8/1959. (TLc) 2 pp. (Enclosed in 590108–012.) MLKP-MBU: Box 69. 590108–011.
1/8/1959	Baker, Ella J. Letter to Martin Luther King, Jr. [*1/8/1959*]. (TLS) 1 p. (Contains enclosures 590108–011 & 590108–013.) MLKP-MBU: Box 69. 590108–012.
1/8/1959	Baker, Ella J. (SCLC). Letter to Kenneth L. Buford. 1/8/1959. (TLc) 2 pp. (Enclosed in 590108–012.) MLKP-MBU: Box 69. 590108–013.
1/9/1959	The Christopher Reynolds Foundation, Inc. Letter to Stephen G. Cary. 1/9/1959. (TLc) 1 p. NNCRF. 590109–005.
1/10/1959	King, Martin Luther, Jr. (Dexter Avenue Baptist Church). Letter to A. Philip (Asa Philip) Randolph. 1/10/1959. Montgomery, Ala. (TLS) 1 p. BSCP-DLC. 590110–000.
1/10/1959	King, Martin Luther, Jr. Letter to V. L. Harris. 1/10/1959. [*Montgomery, Ala.*] (THLc) 2 pp. MLKP-MBU: Box 22A. 590110–003.
1/10/1959	King, Martin Luther, Jr. Letter to H. L. VanDyke and Bessie VanDyke. 1/10/1959. [*Montgomery, Ala.*] (TLc) 1 p. MLKP-MBU: Box 73. 590110–011.
1/11/1959	Dexter Avenue Baptist Church. Program, Sunday services. 1/11/1959. Montgomery, Ala. (TD) 4 pp. DABCC. 590111–000.

1/12/1959 King, Martin Luther, Jr. Letter to Stanley D. Levison. 1/12/1959. [*Montgomery, Ala.*] (TLc) 1 p. MLKP-MBU: Box 2. 590112–002.

1/12/1959 Kaplan, Kivie. Letter to Martin Luther King, Jr. 1/12/1959. Boston, Mass. (TLS) 2 pp. MLKP-MBU. 590112–009.

1/12/1959 King, Martin Luther, Jr., A. Philip (Asa Philip) Randolph, and Ruth H. Bunche. Letter to Eleanor Roosevelt. 1/12/1959. (TLc) 2 pp. APRC-DLC. 590112–012.

1/14/1959 King, Martin Luther, Jr. "The Future of Integration," Address at Yale University. 1/14/1959. New Haven, Conn. (THD) 7 pp. MLKP-MBU: Box 5. 590114–001.

1/15/1959 Randolph, A. Philip (Asa Philip). Letter to Martin Luther King, Jr. 1/15/1959. New York, N.Y. (TLS) 1 p. MLKP-MBU: Box 64. 590115–001.

1/15/1959 MIA. *Newsletter* 1, no. 11. 1/15/1959. Montgomery, Ala. (TD) 3 pp. MLKP-MBU: Box 106. 590115–002.

1/15/1959 Carey, Gordon (CORE). Letter to Martin Luther King, Jr. 1/15/1959. New York, N.Y. (THLS) 1 p. MLKP-MBU: Box 23. 590115–008.

1/15/1959 King, Alfred Daniel, and Naomi King. Telegram to Martin Luther King, Jr. 1/15/1959. Atlanta, Ga. (PWSr) 1 p. CSKC. 590115–009.

1/15/1959 Child, Bob. "Surprise Birthday Party Given Rev. Martin Luther King." 1/15/1959. New Haven, Conn. From: *New Haven Evening Register*, 15 January 1959. (PPh) 1 p. CSKC. 590115–010.

1/16/1959 Bristol, James E. (Quaker Centre). Letter to Corinne B. Johnson. 1/16/1959. New Delhi, India. (TLS) 2 pp. AFSCR-PPAFS. 590116–003.

1/16/1959 [*Meany, George*]. Letter to Martin Luther King, Jr. 1/16/1959. (TLc) 1 p. AFLP-DAFL. 590116–004.

1/18/1959 Dexter Avenue Baptist Church. Program, Sunday services. 1/18/1959. Montgomery, Ala. (TD) 1 p. DABCC. 590118–000.

1/19/1959 Hill, Jesse, Jr. (Atlanta All-Citizens Registration Committee). Letter to Martin Luther King. 1/19/1959. Atlanta, Ga. (TLS) 2 pp. MLKP-MBU: Box 28. 590119–002.

1/20/1959 Mygatt, Tracy D. (Tracy Dickinson) (Campaign for World Government, Inc.). Letter to Martin Luther King, Jr. 1/20/1959. Brewster, N.Y. (THLS) 1 p. MLKP-MBU: Box 22. 590120–001.

1/20/1959 Douglas, Paul Howard (U.S. Congress. Senate). Letter to Martin Luther King, Jr., A. Philip (Asa Philip) Randolph, and Ralph J. (Ralph Johnson) Bunche. 1/20/1959. Washington, D.C. (TLcS) 2 pp. MLKP-MBU: Box 23. 590120–004.

1/21/1959 Dexter Avenue Baptist Church. *Dexter Echo* 3, no. 2. 1/21/1959. Montgomery, Ala. (TD) 6 pp. DABCC. 590121–001.

1/21/1959 Reuther, Walter P. (International Union, United Automobile, Aircraft, and Agricultural Implement Workers of America). Letter to Martin Luther King, Jr. 1/21/1959. Detroit, Mich. (TLS) 1 p. MLKP-MBU: Box 68. 590121–004.

1/21/1959 Hassler, Alfred (FOR). Letter to Martin Luther King, Jr. 1/21/1959. (TLI) 1 p. BRP-DLC. 590121–007.

1/22/1959 King, Martin Luther, Jr. Letter to David George Ball. 1/22/1959. [*Montgomery, Ala.*] (TLc) 1 p. MLKP-MBU: Box 21. 590122–003.

1/23/1959 de L. Maynard, Aubré. Letter to Martin Luther King, Jr. 1/23/1959. (ALS) 2 pp. MLKP-MBU: Box 31A. 590123–002.

1/23/1959 Grant, Joanne (U.S. Festival Committee). Letter to Martin Luther King, Jr. 1/23/1959. New York, N.Y. (THLc) 1 p. MLKP-MBU: Box 72. 590123–010.

1/24/1959 Baker, Ella J. (SCLC). "Agenda, Meeting on registration and voting in Alabama." 1/24/1959. Montgomery, Ala. (TD) 1 p. EJBC-NN-Sc. 590124–002.

1/26/1959 MIA. Program, "Bon voyage to Dr. and Mrs. King and Dr. Reddick." 1/26/1959. Montgomery, Ala. (THD) 1 p. LDRP-NN-Sc: Box 3. 590126–008.

1/27/1959 King, Martin Luther, Jr. Letter to Daniel W. Wynn. 1/27/1959. [*Montgomery, Ala.*] (TLc) 1 p. MLKP-MBU: Box 29A. 590127–006.

1/27/1959 King, Martin Luther, Jr. Telegram to Dwight D. (Dwight David) Eisenhower. 1/27/1959. Atlanta, Ga. (PHWSr) 3 pp. WCFO-KAbE. 590127–009.

1/27/1959 Jackson, Connie. Letter to Martin Luther King, Jr. 1/27/1959. Dahlonega, Ga. (ALS) 1 p. MLKP-MBU. 590127–010.

1/28/1959 Bristol, James E. (Quaker Centre). Letter to Corinne B. Johnson. 1/28/1959. New Delhi, India. (TALS) 2 pp. (Copy to King. Enclosed in 590129–001.) MLKP-MBU: Box 1. 590128–002.

1/28/1959 King, Martin Luther, Jr. "Greetings to West Virginia State College and its sixty-ninth annual commencement." [*1/28/1959*]. [*Montgomery, Ala.*] (THD) 1 p. SCLCR-GAMK: Box 27. 590128–003.

1/28/1959 King, Martin Luther, Jr. Letter to Douglas W. Cook. 1/28/1959. [*Montgomery, Ala.*] (TLc) 1 p. MLKP-MBU: Box 10. 590128–004.

1/28/1959 Rickey, Branch. Letter to Martin Luther King, Jr. 1/28/1959. New York, N.Y. (ALS) 1 p. MLKP-MBU: Box 68. 590128–009.

1/28/1959 SCLC. Press release, "Top leadership meets in Alabama." 1/28/1959. Atlanta, Ga. (TD) 5 pp. MLKP-MBU: Box 70. 590128–010.

1/28/1959 King, Martin Luther, Jr. Letter to Wyatt Tee Walker. 1/28/1959. [*Montgomery, Ala.*] (TLc) 1 p. MLKP-MBU: Box 73. 590128–020.

1/28/1959 King, Martin Luther, Jr. Letter to Kivie Kaplan. 1/28/1959. [*Montgomery, Ala.*] (TLc) 1 p. MLKP-MBU: Box 29. 590128–022.

1/28/1959 King, Martin Luther, Jr. Letter to Samuel McCrea Cavert. 1/28/1959. [*Montgomery, Ala.*] (TLc) 1 p. MLKP-MBU: Box 68. 590128–024.

1/29/1959 Austin, H. Vance (Credit Union National Association). Letter to Martin Luther King, Jr. 1/29/1959. (TLS) 2 pp. MLKP-MBU: Box 1. 590129–000.

1/29/1959 Johnson, Corinne B. (American Friends Service Committee). Letter to Martin Luther King, Jr. 1/29/1959. Philadelphia, Pa. (TLS) 3 pp. (Contains enclosure 590128–002.) MLKP-MBU: Box 1. 590129–001.

1/29/1959 Fair Share Organization. Program, "Dr. Martin Luther King, Jr. in a bon voyage to Europe." 1/29/1959. Gary, Ind. (PD) 26 pp. CSKC: Sermon file. 590129–006.

1/29/1959 Hampton, Robert E. (U.S. White House). Letter to W. C. Patton. 1/29/1959. (TLc) 1 p. WCFO-KAbE. 590129–009.

1/30/1959 Ballou, Maude L. (Dexter Avenue Baptist Church). Letter to Martin Luther King, Jr. 1/30/1959. Montgomery, Ala. (THLS) 2 pp. (Marginal comments by King.) MLKP-MBU: Box 1. 590130–002.

2/1959 SCLC. *The Crusader* 1, no. 1. 2/1959. Atlanta, Ga. (TD) 6 pp. WPRC-MiDW-AL: Box 523. 590200–006.

2/1959 SCLC. "Plans of action for southwide, year-round voter-registration program." 2/1959. Atlanta, Ga. (TD) 8 pp. MLKP-MBU: Box 47A. 590200–011.

2/1/1959 Dexter Avenue Baptist Church. Program, Sunday services. 2/1/1959. Montgomery, Ala. (TD) 4 pp. DABCC. 590201–000.

2/1/1959 King, Martin Luther, Jr. Draft, The Negro is Part of that Huge Community Who Seek New Freedom in Every Area of Life. [*2/1/1959*]. [*Montgomery, Ala.*] (TDd) 8 pp. MLKP-MBU: Box 102. 590201–004.

2/2/1959 Smith, R. Julian (Mt. Moriah Institutional Baptist Church). Letter to Martin Luther King, Jr. 2/2/1959. Atlanta, Ga. (TLS) 1 p. MLKP-MBU: Box 71. 590202–004.

2/2/1959 War Resisters League. Program, "Thirty-sixth annual dinner." 2/2/1959. New York, N.Y. (TD) 3 pp. WRLC-NNWRL. 590202–010.

2/3/1959 Sarah Marquis Travel Service. Itinerary for Martin Luther King, Jr., Coretta Scott King, and Lawrence Dunbar Reddick. 2/3/1959. New York, N.Y. (THD) 4 pp. (Marginal comments by King.) MLKP-MBU: Box 1. 590203–004.

2/3/1959 Desai, Sumant (Indian National Trade Union Congress). Letter to Martin Luther King, Jr. 2/3/1959. New Delhi, India. (TLS) 1 p. MLKP-MBU: Box 47. 590203–010.

2/4/1959 Trent, W. J. (United Negro College Fund). Letter to Martin Luther King, Jr. 2/4/1959. New York, N.Y. (THLS) 3 pp. (Includes enclosures. Marginal comments by King.) MLKP-MBU. 590204–004.

2/4/1959 Jackson, Emory O. (Associated Negro Press). Press release, "Denounce beating of Alabama Negro advocate of voting rights; King, Shuttlesworth send protest letters." 2/4/1959. (TD) 2 pp. CABP-ICHi. 590204–008.

2/6/1959 Gruger, Harriet. Letter to Martin Luther King, Jr. 2/6/1959. New Delhi, India. (ALS) 1 p. MLKP-MBU: Box 1. 590206–001.

2/6/1959 Khan, Ivy (Young Women's Christian Association of India). Letter to Martin Luther King, Jr. and Coretta Scott King. 2/6/1959. New Delhi, India. (TLS) 1 p. MLKP-MBU: Box 1. 590206–002.

2/6/1959 King, Martin Luther, Jr. (Youth March for Integrated Schools). Letter to Ralph Helstein. 2/6/1959. New York, N.Y. (TLS) 2 pp. (Contains enclosure 590100–026.) UPWP-WHi: Box 154. 590206–005.

2/9/1959 Ballou, Maude L. Letter to Martin Luther King, Jr. and Coretta Scott King. 2/9/1959. [*Montgomery, Ala.*] (TLS) 1 p. MLKP-MBU: Box 1. 590209–001.

2/10/1959 Photo of Martin Luther King, Jr., Coretta Scott King, and Jawaharlal Nehru. 2/10/1959. New Delhi, India. (Ph) 1 p. IiNNMML. 590210–004.

2/10/1959 Photo of Martin Luther King, Jr., Rajkumari Amrit Kaur, and Coretta Scott King. 2/10/1959. New Delhi, India. (Ph) 1 p. AFSCR-PPAFS. 590210–008.

2/10/1959 **Photo of Martin Luther King, Jr., James E. Bristol, and G. Ramachandran. 2/10/1959. New Delhi, India. (Ph) 1 p. AFSCR-PPAFS. 590210–011.**

2/10/1959 **Royal Studio. Photo of Martin Luther King, Jr., Lawrence Dunbar Reddick, Coretta Scott King, and Sarvepalli Radhakrishnan. 2/10/1959. New Delhi, India. (Ph) 1 p. AFSCR-PPAFS. 590210–016.**

2/10/1959 **Satakopan, R. Photo of Martin Luther King, Jr., Coretta Scott King, Lawrence Dunbar Reddick, G. Ramachandran, Sucheta Kripalani, and others. 2/10/1959. New Delhi, India. (Ph) 1 p. NNAPWW. 590210–025.**

2/11/1959 Dexter Avenue Baptist Church. *Dexter Echo* 2, no. 3. 2/11/1959. Montgomery, Ala. (TD) 6 pp. DABCC. 590211–002.

2/11/1959 Siddha, Gopal (Shramik Dharma Rajya Parishad). Letter to Martin Luther King, Jr. 2/11/1959. New Delhi, India. (TLS) 1 p. MLKP-MBU: Box 1. 590211–003.

2/11/1959 **Photo of Martin Luther King, Jr., Tina Bristol, James E. Bristol, Swami Vishwananda, Lawrence Dunbar Reddick and Coretta Scott King. 2/11/1959. New Delhi, India. (Ph) 1 p. AFSCR-PPAFS. 590211–010.**

2/11/1959 Trikha, S. K. (Delhi University). Letter to Martin Luther King, Jr. 2/11/1959. New Delhi, India. (ALS) 4 pp. (Includes envelope.) MLKP-MBU: Box 1. 590211–020.

2/12/1959 Joshi, P. S. Letter to Martin Luther King, Jr. 2/12/1959. Rajkot, India. (TLS) 2 pp. MLKP-MBU: Box 1. 590212–012.

2/13/1959 "Martin Luther King, Negro Leader, Pays Tribute To Gandhi." 2/13/1959. New Delhi, India. From: *American Reporter,* 13 February 1959. (PD) 2 pp. MLKP-MBU: Box 1. 590213–001.

2/14/1959 Cady, Lyman V. (Fisk University). Letter to Martin Luther King, Jr. 2/14/1959. Wooster, Ohio. (TLS) 1 p. MLKP-MBU: Box 22. 590214–001.

2/19/1959 Rustin, Bayard (Youth March for Integrated Schools). Form letter to Friend. 2/19/1959. New York, N.Y. (TLS) 1 p. MLKP-MBU: Box 75. 590219–000.

2/19/1959 King, Martin Luther, Jr., Harry Emerson Fosdick, Joachim Prinz, and John LaFarge (Youth March for Integrated Schools). Form letter to Brother. 2/19/1959. New York, N.Y. (TLS) 1 p. APRC-DLC. 590219–003.

2/20/1959 Case, Harold C. (Boston University). Letter to Martin Luther King, Jr. 2/20/1959. Boston, Mass. (TLS) 1 p. MLKP-MBU: Box 20. 590220–004.

2/23/1959 Ballou, Maude L. Letter to Martin Luther King, Jr. and Coretta Scott King. 2/23/1959. [*Montgomery, Ala.*] (TLS) 1 p. MLKP-MBU: Box 1. 590223–000.

2/23/1959 Hukkerikar, R. S. (Gandhi Smarak Nidhi). Letter to Martin Luther King, Jr. 2/23/1959. Dharwar, India. (TLS) 1 p. MLKP-MBU: Box 1. 590223–001.

2/24/1959 Padmore, George (Embassy of Liberia). Letter to Martin Luther King, Jr. 2/24/1959. Washington, D.C. (TLS) 1 p. MLKP-MBU: Box 26. 590224–000.

2/24/1959–2/25/1959 Bristol, James E. (Quaker Centre). Letter to Dorothy Bristol. 2/24/1959–2/25/1959. New Delhi, India. (THLc) 2 pp. AFSCR-PPAFS. 590225–000.

2/25/1959 Bristol, James E. Letter to Dorothy Bristol. 2/25/1959. Bangalore, India. (TAHLc) 2 pp. AFSCR-PPAFS. 590225–001.

2/26/1959 Ballou, Maude L. Letter to Martin Luther King, Jr. and Coretta Scott King. 2/26/1959. [*Montgomery, Ala.*] (TALS) 2 pp. MLKP-MBU: Box 1. 590226–001.

2/26/1959 King, Martin Luther, Jr., Ruth H. Bunche, Harry Emerson Fosdick, Clarence Pickett, John LaFarge, and A. Philip (Asa Philip) Randolph. Letter to Richard M. (Richard Milhous) Nixon. 2/26/1959. (TLc) 2 pp. APRC-DLC. 590226–003.

2/27/1959 **King, Martin Luther, Jr. Letter to Clifford J. (Clifford Judkins) Durr and Virginia Foster Durr. 2/27/1959. Bombay, India. (ALS) 2 pp. CJDP-A-Ar. 590227–001.**

2/28/1959 Guest book from Mani Bhavan Gandhi Sangrahalaya. 2/28/1959. Bombay, India. (PHDS) 2 pp. IiMMBGS. 590228–008.

2/28/1959 **King, Martin Luther, Jr. Guest book entry at Mani Bhavan Gandhi Sangrahalaya. 2/28/1959. Bombay, India. (PHDS) 1 p. IiMMBGS. 590228–009.**

2/1959–3/1959 American Friends Service Committee. "Budget: leadership intervisitation, visit to India by Martin Luther and Coretta King." 2/1959–3/1959. (TD) 1 p. AFSCR-PPAFS. 590300–003.

3/1959 Bunche, Ruth H., Martin Luther King, Jr., and Bayard Rustin (Youth March for Integrated Schools). Form letter to Friend. [*3/1959*]. New York, N.Y. (TLS) 1 p. (Contains enclosures 590100–026 & 590100–032.) NAACPP-DLC: Group III-A334. 590300–028.

1/1959–3/1959 Appan, A. (All India Depressed Classes, Educational, Employment, and Welfare Association). Letter to Martin Luther King, Jr. [*1/1959–3/1959*]. Madras, India. (ALS) 3 pp. MLKP-MBU: Box 1. 590300–036.

3/2/1959 Gray, William H. (William Herbert) (Bright Hope Baptist Church). Letter to Mar-

	tin Luther King, Jr. 3/2/1959. Philadelphia, Pa. (TLS) 1 p. MLKP-MBU: Box 27. 590302–001.
3/3/1959	Ballou, Maude L. Letter to Alberta Williams King. 3/3/1959. [*Montgomery, Ala.*] (THLc) 1 p. MLKP-MBU: Box 29. 590303–004.
3/4/1959	Austin, H. Vance (Credit Union National Association). Letter to Martin Luther King, Jr. 3/4/1959. Madison, Wis. (TLS) 1 p. MLKP-MBU: Box 1. 590304–000.
3/4/1959	Lilly, Eli (Eli Lilly and Company). Letter to Martin Luther King, Jr. 3/4/1959. Indianapolis, Ind. (TLS) 1 p. MLKP-MBU: Box 50. 590304–001.
3/5/1959	Nehru, Jawaharlal. Letter to G. Ramachandran. 3/5/1959. New Delhi, India. (TALS) 2 pp. MLKP-MBU: Box 32. 590305–001.
3/6/1959	King, Martin Luther, Jr. "Impressions of India." 3/6/1959. [*New Delhi, India.*] (TD) 1 p. MLKP-MBU: Box 1. 590306–001.
3/6/1959	Demet, Barton, Harry Lee Senter, Carter Patton, Lawrence T. Hughes, and J. Alan Hanover (Tennessee. Senate). "Committee report to the members of the eighty-first session of the general assembly of the state of Tennessee." 3/6/1959. Nashville, Tenn. (TDS) 14 pp. T. 590306–003.
3/7/1959	King, Martin Luther, Jr., Ruth H. Bunche, Joachim Prinz, and A. Philip (Asa Philip) Randolph. Letter to James Carey. 3/7/1959. (TLc) 2 pp. APRC-DLC. 590307–003.
2/8/1959–3/7/1959	Final program for Martin Luther King, Jr. in New Delhi. 2/8/1959–3/7/1959. (THD) 2 pp. (Marginal comments by King.) MLKP-MBU: Box 54. 590307–005.
3/8/1959	Dexter Avenue Baptist Church. Program, Sunday services. 3/8/1959. Montgomery, Ala. (THD) 4 pp. DABCC. 590308–000.
2/8/1959–3/8/1959	Program for Martin Luther King, Jr.'s trip in India. 2/8/1959–3/8/1959. (THD) 2 pp. (Marginal comments by King.) MLKP-MBU: Box 1. 590308–005.
3/9/1959	King, Martin Luther, Jr. "Farewell statement." 3/9/1959. New Delhi, India. (TD) 1 p. MLKP-MBU: Box 1. 590309–001.
3/9/1959	**Satakopan, R. Photo of Martin Luther King, Jr., Miss Shanta, Tina Bristol, J.B. (Jiwatram Bhagawandas) Kripalani, Coretta Scott King and James E. Bristol. [*3/9/1959*]. New Delhi, India. (Ph) 1 p. NNAPWW. 590309–010.**
2/10/1959–3/10/1959	Bristol, James E. (Quaker Centre). Notes from the tour diary. [*2/10/1959–3/10/1959*]. New Delhi, India. (THD) 9 pp. AFSCR-PPAFS. 590310–006.
3/10/1959	Long, Henry T. Letter to Martin Luther King, Jr. 3/10/1959. Lavonia, Ga. (ALS) 2 pp. MLKP-MBU: Box 10. 590310–007.
3/11/1959	Dexter Avenue Baptist Church. *Dexter Echo* 3, no. 4. 3/11/1959. Montgomery, Ala. (TD) 6 pp. DABCC. 590311–001.
3/11/1959	Bristol, James E. (Quaker Centre). Letter to Corinne B. Johnson. 3/11/1959. New Delhi, India. (TLS) 2 pp. AFSCR-PPAFS. 590311–007.
3/14/1959	Diop, Alione (Societe Africaine De Culture). Letter to Martin Luther King, Jr. 3/14/1959. Paris, France. (TLS) 1 p. MLKP-MBU: Box 26. 590314–001.
3/14/1959	Baker, Ella J., and R.C. Thomas. (SCLC). Form letter to Registered voter. 3/14/1959. Shreveport, La. (TLS) 1 p. EJBC-NN-Sc. 590314–002.
3/15/1959	Grigsby, James O. Letter to Martin Luther King, Jr. 3/15/1959. Kingsport, Tenn. (THLS) 1 p. MLKP-MBU. 590315–001.
3/16/1959	Youth March for Integrated Schools. Press release, U.S. National Student Association endorses Youth March for Integrated Schools. [*3/16/1959*]. New York, N.Y. (TD) 3 pp. LDRP-NN-Sc: Box 3. 590316–001.
3/17/1959	Abernathy, Ralph (SCLC). Form letter to Friend of freedom. 3/17/1959. [*Montgomery, Ala.*] (TLS) 2 pp. SAVFC-WHi. 590317–003.
3/17/1959	Tilley, John Lee (SCLC). Letter to Martin Luther King, Jr. 3/17/1959. Atlanta, Ga. (TLS) 1 p. MLKP-MBU: Box 70. 590317–004.
3/18/1959	Bhave, Vinoba. "Dr. Martin Luther King with Vinoba." 3/18/1959. Varanasi, India. From: *Bhoodan* 3 (18 March 1959): 369–370. (PD) 2 pp. MLKP-MBU: Box 1. 590318–000.
3/18/1959	King, Martin Luther, Jr. "Gandhiji's Principle of Resistance." 3/18/1959. Varanasi, India. From: *Bhoodan* 3 (18 March 1959): 372. (PD) 1 p. (Reprint of 1/31/1958 *Peace News.*) MLKP-MBU: Box 1. 590318–002.
3/19/1959	Williams, G. Mennen (Michigan. Office of the Governor). Letter to Martin Luther King, Jr. 3/19/1959. Lansing, Mich. (TLS) 1 p. MLKP-MBU: Box 31A. 590319–000.
3/19/1959	Winters, Shelley. Letter to Martin Luther King, Jr. 3/19/1959. New York, N.Y. (TLS) 1 p. CSKCH. 590319–002.
3/20/1959	Bristol, James E. (Quaker Centre). Letter to Corinne B. Johnson. 3/20/1959. New Delhi, India. (THLS) 6 pp. AFSCR-PPAFS. 590320–000.

3/20/1959 Johnson, Corinne B. (American Friends Service Committee). Letter to Martin Luther King, Jr. 3/20/1959. Philadelphia, Pa. (TLS) 4 pp. (Includes enclosure.) MLKP-MBU: Box 19. 590320–002.

3/21/1959 Baker, Ella J. Memo to R. C. Thomas. 3/21/1959. (TLc) 3 pp. EJBC-NN-Sc. 590321–002.

3/22/1959 Dexter Avenue Baptist Church. Program, Sunday services. 3/22/1959. Montgomery, Ala. (TD) 4 p. DABCC. 590322–000.

3/22/1959 King, Martin Luther, Jr., Palm Sunday sermon on Mohandas K. Gandhi. 3/22/1959. [*Montgomery, Ala.*] (THTa) 11 pp. MLKJP-GAMK. 590322–001.

3/24/1959 Ballou, Maude L. Letter to Corinne B. Johnson. 3/24/1959. [*Montgomery, Ala.*] (TLc) 1 p. MLKP-MBU: Box 19. 590324–004.

3/24/1959 Daskam, Max F. (Unitarian Church of Germantown). Letter to Martin Luther King, Jr. 3/24/1959. Philadelphia, Pa. (TLS) 1 p. MLKP-MBU: Box 11A. 590324–015.

3/26/1959 Rustin, Bayard (Youth March for Integrated Schools). Letter to Martin Luther King, Jr. 3/26/1959. (TLS) 1 p. MLKP-MBU: Box 5. 590326–000.

3/26/1959 Johnson, Corinne B. Letter to James E. Bristol. 3/26/1959. (TALc) 3 pp. AFSCR-PPAFS. 590326–002.

3/27/1959 Bristol, James E. (Quaker Centre). Letter to Corinne B. Johnson. 3/27/1959. New Delhi, India. (TLS) 1 p. AFSCR-PPAFS. 590327–002.

3/28/1959 Simpkins, Cuthbert O. (United Christian Movement, Inc.). Letter to Martin Luther King, Jr. 3/28/1959. Shreveport, La. (TLS) 1 p. MLKP-MBU: Box 70. 590328–000.

3/28/1959 Wilson, A. W. (Holt Steet Baptist Church). Letter to MIA. 3/28/1959. Montgomery, Ala. (TLS) 1 p. (Copy to King.) MLKP-MBU: Box 73. 590328–001.

3/18/1959–3/28/1959 Press release, "Reddick returns from India; now understands King." [*3/18/1959–3/28/1959*]. Montgomery, Ala. (TD) 1 p. LDRP-NN-Sc: Box 3. 590328–002.

3/29/1959 Dexter Avenue Baptist Church. Program, Sunday services. 3/29/1959. Montgomery, Ala. (THD) 4 pp. DABCC. 590329–000.

3/30/1959 King, Martin Luther, Jr. Letter to Harold Edward Fey. 3/30/1959. [*Montgomery, Ala.*] (TLc) 1 p. MLKP-MBU: Box 22. 590330–000.

3/30/1959 Musselman, Gerald W. Letter to Martin Luther King, Jr. 3/30/1959. Norfolk, Va. (ALS) 1 p. MLKP-MBU: Box 31A. 590330–001.

3/31/1959 Robinson, James R. (CORE). Letter to Martin Luther King, Jr. 3/31/1959. New York, N.Y. (TLS) 1 p. MLKP-MBU: Box 25. 590331–004.

3/1959–4/1959 "Martin Luther King Addresses War Resisters League Dinner," 3/1959–4/1959. New York, N.Y. From: *War Resisters League News*, March 1959-April 1959, p. 1. (PD) 1 p. WRLC-NNWRL. 590400–006.

4/1959 Randolph, A. Philip (Asa Philip), Jackie Robinson, and Bayard Rustin. Memo to All Youth March supporters. [*4/1959*]. (THL) 1 p. (Marginal comments by King.) MLKP-MBU. 590400–011.

4/1959 King, Martin Luther, Jr. "The Future of Integration," Address at Yale University on 1/14/1959. 4/1959. From: *Crises in Modern America*. New Haven: Yale University, April 1959. (PD) 12 pp. MLKP-MBU: Box 102. 590400–013.

4/1959 King, Martin Luther, Jr. Draft, "My trip to India." [*4/1959*]. [*Montgomery, Ala.*] (TADd) 11 pp. MLKP-MBU: Box 1. 590400–017.

4/1959 Youth March for Integrated Schools. Presidential delegation statement. [*4/1959*]. (TD) 2 pp. BRP-DLC. 590400–018.

4/1/1959 Cousins, Norman, and Clarence Pickett (National Committee for a Sane Nuclear Policy (U.S.)). Telegram to Martin Luther King, Jr. 4/1/1959. New York, N.Y. (PWSr) 1 p. MLKP-MBU: Box 22. 590401–001.

4/1/1959 King, Martin Luther, Jr. Telegram to Norman Cousins. 4/1/1959. [*Montgomery, Ala.*] (TWc) 1 p. MLKP-MBU: Box 22. 590401–002.

4/1/1959 Lewis, W. Hallowell. Letter to Martin Luther King, Jr. 4/1/1959. Montgomery, Ala. (TLS) 1 p. MLKP-MBU: Box 29A. 590401–004.

4/2/1959 Abernathy, Ralph (SCLC). Financial report. 4/2/1959. Montgomery, Ala. (THD) 5 pp. (Marginal comments by King.) MLKP-MBU: Box 48. 590402–002.

4/3/1959 King, Martin Luther, Jr. Letter to John L. Sherrill. 4/3/1959. [*Montgomery, Ala.*] (TLc) 1 p. MLKP-MBU: Box 27. 590403–005.

4/3/1959 Arrington, Henry H. Letter to Martin Luther King, Jr. 4/3/1959. Miami, Fla. (TLS) 1 p. MLKP-MBU: Box 44. 590403–010.

4/3/1959 King, Martin Luther, Jr. Letter to John Lee Tilley. 4/3/1959. [*Montgomery, Ala.*] (TALd) 2 pp. MLKP-MBU: Box 72. 590403–012.

4/4/1959 Rodell, Marie F. (Marie Freid) (Marie Rodell and Joan Daves, Inc.). Letter to Martin Luther King, Jr. 4/4/1959. New York, N.Y. (TLSr) 1 p. MLKP-MBU: Box 6. 590404–000.

4/4/1959 Malott, Deane W. (Cornell University). Letter to Martin Luther King, Jr. 4/4/1959. Ithaca, N.Y. (TLS) 1 p. MLKP-MBU. 590404–001.

4/5/1959 Dexter Avenue Baptist Church. Program, Sunday services. 4/5/1959. Montgomery, Ala. (TD) 4 pp. DABCC. 590405–000.

4/5/1959 Anna M. Duncan Club. Program, "Dr. Martin Luther King, Jr., Pastor of Dexter Avenue Baptist Church." 4/5/1959. Montgomery, Ala. (PHD) 2 pp. MLKP-MBU: Box 82. 590405–002.

4/5/1959 King, Martin Luther, Jr. Unfulfilled Hopes, Sermon delivered at Dexter Avenue Baptist Church. [*4/5/1959*]. [*Montgomery, Ala.*] (At) 33 min. (2 sound cassettes: analog.) MLKEC: ET-61. 590405–004.

4/7/1959 King, Martin Luther, Jr. Letter to Marie F. (Marie Freid) Rodell. 4/7/1959. [*Montgomery, Ala.*] (TLc) 1 p. MLKP-MBU: Box 6. 590407–000.

4/7/1959 Merrill, Charles. Letter to Martin Luther King, Jr. 4/7/1959. (AHLS) 1 p. MLKP-MBU: Box 31A. 590407–001.

4/8/1959 Nelson, Reuben E. (American Baptist Convention). Letter to Martin Luther King, Jr. 4/8/1959. New York, N.Y. (TLS) 2 pp. MLKP-MBU: Box 18. 590408–000.

4/8/1959 Randolph, A. Philip (Asa Philip) (Youth March for Integrated Schools). Letter to Roy Wilkins. 4/8/1959. New York, N.Y. (TLS) 2 pp. APRC-DLC. 590408–006.

4/10/1959 King, Martin Luther, Jr. (Dexter Avenue Baptist Church). Letter to Daniel W. Wynn. 4/10/1959. Montgomery, Ala. (TLS) 1 p. DWW-ARC-LNT. 590410–000.

4/10/1959 Huie, William Bradford. Letter to Martin Luther King, Jr. [*4/10/1959*]. Hartselle, Ala. (TLS) 1 p. MLKP-MBU: Box 28. 590410–001.

4/10/1959 Nelson, William Stuart (Howard University). Letter to Martin Luther King, Jr. 4/10/1959. Washington, D.C. (TLS) 2 pp. MLKP-MBU: Box 32A. 590410–003.

4/11/1959 King, Martin Luther, Jr. Letter to Henry H. Arrington. 4/11/1959. [*Montgomery, Ala.*] (TLc) 1 p. MLKP-MBU: Box 44. 590411–004.

4/11/1959 Nixon, Richard M. (Richard Milhous). Letter to Martin Luther King, Jr. 4/11/1959. (THLc) 1 p. PPRN-CYINL. 590411–006.

4/12/1959 Dexter Avenue Baptist Church. Program, Sunday services. 4/12/1959. Montgomery, Ala. (TD) 4 pp. DABCC. 590412–001.

4/12/1959 Mount Vernon First Baptist Church. Program, Installation of Alfred Daniel King. 4/12/1959. Newnan, Ga. (PHD) 4 pp. (Marginal comments by King.) MLKP-MBU: Box 82. 590412–004.

4/13/1959 King, Martin Luther, Jr. (SCLC). Form letter to Friend of freedom. 4/13/1959. Atlanta, Ga. (TLS) 2 pp. NAACPP-DLC: Group III-A177. 590413–006.

4/13/1959 King, Martin Luther, Jr. (Dexter Avenue Baptist Church). Letter to W. J. Trent. 4/13/1959. Montgomery, Ala. (THLS) 1 p. UNCFR-GAU. 590413–007.

4/13/1959 King, Martin Luther, Jr. Letter to A. Franklin Fisher. 4/13/1959. [*Montgomery, Ala.*] (TLc) 1 p. MLKP-MBU: Box 25. 590413–011.

4/14/1959 Wilkins, Roy (NAACP). Letter to A. Philip (Asa Philip) Randolph. 4/14/1959. (TLc) 1 p. APRC-DLC. 590414–004.

4/15/1959 Dexter Avenue Baptist Church. *Dexter Echo* 3, no. 5. 4/15/1959. Montgomery, Ala. (TD) 4 pp. MLKP-MBU: Box 77. 590415–000.

4/15/1959 Ballou, Maude L. Letter to G. Mennen Williams. 4/15/1959. [*Montgomery, Ala.*] (TLS) 1 p. GMWC-MiU-H: Box 719. 590415–002.

4/15/1959 American Committee on Africa. Program, "Africa Freedom Day." 4/15/1959. New York, N.Y. (PD) 2 pp. DBC-WHi: Box 4. 590415–014.

4/15/1959 King, Martin Luther, Jr. Letter to Heinz Kraschutzki. 4/15/1959. [*Montgomery, Ala.*] (TLc) 1 p. MLKP-MBU: Box 26. 590415–017.

4/16/1959 King, Martin Luther, Jr. "To the graduating class of the James G. Blaine Public School." 4/16/1959. [*Montgomery, Ala.*] (TD) 1 p. MLKP-MBU: Box 21. 590416–000.

4/16/1959 [*Bristol, James E.*] (Quaker Centre). Letter to Corinne B. Johnson. 4/16/1959. New Delhi, India. (TAHLfS) 1 p. AFSCR-PPAFS. 590416–003.

4/16/1959 Bristol, James E. (Quaker Centre). Letter to Martin Luther King, Jr. 4/16/1959. New Delhi, India. (TALS) 1 p. MLKP-MBU: Box 21. 590416–009.

4/16/1959 Hoover, J. Edgar (U.S. Federal Bureau of Investigation). Letter to Gordon Gray. 4/16/1959. Washington, D.C. (TLS) 1 p. (Contains enclosure 590416–014.) WONS-KAbE: Box 1. 590416–013.

4/16/1959 [*U.S. Federal Bureau of Investigation*]. "Youth March on Washington" on 4/18/1959. 4/16/1959. (THD) 3 pp. (Enclosed in 590416–013.) WONS-KAbE: Box 1. 590416–014.

4/17/1959 Ballou, Maude L. Letter to Lerone Bennett. 4/17/1959. [*Montgomery, Ala.*] (TLc) 1 p. MLKP-MBU: Box 21. 590417–001.

4/17/1959 Scheinman, William X. Telegram to Martin Luther King, Jr. and Coretta Scott King. 4/17/1959. Littleferry, N.J. (PHWSr) 1 p. MLKP-MBU: Box 31A. 590417–003.

4/17/1959 Nixon, Richard M. (Richard Milhous) (U.S. Office of the Vice President). Letter to Martin Luther King, Jr. 4/17/1959. Washington, D.C. (TLS) 1 p. MLKP-MBU: Box 32. 590417–004.

4/17/1959 Bristol, James E. (Quaker Centre). Letter to Corinne B. Johnson. 4/17/1959. New Delhi, India. (TALS) 2 pp. AFSCR-PPAFS. 590417–006.

4/17/1959 Rogers, T. Y. (Crozer Theological Seminary). Letter to Martin Luther King, Jr. 4/17/1959. Chester, Pa. (TLS) 1 p. MLKP-MBU: Box 68. 590417–011.

4/17/1959 King, Martin Luther, Jr. Statement on science and spiritual ends. 4/17/1959. [*Montgomery, Ala.*] (THD) 1 p. MLKP-MBU: Box 32. 590417–013.

4/17/1959 Youth March for Integrated Schools. "Anti-American groups not invited to Youth March for Integrated Schools." [*4/17/1959*]. (TD) 1 p. NAACPP-DLC: Group III-A334. 590417–015.

4/18/1959 King, Martin Luther, Jr. Address at the Youth March for Integrated Schools. 4/18/1959. Washington, D.C. (TD) 2 pp. APRC-DLC. 590418–000.

4/18/1959 Youth March for Integrated Schools. "Program at the Sylvan Theater." 4/18/1959. (THD) 1 p. APRC-DLC. 590418–004.

4/18/1959 Randolph, A. Philip (Asa Philip). "Statement at Youth March for Integrated Schools." 4/18/1959. Washington, D.C. (TD) 4 pp. APRC-DLC. 590418–008.

4/19/1959 King, Martin Luther, Jr. "The Dimensions of a Complete Life," Address at the Chicago Sunday Evening Club. 4/19/1959. Chicago, Ill. (TD) 5 pp. SCLCR-GAMK: Box 27. 590419–001.

4/20/1959 Gollancz, Victor. Letter to Martin Luther King, Jr. 4/20/1959. London, England. (TLI) 2 pp. MLKP-MBU: Box 2. 590420–009.

4/20/1959 King, Martin Luther, Jr. Letter to Jimmy Beshai. 4/20/1959. [*Montgomery, Ala.*] (TLc) 1 p. MLKP-MBU: Box 26. 590420–010.

4/20/1959 Associated Negro Press. Press release, "Youth marchers on Washington get promise of aid from Eisenhower." 4/20/1959. (TD) 1 p. CABP-ICHi. 590420–014.

4/21/1959 King, Martin Luther, Jr. Letter to Marie F. (Marie Freid) Rodell. 4/21/1959. [*Montgomery, Ala.*] (TLc) 1 p. MLKP-MBU: Box 6. 590421–000.

4/21/1959 King, Martin Luther, Jr. Letter to William Bradford Huie. 4/21/1959. [*Montgomery, Ala.*] (TLc) 1 p. MLKP-MBU: Box 28. 590421–002.

4/21/1959 King, Martin Luther, Jr. Letter to Oscar J. Callender. 4/21/1959. [*Montgomery, Ala.*] (TLc) 1 p. MLKP-MBU: Box 24. 590421–008.

4/21/1959 Bryan, G. McLeod (Wake Forest College). Letter to Martin Luther King, Jr. 4/21/1959. Winston-Salem, N.C. (TLS) 1 p. MLKP-MBU: Box 21. 590421–017.

4/21/1959 King, Martin Luther, Jr. Letter to Deane W. Malott. 4/21/1959. [*Montgomery, Ala.*] (TLc) 1 p. MLKP-MBU: Box 10. 590421–019.

4/22/1959 Bristol, James E. (Quaker Centre). Letter to Corinne B. Johnson. 4/22/1959. New Delhi, India. (TALS) 5 pp. AFSCR-PPAFS. 590422–004.

4/22/1959 Photo of Martin Luther King, Jr. and others. 4/22/1959. Gary, Ind. (Ph) 1 p. GCP-CRA-InU-N: CRA 10, Box 8. 590422–012.

4/23/1959 Hill, Jesse, Jr., (All Citizens Registration Committee). Letter to Martin Luther King, Jr. 4/23/1959. Atlanta, Ga. (TLS) 3 pp. (Includes enclosure.) MLKP-MBU: Box 28. 590423–003.

4/23/1959 Photo of Martin Luther King, Jr., George Sawyer, and audience in Stout Meeting House at Earlham College. 4/23/1959. Richmond, Ind. (Ph) 1 p. Lill-InRE. 590423–006.

4/24/1959 King, Martin Luther, Jr. Letter to William Stuart Nelson. 4/24/1959. [*Montgomery, Ala.*] (TLc) 2 pp. MLKP-MBU: Box 32A. 590424–001.

4/24/1959 King, Martin Luther, Jr. Letter to Richard M. (Richard Milhous) Nixon. 4/24/1959. [*Montgomery, Ala.*] (TLc) 1 p. MLKP-MBU: Box 32. 590424–003.

4/25/1959 Coleman, James P. (Plemon) (Mississippi. Office of the Governor). Telegram to Martin Luther King, Jr. [*4/25/1959*]. Jackson, Miss. (PWSr) 1 p. MLKP-MBU: Box 35. 590425–002.

4/25/1959 King, Martin Luther, Jr. (SCLC). Telegram to William P. (William Pierce) Rogers. 4/25/1959. [*Montgomery, Ala.*] (THWc) 1 p. MLKP-MBU: Box 35. 590425–003.

4/25/1959 Press release, "Charles Parker lynched." 4/25/1959. (TD) 1 p. MLKP-MBU: Box 35. 590425-004.

4/25/1959 King, Martin Luther, Jr. (SCLC). Statement on apparent lynching of Mack Charles Parker. 4/25/1959. [*Montgomery, Ala.*] (TAD) 1 p. MLKP-MBU: Box 35. 590425-005.

4/25/1959 King, Martin Luther, Jr. Letter to O. Clay Maxwell. 4/25/1959. [*Montgomery, Ala.*] (TLc) 1 p. MLKP-MBU: Box 31A. 590425-006.

4/26/1959 Dexter Avenue Baptist Church. Program, Sunday services. 4/26/1959. Montgomery, Ala. (TD) 4 pp. DABCC. 590426-000.

4/27/1959 Reddick, Lawrence Dunbar (Alabama State College). Letter to Martin Luther King, Jr. 4/27/1959. Montgomery, Ala. (TLS) 2 pp. MLKP-MBU: Box 68. 590427-008.

4/27/1959 King, Martin Luther, Jr. Letter to Charlotte Sander. 4/27/1959. [*Montgomery, Ala.*] (TLc) 1 p. MLKJP-GAMK: Box 42. 590427-013.

4/28/1959 King, Martin Luther, Jr. Letter to Samuel J. Long. 4/28/1959. [*Montgomery, Ala.*] (TLc) 1 p. MLKP-MBU: Box 49. 590428-007.

4/28/1959 Photo of Martin Luther King, Jr. on "Front Page Challenge." 4/28/1959. Toronto, Canada (Ph) 1 p. CaOTBC. 590428-013.

4/29/1959 Livingston, Shirley A. Letter to Martin Luther King, Jr. 4/29/1959. Hartford, Conn. (ALS) 1 p. MLKP-MBU. 590429-008.

4/30/1959 MIA. *Newsletter* 1, no. 12. 4/30/1959. Montgomery, Ala. (TD) 3 pp. HG-GAMK. 590430-000.

4/30/1959 King, Martin Luther, Jr. Letter to Jerome Davis. 4/30/1959. Chicago, Ill. (TLc) 2 pp. (Includes envelope.) MLKP-MBU: Box 23. 590430-001.

4/30/1959 Nelson, William Stuart (Howard University). Letter to Martin Luther King, Jr. 4/30/1959. Washington, D.C. (TLS) 1 p. MLKP-MBU: Box 32A. 590430-002.

4/30/1959 King, Martin Luther, Jr. Letter to Julius James. 4/30/1959. [*Montgomery, Ala.*] (TLc) 1 p. MLKP-MBU: Box 28A. 590430-005.

4/30/1959 Braden, Anne (Southern Conference Educational Fund, Inc.). Letter to Martin Luther King, Jr. 4/30/1959. Louisville, Ky. (TLS) 1 p. MLKP-MBU: Box 69. 590430-007.

4/30/1959 King, Martin Luther, Jr. Letter of introduction for G. McLeod Bryan. 4/30/1959. [*Montgomery, Ala.*] (TLc) 1 p. (Enclosed in 590504-011.) MLKP-MBU: Box 21. 590430-014.

5/1959 King, Martin Luther, Jr. "Nonviolence and Racial Justice." 5/1959. Nashville, Tenn. From: *New Christian Advocate*, May 1959, pp. 18-22. (PD) 5 pp. 590500-009.

5/2/1959 Gregg, Richard Bartlett. Letter to Martin Luther King, Jr. 5/2/1959. Chester, N.Y. (TALS) 1 p. MLKP-MBU: Box 27. 590502-000.

5/2/1959 Barden, A. L. (All-African People's Conference). Letter to Martin Luther King, Jr. 5/2/1959. Accra, Ghana. (TLS) 2 pp. MLKP-MBU: Box 26. 590502-001.

5/3/1959 Dexter Avenue Baptist Church. Program, Sunday services. 5/3/1959. Montgomery, Ala. (TD) 4 pp. DABCC. 590503-000.

5/3/1959 Baker, Ella J. (SCLC). Telegram to LeRoy Collins. 5/3/1959. Atlanta, Ga. (TWc) 1 p. MLKP-MBU: Box 70. 590503-001.

5/3/1959 Elizabeth Baptist Church. Program, "Fifty-fourth anniversary of Reverend G.W. Smiley." 5/3/1959. Union Springs, Ala. (TD) 3 pp. MLKP-MBU: Box 82. 590503-002.

5/4/1959 American Friends Service Committee. "Report on Martin Luther King's trip to India." 5/4/1959. (TD) 2 pp. AFSCR-PPAFS. 590504-006.

5/4/1959 Smith, Kelly Miller (First Baptist Church). Letter to Martin Luther King, Jr. 5/4/1959. Nashville, Tenn. (TLS) 1 p. MLKP-MBU: Box 71. 590504-009.

5/4/1959 King, Martin Luther, Jr. Letter to G. McLeod Bryan. 5/4/1959. [*Montgomery, Ala.*] (TLc) 1 p. (Contains enclosure 590430-014.) MLKP-MBU: Box 21. 590504-011.

5/5/1959 King, Martin Luther, Jr. (SCLC). Letter to Jesse Hill, Jr. 5/5/1959. [*Montgomery, Ala.*] (TLc) 1 p. MLKP-MBU: Box 28. 590505-001.

5/5/1959 King, Martin Luther, Jr. Letter to Leo Axlrod. 5/5/1959. [*Montgomery, Ala.*] (TLc) 1 p. MLKJP-GAMK. 590505-010.

5/5/1959 King, Martin Luther, Jr. Letter to William R. Bracy and members of the Guardians Association. 5/5/1959. [*Montgomery, Ala.*] (TLc) 1 p. MLKP-MBU. 590505-012.

5/6/1959 Wilkins, Roy. Telephone conversation with Robert F. Williams. 5/6/1959. (THTa) 4 pp. NAACPP-DLC: Group III-A333. 590506-005.

5/6/1959 United Press International. Press release, Robert F. Williams threatens to meet violence with violence. 5/6/1959. (TD) 2 pp. NAACPP-DLC: Group III-A333. 590506–006.

5/6/1959 Wilkins, Roy (NAACP). Telegram to Robert F. Williams. 5/6/1959. New York, N.Y. (TWc) 1 p. NAACPP-DLC: Group III-A333. 590506–007.

5/7/1959 Jovin, Thomas (California Institute of Technology). Letter to Martin Luther King, Jr. 5/7/1959. Pasadena, Calif. (TLS) 2 pp. MLKP-MBU: Box 28A. 590507–004.

5/7/1959 King, Martin Luther, Jr. "The Future of Integration," Address delivered at the University of Hartford. [*5/7/1959*]. West Hartford, Conn. (At) 47.2 min. (1 sound cassette: analog.) CtWeharU. 590507–007.

5/7/1959 Williams, Robert F. (NAACP). Telegram to Roy Wilkins. 5/7/1959. Monroe, N.C. (TWc) 1 p. NAACPP-DLC. 590507–009.

5/9/1959 Happ, Lewis. Letter to Martin Luther King, Jr. 5/9/1959. Brooklyn, N.Y. (ALS) 2 pp. MLKP-MBU: Box 28. 590509–001.

5/9/1959 Vaughn, Napolean N. (U.S. Air Force). Letter to Martin Luther King, Jr. 5/9/1959. Maxwell Air Force Base, Ala. (TALS) 3 pp. MLKP-MBU: Box 72. 590509–002.

5/10/1959 Dexter Avenue Baptist Church. Program, Sunday services. 5/10/1959. Montgomery, Ala. (TD) 4 pp. DABCC. 590510–000.

5/11/1959 King, Martin Luther, Jr. Address at the Religious Leaders Conference. 5/11/1959. Washington, D.C. (TD) 10 pp. MLKJP-GAMK. 590511–000.

5/11/1959 King, Martin Luther, Jr. Draft, Address at the Religious Leaders Conference. [*5/11/1959*]. [*Montgomery, Ala.*] (THADdf) 5 pp. CSKC: Sermon file. 590511–012.

5/11/1959 President's Committee on Government Contracts. Program, "Religious Leaders Conference." 5/11/1959. Washington, D.C. (TD) 5 pp. MLKJP-GAMK: Box 18. 590511–013.

5/11/1959 King, Martin Luther, Jr. Draft, Address at the Religious Leaders Conference. [*5/11/1959*]. [*Montgomery, Ala.*] (TAHDdf) 4 pp. MLKP-MBU: Box 2. 590511–017.

5/11/1959 Gandhi, Ramdas M. Letter to Martin Luther King, Jr. 5/11/1959. Vardha, India. (TALS) 1 p. MLKP-MBU: Box 26. 590511–020.

5/13/1959 Dexter Avenue Baptist Church. *Dexter Echo* 2, no. 6. 5/13/1959. Montgomery, Ala. (TD) 6 pp. MLKP-MBU: Box 77. 590513–000.

5/13/1959 SCLC. Program, "Africa Freedom Dinner honoring Mr. Tom Mboya." 5/13/1959. Atlanta, Ga. (TD) 5 pp. SCLCR-GAMK: Box 32. 590513–003.

5/14/1959 Ballou, Maude L. Letter to Clarence Pickett. 5/14/1959. [*Montgomery, Ala.*] (TLc) 1 p. MLKP-MBU: Box 19. 590514–008.

5/14/1959 Reddick, Lawrence Dunbar. "Mboya dinner at Atlanta." 5/14/1959. (TD) 5 pp. LDRP-NN-Sc: Box 3. 590514–006.

5/15/1959 Baker, Ella J. (SCLC). "Report of the director to the executive board." 5/15/1959. Atlanta, Ga. (TDS) 4 pp. MLKP-MBU: Box 47A. 590515–001.

5/17/1959 Dexter Avenue Baptist Church. Program, Sunday services. 5/17/1959. Montgomery, Ala. (TD) 3 pp. DABCC. 590517–000.

5/18/1959 King, Martin Luther, Jr. Letter to D. Elton Trueblood. 5/18/1959. [*Montgomery, Ala.*] (TLc) 1 p. MLKP-MBU: Box 38A. 590518–002.

5/19/1959 King, Martin Luther, Jr. Letter to Alan S. Wilson. 5/19/1959. [*Montgomery, Ala.*] (TLc) 1 p. MLKP-MBU: Box 40. 590519–006.

5/19/1959 Moore, Douglas E. Letter to Martin Luther King, Jr. 5/19/1959. Durham, N.C. (TALS) 1 p. MLKP-MBU: Box 31. 590519–011.

5/19/1959 King, Martin Luther, Jr. Letter to Swami Vishwananda. 5/19/1959. [*Montgomery, Ala.*] (TLc) 2 pp. MLKP-MBU. 590519–016.

5/21/1959 Watumull, Ellen J. (Watumull Foundation). Letter to Martin Luther King, Jr. 5/21/1959. Honolulu, Hawaii. (TLS) 1 p. MLKP-MBU: Box 40. 590521–003.

5/21/1959 King, Martin Luther, Jr. Memo to Ralph Abernathy, Ella J. Baker, and Lawrence Dunbar Reddick. 5/21/1959. [*Montgomery, Ala.*] (TLc) 1 p. (Contains enclosure 590521–007.) MLKP-MBU: Box 4. 590521–004.

5/21/1959 Hall, W. H. Letter to Martin Luther King, Jr. 5/21/1959. Hattiesburg, Miss. (TLS) 1 p. MLKP-MBU: Box 41. 590521–005.

5/21/1959 Livingston, Shirley A. Letter to Martin Luther King, Jr. 5/21/1959. Hartford, Conn. (TLS) 1 p. MLKP-MBU: Box 29A. 590521–006.

5/21/1959 [*King, Martin Luther, Jr.*]. Draft, "Proposals for Institute on Nonviolent Resistance to Segregation." [*5/21/1959*]. [*Atlanta, Ga.*] (TADd) 3 pp. (Enclosed in 590521–004.) MLKP-MBU: Box 4. 590521–007.

5/22/1959 Bishop College. Program, "Seventy-eighth annual spring commencement convocation." 5/22/1959. Marshall, Texas. (PD) 4 pp. MLKP-MBU: Box 82. 590522–009.

5/25/1959 King, Martin Luther, Jr. Letter to Gerald W. Musselman. 5/25/1959. [*Montgomery, Ala.*] (TLc) 2 pp. MLKP-MBU: Box 31A. 590525–003.

5/26/1959 Wilkins, Roy (NAACP). Letter to A. Philip (Asa Philip) Randolph. 5/26/1959. New York, N.Y. (TLS) 2 pp. APRC-DLC. 590526–007.

5/28/1959 Baker, Ella J. (SCLC). Letter to Martin Luther King, Jr. 5/28/1959. Atlanta, Ga. (TLS) 2 pp. MLKP-MBU. 590528–000.

5/28/1959 "Facts relating to recent violence inflicted upon Negro citizens of Montgomery, Ala." 5/28/1959. (TD) 1 p. (Enclosed in 590528–001, pp. 216–217 in this volume & 590528–004.) MLKP-MBU: Box 33A. 590528–003.

5/28/1959 King, Martin Luther, Jr., Ralph Abernathy, and S. S. (Solomon Snowden) Seay (SCLC). Letter to William P. (William Pierce) Rogers. [*5/28/1959*]. [*Montgomery, Ala.*] (TWc) 1 p. (Contains enclosure 590528–003.) MLKP-MBU: Box 33A. 590528–004.

5/28/1959 Special Agent in Charge (U.S. Federal Bureau of Investigation). Memo to J. Edgar Hoover. 5/28/1959. Mobile, Ala. (THL) 2 pp. DGFBI-NN-Sc. 590528–011.

5/29/1959 White, W. Wilson (William Wilson) (U.S. Dept. of Justice). Letter to Martin Luther King, Jr. 5/29/1959. Washington, D.C. (TLS) 1 p. MLKP-MBU: Box 23. 590529–003.

5/29/1959 Ballou, Maude L. Letter to Victor Backus. 5/29/1959. [*Montgomery, Ala.*] (TLc) 1 p. (Contains enclosure 590531–002.) MLKP-MBU: Box 38A. 590529–005.

5/29/1959 Sanders, G. W. Letter to Martin Luther King, Jr. 5/29/1959. Jacksonville, Fla. (TLS) 1 p. MLKP-MBU: Box 68. 590529–010.

5/30/1959 King, Martin Luther, Jr. (SCLC). Form letter to Martin Luther King. 5/30/1959. Atlanta, Ga. (TLS) 2 pp. MLKP-MBU: Box 4. 590530–001.

5/30/1959 King, Martin Luther, Jr. Letter to Shirley A. Livingston. 5/30/1959. [*Montgomery, Ala.*] (TLc) 1 p. MLKP-MBU: Box 29A. 590530–004.

5/30/1959 Rodrigues, Deolinda. Letter to Martin Luther King, Jr. 5/30/1959. São Paolo, Brazil. (TLS) 2 pp. MLKP-MBU: Box 25. 590530–006.

5/31/1959 Dexter Avenue Baptist Church. Program, Sunday services. 5/31/1959. Montgomery, Ala. (TD) 4 pp. DABCC. 590531–000.

5/31/1959 King, Martin Luther, Jr. "The Dimensions of a Complete Life," Sermon at Dillard University.[*5/31/1959*]. [*New Orleans, La.*] (TD) 12 pp. (Enclosed in 590529–005.) MLKP-MBU: Box 5. 590531–002.

5/31/1959 Dillard University. Program, "Twenty-fourth annual baccalaureate." 5/31/1959. New Orleans, La. (PD) 3 pp. LND. 590531–004.

6/1959 Barker, Hampton Z. Letter to Martin Luther King, Jr. [*6/1959*]. Atlanta, Ga. (TLS) 1 p. MLKP-MBU: Box 21. 590600–000.

6/1/1959 King, Martin Luther, Jr. Letter to Marguerite Cartwright. 6/1/1959. [*Montgomery, Ala.*] (TLc) 1 p. MLKP-MBU: Box 22. 590601–002.

6/1/1959 King, Martin Luther, Jr. Letter to Sandy F. Ray. 6/1/1959. [*Montgomery, Ala.*] (THLc) 1 p. MLKP-MBU: Box 68. 590601–014.

6/1/1959 King, Martin Luther, Jr. Letter to John Cleopas Miyengi. 6/1/1959. [*Montgomery, Ala.*] (TLc) 1 p. MLKP-MBU: Box 26. 590601–016.

6/1/1959 King, Martin Luther, Jr. Letter to Martin R. R. Goldman. 6/1/1959. [*Montgomery, Ala.*] (TLc) MLKP-MBU. 590601–019.

6/2/1959 King, Martin Luther, Jr. "Remaining Awake Through a Great Revolution," Address at Morehouse College Commencement. [*6/2/1959*]. [*Atlanta, Ga.*] (ADf) 27 pp. MLKP-MBU: Box 119. 590602–005.

6/2/1959 King, Martin Luther, Jr. Remaining Awake Through a Great Revolution, Address at Morehouse College Commencement. [*6/2/1959*]. [*Atlanta, Ga.*] (TDf) 2 pp. MLKP-MBU: Box 29A. 590602–006.

6/2/1959 Morehouse College. Program, "Commencement." 6/2/1959. (PHD) 4 pp. LDRP-NN-Sc: Box 3. 590602–008.

6/3/1959 Dexter Avenue Baptist Church. *Dexter Echo* 2, no. 7. 6/3/1959. Montgomery, Ala. (TD) 6 pp. DABCC. 590603–000.

6/4/1959 King, Martin Luther, Jr. (Dexter Avenue Baptist Church). Letter to Walter G. Muelder. 6/4/1959. Montgomery, Ala. (TLS) 1 p. WMP-MBU. 590604–000.

6/4/1959 King, Martin Luther, Jr. Letter to Herbert Williams. 6/4/1959. [*Montgomery, Ala.*] (TLc) 1 p. MLKP-MBU: Box 73. 590604–010.

6/4/1959 Collins, LeRoy (Florida. Office of the Governor). Letter to Ella J. Baker. 6/4/1959. Tallahassee, Fla. (TLS) 1 p. SCLCR-GAMK. 590604–012.

6/5/1959 Walker, Wyatt Tee (Gilfield Baptist Church). Letter to Martin Luther King, Jr. 6/5/1959. Petersburg, Va. (TLS) 1 p. MLKP-MBU: Box 73. 590605–002.

6/5/1959 King, Martin Luther, Jr. "Statement of southern Negro leaders." 6/5/1959. New Orleans, La. (TD) 1 p. MLKP-MBU: Box 21. 590605–005.

6/5/1959 Randolph, A. Philip (Asa Philip) (Brotherhood of Sleeping Car Porters and Maids). Letter to Roy Wilkins. 6/5/1959. (TLc) 3 pp. APRC-DLC. 590605–006.

6/8/1959 Pickett, Clarence (American Friends Service Committee). Letter to Martin Luther King, Jr. 6/8/1959. Philadelphia, Pa. (TLS) 1 p. MLKP-MBU: Box 19. 590608–005.

6/9/1959 King, Martin Luther, Jr. Letter to Gardner C. Taylor. 6/9/1959. [*Montgomery, Ala.*] (TLc) 1 p. MLKP-MBU: Box 72. 590609–006.

6/9/1959 King, Martin Luther, Jr. Letter to Samuel W. Williams. 6/9/1959. [*Montgomery, Ala.*] (TLc) 1 p. MLKP-MBU: Box 73. 590609–011.

6/10/1959 Muste, A. J. (Abraham Johannes) (*Liberation*). Letter to Martin Luther King, Jr. 6/10/1959. New York, N.Y. (TALS) 2 pp. (Contains enclosure 590610–019.) MLKP-MBU. 590610–000.

6/10/1959 King, Martin Luther, Jr. Letter to Benjamin Elijah Mays. 6/10/1959. [*Montgomery, Ala.*] (TLc) 1 p. MLKP-MBU: Box 31A. 590610–002.

6/10/1959 Norris, Dwight W. (*Newsweek*). Letter to Martin Luther King, Jr. 6/10/1959. New York, N.Y. (TLS) 1 p. MLKP-MBU: Box 32A. 590610–003.

6/10/1959 Blayton, Jesse B. Letter to Martin Luther King, Jr. 6/10/1959. Atlanta, Ga. (TLS) 1 p. MLKP-MBU: Box 4. 590610–006.

6/10/1959 King, Martin Luther, Jr. Letter to Harold C. Case. 6/10/1959. [*Montgomery, Ala.*] (TLc) 1 p. (Contains enclosure 590610–019.) MLKP-MBU: Box 20. 590610–010.

6/10/1959 Ray, Sandy F. (Cornerstone Baptist Church). Letter to Martin Luther King, Jr. 6/10/1959. Brooklyn, N.Y. (TLS) 1 p. MLKP-MBU: Box 68. 590610–011.

6/10/1959 King, Martin Luther, Jr. Letter to Wyatt Tee Walker. 6/10/1959. [*Montgomery, Ala.*] (TLc) 1 p. MLKP-MBU: Box 73. 590610–012.

6/10/1959 "Draft of prospectus for September issue of *Liberation*." [*6/10/1959*]. (TDd) 2 pp. (Enclosed in 590610–000.) MLKP-MBU: Box 20. 590610–019.

6/11/1959 King, Martin Luther, Jr. Letter to Charles C. Diggs. 6/11/1959. [*Montgomery, Ala.*] (TLc) 3 pp. (Includes enclosure.) MLKP-MBU: Box 23. 590611–004.

6/11/1959 King, Martin Luther, Jr. (Dexter Avenue Baptist Church). Letter to Russell R. Lasley. 6/11/1959. Montgomery, Ala. (TLSr) 1 p. (Contains enclosure 590611–009, pp. [illegible] in this volume.) UPWP-WHi: Box 389. 590611–008.

6/12/1959 Smiley, Glenn E. (FOR). Letter to Martin Luther King, Jr. 6/12/1959. Nyack, N.Y. (TALS) 2 pp. MLKP-MBU. 590612–000.

6/12/1959 Feldman, Eugene (*Southern Newsletter*). Letter to Martin Luther King, Jr. 6/12/1959. Louisville, Ky. (TLS) 1 p. MLKP-MBU: Box 70. 590612–004.

6/12/1959 SCLC. "Activities for the next six months." 6/12/1959. Atlanta, Ga. (TD) 2 pp. FJBC-NN-Sc. 590612–007.

6/12/1959 Ballou, Maude L. Letter to Joe N. Ross. 6/12/1959. [*Montgomery, Ala.*] (TLc) 1 p. (Contains enclosure 590612–009.) MLKP-MBU: Box 68. 590612–008.

6/12/1959 King, Martin Luther, Jr. Letter to Conference of deacons and Christian workers. 6/12/1959. [*Montgomery, Ala.*] (TLc) 1 p. (Enclosed in 590612–008.) MLKP-MBU: Box 68. 590612–009.

6/14/1959 Dexter Avenue Baptist Church. Program, Sunday services. 6/14/1959. Montgomery, Ala. (THD) 4 pp. DABCC. 590614–000.

6/15/1959 King, Martin Luther, Jr. Letter to James T. Coats. 6/15/1959. [*Montgomery, Ala.*] (THLc) 2 pp. MLKP-MBU: Box 1. 590615–001.

6/15/1959 King, Martin Luther, Jr. Letter to Paul A. Fullilove. 6/15/1959. [*Montgomery, Ala.*] (TLc) 1 p. MLKP-MBU: Box 25. 590615–004.

6/15/1959 Mays, Benjamin Elijah (Morehouse College). Letter to Martin Luther King, Jr. 6/15/1959. Atlanta, Ga. (TLS) 1 p. MLKP-MBU: Box 44. 590615–005.

6/15/1959 Hester, William H. (Twelfth Baptist Church). Letter to Martin Luther King, Jr. 6/15/1959. Roxbury, Mass. (TALS) 1 p. MLKP-MBU: Box 28. 590615–006.

6/15/1959 Shuttlesworth, Fred L. (Alabama Christian Movement for Human Rights (ACMHR)). Letter to Martin Luther King, Jr. 6/15/1959. Birmingham, Ala. (TLS) 1 p. MLKP-MBU: Box 71. 590615–008.

6/15/1959 King, Martin Luther, Jr. (SCLC). Letter to Martin Luther King. 6/15/1959. [*Montgomery, Ala.*] (TLc) 1 p. SCLCR-GAMK: Box 32. 590615–009.

6/16/1959 Mboya, Tom (Kenya Federation of Labour). Letter to Martin Luther King, Jr. 6/16/1959. Nairobi, Kenya. (TLS) 1 p. MLKP-MBU: Box 32. 590616–000.

6/17/1959 Proctor, Samuel D. Letter to Wyatt Tee Walker. 6/17/1959. (TLc) 2 pp. (Copy to King.) MLKP-MBU: Box 73A. 590617–001.

6/18/1959 Nixon, Richard M. (Richard Milhous) (U.S. Office of the Vice President). Letter to Martin Luther King, Jr. 6/18/1959. Washington, D.C. (TLS) 1 p. MLKJP-GAMK: Box 18. 590618–003.

6/18/1959 Zaugg, Ernest. Letter to Martin Luther King, Jr. 6/18/1959. Munich, Germany. (TLS) 2 pp. MLKP-MBU: Box 26. 590618–007.

6/18/1959 Rickey, Branch. Letter to Martin Luther King, Jr. 6/18/1959. Pittsburgh, Pa. (TLS) 1 p. MLKP-MBU. 590618–011.

6/19/1959 King, Martin Luther, Jr. Letter to Mahomedali Currim Chagla. 6/19/1959. [*Montgomery, Ala.*] (TLc) 2 pp. MLKP-MBU: Box 22. 590619–003.

6/21/1959 Dexter Avenue Baptist Church. Program, Sunday services. 6/21/1959. Montgomery, Ala. (TD) 4 pp. DABCC. 590621–000.

6/22/1959 King, Martin Luther, Jr. Letter to Hampton Z. Barker. 6/22/1959. [*Montgomery, Ala.*] (TLc) 1 p. MLKP-MBU: Box 21. 590622–001.

6/22/1959 King, Martin Luther, Jr. Letter to William Stuart Nelson. 6/22/1959. [*Montgomery, Ala.*] (TLc) 1 p. MLKP-MBU: Box 32A. 590622–004.

6/22/1959 King, Martin Luther, Jr. Letter to May W. Van Meter. 6/22/1959. [*Montgomery, Ala.*] (TLc) 1 p. MLKP-MBU: Box 73. 590622–005.

6/22/1959 King, Martin Luther, Jr. Letter to T. Y. Rogers. 6/22/1959. [*Montgomery, Ala.*] (TLc) 1 p. MLKP-MBU: Box 68. 590622–008.

6/22/1959 King, Martin Luther, Jr. Letter to A. J. (Abraham Johannes) Muste. 6/22/1959. [*Montgomery, Ala.*] (TLc) 1 p. MLKP-MBU: Box 31. 590622–010.

6/22/1959 SCLC. "Revised list of board members." 6/22/1959. Atlanta, Ga. (TD) 2 pp. MLKP-MBU: Box 58. 590622–011.

6/22/1959 King, Martin Luther, Jr. (Dexter Avenue Baptist Church). Letter to Howard Thurman. 6/22/1959. [*Montgomery, Ala.*] (TLc) 1 p. DABCC. 590622–012.

6/24/1959 King, Martin Luther, Jr. Letter to William H. Hester. 6/24/1959. [*Montgomery, Ala.*] (TLc) 1 p. MLKP-MBU: Box 28. 590624–003.

6/26/1959 SCLC. "Institute on Nonviolent Resistance to Segregation information sheet." 6/26/1959. Atlanta, Ga. (TD) 1 p. MLKP-MBU: Box 4. 590626–003.

6/28/1959 Dexter Avenue Baptist Church. Program, Sunday services. 6/28/1959. Montgomery, Ala. (TD) 4 pp. DABCC. 590628–000.

6/29/1959 Taylor, F. W. (Dexter Avenue Baptist Church). "Financial statement for December through May." 6/29/1959. Montgomery, Ala. (TD) 13 pp. CKFC. 590629–000.

6/29/1959 Carter, Harold (Court Street Baptist Church). Letter to Martin Luther King, Jr. 6/29/1959. Lynchburg, Va. (THLS) 1 p. MLKP-MBU: Box 22. 590629–004.

6/29/1959 Crawford, Roger A. (Crawford Studio). Letter to Martin Luther King, Jr. 6/29/1959. Toledo, Ohio (THLS) 1 p. MLKP-MBU: Box 22. 590629–005.

6/30/1959 Cousins, Norman (*Saturday Review*). Letter to Martin Luther King, Jr. 6/30/1959. New York, N.Y. (TLS) 1 p. MLKP-MBU: Box 69. 590630–005.

7/1959 "'Native Son' Delivers Ninety-second Anniversary Commencement Address: Dr. M. L. King, Jr., Makes Epochal Speech." 7/1959. Atlanta, Ga. From: *Morehouse College Bulletin*, July 1959, pp. 3–10. (PD) 8 pp. TAP. 590700–000.

7/1959 Boddie, F. J., J. S. Beane, Elijah Jones, and Wyatt Tee Walker (Virginia Farm and City Enterprises). "Resume, Facts and events pursuant to present condition of Virginia Farm and City Enterprises." [*7/1959*]. (THD) 3 pp. MLKP-MBU: Box 28A. 590700–007.

7/1959 Baker, Ella J. Memo to Martin Luther King, Jr. and Ralph Abernathy. [*7/1959*]. (THL) 3 pp. (Marginal comments by King.) MLKP-MBU: Box 4. 590700–009.

7/1/1959 Bishop, Shelton Hale (St. Elizabeth's Parish). Letter to Martin Luther King, Jr. 7/1/1959. Honolulu, Hawaii. (TLS) 2 pp. MLKP-MBU: Box 40. 590701–002.

7/1/1959 King, Martin Luther, Jr. Letter to William S. Thompson. 7/1/1959. [*Montgomery, Ala.*] (TLc) 2 pp. MLKP-MBU: Box 44. 590701–004.

7/1/1959 King, Martin Luther, Jr. Letter to Douglas E. Moore. 7/1/1959. [*Montgomery, Ala.*] (TLc) 1 p. MLKP-MBU: Box 31. 590701–005.

7/1/1959 Chagla, Mahomedali Currim (Embassy of India). Letter to Martin Luther King, Jr. 7/1/1959. Washington, D.C. (TLS) 1 p. MLKP-MBU: Box 26. 590701–008.

7/1/1959 King, Martin Luther, Jr. Letter to Harold A. Carter. 7/1/1959. [*Montgomery, Ala.*] (TLc) 1 p. MLKP-MBU: Box 22. 590701–009.

7/2/1959 Creecy, Howard W. (First Baptist Church). Letter to Martin Luther King, Jr. 7/2/1959. Dothan, Ala. (TLS) 1 p. MLKP-MBU: Box 22. 590702–006.

7/2/1959 Baker, Ella J. (SCLC). Memo to Martin Luther King, Jr., Ralph Abernathy, Samuel W. Williams, Joseph E. Lowery and Lawrence Dunbar Reddick. 7/2/1959. Atlanta, Ga. (TAL) 3 pp. MLKP-MBU. 590702–007.

7/6/1959 Reddick, Lawrence Dunbar (Alabama State College). Letter to W. E. B. (William

Edward Burghardt) Du Bois. 7/6/1959. Montgomery, Ala. (TLS) 1 p. WEBD-MU. 590706–001.

7/6/1959 King, Martin Luther, Jr. Letter to Fred L. Shuttlesworth. 7/6/1959. [*Montgomery, Ala.*] (TLc) 1 p. MLKP-MBU: Box 70. 590706–007.

7/7/1959 Baker, Ella J. (SCLC). Letter to Martin Luther King, Jr. 7/7/1959. Atlanta, Ga. (TALS) 2 pp. MLKP-MBU. 590707–000.

7/8/1959 Helstein, Ralph (United Packinghouse Workers of America, AFL-CIO). Letter to Martin Luther King, Jr. 7/8/1959. Chicago, Ill. (TLS) 2 pp. MLKP-MBU: Box 6. 590708–000.

7/8/1959 Dexter Avenue Baptist Church. *Dexter Echo* 2, no. 8. 7/8/1959. Montgomery, Ala. (TD) 6 pp. MLKP-MBU: Box 77. 590708–004.

7/8/1959 Wright, Herbert L. Memo to John A. Morsell. 7/8/1959. (THL) 2 pp. (Enclosed in 590708–010.) MLKP-MBU: Box 32. 590708–006.

7/8/1959 Morsell, John A. (NAACP). Letter to Martin Luther King, Jr. 7/8/1959. New York, N.Y. (TLS) 2 pp. (Contains enclosure 590708–006.) MLKP-MBU: Box 121. 590708–010.

7/8/1959 Special Agent in Charge (U.S. Federal Bureau of Investigation). Memo to J. Edgar Hoover. 7/8/1959. (THL) 2 pp. DGFBI-NN-Sc. 590708–014.

7/9/1959 Thomas, Norman. Letter to Martin Luther King, Jr. 7/9/1959. New York, N.Y. (TALS) 1 p. MLKP-MBU: Box 72. 590709–000.

7/10/1959 Fey, Harold Edward (*Christian Century*). Letter to Martin Luther King, Jr. 7/10/1959. Chicago, Ill. (TLS) 2 pp. MLKP-MBU: Box 22. 590710–000.

7/10/1959 Lasley, Russell R. (United Packinghouse Workers of America, AFL-CIO). Form letter to Sir and Brother. 7/10/1959. Chicago, Ill. (TLS) 4 pp. (Includes enclosures.) MLKP-MBU: Box 56. 590710–005.

7/13/1959 Thompson, William S. (National Bar Association). Letter to Martin Luther King, Jr. 7/13/1959. Washington, D.C. (TLS) 1 p. MLKP-MBU: Box 44. 590713–005.

7/14/1959 King, Martin Luther, Jr. Letter to Wonwihari Prasad Bhoop. 7/14/1959. [*Montgomery, Ala.*] (TLc) 2 pp. MLKP-MBU. 590714–006.

7/16/1959 Kalelkar, Dattatraya Balakrishna. Letter to Lawrence Dunbar Reddick. 7/16/1959. New Delhi, India. (TLS) 1 p. LDRP-NN-Sc: Box 3. 590716–000.

7/18/1959 Ajuoga, A. M. (Church of Christ in Africa). Letter to Martin Luther King, Jr. 7/18/1959. Kisumu, Kenya. (TLS) 1 p. MLKP-MBU. 590718–001.

7/19/1959 Dexter Avenue Baptist Church. Program, Sunday services. 7/19/1959. Montgomery, Ala. (TD) 4 pp. DABCC. 590719–000.

7/13/1959–7/19/1959 NAACP. "Fiftieth annual convention resolutions." 7/13/1959–7/19/1959. New York, N.Y. (PD) 37 pp. NAACPP-DLC: Box 2. 590719–001.

7/20/1959 King, Martin Luther, Jr. Letter to Lynward W. Stevenson. 7/20/1959. [*Montgomery, Ala.*] (TLc) 1 p. MLKP-MBU: Box 50. 590720–003.

7/22/1959 King, Martin Luther, Jr. "Proposed schedule for Institute on Nonviolent Resistance to Segregation." 7/22/1959. [*Montgomery, Ala.*] (ADd) 2 pp. MLKP-MBU: Box 4. 590722–000.

7/3/1959–7/22/1959 SCLC. Press release, "Nonviolent Institute features outstanding personalities." [*7/3/1959–7/22/1959*]. Atlanta, Ga. (TD) 2 pp. MLKJP-GAMK: Box 33. 590722–002.

7/23/1959 Randolph, A. Philip (Asa Philip) (Brotherhood of Sleeping Car Porters and Maids). Telegram to Martin Luther King, Jr. [*7/23/1959*]. New York, N.Y. (PWSr) 1 p. MLKP-MBU: Box 71. 590723–000.

7/23/1959 Williams, Chancellor (Tuskegee Institute). Letter to Martin Luther King, Jr. 7/23/1959. Tuskegee, Ala. (TAHLS) 1 p. MLKP-MBU: Box 29A. 590723–005.

7/22/1959–7/24/1959 Palmer, H.J. Notes, Program on First Southwide Institute on Nonviolent Resistance to Segregation. 7/22/1959–7/24/1959. Atlanta, Ga. (THD) 17 pp. HJP-GAMK. 590724–001.

7/24/1959 Bell, Lynn (U.S. Postal Service). Letter to Martin Luther King, Jr. 7/24/1959. Denver, Colo. (TLS) 1 p. MLKP-MBU: Box 34. 590724–011.

7/22/1959–7/24/1959 "Proposals for Southwide Institute on Nonviolent Resistance to Segregation." [*7/22/1959–7/24/1959*]. (TD) 3 pp. MLKP-MBU: Box 4. 590724–020.

7/22/1959–7/24/1959 Lawson, James M. Evaluation, First Southwide Institute on Nonviolent Resistance to Segregation. 7/22/1959–7/24/1959. Atlanta, Ga. (TD) 1 p. MLKJP-GAMK: Box 33. 590724–023.

7/22/1959–7/24/1959 Smiley, Glenn E. Evaluation, First Southwide Institute on Nonviolent Resistance to Segregation. 7/22/1959–7/24/1959. Atlanta, Ga. (TD) 2 pp. MLKJP-GAMK: Box 33. 590724–024.

7/22/1959– SCLC. Program, "First Southwide Institute on Nonviolent Resistance to Segre-

7/24/1959	gation." 7/22/1959–7/24/1959. Atlanta, Ga. (TD) 17 pp. HJP-GAMK. 590724–027.
7/22/1959–7/24/1959	Reddick, Lawrence Dunbar. "Report, Nonviolent Institute." [*7/22/1959–7/24/1959*]. (TD) 4 pp. LDRP-NN-Sc: Box 3. 590724–029.
7/26/1959	Dexter Avenue Baptist Church. Program, Sunday services. 7/26/1959. Montgomery, Ala. (TD) 4 pp. DABCC. 590726–000.
7/27/1959	Ballou, Maude L. Letter to Clarence Pickett. 7/27/1959. [*Montgomery, Ala.*] (TLc) 1 p. MLKP-MBU: Box 33A. 590727–006.
7/27/1959	Muste, A. J. (Abraham Johannes) (*Liberation*). Letter to Martin Luther King, Jr. 7/27/1959. New York, N.Y. (TLS) 1 p. MLKP-MBU: Box 29A. 590727–008.
7/27/1959	King, Martin Luther, Jr. Letter to R. Paul Montgomery. 7/27/1959. [*Montgomery, Ala.*] (TLc) 1 p. MLKP-MBU: Box 31. 590727–014.
7/27/1959	Gaylord, Donald F. (Pearl Harbor Memorial Community Church). Letter to Martin Luther King, Jr. 7/27/1959. Honolulu, Hawaii. (TLS) MLKP-MBU. 590727–018.
7/28/1959	Rutland, J. Theodore (U.S. Dept. of Health, Education and Welfare). Letter to Martin Luther King, Jr. 7/28/1959. Atlanta, Ga. (TLS) 2 pp. MLKP-MBU: Box 1. 590728–000.
7/28/1959	Baker, Ella J. (SCLC). Letter to Martin Luther King, Jr. 7/28/1959. Atlanta, Ga. (TLS) 1 p. MLKP-MBU: Box 70. 590728–002.
7/28/1959	King, Martin Luther, Jr. Letter to Plouis Moore. 7/28/1959. [*Montgomery, Ala.*] (TLc) 1 p. MLKP-MBU: Box 22. 590728–004.
7/25/1959–7/28/1959	SCLC. Press release, "Nonviolent attitude shows strength—not weakness." [*7/25/1959–7/28/1959*]. Atlanta, Ga. (TD) 2 pp. MLKP-MBU: Box 4. 590728–007.
7/30/1959	King, Martin Luther, Jr. Letter to Harold Edward Fey. 7/30/1959. [*Montgomery, Ala.*] (TLc) 1 p. MLKP-MBU: Box 22. 590730–001.
7/30/1959	Williams, M. (Murphy) C. (New Hope Baptist Church). Letter to Martin Luther King, Jr. 7/30/1959. Denver, Colo. (TLS) 1 p. MLKP-MBU: Box 73. 590730–008.
7/31/1959	Mboya, Tom (Kenya Federation of Labour). Letter to Martin Luther King, Jr. 7/31/1959. Nairobi, Kenya. (TLS) 1 p. MLKP-MBU: Box 32. 590731–001.
7/31/1959	Jack, Homer Alexander (American Committee on Africa). Letter to Martin Luther King, Jr. 7/31/1959. New York, N.Y. (TLS) 1 p. MLKP-MBU: Box 19. 590731–002.
7/31/1959	King, Martin Luther, Jr. (Dexter Avenue Baptist Church). Letter to Ella J. Baker. 7/31/1959. Montgomery, Ala. (TLS) 1 p. SCLCR-GAMK: Box 3. 590731–005.
7/31/1959	King, Martin Luther, Jr. Letter to Norman Thomas. 7/31/1959. [*Montgomery, Ala.*] (TLc) 1 p. MLKP-MBU. 590731–009.
8/1959	King, Martin Luther, Jr. Outline, Address on school integration. [*8/1959*]. [*Montgomery, Ala.*] (ADd) 1 p. (Verso of 590828–000 pp. 270–272 in this volume.) MLKP-MBU: Box 6. 590800–005.
8/2/1959	Dexter Avenue Baptist Church. Program, Sunday services. 8/2/1959. Montgomery, Ala. (TD) 4 pp. DABCC. 590802–000.
8/2/1959	Tusiani, Joseph. Letter to Martin Luther King, Jr. 8/2/1959. New York, N.Y. (TLS) 1 p. MLKP-MBU: Box 6. 590802–001.
8/3/1959	King, Martin Luther, Jr. Letter to J. Raymond Henderson. 8/3/1959. [*Montgomery, Ala.*] (TLc) 1 p. MLKP-MBU: Box 28. 590803–000.
8/3/1959	King, Martin Luther, Jr. Letter to Samuel D. Proctor. 8/3/1959. [*Montgomery, Ala.*] (TLc) 1 p. MLKP-MBU: Box 34. 590803–002.
8/3/1959	Wilkins, Roy (NAACP). Letter to Martin Luther King, Jr. 8/3/1959. New York, N.Y. (TLS) 1 p. MLKP-MBU: Box 32A. 590803–003.
8/3/1959	Mygatt, Tracy D. (Tracy Dickinson) (Campaign for World Government, Inc.). Letter to Martin Luther King, Jr. 8/3/1959. Glencoe, Ill. (TLS) 4 pp. (Includes enclosures.) MLKP-MBU: Box 31. 590803–006.
8/3/1959	Gbedemah, K. A. (Ghana. Minister of Finance). Letter to Martin Luther King, Jr. 8/3/1959. Accra, Ghana. (TALS) 1 p. MLKP-MBU: Box 26. 590803–008.
8/3/1959	Helstein, Ralph (United Packinghouse Workers of America, AFL-CIO). Letter to Martin Luther King, Jr. 8/3/1959. Chicago, Ill. (TLS) 9 pp. (Includes enclosures.) MLKP-MBU: Box 6. 590803–012.
8/5/1959	Whitfield, J. Charles (Texas. House of Representatives). Letter to Martin Luther King, Jr. 8/5/1959. Austin, Texas. (TLS) 1 p. MLKP-MBU: Box 73. 590805–003.
8/5/1959	King, Martin Luther, Jr. Letter to Homer Alexander Jack. 8/5/1959. [*Montgomery, Ala.*] (TLc) 1 p. MLKP-MBU. 590805–007.

8/6/1959 Dexter Avenue Baptist Church. *Dexter Echo* 2, no. 9. 8/6/1959. Montgomery, Ala. (TD) 6 pp. MLKP-MBU: Box 77. 590806–001.

8/6/1959 King, Martin Luther, Jr. Letter to Irl G. Whitchurch. 8/6/1959. [*Montgomery, Ala.*] (TLc) 1 p. MLKP-MBU: Box 73. 590806–007.

8/6/1959 King, Martin Luther, Jr. Letter to Hubert W. Siwale. 8/6/1959. [*Montgomery, Ala.*] (TLc) 1 p. MLKP-MBU: Box 26. 590806–008.

8/6/1959 King, Martin Luther, Jr. Letter to Curtis Knox. 8/6/1959. [*Montgomery, Ala.*] (TLc) 2 pp. MLKP-MBU: Box 34A. 590806–009.

8/6/1959 Jelks, Juanita (Citizen's Protective Association). Letter to Martin Luther King, Jr. 8/6/1959. Gadsden, Ala. (TLS) 1 p. MLKP-MBU. 590806–011.

8/8/1959 King, Martin Luther, Jr. Letter to Shelton Hale Bishop. 8/8/1959. [*Montgomery, Ala.*] (TLc) 2 pp. MLKP-MBU: Box 40. 590808–003.

8/8/1959 King, Martin Luther, Jr. Letter to James T. Magruder. 8/8/1959. [*Montgomery, Ala.*] (TLc) 1 p. MLKP-MBU: Box 70. 590808–005.

8/9/1959 Dexter Avenue Baptist Church. Program, Sunday services. 8/9/1959. Montgomery, Ala. (TD) 4 pp. DABCC. 590809–000.

8/10/1959 Austin, H. Vance (Credit Union National Association). Letter to Martin Luther King, Jr. 8/10/1959. Madison, Wisc. (THLS) 2 pp. MLKP-MBU: Box 1. 590810–001.

8/11/1959 Roosevelt, Eleanor. Letter to Martin Luther King, Jr. 8/11/1959. New York, N.Y. (TLS) 1 p. MLKP-MBU: Box 64. 590811–000.

8/11/1959 Proctor, Samuel D. (Virginia Union University). Letter to Martin Luther King, Jr. 8/11/1959. Richmond, Va. (THLS) 1 p. MLKP-MBU: Box 34. 590811–002.

8/11/1959 Jelks, Juanita. Letter to Martin Luther King, Jr. 8/11/1959. Gadsden, Ala. (TLS) 1 p. MLKP-MBU. 590811–005.

8/11/1959 SCLC. "Manifesto, Institute on Nonviolent Resistance to Segregation, 7/22/1959–7/24/1959." 8/11/1959. Atlanta, Ga. (TD) 3 pp. MLKJP-GAMK: Box 33. 590811–006.

8/12/1959 Brown, Aaron (Phelp-Stokes Fund). Letter to Martin Luther King, Jr. 8/12/1959. New York, N.Y. (TLS) 1 p. MLKP-MBU: Box 20. 590812–000.

8/13/1959 Nelson, William Stuart (Howard University). Letter to Martin Luther King, Jr. 8/13/1959. Washington, D.C. (TLS) 1 p. MLKP-MBU: Box 32A. 590813–002.

8/13/1959 Baker, Ella J. Letter to Martin Luther King, Jr. 8/13/1959. (TALS) 3 pp. MLKP-MBU: Box 48. 590813–005.

8/13/1959 National Committee for a Sane Nuclear Policy (U.S.). "Humanity Has a Common Will and Right to Survive!" 8/13/1959. New York, N.Y. From: *New York Times*, 18 August 1959. (PD) 1 p. 590813–007.

8/14/1959 McCollom, Matthew D. Letter to Martin Luther King, Jr. 8/14/1959. Columbia, S.C. (TLS) 2 pp. MLKP-MBU: Box 48. 590814–001.

8/15/1959 Keeling, Bob (*Agapé*). Letter to Martin Luther King, Jr. 8/15/1959. Newton Centre, Mass. (TALS) 7 pp. (Includes enclosures.) MLKP-MBU: Box 29. 590815–003.

8/16/1959 Dexter Avenue Baptist Church. Program, Sunday services. 8/16/1959. Montgomery, Ala. (TD) 4 pp. DABCC. 590816–000.

8/16/1959 King, Martin Luther, Jr. "The Conflict in Human Nature." Sermon at Dexter Avenue Baptist Church. 8/16/1959. Montgomery, Ala. (AD) 3 pp. CSKC: Sermon file. 590816–001.

8/17/1959 Hall, W. H. (Zion Chapel A. M. E. Church). Letter to Fellow minister. 8/17/1959. Hattiesburg, Miss. (TLc) 1 p. (Enclosed in 590903–002.) MLKP-MBU: Box 51. 590817–000.

8/17/1959 King, Martin Luther, Jr. Letter to J. Holmes Ford. 8/17/1959. [*Montgomery, Ala.*] (TLc) 1 p. MLKP-MBU: Box 25. 590817–006.

8/18/1959 King, Martin Luther, Jr. Telegram to William X. Scheinman. 8/18/1959. [*Montgomery, Ala.*] (TWc) 1 p. MLKP-MBU: Box 32. 590818–001.

8/18/1959 Bates, Daisy. Telegram to Martin Luther King, Jr. 8/18/1959. Little Rock, Ark. (PHWSr) 1 p. MLKP-MBU: Box 20. 590818–003.

8/18/1959 Hunter, W. J., and Elliott D. Turnage. Memo to Officers and Members of the Palmetto State Voters Association. 8/18/1959. (TLc) 1 p. MLKP-MBU: Box 48. 590818–005.

8/19/1959 Harrington, Michael (Young People's Socialist League). Letter to Martin Luther King, Jr. 8/19/1959. New York, N.Y. (TLS) 1 p. MLKP-MBU: Box 28. 590819–001.

8/19/1959 King, Martin Luther, Jr. Letter to Julius Gikonyo Kiano. 8/19/1959. [*Montgomery, Ala.*] (TLc) 1 p. MLKP-MBU: Box 26A. 590819–004.

8/20/1959 Davis, Benjamin J. (Benjamin Jefferson). Letter to Martin Luther King, Jr.

8/20/1959. (TLS) 8 pp. (Includes enclosure.) MLKP-MBU: Box 23. 590820-002.

8/20/1959 Mygatt, Tracy D. (Tracy Dickinson) (Campaign for World Government, Inc.). Letter to Martin Luther King, Jr. 8/20/1959. Glencoe, Ill. (TLS) 1 p. MLKP-MBU: Box 31. 590820-007.

8/21/1959 King, Martin Luther, Jr. "The Future of Integration," Address at the National Convention of FOR. 8/21/1959. Green Lake, Wisc. (TAD) 18 pp. MLKP-MBU: Box 2. 590821-000.

8/23/1959 King, Martin Luther, Jr. Loving Your Enemies, Sermon delivered at Central Methodist Church. [*8/23/1959*]. Detroit, Mich. (At) 21.5 min. (1 sound cassette: analog.) MiDCUMA. 590823-002.

8/24/1959 Divers, Arthur J. Letter to Martin Luther King, Jr. 8/24/1959. Detroit, Mich. (ALS) 2 pp. MLKP-MBU: Box 23. 590824-002.

8/24/1959 Craig, L. (Leon) S. (Birmingham Baptist Mission Center). Letter to Martin Luther King, Jr. 8/24/1959. Birmingham, Ala. (TLS) 2 pp. (Includes enclosure.) MLKP-MBU: Box 22. 590824-003.

8/26/1959 King, Martin Luther, Jr. Telegram to Jackie Robinson. 8/26/1959. [*Montgomery, Ala.*] (THWc) 1 p. MLKP-MBU: Box 68. 590826-002.

8/27/1959 Morgan, Gerald D. (U.S. White House). Letter to Martin Luther King, Jr. 8/27/1959. Washington, D.C. (TLS) 1 p. MLKP-MBU. 590827-002.

8/27/1959 Pickett, Clarence. Telegram to Martin Luther King, Jr. 8/27/1959. Philadelphia, Pa. (PHWSr) 4 pp. MLKP-MBU: Box 33A. 590827-004.

8/27/1959 Robinson, Jackie. Telegram to Martin Luther King, Jr. 8/27/1959. New York, N.Y. (TWc) 1 p. MLKP-MBU: Box 68. 590827-005.

8/27/1959 King, Martin Luther, Jr. Letter to Bob Keeling. 8/27/1959. [*Montgomery, Ala.*] (TLc) 1 p. MLKP-MBU: Box 9. 590827-009.

8/28/1959 King, Martin Luther, Jr., Robert E. Dubose, H.J. Palmer, H.H. Hubbard, S.S. (Solomon Snowden) Seay, and Ralph Abernathy (MIA). Letter to the Montgomery County Board of Education. 8/28/1959. Montgomery, Ala. (TLc) 2 pp. (590800-005 on verso.) MLKP-MBU: Box 20. 590828-000.

8/28/1959 King, Martin Luther, Jr. Telegram to Adam Clayton Powell. 8/28/1959. [*Montgomery, Ala.*] (THWc) 1 p. MLKP-MBU: Box 34. 590828-003.

8/28/1959 [*King, Martin Luther, Jr.*]. Draft, Proposed statement to the board of education. [*8/28/1959*]. [*Montgomery, Ala.*] (TDdf) 2 pp. MLKP-MBU: Box 5. 590828-009.

8/28/1959 King, Martin Luther, Jr. "Proposed statement to the board of education." [*8/28/1959*]. [*Montgomery, Ala.*] (TADd) 2 pp. MLKP-MBU: Box 5. 590828-012.

8/30/1959 Dexter Avenue Baptist Church. Program, Sunday services. 8/30/1959. Montgomery, Ala. (TD) 3 pp. DABCC. 590830-000.

8/31/1959 King, Martin Luther, Jr. Letter to Donald L. Hollowell. 8/31/1959. [*Montgomery, Ala.*] (TLc) 1 p. MLKP-MBU: Box 28. 590831-002.

8/31/1959 King, Martin Luther, Jr. Letter to Homer Alexander Jack. 8/31/1959. [*Montgomery, Ala.*] (TLc) 1 p. (Contains enclosure 590831-004.) MLKP-MBU: Box 19. 590831-003.

8/31/1959 King, Martin Luther, Jr. Introduction to pamphlet on South West Africa. [*8/31/1959*]. [*Montgomery, Ala.*] (TD) 2 pp. (Enclosed in 590831-003.) MLKP-MBU: Box 19. 590831-004.

8/31/1959 King, Martin Luther, Jr. Letter to Marshall Shepard. 8/31/1959. [*Montgomery, Ala.*] (TLc) 1 p. MLKP-MBU: Box 70. 590831-006.

9/1/1959 Levison, Stanley D. Letter to Martin Luther King, Jr. 9/1/1959. New York, N.Y. (TLS) 2 pp. MLKP-MBU: Box 2. 590901-000.

9/1/1959 King, Martin Luther, Jr. Letter to Cuthbert O. Simpkins. 9/1/1959. [*Montgomery, Ala.*] (TLc) 1 p. MLKP-MBU: Box 71. 590901-005.

9/1/1959 King, Martin Luther, Jr. Letter to Arthur J. Divers. 9/1/1959. [*Montgomery, Ala.*] (TLc) 2 pp. MLKP-MBU: Box 23. 590901-007.

9/1/1959 "Proposed members of the ad hoc committee on the Eisenhower-Khrushchev talks." [*9/1/1959*]. (TD) 1 p. (Enclosed in 590901-006, pp. 275-276 in this volume.) MLKP-MBU: Box 72. 590901-010.

9/2/1959 Dexter Avenue Baptist Church. *Dexter Echo* 4, no. 1. 9/2/1959. Montgomery, Ala. (TD) 6 pp. DABCC. 590902-004.

9/2/1959 King, Martin Luther, Jr. Letter to Joseph C. Kennedy. 9/2/1959. [*Montgomery, Ala.*] (TLc) 1 p. MLKP-MBU: Box 44. 590902-008.

9/2/1959 King, Martin Luther, Jr. Letter to L. K. Jackson. 9/2/1959. [*Montgomery, Ala.*] (TLc) 1 p. MLKP-MBU. 590902-009.

9/3/1959 Hall, W. H. Letter to Martin Luther King, Jr. 9/3/1959. Hattiesburg, Miss. (TL) 1 p. (Contains enclosure 590817–000.) MLKP-MBU: Box 51. 590903–002.

9/4/1959 King, Martin Luther, Jr. Letter to Chancellor Williams. 9/4/1959. [*Montgomery, Ala.*] (TLc) 1 p. MLKP-MBU: Box 29A. 590904–007.

9/5/1959 King, Martin Luther, Jr. Telegram to Norman Thomas. 9/5/1959. [*Montgomery, Ala.*] (TWc) 1 p. MLKP-MBU: Box 72. 590905–006.

9/6/1959 Dexter Avenue Baptist Church. Program, Sunday services. 9/6/1959. Montgomery, Ala. (TD) 4 pp. DABCC. 590906–000.

9/6/1959 Shuttlesworth, Fred L. (Alabama Christian Movement for Human Rights (ACMHR)). Letter to John Malcolm Patterson. 9/6/1959. Birmingham, Ala. (TLS) 1 p. MLKP-MBU: Box 68. 590906–001.

9/8/1959 King, Martin Luther, Jr. (Dexter Avenue Baptist Church). Letter to L. H. Foster. 9/8/1959. [*Montgomery, Ala.*] (TLc) 1 p. MLKP-MBU: Box 25. 590908–000.

9/8/1959 Stevenson, Adlai E. Letter to Martin Luther King, Jr. 9/8/1959. Chicago, Ill. (TLS) 1 p. MLKP-MBU: Box 69. 590908–001.

9/9/1959 Lenud, Philip. Letter to Martin Luther King, Jr. 9/9/1959. Denver, Colo. (ALS) 3 pp. (Includes envelope.) MLKP-MBU: Box 29A. 590909–002.

9/9/1959 Jelks, Juanita (Citizen's Protective Association). Letter to Martin Luther King, Jr. 9/9/1959. Gadsen, Ala. (TLS) 1 p. MLKP-MBU. 590909–004.

9/10/1959 Kiano, Julius Gikonyo. Letter to Martin Luther King, Jr. 9/10/1959. Nairobi, Kenya. (TLS) 3 pp. MLKP-MBU: Box 26. 590910–000.

9/10/1959 Pickett, Clarence (National Committee for a Sane Nuclear Policy (U.S.)). Form letter to Martin Luther King, Jr. 9/10/1959. New York, N.Y. (TLS) 1 p. (Contains enclosure 590910–007.) MLKP-MBU. 590910–005.

9/10/1959 National Committee for a Sane Nuclear Policy (U.S.) "An open letter to President Eisenhower and Premier Khruschev." [*9/10/1959*]. (TL) 2 pp. (Enclosed in 590910–005.) MLKP-MBU. 590910–007.

9/11/1959 Ballou, Maude L. (Dexter Avenue Baptist Church). Telegram to Norman Cousins. 9/11/1959. [*Montgomery, Ala.*] (TWc) 1 p. MLKP-MBU: Box 22. 590911–001.

9/11/1959 Thurman, Howard (Boston University). Letter to Martin Luther King, Jr. 9/11/1959. Boston, Mass. (TLS) 1 p. MLKP-MBU: Box 72. 590911–003.

9/15/1959 Bailey, Bertha. Letter to Martin Luther King, Jr. 9/15/1959. Vineland, N.J. (ALS) 2 pp. MLKP-MBU: Box 20. 590915–000.

9/16/1959 Hawaii. House of Representatives. "House resolution no. 30." 9/16/1959. (TDS) 1 p. HHSA. 590916–009.

9/18/1959 Thompson, Richard (University of Canterbury). Letter to Martin Luther King, Jr. 9/18/1959. Christchurch, New Zealand. (TALS) 8 pp. (Includes enclosures.) MLKP-MBU: Box 72. 590918–006.

9/21/1959 Proctor, Hilda S. Letter to Martin Luther King, Jr. 9/21/1959. Honolulu, Hawaii. (TLS) 2 pp. (Includes enclosure.) MLKP-MBU: Box 34. 590921–001.

9/21/1959 Steele, C. Kenzie (Inter Civic Council of Tallahassee (ICC)). Letter to Martin Luther King, Jr. 9/21/1959. Tallahassee, Fla. (TLS) 1 p. MLKP-MBU: Box 70. 590921–004.

9/21/1959 Pasternak, Helen. "Segregation Resistance to Collapse, says King." 9/21/1959. Tuscon, Ariz. From: *Citizen*, 21 September 1959. (PD) 1 p. TCCU-AzU: Box 5. 590921–008.

9/22/1959 Powell, Adam Clayton (U.S. Congress. House). Letter to Martin Luther King, Jr. 9/22/1959. Washington, D.C. (TLS) 1 p. MLKP-MBU: Box 33A. 590922–000.

9/22/1959 Kilgore, Thomas (Friendship Baptist Church). Letter to Martin Luther King, Jr. 9/22/1959. New York, N.Y. (TLS) 1 p. MLKP-MBU: Box 29. 590922–004.

9/23/1959 King, Martin Luther, Jr. Draft, Address at public meeting of the Southern Christian Ministers Conference of Mississippi. 9/23/1959. [*Jackson, Miss.*] (ADd) 41 pp. MLKP-MBU: Box 119. 590923–006.

9/24/1959 Hasty, Woodrow W. (Crozer Theological Seminary Alumni Society). Form letter to Crozer alumnus. 9/24/1959. Chester, Pa. (TLS) 2 pp. (Contains enclosure 591104–007.) MLKP-MBU: Box 37A. 590924–001.

9/24/1959 Landis, Paul G. (Mennonite Voluntary Service). Letter to Martin Luther King, Jr. 9/24/1959. Salunga, Pa. (TLS) 5 pp. (Includes enclosures.) MLKP-MBU: Box 31. 590924–002.

9/25/1959 King, Martin Luther, Jr. Letter to Bertha Bailey. 9/25/1959. [*Montgomery, Ala.*] (TLc) 1 p. MLKP-MBU: Box 20. 590925–004.

9/25/1959 King, Martin Luther, Jr. Letter to John J. White. 9/25/1959. [*Montgomery, Ala.*] (TLc) 1 p. MLKP-MBU: Box 73. 590925–005.

9/26/1959	Rodrigues, Deolinda. Letter to Martin Luther King, Jr. 9/26/1959. São Paulo, Brazil. (TLS) 2 pp. MLKP-MBU. 590926–002.
9/27/1959	Dexter Avenue Baptist Church. Program, "The church choir of Ebenezer Baptist Church in concert." 9/27/1959. (TD) 4 pp. DABCC. 590927–000.
9/27/1959	Dexter Avenue Baptist Church. Program, Sunday services. 9/27/1959. Montgomery, Ala. (TD) 4 pp. DABCC. 590927–001.
9/28/1959	Raballa, Nicholas W. (Tuskegee Institute). Letter to Martin Luther King, Jr. 9/28/1959. Tuskegee, Ala. (ALS) 2 pp. MLKP-MBU: Box 35. 590928–001.
9/29/1959	Abernathy, Ralph (SCLC). Financial report, 5/13/1959–9/25/1959. 9/29/1959. Montgomery, Ala. (THD) 6 pp. EJBC-NN-Sc. 590929–006.
5/16/1959–9/29/1959	Baker, Ella J. (SCLC). "Report of the executive director." 5/16/1959–9/29/1959. Atlanta, Ga. (TDS) 5 pp. EJBC-NN-Sc. 590929–007.
9/8/1959–9/29/1959	King, Martin Luther, Jr. (SCLC). Form letter to Friend. [*9/8/1959–9/29/1959*]. (TLS) 1 p. MLKP-MBU: Box 71. 590929–026.
9/29/1959	Wilson, Margaret Bush (NAACP). Letter to Theodore E. Brown. 9/29/1959. St. Louis, Mo. (TLS) 1 p. (Enclosed in 591013–006.) MLKP-MBU: Box 20. 590929–028.
9/30/1959	King, Martin Luther, Jr. Letter to Allen Jordan. 9/30/1959. [*Montgomery, Ala.*] (TLc) 1 p. MLKP-MBU: Box 10. 590930–004.
9/30/1959	King, Martin Luther, Jr. Letter to Shelton Hale Bishop. 9/30/1959. [*Montgomery, Ala.*] (TLc) 1 p. MLKP-MBU: Box 20. 590930–010.
9/30/1959	Smith, Kenneth L. (Crozer Theological Seminary). Letter to Martin Luther King, Jr. 9/30/1959. Chester, Pa. (TLS) 1 p. MLKP-MBU: Box 70. 590930–016.
9/30/1959	King, Martin Luther, Jr. Telegram to Roland Smith. 9/30/1959. [*Montgomery, Ala.*] (TWc) 1 p. MLKP-MBU: Box 70. 590930–017.
9/30/1959	Pickett, Clarence (National Committee for a Sane Nuclear Policy (U.S.)). Letter to Martin Luther King, Jr. 9/30/1959. New York, N.Y. (TLS) 2 pp. (Includes enclosure.) MLKP-MBU: Box 71. 590930–022.
9/30/1959	King, Martin Luther, Jr. Letter to Howard Thurman. 9/30/1959. [*Montgomery, Ala.*] (TLc) 1 p. MLKP-MBU: Box 72. 590930–025.
10/1/1958–9/30/1959	Highlander Folk School. *Highlander Reports.* 10/1/1958–9/30/1959. Monteagle, Tenn. (PD) 4 pp. MLKP-MBU. 590930–029.
9/30/1959	King, Martin Luther, Jr. (SCLC). Recommendations to the board. 9/30/1959. Columbia, S.C. (TD) 4 pp. MLKP-MBU: Box 48. 590930–035.
10/1959	[*King, Martin Luther, Jr.*]. Draft, The Social Organization of Nonviolence. [*10/1959*]. [*Montgomery, Ala.*] (THD) 5 pp. CSKC: Sermon file. 591000–015.
10/1959	Levison, Stanley D. Letter to Bayard Rustin. [*10/1959*]. New York, N.Y. (ALS) 4 pp. BRP-DLC. 591000–016.
10/1959	King, Martin Luther, Jr. Telegram to George M. Houser. [*10/1959*]. [*Montgomery, Ala.*] (TWc) 1 p. MLKP-MBU: Box 19. 591000–017.
10/1/1959	Walker, Wyatt Tee, and Fred L. Shuttlesworth (SCLC). "Resolutions adopted at Fall Session." 10/1/1959. Columbia, S.C. (TD) 2 pp. SCLCR-GAMK. 591001–007.
10/1/1959	Caldwell, Elvin R. (International Opportunity Life Insurance Company). Letter to Martin Luther King, Jr. 10/1/1959. Denver, Colo. (TLS) 1 p. (Contains enclosure 591001–014.) MLKP-MBU: Box 5. 591001–009.
9/30/1959–10/1/1959	Shuttlesworth, Fred L. (SCLC). Minutes, Fall Session. 9/30/1959–10/1/1959. Columbia, S.C. (TD) 2 pp. MLKP-MBU: Box 68. 591001–010.
9/29/1959–10/1/1959	SCLC. Program, "Fall Session." 9/29/1959–10/1/1959. Columbia, S.C. (THD) 10 pp. LDRP-NN-Sc: Box 3. 591001–012.
10/1/1959	International Opportunity Life Insurance Company. Advertisement featuring Martin Luther King, Jr. [*10/1/1959*]. Washington, D.C. (PD) 1 p. (Enclosed in 591001–009.) MLKP-MBU: Box 5. 591001–014.
9/30/1959–10/1/1959	[*Braden, Carl*]. Notes on SCLC Fall Session. [*9/30/1959–10/1/1959*]. (AD) 8 pp. CAABP-WHi. 591001–015.
10/1/1959	SCLC. Recommendations adopted by the executive committee and delegates at Fall Session. 10/1/1959. Columbia, S.C. (TD) 1 p. SCLCR-GAMK. 591001–019.
10/4/1959	Dexter Avenue Baptist Church. Program, Sunday services. 10/4/1959. Montgomery, Ala. (TD) 4 pp. DABCC. 591004–000.
10/5/1959	Nair, K. Krishnan (Gandhi Vijnana Pareshath). Letter to Martin Luther King, Jr. 10/5/1959. Trivandrum, India. (TALS) 2 pp. MLKP-MBU: Box 26. 591005–010.
10/5/1959	Lett, Lottie. Letter to Martin Luther King, Jr. [*10/5/1959*]. Tuscaloosa, Ala. (ALS) 4 pp. MLKP-MBU: Box 29A. 591005–011.

10/6/1959 King, Martin Luther, Jr. Letter to Michael Harrington. 10/6/1959. [*Montgomery, Ala.*] (TLc) 1 p. MLKP-MBU: Box 28. 591006–001.

10/7/1959 Dexter Avenue Baptist Church. *Dexter Echo* 4, no. 2. 10/7/1959. Montgomery, Ala. (TD) 6 pp. MLKP-MBU: Box 77. 591007–000.

10/7/1959 MIA. *Newsletter* 2, no. 1. 10/7/1959. Montgomery, Ala. (TD) 3 pp. MLKP-MBU: Box 106. 591007–001.

10/7/1959 King, Martin Luther, Jr. Letter to Susan S. Wood. 10/7/1959. [*Montgomery, Ala.*] (TLc) 1 p. MLKP-MBU: Box 10. 591007–002.

10/7/1959 Lawson, Marjorie McKenzie (Lawson, McKenzie, and Grillo). Letter to Martin Luther King, Jr. 10/7/1959. Washington, D.C. (TLS) 1 p. MLKP-MBU: Box 29A. 591007–006.

10/7/1959 Program, Dinner in tribute to Eleanor Roosevelt. [*10/7/1959*]. (PD) 4 pp. MLKJP-GAMK: Box 68. 591007–010.

10/8/1959 Horton, Myles (Highlander Folk School). Letter to Martin Luther King, Jr. 10/8/1959. Monteagle, Tenn. (TLS) 1 p. MLKP-MBU: Box 28. 591008–001.

10/8/1959 King, Martin Luther, Jr. Letter to Lottie Lett. 10/8/1959. [*Montgomery, Ala.*] (TLc) 1 p. MLKP-MBU: Box 29A. 591008–004.

10/8/1959 King, Martin Luther, Jr. Letter to Newton Miyagi. 10/8/1959. [*Montgomery, Ala.*] (TLc) 1 p. MLKP-MBU: Box 49A. 591008–005.

10/8/1959 Southern Conference Educational Fund, Inc. Press release, Hearing for Carl Braden and Frank Wilkinson held on 10/7/1959. 10/8/1959. New Orleans, La. (TD) 2 pp. (Enclosed in 591010–005.) MLKP-MBU: Box 20. 591008–011.

10/9/1959 King, Martin Luther, Jr. Letter to Richard Thompson. 10/9/1959. [*Montgomery, Ala.*] (TLc) 1 p. MLKP-MBU: Box 72. 591009–008.

10/10/1959 Braden, Carl (Southern Conference Educational Fund, Inc.). Letter to Martin Luther King, Jr. 10/10/1959. Louisville, Ky. (TLS) 1 p. (Contains enclosure 591008–011.) MLKP-MBU: Box 20. 591010–005.

10/10/1959 Braden, Carl. Letter to Martin Luther King. 10/10/1959. (TLS) 1 p. CAABP-WHi. 591010–007.

10/11/1959 Dexter Avenue Baptist Church. Program, "Annual Women's Day observance." 10/11/1959. Montgomery, Ala. (TD) 4 pp. CKFC. 591011–000.

10/12/1959 King, Martin Luther, Jr. Letter to Hilda S. Proctor. 10/12/1959. [*Montgomery, Ala.*] (TLc) 1 p. MLKP-MBU: Box 34. 591012–002.

10/12/1959 Baker, Ella J. (SCLC). Telegram to John A. Hannah. 10/12/1959. (TWc) 1 p. EJBC-NN-Sc. 591012–003.

10/12/1959 Newgent, William E. Letter to Martin Luther King, Jr. 10/12/1959. Washington, D.C. (TLS) 1 p. MLKP-MBU: Box 32A. 591012–012.

10/13/1959 King, Martin Luther, Jr. (Dexter Avenue Baptist Church). Letter to Myles Horton. 10/13/1959. Montgomery, Ala. (TLS) 1 p. HRECR-WHi. 591013–001.

10/13/1959 King, Martin Luther, Jr. Letter to A. A. Peters. 10/13/1959. [*Montgomery, Ala.*] (TLc) 1 p. MLKP-MBU: Box 34. 591013–003.

10/13/1959 Brown, Theodore E. (American Federation of Labor and Congress of Industrial Organizations (AFL-CIO)). Letter to Martin Luther King, Jr. 10/13/1959. Washington, D.C. (TLS) 1 p. (Contains enclosure 590929–028.) MLKP-MBU: Box 20. 591013–006.

10/13/1959 Kilgore, Thomas (Friendship Baptist Church). Letter to Martin Luther King, Jr. 10/13/1959. New York, N.Y. (TLS) 1 p. MLKP-MBU: Box 29. 591013–011.

10/13/1959 Trenholm, H. Councill (Harper Councill) (Alabama State College). Letter to Julius Gikonyo Kiano. 10/13/1959. Montgomery, Ala. (TLc) 1 p. (Copy to King.) MLKP-MBU. 591013–014.

10/14/1959 Porter, John T. (First Baptist Institutional Church). Letter to Martin Luther King, Jr. 10/14/1959. Hamtramck, Mich. (TLS) 1 p. MLKP-MBU: Box 51. 591014–004.

10/15/1959 Baker, Ella J. (SCLC). Letter to Martin Luther King, Jr. 10/15/1959. Atlanta, Ga. (TALS) 2 pp. MLKP-MBU: Box 20. 591015–002.

10/16/1959 Houser, George M. (American Committee on Africa). Letter to Martin Luther King, Jr. 10/16/1959. New York, N.Y. (TLS) 1 p. (Contains enclosure 591016–011.) MLKP-MBU: Box 19. 591016–000.

10/16/1959 King, Martin Luther, Jr. "The Future of Integration," Address at the American Studies Conference on Civil Rights. 10/16/1959. Minneapolis, Minn. (TAHD) 13 pp. MLKP-MBU: Box 80. 591016–001.

10/16/1959 Holmes, Kirby B. (Upper Room Temple). Letter to Martin Luther King, Jr. 10/16/1959. Fort Worth, Texas. (THLS) 1 p. MLKP-MBU: Box 13. 591016–002.

10/16/1959 King, Martin Luther, Jr. (American Committee on Africa). Draft, Form letter to

Friend. [*10/16/1959*]. New York, N.Y. (THLd) 1 p. (Enclosed in 591016–000.) MLKP-MBU: Box 19. 591016–011.

10/16/1959–10/17/1959 Program, "American studies conference on civil rights." 10/16/1959–10/17/1959. Minneapolis, Minn. (PD) 2 pp. UMR-MnU-Ar. 591017–000.

10/18/1959 Dexter Avenue Baptist Church. Program, Sunday services. 10/18/1959. Montgomery, Ala. (TD) 3 pp. DABCC. 591018–000.

10/19/1959 King, Martin Luther, Jr. (Dexter Avenue Baptist Church). Letter to Myles Horton. 10/19/1959. Montgomery, Ala. (THLS) 1 p. HRECR-WHi. 591019–003.

10/19/1959 King, Martin Luther, Jr. Letter to Thomas Kilgore. 10/19/1959. [*Montgomery, Ala.*] (TLc) 1 p. MLKP-MBU: Box 29. 591019–011.

10/20/1959 Kiano, Julius Gikonyo. Letter to Martin Luther King, Jr. 10/20/1959. Nairobi, Kenya. (TLSr) 2 pp. MLKP-MBU: Box 26. 591020–001.

10/20/1959 Hughes, Robert E. Letter to Martin Luther King, Jr. and Coretta Scott King. 10/20/1959. Birmingham, Ala. (ALS) 1 p. MLKP-MBU: Box 27A. 591020–004.

10/20/1959 King, Martin Luther, Jr. Letter to William E. Newgent. 10/20/1959. [*Montgomery, Ala.*] (TLc) 1 p. MLKP-MBU: Box 32. 591020–010.

10/22/1959 King, Martin Luther, Jr. (Dexter Avenue Baptist Church). Letter to Carl Braden. 10/22/1959. Montgomery, Ala. (THLS) 1 p. CAABP-WHi: Box 53. 591022–003.

10/23/1959 Talley, Cornell E. (Central Baptist Church). Letter to Martin Luther King, Jr. 10/23/1959. Pittsburgh, Pa. (TLS) 2 pp. MLKP-MBU: Box 72. 591023–004.

10/23/1959 Baker, Ella J. (SCLC). Memo to committee on administration. 10/23/1959. (TLc) 3 pp. MLKP-MBU: Box 48. 591023–006.

10/25/1959 University of Chicago. Program, University religious service. 10/25/1959. Chicago, Ill. (PD) 4 pp. MLKP-MBU: Box 82. 591025–001.

10/27/1959 King, Martin Luther, Jr. (SCLC). "Recommendations to committee on future program." 10/27/1959. (TD) 2 pp. MLKP-MBU: Box 48. 591027–003.

10/27/1959 Spilman, Kenneth E. (University of North Dakota, United Campus Christian Fellowship). Letter to Martin Luther King, Jr. 10/27/1959. Grand Forks, N.D. (TALS) 1 p. MLKP-MBU: Box 72. 591027–004.

10/28/1959 Tuggle, Kenneth H. (U.S. Interstate Commerce Commission). Letter to Martin Luther King, Jr. 10/28/1959. Washington, D.C. (TLS) 1 p. SCLCR-GAMK: Box 5. 591028–001.

10/29/1959 Sullivan, Robert E. Letter to Martin Luther King, Jr. 10/29/1959. (THLS) 2 pp. MLKP-MBU: Box 84. 591029–003.

10/29/1959 Hurlburt, Nettie K. Letter to Martin Luther King, Jr. 10/29/1959. Cleveland, Ohio. (THLS) 1 p. MLKP-MBU: Box 27A. 591029–004.

10/29/1959 Durfee, James R. (U.S. Civil Aeronautics Board). Letter to Martin Luther King, Jr. 10/29/1959. Washington D.C. (THLS) 1 p. SCLCR-GAMK: Box 1. 591029–006.

10/29/1959 Federation of Negro Civil Service Organizations, Inc. Flyer, "Rally the Right to Vote." [*10/29/1959*]. New York (PD) 1 p. DBC-WHi: Box 4. 591029–007.

10/29/1959 Braden, Anne (Southern Conference Educational Fund, Inc.). Letter to Martin Luther King, Jr. 10/29/1959. Louisville, Ky. (TLS) 1 p. MLKP-MBU: Box 20. 591029–008.

11/1959 Petition in support of Highlander Folk School. 11/1959. (TD) 1 p. AJMP-PSC-P. 591100–002.

11/1959 SCLC. *The Crusader* 1, no. 2. 11/1959. Atlanta, Ga. (TD) 8 pp. MLKP-MBU: Box 47A. 591100–008.

11/1959 Gibbs, Jewelle Taylor. Letter to Martin Luther King, Jr. [*11/1959*]. Minneapolis, Minn. (AHLS) 2 pp. MLKP-MBU: Box 27. 591100–012.

11/1/1959 Dexter Avenue Baptist Church. Program, Sunday services. 11/1/1959. Montgomery, Ala. (TD) 4 pp. DABCC. 591101–000.

11/1/1959 Levison, Stanley D., Tom Kahn, and Joe Filner. Letter to Bayard Rustin. 11/1/1959. New York, N.Y. (TL) 3 pp. BRP-DLC. 591101–002.

11/2/1959 King, Martin Luther, Jr. (Dexter Avenue Baptist Church). Letter to Anne Braden. 11/2/1959. Montgomery, Ala. (TLS) 1 p. CAABP-WHi: Box 53. 591102–005.

11/2/1959 SCLC. Press release, Expanded program to be implemented in voter registration, leadership training, and nonviolent resistance. 11/2/1959. Atlanta, Ga. (TDf) 1 p. MLKP-MBU: Box 68. 591102–010.

11/2/1959 Teek-Frank, Ingeborg. Letter to Martin Luther King, Jr. 11/2/1959. New York, N.Y. (TLS) 1 p. MLKP-MBU: Box 25. 591102–015.

11/3/1959 King, Martin Luther, Jr. Letter to C. Kenzie Steele. 11/3/1959. [*Montgomery, Ala.*] (TLc) 1 p. MLKP-MBU: Box 69. 591103–002.

11/3/1959 King, Martin Luther, Jr. Letter to Robert E. Hughes. 11/3/1959. [*Montgomery, Ala.*] (TLc) 1 p. MLKP-MBU: Box 27A. 591103-003.

11/3/1959–11/4/1959 Crozer Theological Seminary. Program, "Samuel A. Crozer Lectures." 11/3/1959–11/4/1959. Chester, Pa. (PD) 4 pp. (Enclosed in 590924-001.) MLKP-MBU: Box 37A. 591104-007.

11/4/1959 Dexter Avenue Baptist Church. *Dexter Echo* 4, no. 3. 11/4/1959. Montgomery, Ala. (TD) 8 pp. MLKP-MBU. 591104-000.

11/4/1959 Love, Dois Edward. Letter to Fred L. Shuttlesworth. 11/4/1959. Brooklyn, N.Y. (TLS) 4 pp. (Enclosed in 591217-000.) MLKP-MBU: Box 18. 591104-006.

11/5/1959 King, Martin Luther, Jr. (MIA). Form letter to Friend. 11/5/1959. Montgomery, Ala. (TLc) 1 p. HG-GAMK. 591105-000.

11/5/1959 Baptist Temple Church. Program, "Philadelphia Crusade for Citizenship rally." 11/5/1959. Philadelphia, Pa. (PD) 1 p. MLKP-MBU: Box 82. 591105-004.

11/6/1959 Fletcher, C. Scott (Fund for Adult Education). Letter to Martin Luther King, Jr. 11/6/1959. White Plains, N.Y. (TLS) 2 pp. MLKP-MBU: Box 25. 591106-000.

11/9/1959 Houser, George M. (American Committee on Africa). Letter to Martin Luther King, Jr. 11/9/1959. New York, N.Y. (TLS) 1 p. MLKP-MBU: Box 18. 591109-001.

11/9/1959 DuBois, W.E.B. (William Edward Burghardt). Book review, *Crusader Without Violence* by Lawrence Dunbar Reddick. 11/9/1959. New York, N.Y. From: *National Guardian*, 9 November 1959, p. 8. (PD) 1 p. 591109-004.

11/10/1959 Reddick, Lawrence Dunbar (Alabama State College). Letter to W.E.B. (William Edward Burghardt) Du Bois. 11/10/1959. (TLS) 1 p. WEBD-MU. 591110-000.

11/10/1959 NAACP. Program, "Waterloo NAACP welcome you to hear Dr. Martin Luther King, Jr." 11/10/1959. Waterloo, Iowa (PAD) 4 pp. MLKP-MBU: Box 82. 591110-007.

11/11/1959 King, Martin Luther, Jr. "The Future of Integration," Address at the State University of Iowa. 11/11/1959. Iowa City, Iowa. (TAD) 12 pp. MLKP-MBU. 591111-000.

11/11/1959 King, Martin Luther, Jr. Letter to Marjorie McKenzie Lawson. 11/11/1959. [*Montgomery, Ala.*] (TLc) 1 p. MLKP-MBU: Box 29A. 591111-006.

11/11/1959 King, Martin Luther, Jr. The Montgomery Story, Address delivered at Iowa State Teachers College. [*11/11/1959*]. [*Cedar Falls, Iowa.*] (At) 44.4 min. (1 sound cassette: analog.) MLKJP-GAMK. 591111-012.

11/11/1959 "Work for Humanity, Dr. King Advises." 11/11/1959. Waterloo, Iowa. From: *Waterloo Daily Courier*, 11 November 1959. (PD) 1 p. IaW. 591111-014.

11/12/1959 King, Martin Luther, Jr. (American Committee on Africa). Form letter to Friend. 11/12/1959. New York, N.Y. (TLS) 1 p. MLKP-MBU: Box 88A. 591112-004.

11/12/1959 NAACP. Program, "Reverend Martin Luther King, Jr. at the University Christian Church." 11/12/1959. Des Moines, Iowa (PD) 4 pp. MLKP-MBU: Box 82. 591112-005.

11/13/1959 Belafonte, Harry, Jackie Robinson, and Sidney Poitier (African-American Students Foundation, Inc.). Letter to Martin Luther King, Jr. 11/13/1959. New York, N.Y. (TLS) 2 pp. (Includes enclosure.) MLKP-MBU: Box 19. 591113-003.

11/14/1959 Levison, Stanley D., and A. J. (Abraham Johannes) Muste. Cablegram to Bayard Rustin. 11/14/1959. (AW) 3 pp. BRP-DLC. 591114-004.

11/15/1959 Dexter Avenue Baptist Church. Program, Sunday services. 11/15/1959. Montgomery, Ala. (TD) 4 pp. DABCC. 591115-000.

11/15/1959 Muste, A. J. (Abraham Johannes). Letter to Bayard Rustin. 11/15/1959. (ALS) 10 pp. BRP-DLC. 591115-005.

11/16/1959 King, Martin Luther, Jr. Letter to Linda Carver. 11/16/1959. [*Montgomery, Ala.*] (TLc) 2 pp. MLKP-MBU: Box 22. 591116-001.

11/16/1959 King, Martin Luther, Jr. Letter to Donald L. Parker and Jane Parker. 11/16/1959. [*Montgomery, Ala.*] (TLc) 2 pp. MLKP-MBU: Box 33A. 591116-002.

11/17/1959 Buck, Pearl S. Letter to Martin Luther King, Jr. 11/17/1959. Perkasie, Pa. (TLS) 1 p. MLKP-MBU: Box 20. 591117-004.

11/18/1959 King, Martin Luther, Jr. Letter to Robert E. Sullivan. 11/18/1959. [*Montgomery, Ala.*] (TLc) 2 pp. MLKP-MBU: Box 84. 591118-002.

11/18/1959 Dombrowski, James A. (James Anderson) (Southern Conference Educational Fund, Inc.). Letter to Martin Luther King, Jr. 11/18/1959. New Orleans, La. (TLS) 1 p. MLKP-MBU: Box 69. 591118-003.

11/18/1959 King, Martin Luther, Jr. Telegram to Roy Wilkins. 11/18/1959. Montgomery, Ala. (PWSr) 1 p. NAACPP-DLC. 591118-004.

11/18/1959 Lawson, Marjorie McKenzie (Lawson, McKenzie, and Grillo). Letter to Martin

Luther King, Jr. 11/18/1959. Washington, D.C. (TLS) 1 p. MLKP-MBU: Box 29A. 591118–007.

11/18/1959 Associated Negro Press. Press release, "SCLC urges Martin Luther King to devote more time to its program." 11/18/1959. (TD) 1 p. CABP-ICHi. 591118–011.

11/19/1959 King, Martin Luther, Jr. Letter to Stanley D. Levison. 11/19/1959. [*Montgomery, Ala.*] (TLc) 1 p. MLKP-MBU: Box 2. 591119–001.

11/19/1959 Hicks, James L. (*New York Amsterdam News*). Letter to Martin Luther King, Jr. 11/19/1959. New York, N.Y. (TLS) 1 p. MLKP-MBU: Box 53A. 591119–004.

11/20/1959 Jack, Homer Alexander (American Committee on Africa). Letter to Martin Luther King, Jr. 11/20/1959. New York, N.Y. (TLS) 1 p. (Contains enclosure 591120–001.) MLKP-MBU: Box 18. 591120–000.

11/20/1959 Baldwin, Roger. "A call for peace in Algeria." [*11/20/1959*]. (TD) 1 p. (Enclosed in 591120–000.) MLKP-MBU: Box 18. 591120–001.

11/20/1959 Mays, Benjamin Elijah (Morehouse College). Letter to Alumnus and Friend. 11/20/1959. Atlanta, Ga. (TLS) 4 pp. (Includes enclosure.) MLKP-MBU: Box 31. 591120–007.

11/20/1959 Wofford, Harris. "The Law and Civil Disobedience." 11/20/1959. (THD) 4 pp. (Marginal comments by King.) MLKP-MBU: Box 59. 591120–008.

11/20/1959 King, Martin Luther, Jr. Letter to Ingeborg Teek-Frank. 11/20/1959. [*Montgomery, Ala.*] (TLc) 1 p. MLKP-MBU: Box 25. 591120–009.

11/23/1959 Dellinger, David, A. J. (Abraham Johannes) Muste, and Albert Uhrie (Toll the Bells Committee). Letter to Martin Luther King, Jr. 11/23/1959. New York, N.Y. (TLS) 2 pp. (Enclosed in 591125–003.) MLKP-MBU: Box 25. 591123–003.

11/23/1959 King, Martin Luther, Jr. Letter to James L. Hicks. 11/23/1959. [*Montgomery, Ala.*] (TLc) 1 p. MLKP-MBU: Box 53A. 591123–006.

11/24/1959 Ryan, Joseph M. F. (U.S. Dept. of Justice). Letter to Martin Luther King, Jr. 11/24/1959. Washington, D.C. (TLS) 1 p. MLKP-MBU: Box 24. 591124–000.

11/25/1959 King, Martin Luther, Jr. Letter to Stanley D. Levison. 11/25/1959. [*Montgomery, Ala.*] (TLc) 1 p. MLKP-MBU: Box 2. 591125–000.

11/25/1959 King, Martin Luther, Jr., Joachim Prinz, John LaFarge, and Roy Wilkins. Telegram to Chester Bowles. 11/25/1959. (TWc) 1 p. CB-CtY. 591125–001.

11/25/1959 Muste, A. J. (Abraham Johannes) (FOR). Letter to Martin Luther King, Jr. 11/25/1959. New York, N.Y. (TLSr) 1 p. (Contains enclosure 591123–003.) MLKP-MBU: Box 25. 591125–003.

11/25/1959 Dombrowski, James A. (James Anderson). Memo to Martin Luther King, Jr., Charles G. (Charles Goode) Gomillion, and Cuthbert O. Simpkins. 11/25/1959. (THL) 3 pp. MLKP-MBU: Box 23A. 591125–008.

11/25/1959 King, Martin Luther, Jr. Letter to William J. Shaw. 11/25/1959. [*Montgomery, Ala.*] (TLc) 1 p. MLKP-MBU: Box 47. 591125–017.

11/25/1959 King, Martin Luther, Jr. Letter to Wilbur D. Grose. 11/25/1959. [*Atlanta, Ga.*] (TLc) 1 p. MLKP-MBU: Box 40A. 591125–019.

11/27/1959 King, Martin Luther, Jr. (Dexter Avenue Baptist Church). Letter to Homer Alexander Jack. 11/27/1959. Montgomery, Ala. (TLS) 1 p. ACA-ARC-LNT. 591127–001.

11/27/1959 King, Martin Luther, Jr. Letter to Pearl S. Buck. 11/27/1959. [*Montgomery, Ala.*] (TLc) 1 p. MLKP-MBU: Box 20. 591127–009.

11/28/1959 Rodrigues, Deolinda. Letter to Martin Luther King, Jr. 11/28/1959. São Paulo, Brazil. (AHLS) 2 pp. MLKP-MBU: Box 20. 591128–000.

11/29/1959 Dexter Avenue Baptist Church. Program, Sunday services. 11/29/1959. Montgomery, Ala. (TD) 3 pp. DABCC. 591129–000.

11/30/1959 Dombrowski, James A. (James Anderson). Memo to Charles G. (Charles Goode) Gomillion, Martin Luther King, Jr. and Cuthbert O. Simpkins. 11/30/1959. (THL) 1 p. MLKP-MBU: Box 70. 591130–006.

11/30/1959 Williams, Aubrey Willis. Telegram to Martin Luther King, Jr. 11/30/1959. (PWSr) 1 p. MLKP-MBU: Box 73. 591130–008.

12/1/1958–11/30/1959 King, Martin Luther, Jr. "Annual report, Dexter Avenue Baptist Church." 12/1/1958–11/30/1959. Montgomery, Ala. (TAD) 26 pp. DABCC. 591130–009.

11/11/1959–11/30/1959 SCLC. "Suggested draft for amplifying press release." [*11/11/1959–11/30/1959*]. (THDd) 2 pp. MLKP-MBU: Box 70. 591130–010.

12/1959 Hughes, Langston. "Poem for a Man: to A. Philip (Asa Philip) Randolph on Achieving his Seventieth Year." [*12/1959*]. (TD) 2 pp. (Enclosed in 591222–003.) MLKP-MBU: Box 30A. 591200–004.

12/1959 Yette, S. F. "M. L. King Supports African Student." 12/1959. Tuskegee, Ala. From: *News of Tuskegee Institute*, December 1959. (PD) 1 p. 591200–012.

12/1959 Photo of Martin Luther King, Jr. and Nicholas W. Raballa. [*12/1959*]. Montgomery, Ala. (Ph) 1 p. TIA-ATT. 591200–013.

12/1959 MIA. "Statement about Reverend King's leaving from the MIA executive board." [*12/1959*]. (TD) 2 pp. LDRP-NN-Sc: Box 3. 591200–017.

12/1/1959 Teek-Frank, Ingeborg. Letter to Martin Luther King, Jr. 12/1/1959. New York, N.Y. (TALS) 2 pp. MLKP-MBU: Box 72. 591201–005.

12/1/1959 [*SCLC*]. Draft, Press release, "Dr. King Leaves Montgomery for Atlanta." [*12/1/1959*]. Montgomery, Ala. (THDd) 2 pp. LDRP-NN-Sc: Box 2. 591201–008.

12/2/1959 Peery, Lee. Draft, Letter to S. Ernest (Samuel Ernest) Vandiver. [*12/2/1959*]. Douglasville, Ga. (ALdS) 2 pp. (Copy to King. Includes postscript to King.) MLKP-MBU: Box 33A. 591202–003.

12/2/1959 Bentz, Betty (Hotel and Club Employees Union Local 6). Letter to Martin Luther King, Jr. 12/2/1959. New York, N.Y. (TLS) 1 p. MLKP-MBU: Box 20. 591202–007.

12/3/1959 King, Martin Luther, Jr. (MIA). "Address on the fourth annual anniversary of the MIA at Bethel Baptist Church in Montgomery, Ala." 12/3/1959. From: Los Angeles, Calif.: The Bryant Foundation. (PD) 15 pp. MLKJP-GAMK. 591203–002.

12/3/1959 Smith, Kelly Miller (Nashville Christian Leadership Council). Letter to Martin Luther King, Jr. 12/3/1959. Nashville, Tenn. (TLS) 1 p. MLKP-MBU: Box 70. 591203–006.

12/4/1959 King, Martin Luther, Jr. (Salute to A. Philip Randolph Committee). Letter to Eleanor Roosevelt. 12/4/1959. New York, N.Y. (TLS) 1 p. ERC-NHyF. 591204–003

12/4/1959 Robinson, James R. (CORE). Letter to Martin Luther King, Jr. 12/4/1959. (TLS) 1 p. MLKP-MBU. 591204–007.

12/4/1959 Hocking, Richard (Georgia Council on Human Relations), and Harry Boyte (Greater Atlanta Council on Human Relations). Letter to S. Ernest (Samuel Ernest) Vandiver. 12/4/1959. (THLc) 1 p. LDRP-NN-Sc: Box 2. 591204–008.

12/3/1959–12/6/1959 MIA. Program, "Fourth annual Institute on Nonviolence and Social Change." 12/3/1959–12/6/1959. Montgomery, Ala. (PD) 7 pp. MLKP-MBU: Box 6. 591206–000.

12/7/1959 Baker, Ella J. (SCLC). "Report of the executive director," 9/30/1959–12/8/1959. 12/7/1959. Atlanta, Ga. (TD) 2 pp. EJBC-NN-Sc. 591207–000.

12/8/1959 SCLC. Press release, Annual board meeting held at St. James Baptist Church. 12/8/1959. Birmingham, Ala. (TD) 2 pp. MLKP-MBU: Box 71. 591208–004.

12/8/1959 Poinsett, Alex (*Jet*). Letter to Martin Luther King, Jr. 12/8/1959. Chicago, Ill. (TLS) 1 p. MLKP-MBU: Box 28A. 591208–008.

12/8/1959 Newman, I. DeQuincy (NAACP). Statement regarding meeting and banquet of SCLC. 12/8/1959. (TAHDS) 4 pp. (Enclosed in 591218–000.) NAACPP-DLC. 591208–010.

12/8/1959 Reddick, Lawrence Dunbar. Notes, Executive board meeting of the SCLC. 12/8/1959. Birmingham, Ala. (ATD) 10 pp. LDRP-NN-Sc: Box 2. 591208–012.

12/9/1959 Dexter Avenue Baptist Church. *Dexter Echo* 4, no. 4. 12/9/1959. Montgomery, Ala. (THD) 6 pp. MLKP-MBU: Box 77. 591209–001.

12/9/1959 King, Martin Luther, Jr. Letter to David Dellinger. 12/9/1959. [*Montgomery, Ala.*] (TLc) 1 p. MLKP-MBU: Box 25. 591209–004.

12/9/1959 King, Martin Luther, Jr. Letter to James A. (James Anderson) Dombrowski. 12/9/1959. [*Montgomery, Ala.*] (TLc) 2 pp. MLKP-MBU: Box 32A. 591209–006.

12/10/1959 Morrissett, Ann (American Committee on Africa). Letter to Martin Luther King, Jr. 12/10/1959. New York, N.Y. (TLS) 1 p. MLKP-MBU: Box 19. 591210-002.

12/10/1959 King, Martin Luther, Jr. The Future of Integration, Address delivered at Miami University. [*12/10/1959*]. Oxford, Ohio. (At) 28.1 min. (1 sound cassette: analog.) OOxM. 591210–011.

12/11/1959 Dombrowski, James A. (James Anderson) (Southern Conference Educational Fund, Inc.). Letter to Martin Luther King, Jr. 12/11/1959. New Orleans, La. (TLS) 1 p. MLKP-MBU: Box 23A. 591211–001.

12/14/1959 Mason, E. Harold. Letter to Fred L. Shuttlesworth. 12/14/1959. Alameda, Calif. (ALS) 3 pp. (Enclosed in 591217–000.) MLKP-MBU: Box 18. 591214–011.

12/15/1959 McGill, Ralph (*Atlanta Constitution*). Letter to Harry S. Ashmore. 12/15/1959. Atlanta, Ga. (TLS) 3 pp. RMP-GEU. 591215–007.

12/14/1959–12/15/1959 Inter-Denominational Planning Committee of Chicago. Program, "Martin Luther King, Jr. at Tabernacle Baptist Church and at Stone Temple Baptist Church." 12/14/1959–12/15/1959. Chicago, Ill. (PD) 4 pp. MLKP-MBU: Box 82. 591215–009.

12/17/1959 Shuttlesworth, Fred L. (Alabama Christian Movement for Human Rights (ACMHR)). Letter to Martin Luther King, Jr. 12/17/1959. Birmingham, Ala. (TLS) 1 p. (Contains enclosures 591104–005 & 591214–011.) MLKP-MBU: Box 18. 591217–000.

12/17/1959 Neufeld, Elmer (Mennonite Central Committee). Letter to Martin Luther King, Jr. 12/17/1959. Akron, Pa. (TLS) 1 p. MLKP-MBU: Box 31. 591217–008.

12/18/1959 Wyatt, M. M. (NAACP). Letter to Roy Wilkins. 12/18/1959. New York, N.Y. (TLS) 1 p. (Contains enclosure 591208–010.) NAACPP-DLC. 591218–000.

12/18/1959 Wilkins, Roy (Leadership Conference on Civil Rights). Telegram to Martin Luther King, Jr. 12/18/1959. New York, N.Y. (PHWSr) 2 pp. MLKP-MBU: Box 74. 591218–001.

12/20/1959 Dexter Avenue Baptist Church. Program, Sunday services. 12/20/1959. Montgomery, Ala. (TD) 4 pp. CKFC. 591220–000.

12/21/1959 King, Martin Luther, Jr. Letter to Ralph Abernathy. 12/21/1959. [*Montgomery, Ala.*] (TLc) 1 p. (Contains enclosure 591221–016.) MLKP-MBU: Box 72. 591221–002.

12/21/1959 Menon, M. Gopala (India General Consul). Invitation to Martin Luther King, Jr. in honor of Jawaharlal Nehru and Indira Gandhi. 12/21/1959. New York, N.Y. (PD) 1 p. MLKP-MBU: Box 80. 591221–006.

12/21/1959 King, Martin Luther, Jr. Letter to J. R. Powell. 12/21/1959. [*Montgomery, Ala.*] (TLc) 1 p. (Enclosed in 591221–002.) MLKP-MBU: Box 33A. 591221–016.

12/22/1959 Levison, Stanley D. Letter to Martin Luther King, Jr. 12/22/1959. New York, N.Y. (TLS) 1 p. (Contains enclosure 591200–004.) MLKP-MBU: Box 29A. 591222–003.

12/22/1959 King, Martin Luther, Jr. Letter to Alex Poinsett. 12/22/1959. [*Montgomery, Ala.*] (TLc) 1 p. MLKP-MBU: Box 28A. 591222–005.

12/23/1959 King, Martin Luther, Jr. (Dexter Avenue Baptist Church). Letter to Ann Morrissett. 12/23/1959. Montgomery, Ala. (TLSr) 1 p. ACA-ARC-LNT. 591223–000.

12/23/1959 King, Martin Luther, Jr. Letter to Lee Peery. 12/23/1959. [*Montgomery, Ala.*] (TLc) 2 pp. MLKP-MBU: Box 33A. 591223–001.

12/23/1959 Wilkins, Roy (NAACP). Memo to Gloster B. (Gloster Bryant) Current and John Morsell. 12/23/1959. (TD) 1 p. NAACPP-DLC. 591223–003.

12/23/1959 Muste, A. J. (Abraham Johannes) (Sahara Protest Team). Letter to Martin Luther King, Jr. 12/23/1959. Accra, Ghana. (TALS) 2 pp. (Contains enclosure 591223–010.) MLKP-MBU: Box 71. 591223–009.

12/23/1959 Muste, A. J. (Abraham Johannes). "Proposed statement on Sahara bomb test." [*12/23/1959*]. New York, N.Y. (TAD) 1 p. (Enclosed in 591223–009.) MLKP-MBU: Box 71. 591223–010.

12/27/1959 Dexter Avenue Baptist Church. Program, Sunday services. 12/27/1959. Montgomery, Ala. (TD) 3 pp. CKFC. 591227–000.

12/28/1959 Dombrowski, James A. (James Anderson). Telegram to Martin Luther King, Jr. 12/28/1959. New Orleans, La. (PWSr) 1 p. MLKP-MBU: Box 23A. 591228–001.

12/28/1959 Kaplan, Kivie. Letter to Martin Luther King, Jr. 12/28/1959. Boston, Mass. (TLS) 1 p. MLKP-MBU. 591228–004.

12/30/1959 King, Martin Luther, Jr., A. Philip (Asa Philip) Randolph, and Harry Emerson Fosdick (Salute to A. Philip Randolph Committee). Letter to Dwight D. (Dwight David) Eisenhower. 12/30/1959. New York, N.Y. (TLS) 1 p. MLKJP-GAMK. 591230–002.

12/30/1959 Robinson, James R. (CORE). Letter to Martin Luther King, Jr. 12/30/1959. New York, N.Y. (TLS) 1 p. (Contains enclosure 591230–004.) MLKP-MBU: Box 23. 591230–003.

12/30/1959 [*King, Martin Luther, Jr.*] Introduction, "Cracking the Color Line." 12/30/1959. (TD) 1 p. (Enclosed in 591230–003.) MLKP-MBU: Box 23. 591230–004.

12/30/1959 Rodrigues, Deolinda. Letter to Martin Luther King, Jr. 12/30/1959. (TLS) 1 p. MLKP-MBU: Box 14. 591230–009.

12/31/1959 Fey, Harold Edward (*Christian Century*). Letter to Martin Luther King, Jr. 12/31/1959. Chicago, Ill. (TLS) 1 p. CSKC: Sermon file. 591231–000.

1960 **Uhrbrock, Donald (*Time*). Photo of Martin Luther King, Jr., Coretta Scott King, Yolanda Denise King, and Martin Luther King, III. [*1960*]. Atlanta, Ga. (Ph) 1 p. NNTI. 600000–118.**

1960	Scarsdale Community Baptist Church. Program, Lenten services. 1960. Scarsdale, N.Y. (PD) 3 pp. MLKP-MBU: Box 45A. 600000–142.
1956–1960	King, Martin Luther, Jr. To Win Racial Justice. [*1956–1960*]. [*Montgomery, Ala.*] (PD) 1 p. HJP-GAMK. 600000–176.
1/1960	**King, Martin Luther, Jr. "The Great Debate: Is Violence Necessary to Combat Injustice?" 1/1960. Louisville, Ky. From: *Southern Patriot,* January 1960, p. 3. (PD) 1 p. (Reprint of *Liberation.*) MLKP-MBU: Box 2. 600100–000.**
1/1960	Hughes, Langston. "Prayer for the Mantle-Piece." 1/1960. (TDS) 1 p. (Enclosed in 600118–001.) MLKP-MBU: Box 30A. 600100–002.
1/1960	Hughes, Langston. "Merry-go-Round." [*1/1960*]. (TDS) 1 p. (Enclosed in 600118–001.) MLKP-MBU: Box 30A. 600100–003.
1/1960	Tusiani, Joseph (*Nigrizia*). "La Non Violenza del Dott. King." [*1/1960*]. Rome, Italy. From: *Nigrizia* (January 1960): 23–24. (PD) 3 pp. (In Italian). 600100–014.
1/1/1960	"King to Develop Non-Violent Integration Movement in South." 1/1/1960. Athens, Ohio. From: *Ohio University Post,* 1 January 1960. (PD) 1 p. ASCL-OAU. 600101–004.
1/1/1960	Program, "Second annual Pilgrimage of Prayer for Public Schools." 1/1/1960. Richmond, Va. (TD) 3 pp. CSKC. 600101–045.
1/2/1960	Wofford, Harris (Notre Dame Law School). Letter to Martin Luther King, Jr. [*1/2/1960*]. Notre Dame, Ind. (TALS) 3 pp. CKFC. 600102–003.
1/3/1960	Dexter Avenue Baptist Church. Program, Sunday services. 1/3/1960. Montgomery, Ala. (TD) 4 pp. CKFC. 600103–000.
1/5/1960	King, Martin Luther, Jr. Letter to Stanley D. Levison. 1/5/1960. [*Montgomery, Ala.*] (THLc) 1 p. MLKP-MBU: Box 29A. 600105–004.
1/5/1960	King, Martin Luther, Jr. Telegram to A. J. (Abraham Johannes) Muste. 1/5/1960. [*Montgomery, Ala.*] (TWc) 1 p. MLKP-MBU: Box 71. 600105–006.
1/5/1960	King, Martin Luther, Jr. Letter to John H. Bell. 1/5/1960. [*Montgomery, Ala.*] (TLc) 1 p. (Contains enclosure 600105–011.) MLKP-MBU: Box 20. 600105–010.
1/5/1960	King, Martin Luther, Jr. Tribute to Owen D. Pelt. 1/5/1960. [*Montgomery, Ala.*] (TD) 1 p. (Enclosed in 600105–010.) MLKP-MBU: Box 20. 600105–011.
1/6/1960	King, Martin Luther, Jr. Telegram to James A. (James Anderson) Dombrowski. 1/6/1960. (TWc) 1 p. MLKP-MBU: Box 23A. 600106–001.
1/6/1960	Wilkins, Roy (Leadership Conference on Civil Rights). Letter to Martin Luther King, Jr. 1/6/1960. New York, N.Y. (TLS) 3 pp. (Includes enclosure.) MLKP-MBU. 600106–005.
1/8/1960	King, Martin Luther, Jr. (Salute to A. Philip Randolph Committee). Letter to Eleanor Roosevelt. 1/8/1960. New York, N.Y. (THLS) 1 p. ERC-NHyF. 600108–000.
1/8/1960	Ballou, Maude L. Letter to Marvin Rich. 1/8/1960. [*Atlanta, Ga.*] (TLc) 1 p. MLKP-MBU: Box 35. 600108–005.
1/10/1960	Harvard University Memorial Church. Program, "Order of worship." 1/10/1960. Cambridge, Mass. (PHD) 4 pp. MLKP-MBU: Box 80. 600110–003.
1/10/1960	Cambridge Council of Churches. Program, "Martin Luther King, Jr. in a public worship service at the First Baptist Church." 1/10/1960. Cambridge, Mass. (PD) 4 pp. MLKP-MBU: Box 80. 600110–004.
1/11/1960	King, Martin Luther, Jr. Letter to Nicholas W. Raballa. 1/11/1960. [*Montgomery, Ala.*] (TLc) 1 p. MLKP-MBU: Box 35. 600111–006.
1/11/1960	King, Martin Luther, Jr. Letter to Enoch Dumas. 1/11/1960. [*Montgomery, Ala.*] (TLc) 1 p. LewBP. 600111–007.
1/12/1960	King, Martin Luther, Jr. Letter to Fred L. Shuttlesworth. 1/12/1960. [*Montgomery, Ala.*] (TLc) 1 p. MLKP-MBU: Box 18. 600112–000.
1/12/1960	Baker, Ella J. (SCLC). Memo to Administrative committee. 1/12/1960. (TLc) 1 p. MLKP-MBU: Box 20. 600112–013.
1/12/1960	English, Rose B. Letter to Martin Luther King, Jr. 1/12/1960. Vienna, Austria. (AL) 2 pp. MLKP-MBU: Box 25. 600112–014.
1/13/1960	Dexter Avenue Baptist Church. *Dexter Echo* 4, no. 5. 1/13/1960. Montgomery, Ala. (TD) 6 pp. MLKP-MBU: Box 77. 600113–000.
1/13/1960	Anderson, William F. (Dexter Avenue Baptist Church). Memo to Eleanor Roosevelt. 1/13/1960. Montgomery, Ala. (TL) 1 p. ERC-NHyF. 600113–006.
1/13/1960–1/14/1960	"Participants in civil rights legislative conference." 1/13/1960–1/14/1960. (TD) 1 p. NAACPP-DLC: Box 104. 600114–010.
1/16/1960	[*Rustin, Bayard*]. Telegram to Martin Luther King, Jr. 1/16/1960. New York, N.Y. (PWf) 9 pp. MLKP-MBU: Box 59. 600116–002.

1/17/1960	Dexter Avenue Baptist Church. Program, Sunday services. 1/17/1960. Montgomery, Ala. (THD) 4 pp. (Marginal comments by King.) MLKP-MBU: Box 82. 600117–000.
1/18/1960	Eisenhower, Dwight D. (Dwight David). Letter to A. Philip (Asa Philip) Randolph. 1/18/1960. (TLc) 1 p. (Copy to King.) DDEP-KAbE. 600118–000.
1/18/1960	Hughes, Langston. Letter to Martin Luther King, Jr. 1/18/1960. (TLS) 2 pp. (Contains enclosures 600100–002 & 600100–003.) MLKP-MBU: Box 30A. 600118–001.
1/18/1960	O'Dell, Jack H. Letter to Martin Luther King, Jr. 1/18/1960. New York, N.Y. (THLS) 2 pp. MLKP-MBU: Box 33. 600118–007.
1/20/1960	Abernathy, Ralph. Letter to J. Royster Powell. 1/20/1960. (TLc) 1 p. (Copy to King.) MLKP-MBU: Box 72. 600120–001.
1/20/1960	McKinley, Hamp, and Mary McKinley (First Baptist Parsonage). Letter to Martin Luther King, Jr. 1/20/1960. Rocky Mount, Va. (TLS) 1 p. MLKP-MBU: Box 25. 600120–008.
1/21/1960	Baker, Ella J. (SCLC). Form letter to Executive board member. 1/21/1960. Atlanta, Ga. (TLS) 2 pp. (Includes enclosure.) MLKP-MBU: Box 20. 600121–003.
1/22/1960	King, Martin Luther, Jr. "The Moral Challenges of a New Age," Address at Iowa State University. 1/22/1960. Ames, Iowa (TD) 7 pp. SRCR-IaAS: Box 2. 600122–002.
1/24/1960	Program, "Salute to A. Philip Randolph." 1/24/1960. New York, N.Y. (PD) 1 p. APRC-DLC. 600124–000.
1/24/1960	Chicago Sunday Evening Club. Program, "Order of service." 1/24/1960. Chicago, Ill. (PD) 2 pp. MLKP-MBU: Box 38. 600124–003.
1/25/1960	Hill, Herbert (NAACP). Letter to Martin Luther King, Jr. 1/25/1960. New York, N.Y. (TLS) 1 p. SCLCR-GAMK: Box 5. 600125–007.
1/26/1960	Maxwell, O. Clay (Mount Olivet Baptist Church). Letter to Martin Luther King, Jr. 1/26/1960. New York, N.Y. (TLS) 1 p. MLKP-MBU: Box 31. 600126–005.
1/27/1960	King, Martin Luther, Jr. Letter to George A. Buttrick. 1/27/1960. [*Montgomery, Ala.*] (TLc) 1 p. MLKP-MBU: Box 39A. 600127–004.
1/28/1960	Exman, Eugene (Harper and Brothers). Letter to Martin Luther King, Jr. 1/28/1960. New York, N.Y. (TLS) 1 p. MLKP-MBU: Box 2. 600128–000.
1/28/1960	King, Martin Luther, Jr. Letter to William J. Dawson. 1/28/1960. [*Montgomery, Ala.*] (TLc) 1 p. MLKP-MBU: Box 28A. 600128–003.
1/28/1960	Wilkins, Roy (NAACP). Telegram to Martin Luther King, Jr. 1/28/1960. (PWSr) 2 pp. NAACPP-DLC. 600128–004.
1/30/1960	Wofford, Harris (Notre Dame Law School). Letter to Martin Luther King, Jr. 1/30/1960. Notre Dame, Ind. (ALS) 1 p. MLKP-MBU: Box 74. 600130–000.
1/31/1960	Dexter Avenue Baptist Church. Program, Sunday services. 1/31/1960. Montgomery, Ala. (TD) 4 pp. MLKP-MBU: Box 24. 600131–000.
1/31/1960	[*Dexter Avenue Baptist Church*]. A Salute to Dr. and Mrs. Martin Luther King, Jr. [*1/31/1960*]. (TD) 34 pp. MLKP-MBU: Box 24. 600131–002.
1/31/1960	Dexter Avenue Baptist Church. Program, "A Salute to Dr. and Mrs. Martin Luther King." 1/31/1960. Montgomery, Ala. (TD) 4 pp. MLKP-MBU: Box 24. 600131–003.
1/31/1960	Dexter Avenue Baptist Church. A Salute to Dr. and Mrs. Martin Luther King, Jr. 1/31/1960. Montgomery, Ala. (At) 180 min. (3 sound cassettes: analog.) MLKEC: ET-55 & ET-56. 600131–005.
1/31/1960	"Proceedings before the volunteer Civil Rights Commission." 1/31/1960. Washington, D.C. (THD) 59 pp. SCLCR-GAMK: Box 37. 600131–009.
2/1960	[*King, Martin Luther, Jr.*] Statement on integration of public facilities. [*2/1960*]. Montgomery, Ala. (TDf) 1 p. MLKP-MBU. 600200–004.
2/1/1960	MIA. Program, "A Testimonial of Love and Loyalty." 2/1/1960. Montgomery, Ala. (TD) 4 pp. LDRP-NN-Sc: Box 3. 600201–000.
2/1/1960	Abernathy, Ralph (First Baptist Church). "Inaugural statement upon assumption of the presidency of the MIA." 2/1/1960. Montgomery, Ala. (TDf) 7 pp. MLKP-MBU: Box 6. 600201–002.
2/1/1960	King, Martin Luther, Jr. Address at A Testimonial of Love and Loyalty. 2/1/1960. Montgomery, Ala. (TADd) 1 p. MLKP-MBU: Box 73A. 600201–007.
2/1/1960	MIA. A Testimonial of Love and Loyalty. [*2/1/1960*]. Montgomery, Ala. (At) 140.5 min. (3 sound cassettes: analog.) MLKEC: ET-53 & ET-54. 600201–018.
2/2/1960	Humphrey, Hubert H. (Hubert Horatio) (U.S. Congress. Senate). Letter to Martin Luther King, Jr. 2/2/1960. Washington, D.C. (TLS) 1 p. MLKP-MBU: Box 28. 600202–002.

2/2/1960 Rowan, Carl T. Telegram to Martin Luther King, Jr. 2/2/1960. (TWc) 1 p. CTRP-OO. 600202–012.

2/3/1960 Chalmers, Allan Knight (Boston University). Letter to Martin Luther King, Jr. 2/3/1960. Boston, Mass. (ALS) 1 p. MLKP-MBU: Box 22. 600203–000.

2/3/1960 Duckett, Alfred (Alfred Duckett Associates). Telegram to Martin Luther King, Jr. 2/3/1960. New York, N.Y. (PWSr) 1 p. MLKP-MBU: Box 23A. 600203–003.

2/3/1960 Dexter Avenue Baptist Church. *Dexter Echo* 4, no. 6. 2/3/1960. Montgomery, Ala. (TD) 6 pp. CSKC. 600203–004.

2/5/1960 Nixon, Richard M. (Richard Milhous). Telegram to W. E. Anderson. 2/5/1960. (PWSr) 1 p. PPRN-CYINL. 600205–007.

2/6/1960 King, Martin Luther, Jr. Letter to P. J. Ellis. 2/6/1960. [*Atlanta, Ga.*] (TLc) 2 pp. MLKP-MBU: Box 47A. 600206–001.

2/6/1960 Watson, Melvin H. (Liberty Baptist Church). Telegram to Martin Luther King, Jr. 2/6/1960. Atlanta, Ga. (PWSr) 1 p. MLKP-MBU: Box 29A. 600206–002.

2/9/1960 King, Martin Luther, Jr. Letter to Harry Belafonte. 2/9/1960. [*Atlanta, Ga.*] (TLc) 1 p. MLKP-MBU: Box 21. 600209–002.

2/11/1960 Hunter, Lillie M. Letter to T. H. Randall. 2/11/1960. (TLS) 1 p. DABCC. 600211–000.

2/11/1960 Baker, Ella J. (SCLC). Memo to Martin Luther King, Jr. 2/11/1960. (TL) 1 p. SCLCR-GAMK: Box 32. 600211–004.

2/12/1960 Curry, Constance (U.S. National Student Association). Letter to Martin Luther King, Jr. 2/12/1960. Atlanta, Ga. (TLS) 8 pp. (Includes enclosures.) MLKP-MBU: Box 33. 600212–000.

2/12/1960 Steele, C. Kenzie (Bethel Baptist Church). Letter to Martin Luther King, Jr. 2/12/1960. Tallahassee, Fla. (TLS) 1 p. MLKP-MBU: Box 70. 600212–002.

2/12/1960 Davis, Benjamin J. (Benjamin Jefferson). Letter to Martin Luther King, Jr. 2/12/1960. New York, N.Y. (TLS) 2 pp. (Contains enclosure 600212–008.) MLKP-MBU: Box 23A. 600212–003.

2/12/1960 DeWolf, L. Harold (Lotan Harold) (Boston University). Letter to Martin Luther King, Jr. 2/12/1960. Boston, Mass. (TLS) 2 pp. MLKP-MBU: Box 23A. 600212–004.

2/12/1960 Bronx Committee for the Freedom of Henry Winston. Statement on Henry Winston. [*2/12/1960*]. Bronx, N.Y. (TD) 1 p. (Enclosed in 600212–003.) MLKP-MBU: Box 23A. 600212–008.

2/12/1960 Baker, Ella J. (SCLC). Letter to James F. Estes. 2/12/1960. (TLc) 1 p. MLKJP-GAMK. 600212–009.

2/12/1960 King, Martin Luther, Jr. Defendant. Indictment, *State of Alabama v. Martin Luther King, Jr.* 2/12/1960. Montgomery, Ala. (THFmS) 2 pp. CMCR-AMC. 600212–010.

2/14/1960 Ebenezer Baptist Church. Program, Sunday services. 2/14/1960. Atlanta, Ga. (TD) 4 pp. MLKP-MBU: Box 24. 600214–001.

2/15/1960 Chalmers, Allan Knight (NAACP Legal Defense and Educational Fund). Letter to Martin Luther King, Jr. 2/15/1960. New York, N.Y. (TLS) 2 pp. MLKP-MBU: Box 22. 600215–001.

2/16/1960 Erwin, E. A. (State of Alabama. Dept. of Revenue). Letter to Martin Luther King, Jr. 2/16/1960. Montgomery, Ala. (TLS) 1 p. MLKP-MBU: Box 4. 600216–001.

2/16/1960 Harrington, Donald (American Committee on Africa). Letter to Martin Luther King, Jr. 2/16/1960. New York, N.Y. (THLS) 1 p. MLKP-MBU. 600216–008.

2/16/1960 Thornton, Jim. Photo of Martin Luther King, Jr. touring F. W. Woolworth store. 2/16/1960. Durham, N.C. From: *Durham Herald-Sun*, 16 February 1960. (PPh) NcDurDHS. 600216–013.

2/17/1960 Fauntroy, Walter E. (New Bethel Baptist Church). Letter to Ralph Abernathy. 2/17/1960. Washington, D.C. (TLc) 1 p. (Copy to King.) MLKP-MBU: Box 25. 600217–006.

2/17/1960 King, Martin Luther, Jr. Statement on indictment by grand jury of Montgomery County. 2/17/1960. Atlanta, Ga. (TAD) 1 p. CSKC. 600217–009.

2/17/1960 Associated Press. Photo of Martin Luther King, Jr., Leroy Stynchcombe, Alfred Daniel King, Ralph Grimes and Martin Luther King. 2/17/1960. Fulton County, Ala. (Ph) 1 p. NNAPWW. 600217–013.

2/18/1960 Dobbs, John Wesley (Freemasons. Prince Hall Grand Lodge). Letter to Martin Luther King, Jr. 2/18/1960. Atlanta, Ga. (ALS) 2 pp. MLKP-MBU: Box 23A. 600218–000.

2/18/1960 Wynn, Daniel W. (Tuskegee Institute). Letter to Martin Luther King, Jr. 2/18/1960. Tuskegee, Ala. (TLS) 1 p. MLKP-MBU: Box 74. 600218–002.

2/18/1960 King, Martin Luther, Jr. (Ebenezer Baptist Church). Letter to L. Harold (Lotan Harold) DeWolf. 2/18/1960. Atlanta, Ga. (TLS) 1 p. OGCP-MBU. 600218–003.

2/18/1960 Boyte, Harry Chatten (Greater Atlanta Council on Human Relations). Letter to Martin Luther King, Jr. 2/18/1960. Atlanta, Ga. (TLS) 1 p. MLKP-MBU: Box 20. 600218–005.

2/18/1960 King, Martin Luther, Jr. Letter to O. Clay Maxwell. 2/18/1960. [*Atlanta, Ga.*] (TLc) 1 p. MLKP-MBU: Box 31. 600218–006.

2/18/1960 Moore, Douglas E. Letter to Martin Luther King, Jr. 2/18/1960. Durham, N.C. (TLS) 2 pp. (Includes enclosure.) MLKP-MBU: Box 31. 600218–007.

2/18/1960 Duckett, Alfred (Alfred Duckett Associates). Letter to Martin Luther King, Jr. 2/18/1960. New York, N.Y. (TLS) 2 pp. (Contains enclosure 600218–017.) MLKP-MBU: Box 52A. 600218–013.

2/18/1960 "Martin Luther King Column" V [*2/18/1960*]. (TDd) 3 pp. (Enclosed in 600218–013.) CSKC: Sermon file. 600218–017.

2/19/1960 Randolph, A. Philip (Asa Philip) (Brotherhood of Sleeping Car Porters and Maids). Telegram to Martin Luther King, Jr. 2/19/1960. (PWSr) 2 pp. APRC-DLC. 600219–000.

2/19/1960 [*SCLC*]. Memo regarding retreat meeting at Tuskegee Institute. 2/19/1960. (TL) 1 p. MLKP-MBU: Box 71A. 600219–001.

2/19/1960 Taylor, Gardner C. Telegram to Martin Luther King, Jr. [*2/19/1960*]. Brooklyn, N.Y. (PWSr) 1 p. MLKP-MBU. 600219–007.

2/20/1960 Lewanika, Godwin A. Mbikusita. Letter to Martin Luther King, Jr. 2/20/1960. Kitwe, Northern Rhodesia. (TALS) 1 p. MLKP-MBU: Box 26. 600220–004.

2/21/1960 Burks, Mary Fair. Telegram to Martin Luther King, Jr. and Coretta Scott King. [*2/21/1960*]. Montgomery, Ala. (PHWSr) 1 p. MLKP-MBU: Box 20. 600221–002.

2/21/1960 Chicago Sunday Evening Club. Program, "Order of service." 2/21/1960. Chicago, Ill. (PD) 4 pp. MLKJP-GAMK: Box 123A. 600221–004.

2/21/1960 Quinn Chapel, The Original Forty Club, and Alpha Phi Alpha Fraternity, Inc. Announcement, "A special service of worship in observance of Brotherhood Week." 2/21/1960. Chicago, Ill. (THDc) 1 p. (Contains enclosure 600221–006.) AJC-ICHi: Box 40. 600221–005.

2/21/1960 Quinn Chapel. "The Archibald J. (Archibald James) Carey award." 2/21/1960. (TDc) 1 p. (Enclosed in 600221–005.) AJC-ICHi: Box 40. 600221–006.

2/22/1960 Smith, Kelly Miller (First Baptist Church). Telegram to Martin Luther King, Jr. 2/22/1960. Nashville, Tenn. (PHWSr) 1 p. MLKP-MBU: Box 73A. 600222–006.

2/22/1960 Gay, Eustace (*Philadelphia Tribune*). Letter to Martin Luther King, Jr. 2/22/1960. Philadelphia, Pa. (TLS) 1 p. (Enclosed in 600317–011.) MLKP-MBU: Box 68. 600222–008.

2/24/1960 Smiley, Glenn E. (FOR). Letter to Members and Friends of FOR in North and South Carolina. 2/24/1960. Nyack, N.Y. (TLS) 1 p. FORP-PSC-P. 600224–000.

2/24/1960 Ballou, Maude L. Letter to Donald Harrington. 2/24/1960. [*Atlanta, Ga.*] (TLc) 1 p. MLKP-MBU: Box 19. 600224–002.

2/24/1960 Ballou, Maude L. Letter to Marvin Rich. 2/24/1960. [*Atlanta, Ga.*] (TLc) 1 p. MLKP-MBU: Box 23. 600224–009.

2/24/1960 King, Martin Luther, Jr. Letter to Alabama Bureau of Internal Revenue. 2/24/1960. [*Atlanta, Ga.*] (TLc) 1 p. MLKP-MBU: Box 4. 600224–012.

2/24/1960 King, Martin Luther, Jr. Statement on student sit-ins. [*2/24/1960*]. (F) 1.1 min. WSBA-GU. 600224–018.

2/25/1960 King, Martin Luther, Jr. Letter to L. Venchael Booth. 2/25/1960. [*Atlanta, Ga.*] (TLc) 1 p. MLKP-MBU: Box 47A. 600225–003.

2/25/1960 King, Martin Luther, Jr. Letter to Harry Boyte. 2/25/1960. [*Atlanta, Ga.*] (TLc) 1 p. MLKP-MBU: Box 20. 600225–004.

2/25/1960 Southern Regional Council. "The Student Protest Movement, Winter 1960." 2/25/1960. (TD) 20 pp. CSKC: Sermon file. 600225–006.

2/25/1960 King, Martin Luther, Jr. Letter to Kivie Kaplan. 2/25/1960. [*Atlanta, Ga.*] (TLc) 1 p. MLKP-MBU: Box 29. 600225–007.

2/27/1960 Polier, Justine Wise. Letter to Martin Luther King, Jr. 2/27/1960. New York, N.Y. (TLS) 1 p. MLKP-MBU: Box 33. 600227–000.

2/27/1960 The Church Federation of Los Angeles. Program, "Christian responsibility in a nuclear space age." 2/27/1960. Los Angeles, Calif. (TD) 3 pp. CSKCH. 600227–001.

2/28/1960 Friendship Baptist Church. Program, Sunday services. 2/28/1960. Pasadena, Calif. (TD) 4 pp. MLKP-MBU. 600228–000.

2/28/1960 King, Martin Luther, Jr. "The Three Dimensions of a Complete Life," Sermon delivered at Friendship Baptist Church. [*2/28/1960*]. Pasadena, Calif. (At) 30 min. (1 sound cassette: analog.) JBC. 600228–001.

2/29/1960 King, Martin Luther, Jr. "Integration: Full-Scale Assault." 2/29/1960. New York, N.Y. From: *Newsweek,* 29 February 1960, pp. 24–25. (PD) 2 pp. 600229–008.

2/29/1960 Rodrigues, Deolinda. Letter to Martin Luther King, Jr. 2/29/1960. São Paolo, Brazil (ALS) 2 pp. MLKP-MBU: Box 26. 600229–010.

2/29/1960 King, Martin Luther, Jr., Defendant. "Capias," *State of Alabama v. Martin Luther King, Jr.* 2/29/1960. Montgomery, Ala. (THFmS) 2 pp. CMCR-AMC. 600229–013.

3/1960 King, Martin Luther, Jr., and Ella J. Baker (SCLC). Announcement, "Youth leadership meeting, Shaw University, Raleigh, N.C. 4/15/1960–4/17/1960." [*3/1960*]. Atlanta, Ga. (TD) 1 p. MLKP-MBU: Box 5. 600300–012.

1/1960–3/1960 King, Martin Luther, Jr. "Nonviolence and Racial Justice." 1/1960–3/1960. From: *Current Religious Thought* (Winter 1960): 1. Nashville, Tenn. (PD) 1 p. MLKJP-GAMK. 600300–014.

3/1/1960 Granger, Lester B. (Lester Blackwell) (National Urban League). Letter to Martin Luther King, Jr. 3/1/1960. New York, N.Y. (TLS) 1 p. MLKP-MBU: Box 27. 600301–003.

3/1/1960 Waring, Elizabeth. Letter to Martin Luther King, Jr. 3/1/1960. New York, N.Y. (ALS) 1 p. MLKP-MBU: Box 74. 600301–007.

3/2/1960 Gottlieb, Edward P. (War Resisters League). Letter to Martin Luther King, Jr. 3/2/1960. New York, N.Y. (TLS) 2 pp. MLKP-MBU: Box 27. 600302–001.

3/2/1960 Dexter Avenue Baptist Church. *Dexter Echo* 4, no. 7. 3/2/1960. Montgomery, Ala. (TD) 6 pp. CSKC. 600302–002.

3/2/1960 Gottlieb, Edward P. (War Resisters League). Letter to A. Philip (Asa Philip) Randolph. 3/2/1960. New York, N.Y. (TLS) 2 pp. BRP-DLC. 600302–003.

3/3/1960 Rustin, Bayard (SCLC). Letter to Martin Luther King, Jr. 3/3/1960. Atlanta, Ga. (TALS) 2 pp. MLKP-MBU: Box 4. 600303–001.

3/3/1960 Committee to Defend Martin Luther King and the Struggle for Freedom in the South. Press release, "Statement on the indictment of Martin Luther King, Jr." 3/3/1960. New York, N.Y. (TD) 2 pp. APRC-DLC. 600303–002.

3/3/1960 Committee to Defend Martin Luther King and the Struggle for Freedom in the South. Press release, Committee to undertake fundraising campaign. 3/3/1960. New York, N.Y. (TD) 2 pp. CAABP-WHi. 600303–007.

3/3/1960 Davis, William. Letter to Martin Luther King, Jr. 3/3/1960. Chuckatuck, Va. (ALS) 3 pp. MLKP-MBU: Box 23A. 600303–008.

3/3/1960 Donaldson, James W. Letter to Martin Luther King, Jr. 3/3/1960. Lake Charles, La. (TLc) 4 pp. MLKP-MBU: Box 30. 600303–011.

3/4/1960 Burrows, Ruby Nell (Talladega College). Letter to Martin Luther King, Jr. 3/4/1960. Talladega, Ala. (TLS) 2 pp. MLKP-MBU: Box 20. 600304–000.

3/4/1960 Hendricks, Lola H. (Alabama Christian Movement for Human Rights (ACMHR)). Letter to Martin Luther King, Jr. 3/4/1960. Birmingham, Ala. (TLS) 1 p. MLKP-MBU: Box 72. 600304–001.

3/4/1960 King, Martin Luther, Jr. and Bernard S. Lee. Statement delivered to Alabama State College students at Beulah Baptist Church. [*3/4/1960*]. [*Montgomery, Ala.*] (F) 2.2 min. CLU-FT. 600304–008.

3/5/1960 King, Martin Luther, Jr. Letter to Hubert T. Delany. 3/5/1960. [*Atlanta, Ga.*] (TLc) 1 p. MLKP-MBU: Box 4. 600305–001.

3/5/1960 King, Martin Luther, Jr. Letter to E. A. Erwin. 3/5/1960. [*Atlanta, Ga.*] (TLc) 1 p. MLKP-MBU: Box 4. 600305–002.

3/6/1960 Chalmers, Allan Knight (Boston University). Letter to Martin Luther King, Jr. 3/6/1960. Boston, Mass. (TALS) 3 pp. MLKP-MBU: Box 22. 600306–000.

3/7/1960 Levison, Stanley D. (Committee to Defend Martin Luther King and the Struggle for Freedom in the South). Minutes of board meeting. 3/7/1960. New York, N.Y. (TD) 2 pp. APRC-DLC. 600307–002.

3/7/1960 Delany, Hubert T. Letter to Robert Ming. 3/7/1960. New York, N.Y. (TLS) 3 pp. (Enclosed in 600307–006.) MLKP-MBU: Box 4. 600307–005.

3/7/1960 Delany, Hubert T. Letter to Martin Luther King, Jr. 3/7/1960. New York, N.Y. (TLS) 1 p. (Contains enclosure 600307–005.) MLKP-MBU: Box 4. 600307–006.

3/8/1960 Houston, Hattie M. (U.S. Internal Revenue Service). Letter to Martin Luther King, Jr. 3/8/1960. Birmingham, Ala. (TLS) 1 p. MLKP-MBU. 600308–001.

3/8/1960 King, Martin Luther, Jr. Telegram to Wyatt Tee Walker. 3/8/1960. [*Atlanta, Ga.*] (THWc) 1 p. MLKP-MBU: Box 74. 600308–002.

3/9/1960 King, Martin Luther, Jr. Letter to Harry Belafonte. 3/9/1960. [*Atlanta, Ga.*] (TLc) 1 p. (Contains enclosure 600309–003.) MLKP-MBU: Box 21. 600309–002.

3/9/1960 Chronology of arrests and attacks. [*3/9/1960*]. (TD) 1 p. (Enclosed in 600309-002.) MLKP-MBU: Box 21. 600309-003.

3/9/1960 Dombrowski, James A. (James Anderson) (Southern Conference Educational Fund, Inc.). Letter to Martin Luther King, Jr. 3/9/1960. New Orleans, La. (TLS) 2 pp. MLKP-MBU: Box 69. 600309-006.

3/9/1960 King, Martin Luther, Jr. Telegram to Clarence Pickett. 3/9/1960. [*Atlanta, Ga.*] (TLc) 1 p. MLKP-MBU: Box 71. 600309-008.

3/10/1960 Morgan, Gerald D. (U.S. White House). Memo to William P. (William Pierce) Rogers. 3/10/1960. (TLc) 1 p. WCFG-KAbE: Box 913. 600310-002.

3/10/1960 King, Martin Luther, Jr. Letter to Mary Fair Burks. 3/10/1960. [*Atlanta, Ga.*] (TLc) 1 p. MLKP-MBU: Box 20. 600310-004.

3/10/1960 King, Martin Luther, Jr. Telegram to Jefferson Underwood and Olean Underwood. 3/10/1960. [*Atlanta, Ga.*] (TWc) 1 p. MLKP-MBU: Box 73. 600310-006.

3/10/1960 Randolph, A. Philip (Asa Philip). Telegram to Dwight D. (Dwight David) Eisenhower. 3/10/1960. New York, N.Y. (PWSr) 2 pp. DDEP-KAbE: Box 913. 600310-008.

3/11/1960 Reuther, Walter (International Union, United Automobile Workers of America (CIO)). Telegram to Dwight D. (Dwight David) Eisenhower. 3/11/1960. Detroit, Mich. (PWSr) 3 pp. DDEP-KAbE. 600311-008.

3/13/1960 [*DeWolf, L. Harold (Lotan Harold)*]. Letter to Martin Luther King, Jr. 3/13/1960. (TLc) 1 p. OGCP-MBU. 600313-001.

3/13/1960 Bush, Prescott (U.S. Congress. Senate). Letter to Martin Luther King, Jr. 3/13/1960. Greenwich, Conn. (ALS) 2 pp. MLKP-MBU: Box 8. 600313-002.

3/14/1960 King, Martin Luther, Jr. Letter to Corliss Lamont and Margaret Hayes Irish. 3/14/1960. [*Atlanta, Ga.*] (TLc) 1 p. MLKP-MBU: Box 29A. 600314-002.

3/14/1960 Scheinman, William X. (Arnav Aircraft Associates, Inc.). Letter to Martin Luther King, Jr. 3/14/1960. Little Ferry, N.J. (TLS) 2 pp. MLKP-MBU: Box 70. 600314-003.

3/15/1960 King, Martin Luther, Jr. Letter to P. J. Ellis. 3/15/1960. [*Atlanta, Ga.*] (TLc) 1 p. MLKP-MBU: Box 24. 600315-002.

3/15/1960 King, Martin Luther, Jr. Letter to Yechiael Lander. 3/15/1960. [*Atlanta, Ga.*] (TLc) 1 p. MLKP-MBU: Box 46. 600315-008.

3/15/1960 Butler, George O. (President's Committee on Government Contracts). Letter to Martin Luther King, Jr. 3/15/1960. Washington, D.C. (TLS) 2 pp. MLKP-MBU: Box 74. 600315-010.

3/15/1960 [*National Committee for a Sane Nuclear Policy (U.S.)*]. "Security through arms control." [*3/15/1960*]. New York, N.Y. (TD) 4 pp. MLKP-MBU: Box 71. 600315-011.

3/15/1960 King, Martin Luther, Jr. Letter to H. B. Charles. 3/15/1960. [*Atlanta, Ga.*] (TLc) 1 p. MLKP-MBU: Box 22. 600315-015.

3/15/1960 King, Martin Luther, Jr. Letter to Archibald James Carey. 3/15/1960. [*Atlanta, Ga.*] (TLc) 1 p. MLKP-MBU: Box 22. 600315-016.

3/16/1960 Hassler, Alfred (FOR). Letter to Martin Luther King, Jr. 3/16/1960. Nyack, N.Y. (TLS) 2 pp. FORP-PSC-P. 600316-001.

3/17/1960 King, Martin Luther, Jr. (SCLC). Telegram to Dwight D. (Dwight David) Eisenhower. 3/17/1960. Atlanta, Ga. (PHWSr) 4 pp. WCFG-KAbE. 600317-001.

3/17/1960 Morgan, Gerald D. (U.S. White House). Letter to Martin Luther King, Jr. 3/17/1960. Washington, D.C. (TLS) 1 p. MLKP-MBU: Box 74. 600317-002.

3/17/1960 King, Martin Luther, Jr. (SCLC). Draft, Telegram to Dwight D. (Dwight David) Eisenhower. 3/17/1960. [*Atlanta, Ga.*] (TAHWd) 1 p. MLKP-MBU: Box 74. 600317-005.

3/17/1960 King, Martin Luther, Jr. Letter to Robert Dishman. 3/17/1960. [*Atlanta, Ga.*] (TLc) 1 p. MLKP-MBU: Box 23A. 600317-007.

3/17/1960 King, Martin Luther, Jr. Letter to Bayard Rustin. 3/17/1960. [*Atlanta, Ga.*] (TLc) 1 p. MLKP-MBU: Box 68. 600317-010.

3/17/1960 King, Martin Luther, Jr. Letter to Bayard Rustin. 3/17/1960. [*Atlanta, Ga.*] (TLc) 1 p. (Contains enclosure 600222-008.) MLKP-MBU: Box 68. 600317-011.

3/17/1960 Morgan, Gerald D. (U.S. White House). Letter to A. Philip (Asa Philip) Randolph. 3/17/1960. (THLc) 1 p. WCFG-KAbE: Box 913. 600317-013.

3/19/1960 Niebuhr, Reinhold. Form letter to Friend. 3/19/1960. (TLc) 2 pp. (Includes enclosure.) MLKP-MBU: Box 27A. 600319-000.

3/20/1960 Tabernacle Baptist Church. Program, Sunday services. 3/20/1960. Detroit, Mich. (TD) 6 pp. CSKC. 600320-002.

3/21/1960 Nesbitt, R. D. (Dexter Avenue Baptist Church). Letter to Martin Luther King, Jr. 3/21/1960. Montgomery, Ala. (TALS) 1 p. MLKP-MBU: Box 32. 600321–002.

3/21/1960 King, Martin Luther, Jr. Letter to Elizabeth Waring. 3/21/1960. [*Atlanta, Ga.*] (TLc) 1 p. MLKP-MBU: Box 74. 600321–009.

3/21/1960 King, Martin Luther, Jr. Telegram to Morris H. Rubin. 3/21/1960. Atlanta, Ga. (PHWSr) 1 p. PP-WHi. 600321–015.

3/21/1960 Reddick, Lawrence Dunbar. Notes, Meeting with Martin Luther King, Jr. 3/21/1960. (AD) 8 pp. LDRP-NN-Sc. 600321–017.

3/22/1960 Dixon, Rebecca. Letter to Martin Luther King, Jr. 3/22/1960. Montgomery, Ala. (ALS) 4 pp. MLKP-MBU: Box 23A. 600322–002.

3/22/1960 Barnett, Claude (Associated Negro Press). Telegram to Martin Luther King, Jr. 3/22/1960. Chicago, Ill. (PWSr) 1 p. MLKP-MBU: Box 35. 600322–006.

3/23/1960 Clark, Septima Poinsette (Highlander Folk School). Letter to Martin Luther King, Jr. 3/23/1960. Monteagle, Tenn. (TLS) 1 p. MLKP-MBU: Box 27A. 600323–006.

3/24/1960 Proctor, Hilda S. Letter to Martin Luther King, Jr. 3/24/1960. Los Angeles, Calif. (TLS) 1 p. MLKP-MBU: Box 33A. 600324–001.

3/24/1960 Gray, William H. (William Herbert). Letter to Martin Luther King, Jr. 3/24/1960. Philadelphia, Pa. (TLS) 1 p. MLKP-MBU: Box 27. 600324–003.

3/24/1960 Gray, William H. (William Herbert). Letter to Martin Luther King, Jr. 3/24/1960. (TLS) 1 p. MLKP-MBU: Box 27. 600324–004.

3/25/1960 King, Martin Luther, Jr. Letter to Marvin Robinson. 3/25/1960. [*Atlanta, Ga.*] (TLc) 1 p. MLKP-MBU: Box 68. 600325–004.

3/25/1960 King, Martin Luther, Jr. Letter to Maurice A. Dawkins. 3/25/1960. [*Atlanta, Ga.*] (TLc) 1 p. MLKP-MBU. 600325–005.

3/25/1960 Baker, Ella J. (SCLC). Form letter to Crusader for freedom. 3/25/1960. Atlanta, Ga. (TLS) 1 p. EJBC-NN-Sc. 600325–009.

3/28/1960 O'Dell, Jack H. (Committee to Defend Martin Luther King and the Struggle for Freedom in the South). Minutes of board meeting. 3/28/1960. New York, N.Y. (TD) 2 pp. AJMP-PSC-P. 600328–001.

3/28/1960 Haynes, Roland (Clark College). Letter to Martin Luther King, Jr. and Coretta Scott King. 3/28/1960. Atlanta, Ga. (TLS) 1 p. MLKP-MBU. 600328–004.

3/28/1960 Baker, Ella J. (SCLC). "Ninety years-long enough!" 3/28/1960. Atlanta, Ga. (TDS) 2 pp. MLKP-MBU: Box 35. 600328–005.

3/28/1960 King, Martin Luther, Jr. Letter to Ernest Gordon. 3/28/1960. [*Atlanta, Ga.*] (TLc) 1 p. MLKP-MBU. Box 45. 600328–007.

3/28/1960 Associated Negro Press. Press release, "World leaders send message to ANP Condemning ruthless slaughter of South African natives." 3/28/1960. (TD) 1 p. CABP-ICHi. 600328–009.

3/29/1960 Committee to Defend Martin Luther King and the Struggle for Freedom in the South. "Heed Their Rising Voices." 3/29/1960. New York, N.Y. From: *New York Times*, 29 March 1960. (PD) 1 p. 600329–011.

3/30/1960 Shuttlesworth, Fred L., and N. H. Smith (Alabama Christian Movement for Human Rights (ACMHR)). Press release, Statement in support of lunch counter demonstrations. 3/30/1960. (TDS) 2 pp. FLSC-GAMK: Box 1. 600330–006.

3/30/1960 Baker, Ella J. (SCLC). Telegram to Richard M. (Richard Milhous) Nixon. 3/30/1960. Atlanta, Ga. (TAWc) 1 p. (Enclosed in 600401–016.) WMC-OrU: Box 23. 600330–009.

3/31/1960 Burks, Mary Fair. Letter to Martin Luther King, Jr. 3/31/1960. Montgomery, Ala. (ALS) 2 pp. MLKP-MBU: Box 20. 600331–002.

4/1960 Abernathy, Ralph, Harry Belafonte, A. Philip (Asa Philip) Randolph, Bernard S. Lee, Nat King Cole, and Fred L. Shuttlesworth (Committee to Defend Martin Luther King and the Struggle for Freedom in the South). Form letter to Friend. 4/1960. New York, N.Y. (TLS) 2 pp. ACLUC-NjP. 600400–000.

4/1960 Stephens, Patricia. "Letter from a Jailed Student." 4/1960. New York, N.Y. From: *CORE-lator,* April 1960, pp. 1–2. (PD) 2 pp. 600400–002.

3/1960–4/1960 SCLC. Draft, Appeal letter. [*3/1960–4/1960*]. (TDd) 1 p. (600400–004 on verso.) MLKP-MBU: Box 19. 600400–003.

3/1960–4/1960 King, Martin Luther, Jr. Outline, Appeal for funds. [*3/1960–4/1960*]. [*Atlanta, Ga.*] (AD) 1 p. (Verso of 600400–003.) MLKP-MBU: Box 19. 600400–004.

4/1960 Davis, Benjamin J. (Benjamin Jefferson). Letter to Martin Luther King, Jr. [*4/1960*]. New York, N.Y. (TLS) 2 pp. MLKP-MBU: Box 23A. 600400–008.

4/1960 King, Martin Luther, Jr. Telegram to Norman Cousins. [*4/1960*]. [*Atlanta, Ga.*] (TWc) 1 p. MLKP-MBU: Box 71. 600400–011.

4/1960 King, Martin Luther, Jr. Notes on sit-ins, the presidential election, and Harry S. Truman. [*4/1960*]. [*Atlanta, Ga.*] (AD) 13 pp. CSKC: Sermon file. 600400–017.

4/1960 [*Reddick, Lawrence Dunbar*]. "The Montgomery situation." (TD) 24 pp. LDRP-NN-Sc: Box 2. 600400–023.

4/1960 King, Coretta Scott. Interview by Benita Darby. [*4/1960*]. Atlanta, Ga. (At) 7.8 min. (1 sound cassette: analog.) MLK/OH-GAMK. 600400–025.

4/1/1960 DeWolf, L. Harold (Lotan Harold) (Boston University). Letter to Martin Luther King, Jr. and Coretta Scott King. 4/1/1960. Boston, Mass. (TAHLS) 2 pp. (Marginal comments by King.) MLKP-MBU: Box 23A. 600401–004.

4/1/1960 Announcement, Martin Luther King, Jr. and Bernard S. Lee to speak at protest rally at Salem Methodist Church. 4/1/1960. (TD) 1 p. APRC-DLC. 600401–014.

4/1/1960 Baker, Ella J. (SCLC). Letter to Wayne Morse. 4/1/1960. Atlanta, Ga. (TLS) 1 p. (Contains enclosure 600330–009.) WMC-OrU: Box 23. 600401–016.

4/2/1960 Lawson, Earl Wesley (Emanual Baptist Church). Letter to Martin Luther King, Jr. [*4/2/1960*]. Malden, Mass. (ALS) 1 p. MLKP-MBU: Box 7. 600402–002.

4/3/1960 Ebenezer Baptist Church. Program, Sunday services. 4/3/1960. Atlanta, Ga. (TD) 4 pp. MLKJP-GAMK: Vault Box 9. 600403–000.

4/3/1960 King, Martin Luther, Jr. Love in Action, Sermon outline. [*4/3/1960*]. [*Atlanta, Ga.*] (ADf) 2 pp. MLKJP-GAMK: Box 123. 600403–001.

4/4/1960 King, Martin Luther, Jr. Letter to Morris H. Rubin. 4/4/1960. [*Atlanta, Ga.*] (TLc) 1 p. MLKP-MBU: Box 4. 600404–003.

4/4/1960 Shuttlesworth, Fred L. (Bethel Baptist Church). Letter to William P. (William Pierce) Rogers. 4/4/1960. Birmingham, Ala. (TLS) 2 pp. (Enclosed in 600414–005.) GRDJ-DNA. 600404–013.

4/5/1960 SCLC. Press release, Telegrams sent to national leaders on voting rights; Northern students registered for conference. 4/5/1960. Atlanta, Ga. (THD) 3 pp. EJBC-NN-Sc. 600405–009.

4/6/1960 Gentile, Dolores (Marie Rodell and Joan Daves, Inc.). Letter to Martin Luther King, Jr. 4/6/1960. (TLS) 1 p. MLKP-MBU: Box 6. 600406–001.

4/6/1960 King, Martin Luther, Jr. (Ebenezer Baptist Church). Letter to Lester B. (Lester Blackwell) Granger. 4/6/1960. Atlanta, Ga. (TLS) 1 p. NULR-DLC. 600406–006.

4/6/1960 King, Martin Luther, Jr. Letter to Justus M. Kitonga. 4/6/1960. Atlanta, Ga. (TLc) 2 pp. MLKP-MBU: Box 26. 600406–008.

4/7/1960 Gregg, Richard Bartlett. Letter to Martin Luther King, Jr. 4/7/1960. Chester, N.Y. (TALS) 1 p. MLKP-MBU: Box 27. 600407–012.

4/7/1960 Ballou, Maude L. Letter to Harold E. Fey. 4/7/1960. [*Atlanta, Ga.*] (TLc) 1 p. (Contains enclosure 600407–015.) MLKP-MBU: Box 89. 600407–014.

4/7/1960 King, Martin Luther, Jr. "How My Mind Has Changed in the Last Decade." 4/7/1960. [*Atlanta, Ga.*] (THD) 10 pp. (Enclosed in 600407–014.) MLKP-MBU: Box 89. 600407–015.

4/8/1960 Beer, Samuel H., Robert R. Nathan, and Reinhold Niebuhr (Americans for Democratic Action). Letter to Martin Luther King, Jr. 4/8/1960. Washington, D.C. (THLc) 1 p. (Contains enclosure 600408–004. Marginal comments by King.) MLKP-MBU: Box 18. 600408–003.

4/8/1960 Beer, Samuel H., Robert R. Nathan, and Reinhold Niebuhr (Americans for Democratic Action). Letter to Christian Herter. [*4/8/1960*]. (TLc) 1 p. (Enclosed in 600408–003.) MLKP-MBU: Box 18. 600408–004.

4/8/1960 King, Martin Luther, Jr. Telegram to Irving I. Turner. 4/8/1960. [*Atlanta, Ga.*] (PWc) 1 p. MLKP-MBU: Box 73A. 600408–008.

4/8/1960 Baker, Ella J. (SCLC). Letter to Student leaders. 4/8/1960. Atlanta, Ga. (TLc) 1 p. CSKC: Sermon file. 600408–011.

4/8/1960 "Summary of major provisions of Civil Rights Act of 1960." 4/8/1960. (TD) 1 p. (Enclosed in 600421–004, pp. 439–440 in this volume.) MLKP-MBU. 600408–013.

4/8/1960 Farmer, James. Memo to Roy Wilkins. 4/8/1960. (TLc) 1 p. DJG-GEU. 600408–014.

4/10/1960 Spelman College. Program, "Founders Day, seventy-ninth anniversary." 4/10/1960. Atlanta, Ga. (PD) 4 pp. CSKC. 600410–000.

4/10/1960 King, Martin Luther, Jr. "Founders Day address." [*4/10/1960*]. Atlanta, Ga. (TD) 13 pp. CSKC: Sermon file. 600410–001.

4/10/1960 King, Martin Luther, Jr. Outline, Keep Moving From This Mountain, Founders

Day address. [*4/10/1960*]. [*Atlanta, Ga.*] (AD) 3 pp. CSKC: Sermon file. 600410–002.

4/11/1960 Morgan, Gerald D. (U.S. White House). Letter to Ralph Abernathy. 4/11/1960. (THLc) 1 p. WCFG-KAbE. 600411–003.

4/11/1960 King, Martin Luther, Jr., Joseph E. Lowery, Kelly Miller Smith, C. Kenzie Steele, and Ralph Abernathy (SCLC). Telegram to William P. (William Pierce) Rogers. 4/11/1960. Atlanta, Ga. (PWc) 1 p. GRDJ-DNA. 600411–004.

4/11/1960 Ryan, Joseph M. F., and John L. Murphy. (U.S. Dept. of Justice). Letter to Fred L. Shuttlesworth. 4/11/1960. (THLc) 1 p. (Enclosed in 600414–005.) GRDJ-DNA. 600411–006.

4/11/1960 Baker, Ella J. (SCLC). Memo to *Jet*. 4/11/1960. (TL) 1 p. EJBC-NN-Sc. 600411–007.

4/12/1960 Baker, Ella J. (SCLC). Letter to Martin Luther King, Jr. 4/12/1960. Atlanta, Ga. (TLS) 1 p. MLKP-MBU: Box 71A. 600412–005.

4/12/1960 Reddick, Lawrence Dunbar (Alabama State College). Letter to H. Councill (Harper Councill) Trenholm. 4/12/1960. Montgomery, Ala. (TLc) 2 pp. LDRP-NN-Sc: Box 2. 600412–010.

4/13/1960 King, Martin Luther, Jr. Letter to Ruby Nell Burrows. 4/13/1960. [*Atlanta, Ga.*] (TLc) 2 pp. MLKP-MBU: Box 20. 600413–000.

4/13/1960 Susskind, David (Talent Associates Ltd.). Letter to Martin Luther King, Jr. 4/13/1960. New York, N.Y. (THLS) 1 p. MLKP-MBU: Box 33. 600413–004.

4/13/1960 King, Martin Luther, Jr. Letter to Ernestine Ritter. 4/13/1960. [*Atlanta, Ga.*] (TLc) 2 pp. MLKP-MBU: Box 68. 600413–010.

4/13/1960 Reddick, Lawrence Dunbar (Alabama State College). Letter to Martin Luther King, Jr. 4/13/1960. Montgomery, Ala. (TLS) 1 p. MLKP-MBU: Box 68. 600413–011.

4/13/1960 King, Martin Luther, Jr. Pilgrimage to Nonviolence. [*4/13/1960*]. (TADd) 10 pp. (Verso of 570221–008.) CSKC: Sermon file. 600413–014.

4/13/1960 King, Martin Luther, Jr., and A. Philip (Asa Philip) Randolph. Telegram to Russell R. Lasley. 4/13/1960. New York, N.Y. (PHWSr) 1 p. UPWP-WHi: Box 391. 600413–022.

4/13/1960 King, Martin Luther, Jr. Draft, "How My Mind Has Changed in the Last Decade." [*4/13/1960*]. (ADd) 22 pp. CSKC: Sermon file. 600413–024.

4/13/1960 King, Martin Luther, Jr. Notes, "How My Mind Has Changed" series. [*4/13/1960*]. (AD) 8 pp. CSKC: Sermon file. 600413–025.

4/13/1960 Rubin, Morris H. Letter to Martin Luther King, Jr. 4/13/1960. (TLc) 1 p. PP-WHi. 600413–027.

4/14/1960 Ryan, Joseph M. F. (U.S. Dept. of Justice). Memo to J. Edgar Hoover. 4/14/1960. (TL) 1 p. (Contains enclosures 600411–006 & 600404–013.) GRDJ-DNA. 600414–005.

4/14/1960 Malin, Patrick Murphy (American Civil Liberties Union). Telegram to John Malcolm Patterson. 4/14/1960. New York, N.Y. (THWc) 1 p. MLKP-MBU. 600414–006.

4/14/1960 Rogers, T. Y. (Crozer Theological Seminary). Letter to Martin Luther King, Jr. 4/14/1960. Chester, Pa. (TALS) 1 p. MLKP-MBU: Box 68. 600414–007.

4/14/1960 King, Martin Luther, Jr. (SCLC). Telegram to Frank Stewart. 4/14/1960. Montgomery, Ala. (PWc) 2 pp. MLKP-MBU: Box 21A. 600414–009.

4/15/1960 Rustin, Bayard (SCLC). Letter to Martin Luther King, Jr. 4/15/1960. Atlanta, Ga. (TLS) 1 p. MLKP-MBU: Box 5. 600415–000.

4/16/1960 SCLC, and Raleigh Citizens Association. Program, "Mass meeting featuring Dr. Martin Luther King." 4/16/1960. Raleigh, N.C. (PD) 4 pp. MLKJP-GAMK: Box 123A. 600416–003.

4/15/1960–4/16/1960 Sochurek, Howard (Time Inc.). Photo of Martin Luther King, Jr. and members of SNCC. [*4/15/1960–4/16/1960*]. Raleigh, N.C. (Ph) 1 p. NNTI. 600416–004.

4/17/1960 King, Martin Luther, Jr. Interview on "Meet the Press." 4/17/1960. From: *The Proceedings of Meet the Press* 4 (17 April 1960): 1–12. Washington, D.C. (PHTv) RBOH-DHU. 600417–000.

4/17/1960 [*Lawson, James M.*]. "Statement of purpose." 4/17/1960. Raleigh, N.C. (TD) 1 p. SNCCP-GAMK. 600417–011.

4/15/1960–4/17/1960 Southwide Youth Leadership Conference. "Recommendations of the findings and recommendations committee." 4/15/1960–4/17/1960. Raleigh, N.C. (TD) 2 pp. SNCCP-GAMK. 600417–012.

4/17/1960 Americans for Democratic Action. Press release, "Liberals urge ambassador to

	South Africa be recalled for consultation—suspension of gold purchases." 4/17/1960. Washington, D.C. (TD) 3 pp. MLKJP-GAMK: Box 124. 600417–014.
4/18/1960	King, Martin Luther, Jr. Letter to R. D. (Robert D.) Nesbitt. 4/18/1960. [*Atlanta, Ga.*] (TLc) 1 p. MLKP-MBU: Box 32. 600418–007.
4/18/1960	Spivak, Lawrence E. (Lawrence Edmund) ("Meet the Press"). Letter to Martin Luther King, Jr. 4/18/1960. New York, N.Y. (TLS) 1 p. MLKP-MBU: Box 69. 600418–009.
4/18/1960	King, Martin Luther, Jr. Letter to George O. Butler. 4/18/1960. [*Atlanta, Ga.*] (TLc) 1 p. MLKP-MBU: Box 74. 600418–010.
4/18/1960	King, Martin Luther, Jr. Letter to Rebecca Dixon. 4/18/1960. [*Atlanta, Ga.*] (TLc) 2 pp. MLKP-MBU: Box 23A. 600418–011.
4/18/1960	King, Martin Luther, Jr. (Ebenezer Baptist Church). Letter to William X. Scheinman. 4/18/1960. Atlanta, Ga. (TLS) 1 p. WXSC. 600418–015.
4/18/1960	Moon, Henry Lee (NAACP). Memo to Roy Wilkins. 4/18/1960. (TL) 2 pp. NAACPP-DLC: Group III-A213. 600418–021.
4/18/1960	Wilkins, Roy. Memo to Gloster B. (Gloster Bryant) Current, James Farmer, Henry Lee Moon, John A. Morsell, Herbert Wright, and Herbert Hill. 4/18/1960. (TL) 1 p. NAACPP-DLC: Group III-A213. 600418–022.
4/19/1960	SCLC. "Delegates to Youth Leadership Conference, Shaw University, Raleigh, N.C. on 4/15/1960–4/17/1960." 4/19/1960. Atlanta, Ga. (TD) 9 pp. MLKP-MBU: Box 5. 600419–008.
4/20/1960	Brooks, John M. (NAACP). Memo to Roy Wilkins. 4/20/1960. Richmond, Va. (THL) 2 pp. NAACPP-DLC: Group III-A213. 600420–013.
4/20/1960	Wofford, Harris. Letter to Harry S. Truman. 4/20/1960. (TALc) 3 pp. MLKP-MBU: Box 73A. 600420–014.
4/20/1960	Tusiani, Joseph. Letter to Martin Luther King, Jr. 4/20/1960. New York, N.Y. (TALS) 1 p. MLKP-MBU: Box 72. 600420–015.
4/20/1960	Wofford, Harris. Letter to Martin Luther King, Jr. [*4/20/1960*]. (ALS) 1 p. (Written on 600420–014.) MLKP-MBU: Box 73A. 600420–017.
4/21/1960	Steele, C. Kenzie (Bethel Baptist Church). Letter to Martin Luther King, Jr. 4/21/1960. Tallahassee, Fla. (THLS) 1 p. MLKP-MBU: Box 49. 600421–003.
4/21/1960	Holbrook, Hal. Letter to Martin Luther King, Jr. 4/21/1960. New York, N.Y. (THLS) 1 p. MLKP-MBU: Box 30A. 600421–006.
4/21/1960	SCLC. "Summary, Delegates to Youth Leadership Conference, Shaw University, Raleigh, N.C." 4/21/1960. Atlanta, Ga. (TD) 6 pp. MLKP-MBU: Box 5. 600421–010.
4/22/1960	SCLC. "Northern students and observers to Southwide Youth Leadership Conference Shaw University, Raleigh, N.C." 4/22/1960. Atlanta, Ga. (TD) 4 pp. MLKP-MBU: Box 5. 600422–001.
4/22/1960	Delany, Hubert T. Letter to Fred D. Gray. 4/22/1960. New York, N.Y. (TLS) 4 pp. MLKP-MBU: Box 4. 600422–002.
4/22/1960	SCLC. Adult leaders to Southwide Youth Leadership Conference, Shaw University, Raleigh, N.C. on 4/15/1960–4/17/1960. 4/22/1960. Atlanta, Ga. (TD) 2 pp. MLKP-MBU: Box 5. 600422–007.
4/23/1960	King, Martin Luther, Jr. Letter to George J. Reed. 4/23/1960. [*Atlanta, Ga.*] (TLc) 1 p. BJDP-NN-Sc: Box 1. 600423–001.
4/23/1960	King, Martin Luther, Jr. Letter to Robert E. Hughes. 4/23/1960. [*Atlanta, Ga.*] (TLc) 2 pp. MLKP-MBU: Box 27A. 600423–005.
4/23/1960	Gbedemah, K. A. (Ghana Republic Inauguration Committee). Letter to Martin Luther King, Jr. 4/23/1960. Accra, Ghana. (THLS) 1 p. MLKP-MBU: Box 26. 600423–006.
4/23/1960	King, Martin Luther, Jr. Telegram to Hubert H. (Hubert Horatio) Humphrey. 4/23/1960. [*Atlanta, Ga.*] (PWc) 1 p. MLKP-MBU: Box 73A. 600423–007.
4/24/1960	King, Martin Luther, Jr. Form letter to Brother. 4/24/1960. Atlanta, Ga. (TLS) 1 p. MLKP-MBU: Box 19. 600424–000.
4/18/1960–4/24/1960	[*Wilkins, Roy*]. Letter to Martin Luther King, Jr. [*4/18/1960–4/24/1960*]. (TL) 6 pp. NAACPP-DLC: Group III-A175. 600424–006.
4/25/1960	Ryan, Joseph M. F. (U.S. Dept. of Justice). Letter to Martin Luther King, Jr. 4/25/1960. Washington, D.C. (TLS) 1 p. MLKP-MBU: Box 8. 600425–003.
4/25/1960	Reddick, Lawrence Dunbar (Alabama State College). Letter to Martin Luther King, Jr. 4/25/1960. Montgomery, Ala. (TLS) 1 p. MLKP-MBU: Box 68. 600425–004.
4/25/1960	Kaplan, Kivie. Letter to Martin Luther King, Jr. 4/25/1960. Boston, Mass. (TLS) 1 p. MLKP-MBU: Box 29. 600425–006.

4/25/1960 Wofford, Harris. Memo to Adlai E. (Adlai Ewing) Stevenson. 4/25/1960. (TD) 13 pp. (Enclosed in 600503–011.) MLKP-MBU: Box 59. 600425–009.

4/26/1960 King, Martin Luther, Jr. Letter to Lawrence E. (Lawrence Edmund) Spivak. 4/26/1960. [*Atlanta, Ga.*] (TLc) 1 p. MLKP-MBU: Box 69. 600426–002.

4/27/1960 King, Martin Luther, Jr. Draft, Suffering and Faith. [*4/27/1960*]. [*Atlanta, Ga.*] (AHDd) 6 pp. MLKP-MBU: Box 112. 600427–004.

4/27/1960 Photo of Martin Luther King, Jr. and Martin Luther King III in front of home after cross burning. 4/27/1960. Atlanta, Ga. (Ph) 1 p. UPIR-NNBETT. 600427–014.

4/29/1960 King, Martin Luther, Jr. Letter to Maxcine Young. 4/29/1960. [*Atlanta, Ga.*] (TLc) 2 pp. MLKP-MBU: Box 75. 600429–008.

4/29/1960 First Congregational Church. Program, "The immorality of racial segregation." 4/29/1960. Atlanta, Ga. (THD) 3 pp. CSKC. 600429–011.

5/1960 King, Martin Luther, Jr. Letter to Horace G. Robson. [*5/1960*]. [*Atlanta, Ga.*] (TLc) 1 p. MLKP-MBU: Box 68. 600500–007.

5/1960 Reddick, Lawrence Dunbar. Draft, The State vs. the Student. [*5/1960*]. (THDd) 14 pp. LDRP-NN-Sc: Box 2. 600500–010.

5/1960 Committee to Defend Martin Luther King and the Struggle for Freedom in the South. "The Burning Truth in the South by Martin Luther King." [*5/1960*]. New York, N.Y. (PD) 4 pp. (Reprint of 5/1960 *Progressive*.) MLKP-MBU: Box 85. 600500–017.

4/1960–5/1960 Randolph, A. Philip (Asa Philip), and Gardner C. Taylor (Committee to Defend Martin Luther King and the Struggle for Freedom in the South). Letter to Gentlemen. [*4/1960–5/1960*]. (TLc) 2 pp. APRC-DLC. 600500–019.

5/2/1960 King, Martin Luther, Jr. Letter to James M. Lawson. 5/2/1960. [*Atlanta, Ga.*] (TLc) 1 p. MLKP-MBU: Box 29A. 600502–005.

5/3/1960 King, Martin Luther, Jr. Telegram to Clarence Pickett. 5/3/1960. [*Atlanta, Ga.*] (TW) 1 p. MLKP-MBU: Box 33A. 600503–004.

5/3/1960 Hill, Herbert, and James Farmer. Memo to Roy Wilkins. 5/3/1960. (TL) 3 pp. NAACP-DLC: Group. 600503–010.

5/3/1960 Wofford, Harris (Notre Dame Law School). Letter to Martin Luther King, Jr. 5/3/1960. Notre Dame, Ind. (TLS) 1 p. (Contains enclosure 600425–009.) MLKP-MBU: Box 59. 600503–011.

5/3/1960 McDermott, William K. (U.S. Dept. of Justice). Letter to Martin Luther King, Jr. 5/3/1960. Washington, D.C. (TLSr) 1 p. SCLCR-GAMK: Box 74. 600503–012.

5/5/1960 Brazeal, Brailsford R. (Morehouse College). Letter to Martin Luther King, Jr. 5/5/1960. Atlanta, Ga. (TLS) 1 p. MLKP-MBU: Box 31. 600505–008.

5/5/1960 King, Martin Luther, Jr. Letter to Hal Holbrook. 5/5/1960. [*Atlanta, Ga.*] (TLc) 1 p. MLKP-MBU: Box 30A. 600505–011.

5/5/1960 Eisenstaedt, Alfred (*Life*). Photo of Martin Luther King, Jr. and Kenneth Kaunda. 5/5/1960. Atlanta, Ga. (Ph) 1 p. MLKP-MBU: Box 116. 600505–018.

5/5/1960 Ballou, Maude L. Letter to Joseph Tusiani. 5/5/1960. [*Atlanta, Ga.*] (TLc) 1 p. MLKJP-GAMK: Box 72. 600505–020.

5/6/1960 SCLC. "Persons asked to attend SNCC meeting 5/13/1960–5/14/1960." 5/6/1960. Atlanta, Ga. (TD) 2 pp. MLKP-MBU: Box 5. 600506–001.

5/6/1960 Mays, Benjamin Elijah (Morehouse College). Letter to Martin Luther King, Jr. 5/6/1960. Atlanta, Ga. (THLS) 1 p. MLKP-MBU: Box 31A. 600506–003.

5/6/1960 Kaplan, Kivie. Letter to Martin Luther King, Jr. 5/6/1960. Boston, Mass. (TLS) 1 p. MLKP-MBU: Box 29. 600506–006.

5/8/1960 Johns, Vernon. "Children, Have Ye Any Meat?" [*5/8/1960*]. (PD) 4 pp. (Enclosed in 600508–000, pp. 455–456 in this volume.) MLKP-MBU: Box 28A. 600508–001.

5/9/1960 The Carolina Forum. Announcement, "Rev. Martin Luther King speaking on 'The Struggle for Racial Justice,' Hill Hall." 5/9/1960. (PD) 1 p. MLKP-MBU: Box 37. 600509–003.

5/9/1960 Lawson, James M. (FOR). Letter to Roy Wilkins. 5/9/1960. Nashville, Tenn. (TLS) 2 pp. NAACPP-DLC: Group III-A213. 600509–006.

5/10/1960 Crowther, Frank H. (University of North Carolina). Letter to Martin Luther King, Jr. 5/10/1960. Chapel Hill, N.C. (TLS) 1 p. MLKP-MBU: Box 37. 600510–002.

5/10/1960 King, Martin Luther, Jr. (Ebenezer Baptist Church). Letter to L. Harold (Lotan Harold) DeWolf. 5/10/1960. Atlanta, Ga. (TLSr) 2 pp. OGCP-MBU. 600510–005.

5/10/1960 DeWolf, L. Harold (Lotan Harold) (Boston University). Letter to Martin Luther

King, Jr. 5/10/1960. Boston, Mass. (TALS) 2 pp. MLKP-MBU: Box 23A. 600510–006.

5/10/1960 Jones, Jameson (*Motive*). Letter to Martin Luther King, Jr. 5/10/1960. Nashville, Tenn. (TLS) 1 p. MLKP-MBU: Box 31. 600510–008.

5/10/1960 King, Martin Luther, Jr. Letter to C. Kenzie Steele. 5/10/1960. [*Atlanta, Ga.*] (TLc) 1 p. MLKP-MBU: Box 49. 600510–019.

5/10/1960–5/11/1960 SCLC. Agenda, "Conference on general organization." 5/10/1960–5/11/1960. New York, N.Y. (THD) 3 pp. (Marginal comments by King.) MLKP-MBU: Box 5. 600511–001.

5/12/1960 King, Martin Luther, Jr. Letter to Frank H. Crowther. 5/12/1960. [*Atlanta, Ga.*] (TLc) 1 p. MLKP-MBU: Box 37. 600512–004.

5/12/1960 "Martin Luther King Speaks to Overflow UNC Audience." 5/12/1960. Chapel Hill, N.C. From: *Chapel Hill Weekly*, 12 May 1960. (PD) 600512–007.

5/13/1960 Wilkins, Roy (NAACP). Letter to James M. Lawson. 5/13/1960. (TLc) 4 pp. (Enclosed in 600513–004.) NAACPP-DLC: Group III-A213. 600513–003.

5/13/1960 Wilkins, Roy (NAACP). Letter to Martin Luther King, Jr. 5/13/1960. (TLc) 1 p. (Contains enclosure 600513–003.) NAACPP-DLC: Group III-A213. 600513–004.

5/13/1960–5/14/1960 SNCC. "Report." 5/13/1960–5/14/1960. Atlanta, Ga. (TD) 11 pp. EJBC-NN-Sc. 600514–008.

5/17/1960 King, Martin Luther, Jr. Letter to Benjamin Elijah Mays. 5/17/1960. [*Atlanta, Ga.*] (TLc) 1 p. MLKP-MBU: Box 31. 600517–001.

5/18/1960 Mays, Benjamin Elijah (Morehouse College). Letter to Roy Wilkins. 5/18/1960. Atlanta, Ga. (TLc) 2 pp. MLKP-MBU: Box 31A. 600518–003.

5/18/1960 Robson, Horace G. (Congregational Board of Pastoral Supply). Letter to Martin Luther King, Jr. 5/18/1960. Boston, Mass. (TLSr) 1 p. MLKP-MBU: Box 68. 600518–013.

5/19/1960 Rustin, Bayard (SCLC). Letter to Martin Luther King, Jr. 5/19/1960. Atlanta, Ga. (TLc) 1 p. MLKP-MBU: Box 72. 600519–000.

5/19/1960 Wilkins, Roy (NAACP). Letter to Benjamin Elijah Mays. 5/19/1960. (TLc) 4 pp. NAACPP-DLC: Group III-A213. 600519–005.

5/20/1960 SCLC. Press release, "The slavery of silence—America's liability." 5/20/1960. Atlanta, Ga. (TD) 1 p. EJBC-NN-Sc. 600520–001.

5/20/1960 SNCC. Report, Meeting held at Atlanta University 5/13/1960–5/14/1960. 5/20/1960. Atlanta, Ga. (TD) 11 pp. EJBC-NN-Sc. 600520–007.

5/20/1960 King, Martin Luther, Jr., Defendant. "Demurrer to indictment," *State of Alabama v. Martin Luther King, Jr.* 5/20/1960. Montgomery, Ala. (THFmS) 3 pp. CMCR-AMC. 600520–008.

5/20/1960 King, Martin Luther, Jr., Defendant. "Order on motion to quash indictment," *State of Alabama v. Martin Luther King, Jr.* 5/20/1960. Montgomery, Ala. (TDS) 2 pp. CMCR-AMC. 600520–009.

5/24/1960 King, Martin Luther, Jr. Letter to James A. (James Anderson) Dombrowski. 5/24/1960. [*Atlanta, Ga.*] (TLc) 1 p. MLKP-MBU: Box 69. 600524–000.

5/24/1960 King, Martin Luther, Jr. Letter to James A. Blades. 5/24/1960. [*Atlanta, Ga.*] (TLc) 1 p. MLKP-MBU: Box 20. 600524–001.

5/24/1960 Ballou, Maude L. Letter to Max F. Daskam. 5/24/1960. [*Atlanta, Ga.*] (TLc) 1 p. MLKP-MBU: Box 46. 600524–007.

2/17/1960–5/25/1960 Seay, S. S. (Solomon Snowden) (MIA). Draft, Press release, MIA supports King. [*2/17/1960–5/25/1960*]. Montgomery, Ala. (THDd) 1 p. LDRP-NN-Sc: Box 2. 600525–003.

5/25/1960–5/28/1960 Uhrbrock, Donald (Time Inc.). Photo of Martin Luther King, Jr., Fred D. Gray, and others. [*5/25/1960–5/28/1960*]. Montgomery, Ala. (Ph) 1 p. NNTI. 600528–001.

5/28/1960 King, Martin Luther, Jr. Statement on verdict by jury of Montgomery County. [*5/28/1960*]. [*Montgomery, Ala.*] (F) .6 min. WSBA-GU. 600528–002.

5/28/1960 King, Martin Luther, Jr., Defendant. "Verdict," *State of Alabama v. Martin Luther King, Jr.* 5/28/1960. Montgomery, Ala. (THFmS) 4 pp. CMCR-AMC. 600528–004.

5/29/1960 Wilson, A. W. (Holt Street Baptist Church). Telegram to Martin Luther King, Jr. 5/29/1960. Montgomery, Ala. (PWSr) 1 p. MLKP-MBU: Box 73A. 600529–000.

5/27/1960–5/29/1960 Negro American Labor Council. "Summary of proceedings-the founding convention." 5/27/1960–5/29/1960. (TD) 4 pp. RPP-NN-Sc: Box 3. 600529–008.

5/30/1960 Littell, Franklin H. (Emory University). Letter to Martin Luther King, Jr. 5/30/1960. Atlanta, Ga. (TALS) 1 p. MLKP-MBU: Box 29A. 600530–000.

5/30/1960 Knoxville College. Program, Eighty-fifth annual commencement. 5/30/1960. Knoxville, Tenn. (PD) 4 pp. CSKC. 600530–002.

5/31/1960 Hammerstein, Oscar (National Committee Against Discrimination in Housing). Letter to Martin Luther King, Jr. 5/31/1960. New York, N.Y. (TLS) 1 p. MLKP-MBU: Box 32. 600531–001.

5/31/1960 King, Martin Luther, Jr. Letter to L. H. Foster. 5/31/1960. [*Atlanta, Ga.*] (TLc) 1 p. MLKP-MBU: Box 25. 600531–004.

5/31/1960 Nelson, William Stuart (Howard University). Telegram to Martin Luther King, Jr. 5/31/1960. Washington, D.C. (PWc) 1 p. MLKP-MBU: Box 73A. 600531–006.

5/31/1960 Wheeler, J. H. (Mechanics and Farmers Bank). Letter to Martin Luther King, Jr. 5/31/1960. Durham, N.C. (TLS) 1 p. MLKP-MBU: Box 73A. 600531–007.

5/31/1960 Maxwell, O. Clay. Telegram to Martin Luther King, Jr. 5/31/1960. New York, N.Y. (PWSr) 1 p. MLKP-MBU: Box 73A. 600531–008.

6/1960 Abernathy, Ralph. Press release, Telegram sent to John Malcolm Patterson and Frank Stewart. [*6/1960*]. (TD) 1 p. HG-GAMK. 600600–017.

4/1960–6/1960 King, Martin Luther, Jr. (Ebenezer Baptist Church). "Going Forward By Going Backward," Address at the Chicago Sunday Evening Club on 2/21/1960. Nashville, Tenn. 4/1960–6/1960. From: *A.M.E. Church Review*, April 1960-June 1960, pp. 62–67. (PD) 6 pp. 600600–018.

6/1960 Jabhat al-Tahrir al-Qami. *Algeria: Questions and Answers*. New York: The Algerian Office, June 1960. (PD) CSKCH. 600600–020.

6/1960 King, Martin Luther, Jr. "To Win Racial Justice." 6/1960. Atlanta, Ga. From: *The Student Voice*, June 1960, p. 1. (TD) 1 p. 600600–022.

6/1960 King, Martin Luther, Jr. and A. Philip (Asa Philip) Randolph. Telegram to Los Angeles community leaders. [*6/1960*]. (TWc) 1 p. BRP-DLC. 600600–023.

6/2/1960 SCLC. "Delegates to Youth Leadership Conference," 4/15/1960–4/17/1960. 6/2/1960. Atlanta, Ga. (TD) 10 pp. EJBC-NN-Sc. 600602–006.

6/3/1960 Barry, Marion. Letter to Martin Luther King, Jr. 6/3/1960. Nashville, Tenn. (TLS) 1 p. MLKP-MBU: Box 20. 600603–000.

6/6/1960 Smart-Abbey, A. Q. (Embassy of Ghana). Letter to Martin Luther King, Jr. 6/6/1960. Washington, D.C. (TLS) 1 p. MLKP-MBU: Box 26. 600606–000.

6/6/1960 Rustin, Bayard (SCLC). Letter to Martin Luther King, Jr. [*6/6/1960*]. (TLS) 1 p. (Contains enclosure 600606–012.) MLKP-MBU: Box 5. 600606–011.

6/6/1960 [*Rustin, Bayard*]. Letter to Harry Belafonte. [*6/6/1960*]. (TALd) 1 p. (Enclosed in 600606–011.) MLKP-MBU: Box 5. 600606–012.

6/7/1960 King, Martin Luther, Jr. Telegram to William Stuart Nelson. 6/7/1960. [*Atlanta, Ga.*] (PWc) 1 p. MLKP-MBU: Box 32. 600607–002.

6/8/1960 Abernathy, Ralph. Telegram to FOR. 6/8/1960. Montgomery, Ala. (PHWSr) 1 p. FORP-PSC-P. 600608–004.

6/8/1960 Dexter Avenue Baptist Church. *Dexter Echo* 4, no. 10. 6/8/1960. Montgomery, Ala. (TD) 6 pp. CSKC. 600608–008.

6/8/1960 Press release, "Negro leaders to issue important statement on 1960 elections." 6/8/1960. New York, N.Y. (TD) 1 p. BRP-DLC. 600608–009.

6/8/1960 Rustin, Bayard. Telegram to Press agencies. [*6/8/1960*]. (PWSr) 6 pp. BRP-DLC. 600608–010.

6/9/1960 King, Martin Luther, Jr. Letter to Mildred Scott Olmstead. 6/9/1960. [*Atlanta, Ga.*] (TLc) 1 p. MLKP-MBU: Box 73A. 600609–008.

6/9/1960 Press release, Demonstrations to occur at the Democratic and Republican conventions. [*6/9/1960*]. (TD) 2 pp. BRP-DLC. 600609–011.

6/9/1960 King, Martin Luther, Jr., and A. Philip (Asa Philip) Randolph. Press conference on the March on the Conventions Movement for Freedom Now. [*6/9/1960*]. [*New York, N.Y.*] (F) 2.5 min. CBSNA-NNCBS: 10383. 600609–017.

6/12/1960 Ebenezer Baptist Church. Program, Sunday services. 6/12/1960. Atlanta, Ga. (TD) 4 pp. MLKP-MBU. 600612–003.

6/13/1960 Robinson, James H. (Operation-Crossroads Africa, Inc.). Letter to Martin Luther King, Jr. 6/13/1960. New York, N.Y. (TLS) 1 p. MLKP-MBU: Box 68. 600613–001.

6/14/1960 Sobell, Helen L. Letter to Martin Luther King, Jr. 6/14/1960. New York, N.Y. (THLS) 14 pp. (Includes enclosures.) MLKP-MBU: Box 70. 600614–001.

6/14/1960 Penney, Marjorie (Fellowship House and Farm). Letter to Martin Luther King, Jr. 6/14/1960. Philadelphia, Pa. (TLS) 1 p. MLKP-MBU: Box 70. 600614–002.

6/15/1960 Rustin, Bayard (SCLC). Letter to Martin Luther King, Jr. 6/15/1960. Atlanta, Ga. (TLS) 2 pp. (Includes enclosure.) MLKP-MBU: Box 5. 600615–000.

6/15/1960 Gaston, A. G. (Arthur George) (Citizens Federal Savings and Loan Association).

Letter to Martin Luther King, Jr. 6/15/1960. Birmingham, Ala. (TLS) 1 p. MLKP-MBU: Box 1. 600615–001.

6/16/1960 King, Martin Luther, Jr. Letter to Clarence N. Akpuaka. 6/16/1960. [*Atlanta, Ga.*] (TLc) 1 p. MLKP-MBU: Box 26. 600616–008.

6/16/1960 King, Martin Luther, Jr. Letter to John H. Wheeler. 6/16/1960. [*Atlanta, Ga.*] (TLc) 1 p. MLKP-MBU: Box 73A. 600616–012.

6/16/1960 King, Martin Luther, Jr. (SCLC). Statement on the firing of Lawrence Dunbar Reddick by Alabama State College. 6/16/1960. Atlanta, Ga. (TD) 1 p. MLKP-MBU: Box 35. 600616–014.

6/16/1960 SCLC. Press release, Dismissal of Lawrence Dunbar Reddick. 6/16/1960. Atlanta, Ga. (PD) 2 pp. MLKP-MBU: Box 71. 600616–015.

6/17/1960 Reitman, Alan (American Civil Liberties Union). Letter to Martin Luther King, Jr. 6/17/1960. New York, N.Y. (TLS) 1 p. (Contains enclosure 600617–002.) MLKP-MBU: Box 18. 600617–001.

6/17/1960 American Civil Liberties Union. Press release, Dismissal of Lawrence Dunbar Reddick is a violation of academic freedom. 6/17/1960. New York, N.Y. (TD) 2 pp. (Enclosed in 600617–001.) MLKP-MBU: Box 18. 600617–002.

6/17/1960 King, Martin Luther, Jr. Letter to Maxwell Hahn. 6/17/1960. [*Atlanta, Ga.*] (TLc) 1 p. MLKP-MBU: Box 27A. 600617–004.

6/17/1960 Abernathy, Ralph, S. S. (Solomon Snowden) Seay, R.D. (Robert D.) Nesbitt, and Erna A. Dungee. (MIA). Form letter to the executive board. 6/17/1960. Montgomery, Ala. (TLSr) 1 p. MLKP-MBU: Box 30. 600617–008.

6/17/1960 Barry, Marion, and Jane Stembridge (SNCC). Letter to Martin Luther King, Jr. [*6/17/1960*]. Atlanta, Ga. (TLS) 1 p. MLKP-MBU: Box 6. 600617–011.

6/17/1960 Wilkins, Roy (NAACP). Telegram to John Malcolm Patterson. 6/17/1960. New York, N.Y. (PWSr) 2 pp. MLKJP-GAMK: Box 20. 600617–012.

6/17/1960 Randolph, A. Philip (Asa Philip). Telegram to Maurice Dawkins and Augustus F. Hawkins. [*6/17/1960*]. (TWc) 1 p. (Enclosed in 600617–014.) NAACPP-DLC: Group III-A177. 600617–013.

6/17/1960 Kahn, Tom (SCLC). Letter to John A. Morsell. 6/17/1960. Atlanta, Ga. (TLS) 1 p. (Contains enclosure 600617–013.) NAACPP-DLC: Group III-A175. 600617–014.

6/18/1960 King, Martin Luther, Jr. Letter to Walter E. Fauntroy. 6/18/1960. [*Atlanta, Ga.*] (TLc) 1 p. MLKP-MBU: Box 25. 600618–000.

6/18/1960 King, Martin Luther, Jr. Letter to Douglas E. Moore. 6/18/1960. [*Atlanta, Ga.*] (TLc) 1 p. MLKP-MBU: Box 31. 600618–002.

6/19/1960 Davis, Benjamin J. (Benjamin Jefferson). Letter to Martin Luther King, Jr. 6/19/1960. New York, N.Y. (TLS) 2 pp. MLKP-MBU: Box 23A. 600619–002.

6/19/1960 Central Baptist Church. Program, "Tri-State's Freedom Jubilee." 6/19/1960. Pittsburgh, Pa. (PD) 31 pp. CSKC. 600619–004.

6/19/1960 King, Martin Luther, Jr. Letter to Laurence D. Cundiff. 6/19/1960. [*Atlanta, Ga.*] (TLc) 1 p. MLKP-MBU: Box 22. 600619–005.

6/19/1960 King, Martin Luther, Jr. Letter to John Ruth. 6/19/1960. [*Atlanta, Ga.*] (TLc) 1 p. MLKP-MBU: Box 68. 600619–007.

6/19/1960 "The King-Randolph Call for Freedom March on Conventions." 6/19/1960. New York, N.Y. From: *The Worker,* 19 June 1960. pp. 1, 11. (PD) 2 pp. 600619–009.

6/21/1960 Ryan, Joseph M. F., and Henry Putzel (U.S. Dept. of Justice). Letter to Martin Luther King, Jr. 6/21/1960. Washington, D.C. (TLS) 1 p. MLKP-MBU: Box 24. 600621–000.

6/16/1960–6/22/1960 National Sunday School and Baptist Training Union Congress. Program, "Fifty-fifth annual session." 6/16/1960–6/22/1960. Buffalo, N.Y. (TD) 43 pp. CSKC. 600622–003.

6/23/1960 Swann, Melvin Chester (St. Joseph's African Methodist Episcopal Church). Letter to Martin Luther King, Jr. 6/23/1960. Durham, N.C. (TLS) 1 p. MLKP-MBU: Box 70. 600623–004.

6/23/1960 SNCC. "Report of the Raleigh conference." 6/23/1960. Atlanta, Ga. (TD) 3 pp. EJBC-NN-Sc. 600623–006.

6/24/1960 Thomas, Norman (Reinhold Niebuhr Professorship Fund at Union Theological Seminary). Letter to Martin Luther King, Jr. 6/24/1960. New York, N.Y. (TAHLS) 3 pp. MLKP-MBU: Box 72. 600624–007.

6/24/1960 Ebenezer Baptist Church. Press release, Martin Luther King, Jr. attends the Tenth Baptist World Alliance in Rio de Janeiro, Brazil. 6/24/1960. Atlanta, Ga. (TD) 1 p. MLKP-MBU. 600624–008.

6/27/1960 SCLC. Press release, Bayard Rustin resigns from SCLC. 6/27/1960. New York, N.Y. (THD) 3 pp. SAVFC-WHi. 600627–005.

6/28/1960 Percy, Charles H. (Republican National Committee). Letter to Martin Luther King, Jr. 6/28/1960. Washington, D.C. (TLS) 2 pp. BRP-DLC. 600628–001.

6/29/1960 Bowles, Chester (U.S. Congress. House of Representatives). Letter to Martin Luther King, Jr. 6/29/1960. Washington, D. C. (TLS) 1 p. MLKP-MBU: Box 20. 600629–000.

6/29/1960 Robinson, Jackie (Chock Full O' Nuts). Letter to Martin Luther King, Jr. 6/29/1960. New York, N.Y. (TLS) 1 p. MLKP-MBU: Box 68. 600629–002.

7/1/1960 King, Martin Luther, Jr. Telegram to Bayard Rustin. 7/1/1960. Rio de Janeiro, Brazil. (PWSr) 1 p. BRP-DLC. 600701–001.

6/29/1960–7/4/1960 Republic of Ghana. Invitation to inauguration. 6/29/1960–7/4/1960. Accra, Ghana. (PTD) 1 p. MLKP-MBU: Box 4. 600704–000.

7/6/1960 Dexter Avenue Baptist Church. *Dexter Echo* 5, no. 11. 7/6/1960. Montgomery, Ala. (TDf) 3 pp. CSKC. 600706–008.

7/7/1960 King, Martin Luther, Jr. (SCLC). Introductory remarks to the 1960 Democratic Party platform committee, read by Maurice A. Dawkins. 7/7/1960. Los Angeles, Calif. (TD) 2 pp. OHP-ArU. 600707–004.

7/1/1960–7/7/1960 [*King, Martin Luther, Jr.*]. Draft, "Proposals to both parties." [*7/1/1960–7/7/1960*]. (TAHDd) 2 pp. (Enclosed in 600707–010.) CSKC: Sermon file. 600707–005.

7/1/1960–7/7/1960 [*King, Martin Luther, Jr.*]. Draft, "Introductory remarks to both parties." [*7/1/1960–7/7/1960*]. (TAHDd) 2 pp. (Enclosed in 600707–010.) CSKC: Sermon file. 600707–006.

7/1/1960–7/7/1960 Rustin, Bayard (SCLC). Letter to Martin Luther King, Jr. [*7/1/1960–7/7/1960*]. (TADdI) 1 p. (Enclosed in 600707–010.) CSKC: Sermon file. 600707–009.

7/1/1960–7/7/1960 Rustin, Bayard (SCLC). Letter to Martin Luther King, Jr. [*7/1/1960–7/7/1960*]. (TADdS) 1 p. (Contains enclosures 600707–005, 600707–006 & 600707–009.) CSKC: Sermon file. 600707–010.

7/9/1960 Morton, Thruston B. (Republican National Committee). Letter to Martin Luther King, Jr. 7/9/1960. Washington, D.C. (TLS) 1 p. (Enclosed in 600714–000.) MLKP-MBU: Box 68. 600709–000.

7/11/1960 Clark, Septima Poinsette (Highlander Folk School). Letter to Martin Luther King, Jr. 7/11/1960. Monteagle, Tenn. (TLS) 1 p. MLKP-MBU: Box 12. 600711–000.

7/12/1960 King, Martin Luther, Jr. Form letter to James R. Wood. 7/12/1960. [*Atlanta, Ga.*] (TLc) 1 p. SCLCR-GAMK. 600712–006.

7/13/1960 Lawson, Earl Wesley. Letter to Martin Luther King, Jr. 7/13/1960. Malden, Mass. (AHLS) 2 pp. MLKP-MBU: Box 29A. 600713–001.

7/13/1960 Stembridge, Jane (SNCC). Letter to Martin Luther King, Jr. 7/13/1960. Atlanta, Ga. (TLS) 1 p. MLKP-MBU: Box 6. 600713–003.

7/14/1960 Rustin, Bayard (SCLC). Letter to Martin Luther King, Jr. 7/14/1960. (TLS) 1 p. (Contains enclosures 600709–000 & 600714–001.) MLKP-MBU: Box 72. 600714–000.

7/14/1960 King, Martin Luther, Jr. Telegram to Floyd McCafree. 7/14/1960. New York, N.Y. (TWc) 1 p. (Enclosed in 600714–000.) MLKP-MBU: Box 33A. 600714–001.

7/16/1960 Abernathy, Ralph (First Baptist Church). Letter to Martin Luther King, Jr. 7/16/1960. Montgomery, Ala. (TLS) 2 pp. MLKP-MBU: Box 7. 600716–000.

7/18/1960 King, Martin Luther, Jr. Telegram to Cleveland Robinson and William Michelson. 7/18/1960. Atlanta, Ga. (PWc) 2 pp. MLKP-MBU: Box 73A. 600718–003.

7/18/1960 Dixon, Rebecca. Letter to Martin Luther King, Jr. 7/18/1960. Montgomery, Ala. (ALS) 3 pp. MLKP-MBU: Box 23A. 600718–005.

7/18/1960 King, Martin Luther, Jr. Statement to Al Kuettner. 7/18/1960. [*Atlanta, Ga.*] (THD) 1 p. MLKP-MBU: Box 35. 600718–009.

7/18/1960 King, Martin Luther, Jr. Draft, Form letter to Friend of freedom. [*7/18/1960*]. [*Atlanta, Ga.*] (ALd) 4 pp. MLKP-MBU: Box 19. 600718–012.

7/19/1960 King, Martin Luther, Jr. Telegram to Russell R. Lasley. 7/19/1960. Atlanta, Ga. (PWSr) 2 pp. UPWP-WHi: Box 394. 600719–006.

7/19/1960 Stovall, Edward (Progressive Baptist Church). Letter to Martin Luther King, Jr. 7/19/1960. Berkeley, Calif. (THLS) 1 p. (Marginal comments by King.) MLKJP-GAMK: Box 36. 600719–007.

7/20/1960 King, Martin Luther, Jr. Form letter to Katie Wickham. 7/20/1960. [*Atlanta, Ga.*] (TLc) 1 p. MLKP-MBU: Box 71. 600720–004.

7/20/1960 Brown, Ernestine (SCLC). Memo to Ella J. Baker. 7/20/1960. (TL) 1 p. MLKP-MBU: Box 31. 600720–006.

7/21/1960	Baker, Ella J. (SCLC). Letter to James F. Estes. 7/21/1960. (TLc) 1 p. SCLCR-GAMK. 600721–006.
7/22/1960	Michelson, William (Wholesale and Department Store Union). Letter to Martin Luther King, Jr. 7/22/1960. New York, N.Y. (THLS) 1 p. MLKP-MBU: Box 31. 600722–000.
7/22/1960	Henry, Aaron E. Letter to Martin Luther King, Jr. 7/22/1960. Clarksdale, Miss. (THLS) 1 p. MLKP-MBU: Box 27A. 600722–001.
7/22/1960	King, Martin Luther, Jr. Telegram to Wyatt Tee Walker. 7/22/1960. [*Atlanta, Ga.*] (PWc) 2 pp. MLKP-MBU: Box 73A. 600722–002.
7/24/1960	Ebenezer Baptist Church. Program, Sunday services. 7/24/1960. Atlanta, Ga. (TD) 4 pp. MLKP-MBU: Box 24. 600724–000.
7/25/1960	Barry, Marion (SNCC). Letter to Martin Luther King, Jr. 7/25/1960. Atlanta, Ga. (TLS) 1 p. MLKP-MBU: Box 6. 600725–003.
7/25/1960	King, Martin Luther, Jr. Letter to Allen Jordan. 7/25/1960. [*Atlanta, Ga.*] (TLc) 1 p. MLKP-MBU: Box 44. 600725–004.
7/25/1960	**Miller, Francis (*Time*). Photo of Martin Luther King, Jr. and demonstrators. 7/25/1960. Chicago, Ill. (Ph) 1 p. NNTI. 600725–013.**
7/26/1960	Padmore, George (Liberian Embassy). Invitation to Martin Luther King, Jr. 7/26/1960. Washington, D.C. (PD) 1 p. MLKP-MBU: Box 4. 600726–000.
7/28/1960	King, Martin Luther, Jr. Interview on political nonpartisanship. [*7/28/1960*]. [*Chicago, Ill.*] (F) 1 min. CBSNA-NNCBS. 600728–000.
7/31/1960	Baker, Ella J. (SCLC). Form letter to Friend. 7/31/1960. Atlanta, Ga. (TLS) 2 pp. EJBC-NN-Sc. 600731–001.
7/31/1960	Ebenezer Baptist Church. Program, Sunday services. 7/31/1960. Atlanta, Ga. (TD) 4 pp. MLKP-MBU: Box 24. 600731–002.
8/1960	King, Martin Luther, Jr. Interview by Edwin Randall for "Sit-Ins" radio program. [*8/1960*]. [*Nashville, Tenn.*] (At) 1.8 min. (1 sound cassette: analog.) MLKEC: ET-23. 600800–004.
8/1960	SCLC. Press release, President of Southeastern Greyhound Lines makes statement. [*8/1960*]. [*Atlanta, Ga.*] (THD) 1 p. SCLCR-GAMK: Box 125. 600800–009.
8/1960	*The Lawson-Vanderbilt Affair: Letters to Dean Nelson.* Nashville: Privately printed, August 1960. (PD) 61 pp. FORP-PSC-P. 600800–012.
8/1/1960	King, Martin Luther, Jr. Remarks on civil rights platforms of parties. [*8/1/1960*]. (At) 2 min. (1 sound cassette: analog.) MMFR. 600801–004.
8/2/1960	King, Martin Luther, Jr. Letter to Tom Mboya. 8/2/1960. [*Atlanta, Ga.*] (TLc) 1 p. MLKP-MBU: Box 25. 600802–001.
8/2/1960	Ballou, Maude L. Letter to Pilgrim Health and Life Insurance Company. 8/2/1960. (TLc) 1 p. MLKJP-GAMK: Box 21A. 600802–005.
8/3/1960	King, Martin Luther, Jr. Letter to Jean Berger. 8/3/1960. [*Atlanta, Ga.*] (TLc) 1 p. MLKP-MBU: Box 21. 600803–008.
8/4/1960	Smith, Barry, and Helene Smith. Notes, Workshop by Martin Luther King, Jr., "Nonviolence: its basic precepts." 8/4/1960. Atlanta, Ga. (ADS) 6 pp. SCLCR-GAMK: Box 1. 600804–000.
8/5/1960	[*Smith, Barry*]. Notes, Second Statewide Institute on Nonviolent Resistence to Segregation. 8/5/1960. (AD) 5 pp. SCLCR-GAMK: Box 1. 600805–003.
8/4/1960–8/5/1960	SCLC. Program, "Second Statewide Institute on Nonviolent Resistance to Segregation." 8/4/1960–8/5/1960. Atlanta, Ga. (TD) 5 pp. SCLCR-GAMK: Box 35. 600805–006.
8/7/1960	Ebenezer Baptist Church. Program, Sunday services. 8/7/1960. Atlanta, Ga. (TD) 4 pp. MLKP-MBU: Box 24. 600807–001.
8/8/1960	King, Martin Luther, Jr. Letter to George Wayne High. 8/8/1960. [*Atlanta, Ga.*] (TLc) 1 p. MLKP-MBU: Box 27A. 600808–001.
8/9/1960	King, Martin Luther, Jr. (Ebenezer Baptist Church). Letter to A. Philip (Asa Philip) Randolph. 8/9/1960. Atlanta, Ga. (TLS) 1 p. (Contains enclosure 600809–002, pp. 495–496 in this volume.) EBCR. 600809–000.
8/9/1960	Ballou, Maude L. Letter to Lambert N. Davis. 8/9/1960. [*Atlanta, Ga.*] (TLc) 1 p. MLKP-MBU: Box 23A. 600809–007.
8/9/1960	King, Martin Luther, Jr. (SCLC). Form letter to Friend. 8/9/1960. Atlanta, Ga. (TLS) 1 p. SCLCR-GAMK: Box 35. 600809–008.
8/9/1960	King, Martin Luther, Jr. (Ebenezer Baptist Church). Letter to Roy Wilkins. 8/9/1960. Atlanta, Ga. (TLS) 1 p. (Contains enclosure 600809–002, pp. 495–496 in this volume.) NAACPP-DLC: Group III-A175. 600809–012.
8/9/1960	Ballou, Maude L. Letter to H. Councill (Harper Councill) Trenholm. 8/9/1960.

(TLc) 1 p. (Contains enclosure 600809-002 pp. 495–496 in this volume.) MLKP-MBU: Box 72. 600809-017.

8/10/1960 Ballou, Maude L. Letter to Malcolm X. 8/10/1960. [*Atlanta, Ga.*] (TLc) 1 p. MLKP-MBU. 600810–000.

8/10/1960 Braden, Anne (Southern Conference Educational Fund, Inc.). Letter to Martin Luther King, Jr., and Coretta Scott King. 8/10/1960. New Orleans, La. (TALS) 2 pp. MLKP-MBU: Box 21. 600810–001.

8/10/1960 Maxwell, O. Clay (Mount Olivet Baptist Church). Letter to Martin Luther King, Jr. 8/10/1960. New York, N.Y. (TLS) 1 p. MLKP-MBU: Box 31. 600810–009.

8/10/1960 King, Martin Luther, Jr. Letter to Henry H. Crane. 8/10/1960. [*Atlanta, Ga.*] (TLc) 1 p. MLKP-MBU: Box 22. 600810–012.

8/11/1960 Decter, Moshe (Jewish Minorities Research). Letter to Martin Luther King, Jr. 8/11/1960. New York, N.Y. (TLS) 5 pp. (Includes enclosures.) MLKP-MBU: Box 52A. 600811–001.

8/14/1960 Willoughby, Lillian. Letter to Martin Luther King, Jr. 8/14/1960. Blackwood Terrace, N.J. (TAHLS) 1 p. MLKP-MBU: Box 73A. 600814–000.

8/15/1960 Randolph, A. Philip (Asa Philip) (Negro American Labor Council). Telegram to John Malcolm Patterson. 8/15/1960. (PWSr) 2 pp. MLKP-MBU: Box 72. 600815–001.

8/15/1960 Dombrowski, James A. (James Anderson). Letter to Martin Luther King, Jr. 8/15/1960. (TLS) 6 pp. (Includes enclosures.) MLKP-MBU: Box 23A. 600815–003.

8/16/1960 Randolph, A. Philip (Asa Philip) (Brotherhood of Sleeping Car Porters and Maids). Letter to Martin Luther King, Jr. 8/16/1960. New York, N. Y. (TLSr) 1 p. MLKP-MBU: Box 72. 600816–000.

8/18/1960 King, Martin Luther, Jr. (SCLC). Telegram to John H. Winchel. 8/18/1960. Atlanta, Ga. (TWc) 1 p. RWP-DLC. 600818–003.

8/18/1960 King, Martin Luther, Jr. (SCLC). Telegram to F. W. Ackerman. 8/18/1960. [*Atlanta, Ga.*] (TWc) 1 p. RWP-DLC. 600818–004.

8/17/1960–8/18/1960 SCLC. Program, "Third Statewide Institute on Nonviolent Resistance to Segregation." 8/17/1960–8/18/1960. Birmingham, Ala. (THD) 7 pp. FLSC-GAMK: Box 4. 600818–007.

8/18/1960 Wood, James R. (SCLC). Press release, Martin Luther King, Jr. may call for a boycott of Greyhound Bus Lines. 8/18/1960. (THD) 1 p. SCLCR-GAMK: Box 120. 600818–010.

8/20/1960 Shuttlesworth, Patricia, Ruby Fredericka Shuttlesworth, and Fred L. Shuttlesworth Jr. Interview. [*8/20/1960*] (At) 54.4 min. (1 sound cassette. analog.) HRECR-WHi. 600820-003.

8/21/1960 Gray, William H. (William Herbert). Letter to Martin Luther King, Jr. 8/21/1960. Philadelphia, Pa. (TLS) 1 p. MLKP-MBU: Box 27. 600821–000.

8/22/1960 Barry, Marion, and Jane Stembridge (SNCC). Letter to Martin Luther King, Jr. 8/22/1960. Atlanta, Ga. (THLS) 1 p. MLKP-MBU: Box 6. 600822–002.

8/22/1960 King, Martin Luther, Jr. Telegram to Kelly M. Alexander. 8/22/1960. [*Atlanta, Ga.*] (PWSr) 1 p MLKP-MBU. 600822–007.

8/23/1960 King, Martin Luther, Jr. (SCLC). Excerpts, Address at Jefferson County Armory. 8/23/1960. Louisville, Ky. (TADf) 2 pp. MLKJP-GAMK. 600823–002.

8/24/1960 Walker, Wyatt Tee (SCLC). Letter to Roy Wilkins. 8/24/1960. Atlanta, Ga. (TLS) 2 pp. RWP-DLC. 600824–002.

8/24/1960 Ballou, Maude L. Letter to Jane Stembridge. 8/24/1960. [*Atlanta, Ga.*] (TLc) 1 p. MLKP-MBU: Box 6. 600824–003.

8/25/1960 Ancrum, Charles H. (Holy Covenant Baptist Church). Letter to Martin Luther King, Jr. 8/25/1960. Brooklyn, N.Y. (THLS) 1 p. MLKP-MBU. 600825–006.

8/29/1960 SCLC. Press release, "Shuttlesworth appeals to SCLC." 8/29/1960. (TD) 2 pp. RWP-DLC. 600829–004.

8/30/1960 Ballou, Maude L. Letter to James A. (James Anderson) Dombrowski. 8/30/1960. [*Atlanta, Ga.*] (TLc) 1 p. MLKP-MBU: Box 69. 600830–000.

8/30/1960 King, Martin Luther, Jr. Letter to Charles A. Cowan. 8/30/1960. [*Atlanta, Ga.*] (TLc) 1 p. MLKP-MBU: Box 29. 600830–001.

8/30/1960 Wood, James R. (SCLC). Letter to Helen L. Sobell. 8/30/1960. (TLc) 1 p. MLKP-MBU: Box 70. 600830–002.

8/1/1960–8/31/1960 SCLC. "Monthly budget control sheet." 8/1/1960–8/31/1960. Atlanta, Ga. (PD) 1 p. MLKJP-GAMK: Vault Box 9. 600831–013.

8/31/1960 U.S. Federal Bureau of Investigation. Memo on the Committee to Secure Justice for Morton Sobell. 8/31/1960. New York, N.Y. (THLc) 1 p. DGFBI-NN-Sc. 600831–016.

9/1960 Posey, Barbara Ann. "Why I Sit In." 9/1960. New York, N.Y. (PD) 4 pp. CSKC. 600900–004.

9/1/1960 Stanley, Frank L. (Non-Partisan Registration Committee). Letter to Martin Luther King, Jr. 9/1/1960. Louisville, Ky. (TLS) 1 p. MLKP-MBU: Box 69. 600901–001.

9/2/1960 Tyler, Harold R. (U.S. Dept. of Justice). Letter to Martin Luther King, Jr. 9/2/1960. Washington, D.C. (TLS) 1 p. MLKP-MBU: Box 24. 600902–000.

9/2/1960 Levison, Stanley D. Letter to A. Philip (Asa Philip) Randolph. 9/2/1960. New York, N.Y. (TLS) 1 p. (Contains enclosure 600902–010.) APRC-DLC. 600902–001.

9/2/1960 King, Martin Luther, Jr. Letter to O. Clay Maxwell. 9/2/1960. [*Atlanta, Ga.*] (TLc) 1 p. MLKP-MBU: Box 31. 600902–003.

9/2/1960 Goodson, Johnnie H. (NAACP). Letter to Martin Luther King, Jr. 9/2/1960. Jacksonville, Fla. (TLS) 2 pp. MLKP-MBU: Box 27. 600902–008.

9/2/1960 Committee to Defend Martin Luther King and the Struggle for Freedom in the South. Draft, "Statement of income and expenditure for period ended 7/31/1960." [*9/2/1960*]. (TDd) 2 pp. (Enclosed in 600902–001.) APRC-DLC. 600902–010.

9/3/1960 King, Martin Luther, Jr. Letter to Vernon P. Bodein. 9/3/1960. [*Atlanta, Ga.*] (TLc) 1 p. MLKP-MBU: Box 39A. 600903–001.

6/26/1960–9/4/1960 Central Methodist Church. Announcement, Summer preaching program at Central Methodist Church. 6/26/1960–9/4/1960. Detroit, Mich. (PD) 4 pp. MLKP-MBU: Box 37A. 600904–001.

9/5/1960 King, Martin Luther, Jr. Paul's Letter to American Christians, Sermon delivered at DePauw University's School of the Prophets. 9/5/1960. Greencastle, Ind. (At) 35.9 min. (1 sound cassette: analog.) InGrD. 600905–000.

9/6/1960 King, Martin Luther, Jr. "The Rising Tide of Racial Consciousness," Address at the Golden Anniversary Conference of the National Urban League. 9/6/1960. New York, N.Y. (TAHD) 14 pp. MLKJP-GAMK. 600906-000.

9/7/1960 Robinson, James R. (CORE). Letter to Martin Luther King, Jr. 9/7/1960. New York, N.Y. (TLS) 1 p. MLKP-MBU: Box 23. 600907–001.

9/7/1960 Hadley, William H. (Governmental Affairs Institute). Letter to Martin Luther King, Jr. 9/7/1960. Washington, D.C. (TLS) 8 pp. (Includes enclosures.) MLKP-MBU: Box 27A. 600907–002.

9/7/1960 Ballou, Maude L. Letter to Martin Luther King, Jr. 9/7/1960. [*Atlanta, Ga.*] (TLc) 2 pp. MLKP-MBU. 600907–014.

9/8/1960 O'Dell, Jack H. Letter to Martin Luther King, Jr. 9/8/1960. New York, N.Y. (TLS) 1 p. MLKP-MBU: Box 58. 600908–004.

9/10/1960 Burchfield, Ray A. (Fifth Street Methodist Church). Letter to Martin Luther King, Jr. 9/10/1960. Anderson, Ind. (THALS) 1 p. MLKP-MBU: Box 21. 600910–002.

9/11/1960 Pinn Memorial Baptist Church. Program, Sunday services. 9/11/1960. Philadelphia, Pa. (TD) 4 pp. CSKC. 600911–001.

9/11/1960 Salem Baptist Church. Program, "Annual Men's Day service." 9/11/1960. Jenkintown, Pa. (THD) 4 pp. CSKC. 600911–002.

9/13/1960 Duckett, Alfred (Alfred Duckett Associates). Letter to Martin Luther King, Jr. 9/13/1960. New York, N.Y. (TLS) 1 p. MLKP-MBU: Box 23A. 600913–002.

9/14/1960 King, Martin Luther, Jr. Letter to Claude Thompson. 9/14/1960. [*Atlanta, Ga.*] (TLc) 1 p. MLKP-MBU: Box 72. 600914–001.

9/14/1960 Non-Partisan Crusade to Register One Million New Negro Voters. Press release, Martin Luther King, Jr. and Roy Wilkins announce voter registration campaign. 9/14/1960. New York, N.Y. (TD) 1 p. NAACPP-DLC. 600914–003.

9/14/1960 Photo of Martin Luther King, Jr. and Roy Wilkins at the Overseas Press Club. [*9/14/1960*]. New York, N.Y. (Ph) 1 p. NAACPP-DLC: Group III-A175. 600914–006.

9/16/1960 King, Martin Luther, Jr. Letter to David Livingston. 9/16/1960. [*Atlanta, Ga.*] (TLc) 1 p. MLKP-MBU: Box 29A. 600916–001.

9/19/1960 Wood, James R. Letter to William H. Hadley. [*9/19/1960*]. [*Atlanta, Ga.*] (TLc) 1 p. MLKP-MBU: Box 27A. 600919–001.

9/19/1960 Lee, George W. (Elks Dept. of Education). Letter to Martin Luther King, Jr. 9/19/1960. Memphis, Tenn. (TLS) 1 p. MLKP-MBU: Box 29A. 600919–003.

9/19/1960 King, Martin Luther, Jr. Letter to A.C. Th. Scharten. 9/19/1960. [*Atlanta, Ga.*] (TLc) 1 p. MLKP-MBU: Box 26. 600919–004.

9/20/1960 Wood, James R. Letter to Edith Mackin. 9/20/1960. [*Atlanta, Ga.*] (TLc) 1 p. MLKP-MBU: Box 30A. 600920–004.

9/21/1960 MIA. *Newsletter.* 9/21/1960. Montgomery, Ala. (TD) 3 pp. HG-GAMK. 600921–000.

9/21/1960 DeWolf, L. Harold (Lotan Harold) (Boston University). Letter to Martin Luther King, Jr. 9/21/1960. Boston, Mass. (TLS) 1 p. MLKP-MBU: Box 23. 600921–002.

9/21/1960 King, Martin Luther, Jr. (Ebenezer Baptist Church). Letter to Guichard Parris. 9/21/1960. Atlanta, Ga. (TLS) 1 p. NULR-DLC. 600921–003.

9/22/1960 Robinson, James R. (CORE). Letter to Martin Luther King, Jr. 9/22/1960. New York, N.Y. (TLS) 1 p. (Contains enclosure 600922–001.) MLKP-MBU: Box 23. 600922–000.

9/22/1960 Robinson, James R. (CORE). Letter to Jawaharlal Nehru. 9/22/1960. New York, N.Y. (THLc) 1 p. (Enclosed in 600922–000. Copy to King.) MLKP-MBU: Box 23. 600922–001.

9/22/1960 Eskridge, Chauncey (McCoy, Ming, and Leighton). Letter to Martin Luther King, Jr. 9/22/1960. Chicago, Ill. (THLS) 2 pp. MLKP-MBU: Box 24. 600922–002.

9/23/1960 Wood, James R. Letter to Johnnie H. Goodson. 9/23/1960. (TLc) 1 p. MLKP-MBU. 600923–004.

9/25/1960 King, Martin Luther, Jr. "The Negro and the American Dream," Excerpts of address at the annual Freedom Mass Meeting of the North Carolina State Conference of branches of NAACP. 9/25/1960. Charlotte, N.C. (TADd) 5 pp. CSKC: Sermon file. 600925–000.

9/26/1960 King, Martin Luther, Jr. Letter to Anna Grace Sawyer. 9/26/1960. [*Atlanta, Ga.*] (TLc) 1 p. MLKP-MBU: Box 69. 600926–003.

9/26/1960 King, Martin Luther, Jr. Letter to Lois Doty. 9/26/1960. [*Atlanta, Ga.*] (TLc) 1 p. MLKP-MBU: Box 23A. 600926–007.

9/28/1960 King, Martin Luther, Jr. (Ebenezer Baptist Church). Letter to Lester B. (Lester Blackwell) Granger. 9/28/1960. Atlanta, Ga. (TLS) 2 pp. NULR-DLC. 600928–000.

9/28/1960 Eaton, Herbert H. (Dexter Avenue Baptist Church). Letter to Martin Luther King, Jr. 9/28/1960. Montgomery, Ala. (TLS) 1 p. MLKP-MBU: Box 24. 600928–001.

9/29/1960 King, Martin Luther, Jr. Letter to Phinehas Smith. 9/29/1960. [*Atlanta, Ga.*] (TLc) 1 p. MLKP-MBU: Box 70. 600929–004.

9/29/1960 Stout, Rex (Authors Guild of the Authors League of America, Inc.). Letter to Martin Luther King, Jr. 9/29/1960. New York, N.Y. (TLS) 1 p. MLKP-MBU: Box 70. 600929–007.

9/30/1960 Granger, Lester B. (Lester Blackwell) (National Urban League). Letter to Martin Luther King, Jr. 9/30/1960. New York, N.Y. (TLS) 1 p. MLKP-MBU: Box 27. 600930–001.

9/30/1960 King, Martin Luther, Jr. Letter to Elvin R. Caldwell. 9/30/1960. [*Atlanta, Ga.*] (TLc) 1 p. MLKP-MBU: Box 5. 600930–006.

10/1960 King, Martin Luther, Jr. Why we chose jail rather than bail. [*10/1960*]. (AD) 2 pp. CSKC. 601000–020.

9/1960–10/1960 Uhrbrock, Donald (*Time*). Photo of Martin Luther King, Jr., Lonnie C. King, Julian Bond, and others. [*9/1960–10/1960*]. Atlanta, Ga. (Ph) 1 p. NNTI. 601000–022.

10/1/1960 Stanley, Frank L. (*Louisville Defender*). Letter to Martin Luther King, Jr. 10/1/1960. Louisville, Ky. (TLS) 1 p. MLKP-MBU. 601001–002.

10/4/1960 Chivers, Walter R. (Morehouse College). Letter to Martin Luther King, Jr. 10/4/1960. Atlanta, Ga. (TLS) 1 p. MLKP-MBU: Box 34. 601004–000.

10/4/1960 King, Martin Luther, Jr. (Ebenezer Baptist Church). Letter to William Stuart Nelson. 10/4/1960. Atlanta, Ga. (TLS) 1 p. MWJP-DHU. 601004–002.

10/4/1960 King, Martin Luther, Jr. Letter to Frank L. Stanley. 10/4/1960. [*Atlanta, Ga.*] (TLc) 1 p. MLKP-MBU. 601004–008.

10/6/1960 King, Martin Luther, Jr. Form letter to Friend. 10/6/1960. [*Atlanta, Ga.*] (TLc) 1 p. (Enclosed in 601006–001, pp. 516–517 in this volume.) ERC-NHyF. 601006–000.

10/7/1960 Randolph, A. Philip (Asa Philip), and Gardner C. Taylor (Committee to Defend Martin Luther King and the Struggle for Freedom in the South). Press release, Committee to Defend Martin Luther King and the Struggle for Freedom in the South releases financial statement. 10/7/1960. New York, N.Y. (T (Contains enclosure 601007–004.) APRC-DLC. 601007–003.

10/7/1960 Committee to Defend Martin Luther King and the Struggle for Freedo

South. "Statement of income and expenditure for period ending 7/31/1960." [*10/7/1960*]. (TD) 1 p. (Enclosed in 601007–003.) APRC-DLC. 601007–004.

10/9/1960 Shiloh Baptist Church. Program, "Men's Day." 10/9/1960. Washington, D.C. (PHD) 2 pp. (Marginal comments by King.) SBCC-DSC. 601009–000.

10/10/1960 King, Martin Luther, Jr. Letter to Harold Edward Fey. 10/10/1960. [*Atlanta, Ga.*] (TLc) 1 p. MLKP-MBU: Box 25. 601010–003.

10/11/1960 Abernathy, Ralph (SCLC). Financial report, 12/7/1959–9/30/1960. 10/11/1960. Atlanta, Ga. (TD) 4 pp. MLKP-MBU: Box 5. 601011–005.

10/11/1960 Walker, Wyatt Tee (SCLC). "Report of the director to the executive board." 10/11/1960. Atlanta, Ga. (TD) 7 pp. MLKP-MBU: Box 121. 601011–007.

10/11/1960 Cotton, Dorothy (SCLC). "Minutes of annual board meeting." [*10/11/1960*]. Shreveport, La. (TD) 3 pp. MLKJP-GAMK: Box 29. 601011–008.

10/12/1960 SCLC. Program, "Freedom rally." 10/12/1960. (TD) 1 p. MLKP-MBU: Box 5. 601012–001.

10/12/1960 Allison, Robert (National Broadcasting Company, Inc.). Letter to Martin Luther King, Jr. 10/12/1960. New York, N.Y. (THLS) 2 pp. MLKP-MBU: Box 44. 601012–003.

10/13/1960 Levison, Stanley D. Draft, Letter to Clarence B. Jones. 10/13/1960. (TLc) 1 p. (Enclosed in 601013–002, pp. 518–520 in this volume.) MLKP-MBU. 601013–000.

10/11/1960–10/13/1960 SCLC. Program, "Annual conference." 10/11/1960–10/13/1960. Shreveport, La. (PHD) 14 pp. (Contains enclosure 601013–009, pp. 517–518 in this volume.) PFC-WHi. 601013–005.

10/14/1960–10/16/1960 SNCC. Agenda, "Conference: nonviolence and the achievement of desegregation." 10/14/1960–10/16/1960. Atlanta, Ga. (TD) 3 pp. MLKP-MBU: Box 68. 601016–000.

10/17/1960 Roosevelt, Eleanor. Letter to Martin Luther King, Jr. 10/17/1960. New York, N.Y. (TLS) 1 p. MLKP-MBU: Box 24. 601017–000.

10/17/1960 Tyler, Harold R. (U.S. Dept. of Justice). Letter to Martin Luther King, Jr. 10/17/1960. Washington, D.C. (TLS) 1 p. MLKP-MBU: Box 73. 601017–003.

10/18/1960 Murray, Jack. Letter to Martin Luther King, Jr. 10/18/1960. (TLS) 1 p. MLKP-MBU: Box 24. 601018–000.

10/18/1960 Springfield, Luvenia V. Letter to Martin Luther King, Jr., 10/18/1960. Niles, Mich. (AHLS) 1 p. MLKP-MBU: Box 70. 601018–001.

10/19/1960 Bardacke, Gregory J. (National Committee for Labor Israel). Letter to Martin Luther King, Jr. 10/19/1960. New York, N.Y. (TLS) 2 pp. MLKP-MBU: Box 18. 601019–000.

10/19/1960 Associated Press. Photo of Martin Luther King, Jr., R.E. Little, and Lonnie C. King. 10/19/1960. Atlanta, Ga. (Ph) 1 p. NNAPWW. 601019–002.

10/19/1960 Wood, James R. (SCLC). Telegram to Roy Wilkins. [*10/19/1960*]. Atlanta, Ga. (PHWSr) 1 p. NAACPP-DLC: Group III-A289. 601019–005.

10/19/1960 King, Lonnie C. (Committee on the Appeal for Human Rights). Telegram to Dwight D. (Dwight David) Eisenhower. 10/19/1960. Atlanta, Ga. (TWc) 1 p. SCLCR-GAMK: Box 36. 601019–007.

10/19/1960 King, Lonnie C. (Committee on the Appeals for Human Rights). Telegram to the Managers of major department stores. 10/19/1960. (TWc) 2 pp. SCLCR-GAMK: Box 36. 601019–008.

10/19/1960 King, Martin Luther, Jr. Draft, Statement to Judge James E. Webb after arrest at Rich's Department Store. [*10/19/1960*]. [*Atlanta, Ga.*] (AD) 3 pp. CSKC. 601019–010.

10/19/1960 Wood, James R. (SCLC). Telegram to J. (James) Oscar Lee. 10/19/1960. Atlanta, Ga. (PHWSr) 2 pp. NCCP-PPPrHi: Box 47. 601019–018.

10/20/1960 King, Martin Luther, Jr. Form letter to Friend. 10/20/1960. Atlanta, Ga. (TLS) 1 p. (Enclosed in 601020–001.) WEBD-MU. 601020–000.

10/20/1960 Belafonte, Harry. Form letter to Friend. 10/20/1960. New York, N.Y. (TLS) 1 p. (Contains enclosure 601020–000.) WEBD-MU. 601020–001.

10/20/1960 Gray, William H. (William Herbert). Telegram to William Berry Hartsfield. 10/20/1960. (TWc) 1 p. MLKP-MBU: Box 27. 601020–004.

10/20/1960 Walker, Wyatt Tee (SCLC). Telegram to Eleanor Roosevelt. 10/20/1960. Atlanta, Ga. (PHWSr) 1 p. ERC-NHyF. 601020–006.

10/20/1960 Braden, Anne. Letter to Coretta Scott King. 10/20/1960. (TLc) 1 p. CAABP-WHi. 601020–008.

10/20/1960 King, Martin Luther, Jr. Statement on lunch counter sit-ins arrest. 10/20/1960. Atlanta, Ga. (TTa) 1 p. MLKJP-GAMK. 601020–013.

10/20/1960	Walker, Wyatt Tee (SCLC). Telegram to William Berry Hartsfield. 10/20/1960. Atlanta, Ga. (TWc) 2 pp. SCLCR-GAMK: Box 36. 601020–015.
10/20/1960	Emergency Committee for the Southern Freedom Struggle. Telegram to Martin Luther King, Jr. 10/20/1960. New York, N.Y. (PWSr) 1 p. SCLCR-GAMK: Box 36. 601020–016.
10/20/1960	Shuttlesworth, Fred L. (Alabama Christian Movement for Human Rights (ACMHR)). Telegram to SCLC. 10/20/1960. Birmingham, Ala. (PWSr) 1 p. SCLCR-GAMK: Box 36. 601020–019.
10/20/1960	Walker, Wyatt Tee (SCLC). Telegram to Christian Herter. [*10/20/1960*]. Atlanta, Ga. (TWc) 1 p. SCLCR-GAMK: Box 36. 601020–021.
10/20/1960	Carey, Gordon (CORE). Telegram to Richard M. (Richard Milhous) Nixon. 10/20/1960. New York, N.Y. (PHWSr) 2 pp. PPRN-CYlNL. 601020–025.
10/20/1960	Taylor, Gardner C. Telegram to Martin Luther King, Jr. 10/20/1960. Brooklyn N.Y. (PWSr) 1 p. CSKC. 601020–026.
10/20/1960	Carey, Gordon (CORE). Telegram to Martin Luther King, Jr. [*10/20/1960*]. New York, N.Y. (PWSr) 1 p. CSKC. 601020–027.
10/20/1960	Livingston, David, and Cleveland Robinson (American Federation of Labor and Congress of Industrial Organizations (AFL-CIO)). Telegram to Martin Luther King, Jr. 10/20/1960. New York, N.Y. (PHWSr) 1 p. CSKC. 601020–031.
10/20/1960	Barry, Marion, and Edward B. King (SNCC). Letter to Fellow students. 10/20/1960. Atlanta, Ga. (TLc) 1 p. CSKC. 601020–036.
10/20/1960	King, Martin Luther, Jr. Interview on lunch counter desegregation. [*10/20/1960*]. [*Atlanta, Ga.*] (F) 1 min. WSBA-GU. 601020–037.
10/21/1960	Wilkins, Roy (NAACP). Memo to NAACP branch officers. 10/21/1960. New York, N.Y. (THD) 1 p. NAACPP-DLC: Group III-A177. 601021–007.
10/21/1960	Wilkins, Roy (NAACP). Telegram to Martin Luther King, Jr. 10/21/1960. (PHWSr) 2 pp. SCLCR-GAMK: Box 36. 601021–008.
10/21/1960	Goldburg, Robert E. (Congregation Mishkan Israel). Letter to Martin Luther King, Jr. 10/21/1960. Hamden, Conn. (TLS) 1 p. MLKP-MBU: Box 58. 601021–012.
10/21/1960	Rettig, Dick (U.S. National Student Association). Telegram to Martin Luther King, Jr. 10/21/1960. Philadelphia, Pa. (PWSr) 1 p. CSKC. 601021–014.
10/21/1960	Abernathy, Ralph, S. S. (Solomon Snowden) Seay, and Robert E. Dubose. (MIA) Telegram to Martin Luther King, Jr. [*10/21/1960*]. Montgomery, Ala. (PWSr) 1 p. SCLCR-GAMK: Box 5. 601021–023.
10/22/1960	Steele, C. Kenzie (Bethel Baptist Church). Telegram to Martin Luther King, Jr. 10/22/1960. Tallahassee, Fla. (PWSr) 1 p. CSKC. 601022–001.
10/22/1960	Reddick, Lawrence Dunbar. Telegram to Martin Luther King, Jr. [*10/22/1960*]. Baltimore, Md. (PWSr) 1 p. CSKC. 601022–002.
10/22/1960	Long, Carolyn. Letter to Omega Brothers. 10/22/1960. (ALS) 7 pp. CSKC. 601022–007.
10/22/1960	Ashmore, Ann. Letter to All my friends in the pokey. 10/22/1960. (ALS) 1 p. CSKC. 601022–008.
10/22/1960	Van Arsdale, Harry (New York City Central Labor Council). Telegram to Martin Luther King, Jr. [*10/22/1960*]. New York, N.Y. (PWSr) 1 p. CSKC. 601022–011.
10/23/1960	Cartwright, Marguerite. Letter to Martin Luther King, Jr. 10/23/1960. New York, N. Y. (ALS) 2 pp. (Contains enclosure 601023–001.) MLKP-MBU: Box 22. 601023–000.
10/23/1960	Secretary to the Prime Minister of Nigeria. Telegram to Martin Luther King, Jr. 10/23/1960. Lagos, Nigeria. (PHWSr) 1 p. (Enclosed in 601023–000.) MLKP-MBU: Box 22. 601023–001.
10/19/1960–10/23/1960	Cox, Mattie, Carolyn Long, Wylma Long, and Christine Sparks. Letter to Brothers. [*10/19/1960–10/23/1960*]. Atlanta, Ga. (ALS) 2 pp. CSKC. 601023–007.
10/23/1960	Announcement, "Freedom rally presents Dr. Martin Luther King, Jr." 10/23/1960. Cleveland, Ohio (PD) 1 p. OClWHi: Container 1. 601023–009.
10/19/1960–10/23/1960	**King, Martin Luther, Jr. Letter to female inmates. [*10/19/1960–10/23/1960*]. [*Atlanta, Ga.*] (AL) 1 p. CSKC. 601023–011.**
10/19/1960–10/23/1960	King, Martin Luther, Jr. Draft, Letter to female inmates. [*10/19/1960–10/23/1960*]. (AHLd) 1 p. CSKC. 601023–012.
10/24/1960	Braden, Carl, and Anne Braden. Telegram to Martin Luther King, Jr. [*10/24/1960*]. Louisville, Ky. (PWSr) 1 p. CSKC. 601024–005.
10/24/1960	Kilgore, Thomas (Friendship Baptist Church). Telegram to Martin Luther King, Jr. 10/24/1960. New York, N.Y. (PWSr) 1 p. CSKC: M2. 601024–006.
10/24/1960	Van Arsdale, Harry (American Federation of Labor and Congress of Industrial

Organizations (AFL-CIO)). Telegram to Martin Luther King, Jr. [*10/24/1960*]. New York, N.Y. (PWSr) 1 p. CSKC. 601024–008.

10/24/1960 King, Martin Luther, Jr., and Wyatt Tee Walker (SCLC). Form letter to Pastor and Friends. 10/24/1960. Atlanta, Ga. (TLc) 1 p. SCLCR-GAMK: Box 52. 601024–011.

10/24/1960 Hartsfield, William Berry. Interview on Martin Luther King, Jr.'s arrest and student sit-ins. [*10/24/1960*] (F) 7.2 min. WSBA-GU. 601024-017.

10/25/1960 Cort, Horace (Associated Press). Photo of Martin Luther King, Jr., and two unidentified police officers. 10/25/1960. Atlanta, Ga. (Ph) 1 p. NNAPWW. 601025–003.

10/25/1960 Wilkins, Roy. Press conference. [*10/25/1960*]. (TD) 12 pp. NAACPP-DLC: Group III-A177, A175. 601025–005.

10/26/1960 Granger, Lester B. (Lester Blackwell) (National Urban League). Letter to Martin Luther King, Jr. 10/26/1960. (THLc) 1 p. NULR-DLC. 601026–001.

10/26/1960 SCLC. Press release, Martin Luther King, Jr. sentenced to hard labor. 10/26/1960. Atlanta, Ga. (TD) 2 pp. SAVFC-WHi. 601026–003.

10/26/1960 Prinz, Joachim. Telegram to S. Ernest (Samuel Ernest) Vandiver. 10/26/1960. (TWc) 1 p. NAACPP-DLC. 601026–006.

10/26/1960 Meany, George (American Federation of Labor and Congress of Industrial Organizations (AFL-CIO)). Letter to S. Ernest (Samuel Ernest) Vandiver. 10/26/1960. (TALc) 1 p. ACCP-DAFL. 601026–014.

10/26/1960 Belafonte, Harry. Telegram to Coretta Scott King. 10/26/1960. New York, N.Y. (PWSr) 1 p. MLKJP-GAMK: Vault Box 5. 601026–018.

10/26/1960 Hollowell, Donald. Statement on transfer of Martin Luther King, Jr. to Reidsville State Prison. [*10/26/1960*]. (F) 1.7 min. WSBA-GU. 601026–025.

10/26/1960 Lee, George W. Telegram to Martin Luther King, Jr. [*10/26/1960*]. Memphis, Tenn. (PWSr) 1 p. SCLCR-GAMK: Box 5. 601026–030.

10/26/1960 Walker, Wyatt Tee. Telegram to Martin Luther King, Jr. 10/26/1960. Atlanta, Ga. (PWSr) 1 p. SCLCR-GAMK: Box 5. 601026–035.

10/27/1960 Chalmers, Allan Knight (Boston University). Letter to Martin Luther King, Jr. 10/27/1960. Boston, Mass. (ALS) 1 p. MLKP-MBU: Box 22A. 601027–001.

10/27/1960 SCLC, and Southern Conference Educational Fund, Inc. Telegram to John F. (John Fitzgerald) Kennedy and Richard M. (Richard Milhous) Nixon. 10/27/1960. Montgomery, Ala. (TWc) 4 pp. CAABP-WHi. 601027–004.

10/27/1960 Cort, Horace (Associated Press). Photo of Martin Luther King, Jr., Coretta Scott King, Christine King Farris, Yolanda Denise King, Martin Luther King, III and others. 10/27/1960. Atlanta, Ga. (Ph) 1 p. NNAPWW. 601027–006.

10/27/1960 Dahlberg, Edwin T. (Edwin Theodore) (National Council of the Churches of Christ in the United States of America). Letter to Martin Luther King, Jr. 10/27/1960. St. Louis, Mo. (TALS) 1 p. MLKP-MBU. 601027–019.

10/19/1960–10/27/1960 Tillery, William C. Letter to Martin Luther King, Jr. [*10/19/1960–10/27/1960*]. (ALS) 1 p. CSKC. 601027–022.

10/27/1960 Special Agent in Charge (U.S. Federal Bureau of Investigation). Telegram to J. Edgar Hoover. 10/27/1960. Atlanta, Ga. (PHWSr) 1 p. DGFBI-NN-Sc. 601027–026.

10/27/1960 Bates, Daisy, and L.C. Bates. Telegram to Martin Luther King, Jr. [*10/27/1960*]. Little Rock, Ark. (PWSr) 1 p. SCLCR-GAMK: Box 5. 601027–032.

10/27/1960 Brown, Theodore E. (American Federation of Labor and Congress of Industrial Organizations (AFL-CIO)). Telegram to Martin Luther King, Jr. [*10/27/1960*]. Washington, D.C. (PWSr) 1 p. SCLCR-GAMK: Box 5. 601027–033.

10/27/1960 King, Martin Luther, Jr. Interview on John F. (John Fitzgerald) Kennedy's role in release from prison. [*10/27/1960*]. (F) .8 min. WSBA-GU. 601027–035.

10/28/1960 Burks, Mary Fair (Maryland State College). Letter to Martin Luther King, Jr. and Coretta Scott King. 10/28/1960. Princess Anne, Md. (THLS) 1 p. MLKP-MBU: Box 20. 601028–002.

10/28/1960 Burchfield, Ray A. (Fifth Street Methodist Church). Letter to Martin Luther King, Jr. 10/28/1960. Anderson, Ind. (TALS) 1 p. MLKP-MBU: Box 21. 601028–003.

10/28/1960 Barry, Marion, and Edward B. King (SNCC). Letter to Martin Luther King, Jr. 10/28/1960. Atlanta, Ga. (TLS) 1 p. CSKC. 601028–012.

10/28/1960 Swarthmore College. Minutes, Student council meeting on 10/23/1960. 10/28/1960. Swarthmore, Pa. (TD) 3 pp. PSC-Hi. 601028–014.

10/29/1960 Gray, William H. (William Herbert). Letter to Oscar Mitchell. 10/29/1960. (TLc) 1 p. MLKP-MBU: Box 29A. 601029–000.

10/31/1960 Rodell, Marie F. (Marie Freid) (Marie Rodell and Joan Daves, Inc.). Letter to Martin Luther King, Jr. 10/31/1960. New York, N.Y. (TLSr) 1 p. MLKP-MBU: Box 6. 601031–010.

10/31/1960 Carey, Gordon (CORE). Letter to Martin Luther King, Jr. 10/31/1960. New York, N.Y. (TLS) 2 pp. MLKP-MBU: Box 40. 601031–011.

10/31/1960 Gray, James H. (*Albany Herald*). Telegram to Robert Allison. 10/31/1960. Albany, Ga. (PWSr) 1 p. NBCTV-WHi. 601031–018.

10/31/1960 SCLC. "Statement of receipts and expenditures." 10/31/1960. (TD) 1 p. MLKJP-GAMK: Box 28. 601031–020.

10/31/1960 Walsh, Lawrence E. Suggested statement on arrest of Martin Luther King, Jr. 10/31/1960. (TDd) WCFO-KAbE. 601031–022.

10/31/1960 Jack, Homer Alexander (National Committee for a Sane Nuclear Policy (U.S.)). Letter to Martin Luther King, Jr. 10/31/1960. New York, N.Y. (THLS) 1 p. SCLCR-GAMK: Box 5. 601031–023.

10/1960-11/1960 King, Martin Luther, Jr. Public service announcement on registering and voting. [*10/1960–11/1960*]. [*Atlanta, Ga.*] (TD) 1 p. MLKP-MBU: Box 117. 601100–009.

9/1960-11/1960 King, Martin Luther, Jr. Statement on Negro vote. [*9/1960–11/1960*]. (F) .8 min. WSBA-GU. 601100–011.

10/1960-11/1960 Roosevelt, Eleanor. "The make-up of America: a majority of minorities." [*10/1960–11/1960*]. (At) 3.3 min. (1 sound cassette: analog.) ERC-NHyF. 601100–012.

11/1/1960 SNCC. Form letter to Fellow students. 11/1/1960. Atlanta, Ga. (THL) 1 p. (Marginal comments by King.) MLKP-MBU: Box 68. 601101–003.

11/1/1960 Burchfield, Ray A. (Fifth Street Baptist Church). Letter to Martin Luther King, Jr. 11/1/1960. Anderson, Ind. (TLS) 1 p. MLKP-MBU: Box 21. 601101–004.

11/1/1960 Thompson, Claude (Emory University). Letter to Martin Luther King, Jr. 11/1/1960. (TLS) 1 p. MLKP-MBU: Box 72. 601101–011.

11/1/1960 Randolph, A. Philip (Asa Philip). Telegram to Martin Luther King, Jr. 11/1/1960. New York, N.Y. (PWSr) 1 p. SCLCR-GAMK: Box 5. 601101–015.

11/2/1960 King, Martin Luther, Jr. (Ebenezer Baptist Church). Letter to L. Harold (Lotan Harold) DeWolf. 11/2/1960. Atlanta, Ga. (TLS) 2 pp. OGCP-MBU. 601102–004.

11/2/1960 Teck Frank, Ingeborg. Letter to Martin Luther King, Jr. 11/2/1960. New York, N.Y. (TALS) 58 pp. (Contains 490000–034.) MLKP-MBU: Box 72. 601102–012.

11/2/1960 Coffin, William Sloane (Yale University). Letter to Martin Luther King, Jr. 11/2/1960. New Haven, Conn. (TLS) 1 p. MLKP-MBU: Box 47A. 601102–016.

11/2/1960 Chivers, Walter R. (Morehouse College). Letter to Martin Luther King, Jr. 11/2/1960. Atlanta, Ga. (TLS) 2 pp. MLKP-MBU: Box 34. 601102–017.

11/3/1960 Hollowell, Donald L. Letter to Martin Luther King, Jr. 11/3/1960. Atlanta, Ga. (TLS) 1 p. MLKP-MBU: Box 27A. 601103–000.

11/3/1960 Mays, Benjamin Elijah (Morehouse College). Letter to Martin Luther King, Jr. 11/3/1960. Atlanta, Ga. (TLS) 1 pp. (Contains enclosure 601102–007, pp. 540–541 in this volume.) MLKP-MBU: Box 29. 601103–001.

11/3/1960 Imbrie, James. Letter to Martin Luther King, Jr. 11/3/1960. Lawrenceville, N.J. (THLc) 2 pp. (Includes enclosure.) MLKP-MBU: Box 72. 601103–002.

11/3/1960 Diwakar, R. R. Letter to Martin Luther King, Jr. 11/3/1960. New York, N.Y. (AHLS) 2 pp. MLKP-MBU: Box 73A. 601103–003.

11/3/1960 Burchfield, Ray A. (Fifth Street Baptist Church). Letter to Martin Luther King, Jr. 11/3/1960. Anderson, Ind. (TALS) 1 p. MLKP-MBU: Box 21. 601103–004.

11/3/1960 McWilliams, Carey (*The Nation*). Letter to Martin Luther King, Jr. 11/3/1960. New York, N.Y. (THLS) 1 p. MLKP-MBU. 601103–005.

11/3/1960 King, Martin Luther, Jr. Letter to Ellen M. Kheel. 11/3/1960. [*Atlanta, Ga.*] (TLc) 1 p. MLKP-MBU: Box 36. 601103–007.

11/3/1960 Taylor, Gardner C. (Taylor Team Defense Fund). Letter to Martin Luther King, Jr. 11/3/1960. Brooklyn, N.Y. (TALS) 1 p. MLKP-MBU: Box 11. 601103–008.

11/4/1960 Davis, Benjamin J. (Benjamin Jefferson). Letter to Martin Luther King, Jr. 11/4/1960. New York, N.Y. (THLS) 1 p. SCLCR-GAMK: Box 5. 601104–014.

11/5/1960 Braden, Anne (Southern Conference Educational Fund, Inc.). Letter to Martin Luther King, Jr., and Coretta Scott King. 11/5/1960. Louisville, Ky. (TLS) 2 pp. MLKP-MBU: Box 116. 601105–000.

11/5/1960 King, Martin Luther, Jr. (Ebenezer Baptist Church). Letter to A. Philip (Asa Philip) Randolph. 11/5/1960. Atlanta, Ga. (TLS) 1 p. RPP-NN-Sc: Box 2. 601105–001.

11/5/1960 McDonald, Dora E. Letter to Luvenia V. Springfield. 11/5/1960. [*Atlanta, Ga.*] (TLc) 1 p. MLKP-MBU: Box 70. 601105–005.

11/5/1960 King, Martin Luther, Jr. Letter to Claude Thompson. 11/5/1960. [*Atlanta, Ga.*] (TLc) 1 p. MLKP-MBU: Box 72. 601105–006.

11/5/1960	King, Martin Luther, Jr. Letter to Major J. Jones. 11/5/1960. [*Atlanta, Ga.*] (THLc) 1 p. MLKP-MBU: Box 46. 601105–009.
11/5/1960	King, Martin Luther. Letter to Gardner C. Taylor. 11/5/1960. [*Atlanta, Ga.*] (TLc) 1 p. MLKP-MBU: Box 72. 601105–012.
11/5/1960	King, Martin Luther, Jr. Letter to Robert E. Goldburg. 11/5/1960. [*Atlanta, Ga.*] (TLc) 1 p. MLKP-MBU: Box 58. 601105–017.
11/7/1960	King, Martin Luther, Jr. Letter to Sidney Kaufman. 11/7/1960. [*Atlanta, Ga.*] (TLc) 1 p. MLKP-MBU: Box 29. 601107–001.
11/7/1960	King, Martin Luther, Jr. Letter to Robert Reade. 11/7/1960. [*Atlanta, Ga.*] (TLc) 1 p. MLKP-MBU. 601107–010.
11/7/1960	Kilpatrick, James J. (James Jackson) (*Richmond News Leader*). Letter to Robert Allison. 11/7/1960. Richmond, Va. (THLS) 1 p. NBCTV-WHi. 601107–011.
11/7/1960	Minutes, Meeting on advisory committee on desegregation of lunch counters. 11/7/1960. Atlanta, Ga. (TD) 1 p. (Enclosed in 601108–003.) SWWP-GAU. 601107–012.
10/27/1960–11/7/1960	**The Freedom Crusade Committee. Pamphlet, "The Case of Martin Luther King." [*10/27/1960–11/7/1960*]. Philadelphia, Pa. (PD) 2 pp. 1960CR-MWalK: Box 140. 601107–015.**
11/8/1960	King, Martin Luther, Jr. Letter to Kivie Kaplan. 11/8/1960. [*Atlanta, Ga.*] (TLc) 1 p. MLKP-MBU: Box 29. 601108–001.
11/8/1960	Mays, Benjamin Elijah (Morehouse College). Letter to Samuel W. Williams. 11/8/1960. Atlanta, Ga. (TL) 1 p. (Contains enclosure 601107–012.) SWWP-GAU. 601108–003.
11/8/1960	Committee for Nonviolent Action. Draft, "Statement of purpose for the San Francisco to Moscow peace walk." 11/8/1960. New York, N.Y. (THDd) 2 pp. (Enclosed in 601121–005.) MLKP-MBU: Box 55. 601108–011.
11/9/1960	King, Martin Luther, Jr. Telegram to Geraldine Garrett Fisher. 11/9/1960. [*Atlanta, Ga.*] (PWc) 1 p. MLKP-MBU: Box 25. 601109–000.
11/10/1960	Brown University. Program, "The college convocation." 11/10/1960. Providence, R.I. (PTD) 1 p. CSKC. 601110–018.
11/10/1960	Morrow, E. Frederic (Everett Frederic). Journal entry. 11/10/1960. (TADf) 2 pp. EFMP-KAbE: Box 1. 601110–019.
11/10/1960	Brown University. Letter from Abraham Lincoln to Henry L. Pierce presented to Martin Luther King, Jr. 11/10/1960. (TALS) 6 pp. MLKP-MBU: Box 31. 601110–020.
11/12/1960	Bronner, N. H. (Bronner Bros' Beauty Supply Co.). Letter to Martin Luther King, Jr. 11/12/1960. Atlanta, Ga. (THLS) 1 p. MLKP-MBU: Box 20. 601112–000.
11/13/1960	King, Martin Luther, Jr. The Dimensions of a Complete Life, Sermon at Cornell University. 11/13/1960. Ithaca, N.Y. (TD) 15 pp. MLKJP-GAMK. 601113–000.
11/14/1960	Snyder, Margaret (Planned Parenthood Federation of America, Inc.). Letter to Martin Luther King, Jr. 11/14/1960. New York, N.Y. (TLS) 1 p. MLKP-MBU: Box 34. 601114–000.
11/14/1960	Crane, Henry H. Letter to Martin Luther King, Jr. 11/14/1960. Detroit, Mich. (THLS) 1 p. MLKP-MBU: Box 22. 601114–002.
11/16/1960	Chalmers, Allan Knight (Boston University). Letter to Martin Luther King, Jr. 11/16/1960. Boston, Mass. (THLf) 1 p. MLKP-MBU: Box 21. 601116–002.
11/17/1960	Terrill, L. M. (General Missionary Baptist State Convention of Georgia). "Citation to Dr. Martin Luther King, Jr." 11/17/1960. Athens, Ga. (TADS) 2 pp. MLKP-MBU: Box 121. 601117–003.
11/18/1960	Azikiwe, Nnamdi (Federation of Nigeria). Invitation to a display of national traditional dances. 11/18/1960. (PD) 1 p. MLKP-MBU: Box 26. 601118–002.
11/18/1960	Azikiwe, Nnamdi (Federation of Nigeria). Invitation to the state luncheon. 11/18/1960. (PHD) 1 p. MLKP-MBU: Box 49. 601118–006.
11/9/1960–11/19/1960	Itinerary for Martin Luther King, Jr. 11/9/1960–11/19/1960. (TD) 2 pp. CSKC. 601119–002.
11/19/1960	Mbadiwe, K. O. (Lincoln University Alumni Association). Invitation to Martin Luther King, Jr. 11/19/1960. Ebute Metta, Nigeria. (PHD) 1 p. MLKP-MBU: Box 26. 601119–003.
11/21/1960	Thompson, Era Bell (*Ebony*). Letter to Martin Luther King, Jr. 11/21/1960. Chicago, Ill. (TLS) 1 p. (Contains enclosure 601121–001.) MLKP-MBU: Box 24. 601121–000.
11/21/1960	King, Martin Luther, Jr. Draft, What Happened to Hell? [*11/21/1960*]. (TDd) 1 p. (Enclosed in 601121–000.) MLKP-MBU: Box 24. 601121–001.
11/21/1960	Muste, A. J. (Abraham Johannes) (FOR). Letter to Martin Luther King, Jr.

11/21/1960. New York, N.Y. (TLS) 1 p. (Contains enclosure 601108–011.) MLKP-MBU: Box 55. 601121–005.

11/21/1960 Osibudo, J. S. K. Letter to Martin Luther King, Jr. 11/21/1960. Ibadan, Nigeria. (TLS) 2 pp. MLKP-MBU: Box 53A. 601121–006.

11/22/1960 Randolph, A. Philip (Asa Philip) (Negro American Labor Council). Letter to Martin Luther King, Jr. 11/22/1960. New York, N.Y. (TLS) 1 p. MLKP-MBU: Box 64. 601122–000.

11/22/1960 Wood, James R. Letter to Margrit de Sabloniere. 11/22/1960. [*Atlanta, Ga.*] (TLc) 1 p. MLKP-MBU: Box 70. 601122–003.

11/22/1960 Wood, James R. Letter to Victoria Ashley. 11/22/1960. (TLc) 1 p. MLKP-MBU: Box 26. 601122–010.

11/23/1960 Barry, Marion (SNCC). Letter to Martin Luther King, Jr. 11/23/1960. Atlanta, Ga. (TLS) 1 p. MLKP-MBU: Box 71. 601123–001.

11/23/1960 Wood, James R. (SCLC). Report, "Leadership training program." 11/23/1960. (TD) 2 pp. SCLCR-GAMK: Box 136. 601123–012.

11/24/1960 Cartwright, Marguerite. Letter to Martin Luther King, Jr. 11/24/1960. New York, N.Y. (ALS) 2 pp. MLKP-MBU: Box 53A. 601124–001.

11/26/1960 King, Martin Luther, Jr. Debate with James J. Kilpatrick on "The Nation's Future." 11/26/1960. [*New York, N.Y.*] (TTv) 19 pp. MLKP-MBU: Box 33. 601126–000.

11/26/1960 List of New York audience for "The Nation's Future." 11/26/1960. New York, N.Y. (TD) 1 p. NBCTV-WHi. 601126-001.

11/26/1960 King, Martin Luther, Jr. Notes for debate on "The Nation's Future." [*11/26/1960*]. [*Atlanta, Ga.*] (ADf) 8 pp. CSKC. 601126–002.

11/27/1960 Ebenezer Baptist Church. Press release, Invitation to Sunday services. 11/27/1960. Atlanta, Ga. (TD) 1 p. EBCR. 601127–000.

11/25/1960–11/27/1960 SNCC. Minutes of meeting. 11/25/1960–11/27/1960. Atlanta, Ga. (TD) 4 pp. (Enclosed in 601212–018.) EJBC-NN-Sc. 601127–005.

11/28/1960 Frazier, Edward Franklin (Howard University). Letter to Martin Luther King, Jr. 11/28/1960. Atlanta, Ga. (TLS) 1 p. MLKP-MBU: Box 25. 601128–001.

11/30/1960 Jack, Homer Alexander (National Committee for a Sane Nuclear Policy (U.S.)). Letter to Martin Luther King, Jr. 11/30/1960. New York, N.Y. (TLS) 1 p. (Contains enclosure 601130–003.) MLKP-MBU: Box 71. 601130–002.

11/30/1960 National Committee for a Sane Nuclear Policy (U.S.). Statement on the North Atlantic Treaty Organization as a fourth nuclear power. 11/30/1960. New York, N.Y. (TD) 1 p. (Enclosed in 601130–002.) MLKP-MBU: Box 71. 601130–009

11/30/1960 Fey, Harold Edward (*Christian Century*). Letter to Martin Luther King, Jr. 11/30/1960. Chicago, Ill. (TLS) 1 p. MLKP-MBU: Box 25. 601130–004.

12/1/1959–11/30/1960 King, Martin Luther, Jr., and Martin Luther King (Ebenezer Baptist Church). "Annual report." 12/1/1959–11/30/1960. Atlanta, Ga. (THD) 38 pp. EBCR. 601130–009.

12/1960 King, Martin Luther, Jr. (SCLC). "The Rising Tide of Racial Consciousness," Address on 9/6/1960. 12/1960. New York, N.Y. From: *YWCA Magazine*, December 1960, pp. 4–6. (PD) 3 pp. MLKP-MBU: Box 2. 601200–000.

12/1960 King, Martin Luther, Jr. (SCLC). "The Rising Tide of Racial Consciousness," Address on 9/6/60. [*12/1960*]. (THD) 20 pp. MLKP-MBU: Box 2. 601200–001.

12/1/1960 Rodell, Marie F. (Marie Freid) (Marie Rodell and Joan Daves, Inc.). Letter to Martin Luther King, Jr. 12/1/1960. New York, N. Y. (TLS) 1 p. MLKP-MBU: Box 6. 601201–000.

12/1/1960 King, Martin Luther. Letter to O. Clay Maxwell and Lillie Belle Maxwell. 12/1/1960. [*Atlanta, Ga.*] (TLc) 1 p. MLKP-MBU: Box 24. 601201–003.

12/1/1960 King, Martin Luther, Jr. Letter to John Wesley Dobbs. 12/1/1960. [*Atlanta, Ga.*] (TLc) 1 p. MLKP-MBU: Box 23A. 601201–005.

12/1/1960 King, Martin Luther, Jr. Letter to Maurice A. Dawkins. 12/1/1960. [*Atlanta, Ga.*] (TLc) 1 p. MLKP-MBU: Box 23A. 601201–006.

12/1/1960 Abner, Willoughby (Committee to Defend Martin Luther King and the Struggle for Freedom in the South). Letter to Martin Luther King, Jr. 12/1/1960. Chicago, Ill. (THLS) 1 p. (Marginal comments by King.) MLKP-MBU: Box 7. 601201–008.

12/1/1960 King, Martin Luther, Jr. (Ebenezer Baptist Church). Letter to Roy Wilkins. 12/1/1960. Atlanta, Ga. (TLS) 1 p. NAACPP-DLC: Group III-A175. 601201–014.

12/1/1960 King, Martin Luther. Letter to Sandy F. Ray. 12/1/1960. [*Atlanta, Ga.*] (THLc) 1 p. MLKP-MBU: Box 68. 601201–018.

12/1/1960 Memo, "SCLC-Highlander financial agreements." 12/1/1960. (TL) 1 p. SCLCR-GAMK: Box 136. 601201–024.

12/2/1960 Rodell, Marie F. (Marie Freid) (Marie Rodell and Joan Daves, Inc.). Letter to Martin Luther King, Jr. 12/2/1960. (TLS) 1 p. MLKP-MBU: Box 6. 601202–000.

12/2/1960 Wilkins, Roy (NAACP). Letter to Martin Luther King, Jr. 12/2/1960. New York, N.Y. (ALS) 1 p. MLKP-MBU: Box 32. 601202–001.

12/2/1960 Henry, Aaron E. (NAACP). Letter to Martin Luther King, Jr. 12/2/1960. Clarksdale, Miss. (THLS) 1 p. MLKP-MBU: Box 51. 601202–006.

12/5/1960 Spear, Samuel. Letter to Martin Luther King, Jr. 12/5/1960. Philadelphia, Pa. (ALS) 2 pp. MLKP-MBU: Box 69. 601205–001.

12/5/1960 Levison, Stanley D. (Tribute to Martin Luther King, Jr.). Letter to Martin Luther King, Jr. 12/5/1960. New York, N.Y. (TLS) 1 p. (Contains enclosure 601205–017.) MLKP-MBU: Box 23A. 601205–003.

12/5/1960 Huelle, Marjorie (Bell Gardens School). Letter to Martin Luther King, Jr. 12/5/1960. Bell Gardens, Calif. (AHLS) 1 p. MLKP-MBU: Box 27A. 601205–004.

12/5/1960 Bentz, Betty (Hotel and Club Employees Union Local 6). Letter to Martin Luther King, Jr. 12/5/1960. New York, N.Y. (THLS) 1 p. (Marginal comments by King.) MLKP-MBU: Box 20. 601205–011.

12/5/1960 King, Martin Luther, Jr. Excerpts, The Future of Integration, Address at Ford Hall Forum on 12/11/1960. 12/5/1960. (THD) 1 p. MLKP-MBU: Box 39. 601205–012.

12/5/1960 McDonald, Dora E. Letter to Fred D. Gray. 12/5/1960. [*Atlanta, Ga.*] (TLc) 1 p. MLKP-MBU: Box 7. 601205–016.

12/5/1960 [*Levison, Stanley D.*]. Draft, Letter to Sammy Davis. 12/5/1960. New York, N.Y. (TLd) 1 p. (Enclosed in 601205–003.) MLKP-MBU: Box 23A. 601205–017.

12/7/1960 Wagner, John (National Lutheran Council). Letter to Martin Luther King, Jr. 12/7/1960. Chicago, Ill. (TLS) 1 p. MLKP-MBU: Box 73A. 601207–012.

12/7/1960 Dawkins, Maurice A. (The People's Independent Church of Christ). Letter to Martin Luther King, Jr. 12/7/1960. Los Angeles, Calif. (TLS) 2 pp. MLKP-MBU: Box 52A. 601207–024.

12/8/1960 Abernathy, Ralph (MIA). "Building a Democratic Civilization Amidst World Tensions, Frustrations and Fears," Address at Annual Institute on Nonviolence and Social Change. 12/8/1960. Montgomery, Ala. (TD) 21 pp. HG-GAMK. 601208–000.

12/8/1960 Calhoun, J. H. (Atlanta Student Adult Liaison). "Notes on conference with college presidents." 12/8/1960. (TD) 2 pp. SWWP-GAU. 601208–010.

12/8/1960 King, Martin Luther, Jr. Statement in support of sit-ins. [*12/8/1960*]. [*Atlanta, Ga.*] (TD) 2 pp. NBCTV-WHi. 601208–012.

12/9/1960 Gray, Fred D. Letter to Martin Luther King, Jr. 12/9/1960. Montgomery, Ala. (TLS) 1 p. MLKP-MBU: Box 27. 601209–001.

12/9/1960 King, Martin Luther, Jr. Letter to William Holmes Borders. 12/9/1960. [*Atlanta, Ga.*] (TLc) 2 pp. MLKP-MBU: Box 20. 601209–003.

12/5/1960–12/11/1960 MIA. Program, "Fifth anniversary and the Annual Institute on Nonviolence." 12/5/1960–12/11/1960. Montgomery, Ala. (PHD) 16 pp. HG-GAMK. 601211–000.

12/11/1960 King, Martin Luther, Jr. "The Three Dimensions of a Complete Life," Sermon at Unitarian Church of Germantown. 12/11/1960. [*Philadelphia, Pa.*] (THD) 6 pp. PPUCGC. 601211–003.

12/11/1960 King, Martin Luther, Jr. "The Future of Integration," Address delivered at Ford Hall Forum. [*12/11/1960*]. [*Boston, Mass.*] (At) 38.1 min. (1 sound cassette: analog.) CLPAC. 601211–004.

12/12/1960 Pauling, Linus (California Institute of Technology). Letter to Martin Luther King, Jr. 12/12/1960. Pasadena, Calif. (TLS) 1 p. MLKP-MBU: Box 32A. 601212–000.

12/12/1960 King, Martin Luther, Jr. Letter to Charles A. Baldwin. 12/12/1960. [*Atlanta, Ga.*] (TLc) 1 p. MLKP-MBU: Box 36A. 601212–001.

12/12/1960 King, Martin Luther, Jr. Letter to J. Rupert Picott. 12/12/1960. [*Atlanta, Ga.*] (TLc) 1 p. MLKP-MBU: Box 47. 601212–002.

12/12/1960 King, Martin Luther, Jr. Letter to Henry H. Crane. 12/12/1960. [*Atlanta, Ga.*] (THLc) 1 p. MLKP-MBU: Box 22. 601212–004.

12/12/1960 King, Martin Luther, Jr. Letter to George St. Angelo. 12/12/1960. [*Atlanta, Ga.*] (TLc) 1 p. MLKP-MBU: Box 44. 601212–006.

12/12/1960 King, Martin Luther, Jr. Letter to L. Paul Jaquith. 12/12/1960. [*Atlanta, Ga.*] (THLc) 1 p. MLKP-MBU: Box 38. 601212–007.

12/12/1960 King, Martin Luther, Jr. Letter to Edwin T. (Edwin Theodore) Dahlberg. 12/12/1960. [*Atlanta, Ga.*] (TLc) 2 pp. MLKP-MBU. 601212–010.

12/12/1960 King, Martin Luther, Jr. Letter to Lester I. Levin. 12/12/1960. [*Atlanta, Ga.*] (TLc) 1 p. MLKP-MBU. 601212–012.

12/12/1960 King, Edward B. (SNCC). Form letter to Committee member. 12/12/1960. Atlanta, Ga. (TLc) 1 p. (Contains enclosure 601127–005). EJBC-NN-Sc. 601212–018.

12/14/1960 Stembridge, Jane (SNCC). Letter to Martin Luther King, Jr. 12/14/1960. Atlanta, Ga. (THLS) 1 p. (Marginal comments by King.) MLKP-MBU: Box 6. 601214–000.

12/14/1960 Clareman, Jack (The Christopher Reynolds Foundation, Inc.). Letter to James R. Wood. 12/14/1960. New York, N.Y. (THLS) 1 p. MLKP-MBU: Box 52. 601214–005.

12/14/1960 King, Martin Luther, Jr. Letter to Fred O. Doty. 12/14/1960. [*Atlanta, Ga.*] (TLc) 1 p. MLKP-MBU: Box 47. 601214–007.

12/14/1960 King, Martin Luther, Jr. Letter to Robert Allison. 12/14/1960. Atlanta, Ga. (TLS) 2 pp. NBCTV-WHi. 601214–009.

12/14/1960 King, Martin Luther, Jr. Letter to Betty Bentz. 12/14/1960. [*Atlanta, Ga.*] (TLc) 1 p. MLKP-MBU: Box 20. 601214–013.

12/15/1960 Dobbs, John Wesley (Freemasons. Prince Hall Grand Lodge). Letter to Martin Luther King, Jr. 12/15/1960. Atlanta, Ga. (ALS) 2 pp. MLKP-MBU: Box 23A. 601215–002.

12/15/1960 King, Martin Luther, Jr. Letter to John Wagner. 12/15/1960. [*Atlanta, Ga.*] (THLc) 1 p. MLKP-MBU: Box 73A. 601215–007.

12/15/1960 King, Martin Luther, Jr. Letter to Joseph S. Clark. 12/15/1960. [*Atlanta, Ga.*] (THLc) 1 p. MLKP-MBU: Box 45A. 601215–009.

12/16/1960 King, Martin Luther, Jr. Letter to Richard W. Hostetler. 12/16/1960. [*Atlanta, Ga.*] (TLc) 1 p. MLKP-MBU: Box 46. 601216–004.

12/17/1960 Herriford, John H. Letter to Lucile Bluford. 12/17/1960. Minneapolis, Minn. (TALc) 5 pp. (Enclosed in 601219–006. 610000–053 on verso.) MLKP-MBU: Box 53A. 601217–002.

12/18/1960 Ebenezer Baptist Church. Program, Sunday services. 12/18/1960. Atlanta, Ga. (TD) 4 pp. EBCR. 601218–001.

12/19/1960 King, Martin Luther, Jr. Telegram to Bennie D. Brown. 12/19/1960. [*Atlanta, Ga.*] (TWc) 1 p. MLKP-MBU: Box 37A. 601219–001.

12/19/1960 Meany, George (American Federation of Labor and Congress of Industrial Organizations (AFL-CIO)). Letter to A. Philip (Asa Philip) Randolph and Harry Belafonte. 12/19/1960. Washington, D.C. (TWc) 1 p. ACCP-DAFL. 601219–003.

12/19/1960 King, Martin Luther, Jr. Letter to Maurice A. Dawkins. 12/19/1960. [*Atlanta, Ga.*] (TLc) 2 pp. MLKP-MBU: Box 52A. 601219–005.

12/19/1960 Herriford, John H. Letter to Martin Luther King, Jr. 12/19/1960. (TL) 1 p. (Contains enclosure 601217–002.) MLKP-MBU: Box 53A. 601219–006.

12/21/1960 King, Martin Luther, Jr. Letter to Linus Pauling. 12/21/1960. [*Atlanta, Ga.*] (TLc) 1 p. MLKP-MBU: Box 32A. 601221–000.

12/21/1960 King, Martin Luther, Jr. Letter to Harold Edward Fey. 12/21/1960. [*Atlanta, Ga.*] (TLc) 1 p. MLKP-MBU: Box 25. 601221–001.

12/21/1960 King, Martin Luther, Jr. Letter to Marjorie Huelle. 12/21/1960. [*Atlanta, Ga.*] (TLc) 2 pp. MLKP-MBU: Box 27A. 601221–002.

12/21/1960 King, Martin Luther, Jr. Letter to Jimmie E. Tinsley. 12/21/1960. [*Atlanta, Ga.*] (TLc) 2 pp. MLKP-MBU: Box 72. 601221–004.

12/22/1960 Wood, James R. Letter to John McFerren. 12/22/1960. (TLc) 1 p. MLKP-MBU: Box 32. 601222–002.

12/22/1960 King, Martin Luther, Jr. Letter to Edward E. Hart. 12/22/1960. [*Atlanta, Ga.*] (TLc) 2 pp. MLKP-MBU: Box 40. 601222–006.

12/22/1960 McDonald, Dora E. Letter to Mary I. Jeffries. 12/22/1960. [*Atlanta, Ga.*] (TLc) 1 p. MLKP-MBU: Box 46. 601222–008.

12/27/1960 King, Martin Luther, Jr. Letter to John Young. 12/27/1960. [*Atlanta, Ga.*] (TLc) 1 p. MLKP-MBU: Box 32. 601227–000.

12/29/1960 Gitlin, Irving (National Broadcasting Company, Inc.). Letter to Martin Luther King, Jr. 12/29/1960. New York, N.Y. (TLS) 1 p. MLKP-MBU: Box 32. 601229–001.

12/30/1960 McDonald, Dora E. Letter to Dorothy Norman. 12/30/1960. [*Atlanta, Ga.*] (TLc) 1 p. MLKP-MBU: Box 32. 601230–000.

12/30/1960	Abernathy, Ralph (MIA). Form letter to Friend. 12/30/1960. Montgomery, Ala. (TLS) 1 p. MLKP-MBU: Box 30. 601230–002.
12/30/1960	McDew, Charles E. (SNCC). Letter to Martin Luther King, Jr. 12/30/1960. Atlanta, Ga. (TLS) 1 p. MLKP-MBU: Box 6. 601230–003.
12/30/1960	King, Martin Luther, Jr. "The Negro and the American Dream," Address delivered at the Memorial Auditorium. [*12/30/1960*]. [*Chattanooga, Tenn.*] (At) 34 min. (1 audio cassette: analog.) BTC. 601230–008.
1961	King, Martin Luther, Jr. Notes on sit-ins and nonviolence. [*1961*]. [*Atlanta, Ga.*] (AD) 1 p. (Verso of 601217–002.) MLKP-MBU: Box 53A. 610000–053.
1/12/1961	Gray, Fred D. Letter to Martin Luther King, Jr. 1/12/1961. Montgomery, Ala. (TLS) 1 p. MLKP-MBU: Box 53A. 610112–003.
1/19/1961	Nemiroff, Robert Barron. Letter to Martin Luther King, Jr. 1/19/1961. New York, N.Y. (THLS) 1 p. MLKP-MBU: Box 55A. 610119–006.
1/20/1961	Foley, Edward H. (Inaugural Committee). Invitation to the inauguration of John F. (John Fitzgerald) Kennedy and Lyndon B. (Lyndon Baines) Johnson. 1/20/1961. (TD) 1 p. MLKJP-GAMK: Vault Box 2. 610120–005.
1/20/1961	Woodward, Stanley and Lindy Boggs (Inaugural Ball Committee). Invitation to the inaugural ball of John F. (John Fitzgerald) Kennedy and Lyndon B. (Lyndon Baines) Johnson. 1/20/1961. Washington, D.C. (TD) 1 p. MLKJP-GAMK: Vault Box 2. 610120–006.
1/31/1961	Angelou, Maya. Letter to Martin Luther King, Jr. and Wyatt Tee Walker. 1/31/1961. London, England. (THLS) 2 pp. (Marginal comments by King.) MLKP-MBU. 610131–014.
2/8/1961	King, Martin Luther, Jr. Letter to J. R. Butts. 2/8/1961. [*Atlanta, Ga.*] (TLc) 2 pp. MLKJP-GAMK: Box 1. 610208–019.
2/17/1961–2/18/1961	Negro American Labor Council. Press release, Institute and workshop mark launch of drive against job discrimination. 2/17/1961–2/18/1961. Washington, D.C. (THD) 4 pp. RPP-NN-Sc: Box 3. 610218–002.
2/27/1961	Dawkins, Maurice A. (The People's Independent Church of Christ). Letter to Martin Luther King, Jr. 2/27/1961. Los Angeles, Calif. (TLS) 1 p. MLKP-MBU: Box 45. 610227–005.
3/6/1961	King, Martin Luther, Jr. Letter to Kivie Kaplan. 3/6/1961. [*Atlanta, Ga.*] (TLc) 2 pp. MLKP-MBU: Box 54. 610306–015.
3/31/1961	King, Martin Luther, Jr. Letter to John H. Harriford. 3/31/1961. [*Atlanta, Ga.*] (TLc) 2 pp. MLKP-MBU: Box 53A. 610331–006.
4/1961	King, Martin Luther, Jr. "After Desegregation—What." [*4/1961*]. [*Atlanta, Ga.*] (ADd) 11 pp. MLKJP-GAMK: Vault Box 3. 610400–009.
4/1961	King, Martin Luther, Jr. "After Desegregation—What." [*4/1961*]. [*Atlanta, Ga.*] (TAD) 9 pp. MLKP-MBU: Box 44. 610400–012.
5/31/1961	Williams, Robert F. (NAACP). Telegram to Martin Luther King, Jr. 5/31/1961. Monroe, N.C. (PWSr) 1 p. MLKP-MBU: Box 59. 610531–005.
6/5/1961	*The Crusader.* 6/5/1961. Monroe, N.C. (THD) 8 pp. SCLCR-GAMK: Box 155. 610605–019.
6/18/1961	Western Christian Leadership Conference. Announcement, Martin Luther King, Jr. to speak at freedom rally. 6/18/1961. Los Angeles, Calif. (PD) 1 p. MLKP-MBU: Box 105. 610618–001.
6/21/1961	Rodell, Marie F. (Marie Freid) (Marie Rodell and Joan Daves, Inc.). Letter to Martin Luther King, Jr. 6/21/1961. New York, N.Y. (TLSr) 1 p. MLKP-MBU: Box 57. 610621-002.
9/26/1961	King, Martin Luther, Jr. Letter to James Baldwin. 9/26/1961. [*Atlanta, Ga.*] (TLc) 2 pp. MLKP-MBU: Box 8. 610926–000.
1/26/1962	King, Martin Luther, Jr. Letter to William H. Rhoades. 1/26/1962. [*Atlanta, Ga.*] (TLc) 1 p. MLKJP-GAMK: Box 9. 620126–000.
1/31/1962	Rhoades, William H. (American Baptist Home Mission Societies). Letter to Martin Luther King, Jr. 1/31/1962. New York, N.Y. (TLS) 1 p. MLKJP-GAMK: Box 9. 620131–002.
7/1962–3/1963	King, Martin Luther Jr. Draft of chapter I, "A Tough Mind and a Tender Heart," *Strength to Love.* [*7/1962-3/1963*] [*Atlanta, Ga.*] (AD) 26 pp. CSKC: Sermon file. 630300–071.
8/25/1963	King, Martin Luther, Jr. Interview on "Meet the Press." 8/25/1963. From: *The Proceedings of Meet the Press* 6 (25 August 1963): 1–9. Washington, D.C. (PTv) 10 pp. MLKJP-GAMK: Box 111. 630825–002.
3/9/1964	King, Martin Luther, Jr. Interview by Berl I. Bernhard. 3/9/1964. Atlanta, Ga. (TTa) 26 pp. JFKOH-MWalK. 640309–001.

10/12/1964 King, Martin Luther, Jr., "Remaining Awake Through a Great Revolution" Address delivered to the Sixty-first General Convention of the Episcopal Society for Cultural and Racial Unity. [*10/12/1964*] St. Louis, Mo. (At) 48.4 min. (1 sound cassette: analog.) MLKJP-GAMK. 641012–001.

12/4/1964 Kennedy, Robert F., and Burke Marshall. Interview by Anthony Lewis. 12/4/1964. New York, N.Y. (TD) 164 pp. JFKOH-MWalK. 641204–003.

3/28/1965 King, Martin Luther, Jr. Interview on "Meet the Press." [*3/28/1965*]. [*San Francisco, Calif.*] (At) 5.4 min. (1 sound cassette: analog.) MLKJP-GAMK. 650328–000.

7/4/1965 King, Martin Luther, Jr. "The American Dream," Sermon delivered at Ebenezer Baptist Church. 7/4/1965. Atlanta, Ga. (At) 41 min. (1 sound cassette: analog.) MLKEC: ET-71. 650704–000.

1/6/1966 Hartsfield, William Berry. Interview by Charles T. Morrisey. 1/6/1966. Atlanta, Ga. (TD) 10 pp. JFKOH-MWalK. 660106–001.

1/11/1966 Lawson, Belford V. Interview by Ronald J. Grele. 1/11/1966. Washington, D.C. (TD) 23 pp. JFKOH-MWalK. 660111–000.

8/21/1966 King, Martin Luther, Jr. Interview on "Meet the Press." 8/21/1966. From: *The Proceedings of Meet the Press* (21 August 1966): 1–15. Washington, D.C. (PTvf) 15 pp. CCCSU. 660821–000.

5/22/1967 Vandiver, S. Ernest (Samuel Ernest). Interview by John F. Stewart. 5/22/1967. Atlanta, Ga. (THD) 69 pp. JFKOH-MWalK. 670522–003.

8/13/1967 King, Martin Luther, Jr. Interview on "Meet the Press." 8/13/1967. From: *The Proceedings of Meet the Press* 11 (13 August 1967): 1–8. Washington, D.C. (PTv) 8 pp. MLKJP-GAMK: Box 122. 670813–001.

8/29/1967 King, Lonnie. Interview by John H. Britton. 8/29/1967. Washington D.C. (THTa) 62 pp. RBOH-DHU. 670829–001.

1968 Reddick, Lawrence Dunbar. "With King through India: A personal memoir." [*1968*]. (TD) 14 pp. LDRP-NN-Sc: Box 2. 680000–046.

1968 *Indian Leaders on Martin Luther King, Jr.* New Delhi: Inter-State Cultural League of India, 1968. (PD) (Inscription, 11/21/1968.) CSKCH. 680000–064.

3/31/1968 King, Martin Luther, Jr. "Remaining Awake Through a Great Revolution," Sermon delivered at the National Cathedral. [*3/31/1968*] [*Washington, D.C.*] (At) 47 min. (1 sound cassette: analog.) MLKJP-GAMK: T-60. 680331–000.

12/12/1968 Moore, Douglas E. (Shaw Urban Renewal). Interview by Robert Wright. 12/12/1968. (TTaf) 27 pp. RBOH-DHU. 681212–000.

11/27/1969 Levison, Stanley D. Letter to Lawrence Dunbar Reddick. 11/27/1969. New York, N.Y. (TLS) 2 pp. LDRP-NN-Sc: Box 2. 691127–000.

6/30/1969 Rustin, Bayard. Interview by T. H. Baker. 6/30/1969. (TTa) 38 pp. LBJOH-TxU-J. 690630–000.

11/27/1974 Khazan, Jibreel. Interview by William H. Chafe. 11/27/1974. (TTa) 15 pp. WCOH-NcD. 741127–000.

2/23/1977 Morrow, E. Frederic (Everett Frederic). Interview by Thomas Soapes. 2/23/1977. Abilene, Ka. (TTa) 64 pp. OH-KAbE. 770223–000.

4/19/1977 Baker, Ella J. Interview by Sue Thrasher and Casey Hayden. 4/19/1977. New York, N.Y. (TTa) 72 pp. SOHP-NcU. 770419–000.

3/29/1982 Moses, Robert Parris. Interview by Clayborne Carson. [*3/29/1982*] (At) 210 min. (3 sound cassettes: analog.) CCCSU. 820329–000.

1/25/1994 Vandiver, S. Ernest (Samuel Ernest). Interview by Clifford Kuhn. 1/25/1994. (TTa) 64 pp. GGDP-GASU: Box A. 940125–000.

5/11/1998 Scheinman, William X. (Timings). Letter to Clayborne Carson. 5/11/1998. Reno, Nev. (TLS) 2 pp. WXSC. 980511–000.

INDEX

Boldfaced page numbers in entries indicate that the material can be found in documents authored by Martin Luther King, Jr. Italicized page numbers in entries indicate the location of the main biographical entry for an individual, beginning with the volume number if other than the present volume.

Designer:	Steve Renick
Compositor:	Integrated Composition Systems, Inc.
Indexer:	Towery Indexing Services
Cartographer:	Bill Nelson Maps
Text:	10/12 Baskerville
Display:	Baskerville
Printer and binder:	Thomson-Shore, Inc.